The Facts On File
DICTIONARY
OF
ARCHAEOLOGY

The Facts On File
DICTIONARY
OF
ARCHAEOLOGY

Editor
RUTH D. WHITEHOUSE

Facts On File Publications
New York • Oxford

TO ARCHAEOLOGY STUDENTS

AT THE UNIVERSITY OF LANCASTER

First published in the United States of America in 1983
First paperback edition published in 1988
FACTS ON FILE, INC.
460 Park Avenue South
New York, N.Y. 10016

ISBN 0-87196-048-6 (hc)
ISBN 0-8160-1893-6 (pbk)

Printed in the United States of America

10 9 8 7 6 5 4 3 2

Contents

Tables

Illustrations

Introduction

Archaeology today is both a popular subject for the general public and a flourishing professional discipline. The appeal of the past is manifested by the large numbers who visit sites and museums, watch television programmes, read books and attend educational courses on archaeological subjects. At the same time the professional discipline has made great strides in the last twenty years: not only has there been a quantum leap in the rate of new discoveries, but developments in theory and methodology have provided powerful new interpretative tools for archaeologists. I hope that this Dictionary will be useful to all those interested in the past. Because the subject editors and other contributors are all professional archaeologists at the front of their respective fields, the Dictionary incorporates a body of up-to-date information which should be useful to students and to scholars in areas outside their own particular specializations. However, because the language is where possible non-technical, this information is accessible also to the non-specialist (necessary technical terms are either glossed or cross-referenced to the relevant entry).

The scope of archaeology today is enormous, encompassing the whole world and a timespan of some four million years, from the emergence of man or his immediate ancestors, to the study of recent centuries. It includes also a wide range of relevant approaches from traditional art-history and ancient language studies to modern techniques borrowed from the natural sciences, and the use of statistics and computers. It also involves the practical methods and techniques developed by workers in the field for the recovery, recording, conservation and interpretation of archaeological remains. The Dictionary covers all these aspects of archaeology. I cannot claim, however, that coverage is even. Some areas and periods have received far more study than others and these are inevitably covered more fully in the Dictionary. Moreover, decisions about what to include and exclude are to some extent arbitrary and no two scholars would ever agree entirely. My own prejudices, and to a lesser extent those of my subject editors, have necessarily prevailed.

For me, the most rewarding aspect of this task has been working with my subject editors and other contributors: their enthusiasm and efficiency have made the collaboration a great pleasure. In addition to the listed contributors, many other people have helped with research and advice. I should particularly like to mention Michael Ester, Beryl Smith, Elizabeth Bordt and Dorothy Mancilla, all of Rutgers University, Henry Hurst of Cambridge University and John Salmon of Lancaster University. I offer special thanks to Phil Howard, also of Lancaster University, who has produced the illustrations for publication and has put up with countless changes of content, layout and timetable with great good humour.

Finally, I should like to thank Margot Levy for her splendid work on copy editing, indexing, proof reading and generally making a book out of an amorphous typescript and assorted scribbles.

Lancaster
May 1983

How to use this Dictionary

The Dictionary has been designed to be as simple and convenient to use as possible. A number of points need some explanation.

Name forms, spelling and transliteration

Chinese names are given in the pinyin transliteration, with the form in the earlier Wade-Giles spelling given in brackets (even when the two spellings are the same). In most cases we have not given the Wade-Giles version a separate, cross-referenced entry. The only exceptions are where a site name is very familiar to Western readers in its Wade-Giles form and where this form is significantly different from the pinyin version; for example, we have given Choukoutien a separate cross-referenced entry, since the reader might not recognize the form Zhoukoudian.

Where languages other than Chinese are concerned we have been less consistent in our transliteration. We have chosen the versions that will be most familiar to Western readers. This may offend the purist but will, we believe, achieve the desired objective of getting the reader to the information desired with the minimum of delay.

Similarly, we have not been consistent about the choice of ancient or modern site names for headwords. Again we have chosen the forms which will be most familiar to the reader; the alternative names appear in brackets after the headword and as separate cross-referenced entries.

Cross references

The Dictionary makes extensive use of cross references. When a word that has an entry of its own appears in the text it is normally printed in SMALL CAPITALS the first time it occurs. This is not done, however, in the case of very common words where the general meaning is self-evident, e.g. pottery, bronze, Iron Age. Further cross references appear at the end of many entries.

Dating

Throughout the Dictionary we have employed the convention of using the lower case letters ad, bc and bp (before present) to indicate uncalibrated radiocarbon dates (the problem of radiocarbon calibration is explained in the entry on *radiocarbon dating*, p. 421). The capital letters AD, BC and BP are reserved for dates thought to represent 'real' (i.e. calendar) years: they include corrected radiocarbon dates, dates derived from documentary sources and dates derived from laboratory methods other than radiocarbon, which do not require calibration.

This convention is widely used by British archaeologists working in many different parts of the world; unfortunately, however, it has not been adopted universally. Radiocarbon specialists and the journal *Radiocarbon* publish all dates as 'before present' dates and they use the capitals BP. This practice causes no problems in that context, since everyone knows that they are writing about radiocarbon dates. However, for archaeologists working in fields that draw on a variety of dating methods, there is an urgent need for a method of notation that distinguishes between uncorrected radiocarbon years and dates in real years. The use of lower case letters is the simplest and least confusing convention available and is therefore employed in this Dictionary. When dates appear without associated letters, they refer to years AD, as in normal everyday usage.

While we have used this convention throughout, we have not been consistent in calibrating all radiocarbon dates that can be calibrated (i.e. dates after 7240 bp, 8000 BP). Our usage varies according to the area of the world and the range of dating methods available for the periods in question. For instance, in African archaeology, a high proportion of all dates is derived from radiocarbon; moreover many site sequences run from before 8000 BP to afterwards. Therefore for most African entries we have used uncorrected radiocarbon dates and the ad/bc/bp notation. In China, by contrast, most dates do not come from radiocarbon and it is therefore more convenient to calibrate those radiocarbon dates that do occur, so as to provide direct comparison with dates derived from other sources. Therefore in Chinese entries we use corrected radiocarbon dates and the AD/BC notation.

One other point should be made about dating. When individual radiocarbon dates are quoted, they should strictly be quoted *either* with a central date and a standard deviation *or* as a range of dates. For instance a hypothetical date might be expressed in one of three ways: 2000 ± 100 bc; 2100-1900 bc (68% confidence) or 2200-1800 bc (95% confidence). Because of the awkwardness of such forms in normal text, we have normally used instead *circa* (*c*) symbols or words such as 'approximately' or 'about' to indicate the imprecise nature of the dates. We hope that our professional colleagues will forgive us for this usage; we belive that the general reader will prefer it.

Contributors

Subject editors

Robert Bagley, Fogg Art Museum, Boston.
Peter Bellwood, Australian National University, Canberra.
John Chapman, University of Newcastle.
Valerie Chapman, Australian National University, Canberra.
Desmond Collins
Robert Hebditch, Rutgers University, New Brunswick.
Simon Hillson, University of Lancaster.
Richard Hodges, University of Sheffield.
Fumiko Ikawa-Smith, McGill University, Montreal.
Helmut Loofs-Wissowa, Australian National University, Canberra.
David Phillipson, Museum of Archaeology and Anthropology, Cambridge.
David Whitehouse, British School at Rome.
John Wilkins, University of London.

Other contributors

Royston Clark
Malcolm Colledge, University of London.
Debbie Hodges
Anthony Miller
Graham O'Hare

Illustrations

Philip Howard, University of Lancaster.

A

Aachen [Aix la Chapelle]. One of the finest groups of CAROLINGIAN buildings is the palace complex at Aachen, in particular the chapel built by Odo of Metz for the Emperor CHARLEMAGNE between 792 and 805. The chapel stood on one side of a large courtyard opposite the main palace buildings, and was entered through a high, double-storeyed porch flanked by towers. The plan of the chapel — a tall, domed octagon with vaulted aisles — was evidently influenced by San Vitale in RAVENNA and HAGIA SOPHIA in Constantinople. The sumptuous interior decoration included richly decorated capitals, vault mosaics and walls veneered with coloured marble panels, obviously inspired by the Ravenna and eastern churches, yet overall the chapel has a heavier, northern appearance with solid piers and barrel vaults. The westwork once connected the palace with the royal apartments, and the throne room was situated just inside the vestibule. Many precious relics and objects were brought from afar to adorn the interior of the chapel, and it is still possible to see the exquisite bronze parapet and the gilded pulpit, among other treasures. Unfortunately the mosaic which once lined the dome was replaced by later restorers.

Aardenburg. *See* FLEMISH BLACKWARES.

Abbeville, Abbevillian. One of the key localities where it was first shown that man was of great antiquity. From 1836 onwards BOUCHER DE PERTHES found stone tools in the gravel pits here, and a succession of scholars, especially from England, recognized the significance of these discoveries around 1859. Subsequently, these pits in northern France became one of the richest sources of PALAEOLITHIC tools, especially hand axes, in Europe.

In 1939 Abbé BREUIL proposed the name Abbevillian for both the type of crude hand axe found here and a whole early phase of hand-axe manufacture preceding the ACHEULIAN in Europe. However, many modern prehistorians are not satisfied with the evidence for such a stage either from Abbeville or elsewhere.

abbey. A place where monks or nuns live, work and worship. The concept of monasticism originated in the Near East during the second half of the 4th century, spread to Byzantium, Greece, Italy and France, and seems to have developed independently in the sub-Roman Celtic regions of Britain. The Middle Ages saw the growth of many different religious houses, each observing individual customs and rules; the most important of these was the Benedictine order, founded by St Benedict in the 6th century, which provided the basis for European monasticism. Excavations have helped to show that there was considerable variation between different orders in the layout of abbeys, and how these developed throughout the medieval period. They range from the beehive cells and oratories which typify the Early Celtic monasteries to the mature 12th-century Cistercian plan with cloisters, domestic ranges and large abbey church. Many of the major European monastic complexes have now been excavated, and it is clear from sites such as Monkwearmouth and JARROW in Co. Durham and FARFA and SAN VINCENZO in Central Italy that before the 10th century monasteries were the principal educational, artistic and economic centres of the Christian world.

Abejas. *See* TEHUACAN VALLEY.

Abkan. A stone industry of southern Nubia, believed to have been the work of indigenous peoples who maintained trade contact with more southerly regions of the Nile Valley during the 4th millennium bc. These folk were probably ancestral to the NUBIAN A GROUP.

abri. *See* ROCK SHELTER.

Abri Pataud. A rock shelter in the village of

LES EYZIES in southwest France, hardly known until the major programme of excavation from 1956-64 under Professor H.L. Movius. This revealed 14 main culture layers with radiocarbon ages from c32,500 bc at the bottom to c19,000 bc at the top, which now form the basis of the dating of the French Upper PALAEOLITHIC. The earliest nine levels were AURIGNACIAN followed by PERIGORDIAN stages IV, V and VI. At the top were Proto-MAGDALENIAN and probably Proto-SOLUTRIAN levels. Some art objects were found, and a skeleton was found in the top levels. The different patterns of hearths and living areas have been used to suggest different social groups of smaller and larger size.

absolute pollen counting. POLLEN ANALYSIS may be carried out by determining the number of grains of each pollen type per unit weight (grains/gm) or unit volume (grains/cm^3) of sample. This is called absolute pollen counting, and avoids some of the problems of PROPORTIONAL POLLEN COUNTING, although it is rather more time-consuming. Variation in the rate of sedimentation leads to uncertainty about the number of years each sample represents, and absolute counts for different samples may therefore not be compatible. This has led to the use of pollen influx rates, where a pollen analysis is carefully calibrated by RADIOCARBON DATING, and the number of grains of each pollen type accumulating on a unit area of lake or bog surface in one year (grains/cm^2/year) is calculated for each sample.

Abu Hureyra, Tell. A TELL site on the Euphrates River in Syria, 120 km east of Aleppo. The site was excavated in 1972-3, as a rescue excavation in advance of flooding by the Tabqua Dam. Two major phases of occupation are documented: the first, labelled either EPI-PALAEOLITHIC or MESOLITHIC, dates to the 9th millennium bc; it was later reoccupied after a long period of abandonment in the 7th millennium by a settlement of the PRE-POTTERY NEOLITHIC B culture. It was finally abandoned c5800 bc.

The earlier settlement is particularly important because of the light it sheds on the early development of farming in the Levant. A very large amount of plant material was collected by froth flotation and preliminary results available in 1983 already indicate some very interesting developments. The plant remains include large quantities of einkorn wheat and some grains of barley and rye; there were also pulses such as lentils and vetches, and a wide range of other edible fruits, nuts and seeds. The plant remains were all morphologically wild, but it seems likely that the einkorn at least was being deliberately cultivated: many seeds of weed species were found, typical of cultivated fields in the area today. Most of the meat food came from gazelle and onager and it is suggested that these animals were being either selectively hunted or perhaps herded. It is clear that the 9th-millennium bc community at Abu Hureyra was already involved in incipient farming activities.

The Neolithic settlement of the 7th millennium bc is also of great importance, in this case because of its enormous size: 15 hectares, larger than any other recorded site nof this period (even ÇATAL HÜYÜK). Rectangular houses of pisé were built up into a mound c5 metres high; both floors and walls were sometimes plastered and some wall plaster bears traces of painting. Most of the Neolithic levels were aceramic, but in the uppermost levels after c6000 bc a dark burnished pottery appears.

Abu Shahraim. See ERIDU.

Abu Simbel. A great temple on the west bank of the Nile in northern Nubia, 230 km upstream of Aswan, constructed by RAMESES II in the 13th century BC as part of the cultural Egyptianization of Nubia under the Eighteenth Dynasty (see DYNASTIC EGYPT). The facade of the temple is dominated by four 20-metre-high seated figures of Rameses, and the main part is cut into the solid rock of the hillside, into which it penetrates for 55 metres. The walls of the great hall are decorated with reliefs illustrating the king's military campaigns in Syria and Nubia. To save it from flooding on the completion of the new High Dam at Aswan, the temple was moved under UNESCO auspices to a higher site above the waters of Lake Nasser in 1968.

Abydos. A major town in northern Egypt, which was a centre for the worship of Osiris and the chosen burial place of the pharaohs of the First Dynasty (see DYNASTIC EGYPT). The royal tombs consisted of large underground brick-built rooms lined with wood, covered by a low mound surrounded by a brick wall. Early tombs comprised a single chamber; later developments included stone embellishments to the structure, the addition of a number of surrounding storerooms, and an access stair. Funerary enclosures, perhaps palaces, were also erected. Nearby graves were used for the interment of relatives, court functionaries and retainers; at least some of the retainers were apparently killed to accompany the deceased pharaoh. From the Second Dynasty, the royal graves were at SAQQARA. Under the Old Kingdom, the town of Abydos expanded within its walled enclosure and retained its importance until the Second Intermediate Period. Thereafter it remained a religious centre, and a major temple was constructed by Seti I of the Nineteenth Dynasty.

Acacus. A region of the central Sahara, in what is now southwestern Libya, noted for the presence of rock shelters with occupation deposits and rock paintings. Pottery was made in this region from about 7000 bc: the earliest vessels include examples with the wavy-line decoration typical of the so-called 'AQUATIC CIVILIZATION'. From Uan Muhuggiag comes one of the earliest pieces of dated evidence for animal domestication in the central Sahara, in the form of the skull of a shorthorn ox recovered from a level of c4000 bc which also yielded traces of sheep/goat. At the same site rock paintings of oxen may be shown to pre-date c2700 bc.

Acapana. *See* TIAHUANACO.

acculturation. The adoption of traits characteristic of one culture by another.

Aceramic Neolithic. Term applied to groups demonstrating evidence of a Neolithic economy — that is, an economy based on the cultivation of crops or the rearing of stock or both — but without the use of pottery (which was regarded by an earlier generation of archaeologists as a defining characteristic of the Neolithic). Aceramic Neolithic groups were widespread in Western Asia during the early stages of the development of farming, being found in the Levant (PRE-POTTERY NEOLITHIC A and B), the Zagros area (e.g. KARIM SHAHIR and JARMOAN), in Anatolia (HACILAR Aceramic Neolithic) and probably in other areas also. Outside Western Asia, Aceramic Neolithic groups are rarer; in Europe, for instance, an Aceramic Neolithic phase has been identified only in Greece, where it appears to have been short-lived.

Achaemenid. The Persian dynasty that ruled from its homeland in central and southern Iran from c547 BC, when Cyrus II conquered Lydia, to 331 BC, when the empire fell to ALEXANDER THE GREAT. The Achaemenid Empire reached its height under Darius, who built a splendid new capital at PERSEPOLIS and ruled an area extending from India to Egypt. He was defeated by the Greeks at MARATHON in 490 BC; ten years later his son Xerxes was also defeated by the Greeks at SALAMIS.

Other surviving Achaemenid monuments include the tomb of Cyrus the Great at PASARGADAE, a number of trilingual rock-cut inscriptions of Darius's reign (*see* BISITUN) and the rock-cut tomb of Darius at Naqsh-i Rustam near Persepolis.

Acheulian. The term Epoque de St Acheul was introduced by de MORTILLET in 1872 for a span of prehistoric time, the early part of the PALAEOLITHIC period. This usage is still occasionally found today but after 1925 the idea of epochs began to be supplanted by that of cultures and culture traditions, and it is in this sense that the term Acheulian is more often used today. However, prehistorians are far from unanimous on this question, some still not accepting the usefulness of the notion of traditions or cultures.

The Acheulian is characterized according to most prehistorians by the HAND AXE. In the wider sense now most commonly used, the Acheulian first appeared over a million years ago in Africa, and the earliest assemblages are often rather similar to the OLDOWAN at such sites as OLDUVAI GORGE. Subsequent hand-axe assemblages are found over most of Africa, southern Asia and western and southern Europe. The earliest appearance of hand axes in Europe is still referred to by some workers as ABBEVILLIAN, denoting a stage when hand axes were still made with crude, irregular edges.

The type locality is Saint-Acheul, near Amiens in the Somme valley, in northern France. In Europe, large hand-axe assemblages are mostly found in northern France and England, from around the time of the penultimate interglacial and the succeeding glacial period, perhaps some 200,000 to 300,000 years ago (*see* Tables 4 and 5, pages 418-9). However, Acheulian hand axes are still found around the time of the last interglacial period, and hand axes are common in one part of the succeeding MOUSTERIAN period (the Mousterian of Acheulian tradition) down to as recently as 40,000 years ago.

A number of subdivisions of the Acheulian have been proposed from time to time but none has widespread recognition; it is likely that these subdivisions could only have local validity.

acoustic vessels. From the 9th century large pots were cemented into bell-towers to help boost the chimes of the church bells. A fine 9th-century collection of painted BADORF WARES, for example, was found in the church of Meschede in Westphalia, and larger RELIEF-BAND AMPHORAE were used in 10th- and 11th-century churches. The dating of many pottery types has been helped by architectural studies of the churches into which the pots were cemented.

acropolis [Greek: *akros* (high, top), *polis* (city)]. The higher or citadel section found in a number of Greek cities, notably Corinth and Athens. The name is often used to refer specifically to the Acropolis at Athens, surmounted by the PARTHENON, and the associated complex of monumental public buildings.

acroterion. An end ornament or ornamental figure, mounted with plinth at any of the three corners of the PEDIMENT of a classical building.

AD, ad. Years 'after the birth of Christ' (Anno Domini). The´ lower case 'ad' represents uncalibrated RADIOCARBON years; the capitals AD denote a calibrated radiocarbon date, or a date such as an historically derived one, that does not need CALIBRATION (*see* Table 8, page 422). There is no year 0: AD 1 is the same year as 1 BC.

Addaura. A cave in the Monte Pellegrino group near Palermo, Sicily, with engravings of the Upper PALAEOLITHIC period. The main scene is dominated by human figures. Two in the centre are lying and seem to be bound,

while figures round them seem to be masked and dancing: it may be an initiation or circumcision scene. The carving is attributed to the ROMANELLIAN culture, some 11,000 years ago.

Adena. A widespread native American culture of the Early WOODLAND period, centred on Southern Ohio. It is best known for its ceremonial burial practices, particularly mound building (e.g. GRAVE CREEK MOUND). Adena mounds date from as early as *c*1000 bc, but do not become common until 500 bc. Hunting and gathering was the main subsistence base, but limited horticulture may have been practised. Other characteristic cultural traits include small village dwelling units (possibly seasonally occupied), long-distance trade, and both inhumation and cremation as means of disposal of the dead. A typical artefact inventory would include cord-marked pottery, engraved stone tablets, blocked-end-tube smoking pipes, birdstones, boatstones and hammerstones.

Adichanallur. *See* MEGALITHS (INDIA).

Adlerberg. An Early Bronze Age group in southwest Germany, a variant of the UNĚTICE culture. It is known mainly from a number of flat inhumation cemeteries such as that of Adlerberg itself. The dead were usually accompanied by fairly simple offerings such as copper and bronze daggers and pins, flint tools and one-handled pottery cups. *See also* STRAUBING.

adobe. An American term for sun-dried mud-BRICK.

Adrar Bous. A site in the Air massif, on the edge of the Tenere Desert in Niger, where excavations have revealed a long succession of prehistoric occupation. LEVALLOISO-MOUS-TERIAN settlement was followed by an arid phase when the region was probably uninhabited. The succeeding ATERIAN industry represents a local variant in which bifacial points are a distinct feature. The prolonged post-Aterian arid period is marked by a further hiatus in the archaeological sequence, but by about 10,000 bc there was a rapid return to wetter conditions. Human settlement then resumed: it appears likely that the initial re-occupation of the area was by small mobile groups, perhaps of northerly origin. With increasingly moist conditions, however, the more settled life-style of the so-called 'AQUATIC CIVILIZATION' was soon adopted. By early in the 4th millennium bc techniques of food-production are firmly attested. Adrar Bous is one of the most informative sites of the TENERE NEOLITHIC. The skeleton of a domestic shorthorn ox there dates to 3700 bc. Small stock were also herded, while numerous grindstones suggest that cereals, including sorghum, were intensively exploited if not actually cultivated.

Adria [Atria]. Port in northeast Italy. A principal 6th-5th century BC port on the Adriatic, and important crossover point for Etruscan and Greek trade, linking the sea routes with Etruria, the Po Valley and northern Europe. Variously described as of Venetic, Greek or Etruscan foundation, the town seems to have had a large Greek population. The alternation commonly found between the forms Adria and Atria itself suggests an Etruscan origin at least for the name, there being no separate 'd' in Etruscan script. Less plausible are popular etymologies which attempt to link the name Adria with the Adriatic, variously deriving the one from the other. Silting-up has always caused problems in this area, and it is very likely that the ancient coastline was nearer to Adria. References to a canal being dug at an early stage (possibly 5th century BC) are also credible. Today, flooding, high-water table and a basic bradyseism have covered much of the Roman and pre-Roman evidence with several metres of deposit.

Adulis. Located on the Red Sea coast of Ethiopia, southeast of the modern port of Massawa, Adulis was the principal seaport of AXUM, to which it was linked by a well-travelled trade route. There are indications that Adulis may have been established in Ptolemaic times and, indeed, it must be assumed that ports or other settlements existed on this coast during the PRE-AXUMITE period. However, such excavations as have taken place at Adulis have yielded material which belongs to the 3rd century AD or later.

aerial photography. A technique that has proved to be one of the most successful methods of discovering archaeological sites. Large areas of ground can be covered quickly, and the ground plan of a new site can be plotted from the photographs. Accurate surveys can in fact be made by this method (see PHOTOGRAMMETRY). When viewed from the air, sites may be revealed as SHADOW MARKS, CROP MARKS, SOIL MARKS or FROST MARKS.

Afalou. See MECHTA-AFALOU.

Afanasievo. Culture of southern Siberia, probably beginning in the late 3rd millennium BC. The Afanasievo people were the first food-producers in the area, breeding cattle, sheep and horses, but also practising hunting. There is no direct evidence of agriculture, but it may have been practised. Most known sites are burials under low mounds (*kurgans*). Artefacts include dentate stamped pottery and a few copper ornaments; tools were of stone and bone. The Afanasievo was succeeded by the ANDRONOVO culture in the mid-2nd millennium BC.

Afontova Gora II. See YENISEI.

Afrasiab. See SAMARKAND.

African food-production. The beginnings of food-production in Africa have only been documented with any precision in relatively recent years. Formerly, it was generally believed that techniques of food-production had been introduced into Africa in a relatively developed form, their initiation and formative processes having taken place elsewhere. However, research in the Nile Valley has now shown that the intensive use of cereals, and experimentation with these crops, began there at a rather earlier date than that at which corresponding events are firmly attested elsewhere. At several localities in Upper Egypt and Nubia these processes are now seen to extend back as far as the 16th millennium bc. The best-documented example is at WADI KUBBANIYA. These are, if confirmed, the earliest instances of incipient plant cultivation yet known anywhere in the world, and there can thus be no reasonable doubt that they were indigenous African achievements. They do not seem, however, to have led to the general adoption of such practices at this early date.

Food-production was not generally practised in North Africa before about the 5th millennium bc, and it is as yet unclear to what extent the relevant techniques were derived from a Near Eastern source. The principal crops involved — wheat and barley — are now known to have been present in parts of North Africa before this date. Further south these winter-rainfall crops will not grow satisfactorily, and the cultivated crops are of species indigenous to the immediately sub-Saharan latitudes, notably finger and bulrush millet, sorghum, yams and African rice with, in Ethiopia, teff, enset and noog. It now seems likely that most of these species were brought under cultivation between the 4th and the 2nd millennia bc.

Domestic animals present a somewhat different picture. It appears that domestic sheep and goats cannot be derived from the Barbary sheep, and must therefore be assumed to have been introduced from outside the continent. On the other hand, it is not yet clear whether the early domestic cattle of North Africa could be descended wholly or in part from the local wild species. But south of the Sahara there are no potential wild prototypes, and it is clear that domestic animals must have been introduced to these latitudes from the north. Domestic animals are known from the Sudanese Nile Valley, as at KADERO, as early as the second half of the 4th millennium bc, and from West Africa by the mid-2nd millennium. A gradual introduction of domestic animals into East Africa is now attested from the 3rd millennium onwards, earlier indications being inconclusive. South of the Equator the advent of food-production did not precede the beginnings of the Iron Age.

Afyeh. *See* NUBIAN A GROUP.

Agade. *See* AKKAD.

Agate Basin. *See* PLANO.

ageing of skeletal material. Age at death may be estimated from ancient SKELETONS in a number of ways:
(*a*) *Epiphyseal fusion.* Long bones grow in zones just behind their joint surfaces. Thus a growing bone consists of three elements: the central part, or diaphysis, and the ends, the ephiyses. When the bone reaches adult size, the epiphyses fuse onto the diaphysis. The average age at which this occurs is known for many bones in the skeletons of man and most domestic animals. The stage of epiphyseal

fusion reached in bones from archaeological sites may therefore be used as a guide to age at death. Fusion of other skeletal elements may be used in the same way. There is, however, considerable variation between individuals, and the method has to be used with some caution.
(*b*) *Dental eruption.* Teeth in most animals erupt in a well-established sequence. Average ages for each stage of the sequence are known for man and most domestic animals. The state of eruption of teeth in ancient jaws may therefore be used to estimate age at death.
(*c*) *Dental attrition.* Given a standard diet, teeth of different individuals should wear at roughly the same rate. Degree of wear should therefore represent the age of the animals. Tables of rate of wear have been established for man, but other animals must have this method calibrated by dental eruption.
(*d*) *Antlers.* In the deer, the stage of development of antlers is roughly related to age, but this is not very reliable as an ageing method.
(*e*) *Pubic symphysis.* In man, progressive changes on the joint surfaces of the pubic symphysis occur with age, and can be used successfully to age male individuals.
(*f*) *Dental microstructure.* Counting of incremental structures in teeth may allow estimation of age at death.

Bone microstructure may also prove useful for ageing.

agger. A Latin military term meaning a rampart, earthwork or embankment. The term is applied in a broad way and is used, for instance, for the artificial earthworks erected to support battering engines and for the slightly raised causeway that formed the basis of most Roman roads.

Aghia Triadha. *See* AYIA TRIADHA.

Agop Atas. *See* MADAI CAVES.

agora. An open space in a Greek town, serving as commercial, political and social centre, like the Roman FORUM. The area is often characterized by elaborate architecture, as at classical EPHESUS and at ATHENS, where the agora has been studied in recent excavations.

Agordat. A town in western Eritrea, Ethiopia, best-known archaeologically for the presence of four village sites, never excavated but attributed on the basis of surface collections to about the 3rd millennium bc. The artefacts, notably the stone mace-heads and ground stone axes, show affinities to those of the NUBIAN C GROUP of the Nile Valley. Grindstones and a clay figurine akin to 'C Group' representations of domestic cattle suggest the practice of food-production. The Agordat sites have been proposed as marking an early passage of food-production techniques and associated material culture from the Nile Valley to the Ethiopian highlands (see AFRICAN FOOD-PRODUCTION).

Agrelo. Located in an area 20 km south of the city of Mendoza, Argentina, Agrelo and several related sites are thought to represent the agriculture–pottery threshold in this marginal semi-arid area. No evidence of irrigation is discernible, even though it would have been necessary to any cultivation strategy. Simple pottery, generally in the form of deep, wide-mouthed pots, has been found; it has a rough grey-black body and is usually decorated by incision, punctuation or small appliqué nodes (sometimes in the shape of a human face). Pottery spindle whorls and crude figurines also occur, as do LABRETS, clubheads, triangular projectile points and beads in stone. Pit inhumations were marked by a circle of stones. Nearby coastal pottery styles (e.g. CIENEGA and EL MOLLE) may be precursors to Agrelo and are major factors in dating it to the early centuries of the Christian era.

Agrigento [Greek Akragas]. Modern Agrigento, on the coast of southern Sicily, partially overlies the Greek colony of Akragas, an aggressively expansive and prosperous trading centre during the 6th and 5th centuries BC. There is some evidence for earlier settlement, possibly Neolithic. The classical settlers further strengthened the defences of the site, which is a natural fortress on three sides, by the construction of extensive walls, original sections of which can still be found. Famous as the home of the pre-Socratic poet and philsopher Empedocles (who, however, was subsequently exiled) Akragas also advertised its prosperity and patronage of the arts by the erection of a whole series of public buildings of an especially magnificent nature. Among the remains of classical temples still to be seen, most remarkable are the Temple of Concord (wrongly so called, the original dedication is lost) and the Temple of Olympian Zeus. The Temple of Concord is normally seen as an advanced example of the DORIC order, incorporating mainland sophistications such as 'double contraction', the subtle adjustment of the distances between columns and between the corresponding decoration above, to avoid what were otherwise felt to be infelicitous asymmetries. The Temple of Zeus, unfortunately now ruined, must have been a bizarre and unique structure. Basically a development of the Doric style again, this temple incorporated strange and adventurous modifications. Built on a gigantic ground-plan, it may perhaps have caused some disquiet to its architects and builders even before construction. The usual arrangement of alternating columns and spaces was replaced by a continuous wall, with half-columns of round section at the usual intervals on the outside and of square section on the reverse, thus giving the appearance of the usual Greek peristyle but with walling between the pillars. It is possible that this walling between pillars extended only part way towards the frieze, and that it was in the resulting apertures that 25 gigantic figures were placed to help support, quite literally, the massive entablature. This temple was still incomplete when Akragas was sacked by the Carthaginians in 406 BC.

Resettled later in the 4th century BC (c338), Akragas managed to be on the losing side for most of the Punic Wars. There was some return to commercial prosperity later under Roman administration, when trade seems to have expanded to include textiles and sulphur. The Christian era saw the city abandoned once again, and some church use made of the classical temples, while large areas were utilized as Roman and Christian cemeteries and catacombs. Recent excavations have been quite extensive and have revealed, in the vicinity of the new Museo Nazionale, a network of streets and housing laid out on a grid basis that possibly goes back to the 5th century BC.

Aguada. A culture dominant in the Valliserrana region of northwest Argentina in the period AD 700-1000, and notable for the fine quality of its arts. Incised and polychrome decorated ceramics and ceremonial artefacts of bronze and copper are characteristic and reflect a probable influence from TIAHUAN-

ACO. Feline and dragon motifs are also common, as are depictions of warriors, weaponry and trophy heads. Decapitated burials are a further indication that warfare was a dominant preoccupation of Aguada. Indeed, its sudden disappearance from the archaeological record in c1000 was probably the result of invasion from the east.

Ahar. A site in Rajasthan, western India. Period I is dated c2500-1500 BC and belongs to the Chalcolithic BANAS culture. The population lived by cultivating a cereal crop and hunting deer; there is little evidence of domesticated animals. They used copper and a variety of different types of pottery, including BLACK AND RED WARE. Period II has NORTHERN BLACK POLISHED WARE of the later 1st millennium BC.

Ahichchatra. A large city in northern India, which was occupied from the mid-1st millennium BC to c1100 AD. The city, which occupied several hundred hectares, was the site where PAINTED GREY WARE was first found.

Ahrensburg [Ahrensburgian]. A village close to Hamburg in Schleswig-Holstein, Germany; beside the village are two important late PALAEOLITHIC sites, MEIENDORF and STELL-MOOR, less than a kilometre apart. The main layer at Stellmoor is dated to c8500 bc, and some workers have attributed this to a distinct Ahrensburgian culture; it has tanged points which were possibly arrowheads, for this site has produced the earliest conclusive evidence for the use of the bow and arrow, in the form of a hoard of 50 pine arrow-shafts with bowstring notches ('nocks'). The Ahrensburgians hunted mainly the reindeer.

ahu. A rectangular stone platform, with stepped sides in larger examples, which served as a focus for rituals in the courts of prehistoric Eastern POLYNESIAN temples (marae). Construction of such platforms was most developed in the SOCIETY ISLANDS, and in EASTER ISLAND, where ahu served as statue foundations. See also MARAE, MAEVA, MAHAIATEA, TAPUTAPUATEA, VINAPU.

Ai Bunar. The largest and most completely explored of a group of three copper mines, located near Stara Zagora, central Bulgaria.

The earliest exploitation of the malachite ore beds, by open-cast mining, is dated to the 4th millennium bc KARANOVO VI period, with later utilization in the Late Bronze Age. Although the mines lie close to a row of CHALCOLITHIC tells in the Azmak valley, the copper artefacts from those tells are not made of Ai Bunar copper; however, substantial quantities of this ore have been discovered in settlements in Moldavia and the Ukraine (CUCUTENI-TRIPOLYE culture).

Aichbühl. A Neolithic settlement on the shores of the Federsee in southern Germany, consisting of about 25 houses along the edge of the lake. The houses were built of timber and were rectangular in shape, usually divided into two rooms; the average size was c5 by 8 metres. Most houses contained an oven. The site is not easily assigned to any well-known cultural group, though it shows some features of the MICHELSBERG culture. The commonest artefacts found were SHOE-LAST ADZES and axes of stone and pedestalled pottery bowls.

Aija. See RECUAY.

Ai Khanum. A Hellenistic city (possibly Alexandria Oxiana) occupied between the 4th century and c100 BC, Ai Khanum stands on a naturally defensible site at the confluence of the Oxus and the Koktcha in Afghanistan. The city comprises a citadel, acropolis and lower town, protected by mud-brick walls and ditch. The lower town has an administrative centre, a residential quarter and an open area with few, if any, buildings. In the administrative centre, excavations have revealed an imposing complex containing a courtyard with a peristyle built of columns with pseudo-Corinthian capitals. On one side of the courtyard is a vestibule with Corinthian columns and beyond it is a large rectangular room, perhaps the *bouleuterion* (meeting-place of the city council). Nearby is a 4th-century funerary chapel known (according to an inscription) as the Temenos of Kineas. Kineas, it is suggested, may have been the founder of the city, shortly after ALEXANDER THE GREAT conquered the region in 329 BC. In the same general area, the excavators discovered the so-called temple *à redans*, a building of Mesopotamian type. At the foot of the acropolis is a cemetery. The finds from Ai Khanum, which include an inscription stating that one Clearchus erected a transcript of the precepts at Delphi in the Temenos of Kineas, indicate the persistence of a strong Hellenistic element.

Ain Hanech. A locality in Algeria which has produced some of the earliest evidence of human occupation in north Africa. There is a mammal fauna of Villafranchian type associated with the stone tools, indicating that they were made some 1-1.5 million years ago. The artefacts include choppers and multi-faceted spheroids, which seem to be distinctive of a later OLDOWAN stage, but whose function is not reliably known.

Ain Mallaha [Eynan]. A large village of the early NATUFIAN period by Lake Huleh in Upper Jordan. Each of the three phases contained about 50 substantial circular houses and open areas with storage pits. The size of the settlement (c2000 square metres) and the well-built houses suggest that this settlement was permanently occupied. The economy was based on the hunting or herding of gazelle, as well as hunting other large animals, fishing and harvesting wild cereals. The houses in the lowest level were between 7 and 9 metres in diameter, those from the upper two levels c3-4 metres. They are built in hollows; many had paved stone floors with centrally placed stone-lined hearths, and the superstructures were probably of reeds and branches. One early house, with a paved stone floor and red wall-plaster, was later re-used as a tomb of a man and a woman of some importance, the woman adorned with a shell head-dress. Other graves have also been found, containing single or collective inhumations.

Ainu. The native people of Hokkaido, southern Sakhalin and the Kurile Islands, Japan, who numbered about 17,000 in the 1940s. Before their way of life changed radically in the 19th century, they lived mostly by hunting, fishing and collecting, but they also grew some plants, such as buckwheat.

It was once held that the Ainu were the remnants of the JOMON population, pushed northwards by the YAYOI farmers and their descendants, the Japanese. That the Ainu were pushed and exploited by the Japanese from the early historic period in the 8th century is evident from written records. The Jomon Period, however, is much too long and culturally too diverse to be attributed to a single ethnic group, and the Yayoi development is not the result of mass migration around 300 BC.

The most widely accepted interpretation now is that the Ainu are the descendants of the people who left the Jomon remains in Hokkaido and northern Honshu. Unlike their southern counterparts, they did not go through the socio-cultural changes of the Yayoi and KOFUN periods, but remained what is called the 'Epi-Jomon' until about the end of the 8th century. With the encroachment of the culture based in central Honshu, the Epi-Jomon was transformed into the SATSUMON culture, about the same time as the OKHOTSK culture appeared on the northern and eastern coast of Hokkaido. Some elements of the 19th-century Ainu culture, such as the Bear Ceremonial, find parallels in Okhutsk ceremonialism, while much of the material culture has its origin in the Satsumon culture. Recent work in Hokkaido is filling the gap in our knowledge between the dissolution of the Satsumon culture in the 14th century and the ethnographic descriptions of the Ainu several centuries later.

Aitutaki. *See* COOK ISLANDS.

Ajanta. A Buddhist shrine in central India. A number of cave temples were constructed here from the 1st century BC to the 5th century AD and are famous for their wall paintings, which show scenes from the Jatakas (stories about the lives of the Buddha in earlier incarnations).

Ajdabiyah. An important Islamic town in northern Libya which, in a region of semi-desert, has one invaluable asset: water. Ajda-biyah therefore became an important cara-van town at the junction of the main route from Egypt to the Maghreb and a trans-Saharan route from the Sudan. The town was taken by the FATIMIDS in their advance towards Egypt in 912, and flourished until it was destroyed by the Banu Hilal in 1051. Two monuments belonging to the period 912-1051 are im-portant despite their poor state of preserva-tion: an early congregational mosque and a qasr or fort. The mosque is roughly rect-angular, with maximum dimensions of 47 by 31 metres. The courtyard has a single arcade on all four sides. The plan of the sanctuary is a simple T-shape, with a broad 'nave' and 'transepts' in front of the qibla wall. Stray finds include an inscription of 310 or 320 [AH] (922 or 932 AD). The *qasr* is a rectangular building, 33 metres long and 25 metres wide, with circular towers at the angles and a rectangular salient, including a monumental porch, at each side. The towers and salients appear to be for display rather than effective defence, and since the interior contains little more than reception rooms and magazines, the building has been identified as a rest-house for important travellers between Egypt and the Maghreb rather than a castle or palace.

Ajjul, Tell el-. *See* GAZA.

Ajuerado. *See* TEHUACAN VALLEY.

A-kalam-dug. The name of a king inscribed on a seal in one of the graves (Grave 1050) of the Royal Cemetery at UR, thought to represent a local ruler in a period preceding the First Dynasty of Ur.

Akhenaten. An Egyptian pharaoh of the 18th Dynasty, who reigned from *c*1379 to 1362 BC and is remembered principally for his proscription of the priesthood of AMUN and the adoption of the worship of the sun-disc Aten as the state religion. To facilitate the change, Aten-worship having apparently become of major importance only during the preceding two reigns, the capital was moved from THEBES to a new site at the modern EL-AMARNA in Middle Egypt. Here, at the city of Akhetaten, the new religion was promoted to the neglect of foreign affairs. The art of this period shows a vivid naturalism which contrasts strangely with the stereotyped formality of earlier and later times. On Akhenaten's death a return to the Thebes-based worship of Amun was rapidly accomplished.

Akira. *See* PASTORAL NEOLITHIC OF EAST AFRICA.

Akjoujt. Situated in southern Mauritania, Akjoujt appears to have been an early centre of African copper-working. It is, indeed, one of the few Saharan or sub-Saharan areas where there may have been a distinct 'Copper Age' preceding the local exploitation of iron. Mining of copper ore is indicated from at least the 5th century bc and possibly earlier. Links with other areas of early copper working to the north in Morocco and to the east in Niger (*see*

AZELIK) remain to be demonstrated. Arrowheads are the product most frequently represented, but spearheads, axes, pins and occasional decorative items may also tentatively be attributed to this period.

Akkad [Agade]. Archaeologically unlocated site, near BABYLON (or, possibly, Babylon itself), capital city of the AKKADIAN empire founded by Sargon either in 2370 BC (on the middle chronology, *see* MESOPOTAMIA, Table 3, page 321) or a century earlier (on the high chronology).

Akkadian. (1) Name derived from the city of AKKAD, applied to the northern part of SUMER and to the dynasty that was established by Sargon in the mid-3rd millennium BC. Under Sargon and his grandson Naram-Sin this dynasty established an empire that included northern as well as southern Mesopotamia and neighbouring ELAM to the east.
(2) The Semitic language which was associated with the Akkadian dynasty. Under Sargon and his successors the Akkadian language, written in the CUNEIFORM script which had been devised originally for writing the unrelated and quite different SUMERIAN language, replaced Sumerian as the official language (though Sumerian continued in use for religious purposes) and became the medium for business and international communications throughout the Near and Middle East, from Anatolia to Egypt, as well as in Mesopotamia and ELAM.

Akrotiri. *See* THERA.

Aksum. *See* AXUM.

alabaster. *See* GYPSUM.

alabastron. Greek name for a small jar for perfume or oil, originally of alabaster. The shape is often globular, sometimes tall and narrowing, with narrow mouth, and often without handles. *See also* ARYBALLOS.

Alaca Hüyük. A TELL site in northern Turkey, *c*150 km east of Ankara, occupied in the 4th, 3rd and 2nd millennia BC. A group of 13 extremely rich tombs from the Early Bronze Age II (early 3rd millennium BC) was found outside the town and is thought to represent a royal cemetery. The burials were single and double inhumations in rectangular pits, accompanied by a wealth of fine metalwork. This included two very early iron daggers (made of terrestrial iron) with gold-plated handles; swords, daggers, maceheads, spears and battle-axes of copper and bronze; jugs and goblets of gold, silver, electrum, copper and bronze; diadems, brooches, bracelets, pins and beads in gold; and figurines of bulls and stags in copper, inlaid with electrum, thought to be mounts from funeral standards. The tombs were lined with rough stone walling and roofed with a ceiling of wooden beams, over which skulls and hooves of animals were placed as part of the funeral rite.

The city was reoccupied in the HITTITE period and it has been tentatively identified as the Hittite holy city of Arinna. The best-known monument of this period is a monumental gateway guarded by two great carved sphinxes.

Alacaluf. *See* FUEGIAN TRADITION.

Alaka. A number of shell middens located in the mangrove swamps of the northwest coast of Guyana have been grouped together into the Alaka Phase. An ARCHAIC lifestyle based heavily on shellfish-gathering is indicated throughout. Some crude percussion-made stone tools, MANOS and METATES are present, with crude ceramics appearing in the later stages. These ceramics represent the appearance of intrusive groups and are assumed to mark the passing of Alaka. Dates are hypothetical but range over the period *c*2000 BC to the early Christian era.

Alalakh. Ancient name of the north Syrian city located at TELL ATCHANA.

Alamgirpur. Situated northeast of Delhi in the Ganges Valley, Alamgirpur is the easternmost known site of the HARAPPAN CIVILIZATION. The small late Harappan settlement was succeeded after a gap of unknown duration by an occupation with PAINTED GREY WARE, when iron was in use, and by later phases of occupation.

Alapraia. Site of a group of rock-cut tombs of the Copper Age near Lisbon in Portugal. Simple chambers were entered through smaller vestibules. Finds include ritual objects such as clay sandals, clay LUNULAE and so-called 'pine-cones' (named from their shape; their function is unknown). BEAKER pottery also occurred.

Albany industry. A stone industry of southernmost South Africa, dated between the 11th and 6th millennia bc, best known from stratified assemblages at BOOMPLAAS and ROBBERG. It directly precedes the appearance of the local backed-microlith WILTON industry. Albany assemblages contain few formal tools other than unstandardized flake scrapers. Possibly related and broadly contemporary industries are known from as far afield as southern Namibia and Zimbabwe: some archaeologists have proposed grouping this material together under the name OAKHURST Complex. In the South African coastal region it is perhaps significant that the appearance of the Albany industry broadly coincides with the post-Pleistocene rise in sea-level; marine food-resources were exploited on a larger scale than previously.

albarello. A late medieval Spanish drug-jar with particularly fine TIN GLAZE over typically blue designs that imitate the forms of Arabic script. Early albarelli were made in several parts of Spain and have occasionally been found in Britain and the Netherlands.

Alcala. A cemetery of the early metal ages in southern Portugal containing CORBEL-vaulted tombs of the MEGALITHIC tradition. This site, like LOS MILLARES, was formerly thought to be a colony of Aegean settlers; few now accept this view.

Alchi. A town in Ladakh, Tibet, where A.H. Francke discovered and excavated a number of 'nomads' tombs' between 1900 and 1910. The tombs measured approximately 1.8 by 1.4 metres and were *c*1.8 metres deep; they were lined and covered with undressed stone slabs. Each contained from 3 to 20 long-headed skulls, many small hand-made pottery vessels filled with bones, and grave goods. Some of the pottery was decorated with patterns in dark red, or incised, zig-zagged 'ladders' and possibly stylized leaves or grass. The grave goods included bronze beads, *dril-bu* triangular pendants with triangular apertures and a suspension ring, bracelets, a bronze vessel and glass paste beads. Francke thought that the pottery had originally stood on wooden shelves fixed to the walls of the graves. Other examples were found at Teu-gser-po (near sLeh) and at Ba-lu-mk'ar.

Aleppo. A city in north Syria, covering an ancient city which remains unexcavated. Aleppo is located on the route between the Orontes and the Euphrates Valley, and was important for trade from at least the 2nd millennium BC. Because of its importance it was fought over by Hittites, Egyptians and Assyrians. Subsequently,   as texts from UGARIT, ALALAKH and MARI show, it became part of the Persian trading empire, which stretched from DILMUN via the Persian Gulf and the Euphrates to the Mediterranean.

Alexander the Great. Born in 356 BC, Alexander was tutored for six years by the philosopher Aristotle before he succeeded his father Philip as king of Macedonia and the mainland of Greece. He realized the Greeks' long-felt ambition to be free from Persian domination by crushing Darius, but extended the defeat of Persia into a programme of imperial aggrandizement, emerging as an oriental despot with an empire stretching from India to Egypt. After his death from fever in 323 BC this hastily assembled dominion showed immediate signs of dissolution, but a lasting achievement was the founding of the city of ALEXANDRIA on the Nile Delta.

Alexandria. Founded by ALEXANDER THE GREAT in 331 BC on a narrow strip of land in the northwestern area of the Nile Delta, Alexandria soon replaced MEMPHIS as capital of Egypt. With its double harbour favourably situated at a natural intersection of the shipping lanes of the classical world, the new city rapidly achieved a remarkable prosperity and, subsequently, a reputation for the cosmopolitan life-style of its inhabitants. Its celebrated university and library were of focal importance in the manuscript transmission of earlier classical literature, and Alexandrian editing is inevitably reflected in modern editions. The harbour was well-known in antiquity for its gigantic lighthouse, the Pharos, one of the Seven Wonders of the World. A three-tier structure in glistening white limestone, some 110 metres high, the Pharos was destroyed by an earthquake in the

14th century. During the imperial period Alexandria was notorious for its race and religious riots, notably between the large local Jewish community and the new adherents of Christianity.

Alfred Jewel. An outstanding example of 9th-century Anglo-Saxon craftsmanship found at Newton Park, Somerset, in 1893 and now in the Ashmolean Museum, Oxford. The jewel is a unique piece, about 8 cm long, consisting of an oval portrait (believed to be a personification of sight) executed in different coloured CLOISONNÉ, enhanced with filigree wire and backed by a flat piece of gold engraved with foliate decoration. Engraved around the frame are the words which in translation read 'Alfred had me made', assumed to be King Alfred. The meaning and function of the piece are uncertain; one widely held opinion is that it is the top of an aestal or reading pointer.

Alfred the Great. Our impression of King Alfred is largely gained from two sources: the ANGLO-SAXON CHRONICLE, and the biography written by his friend and teacher Asser. Born in Wantage in 849, Alfred succeeded to the throne of Wessex in 871 and had several encounters with invading Danish forces before whom he was forced to flee to Athelney in the remote western part of Wessex in 877. He returned to drive the invaders from his kingdom and force the DANELAW division upon them. Alfred consolidated his victory by establishing the first English fleet and organizing the chain of fortified BURH towns around the southern coast to protect the civilian population. The king was a considerable scholar and translated works such as the *Curia Pastoralis* from Latin into the vernacular language. He died in 899. The connections between Wessex and Carolingia, together with the demise of the Danish threat in Alfred's time, helped to initiate the artistic renaissance centred on WINCHESTER that flourished for two centuries.

Al Hiba. *See* LAGASH.

alignment. A term referring to single or multiple rows of standing stones (MENHIRS). They occur most frequently in Brittany (*see* CARNAC) and in the British Isles, where they are often found in association with STONE CIRCLES or HENGE monuments. Other examples occur in Corsica. Very little dating evidence has been recovered, but it is thought that many belong to the 3rd millennium BC.

Ali Kosh. A TELL in the Deh Luran plain of Khuzistan, southwest Iran, occupied *c*7500-5600 bc. This site, excavated in the 1960s by a team led by Frank Hole and Kent Flannery, was the first early farming site where significant quantities of plant remains were collected by the FLOTATION technique, representing a landmark in the study of the origins of farming. The earliest phase at Ali Kosh, named Bus Mordeh and dated *c*7500-6750 bc, is characterized by simple rectilinear mud-brick buildings and an economy combining wild and domesticated foods. The population herded goat and a few sheep, hunted a variety of wild animals and caught fish. The plant side of the diet was provided by an enormous variety of grasses and legumes; most of these were wild species, but cultivated two-rowed hulled barley and emmer and einkorn wheats occurred in small quantities.

In the succeeding Ali Kosh phase (*c*6760-6000 bc) the same domesticated plants and animals occurred; hunting and fishing were still of great importance, but there was a decline in the collection of wild plant foods, suggesting that cereal cultivation was proving a more successful way of obtaining plant food. The site of this period was larger than the earlier one and had more substantial buildings.

The final phasee of occupation, named Muhammad Jaffar (*c*6000-5600 bc) saw many innovations, including the introduction of pottery. Farming was firmly established by this phase, but the economic evidence shows signs of strain, perhaps as a result of over-exploitation of an area which was always marginal for agriculture, and in the mid-6th millennium bc the site was abandoned. *See* MESOPOTAMIA, Table 2, page 320.

Alişar. A mount southeast of BOGHAZKÖY in northern Anatolia. The lowest stratum comprises eight CHALCOLITHIC levels, beginning late in the 4th millennium BC. The Early Bronze Age levels are characterized by Alişar painted pottery, which was hand-made with a buff or light red burnish, sometimes with geometric patterns in dark brown or buff. Trading contacts with Assyria were established in the third phase of occupation, early in the 3rd millennium BC, and later a *karum* (*see*

KULTEPE) was built. A small number of Cappadocian tablets were recovered; these are a little later in date than the famous tablets from Kultepe, but their contents are similar.

All Cannings Cross. An important site of the Early Iron Age in Wiltshire, southern England. Within this open settlement were rectangular-built houses and evidence of iron smelting. It is noted especially for its fine haematite-coated bowls with horizontal furrows above the carinations. In the earlier, DIFFUSIONIST, view of British prehistory this site was thought to represent a settlement of HALLSTATT intruders.

allée couverte (Fr.). GALLERY GRAVE.

Allen, Major G. (*d.* 1940). One of the pioneers of AERIAL PHOTOGRAPHY between the two World Wars. Piloting his own aircraft and operating a hand-made camera, he took many thousands of aerial photographs, mostly in southern England. He emphasized the value of oblique aerial photographs, as opposed to the vertical views normally taken at that time.

Allerød interstadial. An INTERSTADIAL of the WEICHSELIAN cold stage. It is dated to between 11,800 and 11,000 bp.

alloy. A mixture of metals. Alloys containing only two major metals are known as binary alloys, those with three major constituents as ternary alloys. BRONZE is a binary alloy of copper and tin; brass a binary alloy of copper and zinc. Alloys are not simple mixtures but complex crystalline structures which may differ considerably from any of their constituents; moreover, slight alterations of the proportions of the constituents can bring about significant changes in the properties of the material. Both bronze and brass are considerably harder than copper.

Almerian. A Neolithic culture of southeast Spain of the 5th and 4th millennia BC. A number of open settlements are known (*see* EL GARCEL), usually on hilltops. The houses were constructed of wattle and daub, and were circular in plan, with hearths and storage pits. This culture is known particularly for its tombs, which were round and built of drystone, and were used for single or multiple inhumations; some authorities believe that they were ancestral to the CORBEL-vaulted tombs of the Copper Age (*see* LOS MILLARES). Almerian pottery was plain, with round or pointed bases. During the later stages of the culture copper came into use.

Al Mina. A site on the coast of Syria near the mouth of the Orontes River. It was at least in part a Greek settlement established from Euboea before the end of the 9th century BC and probably called Posideion. It was an entrepôt site, and excavated buildings were all probably warehouses, built to a standard plan. Material of the 8th to 4th centuries BC has been found, indicating strong trading links between Greece and the Near East. In 413 BC Ptolemy of Egypt sacked and destroyed Al Mina and in the 4th century Seleucus, a few kilometres north, became the new trade centre.

The site of Sabouni nearby has yielded large quantities of imported MYCENEAN pottery of the 14th and 13th centuries BC, showing that the site had a long antiquity as a centre for trade with the Aegean world.

Almizaraque. A settlement site in Almeria, southeast Spain, belonging to the Copper Age LOS MILLARES culture. Houses, oval in plan and with traces of plaster, were surrounded by a ditch. Nearby was a MEGALITHIC tomb, similar to those of Los Millares. The site, which was formerly thought to represent one of a group of colonies from the east Mediterranean, is now recognized as a native settlement. In later phases of the settlement BEAKER pottery appears.

Alpera. The Cueva Vieja at Alpera, southeast Spain, has a fine panel of paintings over the back wall of its shallow rock shelter. They belong to the SPANISH LEVANT cycle, probably of the Mesolithic period between about 8000 bc and 5000 bc. The humans include a group of women and some hunters or warriors with bows and arrows as well as head-dresses probably of feathers. The animals include deer, ox and possibly dog.

alphabet. *See* WRITING.

Alsónémedi. A large cremation cemetery of the Hungarian earlier Bronze Age NAGRÉV group, located 30 km south of Budapest, is found near the same village as a large inhumation cemetery of the Late Copper Age

BADEN culture. The Baden graves yielded cart burials and paired oxen burials, indicating the importance of animal traction in the local economy.

Altai. Mountainous region of southern Siberia which has yielded important prehistoric remains. As well as some possible PALAEOLITHIC deposits at Ulalinka Creek, a late glacial occupation is documented on a number of sites including the Ust'Kanskaia Cave. Food-producing cultures appeared probably in the 3rd millennium BC (*see* AFANASIEVO) and the following millennium saw the development of metallurgy, exploiting the important copper ore sources of the Altai itself (*see* ANDRONOVO, KARASUK). In the 1st millennium BC pastoral nomadism, accompanied by the development of horseback riding, was introduced, and the period from the 7th century BC to the 1st century AD is known as the Early Nomad Period. It is known archaeologically from rich burial remains (*see* PAZYRYK), which document a society characterized by marked social differentiation and dominated by a warrior elite, who enjoyed considerable wealth and acquired prestigious goods from far-flung regions. These communities were initially bronze-using, but in the 4th-2nd centuries BC iron gradually replaced bronze for most purposes. A rich animal art style is characteristic of these groups, as of the culturally very similar SCYTHIANS who occupied the steppes of southern Russia to the west (*see* ANIMAL STYLE).

Altamira. One of the two most famous painted PALAEOLITHIC caves (the other being LASCAUX). Altamira is situated in the Cantabrian Mountains in Santander province, northern Spain. The 280-metre-long cave was investigated by Don Marcelino de Sautola in 1875, but the paintings were only noticed several years later and their authenticity was challenged right up to 1902 when Emile CARTAILHAC finally accepted that they were genuine.

Archaeological deposits of the SOLUTRIAN and MAGDALENIAN periods were found in the entrance of the cave. These included artists' materials from a layer dated by radiocarbon to about 13,000 bc, and it seems likely that most of the art dates from this time or a few thousand years later.

The most famous panel is the ceiling of the

low hall near the entrance. It has some 15 bison as well as deer and horses. The style is referred to as polychrome, for several shades are present, but only two basic pigments are used, namely red iron oxide and manganese. Elsewhere there is a hall with black paintings, and symbols are found in several parts of the cave. Some are simple meanders, others are complex box-shapes.

Altar de Sacrificios. A lowland MAYA site located at the junction of the Pasion and Chixoy Rivers in the southwest Peten province of Guatemala. Its earliest remains (Xe pottery) date to 1000 bc, the Middle PRE-CLASSIC. The beginnings of formal architecture (a ceremonial precinct of three thatch-and-pole buildings on packed lime-and-ash floors on raised platforms) date to c500 bc. Due to its prime commercial position on major water routes joining the interior to the coast, the site flourished in the CLASSIC period as a trade station. Major architecture includes plazas, a BALL COURT and a temple-PYRAMID with STELAE and altars located on its steep stairway.

The intrusion of a Mexican-influenced group (probably the PUTUN) becomes evident in the period AD 800-850. A second invasion of more clearly Mexican-associated groups occurs at the very end of the Classic period in c910 (a LONG COUNT date of 889 is the most recent on the site). After this time power shifted up river to the more defensively positioned site at SEIBAL. Both sites were abandoned by 950.

Altin-depe. A large CHALCOLITHIC and Bronze Age settlement in southern Turkmenia, Soviet Central Asia, similar in nature and history to NAMAZGA-DEPE. In its urban (Namazga V) phase of the early 2nd millennium bc (later 3rd millennium BC), it was smaller in size than Namazga-depe itself, covering c45 hectares, but it has been studied more fully than the larger town. A large artisans' quarter, known as the 'Craftsmen's mound', has been discovered, covering c2.5 hectares, where there is evidence for specialized pottery production. Another area seems to have been the residential quarter of the well-to-do, yielding graves with rich goods, including jewellery of precious metals and semi-precious stones, mostly imported materials. One of the most important discoveries was a complex of monumental structures, showing some similarities with the ZIGGURATS of Mesopotamia and interpreted as a religious building, with three main periods of construction. Altin-depe declined in the earlier 2nd millennium BC and was abandoned by about the middle of the millennium.

Altun Ha. A moderately sized CLASSIC MAYA site, located 10 km inland on the coast of Belize [formerly British Honduras]. It is best known for its numerous caches of OBSIDIAN and JADE and other rich exotic material including the largest piece of worked jade in Mesoamerica — a 4.5 kg head of the Maya sun god.

Surrounding agricultural land is of very poor quality, and excavations by David Prendergast have revealed an extensive exploitation of marine resources. It is thought that control of these resources, which include salt, shells and stingray spines (see PERFORATION) accounts for the extraordinary wealth of such a small centre.

Al 'Ubaid. See UBAID.

Amaravati. (1) An area of southern India with a Buddhist STUPA dating from the period c200 BC to 200 AD. It is built of limestone and finely decorated with scenes from the life of the Buddha.

(2) An archaeologically significant territory of CHAMPA, corresponding roughly to the present central Vietnamese province of Quang-nam, also called the Holy Land of Champa. The name undoubtedly derives from the Amaravati region in southern India, famous for its Buddhist art school (2nd-4th century AD) and denotes the antiquity as well as the origin of Indian influence on the eastern coast of the Indochinese Peninsula. See also DONG-DUONG, MI-SON and TRA-KIEU, the three most important sites in the territory.

amber. Fossilized resin. It is soft and easily carved into jewellery and other artefacts. Amber is normally yellow or orange and transparent, but may be clouded due to the presence of many tiny air bubbles. The main source of European amber is as modular fragments in the Tertiary sand deposits of Prussia. These deposits are eroded by the sea, and the amber washes up on the shores of the Baltic and the coasts of eastern England and the Netherlands. There are other sources in the

Mediterranean, but Baltic and Mediterranean sources may be distinguished by infra-red absorption spectrometry (see CHEMICAL ANALYSIS). Amber was utilized in Europe from the MESOLITHIC period onwards, and was widely traded during the Bronze Age.

Ambrona. One of a pair of Lower PALAEO-LITHIC sites (see TORRALBA) in the province of Soria, central Spain. First discovered by the Marques de Cerralbo before World War I, Ambrona was extensively excavated in the early 1960s. The occupants hunted mainly elephants of the species *Elephas antiquus* and also deer and bovines, but at a higher level the horse was by far the most common animal. The hunters made stone hand axes and cleavers of ACHEULIAN type reminiscent of some African sites. The occupation probably dates from the end of the MINDEL or ELSTER glacial period, possibly some 300,000-400,000 years ago.

Amekni. A site in the Hoggar highlands of southern Algeria, dated to about the 7th millennium bc. Pottery was in use even at this early date, and it shows strong similarities with the 'wavy-line' ware of the 'AQUATIC CIVILIZA-TION' as known from EARLY KHARTOUM. Barbed bone harpoon heads, however, were not represented at Amekni: fishing does not appear to have been an important activity, nor was there any convincing evidence for the practice of food-production.

Amersfoot interstadial. An interstadial of the WEICHSELIAN cold stage. It has been dated by radiocarbon to between 68,000 and 65,000 bp, but this is at the extreme range of the technique (see RADIOCARBON DATING) and it may be earlier.

Amfreville. The find spot in Normandy, northern France, of a helmet of the Early LA TÈNE Iron Age. The helmet is made of bronze sheathed in iron and is richly decorated with scroll patterns on encircling gold-band and enamel ornamentation.

amino acid racemization. After death bones, along with the rest of the body, start to de-compose. In bone this involves breakdown and change of the protein component — principally the COLLAGEN. Like other proteins, collagen is built up from amino acid units, and it is these that are separated and

broken down (this decomposition of collagen gives rise to a dating method, NITROGEN DATING). But besides actual breakdown, the amino acids that remain intact are subject to another change. In life, all amino acids have a particular orientation to their molecular structure (this version is called the L-isomer). After death the amino acids re-align to a mirror-image of this molecular structure (the D-isomer). This reaction is called racemiza-tion (or epimerization) and it occurs at a slow, relatively uniform rate. Measurement of the proportion of the D-isomer to L-isomer should therefore provide a dating method. Unfortunately, racemization is also dependent on temperature, groundwater and the degree of breakdown of the collagen molecules. This makes reliable dates difficult to obtain.

Amlash. A site in northwest Iran, southwest of the Caspian Sea, dating to the late 2nd mil-lennium BC. It has not been excavated scientifically, but systematic looting of rich burials has brought onto the market gold and silver vessels and pottery figurines and animal-shaped RHYTONS, similar to material from MARLIK TEPE. Many forged 'Amlash' goods are also in circulation.

Amorgos. An island in the eastern Cyclades, Greece, known especially for its Early Bronze Age cemetery. Single burials in cist graves were accompanied by pottery, copper weapons and often by fine carved stone figurines of characteristic Early CYCLADIC type. These were usually made of marble and some were almost life-size, although most were about one third this size.

Amorites. An AKKADIAN word meaning 'the west', referring to a group of nomadic tribes in the area west of Mesopotamia. Inscriptions attribute to them the downfall of the Ur III Dynasty in the late 3rd millennium BC, but other texts maintain that they lived peacefully among Babylonians. Economics might origin-ally have forced them to raid settlements or become mercenaries to the Babylonians, receiving payments of land. Eventually they became integrated into the population, as many Amorite names in texts suggest. The first eminent Amorite king, Gungunum, of the late 3rd or early 2nd millennium BC, belonged to the Dynasty of Larsa, and shortly afterwards an Amorite Dynasty emerged at Babylon under Sumuabum, initiating what is known as the Old Babylonian period. *See* Table 3, page 321.

amphitheatre. A characteristically Roman development of ideas derived from the classic Greek THEATRE and STADIUM, the amphitheatre is a large-scale construct with tiers of seats rising from a central space, usually an oval. Designed for events of spectacular complexity, the amphitheatre reveals two typically Roman emphases: the great number of spectators accommodated (possibly more than 50,000 at the Colosseum) and the fact that it was widely copied throughout the Roman empire, since the structure was not dependent on the availability of suitably shaped hills as a backdrop. The new model could thus be erected on any terrain and sited inside an urban centre where required.

An early example from the Republican period is to be found at POMPEII. This represents a transitional stage: the seats are supported by soil, as in the Greek theatre, but the soil itself is kept in place by retaining walls. Presumably to avoid problems with the height and weight of the masonry, the central floor of the arena was excavated below the original ground level.

Typical of the Imperial model is the Colosseum in Rome, the amphitheatrum Flavium, where tiers of seating are supported on an intersecting network of vaulted corridors and arches. Roofing so wide an expanse was beyond Roman technology, but here and elsewhere in the Empire a system of ropes, poles and anchorages was apparently devised so that a canvas could be drawn across at least part of the auditorium. The arena of the Colosseum had a false timber floor, below which there wound a labyrinth of service corridors, probably lit only by crude naked torches. The animal cages were situated here, linked with pre-tensioned lifts and automatic trapdoors with the aim of shooting participants and animals up on to the floor of the arena with unexpected speed and precision. There is evidence that such advanced technical features caused continuous trouble, and many modifications were needed. It is interesting to speculate how the Roman engineers solved the staging of the grand opening, when the arena was flooded for a full-scale sea battle.

amphora. A large two-handled storage jar, made of plain pottery, with a rather plump cross-section. The neck and mouth of the pot are narrow, while at the base there is either a conventional platform, fairly broad and thick for stability, or, perhaps more frequently, a blunt-pointed taper, to facilitate setting the vesseel into the ground or for ease of tipping when used on a flat surface. Plain examples were mass-produced in the Greek and Roman world, and universally used for the bulk transport and storage of liquids, notably wine and olive oil. The container would be sealed when full, and the handle usually carried an amphora stamp, impressed before firing, giving details such as the source, the potter's name, the date and the capacity. Amphorae cannot have been of much commercial value and were probably not normally re-used, as witness for instance the so-called Monte Testaccio (Pot Mountain), the great mound of shattered pottery behind the warehouses that lined the River Tiber in classical times, near the present-day Porta San Paolo.

Ampurias [Roman Emporiae, from the Greek *emporion*: 'market']. A trading and staging post some 40 km northeast of present-day Gerona, in the Gulf of Rosas, Costa Brava, Spain, founded by Greeks from Massalia [now MARSEILLES] in the early 6th century BC. Ampurias was probably at its most prosperous in the 5th to 3rd centuries BC, when it established extensive trading links across the Mediterranean, especially with the towns of Magna Graecia, and marked its commercial achievements by minting its own coinage. The town became an ally of Rome in the 3rd century and was used by Scipio to land his army in 218 BC when he carried his offensive against the Carthaginians into Spain. Here as elsewhere, Greek settlement had from the beginning encountered considerable opposition from an indigenous community, and the new Roman presence seems to have brought some alleviation to the uneasy friction. But Roman reorganization was also instrumental in the town's decline, by shifting the centre of administration to Tarraco. The original harbour had also begun to silt up, and was no doubt inadequate for the increased draught of Roman troops and merchant shipping. The end seems to have come with destruction by the Franks in 265 AD, after which no substantial rebuilding was attempted. Minor Christian communities used the area for burials and possibly settlement, and the deserted site suffered the usual fate of becoming a convenient quarry, in this case eventually for the village of L'Escala and the fortifications of Rosas and Perpignan. The last inhabitants seem to have been the monks of a small monastery, who continued the destruction by attempting to return the site to cultivation. The remains of the church and monastery underlie the present site museum.

Three sites should be distinguished. (*a*) The original Greek settlement on what was an offshore island which, due to geological shift and alluvial silting, is now part of the mainland. It is believed to underlie the present village of Sant Marti d'Empuries. (*b*) The slightly later mainland Greek settlement, overlaid by subsequent Roman development. This site has been extensively excavated, and is now open to the public. (*c*) The indigenous settlement just inland, which was to become the basis for a later colony of Roman veterans. This site has only been partially excavated.

Amratian. *See* PREDYNASTIC EGYPT.

Amri. A site in the Indus Valley in Pakistan, which has given its name to one of a group of pre-HARAPPAN cultures in this area. Periods I and II represent the pre-Harappan settlement of agricultural farmers, who kept cattle, sheep, goat and donkey, but also hunted (or herded) gazelle. The Amri culture is characterized by both hand- and wheel-made pottery, some of it painted in black and red geometric designs. Copper was in use, although stone tools also occur. In the later part of Period II Harappan ceramics appear alongside Amri wares; Period III represents a full mature Harappan occupation. This progressed through three subphases and was finally succeeded by a level (IIID) of the post-Harappan JHUKAR culture.

Amud [Amudian]. A valley close to the Sea of Galilee which contains several important caves. Emireh Cave is the type site of the EMIRAN. Zuttiyeh Cave is the type site of the Amudian, supposed to be an early occurrence of Upper Palaeolithic blade tools earlier than the MOUSTERIAN and its flake tools. The Amud cave is Mousterian or Emiran, and has produced a NEANDERTHAL skeleton with exceptionally large brain (1800 cc). Neither the age of this skeleton nor that of the part skull from Zuttiyeh Cave are well established.

Amun. The supreme state god of Ancient Egypt during the New Empire (*see* DYNASTIC EGYPT), the centre of whose worship was at THEBES, the capital. Depicted in male human form, Amun was frequently identified with RE, the sun-god of Heliopolis, as Amun-Re. The priesthood of Amun achieved very great wealth and influence, especially between the 18th and 21st Dynasties.

Amuq. A plain in northern Syria near the Turkish border east of Antioch. The plain is rich in TELL settlements of the prehistoric and later periods. Excavations at Tell JUDEIDAH and other sites by the Oriental Institute of Chicago University in the 1930s established the basic prehistoric sequence for the area (with phases designated by letters: for instance, Amuq A represents the Early Neolithic). Other important sites on the Amuq plain include Tell ATCHANA and ANTIOCH itself.

Amur Neolithic. The Amur River flows into the Pacific Ocean in eastern Siberia. A number of 'Neolithic' cultures (defined by the presence of pottery, but not necessarily by the practice of farming) have been recognized in the Middle and Lower Amur regions. In the Middle Amur the earliest phase is known as the Novopetrovka blade culture. Rather later is the Gromatukha culture, with heavy unifacially flaked adzes and bifacially flaked arrowheads and laurel-leaf knives or spearheads. Both these early cultures are undated. Probably dating to the 3rd millennium BC are the settlements on Osinovoe Lake, which are characterized by large pit houses. The population lived by cultivating millet, representing the first definite food-production in the area, and by fishing. The fourth Neolithic culture in the area, dating to the mid-2nd millennium BC and also characterized by the combination of farming and fishing, is thought to represent a movement of people from the Lower Amur area.

The Neolithic of the Lower Amur is known from sites such as Kondon, Suchu Island and Voznesenovka. Unfortunately no bone survives on the Amur sites, so precise information on the economy is difficult to obtain. However, the economic basis was certainly provided by the great annual fish runs, leading to the establishment of unusually large sedentary settlements of pit houses; this situation parallels the more famous examples from the Northwest coast of North America (*see* KWAKUITL). Kondon has a single radiocarbon date of *c*2570 bc (*c*3300 BC).

There was considerable continuity from the Neolithic to historic times in the Amur Valley. The 1st millennium BC saw the introduction of iron and the construction of some fortified villages. On the Middle Amur millet farming became the basis of life. Otherwise there was little change.

Ananatuba. *See* MARAJO ISLAND SITES.

Ananda-Temple [from Pali *Anantapaññā*: 'infinite wisdom']. The most famous Buddhist brick monument of PAGAN, northern Burma, built under king Kyanzittha and consecrated in 1090. According to legend, it was modelled after the grotto of Nandamūla on Mount Gandamādana, identified with the Ananta cave-temple of the Udayagiri hills of Orissa, or possibly the temple of Paharpur in northern Bengal. Its plan is cruciform, with the central pillar supporting a STUPA. On the outside of the stucco-decorated monument 1500 glazed terracotta plaques illustrate the Jataka stories (lives of the Buddha).

Anasazi. One of three major cultural traditions in the American Southwest which engaged in sedentary agriculture (*see also* HOHOKAM and MOGOLLON). The core area is on the plateau where the borders of New Mexico, Arizona, Utah and Colorado meet (also known as Four Corners). The generally accepted chronological framework of three BASKETMAKER and five PUEBLO stages was first proposed at the 1927 Pecos Conference.

Anasazi emerged from local ARCHAIC adaptations (e.g. Oshara). Although the practice of agriculture characterizes the tradition, the gathering of wild food-plants and hunting continued to play some part in subsistence activities throughout their history. The traditional starting date for the culture is 1 AD, though this now appears somewhat arbitrary. Distinctive cultural traits, however, occur mostly in the period *c*500-1300. Increasing reliance on cultigens, the replacement of basketry with increasingly complex ceramic technology, and the movement from scattered village life to concentrated Pueblo dwellings are all major trends in this period. By 1200 Anasazi influence was widespread

in the Southwest. Both the Hohokam and Mogollon cultures show an increased adoption of Anasazi traits, leading to the suggestion that the Anasazi actually migrated into these areas. The virtual abandonment of the plateau heartland by 1300 lends credence to this proposition.

Anatolia. A mountainous region of northwest Asia, part of present-day Turkey, it is bounded by the Pontine mountains in the north and the Zagros mountains in the south. Rich alluvial deposits in Pleistocene lakes left much fertile land when the water receded. This fact, combined with the rainfall which was adequate for dry farming, made this a suitable area for the early development of farming and a number of early sites are known with dates from *c*7000 bc. The area was also important for its two main sources of OBSIDIAN, in the Çiftlik area and near Lake Van. This material was exploited from the Upper Palaeolithic onwards and was extensively traded in the Neolithic. The area was an important centre in the Neolithic and Chalcolithic, with sites like ÇATAL HÜYÜK and CAN HASAN, but in the succeeding Bronze Age it was less important, with sites mostly known in the south. It later became the homeland of the HITTITE empire in the 2nd millennium BC.

Anau. A site consisting of two separate tells in the Kara Kum desert of southern Turkmenia, Soviet Central Asia, first excavated in the 1880s and again in 1904. It has given its name to a CHALCOLITHIC culture of the 5th millennium bc, which has been recognized on a number of tell sites. Characteristic material includes fine pottery with geometric painted decoration and simple copper tools. The mixed farming subsistence economy and the building traditions indicate continuity from the preceding DJEITUN culture, but the metal ores were probably imported from the south, where both the SIALK culture of Iran (an early metal-working centre) and the HASSUNA culture of Mesopotamia show connections in pottery styles with the Anau culture.

Ancon Yacht Club. *See* ENCANTO.

Andenne ware. An important medieval glazed ware made at and near Andenne on the River Meuse. The potters at Andenne produced ordinary unglazed wares as well as finer pitchers and bowls, but it is the latter which were widely traded around Western Europe from the late 11th century to the 14th century.

Andersson, J.G. (1874-1960). Swedish geologist who worked in China in the second and third decades of this century. His most important excavations were on sites of the YANGSHAO Neolithic culture, including the type site and other sites of the same culture further west in Kansu. He was also the first excavator in 1921-6 of the famous Palaeolithic cave site of ZHOUKOUDIAN (Choukoutien).

Andrai, Walter (1875-1956). A German scholar who excavated the major Mesopotamian city of ASSUR between 1903 and 1914. These excavations were of very high quality for that period. As well as exposing the major buildings of the ASSYRIAN city, they excavated a sounding beneath the great Temple of Ishtar to expose a series of earlier temples, the first of which belonged to the EARLY DYNASTIC PERIOD.

Andronovo. Culture of southern Siberia of the 2nd millennium BC, which succeeded the AFANASIEVO culture in the same area. The population practised farming — cultivating wheat and millet and breeding cattle, sheep and horses — and lived in settlements of up to ten large semi-subterranean houses of log-cabin construction. The burials, which are the best-known monuments of the culture, were either stone cists or stone enclosures with underground timber chambers. Artefacts include pottery and metal tools, which were derived from the ore sources of the ALTAI. The Andronovo was succeeded by the KARASUK culture.

Ang-ang-hsi. A group of Neolithic sites in Manchuria, showing strong connections with the Novopetrovka and Gromatukha cultures of the Middle AMUR in eastern Siberia, especially in lithic technology. Abundant animal, fish and mollusc remains occur on these sites.

Anghelu Ruju. A cemetery site in northwest Sardinia of the OZIERI Copper Age culture. It contained 36 rock-cut tombs, some very elaborate in plan; some were decorated with carved bulls' heads. They were used for multiple burials and yielded copper and silver objects as well as OZIERI and BEAKER pottery.

Angkor [from Sanskrit *nagara*: 'royal city, the capital']. A complex of more than 250 monuments, dating from the 9th to the 13th century and built almost exclusively in sandstone, on a plain just north of the present town of Siem Reap in northwestern CAMBODIA. Here were the capitals of the KHMER empire from its foundation in 802 to the conquest of Angkor by the Thais (Siamese) in 1431.

Angkor Borei [from Sanskrit *puri*: 'sacred city']. The capital of the kingdom of FUNAN, in the southern part of the Indochinese Peninsula, for some time towards the end of this kingdom in the 6th century. It appears as Na-fu-na in Chinese chronicles, which can be identified with Naravaranagara, and is now a rich archaeological site in Cambodia, south of Phnom Penh near the border with Vietnam. These is much famous statuary in stone, attributable mainly to king Rudravarman; no building of this site and period has as yet been studied.

Angkor Thom [Khmer: 'the big capital']. City situated in the northwestern part of the plain of ANGKOR. It was the capital of the KHMER empire intermittently from the 11th century onward, notably during the reign of king Jayavarman VII (1181-c1218) who surrounded it with walls and moats of 4 by 4 km and built its own TEMPLE-MOUNTAIN, the BAYON, in its very centre.

Angkor Wat [Khmer: 'the capital (which has become a Buddhist) monastery']. The best-known monument of ANGKOR, supposed to be the largest religious structure in the world. Built under king Suryavarman II (1113-1150) as his TEMPLE-MOUNTAIN, it was completed in about 25 years. Situated in an enclosure of 1.5 by 1.3 km, it consists of a three-storeyed pyramid, topped by five towers (symbolizing the five peaks of Mount Meru, the abode of the gods in Hindu cosmology), the central one being 65 metres high. The first storey is devoted to reliefs, of which there are two square kilometres. Angkor Wat is considered to be the highest expression of Khmer classicism, both in architecture and in sculpture-relief.

Angles-sur-l'Anglin. The Roc aux Sourciers at Angles, in the Vienne department, west central France, is a rock shelter with Upper Palaeolithic art. The back wall has fine bas-relief carvings: an outstanding frieze of three female figures in frontal view dominates the shelter, and there are several animal carvings. The occupation deposits are middle and late MAGDALENIAN; the art is dated to c11,000 bc.

Anglian. A group of British QUATERNARY glacial deposits, mainly found in East Anglia; isolated patches of glacial deposits exist elsewhere in Britain which may possibly be correlated with the Anglian. The exact age of the Anglian sediment is unknown, but they are older than the extreme range of RADIO-CARBON DATING (70,000 bp) and can be shown by PALAEOMAGNETISM to be younger than 700,000 BP. Some authorities equate the Anglian with the Elster glacial maximum on the continent and date it to c300,000 to 400,000 years ago. In East Anglia, Anglian deposits are stratified below HOXNIAN and above CROMERIAN interglacial deposits. ACHEULIAN and CLACTONIAN artefacts are found in Anglian sediments, but most evidence of human activity in Britain and in the rest of Europe is later than this time (see Table 6, page 419). It used to be thought that the Anglian represented one glaciation (the antepenultimate) and the term is still frequently used with this meaning. The Quaternary in Britain is now known to be much more complex and such a usage is not advisable; the term Anglian is better confined to the description of a group of deposits.

Anglo-Saxon. A broad term used to describe the majority of the Germanic peoples who settled in England during the 5th and 6th centuries. The name derives from two specific groups — the Angles of Jutland and the Saxons from northern Germany — who were probably among the migrants. Earlier archaeological work concentrated on attempts to recognize separate groups (especially the Angles, Saxons and Jutes mentioned by BEDE) in the archaeological record, but this has now been abandoned as an unprofitable exercise. The term Anglo-Saxon, or simply Saxon, is now generally used as a chronological term, covering the period from the first Germanic invasions of the 5th century up till the Norman invasion of 1066.

During the Early or Pagan Saxon period (up to the mid-7th century) before Christianity was widely adopted, rich grave goods were placed with the dead and most archaeological evidence comes from the cemeteries, including the exceptional ship burial at SUTTON HOO. Settlements of this period are also known, including WEST STOW and MUCKING, where both a settlement and a cemetery have been excavated.

After the adoption of Christianity, following St Augustine's mission in 597 (see CANTERBURY), churches were built and in the Middle and especially the Late Saxon periods form a major focus of Anglo-Saxon studies. Early examples include BRADFORD-UPON-AVON and Deerhurst. Very important monuments of the Middle and Late Saxon periods are the royal palaces at YEAVERING and Cheddar (see CHEDDAR, sense 2).

After the VIKING invasions of the 9th century AD the Late Saxon period saw the growth of the first towns in Britain since the Roman period, following the establishment of BURHS in response to the Scandinavian threat. Large-scale excavations have taken place in the Saxon towns of THETFORD, WINCHESTER and SOUTHAMPTON (Saxon Hamwih). This period is also characterized by wide-ranging trade, a developed coinage and improved levels of craft skills in pottery manufacture and metal-working.

The Anglo-Saxon period saw the emergence of separate British kingdoms, traditionally seven in number, of which the most important were MERCIA, NORTHUMBRIA and WESSEX. These ultimately coalesced in a unified England, with its capital at WINCHESTER in Wessex. The Anglo-Saxons were responsible for the introduction of the English language and for the establishment of the settlement pattern which became characteristic of medieval England.

Anglo-Saxon Chronicle. A compilation of annals, believed to have been initiated around 870, during the reign of ALFRED. The major part was completed by 891, but further accounts were added up until the 12th century. The annals were probably composed in English in the monasteries of Abingdon, Canterbury, Peterborough, Winchester and Worcester. They include particularly vivid accounts of the Viking raids, Alfred's reign and, in the later additions, of the period of anarchy under Stephen.

Animal Style. A term coined by Rostovzteff to describe the horse-trappings and personal regalia of the nomads who inhabited the Eurasian steppes in the 1st millennium BC. The animal themes that dominate this art are treated with widely varying degrees of conventionalization, stylization or abstraction. With a few notable exceptions (e.g. the *animal enroulé*, probably from China), the motifs seem to have originated in the Near East, but the transformations they underwent in the course of their long history on the steppes often leave the sources and affiliations of particular versions obscure. The most popular themes are antlered stags, ibexes, felines, birds of prey and, above all, the animal-combat motif, which shows a predator, usually bird or feline, attacking a herbivore. The joining of different animals and the use of tiny animal figures to decorate the body of an animal are characteristic treatments, both sometimes referred to as 'zoomorphic juncture'. Animal bodies subjected to stylized contortions such as the *animal enroulé* (an animal curved into a circle) and quadrupeds with hindquarters inverted are also typical. The term 'Animal Style' is a convenient shorthand for this complex of motifs and treatments, which for long periods provided the raw materials of art throughout the vast steppe zone of Europe and Asia.

Within the fairly well-defined repertoire of favourite themes, however, Animal Style objects from different regions and periods show an immense diversity of style: a plaque from Scythia and another from the ORDOS may share the animal-combat motif and yet have no other stylistic feature in common. Thus to assume that nomadic cultures are mysteriously linked by the possession of a uniform artistic style, as the name 'Animal Style' unfortunately suggests, raises artificial problems. If the artificiality of the term is kept in mind there will be little occasion to explain the Animal Style as the inevitable artistic expression of shamanistic religion or of the nomadic way of life — interpretations not easily reconciled with the occurrence of the animal-combat motif at PERSEPOLIS or on a Protoliterate vase from URUK or in the DIAN culture of southwest China. Since the present state of archaeological knowledge of the steppes often does not permit the assignment of particular objects to specific tribes or regions, a broadly inclusive term is useful and convenient. If the designation 'Animal Style' is to be at all meaningful, some limits to its scope should be recognized. In particular, it should not be extended to include all art dependent on animal motifs, since this would deprive it of any historical significance ('Animal Style art' would then be found in cultures indebted neither to the steppe nomads nor to the ancient Near East). The bronze decoration of SHANG China is dominated by real and imaginary animals, but Shang decoration originated independently of the Eurasian Animal Style and shares with it neither specific motifs nor treatments of motifs; to call it 'Animal Style art', as some authors have done, is misleading at best.

annealing. *See* COLD WORKING.

antefix. A vertical ornament fixed to the edge of the roof-line of Greek and Roman buildings to provide a decorative cover to the ends of the rain tiles.

Antequera. A town in Malaga, southern Spain, renowned for its three MEGALITHIC tombs, Cueva de Menga, Cueva de Viera and Cueva de Romeral. They are partly cut into the hillside and are constructed in various different ways. The Cueva de Menga has an enormous chamber $c5$ metres wide and $c15$ metres long, roofed by five large CAPSTONES supported by three central pillars and drystone walls. The Cueva de Romeral has a splendid CORBEL vault.

Antioch. An ancient city near the River Orontes in Syria. The plain of Antioch was occupied from the Neolithic onwards (*see* AMUQ), but the city itself was founded in 300 BC by Seleucus I after the death of ALEXANDER THE GREAT. Antioch was one of the two capitals of the PARTHIAN Empire and was populated by indigenous groups and Greek colonists. It became a Roman city in 64 BC and was made capital of the province of Syria.

antlers. Structures of bone-like material on the heads of deer, grown and shed annually. Providing a large enough fragment remains, antlers can frequently be identified to species. The number of points or tines on a pair of antlers generally increases with age, but as it is also dependent on diet and other factors, antlers are not reliable as a method of ageing. They may, however, be used as an indicator of sex: only the male red deer, fallow deer, roe deer or elk (moose) has antlers. Both male and female reindeer (caribou) have antlers, but there is enough difference between them to make identification possible in many cases. Antlers may also be used as an indicator of the seasonal occupation of a site. Most deer shed their antlers naturally in winter, the exception being female reindeer, which shed their antlers in the spring. The quantity of shed as opposed to deliberately severed antler, and of male as opposed to female reindeer, allows the season of occupation to be estimated. Antler has provided a valuable working material for many tools, and roughly trimmed antler picks have been used in construction and FLINT MINING.

Antonine Wall. A short-lived frontier of the Roman Empire in Scotland, spanning the distance between the Firth of Forth and the Firth of Clyde. The wall was probably completed by 143 and abandoned before the end of the century. Erected by the governor Lollius Urbicus for the Emperor Antonius Pius, it was probably a last attempt to secure the Scottish Lowlands. Consisting mainly of turf piled upon a stone foundation, the wall had a defensive ditch to the north (some 12 metres wide and 4 metres deep), a service road to the south, and some 19 forts stationed at regular intervals. The main rampart (*vallum*) was perhaps originally some 4.6 metres high and some 4.3 metres deep. The wall was associated with other forts, notably to the north and along the southern edges of the Forth and the Clyde. The work was executed by men from the legions currently stationed in Britain, and was evidently completed section by section, by different work gangs who left behind a record of their exertions in the form of decorative plaques, a number of which survive. Such a far-flung contract would have required temporary camps for the constructors, and there is perhaps evidence of these in crop markings revealed in aerial photographs. A well-preserved fort site is Rough Castle.

Anu. The SUMERIAN sky god, originally standing at the head of the pantheon, although he was later overtaken by Enlil and Marduk.

He was particularly associated with the city of URUK, where a series of seven superimposed temples were found in a sanctuary dedicated to Anu, but he was eventually overshadowed there by the city's rival deity Inanna, goddess of love, whose Semitic name was Ishtar. Anu's main attribute was royalty, and from him the institution of kingship descended to man.

Anuradhapura. Capital of Sri Lanka from the time of the introduction of Buddhism in the 3rd century BC until it was abandoned in the 8th century AD, as a result of incursions of Tamils from South India. Important Buddhist monuments here include palaces, monasteries and STUPAS, many of which have been conserved and restored. Among the most famous are the Thuparama stupa, originally of the 3rd century BC, the Ruvanveli dagaba (another enormous stupa) and the Lohapasada monastery, both of which were originally built in the 1st century BC.

Anyang [An-yang]. A city in Henan province in North China, near the site of the last capital of the SHANG or Yin dynasty. The site is sometimes referred to as Yinxu, the Waste of Yin, an ancient name for the abandoned capital. At least as early as the SONG dynasty (960-1279) Anyang was known as a source of bronze RITUAL VESSELS prized by antiquarians. At the beginning of the 20th century archaeologists were led there by the discovery that ORACLE BONES found by local farmers carried inscriptions in an archaic form of Chinese. The inscriptions secured the identification of the site as the last Shang capital; according to later texts this capital was the seat of 12 kings who ruled for 273 years, a time referred to as the historical Anyang period (*c*1300-1030 BC on the short chronology; *see* SHANG).

Excavations at Anyang begun in 1928 have continued under the direction of the Academia Sinica to the present day. The Anyang remains are distributed over a large area divided by the Huan River, which has eroded parts of the site. No city wall has been found (*see* ZHENGZHOU). South of the river at Xiaotun were excavated the HANGTU foundations of large buildings and a few associated sacrificial burials, including CHARIOT BURIALS. Very large cruciform SHAFT TOMBS were found north of the river at Xibeigang near the village of Houjiazhuang.

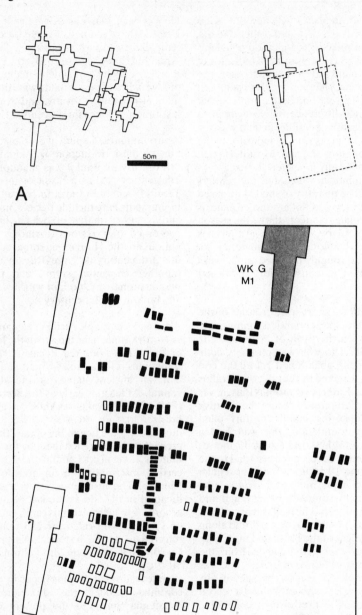

WK G
M1

A) Anyang: plan of Xibeigang royal cemetery
B) Anyang: detail of part of the cemetery

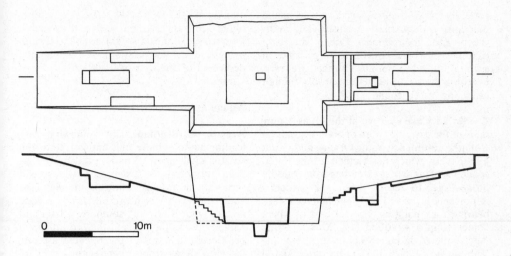

Anyang: plan and section of tomb WK G M1

Because of their size these are assumed to be royal tombs, but all had been stripped by robbers before excavation. There were eight large tombs in the western part of the Xibeigang cemetery and five more in the east (north of the village of Wuguancun). Careful excavation has shown that rows of satellite burials in the eastern section were not laid down at the time of the royal entombments but instead represent later sacrifices offered periodically to the tombs' occupants; these burials correspond precisely with mentions in the oracle texts of victims sacrificed, sometimes by the hundred, to the reigning king's ancestors. The only intact royal tomb yet discovered is that of FU HAO, which is not in the Xibeigang cemetery but across the river at Xiaotun.

The first excavations at Anyang were an unexpected revelation of the antiquity of Chinese civilization. For some years, while Anyang was the only Shang site known, scholars were puzzled by the unheralded appearance of this literate and sophisticated Bronze Age culture, already at a pinnacle of wealth and achievement. Excavations since 1950, however, have established that Anyang was heir to the flourishing civilization of the ERLIGANG PHASE, and the study of Chinese Bronze Age origins now centres on earlier periods and other sites.

Anyathian. A PLEISTOCENE industry of pebble tools and flakes made of silicified tuff and fossil wood, found in terrace deposits of the upper Irrawaddy River in Burma. The earliest assemblages may be of Middle Pleistocene date, and the industry may continue into the early HOLOCENE. *See also* CHOPPER/CHOPPING TOOL.

Anza [Anzabegovo]. A large open settlement of the Macedonian First Neolithic and Early VINČA periods situated on the first terrace of the Bregalnica River in the Ovče Polje basin of eastern Yugoslav Macedonia. Intensive excavations by Korošec, Garašanin and Gimbutas have revealed a four-phase occupation dated c5300-4200 bc. Each successive village cultivated emmer and bread wheat and relied upon caprine herding. Architectural styles were modified from initial use of mudbrick walls to wattle-and-daub timber-framed houses, presumably an adaptation to the temperate climate. Artefactual similarities are found in northern Greece (NEA NIKOMEDEIA), as well as the Anatolian Late Neolithic (HACILAR VI); a life-size fired clay pig was found in the early Neolithic levels.

Apennine Bronze Age. The main Bronze Age culture of the Italian peninsula, lasting from c2000 to c800 BC. It is marked by its distinctive pottery, dark and highly burnished, and decorated with incised and punctuated bands. The handles are elaborate and include tongue, horned and crested types. It is often claimed that the economy was mainly pastoral and certainly many sites, especially those in the Apennine mountains themselves, yield many sheep and goat bones. Other sites, for example, LUNI and NARCE, show evidence of a more mixed economy. Burials are rare, except in the southeast. Bronze tools, though in use, are rarely found.

Apollo 11 Cave. A cave in the Huns Mountains of the extreme south of Namibia, not far from the confluence of the Orange and Great Fish Rivers, which has yielded a long dated sequence of industries extending from 'Middle Stone Age' to recent times. Of particular importance is the series of detached rock slabs bearing rock-paintings, the earliest of which comes from a stratified late 'Middle Stone Age' context dating to about the 25th millennium bc. This is by far the oldest dated attestation of the ROCK ART of southern Africa, and shows for the first time that the duration of this art tradition is of the same order of magnitude as that of European Palaeolithic art. Later horizons at the Apollo 11 Cave yielded a scraper-based industry of the 13th-8th millennia bc akin to the contemporary ALBANY INDUSTRY of the southern Cape Province. True backed microlithic occurrences began in the 8th millennium.

Aq Kupruk. A rock shelter (Aq Kupruk II) and an open site (Aq Kupruk III) on a terrace of the Balkh River. This is one of the richest PALAEOLITHIC sites in Afghanistan, but not the earliest; Lower Palaeolithic material is reported from Dasht-i Nawar and possible Middle Palaeolithic deposits occur at Dara-i Kur, Ghar-i Mordeh Gusfand, Kara Kamar, and other sites. Aq Kupruk II contained a single late Palaeolithic deposit with a blade industry, including microliths, associated with a radiocarbon date of c14,600 bc. Aq Kupruk III yielded two deposits: the upper unit (AK III-A) has the same artefacts as Aq Kupruk II, but the lower unit (AK III-B) lacks the microlithic element. Neither deposit has been dated.

'Aqrab, Tell. A TELL site in the area of the Diyala River in Iraq east of Baghdad, excavated by the Oriental Institute of Chicago University in the 1930s. The mound is now in empty desert, but it was clearly a flourishing city in the 3rd millennium BC. Excavations revealed a temple with building phases spanning the EARLY DYNASTIC period. The temple of ED II was large and included the main sanctuary, two subsidiary shrine chambers and living quarters for priests. It was apparently dedicated to Shara, patron god of the city of Umma.

Aquae Sulis. *See* BATH.

Aquatic Civilization. This somewhat misleading name — more fully and correctly 'the aquatic civilization of middle Africa' — has been proposed to designate a widespread series of cultural adaptations to the high lake and river levels which prevailed over a wide area of what is now the southern Sahara and Sahel between the 8th and the 3rd millennia bc. Certain features of the relevant assemblages do show strong inter-regional similarities, notably the barbed bone harpoon-heads and the pottery, which is characteristically decorated with parallel wavy lines. It is likely that pottery was an independent invention in the southern Sahara in about the 7th millennium, and the harpoons clearly represent a common response to the rich supplies of fish which formed the most readily available source of food. However, other aspects of the assemblages, notably the chipped stone industries, are clearly rooted in local traditions, and the homogeneity of these widespread sites should not be exaggerated. First investigated at EARLY KHARTOUM, sites of this type are now known as far to the southeast as the Lake Turkana basin in Kenya, as at LOWASERA. To the west, related material is found as far distant as KOUROUNKOROKALE in Mali. The greatest significance of the 'aquatic civilization' lies in the settled life-style of its people, for this provided the background for the subsequent adoption of food-production (*see* AFRICAN FOOD-PRODUCTION).

aqueduct. Any channel constructed for the supply of water, but most commonly applied to the massively engineered arched bridges built by the Romans both to carry water supplies over valleys and ravines, and also to maintain correct height and fall across open spaces. The most famous examples are the PONT DU GARD outside Nîmes (Roman Nemausus) in southern France, and the colossal double-tiered example at SEGOVIA in Spain. Building costs were high (Aqua Marcia cost 180,000,000 sesterces) and maintenance was also expensive and demanding. Leakage was a dominant problem, and it is likely that a typical installation operated with high water losses. An aqueduct would usually terminate at a distribution junction (*castellum*) whence public and private supplies would be drawn, with non-essential consumers taking the overflow water, and time limits being generally applied.

Arab'ilu. *See* ERBIL.

Arad. Located in the Negev desert of southern Israel, Arad has revealed evidence of three separate phases of occupation. The first settlement was in the CHALCOLITHIC period and the second in the Early Bronze I and II phases. At this stage, in the later 4th millennium BC, it was a town of *c* nine hectares, initially unwalled, later surrounded by a wall with semicircular bastions. Houses and twin temples of this phase have been excavated. Trading connections with First Dynasty Egypt were apparent from the finds.

The later period of occupation was represented over a smaller area, confined to a citadel on the highest part of the earlier town. It was occupied from the 12th-11th centuries BC and became a southern frontier post of the kingdom of Judah. The most important find of this period is a sanctuary associated with worship of Yahweh. There were citadels on this site also in the Hellenistic and Roman periods and subsequently an Arab *khan.*

Aramagosa. *See* VENTANA CAVE.

Arauquinoid, Arauquin. One of the ceramic series developed by Irving Rouse and José Cruxent to facilitate cultural comparison in the Venezuela/Antilles area. Characterized by soft-textured, grey-coloured vessels tempered with spicules of freshwater sponge, the series flourished in the Orinoco basin from *c*500 to *c*1500 AD. The collared jar with appliquéd human faces with coffee-bean eyes is a common form; fragments of GRIDDLES are also found at most sites. The series replaces SALADOID and BARRANCOID in some places.

Arausio. *See* ORANGE.

Arawak. A number of linguistically associated native groups (e.g. TAINO) which occupied a broad area covering northeastern South America and much of the Caribbean. A southern origin is probable for this skilled pottery-making agricultural group, but a late MESOAMERICAN influence may be inferred from the presence of BALL COURTS and ZEMI worship. Although they were displaced in many areas (especially in the Lesser Antilles) by aggressive CARIB migrants, the Arawak still numbered millions at the time of the arrival of Colombus.

arboreal. To do with trees. In POLLEN ANALYSIS, arboreal pollen types may be distinguished from shrub pollen and herbaceous pollen. Hazel is usually separated from other trees in calculating PROPORTIONAL POLLEN COUNTS.

archaeomagnetism. *See* PALAEOMAGNETISM.

Archaic. In general usage, 'archaic' means primitive or antiquated, but in archaeology the term is used in a number of specific ways.

In American archaeology, the term Archaic has two different usages:
(1) A broad-based way of life with small bands exploiting their environment by means of hunting and gathering in a pattern of seasonal movement linked to the availability of subsistence foods.
(2) A long chronological period, the beginning of which is marked by post-glacial climatic change in association with the disappearance of Late PLEISTOCENE big game animals. It is considered to have ended when sedentary agriculture becomes the favoured means of subsistence. There is considerable local variation in the occurrence of these events, which makes dating difficult. In North American archaeology dates usually fall between *c*8000 and *c*1000 BC. *See* Table 9, page 552.

In Classical archaeology, the term is used to refer to the period of the 8th-6th centuries BC, preceding the CLASSICAL period proper.

archaic maiolica. A great range of jugs and bowls carefully decorated with geometric motifs, leaves and other forms outlined in brown and set in green or brown backgrounds. These wares were made from the early 13th century until the 16th century in many Tuscan and north Italian towns, with certain specialized pots, such as the wares of Montelupo, being sold far afield in Spain, North Africa and even northern Europe. The precise origin of these wares, like the PROTO-MAIOLICAS, is a matter of controversy but it doubtless owes much to the Byzantine and early Persian products of a similar kind although the decorations were clearly designed in Italy.

Arctic Small Tool Tradition. A generalized hunting tradition, evidence of which has been found within a wide geographical band stretching from the Bering Sea across the north Canadian coast as far east as Greenland. The DENBIGH FLINT COMPLEX, named from the type site at Cape Denbigh, Alaska, is the characteristic tool assemblage; tool types include delicately made blades, microblades, BURINS and scrapers, as well as some large bifacial projectile points. Approximate dates are 4000-1000 bc. See Table 9, page 552.

Arcy sur Cure. A group of caves some 160 km southeast of Paris with good examples of Upper Palaeolithic art. The Grotte du Cheval has a series of engravings including a fine mammoth. Archaeologically the most important are the Grotte de l'Hyene and the Grotte du Renne. 'Hyena cave' has early occupation levels of the RISS period, and several MOUSTERIAN levels with NEANDERTHAL remains. The 'reindeer cave' has a long sequence from Mousterian and CHATELPERRONIAN through AURIGNACIAN to later PERIGORDIAN along with radiocarbon dates and pollen evidence. Teeth from the Chatelperronian levels retain archaic features like taurodontism.

ard. A primitive form of plough, pulled by man or beast. It has a simple blade with a share which simply scratches the ground and does not turn a furrow. With this type of plough cross-ploughing is normally necessary, involving two ploughings, the second at right angles to the first.

Ardagh Chalice. One of finest examples of early Christian art known from the British Isles. Found in the last century, its association with another chalice and four brooches suggests that it could be part of the buried loot from a monastery following an Irish or Viking raid. The chalice is an 8th-century piece, in which exceptional artistic and technical skills have been applied to a variety of precious materials to produce an object of rare beauty.

The form is simple: a round silver bowl with two handles standing on a splayed foot, to which it is linked by a band decorated in gilded FILIGREE. The decoration is sumptuous, and strongly resembles Irish ILLUMINATED MANUSCRIPTS of the period as well as ANGLO-SAXON metalwork. On the bowl are bands of gold filigree, and roundels built up of plaques containing enamelling and CLOISONNÉ work, gold wire in the form of Celtic scrolls, and animal interlace. The names of the apostles stand out in embossed silver below the plaques. The flange surrounding the foot of the chalice is heavily ornamented with square blue glass blocks, interspersed with filigree work and geometric interlace ornament.

areca nut. See BETEL NUT.

arena [Latin: 'sand']. The central area in particular of an amphitheatre, which was originally surfaced with a simple sandy floor. When more sophisticated technology was developed 'understage', the surface was often still coated with sand to give an overall uniformity and to conceal trapdoors and other devices; see AMPHITHEATRE.

Arene Candide. A cave site at Finale Ligure on the Italian Riviera, with a stratigraphy extending from the Upper PALAEOLITHIC to the Late Neolithic and, at a poorer level, through to the Roman period. The site was excavated in the 1940s by Bernabò Brea and played an important role in his interpretation of the Neolithic period in the Mediterranean.

Arezzo. See ARRETIUM.

argali. See SHEEP.

Argissa. An important Neolithic settlement site in Thessaly, Northern Greece, which has yielded much evidence of the ACERAMIC NEOLITHIC period. Wheat, barley, lentils and millet were cultivated and sheep, goats, pigs and cattle kept. Houses with timber frames supporting mud walls have been dated before 6000 bc. Tools of flint and obsidian were used.

Argos. City in the northeast Pelopponese, Greece. Ancient Argos, which is mostly covered by the modern city, lay a few miles inland on the Argive plain, overlooked by two hills, the Larissa and the Aspis, both of which show early traces of use as a fortified centre or ACROPOLIS. The city is clearly of central importance in the prehistory of the area, with some evidence of settlement going back to the Neolithic period. Tradition and myth have Argos as a very early Pelasgian foundation, and Homer's *Iliad* describes it as the kingdom of Diomedes, who was second only to Achilles in bravery, and gave his allegiance to Agamemnon (whose capital was at nearby MYCENAE). Dorian association appears to have brought continued ascendancy, and by the 8th-7th centuries BC Argos is credited with the control of the entire eastern Pelopponese. One tyrant, Pheidon, is mentioned by some sources as introducing a primitive form of coinage and a system of weights and measures. The subsequent classical history of Argos is dominated by a power struggle with Sparta, and Argos hastened to join every kind of anti-Spartan conspiracy and alliance.

Material evidence gives Neolithic, Early and Middle Bronze Age remains, a MYCEN-AEAN cemetery with chamber tombs, GEOME-TRIC and ARCHAIC features, and plentiful traces of the classical and Roman city.

Archaic and classical Argos was famed for its connection with the goddess Hera, and for its schools of sculpture. Hera's shrine (Heraeum) lay some 10 km to the north and some 5 km from Mycenae and, for a time, seems to have been jointly maintained by both. The shrine was reputed to be of extreme antiquity, and this is not improbable. A chryselephantine statue of Hera was contributed to a new 5th-century temple by Argos's most celebrated sculptor, Polycleitus, the legendary quality of whose work has reckoned to rival that of Pheidias, the sculptor of the PARTHENON.

Arikamedu. A site on the Madras coast of southern India, excavated by Mortimer WHEELER. A native Iron Age settlement with BLACK AND RED WARES, it yielded evidence of abundant trading contact with the Romans from the mid-1st century BC onwards, attested by finds of ARRETINE WARE, Mediterranean amphorae and Roman coins. During this period it grew into a sizeable town with warehouses and an industrial quarter, and it was clearly an important trading outpost for the Romans.

Arikara. *See* MIDDLE MISSOURI TRADITION.

Arimaddanapura. Original name of the city of PAGAN in northern Burma, founded in 849.

Arinna. *See* ALACA HÜYÜK.

Ariuşd [Erösd]. The eponymous site of a small regional painted ware variant of the CUCU-TENI-TRIPOLYE culture. The site, one of the few TELLS found in southeast Transylvania, is in the catchment of the Upper Olt Valley, Rumania. Excavated by F. László, the site has seven occupation horizons. Levels I-VI contain Ariuşd painted ware, with interesting examples of gold jewellery and copper artefacts (pins, daggers, beads and bracelets); level VII represented a late Copper Age assemblage of Schneckenberg type.

Arkin. A location near Wadi Halfa in the Nubian Nile Valley, where a number of Stone Age sites have been investigated. Of particular interest are factory sites for the preparation of rough-outs for foliate points of the local Later MOUSTERIAN tradition, These factories, the products of which also show affinities to Saharan ATERIAN artefacts, are probably contemporary with the nearby settlements at KHOR MUSA.

Arles [Roman Arelate]. City in southern France. A Celto-Greco-Roman town of Gallia Narbonensis (*see* GAUL) was situated on the left bank of the Rhône, close to the head of the delta. Very little is known of the Celto-Greek settlement, traditionally colonized by the Phocaeans. Significant history probably commences with the construction by Marius in 104 BC of the *fossae Marianae,* a naval canal linking Arles directly with the sea at the Golfe de Fos. Arles soon began to develop what was to be its characteristic role and the basis of its commercial success throughout the Imperial period — the function of service port and naval shipyard. The port was used as naval base by Caesar in 49 BC in his sack of Massilia [MAR-SEILLES], and in 46 BC a colony (*see* COLONIA) was founded for veterans of the 6th legion (Colonia Iulia Paterna Arelate Sextanorum). Romanization in due course provided two aqueducts which brought water from the Alpilles.Christianization saw Arles as the residence of Constantine for a time, and the town became an influential centre for ecclesiastical councils of the 4th and 5th centuries AD.

Remains from the Roman period notably include an imperial Roman theatre, and the largest AMPHITHEATRE north of the Alps (Les Arènes), with seating originally perhaps for more than 20,000 spectators. Both of these buildings have suffered badly as a result of being used as forts during the medieval period — the amphitheatre being converted into a fortified town with watch-towers, three of which survive.

Arlit. *See* TENERE NEOLITHIC.

aroids. The edible tubers of the family *Araceae* were of major importance in prehistoric Oceanic subsistence, and of sporadic importance through South and Southeast Asia. The major species, grown from India to Oceania, is *Colocasia esculenta* (taro), which is irrigated in terraced or bunded fields in many Oceanic regions, especially NEW CALEDONIA, VANATU, HAWAIIAN and COOK ISLANDS). Also important are *Alocasia macrorrhiza*, (India to Oceania) and *Cyrtosperma chamissonis* (grown in INDONESIA and Oceania, and widely cultivated in pits cut to ground water on MICRONESIAN atolls). These Indo-Oceanic species were cultivated by at least 3000 BC according to linguistic evidence, and *Colocasia* had spread from India to Egypt and Africa by the late 1st millennium BC. The aroids are of declining importance today. *See also* HALAWA, KUK, MAKAHA.

Arpachiyah, Tell. A small TELL of the HALAFIAN period near Mosul in Iraq excavated by Mallowan in the 1930s. The site appears to have been a specialized artisan village producing exceptionally fine polychrome pottery. The settlement had cobbled streets, rectangular buildings and other circular buildings with domed vaults, inappropriately compared to Mycenaean THOLOI. Later examples had rectangular anterooms. The function of these buildings is unknown: both religious and secular usages have been suggested. In addition to the painted polychrome wares, other finds include steatite pendants and small stone discs with incised designs, interpreted as early stamp seals.

Arras. A site in Yorkshire, northern England, which has given its name to a local group of the LA TÈNE Iron Age. This site is one of several cemeteries of barrows covering burials, some with chariots. The group is regarded as intrusive and has been associated with the migrations of the Parisii from eastern France.

Arretine ware. *See* ARRETIUM; TERRA SIGILLATA.

Arretium [modern Arezzo]. An Etruscan and Roman city some 80 km southeast of Florence on the Via Cassia, celebrated in antiquity for the fine workmanship of its city walls and its pottery. Remains of the city walls, closely constructed and variously of stone and lightly fired brick, have been discovered; it is likely that these fortifications were destroyed as one of the punishments visited on the town for supporting Marius against Sulla. A considerable degree of industrialization is indicated by the quantity of bronze produced, including the famous chimaera now in Florence and the extensive bronze armaments supplied for Scipio's African expedition, as well as the mass production of pottery. Arretine ware, a glossy red tableware, both plain and relief-decorated, was produced at Arretium from around 30 BC, and came to dominate imperial markets for a century. The designs were imitative of metal vessels and had Hellenistic models: there is evidence that both the technology and the potters were imported from the Hellenistic East. Several factories, notably that of M. Perennius and his school, have been identified within Arretium and outside the city walls. As Arretine output declined, other centres developed to supply the continuing demand for this type of ware, and Arretine became the first example of the whole class of TERRA SIGILLATA pottery.

arrow straightener. A stone with a regular groove on one face, thought to have been used to smooth the wooden shafts of arrows.

arsenic. A metal, found as an impurity or major constituent in COPPER ores. Some Early Bronze Age copper contains more than 1 per cent and up to 7 per cent of arsenic, and should be classed as arsenical copper ALLOYS.

Arthur. There is little resemblance between the legendary chivalric hero of medieval romance and the 5th-century British leader Ambrosius Aurelianus or Arthur. The problem for historians and archaeologists is that there are no contemporary accounts of

King Arthur and his battles, and all the historical references to him in the chronicles of BEDE, Gildas, Nenius, Geoffrey of Monmouth and others were written between 100 and 600 years after the event. By the late 15th century, when Malory's chivalric stories about the Knights of the Round Table and the search for the Holy Grail were written, legend and history had become inseparable.

However, the obsessive search for proof of Arthur's existence and places connected with his name continued. The search probably started with the monks of Glastonbury, who in 1191 claimed to have found the burial of King Arthur and Queen Guinevere inscribed with the words 'Here lies Arthur in the Isle of Avalon buried'. Various locations as far apart as Cornwall and Scotland are claimed as the site of Mount Badon; the refortified Iron Age hillfort of Badbury Rings in Dorset seems the most credible possibility. Serious consideration has also been given to the site of Arthur's court at Camelot, even though the name is undoubtedly an invention of French medieval poets. 'Camelots' exist from Arthur's Seat in Edinburgh to Tintagel in Cornwall. Excavations carried out at SOUTH CADBURY in Somerset in the 1960s revealed an important fortified settlement of the 5th and 6th centuries which could have been the centre from which British resistance to the Saxons was organized.

Aruans. *See* MARAJO ISLAND SITES.

Aryans. A people who called themselves Arya and spoke an Indo-European language, SANSKRIT, known from the RIGVEDA and other early Indian sources. They are thought to have invaded India from the northwest during the 2nd millennium BC and to have spread east and south in the succeeding centuries. By *c*500 BC Aryan speech was probably established over much of the area in which Indo-Aryan languages are now spoken, that is, most of the Indian subcontinent. Archaeologists have devoted much time to the search for archaeological traces of the Aryans, with no very marked degree of success, though many authorities believe that PAINTED GREY WARE marks their presence. The invasion of the Aryans may have been responsible for, or contributed to, the downfall of the HARAPPAN CIVILIZATION.

aryballos [Greek: 'bag, purse']. A small pottery jar used for oil or perfume. The form is normally globular, quasi-spherical or pear-shaped, with narrowing neck and single handle. As with ASKOS, the term perhaps transfers from earlier leather artefacts. The term is also applied to certain INCA pottery forms because of similarity of shape. *See also* ALABASTRON.

Arzawa. *See* BEYCESULTAN.

Ascalon [Askalon, Askelon]. One of the five Philistine cities on the south coast of Palestine, 50 km southwest of Jerusalem. Excavations by Garstang in the early 1920s found mainly remains of the Roman period, though Philistine levels were reached in small soundings. Egyptian texts indicate that Ascalon was one of the cities that revolted against RAMESES II and Merneptah and that it was the centre of worship of the fish god Derhets. In the Roman period, Ascalon was the birthplace of Herod the Great and the city flourished at that time. The city continued to be occupied in the Byzantine and Arab periods and it was famous for the Mosque of Omar.

Ashir. The city of Ashir, 75 km south of Algiers, was founded in 935-6 by Ziri, the ruler of the Sanhaja berbers. Like the FATIMIDS of MAHDIYA, the Sanhaja were Shi'ites and when the Fatimid caliph al-Mu'izz conquered Egypt and established a new capital, CAIRO, in 970, he made the Zirid ruler his governor in the Maghreb. The principal buildings at Ashir were the palace and the congregational mosque. The palace was a rectangular enclosure, 72 metres long and 42 metres wide, with square towers and a monumental entrance. The interior consisted of a central courtyard with four identical apartments at the angles and a throne room preceded by a vestibule opposite the entrance. The plan has much in common with the smaller Fatimid 'palace' at AJDABIYAH. The mosque had a sanctuary seven bays wide, with five transverse aisles.

Ashur. *See* ASSUR.

Asiab, Tepe. A semi-permanent settlement in the Kermanshah valley in the Zagros region of western Iran. Dated between 7100 and 6750 bc, it belongs to the KARIM SHAHIR culture.

Semi-subterranean features may have been the bases of tent-like structures, which animal bone evidence suggests would have been occupied during the spring and summer. Domesticated goats were kept and finds of many horn cores suggest that selective slaughtering of males was practised. Mussels were probably eaten, and the evidence of coprolites indicates that small lizards and frogs were also consumed. As well as flint tools, cones, balls and figurines of lightly baked clay have been found. Two burials have been excavated, both covered in red ochre.

Asikli Hüyük. An ACERAMIC NEOLITHIC site in central Anatolia, located c50 km from the OBSIDIAN source at Ciftlik and probably involved in the extraction and trade in this material. The site has not been excavated, but surface investigation has yielded evidence of mud-brick walls with red lime plaster and of burials under the floors. Finds include greenstone axes, obsidian tools and bone awls, and belt hooks. Animal bones include sheep or goat, cattle, onager, red deer and hare, none certainly domestic. Radiocarbon dates of c7000 and c6660 bc come from unstratified contexts, but suggest that the site is approximately contemporary with aceramic HACILAR, and earlier than ÇATAL HÜYÜK.

askos [Greek: 'bag']. An oil-jug. Normally squat in shape, with convex top and arching handle. Examples are sometimes rather unbalanced with eccentric mouth. As with ARYBALLOS, the term perhaps transfers from earlier leather artefacts.

Aslian. See AUSTRO-ASIATIC.

Asmar, Tell. Modern name of the ancient Mesopotamian city of ESHNUNNA.

Asoka [Asokan]. Head of the MAURYAN empire of India in the 3rd century BC. According to Buddhist tradition he began his career as a fierce tyrant with much bloodshed, but after a spiritual crisis he became a Buddhist and reformed his administration along Buddhist lines. His kingdom included almost all of modern Pakistan and India, except the extreme south. Many monuments survive from this period: STUPAS, rock-cut temples, and commemorative pillars. A series of inscriptions, enshrining Buddhist teaching,

survives on rock faces and stone pillars from widely separated parts of the empire.

Asprochalico. A large rock shelter in Epirus, northwest Greece. There are MOUSTERIAN levels below and a series of Upper PALAEOLITHIC levels above, one radiocarbon-dated to c26,000 bc. Backed blades were common in these levels.

ass. The wild ass was distributed widely in North Africa and Asia. Three races of the African wild ass, *Equus asinus*, existed in northwest Africa, the Nile basin and Ethiopia, and Somaliland. All but the Somali race are now more or less extinct. The Asiatic wild ass, *Equus hemionus*, still survives, but its range is restricted. It used to occupy Syria, Arabia and Mesopotamia. Remaining populations can be found in Iran (where it is called the ONAGER), northwest India (where it is called the ghorkar) and Transcaspia and Mongolia (where it is known as the kiang). Asiatic wild asses as a group may also be called onagers (in a wider sense), kemiones, or half-asses. There is very little osteological evidence for domesticated asses on archaeological sites, but a number of artistic representations have been found. The earliest (securely dated) of these for the African ass is an Egyptian tomb relief of 1650 BC. After this date, domestic asses gradually appear in the Levant, Mesopotamia and finally arrive in Europe during medieval times. The domestic ass, or DONKEY, may be hybridized with the HORSE: a male ass crossed with a female horse produces a mule, and a female ass crossed with a male horse produces a hinny (rather rare); both hybrids are sterile.

assemblage. A group of objects found in ASSOCIATION with each other and therefore thought to be the products of one group of people at one period. An assemblage may contain artefacts of one material only (e.g. flint) or may include objects of many different materials and types (e.g. pottery, stone and metal tools, weapons and ornaments). If an assemblage recurs at a number of sites, it may be regarded as characteristic of a particular CULTURE.

association. The occurrence of objects together in an archaeological context which indicates that they were deposited at the same time. Good examples of associations are grave goods, foundation deposits, hoards and material in destruction levels.

Assur. (1) The old capital of ASSYRIA lies naturally protected on a rock promontory on the bank of the River Tigris in northern Mesopotamia. The earliest levels excavated belong to the first half of the 3rd millennium BC. The remains of a pre-Sargonid temple dedicated to the goddess Ishtar were excavated and SUMERIAN statues were found — among the earliest evidence of Sumerian contact outside the southern plain. It is thought that Assur might originally have been a trading post.

For over 2000 years successive kings built and rebuilt the fortifications, temple and palace complexes: inscriptions associated with these monuments have helped in the construction of the chronology of the site. The fortifications were rebuilt on many occasions, the latest under Shalmaneser III (859-824 BC) who added a new outer wall. Very little is known about the secular buildings at Assur, as most work has been done in the temple and palace complex, with the three large ZIG-GURATS dominating the city. The largest was 60 metres square and was completed by Shamsi Adad I (c1800 BC). It was originally dedicated to Enlil, but later to Assur; the dedication of the other temples also changed through time. Next to the ziggurats, the 'Old Palace' featured a labyrinth of rectangular chambers and storerooms, with private shrines and courtyards. A later 'New Palace' of which only the foundations remain was built by Tukulti-Ninurta I (1244-1208 BC), who also built a residential suburb outside the city. Representations on cylinder seals suggest that many buildings might have had parapets and towers. Assurnasirpal II (883-859 BC) moved the capital to Calah and by 614 BC the city of Assur had fallen to the Median army.

(2) The national god of Assyria, leader of the Assyrian pantheon. The god Assur is represented as a winged sun-disc and was the god most commonly represented on Assyrian reliefs. The emblem suggests that his original nature was a fertility god, rather than the war god he became in the Assyrian state.

Assyria. The northern part of Mesopotamia, with its capital at ASSUR. From c1300 BC the Assyrian kings created an empire which at its maximum extent included Egypt, much of the area to the west as far as the Mediterranean, Elam to the east and parts of Anatolia to the north. Assurnasirpal II (883-859 BC) transferred the centre of government to Calah (NIMRUD), where he rebuilt the city to his own plan; he was also the first Assyrian king to leave pictorial reliefs to supplement CUNEI-FORM inscriptions. The fortunes of the empire waxed and waned under the kings of the 9th-7th centuries: Assurbanipal (668-627 BC) reconquered Egypt, but in 614 the empire fell when the Medes invaded Assyria, captured Calah and destroyed Assur.

astronomy. Most of the ancient civilizations of the world studied the skies and some achieved considerable astronomical knowledge. In the main, ancient astronomy is known from documentary sources rather than material evidence and so falls within the realm of history rather than archaeology. In two cases, however, ancient astronomy has been studied by archaeologists: in prehistoric Europe, where the evidence comes entirely from the monuments themselves, and in central America, where the evidence comes largely from inscriptions and documents, but where there is no separate discipline concerned with the literature (in contrast to Egypt or Meso-potamia, for example).

Prehistoric Europe. Studies of prehistoric astronomy have concentrated on the MEGA-LITHIC MONUMENTS of northwest Europe and especially the STONE CIRCLES of the British Isles and the ALIGNMENTS of Brittany, dating to the Late Neolithic and Early Bronze Age. Research by Alexander Thom and others has shown that many of these monuments incorporate alignments on the rising and setting of the sun, the moon and some of the brighter stars, at various significant points in their respective cycles. Solar alignments are present at the famous sites of NEW GRANGE and STONEHENGE, as well as many others, while a lunar orientation characterizes the RECUMBENT STONE CIRCLES of Aberdeenshire as well as the CARNAC alignments in Brittany. Although most scholars now accept that many monuments reflect a concern with celestial events on the part of the societies that built them, there is considerable disagreement about the accuracy of measurement and the degree of astronomical understanding achieved. Whereas modern astronomers and other scientists have tended to emphasize the accuracy of the prehistoric alignments and to regard the monuments as true observatories, prehistorians have been more sceptical. It may well be that the monuments were temples where astronomical knowledge was exploited by an elite priesthood to produce spectacular theatrical effects such as the lighting-up of the chamber at New Grange at midwinter sunrise, the rising of the midsummer sun behind the Heel Stone at Stonehenge, or the floating of the moon along the top of the recumbent stone in the Scottish recumbent stone circles. The ability to predict astronomical events and produce spectacular effects would certainly enhance political power — a function which is also suggested for the astronomical achievements of Mesoamerica.

Americas. It has long been known that the CALENDAR system of MESOAMERICAN groups (notably the MAYA and the AZTEC) was based on the cyclical nature of the movement of heavenly bodies. Buildings seen as observatories occur at CHICHEN ITZA and at PALENQUE, and the Dresden CODEX is a detailed collection of calculations tracing the eclipses of the moon and the sun and the cycles of Venus and possibly Mars and Jupiter.

Although the solar year incorporated in the Calendar Round was an imprecise 365 days long, the Maya were aware of the error and ultimately initiated a correction factor to account for the quarter day per year discrepancy (*see* SECONDARY SERIES). The cycle of the moon, in comparison, was calculated with astonishing accuracy (29.5302 days compared to the actual figure of 29.5306). Beyond this, the cycle of Venus (calculated at 583.92) was also pinpointed to a degree of accuracy comparable to measurements taken by modern astronomical methods.

Perhaps most spectacular of all is the awareness of long-term astronomical phenomena. Both the central Mexicans and the Maya knew that five Venus cycles were equal to eight earth cycles, but most remarkable was the combination of the periods of Venus, the earth and the Calendar Round into a cycle 104 years long.

Astronomical calculations were long regarded as a curious (although probably religious) obsession with the passage of time; they are now believed to have had a notably secular and practical element to them, namely the use of the ability to predict astronomical

events as an instrument of political control. Concentrated in the hands of the governing elite class, the apparent ability to predict events in the heavens would certainly have increased the credibility of the elite as able rulers.

Asuka. The centre of cultural and political development in the southwestern part of the Nara Basin (also known as the Yamato Plain), Japan, during the 7th century. The Asuka culture and Asuka period are variously defined, emphasizing different aspects of the development. In art history, the Asuka culture refers to early Buddhist art and architecture in the Northern Wei style. The Asuka period refers more specifically to the reign of the Empress Suiko (592-628) when her nephew, as Regent, promoted Buddhism, introduced a formal administrative structure, sought diplomatic relations with the SUI, and began compiling the national history (*see* NIHON SHOKI).

In recent years many sites of old temples and palaces have been added to the surviving examples of Asuka architecture, sculpture and paintings. The original layout of Asukadera, the first formal temple built in Japan, was clarified by excavations in 1956-7. Continuing work at several sites of royal palaces shows a trend towards larger administrative quarters in relation to the private residential areas of the royal family.

Asukadera. *See* ASUKA.

Aswad, Tell. An ACERAMIC NEOLITHIC site in the Damascus basin of Syria, occupied *c*7800-6600 bc, which has produced important evidence on early farming. From the beginning peas, lentils, emmer wheat and probably barley were all cultivated. The presence of both cereals and pulses showing morphological characteristics of domestication suggests that these early farmers might already have discovered that if these two types of crops are grown in rotation soil fertility is renewed.

Aszód. An important early LENGYEL site on a plateau overlooking the Zagyva Valley, 30 km east of Budapest in Hungary, of the Late Neolithic (4th millennium bc). Aszód comprises both settlement and cemetery. Excavated by N. Kalicz, the settlement has over 40 rectangular houses, with rich domestic assemblages including a large collection of bone and antler tools. The medium-sized cemetery is at least partly organized in rows of graves, interpreted as family groupings, with varying degrees of wealth in grave goods. In most periods of Hungarian prehistory, western and eastern Hungary were separated culturally, as physically, by the infertile Danube-Tisza Interfluve. Aszód is one of the rare examples of a site east of the Danube with west Hungarian material culture.

Atchana, Tell. A mound on the AMUQ plain of northern Syria, identified as the ancient city of Alalakh. Excavations by WOOLLEY in the early part of the century revealed occupation levels running from the 4th to the late 2nd millennium BC. In level VII, dated to the 18th and 17th centuries BC, the palace of Yaram-Lim II demonstrates an early form of architecture which was characteristic of Syria, in which stone, timber and mud-brick were all used, as well as basalt for orthostats. Another palace was excavated in level IV, of the late 15th and early 14th centuries, belonging to Niqmepa; this consisted of a number of rooms around a central court. In the official quarters a large quantity of tablets were found. These were written in AKKADIAN CUNEIFORM and demonstrate intense trading with other cities, including UGARIT and the Hittite capital Hattusas, involving food products such as wheat, wine and olive oil. Later in the 14th century the city fell to the HITTITES and became a provincial capital of the Hittite empire. It was eventually abandoned after destruction c1200 BC, perhaps at the hands of the PEOPLES OF THE SEA.

Aterian. A widely distributed Upper PLEISTOCENE stone industry of northern Africa. It appears to have developed, perhaps initially in the Maghreb of Algeria and Morocco, from the local MOUSTERIAN tradition. The date at which the Aterian first appeared is not well attested, but may have been c80,000 BC. The Aterian occurs throughout the Sahara, from near the Atlantic seaboard almost as far east as the Nile. The Sahara at this time was relatively well watered, with Mediterranean evergreen vegetation in many highland areas, whence rivers flowed to the more arid plains.

Aterian assemblages, named after Bir el Ater in Tunisia, are marked by the presence of varied flake tools, many of which possess a marked tang. It is generally assumed, but cannot yet be proven, that such artefacts were hafted. They include not only projectile points but also scrapers and pieces with little retouch other than that forming the tang. In the southern Sahara, as at ADRAR BOUS, as well as in the areas bordering on the Nile Valley, as at BIR TERFAWI, the Aterian industries include fully bifacial points. Later occurrences emphasize parallel-sided blades. The Aterian occupation came to an end c35,000 bc, as increasing aridity resulted in most of the Sahara becoming unsuitable for human settlement.

Ateste. *See* ESTE.

Athens. Major classical Greek city-state in Attica with evidence for continous occupation since the MYCENAEAN period. Most literary sources are decisively pro-Athenian, and Athenian cultural dominance has been such that this bias often still persists in contemporary scholarship. The geographical position in the middle of a seaboard plain some seven km from the sea is no more advantageous than many of the city's ancient rivals, and the immediate neighbourhood was not especially fertile. Marble was available from nearby Mount Pentelikon, silver from the mines of Laurium near Cape Sunium, and there were plentiful local sources for potters' clay.

Some occupation of the ACROPOLIS and the neighbouring area seems likely in the late Neolithic. In the Mycenaean period, legend (and some more recent authorities) would have perhaps a dozen towns or kingdoms in Attica by the time of mythical Cecrops, administered from an Athenian citadel that was strong enough in due course to rival KNOSSOS and, later, to resist successive waves of Dorian invaders. A more sober case, however, might be argued for a modest fortified settlement. Valuable Iron Age material comes from the Kerameikos (Potters' Quarter) cemetery. But it is still not clear how far Athens, with its achievements in GEOMETRIC pottery, and acting perhaps as base for the very early Ionian colonies, managed to ride out the 'Dark Age' that seems to have followed the collapse of Mycenaean civilization elsewhere (*see* MYCENAE).

The tradition of the Attic *synoecism*, in which the small kingdoms supposedly came together to found the city-state of Athens — celebrated in the special festival of the *Synoikeia* — is another which is difficult to convert into a dateable process and awkward to accept without qualification. Athena, the patron goddess of Athens, striking in her fully armed yet female representation, may well be equated with a Mycenaean maiden-protectress of princes and citadels, but such *synoecism* as there may have been seems too early to have been associated with the legendary Theseus. If the tradition does conceal a reality, perhaps the process should be placed much later, and relate rather to the expansionism that begins to appear from the 7th century onward.

With the 7th and 6th centuries BC we have evidence for a cultural and commercial renaissance, partly home-grown and partly recrossing the Aegean sea from the Ionian settlements. A major component in this socio-economic revolution was undoubtedly the borrowing of the PHOENICIAN alphabet for the writing of Greek. Athens entered directly upon a process of alternating success and failure that was to last right up to the Roman Imperial period. Commerical success against rival CORINTH and further afield brought rapid economic growth and a population explosion. New ideas were imported, and political upheaval led to experiments in government which slowly democratized an entrenched aristocracy.

In 490 at MARATHON and again in 480 at SALAMIS, Athens was able to act as focus for Greek national resistance to the Persian invaders, and the prestige derived from these victories led directly to the Delian League and the greatest ever extension of her political power — the Athenian empire. The new imperial status gave a boost to conservative idealism in the city (as may be seen very clearly, for example, in Pericles' Funeral Speech in Thucydides II), and ushered in what later writers such as Plato, and antiquity and the western world in general, always were to look back to as the Golden Age of Greek civilization. In the years 447-431 BC, under the unwavering leadership of Pericles, vast sums were spent on grandiose schemes of public works, such as the new group of buildings on the Acropolis including the PARTHENON. Athenian pretensions, however, were widely resented, and it fell to SPARTA and Boeotia to make sure that they were short-lived. The final

Spartan embassy to Athens simply said: 'Sparta wants peace. Peace is still possible if you will give the Hellenes back their freedom.' Pericles advised no concession, and Athens began the long catalogue of misdirected strategy and disaster that was to be the Peloponnesian War (431-404 BC). The end of the war brought Athens the ignominy of dependency under Sparta.

The 4th century BC saw Athens returning to commercial success but pursuing an uncertain foreign policy. Escape from Spartan imperialism brought an uneasy autonomy, to be followed by the successive threats of Philip of Macedon and Alexander the Great. By the end of the century, Macedonian domination had arrived, and with it the final end to any Athenian claim to the status of a leading power.

Athens made determined efforts to shake off Macedon during the 3rd century BC and was rewarded with the achievement of independence once again by 228 BC. The 2nd and 1st centuries, however, saw Athens facing yet another intruder, Rome, and having to endure siege and plunder at the hands of the arch-philistine Roman, Sulla.   During the Imperial period, Athens was confined quietly to her remaining role of cultural centre and fashionable seat of learning for the sons of the rich (though even in this there was now competition from cultural rivals, such as Alexandria). The cultural function lasted into the 6th century AD, until the edict of Justinian in 529 closed down the schools of philosophy. By the Byzantine period Athens had become a modest provincial town.

What remains today of the monuments of classical Athens was, until very recently, more the outcome of chance than conscious management. In the case of the Temple of Hephaestus and Athena (so-called Theseion), use as a church up to 1834 contributed to its preservation. The major buildings on the Acropolis, however, all suffered variously from the vicissitudes of Christian re-use and Turkish occupation. The ERECHTHEUM, for instance, was converted into an harem for a time, while the Turks' use of the Propylaea and the Parthenon as powder magazines led to massive damage to both. The colossal explosion after the magazine in the Parthenon was hit by mortar fire from Mouseion Hill in 1687 left the temple a smouldering ruin, torn into two gutted halves. To this sorry history have now been added two modern evils — the corrosive present-day atmosphere of Athens and Attica, and the unending attrition of visiting tourists. Removal of the surviving sculptures from the buildings before they deteriorate further is a sensible act of management, but unfortunately longer-term solutions will be complex and costly.

Atlantic. A climatic division of the FLANDRIAN period. Godwin's POLLEN ZONE VIIa corresponds to the Atlantic period in Britain. On botanical grounds, the Atlantic period is supposed to have represented a maximum of temperature, the 'climatic optimum' of the Flandrian. Evidence from beetles, however, suggests that it may have been little warmer than average for the interglacial. Zone VIIa is dominated by trees of the Mixed Oak Forest: oak, elm, alder and lime. It is initiated by the rise of alder pollen, supposed to take place at about 7000 bp, but with radiocarbon dates varying over a range of some 2000 years. Zone VIIa ends with the ELM DECLINE, radiocarbon dates for which vary between 5300 and 6200 bp. Throughout the zone there is evidence, particularly in today's moorland and heathland areas, that transient woodland clearance by MESOLITHIC man continued (*see* BOREAL).

Atlantic Bronze Age. A late Bronze Age metal-working tradition found on the west coast of France, spreading to southern England and Iberia; alternatively known as the CARP'S TONGUE SWORD complex. It is known mainly from a large number of hoards, which include not only the characteristic swords, but also end-winged axes, hog-backed razors and bugle-shaped objects of uncertain function. The widespread distribution of these metal types indicates extensive trade along the Atlantic coasts of Europe; the tradition flourished west of the area dominated by the central European URNFIELD cultures.

atlatl. An American term for a spear-thrower, or device for increasing thrust when throwing a spear or similar projectile, by extending the length of the thrower's arm. Usually it consists of a flat board or rod with a means of gripping at one end and a notch or hook to retain the projectile at the other. It was often used in conjunction with weights such as bannerstones, the precise purpose of which is uncertain.

Atlitian. An Upper PALAEOLITHIC assemblage named after the site of Atlit in the MOUNT CARMEL area of Israel. The sequence of Upper Palaeolithic deposits in the east Mediterranean includes several layers with AURIGNACIAN-like assemblages. The level which followed these in the Mount Carmel sequence was termed Atlitian by Garrod; the name is little used today.

atomic absorption spectrometry. A technique of CHEMICAL ANALYSIS.

Principles. A sample is dissolved and then atomized in a flame. A beam of light, of carefully controlled wavelength, is shone through the flame to a detector on the other side. The wavelength is selected so that atoms of the element under study will absorb some of the light. Concentrations of this element in the sample can then be calculated from the degree of absorption.

Materials. A powdered sample of between 10 and 100mg is required. The technique has so far been used to analyse FLINT and BRONZE.

Applications. Atomic absorption spectrometry has been used to investigate TRACE ELEMENTS in flint. It is possible to trace the origin of some flint artefacts by matching their trace element concentrations with those of various sources of the material.

Atranjikhera. A settlement site in Uttar Pradesh in northern India with a series of occupation levels. The earliest level had OCHRE-COLOURED POTTERY; this was succeeded by a level with BLACK AND RED WARE, which was itself followed by a series of layers with PAINTED GREY WARE, which also produced iron tools and weapons and an associated radiocarbon date of *c*1025 bc (*c*1280 BC) which, however, is thought by many authorities to be too early.

Atria. *See* ADRIA.

atrium. Latin term for the entrance-hall of a Roman house, as seen, for instance, in the many examples at POMPEII. Early versions may have been roofed over, but the pattern soon established was of *compluvium* (a rectangular opening in the roof) over a central *impluvium* (shallow pool in the floor, drained to a cistern). Vitruvius draws a parallel with Etruscan house layout (*atrium tuscanicum*), and an Etruscan indebtedness is not implausible. The inward-sloping roof arrangement around the *compluvium* is echoed in some Etruscan house-shaped urns, and Varro derives the word *atrium* from Etruscan Atria (*see* ADRIA) on the grounds of architectural parallels. Greek influence is also visible in the use of *tetrastyle* (four columns to support the roof), and *peristyle* in some examples. The walls of the *atrium* would be decorated, sometimes with painted panels or family portraits, and a shrine to the Lares and Penates (household gods, also probably of Etruscan derivation) is sometimes found in the general area. Above the *atrium* were typically grouped the *cubicula* (bedrooms) and beyond lay the *tablinum* (family room and study), *triclinium* (dining room) and *hortus* (garden).

Attic. (1) Relating to ATHENS, or the surrounding area of Attica.

(2) The particular dialect of Greek spoken and written in classical ATHENS, especially in the 5th century BC. This dialect was originally only one of a number of differing regional forms, but, by the accident of Athenian cultural history, has come to be regarded in time as standard classical Greek.

Aubrey, John (1626-97). British antiquary who worked mainly in southern England and produced detailed accounts of the monuments of AVEBURY and STONEHENGE. The 56 pits inside the bank of the first phase of Stonehenge are known as the Aubrey holes, after their discoverer.

auger. An implement for obtaining samples of buried SOIL HORIZONS and deposits. Augers are widely used in soil science, but less so on archaeological sites, due to the disturbance of features, layers and artefacts that may be caused.

Augst [Roman Augusta Rauricorum]. A Roman COLONIA and frontier post of the Upper Rhine valley near Basel, Switzerland. Although founded in 44 BC by Caesar and L. Munatius Plancus in the territory of the tribe of the Raurici, there seems to be no evidence for occupation before 15 BC. In this year, Tiberius and Drusus completed their campaign in the Central Alps, and a military post was established at Augst. The town flourished until an attack by the Alamanni in 260 AD. After this,

settlement appears to have been disturbed and sporadic, and it appears that the population eventually moved to the vincinity of the new fort of Castrum Rauracense, also on the Rhine. Early structures were in the familiar Roman military style, constructed of earth and timber. Evidence of stone structures survives for many features of the town, including the CURIA, BASILICA, and a THEATRE complex which may have included a phase of combined theatre/amphitheatre use.

Âu-lac. A kingdom in northern Vietnam, founded by the king of Thuc (an unidentified country to the north) in 258 BC on the ruins of the kingdom of Văn-lang. Its capital was at CÔ-LOA, near present-day Hanoi. It was incorporated in 207 BC into the kingdom of NAM-VIÊT.

Aunjetitz. Earlier name for the Czechoslovakian site and Early Bronze Age culture of ÚNĚTICE.

Aurignacian. In the classic French Upper PALAEOLITHIC sequence, the Aurignacian falls before the SOLUTRIAN and the MAGDALENIAN. In modern usage only the old 'middle Aurignacian' is still called Aurignacian. In France, radiocarbon dates place it mainly between about 35,000 and 25,000 years ago. However, there are a number of different types of Aurignacian, and in central Europe a related form may be considerably older. There is still considerable dispute about the extent to which the Aurignacian is contemporary with the cultures of the PERIGORDIAN group in southwest France. The first representational art and the earliest bone flutes appear in the Aurignacian, and it is also important as the most distinctive and abundantly represented of the early Upper Palaeolithic groups. The most characteristic artefacts are carinates (steep end scrapers), Aurignac blades (with heavy marginal retouch) and split-based bone points.

aurochs. Also known as urus, or wild cattle; classified as *Bos primigenius. See* CATTLE.

Australian Core Tool and Scraper Tradition. A late PLEISTOCENE and HOLOCENE stone industry characterized by high-domed chunky cores (sometimes termed 'HORSEHOOF CORES') and steep-edge flake scrapers. Artefacts have been found in all areas of the mainland and Tasmania, dating from 30,000 bc at LAKE MUNGO until the recent past. This industry has close parallels in industries of similar date in Island Southeast Asia. *See also* CAGAYAN, KAFIAVANA, LEANG BURUNG, MADAI, NEW GUINEA, TABON.

Australian Small Tool Tradition. A Mid-HOLOCENE suite of stone tool types comprising backed blades and flakes, unifacial and bifacial points and small adze flakes. Tools with regional distributions include BONDI POINTS, geometric microliths, PIRRI POINTS and TULA ADZES. All except the Bondi points and geometric microliths were still in use as stone components of wooden weapons and tools at the time of European contact, and the exceptions were not recognized as artefacts by Aborigines. Earliest dates for most of the small tools are around 3000 bc, although adze flakes first appeared possibly 2000 years earlier. Debate centres on the question of whether the tradition developed locally or was introduced from Indonesia, where there are technological parallels in the microliths of southwestern Sulawesi from 4000 bc (*see* TOALIAN).

Australopithecus. The baby skull found at TAUNG in 1924 was named *Australopithecus africanus* (southern ape of Africa) by Dart in 1925. A number of African fossil hominids have subsequently been included in this genus, and since 1962 many authorities have recognized two species: *A. africanus*, a gracile form best-known from STERKFONTEIN and MAKAPAN in South Africa, and a larger species, *A. robustus*, represented by fossils from SWARTKRANS and KROMDRAAI. All these fossils have a small brain (400-600 cc) and large molar teeth; beyond this their differences tend to be more important than their similarities.

East African finds since 1959 are often compared with the two South African species, and representatives of both species seem to be present in Tanzania, Kenya and Ethiopia. The robust type, often called *A. boisei* in East Africa, seems to date from c2.1 to 1.1 million years ago, and is thus contemporary with HOMO ERECTUS and HOMO HABILIS. This form can probably be excluded from direct human ancestry and placed in a cousin lineage. *A. africanus* seems to date mainly to before 2.5 million years ago, and may be a direct human

ancestor. Fossils from HADAR and LAETOLI have been placed in a new species, *A. afarensis*, but may nevertheless be *A. africanus*. At c3.75 million years, the Laetoli find is the earliest good sample of the genus, but some fragments from LOTHAGAM at c5.5 million years may also be *Australopithecus*. *See also* HUMAN EVOLUTION.

Austro-Asiatic. A linguistic family which includes Munda (eastern India), Mon (southwest Burma), Khmer (Kampuchea), Vietnamese and several minor language groups including Nicobarese, and Aslian of peninsular Malaysia. Once the major linguistic family of mainland Southeast Asia, its speakers have become geographically fragmented owing to the expansion, mainly during the past two millennia, of the Tibeto-Burman, Thai and AUSTRONESIAN (Cham and Malay) languages.

Austronesian. The major language family of Island Southeast Asia and the Pacific: TAIWAN, PHILIPPINES, MALAYSIA, INDONESIA, parts of southern VIETNAM, MADAGASCAR, MELANESIA (excluding most of NEW GUINEA), MICRONESIA and POLYNESIA. Proto-Austronesian was probably located in southern China or Taiwan before 3000 BC and geographical expansion of the family has been by horticultural, canoe-using peoples with pottery, perhaps commencing with rice cultivation in southern China and Taiwan, but turning to fruits and tubers in eastern Indonesia and Oceania. Austronesian speakers were the first humans to settle the Pacific islands beyond western Melanesia. Expansion reached its limits in Madagascar (early centuries AD) and New Zealand (cAD 900); prior to European expansion, Austronesians were the most widely spread ethno-linguistic group on earth, the distance from Madagascar to Easter Island being 210 degrees of longitude.

Austro-Thai. A hypothetical linguistic family proposed by linguist Paul Benedict to include the present (and now geographically separated) Thai-Kadai and AUSTRONESIAN families. It is possible that these two major linguistic groups could have shared a common origin area in southern China, probably in excess of 5000 years ago.

Autun [Roman Augustodunum]. City in Saône-et-Loire, Central France. It was a fortified town of Gallia Belgica (*see* GAUL) built for Augustus sometime in the last decade BC as a replacement capital for the Celtic tribe of the Aedui. (The site of their previous capital is known at nearby Mont Beuvray; *see* BIBRACTE). An expansive concept (some 200 hectares), it was clearly designed to give strong representation to Rome's interests in the area. The importance of Romanization and favourable propaganda is also seen in the investment made in local education. Tacitus notes the town as a centre of learning only a few decades after its foundation, and from the end of the 3rd century AD we have the eloquent witness of Eumenius, schools principal. The city's prosperity was finally ruined by supporting the wrong side (Claudius II) in 269 AD and it never recovered its size or wealth. Two of the city's original gateways (Porte d'Arroux and Porte St André) are well preserved and probably date in their original construction from early imperial times. Also interesting are the remains of the THEATRE, one of the largest in Gaul and probably begun in the 1st century AD.

Avebury. A HENGE in Wiltshire, one of the most impressive British Neolithic monuments. It consists of a large bank with internal ditch (1.2 km long) with four entrances. Inside the ditch was set a circle of 98 SARSEN stones, weighing as much as 40 tonnes each. In the central area were two smaller stone circles, each c100 metres in diameter. From the south entrance the Kennet Avenue leads to another stone circle site on Overton Hill. Traces of a second avenue remain on the opposite, Beckhampton, side of the monument. In recent years, much work has been devoted to studying the complex geometry of this site, possible astronomical alignments built into it, and the number of man-hours required for its construction.

Avebury, Lord [Sir John Lubbock] (1834-1913). Distinguished British archaeologist, whose book *Prehistoric Times*, first published in 1865, went into seven editions, the last in 1913, and achieved wide popularity. He was an early convert to DARWIN's theory of evolution and the acceptance of the antiquity of man. One of his innovations was the introduction of the terms Palaeolithic and Neolithic

as subdivisions of the Stone Age (*see* THREE AGE SYSTEM).

Awdaghast. The site of a major trading centre in southern Mauritania, at the southern end of the main caravan route leading across the Sahara to the ancient Kingdom of GHANA. It was probably through this route that much of the gold of BAMBUK was exported northwards from at least the closing centuries of the 1st millennium AD.

Axayacatl. *See* CALENDAR STONE.

axe factory. During the Neolithic period in Europe certain outcrops of fine-grained rock were exploited for the production of polished axes. Microscopic analysis of the rock allows the sources to be identified, as each type of rock has its own distinctive crystalline structure; this enables the trading networks to be reconstructed. In the British Isles important factories have been identified at GREAT LANGDALE, GRAIG LLWYD, PENWITH and TIEVEBULLIAGH.

Axum [Aksum]. From at least the 3rd century AD, this city in the highlands of northern Ethiopia, rose to be the centre of an important kingdom. Its antecedents are clearly rooted in the PRE-AXUMITE culture of the area, but the origins of the city itself remain uncertain. The political history of Axum is best known from its coins: the series runs from approximately the 3rd century until the 7th century. Inscriptions were first in Greek, latterly in Ethiopic. Religious symbols on the coins reflect the early 4th-century adoption of Christianity in place of the worship of the South Arabian moon god. Archaeologically, Axum has yielded evidence for large multi-storey stone buildings and for an impressive series of monolithic funerary stelae up to 33 metres in height, some of which were carved into schematized representations of multi-storey buildings. The local economic base of the kingdom is poorly known, but on a wider front its prosperity was clearly based upon control of trade between an extensive interior area including the Butana plain to the west and the outside, principally Mediterranean, world via the Red Sea port of ADULIS. Ivory was probably the export on which this trade depended. Through the development of this trade Axum's rise to prosperity was at the expense of MEROE, believed to have been finally conquered by the Axumites in the 4th century. For brief periods in the 3rd and 6th centuries Axum achieved political control over parts of southern Arabia. Thereafter it declined, and was sacked in the 10th century; it remains an important centre of the Ethiopian church.

Ayacucho. A valley in southern Peru at which a number of caves (notably Pikimachay or Flea Cave and Jayamachay or Pepper Cave) have evidence of a long sequence of human occupation. Excavated by Richard McNeish, the remains at these caves have produced a series of radiocarbon dates which push the presence of man in South America back to c20,000 years ago. The earliest level, PACCAICASA, is dated 18,000-14,000 bc and is followed by the Ayacucho complex (14,000-11,000 bc) which contains basalt and chert core tools, choppers and unifacial projectile points. Succeeding levels contain burins, blades, fishtail points and MANOS and METATES, and thus conform to the generally held succession of BIG GAME HUNTING followed by hunting and gathering. It should be noted that in spite of the radiocarbon dates McNeish's arguments for man's presence at such early times present many problems. Chief among these are: (1) the possibility that many of the early 'tools' are not actually man-made; (2) the possibility that the sloth bones (from which the earlier dates derive) are natural occurrences and not the remnants of man's hunting activities; (3) the fact that McNeish's construction hinges on the unlikely proposition that South American glacial periods alternate rather than coincide with those in the Northern Hemisphere.

Ayampitin. An open camp-site in the province of Cordoba in northwest Argentina containing evidence which implies a transition from generalized BIG GAME HUNTING to a more specialized, regionally oriented hunting and gathering economy. The assemblage contains lithic hunting tools and tool-manufacturing debris in association with MANOS and milling stones, and is noticeably similar to Level IV at INTIHUASI CAVE. The willow-leaf projectile point is particularly characteristic, and has cognates over a wide area of the region. There are no radiocarbon dates, but comparison with Intihuasi, LAURICOCHA CAVES and elsewhere suggests a period of occupation in the early 6th millenium bc.

Ayia Triada. A MINOAN villa in southern Crete, built around 2200 BC and inhabited until its destruction c1450 BC. It was connected by a road to the palace at PHAESTOS. One room contained many clay tablets with LINEAR A inscriptions. Subsequently a MEGARON was built on the site.

Aylesford. A cremation cemetery of the 1st century BC in Kent, this site has given its name to the Aylesford-Swarling culture. It is often thought to represent the arrival in Britain of Belgic peoples fleeing from Gaul in advance of Caesar's army (see BELGAE).

Aymara. The Aymara language, still spoken and once widespread in southern Peru and the Bolivian Highlands, is one of the defining characteristics of numerous polities in and around the Lake Titicaca basin in the Late INTERMEDIATE PERIOD. These 'Aymara Kingdoms' (the largest being Colla and Lupaqa) were frequently involved in internecine hostilities, but shared a number of cultural characteristics which indicate political units of some sophistication. Some of these appear to have been incorporated into the INCA political system, such as class stratification, a powerful ruling class and CHULLPA burials. The common subsistence base appears to have been cultivation of tubers and the herding of alpaca and LLAMA, but it appears that MAIZE (which could not be grown in the highland climate) was imported, possibly from lowland colonies some distance from the major centres.

Ayutthaya [Ayut'ia, Ayuthya, Ayudha]. A city in southern central Thailand, about 75 km north of Bangkok, founded in 1350 by king Rāmādhipati to unify the countries of Syām (Sukhothai) and Lavo (Lopburi). It became the capital of the powerful Thai kingdom of the same name for more than four centuries until its destruction by the Burmese in 1767. Having recently been greatly restored, Ayutthaya, with its hundreds of brick monuments, is now a major tourist attraction of Thailand. See also LAVO, SUKHOTHAI and SYĀM.

Azcapotzalco. See AZTEC, TRIPLE ALLIANCE.

Azelik. A number of sites around Azelik in Niger have yielded evidence for metal working at a very early date, with copper smelting firmly attested by the 5th century bc and possibly extending back to the late 2nd millennium. It appears that iron was not worked until somewhat later, although its presence in southern Air, also in Niger, is dated to the last three centuries bc. Here, as at AKJOUJT, there may be evidence, rare in sub-Saharan Africa, for a brief 'Copper Age' preceding the adoption of iron.

Azilian. The culture or stage which follows the MAGDALENIAN in France. It is now known to date from c9000 to 8000 bc, the closing millennia of the last ice age. According to some definitions this would make it late Palaeolithic, but traditionally it has often been regarded as Mesolithic. Red deer has replaced reindeer as the principal quarry; indeed, the reindeer had probably already become extinct in southern France by this time. The type site of the Azilian is Mas d'Azil in the Pyrenees. The distinctive tool types are the Azilian point (a double-pointed backed blade) and a flat red deer antler harpoon.

Azmak, Tell [Asmaska Moghila]. A TELL site of the Bulgarian Neolithic and Copper Age, located near Stara Zagora in south Bulgaria. In the 7.5-metre stratigraphy, five settlement horizons were distinguished by the excavator, G. Georgiev: five building levels of the early Neolithic KARANOVO I culture, one building level of the VESELINOVO culture; after a stratigraphic break four building levels of both Karanovo V and VI cultures and, after another break, building phases of the Early Bronze Age Karanovo VII culture. Complete village plans for these layers can yield fascinating architectural detail for the whole sequence.

Aztec. Centred on the Basin of Mexico, the NAHUATL-speaking Aztec, also known as the Mexica, were the dominant polity of the Late POST-CLASSIC PERIOD. Their origin is obscure, partly because of the deliberate destruction of their own records, but tradition holds that in 1193 AD the last of seven CHICHIMEC tribes left Aztlan, a mythical birthplace somewhere north or west of Mexico, and filtered south. They founded their capital, TENOCHTITLAN, on an island on Lake Texcoco c1345, having subsisted in the area for most of the intervening years.

The rise of Aztec power is marked by the victory at Azcapotzalco and the formation and ultimate domination of the TRIPLE ALLIANCE. By the early 16th century the Aztec had established hegemony over most of present-day Mexico. The empire was maintained through a system of tribute rather than direct administrative control, and some city-states, such as the TARASCANS and Tlaxcalans, managed to maintain their independence despite persistent pressure.

Aztec society was characterized by a clearly defined hierarchical class system. At the top was the ruling class (Pipil) from whom and by whom the emperors were chosen. The mass of the population were freeman (machuale); under them were the serfs (mayeques) and at the bottom the slaves. Most members of society also belonged to a kin-based land-holding group called the Calpulli, which itself had an internal hierarchy. Social mobility seems to have been possible through state service in either military or mercantile activity. Most prestige was gained through military service, possibly because blood and SACRIFICE had great religious significance. However, the merchants (pochteca) also served as early-reconnaisance and espionage groups, whose members were both plebeian and aristocratic.

Religious activities were to a great degree regulated by the CALENDAR. Ritual human sacrifice was a common event, necessary in ensuring the daily rising of the sun. The Aztec pantheon is dominated by gods of multiple aspects, usually of a stern or warlike attitude. Of the major deities Huitzilpotchtli (the warrior god and chief deity of Tenochtitlan), Texcatlipoca (god of night, death and destruction), Xipe Totec (god of spring and renewal) and QUETZACOATL, the plumed serpent (god of self-sacrifice and inventor of agriculture and the calendar) only the last-named seems not to have been involved in rituals of blood sacrifice.

The arrival of the Spaniards in 1519 and the fall of Tenochtitlan in 1520 after a 90-day siege marks the end of Aztec dominance.

Aztlan. *See* AZTEC.

B

Baal. An ancient CANAANITE god, first appearing in inscriptions of the early Middle Bronze Age (*c*2000 BC). An important temple dedicated to Baal has been excavated at UGARIT. One of his main roles was as a god of fertility. The worship of Baal continued into PHOENICIAN times and also appears in the Punic west, especially at CARTHAGE.

Baalbek. A settlement in the Lebanon, which achieved importance in late Hellenistic and Roman times, especially as holy city for the predatory Ituraean tetrarchs, and as religious centre of the Beqa'a region. Often known by its Greek name of Heliopolis (City of the Sun), it shows magnificent ruins of the Roman imperial period, particularly the Temples of Jupiter and Bacchus.

Ba and Shu [Pa-Shu]. Ba and Shu, names often coupled in Chinese texts, were kingdoms ruling the area of modern Sichuan during the Eastern ZHOU period, Ba dominating the eastern half of the province and Shu the plain of CHENGDU (the word Shu survives today as the literary name for Sichuan). Under pressure from the CHU state, Ba conquered Shu in the 5th century BC but was itself overrun by Chu and finally by QIN in the 4th century. Ba and Shu cultural remains are similar; especially characteristic are boat-coffin burials set on river terraces, and tanged willow-leaf-shaped bronze swords. The swords, which perpetuate an archaic (Western Zhou) form long since superseded elsewhere in China (*see* SWORDS), often bear a sort of pictogram that combines a hand, the head of a snake, and sometimes a tiger. *See also* BELLS (CHINA).

Babadag. A TELL settlement site of the Late Bronze Age, located on a fortified promontory in the middle of Lake Babadag, in the Rumanian Dobrogea. Six levels of occupation have been identified in a two-metre stratigraphy, all of which are associated with rich assemblages of pottery, bones, carbonized cereals, iron and bronze tools. The site gives its name to the local Late Bronze Age group.

Babylon. The capital of BABYLONIA, situated on the Euphrates River south of Baghdad in modern Iraq. The city was occupied from the 3rd millennium BC but became important early in the 2nd millennium under the kings of Babylon's First Dynasty (*see* Table 3, page 321). The sixth king of this dynasty was Hammurabi (*c*1792-1750 BC) who made Babylon the capital of a vast empire, and is best remembered for his code of laws (*see* SUSA). This period was brought to an end by an attack by HITTITES, and the city had a mixed history until the Neo-Babylonian period of 7th-6th centuries BC — it once again achieved preeminence when Nebuchadnezzar extended the Babylonian Empire over most of Western Asia. Babylon fell to Cyrus in 539 BC; occupation continued in the ACHAEMENID period. The city was taken by ALEXANDER in 331 BC; indeed, Alexander died in Babylon in 323. Babylon subsequently declined and was eventually abandoned after the Muslim conquest of AD 641.

Because of the high water table, which has risen in the last few millennia, only buildings of the Neo-Babylonian period were accessible to the German excavators of Babylon in the first decades of this century. The city of this period covered *c*200 hectares, divided into two by the River Euphrates. Most work was conducted in the part of the Inner City on the east bank, which housed the palace and several important temples. The fortifications consisted of a double line of walls and a moat connected to the Euphrates, allowing boats to enter under the gatehouse bridges. The most impressive surviving monument is the Ishtar Gate on the north side of the city, approached by a processional way, and decorated with glazed bricks bearing relief figures of lions, bulls and dragons. Important buildings excavated include Nebuchadnezzar's palace, close to the Ishtar Gate, a colossal building with many rooms arranged around five different courtyards; the vaulted store rooms of this palace were formerly interpreted as the base of the 'Hanging Gardens' of ancient repute. Another huge palace of Nebuchadnezzar's reign (605-562 BC) — the so-called 'Summer Palace' — was constructed to the northwest of the Inner City and was enclosed by a triangular outer wall. A number of temples were excavated, including the temple and ZIGGURAT of the city's patron deity, Marduk, which was the original 'Tower of Babel'; little of the structure survives today after centuries of brick-robbing by later Mesopotamians.

Babylonia. Geographically, Babylonia refers to southern Mesopotamia, the southern part of modern Iraq, lying between Baghdad and the Gulf. Babylonia is a flat alluvial plain formed by the two great rivers, the Tigris and the Euphrates, which made this arid region one of the richest agricultural areas of the ancient world. The world's earliest civilization — that of SUMER — arose in this area in the late 4th millennium BC, but historians usually restrict the use of the term Babylonia to a later period, following the unification of the country under Babylon's First Dynasty in the 2nd millennium BC (*see* Table 3, page 321).

Bacho Kiro. A cave in central Bulgaria with a series of MOUSTERIAN levels (14 to 12) and then Upper PALAEOLITHIC levels (11 to 3). The earliest Upper Palaeolithic levels have AURIGNACIAN features. Backed blades appear towards the top. On the basis of radiocarbon and other indications, the earliest Upper Palaeolithic levels seem to be c43,000 bc, earlier than any known elsewhere.

bacini. Pottery vessels that were placed for decorative purposes high in the walls of churches, over church doorways or in church towers. The best-known group occurs in northern Italy, where several hundred later medieval churches have such vessels, ranging in date from the 11th century to the 15th century. The Italian examples were imported from the Byzantine and Arabic world to begin with, but in the later medieval period north Italian MAIOLICAS were regularly used as well. Bacini were probably also employed in southern Italian, Greek and western European churches, but little is known about these.

Bacsonian. An early HOLOCENE (c8000-4000 bc) stone tool industry of northern Vietnam, normally regarded as a late variant of the more widespread Southeast Asian HOABINHIAN industry. The Bacsonian industry is characterized by a high proportion of edge-ground pebble tools, and some sites have produced cord- or basket-marked pottery. The industry could have incipient horticultural associations, but this is the subject of an unresolved current debate. *See also* DA BUT.

Bactria. The fertile region of Afghan Turkestan, south of the River Oxus. Its earliest significance was as one of the 20 satrapies of the ACHAEMENID empire. Bactria remained important after its conquest by ALEXANDER in 329 BC and subsequently as part of the PARTHIAN empire. Its wealth and importance depended on the east-west trade routes that passed through it, linking China in the east with the Mediterranean world in the west. Many Greeks settled in Bactria in the Seleucid period and through this province and its neighbour to the south, GANDHARA, Greek ideas reached the civilizations of India.

Badarian. An early predynastic industry of Upper Egypt, dating from the early 4th millennium BC. Settlement sites have proved elusive, and much of the available information comes from graves. Badarian material culture was essentially Neolithic, the only metal objects being beads made of native, that is not smelted, copper. The characteristic pottery is red with black tops to the vessel walls; a range of vessels was also hollowed from basalt and alabaster. Barley and emmer wheat were cultivated, while cattle and sheep or goats were herded. Flax was grown and woven into linen cloth. Recent research tends to emphasize the continuity of cultural development in PREDYNASTIC EGYPT, and the Badarian is no longer regarded as the distinctive entity it once appeared to be.

Badbury Rings. *See* ARTHUR.

Baden culture. A 3rd millennium bc Copper Age culture group of vast extent, covering northern Yugoslavia, all of Hungary, most of Czechoslovakia, southern Poland and part of the east Alpine zone. On the basis of E. Neustupny's radiocarbon chronology, the

Baden culture is divided into three phases : Early (2750-2450 bc), Classic (2600-2250 bc) and Late (2400-2200 bc). The most complete sequences are represented in Hungary and Czechoslovakia. Baden marks a strong contrast with the rich TELL settlements of the preceding Chalcolithic, embodying a highly dispersed settlement pattern, a nucleated cemetery pattern (e.g. ALSONE-MEDI) and absence of highly decorated pottery. The paucity of Baden metalwork reflects the period between the decline of Carpathian surface ores and the onset of the Alpine 'Fahlerz' boom.

Badorf ware. A distinctive type of pottery dating to the later 8th century and the 9th century, made in the Vorgebirge hills west of Cologne. The pottery was probably produced in the typical cream fabric as early as the 7th century, but the globular pitchers and bowls of the Carolingian period are the best known. Badorf-ware kilns have been excavated at Bruhl-Eckdorf and Walberberg in recent years; the products of these workshops have been found in the Netherlands, eastern England, and as far north as Denmark. At some time in the 9th century the pots were first decorated with red paint, and gradually the new forms and styles known as PINGSDORF WARES evolved.

Baghdad. The present-day capital of Iraq and the Islamic capital from the 8th century to the 13th century. When the Abbasids overthrew the last Umayyad caliph in 750, they decided to move the Islamic capital from DAMASCUS, which was full of Umayyad sympathizers and too close to the Byzantine frontier. Two replacements were chosen and rejected before al-Mansur selected Baghdad in 762. The site is on the River Tigris, at a point scarcely 40 km from the Euphrates, and where the two rivers were connected by canals. Moreover, Baghdad lay on the 'Khorasan road', part of the SILK ROUTE leading eastwards to BUK-HARA, SAMARKAND and China. The site was therefore well-watered, defensible and well-placed for communications by road and river. Abbassid Baghdad is buried beneath the modern city, and almost all we know of it comes from contemporary writers, such as Ya'qubi and al-Khatib. The focal point was the 'round city', a royal precinct containing the palace, a congregational mosque, ministries and barracks, surrounded by walls and a moat. According to al-Khatib, the architect Rabah recorded the diameter of the city as 2640 metres. To the south lay al-Karkh, a township which already existed in 762, while to the north was al-Harbiyah, a quarter dominated by army officers. Across the Tigris lay the quarters of Rasafah (begun in 769), ash-Shammasyah and al-Mukharrim. In the late 8th and early 9th centuries Baghdad was large and wealthy, and under rulers such as Harun al-Rashid (d. 809) the court had a reputation for gross extravagance. The caliph abandoned Baghdad in favour of SAMARRA in 836, but returned in 882. The city was burnt by the Mongols in 1258, rebuilt and sacked by TIMUR in 1400.

Bahia. A regional development on the central coast of Ecuador which flourished from c500 BC to AD500.Characterized by large stone-lined platform mounds and unique pottery forms, Bahia represents a well developed socio-political and religious unit. Some continuities with earlier FORMATIVE PERIOD ceramics are evident (e.g. MACHALILLA) but new elements such as the everted, perforated rim and polypod legs are introduced. Particularly elaborate anthropomorphic vessels give information on dress and ornamentation (nose discs and tusk-like pendants). A possible MESOAMERICAN influence can be discerned in these motifs.

The La Plata Island site is almost certainly a CEREMONIAL CENTRE, with huge volumes of figurines, geometrically incised blocks of volcanic material and hardly any evidence of day-to-day living. Ceramic models of houses with high gables and low down-curving roof ridges together with elaborately carved head or neck rests have a notably exotic flavour and indicate possible contact with Asia.

Unfortunately, Bahia centres are located close to present-day centres of population and many sites have already been lost to modern development.

Bahrain. The island of Bahrain in the Arabian Gulf has been identified plausibly with the land of DILMUN, mentioned in Mesopotamian documents of the second half of the 3rd millennium BC. A Danish expedition has investigated sites ranging in date from prehistoric to the 16th century AD. Two important sites in the north of the island belong to the

'Dilmun period', when the island was acting as an entrepôt in trade between Mesopotamia and the HARAPPAN CIVILIZATION of the Indus Valley. One site is a walled town covering *c*17 hectares at Qala'at al-Bahrain; the other a complex temple building a few kilometres away at Barbar. Among the finds of this period are circular steatite stamp seals of the type labelled 'Persian Gulf seals', related to Indus Valley seals, but probably made locally in the Gulf area.

Baikal Neolithic. The Neolithic of the Lake Baikal region in eastern Siberia is relatively well known (the term Neolithic being used here to refer to communities that used pottery, rather than those that practised farming). The first stage is called after the site of Isakovo and is known only from a small number of burials in cemeteries mostly of later date. There is no dating evidence, but guess dates put this stage in the 4th millennium BC. The succeeding Serovo stage, guess-dated to the following millennium, is also known mainly from burials; the most important new artefact of this period is the compound bow, backed with bone plates. The third phase, named Kitoi, has burials with red ochre; composite fish hooks appear, which may indicate greater emphasis on fishing. All three stages seems to have been based on hunting and fishing. The succeeding Glazkovo phase of the 2nd millennium BC saw the beginnings of metal-using, but generally showed continuity in artefact and burial types.

Băile Herculane. A large cave site with an important Palaeolithic, Mesolithic, Neolithic and Copper Age stratigraphy, located in a side valley 10 km north of the Iron Gates gorge of the river Danube in the Rumanian Banat. The long stratigraphy comprises three main occupation horizons: I, Upper Palaeolithic levels corresponding to the WÜRM II phase and defined by a quartzite industry with a lot of end scrapers; II, a thin late Mesolithic level with microlithic flints and crude quartzite tools and Danube fish bones. This is separated by a 60-cm deposit containing Neolithic stray finds (VINČA and TISZA pottery) from III, at least six levels of Late Copper Age occupation, with SALCUŢA IV levels stratified below a long COTOFENI sequence.

Bakers Hole. A chalk pit at Northfleet close to the SWANSCOMBE sites of northwest Kent. Its

'coombe rock' deposits are geologically a little later than the Swanscombe high terrace deposits, and contain a large series of LEVALLOIS flakes and cores.

Bakong. A monument in the southeastern part of ANGKOR, in Roluos, just east of present Siem Reap, Cambodia. Founded by king Indravarman in 881, it is the first KHMER monument to represent a TEMPLE-MOUNTAIN and the first to be built in sandstone (earlier ones having been built of brick). The central tower is 34 metres high.

Baktun. *See* CALENDAR (AMERICAS).

Bakun, Tall i. A TELL site near PERSEPOLIS in southern Iran, occupied in the CHALCOLITHIC period, probably from the early 5th millennium bc. The site consisted of 12 mud-brick buildings with from one to seven rooms each; it was occupied by a simple agricultural community, that excelled in the production of fine painted pottery, related to SUSA A wares. Vessels included conical bowls and goblets with stylized designs including mouflon horns, birds, demons and plants. Other finds include vessels of calcite and alabaster and figurines of women and of oxen.

Bala Hisar. *See* CHARSADA.

Bala Kot. A site of the HARAPPAN CIVILIZATION on the Makran coast of Baluchistan, Pakistan.

Balanovo. The eponymous cemetery of a regional group of the CORDED WARE culture group, distributed in the Volga-Oka area of south central Russia in the early 2nd millennium bc. Most sites are cemeteries, the majority using flat inhumation rites as at the type site. At Balanovo some 120 graves are known, including double burials and some rich graves with copper battle-axes. A broad-spectrum economy is attested at the short-lived settlement sites, confined largely to the main river valleys. Corded beakers, stone battle-axes and fired clay model wheels are characteristic finds.

Bali. Archaeologically, the island of Bali has always lived in the shadow of its bigger neighbour JAVA. The earliest inscriptions, dating from the end of the 9th and the 10th century, reveal an independent INDIANIZED Balinese society practising Buddhism and Sivaism at the same time. The marriage of the king of Bali to a Javanese princess in the late 10th century resulted in the introduction of Javanese culture into the island. Javanese political control was established by the conquest of the island in 1284 and again in 1343; mass immigration of Javanese intensified the Javanization of Bali. From the middle of the 15th century on, when the Indian cults in their old form (Sivaism, Vishnuism, Theravada Buddhism using Sanskrit, and Mahayana Buddhism) retreated before the advance of Islam in Java, Bali became the intellectual centre preserving the essentials of Indo-Javanese culture. However, the fact that at present only seven per cent of the population belong to the *trivamsa* (castes) shows that Indianization did not percolate to the masses.

Balkh. Known to its Arab conquerors as the 'Mother of Cities', the city of Balkh in Afghanistan was occupied long before the arrival of Islam. In the 1st millennium BC it was associated with Zoroaster, and ALEXANDER THE GREAT made it his base for operations in 329-327 BC. Balkh was a caravan city on the SILK ROUTE from the east and a major outpost of Buddhism. Islamic Balkh flourished under the Samanids of BUKHARA (873-999) and contemporary visitors mention two congregational mosques. The city was devastated by the Mongols in 1220 and Ibn Battuta reported that it was still in ruins a hundred years later. Balkh revived in the 15th century under the Timurid rulers of HERAT. Although a section through the massive mud-brick defences revealed a long history of construction, we know very little about the pre-Islamic city. Two Islamic monuments survive: the Masjid-i No Gunbad and the shrine of Khwaja Abu Masar Parsa. The mosque is a mud-brick building, now roofless, with a square plan, 20 metres across, divided by piers into nine square compartments, each originally with a dome (hence the name 'Mosque of the Nine Domes'). The interior contains exquisitely carved stucco decorated with vine scrolls, palmettes etc, reminiscent of 9th and 10th century stucco at SAMARRA, SIRAF, and elsewhere in Iran and Iraq. The shrine, which commemorates a local theologian who died in 1460, has typical Timurid tilework.

ball court. *See* BALL GAME.

ball game. A game both recreational and of ritual significance, originating in MESO-AMERICA and ultimately spreading over wide areas of the Americas; it is also known by the NAHUATL word *tlatchli*. Stone reliefs at Dainzu and the possible remains of a ball court at SAN LORENZO TENOCHTITLAN indicate that the game existed as early as PRE-CLASSIC times. There is considerable diversity in the rules both over time and across cultures, but typically, opposing teams or individuals played on a court, classically (but not necessarily) in the shape of an elongated H. Players wearing special equipment (*see* YOKE) would attempt to keep a solid rubber ball (sometimes 30 cm in diameter and more than 2 kilos in weight) in motion without the use of hands or feet. Some courts, especially in the POST-CLASSIC, had a series of stone rings set high in the court wall; if a team managed to pass the ball through one of these (a rare event indeed) the game was immediately won. Death through injury was not unusual and the loss of a game could sometimes result in the SACRIFICE of the losing team. There is a considerable inventory of artefacts associated with the ball game, including hachas, palmas, court markers, elbow stones and yokes.

ballista. Of the numerous pieces of artillery (possibly about 55) available to the Roman legionary, remarkable were two large torsion engines, the *ballista* for projecting large boulders, and the *catapulta* for firing bolts and other arrow-like missiles. A *ballista* survives at HATRA. The two terms are often used interchangeably.

Balof Cave. A coral rock shelter on New Ireland, Oceania, with a preceramic industry of TALASEA (New Britain) obsidian and bone points in its lower levels, dating from c5000 bc. This site has one of the earliest dates for human settlement (presumably by PAPUAN-language speakers) in Oceania east of New Guinea, at a date long prior to that normally accepted for AUSTRONESIAN expansion in this area. *See also* MISISIL CAVE.

Bambandyanalo. A site in the Limpopo Valley, northern Transvaal, South Africa, where Iron Age occupation is dated to the 11th and 12th centuries ad. A large mound represents the debris of successive substantial settlements, the economy of which was evidently based upon the herding of cattle. The pottery and other artefacts show strong affinities with those from contemporary sites in the Bulawayo area of Zimbabwe. Controversy has surrounded the significance of some 70 human skeletons interred at Bambandyanalo: it was formerly believed that these indicated a non-negroid population, but the supposition is no longer maintained.

Bambata. A cave in the Matopo Hills of south-western Zimbabwe, where excavations have revealed a long sequence of occupations probably covering most of the past 50,000 years. The cave walls also bear an interesting series of rock paintings. The site has given its name to a stone industry and a pottery type which should not be confused as they belong to widely separated periods. The Bambata industry, also referred to in some older works as 'Stillbay' is based upon the use of prepared cores to produce flakes that were retouched into a veriety of scrapers and unifacial or bifacial points. Dated between the 50th and 20th millennia bc, its distribution extends northwards into Zambia and southwards to the Orange Free State and perhaps the Cape. Bambata ware is known only from contexts of the 1st millennium ad in Zimbabwe. It is elaborately decorated with overall stamped designs, and opinion is divided as to whether it should be attributed to the Early Iron Age complex or to a late hunter-gatherer population.

Bambuk. The gold-yielding area of Guinea, near the headwaters of the Niger and Senegal Rivers. Through long-distance trade, the metal obtained here provided much of the wealth of the empires of GHANA and MALI. Significantly, neither of these empires appears to have incorporated the Bambuk area; instead they exploited their intermediate position between Bambuk and the trans-Saharan gold markets. The Bambuk area awaits full archaeological investigation.

Bamiyan. A high valley (2500 metres) in the Hindu Kush, which formed a corridor for the caravan route from BEGRAM and the east to BALKH and the west. In the early centuries AD it was an important Buddist centre, and pilgrims such as Hiuen-Tsang (7th century)

described the numerous rock-cut monasteries, which extend for several kilometres along the cliffs on the north side of the valley. Dominating the scene are two standing Buddhas, carved in the face of the cliff. The smaller (35 metre) Buddha may date from the 3rd century, while the larger (53 metre) statue belongs to the 5th or 6th century. Details of drapery etc were added in plaster, and both the statues and the niches in which they stand were painted. The paintings are in a hybrid style, containing SASSANIAN, GANDHARAN and Indian elements.

Bamiyan remained a Buddhist enclave until its conquest by the Muslim ruler of Sistan, Yaqub b. Layth Saffari, in 870. The citadel of the Islamic town, known today as Shahr-i Gholghola, overlooks the valley from the south. The town and the fortress guarding the eastern approaches to the valley, Shahr-i Zohak, were destroyed by Genghiz Khan in 1221.

banana. The edible fruit-bearing bananas belong to the genus *Musa*, and have been classified into two sections, termed Australimusa and Eumusa. The major cultivar in the Australimusa section (the Fei'i banana, *Musa troglodytarum*) probably originated in the New Guinea-Solomons area, and was spread into tropical Polynesia by AUSTRONESIAN colonists. The Eumusa section contains the bananas of economic importance today, and the major cultivars evolved in the region of Malaysia and Indonesia, to be carried by Austronesian settlers into Oceania, and westwards to Madagascar and Africa. On linguistic grounds it seems probable that bananas were being cultivated by Austronesians in Island Southeast Asia by 3000 BC. Claims for a prehistoric introduction into South America across the Pacific are still under debate.

Banas. A CHALCOLITHIC culture of Rajasthan, western India, of the 3rd and 2nd millennia BC. The most important sites are AHAR and GILUND.

Banaue. A region of spectacular rice-terracing, belonging to the Ifugao people of the Mountain Province of northern Luzon, Philippines. The terraces extend like giant steps up mountain sides and are of unknown antiquity, although they were considered by anthropologist Felix Keesing to have been constructed after Spanish penetration of the

Philippines (commencing 1571). However, more recent excavations suggest that some house terraces in the region could date back to 1000 BC.

Banbhore. Standing among desolate salt flats on a former mouth of the Indus and the only major site in a sparsely populated region, Banbhore is plausibly identified as Daibal, the first town in Sind to fall to the Moslems, in 712. Excavations revealed that occupation began in the Scytho-Parthian period (1st century BC to 2nd century AD) and ended in the 13th century. Like SIRAF, the city was located on a barren coast, which could not have supported a town without the wealth generated by trade. It was a port of call for ships voyaging between India and the Persian Gulf and an outlet for commodities from the interior; in the 2nd century, the *Periplus of the Erythraean Sea* mentions an entrepôt in the Indus delta which exported lapis lazuli from the Hindu Kush, musk from the Himalayas etc. In the Islamic period, Banbhore was a walled town, just over 500 metres across. Within the walls, the most imposing building was the congregational mosque. Outside the walls, the excavators found an industrial quarter and a reservoir or enclosed harbour.

Ban Chiang. A site of major importance in northeast THAILAND, containing 4.5 metres of burial deposits spanning the period 3600 BC to AD 1800. The basal burials are associated with incised and cord-marked pottery, copper and bronze artefacts, and evidence for rice cultivation and domesticated cattle, probably in a regime of shifting agriculture. From levels dated to the late 2nd and 1st millennia BC, the site has produced a famous variety of curvilinear painted red-on-buff pottery, together with iron, bones of water buffalo, and palaeoecological evidence suggesting the practice of wet-rice agriculture. However, there is now disagreement over the dating of Ban Chiang, and from recent excavations at the nearby site of Ban Nadi it is apparent that the dates claimed for the appearances of iron and the painted pottery may be too old by a millennium or more, and the true antiquity of bronze prior to 1500 bc is still unclear. *See also* BAN KAO, KOK CHAROEN, NON NOK THA.

Banjica. An early and late VINČA open settlement on the northern slopes of the Avala Hills in Belgrade, Yugoslavia. The third of five occupation horizons has been dated to c3760 bc. During excavations by Todorović and Cermanović, complete late Vinča house plans were recovered, which yielded detailed information on domestic activities. Food-preparation and cooking, flint-knapping, weaving and storage are all attested inside the houses, while other industrial tasks are documented in working pits in yards. A large collection of signs incised on pottery indicates ritual activity in the village community, which reflects domestic rather than public religious activity.

Ban Kao. A burial site in Kanchanaburi Province, western Thailand, Ban Kao spans mainly the period 2500-1600 bc, and the burials have produced elaborately shaped unpainted pottery with a range of bone, stone and shell artefacts. The site has produced no bronze, despite claims for use of this metal in northeastern Thailand before 3000 BC. *See also* BAN CHIANG, GUA CHA, KOK CHAROEN, NON NOK THA.

Bann point. *See* LARNIAN.

Banpo [Pan-p'o]. Site of an early YANGSHAO Neolithic village, now preserved as a museum, at Xi'an in Shaanxi province, China. Four radiocarbon dates from Banpo range from c4800 to c4300 BC. The settlement occupied about 50,000 square metres and included a cemetery and pottery kilns outside a ditch that surrounded the residential area. Dogs and pigs were domesticated, and millet was the staple crop. Unpainted pottery was cord-marked or stamped, while the finest pottery was painted in black or red with a limited range of simple geometric patterns and drawings of fish, turtles, deer and masked or stylized faces, pictorial motifs rarely encountered elsewhere in Chinese Neolithic pottery.

Remains comparable to those from Banpo have been unearthed nearby at Jiangzhai in Lintong Xian and at Baoji Beishouling and Hua Xian Yuanjunmiao, all in Shaanxi. At Beishouling and Yuanjunmiao, Banpo-type remains overlie older Neolithic levels in which all the pottery is unpainted; a radiocarbon date late in the 6th millennium BC has been obtained for an equivalent stratum at Hua Xian Laoguantai. Dates in the same range have come from Neolithic sites at Wuan

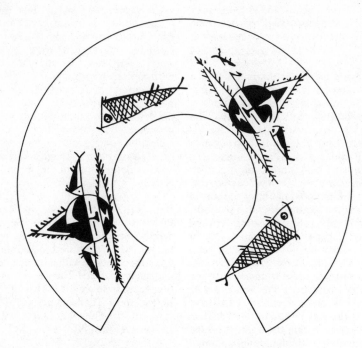

Design painted inside a pottery bowl from Banpo

Cishan in southern Hebei and Xinzheng Peiligang in Henan, both with evidence of millet cultivation and domesticated pigs and dogs.

Banshan [Pan-shan]. Site of a Neolithic cemetery in the Tao River valley south of Lanzhou in Gansu province, China. It is the type site of the Banshan culture, which belongs to the western or Gansu branch of the YANG-SHAO Neolithic. Banshan is best known for its pottery urns with painted designs in black and brown, which are well represented in Western museums. Banshan and MAJIAYAO pottery designs have a common starting point in simple running spirals, but in Majiayao these are elaborated to a degree of complexity never seen in Banshan wares. Banshan designs have loose parallels in spiral designs from other parts of the world (most of them well beyond the reach of DIFFUSIONIST explanations) while Majiayao is isolated and highly distinctive. A few radiocarbon dates for Banshan in the 3rd millennium BC have been taken as evidence that it derives from the earlier Majiayao culture, though the relationship between the

two need not be so direct. A late stage of Banshan is named after the site of MACHANG.

Banteay Ch'mar [Khmer: 'the narrow citadel']. A huge stone monument near the Dangrek mountains in northwestern Cambodia, erected by king Jayavarman VII towards the end of the 12th century to the memory of one of his sons killed in action. It has historically important reliefs.

Banteay Srei. [Khmer: 'the citadel of the ladies']. A comparatively small, but very beautiful monument in pink sandstone to the east of the main group of ANGKOR in Cambodia, built in 967 by the Brahman Yajñavarāha, preceptor of the king, in honour of Siva. Famous in particular for its elaborate relief decoration, the monument forms an architectural and art style in its own right.

Bantu. A linguistic term, applied to a widely distributed group of closely interrelated languages in sub-Saharan Africa. It has long been believed that the distribution of these languages, which form part of the Niger-

Congo linguistic family, indicates a relatively recent expansion of population from a single source area, which linguistic evidence locates in the modern eastern Nigeria/Cameroon area, at the extreme northwestern limit of the Bantu-speaking zone. Beyond this area Bantu languages are today spoken over the whole of the continent south of a line which closely follows the northern margin of the equatorial forest, with the exception of the San people now concentrated in Botswana and Namibia.

Despite the manifest dangers in assuming a correlation between archaeological and linguistic reconstructions of the past, several prehistorians have attempted to trace parallels between the linguistically indicated Bantu language dispersal and the archaeological evidence for the rapid appearance of metal-working mixed-farming peoples over the greater part of sub-Saharan Africa during the first few centuries of the Christian era. Whatever the linguistic attributions of the people concerned, it is clear that this period saw a pronounced change in the life-style prevailing over the eastern and southern parts of the subcontinent. Villages of mixed-farmers who made pottery and worked metals were established in areas which appear previously to have been occupied solely by hunter-gatherers using stone tools. It seems probable that this change was due to the physical arrival of a new population element, particularly since both life-styles seem to have flourished side by side in many areas throughout and beyond the 1st millennium ad. Throughout the region these first farming settlements are marked by a common pottery tradition, seen as the hallmark of a single 'Early Iron Age' complex. This complex is represented first during the last few centuries bc in the Lake Victoria basin, where its characteristic pottery is known as UREWE WARE. Related wares are attested near the Kenya and Tanzania coasts by the 2nd century ad, and as far south as the Transvaal and Natal by the 4th century.

Baoji [Pao-chi]. A district on the Wei River in western Shaanxi province, China. Neolithic remains at Baoji Beishouling may represent antecedents of the BANPO culture. Western ZHOU bronzes have been unearthed repeatedly in the Baoji area, including notably an altar set found in 1901 and now in the Metropolitan Museum in New York. Two tombs of the 19th century bc excavated at Baoji Rujiazhuang in 1975 contained bronze RITUAL VESSELS, some with stylistic eccentricities that point to contacts with non-Chinese (or at any rate less Chinese) populations farther west in Gansu. The Rujiazhuang tombs also yielded the earliest known evidence of SILK embroidery.

Baphuon. An enormous sandstone monument in the northwestern part of ANGKOR, Cambodia, built by king Udayadityavarman II (1050-66) as his TEMPLE-MOUNTAIN and the centre of his capital. With its dimensions of 120 by 100 metres at the base and a height of 24 metres, this five-storeyed pyramid (topped originally by a tower of about the same height again) is the most massive artificial mountain of classical CAMBODIA and its second largest monument, after ANGKOR WAT. There are vigorous reliefs on the walls of the first and second storeys.

Baradostian. The name given to the earlier Upper PALAEOLITHIC levels of the cave of SHANIDAR in northern Iraq, also applied to other assemblages in Iraq and Iran. It has radiocarbon dates centring on about 30,000 bc.

Baray [Khmer: 'artificial lake']. Large rectangular water reservoirs in Cambodia; notable examples at ANGKOR are the Eastern (Oriental) Baray, originally called Yaśodharatataka, 7 by 1.8 km, built by king Yaśovarman (889-900), and the Western (Occidental) Baray, 8 by 2.2 km, built by king Udayadityavarman II (1050-66).

Barbar. *See* BAHRAIN.

barbotine. A method of decorating pottery, particularly popular in Roman Gaul and Britain, in which very soft clay was piped on to the surface of coloured wares before firing, giving an effect rather like that of icing upon a cake.

Barche di Solferino. A settlement at the southern end of Lake Garda in northern Italy belonging to the Bronze Age POLADA culture of the 2nd millennium BC. The houses were raised off the ground on a framework of timbers covered by brushwood. Finds, including those made of organic materials such as wood, were well preserved by the mud and include wooden vessels, wheels and a dugout canoe.

Barclodiad Y Gawres. A PASSAGE GRAVE on the island of Anglesey in Wales related to those of the BOYNE CULTURE and the nearby tomb of BRYN CELLI DDU. It consists of a chamber and passage, surrounded by a ring of stones, many decorated in a style similar to that of the Boyne tombs, all under a round barrow, c30 metres in diameter.

Barkaer. A site of the later Early Neolithic (TRB CULTURE) in east Jutland. Two large rectangular structures of timber were excavated, each divided up into smaller units. These were originally interpreted as houses, but recently it has been suggested that they were in fact burial structures. Apparent offerings of amber beads and pottery were found in pits below floor level.

barley. A group of cereals, members of the genus *Hordeum*. Wild two-row barley (*H. spontaneum*) occurs today in a similar area of the Near East to the WHEATS. This species seems to be the ancestor of all domestic forms of barley. *H. spontaneum* appears in the early Neolithic of the Near East by 7000 bc, as early as the wheats, but domesticated two-row barley does not appear until slightly later in the Neolithic. Six-row barleys, with six vertical rows of grains up the ear, appeared as a result of domestication at about the same time. Barley spread into Asia and Europe mainly in the six-row form. All the domestic barleys are closely related and their nomenclature is in some disarray. Some authors include them all in one species, under the heading *H. vulgare sensu lato*, or another name, *H. sativum*. Two-row barleys are sometimes distinguished as *H. distichum* or *distichon*. Six-row barleys are variously called *H. polystichum*, *H. hexastichum* or, confusingly, *H. vulgare sensu strictu*. Both two-row and six-row forms have varieties that thresh free from the chaff (naked barleys) and that do not (hulled barleys).

Barnenez. A Neolithic site in Brittany, consisting of two long CAIRNS, one of which contained 11 PASSAGE GRAVES, placed side by side. They display a range of architectural techniques, using both large megalithic slabs and drystone walling; some chambers had corbelled vaults. Corrected radiocarbon dates

suggest that the site was used in the 5th millennium BC, making it one of the earliest megalithic tombs in Europe. *See also* CORBEL, MEGALITHIC MONUMENTS.

Barrancoid [Barrancas]. One of the major ceramic series developed by Irving Rouse and José Cruxent to facilitate cultural comparison in the northeast South America / Antilles area. Possibly originating on the Caribbean coast of Colombia, the series was established on the Orinoco Delta by c1000 BC and continued in some areas as late as AD 1000. (This period is also known as the Neo-Indian epoch.) Its best-known features are skilfully modelled, biomorphic ornamentation and broad-lined incised patterns. Although roughly contemporary with the SALADOID series in other areas, Barrancoid replaced Saladoid in the delta area. The type site is Barrancas.

barrow. A mound, usually of earth and rubble, and occurring in a variety of shapes and sizes, which was raised to cover either single or multiple burials. The term 'tumulus' is used synonymously with barrow, while the related term 'cairn' is used to describe a mound constructed exclusively of stone. The term 'barrow' is used widely in European prehistory but most commonly in Britain, where it originated. In Britain most barrows of the Neolithic period were long, either oval or trapezoidal in shape, and usually covered either mortuary houses or other timber structures, or MEGALITHIC chambers (*see also* PASSAGE GRAVE, GALLERY GRAVE). In the BEAKER period and subsequent Bronze Age, round barrows became the dominant form and generally covered single burials, rather than the collective inhumations of the Neolithic. Bowl barrows — simple round mounds, often surrounded by a ditch — were the most common form, used throughout the Bronze Age and sporadically also in the Iron Age. The WESSEX CULTURE of the southern English Early Bronze Age was characterized by special types of barrows: bell, disc, saucer and pond barrows. Bell barrows have relatively small mounds and a berm or gap between the mound and the ditch; disc barrows are very small mounds in the centre of a circular open space, surrounded by a ditch; saucer barrows are low disc-like mounds occupying the entire space up to the ditch; while the misleadingly named pond barrows are not mounds at all, but circular dish-shaped enclosures surrounded by an external bank.

On the continent of Europe both long and round barrows are found in association with megalithic tombs during the Neolithic and Copper Age, while round barrows covering single inhumations or cremations occur in a number of different areas in the Bronze Age and Iron Age. Indeed, barrow burials occur also in Roman and post-Roman times: one of the most famous of all barrows in Britain is that covering the Anglo-Saxon boat burial at SUTTON HOO.

Barton Ramie. A site located on the Belize River in eastern Belize [formerly British Honduras] and notable for its sudden influx of foreign materials shortly before the opening of the CLASSIC PERIOD. This new ceramic complex, called Floral Park, while not completely eclipsing earlier local material, is virtually indistinguishable from ceramics found at CHALCHUAPA in El Salvador. Some archaeologists have proposed that this intrusive complex represents the immigration of groups fleeing the disastrous effects of the Mount ILOPANGO eruptions in *c*260.

Barumini. Site of a NURAGHE, named Su Nuraxi, in southern Sardinia. It began with a single tower *c*17 metres high, with two upper storeys containing niches, apparently for sleeping. It was later surrounded by a wall with smaller towers in it and an outer circle of free-standing towers; these too were soon linked to provide a double wall for the original tower, and the whole complex was associated with a village of stone huts. There is a radiocarbon date for an early stage of *c*1450 bc (*c*1800 BC) and the site remained in occupation until the Roman period, although it was temporarily deserted after an attack by CARTHAGINIANS in the 6th century BC.

Basatanya. *See* TISZAPOLGÁR.

basilica [Greek: 'royal building']. The Romans applied this name to a range of rectangular roofed buildings, with or without apse, subdivided internally by single or double rows of columns, roughly in the manner of the nave and aisles now familiar from church architecture. There was usually a clerestorey (a series of windows piercing the upper part of the nave wall to give extra light) above which

rose the roof, sometimes vaulted but more commonly of timber. The building was usually entered through a covered entrance porch (narthex). One such building is the Basilica of Maxentius, which has survived in the ruins of the Forum in Rome. However, in ancient Rome the term 'basilica' applies to the function rather than the form of the building: the Roman buildings normally adjoined the FORUM and functioned as public meeting halls, courts and even markets.

In the early medieval period, the basilican form was adapted for Christian use. In several instances, Roman basilicas were refashioned for Christian worship, and the form of construction remained popular for a variety of religious purposes in ROME, RAVENNA and the Latin West as well as in BYZANTIUM and North Africa from the 4th century to the 12th century. Constantine, the first Christian emperor, constructed several basilican churches in the 4th century, including the first St Peters and the Lateran. The finest early Christian basilicas — S. Apollinare Nuovo and S. Apollinare in Classe — are to be seen in Ravenna, with their marble columns and marvellous Byzantine mosaics intact. The true basilican church belongs to the Mediterranean, North Africa and Byzantium in the early Christian era between the demise of the Roman empire and the emergence of the Romanesque style. The longitudinal aisled hall remained in the minds of the architects of the great Romanesque and Gothic cathedrals of Western Europe, but by the later medieval period the essential simplicity of the basilican design had been submerged in elaborate bayed and vaulted schemes with transepts, towers and elaborate facades.

Basketmaker. The earliest of two major chronological periods of the ANASAZI tradition, the more recent being PUEBLO. The whole period is characterized by transition from Late ARCHAIC life-styles to sedentary agriculture with characteristics such as pottery, pit houses, cist storage and grinding tools becoming increasingly apparent as time progresses. Three Basketmaker stages were recognized at the 1927 Pecos Conference of Southwesternists (*see* KIDDER). Basketmaker I is purely hypothetical and was based on the supposition that evidence of an early Anasazi stage would eventually come to light; so far it has not. The typical settlement pattern for

Basketmaker II (AD 1-450) was a large base camp and widely scattered seasonal camps, where the preferred container was the basket (hence the name). Limited maize and squash cultivation and the rare occurrence of crude pottery also indicate a largely Archaic lifestyle. Basketmaker III (450-700/750) saw a shift in settlement patterns. Small villages of pit houses became increasingly common and the preferred locus was the well-watered valley bottom. Specialized structures such as wattle-and-daub storage bins and large rooms for communal activity (possibly early KIVAS) also began to occur more frequently.

Basra. The city of Basra stands near the west bank of the Shatt al-Arab, in modern Iraq, through which the Tigris and Euphrates reach the Gulf. Founded in 637/8 by the caliph Omar as a military base, Basra rapidly became a thriving city. In due course, ships supplying BAGHDAD with goods from Africa, India and beyond used Basra as a port-of-call and its bazaars became famous. Its was also an important centre of learning. From the late 9th century Basra suffered a series of disasters and gradually declined. The Zanj (negro slaves who worked in the fields and plantations of southern Iraq) revolted in 869-73 and sacked the city, and in 923 it was plundered by the Qarmarthians. In 1050, parts of the city were in ruins, although the bazaars were still doing business.

Basse Yutz. The find-spot in Lorraine, eastern France, of a pair of bronze wine flagons, regarded as among the finest examples of early CELTIC ART, dating to the early 4th century BC.

Batalimo. One of the very few later prehistoric settlement sites so far investigated in the Central African Republic, dated to early in the 1st millennium ad. Artefacts of chipped and ground stone were recovered, but although no trace of metal was found, the possibility remains that Batalimo was in fact an Iron Age settlement.

Bat Cave. A site in southwestern New Mexico, USA, notable for its evidence of prehistoric plant cultivation. Early levels indicate the use of primitive pod corn (dated c3500 bc), but a cultivated form of MAIZE was in use by 2500 bc, the earliest date for cultigens in the American Southwest. Both maize and squash remains were found in association with COCHISE materials of the CHIRICAHUA stage, and evidence of beans (dated to 1000-400 bc) was found in association with SAN PEDRO materials. These plants represent the three basic staples which underlie North American agriculture, although a cave location seems far more appropriate to the earlier ARCHAIC lifestyle, based on hunting and gathering.

Bath [Aquae Sulis]. The emergence from the ground of natural hot springs at a temperature of 120°F attracted the bath-loving Romans here after their invasion of Britain. The springs were sacred to the local goddess Sulis (equated by the Romans with Minerva), hence the Roman name Aquae Sulis [Waters of Sulis]. From the late 1st century AD onwards the springs became the centre for a complex of monumental buildings unparalleled for their lavish extent and sophistication elsewhere in Roman Britain. These include the Temple of Sulis Minerva with Corinthian pilasters and a medusa-head relief on the pediment, and an extensive collection of baths, the most notable being the vaulted Great Bath, originally over 17 metres high.

baths, Roman. From the 1st century BC onwards the Romans turned bathing into a highly civilized and essentially communal activity. Establishments called *balneae* or, later, *thermae* incorporating suites of rooms at different temperatures became a feature both of private and public building. A typical installation would include a *tepidarium* (warm room, probably without bath), a *caldarium* (hot, with plunge bath), a *frigidarium* (cold, also with bath), and an *apodyterium* (changing-room). Elaborate examples might also include a *laconicum* (room with dry heat), a swimming bath, an exercise area (*palaestra*), gardens and a library. Such a complex provided a central and important social meeting-point, and it seems that access was enjoyed by a wide cross-section of society. The swift expansion of this type of building, both in individual size and geographically across the Roman empire, was undoubtedly helped by the development of new technologies such as the use of concrete to construct wider and higher vaults, and the installation of underfloor and ducted hot-air heating systems (*see* HYPOCAUST).

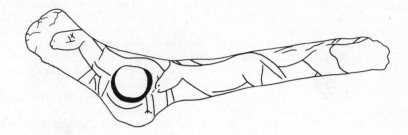

Bâton de commandement

bâton de commandement. A name given to perforated batons made of antler of the Upper PALAEOLITHIC period in western Europe. They are usually some 30 cm long, but are often broken. The perforation is smooth and round, usually a few centimetres in diameter. The antler widens out at the point of branching and this is where the hole is usually made. They are typical of the MAGDALENIAN period, but are found as early as the AURIGNACIAN, some 30,000 years ago. A number of explanations of their function have been offered; 'staffs of office', as implied by the French name, is not a likely explanation. They are more likely to have been used as straighteners of wood and antler strips for use in composite spears.

Battersea Shield. A late Iron Age parade shield found in the River Thames at Battersea. A fine example of insular CELTIC ART, the shield is elongated with rounded ends and a slight waisting in the middle; it is made of bronze and decorated in relief and with red glass inlay.

battle-axe. A type of shaft-hole axe designed for use in warfare, made of either stone or metal. Stone battle-axes were widely used in prehistoric Europe from the Late Neolithic onwards; they were so ubiquitous in the later Neolithic of northern Europe that the term Battle-axe culture is often used as a synonym for CORDED WARE or SINGLE GRAVE culture. Copper and bronze examples are common in the Copper and Bronze Ages of eastern Europe, while the VIKINGS also made use of battle-axes, normally made of iron.

Battle-axe culture. *See* BATTLE-AXE, CORDED WARE, SINGLE GRAVE.

baulk. A section of unexcavated material left standing between different parts of an excavation. The main purpose of baulks is the retention of a visible record of stratification, but they also serve to facilitate access to different areas of the excavation.

Bayeux Tapestry. This famous tapestry, 70.34 metres long and 50 cm deep, is worked in coloured wools on a background of bleached linen. The work was probably commissioned by Bishop Odo of Bayeux (1036-97) a half-brother of William the Conquerer, and took about two years to complete. The tapestry depicts the events leading up to the invasion of England by William Duke of Normandy and the Battle of Hastings on 14 October 1066, when the English King Harold was defeated and killed. The tapestry was almost certainly designed and embroidered in England; its purpose is not certain but it may well have been used to adorn the walls of a royal hall (the bawdy scenes often occurring along the border of the tapestry would argue against it being a hanging for the cathedral). The themes are enacted very much in the manner of a feudal drama or *chanson de geste*.

The technical detail and iconography in the Bayeux Tapestry is of unparalleled importance to the social historian and medieval archaeologist; for instance, 33 buildings depicted in highly stylized form offer an impression of contemporary churches, castles, towers and hastily constructed MOTTE AND BAILEY castles. The battle scenes provide a detailed contemporary impression of infantry and cavalry formations, Norman armour and weapons as well as the clothing and hairstyles of both men and women. The invasion fleet is a readily identifiable collection of 'Viking double enders' (clinker-built long boats probably varying in length from about 25 to 30 metres, propelled by oars and a single mast). The Norman invasion of England was by the standards of the time a gigantic military operation, involving 7000 men including 2000 cavalry, and the tapestry captures some of the excitement and drama of the event.

Bayon. A majestic monument in sandstone in the northwestern part of ANGKOR, Cambodia, built c1200 by the last great ruler of the KHMER empire, the Buddhist king Jayavarman VII (1181-c1218) as his TEMPLE-MOUNTAIN and the centre of his restored capital ANGKOR THOM. It consists of a central circular sanctuary representing a mountain, situated within two relief-covered rectangular galleries, the outer one measuring 160 by 140 metres. This architectural ensemble is crowned by 54 towers, the central tower reaching a height of 43 metres. Each tower is decorated with four enigmatically smiling faces, representing the king himself in the form of the compassionate Bodhisattva Lokeśvara. Moreover, the monument is also integrated in the general architectural symbolism of Angkor Thom — the Churning of the Ocean, according to Hindu mythology — with the central mountain serving as the churn.

BC, bc. Years before Christ. The lower case 'bc' represents uncalibrated RADIOCARBON years; the capitals BC denote a calibrated radiocarbon date, or a date such as an historically derived one, that does not need CALIBRATION (*see* Table 8, p. 422). There is no year 0: 1 BC is the same year as AD 1.

Beaker. A general term to describe a simple type of drinking vessel without handles. Specifically, the term Beaker or Bell Beaker is applied to a particular type of vessel made of fine red or brown burnished ware, decorated with horizontal panels of comb- or cord-impressed designs, found in the 3rd millenium BC in many parts of Europe, from Spain to Czechoslovakia and Hungary, and from Italy to Britain. Beaker pots are commonly found in graves, which were often single inhumations under round BARROWS; commonly associated finds include copper or bronze daggers and ornaments, flint arrowheads and stone wristguards and stone battle-axes.

The widespread distribution of Beaker finds has led to the frequent identification of a Beaker people and many speculations about their possible origins. The most popular view has favoured an Iberian origin, but there have also been proponents of an east or north European origin, and David Clarke favoured a south French origin. The most complicated view, propounded by E. Sangmeister, involved an original spread from Iberia and a later reflux movement of an allegedly hybrid Beaker/CORDED-WARE group back from the Low Countries, and is not much favoured today. More recently, workers such as Richard Harrison and Robert Chapman have suggested dual or multiple origins for the Beaker culture, while Stephen Shennan has suggested that Beaker finds do not represent a migrating people at all, but are a 'status kit' acquired through trade or exchange by individuals of high status in different parts of Europe. The 'Beaker problem' is likely to remain a focus of discussion in European prehistory for some time to come.

bean. The general term 'beans' includes two genera of plants: *Phaseolus* and *Vicia*. *Phaseolus* comprises a number of species, varieties of which include the haricot bean, french bean, runner bean, butter bean etc. These species all originated in Mexico and South America, only spreading to the Old World after Columbus. The earliest finds of cultivated *Phaseolus* beans are from Peru and Mexico, during the 6th millenium bc. *Vicia*, on the other hand, includes only one cultivated species, *Vicia faba*, the horsebean, field bean or broad bean. This species originated in the Old World. The earliest finds are from early Neolithic sites in the Near East. Later in the Neolithic, the species appeared in Spain and Portugal, and eastern Europe. During the Bronze Age, the field bean occurred in southern and central Europe, and by the Iron Age it appeared as far north as Britain.

bear. Today's bears can be split into three groups: the brown bears, typified by the European brown bear (*Ursus arctos*), the black bears and the polar bear (*Thalarctos maritimus*). Occasional finds of fossil polar bear bones outside the Arctic Circle are presumably related to the presence of pack ice and ice shelves at the edges of ice sheets during glaciations. Brown bears have existed in Europe and Asia for much of the later

QUATERNARY period. Today they inhabit woodland, eating large quantities of vegetable matter as well as meat. In Europe, there evolved a much larger variant, the 'Cave Bear' (often differentiated as *Ursus spelaeus*). Fossils of this giant bear are quite common in Quaternary cave deposits. The animal appears to have become rare by the middle of the last glaciation.

Bede. The Venerable Bede was born in 673 and spent most of his life in the monastery founded by Benedict Biscop at JARROW, Co. Durham. He is known for his prolific writings and his energetic promotion of Christian learning. The *Ecclesiastical History of the English People*, written towards the end of his life, is a monumental work in Latin describing the history of the nation from the time of the Anglo-Saxon invasions, through the legendary period of ARTHUR and the Battle of Mons Badonicus, into the era of the conversion to Christianity and the foundation of the Roman Church. At the time of his death in 735 Bede was working on a translation of the Gospels of St John.

Bedsa. A rock-cut Buddhist temple in western Deccan, India, of the 1st century BC. The interior is elaborately decorated; the pillars have vase-shaped bases and bell-shaped capitals surmounted by sculpted human and animal groups. In front of the temple is a facade and a large entrance with decorated pillars.

Beersheba. A Palestinian site in southern Israel, which formed one of the desert frontier posts. The earliest occupation belongs to the 12th and 11th centuries BC, but the first town belonged to the period of the United Monarchy (10th century). The only phase which has been excavated on any scale is Stratum II, of the 8th century BC. The town wall of this period was a casemate wall, with a great gateway flanked by double guard chambers and external towers. A ring road 15 metres inside the wall divided the inner and outer towns. Between the wall and the road were radially planned buildings including, to the right of the gateway, structures interpreted as storerooms. Inside the ring road there were mostly domestic buildings arranged in blocks. Beersheba may have been the adminstrative centre of the region and the storerooms may

have contained the royal stores for the collection of taxes in kind (grain, wine, oil etc). The town was destroyed in the mid-7th century BC.

beetles. More than 250,000 different species of beetle are known. A great variety of forms exists, inhabiting a wide variety of habitats. Many beetles are very dependent on particular features of their environment; some, for example, live only in the bark of a particular tree. It is this 'fastidiousness' that makes beetles useful for reconstructing ancient environments. Parts of the tough beetle exoskeleton may be well preserved in acid and waterlogged conditions, not only on archaeological sites, but also in peats, silts and lake clays outside human habitation. Using such fossils, the known temperature preferences of beetles have made it possible to reconstruct climatic changes during the DEVENSIAN cold stage and the FLANDRIAN interglacial. Beetles can also be used to investigate changes in vegetation, conditions in towns, and problems with storage of food.

Begho. Located near the northern edge of the forest in the west of the modern Ghana, Begho was a major trading centre around the middle of the 2nd millennium AD, and by the 5th century a pottery style had been established which appears to be ancestral to that practised into historical times by Akan groups who traditionally trace their origin to this area. It has been shown by excavation that Begho in its heyday was an extensive town, with distinct quarters occupied by artisans and traders. It maintained close trade contact with JENNE near the inland Niger delta, by which route gold derived from the forest areas to the south was exported. Begho was eclipsed around the start of the 18th century by the rise of the Asante kingdom in the gold-producing area itself.

Begram. A site in Afghanistan, confidently identified as Kapisa, the capital of several Indo-Greek rulers in the 3rd — 2nd centuries BC, a summer residence of the Kushan Kings (1st century BC to 3rd century AD) and an important town on the caravan route between India and the West. Excavations in the so-called 'palace' yielded an astonishing collection of *objets de luxe*, which range in date from the late 1st to the early 3rd century AD: Chinese lacquer, Indian ivories and Roman bronzes, glass vessels and plaster models, presumably intended to serve as exemplars for non-Roman craftsmen. The objects were found in two rooms, the doorways of which had been walled-up in a (successful) attempt to prevent discovery by looters. Although the nature of the collection is uncertain — the stock of a merchant-manufacturer, perhaps — it provides a vivid reminder of the range of contacts enjoyed by the cities of the inter-national caravan routes.

Behistun. *See* BISITUN.

Beidha. A NATUFIAN and ACERAMIC NEO-LITHIC site near PETRA in southern Jordan. It was first occupied for a short period as a semi-permanent camp in the Early Natufian period. The community of this time lived off ibex and goat; 75 per cent of the goats were immature animals, suggesting that selective hunting or perhaps herding was practised.

Beidha was reoccupied *c*7000 bc by a PRE-POTTERY NEOLITHIC A [PPNA] group, who lived in a planned village of roughly circular semi-subterranean houses, arranged in clus-ters. The main meat food came from domesti-cated goats, while the villagers also cultivated emmer WHEAT and BARLEY, both still in an early stage of domestication, and collected a number of wild plants. In the succeeding PPNB phase there was little change in the sub-sistence economy, but the form of the build-ings changed: in this stage there were com-plexes of large rectangular rooms, each with small workshops attached. Floors and walls were plastered. There is some evidence that there may have been upper storeys.

Burials without skulls were found in the settlement and there was also a separate ritual area away from the village, where three apparently ritual buildings have been excavated.

Finds from the site include materials that had come from great distances, including obsidian from Anatolia and cowries and mother-of-pearl from the Red Sea.

Beijing [Pei-ching, Peking]. Present-day capital of China. The SHANG civilization reached this area in the early part of the dynasty; a grave of about the 14th century BC at Pinggu Liujiacun contained bronze RITUAL VESSELS and a bronze axe with a blade of forged meteoritic iron. Many early ZHOU finds have been made in the city, notably at the cemetery site of Fangshan Liulihe. These are connected with the YAN fief, whose capital may have been at Beijing (the old literary name of the city is Yanjing, 'the Yan capital'). In later times the YUAN, MING and QING dynasties had capitals at Beijing, which apart from short interruptions has been the capital of China since the 13th century AD.

Beishouling [Pei-shou-ling]. *See* BANPO.

Beit Mirsim, Tell. A three-hectare mound in the low hill country southwest of Hebron, on the west bank of the Jordan. This fortified settlement has been identified as the biblical town of Kirjath-sepher. Successive occupation layers from the 3rd millennium BC to the Babylonian destruction in 588 BC (with a gap from the end of the Middle Bronze Age, in the later 16th century BC until the second half of the 15th century BC) have helped establish a chronology for the Levant, especially through the detailed analysis of pottery. The town seems to have been prosperous, and stone dye vats indicate that one industry practised here was the manufacture of textiles.

Beiyinyangying [Pei-yin-yang-ying]. Neo-lithic cemetery site at Nanjing in Jiangsu province, China. The finds probably belong to the latter part of the 4th millennium BC; most notable among them are finely polished jade ornaments and disc-like axes. *See also* MAJIABANG.

Belbasi. A cave on the southern coast of Anatolia which has given its name to a late Palaeolithic culture. The tool kit includes tanged arrowheads, triangular points and obliquely truncated blades. The most interest-ing feature of this group is its rock engravings, the only known cave art in western Asia. The best-known site is BELDIBI.

Beldibi. A rock shelter which has given its name to a Mesolithic or 'Proto-Neolithic' culture which succeeds the BELBASI culture in the Antalya region of southern Anatolia. The lower levels belong to the Belbasi culture and rock carvings of a bull and a stag are probably associated with this phase. Later phases contained imported obsidian and, later still, early forms of pottery. There is no evidence in the Beldibi culture of food production or herding. Bones of deer, ibex and cattle occur, while coastal fishing and the gathering of wild grain were probably practised in suitable areas.

Belgae. A basically Celtic tribal group known mostly from Caesar's account, found in northern France in the last few centuries BC. During the 1st century BC the Belgae expanded into southeast England in advance of the Roman armies (*see* AYLESFORD). They introduced the potter's wheel and coinage to Britain, and lived in large fortified settlements known as OPPIDA. The Belgae were the only prehistoric inhabitants of Britain whose life-style can be regarded as urban or proto-urban.

Bel'kachi I. An important settlement site on the Aldan River in central Siberia, occupied during the Neolithic (defined by the use of pottery, rather than the practice of farming). The lowest level has a radiocarbon date of *c*4020 bc (*c*4920 BC), which is the earliest date for pottery in Siberia, for a hand-moulded, sand-tempered ware decorated with net or mat impressions. The succeeding phase, often known as the Bel'kachinsk culture after this site, has another distinctive pottery style, decorated with impressions made with a cord-wrapped paddle. It is thought to date to the 3rd millennium BC. In the Late Neolithic, probably belonging to the 2nd millennium BC, a new type of pottery appeared: check-stamped ware, made by beating with a grooved paddle. Changes in stone and bone tools occurred during the development of the Neolithic, but throughout the economic basis remained hunting and fishing. The modern Yukagir population may be direct descendants of the Neolithic groups in this area.

bell barrow. *See* BARROW.

Bell Beaker. *See* BEAKER.

Bellows Beach. A coastal occupation site on Oahu, Hawaiian Islands, which has produced some of the earliest dates (AD 600-1000) for occupation of this island group. The assemblage is of Early Eastern POLYNESIAN type: shell fishhooks, stone adzes and bones of pig, dog and rat. *See also* HALAWA.

bells. *China*. Chinese bells of the SHANG and ZHOU dynasties have two peculiarities: they seldom have clappers — they are struck on the outside with a mallet — and they are not round but have a pointed-oval cross-section. The cusped cross-section, known from the earliest examples (a small and primitive bell from ERLITOU, mid-2nd millennium BC, and its descendants from ANYANG), makes it possible to obtain two distinct pitches from a large bell, depending on where the bell is struck. Whether this property was exploited in Shang times is uncertain, but the scales played by some Eastern Zhou chimes of bells incorporate both pitches of each bell.

The nomenclature of Chinese bells is confused, partly because the conventional names do not reflect the actual affiliations of the various types and partly because individual bells are sometimes classified differently by different scholars. The major types all descend from two bells of the Shang period, the *ling* (suspended by a loop) and the *nao* (supported mouth-upward on a stem or *yong*). In Shang finds *ling* and *nao* occur singly or in graduated sets of at most five bells. At metropolitan Shang sites such as Erlitou and Anyang they are not very common; the *ling* often has a clapper, and both *ling* and *nao* are small and insignificant objects, easily held in the hand. At Shang-period sites in the middle and lower Yangzi region, however, bells of the same two types are the defining artefact of local bronze-using cultures, and here they are finely decorated and very large: an example from NINGXIANG weighs 154 kg. Most of these monumental provincial bells are *nao*. The few provincial versions of the *ling*, lacking clappers, are usually distinguished from their small metropolitan prototypes by the name *zhong* (a general term for bells).

In the Western Zhou period large bells, often made in sets, begin to appear at northern sites. By their size alone these are related to bells from the Yangzi region rather than to metropolitan Shang bells, a descent confirmed by other stylistic features. The Western Zhou flanged bell supported vertically from a loop is particularly close to *zhong* from the Yangzi region: this type underwent no fundamental change in the Western Zhou period. The large *nao*, however, designed originally to stand upright on its hollow stem, was adapted by the Western Zhou caster for suspension mouth downward. This was managed by adding a small suspension loop at the point where the stem joins the bell proper; the bell supported by this loop hangs obliquely and is called a *yong*, short for *yong zhong* (i.e. a bell [*zhong*] with a stem [*yong*]. Examples found at PUDUCUN date this innovation to the 10th century BC or earlier.

In the Eastern Zhou period the most common types of bell are the *yong* (the inverted *nao*) and the *bo* (descended from the *zhong* and thus ultimately from the *ling*, but now usually without flanges). Both types are found increasingly often in tuned sets called *bianzhong*, the largest and most extraordinary of such sets being the 5th-century BC chime of 64 bells from SUI XIAN (*see also* XINYANG). *Bianzhong*, frequently accompanied by other musical instruments, occur primarily in tombs in or near the territory of the CHU state. This is the same area of central China where Shang-period finds regularly include large *nao*: the Yangzi region seems to have been the home of a musical tradition, no doubt serving a ritual purpose at least at first, for which there is little parallel at northern sites of any stage; *see also* DRUMS (CHINA).

One provincial Eastern Zhou bell type stands outside the main classes. The *chunyu*, a fairly small bell made for use in war, is a slender relative of a kind of bronze drum characteristic of the DIAN civilization of southwest China. Early versions of the *chunyu* are known from the lower Yangzi region. The type seems to have spread westward along the Yangzi valley to Sichuan, where it is associated with the BA AND SHU cultures and typically carries a small three-dimensional tiger on its flat upper surface.

Japan. Unique among bells are the *dotaku* of Japan, attributed to the latter half of the YAYOI period, in the first three centuries AD. More than 350 of these bronze bells, ranging from 13 to 135 cm in height, have been found in western and central Honshu, with the centre of distribution in the Osaka-Kyoto area. Several stone moulds for casting them have been found at Yayoi settlement sites, but the bells themselves come from isolated places on hills, singly or in groups and often in a damaged state. The unusual manner of disposal, as well as the elaborate decoration, suggests ritual significance. Later *dotaku* tend to be larger and often lack the inside clapper necessary to make sound. It is believed that the *dotaku* developed out of the smaller bronze bells found in Korean graves into ceremonial

objects with more emphasis on size and exterior decoration.

Belt Cave. *See* GHAR-I KAMARBAND.

belt hook [or toggle]. Names applied to various garment hooks made in China as early as the 7th or 6th century BC (a date resting partly on finds from LUOYANG Zhongzhoulu and the HOUMA foundry site). Belt hooks have been found in HAN tombs at places as widely scattered as LELANG in Korea and the DIAN kingdom in southwestern China, but this luxury item enjoyed its greatest vogue during the WARRING STATES period (5th-3rd centuries BC). Most examples are bronze, often lavishly decorated with inlays, but a few are made of jade, gold, or iron. As a rule the belt hook consists of a bar or flattish strip curving into a hook at one end and carrying at the other end, on the back, a button for securing it to the belt. The hooks vary widely in size, shape, and design, and although contemporary sculptures sometimes show them at the waists of human figures, some examples are far too large to have been worn and their function is unclear. Textual evidence hints that the belt hook was adopted by the Chinese from the mounted nomads of the northern frontier, perhaps along with other articles of the horseman's costume.

Belverde. A site of the APENNINE BRONZE AGE near Cetona in Tuscany, central Italy. It may have been a ritual site, as it is characterized by rocks carved to form tiers of seats, as well as into other shapes. Moreover, complete pottery vessels filled with carbonized grain, acorns and beans had been placed into fissures in the rocks, perhaps as offerings to a deity.

Belzoni, Giovanni Battista (1778-1823). An Italian by birth, Belzoni made a reputation as an unscrupulous robber of Egyptian tombs for their antiquities, both on his own account and for the British Consul-General, who collected on behalf of the British Museum. An account of his colourful and bizarre adventures was published in the year of his death under the title *Narrative of the Operations and Recent Discoveries within the Pyramids, Temples, Tombs and Excavations in Egypt and Nubia.*

Benfica. A location near Luanda on the coast of Angola where chipped stone artefacts are associated with pottery apparently of Early Iron Age type, in a context dated to the 2nd century ad. This is one of very few dated occurrences of this period yet known from Angola.

Benghazi [ancient Euesperides; later Berenice]. Situated on the coast of Cyrenaica in Libya, the first city, Euesperides, was probably founded from CYRENE in the 6th century BC; it was replaced in the mid-3rd century by a new city to the southwest, named Berenice after the wife of Ptolemy III. It continued in occupation until the 10th or 11th century AD and was ultimately replaced by the city of Benghazi.

Excavations at various times have revealed evidence of the classical and Hellenistic levels, while British excavations in the 1970s have revealed the final phase of occupation prior to the town's capture by the Arabs in AD 642-5. The excavations confirmed the refurbishing of the enclosing walls during Justinian's time (*r.* 527-565). They also charted the evolution and later decay of a Christian basilica, which was used for some secondary purpose after the capture of the town by the Arabs.

Benin. This southern Nigerian city had already risen to prominence before the first visit by the Portuguese in 1485. It was probably shortly before that date that the massive series of city walls, over 100 km in total length, was constructed. Benin is best known to the outside world for the fine CIRE PERDUE bronze castings, mostly relief plaques and near life-size human heads produced there over a long period; the heads show significant stylistic development until the 19th century. It has been suggested that the origins of the Benin bronze casting tradition may be traced to IFE, but the connection is disputed.

Bennett, Wendell (1905-53). American archaeologist who excavated many important sites in Peru. His studies of Peruvian ceramics made major contributions to the establishment of the prehistoric sequences of both coastal and highland Peru.

Benty Grange Helmet. During the 19th century most of the prehistoric barrows in Derbyshire were excavated, and secondary burials of Anglo-Saxon date were found in a number of them. In 1848 the most spectacular

of these was opened at Benty Grange, and an Anglo-Saxon ceremonial helmet was found. Unlike the SUTTON HOO helmet, which has similarities to Swedish helmets, the Benty Grange example is undoubtedly of native workmanship. The helmet is an elaborate object combining the pagan boar symbol with Christian crosses on the nail heads.

Beowulf. One of the earliest, longest and most complete examples of ANGLO-SAXON verse. It takes the form of a heroic epic and was probably written sometime during the 8th century. The poem is of singular historical and social importance as well as being an outstanding literary document of the period. Its themes are essentially the conflict between good and evil and the nature of heroism; fantasy and reality are intertwined as the hero Beowulf fights Grendel and other semi-mythological monsters. The poem gives an impression of Scandinavian nobility, warriors and lesser mortals, describing their customs, weapons, armour, dress and even the timber banqueting halls.

Perhaps *Beowulf's* greatest contribution to archaeology is the light the poem has shed on the funerary customs displayed in the SUTTON HOO ship burial (*see* BOAT BURIAL). The opening passages describe how the dead King Scyld Scefing was borne out to sea in a ship; jewels were placed on his chest, armour and treasure heaped around his body, and a standard was hoisted overhead.

Bergen. A Norwegian royal foundation dating back to 1070 and the reign of King Olaf. The town occupies a sheltered position on Norway's western coast, and was from the beginning an important trading port famous for its role in the North Atlantic fishing industry. Excavations begun in the Bryggen, the harbour area, in the mid-1950s revealed a sequence of levels that illustrate the evolution of the waterfront and its hinterland from the 11th century onwards. These levels have been accurately dated by a series of fires which occurred at various stages of Bergen's history. The waterlogged conditions have preserved many of the timber buildings, streets and quays, and it seems that building styles changed considerably over 400 years. The 11th-century houses and warehouses were carried on piles and had sills at ground level, while in the Hanseatic period during the 14th and 15th centuries jetties became popular. The Bryggen excavations revealed a remarkable collection of imported pottery from all over Europe as well as quantities of leather and wooden objects. Parts of three trading ships or freighters were also found in the excavations, their timbers having been re-used in the buildings.

Bering Land Bridge. The present-day floor of the Chukchi and Bering Seas, which emerged as dry land during Late Pleistocene glacial advances. Asian hunters, probably following migrating big game herds, are thought to have entered the Americas by this route. During the most recent major advance (Late WISCONSIN) the ice-free bridge was open, to a maximum width of 2000 km, for most of the period 25,000 to 10,000 bp. The weight of the archaeological evidence shows this to be the most likely period for transmigration, although crossing during an earlier advance cannot be completely ruled out.

berm. Flat area left between an earthwork such as a bank or BARROW and the top of an associated ditch.

betel nut. The hard nut of the areca palm, *Areca catechu*, is chewed together with powdered lime and pepper leaves (normally of Piper *betle*) as a stimulant from India through Southeast Asia to the Santa Cruz Islands of MELANESIA. Archaeological occurrences include SPIRIT CAVE (c10,000-7000 bc), eastern Timor (early HOLOCENE) and several sites in the Philippines, where characteristically stained teeth have been found from c3000 BC onwards. Oceanic peoples beyond Santa Cruz used a different stimulant made from roots of *Piper methysticum* (KAVA).

Beth Shan. A Palestinian mound with an occupation depth of 21.5 metres. A sounding down to bedrock found traces of occupation from the 4th millennium bc onwards. Very little is known about the earliest levels, although rectangular houses with apsidal ends of the late CHALCOLITHIC or Early Bronze Age are documented. Most work was concentrated in an area containing superimposed temples from the Early Iron Age through to the Hellenistic and Byzantine periods. A series of fortresses of the 14th-12th centuries BC attests a strong Egyptian presence, and finds

include a stone stele of the pharaoh Sether. Large numbers of tombs were excavated, representing all periods from the Early Bronze Age to the Byzantine period.

Bewcastle Cross. A standing cross situated in the churchyard of Bewcastle, Northumberland, northern England, and one of the finest examples of Early Christian NORTHUMBRIAN art. The headless sandstone column stands 4.42 metres high and is profusely decorated in the classically derived style typical of the period, probably transmitted to the British Isles by interchanges of missionaries and imported manuscripts. The decoration is contained within distinct panels, and the figures include Christ in Majesty, St John the Baptist and St John the Evangelist, while on the back there is an inhabited vinescroll. Like the RUTHWELL CROSS, that at Bewcastle possesses a poem inscribed in Runic script (*see* RUNES). Considerable debate surrounds the dating of Northumbrian sculpture, but current opinion places this cross in the late 7th or early 8th century.

Beycesultan. A TELL site on the Meander River in southwestern Anatolia, with a long occupation sequence through the CHALCOLITHIC and Bronze Age. The most prosperous period for Beycesultan was the Middle Bronze Age (early 2nd millennium BC), with a large and elaborate palace, rather like those of the MINOANS in Crete. A separate enclosure housed other public buildings, and a temple of this phase has also been excavated. The whole settlement and a lower terrace on the river was enclosed by a perimeter wall. This town was violently destroyed and although the settlement was rebuilt it remained relatively poor into the Late Bronze Age. It is likely that Beycesultan was a major city of the state known to the HITTITES as Arzawa.

Bhaja. A Buddhist site in western Deccan, India. In the 2nd and 1st centuries BC, STUPAS and rock-cut temples and monasteries were excavated and decorated with sculpture in relief. The early 2nd-century BC *vihara* [monastery] has decoration which figures VEDIC deities, appearing here as symbols of the Buddha who has assimilated their powers.

Bharhut. A Buddhist STUPA in central India. The stupa may have been constructed in the

ASOKAN period but the surviving structure belongs to the 2nd century BC. The railing surrounding the stupa is decorated with scenes from the Jataka stories.

Bhir Mound. *See* TAXILA.

bi [*pi*]. A JADE disc with circular central perforation. In Chinese texts of the Eastern ZHOU period the word is used in this sense, but can also refer more generally to any precious jade. Jade discs and disc-like axes have come from 4th- and 3rd-millennium BC graves at east-coast Neolithic sites such as BEIYINYANG-YING (*see also* LIANGZHU). Polished stone disc segments are known still earlier at BANPO. The traditional interpretation of *bi* discs as 'symbols of heaven' is a late invention unsupported by archaeology or early texts.

bianzhong [*pien-chung*]. *See* BELLS (CHINA).

Bible. The holy book of the Jewish (Old Testament only) and Christian (Old and New Testaments) faiths. The Old Testament, written in Hebrew, represents a history of the Jewish people, beginning with the creation of the world. The New Testament records the life and teachings of Christ. Much of early archaeological work in the Near East was designed to illustrate or defend the biblical account but today the Bible is used as a historical source in a more critical and objective way and is recognized as a collection of legends, myths and stories collected together long after events occurred. However archaeology has lent support to some biblical accounts, such as the population movements of the biblical Patriarchs who moved into Canaan during the 19th and 18th centuries BC. Moreover, the Bible has provided information on aspects of society such as marriage customs, inheritance and land ownership which are difficult to recreate from archaeological evidence.

Bibracte [modern Mont Beuvray]. An Iron Age OPPIDUM near Bourges in central France. The site of Mont Beuvray has been clearly identified as Bibracte, capital of the Aedui tribe before the foundation of Augustodunum (AUTUN) some 30 km away *c*5 BC. Bibracte is known from Caesar's account as a major Aeduan stronghold and scene of one of the fiercest battles against him. Led by Vercinget-orix, the defenders held on for 27 days before the town was captured and the inhabitants slaughtered by the Romans. The ramparts were of MURUS GALLICUS type and run for nearly five km around the hilltop. Excavations in the 19th century revealed remains of both the Iron Age settlement and of the Roman period, including a large temple, houses and metal-working workshops. As well as local products, many imported objects were found, dating to before the Roman conquest — coins, amphorae, 'Campanian' black glaze and ARRETINE red glaze pottery — and it is clear that Bibracte was a major trading and production centre in the late Iron Age.

Big Game Hunting tradition. An adaptation to the grasslands environment of the Late Pleistocene period in North America, especially evident in the Great Plains. Large game animals (megafauna) were hunted as the primary means of subsistence. Lanceolate projectile points, such as CLOVIS and FOLSOM, characterize the tradition. Approximate dates are from 12,500 bp to 8000 bp, with considerable local variation. *See* Table 9, page 552.

Bigo. A site in southwestern Uganda marked by massive linear earthworks and recalled in oral historical tradition as a former capital. The earthworks, over 10 km in total length, attest to the organizational capabilities of the early interlacustrine kingdoms. The site has also yielded an early 13th-15th century ad occurrence of the roulette-decorated pottery which is characteristic of the later Iron Age over much of East Africa.

Bilzingsleben. Recent excavations on this travertine site in East Germany, not far from Halle, have revealed thousands of stone tools of a Lower Palaeolithic CLACTONIAN-type culture. A few human fossil skull pieces are known. Numerous lines of evidence indicate the interglacial environment and a date in the penultimate or HOLSTEIN interglacial, perhaps some 250,000-350,000 years ago.

bird bones. These are quite commonly preserved on archaeological sites. Identification is a very specialized skill, but considerable precision is often possible. Interpretation may then be carried out in terms of diet and reconstruction of the ancient environment.

Birdlip. A site near Gloucester with four CIST GRAVES of the 1st century BC. One cist contained the skeleton of a woman together with bronze bowls, silver and gold bracelets, a bronze brooch and a bronze mirror with incised and enamel decoration, a fine example of insular CELTIC ART.

Birsmatten. The Basis-Grotte at Birsmatten in the Bern district of Switzerland has one of the longest known sequences of MESOLITHIC deposits. There are several levels of SAUVE-TERRIAN and TARDENOISIAN occupation and extensive human remains of Mesolithic man.

Bir Terfawi. A late ATERIAN site in the Egyptian Western Desert, dated to about 42,000 bc. The shores of a shallow lake were settled by hunters who preyed on a varied fauna including species of both Mediterranean and more southerly affinities.

Bisitun [Behistun]. A rock face in northwest Iran on which Darius I placed a trilingual inscription recording his military victories in 516 BC. The inscription was in Old Persian, Elamite and Babylonian, all three written in the CUNEIFORM script. In spite of the difficulty of gaining access to the high vertical face and of copying the inscriptions, this feat was accomplished by Henry RAWLINSON between 1835 and 1844. It enabled him subsequently to understand the cuneiform script and to decipher the languages of the inscription. This provided the breakthrough to the decipherment later of other languages in the cuneiform script, including SUMERIAN.

Biskupin. An Iron Age settlement belonging to the late LAUSITZ culture in northwest Poland. It was situated on an island and defended with timber breakwaters and box ramparts. More than 100 rectangular timber houses were laid out on a regular street system and may have housed up to 1000 people. Workshops for craftsmen in bronze, horn and bone were excavated.

Bismarck Archipelago. *See* MELANESIA, NEW BRITAIN.

bison. Two species of bison survive today: the European bison or wisent (*Bison bonasus*) and the American bison (*Bison bison*). Only a small number of European bison now exist,

bred from zoo specimens. Two further species, now extinct, inhabited Europe for much of the QUATERNARY period. The great steppe wisent (*Bison priscus*) was present during both INTERGLACIALS and cold periods. It was particularly common in Britain during the DEVENSIAN cold stage. *Bison schetensacki*, the smaller wood wisent, was only present in Europe during interglacials. In America, a number of species preceded today's American bison.

Black and Red ware. An Indian pottery type, red on the outside, but black on the inside and round the rim, due to firing in the inverted position. Characteristic forms include shallow dishes and deeper bowls. In one form or another this ware is found throughout much of the Indian peninsula in the later 2nd and early 1st millennium BC. In the Ganges Valley it post-dates OCHRE-COLOURED POTTERY and generally precedes PAINTED GREY WARE, although on some sites it continues in use alongside the latter.

Black-figure ware. A phase in Greek vase painting. From about 720 BC vase-painters, especially in Corinth and Athens, developed a characteristic style, in which one or more bands of human and animal figures are silhouetted in black against a red background. The red colour is given by the fabric of the pot when fired, but the exact details of the technical process used are still unclear. The delineation of the figures is often heightened by the use of incised lines and the addition of white or purple colouring material. This style was gradually succeeded, from *c*530 BC, by its inverse, RED-FIGURE.

Black Pottery cultures. *See* LONGSHAN.

Blackwater Draw. A deeply stratified site in eastern New Mexico, USA, with evidence of occupation from earliest PALEO-INDIAN through ARCHAIC times. Stratigraphic evidence has established unequivocally that the LLANO culture was earlier than FOLSOM, and showed a clear association between CLOVIS projectile points and mammoth kills. Blackwater Draw is the type site for Clovis, and has also become a major yardstick for evaluating chronological sequences at other sites.

Blade

blade. The basis of stone technology is the removal of pieces of flint or other stone by striking the parent nodule or CORE with a hammer. When the flakes removed are elongated so as to be at least twice as long as they are wide, they are called blades. A typical blade has parallel sides and regular scars running down its back parallel with the sides. The prerequisite for blade production is the preparation of a blade core of elongated or prismatic shape. Blades appear at an early stage of technological development, but they become important from the Upper PALAEO-LITHIC onwards.

bleeper. A type of proton GRADIOMETER, in which the reading is given as a series of bleeps. This design of MAGNETOMETER is very cheap to produce, and has therefore been widely used in archaeology.

bloodletting. *See* PERFORATION.

bloom. A spongy mass of IRON and SLAG, resulting from the initial SMELTING of iron ore.

bo [*po*]. *See* BELLS (CHINA).

Boadicea. *See* BOUDICCA.

boat axe. A special type of stone BATTLE-AXE

found in eastern Scandinavia in the late Neolithic, so named because it resembles a simple boat with upturned ends. The term 'Boat-axe culture' is sometimes used for the east Scandinavian variant of the SINGLE GRAVE or CORDED WARE culture in which these axes occur.

boat burial. A pagan burial ritual widely adopted by the VIKINGS, and practised to a lesser extent by the ANGLO-SAXON and Germanic races before them. The Anglo-Saxon poem BEOWULF demonstrates the belief that the journey to the afterlife could be achieved in a vessel, and indeed the Saxon boat graves excavated beneath the barrows at SUTTON HOO and Snape in East Anglia provide physical evidence to bear out the literature. But, although boat burials are known from Europe at this time, they are a fairly rare phenomenon and it was the Vikings who from the 9th century onwards developed boat burial into a cult. In Norway alone there are 500 known boat graves, and many more from the rest of Scandinavia and other Viking colonies. To these seafaring people, ships were a means of transport, a way of life, and symbols of power and prestige, in death as in life. Usually the body or cremated remains were placed in a vessel which was then deposited under a mound; when excavated, only traces of planks in the soil and a few iron clamps tend to remain. The best-known burials after Sutton Hoo are the 9th-century barrows of OSEBERG and GOKSTAD in Norway, and the 10th-century barrow at Ladby in Denmark. These boats have been a major source of evidence for the history of seafaring.

boat-shaped buildings. A variety of long house with bowed sides, known from Scandinavia and Scandinavian colonies in other parts of Europe throughout the VIKING period. The finest examples have been excavated at 11th-century Viking camps such as TRELLEBORG in southern Jutland. A typical example has been reconstructed at Trelleborg with walls made of halved tree-trunks set in rows, with the curved face outwards as in stave churches. In this case there seems to have been a series of angled posts around the outside acting rather like buttresses and giving additional support to the gabled roof with its curved ridge. The roof may have been covered in wooden shingles, thatch or turf.

Archaeological investigations of the Viking Age royal sites in Denmark as well as other settlements have revealed considerable variations in boat-shaped houses according to function and locality. There are examples built in dry stone with internal aisles, or dry-stone and turf, or half-timbered types, but most of them do not have provision for an animal byre, which is the essence of the true European LONG HOUSE. A few examples have been discovered in English contexts, notably one possible boat-shaped building from HAMWIH and another from Bucken, Huntingdonshire.

Boca Chica. *See* CHICOID.

Bochica *See* CHIBCHA.

Bodh Gaya. A site in northeast India, famous as the scene of the Buddha's enlightenment. Archaeological remains include an ASOKAN pillar, erected by the emperor on his pilgrimage of 249 BC, and a railing surrounding the tree beneath which the Buddha meditated for six years before his enlightenment (perhaps 2nd century BC).

Bodrogkeresztur. The eponymous site of the Middle Copper Age culture of eastern Hungary comprises a LINEAR POTTERY domestic occupation stratified below a medium-sized Copper Age inhumation cemetery. The Bodrogkeresztur culture represents the first peak of metallurgical development in Hungarian prehistory, defined by large-scale production of gold ornaments and heavy shaft-hole copper tools (axes, adzes and hammer-axes). The principal landscape feature was the nucleated cemetery which served dispersed hamlets. Long-distance exchange is witnessed by the occurrence in the Pannonian Basin of Transylvanian gold, Slovakian copper and flint from Poland and the Dniester valley.

bog. A term generally used to describe communities of plants growing on acid water-logged ground, as opposed to FEN. Three main types of bog can be distinguished: valley bogs remain waterlogged due to the concentration of drainage into a valley; raised bogs form as large pillows of PEAT, and are kept water-logged by high rainfall; blanket bogs form through the growth of the organic horizons of GLEYED PODZOLS.

bog burials. Name given to the human bodies found in peat bogs in Scandinavia and northern Europe, including more than 160 from Denmark. They are renowned for the remarkable preservation of the bodies caused by the chemicals in the peat, which has allowed archaeologists to study aspects of past life usually lost, including the soft tissues of the bodies themselves and the contents of the stomachs. Most of the bodies apparently date to the first few centuries of the present era and had been deliberately killed. It is not clear whether they represent executed criminals or sacrificial victims, or both. *See also* GRAU-BALLE MAN, TOLLUND MAN.

Boghazköy. The site of the HITTITE New Kingdom capital, Hattusas, occupying a rock citadel called Büyükkale in central Turkey. Little is known of the CHALCOLITHIC or Hittite Old Kingdom phases on the site; excavation has in the main concentrated on the monuments of the New Kingdom city, after c1400 BC, which covered c120 hectares and was defended by a stone and mud-brick city wall. A series of major buildings on the citadel represents administrative quarters and royal buildings, including an audience hall. Two of these buildings housed archives of clay tablets inscribed in the CUNEIFORM script and Hittite language; there were more than 10,000 of these tablets and they have provided much information about the Hittites. Another important building was Temple I, not on the citadel, but in the lower town, which consisted of a series of rooms around three sides of a court with a colonnade on the fourth. Other temples have been excavated on the citadel and in the lower town and there is a rock-cut sanctuary c2 km away at YAZILIKAYA. There were at least six gateways in the city wall and three of these were decorated with impressive carved reliefs. The city fell at the same time as the Hittite empire, in the early 12th century BC.

Boian. After the excavations of I.Nestor in 1925 at the Boian A tell, it became possible to divide the Rumanian Neolithic into two phases: an earlier, Boian, phase and a later GUMELNIŢA, phase. The Boian culture is now recognized as the principal Middle Neolithic culture in Muntenia, in the lower Danube valley of Rumania c4200-3700 bc. During the Boian period, settlement became more long-lived and spread from the hitherto favoured first terrace-floodplain ecotone into the fertile interfluve zone. While intramural burial is most common, occasional large inhumation cemeteries are known (*see* CERNICA). Flourishing exchange networks are known to involve Prut Valley flint, SPONDYLUS shells from the Black Sea, and copper.

Bølling interstadial. An INTERSTADIAL of the WEICHSELIAN cold stage. It is dated to between 13,000 and 12,000 bp.

Bologna [Bononia]. The general area at the eastern end of the Po Valley now covered by the sprawl of modern Bologna, is naturally favourable to agriculture, and straddles obvious lines of communication between plain, mountain and seaboard. Evidence for settlement is often virtually obliterated by successive re-use. In the earliest phases, we have transient Bronze Age groups, followed by many traces of Iron Age huts and tombs (VILLANOVAN). From the 6th century BC urbanization arrived with the Etruscans, for whom the city became the capital of the Po Valley, under the name of Felsina, with important trade links with Spina on the Adriatic coast. Traces of street plans survive, as do cemeteries with trench-type inhumation and cremation. Finds include sandstone grave stelae and many grave goods. Subsequently occupied by the Boii, a Celtic tribe who invaded the area and established themselves in the Po Valley, the city became the regional capital for the invaders and, presumably from them, gained its new name, Bononia. Taken by the Romans in 196 BC and declared a COLONIA, the city enjoyed considerable importance and success.

Bonampak. A MAYA CEREMONIAL CENTRE located close to the Lacanha River in the tropical rain-forest of northeast Chiapas, Mexico. Dating to the Late CLASSIC PERIOD (*c*450-750), it is most notable for its polychrome murals which can be tightly dated to 800 on the basis of LONG COUNT inscriptions. The so-called Temple of the Paintings consists of three rooms, painted from floor to ceiling with scenes of ceremony, battle and sacrifice. Hieroglyphs also occur frequently and the whole collection is seen as a continuous narrative (showing the battle itself, the disposal of the captives and the victory celebration). Aside from the artistic achievement, the murals provide remarkably detailed information on Maya dress, music and weaponry.

Bondi point. A small asymmetric backed point, named after a site at Bondi, Sydney, Australia. It is usually less than 5 cm long and is sometimes described as a backed blade. A component of the AUSTRALIAN SMALL TOOL TRADITON, it occurs on coastal and inland sites across Australia, generally south of the Tropic of Capricorn. The oldest examples come from southeast Australia, dating from about 3000 bc, and the most recent are 300-500 years old. The Bondi point was not being used by Aborigines when Europeans arrived, but traces of resin on the backed margins of several examples suggest that the points were set in wooden handles or shafts.

bone. In life, bone is one of the connective tissues of the body and consists of crystallites of the mineral hydroxyapatite, deposited on a fibrous matrix of the protein COLLAGEN. Mineral occupies 71 per cent of the volume, collagen 19 per cent, other proteins 2 per cent, and water 8 per cent. After death, the proteins slowly decompose (this gradual decomposition forms the basis of a BONE DATING method — nitrogen analysis). The remaining mineral is subject to solution in acid soil conditions. Bones are preserved on a wide variety of archaeological sites, and the state of bone preservation varies widely. Two main types of bone are found in mature animals: compact, or cortical bone and cancellous, spongy or trabecular bone. Compact bone forms the dense outer layer in a particular structure of the skeleton. Cancellous bone is found inside, forming a light internal framework. Bones as elements of the skeleton have a number of forms: long bones — as in the limbs; flat bones — as in the cranial vault of the skull; cuboidal bones — as in the wrists and ankles; irregular bones — vertebrae and bones of the face and jaws. For the study of bones from archaeological sites, *see* SKELETON.

Bone was also used as a raw material for making artefacts.

bone dating. BONE may be dated in a number of ways. The most commonly used is RADIOCARBON DATING: both the COLLAGEN and mineral components of bone are dateable.

Recently a number of bone samples have been dated by a URANIUM SERIES method. Relative dates may be obtained from time-related chemical changes which occur in bone after burial. In particular, these include FLUORINE DATING, NITROGEN DATING and AMINO ACID RACEMIZATION.

bone measurement. Dimensions of skeletal structures can be taken using a variety of calipers and other measuring equipment. The aim of such work is to compare the size and shape of BONES between many different individuals. This is done by statistical methods, nowadays using MULTIVARIATE ANALYSIS to compare many measurements at once. Comparisons of this kind can help in identifying bones (for example in distinguishing SHEEP from GOAT), in sex determination and in studying the genetics of groups of animals. Much work has been carried out with human skull measurements to investigate the genetical relationships of ancient populations.

Bonfire Shelter. *See* PLANO.

Bongkisam. *See* SANTUBONG.

Bon-po religion. The ancient shamanic religion of pre-Buddhist Tibet. Many small bronze artefacts found throughout Tibet — evidently amulets, decorations for clothing and horse harness, and jewellery — incorporate its symbolism of significant numbers (three, seven, thirteen) and mythical animals, especially the benevolent *k'yun,* a bird with horns, and the demoniac *mk'a'-Idin.*

The royal tombs at AP'YON-RGYAS are entirely a product of Bon-po ritual, despite the fact that the kings buried within them had introduced Buddhism to Tibet. The kings of the Royal Dynastic period (c620-842) were all given traditional pre-Buddhist funerals, conducted by Bon-po priests or shamans, in tombs incorporating Bon-po symbolism.

Book of Kells. One of the earliest ILLUMINATED MANUSCRIPTS of Europe, produced either at Kells (the Columban monastery founded by the monks of IONA when they fled from the Vikings in 806) or at Iona itself. Its appearance bears a strong resemblance to Irish manuscripts and metalwork of the early part of the 8th century, with vibrant complex designs of Celtic spirals and scrolls intermixed with Germanic interlace. The script is an Irish minuscule combining elements of Latin, and is written on vellum. The contents of the work include gospels, prefaces, summaries and concordances, with a large portion of 11th-century legal documents relating to the abbey of Kells.

The decorative style of the Book of Kells owes something to the Book of Durrow and other earlier Irish manuscripts, but the tightly packed repetitious motifs are a new advance, as are the interlinear drawings. The dazzling colours and profuse ornament range across the carpet pages and large decorated monograms, while the many portrait pages display very stylized versions of Christ, the Evangelists and the Virgin and Child, all with elaborate hairstyles and stiffly folded garments. Much of the decorative inspiration for this work could have come from the metalwork produced at the beginning of the 8th century.

boomerang. A curved wooden throwing stick of thin bi-convex or semi-oval cross-section, distributed widely over Australia but unknown in Tasmania. The boomerang was most frequently used as a fighting or hunting weapon, with marked regional variations in design and decoration. The returning type was usually regarded as a plaything. Boomerangs excavated from peat deposits in Wyrie Swamp, South Australia, have been dated to c8000 bc.

Boomplaas. A cave near Oudtshoorn in the Folded Mountain Belt of the Cape Province, South Africa, containing a long sequence of Upper PLEISTOCENE and HOLOCENE deposits. The earliest occupation probably took place some 80,000 years ago. Following a long 'Middle Stone Age' sequence which has not yet been reported in detail, there are successive occupations attributed to the ROBBERG, ALBANY and WILTON industries. Excellent conditions of preservation combined with meticulous excavation methods have yielded a wealth of information concerning the exploitation of vegetable and animal foods through this long sequence. By the 3rd century ad domestic small stock are attested.

Boreal. A climatic sub-division of the FLANDRIAN period, supposed to be warm and dry. Godwin's POLLEN ZONES V and VI correspond to the Boreal period in the British Isles. Zone V was dominated by birch and hazel, the latter rising through the zone to dominate Zone VI. The forest trees, elm, oak, alder and lime rose through Zone VI, to dominate in the succeeding Zone VIIa, the ATLANTIC period. In some areas, notably the North York moors, southern Pennines and lowland heaths, MESOLITHIC man appears to have been responsible for temporary clearances by fire, even before forest became established, and initiated the growth of moor and heath vegetation.

Borg-in-Nadur. A fortified promontory site in southeast Malta, which has given its name to the later Bronze Age culture of the island. The settlement was surrounded by walls of CYCLOPEAN MASONRY and enclosed oval huts. The discovery of a sherd of MYCENAEAN pottery points to long-distance trading contacts.

Borneo. The largest island of Southeast Asia, situated at the eastern edge of the SUNDA SHELF. Borneo, with SUMATRA and JAVA, was joined to mainland Southeast Asia during PLEISTOCENE periods of low sea-level, but so far no traces of settlement by *Homo erectus*, attested from 2 million years ago on Java, have been found. Archaeological sequences so far come from purely coastal locations, particularly the NIAH CAVES of Sarawak, and the MADAI-Tingkayu region of Sabah (all in East Malaysia). The Niah Great Cave sequence suggests the presence of a population of early Australoid affinity from about 40,000 years ago, and all the sites mentioned, together with linguistic evidence, suggest that the ancestors of the present AUSTRONESIAN-speaking populations of Borneo arrived with a horticultural economy soon after 3000 bc, probably from the Philippines. No traces now survive in Borneo of earlier Australoid or Negrito populations. For protohistoric sites and trade with China, *see* KOTA BATU, SANTUBONG, TANJONG KUBOR.

The island does not seem to have played a significant part in the early history of Southeast Asia. The very few Brahmanic or Buddhist images found along the major rivers do not prove an Indian cultural influence. Some small INDIANIZED kingdoms must nevertheless have existed from the 4th century in coastal areas. A Sanskrit inscription, dated to *c*400 and thus being the earliest historical document on the island, found in the present Sultanate of Kutei, emanates from an obviously Indianized king. The earliest secure Chinese information concerning Borneo (P'o-ni) is only from 977, and in 1082 the *History of the Sung* records an embassy from the Mahārāja of Borneo. But in a 13th-century Chinese source a country called Tan-jung-wu-lo (Tanjang Pura) in southwestern Borneo is mentioned as the dependency of a Javanese kingdom. From this time on, Borneo has to be seen politically as an extended part of JAVA.

Borobudur. A Mahayana Buddhist monument near Yogyakarta in Central Java, Indonesia, which is the largest Buddhist monument in the world. In the form of a stepped pyramid, constructed of local volcanic stone around and over a natural hill, it consists of six square and three circular superimposed terraces, crowned by a large STUPA; measuring 123 metres square at the base and with a height of 35 metres to the top of the stupa. The monument was built as a place of meditation by SAILENDRA kings from *c*780 onward and was completed about 80 years later by SANJAYA kings. The lower, square terraces, with their galleries containing 1300 reliefs, represent the World of Form (*Rupadhatu*), whereas the unadorned circular terraces above symbolize the World of Formlessness (*Arupadhatu*). There are 504 statues of the Buddha on the Borobudur.

boshanlu [po-shan-lu]. A Chinese incense burner (*lu*) with a lid designed to represent mountain peaks (Boshan is a mountain in Shandong province). Made either of pottery or bronze, the *boshanlu* takes the form of a stemmed bowl with a perforated conical lid. Most examples date from the Western HAN period. One of the finest, from the tomb of Liu Sheng (*d*.113 BC) at MANCHENG, is inlaid with gold, and shows the mountain, populated by animals and men, rising from swirling ocean waves. These censers may depict a mythical Isle of the Immortals where elixirs of immortality were supposedly to be found.

bosing. A method of detecting buried features of archaeological sites. The fill of pits and ditches, or hollow chambers, may resonate if the ground is struck with a heavy implement. Bosing has been successful in finding sites (particularly tomb chambers), but it is not as objective as other geophysical methods of investigation.

bossed bone plaque. Objects of unknown function made of bone and carved with a row of adjacent round bosses; incised decoration may occur on the background and sometimes on the bosses themselves. Bossed bone plaques have been found in the eastern and central Mediterranean at TROY, LERNA, Altamura in southern Italy, CASTELLUCCIO in Sicily and on Malta. They all date to the later 3rd millennium bc (earlier 3rd millenium BC) and because of their close similarity are thought to represent traded objects.

Bosumpra. A cave site near Abetifi in southern Ghana which yielded one of the first scientifically excavated assemblages of a West African Neolithic industry. More recent investigations have provided a radiocarbon chronology, showing that the site's occupation began around the middle of the 4th millennium bc and continued for at least 3000 years. Throughout the sequence a microlithic chipped-stone industry was associated with simple pottery and with ground stone implements of axe-like or hoe-like form; the last two categories of artefact became progressively more common through the occupation. The site has yielded no conclusive evidence for the practice of food production which is, however, attested elsewhere in Ghana from the 2nd millennium bc (*see* KINTAMPO).

Botta, Paul-Emile (1802-70). French consular agent in Iraq from 1840 to 1843 who conducted excavations on the Mesopotamian sites of Kuyunjik (NINEVEH) and KHORSABAD. These were the earliest excavations in Mesopotamia and were conducted without any kind of scientific method, with the sole object of unearthing, and where possible removing, antiquities; many of the Khorsabad sculptures are now in the Louvre in Paris.

Bouar. A numerous series of megalithic monuments in a restricted area of the Central African Republic, consisting of settings of standing stones associated with tumuli. Dating evidence derived from such excavations as have yet taken place is hard to interpret, but it is possible that some of the monuments were erected as early as the 6th or 5th millennium bc.

Boucher de Perthes, Jacques (1788-1868). A customs officer from Abbeville in northern France who collected stone tools of the type now known as HAND AXES from the gravels of the River Somme in the 1830s, 1840s and 1850s. His claims that these objects were indeed the tools of ancient man and that they occurred in association with the bones of extinct animals were ridiculed by scholars of the time and his three-volume work *Antiquités Celtiques et Antédiluviennes*, the first volume of which was published in 1847, was largely ignored. However in the 1850s scholars were gradually converted to his views and in 1859 his excavations were visited by three distinguished Britons — Hugh Falconer, John Prestwich and John EVANS — who were convinced by what they saw. From that point on the antiquity of man was widely accepted in the scholarly world.

Boudicca [inaccurately Boadicea]. Queen of the Iceni, a British tribe inhabiting a large area of East Anglia. Under a special client-king agreement (dependent sovereignty), their King Prasutagus was permitted to continue ruling after the Romans began to occupy Britain in AD 43. Upon his death (*c*60), Rome took advantage of the King's ill-advised will, under which he left his kingdom jointly to the Emperor and his own daughters, and moved directly to annex the territory. Apparently for daring to object Queen Boudicca was savagely beaten and her daughters raped. This provocation, coming on top of excessive taxation and other forms of harassment, goaded Boudicca into leading a massive rebellion involving the entire southeast of the province. TACITUS relates the burning of COLCHESTER [*Camoludunum*], LONDON [*Londinium*] and St Albans [VERULAMIUM]. The rebellion was eventually crushed by the governor Suetonius Paulinus, and Boudicca committed suicide by taking poison.

boulder clay. A type of TILL. The term is sometimes (erroneously) used to mean all kinds of till.

bouleuterion. Council-house for the meetings of the Greek city council (*boule*). Probably not originally distinctive in architecture, it seems to be one of a range of straightforward rectangular civic buildings. The internal space was probably undivided, except by a number of columns to hold up the roof structure, and seating would normally be provided. ARCHAIC and CLASSICAL examples have been found at ATHENS, and a large elaborate HELLENISTIC example (c170 BC) at MILETUS.

Bouqras. A 7th-millennium bc PRE-POTTERY NEOLITHIC B village site near the River Euphrates in Syria. The first occupation phase had two levels with rectangular mud-brick houses. The next four levels had more solid mud-brick houses, some with plastered floors, benches and pillars. The animal economy was based on the hunting of wild animals except in the final phase, when sheep and cattle were bred. On the plant side, sickle blades, pounders and querns — used either for wild or cultivated plants — appear in the first phase, but afterwards disappear from the toolkit. Artefacts include a 'white ware', made of mixed lime and ash and used to cover baskets, producing watertight vessels. Obsidian occurs in large quantities, indicating extensive trade networks linking Bouqras with the source sites in Anatolia.

bowl barrow. *See* BARROW.

box flue. [Latin *tubulus*: box tile]. A term denoting the hollow box-shaped TERRACOTTA tiles which were joined together to form passages in the walls and roofing of Roman imperial buildings, especially BATHS, to carry furnace-heated hot air up from the hollow HYPOCAUST floors.

Boyne culture. The term used for the PASSAGE GRAVES of the Boyne Valley in Ireland, dated to the 4th millennium BC. They are notable for their size, the architectural expertise shown in their construction, and their decoration. The area must have been a centre of some importance, as five HENGES have been found, as well as a number of large mounds covering passage graves, including KNOWTH and NEW GRANGE.

BP, bp. Years before present. The 'present' referred to is the year AD 1950, the latest that the atmosphere was sufficiently uncontaminated to act as a standard for RADIOCARBON DATING. The lower case 'bp' represents uncalibrated radiocarbon years; the capitals BP denote a calibrated radiocarbon date, or a date derived from some other dating method, such as POTASSIUM-ARGON, that does not need CALIBRATION (*see* Table 8, page 422).

brachycephalic. Broad headed, having a CEPHALIC INDEX of 80 to 84.9.

Bradford-on-Avon. St Lawrence Church in Bradford-on-Avon in Somerset, is possibly the finest and best-preserved AANGLO-SAXON church in England. The church is a small chapel, with a tall nave and chancel flanked by two side-porticos. There is some controversy as to its date, but it is likely that the major part of the present building is the one that St Aldhelm founded in the early 8th century. The interior is enhanced by two 10th-century angels in WINCHESTER style carved over the chancel arch, by the perfect examples of double-splayed windows, and the decorated stone altar. The exterior walls of the nave and chancel are embellished by an unusual form of arcading which stands out in relief from the ashlar walls.

Brahmagiri. *See* MEGALITHS (INDIA).

Brak, Tell. A TELL site of c30 hectares on the Khabur River in northeast Syria overlooking an important river crossing. Material from the HALAF and UBAID periods indicates a long history, but the site is best known for its sequence of rich temples of the late URUK and JEMDET NASR periods, when it was clearly an important centre. Most famous of all is the so-called Eye Temple, richly decorated with clay cones, copper panels and gold work, in a style very similar to that found in the contemporary temples of SUMER (southern Mesopotamia). Later, in the 3rd millennium BC, Tell Brak became a provincial capital of the AKKADIAN empire; the palace of Naramsin of this period was more of a depot for the storage of tribute and loot than a residential seat. The city was plundered after the fall of the Akkadian empire, but the palace was rebuilt in the UR III period by Ur Nammu.

Branč. Cemetery of the Early Bronze Age Nitra group in southwest Slovakia. 308 graves have been excavated by J. Vladár, mostly simple rectangular pits, sometimes with a wooden lining, containing inhumation burials.

An interesting study of the grave goods by Susan Shennan suggests that certain burials stand out as noticeably rich, on the basis of the rarity of the raw materials employed and the amount of time taken to produce the goods. Both males and females were buried with rich goods (more females) and it is suggested that women may have achieved their wealth through marriage. Some children's burials were rich, suggesting that wealth was ascribed (inherited) rather than achieved.

Brassempouy. The Grotte du Pape near Brassempouy in the Landes, southwest France, had a long series of early Upper PALAEOLITHIC deposits, but the early excavations by PIETTE do not enable the exact sequence to be reconstructed. The site is famous for a series of carved ivories, broken statuettes of the 'venus' (*see* VENUS FIGURINES) type and a head with some facial features.

Bratthalio. *See* GREENLAND.

breadfruit. The breadfruit tree (*Artocarpus altilis*) provides a large, starchy fruit which requires cooking before it can be eaten. The tree was probably first brought into cultivation in a region extending from the Philippines to New Guinea, and attained its greatest economic importance in the Polynesian Islands, especially the Marquesas and Tahiti, whither it was presumably carried by the first settlers c1500-2000 years ago. The fruit was also dried or allowed to ferment, and could then be stored for several years in underground pits (especially in the Marquesas). In 1788 Captain William Bligh was attempting to take breadfruit saplings from Tahiti to the West Indies when the famous mutiny on HMS *Bounty* occurred.

breccia. A SEDIMENT composed of angular fragments of gravel.

Breuil, Abbé Henri (1877-1961). French Catholic priest who made major contributions to PALAEOLITHIC archaeology and especially to the study of the Upper Palaeolithic CAVE ART of France and northern Spain. He made detailed studies of nearly all the known decorated caves and to this day many of the illustrations of cave paintings published are derived from Breuil's copies of the originals.

He proposed a series of four successive art styles, based on the superposition of paintings found in many caves, and held the view that the purpose of the paintings was sympathetic magic, to ensure success in hunting.

brick. A shaped CLAY block, used in building, or the material from which such blocks are made. The brick clay may be hardened by baking in a kiln, in which case it may be termed TERRACOTTA. In drier climates, such baking is not so necessary and bricks may be dried in the sun; such bricks may be called mud-brick or adobe.

Bristlecone Pine. *See* DENDROCHRONOLOGY.

Britannia. Name given by the Romans to the imperial province of Britain, occupied from 43 to 410, and comprising England, Wales and (for much of the 2nd century) lowland Scotland. In 197 the province was divided into two, c300 into four, and in 369 into five smaller provinces.

Brno [German: Brünn]. The capital of Moravia, the central province of Czechoslovakia. Important PALAEOLITHIC and geological sites surround the town, and are illustrated in a fine regional museum. Several interesting Palaeolithic discoveries have been found in the confines of the town. The most important was a burial found in Francouzska Street in 1891. Covered in red ochre and with mammoth tusks and ornaments,it is one of the earliest Upper Palaeolithic burials known, possibly c30,000 bc. The skull retains such primitive features as large brow ridges.

Broadbeach. A burial ground in coastal dunes south of Brisbane, Queensland, Australia. Excavations indicated that during the last 1300 years about 200 individuals may have been buried there. There were wide variations in burial practices, possibly related to age, sex and status; they included primary, secondary, single and multiple burials, as well as cremations. Skeletons were extended, flexed or wrapped in bundles, and deposited in vertical or horizontal pits. Red ochre was present in nearly all graves, while grave goods included stone and shell arrangements, and bone and shell tools. Evidence of charcoal and food remains in and on top of the filled graves suggested that a cooked meal was part of the burial ritual.

broch. A type of circular building found in north Scotland and the Isles from around the turn of the Christian era. Brochs were built of drystone walling, up to *c*4 metres thick; the brochs themselves may be up to 12 metres in diameter. They contained many chambers and stone stairways leading up to tiers of galleries above, and may have been fortified home-steads, since good arable land is usually to be found in the vicinity.

Broederstroom. An extensive Early Iron Age village site west of Pretoria, South Africa, which has yielded an unusually complete picture of village life in the mid-1st millennium ad. Remains of 13 circular houses, spread over an area of some two hectares, have been investigated. Iron-smelting is attested, as is the herding of cattle, sheep and goats. The typology of the Broederstroom pottery suggests that the Early Iron Age population of this area had connections with contempor-aneous peoples further to the northwest.

Broken Hill. A mine at Kabwe in central Zambia, exploited from the early years of the present century. Mining operations have exposed a long series of stone industries extending from the ACHEULIAN to the CHARAMAN. Particular interest attaches to a cave, now completely quarried away, from which abundant faunal remains were recovered in association with a Charaman stone industry and perhaps with earlier artefacts also. In 1922, fossil human remains were discovered, including a complete skull in a remarkably fine state of preservation. Generally attributed to a sub-group of HOMO SAPIENS, *H. s. rhodesiensis* [RHODESIAN MAN], the skull has marked brow ridges, a sharply receding forehead and a cranial capacity of 1280 cubic centimetres. Different authorities have varyingly emphasized the specimen's affinity to the European and Near Eastern neanderthaloids, or the features which are reminiscent of HOMO ERECTUS. Dating by the AMINO-ACID RACEMIZATION technique indicates an age of more than 100,000 years. Together with the fact that over 25 per cent of the species represented by the associated faunal remains are now extinct, this suggests that the skull is that of the maker not

of the Charaman industry but of the SANGOAN or late Acheulian material also found in the vicinity.

Broken K Pueblo. A single-storey masonry PUEBLO located 18 km east of Snowflake, Arizona, and one of the exemplary models of the practice of NEW ARCHAEOLOGY along with William Longacre's Carter Ranch excavations and James Deetz's Arikara study. Using pollen evidence, James N. Hill was able to isolate the function of several room types, and with detailed analysis of style based on computer-related statistical techniques he extrapolated details of the social systems which operated at the site, such as division of labour and post-marital domicile.

bronze. An ALLOY of COPPER. Tin bronzes are copper alloys that contain more than 1 per cent TIN. Most Bronze Age bronzes contained around 10 or 12 per cent tin, but some have as much as 37 per cent. Bronzes, like copper, are relatively soft and can be COLD WORKED. Similarly, they have a relatively low melting point, and could be melted and CAST in antiquity. The advantage of tin bronze over copper lies in ease of casting and in increased hardness. Many of the first bronzes to appear in the European Early Bronze Age had a lower tin content and a high ARSENIC content (*see* COPPER). These may be regarded as transitional between copper and bronze. Bronzes can be made by SMELTING copper and tin ores together in a simple furnace, but better control of the proportions can be obtained by smelting the two metals separately and subsequently remelting and mixing them. During the Late Bronze Age LEAD, which had hitherto been present at less than 1 per cent, was added at around 4 to 7 per cent (up to 15 per cent). The reason for this is unclear.

Bronze Age. Second age of the THREE AGE SYSTEM, defined by the use of bronze as the main material for making tools. The term is still widely used in West Asiatic and European prehistory. The dates of the Bronze Age vary from area to area, but in general terms it belongs to the 3rd and 2nd millennia BC in Western Asia, the 2nd and early 1st millennia BC in Europe.

bronzes (China). *See* RITUAL VESSELS (CHINA), BELLS (CHINA), MIRRORS, DRUMS (CHINA).

Brook Street. *See* WINCHESTER.

Brørup interstadial. An interstadial of the WEICHSELIAN cold stage. It has been dated by radiocarbon to between 63,000 and 61,000 bp, but this is at the extreme range of the technique (*see* RADIOCARBON DATING) and it may be earlier.

Brown Forest soil. The type of SOIL which develops under mature deciduous woodland. Variants of the Brown Forest soil are thought to have covered most of the British Isles and temperate Europe under the great forests which existed during the middle of the present INTERGLACIAL (*see* ATLANTIC). The soil type is characteristically penetrated by tree roots, and actively worked by EARTHWORMS to a considerable depth, so that litter from the trees which falls on to the surface is rapidly incorporated into the soil. The top of the PROFILE is marked by a thick, strongly structured and well-mixed HORIZON of mineral material and HUMUS. Brown Forest soils are fertile and stable, but if the woodland cover is removed repeatedly, or nutrients are removed from the soil by agriculture and animal feeding, they may degrade. In those areas where there is relatively low annual rainfall, a SOL LESSIVÉ profile may develop. In areas of higher rainfall, or under heath vegetation or coniferous woodland, a PODZOL may develop. As a result of such changes, true Brown Forest soils are rare today.

Brucato. *See* DESERTED MEDIEVAL VILLAGES.

Bruniquel. A cave and a rock shelter at Bruniquel in the Tarn department, southwest France, have revealed MAGDALENIAN deposits, including the remains of two or three well-preserved skulls and skeletal parts, and mixed fragmentary remains of over a dozen more individuals. Carved bone and antler art objects are known.

Bryggen. *See* BERGEN.

Bryn Celli Ddu. A PASSAGE GRAVE in Anglesey, Wales, under a cairn *c*50 metres in diameter. This tomb is linked to the BOYNE CULTURE by the decoration on the underside of the capstone; such decoration is rare outside Ireland, although it occurs on another Anglesey passage grave, at BARCLODIAD Y GAWRES. Another distinctive feature of this tomb is the four concentric STONE CIRCLES surrounding the chamber, the outer one surrounding the base of the cairn.

Brześć Kujawski. A multi-focal site of the LENGYEL culture located in the Blackearth region of Kujavia, central Poland, and dated to the early 4th millennium bc. Brześć Kujawski comprises a large settlement site of *c*60 trapezoidal LONG HOUSES, smaller sites of one or more house clusters and a large flat inhumation cemetery with double graves, animal burials and rich copper grave goods. The Lengyel village has four phases of occupation, indicated by overlapping house plans and suggestive of cyclic agriculture.

Bubanj-hum. A poorly understood group dated to the late 4th to early 3rd millennia bc in the Morava valley of eastern Yugoslavia. The eponymous site, on a gravel terrace of the Nišava river outside Niš, was excavated by Garašanin in the 1950s. Four main periods are recognized, after surface finds of the early Neolithic STARČEVO culture; IA: four building phases with graphite painted ware and VINČA-derived dark burnished ware; IB: a short phase with BADEN pottery; II: a short phase with material like COȚOFENI and SALCUȚA IV; and III: a full Early Bronze Age occupation. The ceramic developments of Period IA reflect the diffusion of graphite painted ware from Bulgaria into the west Balkans, together with the gradual decline in popularity of dark burnished wares on the periphery of the late Vinča culture.

bucchero. Pottery fired so as to be grey throughout the fabric with a slight surface sheen. It was inspired by earlier near-eastern models, and occurs principally in Greek-speaking and Etruscan areas between the 8th and 5th centuries BC. Shapes vary greatly as do styles of decoration (incised, stamped and applied).

Buccino. A group of sites within the comune of Buccino in southwest Italy. In the San Antonio area, a cemetery of six rock-cut tombs of the Copper Age GAUDO group, with radiocarbon dates of 2580-1970 bc (c3350-2500 BC) has been found. In the Tufariello area there is a settlement site of the Early Bronze Age, belonging to an early stage of the APENNINE culture. The site was surrounded by a stone wall and contained rectangular stone-built huts.

Buddhism. The Buddha, who lived in India in the 6th century BC, challenged the religious teachings of the Brahmans, who dominated Indian civilization at the time. An early convert to Buddhism was Bimbisara, king of Magadha, but its most extensive development was under the MAURYAN empire of ASOKA in the 3rd century BC, when there existed what has reasonably been described as a Buddhist civilization. By the end of the Mauryan empire in the early 2nd century BC, Buddhism had already developed internal divisions in its beliefs and practices and, although in the subsequent centuries it both spread to other areas and continued to contribute to Indian civilization, it lost its dominant role in that development. Early in the present era a new form of Buddhism appeared, known as the Mahayana or 'Great Vehicle', which had a more flexible doctrine. It was this form of Buddhism that found its way from India through Central Asia to China in the 1st or 2nd century AD. Very large numbers of Buddhist monuments survive in India itself, including STUPAS and rock-cut cave temples.

Tibet also has large numbers of Buddhist monuments. Buddhism was first introduced to Tibet from India during the reign of king Sron-brtsan-sgam-po (c620-649) and revived in the late 10th century by Rin-c'en-bzan-po (958-1055) and the Indian teacher Atiśa. Its archaeological manifestations are the numerous temples, monasteries and shrines found throughout the Tibetan cultural area. The earliest temples (Iha-k'an) are small, rectangular in plan and have massive inward sloping walls and flat roofs. The original foundations of the Royal Dynastic period (c620-842) are usually distinguished by tall dressed stone pillars topped by a roof-like canopy and sometimes bearing a dedicatory incription. The first true monastery in Tibet was that of bSam-yas, built by K'ri-sron-Ide-brtsan (755-?797). In its original form it had a large seven-storey temple surrounded by eight ancillary buildings to house the monks. mC'od-rten, a type of shrine very common in Tibet, are symbolic buildings modelled on the Indian stupa. They are psycho-cosmograms, representing the Buddhas and their teachings, and are made of dressed stone or sun-dried brick with a plaster facing. They normally contain a cavity for religious relics and the largest examples contain actual rooms.

Buddhism reached Southeast Asia in the early centuries of the Christian era as part of the process of INDIANIZATION. It reached Japan rather later: the Mahayana Buddhism was officially introduced to the Japanese court in 538, but it had probably been known in the country for some time before that. After an internal struggle over its acceptance, Buddhism became part of the adminstrative measures which the emerging central government adopted to tighten its control over the provinces. Syncretism with the indigenous nature worship began by the 8th century, but Buddhism remained the religion of the elite until the 14th century, when Pure Land Buddhism met an enthusiastic reception from the masses.

Bug-Dniester. The names of these two river valleys in southwest European Russia define the distribution of a long-lived culture which developed throughout the 5th millennium bc. Three phases are recognized: Early (Sokoletz), Middle (Samtčin) and Late (Savran). Each phase is typified by short-lived sites on the edge of river terraces, occupied all the year round, perhaps for five to ten years. Subsistence strategies changed little from the preceding Mesolithic hunting, fishing and shell-collecting, with the minor addition of small quantities of domesticated pig, cattle and einkorn wheat. Demand for increased storage capacity led to the apparently independent evolution of pointed-base pottery, although local FIRST TEMPERATE NEOLITHIC (Criş) pottery occurs in the early phase.

Buhen. A fort on the west bank of the Nile, 260 km upstream of Aswan, erected during the Middle Kingdom (see DYNASTIC EGYPT) to secure Egyptian control of trade in gold and other commodities during the military occupation of Nubia.

Buka. See SOLOMON ISLANDS.

Bukhara. A city in Soviet Central Asia, already an important town before the Arab conquest in 713. Bukhara flourished after the conquest, becoming the capital of the Samanid dynasty from 875 to 999. In 1220 the city was sacked by Chingiz Khan. The best-known monument is the Mausoleum of Ismael the Samanid, built shortly before the ruler's death in 907. It is a domed cubic structure, 9.5 metres across, decorated both inside and out with elaborate brick ornament. The minaret of the Masjid-i Kalan, completed in 1127, also has brick patterns, enlivened with an inscription made of bricks with turquoise glaze, one of the earliest examples of coloured architectural ornament in Central Asia. The mosque itself belongs to the 15th century, while the adjacent Madrasa Mir-i Arab was founded in 1535 (a madrasa is a school for Quranic studies). The oldest surviving mosque is the 12th-century Masjid Magoki Attari.

Bükk. This mountain range in the north of Hungary gives its name to a Middle Neolithic regional group of the Alföld LINEAR POTTERY culture of the late 5th millennium bc. The appreciable number of cave sites in upland locations indicates a seasonal focus on transhumance, as well as the exploitation of rocks for axes and other tools. Within the Bükk culture are sites with hoards of axes and half-finished unused flint blades. While the distinctive painted and incised Bükk pottery and obsidian was introduced into exchange networks north and south of the Carpathians, it should be noted that, contrary to the claims of V.G. CHILDE, there are no obsidian sources in the Bükk Mountains themselves.

bulb of percussion. When a FLAKE is removed from a CORE by striking with a hammer, the flake has a swelling adjacent to the point where it was hit, and spreading over part of the newly exposed flake surface. This is called the bulb of percussion and usually indicates human manufacture.

Buret'. A site in southern Siberia near Lake Baikal, occupied in late PALAEOLITHIC times, famous for some peg-like female figurines dressed apparently in fur suits.

Burgäschi-See Sud. Lakeside settlement site of the Neolithic CORTAILLOD culture in Switzerland, dated to the mid-4th millennium BC. Like other Cortaillod sites, Burgäschi-See Sud has excellent preservation of organic

remains. Unlike other sites of the period the fauna consisted of 90 per cent wild species, of which the most important were red deer, roe deer, aurochs and wild boar. Domesticated cattle, sheep, goat and pig were kept, but clearly most meat food was obtained from hunting. Among the artefactual material was a number of copper beads, probably imported from eastern Europe.

burh. A small fortified town, found in later Anglo-Saxon England, where the population could take refuge during times of threat. Burhs were established as a national system of defence in the later 9th century by King ALFRED of Wessex in response to the persistent threat of Viking incursions. This defensive system is known as the burghal system. Excavations in many burhs, such as Wareham, Tamworth, Wallingford and Cricklade, have revealed that the initial burghal defences consisted of a wide palisaded bank and v-shaped ditch with turf and timber revetments. Many of these burhs were also developed as market towns and gridded streets were laid out within a number of them. These centres became the foci of the 10th-century urban revival in Anglo-Saxon England.

Burial Mound Period. The penultimate period of a chronological construction relating to the whole of eastern North American prehistory. Formulated in 1941 by J.A.Ford and Gordon Willey, the total chronology, from early to late, runs PALEO-INDIAN, ARCHAIC, Burial Mound, TEMPLE MOUND. The Burial Mound Period is divided into two sub-periods. Burial Mound I (1000-300 BC) covers the period of transition from Late Archaic to Early WOODLAND ways of life and is associated especially with the ADENA culture. Burial Mound II (300 BC-AD 700) is characterized by the dominance of Middle and Late Woodland groups, especially HOPEWELL.

buried soils. Soils may be buried by structures and deposits on archaeological sites. Such soils are frequently preserved under RAMPARTS, BARROWS and other mounds, or buried within the fill of a DITCH. Turves, and the upper HORIZONS of the soil PROFILE which may have been cut with them, can also be preserved within mounds. The study of buried soils yields valuable information about environmental change in the area. Sometimes the marks made by

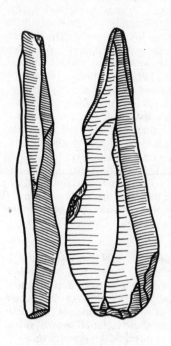

Burin

move from eastern Tibet they had been preceded by the PYU, who had established a kingdom there as early as the 3rd century. The original historical inhabitants of Lower Burma were the staunchly Theravada Buddhist MON, with their centres at Thaton, at the mouth of the Sittang (often identified with SURVARNAB-HŪMI), and at Pegu, former HAMSAVATĪ. It was only in the 11th century that the Burman kingdom of PAGAN established Burman suzerainty over the Mon south, absorbing in the process many Mon cultural elements which now form the basis of the Burmese civilization. The Pyus, whose kingdom of ŚRĪKSHETRA (Prome) was thus sandwiched between the Mons and the Burmans, were eventually assimilated by the latter. But the kingdom of Pagan was to last only to the end of the 13th century when it was conquered by the Mongols, in the wake of whom the Shan (i.e. Thais) rules over the area for such a long time that it could have become another 'Thailand' had not the Burmans once again taken the political lead in the 16th century.

burnish. A polish given to the surface of a pottery vessel, usually with a bone or wooden implement, and carried out after drying but before firing. The purpose is usually to make the vessel less porous and more watertight, but burnishing is sometimes used for decorative purposes. For instance, areas are sometimes left matt to contrast with the shiny burnished areas, producing a decorative effect known as pattern burnish.

Burrill Lake rock shelter. A rock shelter situated on the southeast coast of New South Wales, Australia, with basal deposits dated to c18,000 bc. Stone artefacts in these Pleistocene levels included flake scrapers and dentated saws. At about 3000 bc BONDI POINTS and other tools of the AUSTRALIAN SMALL TOOL TRADITION appeared. This is one of the earliest dates for Bondi points.

Burzahom. A prehistoric site in Kashmir. Four phases of occupation have been identified, ranging in date from the 3rd-2nd millennium BC to the 3rd-4th centuries AD. Phase I is characterized by pit-dwellings, while Phase II has houses of mud and mudbrick, as well as burials of both humans and animals (dog, wolf and ibex) in pits. To Phase III

ancient ploughing are preserved in the ancient profile. In addition, the POLLEN or SNAIL shells which became incorporated into the soil by EARTHWORM sorting, and are preserved by burial, may be used for environmental investigations. Soil profiles may be altered as a result of their burial and care needs to be taken when studying them.

burin. A kind of stone tool often made on a BLADE. At one end, slivers or spalls of stone have been removed to make a kind of chisel edge, probably used for carving antler and bone tools, as well as art objects. There are many kinds of burin and they are often multiple. Burins are typical of sites of the Upper Palaeolithic stage and especially typical of the MAGDALENIAN.

Burma. The history of the Irrawaddy basin is that of several peoples, the ethnic Burmans being only one of them. On their southward belongs a group of large stones arranged in a rough semicircle. Parallels for this stone ring, as well as for the pit-houses of Phase I and some of the associated artefacts of Phases I-III (pottery, polished stone and polished bone tools) occur in Central and Northern Asia, rather than in the Indian subcontinent.

Bush Barrow. A rich grave under a BARROW, belonging to the WESSEX CULTURE of southern England. It contained a single male inhumation with grave goods, including a bronze axe, two bronze daggers of 'Bush Barrow' type, one of which had a hilt decorated with many tiny gold pins, a belt-hook and two lozenge-shaped plaques of gold with incised decoration, in addition to a stone macehead and zig-zag shaped bone mountings for the mace shaft; these have often been compared to similar mountings from MYCENAE, but the Bush Barrow examples are probably several centuries earlier.

Bus Mordeh. *See* ALI KOSH.

Butmir. As with many type sites excavated in the early 20th century and before, Butmir, situated near Sarajevo in Bosnia, Yugoslavia, is not characteristic of the whole of the Butmir culture. The site represents a classic, or late, phase of the culture, defined by richly decorated ceramics (especially spiral and meander motifs) and a wide range of fired clay anthropomorphic figurines, depicting several physical types, varied costume and even pathological conditions. The Butmir culture comprises the Middle and Late Neolithic of central Bosnia, in the period c4350-3700 bc. An autochthonous local origin for this culture from the preceding KAKANJ stage has recently been demonstrated (*see* OBRE).

Byblos [Gebal, Gebail]. An important coastal settlement in Lebanon, north of Beirut, occupied for approximately 5000 years. The earliest settlement was a modest Neolithic village of the 6th millennium bc with rectangular mud-brick houses with plastered floors. This settlement developed through several phases, throughout the 5th and into the 4th millennium bc. It was then abandoned for a period of unknown length and when it was reoccupied before 3000 BC it was as a town with rectangular houses and paved streets. This town went through several phases of development in its turn, with later phases having houses of stone instead of mud-brick and a well-built city wall. The city was violently destroyed, perhaps by the AMORITES, late in the 3rd millennium BC. It was rebuilt, however, and urban life continued. The importance of the site lay in its commercial role: its extensive contacts with Egypt (which imported the famous Lebanese timber mostly through Byblos) and trade with many areas of inland western Asia, including southern Meso-potamia. Byblos dominated eastern Mediter-ranean trade in the 3rd and early 2nd millennia, but its role declined later in the millennium and UGARIT, SIDON and TYRE became the great port sites of the later Bronze Age. The most famous monument of the city was the temple of the 'Lady of Byblos' (Ba'alat Gebal), a local variant of Astarte or Ishtar, the Semitic goddess of love.

Bygland. A site in Norway where the grave of a Viking Age smith was discovered. The cremated remains were accompanied by an outstanding collection of 25 iron-working tools, as well as some of the craftsman's products: these included swords, shield bosses and axes of mid-10th century date.

Bylany. A large village settlement of the Bohemian regional group of the LINEAR POTTERY culture, located on the fertile loess-lands of the Bohemian plain in Czecho-slovakia. This 6.5-hectare site comprises timber-framed LONG HOUSES from three main phases (2-4) of the Linear Pottery sequence. According to the excavator, the late B. Soudsky, each occupation phase comprised a small number of houses centred on a large long house (or 'clubhouse') and associated with a stock enclosure. Subsistence strategies were based on the cultivation of emmer wheat and cattle husbandry; the excavator has hypothes-ized a form of cyclic agriculture.

Byzantium [later Constantinople, now Istanbul], **Byzantine**. In the 7th century BC Dorian Greeks founded the settlement of Byzantium on a trapezoidal promontory on the European side of the Bosporus channel which leads from the Mediterranean to the Black Sea and separates Europe from Asia. Thus began a city which has been occupied to the present day and which was the successor of Rome as the capital of both an empire and a civilization.

The city's first millennium is known mainly from literary evidence. It prospered from its strategic position, but fell successively under the domination of ACHAEMENID Persians (c512-478 BC), Athenian Greeks (478-339 BC), Hellenistic Greek kings (until 2nd century BC), the Roman Republic (up to 30 BC) and thereafter Roman emperors. One of these, Septimus Severus (AD 193-211), after initially damaging it, was responsible for restoring the city, re-walling it and beginning the construction of the limestone racecourse (Hippodrome).

The greatest period of the city's existence followed the year 330 AD when the first Christian emperor, Constantine, inaugurated Byzantium, now renamed Constantinopolis, as the new capital of the Eastern Roman Empire. The 'new Rome' became the inspirational force of the Christian Byzantine Empire, with its unique blend of late Roman and Greek culture. The city flourished over the succeeding centuries and in terms of its architecture and other aspects of civilized life became one of the finest cities in the world. Constantine himself erected new walls, churches and (in his Forum) a porphyry ('Burnt') column with relief sculture; he founded the imperial palace and finished Severus' Hippodrome. His successors continued its embellishment. In 368 Valens raised his still impressive aqueduct. Theodosius I 'the Great' (379-395) adorned the Hippodrome with an Egyptian granite obelisk on a base with reliefs, still standing; in 400-401 his son Arcadius erected a column. In 413 Theodosius

II built the colossal surviving walls of stone and brick-faced concrete, 19 km long with 96 variously shaped towers and the principal entrance at the Golden Gate. A column and church of Marcianus (450-457) remain. Even more splendid were the works of Justinian (527-565). Probably his were the marble Hippodrome seating, great cisterns and realistic white-ground palace mosaics; certainly his were several churches, above all the domed, richly embellished HAGIA SOPHIA.

Constantinople withstood successive outside attacks throughout its history and was once conquered by Frankish knights during the Fourth Crusade in 1204; it was finally lost to Christendom when it was besieged and captured by the Turks in 1453.

In spite of the renaming of the city by Constantine, it is the older name that survives in the term Byzantine, used to describe the Eastern Christian Empire and the civilization that developed under the inspiration of the new faith. The Byzantines were responsible for preserving much of Greek and Roman culture, but they also provided an avenue for eastern ideas to reach the west. Mixed eastern and western influences are most clearly seen in the field of architecture: the great domed churches of 6th-century Constantinople — Hagia Sophia, SS Sergius and Bacchus and St Eirene — reflect Persian as well as Roman building traditions. In decorative art, the Byzantines excelled at mosaics, which they used mainly for walls and ceilings, rather than for floors. Fine Byzantine mosaics, using, among other materials, gilt glass, survive in Asia Minor and in Greece, but some of the finest examples of all are found in the West in PALERMO and RAVENNA.

C

Cabenge [Tjabenge]. A river terrace site in the Walarae valley of southwestern SULAWESI, Indonesia, which has produced a pebble tool and flake industry of presumed Upper PLEISTOCENE date. An archaic fauna (with *Stegodon* and *Archidiskodon*) thought to be contemporary with the tools is now known to be of separate origin and of Late PLIOCENE date.

cacao. The crop from which chocolate, the favoured drink of the nobility of many Mesoamerican cultures, is produced. Because its production is limited by the environmental setting in which it will flourish (that is, tropical lowlands), cacao attained considerable importance as a luxury item in the economies of the MAYA, TEOTIHUACAN and AZTEC. Depictions on IZAPAN sculpture show that it was first used in the PRE-CLASSIC period. The CODEX Mendoza indicates that by Aztec times it had become a medium of exchange and that tribute was commonly paid in this commodity.

Caddoan. *See* SPIRO.

Caere. *See* CERVETERI.

Caerleon [Isca]. The Romans established this 20-hectare fort, named Isca, with its 64 barrack blocks, during the pacification of Wales, which was finally achieved in AD 78. The fort is one of three major legionary fortresses, the other two being at CHESTER and YORK. Originally constructed of timber and earth, it had been largely rebuilt in stone before the garrison finally left for home during the abandonment of the province. Evidence has been found for centurion houses, workshops, barracks, stores, ovens, hospital, baths and latrines. Outside the immediate fortification, in an associated civic settlement, lies an amphitheatre (built *c*80 AD of earth, timber and masonry) now fully excavated, traces of two bath buildings, and of extensive cemeteries.

Caesarea. A coastal city in Israel, founded in the 4th century BC. It flourished under Herod the Great, who enlarged the city and rebuilt its harbour. After the death of Herod it became the capital of the Roman province of Judaea. An inscription naming Pontius Pilate is one of the best-known finds from this site.

The town became important again during the Crusades of the 12th and 13th centuries; the still impressive defences date to this period.

Cagayan Valley. A broad valley in northern Luzon, Philippines, containing several open sites from which, according to some claims, comes an association of a pebble and flake industry with a Middle PLEISTOCENE fauna which includes *Elephas*, *Stegodon*, rhinoceros and bovids. Recent geomorphological studies have established the authenticity of the fauna, but there is still debate as to the precise stratigraphic occurrence of the tools, which may be later.

Cahokia. Located in an alluvial valley near East St Louis, Illinois, USA, Cahokia is easily the most spectacular of the MISSISSIPPIAN centres. The site is 15-20 square kilometres in area, and at its height (1050-1250) had a population estimated variously between 10,000 and 38,000. It includes more than 100 man-made mounds (both burial and platform types) built over the period 700-1600 (*see* TEMPLE MOUND PERIOD). Monk's Mound, the largest of these, measures 330 metres long by 218 metres wide and reaches a maximum height of 30 metres. As is typical of flat-topped temple mounds, it served as base upon which civic buildings were erected. Its four terraces underwent at least seven periods of reconstruction, during each of which the surmounting buildings were completely razed. Portions of a wall or palisade have already been uncovered and indications are that it probably enclosed some 120 hectares including Monk's and 16 other large mounds.

In addition to construction on a grand

scale, evidence of long-distance trade, elaborate ceremonial activity and possibly astronomical observation indicate a centre of notable social complexity. Artefacts include flint hoes (the characteristic Mississippian artefact), shell and limestone-tempered pottery, and engraved stone tablets sometimes etched with the motifs of the SOUTHERN CULT.

Cahuachi. *See* NASCA.

Cai [Ts'ai]. *See* SHOU XIAN.

Caimito. *See* TUTISHCAINYO.

cairn. *See* BARROW.

Cairo. The capital of modern Egypt. In 641, the Arab conqueror of Egypt, Amr Ibn al-As, built a new quarter, Fustat ['The Tents'], outside the old town of Cairo. Among the first monuments erected in Fustat was the Mosque of Amr; the present structure, however, is almost entirely of the 19th century. New suburbs were added in the 8th and 9th centuries, making Fustat a large city. Ahmad ibn Tulun, governor from 869, chose it as his capital. Two buildings are associated with ibn Tulun: the Nilometer on Roda Island, which he restored in 872-3, and a mosque, finished in 879. The mosque is well preserved. It stands in a precinct and consists of a rectangular building, 140 metres long and 122 metres wide, with a courtyard surrounded on three sides by double arcades and a sanctuary five bays deep. The interior is richly decorated with stucco. In 969, the FATIMIDs arrived in Egypt and established another new town, al-Qahira ['The Visitors'] nearby. Cairo contains two major 10th-century monuments: the Mosque of al-Azhar, completed in 972, and the Mosque of al-Hakim, begun in 990. The original appearance of the former virtually disappeared in the course of alterations associated with the University of al-Azhar, founded in 988. The latter has a monumental entrance and sanctuary with a T-shaped plan recalling the first Fatimid mosque at MAHD-IYA. In 1087, the caliph al-Mustansir strengthened the walls of Cairo, employing Armenian architects for such features as Bab al-Futuh. Fustat, gradually abandoned in the Fatimid period, has been excavated on several occasions and became a hunting-ground for

dealers, providing the large collections in museums all over the world.

Calatagan. A peninsula in Batanga Province, about 100 km south of Manila in the Philippines, containing several burial grounds of the late 14th century to early 16th century. Burials are normally extended (some children were placed in urns); goods comprise local earthenware pottery, beads, glass bracelets, iron and brass goods, and a large and important range of imported pots from Thailand and MING Dynasty China. Calatagan is the best reported site of this period in the Philippines. *See also* SANTA ANA.

calendar, calendrics. Most ancient civilizations (and perhaps some non-literate prehistoric societies) developed calendrical systems to mark the passage of time. Where these were both carefully calculated and written down, as in Egypt, Mesopotamia and Mesoamerica, they are of considerable assistance to archaeologists for dating purposes.

The Egyptians employed a solar calendar of 365 days in a year (divided into 12 months of 30 days plus 5 intercalary days) for civil purposes. This civil calendar naturally diverged from the real solar year (which has 365.2422 days) by increasing amounts. For agricultural purposes and for determining the dates of religious festivals they used a different calendar based on observations of the dog star Sirius, known to them as Sothis, whose annual heliacal rising (i.e. rising at the same time as the sun) conveniently preceded the Nile Flood. The two calendars would coincide every 1,460 years (known as the Sothic cycle). The fortunate survival of three texts which record the date in the civil year on which Sirius rose heliacally on three different occasions (probably in 1469, 1537 and 1872 BC) has assisted in the reconstruction of ancient Egyptian chronology.

The calendar in use in ancient Mesopotamia and the Levant was lunar, based on twelve months of 30 days each. This produced a year of only 354 days, about 11¼ days short of the true solar year; the necessary correction was made by the addition of seven months over a period of 19 years. This type of calendar is still used in both Judaism and Islam for religious purposes, though many countries now also employ the Gregorian solar calendar for secular purposes.

Among the Greeks almost every community had a calendar of its own, but all were lunar calendars. Some of the Greek month names occur in LINEAR B, indicating that a calendar of this type was already in use in MYCENAEAN times. Ordinary years in Greek calendars consisted of 12 months of 29 or 30 days; leap years of 13 months were inserted from time to time (but not apparently according to any organized system). The Romans originally had a calendar of 10 months, but subsequently adopted the ETRUSCAN calendar of 12 months, with 28, 29 or 31 days each; corrections were made by intercalating a 'month' of 22 or 23 days between the 23rd and 24th February. However, this was so inefficient that by the time of Julius Caesar the civil calendar was three months ahead of the solar calendar. In the year 46 BC Caesar corrected this by having a year of 445 days (known as the 'ultimus annus confusionis' or 'the last year of the muddled reckoning'). He then adapted the Egyptian solar calendar for Roman use, inserting extra days in the shorter months to bring the total up to 365, with the addition of a single day between the 23rd and 24th February in leap years. This calendar, known as the Julian Calendar, remained in use until the time of Gregory XIII in 1582, who made a further correction (of eleven days) and instituted the calendar which is in general use today.

A complex calendrical system was the hallmark of many MESOAMERICAN societies, but it found its extreme expression among the MAYA. It seems, however, to have been introduced by the OLMEC some time in the PRE-CLASSIC (see TRES ZAPOTES and CHIAPA DE CORZO). Two calendars were in use in both the Maya and later the AZTEC cultures. The Sacred Calendar was 260 days long and consisted of 13 months of 20 days; the Solar Calendar of 365 days was made up of 18 months of 20 days plus five extra (regarded as unlucky) days. These two calendars were integrated so that any given day would only occur once in 52 years. Known as the Calendar Round, it is best visualized as a pair of meshing gears of 260 and 365 teeth respectively, where, if a line were marked on them at the initial point of their meshing, it would take 52 revolutions of the larger one to restore the gears to their original relationship.

Far more useful to archaeologists is the Maya Long Count or Initial Series, which was a means of recording absolute time. Its starting date of 3113 BC (using the Goodman-Thompson-Martinez correlation) marks some mythical event in Maya history and itself stands at the beginning of a cycle 13 Baktuns long. A Baktun at 144,000 days is the largest unit of time in the calendar. This is further divided into smaller units: the Katun (7200 days); the Tun (360 days); the Uinal (20 days) and the Kin (a single day). Thus Long Count dates are expressed in terms of these units in a five place notation. Therefore the date 9.18.0.0.0. indicates the passage of 9 × 144,000 plus 18 × 7200 days since the initial date of 3113 BC. In cultural contexts, however, the dates are inscribed as a series of hieroglyphs which incorporate numeration via bars (units of five) and dots (units of one).

Short Count dating replaces the Long Count after AD 900 and although based on a similar system, the Katun replaces the Baktun as the largest unit. Unfortunately, it is a good deal less precise from the point of view of the archaeologist. Its imprecise nature is best understood by analogy with our own habit of recording only the last two digits of the year, for example '82: such a date, of course, can be interpreted as 1882 or 1982.

The Secondary Series is a means of correcting the quarter day error in the 365-day Solar Year (i.e. the equivalent of our leap year). As an addendum to calendar dates inscribed on STELAE, the Secondary Series records the number of days by which the inscribed date was out of synchronization with the actual 52-year cycle of the Calendar Round.

Other calendars, based on long-term observations of heavenly bodies (see ASTRONOMY), were used as a means of predicting events. Many aspects of daily life were regulated by the calendar, with certain periods being considered dangerous or unlucky. The five odd days of the Solar Year, for instance, were unlucky days, while the completion of any Calendar Round was a particularly dangerous time, since it was believed that the end of the world would come at just such a time.

Calendar Stone. A 20-tonne, 4-metre diameter, carved monolith, commissioned by the emperor Axayacatl in 1479, which symbolizes the AZTEC universe. The populations of central Mexico believed that they were living in the fifth epoch of a series of worlds (or suns) marked by cyclical generation and destruction (*see* CALENDAR). The central figure of the stone is this fifth sun, Tonatuih. Surrounding this are four rectangular cartouches containing dates and symbols for the gods Ehecatl, Texcatlipoca, TLALOC and Chilchihuitlicue who represent the four worlds previously destroyed. In a series of increasingly larger concentric bands, symbols for the 20 days of the month, precious materials and certain stars are represented. The outermost band depicts two massive serpents whose heads meet at the stone's base.

calibration. *See* RADIOCARBON CALIBRATION.

Callanish. An important group of MEGA-LITHIC monuments on the island of Lewis in the Outer Hebrides. The main monument is a STONE CIRCLE with an avenue to the north and ALIGNMENTS to the south, east and west. In the middle, and probably of a later date, is a small PASSAGE GRAVE under a round cairn. The alignments are thought to have had an astronomical role.

Callejon de Loreto. *See* CUZCO.

Calowanie. *See* SWIDERIAN.

Camaracayu. *See* TUTISHCAINYO.

Camare. *See* EL JOBO.

Cambodia [present-day Kampuchea].

Prehistory. Lying between THAILAND and VIETNAM on the Southeast Asian mainland, Cambodia has important remains of both the prehistoric and historic periods. Stone tools have been found in terraces of the Mekong River in possible association with tektites from a shower that fell c600,000 to 700,000 years ago. In western Cambodia there is an important HOABINHIAN sequence from the cave of LAANG SPEAN, with cord-marked and incised pottery in upper levels by 4300 bc. The major NEOLITHIC site is the 4.5 metre-thick occupation mound at SOMRONG SEN near the Tonle Sap lake, which has produced an elaborate assemblage which seems to predate 1000 bc. A number of DONG-SON drums and bronze assemblages have also been found in the country.

Classical. In spite of its relative distance from India, it was on the Indochinese Peninsula that the earliest known INDIANIZED kingdom developed, that of FUNAN. From small beginnings in the 1st century AD somewhere on the Lower Mekong it rapidly became the leading power of the region, with far-reaching trade connections. In the 6th century Funan declined; it was succeeded in its eastern part, corresponding to present Cambodia, southern LAOS and southern VIETNAM, by its former vassal CHENLA, while other former possessions became independent. Chenla in turn ceased to exist when, after having become a JAVANESE vassal in the late 8th century, the independent KHMER kingdom of ANGKOR was declared in 802. This kingdom developed once again into the most powerful state on the Indochinese Peninsula, at its apogee in the early 13th century occupying all but the most northeastern parts (the newly independent state of Vietnam) and most western parts (PAGAN), as well as much of the Malay Peninsula. The decline of the Angkorian empire was heralded by the achievement of independence of SUKHOTHAI in the middle of the 13th century, accentuated by the establishment of the kingdom of AYUTTHAYA in 1350 and consummated by the conquest of Angkor by the Thais in 1431. *See also* DVĀRAVATĪ, OC-ÈO, VYĀDHAPURA.

Camden, William (1557-1623). British antiquary who was among the first to describe the visible antiquities of Britain. HADRIAN'S WALL and STONEHENGE are among the sites described in his book *Britannia*, published in 1586.

camel. There are two surviving species of the genus *Camelus*, both domesticated: the two-humped Bactrian camel (*C. bactrianus*) and the single-humped dromedary (*C. dromedarius*).

Archaeological evidence is hard to obtain but the domestication of the Bactrian camel must have taken place within a broad area of central Asia, bounded by the Caspian Sea on one side and the Indus Valley on the other. The earliest evidence comes from the site of SHAHR-I SOKHTA in eastern Iran, where camel dung (presumably from domesticated animals) was found in levels of the first half of the 3rd millennium BC. The dromedary was probably domesticated somewhere in the Arabian peninsula; it is recorded from UMM

AN-NAR in Oman, which should perhaps be dated to the early 3rd millennium BC.

Although some communities exploit camels for milk, meat and wool, they were almost certainly domesticated for use as pack animals and this has always been their main function. Alexander the Great is said to have employed 5000 Bactrian camels, as well as other pack animals, to carry away the loot from PERSEPOLIS after he sacked the city in 330 BC.

Camelot. *See* ARTHUR, SOUTH CADBURY.

Camerton-Snowshill. The name, derived from two burial sites, given to a form of ogival bronze dagger of the later part of the WESSEX CULTURE of southern England. The name is also sometimes used for the whole phase of the culture, during which cremation gradually replaced inhumation as the dominant burial rite and there were changes in the goods placed with burials. This phase is dated to c1500 BC by corrected radiocarbon dates.

Camulodunum. *See* COLCHESTER.

Canaanites. A people who occupied Palestine in the 2nd millennium BC, the ancestors of the PHOENICIANS. The most important Canaanite towns were JERUSALEM, GEZER, HAZOR, LACHISH, MEGIDDO and, further north, BYBLOS and UGARIT. Excavations of temples and the cemetery of Minet el Beidha near Ugarit have revealed something of Canaanite religion and society. The Canaanites were responsible for the invention of the first alphabetic writing system (*see* WRITING).

Canegrate. A group of urnfields in northern Italy which have given their name to a Late Bronze Age group. This culture was probably ancestral to the GOLASECCA culture of the Iron Age.

Can Hasan. Site of a number of TELLS in the Konya plain of southern Turkey. Can Hasan III was an ACERAMIC NEOLITHIC settlement, perhaps of the 7th millennium bc. It had at least seven structural phases of small rect-angular buildings abutting on to each other. These were built mainly of slab pisé coated with mud plaster and sometimes painted red. The villagers were agriculturalists, growing einkorn and emmer WHEATS, lentil and vetch in the earlier phases, hexaploid bread and club wheats in the later phases. Cattle, sheep, goat and pig were all eaten, but it is not clear whether these were domesticated.

The main Can Hasan mound was occupied in the late Neolithic and CHALCOLITHIC periods. Several phases of occupation are documented, but the best explored is phase 2B which was destroyed by fire, carbon-dated to c4900 bc. This phase was characterized by rectangular mud-brick buildings, fine painted wares mainly in red on cream, and the use of copper. In the succeeding 2A phase poly-chrome wares were made. The site was subsequently abandoned but reoccupied in the Late Chalcolithic, late in the 5th millennium bc.

Canterbury [Durovernum Cantiacorum]. Town in Kent, southeast England, occupied from the later IRON AGE to the present day. Strategically well-sited at a crossing of the River Stour, and at the intersection of important land routes, Canterbury already had a sizeable BELGIC settlement before the arrival of the Romans in AD 43. The town was refounded soon after the invasion as Dur-overnum, the tribal capital (*civitas*) of the Cantiaci, probably c49. After a slow start, urbanization went ahead dramatically from the Flavian period (69-96) onwards. Traces have been found of a THEATRE (rebuilt c210-220), a FORUM, houses, streets and local industries; a stone wall with earth bank was added as fortification c270-290. There is some evidence of Christian occupation from the 4th century and prosperity seems to have declined sharply after 400, probably following the withdrawal of Roman forces.

Canterbury is also an important medieval town, famous firstly as the place to which Saint Augustine came in 597 on his mission to convert the English, and secondly as the greatest pilgrimage centre in the British Isles to which millions flocked throughout the Middle Ages to worship at the shrine of Thomas à Becket, the Archbishop who was murdered in Canterbury in 1170.

Archaeological investigations in Canter-bury have contributed to our understanding of the continuity of secular occupation in Roman towns after the imperial withdrawal from Britain; in particular, sunken huts and other evidence of the Early Saxon period have been found to overlie the Roman buildings. Excavations have also been carried out on the unique group of churches which may date to the late 6th or 7th century; these are St Augustine's Abbey, St Martin's and St Pancras, all of which were built in the Roman as opposed to the insular tradition, with flanking porticuses and apsidal chancels. The later medieval town boasts the magnificent medieval cathedral, an impressive circuit of town walls, a large 12th-century castle and some of the best preserved timber-framed buildings in England.

cantharus. A type of pottery cup made in Greek-speaking areas and in Etruria between the 8th and the 1st centuries BC, with a deep bowl, a foot, and characteristic pair of high vertical handles. Related Roman forms occur.

Cape Gelidonya. Part of the rugged coast of southwestern Turkey, famous for the underwater excavation of a very early ship, wrecked off this coast in the late Bronze Age (13th century BC). The small merchant ship was carrying a cargo of copper and bronze ingots, still wrapped in basketry. The presence of tin oxide suggests that the merchant himself may have been involved in the manufacture of bronze. Half a tonne of bronze ingots, some lettered, was removed from the wreck by the archaeologists. The excavation also produced a structural plan of the ship, including evidence of a grill of twigs on the bows to keep water off the deck — a technique still in use today. As well as the ingots, finds included pottery and three scarabs, one of which was of FAIENCE and another of ivory.

Cape Krusenstern. A site with evidence of long occupation on the north Alaskan coast, at which chronological associations have been uniquely preserved. The major cultures of Arctic prehistory, spanning a period from c3000 BC to historic times, are represented here. (The Palisades complex at nearby Ingitkalik Mountain may yet extend this continuum further into the past, possibly as early as 8000 BC.) Cultural debris left from the exploitation of marine resources by successive cultures, in combination with the seaward movement of the shoreline, has produced a 'horizontal stratigraphy'. This stratigraphy is visible as a sequence of strips, roughly parallel to the shoreline, with the oldest, DENBIGH, being furthest from the present-day shoreline. Old Whaling, CHORIS, NORTON, IPIUTAK and western THULE follow in chronological order. This horizontal sequence, in combination with the vertical stratigraphy of ONION PORTAGE, forms the most reliable chronological framework in Western Arctic prehistory.

Capeletti. A cave in the Aures Mountains of eastern Algeria which has yielded the clearest picture yet available of early North African pastoralism by a 'CAPSIAN NEOLITHIC' population. The first appearance of small stock (sheep and/or goats) appears broadly to have coincided with the beginning of pottery manufacture. Small stock were kept by transhumant herders in the Aures from the 5th millennium bc. By the 3rd millennium small domestic cattle are also attested.

capital. In architecture, the decorative top-member of a column, usually made of wood or stone. Portraying a moulded part (*echinus*) below, and a flat slab (*abacus*) above, it eases the visual transition from column shaft to the roofing beam (*architrave*) above. Decoration was normally according to one of the so-called orders, such as CORINTHIAN, DORIC or IONIC.

Capitol [Capitolium]. The Capitol in Rome acted as citadel and religious centre for the city from its beginnings. The Capitol comprised twin hillocks overlooking the FORUM. On the northern of the two hills was a citadel, and on the southern the great temple of Jupiter Capitolinus. The temple, whose founding is traditionally attributed to the early king Tarquin, seems to have preserved its original 6th-century plan through successive rebuildings. The capitol was approached by its own street, the Clivus Capitolinus. The Sibylline books were kept here, and rock-cut chambers underneath were apparently used as secret treasuries. Here too the consuls made their sacrifices and took their vows upon taking up office, and generals returning in triumph came to give thanks for their victory. The northern site, that of the citadel, is now covered by the church of Santa Maria in Aracoeli, while the site of the great temple is partly covered by the Palazzo Caffarelli.

caprovine. *See* SHEEP.

Capsian. A post-PLEISTOCENE industry of North Africa which occurs in several facies.

The Typical Capsian, dated to c6500 bc, characteristically occurs on shell middens and has large burins, backed blades and other implements. It is restricted to a limited area south of Tebessa near the present border between Tunisia and Algeria. The so-called Upper Capsian is more widespread, its distribution extending into western Algeria. Since it has now been dated to the 8th and 7th millennia bc, it can no longer be interpreted as derived from the Typical Capsian, although at Relilai it does overlie a deposit of the latter industry c5800 bc. Backed microliths are accompanied in the Upper Capsian by varied bone tools. Hunting and snail-collecting seem to have formed the basis of the economy. Human remains from Capsian sites are mostly of MECHTA-AFALOU type.

'Capsian Neolithic' The CAPSIAN industries of the Maghreb were succeeded by a somewhat heterogeneous series of assemblages, including pottery and — in some cases — evidence for the practice of food-production, to which the name 'Capsian Neolithic' [*Néolithique de tradition capsienne*] has generally been given. Pottery first appears in this region in the 5th millennium bc, by which time domestic small stock were herded. There is as yet no conclusive evidence for domestic cattle before the 3rd millennium. In fact, several local Neolithic traditions may be recognized in the Maghreb, as at EL KHRIL near Tangier, where the pottery shows affinities to Iberian wares, at Oued Guettara in northern Algeria, and at CAPELETTI in the Aures Mountains.

capstone. A large slab of stone set horizontally to cover a MEGALITHIC tomb or CIST GRAVE.

Capua [present-day Santa Maria di Capua Vetere]. This important coastal town in Campania, southern Italy, already had an early Iron Age settlement in the 9th century BC. Some time towards the end of the 7th century BC it was occupied by the ETRUSCANS, who transformed it into a very prosperous city, famous for its bronzes and notorious for the luxury of its life-style. The Etruscan period has left behind characteristic pottery, bronzes and tombs, and one of the principal pieces of evidence for the still little-understood Etruscan language — the so-called Capua Tile, an inscription of some 62 lines. Majority

orthodox opinion, if there is such a thing in Etruscan language scholarship, would regard it as a religious or ritual text. In the 5th century BC Capua was taken over by the Samnites, and from 338 BC it became Roman, apart from a brief period of secession after Rome's defeat at Cannae. The reputation for high living seems to have survived into the imperial period, when its AMPHITHEATRE (associated with a notorious gladiatorial school) rivalled the COLOSSEUM at Rome for magnificence. Still listed by Ausonius Magnus as a great city in the 4th century AD, Capua was sacked by the Vandals in 456 and virtually destroyed by the Saracens in 840. The modern name would perhaps confirm that only the church survived, the remnant of the population fleeing to nearby Casilinum. Besides the fine amphitheatre, imperial remains include a THEATRE, a ceremonial arch of Hadrian, and a MITHRAEUM.

Carbon 14. *See* RADIOCARBON.

carbonization, carbonized. Terms often used by archaeologists to describe organic materials preserved in a carbon-rich form, as a result of partial burning. CHARRING is a more precise word for this process.

carburization. *See* STEEL.

Carchemish. A TELL site on the Euphrates River on the Turkish-Syrian border. It was occupied from the 5th millennium bc, but became an important city only after the HITTITE conquest in the 14th century BC. Carchemish remained important after the fall of the Hittite empire, during the period of the Syro-Hittite city states (12th-8th centuries BC). The city consisted of a heavily fortified citadel and a large walled town adjacent to it. It is famous for the carved reliefs and inscriptions in 'Hittite hieroglyphics' decorating the great gateways and the monumental buildings of the city. Carchemish was conquered by the Assyrians under Sargon II in 716 BC.

Cardial ware. *See* IMPRESSED WARE.

cardo [Latin: 'hinge']. Term for the main north-south axis of Roman towns and military forts and camps. Technical use of the term seems to originate with Roman agricultural surveying practice, where *cardo* denotes the principal north-south axis of the site, about which other measurements 'hinge'. In a typical process of CENTURIATION (division into a hundred parts), the *cardo* is used with the other principal axis, the *decumanus* (properly due east-west) to divide a given area up into squares (reckoned to be 2400 Roman feet square), each of which is subsequently to be divided into one hundred smallholdings. It is likely that this agricultural technique underlies what from the 4th century BC onwards became the characteristic Roman grid system that Roman planners gave to so many army camps and new towns. For the technique itself, it is likely that the Romans were indebted to the Etruscans (though probably not so slavishly as Roman writers would themselves suggest) and to the Greeks, both of whom seem to have used grid town-planning, but almost exclusively only for colonial rapid expansion. The *cardo* need not be precisely aligned north-south, nor the *decumanus* east-west; what matters for the grid is the right-angle contained, and the subdivision into squares. The actual superimposition of the grid upon the terrain might be varied for all kinds of reasons, some perhaps religious, and some practical, such as the natural fall of the ground. The convention of referring to these urban axes as *cardo maximus* and *decumanus maximus* does not have direct classical authority.

Carib. A native group occupying the Lesser Antilles at the time of Columbus. Originating somewhere on mainland South America, they migrated along the islands, displacing the ARAWAK, probably by force. The Arawak language, however, remained; and the new group is distinguished from the old by the absence of ZEMI worship. Even though they were skilled pottery-makers and agriculturalists, the Carib's spiritual emphasis seems to have focussed on warfare and the ritual eating of human flesh (the word cannibal is derived from Carib).

carination. A sharp angle in the profile of a pottery or metal vessel.

Carnac. A region of south Brittany, northern France, famous for its stone ALIGNMENTS. Each group consists of 10-13 parallel rows several kilometres long, some ending in semicircular or rectangular enclosures. The stones, nearly 3000 in number, were chosen carefully

and planned so that they decreased steadily in size along the lines. The area was clearly an important ritual centre, as there are MEGALITHIC tombs nearby and stone boxes containing charcoal, cattle bones, polished axes and pottery. One suggestion is that the area was a lunar observatory. The largest stone — the Grand Menhir Brisé — weighed 345 tonnes; it is now recumbent, broken into three pieces and may in fact have fallen when the Neolithic builders first tried to erect it.

carnyx. A Celtic war-trumpet used in battle to produce noise and panic. It was constructed with a straight body of bronze, topped by a bronze animal head, usually that of a boar, with the tongue acting as a clapper. The carnyx was in use from the 2nd century BC to the first century AD and is known mostly from representations (*see* GUNDESTRUP).

Caroline Islands. *See* MICRONESIA.

Carolingian. This adjective stems from Charles the Great [CHARLEMAGNE] (771-814) and is used to describe the imperial territory, concepts and cultural renaissance for which he was responsible. The term is also used more generally to include the reign of his son, Louis the Pious, and less specifically the remainder of the 9th century in Western Europe, but in an archaeological and architectural sense, it is used to describe the period *c*750-*c*900.

carp's tongue sword. A type of bronze sword found mostly in north-west France and southern England in the Late Bronze Age (early 1st millennium BC). It had a flange hilt, a broad slashing blade and a long projecting point, which has given the type its name. *See* ATLANTIC BRONZE AGE, HUELVA.

Cartailhac, Emile (1843-1921). Eminent French prehistorian of the 19th century. Although he made many contributions to French archaeology, he is best remembered today for his long refusal to accept the authenticity of CAVE ART. When he was finally convinced, after a visit to the Spanish site of ALTAMIRA, he wrote an article for the journal *L'Anthropologie* in 1902, subtitled 'Mea culpa d'un sceptique', which helped to convince many scholars of the day that these and other cave paintings were indeed genuine and the earliest manifestations of art in the world.

Carter, Howard (1874-1939). Egyptologist famous above all for his discovery in 1922 and subsequent excavation (in an expedition organized by Lord Carnarvon) of the tomb of TUTANKHAMUN in the Valley of the Kings at THEBES.

Carthage. The city of Carthage was founded as a colony from the PHOENICIAN city of Tyre (the Phoenician name Qart Hadasht means 'new city'); traditionally this occurred in 814 BC, although Phoenician occupation on the site is archaeologically attested from about a century later. The new city rapidly prospered from its position overlooking the straits which divide the eastern and western seas of the Mediterranean: by the mid-7th century BC it had planted its first colony at Ibiza in the Balearics. The ASSYRIAN takeover of the Phoenician cities in the east had meanwhile cut the western Phoenicians off from their motherland. Until around 500 BC Carthage was one of three great mercantile powers in the central Mediterranean, together with the ETRUSCANS and Western Greeks. Carthaginian wealth must have been derived mainly from activities as a middle-man, possibly supported (as was certainly the case in the 4th century) by a trade monopoly over certain areas, and the city had direct access to the mineral-rich areas of southwest Spain.

In the 5th century BC Etruscan power was in decline and Carthage embarked on more than a century of fighting with the Greeks over control of Sicily. The Carthaginians then moved to establish a West Mediterranean empire out of a string of Phoenician trading stations along the southern and western coasts of the Mediterranean, extending also through the Straits of Gibraltar to Mogador, southern Morocco, in the south and Cadiz in the north. The previously small and seaward-facing city of Carthage turned to exploiting the fertile agricultural land of northern Tunisia and developed rapidly, so that in the 3rd and 2nd centuries it had become a Greek-style metropolis with a six-figure population.

The emergence of Rome as a power throughout Italy led eventually to a clash with Carthage. Three great wars in the 3rd and 2nd centuries culminated in the obliteration of Carthaginian power and destruction of the city in 146 BC.

Carthage was re-established as a Roman colony by Julius Caesar and his heir Octavian, who sent 3000 settlers in 29 BC. The Roman city prospered as the port from which the grain and olive oil of Africa, on which Rome increasingly depended, were shipped overseas to Italy. Carthage replaced Utica as the capital of the province of Africa and became the second largest city in the western part of the empire after Rome itself. In the 4th and early 5th centuries it was a notable centre for Christianity and the home of St Augustine.

The VANDALS, who had moved first to Spain and then across North Africa with the break-up of the western Roman empire, took Carthage in 439 and retained control until the BYZANTINE invasion under Belisarius in 533. Carthage was the capital of the Byzantine empire in Africa until the Arab take-over of 698, but with the reduction in Mediterranean trade in the 7th century the city had been in severe decline for some years before the Arab conquest.

The site of ancient Carthage is now a suburb of Tunis but among the modern buildings there are remains of all periods: houses on the Byrsa hill, the Sanctuary of Tanit (or 'Tophet') and the two manmade harbours survive from the Punic (pre-146 BC) period; Roman monuments include the Antonine Baths, fourth largest in the empire, the circus, a theatre and amphitheatre and areas of streets and houses, together with a number of early Christian churches, but are poorly preserved or heavily restored.

caryatid. Properly, a standing female figure sometimes substituted in a classical building for a column (usually of the IONIC order). Notable examples are to be found in the Cnidian and Siphnian Treasuries (6th century BC) at Delphi in Greece, and one porch of the ERECHTHEUM temple on the ACROPOLIS at ATHENS (late 5th century BC).

Casamance. A river in Senegal around the estuary of which are grouped several extensive shell middens where occupation is dated between the last centuries bc and the 17th century ad. The later phases are linked with a cultural pattern related to that of the recent Diola.

Cascade point. *See* OLD CORDILLERAN CULTURE.

Căscioarele. A small long-lived settlement on an island in a former loop of the lower Danube, in southern Rumania. Excavations by V. Dumitrescu have revealed multiple occupation layers of the Middle Neolithic BOIAN and later Neolithic GUMELNIŢA cultures. The former is dated *c*3900-3700 bc, the latter *c*3700-3500 bc, making Căscioarele the only site with a clearly dated middle-late Neolithic transition. A complete village plan is available from the Gumelniţa occupation, consisting of one large central structure surrounded by six smaller structures. The Gumelniţa finds are as remarkable for their ritual implications — a large and elaborate fired clay model dubbed a 'shrine' — as for their technological importance: a rare surviving fragment of an antler plough. Another surprise is the heavy reliance on wild animal meat, including 40 per cent red deer.

Cashel. A rock in Co. Tipperary, Ireland, which rises dramatically above the surrounding plain, and houses a cluster of important ecclesiastical buildings of the medieval period. St Patrick consecrated Cashel as a bishopric and it later bcame the see of the infamous Bishop Cormac who was killed at the battle of Ballaghmoon in 908 while attempting to make himself the king of Ireland.

The earliest and finest church on the rock is known as Cormac's Chapel and was built by Bishop Cormac MacCarthy in 1134, its style is heavily influenced by the German Romanesque with square flanking towers, but the blind arcading is a feature commonly employed on Norman churches in France and England. The cathedral dates to the 13th century and later, and stands near to the attractive perpendicular Gothic choral building. Beside the cathedral is a round tower of contemporary date. Other monuments of interest include a large sarcophagus carved in devolved Scandinavian styles and a Christian standing cross which depicts the Crucifixion on one face and St Patrick on the other.

Cassibile. A Late Bronze Age settlement and large cemetery of rock-cut chamber tombs in southeast Sicily, of the early 1st millennium BC. It belongs to the PANTALICA culture, which is characterized by large urban settlements, of which Cassibile was presumably one, since although the settlement site itself has not been securely identified, some 2000 tombs have been found. Characteristic artefacts include a distinctive painted ware with plume motifs and a number of typical bronze types, including stilted and thick arc fibulae and shaft-hole axes.

Castanet. An Upper PALAEOLITHIC rock shelter at Castelmerle, situated at the foot of cliffs overlooking the Vezère River of the Dordogne, southwest France. Two levels of AURIGNACIAN type are present, containing art objects of carved or painted stone. The art from Castanet and the neighbouring Blanchard rock shelter is amongst the earliest known and, at *c*33,000 bc, perhaps actually the earliest ever executed.

Castelluccio. A settlement and cemetery site in southeast Sicily which has given its name to an Early Bronze Age culture. The cemetery contained several hundred rock-cut tombs used for collective burial; the tombs were sometimes closed with rock slabs and these were occasionally decorated with carved spirals, which were at one time compared to those found in the Mycenaean world; they are now thought to be of considerably earlier date. Grave goods include a fine buff ware painted with black or green designs, and BOSSED BONE PLAQUES demonstrating connections with the Aegean world well before 2000 BC.

casting. METALS with a low enough melting point can be melted in a crucible on a simple hearth, and cast in a MOULD. COPPER, BRONZE, GOLD and SILVER were all commonly cast in antiquity. IRON and STEEL could not be melted by ancient hearths and furnaces. Metal melted over fire absorbs gas resulting from combustion of the fuel. Moulds have to be carefully designed to make sure that bubbles of gas do not spoil the casting.

casting jet. *See* MOULD.

casting seam. *See* MOULD.

castle. The castle has many different meanings in European history and archaeology. Its most familiar use is to describe a fortified residence, but it is sometimes used to refer to later medieval fortified villages. The evolution of the castle has been well documented by European archaeologists. The first late CAROLINGIAN types were possibly modelled on the fortified homesteads of the SLAVS, but in the 10th century the manor or principal house was set up on a raised mound within the enclosure. This MOTTE AND BAILEY type was introduced to central and northern France in the 11th century, whereas previously only simple enclosures had existed. The NORMANS then introduced this type to the British Isles and to Southern Italy, and also built stone keeps within their enclosures, using their experiences in the Crusades to accelerate castle design. Hence later 12th-century castles in France and England comprise large stone walls, inturned gateways modelled on Arabic and Byzantine forts, and massive circular central keeps. Multiple walls with strengthened gateways are an invention of the mid-13th century, and splendid examples are still to be seen at Angers in France or in the Edwardian castles of North Wales. During the 14th century the interior buildings within the walls were formed into rational plans to make these quarters more tolerable to live in for longer periods, while at the same time reinforcing their defensive properties. In the later 14th and 15th centuries the introduction of the cannon effectively undermined the value of castles. Spanish and Italian builders compensated by constructing yet more formidable multiple ramparts, while Rhenish castles were sited on high precipitous positions, out of the range of cannon. Henry VIII of England developed a very low form of castle with multiple bastions to hold cannon which was the forerunner of the bunker used until recent times.

castro. Portuguese term for a defended site, most commonly applied to the local Iron Age HILLFORTS.

catacomb. A name of obscure origin, perhaps first given to the extensive subterranean Christian cemetery in the vicinity of the church of San Sebastian on the Via Appia Antica, south of Rome, and then generally to a large number of similar complexes around Rome and elsewhere. Characteristically, a labyrinthine succession of narrow galleries and chambers are cut into the soft bedrock. Rows of horizontal slots (*loculi*) are provided in the walls for single or multiple burials, the niche being subsequently sealed. Walls and ceilings are decorated with a variety of pagan and Christian motifs. Catacombs are generally to be found in areas that were already in use as cemeteries, outside the city proper, and their subterranean nature is usually explained on the basis of the need for security and secrecy on the part of a religion that was at worst banned and at best tolerated. Certainly they appear to decline in use soon after the official recognition of the Church. Other parallels, for instance the multiple family nature of the burials, may perhaps be drawn with Jewish examples, Etruscan family/freedmen/slaves burials, and the 'pigeon-hole' approach of the Roman COLUMBARIUM.

Çatal Hüyük. A site located south-east of Konya in ANATOLIA, and one of the largest Neolithic settlement known in Western Asia, covering $c13$ hectares. In the small part excavated, 14 building levels were found, without undisturbed deposits being reached. Radiocarbon dates cover the period $c6250$-5400 bc. Cereals were cultivated, and cattle, perhaps domesticated locally, were bred; in fact 90 per cent of the animal bones came from cattle and these animals were clearly of ritual as well as economic importance to the community, as bull horns and skulls form the dominant motif in the many shrines on the site. Sheep and goats were hunted and may have been domesticated in later levels.

The houses were built of mud-brick and were of a standard type, $c25$ square metres with kitchens, living and storage rooms. The houses were built against each other, with no streets or courtyards, suggesting rooftop walkways and access from the roof. Built-in furniture includes benches and platforms. The buildings designated shrines were identical in form, but decorated with remarkable painted and relief ornamentation, figuring bull motifs predominantly,but also other animal hunting scenes, and figures of the 'mother goddess', sometimes giving birth. Burials under the floors and platforms were common; those under the shrines were often accompanied by precious objects.

As well as the unique shrines, this site is remarkable for its advanced technology in the crafts of OBSIDIAN working, weaving and woodwork and even in incipient metallurgy (copper and lead). The evidence suggests both craft specialization and social stratification.

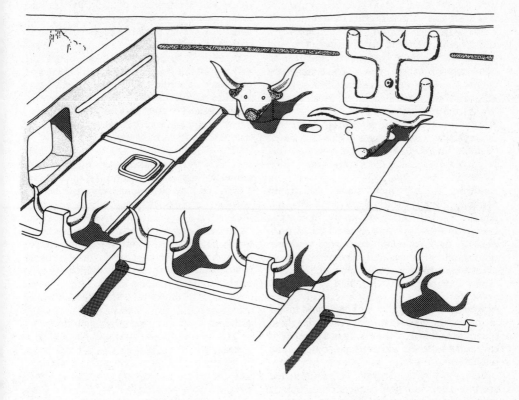

Çatal Hüyük: reconstruction of a decorated shrine

The great wealth and precocious development of this settlement may have arisen through control of the trade in obsidian from central Anatolian sources throughout the Near East.

catapulta. *See* BALLISTA.

Catfish Cave. *See* SHAMARKIAN.

cattle. Members of the genus *Bos*. Wild and domestic cattle are classified separately as *Bos primigenius* (wild cattle or aurochs) and *Bos taurus* (domestic), but they apparently represent only one species. They differ mostly in size — the wild form being very much larger — but there are other, more detailed differences in form. *Bos primigenius* is now extinct, the last record being AD 1627 in Poland. It was, however, uncommon long before then (by c1000 bc in Britain) and it is unclear whether the historical accounts refer to feral animals or

truly wild ones. Fossils of *Bos primigenius* are found right across Europe, Asia and into North Africa, and are present from the Middle PLEISTOCENE. They appear to have been mainly forest dwellers, presumably browsing foliage in the clearings. They are absent or rare during colder periods (*see* QUATERNARY) in northern latitudes, when deciduous forest would have been excluded. Wild cattle formed a major component of the diet of Palaeolithic and Mesolithic hunters throughout Eurasia. Two forms have been recognized, one rather smaller than the other (and classified by some as *Bos brachyceros*), but it is likely that they represent sexual dimorphism. The earliest evidence of domestication occurs at ÇATAL HÜYÜK in Anatolia. The lowest levels so far excavated at this site (c6400 bc) show some evidence of 'interference' by man. A reduction in size of cattle bones occurs further up the sequence (c5800 bc) and this is taken as the first morphological evidence of domestication. Cattle have usually been thought to have been imported ready domesticated into Europe, although wild cattle would have been present throughout and could have been domesticated early. In fact domestic cattle appear almost as early as at Çatal Hüyük at a number of sites in Greece: NEA NIKOMEDEIA in Macedonia, ARGISSA in Thessaly and KNOSSOS in Crete. The small domestic cattle of the Bronze and Iron Ages in Europe used to be differentiated as *Bos longifrons*, but there is no reason to separate them from other cattle.

cauldron. A large metal vessel for use in cooking, usually with a round base and handles for suspending over a fire. In Europe, cauldrons first appeared in the Late Bronze Age. In the later Iron Age they were sometimes made of silver, and became objects of great wealth and prestige. One of the most famous comes from GUNDESTRUP.

causewayed camp. A type of enclosure found in the earlier Neolithic of southern England (4th millennium BC), consisting of a number of concentric ditches with internal banks. The ditches were rarely continuous, but were interrupted by causeways of untouched ground. Their function is unclear, as there is little evidence of permanent or seasonal occupation. They may have been tribal meeting-places for annual or more frequent fairs, or, alternatively, they may have been ritual sites, as some have evidence for disposal of the dead. *See also* WINDMILL HILL.

Čavdar [Čevdar]. One of the few TELL sites of the west Bulgarian regional group of the FIRST TEMPERATE NEOLITHIC, located in the southern part of the upland Sofia basin and dated *c*5100-4700 bc. Five Kremikovci occupation levels are stratified below a KARANOVO VI level. The mainstays of the mixed farming economy were emmer wheat and six-row barley, cattle and caprine husbandry. Kremikovci painted wares include a rich polychrome assemblage dating to the end of the Early Neolithic.

cave art. Possibly the best-known feature of the Upper PALAEOLITHIC of Western Europe is the painted caves. Some caves contain extensive paintings, some only a few. Only two pigments are known to have been used: iron

oxide and manganese dioxide. In addition many caves have engraved figures on their walls. Altogether over 150 caves have wall art dated to Palaeolithic times, although such art is very difficult to date, except by comparison with MOBILIARY ART. Most of the decorated caves are in southern France, though Spain also has a large number. Some examples are known from Portugal and Italy, but there is a big geographical gap between Italy and the only known Russian site, KAPOVO CAVE.

The main subject matter is animals, especially the horse and bison; there are also numerous signs and symbols. Human figures are exceedingly rare and usually hard to make out. The purpose of the art is largely unknown, though it is likely that the caves were used for ceremonies of a magic or ritual kind, perhaps for initiation rites. Youthful footprints are found in some caves and hand silhouettes were made on the walls round hands which were too small to belong to adult males. Occupational evidence is rarely found with the art and there are major problems in investigating it; even the authenticity of some examples is in doubt.

See ADDAURA, ALTAMIRA, ANGLES SUR L'ANGLIN, ARCY-SUR-CURE, COVALANAS, FONT DE GAUME, GABILLOU, LASCAUX, LAUSSEL, LES COMBARELLES, LES EYZIES, NIAUX, PAIR-NON-PAIR, ROC DE SERS, TEYJAT, TUC D'AUDOUBERT.

Cave Bay Cave. *See* TASMANIA.

cave dwelling. Especially during the colder periods of the ice ages, caves were frequently occupied by PALAEOLITHIC man. The dwelling was usually sited in the mouth of the cave or even outside under a rock overhang. Cave dwelling was rare or unknown before the penultimate glacial period. Caves continued to be used for settlement and other purposes in some areas in later prehistoric periods and occasionally into recent times.

cave earth. The name given to cave deposits composed of shattered boulders and pebbles, arising from frost action and thermal weathering.

Cave of Hearths. A cave near Pietersburg in the northern Transvaal, South Africa, located close to the MAKAPANSGAT australopithecine site. The earliest deposits are ACHEULIAN, followed by a thick sterile horizon representing a long period of abandonment. Next comes a long succession of PIETERSBURG industries. Despite the hiatus between them, there are some signs of typological continuity between the Acheulian and the Pietersburg assemblages at the Cave of Hearths, notably the tendency in the final stages of the Acheulian to the production of elongated blades. The Pietersburg industry was succeeded by one of sub-triangular points and flake scrapers akin to the BAMBATA industry of Zimbabwe.

Cayla de Mailhac. *See* MAILHAC.

Çayönü Tepesi. An important early farming site on a tributary of the Tigris River in eastern Turkey, occupied for about a millennium $c7500$-6500 bc. The site had five major levels, all characterized by impressive architectural remains with stone foundations. The economic evidence has shown that the community depended initially on hunting large game animals (auroch and red deer), but by the latest phase concentrated on domesticated sheep and goats; pigs may also have been domesticated by this stage. On the plant side, einkorn wheat was cultivated from the beginning, and later emmer wheat; peas and lentils were also cultivated. Wild plants collected include pistachio nuts, almonds, hackberries and acorns. Another important feature of this site was the very early appearance of simple copper objects, derived from the Ergani Maden lodes, $c20$ km away.

Cazador. *See* COCHISE, SULPHUR SPRINGS.

Celebes. Surprisingly, this Indonesian island, situated east of Borneo, has produced the oldest Buddhist image known in the Archipelago. The image is dated to the 4th century, and although not proof of the Indianization of the area it is at least evidence of some connections with India at an early date. In the late 14th century the island, perhaps with the exception of the north, became part of the JAVA-based Indianized kingdom of MAJAPAHIT.

cella [Latin; Greek: *naos*]. Architectural term used to describe either the whole of a temple apart from its outer colonnade or, in a more restricted sense, only the main hall, in which the cult statues were placed.

celt. An antiquated 19th-century term for an axe or adze.

Celt, Celtic. Term used in a number of different ways. In language studies it refers to a branch of INDOEUROPEAN languages found now only in the far northwest of Europe (Gaelic, Welsh, Cornish and Breton) but once much more widespread.

As an ethnic group Celts were described by classical writers such as Herodotus who placed their homeland — rather ambiguously — somewhere in central or western Europe. They are known to have invaded Italy and sacked Rome itself in the early 4th century BC, while in the following century groups of Celts invaded Greece, sacking Delphi, and others invaded Anatolia.

In archaeology the term Celtic is often used to denote the peoples of the European Iron Age, and it is hard to dispute the likelihood that many of these peoples would indeed have been of Celtic ethnic stock and doubtless would have spoken a Celtic language. However, archaeological cultures do not necessarily coincide with ethnic or linguistic groups and it is preferable to use the cultural terms HALLSTATT and LA TÈNE when describing archaeological remains.

Celtic art. Name given to the art of the European Iron Age, which developed in central and western Europe from the 5th century BC, among presumed CELTIC peoples. The term LA TÈNE art is also used.

Celtic art developed in the courts of the La Tène chieftains and it seems likely that the craftsmen worked under the direct patronage of the chiefs themselves. It is primarily a metalworker's art, found on vessels associated with drinking (jugs, buckets, bowls, cups and tankards); on weapons (swords, daggers, scabbards, helmets and shields) and horse and chariot fittings; and on personal ornaments (torcs, bracelets, armlets, brooches etc). Techniques employed include decoration in relief, engraving and inlay (in coral or, later, enamel); two or more techniques are commonly applied on the same article. Although it is most commonly found on metal objects, it appears sometimes in other media, such as pottery and stone sculpture.

Stylistically, Celtic art combines elements taken from the classical world (especially plant motifs), from the Scythians to the east (animal motifs) and from the local earlier HALLSTATT Iron Age (geometric designs), to produce a strong curvilinear style, non-naturalistic, but incorporating plant and especially animal and human motifs in stylized and sometimes grotesque form. The art developed through several styles on the Continent (Early, WALDALGESHEIM, Plastic and Sword styles) but came to an end with the Roman occupation. In Britain an insular style developed in the last 100 years before the Claudian invasion, producing, inter alia, a fine series of engraved bronze mirrors and splendid gold, silver and electrum TORCS. On the fringes of the Roman world in Britain, Celtic art survived throughout the period of the occupation and the style of the early Christian ILLUMINATED MANUSCRIPTS is still recognizably in the same tradition (*see* BOOK OF KELLS, LINDISFARNE).

Celtic field. Term used for the remains of field systems of pre-Roman times in Britain and northwest Europe. The earliest are certainly Bronze Age in date, and it is misleading to associate them with the Celts. The fields are small and more or less square, and are visible because of the LYNCHETS formed by cross-ploughing with a light ard.

cenote. The limestone formations of the arid Yucatan peninsula in Mexico are honeycombed with water-filled underground caves. The collapse of the roofs of some of these caves causes a kind of natural well, or cenote. These became the major source of water for MAYAN and subsequent groups in the area. These formations also had some ritual significance. The Sacred Cenote at CHICHEN ITZA, for example, contained a considerable amount of skeletal material together with luxury items such as jade, gold and copper. This material seems to confirm legendary accounts of human SACRIFICE.

centuration. Term used by the Romans to describe a method of land surveying, used in the area (*territorium*) surrounding a town, especially a colony. *See* CARDO.

cephalic index. A combination of two skull measurements, L (maximum cranial length) and B (maximum cranial breadth).

$$\text{Cranial Index} = \frac{B \times 100}{L}$$

The index describes the overall proportions of the cranium (brain box); *see* BRACHYCEPHALIC, DOLICHOCEPHALIC. In the past, it was used alone to assess genetic differences between groups of human skeletal material (*see* SKELETON). Nowadays it is recognized that far more measurements are needed to compare skull shapes adequately.

ceramic. A material, usually clay, which can be moulded when in a soft, plastic state and is then hardened by heat. *See* POTTERY.

ceramics (China). The Western world's awareness of China has, throughout most of history, centred on two export commodities: the Romans knew China as Serica, the place from which SILK came, while for Europeans of more recent centuries the country was synonymous with the porcelain it produced. China began to export pottery on a large scale not much before the TANG dynasty (AD 618-907), a date secured by the vast deposits of sherds at sites such as Fustat (Old CAIRO), but the qualities that made Tang stonewares sought-after rested on the technical achievements of a long ceramic tradition notable for its sophistication even in Neolithic times. Painted pots of the YANGSHAO Neolithic were fired at temperatures sometimes exceeding 1000°C; unpainted LONGSHAN pots fired under reducing conditions show expert control of kiln atmospheres as well as occasional use of the potter's wheel. Glazed stonewares appeared in SHANG times, shortly after the middle of the 2nd millennium BC (*see* WUCHENG), and kaolin, an important ingredient of later porcelains, was used to make the Shang WHITE POTTERY. The glaze of the Shang stonewares and their ZHOU descendants (*see* TUNXI) was high-fired and leadless. Lead-glazed earthenwares came into use just before the HAN dynasty, later enjoying a special vogue in the gaudy 'three-colour' pots and figurines of the Tang period. Stonewares with high-fired leadless glazes continued to be made, however, the gradual perfection of these wares being associated with the YUE region in the southeast. Growing experience with white-bodied stonewares led eventually to the production of true porcelain around the 9th century AD.

The term 'porcelain' is generally reserved for a vitrified ceramic material prized for its extremely hard white body; it can be so thin as to be translucent and to make a ringing tone when struck. The main constituent of Chinese porcelain is porcelain stone, which occurs in large deposits in several places in China, notably at Jingdezhen in Jiangxi province. Porcelain stone consists chiefly of sericite, hydromica, and quartz (and differs in composition from European porcelain stones); after crushing, washing, and precipitation it is plastic enough to be thrown, and on firing above 1200°C it becomes porcelain. In the SONG period the *yingqing* porcelains of Jingdezhen and the Longquan celadons of Zhejiang province were made of porcelain stone. From the 14th century kaolin was added, as the mixture of kaolin and porcelain stone gives a higher degree of vitrification and a stronger body.

Glazes that fire at the same high temperature as the porcelain body are by and large limited to the soft muted colours for which SONG porcelains are noted. Early in the 14th century, however, it was discovered that cobalt can give an intense blue to such glazes; this discovery was exploited in the immensely popular blue and white ware, blue decoration being applied to the white porcelain body and covered with a colourless or very pale bluish glaze. Polychrome effects, in vogue from the 15th century onwards, were achieved by applying enamels over the glaze; overglaze enamels include the *famille rose* and *famille verte* wares of the QING period.

The unmatched technical quality of Chinese porcelain caused it to be imported and imitated in Korea, Japan, Southeast Asia and the Philippines, India, throughout the Moslem world, and in Europe from the time of the Crusades (*see* SINAN). Unable to duplicate the hard porcelain body, potters from Iran to Delft copied the outward appearance of Chinese blue-and-white, whose decoration might be said to have enjoyed a worldwide influence out of all proportion to its intrinsic merit. The extent of the trade in Chinese porcelain can be suggested by a single statistic derived from the records of the Swedish East India Company, one of the smaller European companies engaged in the China trade: between 1766 and 1786, when the population of Sweden was about 2 million, more than 20 million pieces of Chinese porcelain were imported into Sweden alone. The imperial kilns at Jingdezhen, which supplied this enormous trade, were described in letters written from China by the Jesuit Père d'Entrecolles in 1712 and 1722. At about the same time European experimenters managed to produce ceramic materials that fire at temperatures in the same range as porcelain, and factories at Meissen and elsewhere began to manufacture European porcelains not as a rule identical to Chinese porcelain in composition, but able to compete with it.

céramique onctueuse. A distinctive type of medieval pottery made in western Brittany. *Céramique onctueuse* is typically very soft and has an unusual tempering material, talc, which only occurs in a small region of Finistère. It was first made in the 10th century and production of fish-platters and bowls continued until the 18th century. This unusual pottery appears to be a distinctive product of the Breton culture.

Cerbat. *See* HAKATAYA.

Cerca Grande. *See* LAGOA SANTA.

ceremonial centre. A complex of monumental buildings which formed the hub of religious and civic activities in the prehistoric New World. Permanent residence was restricted to a very few, usually the elite and their retainers, and a regionally dispersed population visited the site on a periodic (possibly seasonal) basis. Many prominent sites in Mesoamerica, such as TEOTIHUACAN, TIKAL and MONTE ALBAN, have been interpreted as ceremonial centres. However, subsequent fieldwork beyond the major architectural features has shown that many sites were directly associated with large populations and thus challenges the original premise of the ceremonial centre. Although the term is employed a good deal less frequently today, there are nonetheless important sites to which it may still apply, for example LA VENTA and SAN LORENZO.

Cernavoda. (1) An important cemetery site of the Late Neolithic HAMANGIA culture, dated to the mid-4th millennium bc and located near the Black Sea coast of the Rumanian Dobrogea. Over 300 extended inhumations are known, clustered in groups, some with richer grave goods. (2) The eponymous site of a Late Copper Age culture of the 3rd millennium bc, distributed over much of the Black Sea coastal zone in Rumania and Bulgaria and closely related in the latter zone to the EZERO group. Most sites are short-lived occupation sites, with a small number of cemeteries with contracted inhumations.

Cernica. An important Neolithic site, comprising both settlement and cemetery, dated to the late 5th millennium bc and lying south of Bucureşti, Rumania. In the settlement, a BOIAN II pit cuts superposed levels of the late DUDEŞTI and Boian I phases — one of the few such stratigraphic relationships noted in Muntenia. Adjoining the settlement is the key Boian I cemetery, the largest inhumation cemetery in the Balkan Middle Neolithic. Comprising over 350 graves, the Cernica cemetery contains zones of graves with richer grave goods, interspersed with 'poorer' grave goods. Richer graves contained marble, shell and bone beads, as well as some of the earliest copper ornaments in the Balkans. In contrast to most other Balkan burial rites of crouched inhumation, the Cernica burial rite is almost exclusively extended inhumation.

Cerro de las Mesas. A site in southern Veracruz, Mexico on the northern edge of the Tuxtla Mountains. Although there is a PRE-CLASSIC component to the site (possibly associated with IZAPA), the major occupation was in the CLASSIC PERIOD. An inheritor of OLMEC traditions, along with nearby TRES ZAPOTES, Cerro survived long after the demise of the latter. The Classic occupation contains abundant TEOTIHUACAN materials and two MAYA LONG COUNT dates (AD 468 and AD 533). Thus it is usually interpreted as a redistribution point for materials from both Mexico and the Maya lowlands. It is also well known for its cache of some 782 jade objects.

Cerro Sechin. A site in the Casma Valley on the north-central coast of Peru and probably dating to the INITIAL PERIOD (1800-900 bc). The primary construction of this CEREMONIAL CENTRE is a rectangular platform mound with an enclosing wall of decorated monoliths. Carvings of warriors, dismembered humans and individual heads are incised in an 'economy of line' rather than simple, crude style, implying an earlier artistic tradition. Dating is tenuous, but cross comparison suggests that the Sechin style is a precursor of CHAVIN; in any event the site does represent an early appearance of monumental art.

Cerveteri [Roman Caere vetus, Etruscan Xaire, Greek Agylla]. A town in central Italy, some 48 km north-west of Rome, Caere was one of the 12 great cities of the ETRUSCAN federation. Earliest occupation seems to be Iron Age VILLANOVAN of 9th to 8th centuries BC. Two necropoleis from this period have been identified, with evidence for pit, trench and chamber tombs (some of the latter large and rich). The town's most splendid phase, however, was the Etruscan, which spans the 7th-5th centuries BC. Communications and commercial prosperity clearly expanded (as witness the large quantity of imported Greek pottery), and the accumulating wealth is reflected in the grandeur of many surviving tombs. Tomb architecture developed rapidly, with the grand tumulus-type chamber tombs, containing several rooms or indeed several separate tombs, becoming common. In the more elaborate examples, the internal tufa may be sculpted in imitation of (presumably contemporary) roof and ceiling structures, architectural features, weapons and domestic objects; and thrones and couches are carved out. Decoration may be by painting and/or relief-work. The road network which is so striking a feature of the necropoleis as seen today may be a relatively late aspect of re-organization, when streets of repetitive facades perhaps betray middle-class pressure for fashionable burial. Of Caere's two ports, Pyrgi and Alsium, the former has yielded evidence of temples, and given scholars of the Etruscan language one of their most important pieces of evidence — a temple text on gold laminae. Unfortunately this bilingual text (one version in Punic, and two different ones in Etruscan) has perhaps created more problems than it has solved. One result is noteworthy: the confirmation of the value 3 for the Etruscan numeral *ci*. Caere lost importance during the Roman period, and by the early Empire was reported to be no more than a village.

Chac. *See* TLALOC.

Chacmool. A life-sized sculpted stone figure in the standardized form of a reclining human, with flexed legs and head gazing to one side, holding a plate-like receptacle flat on the stomach. A widespread phenomenon in the POST-CLASSIC PERIOD of Mesoamerica, it is particularly associated with the TOLTEC. The precise purpose of the figure is uncertain, but since it is invariably located at the entrance way to a temple it was probably a repository for offerings.

Chaco Canyon. An alluvium-filled canyon in northwest New Mexico, USA, occupied by the ANASAZI during PUEBLO I and II times. Between 850 and 1150 it supported at least a dozen pueblo-type towns, such as PUEBLO BONITO, as well as hundreds of small villages. Evidence of town planning, water control systems, inter-community roadways and long-distance trade indicates that this was a well-organized centre of commercial and political activity.

Chagar Bazar. A TELL site in the upper Khabur valley in northeast Syria, occupied from the HALAF period (5th millennium bc) to the mid-2nd millennium BC. It gradually grew in size and importance and during the reign of the Assyrian king, Shamsi Adad I (early 2nd millennium BC) it was an administrative centre and possibly one of the king's ruling seats.

Chakipampa. *See* HUARI.

Chalandriani. An Early Bronze Age (3rd millennium BC) settlement and cemetery on Syros in the Cyclades. The settlement was surrounded by dry-stone defences with six semi-circular bastions; inside were a number of small rooms, separated by narrrow paths. The cemetery of *c*500 tombs, built of dry-stone walling and housing one or two bodies, produced material of the so-called Keros-Syros culture, including the highly decorated dishes known as FRYING PANS.

Chalcatzingo. *See* LAS BOCAS.

chalcedony. A very finely crystalline form of the mineral silica, rather similar to CHERT. There are many varieties, several of which are prized as semi-precious stone — agate, onyx, cornelian and jasper, for example. These may be used in making beads and other jewellery.

Chalchuapa. *See* BARTON RAMIE.

Chalcolithic. A term used, like its alternatives Eneolithic and Copper Age, to refer to a period between the NEOLITHIC and the BRONZE AGE when copper was used for tools,

but not bronze (an alloy of copper and tin). The term is much less widely used than other divisions and subdivisions of the THREE AGE SYSTEM, partly because of the difficulty in distinguishing copper from bronze without chemical analysis, partly because many areas did not have a Chalcolithic period at all. Different usages have grown up in different areas and this can cause confusion: for instance, the Italian and Spanish Chalcolithic or Copper Age cultures are equivalent — both chronologically and technically — to the Early Bronze Age in the Aegean.

Chaldea. The Chaldean (Kaldu) tribes occupied the swamp area of the lower courses of the Tigris and Euphrates in southern BABYLONIA. They were controlled by sheikhs who assumed the kingship of Babylonia in the 7th century BC. The Chaldean Dynasty was founded in 625 BC by Nabopolassar and continued with his son Nebuchadnezzar II. During this period Babylonia became known as Chaldea, and replaced Assyria as the main power in the Near East. In 539 BC, in the reign of Nabonidus, the Empire fell to the Persians under Cyrus.

chaltoon [choltun, chultun]. A bottle-shaped underground chamber or series of chambers, found in MESOAMERICA. Principally for storage, they may also have been used as sweat baths or burial chambers. In the southern Maya Lowlands they were most often used to store dry foods especially ramon (bread) nuts. In the northern Yucatan, however, they were more frequently used as water cisterns, in which case they were usually lined with stucco to prevent seepage.

chamber tomb. Term for any tomb, whether rock-cut or built above ground, with a large or fairly large chamber to contain the dead and accompanying grave goods. Chamber tombs were often, but by no means always, used for collective burial over long periods of time. They occur in many parts of the world at different times, but the term is particularly widely used in Europe to describe tombs of the prehistoric and classical periods. *See also* MEGALITHIC MONUMENTS.

Champa. A now-vanished Indianized kingdom on the eastern coast of the Indochinese Peninsula, corresponding roughly to present central Vietnam. There, to the south of their own province of CHIAO-CHIH, the Chinese mentioned the foundation of the kingdom of LIN-YI in 192 AD, later called Champa (unknown etymology) in Sanskrit sources. Well-developed sculpture and reliefs occur from the 7th century and impressive architecture in the form of brick towers from the 9th century; both art forms eventually vanish in the 13th century. After unsuccessful attempts to expand towards the north, into Chinese-held territory, Champa itself lost ground from the time Vietnam gained independence from China in 939. Lacking a solid economic basis, the Chams could not prevent their country from being absorbed little by little by the southward-expanding Vietnamese. In 1471 the then capital VIJAYA was taken, and by the end of the 18th century Champa had ceased to exist, even as a nominal vassal of Vietnam. *See* AMARAVATI, KHAUTHARA, PANDURANGA and VIJAYA.

champlevé enamelling. An effective enamelling technique which was probably developed by CELTIC metal-workers and afterwards copied by the ANGLO-SAXONS. The process involved the melting of enamel into the incised hollows in a piece of metal. It was often employed in the decoration of the escutcheons on hanging bowls, on the roundels which supported the handles of the bowls.

Champollion, Jean-François (1790-1832). French scholar, one of a number brought to Egypt under the French occupation of Napoleon Bonaparte, who accomplished the decipherment of the Egyptian HIEROGLYPHIC writing system. His work, which was published in 1822, was based largely on the ROSETTA Stone, which has inscriptions in Greek, hieroglyphs, and in the Egyptian demotic script.

Chams. An AUSTRONESIAN-speaking population of unknown origin (possibly Borneo or the Philippines) who settled Vietnam from about 1000 BC. Their early prehistory appears to be associated with the SA-HUYNH culture, with its strong Philippine connections. From the 2nd century AD the Chams developed the powerful Indianized kingdom of CHAMPA on the east coast of the Indochinese Peninsula. This lasted until 1471, when it was overrun by the southward-

expanding Vietnamese. Chams continued to occupy the Mekong Delta until the 17th century. In the 1950s there were about 105,000 Chams left, of whom about 70,000 lived in Cambodia; their present fate is unknown.

Chancay. A cultural entity which arose in the Late INTERMEDIATE PERIOD in the northern area of the Peruvian central coast. Found in the Huara, Chancay, Ancon and Chillon valleys, it is characterized especially by a unique black-on-white pottery style. It has a white (often yellowish) slip and black line geometric decoration, usually of parallel lines or chequered design, which is sometimes augmented by small appliqué biomorphic figures. The most common forms were tall, two-handled collared jars and large figurines. Regional expressions such as Chancay came about in the political vacuum left after the decline of HUARI and TIAHUANACO.

Chanchan. *See* CHIMU.

Chandoli. A site in southern India occupied in the 2nd millennium BC. Ground stone axes, copper objects (flat axes and antenna swords or daggers) and pottery of MALWA type were found. Urn burials also occur.

Chandragupta *See* MAURYAS.

Chang'an [Ch'ang-an]. Capital of the Western HAN dynasty in China and, moved to a site just southeast of the Han city, of the TANG dynasty; the modern city of Xi'an, capital of Shaanxi province, occupies the latter site. In the Tang period, Chang'an was the eastern terminus of the SILK ROUTE and one of the world's great cities, its walls enclosing an area of 84 square kilometres. The site of the QIN capital Xianyang is near Xi'an, and the Western ZHOU CAPITALS Feng and Hao are supposed to have been in this area as well, possibly lying within the boundaries of the modern Chang'an district southwest of Xi'an (*see* ZHANGJIAPO, KEXINGZHUANG).

Changsha [Ch'ang-sha]. Present-day capital of Hunan province, China. Only a few isolated finds hint at SHANG and Western ZHOU settlement in this area, but in Eastern Zhou and HAN times Changsha was a major centre of the CHU culture. Well over a thousand Chu burials have been excavated in the neighbourhood, the richest by far being the early 2nd century BC tombs at MAWANGDUI. Changsha lay in the southern part of the Chu state; finds made at the Chu capital 250 km to the north at JIANG-LING are comparable in date and importance.

Changtaiguan [Ch'ang-t'ai-kuan]. *See* XIN-YANG.

Changzhi [Ch'ang-chih]. *See* LIYU.

Chanhu-Daro. A town of the HARAPPAN CIVILIZATION of the 3rd millennium BC. Situated on the eastern side of the Indus Valley, *c*130 km south of MOHENJO-DARO, Chanhu-Daro covered *c*6.5 hectares, and was characterized by the typical gridiron street plan and well-built drainage system of Harappan towns. The most interesting discovery was a bead-maker's workshop, where evidence was found for the processes of sawing, flaking, grinding and boring of stone beads. Excavation has shown that, like Mohenjo-Daro, Chanhu-Daro had been inundated by floods: it was twice destroyed and subsequently rebuilt on a different plan. Finally, after the end of the Indus Valley civilization, it was reoccupied by representatives of the JHUKAR culture, living in village rather than urban style.

Chanka. *See* INCA.

Charaman. A stone industry of Zimbabwe, parts of southern and central Zambia and adjacent areas, where it was the local successor of the SANGOAN. Formerly often referred to as 'Proto-Stillbay', its connections with the Sangoan are now seen to have been stronger than was previously implied. Many Charaman assemblages come from surface or river-gravel occurrences, as at VICTORIA FALLS. In contrast with the Sangoan, large picks and core-axes are rare and there are many scrapers, sub-triangular points and other flake tools. Of cave sites with Charaman deposits the most important, now destroyed, was at BROKEN HILL, which yielded the remains of *Homo sapiens rhodesiensis*.

charcoal. Partly burned ('charred') wood, consisting mostly of carbon, sometimes found *in situ* as burned timbers of buildings and other structures or in hearths, but more frequently widely disseminated through the deposits of an archaeological site. Charcoal survives because carbon cannot be utilized by the organisms of decomposition, and it is the best material for RADIOCARBON DATING. Fragments of reasonable size and preservation may be identified to the tree of origin.

Charentian. After a detailed analysis of the Middle Palaeolithic MOUSTERIAN culture, F. Bordes and his collaborators suggested that it had two distinct components: a Charentian group characterized by the dominance of *racloirs* (side scrapers) and QUINA retouch, and another 'true' Mousterian group including the Mousterian with Handaxes. The Charentian seems to originate in the penultimate glacial period, and has a distribution across Europe and Russia. It is least typical of northwest Europe. In most of the cases where classic NEANDERTHAL man is known to have come from a definite archaeological context, that context is Charentian. Two types were recognized by Bordes: the Quina and the Ferrassie (*see* LA FERRASSIE).

chariot burials (China). Chariots and chariot burials provide the earliest generally acknowledged evidence of foreign influence on Chinese Bronze Age civilization. The first Chinese chariot burials are at the ANYANG site (at Xiaotun, Dasikongcun, and Xiaomintun) and belong to the latter part of the SHANG dynasty. The large Anyang tomb WKGM 1 near Wuguancun, dating from the 13th century BC, lacked clear evidence of chariots but contained skeletons of 27 horses. Shang chariot burials usually include horses and charioteers, and often also contain certain distinctive bronze fittings ('bow-shaped ornaments') and knives that, like the chariot itself, have not yet been found at pre-Anyang sites. Chariot burials occur throughout the ZHOU period, at BAOJI, BEIJING, LINGTAI, XINCUN, and ZHANGJIAPO in Western Zhou, and at LIULIGE, LUOYANG and SHANGCUN-LING in Eastern Zhou. At Liulige, 19 chariots were buried in a single pit. The mausoleum complex of QIN SHI HUANGDI (*r*.221-210 BC) included not only burials of real chariots drawn by pottery horses but also a pair of nearly life-sized four-horse chariots, the horses, chariots, and drivers all made of bronze.

Chariots thus seem to have arrived in China

midway through the Shang period, perhaps in the 13th century BC. Thereafter they formed an important part of Chinese armies; the power of an Eastern Zhou state was measured in chariots. In Chinese histories the abandonment of chariots in favour of cavalry is associated with a king of the northern state of Zhao (r.325-299 BC) who adopted tactics and equipment from his steppe-nomadic adversaries; the QIN state's reliance on large armies of infantry may, however, have been a more significant change. Lavish bronze chariot fittings, during Eastern Zhou often inlaid with gold and silver, hint that in addition to their military function chariots always had a role in ceremony or pageantry. In this role they survived to later periods, as shown for instance by bronze miniatures of chariots found in HAN tombs (see WUWEI).

Charlemagne. Charles the Great [Charlemagne] is one of the greatest historical and legendary heroes of western romance. The son of Pepin the Short, he became sole king of the FRANKS and leader of the Arnulfing dynasty in 771. The monk Einhard, Charlemagne's court biographer, gives the impression of a cultured, intelligent, charismatic figure blessed with outstanding ability and strength. It was Charlemagne who finally united the Frankish kingdom, restoring its laws and economy, and re-establishing the institutions of the Western Church. Charlemagne was also an able military leader, and extended his kingdom to encompass most of western Europe, except Spain and southern Italy. Charlemagne gathered men of culture and learning at his court, and through his patronage and energy the late 8th and 9th centuries have become known as the period of the CAROLINGIAN Renaissance. The emperor died in 814 and was succeeded by his son, Louis the Pious. The images that survive portray Charlemagne as the Christian successor to the Roman emperors. The same image is to be found in his palatial complex at AACHEN, and on his reformed coinage, where he sometimes appears with a laurel wreath around his head.

charred, charring. Organic materials may be preserved as a result of charring. Partial burning reduces the material to a carbon-rich residue. In the case of WOOD, this residue is familiar as CHARCOAL. Other parts of plants may also be charred — SEEDS, GRAIN, twigs, etc. Many organic materials may not retain their structure, and become an amorphous charred residue in the ashes of a fire. Charred remains are preserved on archaeological sites because carbon on its own, as an element, is relatively inert in the soil. The micro-organisms which would normally break down organic material are unable to make use of carbon in this form. Charcoal and charred seeds are therefore preserved for many thousands of years. They are a particularly good material for RADIOCARBON DATING.

Charsada. This site on the plain of Peshawar, at the foot of the Khyber Pass in Pakistan, is a series of mounds, up to 20 metres high, concealing the caravan city of Pushkalavati [Peukolaotis], one of the capitals of GANDHARA. Occupation extended from the 6th century BC, when the Achaemenians occupied Gandhara, to the 2nd or 1st century BC. A rampart and ditch at the foot of the largest mound, the Bala Hisar, are identified as defences against ALEXANDER THE GREAT, who took the town in 327 BC. Not far from the Bala Hisar, in an area known as Shaikhan, aerial photography revealed the rectilinear street-plan of an Indo-Greek city of the last two centuries BC.

Chartres. A city in Eure, northern France, where since the Carolingian period there has always been an important pilgrimage church holding relics of the Virgin Mary. A series of disastrous fires destroyed the earlier churches, although part of the Ottonian period (10th century) ambulatory crypt still survives below the present east end. After 1145, dedicated townsfolk helped to reconstruct the church as one of Europe's greatest Gothic cathedrals. The late 12th- and 13th-century building was constructed out of Bercheres stone to an advanced Gothic design, starting with its twin-towered facade containing three magnificent portals. The long nave terminates in an advanced chavet with aisled transepts and an ambulatory apse with radiating chapels. The nave is very high, and has ribbed quadripartite vaults supported externally by flying buttresses and internally by slender piers surrounded by columns. The most outstanding feature of Chartres Cathedral is its series of 173 stained glass windows dating from the 12th and 13th centuries; indeed the town itself became a centre for stained glass production, and the interior of the building mirrors the great regard that local businesses and shops held for their church. Almost as famous as the cathedral's stained glass is its school of sculpture, examples of which can be seen around the portals and entrance ways of the exterior.

chasing. One of the methods used in RE-POUSSÉ metal-work. The term 'chasing' may also be used in a more general way, to describe any decorative work on metal employing hammer or punch.

Chassey. A Neolithic culture of France, named after the site of Camp de Chassey in Burgundy. In southern France, the Chassey culure succeeded the IMPRESSED WARE culture after *c*4000 bc, but in much of central and northern France the Chassey culture represents the earliest NEOLITHIC, and has radiocarbon dates after 3000 bc. Both cave and open settlements were occupied, and a well-established mixed farming economy was practised. Burials in pits, in CIST GRAVES and in MEGALITHIC CHAMBER TOMBS occur. The characteristic pottery is dark, burnished and round-based; in the southern Chassey version incised decoration often occurs. VASE SUP-PORTS and PAN-PIPE LUGS also occur.

Château Gaillard. The magnificent castle of Château Gaillard was built at Les Andelys in Normandy by Richard Coeur de Lion, King of England and Duke of Normandy, on his return from the Third Crusade in 1196. It was situated on a promontory overlooking the Seine to control the approach to Rouen, the capital of Normandy, and its natural defensive position meant that it need only be protected on one side. The design of Chateau Gaillard, which probably took its inspiration from KRAK DES CHEVALIERS and other major fortifications in the Holy Land, was soon to become outmoded: its first defence was a wide ditch cut across the spur, then came an outer bailey, and then a moat between the inner bailey and the so-called chemise wall protect-ing the keep. The chemise wall had a series of round towers at extremely short intervals, while the walls of the keep were 3.6 metres thick. Although a massive and impressive construction it was successfully besieged by Philip Augustus in 1203: the French king merely starved the defenders, who in the last resort surrendered.

Châteauneuf-les-Martigues. A large rock shelter north-west of Marseilles in southern France, with a series of deposits from the Upper PALAEOLITHIC to the NEOLITHIC. Particular interest has focused on a level with IMPRESSED WARE, possibly domesticated sheep and a radiocarbon date in the early 6th millennium bc; however, another date from this level is much later, and the true date is uncertain.

Chatelperron, Chatelperronian. A cave site in Allier, central France, which has given its name to the Chatelperron point, a curved backed blade point typical of the PERIGORD-IAN I stage of the initial French Upper PALAEOLITHIC. The phase is also called Chatelperronian.

Chatham Islands. Occupying an isolated position in the South Pacific, 860 km east of Christchurch, New Zealand, these islands were settled by POLYNESIANS from NEW ZEA-LAND about AD 1000-1200. They are of great interest because they lie climatically beyond the limits of prehistoric Polynesian horticul-ture, and thus supported a fishing and collect-ing Polynesian population until European contact (1791). Material culture remained similar to Archaic MAORI throughout. The original inhabitants, called Moriorios, died out following contact with Europeans and con-quest by New Zealand Maoris in 1835.

Chavin [Chavin de Huantar]. In the period 900-200 BC (*see* EARLY HORIZON), the Chavin Horizon art style became the dominant cultural influence in Peru. Probably developed in the medium of low-relief stone carving, it was ultimately expressed in other media as well, for instance, pottery, metals and bone. A highly distinctive style, its themes are bio-morphic (especially feline) and are executed in flowing curvilinear lines. The eye with an eccentric pupil is a highly characteristic motif. Origins are obscure, but the frequent depic-tions of the jaguar, a tropical lowland animal, imply a non-Andean beginning. Some archaeologists propose CERRO SECHIN as a possible precursor.

The art style takes its name from the type site at Chavin de Huantar, which is located at a

3200-metre elevation on a tributary of the Rio Maranon in the Cordillera Blanca of north-central Peru. The main structures of the site, originally decorated with carved relief sculpture, are a complex of platforms faced with cut stone blocks. Two major building phases are evident. The earlier Old Temple, built on a U-shaped plan similar to EL PARAISO, was enlarged and altered to form the New Temple or Castillo. Despite the solid external appearance of the structures, one third of their total volume is a honeycomb of stone-lined galleries and rectangular rooms.

The most famous examples of elaborate Chavin carving are the great image or Lanzon, a 4.5-metre high sculpted megalith located in the central gallery of the Old Temple, and the Raimondi Stone, which is associated with the New Temple. Pottery is typically black or brown, dark fired and finished by polishing, incision or rocker stamping (*see also* CUPISNIQUE).

Although Chavin de Huantar was a CEREMONIAL CENTRE of some importance, a number of nearby sites appear to be associated, indicating that it was also a population centre of some size.

Cheddar. (1) Gough's Cave in the Cheddar Gorge in the Mendips, southwest England, has produced late PALAEOLITHIC remains, comprising bone and stone tools and skeletal remains which include the nearly complete skeleton of Cheddar man. These finds probably date from about 8000 to 10,000 bc and are often called CRESWELLIAN or Cheddarian, being a kind of late MAGDALENIAN.

(2) The site of the palace complex of the kings of WESSEX. The Cheddar site is well documented from the reigns of ALFRED, Edmund, Edwin and Edgar, and is described in charters and chronicles. Excavations have revealed a sequence of wooden halls and outbuildings representing the nucleus of the complex, with no obvious residential quarters. One of the most interesting features was the elaborate drainage system, constructed prior to 930 to protect the long hall and outbuildings from flood waters. After 930 a new west hall was built, with a small stone private chapel and ancillary agricultural buildings nearby. The entrance to the palace was protected by a timber stockade and ditch, and the foundations for a timber pole or flagstaff were located beyond this. Extensive rebuilding was carried out during the 11th century, but the layout remained essentially the same.

Chedworth. Here, in idyllic surroundings in the Cotswold area of southern England, stand the ruins of a large Roman villa, one of the best-preserved in Britain and probably, in its final phase, typical of a whole group of rich villas that characterized the last years of the Roman occupation. At Chedworth three phases may be distinguished: in the first (c100-150 AD) there were two buildings and a separate bath block; in the second (early 3rd century) there seems to have been rebuilding and enlargement after a fire; and in the third (early 4th century) the villa acquired its present-day layout, with the various elements united by a verandah. Notable features include a fine dining-room with mosaic floor depicting the seasons personified, a nymphaeum, and a modest Romano-Celtic temple

Chelford. An INTERSTADIAL of the DEVENSIAN cold stage. It has been dated by radiocarbon to *c*61,000 bp, but this is near the present extreme range of the technique (*see* RADIOCARBON DATING) and the date may be older.

Chellian. The name given by de MORTILLET in the 1880s to the epoch characterized by hand axes in his classification, equivalent to the Lower PALAEOLITHIC. It replaced the term ACHEULIAN, which was eventually reinstated after a long and confused debate. The concept of epochs, favoured by de Mortillet, has now generally been abandoned, and the term Acheulian is normally used for hand-axe assemblages. Chelles sur Marne, after which the Chellian was named, is a site near Paris.

chemical analysis. Archaeological artefacts and materials can be analysed to determine concentrations of major, minor and TRACE ELEMENTS. The methods used for this include X-RAY FLUORESCENCE SPECTROMETRY, OPTICAL EMISSION SPECTROMETRY, ATOMIC ABSORPTION SPECTROMETRY and NEUTRON ACTIVATION ANALYSIS. This information can be used in the study of technology, trade and distribution.

Chenes. One of three architectural styles occurring in the Lowland MAYA area of north-central Yucatan. Its hallmark is the employment of elaborately decorated pre-cut veneer masonry, but it is distinguished from both RIO BEC and PUUC by its concentration on towerless, low, single-storey buildings and a preference for certain motifs, notably the earth monster. As with other styles, the Chenes dates to AD 800-1000, a period which overlaps the CLASSIC and the POST-CLASSIC, but stylistically it is often viewed as intermediate between Rio Bec and Puuc. Its best expression is found at Hochob.

Chengdu [Ch'eng-tu]. Capital of Sichuan province, China. The material culture of the Chengdu plain kept a strong local flavour long after its first contact with the Bronze Age civilizations of North China, which on the evidence of RITUAL VESSELS found in nearby PENG XIAN must be dated no later than the beginning of the Western ZHOU period. Apart from the Peng Xian bronzes there is little sign that Western Zhou influence in Sichuan went beyond the introduction of bronze weapons; in the course of the Zhou period these weapons evolved local forms that often appear peculiar or archaic by comparison with counterparts from more metropolitan centres. In the late Eastern Zhou period, when Sichuan was the route by which influences from the northern steppes reached the DIAN KINGDOM in southwestern China, the Chengdu plain was occupied by the kingdom of Shu (*see* BA AND SHU). Though still a cultural backwater, Chengdu at this time seems to have been a major centre for the manufacture of painted LACQUERS. In the HAN period state-operated workshops at Chengdu and nearby Guanghan dominated the lacquer industry, and their products have been found as far away as JIANGLING and MAWANGDUI in Hunan province, NOIN ULA in Outer Mongolia, and LELANG in Korea.

Cheng Zhou [Ch'eng Chou] (*distinguish from* ZHENGZHOU). *See* ZHOU CAPITALS.

Chengziyai [Ch'eng-tzu-yai]. *See* LONGSHAN.

Chenla. The first kingdom of the KHMERS which came into being in what is now southern LAOS in the middle of the 6th century. Its etymology is not known. It gradually expanded towards the south to absorb the territories formerly occupied by FUNAN (i.e. present CAMBODIA). At the beginning of the

8th century it split into Upper (or Land) and Lower (or Water) Chenla, the latter part coming under Javanese suzerainty towards the end of the same century. Chenla ceased to exist with the establishment, in 802, of the kingdom of ANGKOR which succeeded it. As no site of this period has so far been excavated, the material culture of Chenla is little known, but from local inscriptions, architectural remains and Chinese sources it is clear, that it was a so-called INDIANIZED kingdom. In art history the time is known as the 'pre-Angkor' period. *See also* ÎSÄNAPURA.

Chernigov. A town on the River Dnieper in the western Soviet Union, probably founded by the Swedish Vikings between the 9th and 11th centuries. It was principally a trading town on the north-south route across eastern Europe between the Black Sea and Baltic areas.

chert. A very finely crystalline form of the mineral silica, found as nodules in limestones. Many cherts are so fine-grained that they behave like a GLASS — they fracture almost as sharply as OBSIDIAN, and may be chipped or flaked to make artefacts. All have been used as materials for making artefacts, but the most commonly used has been the particularly glassy variety called FLINT, which is found in the chalk of England and Europe.

Chesowanja. An open site in Kenya, which has produced the earliest evidence yet recorded of fire in association with tools. The site is dated to 1.4 million years ago and predates the previous earliest evidence for fire — at ZHOUKOUTIEN — by nearly 1 million years. However, it has been suggested that the burning documented at Chesowanja was produced not by man, but by some natural cause such as lightning. If it was man-made, the problem arises as to which hominid was responsible. At a date of 1.4 million years the most plausible candidate is *Homo erectus*, but the only hominid actually documented at Chesowanja is *Australopithecus robustus*, normally regarded as neither a tool-maker nor a meat-eater (and therefore an implausible candidate for a fire-maker). One view that has been expressed is that *A. robustus* was the victim of the fire-making *Homo erectus*, but in the absence of actual *H. erectus* fossils, this seems like special pleading. *See also*

AUSTRALOPITHECUS,   HOMO   ERECTUS,
HUMAN EVOLUTION.

Chester [Roman Deva]. City in northwest England. Modern Chester overlies a massive Roman camp (*castra*) of some 24 hectares, sited strategically on the River Dee to control communications with the Northwest and Wales, to separate the warring tribes of the Brigantes and the Ordovices, and to assist the sister camp at CAERLEON in the continuing programme of subjugation in Wales. Perhaps already a small fort by AD 60, the fortress was firmly established, as inscriptions show, in a surge of construction in the years 76-79. This initial phase of timber and earthworks was itself subsequently renewed in stone. Water supply by aqueduct was also laid on by 79. The layout, externally and internally, was typically rectilinear, with perimeter wall and ditch, corner towers, a gateway in each side, and intermediate towers. A street grid linked the principal quarters of the camp. Outside the fortifications lay a civilian settlement, an amphitheatre, cemeteries and quarries. Abandonment came about 380.

chevaux de frise. A form of defence developed especially to break cavalry charges, although also effective against foot soldiers; consisting of closely spaced stakes or stones placed on end, *chevaux de frises* are sometimes associated with HILLFORTS in prehistoric Europe.

Chiao [also Giao]. Name of the formerly independent kingdom of NAM-VIÊT (Chinese Nan-yüeh) when it was incorporated as a province into the Han empire in 111 BC. The province of Chiao consisted of nine commanderies, six of which correspond to the present Chinese provinces of Kwangtung and Kwangsi and the island of Hainan, while the other three formed the northern half of present Vietnam which gained independence from China in 939. *See also* CHIAO-CHIH.

Chiao-chih [Giao-chi]. One of the nine commanderies of the Han Chinese province of CHIAO which corresponded to the region of the Red River delta, the heartland of the later (10th-century) independent state of VIET-NAM. The name was used by early European and West Asian traders to designate this state long after it had gained independence from China and possibly survives in 'Cochin-China'.

Chiapa de Corzo. Located on the banks of the Grijalva River in the central depression of the state of Chiapas, Mexico, Chiapa de Corzo has one of the longest occupational sequences in Mesoamerica. Although it spans the period *c*1500 BC to the present, it is most interesting for its coverage of Late PRE-CLASSIC to Early CLASSIC times. Evidence of construction (adobe fragments), utilitarian ceramics and figurines occur at the earliest level; PYRAMIDS date to 550 BC and residential complexes of cut stone to 150 BC.

The site is particularly notable for its record of constantly changing external influences. Elements of style and iconography in certain artefacts indicate contact with IZAPA and KAMINALJUYU in the Late Pre-Classic. Hundreds of broken sherds found in Mound 5 tell of trade contact with sites in the Peten, MONTE ALBAN and TEOTIHUACAN in the Early CLASSIC. Deliberate destruction of Mound 5 occurred in AD 500 and was followed by a brief period of abandonment. Reoccupation appears to have been by an entirely new group, possibly the Zoque.

Chibcha. A culture centred on the eastern cordillera of Colombia, near to present-day Bogota, which was still flourishing in the 16th century at the time of Spanish contact. Much of what is known comes from historical documents of that time, although excavations at the huge site of La Ramada have provided some archaeological information.

Large populations living in palisaded towns were governed as autonomous chiefdoms by an absolute ruler. (The ceremonial coating of the chief's body with gold leaf may well be the origin of the El Dorado legend.) Ceremonial practice centred around sun-worship and included human sacrifice. Rituals associated with the culture hero/god Bochica show marked similarities to rituals connected with Mesoamerican deities.

The Chibcha were successful agriculturalists, farming, among other things, MAIZE and POTATOES. As such, their artefact inventory (especially ceramics) tends to be utilitarian; distinctive human effigy vessels, however, may have some ritual significance. Gold, copper and tumbaga (a copper-gold alloy) were also worked in a variety of techniques — soldered wire embellishments are characteristic — but the art style is rather crude compared to contemporary Columbian cultures such as TAIRONA.

Chicanel. A phase of the Lowland MAYA PRE-CLASSIC dated 300 BC to AD 150. It is characterized by a complex of architectural and ceramic traits which presage the rise of CLASSIC Maya civilization, for instance temple-pyramids, corbelled arches and painted murals. Also notable is increasing uniformity between sites, a growing variety of ceramic forms and the disappearance of figurines. *See also* MAMON.

Chichen Itza. The primary centre of power in the northern Yucatan during the Early POST-CLASSIC PERIOD. Although there is a PRE-CLASSIC occupation and Chichen Itza functioned as a minor CEREMONIAL CENTRE in the CLASSIC PERIOD, its major occupation was between c1000 and 1250. From historical sources it seems likely that the Itza (*see also* COZUMEL) arrived in 918 and were responsible for the early structures, some of which are in the PUUC style, for example the High Priest's Grave, the inner structures of the Castillo and the Caracol (the Observatory). There is a good deal of confusion over who the Itza were and how they relate to the TOLTEC, but they were probably a Mexican-influenced PUTUN group.

The arrival of the Toltecs at Chichen Itza is coincident with the banishment of QUETZA-COATL from TULA in 987; indeed, representations of the feathered serpent abound after this time. This second building phase, although clearly Toltec-inspired (several buildings are markedly similar to structures at TULA) also incorporates strong MAYAN elements. At the centre of the site is the Castillo or temple-PYRAMID of Kulkulkan, the Maya equivalent of Quetzacoatl; this is linked by a causeway to the nearby Sacred CENOTE. Other major structures include the Temple of the Warriors (in front of which stands a CHAC-MOOL), large 'dance platforms', the Group of a Thousand Columns, the Temple of the Jaguars and, at 150 metres long, the largest BALL COURT in Mesoamerica. Bas-relief carvings on a massive skull rack (*tzompantli*) shows the BALL GAME to be associated with scenes of sacrifice. Relief carvings with themes of conquest and violence abound, and representations of

Maya warriors submitting to Toltec warriors have been found on gold discs recovered from the Sacred Cenote.

The terminal date for Chichen Itza is uncertain but the chronicles indicate either 1187 or 1227 as the time of the disappearance of the Toltec. Certainly by the mid-13th century power had shifted to the Late Post-Classic centre at MAYAPAN.

Chichimec. In the Early POST-CLASSIC PERIOD, mixed groups of nomadic hunters and gatherers and displaced farmers began drifting south from the northernmost margins of Mesoamerica. The reasons for this migration are uncertain, but it is thought that these northern areas were subject to sustained climatic deterioration, reducing available subsistence resources below critical levels. Revered as warriors, they were claimed as antecedents by numerous Mesoamerican groups including the TARASCANS and the AZTECS. The TOLTECS also claimed to be descendants, but it has been shown that the Chichimecs did not establish their major centre at TENAYUCA until 1224, after the fall of TULA, for which they were supposedly responsible. The Chichimecs are also associated with the introduction of the bow and arrow into the Valley of Mexico.

Chicoid [Boca Chica]. One of two ceramic series (the other being MEILLACOID) that appear to have developed out of the OSTINOID series. Originating in eastern Hispaniola — the type site is at Boca Chica in the Dominican Republic — Chicoid influence spread over much of the eastern Antilles, probably by diffusion of ideas rather than actual migration. The artistic and ceremonial traits with which Chicoid materials are associated represent the cultural climax of the Caribbean area. Paraphernalia of the BALL GAME, ZEMIS and a variety of wood and stone carvings are among these traits. A strong BARRANCOID influence is evident in the ceramics, especially modelled ornamentation and incision, although the painted decoration normally associated with Ostionoid is replaced by curvilinear incision. The series first appears in c1000 AD and continues into the time of European contact.

Chilam Balam. *See* CODEX.

Chilca. Dating to the PRE-CERAMIC PERIOD

V (4200-2500 bc), the Chilca site, 67 km south of Lima, Peru, was originally a summer camp for ARCHAIC groups. An increasingly warmer climate, however, caused the drying up of the LOMAS and coastal sites such as Chilca became favourable loci for a new subsistence pattern (see ENCANTO). Remains of semi-subterranean cane and grass houses, coupled with increasing evidence of exploitation of marine resources and of wild and domesticated plants, such as beans, emphasize the tendency to sedentary life. Radiocarbon dates for the early period of occupation are in the range 3800 to 2650 bc. DOLICHO-CEPHALIC human remains date to this period but appear ultimately to have been replaced by BRACHYCEPHALIC types some time after 2500 bc.

Chilchihuitlicue. *See* CALENDAR STONE.

Childe, Vere Gordon (1892-1957). Australian by birth, Childe spent most of his life in Britain, where he was successively Abercromby Professor of Archaeology at Edinburgh and first Professor of European Prehistory in the Institute of Archaeology at London University. For more than 30 years Childe dominated European prehistory. He was the chief proponent of the DIFFUSIONIST view which interpreted all major developments in prehistoric Europe in terms of the spread of either people or ideas from the Near East. He developed this theme in great detail in a number of seminal works, among the most important of which were *The Danube in Prehistory*(1929) and *The Dawn of European Civilization*(1925, 7th ed. 1957). Although in European archaeology Childe is associated with the idea of diffusion, he also studied Near Eastern prehistory and in that context he studied developments occurring locally — what today is often called processual archaeology. In his books *The Most Ancient East*(1928) and its later edition *New Light on the Most Ancient East* (1934) he emphasized the importance of the change from hunting and gathering to farming as the basis of life, which he called the Neolithic or Food-producing Revolution, and the later development of civilization, which he called the Second or Urban Revolution. Though the term 'revolution' is rarely used in these contexts today, these developments remain a major focus of study for scholars of the 1980s.

In addition to a very large number of technical books and articles, Childe wrote many books about archaeology for the general public.

Chimu. Centred on the north coast of Peru, the Chimu kingdom was the largest of the independent states to appear in the Late INTERMEDIATE PERIOD. Developing out of MOCHE, the kingdom at its zenith stretched from the borders of Ecuador to the Chillon Valley. The capital, Chanchan, was located in the Moche Valley and consisted of nucleated monumental architecture covering an area of over six square kilometres. The site is dominated by ten rectangular enclosures with walls from 200 to 600 metres long and up to 10 metres high. The nature of the complexes within these enclosures — large rooms, courtyards, sunken gardens, rich tombs — suggest that they were occupied by the ruling elite of Chimu society. (Although an alternative interpretation is that they were occupied by groups defined either by kinship or craft specialization.)

A system of inter-valley highways (popularly supposed to be INCA) confirms the likelihood of a widespread trade network. Such roads, in company with garrisons and fortified posts, would also have been a factor in the maintenance of control by a strong central government. Canal irrigation on a grand scale was also practised.

Mould-made, burnished black ware, decorated in low-relief, was the characteristic Chimu pottery, although polychromes displaying HUARI-inspired designs occurred in earlier contexts. The STIRRUP-SPOUT and SPOUT-AND-BRIDGE vessels are the most common forms.

Although Chimu characteristics are still distinguishable as late as 1600, the culture was effectively absorbed into the Inca empire some time in the mid-15th century.

chinampa. An extremely productive method of agriculture practised in MESOAMERICA, especially by the AZTEC. Although often incorrectly called 'floating gardens', the method is rather similar to a system of land reclamation. Successive rectangular mats of marsh vegetation were floated to suitable shallow-water sites and anchored first to the lake bottom and then successively to each other. Once built up above the water level, nutrient-rich lake mud was dredged up and piled on top. Periodic renewal of this mud layer created a permanent supply of fertile soil so that as one crop was harvested it could be immediately replaced with another. The chinampas were normally separated by a system of canals which allowed both access and water circulation. A carrying capacity of 60 to 100 persons per hectare is estimated for the system at TENOCHTITLAN.

Chincha. A small autonomous state of the Late INTERMEDIATE PERIOD, centred on the Chincha Valley in south coast Peru. Although known mostly from its pottery, some sites do exist: notably the administrative complex at Tambo de Mora (probably the capital), La Centinela and La Cumbe. Chincha pottery was widely traded and is typically a smoked black ware, although there were some polychromes. A reputation for military prowess appears to derive from the early (and probably exaggerated) reports of the Spanish conquistadores. Whatever their fighting ability, the Chincha were ultimately incorporated into the INCA empire.

Chiozza. A Neolithic settlement site in Emilia, northern Italy, of the later 5th or early 4th millennium bc. The only structural remains were oval and circular pits, possibly the floors of sunken huts, but more probably storage pits. Pottery was of the SQUARE-MOUTHED type and indeed the term Chiozza is sometimes used as an alternative name for this type of pottery, or sometimes just for a later phase of it.

chip carving. A technique that probably originated in the Roman and Celtic world. The method required an incised strip to be drawn across the surface of the piece to be decorated, and then a series of lozenges were cut inside the borders of the strip; each lozenge section was individually eased out with a chisel in such a way that the resulting cavity sloped in towards the centre in a pyramidal depression. The end result was a pattern of combined V-shaped incisions, with a glittering faceted appearance. The technique was effectively adapted by Germanic wood-carvers to make animal ornaments, and by metalsmiths of the Migration Period to produce objects of unparalleled skill.

chipping floor. In the process of flaking stone tools, large quantities of waste chips are produced. A land surface on which a scatter of these is found is a chipping floor. At least from the earlier stone age, it is rare to discover a chipping floor where finished tools and indications of other activities are absent.

Chiricahua. The second of three chronological stages of the COCHISE culture, with dates clustering between 3500 and 1500 bc. A mixed foraging economy is indicated by assemblages commonly including cobble MANOS, shallow basin grinding slabs, choppers, scrapers and distinctive, side-notched projectile points. Some degree of permanence can be inferred from the occurrence of large base camps, storage pits and outlying specialized-activity camps. Evidence from BAT CAVE indicates that primitive MAIZE was also being cultivated during this period, although botanical remains are rare at other sites.

Chiripa. A site located at the south end of Lake Titicaca in Bolivia and dating to the MIDDLE HORIZON. It consists of a series of rectangular rooms, some with underfloor stone-lined graves, arranged around a rectangular plaza. An unusual feature is the use of the space between the double walls of some of these structures for storage. Chiripa's distinctive ceramics are part of a region-wide artistic tradition linked both to PUCARA and the beginnings of TIAHUANACO. Typical pottery is a cream-on-white ware, decorated with geometric designs (usually broad steps or serrations); modelled and incised felines are another favoured motif. The common form is a flat-bottomed, vertical-sided open bowl.

Chitope. A village site in northern Mashonaland, Zimbabwe, occupied briefly during a final phase of the local Early Iron Age in the 11th or 12th century ad. The presence of a single glass bead suggests that this period saw the beginning of contact with the coastal trade, which greatly developed during the succeeding later Iron Age.

Chiusi [Roman Clusium]. Town in central Italy. Situated on a hill commanding the southern end of the Val di Chiana, Clusium enjoyed in antiquity good agricultural fertility, deposits of iron and copper ore, natural hot springs, and a key position on trade routes. Settlement appears to be unbroken and successful from the first VILLANOVAN dwellers onwards. Under ETRUSCAN rule (6th-4th centuries BC), Clusium prospered as one of the great 12 cities of the confederation, and gained a reputation for bronze and stone craftsmanship. Numerous Etruscan tombs, mostly cut into the soft tufa rock and dating from the 7th to the 1st centuries BC, some richly decorated, some with rich contents of vases, sarcophagi, sculpture and CIPPI, bear eloquent witness to this wealth. In general, the great preponderance of material originating from tombs and cemeteries (both Villanovan and Etruscan) gives the evidence a funerary imbalance that needs cautious interpretation. There is the impression of a continuous Villanovan-Etruscan settlement that was slow to admit other influences. In particular, there is evidence for a marked persistence of the cremation rite, a continuity that produces a wide variety of cinerary urns, 'canopic' jars (with human representation), and the characteristic hollow seated figures (hollowed out from so-called *pietra fetida* limestone, to act as cinerary containers). By contrast, although contact with Rome came early, Roman influence seems to exert very little effect.

Chivateros. A stratified site in the coastal Chillon Valley of central Peru, which has produced a lithic flake industry dating to as early as the Late PLEISTOCENE. Radiocarbon dates of *c*8500 bc, taken from wood fragments, have helped to define Chivateros I as the period *c*9500 to 8000 bc. By cross-comparison of artefacts with a nearby workshop (designated the Oquendo complex) a date of pre-10,500 bc has been convincingly postulated for the underlying Red Zone. The whole industry is characterized by burins and bifaces with the upper level (Chivateros II) containing long, keeled, leaf-shaped projectile points which resemble points from both LAURICOCHA II and EL JOBO.

Dating has also been aided by the deposition of both LOESS and salt crust layers which seem to suggest alternating periods of dryness and humidity, and which furthermore can be synchronized with glacial activity in the northern hemisphere. (Note, however, that our knowledge of the glacial stages in the southern hemisphere is still highly speculative: *see also* AYACUCHO.)

Although these assemblages are clearly hunting-oriented, no bone survives at Chivateros and it is supposed that the population lived away from this workshop site.

chloromelanite. A form of JADEITE.

Chodo. *See* PUSAN.

Choga Mami. A settlement site of the SAMARRA culture near Mandali in southeast Iraq. The site which has radiocarbon dates of the late 6th millennium bc, has several occupation phases spanning the transition from the Samarran to the UBAID culture. The subsistence economy of Choga Mami was based on mixed farming, involving the rearing of cattle, sheep and goats and the cultivation of wheat, barley and flax. These crops were cultivated with the help of irrigation, for which unequivocal evidence survives in the form of a series of ditches on the edge of the settlement. The site covers *c*3500 square metres and contains buildings of mud-brick with external buttresses; houses were rectangular and consisted of ranges of rooms, in two or three rows. A mud-brick tower guarded the entrance to the settlement. Artefacts from the site include the typical Samarran painted pottery and elaborate female figurines of clay.

Choga Mish. A site in southwest Iran occupied in the 6th millennium bc. The earliest layers have painted pottery related to that from MUHAMMED JAFFAR, followed by pottery of Tepe SABZ and Susiana A (*see* SUSA) types.

Choga Zanbil. City near SUSA in southwest Iran which was founded as a second capital of ELAM in the 13th century BC by Untash-Gal, from whom it took its ancient name, Dur-Untash. The city was lavishly laid out but never completed; it declined in importance after the death of Untash-Gal. Excavations have exposed three concentric city walls, three palaces, a huge central ZIGGURAT still surviving to a height of *c*28 metres but probably originally almost twice that height, other associated temples in the same complex and a reservoir.

Cholula. One of the independent POST-CLASSIC centres of Mexico to survive after the fall of TEOTIHUACAN, and the major locus for the production of the elaborate polychrome wares of the Mixteca-Puebla art style (*see* MIXTEC). Located in the state of Puebla in Mexico, it is dominated by the largest PYRAMID in MESOAMERICA. This structure covers an area of 16 hectares and rises to a height of more than 30 metres.

Limited excavation via tunnelling shows four earlier pyramids nested inside the Great Pyramid, the earliest of which goes back to the PRE-CLASSIC PERIOD when the site was first occupied. Cholula survived as a political and mercantile centre until the time of the Spanish and appears to have flourished in spite of having been dominated by a series of conquering groups including the historic OLMEC, Tolteca-Chichimec and the AZTEC.

Chondwe. An Iron Age site on the Zambian Copperbelt. It has given its name to the local manifestation of the Early Iron Age complex apparently established in the 4th or 5th century ad. Its closest affinities at this time were with the Lusaka area (compare KAPWIRIMBWE) and, probably, with areas further to the west. Smallscale exploitation of the region's copper deposits dates from the time of this Early Iron Age occupation, when there is also some evidence for the growth of inter-regional trade.

Chono. *See* FUEGIAN TRADITION.

chopper/chopping tool. These names are given to simple forms of stone tool made on a nodule or cobble with a roughly flaked sharp edge. By convention, tools with the cutting edge flaked from one direction are called choppers and those flaked from two directions are called chopping tools. Their use is generally unknown, though a few examples from the CLACTONIAN in England are believed, on the basis of wear traces, to have been used for chopping wood. The term chopper/chopping tool tradition is frequently applied to the Pleistocene pebble and flake industries of eastern Asia, to differentiate them from the HAND AXE industries of western Eurasia and Africa (*see* ANYATHIAN, PACITANIAN, ZHOUKOUDIAN) although their distribution is by no means restricted to eastern Asia.

Choris. The earliest manifestation of the NORTON tradition of Western Arctic prehistory. The most characteristic artefact is coarse stamped pottery, the technology for which was probably imported from Asia. Tool assemblages are usually diverse and clearly different from earlier levels, for example at Point Barrow. Tools of polished slate and oil lamps first appear in Choris times. Considerable local variation in assemblages at Choris sites makes it difficult to generalize about this tradition. The type site is at Kotsebue Sound but there are Choris components at CAPE KRUSENSTERN and ONION PORTAGE as well as other Arctic sites. The most characteristic dates are *c*1500-500 bc.

Chotnica [Hotnica]. A long-lived TELL settlement site of the later Neolithic period, located in the Yantra Valley in north Bulgaria and dated to the late 5th to early 4th millennium bc. The cultures found represent regional variants on Rumanian groups of the lower Danube valley and occur in three main occupation horizons: I, a thin DUDEŞTI level with pits and post holes, associated with a rich pottery assemblage; II, a BOIAN level with ceramics of the Boian II phase; and III, a thick horizon of the GUMELNIŢA culture, in which a complete village plan with over 15 houses is known. In the smallest structure in the Gumelniţa village was found the Chotnica hoard of 44 or 48 gold ornaments (4 pendants and 40 or 44 bracelets). The exact context of the hoard inside the building is still unknown.

Choukoutien. *See* ZHOUKOUDIAN.

Christy, Henry (1810-65). English banker who in the last three years of his life supported financially and assisted in person the French archaeologist Edouard LARTET in excavations in many of the great caves of southwest France, including LAUGERIE HAUTE, LA MADELEINE and LE MOUSTIER. Christy left money for the publication of his and Lartet's work, which was eventually produced serially under the title *Reliquiae Aquitanicae* and finally completed in 1875.

chronology. A related sequence of dates. Chronologies may be built up on archaeological grounds (e.g. CROSS DATING, STRATIGRAPHY or TYPOLOGY) or from independent dating techniques (e.g. RADIOCARBON, ARCHAEOMAGNETISM etc).

Chu [Ch'u]. A state that ruled a large area of

central China during the ZHOU period. According to tradition a Chu ruler was given a title by the second Western Zhou king, implying that a Chu kingdom existed as early as c1000 BC. Little is known of this kingdom until the Eastern Zhou period, however, when archaeology and historical sources reveal it as a distinctive, highly civilized cultural and political entity. From the 8th century until its destruction by QIN in the 3rd century BC Chu was the largest and most powerful of the Eastern Zhou states, presenting a constant threat to its neighbours on the west, north, and east.

Chu occupied modern Hubei province and adjacent parts of Hunan, Jiangxi, Anhui, and Henan. The distribution of Chu sites suggests that the main settlements lay on the shores of a great lake called Yunmeng in ancient texts, of which Lake Dongting is today the remnant, and along the rivers that flowed into or out of the lake (Xiang, Han and Yangzi). Major finds have also been made to the north of this region (see XIASI) and northeast across the Dabieshan mountains in the Huai River valley (see XINYANG), but Chu remains are most densely concentrated at JIANGLING in southern Hubei and CHANGSHA in northern Hunan. The Chu capital was at Jiangling from 689 to 278 BC, when the city fell to Qin. The Chu court then retreated to the Huai valley, remaining there until its final overthrow in 223 BC (see SHOU XIAN).

Although surviving documents show that the Chu people wrote and thus presumably spoke Chinese, the contemporary states in the north, direct heirs of the SHANG and Western Zhou empires, always regarded themselves as 'more Chinese'. The cultural differences that set Chu apart are clearly visible in the archaeological record and also in ancient texts such as the *Chu ci* or *Songs of Chu*, a remarkable collection of Chu poems. These differences are of special interest to the historian, for much in Chu culture that was exotic by comparison with the Shang and Zhou tradition had by the end of the HAN period entered the mainstream of Chinese civilization.

Few Chu habitation sites have been excavated. Evidence for the material culture of Chu comes instead from countless tombs, including some that date from the Han dynasty (see MAWANGDUI). Chu bronze-casting was highly developed and idiosyncratic (see XIASI, SUI XIAN), but the Chu art form *par excellence*

was painted LACQUER. Lacquered objects range from containers of all sorts to strange wooden effigies, musical instruments, coffins, and other wooden tomb furniture. Paintings on lacquer and SILK together with a few illustrated silk manuscripts hint at a rich mythology made explicit in the *Chu ci*, whose shamans and weird demons have no parallel in contemporary texts originating outside the Chu sphere. The bronze RITUAL VESSELS essential to the religious observances of the northern states seem to have been less important to Chu ceremony than the musical instruments, especially BELLS and DRUMS, found in large numbers in Chu tombs. The bells and also certain animal motifs ubiquitous in Chu art — birds, snakes, tigers — argue for continuity with Shang-period local cultures of the Yangzi region (see NINGXIANG). Silk, lacquer, and IRON were all Chu specialities, and the northern states felt the appeal of Chu material culture long before the Han dynasty (see YUNMENG). With the incorporation of Chu into the Han empire — whose founder was of Chu descent — the influence of Chu art throughout China became overwhelming. The contributions made by Chu literature, philosophy, and government administration seem to have been equally crucial for the genesis of Han civilization.

chullpa. A burial tower commonly found in the southern Peruvian Andes, especially in the Lake Titicaca basin. Of either circular or rectangular plan, *chullpa* are built from adobe or from a variety of natural or dressed stone. Often associated with the INCA, they were already being built and used in the Late INTERMEDIATE PERIOD, especially by the Colla (see AYMARA).

Chunqiu [Ch'un-ch'iu]. The SPRING AND AUTUMN PERIOD, 770-476 BC. See ZHOU.

chunyu [*ch'un-yü*]. See BELLS (CHINA).

Chuqitanta. See EL PARAISO.

church. A building used for collective Christian worship, the performance of ceremonies, pilgrimages and the veneration of relics. The earliest churches were hidden in caves and CATACOMBS but with the official acceptance of Christianity in the 4th century larger buildings, typically the BASILICAN halls, were built specifically for communal worship. In the early Christian period, baptistries, martyria, and covered cemeteries often remained separate to one side of the building for worship.

Although the usual form of churches has been the hall or axial plan, other forms have also been used: circular, polygonal or cross-shaped. However, the plan and appearance of a church is not determined only by its liturgical and ceremonial functions, but by other symbolic and spiritual considerations. All the details and proportions in a medieval church are to some extent a material reflection of deeper spiritual and symbolic meanings.

Ciempozuelos. A Copper Age cemetery near Madrid in central Spain, which has given its name to a late variety of Spanish BEAKER. Most of the burials were flexed inhumations in cists. The Ciempozuelos beakers and other pots are of high quality with a red or brown burnished slip and incised decoration; they belong to the 2nd millennium BC.

Cieneza. *See* AGRELO.

Cimmerians. A nomadic people of the south Russian steppes, known to us through the writings of Herodotus and the ASSYRIAN records. In the 8th century BC, under pressure from the SCYTHIANS, they moved into Anatolia, while a related group called Thracians moved north-west into Europe. They may have played a part in the spread of iron technology to the west, though this view has fewer adherents today than formerly. The name Thraco-Cimmerian has been attached to a particular kind of horse-bit found widely in Europe, but its real association with either Thracians or Cimmerians is not well established.

cippus [*pl*: cippi]. A short pillar of stone, usually rectangular or cylindrical, and often with mouldings at top and bottom. Often inscribed, it is normally associated with burials or tombs, and essentially serves as a gravestone.

Circea. A multi-level settlement site of the Early Neolithic CRIŞ culture, located in the Olt Valley of southwesten Rumania and dated from the late 6th-mid—5th millennia bc. Four main occupation phases have been disting-

uished in a three-metre stratigraphy, all of which are defined by rich painted ware assemblages. Level I includes some of the earliest white-on-red painted pottery of the FIRST TEMPERATE NEOLITHIC, with affinities in the Proto-Sesklo repertoire of Greece, whilst in the latest level (IV) the latest style of STARČEVO-CRIŞ polychrome painted pottery in Rumania is found.

Circumpolar cultures. Alternatively labelled Arctic Stone Age, these cultures are found in the most northerly regions of Eurasia. The population remained hunter-gatherers long after farming had been established further south, exploiting food sources such as elk, reindeer and seal. In some areas, a lively rock art is found, depicting scenes of hunting and fishing, as well as equipment such as skis, sledges and skin boats. Tools were often made of slate, and amber was widely used for ornaments. Trading connections with farming groups to the south were well established and amber may have been the main commodity traded. The practice of pottery-making was acquired through these contacts.

circus. An oval race-course with a central wall (*spina*) and columned turning points (*metae*), particularly for chariot races. There were several examples in ancient Rome, the greatest being the Circus Maximus. It is essentially a Roman development from the Greek STADIUM or HIPPODROME.

Cirencester [Corinium Dobunnorum]. Situated in Gloucestershire, southwest England, Cirencester was the site of a cavalry fort during the period AD 43-70. It subsequently became the CIVITAS capital of the Dobunni tribe and by the 3rd century the town walls enclosed *c*100 hectares. Occupation continued well into the Anglo-Saxon period. Most of ancient Corinium lies under modern Cirencester, but part of the wall can still be seen and an amphitheatre to the southwest of the town. Excavations have revealed much of the layout of the town and the plan of the forum and basilica, a market hall, shops and houses.

Work on the cemetery containing *c*450 individuals, published in 1982, has cast interesting light on the health of the population of Cirencester. The skeletons contained high levels of lead, lending suppport to the view that lead poisoning contributed to the decline of the Roman Empire. The lead level in the bones of some children was so high that they may have actually died of lead poisoning, although this cannot be ascertained from the skeletons. Other conditions identified in the skeletons include arthritis and gout.

cire perdue[lost wax] **method**. A method of constructing moulds for metal casting. In the lost-wax method, a model of the object to be cast is made in wax and then invested with clay; when the clay is baked the wax runs out, leaving a clay envelope in which an exact metal replica of the wax model can be cast. If the metal object is to be hollow, it is only necessary to give the wax model a clay core (which will become the core of the casting and may be seen in X-rays of ancient artefacts). The lost-wax method is well-suited to produce objects of irregular or undercut shape. Since the thickness of wax applied to the clay core is easily controlled, it also helps the craftsman to keep the walls of a hollow casting uniformly thin, saving metal and reducing the risk of flaws due to uneven cooling. The earliest lost-wax castings yet identified come from a 4th millennium BC hoard of copper and arsenical copper objects, some cast around clay cores, found in Nahal Mishmar near the Dead Sea.

The main alternative to the lost-wax process, called the piece-mould or section-mould technique, constructs the mould without the aid of an evanescent model. In this technique, clay is packed around a permanent model, not of wax, and then removed from the model in sections, the sections being re-assembled to form the mould. The number of sections into which the mould must be divided in order to free it from the model depends on how intricate or undercut the shape of the model is. Bivalve moulds, the simplest of section moulds, are adequate to produce many weapons and tools. Castings with mould marks corresponding to the divisions of three- or four-part moulds were among the metal objects unearthed by WOOLLEY in the Royal Cemetery at UR. For shapes that are not excessively complicated, the section-mould method is practical and straightforward (see RITUAL VESSELS, CHINA).

The section-mould method was used extensively in ancient China, where lost-wax casting did not appear until about the 6th century BC (see XIASI). Outside China, however, perhaps its main use has been as an adjunct to lost-wax casting. The lost-wax method suffers from the drawback that the model is destroyed in the process of making the mould, so that only one casting can be obtained from each model; moreover any accident to model or mould can mean the loss of all the effort invested in preparing the wax model. The solution to this problem, exploited in Greek foundries in the 5th century BC if not before, is to begin with a permanent model that is not of wax and to form a section mould on this; the section mould is then used to shape duplicate wax models, each of which can be used to make a casting mould. Modern art-foundry work generally relies on some such combination of the section-mould and lost-wax techniques, using first the section-mould method to make a wax model and then the lost-wax method to cast a metal replica of the wax model. The procedure necessarily sacrifices some of the freedom of shape offered by the lost-wax method, since the model must not be so complicated that a mould cannot be conveniently removed from it in sections. By way of compensation, it allows duplicate castings and keeps the original model intact. The expression 'lost-wax process' in many contexts refers to the entire procedure just described, including the first step in which a section mould is formed on the permanent model.

Cishan [Tz'u-shan]. *See* BANPO.

cist. A simple square or rectangular tomb made of stone slabs set on edge and covered by a CAPSTONE. Cists may be sunk into the ground or built above it and they may be free-standing or covered by a BARROW.

Cistercian ware. A distinctive 15th-16th-century manganese glazed ware commonly associated with Cistercian sites in pre-Reformation times. This type of pottery marks a break with earlier traditions of LEAD GLAZED wares, and the various forms were produced in many kilns. Production was concentrated in Yorkshire, and the unusual two-handled cup forms found favour not only with monks but with households of all kinds.

Ciumeşti. A small cluster of Mesolithic and Neolithic settlement sites, located on the sand dune zone of the upper Crasna River in the

Maramureş area, northwest Rumania. Within a radius of 10 km short-term Late Mesolithic, Early Neolithic CRIŞ and later Neolithic LINEAR POTTERY sites are found, sometimes with superimposed culture levels. The chipped stone assemblages are distinguished by a high percentage of obsidian, procured from the Tokaj Mountains some 180 km away in northeastern Hungary.

Cividale. The little church of Santa Maria in Valle or the 'Tempietto' at Cividale, near Friuli in northeast Italy, is one of the finest surviving examples of LOMBARDIC architecture. It was built between 762 and 776 and combines elements of Lombardic 'proto-Romanesque' with Arabic and Byzantine influences. The groin-vaulted nave is carried on columns and leads to a small sanctuary. The plainness of the exterior greatly contrasts with the abundant carved decoration and sculpture which adorns the inside; most of which is carried out in the unusual medium of stucco. The most impressive feature of all is the frieze of six full-length stucco figures, whose graceful poses resemble mature Romanesque sculpture.

civitas. A term used in the later Roman Republic and under the Roman Empire, to describe certain self-governing communities, which comprised a town with its local citizens and magistrates together with its surrounding territory. *See also* COLONIA, MUNICIPIUM.

Clactonian. A series of river and estuarine deposits on the Essex coast near Clacton, southeast England, date from the HOXNIAN or MINDEL-RISS period, and contain stone tools and animal and plant remains. There is one URANIUM SERIES date of about 250,000 years. The stone artefacts consist of thick flakes and rough cores, but typical hand axes are not found. The type of assemblage or culture is called Clactonian. *See* Tables 5 and 6, pages 418-9.

Clarke, David (1938-76). A British archaeologist who made major contributions to archaeological methodology and theory before his death at a tragically early age. His seminal book *Analytical Archaeology*, published in 1968, is sometimes regarded as heralding in a new era in the development of archaeology, equivalent to the so-called NEW

ARCHAEOLOGY of the United States. Clarke emphasized the need for an explicit theory and a more rigorous methodology in archaeology — both of which are now widely accepted by the new generation of archaeologists.

Classical. A term derived from the Latin *classicus* ('of the highest class'), used to designate a supposedly high point of a civilization. It is frequently the central term in a three-tier series: ARCHAIC (for preceding periods, with implications of primitivity), Classical (central period of greatest achievement), and 'late' (of subsequent periods, with implications of degeneracy and breakdown). In a broader sense, the term often describes the whole period of Greek and Roman antiquity.

Classic Period. Conceived as the period of florescence of the great civilizations of MESOAMERICA, initially defined by the earliest and most recent LONG COUNT dates found on MAYA stelae, AD 300-900. As more sites came to light, it became increasingly clear that many well-developed cultures did not fit comfortably into this dating scheme (e.g. OLMEC, MONTE ALBAN). While the period largely applies to those civilizations which arose in central and southern Mesoamerica, the notion of an area-wide florescence is now untenable. A division between Early and Late Classic was arbitrarily set at AD 600, but since in some areas, e.g. TEOTIHUACAN, great civilizations had already collapsed, some scholars regard this date as marking the end of the Classic Period. The term is also adopted in other areas of the New World, but it is in Mesoamerica that it is most widely used. *See* Table 9, page 552.

classis Britannica [Latin: British fleet]. The fleet based at Boulogne during the Roman occupation of Britain (43-410). With its captains (*trierarchi*) and marines (*milites*), its responsibilities were the transporting of supplies, military activities and, later, the patrolling of the Channel, when its scout craft were painted sea-blue.

claw beaker. Glass claw beakers date from the late 6th-7th centuries and occur in Early Saxon graves and Frankish burials. In form they are similar to free-standing conical beakers, but they are embellished by a series of unusual claw-like protrusions, and in many

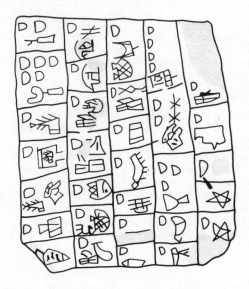

Archaic Uruk clay tablet

cases the glass is tinted in shades of brown, blue and yellow. These beakers were probably made in glasshouses either in Cologne or Trier in Germany.

clay. Strictly, the word clay describes the size of the particles which go to make up a SEDIMENT, soil or similar material. Clay particles are those that are less than 0.002 mm (BS 1377) in diameter (*see* PARTICLE SIZE). Thus a clay is a sediment consisting largely of clay-sized particles; strictly used, the term has no implications about colour, organic content or any property other than particle size or TEXTURE. However, there may be other connotations. The minerals most frequently found as clay-sized particles are the 'clay minerals' such as kaolinite, illite or montmorillonite. Clay as a material frequently consists largely of one or more of these clay minerals. In general usage, 'clay' may imply the material used for making POTTERY, BRICKS or tiles. These, however, frequently contain large quantities of other particle sizes, such as SILT or SAND. 'Clay' in this context merely implies that the material is more or less mouldable when wet, but on drying out becomes hard. This property is shared by most materials that contain any significant quantity of clay-sized particles (*see* POTTERY).

clay tablets. The main writing material employed by the scribes of the early civilizations of Western Asia. Signs were inscribed or, more usually, impressed on the soft clay, which was then dried in the sun. *See also* CUNEIFORM.

cleaver. A large flake tool of the PALAEOLITHIC period. The butt end is often worked into the approximate shape of a hand axe butt, but the other end always has a wide axe-like cutting edge. In the typical African form, much of the flake surface is left unretouched. On some hand axes the tip is flaked into cleaver form.

Cleland Hills. A PANARAMITEE-style rock-art site 320 km west of Alice Springs in central Australia. In addition to the usual Panaramitee motifs, there are 16 deeply engraved and weathered heart-shaped 'faces' with concentric circle 'eyes', unique in Australian rock art.

Cloggs Cave. A limestone cave in the lower Snowy River valley, northeastern Victoria, Australia, with human occupation deposits which included ochre and hearths and are dated from about 16,000 to 7000 bc. Stone tools belonging to the AUSTRALIAN CORE TOOL AND SCRAPER TRADITION showed use-wear interpreted as resulting from skin-working, and resembled similar Tasmanian artefacts. Bones of extinct animals (*Sthenurus orientalis*) were excavated from deposits more than 20,000 years old and separated from the human deposits. AUSTRALIAN SMALL TOOL TRADITION artefacts were excavated from late HOLOCENE deposits in a rock shelter outside the main cave.

cloisonné. A technique used in Anglo-Saxon England and by other Germanic metalsmiths as a means of decorating POLYCHROME JEWELLERY and metalwork with inlaid stones of glass. The cloison (or cell) into which the jewel was set is fabricated from bands of thin metal attached to a base plate, and these were often separated from each other by FILIGREE wire. A piece of stamped metal was placed at the bottom of each cell to reflect back through the stone and enhance its beauty.

Clovis. A complex of cultural traits from the PALEO-INDIAN period which characterize the LLANO culture of North America. A distinctive, fluted, lanceolate projectile point, especially when found in association with mammoth bones, is particularly diagnostic. The type site for this complex is BLACKWATER DRAW. Numerous sites throughout North America have a Clovis component that usually falls within the date range 10,000 to 9000 bc.

cluster analysis. A technique of MULTI-VARIATE ANALYSIS, which compares the distances between points, objects or items, distributed in a hyperspace whose dimensions are measurements or scores for a number of VARIABLES. Cluster analysis results are normally plotted as a 'dendrogram', a tree-like representation of the distances between objects in hyperspace. Items that are closer together in hyperspace are deemed to be more closely related, and are linked more closely in the dendrogram. Like any other multivariate technique, cluster analysis could conceivably be done by 'pencil-and-paper' methods; it is the number of calculations involved that usually necessitates the use of a digital COMPUTER.

Clyde-Carlingford tombs. A group of MEGA-LITHIC CHAMBER TOMBS found in southwest Scotland and northern Ireland. They are sometimes described as segmented GALLERY GRAVES, since they consist of rectangular chambers subdivided into a number of segments. Another important characteristic was the forecourt, concave or semicircular in shape; in some of the Irish examples this may be oval or circular and the term 'court cairn' is sometimes used for these tombs. The overlying cairns are normally long, but may be oval, rectangular or trapezoidal in shape. Collective inhumation was the normal practice, although cremation sometimes occurs in Ireland. Two sites have produced radiocarbon dates before 3000 bc, demonstrating that these tombs were constructed from an early stage of the Neolithic.

coatepantli. A precinct wall elaborately decorated with a serpent motif and used principally as a means of demarcation separating ceremonial buildings from other civic architecture in Mesoamerica. It is associated especially with Late POST-CLASSIC cultures such as the TOLTEC and the AZTEC and was employed at both TULA and TENOCH-

TITLAN. A fine example still stands at TENAYUCA.

Cochise. A manifestation of the DESERT TRADITION, the locus of which was an area spanning the common borders of southwestern New Mexico and southeastern Arizona, USA. Its origins are obscure but a largely ARCHAIC lifestyle is indicated throughout its three-stage sequence. Evidence from BAT CAVE, however, indicates that some horticulture was practised in its later stages. The earliest stage, SULPHUR SPRINGS (7300-6000 bc), is followed by CHIRICAHUA (3500-1500 bc) and then by SAN PEDRO (1500-200 bc). The poorly understood Cazador phase may bridge the long hiatus between Sulphur Springs and Chiricahua, but as yet the evidence is inconclusive.

Cocijo. *See* TLALOC.

Cocle. A province on the Pacific coast of Panama where deep rectangular tombs — especially at the type site of Sitio Conte — have yielded grave goods evidencing a rich ceramic and metallurgical tradition. The extremely fine polychrome pottery is characterized by decoration of intricate geometric patterns and by stylized biomorphic forms. Gold- and tumbaga-working techniques, probably imported from Columbia, include CIRE PERDUE casting. Some stylistic congruence with TAIRONA is recognized in some artefacts, especially in the wing-shaped pendants. In addition to these grave goods, faunal evidence indicates that wife and servant sacrifice took place at the death of an important personage. Dates are largely hypothetical, but Cocle's estimated time-span is from *c*500-1000 AD with some survivals up to the time of the Spanish Conquest.

coconut. *Cocos nucifera* was probably being cultivated by AUSTRONESIAN-speakers in Island Southeast Asia by 3000 BC, although early history is obscure owing to the absence of a wild ancestral form. The palm was undoubtedly spread by Austronesians through the Pacific, perhaps eventually to the Pacific coast of central America, and westwards to India and East Africa. Charred fruits occur in Western Melanesian sites back to *c*3000 BC, and the coconut must always have been of importance in coastal tropical economies owing to its enormous range of uses. It has high salt-tolerance and the seed (the coconut itself) is easy to transport.

codex. (1) An early Christian gospel book, in the form of a handwritten manuscript, produced in one of the monastic establishments of the Post-Roman era..

(2) A type of Mesoamerican document, made of folded strips of bark or deer skin, on which various aspects of life are recorded. The information, in hieroglyphic or pictographic form, concerned astronomy, religious ceremonies, calendrics, genealogy or simple accounting. Very few pre-Conquest codices survive; the best example of these is the Codex Dresden. A number were commissioned by the Spanish, and at least some are copies of earlier works. The best known of these are the MAYAN Book of Chilam Balam, the Popol Vuh, and the AZTEC tribute lists of the Codex Mendoza.

Cody. A late PLANO tool assemblage which probably represents the last of the plains-based hunting groups. First identified at the Horner site in Cody, Wyoming, USA, it is characterized by finely-worked lanceolate blades and projectile points (e.g. Eden and Scottsbluff) and by the unique asymmetrical Cody knife.

Coedès, George (1886-1969). A French scholar who has been hailed by his colleagues as the unchallenged dean of Southeast Asian classicial scholarship. Coedès spent most of his career in French Indochina and Siam. He is best known for his major work of synthesis *The Indianized States of Southeast Asia*, first published in French in 1944 and re-edited three times; it was translated into English in 1968. The most significant of his many original contributions, published in more than 300 papers from 1904, was the discovery in 1918 of the Indonesian empire of SRĪVIJAYA.

Cohohina. *See* HAKATAYA.

Cohuna. The site of the discovery in 1925 of a cranium with morphologically robust features, excavated from a swamp close to Murray River, Victoria, Southern Australia. The age of the specimen is unknown, but it closely resembles the nearby KOW SWAMP skulls, which have dates of 11,000-7000 bc.

coinage.

Western Asia. The earliest true coins were minted in the kingdom of LYDIA in Asia Minor in the 7th century BC and were made of the gold-silver alloy electrum. In the 6th century the legendary King Kroisos (Croesus) introduced coinage of pure silver and, to a lesser extent, gold. The coins were in origin simply pieces of metal of standardized weight and stamped with designs — and later, inscriptions — identifying the issuing authority. They were almost certainly used, like most early coinage, for specialized, prestigious purposes, and not for everyday exchange. The principal Lydian mint was at the capital SARDIS. After Cyrus the Great gained control of Lydia in the 6th century, the ACHAEMENID Persians adopted a gold currency; their coins usually bear a punch mark on one side and a portrait of the king on the other. It was probably through the Achaemenid satrapy of GANDHARA that coinage was introduced to India.

Greece and Rome. The eastern Greek cities of Asia Minor adopted the new invention of coinage from their Lydian neighbours at an early stage and thereafter it spread rapidly throughout the Greek world. The early Greek coins were also made of electrum, silver or gold and were produced by the individual city states; the Greeks never adopted a copper or bronze coinage. The earliest coins were struck on one side only; then the same design appears on both sides; then, in the 6th century, separate obverse and reverse designs become common. Later the reverse often bore an inscription showing the coin's place of origin.

The first Roman coins were produced in the early 3rd century BC and were also made of precious metals. Later in that century the first bronze coin — the *as* — was introduced and this was followed by the silver *denarius* (equivalent to 10 *as*). Under the Republic coins were usually issued by senatorial decree, but in the imperial period they came under the close control of the emperors themselves, who used them for propaganda as well as economic purposes (for instance, designs commemorating important events often appeared on the reverse of the coin, while the emperor's head appeared on the obverse). The coinage was altered and devalued several times during the Empire in response to inflation and other economic pressures.

Prehistoric Europe. In the last two centuries BC, prehistoric communities in several parts of Europe, in close contact with the Romans, started to produce coins of their own. This coinage, labelled CELTIC, was produced in Austria, Switzerland, Czechoslovakia, Germany, France and southern England (associated with BELGIC groups). These coins were normally of precious metals, although some copper coins do appear. They are derived from Greek and Roman prototypes — most commonly the 4th-century gold staters of Philip II and Alexander III of Macedon — but the designs were developed by the European Iron Age craftsmen according to their own artistic traditions (*see* CELTIC ART): the naturalistic human heads and animals of the classical coins appear in highly stylized versions or are entirely transformed into complex abstract designs.

India. The earliest Indian coins were produced by the cities of the GANGES CIVILIZATION in the 5th century BC; they take the form of small bent bars or circular pieces, both made of silver and with symbols punched on both sides. The symbols show connections with ACHAEMENID Persia — the most likely source of Indian coinage. Copper coinage was only introduced in the MAURYAN period (with coins cast in moulds), whereas die-struck coins appear only in the post-Mauryan period, introduced by Indo-Greeks from Bactria. These coins established the standard type for much of the later coinage of north India, carrying representations of the king and a deity and a legend, usually including a royal title. The KUSHANS produced gold coins, as well as the more common copper and silver coinage.

China. Cowrie shells were used as money in China at least as early as the SHANG dynasty; inscriptions name them as royal gifts, and the tomb of FU HAO contained nearly 7000 cowries. Hoards of miniature bronze axes suggest that these also served as money in Shang times, at least in the Yangzi region. A few bronze copies of cowries are known from the latter part of the Shang dynasty (12th-11th centuries BC) but metal coins were not in wide use until the EASTERN ZHOU period, and even then did not replace cowries altogether. Eastern Zhou coins were usually of bronze, though a few silver coins have been found; they fall into two main categories, spade-shaped and knife-shaped, varying in size,

shape and inscription according to the issuing state or city. Unlike coins made in the West, Chinese coins were not as a rule minted (i.e. struck) but nearly always cast, inscription and all. In the Yangzi region, however, the Eastern Zhou state of CHU circulated both bronze cowries and gold bars, the latter stamped with mint marks. Towards the end of Eastern Zhou several states began issuing round coins provided with holes for stringing, and such coins were made standard throughout the country after the QIN unification in 221 BC. The Qin coin, round with a square hole, remained the pattern for Chinese coins until the 19th century.

Coixtlahuaca. *See* MIXTEC.

Čoka [Csóka]. A TELL settlement of the later Neolithic period, located in the middle Tisa Valley in the Yugoslav Banat and dated to the late 5th to early 4th millennium bc. Totally excavated by F. Móra in the first decade of this century, the site has two main chronological phases: a mixed SZAKALHÁT-Early VINČA horizon, and a mixed TISZA-Late Vinča horizon. These 'mixed' assemblages denote overlap zones in pottery consumption rather than ethnic differences and occur throughout the Neolithic of the north Banat. Two of the earliest hoards of jewellery in the Balkan Neolithic occur in the Szakalhát layers and include shell, bone and stone ornaments and malachite rings. Workshops for making antler harpoons and bone finger rings are known from the Tisza levels.

Colchaqui. *See* DIAGUITA.

Colchester [Roman Camulodunum]. A city in southeast England, some 80 km northeast of London, formerly an Iron Age Celtic settlement (*oppidum*) surrounded by dykes. It was the capital of the tribal chieftain, Cunobelinus, who seems to have been known to the Romans as King of the Britons. This local importance probably made the site a principal objective for the Romans in their invasion of 43 AD, and it is possible that some kind of military camp was established here almost at once. Certainly, in the year 49 the Romans built here their first colonial town (COLONIA), alongside the town of Cunobelinus, and they may have intended this as their capital for the new province, since a huge temple was erected to the Emperor

Claudius, in Roman style, and with massive vaulted substructures which still survive. Destroyed in BOUDICCA'S rebellion of 60-61, the site was subsequently rebuilt as a pleasant Roman provincial town, eventually extending to some 44 hectares with stone walls (partly surviving, as at the Balkerne Gate), houses with painted wall plaster and mosaics, and sizeable cemeteries.

Coldstream Cave. A cave near Humansdorp on the southern Cape coast of South Africa. Particular interest attaches to a painted stone from a grave associated with a microlithic industry of WILTON type. The stone, some 300 mm across, depicts three human figures in polychrome, one of which appears to be holding a palette and painting utensils.

cold working. Most METALS, such as COPPER, BRONZE, GOLD and SILVER, are soft enough to be worked whilst cold. Operations such as hammering and beating (including REPOUSSÉ and CHASING), cutting and engraving could be carried out without any heating to make the metal softer. IRON and STEEL, by contrast, have to be heated before they can be shaped (*see* FORGING). Most of the softer metals, however, cannot be cold worked indefinitely. With continous working, the metal becomes brittle and eventually fractures. This has to be counteracted by periodic gentle heating of the metal, called ANNEALING. If the annealing is carried out correctly, it allows crystals within the metal to recrystallize and so distribute the stress that has built up. Cold working can then go on until the metal becomes brittle again. METALLOGRAPHIC EXAMINATION, by study of the crystal structure, can yield information about the cold working and annealing processes in the last stages of making an artefact. Pure gold is one of the few metals that can be cold worked indefinitely without annealing.

coleoptera. An order of the class Insecta, comprising the BEETLES.

Colla. *See* AYMARA.

collagen. The major organic component of BONE. It is the best part of bone for RADIO-CARBON DATING and can be extracted by dissolving the mineral component of bone with an acid. Very old bone may need a large sample to produce enough collagen for a date.

collared urn. A special type of URN used in the British Early Bronze Age. Previously called an 'overhanging rim urn', the collared urn has a developed rim which may be straight, convex or slightly concave in profile. Decoration is normally confined either to the rim alone or to the upper half of the vessel. Collared urns were normally used to contain cremation burials, though some have been found in apparently domestic contexts.

Collingwood Bay. *See* NEW GUINEA.

colluvial. Resulting from SOIL erosion. Colluvial deposits accumulate at the bottom of slopes, where soils above have lost their structure and are being eroded. This is frequently caused by man's clearance of forest, ploughing and cultivation. Typically, colluvial material has gathered in the dry valleys of the chalklands. Fans of colluvial material may be found at the foot of escarpments or valley sides. Where field boundaries present a barrier to downslope movement, step-like features called LYNCHETS develop.

Cô-loa. Capital of the kingdom of ÂU-LAC which existed from 258 to 207 BC. Situated about 20 km northwest of Hanoi in northern Vietnam, it comprised three walls more than 4 km long which surrounded the city in a spiral; hence the nick-name of 'Conch-City'. When Vietnam became independent from China in the 10th century, Cô-loa was again chosen as the site of the capital in order to renew links with the pre-Chinese past. *See also* DONG-SON.

Cologne [Roman Colonia Agrippinensis]. City on the left bank of the Rhine, West Germany. In about AD 50 a Roman COLONIA was founded here by the emperor Claudius at the prompting of his wife Agrippina who, Tacitus tells us, was connected with the area by birth. Formerly, from 38 BC, there had been a modest town, established for the local (and co-operative) tribe of the Ubii by Agrippa. Later (perhaps 5-9 AD) a ceremonial altar to Rome and Augustus (*ara Romae et Augusti*) had been added, and the area strengthened by a legionary camp. Now the new *colonia* became the capital of the province of Lower Germania, an important commercial centre and the regional mint. Numerous, if unspectacular, traces of the Roman period survive, including the principal elements of the street plan, town walls and gates, Roman and 'Gallo-Roman' temples, water installations, Rhine port, bridges and fort, pottery and glass factories, villas and cemeteries.

In the 5th century, the Roman town was overrun by the FRANKS and their famous leader Clovis was baptized here. Throughout the Frankish and CAROLINGIAN periods and during much of the Middle Ages Cologne was a major bishopric and a leading commercial and cultural centre.

Cologne suffered enormous devastation in World War II and the destruction provided an opportunity for large-scale archaeological investigation. The impressive Roman praetorium and two early extra-mural martyr churches of St Gereon and St Severin were excavated, but the investigations in and around the cathedral have proved of the greatest interest. These established that the Gothic cathedral overlies a Roman temple and a complex sequence of Merovingian and Carolingian churches. In the course of the excavations, two spectacular Frankish royal graves dating to the mid-6th century were uncovered. The first of these belonged to a woman buried with fine garments, gold belt, fibula and head band, a bucket, glasses and flask of wine. The second was of a small boy laid to rest in the manner of a warrior; he was clothed in finery and lay on a wooden bed, wearing a miniature helmet and surrounded by full-size ceremonial weapons. These internments were placed in a small eastern chapel which was later converted into the ambo of the mid-8th-century church. This first Carolingian church had a ring crypt at its eastern end and an open ambulatory at the west end, both of which contained altars. The west end was embellished by a magnificent west work. This church was soon replaced by a larger building constructed by Bishop Willibert in 870 with two choirs, transepts, and an apse flanked by two round towers with a lower ring crypt. This church remained until 1248, when work on the present Gothic cathedral commenced.

colonia. The Latin name given in the later Republican and imperial Roman periods to a township, often of retired veteran soliders, strategically placed to defend imperial interests. A self-governing constitution imitated that of Rome, and the citizens had either full (Roman) citizenship or limited (Latin) citizenship.

Colosseum. Ancient and modern nick-name for the Flavian Amphitheatre in Rome, construction of which began under the reign of the emperor Vespasian (AD 69-79). The name apparently derived from an adjacent colossal statue. *See* AMPHITHEATRE.

colour-coated wares. Many kinds of pottery in the Greek and Roman periods were given an extra surface coating, usually slightly glossy and most often red. Recent research suggests that the coating was made from fine clay particles suspended in water with a peptizing agent added; iron oxide produced the red, and illite the gloss.

Colt Hoare, Sir Richard (1758-1838). British antiquary who excavated a large number of BARROWS mostly on Salisbury plain. His excavation techniques were relatively good for his time, but due to the undeveloped state of the study he was unable to date any of the material he found.

columbarium [Latin: dovecot]. The name derives from the pigeon-holes (*loculi*) provided for cinerary urns and other ash containers, which characteristically lined the funerary complexes of certain large Roman households. This type of burial is typically afforded to the large staff of slaves and freedmen, and probably derives ultimately from ETRUSCAN examples. *See also* CATACOMB.

column. A Latin architectural term denoting a cylindrical pillar, usually of wood or stone. In classical architecture a column is visually composed of three parts, the base (not always present), shaft and CAPITAL. The shaft, when of stone, would typically be made up of several superimposed drums, so jointed and pinned together as to appear completely flush. The column was normally tapered upwards (though not always uniformly, as bulging 'cigar'-shapes, *entasis*, are also found) and the surface was finished with vertical fluting.

Columnata. A site some 200 km southwest of Algiers which has yielded human skeletons of MECHTA-AFALOU type associated with a stone industry of IBEROMAURUSIAN affinities. Some of the burials were accompanied by red ochre and perforated shell ornaments, often covered with settings of stones and, in one case, bones of wild cattle. By about 8000 bc the Iberomaurusian was replaced by a local blade industry which has been named Columnatan.

Combe Grenal. A site near Domme on the Dordogne River, southwest France. With some 64 archaeological levels, the large rock shelter and small cave have the largest number of culture levels of any PALAEOLITHIC site known to date. The 55 MOUSTERIAN levels have formed the basis for the analysis of the Mousterian into five main types. The bottom nine levels are ACHEULIAN and are believed to precede the last interglacial. A burial pit has been recognized in the Mousterian levels, and some human bones are also known. The site has fauna and pollen evidence from all levels.

computers. Machines which can be programmed to calculate and compare, store and manipulate information. They consist of four main components: (1) a central processing unit, in which program instructions are interpreted and calculations carried out; (2) storage units, where information may be held temporarily or permanently; (3) input facilities, into which are fed instructions and information; (4) output units, from which the results can be obtained.

Computers are controlled by a program called the operating system. Instructions are input as a series of codes and key words that the system interprets and causes the computer to obey. Additional programs can be written in a number of international 'high level' languages, which the system converts to a code that the computer can 'understand'. Such programs may then be run by issuing the appropriate commands to the operating system. Programs have been written to carry out, for example, STATISTICAL calculations, MULTI-VARIATE ANALYSIS, DATABASE MANAGE-MENT, SIMULATION and GRAPHICS.

Computers may be of any size, from the vast 'mainframe' machines, to microprocessors and small programmable calculators. Mainframe computers are normally shared between a large number of activities. Microprocessors are so cheap that they can be dedicated to one user or one operation. Archaeology already uses computers widely. Microprocessors have started to make their appearances as finds- and site-recording

systems, controllers of measuring devices etc.

Conca d'Oro. A Copper Age culture in northwest Sicily, which takes its name from the area around Palermo. A number of cemeteries of rock-cut tombs of the *a forno* or oven-shaped type have been investigated. They were used for collective burial, and the associated grave goods include pottery vessels and stone and occasional metal tools and weapons. As well as pottery of purely local style, imported BEAKER pottery occurs, as well as a local imitation known as the 'Carini beaker'. A 3rd millennium BC date seems likely, although we lack radiocarbon dates.

Conchopata. A site dating to the Early MIDDLE HORIZON, located in the Ayacucho Valley near HUARI, Peru, and probably the site of a religious shrine. Large beaker-shaped urns, intentionally smashed and concentrated in only a few locations, appear to have votive or some other ceremonial significance. The polychrome decoration is distinctive but is clearly TIAHUANACO-influenced: depictions of the 'Gateway God' are common. Concho-pata materials frequently appear in early Huari contexts.

Conelle. Ditched settlement site near Arcevia in the Marche, which, together with the site of Ortucchio in Abruzzo, has given its name to a Copper Age culture of east central Italy (Conelle-Ortucchio group). The characteristic pottery is decorated with bands of impressed dots.

Constantinople. *See* BYZANTIUM.

contamination. In general, the term contamination is applied to SAMPLES of archaeological deposits or materials which have been affected by contact with other matter. In particular the term is often applied to samples taken for RADIOCARBON DATING which have been affected by their environment. For instance, they may have been contaminated by HUMUS. The humus, which also contains carbon, may be much younger than the sample, thus resulting in an inaccurate date. Samples that have been contaminated in this way can be treated with sodium hydroxide to dissolve out the humus. Dates are then determined for the treated sample and the dissolved 'humate' separately. This makes it possible to see how much contamination has occurred.

convergence. Term used to describe the appearance of similar traits or techniques in different contexts, as a result of parallel or converging evolution (in contrast to DIFFUSION).

Cook, Captain James (1728-79). From 1769 until his death in the HAWAIIAN ISLANDS in 1779, the great English navigator made three voyages of exploration in the Pacific and made many discoveries in POLYNESIA and Australia. Cook was not the first European to discover most of the islands he visited, but his accounts of the native peoples of Polynesia, MELANESIA and Australia at the crucial point of first European contact are by far the most important in maritime history. His journals are used constantly by archaeologists who work in the Pacific region.

Cook Islands. An extensive island group in the central Pacific, settled by POLYNESIANS about 1000 to 1500 years ago. Archaeological excavations have been undertaken on Rarotonga, Aitutaki and Penrhyn, and many islands of the group have well-preserved examples of Polynesian temples (MARAE).

coombe rock. A PERIGLACIAL deposit that results from solifluction (*see* PERIGLACIAL).

Copan. An important CLASSIC PERIOD centre of the Southern MAYA located in western Honduras on the Rio Copan, a tributary of the Rio Motagua. Although it is a CEREMONIAL CENTRE of massive proportions, including temple-PYRAMIDS, plazas and a BALL COURT, Copan is best known for its ornate stone carving. 20 elaborately carved STELAE, unusual in that they are carved in the round, are clustered in the north end of the site.

Buildings are constructed in a locally available greenish volcanic tuff, and almost all have some heavy relief carving in this unique regional style. Access to the Acropolis (the central complex of the site) is gained via the Hieroglyphic Stairway, the 63 risers of which are carved with some 2500 hieroglyphs.

J.L. Stephens visited the site in 1839 and 'purchased' it for a mere $50. Since then much of the beautiful carving has deteriorated, but the highly detailed pen-and-ink drawings of his colleague Frederick Catherwood still survive and are a great source of iconographic detail.

Coppa Nevigata. A site on the coast of southeast Italy. The first occupation was by a community of shellfish-gatherers, who have left us no trace of other economic activities, though these may well have been practised; they used IMPRESSED WARE and a specialized microlithic flint industry, and may have been present as early as the 7th millennium bc. A later occupation belongs to the APENNINE BRONZE AGE. At this stage the site was defended by a substantial stone wall.

copper. A relatively soft metal, which can be COLD WORKED and melts at a low enough temperature to be cast using the technology available in antiquity. The metal occurs, rarely, as nuggets of native copper; it is in this form that it was first worked by man. More frequently, copper is obtained from ores. These are quite widely found, and may be oxide ores (including MALACHITE) or sulphide ores. SMELTING of these ores can be accomplished in a simple furnace, assisted by bellows. The oxide ores involve the least complicated smelting process. The resulting copper ingot could be cold worked or remelted and cast in a MOULD. 'Pure' copper may contain up to one per cent of impurities. The concentrations of these impurities may indicate the source of the ore. The metal is said to be an ALLOY when it contains more than one per cent of another element. Tin BRONZE thus contains more than one per cent TIN. European Early Bronze Age copper-based artefacts may also contain quantities of ARSENIC. These fall into two groups. Those with one per cent or less arsenic are classed as 'pure' copper. Others, which commonly have two or three per cent arsenic (sometimes as much as seven per cent) can be classed as arsenical copper alloys. These may come from an ore body particularly rich in arsenic or may be deliberate alloys. Arsenical copper alloys have some advantages over pure copper in ease of casting and in the hardness of a hammered edge.

Copper occurs fairly widely in the Old World, and was first used in Western Asia before 6000 bc, though it did not come into common use until after 4000 bc. It was also used by prehistoric communities in the New

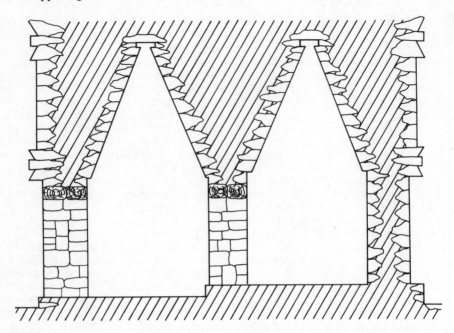

Maya corbelled arch

World, both in the Arctic area and in South America.

Copper Age. Another term for CHALCO-LITHIC. *See also* THREE AGE SYSTEM.

Coppergate. *See* YORK.

coprolite. Fossilized animal droppings. These are preserved on a variety of archaeological sites, coming from a whole range of animals, including man. The contents can be analysed and food plants, animals and parasites identified.

corbel, corbelling. A way of building in stone that can be used to bridge columns or walls or to roof chambers, but which lacks the keystones of the true arch or vault. It is built up of successive stones each of which juts out over the one below until the gap can be closed by a simple CAPSTONE. This method of roofing, sometimes labelled a false vault, was used in some of the PASSAGE GRAVES of prehistoric Western Europe, such as NEW GRANGE and MAES HOWE, and in the THOLOS tombs of the MYCENAEAN world. The corbelled arch was also a hallmark of Classic MAYA architecture in Central America. Its earliest expression is in Late CHICANEL tombs at TIKAL and ALTAR DE SACRIFICIOS.

Corbridge [Roman Corstopitum]. A Roman fort in northeast England, situated on the north bank of the River Tyne at the point where the Roman York-Scotland road (Dere Street) forked for Carlisle (the so-called STANEGATE road). Probably first established by the governor Agricola in 79-80 AD, it was burnt and re-erected in *c*105, only to be neglected once more *c*124, when HADRIAN'S WALL with its own forts was built not far to the north. In about 139, when the Roman frontier was pushed further north, the fort was reconstructed in stone, presumably reflecting increased strategic importance. Later, when the frontier fell back to Hadrian's Wall once again, Corbridge flourished as a market town and a military supply depot. Remains of military quarters, granaries and temples may still be seen.

Corded Ware. A culture found over large parts of the north European plain in the earlier

3rd millennium BC. The characteristic pottery, which has given its name to the culture, is decorated with twisted cord impressions; the most common forms are beakers and amphorae. Associated characteristics are stone battle-axes and the practice of single burial under round barrows; some groups also had metal artefacts. There is some evidence that Corded Ware people had domesticated horses and wheeled vehicles, and they are sometimes interpreted as nomadic groups — possibly Indo-European speaking — who spread across northern Europe from the east. A closely related group is the GLOBULAR AMPHORA culture.

Cordoba. Early in the 8th century, Visigothic Spain was conquered by the Arabs and became the independent caliphate of Al Andalus with its capital at Cordoba. The city quickly rose to become one of the finest in Europe, rivalled only by Baghdad and Constantinople for its wealth and splendour. Cordoba was a centre of culture and learning where the arts and sciences flourished; by the 10th century it was described as the 'Jewel of the World' because of its schools, libraries and mosques. In 785 the Emir Abd al Rahman built his great mosque, which remains as testimony to the glory of Muslim Spain; the mosque is square in plan, with an outer court-yard and an interior hall divided by parallel arcades supported on slender columns. In the 10th century, one of the rulers of Cordoba built a pleasure-city outside its walls known as Medina al Zahara; this is now an archaeological site, where the remains give an impression of buildings adorned with luxurious and costly materials.

core. Any lump or nodule of stone from which FLAKES have been intentionally removed. Frequently, cores are of special types, shaped to facilitate the removal of particular blanks like BLADES or bladelets, or large oval flakes with a sharp edge all round. The most distinctive cores of the last-mentioned kind are called tortoise cores, from their resemblance to that animal, and are associated with LEVAL-LOISIAN technology.

Corinth. Major ancient Greek city on the Isthmus of Corinth, excavated since 1896 by the American School of Classical Studies at Athens. The city, with its exceptionally high acropolis on Acrocorinth Hill, profited from having ports on both the Corinthian and Saronic Gulfs and was an important trading city at most periods.

Prehistoric settlement is well documented and there is evidence of a Neolithic and an Early Bronze Age settlement at Corinth, both apparently of considerable size. By contrast, there is rather little evidence of MYCENAEAN settlement and, although enough has been found to indicate some activity at this period, Corinth was clearly not a major Mycenaean site. The next major settlement belongs to the Dark Age, beginning perhaps in the late 10th century BC. Thereafter Corinth was a very

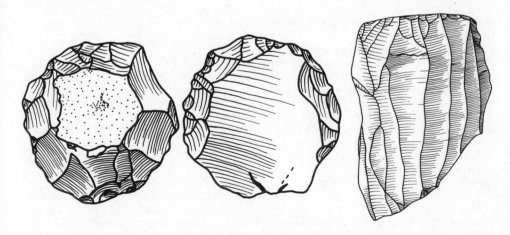

Cores: prepared core (left and centre) and blade core (right)

important city throughout the Archaic, Classical and Hellenistic periods.

During the period of Greek colonization Corinth founded colonies at Corcyra and SYRACUSE. From c720-570 BC Corinthian painted vases in the BLACK-FIGURE technique (which the Corinthians invented, although it is best known in the Athenian or ATTIC version) were exported all over the Greek world. Workshops dating to this period have been excavated in the potters' quarter at Corinth, producing both pottery and terracottas. Corinthian pottery provides the most useful dating method available to archaeologists studying this period.

In the 6th century BC a fine limestone Doric temple, which is still standing, was raised to Apollo; this replaced an earlier temple, built in the early 7th century. The Pirene fountain may also have been built in the 6th century.In the next century Callimachus is said to have invented the CORINTHIAN column capital here c 450-425 BC. The city flourished until a Roman punitive destruction in 146 BC. In 44 BC it was re-founded as a Roman colony and flourished again.

Many of the visible remains date from the classical Greek and especially the early Roman periods. These include Lechaion Street; the Roman market place (agora) with vaulted shops where St Paul doubtless spoke in AD 51-2; the Odeon and the refurbished Pirene fountain; the Glauke fountain; temples; baths; a basilica; a theatre and amphitheatre; houses with mosaics and (in the Museum) sculptures. Parts of the classical fortifications on the acropolis survive, re-used in the medieval period: the defences of this time are well-preserved.

The American expedition's work included valuable studies of the Byzantine and later periods at Corinth. Various buildings, for example, betray a violent phase towards the end of the 6th century AD, while the hypothetical Metropolitan Church in the Julian Basilica decayed and disappeared. The buildings in the South Stoa area became ruinous while the Central Stairway in this monumental complex was pulled apart. There are clear signs of urban revival in the 10-12th centuries and among the structures from this period there were several churches, town houses and a pottery kiln. In 1082 the Venetians were allowed to use the port and from then on its buildings take on a grander air. In the later medieval period it then passed from Frankish to Venetian and eventually to Turkish hands. Substantial buildings from all these periods were found in these excavations.

Corinthian. In traditional classical archaeology, used principally of:
(1) an important stage of Greek vase-painting, notably the Proto-Corinthian and Corinthian schools of c720-550 BC, to which may be attributed perhaps the invention of BLACK-FIGURE technique, and some new shapes, such as the graceful ARYBALLOS;
(2) the Corinthian 'order' in classical architecture, characterized by a capital having a bell-shaped echinus (see CAPITAL) decorated with a combination of spiral and plant (especially acanthus) motifs. The innovation is traditionally ascribed to Callimachus of Corinth (c450-425 BC). The Corinthian capital became very popular with Roman architects, who adapted it in many free variations, and reappears again in the so-called 'composite' order — a combination of four-sided IONIC and Corinthian. See also CORINTH.

correlation. (1) In STATISTICS, correlation means the degree of relation between VARIABLES. Correlations between pairs of variables may be calculated using a correlation coefficient. MULTIVARIATE techniques for assessing correlation also exist.

(2) In geology, the term correlation refers to the relation of one stratigraphical unit with another, by petrological, osteological or palaeontological means. It may also be used in this way to refer to stratigraphical units on archaeological sites.

Cortaillod. A LAKE VILLAGE on the edge of Lake Neuchâtel, and type site of the earliest NEOLITHIC culture in western Switzerland. The houses were built on wooden frames with walls of clay set on closely spaced timbers; the roofs were probably thatched. The inhabitants practised mixed farming, but supplemented their diet with the products of hunting and fishing. The round-based dark burnished pottery demonstrates connections with the CHASSEY culture of France. The lakeside positions of many Cortaillod sites has ensured the survival of a large number of wooden and birch-bark utensils and containers, and also many plant remains, including fruits and nuts, as well as cereals, pulses and flax. Dates for the Cortaillod culture begin *c*3000 bc (*c*3800 BC).

Cortes de Navarra. A settlement site in the Ebro valley, northern Spain, occupied during the 1st millennium BC. The site is really a TELL, as the building material used was mud-brick and successive rebuildings raised the level of the site. The houses were rectangular and arranged in rows. The cultural material is said to show some URNFIELD characteristics and some archaeologists regard the appearance of such traits in southern France and northern Spain in the early 1st millennium BC as indicating the movement of CELTIC groups into the area.

Cosa [Modern Ansedonia]. A town on the west coast of Italy, some 140 km north of Rome. Cosa was a Latin colony, founded on a coastal crag in 273 BC to confirm Roman domination in an area that was still felt to be too strongly ETRUSCAN. The fate of Etruscan Cusi (from which the Roman name derives) is obscure, and the site has not been identified. Roman Cosa enjoyed its greatest prosperity under the later Republic. Massive polygonal masonry survives, as do remains of the grid street-plan, FORUM, BASILICA and citadel. Some of the engineering in the port area may be Etruscan. The Imperial period brought a decline, although there is some use into the 3rd century AD. Later, in the 4th-5th centuries, the ruins of the forum became the centre of a large estate.

costrel. A medieval pottery flask. Flasks were probably very common in the Middle Ages, but most were made of leather and have not survived. MEROVINGIAN and CAROLINGIAN pottery costrels tend to be roughly round in shap, with a slight neck into which a stopper was rammed. The best-known is the Zelzate costrel, made in the 'BADORF-type' industries of the central Rhineland, which contained a Viking-period hoard dating to 870. The other well-known type is the barrel variant found in 13th—16th-century contexts, and probably made in northern and western France. Barrel costrels were in great demand and were widely traded; a hoard of them was found in Winchester.

Coţofeni. Eponymous site of a widespread Late Copper Age culture distributed over most of Rumania and dated to the 3rd millennium bc. The preponderance of sites are small, short-lived settlements with an altitudinal range from the lowest Danube flood plain to high mountain plateaux. Seasonality and presumably pastoralism was important in Coţofeni economies, although agriculture and fishing is also evidenced. Most burial sites used inhumation rites, although cremation is found. Although poor in metal, Coţofeni sites have a rich pottery assemblage with *Furstenstich* and lentil-impressed decoration (*Linsenkeramik*).

Cotte de St Brelade. A cave with PALAEO-LITHIC occupation in the granite of St Brelade's Bay, Jersey. A long sequence of MOUSTERIAN levels is known, and beach deposits possibly of last interglacial date intervene in the sequence, suggesting a pre-Mousterian age for the first occupation levels. Human remains include large teeth and a piece of a child's skull, presumed to be NEANDER-THAL.

cotton. Plants of the genus *Gossypium*, cultivated for their hairy flowering heads, from which come fibres widely used in textiles. There are some 30 diploid (with two sets of chromosones) members of the genus — all of which originated in the Old World — and 4 tetraploid (four sets of chromosones) species, originating in the New World. Most of today's cotton is produced from the cultivated tetraploid species *G. hirsutum* and *G. barbadense*; very little is grown of the cultivated diploids *G. herbaceum* and *G. arboreum*. The earliest cotton yet found comes from the site of MEHR-GARH in Pakistan, where it was probably being cultivated before 4000 BC. Actual cotton fabrics appear in the same area at MOHENJO-DARO at about 2500 BC. The earliest finds of cotton in the New World are from Mexico and Peru, at about 3500 BC. The Mexican finds are of domestic *G. hirsutum*, already considerably different from the wild hirsutum which is found today through Mexico and the Caribbean. The Peruvian finds are intermediate between the wild and domestic forms of *G. barbadense* found in the area today.

counterscarp bank. Low bank found on the outer side of a defensive ditch, most of the material from which has gone into the main bank on the inner side. The purpose of counterscarp banks is unclear, since they do not enhance the defensive value of the earthwork; they may have served to provide visual emphasis for the main bank and ditch. They are commonly found on the HILLFORTS of the British Iron Age, but also occur on earthworks of other periods and in other areas.

coup de poing. French name for the PALAEOLITHIC tool type known in English as a HAND AXE.

court cairn. *See* CLYDE-CARLINGFORD TOMBS.

court markers. *See* BALL GAME.

Covalanas. An Upper PALAEOLITHIC painted cave in the Cantabrian region of northern Spain. The style, including a finger-blob technique, suggests that it belongs to a primitive stage of cave art, possibly preceding the SOLUTRIAN.

cover-sand. *See* LOESS.

Coveta de l'Or. A cave in eastern Spain near Valencia. An Early NEOLITHIC level with IMPRESSED WARE has produced remains of einkorn, emmer and bread wheats, and naked barley, together with radiocarbon dates of the mid-5th millennium bc. Large deep pottery jars may have been used for grain storage.

Coxcatlan. *See* TEHUACAN VALLEY.

Coyotlatelco. A ceramic horizon of the Early POST-CLASSIC PERIOD which begins to occur in central Mexican Mesoamerica following the fall of TEOTIHUACAN. A distinctive red-on-buff painted ware, it appears in the early phases of both TULA and CHOLULA, and is a forerunner of the late MAZAPAN style.

Cozumel. An island located 16 km off the east coast of the northern Yucatan Peninsula in Mexico. Although its earliest artefacts date to *c* 1000 bc, its major period of occupation was in the POST-CLASSIC. Important as a redistribution centre in coastal trade networks, it was coincidentally a place of pilgrimage to the MAYAN moon goddess Ix Chel. Its ceremonial architecture, however, is considerably more modest than the great CLASSIC centres of the mainland. Under the control of the PUTUN for some time, Cozumel is the putative starting-point for the Itza migrations into the northern Yucatan.

The Conquistadore Hernan Cortes briefly reviewed his small army here in February 1519.

Cracow [Kraków]. A city in western Poland, situated on the once-great trade route which ran across Europe to BYZANTIUM in the early middle ages. Excavations have revealed that by the 10th century there was a well-established trading centre here, with a large fortified acropolis containing stone palaces and churches. The lower part of the town was mostly devoted to artisans' workshops.

crannog. A small artificial island constructed beside or in the middle of a lake, usually defended by a wooden palisade and supporting houses. Crannogs are confined to Ireland and Scotland; their origins are believed to go back to the pre-Roman Iron Age period, and on many of them occupation continued throughout the medieval period. As monuments, crannogs are not very impressive, and perhaps the most interesting is that in LOUGH GUR, Co. Limerick. Excavations at Lagore crannog revealed an extremely rich royal site of Early Christian date.

crater [Greek: 'mixing bowl']. Originally a vessel for the mixing of wine with water, the normal custom in antiquity. In the study of classical Greek vases, the term is usually applied to a fairly large vessel with deep round bowl and wide mouth, standing on a broad base. The classification is normally subdivided into four types: column crater, volute crater, calyx crater and bell crater, which take their names from the characteristic shape either of the handle or of the body of the vase.

Crawford, O.G.S. (1886-1957). British archaeologist who made many contributions to the development of archaeology. Like Cyril FOX, Crawford brought a geographical approach to his studies; as Archaeological Officer of the Ordnance Survey, he was largely responsible for the high standard of mapping of archaeological sites in Britain. He made major contributions to the development of AERIAL PHOTOGRAPHY for archaeological purposes. Another interest was the dissemination of the results of archaeological research to a wider public; in 1927 he founded the journal *Antiquity*, which he edited until his death in 1957.

Creswell. The Creswell Crags group in a limestone gorge in Derbyshire, northern England, includes two caves with MOUSTERIAN levels, Robin Hood's Cave and Pin Hole Cave. In addition, Pin Hole has an early Upper PALAEOLITHIC level and all the caves in the gorge have a late Upper Palaeolithic usually called Creswellian, with some points of similarity to the latest MAGDALENIAN. Two engraved art objects are known, and there are miscellaneous and poorly documented human remains.

Crickley Hill. Neolithic CAUSEWAYED CAMP and Iron Age HILLFORT in Gloucestershire, southwest England. The Neolithic site was used for several centuries and the ditches and banks were refurbished several times. The final Neolithic phase had deeper quarry ditches and a rampart faced with drystone walling at the front and a timber stockade at the back and a wooden fence on the top. This substantial defensive work was pierced by two gateways; evidence of burning and finds of many flint arrowheads indicate that the site was attacked and burnt down around 2500 BC. The site was abandoned for nearly two millennia, when it was once again used for a defended settlement. Two phases of Iron Age occupation are represented, probably falling between 700 and 500 BC. The site was defended by a substantial drystone wall and ditch, with a single entrance. The earlier phase was characterized by rectangular houses and square storage huts, while the second phase had one large round house, smaller round buildings and more small square huts, perhaps granaries. The site was burned down for the last time *c*500 BC and never reoccupied.

Criş. *See* FIRST TEMPERATE NEOLITHIC.

Crnolačka Bara. A three-level occupation site of the late STARČEVO, early and late VINČA periods, located in the low foothills east of the middle Morava valley in Serbia, Yugoslavia. The site indicates repeated, intermittent occupation rather than continuous settlement of a preferred long-term site.

Cromagnon. A small cave at the edge of the village of LES EYZIES in the Dordogne, southwest France. In 1868 several skeletons were found here, resting on the Upper PALAEOLITHIC levels. Their exact age is not well established, and might be anything in the range 28,000 to 10,000 bc. Nevertheless, these finds have given their name to the type of fossil man found in the European Upper Palaeolithic, which in turn is usually grouped with modern man.

Cromerian. The Cromerian stage is a group of INTERGLACIAL deposits of the QUATERNARY system in Britain. These deposits are stratified under ANGLIAN glacial deposits and above an extensive sequence of earlier Quaternary deposits. The type site of the stage is at West Runton, Norfolk, but a number of other deposits have been correlated with it — from Suffolk, Oxfordshire and Somerset.

Confusion may arise from the use of 'Cromerian Complex' to describe part of the Quaternary succession in northwest Europe. In this case, the term is used to describe a group of deposits representing several interglacials and intervening cold stages. These deposits are stratified below ELSTER glacial deposits and above a sequence extending back into the PLIOCENE. The Brunhes/Matuyama boundary of *c*700,000 BP (*see* PALAEOMAGNETISM) occurs within the European 'Cromerian Complex', but it is unclear how these deposits should be correlated with the Quaternary of Britain. *See* Tables 5 and 6, pages 418-9.

cromlech. A Welsh term applied to all MEGALITHIC tombs, sometimes used in France to apply to STONE CIRCLES as well. The term is no longer used by archaeologists, but persists in popular usage in Wales.

crop marks. Variations in the colour or growth of a crop or other vegetation, shown on an aerial photograph, may reveal the buried walls, ditches and pits of an archaeological site. In particular, buried pits and ditches may retain moisture better than the surrounding subsoil, and during a dry spell plant growth is often enhanced over such features. Crop marks of this kind are best seen during a dry summer, and in drier areas.

crossbow. A bow made with a crossbow parallel to the arrow and operated by a mechanical trigger release. The crossbow appeared in China no later than the 4th century BC (some scholars say far earlier) and may be a Chinese invention. Cast-bronze trigger mechanisms are commonly found in late Eastern ZHOU burials along with inlaid bronze bow fittings and bronze arrow points; the arrow points, sometimes fitted to IRON shanks, either carry three low fins or are round in cross-section, without fins.

cross dating. DATING by relation to established chronologies. Artefacts from an archaeological site are often dated by correlation with typologies of similar artefacts in the surrounding area. The method is based on the assumption that typologies evolved at the same rate and in the same way over a wide area or alternatively on assumptions of DIFFUSION. By itself, a cross-dated chronology does not give absolute dates (*see* SEQUENCE DATING), but it may be calibrated by reference to other dating methods. The Swedish prehistorian Oscar MONTELIUS built up a chronology for prehistoric Europe by cross dating to the historical chronologies of Egypt and Mesopotamia, and this was further developed by Gordon CHILDE. Unfortunately, RADIO-CARBON DATES have demonstrated that these chronologies for Europe were in many cases erroneous (in some cases by a millennium or more) and it seems that the typological comparisons on which they were based were insufficiently rigorous. A kind of cross dating has always been used in geology, and stratigraphical sequences are often correlated by the assemblages of fossils they contain; this is known as biostratigraphy. The archaeological version of cross dating may have been developed directly out of the geological method and may have been' based on a false analogy between biological fossils and archaeological artefacts.

crucible. A vessel, usually of pottery, in which METAL may be melted. This process may be carried out for extraction, ALLOYING or CASTING.

cruck. A simple, easily constructed form of timber-framed building, well known from the 13th century onwards and most commonly used for barns, farm buildings and dwellings. The distinguishing feature of the cruck, as opposed to box-frame construction, is that the essential longitudinal supports take the form of a series of curved, triangular trusses, connected by purlins and provided with vertical in-filled walls. The main paired timbers are usually the identical halves of one tree trunk. Not only was this form of building easy to design and raise but it proved a very effective means of distributing the load of the roof through the walls down to the ground. True crucks have no break between the wall timbers and those of the roof, but there are many variations and adaptions of this particular idea, for example, what are known as base crucks, half crucks, raised crucks and upper crucks, all of which contain some element of the curved, paired truss.

Crvena Stijena. A long-lived cave site in the karstlands of the southern Dinaric mountains, located in the Trebišnjica Valley 20 km inland from Dubrovnik, in Dalmatia, Yugoslavia. 31 levels have been distinguished in a 20-metre stratigraphy: XXXI-V, Palaeolithic, with deposits of the MOUSTERIAN and Upper Palaeolithic covering the last two major glaciations; IVb-IVa, Early and Late Mesolithic respectively, with microlithic flint industries and a large faunal sample dominated by red deer and chamois; III, pottery of Early Neolithic IMPRESSED WARE type associated with a fauna dominated by hunted mammals; II, pottery of DANILO-KAKANJ style associated with wild mammal bones and a macrolithic flint industry; I, a Late Bronze Age level with HALLSTATT A-B metalwork.

cryoturbation. *See* PERIGLACIAL

Cucuteni-Tripolye. The double-barrelled name indicates national terminology for a more-or-less identical cultural assemblage. Cucuteni, the Rumanian version, distributed over Moldavia, is divided into stages: Pre-Cucuteni, Cucuteni A, AB and B, dating *c*4200-3000 bc. Tripolye, the Russian version, spreading eastwards across the Ukraine to the edge of the forest steppe zone near Kiev, is divided into five phases — A, B1, B2, C1 and C2 — the latest dating to the full Early Bronze Age in the 3rd millennium bc. The late Cucuteni-Tripolye phase is regarded as the local climax of Neolithic cultural development. Beside the achievement of large-scale production of fine wares and long chipped stone blades stands the technological mastery of metallurgical techniques such as alloying, casting and welding. Such craft specialization evolved in large nucleated villages, the largest covering over one square kilometre. The subsistence economy is as remarkable for its range of fruits (including the hybrid apricot) as for the earliest recorded domestication in Europe of the horse.

Cuello. A site located on a ridge between the Rios Hondo and Nuevo in northern Belize [formerly British Honduras] which is notable for its evidence of early settlement in the MAYA Lowlands. Its long stratigraphic and ceramic sequences cover the period from the Early FORMATIVE to the Late CLASSIC. The earliest Swasey Phase (radiocarbon dated to c1950 bc) has evidence of MAIZE cultivation and a unique, fully developed ceramic complex of great variety.

The site operated as a minor CEREMONIAL CENTRE in the Late Classic Period.

Cueva de la Sarsa. A cave near Valencia in southeast Spain with Neolithic settlement of the IMPRESSED WARE phase. As well as pottery, finds include polished stone axes, flint tools, bone spatulae and spoons, and stone and bone jewellery. Evidence on the subsistence economy is provided by the remains of carbonized wheat, shellfish and bones of sheep, goat, cattle and pig.

Cuicuilco. Located at the southern end of ancient Lake Texcoco, Cuicuilco was the largest and most important centre of the Basin of Mexico in the Late PRE-CLASSIC PERIOD. Early large-scale construction in the form of adobe and stone-faced platforms occur in c400 BC. Cuicuilco appears to have been a thriving centre and an early rival of TEOTIHUACAN. An eruption of the Xitle volcano in c150 BC destroyed not only Cuicuilco but much of the surrounding agricultural land. It was never reoccupied and its destruction probably gave a considerable impetus to the growth of its rival at the nothern end of the lake.

Cuidadela. *See* TEOTIHUACAN.

Cuivier, Baron Georges (1769-1832). Eminent French geologist (nicknamed the 'Pope of Bones') who was one of the foremost proponents of the catastrophist geological theory, which held that the record of the earth's surface could only be interpreted in terms of a series of great catastrophes, of which Noah's Flood was the last. For a contrasting view, see LYELL, Sir Charles.

culture. As used by archaeologists, the term has two separate meanings. In the more general sense it refers to everything that man does that derives from 'nurture rather than nature' (V.G. CHILDE), that is, behaviour that is learned rather than genetically controlled. An alternative definition of culture in this sense is man's 'extra-somatic means of adaptation' (L. Binford).

The second and more restricted use of the term refers to an ASSEMBLAGE of artefacts and other traits (e.g. house plans or burial rites) that regularly occur together within a restricted area and are thought to represent the physical remains of a particular group of people. Cultures are usually named after either a type site (e.g. STARČEVO CULTURE) or after a characteristic artefact (e.g. LINEAR POTTERY CULTURE). The use of the concept of cultures was popularized by Childe and it is still widely used today, although there is considerable controversy over the nature of the social groups that they are thought to represent.

Cumae. A town in Campania, southwest Italy, best known as one of the first Greek colonies in Italy and the home of the Sibylline oracle. Evidence exists for earlier (Bronze Age) occupation. Lying in the area known to antiquity as the *campi phlegraei* ('fiery fields') because of the volcanic and hot-spring activity, the site probably appealed to Greek colonists (from Colchis, c750 BC) by virtue of its fertility and the natural advantages of the port, land defences and citadel. Prosperity was rapidly established, and Cumae went on to found daughter colonies, most notably Neapolis (which was to become NAPLES) and probably Puteoli. Aided by Syracuse, Cumae finally ousted the Etruscans from Campania in 474 BC, only to fall under Oscan control from c420 BC and Roman domination from 338 BC. As a port, Cumae always had problems with silting-up, and the whole installation was radically re-engineered by Agrippa in 36 BC. A popular tourist resort for upper-class Romans of the late Republic and early Empire, Cumae was one of a trio of such watering-places, with Baiae and Puteoli; Cumae was gradually eclipsed by Puteoli, possibly because of the latter's greater proximity to the ever-popular Baiae.

It is probably through 7th-century Cumae that a Chalcidaean version of the Greek alphabet was transmitted to the Etruscans and thence eventually to the Italian peninsula. Also notable is the spectacular nature of the tunnels, grottos and cuttings which characterize the area, especially Agrippa's supply tunnel under Monte Grillo, Domitian's cutting through the same hill (spanned by a high-level bridge) and the famous grotto of the oracular Sibyl, described with apparently eye-witness accuracy by Virgil in the opening of the sixth book of the *Aeneid.*

cuneiform. Writing system developed in SUMER in the early 3rd millennium BC and used in many areas of western Asia until the last few centuries BC. The system involved making impressions on CLAY TABLETS with a wedge-shaped stylus, which has given the script its name (from the Latin *cuneus*, a wedge, and *forma*, shape). Cuneiform developed out of the simple pictographic script of the late URUK period, which is the earliest known writing in the world and evolved as a response to the demands of the growing temple administration, in order to cope with the necessary book-keeping. The fully developed cuneiform writing was no longer pictographic, but a partly syllabic script of several hundred signs, consisting of a mixture of ideograms, phonograms and determinatives. The cuneiform script was evolved for the SUMERIAN language, but it was subsequently adapted for many other languages, including AKKADIAN, ELAMITE, HITTITE and Old Persian. The decipherment of cuneiform was the work of a number of scholars of the 19th century, including GROTEFEND and Sir Henry RAWLINSON, whose transcription of the massive trilingual inscription at BISITUN in western Iran provided the key to the decipherment.

cuniculus [Latin: 'a mine']. Latin military term, usually an area of excavation by a besieging force beneath a fortification wall with the aim of undermining the structure and/or gaining access. The digging soldiers (*cunicul022arii*) would normally be protected by various structures of wooden posts, shields, arrangements of chariots etc, variously called *testudo* (tortoise) and *vinea* (vine). Countermeasures by the defenders, apart from building very massive walls with very deep foundations, included laying a bronze shield on the ground to track vibrations, digging counter-mines, and smoking out the diggers.

Cunnington, William (1754-1810). British antiquary who, like his contemporary COLT HOARE, recorded and excavated many barrows and other prehistoric monuments in southern England, especially on Salisbury Plain. His excavations were of good quality for the time, but his work lacked the framework of a classificatory system, such as was later provided by the THREE AGE SYSTEM.

cup and ring mark. The commonest form of rock carving in the British Isles, consisting of a cup-like depression surrounded by one or more concentric grooves. Cup and ring marks are found on standing stones, on their own or in STONE CIRCLES, and on the slabs of burial cists, as well as on natural rock surfaces. The majority are thought to belong to the Bronze Age; their function is unknown.

Cupisnique. Centred on the Chicama Valley in north coast Peru, Cupisnique is characterized by CHAVIN-like pottery, so much so that it is sometimes referred to as Coastal Chavin. Most often associated with graves, pottery is typically a polished grey-black ware and STIRRUP-SPOUT vessels are a common form. There is, however, considerable variety in both technique and form. Early Cupisnique tends to be strongly modelled by plastic manipulation of the surface. In later phases red and black banding, separated by incision and life modelling, especially stylized felines, appear increasingly.

Curacchiaghiu. A rock shelter in southern Corsica with a sequence of deposits from a pre-NEOLITHIC level dated to the 7th millennium bc (the earliest evidence of man in Corsica) to the Late Neolithic. A level with 6th millennium bc dates had pottery with punctated and incised decoration, and a lithic industry with geometric trapezes on hard rock and obsidian imported from Sardinia. Because of the conditions in the rock shelter no bones survived and unfortunately we have no evidence about the subsistence economy of this community.

curia. A Latin term used in the early period of Rome's history to denote a principal subdivision of the Roman people. Each of the original three tribes of Romulus were subdivided into ten *curiae*. This division was important for military organization, and for political representation — an early assembly is called the *comitia curiata*. From this association with political meetings comes the more general use of *curia* for 'senate' — often, under the Empire, a municipal senate. The term is also used for the senate house itself, and particularly of the Senate House at Rome. Rebuilt many times, this building now survives in a version restored by Diocletian in 303 AD, and owes its survival to Church use.

Curicamcha. *See* CUZCO.

currency bar. A term used to describe long iron objects found in the British late Iron Age and thought to represent a form of currency. Three standard types have been identified — sword, spit and ploughshare; they are thought to represent regional preferences rather than different values.

cursus. A type of NEOLITHIC earthen monument found in Britain, consisting of a long narrow enclosure or avenue delineated by banks and external ditches. The antiquary William STUKELY was the first to identify a monument of this type, near STONEHENGE, and he is responsible for the name: he compared the monument to a Roman racetrack. The Stonehenge example is more than 3 km long, but the longest known example, the Dorset cursus, is nearly 10 km in length. These monuments clearly represent a very considerable investment of labour for Neolithic communities; their function is unknown.

Cuzco. Still a thriving community, this site of the INCA capital is located in the Urubamba Valley in Peru at an elevation of 3500 metres. A CEREMONIAL CENTRE rather than a population centre, it stood at the intersection of the four administrative quarters of the empire (called Tawantinguyu). Although a pre-Inca ceramic complex has been defined (named Killke, a fusion of HUARI and other elements), legend has it that the capital was founded by the first emperor Manco Capac in c1200 AD. The major public works, however, were completed by Pachacuti some time after 1440.

The city was planned on a grid system and the CYCLOPEAN masonry walls of some streets, such as Callejon de Loreto, still exist, as do those of the nearby fortress of SACSAHUAMAN. A system of stone conduits set in the centre of the streets assured residents of a good water supply from diverted river sources. Though the Spanish built the Church of Santo Domingo over it in 1534, the lower walls of the massive Temple of the Sun (Curicancha) also still remain. Excavations after the collapse of the church in 1950 due to an earthquake did uncover a small gold statuette, but nothing remains of the fabulous gold-clad buildings and monumental statues of Spanish report.

Cuzoul. The rock shelter of Le Cuzoul de Gramat in Lot, southwest France, has a series of Mesolithic levels, mostly TARDENOISIAN. Well-preserved human remains including a skeleton came from these deposits.

Cycladic. Term for the Bronze Age of the Aegean Islands, equivalent to HELLADIC on the Greek mainland and MINOAN in Crete. It is usually divided into three major divisions: Early, Middle and Late. In the earlier Bronze Age, Cycladic culture seems to be largely independent, but in the late Middle Cycladic to early Late Cycladic (mid-2nd millennium BC) Minoan influence becomes important. After c1400 BC mainland (MYCENAEAN) influence replaces the Minoan and indeed many islands may have been colonized by the Mycenaeans.

Cyclopean masonry. A style of building with large, irregular blocks of stone fitted closely together. It is named after the Greek mythical character Cyclops, thought by the Greeks to have built the walls of TIRYNS, which are constructed in this way.

cylindrical tripod vase. A ceramic form popular in the Early CLASSIC PERIOD in Mesoamerica and a hallmark artefact of TEOTIHUACAN. As the name suggests, it is cylindrical in shape and stands on three slab or cylindrical legs; it frequently has a knobbed lid.

Cyrene. A Greek colony in Libya founded c630 BC by settlers from Thera who, according to a standard explanation by Herodotus, had been driven from home by shortage of food.

Later, as capital of the imperial province of Cyrenaica, it was important enough to merit being given the title of *metropolis*. It is likely, however, that Cyrene was always a cultural and commercial outpost, isolated by large tracts of desert from Egypt to the east and CARTHAGE to the west, and looked north across the sea for its communications and trade. The site, on a raised plateau some 8 km inland, was perhaps chosen for its water supply, the so-called Fountain of Apollo, and overseas contact was maintained by a separate port, Apollonio. The foundation of the city's prosperity was probably largely agricultural, based on the staple products of corn, oil and wool. Cyrene was also famous in antiquity for its horses, and the production of the plant *silphium* (possibly laserwort) which was a favourite with the Greeks in the preparation of certain medicines and dishes. The extensive remains still visible today are mostly Roman, laid out on an Hellenistic plan. Evidence exists for earlier buildings, as for instance the important 6th-century BC Temple of Apollo with stone columns and mainly mud-brick walls.

D

Dabar Kot. A large site in the Loralai Valley in northern Baluchistan, Pakistan, probably occupied from the 5th millenniuum BC. In later levels, material of HARAPPAN type was associated with local artefacts such as figurines of ZHOB type. The latest occupation of the site is represented by a large Buddhist structure.

Dabban. A blade industry of Cyrenaician Libya, named after the site of HAGFET ED DABBA but best known at HAUA FTEAH. At the latter cave it appears in the sequence *c*40,000 bc, making a sharp break with the preceding Libyan Pre-AURIGNACIAN. The Dabban is clearly related in some way to the broadly contemporary Upper PALAEOLITHIC complex of Europe and the Near East, backed blades, burins and endscrapers being its most characteristic artefacts. Dabban occupation of Haua Fteah continued until *c*12,000 bc.

Da But. A five-metre deep marine shell midden near Thanh-hoa in northern Vietnam, which has produced a mixed BACSONIAN and NEOLITHIC stone industry together with ochre-stained burials and pottery. Excavated in the 1920s, the site has recently been dated to *c*4000 bc.

Dacia. A Roman frontier province held from *c*106-270 AD, comprising an area to the north of the Danube and roughly equivalent to modern Rumania. The Dacians had constituted a threat to Rome for some time, and their leader Decebalus had to be recognized as a client king by Domitian. A more determined and successful onslaught was made by Trajan, who may also have been attracted by mineral deposits. Trajan celebrated his triumph on the spiral frieze of a ceremonial column at Rome (*see* TRAJAN'S COLUMN). Colonies were planted at Sarmizegethusa and Apulum. The province was abandoned by Aurelian in 270.

Dadunzi [Ta-tun-tzu]. A Neolithic site in Pei Xian, northern Jiangsu province, China, with three main levels named after the nearby sites of Qinglian'gang, Liulin, and Huating. Archaeologists commonly refer to these three levels as successive phases of the QING-LIAN'GANG culture. The lowest (Qinglian'gang) level at Dadunzi yielded a radiocarbon date of *c*4500 BC. In the middle (Liulin) level, extraordinary painted pottery was found side-by-side with the usual undecorated pots native to the local Qinglian'gang tradition. Both the shapes and the painted designs copy the YANGSHAO pottery of MIAODIGOU; radiocarbon dates from Miaodigou (*c*3900 BC) and also from DAHE (*c*3700 to *c*3050 BC) can therefore be taken to suggest that the Liulin phase belongs in the 4th millennium BC. The intrusive Miaodigou-style ware at Dadunzi, occurring in the middle of the Qinglian'gang-Liulin-Huating sequence, argues against the so-called nuclear theory, according to which the painted pottery of Miaodigou should antedate the entire east-coast Neolithic (*see* LONGSHAN).

Some graves of the Liulin phase at Dadunzi contained sacrificed dogs. At Dawenkou in Shandong, where the lower level belongs to the Huating phase, pigs appear instead, and the graves often take the form of a stepped pit (i.e. they have *ercengtai*; *see* SHAFT TOMBS). These features are significant as early forerunners of characteristic SHANG burial practices. Perforated tortoise shells from Liulin graves may likewise foreshadow the use of tortoise plastrons in Shang scapulimancy (*see* ORACLE BONES) and the pottery drinking vessels found in Liulin and later graves are so impractical as to suggest a ceremonial purpose like that served by Shang bronze RITUAL VESSELS.

Dahe [Ta-ho]. The site of a Neolithic village, now preserved as a museum, at Zhengzhou in Henan province, China. Several YANGSHAO levels are overlaid by HOUGANG II and SHANG remains; four radiocarbon dates for the Yangshao levels range from *c*3700 to *c*3050 BC. The uppermost Yangshao level represents a late stage of the MIAODIGOU I culture, known also from Guangwu Qinwangzhai and seen here at the eastern limit of its distribution. In this level at Dahe the expected painted pottery is found alongside unpainted pots, including DING and *dou* shapes, that recall the Huating-Dawenkou phase of the east-coast QINGLIAN'GANG culture. Apparently intrusive at Dahe, this pottery may represent the beginnings of a westward movement of east-coast influences that eventually transformed the Yangshao tradition, in Henan giving rise to the Hougan II culture (*see* LONGSHAN).

Daima. A large occupation mound in the extreme northeast of Nigeria, on the seasonally inundated plains adjacent to Lake Chad. The site's occupation began shortly before the middle of the last millennium bc, but reflected the continuation of a life-style that had been established in the area at least 500 years earlier. Herding of cattle and cultivation of sorghum were the joint bases of the econmy. Stone for tool manufacture had to be imported, but iron was introduced at some as yet poorly defined time between the 1st and 6th centuries ad. The adoption of iron was apparently not marked by any discontinuity in the archaeological sequence. Some centuries later, however, more pronounced change took place as Daima became part of a more wideranging trade system; it is tempting to link this phenomenon with the rise of the kingdom of KANEM.

Dainzu. *See* BALL GAME.

Dai Viêt. [Sino-Vietnamese: 'Great Viet']. Name of VIETNAM during certain periods of its history, notably from the 11th century to the 14th century, when the expansion towards the south and the absorption of the kingdom of CHAMPA began.

Dalmatia. A Roman province, called after the local tribe of the Delmatae, which corresponds partly to modern Yugoslavia. The whole eastern Adriatic area, roughly equivalent to present-day Yugoslavia and Albania put together, was finally annexed by Rome in 9 AD and became the province of Illyricum, valuable to Rome for its mineral deposits, land routes and harbours, and the legendary fighting qualities of its soldiers. Illyricum was soon sub-divided into two provinces, known by the Flavian period as Dalmatia and Pannonia.

Dalriada. In the later 5th century a group of Gaelic-speaking people known as the Scotti travelled from western Ireland to the northeast coast of Scotland (modern Argyllshire). There they founded the kingdom of Dalriada, which was imposed upon a native Pictish population. The Dalriada introduced the PICTS to their version of the OGHAM script as well as the Scottish/Gaelic language.

There are secure place-name and linguistic links between this part of Scotland and Ireland, and the history and royal successions of Dalriada are recorded in *The Chronicle of Dalriada* and elsewhere. However, there is little archaeology to illuminate this migration. The one site of real importance is DUNADD in Crianan Moss, a nucleated fortified citadel dating to around 500 and thought to be the capital of Dalriada. It consists of a dry-stone central stronghold with two outer walled enclosures, and was extensively excavated in 1929.

Dalton. A complex of cultural traits from the late PALEO-INDIAN period, centred on the Southeastern United States. It is characterized by the Dalton point, a fish-tailed variation of the CLOVIS point. Most Dalton sites indicate that major subsistence effort was in hunting deer. There is inconclusive evidence that gathering of plant food may also have been a subsistence activity. Brand in northeast Arkansas and Stanfield-Worley Bluff in Alabama are the best-known sites.

Damascus. Modern capital of Syria. A rich oasis city, Damascus was occupied by the 3rd millennium BC, but the settlements of the prehistoric, biblical and Roman periods underlie the modern and medieval city and are therefore not readily available for excavation. Egyptian texts and references in the Bible attest the city's importance in international trade from the 16th century BC; it appears as Damashqa in the Tell EL-AMARNA documents. The Aramaeans conquered Damascus in the late 2nd millennium BC and it was subsequently annexed by the ISRAELITES (10th century BC) and later the ASSYRIANS (8th century BC). By 85 BC it had become capital of Nabatean kingdom; by 64 BC it was a Roman city of commercial and strategic importance, and subsequently a major Byzantine garrison.

Damascus was captured by the Arabs in 635 and chosen as their capital by the Ummayads, who formed the first Islamic dynasty and ruled from 661 to 750. Its most famous Islamic monument is the Great Mosque of the caliph al-Walid, built in 706-714/5 in the *temenos* of a Roman temple which at the time of the Arab conquest contained a church. On the south side of the temenos, al-Walid erected a sanctuary with three aisles bisected by a tall nave with clerestory windows and a dome over the central bay. Single arcades surrounded the courtyard in front of the sanctuary and the corner towers of the temenos were converted into minarets. The mosque was adorned with mosaics and marble panels, some of which survive.

Damb Buthi. A prehistoric site in south-western Sind, Pakistan, which has produced material of both AMRI and HARAPPAN types, but from separate locations on the hill.

Damb Sadaat. A prehistoric site in the QUETTA valley of West Pakistan which was occupied during the 3rd millennium BC. The population of this period lived in well-built mud-brick houses consisting of several small rooms, used tools of copper, and had wheel-turned pottery painted in black designs on a buff or greenish ground known as Quetta ware. In Period III there was an interesting structure on the highest part of the mound: it was built on a brick platform and had thick spur walls leading to the lower parts of the mound. This building may have had some special function, as eight female figurines were found in its vicinity and underneath the main wall was a stone-built hollow containing a human skull.

Dammayan Temple [Dhammayazika, Dhammaramshi]. One of the largest Buddhist brick monuments in PAGAN, northern BURMA, built under king Narapatisithu in the late 12th century. It is similar in style to the ANANDA TEMPLE.

Danekirke. A 5th-century site situated outside Ribe in Western Jutland. It poses interesting archaeological problems as the excavators found traces of only one large timber hall, associated with enormous quantities of imported luxury items including a great deal of West European glass. It may well be a MIGRATION PERIOD royal site.

Danelaw. An agreement by formal treaty between King ALFRED of Wessex and the Danish leader Guthram in 878, establishing a political boundary along the line of the old Roman road, Watling Street, from Chester through Lichfield and Hertford to London. The Danes were given the large area to the east of the line, which was known as the Danelaw. This division only lasted until the early 10th century, when Alfred's son Edward began the process of reconquering the area for the English monarchy.

Danger Cave. A site of long occupation in northwest Utah, USA, containing one of the most complete inventories of material from the DESERT TRADITION. Characteristic artefacts, such as baskets, MANOS, METATES and small projectile points, were found in abundance. The earliest evidence of human occupation dates to 9500-9000 bc. Subsequent levels, although discontinuous, are evidence of occupation into the Christian era.

Danilo. The eponymous site for the Danilo culture, distributed over central and southern Dalmatia from c4700 bc to the early 4th millennium bc. Excavated by D. Rendić-Miocević and J.Korošec, the site, near Sibenik, consists of large numbers of pits and post holes, whose associated material has been subdivided typologically into five phases. Typical finds include incised and encrusted wares, bichrome and trichrome painted wares and a long blade and tanged point stone industry closely related to fishing practices. The economic base of the Danilo culture is broad spectrum in nature, with mixed farming supplemented by fishing, hunting and shell-collecting. The so-called 'cult rhyton' (resembling a miniature coal-scuttle in appearance), a form characteristic of the culture, is more plausibly interpreted as a salt-pot.

Dantu [Tan-t'u]. A district just south of the Yangzi River in Jiangsu province, China. A Western ZHOU tomb found in 1954 at Dantu Yandunshan contained a few pieces of glazed pottery and 12 bronze RITUAL VESSELS. The inscription on one of the bronzes, a GUI of conventional early Western Zhou style, names the marquis of a fief called Yi, which may have been located on this remote frontier of the Zhou empire. The other bronzes are evidently local products; their decoration is copied in some cases from the repertoire of the native GEOMETRIC POTTERY tradition, an influence more pronounced in later bronzes from the same region (*see* TUNXI).

Danubian culture. Term used by Gordon CHILDE to describe the sequence of prehistoric cultures found in central Europe, along the valley of the Danube and other rivers; it is not often used today. Danubian I is the LINEAR POTTERY culture; Danubian II the later Neolithic cultures, such as TISZA, LENGYEL, STROKE-ORNAMENTED WARE and RÖSSEN; Danubian III-VI were used by Childe to describe the various phases of the Copper and Bronze Ages in the area, but were never widely adopted by other scholars.

Danzantes. Stone slab, bas-relief carvings dating to *c*100 BC – AD 100 (*see also* PRE-CLASSIC) that flank the earliest flat-topped mound at MONTE ALBAN, Mexico. They depict nude male figures, some with mutilated or elaborately emphasized sexual organs, in unnatural dancing or possible swimming poses. Sometimes interpreted as dead, possibly sacrificed captives, certain elements of the iconography, such as thick lips and downturned mouths, indicate an OLMEC origin. Associated hieroglyphs and CALENDAR dates also tend to confirm this.

Dapenkeng [Ta-p'en-k'eng]. A Neolithic site in Taiwan, near Taibei, characterized by coarse cord-marked pottery of a kind widely represented at sites in south and southeastern China that fall somewhere between the late 5th and the 3rd millennium BC. The relationship of this corded-ware Neolithic, sometimes called the Yue Coastal Neolithic, to the Neolithic cultures of the lower Yangzi region (*see* LONGSHAN, sense 2) is not clear. At a later stage the corded ware gave way to GEOMETRIC POTTERY.

Dapona [Ta-p'o-na]. *See* DIAN KINGDOM.

Dara-i Kur. *See* AQ KUPRUK.

Dar es Soltan. A cave on the Atlantic coast of

Morocco, some 200 km south of Tangier, where excavation has revealed a late ATERIAN industry associated with human remains of MECHTA-AFALOU type. Later levels contain a long sequence of IBEROMAURUSIAN-related industries.

Darwin, Charles (1809-82). The founder of evolutionary theory, which he expounded in his seminal work *Origin of Species by Means of Natural Selection or the Preservation of Favoured Races in the Struggle for Life*, published in 1859. Its particular relevance for archaeology was to boost the acceptance of the antiquity of man, which had already gained the support of some scholars by 1859 (*see* BOUCHER DE PERTHES, MACENERY, PENGELLY). In a later work, *The Descent of Man* (1871) Darwin spelled out the implication of his theory for man's origins and suggested that man evolved from some ape-like ancestor, probably in Africa.

Dasht-i Nawar. *See* AQ KUPRUK.

Dasikongcun [Ta-ssu-k'ung-ts'un]. *See* CHARIOT BURIALS (CHINA).

database management system. A COMPUTER program that stores information and allows it to be retrieved in any desired combination or order. Filing systems of various kind are already widely used in archaeology; database management systems are merely an extension of these.

dating. The determination of a date for objects, deposits and buildings is at the centre of all archaeology. In later periods this may be accomplished by historical methods (e.g. coin dating) but if such evidence is not available other methods have to be used. CROSS DATING and SERIATION or SEQUENCE DATING are the traditional approaches. Since 1948, independent methods have become available, including RADIOMETRIC dating, THERMOLUMINESCENCE, ARCHAEOMAGNETISM, DENDROCHRONOLOGY, FLUORINE and NITROGEN DATING, OBSIDIAN HYDRATION and dating from AMINO-ACID RACEMIZATION. These methods have varying applications, accuracy, range and cost.

daub. A clay-based material, acting as the matrix in a WATTLE and daub wall. The daub is plastered on to the wattle framework and allowed to dry, forming a quick and relatively weathertight structure. The imprint of wattle has survived on some ancient daub from archaeological sites.

Davis, E.H. (1811-88). American doctor who together with E.G. SQUIER studied the prehistoric mounds of the eastern USA.

Dawenkou [Ta-wen-k'ou]. *See* DADUNZI, QINGLIAN'GANG, LONGSHAN (sense 2), GUI.

Dazaifu. The remains of the centre of frontier adminstration near Fukuoka, Japan. Established shortly after Japan's spectacular defeat in the Korean campaign of 663, Dazaifu remained an important outpost of the government in the western frontier for the next few centuries. The Dazaifu area, with adminstrative buildings and temples, has been investigated since 1968.

Dead Sea Scrolls. Ancient Hebrew manuscripts found in a cave near the ruin of Khirbet Qumran, north-west of the Dead Sea, in 1947. They are believed to be the library of the monastery at Qumran, occupied by an extreme religious sect known as the Essenes between 100 BC and AD 100. The library included all the Old Testament texts as well as sectarian works. The scrolls, together with the excavations at Qumran, have provided much information about the beliefs and way of life of the Essenes. It is thought that the library was hidden in the cave in anticipation of the destruction of Khirbet Qumran by the Romans, which occurred in AD 66-70.

Debeira West. An extensive village site in Nubia, occupied between the 7th and 13th centuries. Excavation of its two-storey brick buildings has yielded a clear picture of its inhabitants' life-style. Dates and sorghum were cultivated with the aid of irrigation; cattle, pigs, sheep and goats were herded. The village had its own church with associated cemetery.

Déchelette, Joseph (1862-1914). French archaeologist who produced a masterly synthesis of European prehistory in the early part of this century. Entitled *Manuel d'Archéologie Préhistorique, Celtique et Gallo-romaine*, the first volume — on prehistory —

was published in 1908; the second part came out in separate volumes, that on the Bronze Age in 1910, on HALLSTATT in 1913, and LA TÈNE in 1915 (completed by Albert Grenier after Déchelette's death early in World War I).

decumanus. *See* CARDO.

deep sea cores. Since the development of the piston corer in 1947, it has been possible to take long cores of SEDIMENT from the ocean bottom. A wide variety of such sediment exists, but those most studied have been the oozes. Oozes form by accumulation of the dead skeletons of foraminifera and radiolaria, together with a variable amount of inorganic material. These sediments build up very slowly, from 10 mm per 1000 years up to 50 mm per 1000 years, but their sequence is uninterrupted. Some cores have provided an unbroken record for the whole of the QUATERNARY. The main problem with such sequences is disturbance by animals living on the ocean bottom. Dating of the succession is accomplished by RADIOCARBON, which covers the last 70,000 years (the top 400 mm or so of most cores) and by PALAEOMAGNETISM, which provides fixed points of known date, between which further dates have to be interpolated. There are still problems with the detailed dating of cores. Two main types of investigation have been carried out:

(*a*) *Faunal variation*. Foraminifera can be identified from their skeletons. Changes occur in the relative proportions of different species, through the sequence shown in the cores. Such variation is compared mathematically with the known ecology of today's foraminifera. This allows the reconstruction of variation in such factors as surface temperature and salinity throughout the time which the cores represent.

(*b*) *Oxygen isotope ratios*. Sea water contains a number of isotopes of oxygen, the most common being ^{18}O and ^{16}O. During periods of growing ICE-SHEETS, water rich in ^{16}O is preferentially bound up in ice-sheets. Conversely, sea water becomes relatively rich in ^{18}O. Thus the $^{18}O/^{16}O$ ratio is an indicator of the global extent of ice-sheets. Both isotopes are incorporated into the skeletons of foraminifera. These skeletons then become deposited as ocean-bottom ooze, appear in cores and can be analysed for $^{18}O/^{16}O$ content. Temperature may also affect the rate at which either isotope is taken up by the foraminifera. This effect can be eliminated by studying only species that live deep in the water, where temperature varies little. This technique has been combined most successfully with palaeomagnetism by Shackleton and Opdyke, on core number V28-238 from the south Pacific. Numbered stages are assigned to the fluctuations in isotope ratio up the core. At least eight major glacial episodes are shown to have occurred during the past 700,000 years. This is difficult to correlate with terrestrial sequences of Quaternary deposits.

Deir el Bahari. A location at Thebes in Upper Egypt, the site of several temples, notably the funerary temple of Queen Hatshepsut, daughter of the Eighteenth Dynasty pharaoh Thutmosis I, who reigned over Egypt in her own right 1511-1480 BC. The temple includes a series of colonnaded terraces. Particular interest attaches to the fine relief carvings, one of which illustrates an Egyptian trading expedition to the Land of Punt, believed to have been part of the African coast near the southern end of the Red Sea.

Deir el-Daleh. *See* GAZA.

Dejbjerg. A bog site in west Jutland, where two pre-Roman Iron Age vehicles were found, believed to be imports from South Gaul. They were decorated with openwork bronze, bronze masks, bosses and lattice work. The wheels had iron tyres and pegs of hard wood to act as ball-bearings.

Deloraine Farm. A site near Rongai in the Rift Valley highlands of central Kenya, dated late in the 1st millennium ad. Domestic cattle were herded in large numbers. The associated pottery is unlike that found on PASTORAL NEOLITHIC sites: the relatively small number of chipped obsidian artefacts recovered suggests that iron may have been known to the site's inhabitants.

Delos. Tiny central member of a group of islands in the central Aegean known to antiquity as the Cyclades (from the Greek *kuklos*, 'circle') because they encircled the holy island of Delos. There is evidence for some late Neolithic and some MYCENAEAN settlement. Sometime early in the 1st millennium BC association with the worship of Apollo is

established, and myth claimed the island as his birthplace. This religious link, coupled with vigorous promotion by Athens from the middle of the 6th century to the end of the 4th century BC, turned the island into a populous religious and political centre for the Aegean, with an oracle that was perhaps second only to Delphi. Delos was also chosen as the headquarters and treasury for the important maritime alliance against the Persians, the Delian League. After 314 BC a period of neutrality brought commercial prosperity, and Hellenistic kings contributed towards its monuments. Further success came with the status of free port from 166 BC, and a cosmopolitan community helped to create fine streets, Greek and oriental temples, meetinghouses for the merchant guilds, a unique colonnaded ('hypostyle') hall, and splendid houses. From 88 BC various pirate attacks indicate a lessening investment and this, combined with the general westward shift in commercial and political focus which had come with Roman domination of the eastern Mediterranean, eventually led to the abandonment of the island. Excavations have been conducted since 1873 by the French School (Athens).

Delphi. A dramatic site on the steep slopes of Mount Parnassus, central Greece, famous in classical antiquity as the home of the Delphic oracle. It is likely that there was pre-Hellenic use as an earth deity shrine, and the setting, with its striking backdrop of cliff-face, rock fissures and springs, was no doubt deliberately chosen. In addition to answering consultations by states and individuals (the answers were often couched in obscure hexameter verses which left the enquirer none the wiser) Delphi seems to have acted as a religious and festival centre for the different Greek city states who organized themselves into the so-called Amphictyonic League. The Pythian Games, held at Delphi, became a great national festival, and over the years an elaborate complex of religious and ceremonial buildings grew up. Along a Sacred Way were placed some 20 temple-like treasuries, erected by member states to house valuable offerings. Above, on a terrace supported by a wall of unusual polygonal masonry, stood the great Temple of Apollo, containing in a holy of holies (*adyton*) a navel-shaped stone (*omphalos*) marking the centre of the earth, and a rock fissure from which emanations were supposed to inspire the Pythian priestess. The virgin priestess would fall into a trance to give (inarticulate) answers to male priests (women were not admitted). The temple was reconstructed after earthquake damage in c350 BC, and a theatre and stadium were added. After c300 BC the oracle began a slow decline in authority, and Roman rule, sceptical of its value, brought further deteroriation, with some prominent Romans plundering the site for its art treasures — the emperor Nero, in a fit of pique at the oracle's comments on his murder of his mother, is said to have carried off five hundred statues. The oracle was finally closed by the Emperor Theodosius in 390 AD as anti-Christian.

demography. The study of population. It is difficult to study the size of ancient human populations, since it is most unlikely that skeletons excavated from sites in a given area represent the local population size reliably. However, age and sex may be determined from most human skeletons, and study of the proportions of different age-groups and sexes may yield valuable information about the way of life of an ancient population. *See* AGEING OF SKELETAL MATERIALS.

Denbigh Flint Complex. The type collection for the ARCTIC SMALL TOOL TRADITION which was first excavated at Cape Denbigh on Norton Bay, Alaska. The site yielded a radiocarbon date of 2000 bc, which became a landmark in the chronology of Arctic cultures. Denbigh artefacts have been found at numerous Arctic sites, notably at ONION PORTAGE, CAPE KRUSENSTERN and Ityatet. Finely worked microblade tools are characteristic, and land mammals seem to have been the primary focus of subsistence activity.

dendrochronology. The construction of chronologies from tree-ring sequences. Dendrochronology can be used as a dating method for timbers in buildings and other archaeological sites. It has also been used with great success for the calibration of RADIO-CARBON DATES. Tree-ring sequences are also used as indicators of environmental change.

Principles. It is common knowledge that the age of a tree may be determined by counting the number of tree rings. Depending on the growing conditions in the particular years of their growth, tree rings differ in width and structure; for instance, during good growing years a thicker ring is added than in poorer years. Trees of a similar age in the same area will all be similarly affected and so will have similar sequences of ring widths; therefore sequences can be correlated btween trees. Correlation can also be carried out with overlapping parts of tree-ring sequences from older trees, dead trees and timbers preserved on archaeological sites, In this way, an overlapping sequence of tree-ring widths can be built up and ideally such a sequence would extend back unbroken from the present day. However, timbers linking parts of the sequence may be missing and in these cases 'floating chronologies' are built up. Floating chronologies have to be dated approximately by radiocarbon, but as more timbers are found, it is hoped to join them to the sequence which is anchored in the present day, thus providing an absolute chronology. Once a master chronology has been constructed, other timbers from buildings and sites can be dated by matching them into the sequence.

Range. The long-living Bristlecone Pine (*Pinus aristata*) of California has yielded a sequence extending back to c9000 BP. In Ireland, oak preserved in bogs has produced a floating chronology from c2850-5950 BP. Similar chronologies are being built up throughout Europe.

Accuracy. Correlation between sequences is never perfect and has to be accomplished statistically. In addition, rings may be missed out in some years (between 3.4 per cent and 0.86 per cent of rings may be missing in one tree); other years may produce multiple rings (this is much rarer). Accuracy therefore varies, but the method appears to be much more accurate than any of the other dating methods.

Problems. To use dendrochronology as a dating method, a sequence has to be built up for the area in which sites exist. This chronology will then apply to only one species of tree in one particular area. The size of the area will vary, but Bristlecone Pine sequences can be correlated between trees up to 1600 km apart.

Radiocarbon calibration. Once the Bristlecone Pine absolute chronology had been established, small blocks of wood (c10 rings) were sampled at intervals down the sequence. These were dated by radiocarbon and the difference between the two sets of dates used to construct calibration tables.

Dendrochoronology and climate. Since tree ring widths are dependent on environment, it is possible to use the sequence of width changes to reconstruct environmental (particularly climatic) history for an area.

Denekamp interstadial. An interstadial of the WEICHSELIAN cold stage. It is dated to around 28,000 bc.

Dereivca [Dereivka]. A late Neolithic site located on the river Omifinev, some 25 km south of Kremenčug in the Ukraine, USSR, and dated to the 3rd millennium bc. The main site component is a cemetery of the Mariupol type, with 106 extended inhumations arranged in groups. Adjacent to the cemetery is a settlement site with DNIEPER-DONETS pottery associated with a 10-metre-long timber-framed house.

Desborough. The find spot in central England of a 1st-century BC bronze mirror, with fine engraved decoration in the insular British LA TÈNE art style.

deserted medieval village. The fossilized remains of hamlets and villages in Western Europe with earthworks or walls representing the church, the MANOR, the dwellings, and other features associated with medieval rural life. Some settlements were deserted each century, but many of these villages were abandoned following the series of plagues in the 14th and 15th centuries.

Excavations have been carried out in many villages, and the density of deserted villages in certain regions has been accurately recorded. The most extensive excavations in the British Isles are at WHARRAM PERCY in North Yorkshire, but sites such as Goltho in Lincolnshire and Hound Tor, Devon, illustrate the wide variety of settlements that can readily be found. Sites have been excavated in every region of France; the settlement at Rougiers is possibly the best-known. French archaeologists have excavated Brucato in Sicily, and comparable sites are under investigation in Tuscany. Lowland sites have been excavated in Holland and North Germany, and a detailed survey has been made of the large number of sites in the Eifel Mountains. Scandinavian sites stemming from later Viking times have also been surveyed or partially excavated.

Deserted villages are perhaps the most common archaeological sites of the medieval period, and their investigation has become fundamental to the modern study of medieval archaeology in Western Europe.

Desert Tradition. A post-PLEISTOCENE adaptation to the arid environment of the Great Basin area of the western USA, which continues to be practised in some areas to this day. It is characterized by the utilization of a wide variety of food sources. Both big and small game animals as well as numerous plant species were exploited in a cyclical pattern typical of the ARCHAIC lifestyle. The hallmark artefacts are the basket and the flat milling stone. Evidence of the Desert Tradition has been found not only in much of the western USA, for example VENTANA CAVE and DANGER CAVE, but also in northern Mexico. Probably its best known manifestation is COCHISE. *See* Table 9, page 552.

Deva. *See* CHESTER.

Devarāja [Sanskrit: 'God-King']. Name of a Hindu religious mode, known as the Devarāja cult, which prevailed in the kingdom of ANGKOR, Cambodia, from the 9th to the 13th centuries. It was based on the belief that during his lifetime the king was the incarnation or representation of a Hindu god, with whom he became one after his death. This interpretation has lately been contested; however, it seems certain that some form of apotheosis of kings was a characteristic element of Angkorian civilization.

Devensian. A group of British, mainly GLACIAL, deposits, stratified above IPSWICHIAN INTERGLACIAL deposits (*see* Table 6, page 419). Much of northern England, Scotland and Wales is covered by a blanket of Devensian TILLS, sands and gravels. These SEDIMENTS were deposited by an ice-sheet which spread out from centres in Wales, the Lake District, the Pennines and southern and highland Scotland. South of the ice-sheet margin is a series of related PRO-GLACIAL and PERIGLACIAL deposits. Most of the Devensian stage can be dated using RADIOCARBON, and by this means it has been correlated with the WEICHSELIAN in northwest Europe and the WISCON-

SIN in North America. All these formations represent one cold stage, which lasted from c120,000 bp until 10,000 bp and directly preceded our present period of predominantly warm climate (the FLANDRIAN or HOLOCENE). Not all of the Devensian deposits are strictly glacial. Some contain abundant fossils which can be used as ENVIRONMENTAL INDICATORS. The species present in various of such deposits indicate warmer INTERSTADIAL periods amongst the generally cold Devensian climate. Three interstadials have been defined in Britain, using BEETLES as environmental indicators for temperature: the CHELFORD INTERSTADIAL (c61,000 bp); the UPTON WARREN INTERSTADIAL complex (45-25,000 bp) and the WINDERMERE INTERSTADIAL (13-11,000 bp). PALAEOBOTANY supports the beetle evidence for Chelford and Windermere, where the existence of deciduous trees (birch and pine) suggests warmer temperatures. There is, however, no evidence of trees for Upton Warren, which had a tundra flora similar to the older parts of the Devensian. Britain was by no means ice-covered throughout the Devensian cold stage. Ice-sheets seem to have appeared only during the cold STADIAL between 26,000 and 13,000 bp. These sheets were lost completely during the Windermere interstadial; then during the cold LOCH LOMOND STADIAL that followed only one ice cap and small glaciers were formed in the highest hills. SEA LEVEL fell during the colder parts of the Devensian, exposing the bottom of the Irish Sea, North Sea and the Channel and connecting Britain to the Continent. LEVALLOISIAN, MOUSTERIAN and Upper PALAEOLITHIC artefacts are found in Devensian deposits. In addition, bones of HOMO SAPIENS have been found in Devensian cave sediments.

Deverel-Rimbury. Middle to Late Bronze Age culture of southern England, named after two burial sites in Dorset. Palisaded farmsteads, nucleated settlements and some HILLFORTS of this culture are known and many CELTIC FIELD systems are recorded. The dead were cremated and placed in globular, barrel- or bucket-shaped urns either under BARROWS or in flat cemeteries.

Devils Lair. A limestone cave near the southwest coast of Western Australia, containing deep, well-preserved organic and stone deposits dating from the late PLEISTOCENE. Human occupation debris was relatively sparse and occurred mainly between levels dated to 27,000 and 10,000 bc. The stone assemblage included cores, scrapers, denticulated flakes and adze flakes. Several artefacts carried tracers of resin, suggesting use in composite tools. Three unifacially incised limestone plaques (10,000-18,400 bc) and a piece of artificially perforated marl were interpreted as ritual items or adornments. CHERT sources for some of the artefacts are not evident on the present coastline, but undersea-drill cores from the nearby continental shelf have produced the same Eocene fossiliferous chert from a zone which would have been exposed during Pleistocene low sea-levels. Bone artefacts included points dated c27,000 bc and beads between 13,000 and 10,000 bc, claimed to be the oldest known ornaments in Australia.

Devon Downs. A limestone shelter in cliffs beside the lower Murray River in South Australia. The two-metre deep deposit, rich in faunal material as well as stone and bone tools, was excavated by H. Hale and N.B. Tindale in 1929, as was the nearby open site of TARTANGA. This was the first systematic archaeological excavation in Australia. Later radiocarbon dating of samples from the excavation estimated human occupation of the shelter from 3000 bc.Interpretation of the STRATIGRAPHY and stone tool sequence at the two sites introduced concepts of antiquity and cultural change in Aboriginal prehistory which had previously been denied in Australian anthropology.

Dharmarajika. See TAXILA.

Dhar Tichitt. Located in south-central Mauritania on the southern edge of the Sahara Desert, the Dhar Tichitt sites provide a clear, dated picture of the local beginings of cereal cultivation. Wild sorghum and bulrush millet are indigenous to the area. Around 2000 bc there were extensive lakes at Dhar Tichitt, supporting a population which relied for its livelihood on collecting, hunting and fishing. By c1500 bc the inhabitants had obtained domestic cattle and goats. Desiccation resulted in marked shrinkage of the lakes at the close of the 2nd millennium, by which time a number of species of wild grass, still used in the southern Sahara in times of famine, were being collected. Shortly after 1000 bc, in the so-called Chebka phase, bulrush millet of a clearly domesticated type was the cereal most frequently represented. Villages at this time were no longer situated beside the lakes but in defensive positions on the adjacent escarpment; they were also larger than their predecessors. Increases both in population and perhaps also in competition for control of resources may be indicated. By the 4th century bc bulrush millet clearly formed the staple diet of the inhabitants of the area.

Dhimini. A small fortified settlement in Thessaly, northern Greece, which has given its name to the local late Neolithic. The settlement occupied c0.5 hectares and contains houses and a larger building in MEGARON form. The finely decorated pottery is painted in black or sometimes white on a yellow or buff surface and the motifs include spirals and meanders.

Dhlo Dhlo. A later Iron Age site located northeast of Bulawayo, Zimbabwe. Occupation probably began during the 16th century and was marked by the erection of elaborate dry-stone terrace-retaining walls surrounding extensive house-platforms. The foundation of this site, like that of comparable stone structures at KHAMI and Naletale, is traditionally attributed to the Rozwi, following the decline of the Monomotapa empire. Throughout its occupation, the inhabitants of Dhlo Dhlo appear to have had access to imported luxury goods derived from the African east coast trade.

Di [Ti]. *See* RONG AND DI.

Diablo. *See* TAMAULIPAS.

Diaguita. A cultural group of the south-central Andes characterized by distinctive ceramic complexes. Two principal sub-groups have been defined: the Argentinian, on the eastern side of the Andes and the Chilean, centred on the western side. Although they have some cultural traits in common (funerary practices, use of bronze and probably language), there are grounds for regarding them as being only marginally related.

Argentine Diaguita replace AGUADA in the Valliserana region. The new pottery tradition (Colchaqui) is distinguished by its introduction of new motifs, such as stylized reptiles, avia and humans, and is characterized by its polychrome funerary urns — the preferred method of burial for children; adult burials were stone-lined pit inhumations.

Chilean Diaguita ceramics are, on the whole, smaller and more delicately decorated. In its later stages especially, new forms make their appearance, for instance shoe- or duck-shaped vessels and bird effigy jars. Influence from the north (TIAHUANACO in the early stages and INCA later) is also apparent. Petroglyphs are common throughout the Diaguita area, but it is doubtful whether they are related to the ceramic tradition. The early date for Diaguita is c900 AD and it continued into Conquest times, at which time forced relocation of the natives dispersed the tradition.

Diana. A site on the island of Lipari, one of the Aeolian Islands north of Sicily, which has given its name to a local Final NEOLITHIC culture, with dates in the early 4th millennium BC. Diana had a very distinctive pottery with a glossy red slip and splayed lugs or tubular handles, which has also been found on Sicily and mainland Italy. The Diana culture is associated with the last phase of intensive exploitation of the Lipari OBSIDIAN source.

Dian [Tien] **kingdom**. A barbarian kingdom in southwest China centred on Lake Dian in Yunnan province. According to Chinese sources the Dian royal house traced its descent from a CHU general who invaded Yunnan in the late 4th century BC and remained to rule the local tribes. In 109 BC Dian surrendered to HAN armies and the Dian king was enrolled as a Han vessal. A generation later the kingdom was destroyed after a revolt.

The highly distinctive culture of the Dian kingdom is known mainly from cemetery sites excavated since 1955 near Lake Dian. Of these the richest is Shizhaishan in the Jinning district, where the burials date from the Han occupation (2nd-1st centuries BC). Earlier burials of the period c600-300 BC have been excavated at Dapona and Wanjiaba. Many of the objects unearthed at Shizhaishan were imports from China: coins, mirrors, belt hooks, silk, crossbow mechanisms, and a gold seal, the gift of the Han court, that reads 'Seal of the King of Dian'. Other finds, such as lacquer coffins and eccentric GE blades, seem to represent local adaptations of prototypes originating in the state of Chu, the likely source also of certain ornamental motifs (e.g. combinations of birds and snakes).

Chu and Sichun were the intermediaries by which influences reached Dian not only from Chinese civilization but also from the northern steppes. Dian bronze plaques copying ANIMAL STYLE models show the animal-combat motif in the most animated and realistic versions known in the full range of Animal Style art and indeed in the entire history of this very ancient motif. The vivid narrative art and mastery of lost-wax casting (*see* CIRE PERDUE) seen in these plaques are the salient features of Dian material culture. Both are illustrated again in the characteristic drum-shaped containers for cowrie shells found regularly in Dian burials. Three-dimensional figures grouped on the tops of these containers portray scenes of ritual, war and daily life with a lively movement and enthusiam for realistic detail unmatched in contemporary Chinese art. Prominent in nearly all the scenes are bronze drums, the same drums that the cowrie containers themselves imitate. Similar in shape to the *chunyu* bells of Sichuan, the Dian drums are regarded by many scholars as prototypes of those found in neighbouring Guangxi province and in Vietnam, where they are the defining artefact of the DONG-SON culture. *See* BELLS (CHINA), DRUMS (CHINA).

diffusion [diffusionist]. The spread of a technique or cultural trait or a complete way of life from on area to another. This can take place through the movement of people or through the spread of ideas (sometimes known as stimulus diffusion). It is clear that diffusion has often taken place in the past and that it has sometimes been a potent force for change. However, general interpretative frameworks based on diffusion are now less popular than they once were.

In the early part of this century Sir Grafton ELLIOT SMITH and his followers, like William Perry, expounded a view which is often described as 'hyperdiffusionist'; they believed that all inventions had taken place only once, in ancient Egypt, and that the knowledge of these inventions and practices had spread outwards from Egypt, carried by crusading missionaries, the 'Children of the Sun'. To take a single example, every mound-like structure

from European MEGALITHIC tombs to central American platform mounds was regarded as derivative of the Egyptian pyramids. This view was never widely accepted by scholars, but a modified version — often known as 'modified diffusionism' and associated especially with Gordon CHILDE — gained support. This version did not accept far-fetched connections and allowed for the possibility of independent invention in more than one area, but nonetheless accounted for most major developments in European prehistory in terms of diffusion from the Near East. Until relatively recently this was the standard interpretative framework for European prehistory, but in the last 10-15 years many of its tenets have been challenged, partly as a result of radiocarbon dates and the tree-ring calibration(*see* DENDROCHRONOLOGY, RADIOCARBON DATING), partly on theoretical grounds.

Dilmun. A name appearing in Mesopotamian texts of the EARLY DYNASTIC, AKKADIAN and UR III periods. It seems to be used in two ways, referring sometimes to a mythical land, a sort of Paradise; the epic hero GILGAMESH visited Dilmun in his search for immortality. On other occasions, however, the name Dilmun appears in economic documents and clearly refers to a real land, with which the cities of Mesopotamia traded. In recent years it has been identified with the island of BAHRAIN, or, perhaps more probably, with a larger area including the Arabian coast from the head of the Gulf to Bahrain. From the Mesopotamian documents it seems that Dilmun served mainly as an entrepôt for trade between the Indus Valley civilization and Mesopotamia, but it is also recorded as exporting dates and pearls of its own.

Dimolit. A site in Isabela Province, northern Luzon, and one of the earliest Neolithic open sites to have been excavated in the Philippines. The occupation, with pottery, flakes with edge-gloss and postholes of small square houses, probably dates from between 2100 and 1200 bc.

Dinas Powys. An Iron Age HILL FORT near Cardiff, Wales, which was refurbished in the sub-Roman and medieval periods. Some time in the 5th or 6th century the northern end of the hill was cut off by a modest bank *c*3 metres wide and 1.5 metres high and a rock-cut ditch.

Inside the enclosed area the excavators found the traces of a dwelling in the form of hearths, a collection of Mediterranean imported pottery, and metal-working debris such as moulds, furnaces and ovens. Very fragmentary outlines were found of two main structures including one possible hall, though it seems that dry stone used for these Dark Age buildings was re-used in the construction of the 11th-century rampart. This important sub-Roman phase at Dinas Powys has been attributed to a petty chief engaged in localized industrial activities. The small Norman ringwork is also of interest.

ding [ting]. A Chinese tripod bowl with solid legs (compare LI). The *ding* is almost unknown at YANGSHAO sites but is ubiquitous in pottery of the east-coast Neolithic and of the Henan Longshan culture (*see* LONGSHAN, HEMUDU). It was made in both pottery and bronze versions throughout the Chinese Bronze Age (*see* RITUAL VESSELS).

dingo. Australia's native dog (*Canis familiaris*) and only terrestrial non-marsupial carnivore. Distributed widely on the continent, it does not occur in Tasmania. The oldest well-authenticated dates for dingo bones come from the sites of FROMMS LANDING (South Australia), Madura Cave, (Western Australia) and Wombah (coastal New South Wales), between 1000 and 1500 bc. At present the dingo's external origins are unknown, but the answer to this question will have implications for the investigation of human migrations and contacts between Australia and Asia in the mid-Holocene.

disc barrow. *See* BARROW.

discriminant analysis. A technque of MULTIVARIATE ANALYSIS. Most discriminant analysis programs perform two operations. One is to calculate discriminant functions and the other is known as 'classification'.

Discriminant Functions. New VARIABLES which are calculated from the original, large number of variables. The discriminant functions are somewhat akin to PRINCIPAL COMPONENTS — calculated so that most of the variation in the original DISTRIBUTION is squeezed into the first few functions, which can then be plotted or analysed statistically. The differ-

ence between the two methods is that discriminant functions are specially calculated to show up differences between previously defined groups of items (for instance artefacts from several different sites), whereas principal components do not make any distinction between groups.

Classification. The object of this operation is to see how widely separated are the multivariate distributions of a number of previously defined groups of items in hyperspace. Each item is taken in turn, and the likelihood of its belonging to a group is calculated for each of the group distributions. The results are presented as a 'classification results table' in which the known grouping of items is compared with the most likely grouping, calculated from the variables supplied to the analysis. The smaller the proportion of items 'correctly classified' in this way, the more overlapping are the previously defined groups. Conversely, the larger the proportion 'correctly classified' the less the groups overlap. Classification is, for example, particularly useful in comparing groups of skulls from different sites, on the basis of their measurements.

Discriminant analysis can be, and was originally, done by 'pencil-and-paper' methods, but nowadays it is usually carried out by digital computer. *See also* COMPUTER, STATISTICS.

distribution. This term is used in two different ways in archaeology.

(1) In general it refers to the spatial location of archaeological sites or artefacts. These are usually plotted on one or more distribution maps, which are used in a number of ways. For instance, they may simply indicate the spatial extent of the items in question, or they may be used to indicate the distribution of material from a source, or to suggest relationships between one archaeological feature and another or between archaeological features and topography or other aspects of the natural environment.

(2) The second use of the term relates to STATISTICS. In this context distribution refers to the way in which values of VARIABLES are spread throughout a group of cases, objects or items. Distributions for one variable are easily represented by histograms (bar-charts). It is, however, just as possible to have a distribution for two, three or many more variables (*see* MULTIVARIATE ANALYSIS).

ditch. A common feature of archaeological sites, not only as defensive structures in association with RAMPARTS and walls, but also as a means of drainage or as a construction trench. Large ditches which are allowed to erode, without much interference from man, go through three phases of infilling. Primary fill accumulates rapidly as the sides of the ditch collapse. When the sides reach their angle of rest, the rate of deposition slows down, vegetation colonizes the bottom of the ditch and the secondary fill starts to build up. This material has a much finer texture than primary fill; it accumulates by inwash and from wind-borne particles trapped in the ditch bottom vegetation, and is subject to SOIL-forming processes. The rate of secondary fill deposition is related to soil erosion in the surrounding area. Finally, if the land adjacent to the ditch is being ploughed, thick COLLUVIAL deposits, called tertiary fill, may bury the secondary fill. This sequence may be interrupted by tipping-in of additional material by man. The smaller drainage ditches within a site tend to be filled by the tipping of rubbish and similar material rather than by the sequence of fills seen in larger ditches. EXPERIMENTAL ARCHAE-OLOGY has shown that as a result of erosion the excavated PROFILE of the ditch may bear little relation to the original form, and that LAYERS within the fill of a ditch may be more related to erosion and soil-forming processes than to human activity.

Divostin. A three-level site of the Early STARČEVO phase and early and late parts of the Late VINČA phase, west of Kragiyerac in central Serbia, Yugoslavia. The occupations date from *c*5250-4960 bc (Starčevo) to *c*3900 bc and *c*3300 bc (Late Vinča). Open excavation uncovered seven complete house-plans of the Late Vinča village, including one house containing 100 pots. The subsistence economy was based on cattle husbandry and plough agriculture. A wide range of cult objects included a model ritual scene and many fired clay anthropomorphic figurines.

Diyala. A tributary of the Tigris River, east of Baghdad in Iraq. In the 1930s important excavations were carried out in this area by the University of Chicago on four sites: Tell Asmar (ESHNUNNA), Tell AQRAB, KHAFAJE and Ischali. This allowed the establishment of a pottery sequence for this part of Mesopo-tamia, from the late 4th to the early 2nd millennium BC and the investigation of a number of important buildings of the JEMDET NASR and EARLY DYNASTIC periods.

Djeitun. The type site of a 6th millennium bc Neolithic culture of Turkmenia, Soviet Central Asia. Characteristic settlements were villages of up to 30 one-roomed houses, built of mud-brick with lime-plastered floors. Both floors and walls were sometimes painted. The subsistence economy was based on cereal agriculture, probably employing simple irrigation techniques, accompanied by the rearing of sheep and goats and the hunting of gazelle, onager, wild pig and sheep and a variety of smaller animals. The equipment of the Djeitun culture includes a microlithic flint industry and chaff-tempered pottery, decorated with simple painted designs.

Djoser. Either the first or the second pharaoh of the Third Egyptian Dynasty, *c*2660 BC. Later tradition was probably correct in regarding him as the effective founder of the Old Kingdom. His most lasting monument is his burial place, the step pyramid complex at SAQQARA, designed by the royal architect Imhotep.

Dnieper-Donets. Denotes a long-lived 3rd-2nd millennium bc Late Neolithic culture of these two valleys in southwest Russia. Large numbers of small settlements are known, employing largely fishing and hunting strate-gies. Large quantities of comb-pricked pots are known, especially from a series of rich cemeteries concentrated on the Dnieper rapids area, in which 30-130 burials are found. Extended inhumation is the norm, with grave goods rare except for copper rings and deer- and carp-tooth necklaces. The physical type in these burials is identified as CROMAGNON.

Dniester-Bug. *See* BUG-DNIESTER.

Dôc Chua. [Vietnamese: 'Pagoda Point']. A recently discovered rich Bronze Age site in southern Vietnam, near Xuân-lôc, north of Ho Chi Minh City (former Saigon). Many finds typical of the so-called DONG-SON culture have been made here including Chinese-style *ko*-axes; the presence of these so far south on the Indochinese Peninsula is an enigma.

dog. All domestic dogs appear ultimately to have been derived from the wolf. Today's dogs are the product of very intensive artificial selection and show exceptional variation in size and shape. Selection for particular forms has been so intense that in many breeds of dog it has led to physical deformity. Snouts, in some breeds, have become so excessively shortened as to cause dental and respiratory problems. In some of the extreme variation in size, there seems to be a link with congenital deformities such as achondroplasia and acromegaly.

By contrast with the enormous variation of today, the early domestic dogs are difficult to distinguish from wolves. In general, dogs are smaller than wolves, have shortened snouts and jaws, and crowded teeth which are themselves decreased in size. There is, however, considerable variation in wolf populations — European wolves being larger than Asian and Indian wolves — and there is overlap between dog and wolf in many characteristics. A number of PALAEOLITHIC, MESOLITHIC and NEOLITHIC sites have yielded skeletal remains which may be of dog or wolf. At many of these, it is not possible to determine the extent of domestication. There must have been considerable interchange of genes between the animals kept by man and those of the wild population. But at several of the sites, the skeletal material is sufficiently different to allow it to be distinguished as dog. The earliest such site is the Upper Palaeolithic cave of PALEGAWRA in Iraq, with a date of c10,000 bc. Other early sites are STAR CARR, England (c7500 bc) and CAYÖNÜ, Turkey (c7000 bc). The dog is thus among the earliest of domestic animals, and is found in hunter-gatherer communities as well as early farming communities.

Doian. A stone industry found exclusively in the southern and eastern areas of Somalia and, perhaps, in the adjacent northeastern part of Kenya. Doian assemblages contain backed microliths and flake scrapers with both unifacial and bifacial points. The industry has not been subjected to recent research and no radiocarbon dates are available. A post-Pleistocene age is, however, probable.

Doigahama. A YAYOI cemetery in Yamaguchi prefecture, Japan. The remains of at least 200 men and women of various ages were found buried in pits, in extended or flexed position. The presence of iron nails suggests the use of wooden coffins in some cases, while in others a stone was placed at each side of the head and feet of the body. In a few instances the walls and the top of the pit were covered with stone slabs. Burial jars were not used. Apart from personal ornaments of glass, stone and shell, the burials were sparsely furnished, unlike the Middle Yayoi burials, such as SUGU, in Kyushu.

dolichocephalic. Long-headed, that is, having a CEPHALIC INDEX greater than 75.

dolmen. A term once used to describe any MEGALITHIC CHAMBER TOMB. Today it is used by French archaeologists to describe a megalithic tomb of simple form, whereas in England its use is retained only in the specialized term PORTAL DOLMEN. In other areas of the world the term is still used in the general sense.

Dolní Věstonice. Perhaps the most important of the central European mammoth-hunters camps of the Upper PALAEOLITHIC. Like PAVLOV, it is situated on the loess plains of southern Moravia. The main occupation level dates from the end of an INTERSTADIAL period when climate was less intensively cold, about 26000 bc on the radiocarbon time-scale, although the thermoluminescence dates come out higher. The culture has been called Pavlovian or eastern GRAVETTIAN. A series of human remains has been found, including a female burial under a mammoth scapula. Several huts were excavated, and one seems to have had an oven inside, where clay figurines were fired. One of these is the famous venus of Dolní Věstonice (see VENUS FIGURINES).

Domburg. The 7th-9th century trading settlement of Domburg was situated upon the sand dunes of the island of Walcheren, north of the Scheldt estuary in the Netherlands. Nothing now remains of the settlement, but plans of the site made in the 19th century and the rich unstratified collection of pottery, metalwork, worked bone and English SCEATTAS suggest that it once flourished as an important trading site.

Domesday Book. A survey of land ownership in England after the Norman Conquest. The ANGLO-SAXON CHRONICLE relates how at a council held in Gloucester at Christmas 1085 it was decided to make a record of the number of hides in land existing in each English shire and to establish the amount and value of acreage and livestock possessed by individual landowners. The idea behind this was to untangle the complexities of tenure in post-Conquest England, and lay down the terms for a new rating system which would protect and enlarge the king's revenue. The resulting document — a two-volume survey of land ownership arranged under tenurial rather than territorial headings — is the great testament of feudal England. Domesday Book is of fundamental importance to both historians and archaeologists of the Late Saxon and early Norman periods, as it gives the names and sizes of villages, farms, manors, churches and other properties that existed at the time as well as certain sales and transactions. It has some limitations, not only because there are a number of omissions and errors but because the country as a whole is viewed as a collection of manors, sokes and berewicks. As a result it is sometimes difficult to gain from its pages a completely clear impression of village structures or population density. Domesday lists 13,000 pre-existing units or vills and even by the time of its compilation the rapid spread of manorialization and deliberate afforestation were evident.

domestication. The process by which wild plants and animals have been adapted to man's needs and methods of husbandry. The division between domestic and wild is not clear-cut. Many domestic plants and animals differ markedly from their wild relatives, others are very similar; several have no living wild relative at all. Some plants and animals are not 'farmed' by man in the sense of deliberately being bred or cultivated, but are still very closely associated with man. To add to the confusion, many of today's 'wild' stocks may, in fact, be feral.

Domestication involves a process of selection. It may be seen as part of evolution. Selection for particular features of shape, size and behaviour causes domestic animals and plants to diverge from their wild progenitor. Selection of this kind also leads to the establishment of varieties and breeds. The enormous range of breeds in animals such as the dog is probably due to selection for congenital deformities.

See, for example, CATTLE, DOG, DONKEY, GOAT, HORSE, PIG, SHEEP; BARLEY, BEAN, MILLET, MAIZE, OATS, RICE, RYE, WHEAT.

domus de janas. Sardinian name for the type of rock-cut tomb found in the island during the Copper Age and Bronze Age. The term means 'house of the fairies' and describes often complex, multi-chambered tombs. *See also* ANGHELU RUJU.

Dong-dau. The second Bronze Age phase of North VIETNAM (*bronze moyen*), dated to the second half of the 2nd millennium BC. Bronzes contain about 20 per cent tin, and forms and casting methods are ancestral to those of the classic DONG-SON (*bronze final*) phase. The Dong-dau phase is also classified as a late phase of the PHUNG-NGUYEN culture.

Dông-duong. Important archaeological site in the AMARĀVATĪ region of northern CHAMPA, now central Vietnam. The main building is a big monastery built in brick and dedicated to Lokeśvara by king Indravarman II in 875. This is the first evidence of the existence of Mahayana Buddhism in Champa; it is also recognized as a particular style in Cham art. A bronze Buddha figure of the Amarāvatī-style (2nd-4th century) has been found on the site. *See also* BUDDHISM.

Dong-son. The classic Bronze Age of North VIETNAM (*bronze final*), dated *c*500 bc to ad 100 and preceded by the GO BONG (*c*2000-1500 bc), DONG-DAU (*c*1500-100 bc) and GO MUN (*c*1000-500 bc) phases of the Vietnamese Bronze Age. The Dong-son culture thus overlaps the Chinese conquest of northern Vietnam in 111 BC. Characteristic are large incised bronze drums, rich burial assemblages (in lacquered wood coffins at Viet-khe) and evidence for developing urbanism (defensive earthworks at CÔ-LOA) based on wet rice cultivation. Dong-son drums of presumed Vietnamese manufacture were traded through vast areas of south China and Southeast Asia to as far as New Guinea, and the Dong-son bronze-working tradition was by far the richest and most advanced ever to develop in Southeast Asia. Most Vietnamese assemblages contain iron, although the culture is termed *bronze final* by Vietnamese archaeologists.

donkey. A domesticated ASS.

Dorestad. An early medieval trading site advantageously situated on the confluence of the Rivers Lek and Rhine in central Holland. Although it was first recognized in the 19th century it was not until the 1960s that excavations established the true extent and importance of this 7th-9th-century emporium which conducted trade with the Viking and Anglo-Saxon worlds.

The recent extensive excavations have shown that the medieval settlement of Wijk bij Duurstede lies close to a possible Roman LIMES fort, and that the emporium probably covered an area of more than 50 hectares. The shifting river-bank was flanked by timber walkways and jetties constructed on piles which seem to have been individually owned by the occupants of nearby rectangular structures. In contrast, the central area of the settlement was occupied by a series of FRISIAN-type farm units comprising a LONG HOUSE often accompanied by wells and granaries set within fenced enclosures. One of Dorestad's two cemeteries was fenced off in the centre of the farms and this incorporated an interesting timber structure and possible bell-tower. The modern excavations have produced enormous quantities of occupation debris including large amounts of imported Rhenish and local pottery, wine casks from the Mainz area (which were often re-used as wells), Niedermendig lava QUERNS, and stone mortars made in eastern Belgium. The Rhenish glassware and the great variety of metalwork and coin assemblages from Dorestad are also of singular importance, while the faunal assemblages include substantial numbers of fresh- and sea-water fishes. There is also evidence of industrial activities like weaving, ship-building, bone and metal-working. Dorestad is the best-excavated and finest example of a CAROLINGIAN emporium and illustrates the scale of commerce between the imperial estates in the Rhineland and other North Sea communities.

Doric. (1) One of the principal regional dialects of ancient Greece, traditionally named after the tribe of the Dorians.

(2) In classical architecture, the 'Doric order', a plain, early Classical, Greek style characterized by a simple, often rather stubby COLUMN, fluted but without base, with a CAPITAL with shallow bowl-shaped *echinus* and slab-like *abacus*. Over the columns were placed directly the linking beams (*architrave*), and over these, a frieze of alternating *triglyph* ('triple groove') and *metope* ('brow') — a pattern generally believed to originate from a decorative treatment of beam-ends and spaces.

rDo-riṅ. The megalithic ALIGNMENTS at rDo-riṅ, *c*50 km south of the sPaṅ-groṅ-mts'o-sha salt lake in Tibet were discovered by J.N. Roerich in the 1920s. There were 18 parallel rows of upright stone slabs, aligned east-west. At the west end were two concentric semi-circles of slabs, within which were three large standing stones, the central one *c*2.75 metres high, with a stone table or *Iha-t'o* in front of them. This standing stone showed traces of butter libations and was said to be the home of a local god. At the east end there was a huge arrow-shaped figure marked out with large slabs, pointing west. Roerich does not, unfortunately, record any overall measurements. Very similar sites were also found at RATI (in Nag-tshan), at Lap-c'un and at Tsuk-c'uṅ.

Dörpfeld, Wilhelm (1853-1940). German archaeologist who excavated many important sites in the Greek world, both prehistoric and classical. He worked under Ernst Curtius on the excavations by the German Archaeological Institute at OLYMPIA in the late 1870s and then assisted SCHLIEMANN on his third and fourth seasons at TROY in 1882-3 and 1889-90, bringing to this work the careful digging and recording techniques worked out at Olympia. After Schliemann's death he continued work at Troy in 1893-4. He later lived and worked on the Ionian island of Levkas, off the west coast of Greece which, contrary to most other authorities, he believed to be Homer's Ithaka; he excavated many sites on the island.

Dorset tradition. An eastern Arctic tradition whose stone-working technology is clearly related to the ARCTIC SMALL TOOL TRADITION. Its core area was centred on the North Foxe Basin in northern Canada, but ultimately its influence spread as far as Greenland. Whether the culture originated in Alaska or from a point somewhere south is still uncertain. The earliest manifestation, known as pre-Dorset (in some areas as Sarqaq) is represented at sites on Baffin Island and dates from *c*2400 bc. A slow and steady transition marked the passage from pre-Dorset to Dorset, and by 700 bc the latter is distinctly different from the former. By *c*1000 ad Dorset had almost universally been replaced by THULE.

Dos Aguas. A rock shelter with paintings of the SPANISH LEVANTINE (Mesolithic) type situated in Valencia province, southeast Spain.

dotaku. *See* BELLS (JAPAN).

dou [*tou*]. *See* RITUAL VESSELS (CHINA).

Douar Doum. A site outside Rabat in Morocco which has revealed some of the earliest stone tools in Africa. The tools are in rough stone and include a variety of pebble tools, but no hand axes. They are typical of the OLDOWAN or pebble culture of Africa, and are contemporary with the Moulouyan dunes of about 2 million years old or more. Earlier levels are devoid of stone tools, but tools are associated with later beaches at around 100 metres above modern sea-level.

double axe. A shaft-hole tool with symmetrical double axe blades. It can be made of stone or copper or bronze. In MINOAN Crete it was an important cult symbol, as well as a practical tool.

Douglass, A.E. (1867-1962). American astronomer who developed the DENDRO-CHRONOLOGY dating method. He outlined the method as early as 1901, but it was not until 1929 that he was able to publish an unbroken sequence of tree-rings for the Southwest USA extending back from the present day to the early years of the present era. This provided a dating method for the PUEBLO villages of that area.

Dou Wan [Tou Wan]. *See* MANCHENG.

dowsing. A practice similar to water divining. There have been a number of claims for the detection of archaeological sites by dowsing, but until the explanation of such phenomena is established it is difficult to assess the application of dowsing to archaeology.

Drachmani. *See* ELATEIA.

Dralang. A MEGALITHIC site at Dralang in southwestern Tibet, discovered by A.H.Francke between 1900 and 1910. It consisted of a cleared space with a stake in the centre, flanked on two sides by *lha-t'o*, arrangements of two stones supporting a third flat slab to form a small table-like structure. Within the space were three large standing stones or *rdo-riṅ*, the middle one bearing an inscription *Om a huṅ*, which is probably much later than the monument's construction and use. Pits not far away were supposedly for infant sacrifices. According to inhabitants of the area, the site had formerly been used for an annual *Shar-rgan* festival at which dances were performed in the cleared space and human sacrifices were offered to the goddess Tārā.

drift. The name given to all unconsolidated sediments which lie on the top of the 'solid' geology. This term originates from the belief that such deposits were transported across the waters of the Catastrophists' 'Flood', frozen into drifting icebergs. The Catastrophist view of geology held that the observable changes in the earth's surface had come about as a result of a series of natural catastrophes, of which Noah's FLOOD was the latest. (*See also* CUIVIER and LYELL). The term 'drift' remains in common usage and includes alluvium, PRO-GLACIAL deposits, TILL and ice-contact stratified drift (forming against the edge of ICE-SHEETS and GLACIERS).

dromos. [Greek: 'course', 'avenue']. A ceremonial corridor or avenue, often fairly long, and sometimes on a descending ramp, that leads to the entrance of certain types of 'room-like' tomb; *see* CHAMBER TOMB, THOLOS.

Druids. A powerful Celtic priesthood, evidence for which we derive mostly from late Roman Replublican and Imperial literary sources. Since they provided a focus of opposition to Roman expansionist aims, Druids tend to be viewed with hostility by Latin authors, and are credited with various barbarisms, such as the practice of human sacrifice. Led by an arch-Druid, their tribal responsibilities seem to have included functions that were social (e.g. calling the annual assembly), juridical (e.g. holding court and issuing sentences) and scholarly/archivist (e.g. the maintenance and transmission of knowledge in subjects such as physics, astronomy and theology). Archaeological evidence with direct named connection is lean, but Druids are, for instance, thought to be associated with a hoard of bronze and iron at Llyn Cerrig Bach in Anglesey. Supposed association with the stone circles of Stonehenge and Avebury should be consigned where they belong — to the world of popular myth.

drums (China). Traces of a wooden drum were found in a SHANG tomb at ANYANG, and drums are mentioned in a poem of the *Shi jing* anthology, which purports to be Western ZHOU. Only two bronze drums as early as the Shang period are known, however, and they do not belong to the metropolitan Shang culture of Anyang but instead to a provincial Shang culture of the Yangzi region (*see* NINGXIANG). Leaving aside these few examples from the late 2nd millennium BC, the earliest Chinese drums come from the Eastern Zhou period: wooden drums supported on lacquer stands are regular furnishings in CHU tombs of the 6th century BC and later (*see* XIANYANG, SUI XIAN). These Chu drums are found in the same region of central China as the provincial Shang examples and they are loosely comparable in type (barrel-shaped and supported with the drum heads to the side). Drums of the same variety may have been known as far south as Guangxi province, for a drum on a stand similar to the one from the Sui Xian tomb is depicted in the decoration of a locally cast early Eastern Zhou bronze vessel found in the Gongcheng district of Guangxi. This is an isolated find, however, and Guangxi lies in the sphere of a very different and far more common bronze drum, the defining artefact of the DIAN and DONG-SON cultures of Yunnan, Guangxi, and Vietnam. These drums from the southwest, which stand with the single drum head horizontal, have no obvious connection with the much rarer drums of central China. Their profile, which bulges just beneath the drum head, seems to relate them instead to the *chunyu*, an eccentric form of bronze bell common just to the north in Sichuan province; *see* BELLS (CHINA).

Dublin. The city of Dublin, the modern capital of Eire, was founded by Norse settlers in the 9th century. Its position near the Liffey estuary provides a sheltered and defensible harbour, and througout much of the Middle Ages it remained one of the foremost sea ports in the British Isles. Excavations have been continuing for over a decade in many parts of the town. Remarkable waterlogged conditions have preserved organic material from levels dating to between the 9th and 14th centuries. The footings of wattle-and-daub and timber-framed buildings have been recovered, with door posts, screens and hearths, as well as timber streets. There is also abundant evidence of the crafts and industries practised in the Hiberno-Scandinavian and Anglo-Norman periods; these include woodworking, metal-working, hooping, comb-making, leather-working and cobbling. Associated with these crafts were numerous items such as shoes, wooden bowls, soapstone bowls, and ornate objects like bone trial pieces decorated in URNES and RINGERIKE STYLE, a highly ornate Borre style disc brooch with pin, and an incised drawing of a ship on a piece of wood dating to the 11th century.

Dudeşti. Type site of a Middle Neolithic culture distributed in Oltenia and Muntenia, Rumania, in the late 5th millennium bc. Dudeşti sites are typically single period, short-lived occupations, defined by storage pits and post-holes. Most sites are limited to the first terraces of major Wallachian river-valleys. The largely undecorated pottery is a derivative of the dark burnished ware tradition of the south Balkans.

Duff, Sir Roger (1912-78). Leading New Zealand archaeologist, best known for his excavations at the site of WAIRAU BAR, his classification of Polynesian and Southeast Asian stone adzes, and his fundamental work *The Moa-hunter Period of Maori Culture*, first published in 1950.

dui [*tui*]. *See* RITUAL VESSELS (CHINA).

dun. Term used for stone-built fortified settlements found in western and northern Scotland. Most are quite small, representing an individual homestead, but the term is sometimes applied to larger settlements defended with stone walls. Many duns were built in the later Iron Age, but they continued to be built in the post-Roman period. Characteristic features are very thick stone walls with internal rooms and galleries.

Dunadd. A site in Argyllshire, Scotland, which was a nuclear fort of the Kingdom of DALRIADA, besieged by the PICTS in 683 and 736. Unfortunately, excavations carried out at the beginning of the present century ruined much of the internal plan, but the more recent investigations succeeded in establishing that the main citadel measured *c*30 by 12 metres and that it was connected to a middle courtyard by a stone wall. At the bottom of the slope was a lower enclosure with the remains of later houses inside it. The most important finds from Dunadd are several carved stones and imported Mediterranean pottery.

Dundo. A town of northeastern Angola, the centre of extensive mines where alluvial deposits of the northwards-flowing Congo tributaries are worked for diamonds. The nature of the deposits and the circumstances of the recovery of the prehistoric artefacts which they contain have ensured that little archaeological material has been discovered in undisturbed contexts. It has nevertheless proved possible to establish a sequence of stone industries, for part of which radiocarbon dates are available. Sparse ACHEULIAN occupation of the area was succeeded by SANGOAN and then by LUPEMBAN industries, the last being dated at Mufo near Dundo to before 30,000 bc. The Lupemban continued, with reduced artefact size, until *c*13,000 bc. Throughout this period it seems likely that the local climate was not significantly different from that of the present. From *c*12,000 bc TSHITOLIAN industries developed and appear to have continued in vogue until after the introduction of iron-working technology around the beginning of the Christian era.

Dunhuang [Tun-huang]. A Chinese frontier outpost at the western end of the Gansu Corridor where the SILK ROUTE branches before crossing Central Asia. Dunhuang was established as a HAN military commandery in 111 BC and many documents and manuscripts dating from the Han dynasty have been found there. It was a flourishing Buddhist centre from the 4th to the 13th century AD, when the Silk Route was the main path taken by Buddhist missionaries and pilgrims between China and Central Asia and India. To this long period belongs a complex of nearly 500 Buddhist cave temples with well-preserved paintings and sculptures. A Buddhist library walled up in a cave around 1035 and rediscovered only in 1900 contained thousands of manuscripts written in Chinese and various Central Asian scripts, some with dates ranging from 406 to 996. Manuscripts and paintings on silk and paper from the Dunhuang library were obtained by Aurel STEIN for the British Museum and Paul Pelliot for the Bibliothèque Nationale; others are now in Beijing and Japan. Among the material in the British Museum is the oldest extant printed book in the world, a Chinese translation of the *Diamond Sūtra*, a Buddhist text, dated 868.

Dura Europus. A TELL site on the middle Euphrates River in Syria, which was an important PARTHIAN city, serving as a centre for trade, where merchants from areas as far apart as Palestine and Mesopotamia met. The site was occupied from its foundation by the SELEUCIDS in the late 4th century BC, until its destruction by SASSANIANS in AD 256. The walled city was laid out on a grid plan and excavations have revealed many sanctuaries and temples dedicated to the manifold deities of the mixed population that lived there, including Christians and Jews as well as others. Architectural styles, burials, frescoes and reliefs all demonstrate a wide range of cultural and artistic influences.

Durrington Walls. A very large HENGE monument in southern England, belonging to the Late Neolithic period and dated to the later 3rd millennium BC. The monument has a diameter of nearly 500 metres and encloses an area of *c*10 hectares. Inside, the excavators found remains of two large circular timber structures, each of which had evidence for several different phases of construction. The pottery associated with the henge monument was GROOVED WARE and BEAKER wares, but there was also an earlier occupation, predating the construction of the henge, which yielded pottery of WINDMILL HILL type.

Duyong Cave. *See* TABON CAVES.

Dvāravati. A Buddhist kingdom in present-day Thailand, first mentioned in Chinese sources as T'o-lo-po-ti in the middle of the 7th century; it is believed that the kingdom came into being as a result of the dismemberment of the far-flung empire of FUNAN. Its centre was probably in the Suphanburi area of southwestern central Thailand, but its territory must have comprised almost all present Thailand. The population of the kingdom seems to have been predominantly MON. Apart from architectural remains, the art of Dvāravatī consists mainly of a Buddhist statuary in bronze or stone. The kingdom came to an end when the KHMERS under king Sūryavarman I (1002-50) expanded into the Menam basin and incorporated the area in the empire of ANGKOR. *See also* LAVO.

dyke. A linear earthwork, consisting of a bank and ditch, running across country. They may be defensive structures or territorial boundaries. *See* OFFA'S DYKE.

Dynastic Egypt. The history of ancient Egypt is traditionally tied to a framework of 30 dynasties of kings, or pharaohs, who ruled over the country from the time of its unification into a single kingdom in about 3100 BC until its conquest by ALEXANDER THE GREAT in 332 BC. This scheme, summarized below, is based upon the records of the historian Manetho who wrote in Greek during the 3rd century BC.

The great wealth of ancient Egypt was based primarily upon the annual Nile flood which deposited fertile silts of high agricultural productivity: thus crop yields were sufficient to support a substantial population concentrated in the narrow Nile Valley. Secondly, control was exercised over valuable natural resources, and these were supplemented by extensive foreign trade.

The pharaohs of the 1st Dynasty are frequently depicted as conquerors, and it appears that unification of the kingdom was brought about by means of conflict. These political developments were accompanied by major growths in craftsmanship, industry and trade in raw materials. It has been claimed that these developments owed much to contact with Mesopotamia, and certainly some innovations may have been so derived, although there is no reason to suggest that the Egyptian state-system itself was of foreign inspiration.

The Egyptian state was headed by the divine ruler, the pharaoh, to whom the whole of its complex bureaucracy was ultimately resposible. In the earlier periods, the pharaoh's position was strengthened by the appointment of members of the royal family as senior officials. The pharaoh was also the figurehead of the official religion, the personification of the sun god Ra, counterpart of Osiris, the god of the land of the dead.

Preparation for life after death was of very great importance to the ancient Egyptians, as is shown by the complex and costly efforts made to protect the bodies of the dead by mummification and secure entombment. It is thus hardly surprising, but nevertheless unfortunate, that archaeological research has for many years tended to concentrate on the tombs of the dead rather than on the settlements of the living. The royal tombs in particular reflect the great wealth and concentration of resources, both human and material, at the pharaoh's disposal, whether at the Old Kingdom pyramids at GIZA or in the underground chambers of the Valley of the Kings at THEBES.

In evaluating the technological achievements of the ancient Egyptians it is necessary to remember the limitations under which they worked. The wheel was unknown before the New Kingdom; the pyramids, for example, were built of stone blocks weighing over 2.5 tonnes which were presumably moved and erected with the aid of levers and rollers. Copper, bronze and gold were effectively the only metals used, for iron did not come into regular use before the 26th Dynasty in the 8th century BC.

Much of our information about ancient Egyptian history comes from the records that were carefully maintained by the Egyptians themselves, notably by the priests who were regarded as the guardians of the state's accumulated wisdom. Scenes of everyday life, at least for the upper classes of society, were often depicted on the walls of tombs. The political history, largely derived from written sources, has a detailed and, for the most part, precise chronology.

After the Early Dynastic period, during which the unification of the Egyptian state was consolidated, the accession of the 3rd Dynasty in about 2700 BC marks the start of the first major period of prosperity, the Old Kingdom. Through patronage and the control of trade, power and wealth were effectively concentrated in the hands of the ruling dynasty. This is reflected most clearly in the scale at which resources and manpower were devoted to state works, notably to the construction of pyramids for the burial of deceased pharaohs. By later Old Kingdom times the pharaoh's

Table 1. Dynastic Egypt

Period	Dynasty	Date BC
Early Dynastic	I	c3100-2890
	II	c2890-2686
Old Kingdom	III	c2686-2613
	IV	c2613-2494
	V	c2494-2345
	VI	c2345-2181
First Intermediate	VII-XI	c2181-1991
Middle Kingdom	XII	1991-1786
	XIII	1786-1633
Second Intermediate	XIV-XVII	1633-1567
New Kingdom	XVIII	157-1320
	XIX	1320-1200
	XX	1200-1085
Late Dynastic	XXI	1085-945
	XXII-XXIII	945-730
	XXIV-XXV	730-668
	XXVI-XXXI	664-332

control over the state bureaucracy seems to have weakened, and the proportion of the state's resources devoted to royal works was consequently diminished. This process may be seen reflected in the smaller size of the 5th Dynasty pyramids after those of the 4th Dynasty. Shortly after 2000 BC, following a period of contraction from the peak of Old Kingdom prosperity and wide-ranging trade, Egyptian political unity broke down for some 200 years during the First Intermediate period. Famine may have added to the general impoverishment of this time. Reunification under the 11th Dynasty heralded the Middle Kingdom, based at a new capital at Thebes.

The new-found stability was short-lived, however, and during the 13th and 14th Dynasties there was a rapid succession of pharaohs as different factions competed for supremacy. Early in the resultant Second Intermediate period a group of invaders from Palestine, the so-called HYKSOS rulers, took advantage of Egypt's weakness and established themselves in Lower Egypt as the 15th Dynasty in about 1670 BC. Increased fre-

quency of trade-goods of Palestinian origin, particularly in the Nile Delta, indicates greater contact with southwest Asia during the period of Hyksos rule.

Eventually, a dynasty (the 17th) from Thebes achieved the expulsion of the Hyksos rulers and the re-establishment of Egyptian unity and independence. From this base developed the greatest florescence of ancient Egyptian power and prosperity in the New Kingdom. Egyptian control was established over Nubia and substantial areas of the Near East, all governed by a complex imperial bureaucracy set up by the pharaoh Tuthmosis III. Egyptian trade ranged far and wide, even to the Land of Punt in eastern Africa. During the 18th Dynasty occurred the remarkable reign of the pharaoh AKHENATEN who, from his new but short-lived capital at EL-AMARNA, attempted to impose monotheism in place of the traditional religion. Akhenaten's successor was the young TUTAN-KHAMUN, the only pharaoh whose grave, near Thebes, has survived virtually undisturbed and unrobbed to reveal the full richness and splendour which surrounded the New Kingdom rulers.

From the 21st Dynasty onwards, Egypt's cohesion once again broke down, and from the 11th to the 7th centuries BC Libyan, Asian and Nubian contenders vied with Egyptians for control of the state. The 25th Dynasty originated in Nubia and finally lost control of Egypt to an invasion from Assyria, after which ancient Egypt never regained its independence.

dyss [plural: *dysser*]. Danish name for the earliest type of megalithic CHAMBER TOMB found in Scandinavia. *Dysser* are simple rectangular chambers containing one to six bodies; one or more such chambers may be found under the characteristic rectangular mounds, surrounded by a kerb of stones. Dysser are associated with an early phase of the TRB CULTURE.

Dzibilchaltun. A MAYA site of long occupation located close to the ocean in the northeastern corner of the Yucatan Peninsula in Mexico. Its earliest occupation is denoted by MAMON ceramics and CHICANEL structures, although there are no corbelled arches. The site centres around the CENOTE Xlacah, with major plazas and associated civic architecture nearby; numerous causeways (*sacbe*) converge in the middle of the site. Although the main structures, dating to the PUUC period, are unprepossessing, archaeological remains cover an area larger than 46 square kilometres, indicating a population of 10-20,000 — a huge population for the time.

E

Early Dynastic Period(Mesopotamia). Term describing the earliest historical period in Mesopotamia, dated 2900-2370 BC on the middle chronology, 3100-2450 BC on the high chronology (*see* Table 3, page 321). The term is derived from the Sumerian 'king list' which implies that Sumer was ruled by kings at this stage, although archaeological evidence for the existence of kingship is meagre before the middle of the period. Traditionally the period is divided by archaeologists into three — ED I, II and III — each of approximately 200 years duration. The Royal Tombs of UR belong the the ED III period. The Early Dynastic phase shows clear continuity from the preceding JEMDET NASR, and represents a period of rapid political, cultural and artistic development which saw the establishment of independent states governed — ultimately at least — by kings. Within this period the pictographic writing of the earlier period developed into the standardized CUNEIFORM script.

Early Horizon. One of a seven-period chronological construction used in Peruvian archaeology. It runs from 900 to 200 BC and coincides with the duration of the CHAVIN style and its derivatives, such as CUPISNIQUE. *See* Table 9, page 552.

Early Khartoum. A site within the area of the modern Khartoum conurbation which provided the first clear picture of the so-called 'AQUATIC CIVILIZATION'. The site was evidently a substantial base-camp, and traces of sun-dried daub suggest the presence of structures which would have been occupied on more than a temporary basis. Fishing by means of bone-headed harpoons, in a Nile flowing at a higher level than the present, formed the economic basis of the settlement. Nets were probably also used. Other artefacts include chipped and ground stone, and pottery with 'wavy-line' decoration. No radiocarbon dates are available for this settlement, but an age in the 6th or 5th millennium bc seems probable: at Tagra, 200 km to the south, similar harpoons occur in an aceramic context dated to *c*6300 bc.

Early Man Shelter. An Australian rock shelter at Laura, Cape York, containing paintings and engravings of humans, animals, tracks and abstract motifs. Charcoal from occupation deposits covering wall engravings yielded radiocarbon dates between 10,000 and 13,000 bc, which are the earliest for rock art in Australia, other than the engravings at KOON-ALDA Cave, dated to *c*18,000 bc. The shelter also contained the oldest known remains of *Sarcophilus harrisii* (Tasmanian devil) in tropical Australia: it is now found only in Tasmania.

Early Nomad Period. *See* ALTAI.

Early Shang. *See* ERLIGANG PHASE.

earth. A rather general term, best used to describe mixed material which is cast up from an excavation. Earth is not really the same as SOIL, which has a more precise definition, although earth may include material from soils in addition to material from other sources.

earthworms. One of the main agents by which plant litter, HUMUS and minerals are incorporated and mixed in SOIL. Earthworms are responsible for the maintenance and stability of various types of soil, especially the BROWN FOREST SOILS. The character of a soil may change markedly if the plant litter produced by the vegetation changes to a kind which is unpalatable to earthworms (*see* PODZOL). The effects of earthworm sorting may be seen on archaeological sites in the blurring of LAYERS and the development of worm-sorted layers in the top of BURIED SOILS, where a line of stones marks the lower limit of worm activity.

Easter Island. 4000 km from South America and 2000 km from the closest inhabited islands of POLYNESIA, Easter Island was settled by Polynesians by about AD 400. The MEGA-

LITHIC stone platforms and statues were constructed between 700 and 1700, after which the culture and population declined, virtually to die out after European contact. Only occasional contacts occurred with South America (see SWEET POTATO, VINAPU). The islanders erected stone statues weighing up to 100 tonnes and also carved on wooden boards in an undeciphered script (RONGORONGO). Easter Island culture represents perhaps the most bizarre cultural development ever to occur in an isolated human community, and its decline may have been purely internal (through overpopulation or warfare for example). See also ORONGO, PURAPAU, RANO RARAKU.

Eastern Zhou [Chou] period. The latter part of the Zhou dynasty, from 770 BC to the extinction of the Zhou royal house in 256 BC (or, more loosely, to the founding of the QIN dynasty in 221 BC). See ZHOU.

East Rudolf. See TURKANA.

East Spanish rock art. See SPANISH LEVANT ART.

Ebbsfleet. A small valley close to SWANS-COMBE and BAKERS HOLE in southern England with an important series of loams and gravels later than the Swanscombe high-terrace deposits, spanning the last two glacial periods and intervening interglacial. Stone tools included LEVALLOIS flakes, but only a few hand axes and other tool types were found in the various levels. Both warm- and cold-indicating animal fossils were found at different levels.

The area has also given its name to a decorated pottery style of the Neolithic period.

Ebla, Eblaite. Ancient city excavated at the site of Tell Mardikh on the River Orontes in Syria. Recent excavations have yielded evidence of the previously unknown language and history of a powerful state of the 3rd millennium BC. Although the site was occupied from the 4th millennium BC onwards, the period of its greatest wealth and power was in the mid-3rd millennium; a large royal palace of this period has yielded an archive of more than 15,000 CLAY TABLETS inscribed in the CUNEIFORM script in two languages, SUMERIAN and the local language, a Semitic tongue now labelled Eblaite. Work is still continuing on the tablets, but they have already revealed a wealth of information about the economy, political organization and religion of Ebla. The city was clearly an important commercial centre, exporting woollen cloth, wood and furniture to areas as far flung as ASSUR in Mesopotamia and KANESH in Anatolia. The settlement of this period was destroyed, probably by the AKKADIAN ruler Naram-Sin, but the city was rebuilt and a great palace complex and some wealthy burials of the early 2nd millennium BC have been excavated. The Ebla texts include many Semitic names which recall those of the Old Testament, but extravagant claims of a cult of Yahweh at Ebla and of texts mentioning the biblical patriarchs, the cities of Sodom and Gomorrah, and the Flood story are without foundation.

Eburran. A recently proposed name for an idiosyncratic obsidian industry of the central Rift Valley, Kenya, previously known as the 'Kenya Capsian' and before that as the 'Kenya Aurignacian'. Both these former names implied a connection with distant industries which is not upheld by recent research. The distribution of the Eburran is restricted to a small area around Lake Nakuru, and its time-span to between the 11th and the 8th millennia bc. The assemblages, as recovered from GAMBLE'S CAVE and NDERIT DRIFT, comprise large backed blades, crescentic microliths, burins and end-scrapers.

ecology. The relationship of plants and animals with their environment. The environment in this sense consists not only of climate, but also geology, soils, vegetation, other animals, man-made structures — anything that impinges on the organism being studied. ENVIRONMENTAL ARCHAEOLOGY is concerned not only with the ecology of man himself, but also with the ecology of other animals and plants living in the same environment.

Eden. See CODY.

edge-ground axes (Australian). See OEN-PELLI SHELTERS.

Edo. See MIRRORS (JAPAN).

Eemian. A group of QUARTERNARY INTER-GLACIAL deposits in northern Europe (*see* Table 5, page 418). They are found right across Europe from the Netherlands to the USSR, containing FOSSILS that indicate warm conditions. Their exact age is unknown, but they are older than the extreme range of RADIOCARBON dating (*c*70,000 bp) and can be shown by PALAEOMAGNETISM to be younger than 700,000 BP. They are directly overlain by WEICHSELIAN glacial deposits. In the Netherlands and north Germany, SEA LEVEL rise caused the deposition of Eemian marine sediments. Recent evidence from a borehole in northern Germany has shown that there are, in fact, two sets of marine deposits — one stratified underneath WARTHE glacial deposits and the other stratified above the Warthe deposits. Thus the Eemian appears to represent at least two interglacial stages. Further recent evidence suggests that there may even be three. Despite this, the term 'Eemian' is still frequently used to mean the 'last' interglacial only. LEVALLOISIAN and MOUSTERIAN artefacts are found in Eemian deposits.

Efate. *See* ROY MATA.

Effigy Mound culture. A Middle/Late WOODLAND group (possibly an extension of HOPEWELL) centred on the upper Mississippi Valley to the west of Lake Michigan, USA. It is characterized by the construction of low mounds of various shapes, especially (though not always) life forms. Bundled, flexed and cremated burials are common, with certain locations within the life-form mounds being preferred (e.g. the head, heart and hips). Grave goods, if they occur at all, are very simple. No clear chronology has emerged for this culture, but evidence indicates continuing activity beyond AD 1000.

Egolzwil. A series of Neolithic sites around the shores of Lake Wauwil in Switzerland. Most of them belong to the CORTAILLOD culture and, like so many of the lakeside settlements of this culture, have produced very well-preserved organic material. The site of Egolzwil 4 had ten rectangular wooden houses placed close together. Each house probably contained a nuclear family of about five people, giving an overall population for the settlement of not more than 50 people. Surviving food remains include cereals, lentils, beans and flax, presumably all cultivated, and also wild strawberries and chestnuts; animal remains include both domesticated and wild animals, duck, and salmon, perch and carp from the lake. The site also produced evidence about the nature of farming at this time: a building near the village entrance contained layers of vegetable matter and many pupae of the common housefly. It is suggested that this building served as a stall for cattle during the winter and that flies laid their eggs in the accumulated dung. Stacks of leaves, mistletoe twigs and hay probably represent collected winter fodder for the cattle.

Egtved. An Early Bronze Age burial in east Jutland, Denmark. A round BARROW covered the remains of a young woman in an oak coffin. The acid soil had destroyed all bones but, as in other oak coffin burials of this kind, remains such as skin and hair, as well as clothing, survived. She was wearing a woollen jacket and skirt and was covered by an ox-hide shroud. Bronze bracelets and a bronze disc on her belt also survived. The grave also contained a birch-bark box containing an awl and a hairnet. Beneath the woman's body were the cremated remains of a child.

Ehecati. *See* CALENDAR STONE, QUETZA-COATL.

Ehringsdorf. A travertine quarry in central Germany near Weimar. A badly broken skull and other human remains have been found here with stone tools resembling the MOUSTERIAN. The fossil man is of generalized NEANDERTHAL type, but earlier than the usual Mousterian and classic Neanderthal finds. Often ascribed to the last interglacial (about 120,000 years ago), the remains have also been dated by the URANIUM SERIES method to about 220,000 years ago and may really date to a temperate period before the last interglacial.

einkorn. *See* WHEAT.

Elam, Elamite. Important state in southern Iran with its capital at SUSA. The development of civilization in this area closely paralleled that in Mesopotamia proper; for instance, writing appeared almost as early (*see* PROTO-ELAMITE), before 3000 BC, though later the

Elamites were to take over CUNEIFORM and adapt it to their language. The Elamites usually appear in the Mesopotamian texts as enemies, and indeed it was Elamite incursions that brought down the Third Dynasty of UR late in the 3rd millennium BC. The high point of Elamite civilization was reached in the reign of Untash-gal, who extended the kingdom and invaded KASSITE Babylonia. He also built a royal city at CHOGA ZANBIL. The kingdom of Elam fell to the ASSYRIANS when Ashurbanipal sacked the city of Susa, c640 BC.

The sculpture, bronze work and jewellery of the Elamites were of a high standard and demonstrate strong local styles, while sharing an overall similarity with Mesopotamian work. Little is known about the Elamite language, which is not related to any known tongue and still not fully deciphered.

El-Amarna. A city in Upper Egypt built as his capital by the Eighteenth Dynasty pharaoh AKHENATEN during the 14th century BC. Palaces and temples, erected to support the worship of the divine sun-disc Aten, were abandoned and largely destroyed on Akhenaten's death. The art of this brief period of monotheism was realistic and unrestrained, in contrast with the stereotyped art-style of other periods in ancient Egypt. Important diplomatic correspondence has also been recovered during excavations at El-Amarna.

Elandsfontein. A farm southwest of Hopefield in Cape Province, South Africa, and 25 km southeast of Saldanha Bay, which has produced several Palaeolithic cultures and a human skull somewhat like that of BROKEN HILL. The skull is believed to be associated with late ACHEULIAN tools and may be 100,000 or so years old. Traces of 'Middle Stone Age' and 'Late Stone Age' tools were also found.

El Argar. Situated on a hilltop near Almeria in southeast Spain, El Argar is the type site and largest known settlement of the Argaric Bronze Age of the 2nd millennium BC. The settlement was fortified and contained rectangular stone houses, though these are less well preserved than at other Argaric settlement sites such as at Ifre and EL OFICIO. The settlement also contained 950 burials, the earlier ones in cists, later ones in large jars. Grave goods include plain burnished pottery in simple shapes, including pedestalled bowls and cups, and a variety of metal goods, including daggers, swords and axes of copper or bronze and ornaments of gold and silver. Silver was particularly common, perhaps more common than anywhere else in Europe at this time, and was used especially for diadems.

Elateia. The earliest known Neolithic settlement in central Greece, near Phocis, dated to the mid-6th millennium bc. Rectangular houses were built of timber with earthen floors. A series of pottery styles has been recognized, starting with undecorated dark- and light-surfaced wares, later replaced by black polished and polychrome painted wares. Coal-scuttle shaped vessels, presumably for ritual use, show connections with the DANILO culture of Yugoslavia. This site is also known as Drachmani.

El Baul. *See* IZAPA.

elbow stones. *See* BALL GAME.

Ele Bor. A group of rocky outcrops in the north Kenya plains, not far from the foothills of the Ethiopian escarpment. A group of rock shelters yielded a composite sequence extending from 'Middle Stone Age' into recent times. A backed-microlith industry appeared at an as yet unknown date and continued in use by hunter-gatherers into the period when fishermen of the 'AQUATIC CIVILIZATION' were established beside Lake Turkana to the west. Domestic sheep/goat and, it appears, camel were present in small numbers from about the 3rd millennium bc, at which time pottery also came into use. Seeds and numerous grindstones suggest intensive exploitation of — presumably wild — cereals. The climate at this time was somewhat moister than that of the present. With subsequent desiccation, cereal use was abandoned, but both hunting and small-scale pastoralism continued into the present millennium.

electromagnetic surveying. A GEOPHYSICAL surveying method. Instruments designed for this technique have two coils. One, through which an alternating electric current passes, produces a magnetic field. This field induces electrical currents in buried objects, which are detected in the second coil of the apparatus. It is possible to detect buried features of archaeological sites by this method, due to differences in electrical and magnetic properties between the fill of the features and the subsoil. Electromagnetic systems are, however, more widely used in METAL DETECTORS.

elephant. A group of the order *Proboscidea*. The living elephants are confined to Africa — *Loxondonta africanus* (*Elephas africanus*) — and India — *Elephas maximus* (*indicus*). The African elephant is adapted to a savanna environment and formerly occupied a far larger area, as is attested by skeletal evidence and cave paintings in North Africa. The reduction in its range is probably due to the combined effects of climatic change, human hunting and cattle-grazing. Other species of elephant are now known to have existed. The straight-tusked elephant, *Elephas* (*Palaeoloxodon*) *antiquus*, apparently adapted to the open deciduous woodlands of interglacials in Europe, became extinct at the end of the IPSWICHIAN interglacial. Related forms existed in Asia, North Africa and East Africa. Dwarf forms of the straight-tusked elephant evolved on islands of the Mediterranean. MAMMOTHS seem to have been adapted to more open conditions, and although present during interglacials were particularly common during colder periods.

Elephantine. An island in the Nile near Aswan on the ancient boundary between Egypt and Nubia. The area was famed for its quarries, which yielded the granite extensively used throughout ancient Egypt.

Eleusis. Greek city, some 22 km west of Athens, famous in antiquity as the home of the Eleusinian Mysteries, a mystery cult in honour of Demeter and Persephone. Situated on a bay that is virtually an inland lake, the town enjoys good protection from the sea. This advantage, coupled with a naturally defensible acropolis, would have made the site attractive, and occupation is attested from the early Bronze Age onwards. Use as a sanctuary seems to go back at least to MYCENAEAN times. The major ritual building of the sanctuary, the so-called *telesterion* (Hall of Initiation), was a temple of unusual design dedicated to Demeter, incorporating such rare features as a lantern over the *anaktoron* (holy of holies) and built-in seating to the main hall. Interpretation of the site is not straightforward, with some evidence

for one or more archaic temples and possibly a Mycenaean-type MEGARON. The sanctuary continued to enjoy great popularity into Roman times, and it was only devastation by Alaric and his hordes (*see* GOTHS) and the edicts of the emperor Theodosius that finally led to its abandonment.

El Garcel. A settlement of the 4th millennium bc ALMERIAN Neolithic culture of southeast Spain. Excavations in the 19th century produced evidence of round houses, storage pits, undecorated round-based pottery and, before the end of the settlement, copper slag, suggesting the local development of metallurgy.

Elgin, Lord (1766-1841). British diplomat best known for transporting the marble sculptures from the Parthenon in ATHENS to London. Since 1816 these sculptures, known as the 'Elgin Marbles', have been among the prime exhibits of the Department of Greek and Roman Antiquities of the British Museum. The removal of these sculptures from their source has often been criticized and the issue of their possible return to Greece is raised from time to time, most recently in the early 1980s, though it is not easy to foresee a mutually agreed solution to the problem.

El Guettar. An ATERIAN site in southern Tunisia. The relatively moist climate of the Sahara at this time is demonstrated by the presence of rhinoceros remains in these northerly latitudes.

El Inga. A PALEO-INDIAN site in highland Ecuador, 24 km south of Quito, at which a large and varied inventory of flint and OBSIDIAN tools provides evidence for man's southward passage through South America. Fishtail points from El Inga level I show technological and morphological similarities to CLOVIS/FOLSOM points and to the fishtail points of MAGELLAN I. Levels II and III contain willow-leaf points similar to those at AYAMPITIN, LAURICOCHA CAVES and elsewhere, as well as stemmed points, flaked knives and scrapers.

Although El Inga seems to represent a hunting-based society and some bone was found nearby, no faunal remains or hearths were associated with stone tools. Absolute dates are rare. but the earliest radiocarbon date is *c*7000 bc and a 4000-5000-year period of occupation is postulated.

El Jobo. One of a series of stone tool complexes found at a group of sites in northwestern Venezuela. Designated the Joboid series, they appear to span a considerable time period. There are no absolute dates but ancient erosional episodes have defined a series of terraces upon which man-made lithics were deposited and which seem to represent successive complexes. The highest, and also the oldest, is Camare, which contains crude chopping tools; next is Las Lagunas, which contains bifaces. This is followed by El Jobo, characterized by lanceolate leaf-shaped points; El Jobo is followed by Las Casitas, the lowest and most recent terrace, containing stemmed points. The leaf-shaped points of El Jobo resemble tools elsewhere, especially at LERMA and SANTA ISABEL IZTAPAN and thus may indicate the presence of intrusive PALEO-INDIAN groups. Comparison with these and other sites has led to an estimated age of 8000-9000 bc. Some archaeologists, however, prefer to see the complex as a local development unassociated with the movement of BIG GAME HUNTERS into South America.

El Khril. A CAPSIAN NEOLITHIC site near Tangier in northern Morocco. The pottery is of cardial type, akin to contemporary Iberian wares, and is associated with evidence for the herding of small stock.

Elliot Smith, Sir Grafton (1871-1937). An anatomist by training, who became interested in many aspects of archaeology. He was involved, for instance, in the examination of the remains from PILTDOWN and it has even been suggested that he may have been implicated in the forgery. He is best known, however, for his espousal of the exaggerated form of DIFFUSIONISM, sometimes called 'hyper-diffusionism', which interpreted the appearance of new developments anywhere in the world in terms of a spread from Egypt.

Ellora. A site in central India with several rock-cut Buddhist, Jain and Hindu temples, mainly of the 6th-8th centuries AD. Many of them have fine sculptures.

elm decline. A permanent fall in elm pollen, seen in POLLEN DIAGRAMS from Britain and Northern Europe. In diagrams plotted from PROPORTIONAL POLLEN COUNTS, other trees are largely unaffected. Radiocarbon dates for the elm decline in Britain mostly fall between 3300 and 3100 bc, some time after the first appearance of Neolithic culture. Explanations for the decline include climatic change, a rapidly spreading selective disease, and human interference. But in a number of diagrams plotted from ABSOLUTE POLLEN COUNTS it has been shown that although elm declines most markedly other trees are affected as well. This makes disease a far less likely cause. In addition, small transient forest clearances are increasingly being shown in pollen diagrams, just before and during the elm decline. It is therefore quite reasonable to suggest that elm may have been particularly affected by man's activities in the forest. Elm is among the most palatable of tree foliage, and it may be that Neolithic cattle browsing in the forest, and the gathering of foliage for their winter fodder, caused the selective decline of the elm.

Elmenteitan. A Neolithic industry which occurs in a restricted, well-watered highland area on the west side of the central Rift Valley in Kenya. Typical artefact assemblages include large double-edged obsidian blades, plain pottery bowls and shallow stone vessels of unknown function. Domestic cattle and small stock were herded; it is not yet known whether cereal agriculture was also practised. The dead were cremated, as at the mass-burial site at NJORO RIVER CAVE. The latter, dated to *c*1000 bc, appears to be one of the earliest Elmenteitan sites; but the industry continued into the 1st millennium ad. The Elmenteitan is best regarded as a localized and specialized facies of the PASTORAL NEOLITHIC complex of East Africa.

El Molle. *See* AGRELO.

El Oficio. A hilltop settlement of the ARGARIC Early Bronze Age in Almeria, northeast Spain. The site was surrounded by a thick defensive wall. Inside were rectangular houses of stone, some with evidence of wooden upper storeys, packed tightly together. 200 burials were found within the settlement, some under the floors of houses.

El Paraiso. Located in the flood plain of the lower Chillon Valley on the central coast of Peru, El Paraiso (also known as Chuquitanta) dates to PRECERAMIC PERIOD VI. Considerably larger than other contemporary sites, its massive architectural complex of mounds, courts and rooms interconnected by corridors covers an area of 50 to 60 hectares. Five to six building phases are evident in the constructions of fieldstone masonry laid in clay (some with mud-plastered walls). Although the population at its maximum is estimated at only 1500, the whole complex represents an investment of labour considerably beyond what could be expected of such a population. The low population figure (confirmed to a great extent by the small amount of cultural refuse) suggests that El Paraiso was an early CEREMONIAL CENTRE. No pottery or maize was found at any level, but twined and woven textiles are common (found in fabric-wrapped burials) and domesticated beans and squash remains were also recovered.

El Riego. See TEHUACAN VALLEY.

Elsloo. A settlement of the Neolithic LINEAR POTTERY culture in southern Holland. Long houses of various types have been found, as in the other Dutch sites of this culture, such as GELEEN, SITTARD and Stein.

Elster. See ANGLIAN.

Els Tudons [Es Tudons]. A tomb of NAVETA type on the island of Minorca. It is c14 metres long and contains a two-storeyed chamber originally housing the remains of many individuals. It is built in CYCLOPEAN MASONRY and, as the term *naveta* implies, is vaguely boat-shaped in plan. Like the other *navetas* on the island, Els Tudons belongs to the TALAYOTIC culture of the 2nd millennium BC.

El Tajin. The major CLASSIC PERIOD centre located in a rain forest valley in northern Veracruz, Mexico. Its central structures are very tightly grouped but there are hundreds of other structures spread about the valley which remain to be investigated. The art style of the site was subject to many influences including MAYAN, IZAPAN and OLMEC, but TEOTIHUACAN influence dominates the early period; the central structure, the Temple of the Niches, for example, is constructed in a modified TALUD-TABLERO style.

El Tajin, however, rose to prominence after the fall of Teotihuacan. Its location in an area where rubber grows naturally and its unusually high number of ball courts (at least seven) indicates that it may have been a centre for the BALL GAME. In addition, vast quantities of ball game paraphernalia (YOKES, *hachas* and *palmas*) have been uncovered.

The artefact most commonly associated with Classic Veracruz culture is the hollow, clay 'smiling face' figurine; but the main centre for its manufacture lies to the south at REMOJADES. El Tajin's final destruction by fire was probably at the hands of the CHICHIMECS. The site was abandoned in c1100.

eluvial horizon. A SOIL HORIZON from which minerals, HUMUS or plant nutrients have been lost. See ILLUVIAL HORIZON.

El Zacpool. See JAINA.

Emery, Walter Bryan (1903-1971). British Egyptologist whose long career involved more than 40 years of fieldwork, as well as the production of general books and technical articles. His most important excavations were at EL-AMARNA and SAQQARA.

Emiran. Named after the Emireh ['princess'] cave north of the Sea of Galilee in northern Israel, this is the earliest stage of the Upper Palaeolithic recognized in the east Mediterranean region. It is characterized by Emireh points, a kind of elongated MOUSTERIAN point with the bulb thinned away by retouch. The Emiran is believed to date from about 30,000 bc and may be transitional from the Mousterian.

emmer. See WHEAT.

Emporiae. See AMPURIAS.

enamel. A decorative coating of glassy material which is fused to the surface of a metal artefact.

Encanto. A complex of 13 sites concentrated on the Peruvian central coast, including CHILCA and Ancon Yacht Club, which demonstrate the changing subsistence patterns resulting from the decreasing availability of LOMAS vegetation. Dating to the PRE-CER-

AMIC PERIOD V, the Encanto phase is characterized by the gradual abandonment of ARCHAIC subsistence practices in favour of sedentary ways of life, particularly increased exploitation of marine resources and the practice of limited agriculture.

end scraper. *See* SCRAPER.

Eneolithic. Another term for CHALCOLITHIC. *See also* THREE AGE SYSTEM.

Engaruka. Located on the western side of the Eastern Rift Valley between Lake Manyara and Lake Natron in northern Tanzania, Engaruka preserves the remains of an Iron Age irrigation system covering more than 20 square kilometres. There are indications that settlement of the area began by the mid-1st millennium ad, but the major irrigation developments are probably subsequent to the 14th century. Water from streams flowing into the valley was dispersed through an elaborate network of stone-lined furrows to serve a large number of small stone-terraced fields. Sorghum was one of the crops that was cultivated. The affinities of the Engaruka people to any contemporary later Iron Age populations in East Africa remain to be demonstrated satisfactorily.

Englefield Island. *See* FUEGIAN TRADITION.

Enkomi. A Middle and Late Bronze Age settlement on the Bay of Salamis in Cyprus. First settled early in the 2nd millennium BC, by c1500 BC it had become a major metal-working and trading settlement; many copper ingots have been found on the site and it is clear that Enkomi was involved in trading the metal from which Cyprus derives its name throughout the east Mediterranean. In the 13th century BC Enkomi seems to have been taken over by MYCENAEANS, perhaps refugees from the Mycenaean collapse on the Greek mainland. The site continued to flourish as a trading centre until c1200 BC when it was attacked again, perhaps by the PEOPLES OF THE SEA. It was not abandoned, but started to decline from this point and by c1000 BC the site was deserted.

Enlil. The SUMERIAN god of air or 'Lord Wind', the patron deity of the city of NIPPUR. He was the son of Anu and inherited his father's title of 'father' or 'king' of the pantheon. Like Anu, he is credited with giving kingship to man, and the Tablet of Destiny, through which the fate of man and gods was decreed, also belonged to Enlil. The god was thought to have been responsible for the downfall of AKKAD: because of the desecration of his shrine at Nippur by Naram-Sin, he called on the Gutians to invade. Enlil was ultimately dislodged from his prime position in the pantheon by the god of Babylon, Marduk, but this did not occur till late in the 2nd millennium BC.

Ensérune. An Iron Age promontory fort in Languedoc, southern France. It had defences of CYCLOPEAN MASONRY from the early 4th century BC and well laid-out stone houses. Both defences and houses are very similar to those found on Greek settlements in the area (*see* MARSEILLES). Large storage jars and silos excavated into the tufa were probably for grain or water. Nearby is a large cremation cemetery of the 3rd century, with the cremated remains placed in urns.

entrance grave. A type of MEGALITHIC tomb characterized by a chamber without separate passage, under a round BARROW. Although the chamber form is similar to that of the GALLERY GRAVE, the round barrow is more characteristic of the PASSAGE GRAVE tradition. Entrance graves are found in southern Spain and along the Atlantic seaboard to Brittany and southwest Britain, and on the other side of the Irish Sea in southeast Ireland.

Entremont. An important OPPIDUM near Aix-en-Provence, southern France, which was the capital of the Salyes from the 4th century BC until it was taken by the Romans in 123 BC. It had ramparts built of large stone blocks, with watch towers. Inside were streets, houses of dry stone, drainage and water systems, all laid out on a rectilinear system. It also had a sanctuary of the SEVERED HEAD CULT, with four-sided pillars of stone carved with severed heads, separate carved stone heads and torsos and actual human skulls in niches, supported by iron nails.

environmental archaeology. The aspect of archaeology that is concerned with reconstructing past environments and understanding the ECOLOGY of man and other animals and plants living in the same environment. Many disciplines are involved in this study: climatology, QUATERNARY geology, SOIL SCIENCE, PALAEOBOTANY, zoology (*see* SKELETON, MOLLUSCS, BEETLES) and human biology.

environmental indicators. Species of plants and animals that are used to indicate a feature of the environment. If the modern environmental requirements are known, the presence of preserved remains of the same species in ancient deposits and soils may suggest that similar conditions prevailed in the past. Many such indicator fossils are used to reconstruct temperature. Ivy is a well-known example: this plant is particularly susceptible to hard winters and autumn frosts, and is today restricted to areas of moderately high summer temperature and average temperature in the coldest winter month above −1.5°C; the appearance of ivy in a POLLEN DIAGRAM is thus often taken to be evidence of an amelioration of climate. There are, however, pitfalls with these methods. Many other factors of ecology may also exert control over the distribution of a species, and the absence of an environmental indicator does not imply lack of the conditions which it is supposed to indicate. In addition, the ECOLOGY of the species may have changed. The method only becomes reliable when whole communities, comprising many different species, all indicate the existence of a particular environment.

eolith. A roughly chipped stone widely claimed in the past to be evidence of man's most primitive handiwork during a remote eolithic period. Most eoliths were frost-split chunks with irregular chipping round the edge, now generally thought to be natural in origin.

Ephesus. One of the richest and most splendid cities of the classical world, on the west coast of Turkey, famous in antiquity for its colossal temple of Artemis (one of the SEVEN WONDERS OF THE WORLD). The town was situated strategically in the delta area of the River Cayster, and there is some evidence for occupation from MYCENAEAN times. Tradition, however, describes the settlement as founded from Athens by King Androklos. It is likely that Ephesus soon took on the uneasy balancing role — familiar to the major cities and ports along this seaboard — between influences from mainland Greece and pressures from the hinterland of Asia Minor, notably in this case from Lydia and Persia. Artemis herself, for instance (Diana to the Romans), may be seen as a Greek equivalent for the Anatolian goddess, Cybele. Supreme prosperity, however, only arrived once general conditions in the eastern end of the Mediterranean had stabilized under the Hellenistic kings and Roman rule. Apart from the great temple, this later Greco-Roman city boasted a generalized magnificence, as, for instance, in the grand scale of its AGORAS, BATHS, THEATRE (the setting for Paul's address, Acts of the Apostles XIX), the Library of Celsus, the Gymnasium of Vedius, and the arcaded streets, notably the Arkadiane (whose visible remains date from the period of the Emperor Arcadius AD 395 onwards), running more than 500 metres from the theatre to the harbour, and equipped with a central vehicular lane, mosaic pavements, shops, and even street-lighting.

Epi-Palaeolithic. This name is sometimes given to the cultures of the very end of the Palaeolithic, such as the FEDERMESSER or AHRENSBURG groups, or even to post-glacial cultures more usually described as Mesolithic. Because of this confusion and imprecision, the term is better avoided.

Epidauros. Classical Greek city on the east coast of Argolis with site close to that of present-day Palaia Epidavros. The lower city and harbour are now submerged, while sections of Cyclopean wall (*see* CYCLOPEAN MASONRY) are still visible. Epidauros was famous, especially from the 4th century BC onwards, for its sanctuary (*hieron*) of Asclepius, the god of healing, and mythical saviour/doctor figure. The sanctuary lay in a broad valley some 13 km inland, where a network of buildings grew up to serve the twin functions of faith-healing and general spa-type recreation. The centrepiece was the Temple of Asclepius itself. This modest-scale DORIC building seems to have been strikingly decorated, with black-and-white marble floor, and the widespread use of inlays of ivory, ebony and gold. The cult figure was similarly chryselephantine. A second cult building was the *enkoimeterion* or *adyton*, in which visiting sufferers might hope to obtain a cure by sleeping and dreaming. Also probably associated with the cult, but of obscure function, was a fine Doric rotunda with labyrinth. Facilities seem to have been comprehensive, including baths, gymnasium and palaestra for exercise, hospitals for the sick and sanatoria for the convalescent, accommodation for the priest-doctors and a magnificent (4th-century BC) theatre for cultural recreation, which is exceptionally well preserved.

Erbil. The ancient Assyrian city of Arab'ilu and a modern town in Iraq. It has been continuously inhabited for about 8000 years and provides a living example of the formation of a TELL. Because it lies under the modern city there has been little excavation, but it is known from texts that it had a temple dedicated to Ishtar and was a cult centre of importance, second only to ASSUR itself. The earliest records referring to Arab'ilu belong to the late 3rd millennium BC.

ercengtai [*erh-ts'eng-t'ai*]. *See* SHAFT TOMBS (CHINA).

Erd. A recently excavated MOUSTERIAN site in Hungary near Budapest. Radiocarbon dates suggest that it was occupied by bear-hunters in the later part of the Mousterian period.

Erech. Biblical name for the Mesopotamian city of URUK.

Erechtheum. A religious building on the North side of the ACROPOLIS at ATHENS, named after the legendary King Erechtheus of Athens, and put up in the name of various cults to house cult objects and to cover cult areas. It is a large and complex rectangular building in the IONIC style, built of white Pantelic marble and dark Eleusis stone, and was erected in the period c421-407 BC. Architecturally it is most noteworthy for the Porch of the Maidens on its south side, with its delightful marble CARYATIDS.

Eridu. The most southerly and possibly also the earliest city of SUMER in southern Mesopotamia. A sounding excavated underneath a ZIGGURAT of the late 3rd millennium BC revealed a sequence of 18 religious buildings. The earliest building was a simple mud-brick shrine resting on virgin sand. By the time of its tenth rebuilding it had acquired the standard form of the Sumerian temple, with tripartite plan consisting of a long central room, flanked by symmetrically grouped side chambers, and was built on a substantial platform.

The earliest phase of occupation, named the Eridu phase, is dated to c5000 bc; this is followed by the Hajji Muhammed phase and both of these precede the UBAID culture proper; they are often regarded as early or proto-Ubaid. The settlement at Eridu can be regarded as proto-urban from the beginning; it grew into a substantial city by the EARLY DYNASTIC period; and two royal palaces of this period have been excavated.

Outside the temple precinct a large cemetery of the late Ubaid period was found; this contained perhaps 1000 graves, of which c200 were excavated. Grave goods include painted pottery vessels, terracotta figurines and baked clay tools, such as sickles and shaft-hole axes. One contained a model of a sailing boat, and is a very early indication of the use of wind power to propel boats.

Erimi. A deeply stratified site in southern Cyprus, which has produced evidence of a sequence of pottery styles covering most of the 4th millennium BC. To begin with houses were cut into the rock, but were later built free-standing. The site is best known for its single copper chisel, the earliest evidence on the island for the use of the metal from which it derives its name and for which it was famous in the ancient world.

Erligang [Erh-li-kang] **phase**. A stage of the early Bronze Age in North China defined by two strata at ZHENGZHOU Erligang in Henan province. The Erligang phase is assumed to belong to the earlier part of the SHANG dynasty. It follows immediately on the ERLITOU phase and precedes the historical ANYANG period (c1300-c1030 BC; *see* SHANG, GAOCHENG). Two radiocarbon dates obtained from the Lower and Upper Erligang levels at Zhengzhou are c1600 BC and c1550 BC respectively. Remains comparable to those from Erligang are very widely distributed in North China, reaching from the Wei River valley in the west to Shandong in the east, as far south as PANLONGCHENG near the Yangzi River, and in the north to parts of Shanxi and Hebei provinces and to BEIJING. The Erligang phase may correspond to the widest sway of the Shang empire. The period is notable for its highly developed bronze-casting industry.

Until recently the Erlitou and Erligang phases were often referred to as Early Shang and Middle Shang respectively; these terms have gone out of use since radiocarbon dates raised doubts as to whether Erlitou is a Shang site. Some Chinese archaeologists have even begun calling the Erligang phase Early Shang.

Erlitou [Erh-li-t'ou]. Type site of the Erlitou phase, near Luoyang in Yanshi, Henan province, north China. The Erlitou phase represents the earliest known stage of the Chinese Bronze Age. Radiocarbon dates suggest that the four levels at the Erlitou site span the first half of the 2nd millennium BC. The two lowest levels have yielded only insignificant metal remains, but in the third and most important level were found the earliest bronze RITUAL VESSELS yet known from China, along with bronze GE blades and fine jades. To the same level belongs a very large HANGTU palace compound whose pillared hall and south-facing plan establish the norm of later Chinese palace architecture. The hall, raised on its own *hangtu* podium, stood on a square *hangtu* terrace 100 metres on a side; the terrace was enclosed by a corridor-like structure.

Archeaologists at first assigned the Erlitou site to the early SHANG dynasty, some identifying it as the capital of the dynasty's founder; current opinion holds that it is probably too early to fall within the Shang period and might instead belong, at least in part, to the preceding XIA dynasty. The fourth level at the site is described as transitional to the full-fledged Bronze Age culture of the ERLIGANG PHASE, which is generally believed to correspond to the earlier part of the Shang dynasty. Thus whatever the political status of the city may have been, the Erlitou remains provide the fullest evidence now available for the emergence of the Shang civilization from its local forbears.

Ermine Street. Name given to the Roman road that ran north from LONDON to LINCOLN. Doubtless following more ancient tracks, it was most likely established very soon after the Roman invasion of Britian in AD 43, to provide communications with the legionary fortress at Lincoln. Later, when Lincoln became a colonial town *c*90, it retained its importance as a trunk route, running on north to reach the Humber at Winteringham.

Erösd. *See* ARIUŞD.

Ertebølle. A coastal shell-mound site in Jutland which has given its name to a late Mesolithic culture in Denmark. Pottery was apparently introduced in this culture.

Escomb. A village in Co.Durham which contains one of the most complete upstanding Anglo-Saxon churches in England, the small chapel of St John. A simple double-celled building, its square-ended chancel has a tall narrow chancel arch with jambs formed of monolithic blocks laid in 'long and short' style that have given their name to the term 'Escomb fashion'. The church, which dates from the early to mid-8th century, has several early constructional features such as roughly coursed masonry (including a great many re-used Roman stones), side alternate quoining, and round-headed, single-splayed windows. Excavations here have shown that at one stage in its history Escomb had a pair of flanking side chapels or porticos, and that the windows were glazed from an early stage.

Eshnunna. The ancient name of a city under the mound of Tell Asmar, excavated by an American team led by Henri Frankfort in the 1930s. Situated in the Diyala area, to the northeast of SUMER proper, Eshnunna was nonetheless to all intents and purposes a Sumerian city. Although it was occupied from the EARLY DYNASTIC PERIOD onwards, politically it was most important in the period after the fall of the Third Dynasty of UR, in the first two centuries of the 2nd millennium BC, when it was the centre of an independent kingdom of some size and importance. Subsequently it was conquered by Hammurabi and absorbed into the growing power of BABYLON, after which it rarely appears in the texts and presumably declined in importance.

Esh Shaheinab. A site near the eastern bank of the Nile, 50 km downstream from Khartoum, dated to the second half of the 4th millennium bc. For long the only fully investigated manifestation of the so-called 'Khartoum Neolithic', the site was held to illustrate the small-scale beginnings of food-production in the Sudanese Nile Valley. New excavations, as at KADERO, show that Esh Shaheinab represents only one, possibly atypical, aspect of a complex economic system. The material culture of Esh Shaheinab, together with the general life-style of the site's inhabitants, shows much continuity from the older occurrence of EARLY KHARTOUM. Fishing was evidently of major importance and was conducted both by means of shell fish-hooks and with harpoons whose barbed bone points were now pierced for the attachment of the line. Edge-ground axes and adzes were made both from bone and stone. The microlithic stone industry and the pottery were very similar to those from Early Khartoum. The animals slaughtered by the Esh Shaheinab people were mostly wild but included a few examples of small domestic goat.

Eskimo [Inuit]. A long-standing and widely used term for the Arctic hunting peoples. It is a French transliteration of an Algonquin word meanin 'raw flesh eaters'. Inuit, a native Eskimo word meaning simply 'the people', is the term currently favoured to describe the same group.

Essenes. *See* DEAD SEA SCROLLS.

Este. The ancient name of this town standing in antiquity on the River Adige in northeast Italy was Ateste, which is now used to denote the striking Iron Age culture of the area from the 9th century BC. Profiting from its position, its maritime trade connections and its contacts with Greek and Etruscan cultures, the town became the leading centre of the area. Its craftsmen produced a variety of pottery types, including red and black cordoned wares made on a wheel (from the 6th century BC), and much fine sheet bronze work. The most impressive products of the bronzesmiths are the sheet bronze SITULAE, some plain, but others decorated in repoussé with zones of figures in scenes of feasting, sporting and warfare; the scenes indicate a mixture of local and Greek elements. Situlae and other decorated bronze objects were traded to the other side of the Adriatic, to the BOLOGNA area and over the Alps into the eastern part of the HALLSTATT Iron Age area.

The florescence of the culture was from the 6th century to the mid-4th century, when northern Italy was invaded by CELTS, but it continued until the area was annexed by Rome in 184 BC. It is likely that the Atestine culture is the archaeological manifestation of the Veneti, the tribe recorded as occupying this area in the classical sources.

ethnoarchaeology. The study of living societies from an archaeological point of view. The ethnoarchaeologist studies the material remains of such societies with the aim of furthering understanding of the patterns of material remains that emerge from archaeological contexts. In particular, ethnoarchaeology is concerned with establishing systematic relationships between patterns of material culture and other aspects of society, as, for instance, residence patterns or systems of inheritance, which do not leave very direct indications in the archaeological record. Lewis Binford's study of the Nunamiut Eskimo is one of the best known studies in ethnoarchaeology, which represents a relatively new development in archaeology generally.

Etowah. A large MISSISSIPPIAN site located on the north bank of the Etowah River in northern Georgia, USA, which appears to have functioned as a CEREMONIAL CENTRE rather than a centre for population. Its major features are three truncated pyramid mounds, surrounded by a ditch and palisade. The largest mound contains over 125,000 cubic metres of earth; in North America only Monk's Mound at CAHOKIA contains a greater volume. The artefact inventory includes Lamar pottery (an elaborately stamped or incised utilitarian ware), under life-size stone statues of humans usually in a sitting or kneeling position, and large quantities of the paraphernalia of the SOUTHERN CULT. The site's florescence is strongly linked to that of the Cult and dates to c1200-1700 AD.

Etruscan. An important culture, dominant in west central Italy (approximately the area of present-day Tuscany) from about the 8th to 5th centuries BC, with decisive influence upon its direct successor, Rome. Literary sources give a picture of a loosely structured but powerful confederacy of city-states (such as TARQUINIA, CAERE, VEII, Clusium [CHIUSI], Populonia) combining to push their dominion north into the Po Valley, and south into Campania. Roman sources are generally hostile, and rehearse the standard clichés of extreme luxury, moral decadence and sexual licence. Recent thinking suggests some kind of continuity with Iron Age VILLANOVAN culture, with no clear breaks in settlement patterns. The striking, especially oriental, developments in art, pottery, metalwork, tomb and temple architecture are then accounted for as bought-in acquisitions or expertise, purchased by a rising élite out of commercial success and vigorously expansive trade. Alternatively, an add-on intrusive aristocracy is suggested.

Antiquity, on the other hand, particularly antiquarians such as Varro and the emperor Claudius (a considerable Etruscologist whose work, including a treatise on language, is unfortunately lost) tended to see an enigmatic opposition between two traditional literary viewpoints, represented by Herodotus — who derived the Etruscans from Lydia in Asia Minor(modern Turkey) — and Dionysius of Halicarnassus, who claimed that they were indigenous.

For the ancients, the mystery was compounded by the Etruscan language, whose affinity is still undecided. The letters of the script may be read easily enough, since the Etruscans used a Western Greek alphabet (which, through Etruscan, is the precursor of all subsequent Western forms of the alphabet). Clear too is the context of the vast majority of the inscriptions, which is funerary. There is no real doubt that a parallel can be sought with Oscan, Umbrian and Latin inscriptions of a similar period giving, for example, name and family of deceased, offices and honours, and age at death. Difficulties, however, immediately multiply with the few longer texts, once any effort is made at an unambiguous identification of vocabulary items or, worse, aspects of syntax and morphology. Just how severe the complexities remain may be judged from the failure to establish any exact correspondences in the Pyrgi so-called bilingual — a temple dedication with three parallel texts, one in Punic and two (different) ones in Etruscan.

The 'colourful and mysterious' image commonly ascribed to Etruscan civilization also needs to be handled with some caution. The 'goody-hunting' approach of 19th-century antiquarians and some 20th-century archaeologists has produced a body of evidence that is almost entirely derived from cemeteries and grave goods. Apart from the exception of MARZABOTTO (a 'colonial' town site near Bologna), there has been little excavation or study of occupation sites. This weighted evidence shows a surge in wealth, with a high preponderance of imports, especially metalwork and Greek painted pottery. The market for such products encouraged local copies, and the growth of a home industry. Typical products are the ubiquitous decorated bronze mirror, BUCCHERO pottery, and sophisticated filigree jewellery. Inhumation tends to replace cremation, and characteristic are the stone sarcophagi with reclining figures, chamber tombs (with or without decoration) and the rounded tumuli often heaped over them (e.g. CAERE, CHIUSI, TARQUINIA).

Rome is indebted to the Etruscans not only for its early kings, such as the notorious Tarquin, but virtually for the total infrastructure of its civilization. The debt is such that maybe the inverse picture is the true one, Roman culture being essentially the continuation of Etruscan under another name and language. Among areas of continuity too numerous and complex to list, notable are religion (e.g. Etruscan *haruspex* and Roman augury), political and social organization, strategic arts, architecture, art, drama, theatre and civil engineering (notably hydraulics, such as aqueducts and drainage systems).

Euesperides. *See* BENGHAZI.

eustatic. Eustatic sea level changes are long-term fluctuations in the absolute volume of sea water held in the oceans of the earth. Such fluctuations have occurred throughout the QUATERNARY, due to changes in the extent of ice-sheets and thus in the volume of water locked up as ice. The larger the ice-sheets, the less water available to the sea, and so sea level is lower during GLACIALS than during INTERGLACIALS. Evidence exists for a whole series of eustatic sea level fluctuations, but the most widespread is the 'high stand' on c120,000 BP, just before the start of the last cold stage (DEVENSIAN, WEICHSELIAN, WISCONSIN), when sea levels were between two and ten metres higher than at the present day. During the maximum extent of the ice-sheets of the last cold stage, eustatic sea level was much lower than that of today. Large areas of continental shelf were exposed, some being occupied by the ice-sheets themselves. Recovery of sea level at the end of the last cold stage is relatively well known from deposits in the Netherlands, Scandinavia and Scotland, but is complicated by isostatic changes. The North Sea and English Channel flooded, separating Britain from the Continent, by about 7000 bp. Ireland became a separate island at about the same time. Scandinavia had a complicated series of different seas and lakes, until a sea similar to today's Baltic became established around 7000 bp.

Evans, Sir Arthur (1851-1941). British archaeologist, son of Sir John EVANS. His main contribution was in the field of Cretan studies, through his excavations at KNOSSOS for than 30 years from 1899. He was largely responsible for demonstrating the existence of a pre-MYCENAEAN Aegean civilization, for naming it MINOAN (after the legendary King Minos of Crete) and for revealing most of its characteristics. Not surprisingly, some aspects of his work have been criticized in the years since his death, but in the main his conclusions have stood the test of time and remain the basis of Minoan studies today.

Evans, Sir John (1823-1908). British scholar, collector and antiquary. He published three major works on British prehistoric artefacts: on coinage (pre-Roman), stone implements and bronze implements. He was keenly interested in the archaeological issues of the day and played an important role in support of those scholars who were arguing for the great antiquity of man (*see* BOUCHER DE PERTHES).

evolution. The idea that the animals and plants of today originated from ancestors of a different kind goes back at least to early Greek philosophers, but it was Charles DARWIN who provided the first satisfactory account of a mechanism which would cause this to happen. The *Origin of Species* was published in 1859, the year after Darwin and Alfred Wallace had briefly presented the theory of evolution by Natural Selection, and it had an immediate impact on prehistory and the question of the antiquity of man (*see* HUMAN EVOLUTION). The Darwinian idea — of species generally over-reproducing themselves and only the better-fitted surviving to pass on their superior adaptation to the next generation — has been modified and amplified in the 20th century by new knowledge of genetics, and especially of mutation and re-combination of genes. The newer view is often called Neo-Darwinism.

experimental archaeology. A term used to describe experiments carried out to test hypotheses about practical aspects of past societies, such as how tools were made and used, how buildings and other structures were constructed and how long the construction would have taken, how ancient crops were planted, harvested and stored, or how boats were made and used. The journey of the KON TIKI in 1947 is one of the best-known of all archaeological experiments. One of the most important projects still in progress is the experimental farm at Butser Hill in Hampshire, southern England, where hypotheses about Iron Age farming practices are tested. Another type of experiment is aimed at discovering information about how structures, artefacts and materials decay over time; two experimental earthworks in southern England (Overton Down in Wiltshire and Wareham in Dorset) are being excavated at intervals to monitor processes of collapse and silting of the structures, and the movement and decay of various buried materials.

Eye Temple. *See* BRAK, TELL.

Eynan. *See* AIN MALLAHA.

Ezero. Denotes the Dipsis TELL near Nova Zagora, the eponymous site of the Early Bronze Age culture in south Bulgaria. Excavated by G. Georgiev and N. Merpert, the site comprises a 9-metre stratigraphy with four main building phases. These include at least two building levels of the VESELINOVO culture (KARANOVO III), dated *c*4320 bc; a single level with Karanovo IV pottery; eight building levels of the Copper Age (Karanovo V-VII) dated *c*3630 bc, and four metres comprising nine building levels of the Early Bronze Age. The Bronze Age levels have radiocarbon dates of *c*2500-2200 bc, the pottery has affinities in the Early Bronze Age of TROY and there is a very rich bone, antler and stone industry. The subsistence strategies favoured were the cultivation of emmer wheat and six-row barley, and cattle husbandry.

F

fabric. The material of which POTTERY is composed.

fabricator. A piece of stone or bone used for detaching FLAKES from a CORE or tool. Fabricators are usually heavily worn at one end.

Fafos. An early VINČA settlement with two horizontally distinct settlement foci, located in Kosovo, south Serbia, Yugoslavia. Fafos I, the earlier of the two, consists of three occupation levels with pits and post-holes, covering 2.5 hectares, while Fafos II is smaller, less prolific in artefacts and shorter-lived. The site is characterized by particularly rich ritual equipment, chiefly fired clay figurines in the local Kosovo style. Powdering of azurite and malachite is also known.

faience. Properly a type of medieval pottery manufactured at Faenza in northern Italy. The term is, however, more widely used to describe the turquoise-blue or greenish glazed material used to make small objects such as beads and seals. This material appeared first in Mesopotamia in the 3rd millennium BC and then, almost as early, in Egypt; it is sometimes called Egyptian faience. It is made with a core of quartz, or quartz and soda-lime, fired so that the surface fuses into a glassy coating; the characteristic colour is achieved by the addition of copper salts. It was widely produced and traded throughout the Near East in the 2nd millennium BC. Examples occur also in Bronze Age contexts in Europe, including the WESSEX CULTURE and opinion is divided as to whether these represent items traded from the east Mediterranean or whether there were independent centres of manufacture in several parts of Europe.

false entrance. Term for a phenomenon most commonly found in MEGALITHIC tombs in the British Isles, where an apparent entrance to a chamber, often leading from a forecourt, is in fact a dummy and the real chambers open not from the end but the side of the mound.

fang ding [*fang-ting*]. *See* RITUAL VESSELS (CHINA).

fang yi [*fang-i*]. *See* RITUAL VESSELS (CHINA).

Fara. *See* SHURUPPAK.

Far'ah, Tell el [Fara] (1). Site on the Wadi Ghazzeh in southern Palestine, excavated by Flinders PETRIE in 1928-30. Occupation levels and tombs dating from the Middle Bronze Age to the Iron Age were excavated. The most impressive material came from five rich PHILISTINE tombs containing characteristic Philistine decorated pottery, native Late Bronze Age undecorated wares, bronze bowls, daggers and spears; an iron dagger and an iron knife were also found, among the earliest finds of this metal in Palestine.

Far'ah, Tell el [Fara] (2). Site in central Palestine near the head of the Wadi Far'ah. The site was occupied from the Chalcolithic (5th millennium BC) to c600 BC, with a major gap in the later 3rd and early 2nd millennium BC. In the 9th century the site is identified as TIRZAH, the capital of Omri before he moved to SAMARIA.

Faras. A former capital of the Nubian kingdom of Nobatia on the west bank of the Nile near Wadi Halfa, Faras is best known for the magnificent cathedral which was erected there in the 7th century and flourished until the 12th century. Fine mural paintings were recovered during excavation, together with inscriptions of major historical value; the study of superimpositions has enabled a detailed record of stylistic development to be established.

Farfa. One of the richest Benedictine monasteries in Italy in the early Middle Ages, situated northeast of Rome. The scriptorium was famous and the *Farfa Chronicle* was widely imitated. Founded c680-700, Farfa came under the protection of the Lombard duke of Spoleto in 705 and, with the Carolingian conquest of 774, passed into the hands of CHARLEMAGNE. An ambitious programme of building took place under Abbot Siccard (830-42). The monastery was burnt during the Moslem incursion of 897, but restored by later abbots, notably Ratfred (in 933) and Hugo (998-1039). Very little of the medieval complex survives above ground, but a series of excavations has revealed remains of the principal church (perhaps of the 8th century, with transepts and a crypt added by Siccard); one of the five minor churches mentioned in medieval descriptions at Farfa; the cemetery and other structures including a concentric ambulatory outside the crypt. This last feature recalls the early 9th-century arrangement at Fulda in Germany, and suggests that the abbots of Farfa were as aware of the latest architectural developments north of the Alps as of those in Rome.

Fatimid. An Islamic dynasty that seized power from the earlier Abbasid dynasty in Tunisia in 909. The Fatimids subsequently conquered Egypt (in 969), which they then dominated for some two centuries. Much Fatimid architecture survives, including mosques, palaces and elaborately decorated chamber tombs. *See also* AJDABIYAH, CAIRO and MAHDIYA.

Fatyanovo. A cemetery on the upper Volga, USSR, representing part of the Copper Age SINGLE GRAVE tradition. The burials were crouched inhumations in shallow pits; grave goods included globular pottery vessels (some with cord ornament), stone battle-axes and ornaments of copper and bone.

Fauresmith. The name formerly given to a stone industry now recognized as a final phase of the South African ACHEULIAN. Named after a town in the Orange Free State, the 'Fauresmith industry' was characterized by the presence of small, neatly made, pointed hand axes.

Fayum. A low-lying lake-basin in Lower Egypt to the west of the Nile, to which it was formerly connected by a channel. The Fayum Depression has yielded a long sequence of archaeological occurrences, but is primarily known for Neolithic sites illustrating the earliest farming communities yet recognized in the Nile Delta region, dating from c5000 bc. In contrast to their counterparts at Helwan and MERIMDE, the Fayum Neolithic sites appear to have been only briefly occupied. The fine workmanship of the chipped stone industry, including many bifacial implements, contrasts markedly with the crude undecorated pottery. Artefacts of special note include a threshing flail and a wooden sickle set with flint teeth. The grain so processed was stored in mat-lined pits. Barley, emmer wheat and flax were the principal crops, the latter being used for the production of linen cloth. Cattle, sheep, goats and pigs were herded, while hunting and fishing continued to be practised.

feature. On archaeological excavations the term is used for any recorded remain that is not classified as a structure, a layer or a small find. For instance, pits and post-holes are features, as is anything of uncertain nature or function.

Feddersen Wierde. The most thoroughly excavated and best-preserved of the TERP settlements on the North Sea German littoral. Lack of space necessitated that the internal layout of the village was carefully planned, and so it was divided into segments radiating like spokes of a wheel from a central open area, separating farm and dwelling units from the industrial areas where leather- and bone-working was carried out. All the buildings at Feddersen Wierde were constructed of timber, the usual type being an aisled LONG HOUSE infilled with wattle walls that incorporated a byre with stalls and a central drain at one end. The settlement was occupied between about the 1st century and the early 5th century and was involved in a certain amount of foreign trade.

Federmesser. Literally, a pen-knife point. Points of this type are a typical constituent of assemblages of flint tools in northern Europe dating from the last few millennia of the last ice age. They are backed blades tapering to a point, and were probably used as arrowheads. They tend to have curved or angled backs unlike the earlier Gravette points (*see* GRAVETTIAN). A group of cultures is named after them.

Fell's Cave. Located on mainland Chile near the Straits of Magellan, this is one of the principal sites used in defining the MAGELLAN

COMPLEX (the other being Palli Aike). A radiocarbon date of 8700 bc taken from its earliest level has helped make credible the widely accepted minimal date of 9000 bc for the presence of man in South America.

fen. A community of plants growing in basic or neutral waterlogged conditions, as opposed to BOG. Fens represent a stage in the progressive colonization of shallow water; this plant succession continues with the colonization by trees (the 'carr' stage) followed in some areas by the growth of a raised bog on top of the fen and carr.

Feng [Feng]. *See* ZHOU CAPITALS.

Fenghuangshan [Feng-huang-shan]. *See* JIANGLING.

Fenshuiling [Fen-shui-ling]. *See* LIYU.

Fernando Po. Island off the coast of Equatorial Guinea, of particular archaeological interest since (presumably due to the absence of sources of metal) a NEOLITHIC technology and life-style appear to have continued until at least the early centuries of the 2nd millennium ad. A similar situation seems to have prevailed on the Canary Islands.

Ferrières. A PASSAGE GRAVE in Languedoc, southern France, which has given its name to a cultural group of the Late Neolithic and Copper Age (3rd millennium BC). It is characterized by pottery with incised decoration.

Fertile Crescent. A term invented in 1916 by James Breasted, first Director of the Oriental Institute of Chicago. The term was applied to a crescent-shaped area of cultivable land between the highland zones and the West Asian desert, stretching from Egypt through the Levant to southern Anatolia and northern Mesopotamia, and eastwards to the flanks of the Zagros Mountains. Conditions in this area were favourable for the early development of farming, and all the earliest farming communities were thought to lie within it. We now know that some early domestication of plants and animals took place in more marginal areas, and the term is rarely used today.

fibula. Latin word for a common type of brooch, usually made of bronze, resembling the modern safety-pin and used in the fastening of such clothes as tunics and cloaks. The fibula essentially comprises a pin bent round (often with a spiral at the angle) with a catch to hold the point. Alternative forms have the pin made separately from the bow (northern Europe) or have a hinge instead of a spiral (introduced by the Romans). The first fibulae appear in prehistoric Europe *c*1300 BC, with the earliest forms appearing in northern Italy (*see* PESCHIERA) and MYCENAEAN Greece; there is no agreement as to which area first developed these brooches. At approximately the same time there was an apparently independent development in northern Europe of the two-piece variety. An enormous number of different types of fibulae were made and they can often be a useful guide to dating.

Fiji. An archipelago in eastern MELANESIA, centred on the large islands of Viti Levu and Vanua Levu. A rich archaeological sequence begins with the Lapita culture from about 1300 bc, and progresses through successive ceramic phases (*see* SIGATOKA) to a period of earthwork fort construction and warfare, perhaps starting after ad 1100. Fijians are an intermediate Melanesian/Polynesian population, and their islands formed the main bridgehead for the Polynesian settlement of western POLYNESIA soon after 1300 bc. Fiji is the most easterly point in Oceania to have maintained production of pottery throughout its prehistory.

filigree. A technique of decorating gold and silver jewellery: designs formed by thin wire are soldered on to the part to be decorated. The technique had been mastered by the Early Dynastic SUMERIAN craftsmen of the 3rd millennium BC and fine jewellery decorated in this way appears in the Royal Tombs of UR. One of the greatest developments of this technique was by ANGLO-SAXON and Germanic metalworkers, who used it to decorate gold jewellery and other objects. The wire was produced by hammering, rolling, twisting and coiling, and then threaded, pearled and beaded into delicate granulated and plaited patterns. The main function of filigree at this period was to soften hard edges and fill in blank spaces; it is extensively used on such pieces as the ALFRED JEWEL and the Kingston Brooch.

Filitosa. A defended promontory site in southern Corsica, belonging to the TORRE culture. The walls are built of CYCLOPEAN MASONRY and incorporate broken STATUE-MENHIRS; these and others in the area apparently represent male figures equipped with daggers and swords. There is a radiocarbon date of c1200 bc (c1500 BC) for one of the three *torri* inside the defences.

Finglesham. An early Saxon cemetery situated close to the former mouth of the Wansum estuary in Kent, in use between the early 6th and mid-7th centuries. The large inhumation cemetery was partially excavated at the beginning of this century; the main research excavation took place in the 1960s, and over 40 graves have been investigated. These have produced an impressive collection of material including a PATTERN-WELDED sword, rich garnet-inlaid bird brooches made in Kent, Continental radiate brooches and a magnificently decorated square-headed brooch. Wooden boxes with bronze binding, strings of beads, corroded buckets and bone objects of the period were also found. One gruesome aspect is that some of the female burials seem to have been interred alive.

Fiorelli, Giuseppe (1823-96). The most important of the 19th-century archaeologists to excavate at POMPEII. He set up a training school based at Pompeii, where many other archaeologists learnt the techniques of stratigraphical excavation.

fire. Possibly the most important single discovery made by early man was how to produce fire at will. Fire is first found on occupation sites of the Lower PALAEOLITHIC period, approximately half a million years ago, although true hearths do not become typical until the penultimate glacial period, perhaps 200,000 years ago. Hearths and thick deposits of burnt material are typical of the last glacial period, by which time it is likely that the two main methods of making fire (the friction method of rubbing or rotating sticks to generate heat and the percussion method of striking sparks with iron and flint) were both in use. *See also* CHESOWANJA.

firedog. An instrument to ensure the proper burning of a fire, alternatively known as an andiron. The end of a log could rest on the crosspiece, which was supported by two uprights. Decorative iron examples come from LA TÈNE Iron Age contexts, mostly graves. There are several examples from the British Isles, all with their uprights adorned with animal heads.

First Northern Culture. *See* TRB CULTURE.

First Temperate Neolithic [FTN]. Generic term for the earliest farming cultures in the temperate zone of Europe (and sometimes applied in other areas also). In southeast Europe from c5400-4500 / 4300 bc the following regional groups have been identified: STARČEVO (eastern and northern Yugoslavia), KÖRÖS (eastern and southwest Hungary), CRIŞ (west of lowland Rumania), KREMIKOVCI (northwest Bulgaria) and KARANOVO (central and southern Bulgaria). While the regional groups are differentiated by their individual painted wares, the whole FTN group is unified by non-ceramic traits such as miniature polished stone axes, slotted antler sickles, polished bone spoons, fired clay lip-plugs, rod-head figurines and stamp seals. The vast majority of early FTN sites are located in the major river valleys of the Balkans, either as TELL settlements (in Macedonia and south Bulgaria) or as short-lived flat sites (other areas). Hoe or digging-stick agriculture combined with cattle husbandry forms the economic base of most FTN settlements.

fish bones. Fish have a markedly different skeleton to mammals. Many of the bones are very small and thin, and so do not survive very well on archaeological sites. However, some bones are commonly preserved, notably the jaws and some other head bones, OTOLITHS and the centra of vertebrae. They usually accumulate in refuse deposits and may be interpreted in terms of diet and fishing on the site or in the area that supplied it.

Fishbourne. Town in Sussex, southeast England, best known for its Roman-style villa/palace of the 1st century AD, a four-hectare extravaganza, possibly put up for and by the British king (of the tribe of the Regni) Cogidubnus, a noted Romanophile. The site lies near to Chichester, which was first fort and then CIVITAS capital of the Regni. Earlier buildings at Fishbourne include a sizeable stone mansion with baths, garden and rich decoration, possibly dating from the 60s AD, which some take to be an earlier palace. Soon after 75 AD came the palace itself, consisting of four colonnaded wings around an oblong formal garden. Apart from the evident luxury of the scale and standard of decoration, the presence of an assembly hall and a separate audience hall approached through a monumental entrance (across the formal garden) suggest a palatial function. Alterations and rebuilding during the 2nd century, after the death of Cogidubnus, imply continued use at least as a very important villa. The late 3rd and early 4th centuries brought more modest use and some limited new adaptations, but a serious fire seems to have caused damage that was uneconomic to repair. Notable features include the discovery of bedding trenches for hedges, terracotta pipelines to fountains, a black-and-white geometric mosaic, and another with Cupid riding centrepiece to a medley of marine creatures.

fishing. Fishing probably did not become a major source of food until quite late in man's evolution, although fish remains are occasionally found on early PALAEOLITHIC sites, such as OLDUVAI. Fish and other sea food were a more important part of the diet for coastal peoples and in the poleward latitudes. In some areas, late Palaeolithic man may have specialized in salmon fishing. Only in the MESOLITHIC, from c6000 bc onwards, when coastal and lakeside sites became common, did fishing become a major part of the economy, and fishing gear such as hooks and nets is known from this period. Boats are also likely to have come into general use at about this time.

fission track dating. A RADIOMETRIC DATING method for mineral materials.

Principle. One of the isotopes of uranium, ^{238}U, spontaneously undergoes nuclear fission to produce two heavy 'fragment' nuclei. This happens at a very slow, but known, rate. The fission fragments are released with great energy and create tracks of damage through the mineral in which the uranium is contained. Such fission tracks are very small, but can be identified by etching and microscopic examination. A count of the tracks is made for a unit area of mineral, and since this represents the number of fissions that has occurred, an age can be calculated from the known rate of uranium fission. The method depends on there being enough uranium and a large enough piece of mineral for the tracks to be counted successfully. In archaeology, it is also essential that the mineral has been heated, annealing any previous tracks, otherwise the date produced will only be that of the original formation of the mineral. Fission track dating is therefore confined to pottery or the rare occasions where stone objects can be proved to have been heated.

Range. Maximum age is almost unlimited; minimum age depends on the uranium content, the area of mineral available for examination and the time available for counting tracks.

Accuracy. Again dependent upon uranium content and the size of the piece of mineral. For most practical purposes the method is limited to samples that are very old or have a high uranium content.

Materials. OBSIDIAN contains relatively large quantities of uranium and can provide a large area for counting, but it must have been reheated in antiquity for the date to be useful. POTTERY in general has a low uranium content, but some of its mineral inclusions contain adequate uranium for a reasonable dating accuracy. Zircon is the most common of these, having a uranium content between 1000 ppm and 1 per cent. Grains of zircon can be separated from crushed pottery by standard heavy mineral flotation techniques. The grain must, however be large enough for there to be a chance of counting tracks over a large enough area for reasonable dating accuracy. The size of this area depends on the uranium content, the age of the sample and the accuracy required. Small grains may be ground down in stages to provide a whole series of surfaces for counting, to make up the required area.

Problems. Fission track dating has proved very useful for geology, but its time-consuming nature for many archaeological applications has resulted in little work being done with it. Where pottery contains sufficient zircon, fission track is potentially very useful as a cheap, reliable and independent method of dating. It could easily be combined, for example, with a petrological study of pottery inclusions.

Five Dynasties period. The period of Chinese history between the fall of the TANG dynasty in 907 and the founding of the SONG dynasty in 960. The name refers to a series of dynasties that ruled North China; in the same period the south was divided among the Ten Kingdoms.

flake. The removal of a flake from a block of raw material is the basis of flint, and other stone, technology. Flakes vary greatly in shape and size, according to the technique used to remove them. They are generally used as blanks for the manufacture of tools, which is done by the removal of further small flakes.

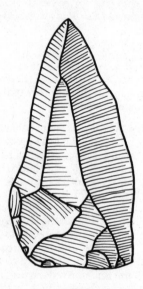

Primary flake

Flandrian. A group of British QUATERNARY INTERGLACIAL deposits. The Flandrian can be dated by radiocarbon, and ranges from 10,000 bp (the end of the DEVENSIAN) up to the present day (*see* Table 6, page 419). These deposits represent the latest Quaternary interglacial stage, equivalent to the HOLOCENE epoch. As well as SEDIMENTS similar to those of previous interglacials, the Flandrian includes deposits on archaeological sites which contain Mesolithic, Neolithic, Bronze Age, Iron Age, Roman, Dark Age, medieval and more recent artefacts.

Flemish blackwares. Later medieval Flemish pottery is well-known from paintings of the Renaissance period. Some of these wares were especially well-decorated, such as the so-called Aardenburg type, which has applied floral decorations. However, the majority of the Flemish wares were coarse black wares with pinched bases, usually black or grey in colour. These wares stem from a Roman tradition of potting in Flanders, and although they took local forms the reduced fabric was widely imitated between the Rhine and the Seine.

flint. *See* CHERT.

flint mine. During the Neolithic and Copper Age of Europe, flint workers recognized that flint from beds below ground was of much superior quality to surface flint, especially for the manufacture of large tools such as axes. These beds were exploited by sinking shafts and then excavating galleries outwards. Flint mines are known from many areas of Europe and good examples occur in Poland (e.g. Krzemionki), Holland, Belgium (*see* SPIENNES) and England (*see* GRIMES GRAVES).

Flood, the. 'Flood stories' appear in the literature of many of the civilizations of western Asia. The discovery by George Smith in 1872 of a Babylonian version among the tablets of Ashurbanipal's library in NINEVEH aroused great public interest because of its similarity to the biblical account. In this version, the Noah-figure is called Uta-Napishtim; more recently an even older — SUMERIAN — flood story has been found in which the Noah-figure has the name Ziusudra. Archaeological stratigraphies on sites in Mesopotamia have often found traces of water-laid sand and clay deposits, demonstrating that floods were a frequent occurrence. When Leonard WOOLLEY found such a deposit in a deep sounding at UR in 1929 he believed that he had found evidence of Noah's Flood. Today most archaeologists believe that the various flood stories do not represent the record of a single event, but rather a whole series of natural disasters which affected the low-lying alluvial plain of southern Mesopotamia.

Floral Park. *See* BARTON RAMIE.

Florence [Roman Florentia, modern Italian Firenze]. City in Tuscany, central Italy, a rich and important town since later Roman imperial times. Little is known of earlier settlement on this favourable site on the junction of the Arno and the Mignone, but recently discovered VILLANOVAN material suggests occupation from the 8th or 9th centuries BC. It is probably not an Etruscan town. The Etruscan town which we would expect to find serving the same function as present-day Florence (i.e. major staging-post between Etruria and the Po plain) is possibly to be seen at Fiesole (Roman Faesulae) situated upon a neighbouring hill, although even there the bulk of the material evidence (e.g. walls, temple and cemetery) date only from the early 3rd century BC. Present-day Florence would seem to date only from the establishment of a Roman COLONIA in the mid-1st century BC. Evidence for the Roman period include remains of a couple of bath buildings, theatre and amphitheatre and a temple to Isis, but very little is still to be seen *in situ.*

Florentine Valley. *See* TASMANIA.

Florisbad. A spring deposit in the Orange Free State, South Africa, which preserved a human cranium attributed to an early form of modern man, HOMO SAPIENS SAPIENS. Its brow ridges, while pronounced, are markedly less prominent than those of the (presumably earlier) skull from BROKEN HILL in Zambia. The Florisbad specimen is best dated to c50,000 bc and appears to be associated with a 'Middle Stone Age' industry of PIETERSBURG type.

flotation. A method of extracting fossil plant remains (especially seeds), shells, small bones and insects from ancient soils and sediments. At its simplest, the method involves mixing the material with water and skimming off the organic fragments that float to the surface. Organic remains may be rendered more buoyant by mixing the material with paraffin beforehand. Froth flotation involves placing the material in a tank of water, to which a frothing agent has been added, and through which bubbles are blown. The organic remains accumulate in the resulting froth and are washed into a sieve over a lip at the side of the tank. There are several designs for froth flotation machines, often referred to as seed machines.

fluorine dating. One of the methods of BONE DATING. Fluorine-containing groundwater percolates through deposits, its fluorine becoming absorbed onto the crystal lattice of the mineral component of buried bones (in the same way that fluorine is adsorbed into the surface layers of teeth from repeated brushing with fluoride toothpaste). Given a constant rate of groundwater percolation, the concentration of fluorine in the bone should be proportional to its age. Bones from the same STRATIGRAPHICAL context can be dated relatively by comparison of their fluorine content. The PILTDOWN forgery was finally exposed by this method.

flûte de Pan. *See* PAN PIPE LUG.

Fluxgate magnetometer. *See* MAGNETO-METER.

foederati. Roman technical term (from Latin *foedus*, 'treaty') denoting tribes external to the Empire who were under a treaty relationship with Rome. The conditions usually involved co-existence and military help to Rome in time of need. Sometimes also used of mercenaries in general.

fogou [fougou]. Name for an Iron Age structure found in Cornwall, southwest England, constructed like a gallery partially or mostly under ground, usually covered by a mound of earth and stones. They are generally found near settlements and may have been used as storerooms or as refuges, or both.

Folsom. A kill site discovered in the plains area of New Mexico, USA, in 1926. Distinctive man-made weapons found in assocation with the remains of the now extinct *Bison antiquus* established beyond doubt the antiquity of the native American. Based on this association, further sites were designated Folsom (or as having a Folsom component). The Folsom fluted point, although similar to CLOVIS, is usually smaller with finely retouched edges and characteristic ear-like projections at the base. The term Folsom is still retained, especially in the typology of projectile points, but is now viewed less as a cultural entity than as a variation in a cultural continuum. Dates for Folsom material are usually within the period 9000-8000 bc.

Fontbouisse. A Copper Age settlement in Languedoc, southern France, which has given its name to a cultural group. It is known for settlement sites, MEGALITHIC tombs and caves used for burials, and is associated with both extensive flint mining and the first evidence of copper working in this area. The economy seems to have been based on mixed farming, with a pastoral element. The characteristic pottery has channelled decoration.

Font de Gaume. A painted cave close to LES EYZIES in the Dordogne region, southwest France. Recent excavations have revealed archaeological levels deep in the interior spanning several earlier Upper PALAEOLITHIC phases, but the polychrome paintings of bison and other animals almost certainly date from the late MAGDALENIAN at the end of the Palaeolithic.

Fontéchevade. A cave in Charente, west-central France, where in 1946 a small piece of human frontal bone and a skull cap were found in 'Tayacian' levels, believed to be earlier than the MOUSTERIAN or classic NEANDERTHAL period, and now thought to precede the last interglacial. According to Vallois, the Fontéchevade fossils proved that 'Praesapiens' [looking like modern man] existed before and during the Neanderthal period as representatives of our direct ancestors and contemporaries of the extinct Neanderthals. Most modern workers doubt the significance of the Fontéchevade fragments. The frontal fragment may be juvenile, accounting for its small brow ridge, and the skull top may well be within the range of known early Neanderthals.

food vessel. The name given to a series of pottery vessels of the earlier Bronze Age in northern Britain and Ireland. They are normally found in burials under round cairns, and are more frequently associated with inhumation than cremation. Associated vessels include plano-convex flint knives and, sometimes, crescentic necklaces of jet beads.

forging. The process of working hot metal:IRON and STEEL are too hard to be COLD WORKED and must be heated before they can be shaped. Techniques include hammering, cutting, drawing-out, hole-punching and welding. Forging was not only used to shape metal, but was also part of the refining process

for iron, where the BLOOM produced bySMELTING had to have the SLAG impurities forged out of it.

Formative Period. A term used in many chronological constructions in New World archaeology. The Formative Period is characterized by the appearance of traits that indicate a sedentary way of life and have the potential for the development of civilization. Chief among these traits are the development of agriculture, the introduction of pottery, and the building of urban or CEREMONIAL CENTRES. Since the appearance of these traits is not conditioned by the passage of time, the Formative is best understood as a concept rather than a fixed period. Even so, it is usually framed within the period 1800 BC to AD 100 in South America. In Mesoamerica, it is more often referred to as the PRE-CLASSIC and divided into Early (2000-1000 BC), Middle (1000-300 BC) and Late (300 BC-AD 300). *See* Table 9, page 552.

Fort Rock Basin sites. A cluster of associated sites with a long sequence of occupation, located in an ancient PLEISTOCENE lake basin in south-central Oregon, USA. Deposits of pumice from an eruption of nearby Mount Mazama in *c*5000 bc have provided excellent chronological control for these sites. The earliest date, 11,200 ± 720 bc, taken from hearth charcoal, confirms the presence of man below the WISCONSIN glacial ice (*see also* WILSON BUTTE CAVE). Associated artefacts, including a MANO, indicate an early hunting and gathering rather than a BIG GAME HUNTING subsistence pattern for this period. Later contexts contain artefacts of the DESERT TRADITION. Occupation continued into historic times, but looting has caused the archaeological record to be wholly unreliable after *c*1000 bc.

forum. Generally, any large open space in a Roman town. Often used specifically of the main square which, like the Greek AGORA, served as commercial, social, legal and political centre. It was usually rectangular, colonnaded, and lined with public buildings, including typically a temple and a BASILICA. A largish town might have more than one such forum and a number of minor *fora* or 'markets' devoted to particular purposes, as, for example, *forum piscarium* (fish-market), *forum olitorium* (vegetable market) or *forum cuppedinis* ('dainties-market'). 'Forum' in the sense of 'market' or legal 'assize' is also common in place names as, for instance, Forum Appii, Forum Julii etc.

Forum ware. A distinctive green glazed pottery that came to light in the 19th-century excavations of the forum in Rome. This ware has since been found on many sites close to Rome, and in settlements of all types in southern Etruria. It typically comprises pitchers, often with incised wavy-line decoration around the body of the pot. Some scholars regarded these pots as later medieval, but it has now been proved that the ware belongs to the 6th or early 7th century and, therefore, reflects the latest phase of Late Roman activity.

Fossellone Cave. *See* MONTE CIRCEO.

Fosse Way. Roman road in England stretching from Exeter to LINCOLN. The road marks the line originally chosen by the invading Romans as frontier (*limes*) for the new province. A service road was needed to link a line of forts. The line, however, rapidly proved unsatisfactory, and the frontier was soon pushed forward, leaving the Fosse Way to become a major cross-country trunk route of the expanded province.

Fourneau du Diable. A cave in the northern part of the Dordogne, southwest France, occupied during the Upper PALAEOLITHIC, with PERIGORDIAN, SOLUTRIAN and MAGDALENIAN deposits. It is one of only two sites where Solutrian art is well-exemplified, in the form of a fine limestone bas-relief of wild oxen.

Fox, Sir Cyril (1882-1967). British archaeologist who made important contributions to the development of field archaeology in the 1920s and 1930s. He also contributed to theoretical archaeology, especially in introducing geographical approaches. The concept of a division of Britain into Highland and Lowland Zones, which he outlined in *Personality of Britain* (1932) is still useful today.

Franchthi Cave. A cave in the Argolid, southern Greece, with a long stratigraphy covering the period which saw the transition from hunting and gathering to farming as the basis of life. A late Palaeolithic occupation of the 10th millennium bc was followed by an 8th-millennium bc Mesolithic deposit, when obsidian from MELOS was already being imported. The economy was based on the hunting of forest animals — red deer, wild pig and a few wild cattle — fishing and the collection of wild plant foods (nuts such as almonds and pistachios, as well as leguminous plants such as vetch and even wild barley). An abrupt transition shortly after 6000 bc saw the introduction of domesticated sheep and goat, and a little later cultivated barley and the first pottery appeared.

Franks. A Germanic tribe who crossed the Rhine in the later 3rd and 4th centuries. The Salian Franks settled in Flanders around the Gallo-Roman centre of Tournai, while the Ripurian Franks penetrated the central Rhineland and Cologne, Bonn and Mainz. Both tribes rose to dominate early medieval politics. The territory of the Salian Franks was greatly increased by their great king Clovis at the end of the 5th century, when much of northern France was drawn within their hegemony. Meanwhile, the Ripurian Franks consolidated their hold over the Rhineland, and provided the basis for the Austrasian kingdom. The archaeology of the Franks is best known from their cemeteries (*see* REIHENGRABERFELD) and the goods interred within them. Many Roman manufacturing industries were preserved by the Franks, but they introduced Germanic craftsmanship, arts and building techniques.

Fraser Cave. *See* TASMANIA.

Fraser River sites. A complex of sites centred on the Fraser River system in southern British Columbia, Canada. Three culturally distinct areas (the Canyon, the Plateau and the Delta) contain evidence of the differing influences which ultimately coalesced into the NORTHWEST COAST TRADITION. Artefacts from the Plateau have a strong Alaskan component (e.g. ARCTIC SMALL TOOL TRADITION materials) and are loosely dated from post-PLEISTOCENE to historic times. Canyon sites provide evidence of a long occupation covering BIG GAME HUNTING TRADITION, OLD CORDILLERAN CULTURE and ARCHAIC, with evidence of incipient woodworking apparent in the later stages. The Delta sites are generally later than those inland. Taken together, all the sites indicate a movement from inland to the coast beginning c2000 bc.

Frere, John (1740-1807). English antiquary famous for his precocious recognition of the antiquity of man. In 1797 he wrote to the Society of Antiquaries reporting on the discovery of flint implements found in association with bones of extinct animals in a brickearth pit at HOXNE, Suffolk. Frere recognized that the implements were man-made, 'fabricated and used by a people who had not the use of metals', and suggested that they should be referred to 'a very remote period indeed; even beyond that of the present world'.

Frisians. A loose-knit collection of tribes who inhabited the North Sea littoral between the Rhine and the Elbe from later Roman times. These communities traditionally lived in nucleated villages constructed on mounds (TERPS), safe from sudden inundations by the sea. The Frisians stubbornly resisted the annexation of their eastern territory by the Merovingian kings of Austrasia in the 7th century, but Charles Martel succeeded in bringing most of the area under early CAROL-INGIAN hegemony, and CHARLEMAGNE completed the conquest. The area was only slowly brought within the Christain orbit during the second half of the 8th century, when Anglo-Saxon missionaries penetrated the archipelago. The Frisians are best known as adventurous traders, true ancestors of the Amsterdammers. Documentary references to their trading exploits in the Rhineland, northern France, London and York, and even in Rome have made them the most frequently cited merchants of the Dark Ages. The archaeological evidence of these trading ventures is to be seen at DORESTAD, where extensive excavations have revealed the entrepôt handling the Rhenish trade of the Carolingian period. Yet at an even earlier date the mounded villages betray signs of long-distance trade contacts, suggesting that the Frisians linked the Rhineland to the northern world from the beginning of the Roman period until modern times.

Fromms Landing. A rock shelter on the banks of the lower Murray River, South Australia, 16 km from DEVON DOWNS. Human occupation lasted about 2000 years from c3000 bc. Stone artefacts included PIRRI POINTS and microliths in the same layers down to the earliest levels. A well preserved DINGO skeleton was dated to between 1000 and 1200 bc.

frost marks. The features of an archaeological site may be revealed on an AERIAL PHOTO-GRAPH by the differential retention of frost in hollows and over different types of material.

froth flotation. A method of FLOTATION.

frying pan. A special type of shallow pottery bowl found in the Cycladic Early Bronze Age. It is characterized by low sides, a highly decorated base and a handle split into two knob-like projections. The resemblance to a frying pan is superficial and certainly misleading. The vessels were probably used for ritual purposes: the frequent occurrence of vulva symbols suggests that the ritual may have been connected with fertility and childbirth.

fu [*fu*]. *See* RITUAL VESSELS (CHINA).

Fuegian tradition. A tradition based on the exploitation of marine resources and operative on the southern coast and offshore islands of southern Chile. Although a shell-midden site at Englefield Island has provided radiocarbon dates in the range 7200-6500 bc (± 1500 years) they are generally thought to be too early. The inception of the tradition, marked by a change from land-oriented hunting and gathering, is more likely to be c4000 bc. Bone and stone tool technology persisted well into historic times, and ethnographic studies of the Chono, Alacaluf and Yaghan tribes are the most valuable sources for the tradition.

Fufeng [Fu-feng]. District just north of the Wei River in central Shaanxi province, China. The Zhouyuan region, comprising Fufeng and neighbouring QISHAN, is exceptionally rich in Western ZHOU remains; this area was the centre of Zhou power for several generations preceding the founding of the Zhou dynasty, and the dynastic capital Zong Zhou may also have been here (*see* ZHOU CAPITALS). Excavations underway since 1976 at Fufeng Shaochen have revealed a palace complex dating from the early and middle Western Zhou; the remains of eight tile-roofed buildings are spread over nearly 6000 square metres. A hoard of 103 RITUAL VESSELS and BELLS discovered at Fufeng Zhuangbo in 1976 is the single most important find of Western Zhou bronzes ever made; the contents of the hoard span nearly the whole of the Western Zhou period.

Fu Hao [Fu Hao]. A consort of Wu Ding, the fourth SHANG king to rule at ANYANG. Fu Hao is mentioned in many ORACLE BONE texts. Her tomb, discovered at Anyang Xiaotun in 1976, is the only royal tomb of the Shang period found intact and the only one whose occupant could be identified: many bronzes from the tomb are inscribed with the name Fu Hao. The tomb was a small pit without entrance ramps, 8 metres deep and 5.6 by 4 metres on the sides, a size modest by comparison with the large cruciform royal tombs at Anyang (*see* SHAFT TOMBS, CHINA). Its furnishings, however, were astonishingly rich, including more than 200 bronze ritual vessels, 200 bronze weapons and tools, 600 jades and stone carvings, 500 objects of carved bone and ivory, 4 bronze mirrors, 7000 cowrie shells (used as money), and 16 sacrificial victims. The discovery has an important bearing on the chronology of Shang art and the periodization of oracle bone texts.

Fukui. A deep stratified rock shelter in Nagasaki prefecture on Kyushu, Japan. The unmistakable stone tools from the oldest layer, dated older than 31,900 years, are among the earliest convincing evidence of human occupation of Japan. Microblades appear in the last Palaeolithic layer, and continue in the two early ceramic layers, suggesting a continuity in stone tools at the time when pottery-making began in Japan. The older ceramic layer, dated to 10,650 bc, contained linear-relief pottery, while the younger one, dated to 10,450 bc, included fingernail-impressed ware. These were succeeded by a layer with arrowheads and Initial JOMON pottery, with geometric designs made by rolling a notched stick.

Funan (probably a transcription of the Chinese rendering of the Old Khmer word for 'mountain'). The first INDIANIZED kingdom of Southeast Asia, founded in the 1st century AD in the lower valley of the Mekong in present Cambodia. According to legend it came into being as a result of the union of an Indian

Brahman and the daughter of a local chief. From Chinese sources and archaeological evidence it appears that in the 3rd century Funan extended its power over much of the southern part of the Indochinese Peninsula, around the Gulf of Siam into the Malay Peninsula and possibly even across into Lower Burma. Strategically situated on the trade routes between India and China, Funan became for several centuries the most important maritime power in Southeast Asia. During the 6th century Funan broke up, being gradually taken over by its former vassal CHENLA, which became its successor state. There is abundant information about the material culture of Funan from excavations, notably those of OC-ÈO, thought to have been its main port.

funnel beaker. *See* TRB CULTURE.

Fustat. *See* CAIRO.

Füzesabony. An earlier Bronze Age group of the early 2nd millennium bc, located on and around the Tisza Valley in eastern Hungary and closely related to the Rumanian OTOMANI group. Most known settlements are unfortified TELLS with wattle-and-daub timber-framed houses, sometimes with plank and beam floors. HILLFORTS are rare. Another important landscape feature is the large cemetery, usually with inhumation burial but sometimes bi-ritual in nature. Subsistence evidence from this primarily lowland group indicates a broad-spectrum economy with hunting and fishing as important as mixed farming.

Fyrkat. A fortress similar to TRELLEBORG in northern Jutland which dates to the mid-10th century. Recent investigations have revealed the perfect circular rampart and ditch enclosing four blocks of boat-shaped buildings. Fyrkat is a few kilometres from open sea, and it is now generally believed that it was a royal centre rather than the encampment for warriors bound on some raid to England. DENDROCHRONOLOGY has shown that repairs to the fortress were made about 980. Like the other Trelleborg-type fortresses, the site was probably abandoned early in the 11th century as the Danish kings founded new towns and built small palaces in them.

G

Gabillou. A cave with Upper PALAEOLITHIC occupation close to Mussidan in the Dordogne, southwest France. Levels of MAGDALENIAN type were found in the cave. Numerous engravings are believed to be of the same date. They are amongst the finest and most delicate ever found from the Palaeolithic period.

Gades [Phoenician Gadir, modern Spanish Cadiz]. City in southwest Spain. In antiquity Gades enjoyed great prosperity for more than a millenium as a commercial port. Tradition dates its foundation (by PHOENICIANS from Tyre) to 1100 BC, but a date in the 7th or 8th century BC is perhaps more plausible. Prosperity only declines with the rise of nearby Hispalis (Seville) from the 2nd century AD.

The town's twin bases of success, adventurous sea-borne trade and fishing, are well reflected by early coins which show Phoenician Hercules backed by the tuna fish. The trade portrays a dominant association with metals and metallurgy, and by the 1st century BC Gades seems to have cornered a significant market in tin-mining and the tin trade generally. The link with tin may indeed go back much further, since Phoenician sailors from Gades are credited with the discovery (and no doubt the keeping secret) of a direct trade-route with the so-called Cassiterides ('Tin Islands' — usually interpreted as the Scilly Isles in this context), and some sources would put this connection back to the 7th century.

Defection from the Carthaginian side to Rome in 206 BC clearly gave a new impetus to this East-West melange of cultures at the western end of the Mediterranean, and it is no surprise that Gades (*Gades iocosae*, 'merry Gades') with its *puellae Gaditanae* ('dancing girls of Gades') became proverbial to the Romans for its colourful gaiety and exotic pleasures.

Gagarino. A late PALAEOLITHIC site in the Don basin of European Russia. Mammoth hunters of this Kostenkian or east GRAVETTIAN group carved bone and ivory copiously, including female figurines of the 'VENUS' type. Huts were also discovered.

gallery grave. One of the major categories of MEGALITHIC tomb in prehistoric Europe, characterized by a rectangular chamber with no separate entrance passage. Gallery graves are frequently but not always found under long BARROWS; they may be subdivided (SEGMENTED) or have additional side chambers (TRANSEPTED); they are sometimes associated with elaborate facades and forecourts. They occur throughout the area where megalithic tombs occur in Europe and were constructed from the Early Neolithic into the Bronze Age.

Gallinazo. A culture that flourished in the VIRU VALLEY in Peru between *c*200 BC and AD 200 (*see* Early INTERMEDIATE PERIOD). Together with the slightly earlier SALINAR, the Gallinazo culture is seen as transitional from CHAVIN-associated groups, such as CUPISNIQUE, to the rise of the MOCHE state. Some decorative techniques employed on the widely used oxidized red-ware can be traced to Salinar, and some life-modelling is reminiscent of Cupisnique. The best-known Gallinazo pottery, however, is black-on-orange negative resist decorated ware, probably related to RECUAY.

The type site appears to have been a CEREMONIAL CENTRE with a central nucleus of adobe mounds and walled courtyards. Residential apartment complexes are scattered over an area of two square kilometres around this centre; it was abandoned some time after the rise of Moche.

Gallurus Oratory. A boat-shaped oratory situated on the Dingle peninsula in Co. Kerry, Ireland. Few examples of pre-11th century Irish ecclesiastical architecture have survived, since most early Celtic monastic buildings were primitive constructions of timber or dry stone, but there are a few remaining beehive cells (known as clochains) and a group of roughly boat-shaped oratories, of which Gallurus is the most sophisticated.

It is impossible to date the oratory precisely, but it must belong to a building tradition that falls between the beehives of the 6th and 7th centuries and the first stone churches of the 11th or 12th century. The building is constructed of large, flat CORBELLED stones, with inward-sloping walls apexing in a gable at each end. Inserted into the western end is a doorway with a lintel and sloping jambs, while the eastern gable is penetrated by a small round-headed window, splayed internally. The building measures 4.6 by 3.1 metres and has no interior divisions.

Gamble's Cave. Situated in the central Rift Valley of Kenya, adjacent to a high beach level of the formerly combined lakes Nakuru and Elmenteita, this cave contains a long sequence attributed to the EBURRAN industry (formerly known as the Upper Kenya Capsian). A later horizon contains an ELMENTEITAN occurrence.

Gandhara. An area on the northwest frontier of Pakistan which from the 6th century BC formed a satrapy of the ACHAEMENID (Persian) empire. Through this province Western influences, and perhaps actual craftsmen, reached India. Gandharan art reflects these Western (provincial Hellenistic) influences, alongside other elements of purely Indian origin. Western influence is apparent also in the grid-iron town planning found at the important Gandharan cities of CHARSADA and TAXILA.

Gandhara Grave culture. A culture of the 2nd and 1st millennia BC found in northwestern Pakistan. Characteristic burials are in tombs consisting of two small chambers, one on top of the other; the lower chamber contained both the burial (either inhumed or cremated) and the grave goods, while the upper chamber was empty. The population seem to have been cattle- and later horse-breeders and to have practised some agriculture. They were accomplished metal-workers, producing tools, weapons and ornaments of copper or bronze, gold, silver and iron by the later phases. Their culture demonstrates connections with eastern Iran and central Asia.

Ganges civilization. In the 7th-6th centuries BC the villages of the central Ganges and the Ganges-Jamuna Doab developed into true city-states, characterized by extensive urban settlement and a developed social organization. The states engaged in long struggles for power, which ended in the 4th century BC with the establishment of the MAURYAN empire under Chandragupta. Much of the information about the Ganges civilization comes from literary sources, including a few contemporary writings, but mostly from texts written at a later date which paint an idealized picture of these early cities. Archaeological information is restricted since excavations have usually been on a small scale. We know that the cities were large and usually fortified, often with massive mud ramparts. The characteristic pottery is NORTHERN BLACK POLISHED WARE. *See also* MAGADHA, PATNA, UJJAIN.

Gangetic hoards. Hoards of copper objects found in the Ganges basin in India. The main types of objects found are flat and shouldered axes, bar chisels, barbed harpoons, antenna-hilted swords and anthropomorphic objects. Associations with OCHRE-COLOURED POTTERY suggest a date of the 2nd millennium BC. Most authorities today believe that the metal types in these hoards represent an indigenous development and are not connected with the ARYAN invaders, as was sometimes suggested in the past.

Ganj Dareh, Tepe. A small mound in the Kermanshah region of western Iran, which has yielded five occupation levels with radiocarbon dates ranging from 8400 to 6800 bc. The lowest level had no permanent architecture, but only shallow pits and hollows. The next level, however, had mud-brick structures, mostly very small adjoining cubicles, perhaps used for storage. The village of this level was destroyed by fire, which appears to have preserved containers made of sun-dried clay by 'firing' them. Animal and human figurines of clay were also found. Preliminary studies suggest that the stone industry remained largely the same throughout the occupation and neither polished stone tools nor obsidian have been found. The economic evidence has not yet been fully published, but it seems that domestic goats were kept and some plants may have been cultivated.

Gaocheng [Kao-ch'eng]. County in southern Hebei province, China, with widely scattered SHANG remains, of which the most notable are those near the village of Taixicun. The main occupation at Taixicun postdates the ERLI-GANG PHASE and is either coeval with or, more probably, a little earlier than the historical ANYANG period; a single radiocarbon date of *c*1500 BC has been reported from Taixicun. The site is dominated by three large rect-angular HANGTU platforms, 6-7 metres high, 100 metres long and 60-80 metres wide. A large house foundation had sacrificial burials associated with it; other graves yielded bronze RITUAL VESSELS, fragments of lacquer, and a bronze axe with a blade forged from meteoritic iron. The early date and evident importance of the site suggest that it may be the location of a Shang capital occupied after ZHENGZHOU but before Anyang.

Garstang, John (1876-1956). Distinguished British archaeologist who worked for more than 30 years on prehistoric sites in Anatolia and the Levant. His excavations at SAKCE GÖZÜ, JERICHO and MERSIN made major contributions to the development of Near Eastern prehistory.

garum. Many Romans greatly appreciated good cooking, and several writers mention a rich fish sauce (*garon* in Greek and *garum* in Latin) made from small fish, and a speciality of the provinces of Greece, North Africa and Spain.

Gatung'ang'a. A site in the eastern highlands of Kenya which illustrates the Early Iron Age settlement of that region during the second half of the 1st millennium ad. The pottery shows similarities with KWALE ware and it seems probable that the Early Iron Age population of the eastern highlands derived from the coastal regions to the southeast.

Gaudo. A cemetery site in Campania, south-west Italy, which has given its name to the local Copper Age culture of the 4th-3rd millennia BC. Gaudo sites are characterized by rock-cut tombs used for collective burial. Grave goods include abundant pottery — assymmetrical jars with strap handles sometimes called *askoi* (on analogy with the classical pottery form), double dishes linked by strap handles, and a variety of bowls and cups — and flint arrow-heads and daggers; metalwork is rare, but some copper daggers and awls occur and one or two small objects of silver.

Gaul [Latin Gallia]. The Romans regarded France and Germany west of the Rhine as a unity, inhabited primarily by Galli. In 121 BC they annexed the southernmost strip as Gallia Transalpina. Caesar's conquests (58-51 BC) and Augustus's organization (30 BC-14 AD) resulted in four Gallic provinces: the southern or 'senatorial' Narbonensis, and the 'imperial' Aquitania, Lugdunensis and Belgica.

Gavrinis. An early Neolithic PASSAGE GRAVE on an island in the Gulf of Morbihan, Brittany. It is very elaborately decorated with pecked designs, mostly abstract, over most available surfaces.

Gawra, Tepe. A TELL, northeast of NINEVEH in Iraq, which has provided a cultural sequence from the 6th millennium bc to the mid-2nd millennium BC. The earliest material was of the HALAF period, while the succeeding period shows increasing contacts with the southern Mesopotamian UBAID culture. Belonging to this period is a group of three tripartite temples facing on to an open courtyard, very similar to those of the south. The succeeding period is contemporary with the URUK and JEMDET NASR periods further south, but is culturally distinctive; this is often described as the 'Gawra period'. In this period (later 4th millennium BC) there is abundant evidence for differential wealth and social position, manifest in the grave goods found in a number of tombs built of mud-brick or stone. Three of these tombs were particularly rich, containing many goods of gold, electrum, lapis lazuli and ivory, all materials that had to be imported. Several temples of the 'Gawra period' have been excavated; they are of an unusual form with separate portico, not unlike the MEGA-RON plan. The most distinctive building of this phase, however, is a circular structure known to the excavators as the 'Round House'; it has a diameter of *c*18 metres, a thick outer wall and 17 rooms; its function is unknown.

Gaza. A Palestinian site underlying the modern town of Gaza. No excavations have taken place, but it is known to have had PHIL-ISTINE, Egyptian and 'PEOPLES OF THE SEA' occupation. The nearby cemetery of Deir el-Daleh has produced Egyptian material.

Ten km south is the mound of Tell el-Ajjul, which was excavated by Flinders PETRIE in the 1930s. The earliest evidence comes from two cemeteries, one to the north and one to the east of the main mound, with shaft graves containing pottery and daggers of the late 3rd millennium BC. On the tell itself the earliest excavated remains are of the Middle Bronze Age (2nd millennium BC); earliest of all was a cemetery, underlying a large building interpreted by Petrie as a palace of the Middle Bronze Age II period. This was succeeded by four other large buildings, of the later Bronze Age and early Iron Age. In the Middle Bronze Age the town was defended by a great ditch, of a type often associated with the HYKSOS.

Gdansk. A city situated on the Vistula estuary in Poland, which evolved from the 12th century to become one of the most important trading centres of eastern Europe. The town controlled the overland timber trade and its access to the northern-flowing rivers gave good access to the Baltic. Some of the most spectacular archaeological finds are a collection of Byzantine silks.

ge [*ko*]. A halberd or dagger-axe, the characteristic weapon of the Chinese Bronze Age. The dagger-shaped bronze blade, usually with a flat tang but occasionally with a shaft hole, was mounted perpendicular to the wooden shaft. The blade had a crosspiece parallel to the shaft to help secure it in place; in later versions this crosspiece reached increasingly far down the shaft. Bronze *ge* blades and non-functional jade replicas of blades often appear as mortuary gifts in SHANG tombs. The earliest *ge* yet known have come from the third stratum at ERLITOU (mid-2nd millennium BC).

In the Eastern ZHOU period the *ge* was sometimes combined with a spear, the *ge* blade at right angles to the spearhead, to form a *ji*. The *ji* was in existence by the late 6th or early 5th century BC, as it is depicted in battle scenes on bronze vessels of that time. Extravagant *ji* carrying three *ge* blades were found in the late 5th-century BC tomb of the Marquis Yi in SUI XIAN.

Gebal [modern Gebail]. Ancient name of the east Mediterranean town known by the Greek name of BYBLOS.

Gedi. Archaeologically, this is the most intensively excavated of the early towns of the East African coast; it does not, however, receive mention in any of the relevant written records. Located on a now abandoned site beside a tidal inlet south of Malindi, Kenya, Gedi was probably founded around 1300. Stone buildings continued to be erected into at least the 16th century. These three centuries probably saw the greatest prosperity of the Indian Ocean trade which nurtured the coastal town and was drawn southwards by the greatly increased exploitation of Zimbabwean gold. At Gedi the ruins of the houses and Great Mosque are well preserved. Although the remains of any associated mud buildings have not been investigated, Gedi provides a useful basis for comparison with the richer contemporary cities such as KILWA and with later Swahili urban settlements.

de Geer, Baron Gerhard (1858-1943). Swedish scholar who developed the technique of dating by counting VARVES, first published in a paper of 1910 entitled 'A Geochronology of the last 12,000 years'.

Geleen. A settlement of the Neolithic LINEAR POTTERY culture in southern Holland, which has produced house types similar to those of other Dutch sites of this culture, including ELSLOO, SITTARD and Stein.

Gelidonya. *See* CAPE GELIDONYA.

Genoa. A major medieval port which competed with Venice, Pisa and Florence for the trade of the Mediterranean. Genoa's importance dates back to Byzantine times, when it was a small fort. The medieval city wall enclosing a substantial area by the seashore probably dates to the 12th century, when the city was fast approaching its zenith. Excavations in the town have demonstrated the wealth of the late medieval deposits. The notable project at the Cloister of San Silvestro, for example, revealed not only well-preserved buildings but a rich range of pottery from many parts of Italy and Spain reflecting some of Genoa's trading contacts.

geochronology. A geologically based chronology, into which archaeological events can be fitted. For example, QUATERNARY chronologies form the basis of PALAEOLITHIC archaeology (*see* Tables 5-7, pages 418-20). Late TERTIARY chronologies give a framework to hominid evolution. Geological chronologies are based on the STRATIGRAPHY of deposits in a given area, supported by independent dating methods such as RADIOCARBON, PALAEOMAGNETISM or POTASSIUM-ARGON. Such chronologies should not be applied outside the area for which they were developed.

Geoksyur. An oasis in the ancient delta of the Tedjen River in southeast Turkmenia, Soviet Central Asia, which was first settled in the early CHALCOLITHIC period, in the phase designated ANAU I or NAMAZGA I. At this stage typical settlements were small villages of mud-brick houses, though the central settlement of Geoksyur itself seems to have been much larger. The exploitation of this oasis indicates the existence of a developed agricultural economy involving the cultivation of both wheat and barley with the help of irrigation. Domesticated animals were kept and sheep seem to have been bred partly for their wool. Hunting played only a subsidiary role.

geology. The study of the earth and its history. Geology's aims overlap considerably with those of archaeology, particularly in the prehistoric periods. Even in later periods, the study of environmental archaeology could be described as the 'geology of the Holocene'. Work on the stratigraphy of the QUATERNARY is essential to provide a geological chronology (GEOCHRONOLOGY) for the study of the PALAEOLITHIC and MESOLITHIC. Similarly, reconstructions of environmental changes throughout the Quaternary form an essential background to all archaeology. The palaeontology of fossil hominids and the other animals that lived at the same time is another area in which geology and archaeology overlap. Primarily geological methods of dating such as RADIOCARBON, PALAEOMAGNETISM and POTASSIUM-ARGON form the basis of most prehistoric chronologies. GEOPHYSICAL techniques are used for the location of sites, and PETROLOGY traces the origins of stone implements and inclusions in pottery.

geometric. Used generally of any style of decoration that characteristically makes use only of 'geometric' shapes, such as circles, squares, triangles, lozenges and running linear patterns etc and, where it does admit human and animal figures, treats them also in a linear schematic way. In classical Greek art history, the term is used specifically of the early phases of vase-painting as, for example, Protogeometric (c1050-900 BC), Geometric (c900-750 BC) and Late Geometric (c750-700 BC).

Geometric pottery (China). Well-fired, stamp-impressed pottery characteristic of 2nd-millennium BC sites in south and southeastern China. The 'Geometric pottery cultures' seem to have grown out of local Neolithic predecessors; in and near Shanghai, for instance, Geometric pottery levels overlie LIANGZHU remains. These cultures probably arose too early to have been formed under SHANG influence, as was once assumed, but they were partly coeval with the Bronze Age of North China. The Geometric pottery culture of southern Jiangsu and central Anhui, known as the Hushu culture, clearly borrowed its primitive bronze metallurgy from more civilized Shang centres, and in the same region the characteristic pottery designs were copied in metal on a few bronze vessels of Western ZHOU date (*see* TUNXI).

geophysics. The physics of the earth. Many archaeological DATING methods may be said to be based on geophysical principles. Geophysical methods are often used to investigate archaeological sites without (or prior to) excavation. Features of a buried site may change the physical properties of the earth. Electricity (*see* RESISTIVITY) and magnetism (*see* MAGNETIC SURVEYING) or both (*see* ELECTROMAGNETIC SURVEYING) are the properties most often investigated in archaeology.

Gerzean. *See* PRE-DYNASTIC EGYPT.

Gezer. An important Palestinian site northwest of JERUSALEM. The results of excavations early this century have been clarified by new work in the 1960s and 1970s. The site was occupied from the Chalcolithic (5th millennium BC) to the Hellenistic period and perhaps as late as Byzantine times. The first fortified town belonged to the Middle Bronze Age (early 2nd millennium BC); an important discovery of this phase was a 'High Place' — a ceremonial meeting place for the renewal of treaties — consisting of a row of ten tall monoliths. Gezer was destroyed early in the 15th century BC, perhaps by Thotmes III, but there were later important phases of occupation in the Late Bronze Age and in the PHILISTINE period. In the Solomonic period the site had a splendid gateway like those at MEGIDDO and HAZOR. Succeeding levels show a decline, with destruction attributed to Assyrians and, later, Babylonians. The city became important again in the Hellenistic period.

Ghana. Ancient Ghana, possibly the earliest, and certainly one of the most important of the early African sudanic states, is not to be confused with the modern republic of the same name, being centred in southern Mauritania and southwestern Mali between the upper reaches of the Rivers Niger and Senegal. Ancient Ghana was established well before the middle of the 8th century, when it was first visited by Muslims from north of the Sahara. Its capital is believed to have been at KUMBI SALEH, where ruins of a large stone-built town have been investigated. Ghana also controlled the trading centre at AWDAGHAST, at the southern end of one of the major trans-Saharan caravan routes. The state was thus in a position to regulate and profit from trade in the products of the BAMBUK gold-field, further to the south. From the 11th century Arabic written accounts are an important source for the history of ancient Ghana: late in that century the state was conquered by the Almoravids, who imposed Islam. Ghana was effectively eclipsed by MALI during the 13th century.

Ghar Dalam. Cave site in the south of the island of Malta which has given its name to the island's earliest Neolithic phase, and indeed the earliest evidence of occupation of any kind. The culture, which is dated to the late 5th millennium bc, is characterized by evidence of domesticated animals and cultivated plants and by the use of IMPRESSED WARE, quite similar to the Sicilian STENTINELLO type, and of obsidian from LIPARI. As well as at the type site, the culture is well represented in the lower levels of SKORBA.

Ghar-i Kamarband [Belt Cave]. Cave situated near the southeast corner of the Caspian Sea in northern Iran. Occupation levels demonstrate settlement spanning the late PALAEOLITHIC to early farming period

(c10,000-5000 bc). After c6000 bc there is evidence of increasing concentration on caprines (sheep and goat) in the diet and it is possible that herding or incipient domestication was practised. At the same time there is also evidence of harvesting of wild cereals. Pottery appears in a level dated c5300 bc and shortly afterwards the cave was abandoned.

Ghar-i Khar [Donkey Cave]. A cave in the mountain zone of western Iran, occupied from the Middle PALAEOLITHIC onwards. The Upper Palaeolithic industry is similar to the BARADOSTIAN at SHANIDAR Cave. The cave has also yielded a NEOLITHIC level with pottery, probably associated with a food-producing community. Rare finds of later periods probably indicate sporadic visits by shepherds.

Ghar-i Mordeh Gusfand. *See* AQ KUPRUK.

Ghassul, Teleilat el. A Palestinian site northeast of the Dead Sea, consisting of several low mounds. Four main occupation layers were revealed by excavation, all belonging to the CHALCOLITHIC period of the 5th and early 4th millennia bc. This site has given its name to the local Chalcolithic culture, which is known as the Ghassulian. The settlement consisted of simple mud-brick houses, irregular in plan, built on stone foundations. Some walls were decorated with remarkable painted wall plaster; the motifs include geometric designs and representations of stylized dragons, human figures and birds, and a sailing boat with oars. Burials were in cists, made of stone slabs and covered by stone cairns.

Ghazni. A major pre-Islamic settlement in Afghanistan, the most spectacular remains of which are the Buddhist monastery at Tapa Sardar. In the Islamic period, it became the capital of the Ghaznavids, a dynasty of Turkish origin which ruled from 977-1186 and for a time controlled large parts of Afghanistan, western Iran and northwest India. The town has two stunning Ghaznavid monuments: the minarets built by Masud III (1099-1114) and Bahram Shah (1117-53). Each has a star-shaped plan and is of fired brick, with elaborate kufic inscriptions and geometric ornament. Excavation has revealed part of the palace of Masud III, which contemporary writers described as filled with booty from India. The central courtyard contains a magnificently carved inscription, 250 metres long, in Persian rather than the customary Arabic — one of the oldest examples of Persian epigraphy. Nearby is the mausoleum of Sultan Abdur Razaq, a fine TIMURID building which contains a museum of Ghaznavid epigraphy, ceramics and metalware.

giant's grave [Italian: *tomba di giganti*]. Local name for the MEGALITHIC tombs of the island of Sardinia. The tombs are of GALLERY GRAVE type, with curved facades and forecourts and are set in long CAIRNS. They belong to the NURAGHIC Bronze Age culture of the 2nd millennium bc.

Gibraltar. Cave sites on the island of Gibraltar in the western Mediterranean have revealed remains of NEANDERTHAL man and stone tools. The first Neanderthal skull ever found came from Forbes Quarry, Gibraltar, in 1848. A second, juvenile, Neanderthal was found in 1926 at Devil's Tower. A third cave revealed MOUSTERIAN and Upper PALAEOLITHIC levels.

Gilgamesh. Heroic king of the ancient Mesopotamian city of URUK who appears in a number of epic tales, collectively labelled the *Epic of Gilgamesh*. He is now thought to have been a real historical king belonging to the First Dynasty of Uruk (in the Early Dynastic III phase, *c*2650-2550 BC). The epics credit him with the construction of two temples and the city wall at Uruk and archaeological excavations have shown that these are real structures.

Gilgamesh is best known through the epics, written originally in SUMERIAN but surviving through copies in AKKADIAN and later languages. Out of the nine Sumerian epics known, four are about Gilgamesh and cover a wide variety of topics, including man and nature, love and adventure, and friendship and combat. The desire for immortality is a central theme which carries Gilgamesh to the mythical land of DILMUN (perhaps also the real land of Bahrein) and brings him into contact with the BÁBYLONIAN Noah-figure, Utanapishtim.

Gilimanuk. An important burial site of perhaps the early 1st millennium in western Bali, Indonesia. The burial goods appear to be pre-Hindu/Buddhist, and include bronze and iron artefacts, beads, and a gold eye-cover of probable south Indian origin. Burials are primary, secondary or urned.

Gilund. A site of the BANAS culture in Rajasthan, western India. It was a substantial farming village, with four major phases of occupation. Pottery types include BLACK AND RED WARE and a fine black, red and white polychrome ware.

Gilyak. *See* OKHOTSK CULTURE.

Giyan, Tepe. A TELL site in west-central Iran, whose long occupation sequence has yielded an important pottery typology spanning the period from the late 6th millennium bc until the Iron Age. The latest phase belongs to the ASSYRIAN period, when the site seems to have been an outpost of the empire.

Giza. The royal pyramid cemetery of the Fourth Dynasty of ancient Egypt (*see* DYNASTIC EGYPT), near modern Cairo. Derived from earlier tomb types as seen at SAQQARA, the Giza pyramids represent the peak of the concentration of resources on pharaonic funerary monuments. The largest pyramid, that of Khufu, was 148 metres high and covered an area of more than 5 hectares, having been laid out with very great accuracy. Elaborate measures were adopted to prevent disturbance of the royal burials, but despite this all pyramids were looted in antiquity. Associated with Khafra's pyramid complex at Giza is the great Sphinx, an 80-metre-long statue of a human-headed lion.

glacial [glaciation]. (1) *Noun*: Strictly, a glacial or glaciation is a period during which ice-sheets, ice-caps and glaciers grow. The term has also commonly been used to describe the periods of generally cold climate which occurred at intervals during the QUATERNARY period (*see* Tables 5-7, pages 418-20). It is, however, now becoming clear that ice-sheets grew only during parts of these so-called 'glacials' (for example, the DEVENSIAN). For this reason, the term 'cold stage' is preferable. *See* INTERGLACIAL, INTERSTADIAL, STADIAL.

(2) *Adjective*: Appertaining to erosion and deposition by ice-sheets, ice-caps and glaciers, their associated PROGLACIAL streams and

lakes, and PERIGLACIAL activity outside the ice margin.

Gladkaia I. A site in eastern Siberia which has yielded evidence of a NEOLITHIC occupation (defined by the use of pottery rather than the practice of farming), dating probably to the 2nd millennium BC. The population of Gladkaia I lived by hunting and fishing, and used pottery and tools made of obsidian.

glans plumbea [Latin: 'lead acorn']. A slug of lead, an item of hand ammunition in the Roman army. They were used in quantity and at high velocity (mostly by specialized corps of *funditores*, 'slingsmen') and as an alternative to stones. Both stone and lead missiles are found inscribed with epigrammatic wishes or instructions as to their lethal intent.

Glanum. A settlement in southern France, some 24 km northeast of ARLES, with three phases of occupation — native Ligurian, Hellenistic and Roman. It is likely that the dominant early association is that of religious shrine, dedicated perhaps to a healing deity. The Hellenistic phase still shows religious connections, with some evidence for cult structures and the practice of a SEVERED HEAD CULT. With Romanization from the 1st century BC onwards, Glanum became a prosperous provincial town, and the religious associations may have weakened. The Roman town shows Republican-period baths, imperial forum, temples and shrines; at the entrance to the town, a splendid triumphal arch with decorative panels involving groups of Gallic prisoners; and the so-called Mausoleum of the Julii. German attack in 270 AD brought an end to the occupation of the site, which was subsequently hidden by a slide of alluvium from the nearby hills. The triumphal arch and the mausoleum stood clear of this fate, and came to be known as Les Antiques.

Glasinac. A valley in Bosnia, Yugoslavia, containing an estimated 20,000 graves, spanning the 10th to 1st centuries BC, including 25 groups of tumuli. Inhumation was the dominant rite and some graves were very richly equipped. Local sources of gold, silver, copper and iron were exploited, and the communities here were involved in trade with Greece, Italy and the Danube Valley.

glass. A mineral material that has been cooled so quickly that a crystal structure has not had time to form. Glasses are brittle and, when broken, fracture along curved lines, to produce shell-like scars and sharp edges. This property of so-called conchoidal fracture was used in antiquity to make sharp tools. Natural glasses, such as OBSIDIAN, are rare, but cryptocrystalline materials, with so fine a crystal structure that they behave somewhat like glasses, are relatively common (e.g. flint). Man-made glasses are formed from the heating and fusing of quartz sands, which on rapid cooling take on a glassy texture. FAIENCE beads (and similar objects) which have a fused, glassy surface were made both in Early DYNASTIC EGYPT and SUMER, and true glass was in use in Mesopotamia by the Sargonid (AKKADIAN) period.

glass (China). Glass appeared in China far later than in the Near East and has played a comparatively minor role in Chinese material culture. High-fired glazes were known in China by about the 14th century BC (*see* WUCHENG), and a few pale green glass beads have reportedly been found in 9th-8th century BC contexts at ZHANGJIAPO and LUOYANG Zhongzhoulu. When glass begins to occur at Chinese sites with some regularity, around the 5th century BC, it is mainly in the form of coloured beads that copy imports from Western Asia or Europe. The imports as well as the copies have been found in China, the latter being distinguished by their high lead and barium oxide content. Fine examples from JINCUN (5th-3rd centuries BC) are of two types, beads of solid glass and cored beads with glazed exterior and quartz or clay interior; the cored variety is sometimes described as FAIENCE. Like jade, glass was occasionally used as a decorative inlay, for example on a mirror of Jincun style in the Fogg Art Museum and on a bronze *hu* from one of the HAN tombs at MANCHENG. In the Han period green glass served commonly as a cheap substitute for mortuary jades. In later times the high development of CERAMICS in China forestalled any extensive exploitation of glass for vessels.

Glass Palace Chronicles [Hmannan Yazawin]. The Burmese Royal Chronicle of the 19th century, based on earlier versions. It relates events from the creation of the world, according to Buddhist cosmogony, to the early and later history of BURMA up to the time of its final compilation.

Glastonbury. (1) An Iron Age LAKE VILLAGE on the SOMERSET LEVELS, southwest England, occupied from the 3rd century BC until the Roman period. Excavations between 1892 and 1907 were not of modern standard, but because of the excellent preservation conditions a great deal of information has been gained about the community that lived here. The settlement was surrounded by a wooden palisade and contained more than 60 circular huts with clay and wood floors. Finds include a great deal of woodwork (vessels and parts of wooden wheels and dug-out canoes), pottery decorated with incised curvilinear designs (labelled 'Glastonbury style'), iron objects, including CURRENCY BARS, and much bonework, mostly connected with the production of woven woollen textiles (weaving combs, shuttles etc). The village may have concentrated on the production of woollen cloth, since the faunal remains were dominated by sheep (between 80 and 90 per cent of the total fauna). Pottery and metalwork were also produced in the village.

(2) The monastic foundation of Glastonbury often features in the history and legends of the Early Christian period. The monastery was probably in existence as early as 600, at a time when Saxons and Britons were fighting for control of the region, and it has thus inevitably been linked with King ARTHUR. In about 705 King Ine of Wessex was persuaded by Bishop Aldhelm to build a church at Glastonbury, and under Bishop (later Archbishop) Dunstan in the mid-10th century it became one of the richest and most influential monasteries in England.

Excavations in the 1950s demonstrated the growth of the pre-Conquest abbey, revealing a particularly interesting sequence of buildings. The primary church and its ancillary buildings were of wattle construction; in the next phase, traces of Ine's stone church were found, with flanking chapels which had painted wall plaster and OPUS SIGNINUM floors. Under Dunstan, large-scale replanning and enlargement of the complex were carried out. The only known examples of Anglo-Saxon glass furnaces were discovered during the excavations.

glaze. A glassy coating for pottery. Glazes are most commonly applied as a mixture of fine particles suspended in water, with which the pottery is coated. On firing, the particles fuse and as the pottery cools the material forms a glassy layer. A large variety of glazes may be used, varying in colour, texture and suitability for different types of pottery. SeeLEAD GLAZE, TIN-GLAZED POTTERY.

Glazkovo. See BAIKAL NEOLITHIC.

Glevum. See GLOUCESTER.

gleying. Waterlogging of SOILS. Gleying may result from a raised water table, or from drainage impedance within the soil PROFILE; the latter condition occurs in some PODZOLS.

Globular Amphora. Type of pottery vessel which has given its name to a Late Neolithic or Copper Age culture of the 3rd millennium bc in much of Germany and Poland and extending into the western USSR. It is characterized by single burials, often in stone cists under barrows, usually accompanied by the characteristic pottery vessel, which is bulbous in shape with a narrow neck and suspension handles; some examples are undecorated, while others have incised, stamped or cord-impressed ornament on the upper part of the vessel. The Globular Amphora group may have developed out of the TRB CULTURE and may be a parallel development to the SINGLE GRAVE group in Scandinavia.

Gloucester [Roman Glevum]. A Roman COLONIA in southwest England founded officially under Nerva (96-98 AD). Some six years after the invasion of 43 AD and as part of their conquest of southern England, the Romans established a legionary fortress in this general area, although its precise location is uncertain. Around 67 this was followed by a second fortress, this time on the site of Glevum itself. Probably during the 80s (certainly by 87) this was being converted into a town for veterans, later to become the official Colonia Nervia(na) Glevi. It achieved reasonable prosperity with a colonnaded forum, a basilica and pleasing houses with mosaic floors, and was still occupied in the early 5th century. Unfortunately very little survives *in situ*, but there is a good collection of material in the Gloucester City Museum, notable being the tombstone of Rufus Sita, an auxiliary cavalry-man from Thrace.

Gnezdovo. A site outside Smolensk on the River Volga, where excavations have revealed one of the largest Viking Age gravefields known from Russia. Most of the grave mounds contained cremations associated with oval brooches and other objects dating from the 9th and 10th centuries. The burial area itself seems to be associated with a very large trading station which controlled an area of the Baltic.

Gniezno. A town in Poland formally established during the 960s when Mieszko I united bands of Slavic tribes to form the Polish state. Excavations have been carried out on the earliest timber fortress with its impressive system of double defences. The old town has many interesting buildings including the cathedral, which has 12th-century carved bronze doors.

goat. Members of the genus *Capra*, distinguished from *Ovis* (the SHEEP) by differences in scent glands, possession of a beard, number of chromosomes and possession of scimitar-like horns, sweeping back from the forehead. For archaeologists goats may be hard to differentiate from sheep, especially in the skeleton. *Capra* includes three groups of animals. (*a*) The wild goat and its domestic relatives. These are not really separate species, but are frequently classified apart. *Capra aegagrus*, the wild goat, lives as isolated communities, widely distributed through rocky, mountainous terrain around the easten Mediterranean and Asia. The domestic goat, in all its varieties, is often distinguished as *Capra hircus*. (*b*) Ibexes. Many species and subspecies, found in the most precipitous mountain areas of central Europe, Asia and northeast Africa. Difficult to distinguish in the skeleton from goat. (*c*) Markhor. The large, screw-horned goat of Afghanistan and the Himalayas.

Goat bones first appear in Middle PALAEO-LITHIC levels of caves. Ibexes seem to have been hunted extensively by Upper Palaeolithic man in the Pyrenees and in parts of Italy. *Capra aegagrus* is identified first in MOUSTER-IAN levels of caves in the Near East. The first evidence for possible human management is at SHANIDAR Cave, Kurdistan, where there are high proportions of juvenile goats and sheep at c8500 bc. The earliest morphological change

possibly due to domestication is shown at ALI KOSH (6750-6000 bc), further south in the Zagros mountains, where goat horn cores take on a form more like that of domestic animals. Goats seem to have been imported into Europe already domesticated — they appear in the Aegean before 6000 bc.

Gobedra. A small rock shelter near AXUM in northern Ethiopia which has yielded a stratified sequence of industries covering the last ten millennia bc. The earliest occurrence was of large blades, replaced c8000 bc by an industry dominated by backed microliths. Pottery first appeared at a level tentatively dated to the 3rd millennium which also yielded seeds of cultivated finger millet, *Eleusine coracana*. The latest stone industry was a specialized one of small steep scrapers of a type commonly found on Axumite sites.

Go Bong. (1) The earliest phase of the Bronze Age of north Vietnam (*bronze inférieur*), with dates estimated at 2000-1500 bc.
(2) An early site within the PHUNG-NGUYEN culture.

Godin Tepe. A site on the Gamur Ab river system of western Iran, with a continuous occupation from the 6th millennium bc to c1600 BC, when it was abandoned following an earthquake and not reoccupied for c800 years. Soundings to the earliest levels (Godin VII) revealed two building levels associated with straw-tempered, poorly fired pottery and a stone industry that lacked obsidian and ground stone, but yielded many blades with extensive retouch.

A later phase, Godin V (late 4th millennium BC) shows trading connections both with Mesopotamia (bevel-rim bowls) and with other parts of Iran (CLAY TABLETS in the PROTO-ELAMITE script). In Godin II (c750 BC) the site was a fortified town of the MEDES, and an important building with three colonnaded halls and a throne room has been excavated.

Gogo Falls. *See* KANSYORE WARE.

Gokomere. A site in south-central Zimbabwe where Early Iron Age settlement is attested from the 5th century to the 7th century ad. Through its characteristic pottery, Gokomere ware, the site has given its name to the archaeological industry representing the Early Iron Age occupation of central and eastern Zimbabwe and the northern Transvaal.

Gokstad Ship. Discovered in 1880 under a large tumulus near Oseberg on the Oslo Fjord, Norway, the Gokstad Ship is the most impressing VIKING vessel ever found. Much of its original timber was preserved by the clay in which it was set. In the middle of the ship a special platform had been constructed to hold the funerary chamber, which contained the skeleton of a man (possibly King Olaf of Vestfold who died in 890) surrounded by weapons, slaughtered animals and other objects (see BOAT BURIAL).

The Gokstad Ship is the ultimate Viking war machine — a slender oak-built vessel made for strength and speed, propelled by a large square sail and 16 pairs of oars for manoeuvring. It would have been equally navigable in open seas or in shallow inland waters, and in 1893 a replica successfully crossed the Atlantic.

Golasecca. An Iron Age culture of Lombardy, northwest Italy, from the 9th century to the 1st century BC. A few defended hilltop settlements are known, but the culture is known mainly from its cemeteries of inurned cremations, containing tens, hundreds or sometimes, as at the type site, thousands of burials. Grave goods are generally modest, but a number of outstandingly rich graves, interpreted as chieftains' burials, are known. These include wagon and chariot burials and contain rich grave goods of metal, showing connections both with the HALLSTATT Iron Age culture of central Europe and with the ETRUSCANS in central Italy.

gold. The most common source of ancient gold would have been nuggets or fine particles of native METAL, not ore. Gold in this form usually occurs ALLOYED with other metals. To make pure gold, these impurities have to be removed by a complex refining process. In any case, the remarkable malleability of pure gold (which allows it to be COLD WORKED without ANNEALING) would usually be undesirable in artefacts. The metal therefore appears most often as a gold alloy. Gold, like COPPER, was one of the earliest metals to be exploited by man, due to its natural occurrence as nuggets of native metal.

Goljamo Delčevo. An important Neolithic and Copper Age site located 30 km inland from the Black Sea in northeast Bulgaria and comprising a TELL settlement with adjoining cemetery. The tell, dated pre-4000 to 3600 bc, has 16 occupation layers with many complete house-plans. All categories of find, even metal and especially ornaments, are more common on the tell than in the cemetery. In the small Copper Age cemetery of 30 graves, contracted inhumation is the norm, with occasional cenotaph graves. The subsistence is based on mixed farming, specializing in cattle husbandry and the cultivation of einkorn and emmer wheat.

Goltho. See DESERTED MEDIEVAL VILLAGES, MANOR.

Gombe Point [formerly known as Kalina Point]. A site overlooking the Congo River in Kinshasa, which has yielded a long series of stone industries best regarded as local variants of the LUPEMBAN-TSHITOLIAN sequence of west-central Africa. Although apparently stratified, the succession is now believed to have suffered a considerable degree of post-depositional re-sorting.

Gomolava. A large, frequently occupied, site comprising two TELLS, formerly on an island in the Sava River in Srem, northern Yugoslavia. On both tells, the prehistoric sequence is broadly similar and divided into eight levels. Level I has Late VINČA houses and pits (on the south tell, a cemetery with copper grave goods). II is a prehistoric buried soil, which built up when the tell was unoccupied and which contains late LENGYEL, SOPOT-LENGYEL III and TISZAPOLGÁR sherds. III has pits with pottery of Middle and Late BADEN and VUČEDOL types. IV has pits with pottery of the Bronze Age Omoljica-Vatin and Belegiš groups. V is an occupation level of the Early Iron Age Bosut group; VI a Late Iron Age (Celtic) occupation level; VII a Roman building level and VIII a medieval cemetery. The subsistence economy of most levels indicates reliance on einkorn wheat and cattle husbandry.

Go Mun. (1) The third phase of the Bronze Age of north Vietnam (*bronze supérieur*), dated c1000-500 bc and immediately preceding the classic DONG-SON phase.

(2) A late site within the PHUNG-NGUYEN culture.

Gordion [Gordium]. A city occupying the mound of Yasi Hüyük, 90 km west of Ankara in Turkey, capital of the PHRYGIAN kingdom in the 8th century BC and sacked by CIMMERIAN nomads in 685 BC. Gordion occupied *c*8 hectares, surrounded by a massive mud-brick wall with a monumental gateway. The city was dominated by about ten important buildings built on the MEGARON plan and a palace complex. Outside the city gate was a cemetery of nearly 80 large tumuli, which have yielded a wealth of material of the 8th-6th centuries BC. The 'Great Tumulus' was *c*300 metres in diameter and *c*53 metres high; it covered a wooden chamber with a double-pitched roof and contained the extended burial of an old man lying on a bed. Some authorities identify the occupant as King Midas, who allegedly committed suicide when the Cimmerians attacked the city. The tomb also contained nine tables and two screens of wood, three bronze cauldrons, 166 other bronze vessels and 146 bronze fibulae [brooches]. Traces of linen and woollen textiles were found on the bed, and traces of purple cloth were also found on the throne in another rich tumulus, Tumulus P.

Gornja Tuzla. A TELL settlement of the STARČEVO, Early and Late VINČA and Late Copper Age periods, located near a narrow valley in upland north Bosnia, Yugoslavia. Pottery typology and radiocarbon dates for levels VI (*c*4690 — Starčevo) and III (*c*3760-3630 bc — Late Vinča) indicate sporadic occupation interspersed with long breaks. In the Late Vinča levels evidence of copper-smelting is known from within a house. The pottery characterizing the latest level (I) still lacks close affinities in the Balkan area.

Gorods'ke. The latest phase of the CUCUTENI-TRIPOLYE culture development (Tripolye C2) dated to the late 3rd millennium bc and centred on Volhynia, northeast of the Carpathians. Most settlements are located on high plateaux above river valleys, with rich household assemblages of bone and stone work. Metal is plentiful in Gorods'ke cremation cemeteries; some metal tools and weapons indicate a date in the Early Bronze Age.

Gortyn. An important ancient Dorian Greek city in southern Crete, later to become capital of the Roman province of Crete and Cyrenaica. It is perhaps most famous for the Gortynian Law Code, a 5th or 6th century BC inscription incorporated by the Romans into the back wall of an ODEUM when this was being reconstructed in 100 AD under Trajan. The Code, written *boustrophedon* (alternately from left and right), contains rules of civil law concerning such matters as family, adultery, divorce, property, mortgage and the rights of slaves (who were permitted *inter alia* to own property and to marry free women).

The site is rich in occupational evidence, much of which remains to be excavated. The acropolis appears to have Neolithic and Late Bronze Age evidence, and traces of a temple of the 8th-7th centuries BC. Homer refers to the city, and describes it as walled (presumably the acropolis) though no walls survive. A votive deposit associated with an altar on the slope of the hill contained a wide selection of objects from all periods from Late Minoan III through to Roman. Many of the major buildings date from after the Roman conquest in 67 BC, notably from the 2nd century AD. Identifiable are a *praetorium* (governor's residence), AGORA buildings, and odeum. Gortyn maintained its importance through early Christian times, becoming an early Byzantine religious centre.

Goths [Ostrogoth, Visigoth]. A group of Germanic tribes from the steppes of southeast Europe and southern Russia. In the 4th century food shortages and pressure from the HUNS to their east caused the Goths to join other Barbarian tribes in attacks on the outlying Roman and Byzantine provinces. They comprised two distinct groups — the easternmost tribes known as the Ostrogoths who controlled the steppe lands between the Crimea and Rivers Don and Dniester, and the western tribes known as the Visigoths who came from between the Dniester and the Danube.

Under their king Alaric the Visigoths sacked Rome in 410. Later they moved to southern France and settled in Aquitaine before seizing control of Spain. The material culture of the Visigoths is best exemplified by the Guarrazar and Torredonjimeno treasure hoards, which include a number of richly encrusted gold object such as the distinctive hanging crowns and pectoral crosses. Although Christians, both the Ostrogoths and Visigoths subscribed to the Arian sect. This was a matter of great contention with the Orthodox church of the Byzantine world and was possibly one reason why no help was given to the Visigoths in 711 when the Arabs invaded Spain and seized most of their kingdom.

After a period of intermittent war with the Eastern Empire, the Ostrogoths helped the Imperial forces to defeat the Huns in Italy in 454, and under their leader Oadacer were asked by the eastern Emperor Zeno to take control of the country. Under Oadacer and Theodoric there was a period of comparative peace until they were challenged and defeated by JUSTINIAN. The Ostrogothic culture blended in with the Byzantine and as a result is virtually indistinguishable. However, since they were Arians their religious art banned the portrayal of the Virgin; examples are to be found in some of the mosaics at RAVENNA.

gourd. The cucurbit *Lagenaria siceraria* produces a large fruit with a hard rind which was widely used for containers in Africa, southern Asia, the Pacific Islands and the Americas. Attested in South America and Thailand (SPIRIT CAVE) prior to 7000 bc, the plant is perhaps the most widespread of all the ancient cultigens. Thought to be of African origin, the dates and routes of its spread are unknown.

Gournia. A MINOAN settlement in eastern Crete, interesting because, unlike most other Minoan sites, it is not dominated by a palace, but appears to be a civilian town with narrow curving streets and many small houses. There *was* a small palace here, constructed in the Middle Minoan period, but in the Late Bronze Age, after *c*1550 BC, it was turned into small domestic dwellings. The only public building of this stage was a modest shrine.

Grächwil. A group of HALLSTATT barrows in the canton of Berne, Switzerland. Rich grave goods were recovered, including a fine imported Greek bronze HYDRIA of the early 6th century BC. It is decorated with scenes showing the 'mistress of animals', surrounded by four lions, crowned with eagles and snakes and holding a hare in each hand.

Gradešnica. A TELL site with KARANOVO I and Copper Age (cf Karanovo V) layers, situated in the upland Vraca Basin in northwest Bulgaria. Large-scale excavations by B. Nikolov have revealed complete early Neolithic house-plans, succeeded in the Copper Age by a large village of three occupational phases with houses arranged in streets. Among the rich Copper Age ritual assemblage is a house model inscribed with signs and the so-called Gradešnica plaque — a fired clay disc covered in elaborate incised symbols.

gradiometer. *See* MAGNETOMETER.

Graig Llwyd. An AXE-FACTORY in North Wales, chosen for its fine-grained igneous rock, suitable for polishing. Axes from this factory were in use during the Neolithic and Bronze Age and were widely traded: they have been found as far away as southern England, Yorkshire and east Lothian.

grain. *See* SEED.

grain impressions. Grain, other seeds, other parts of plants, and also small animals, such as insects, may become incorporated in pottery, bricks, daub or other clay materials. On firing, or as a result of decomposition over time, the organic material itself is lost, but the outline remains as an impression within the clay. Casts of these impressions are taken using latex rubber, and the original plant or animal may be identified.

Graman. A group of sandstone rock shelters in a small, well-watered valley on the western slopes of the Northern Tablelands of New South Wales, Australia. Human occupation has been dated between *c*3000 and 1000 bc. Stone artefacts included some of the earliest BONDI POINTS and geometric microliths found in Australia, dated to *c*3000 bc. Some have traces of resin along backed margins. Stratigraphic changes occurred, with a predominance of microliths in the lower levels being replaced by edge-ground tools in the upper levels; this change was paralleled in the faunal remains as macropod bones were replaced by possum bones. This was interpreted as a technological change from stone barbed spears used for hunting kangaroos and wallabies to axes used for extracting possums from trees. Other artefacts included grinding slabs, adze flakes, awls, perforated pendant fragments and bone points.

Granada. The most complete and spectacular Muslim city in Spain. Although its origins go back to the early years of the Moorish occupation in the 8th century, Granada rose to importance after the mid-13th century when it became the capital of a new state founded by Mohammad Al Ahmar. It was a large city dominated by the fortified citadel and Alcazaba, Medinat-al-Hamra, now known as the Alhambra. The Alhambra was defended by a massive towered enceinte enclosing a series of magnificent palaces linked by tranquil courtyards and gardens, much of which still remains. Apart from the Alhambra, Granada also preserves many examples of Islamic architecture in the older quarters of the city, including traces of the first western Muslim university. After the Catholic conquest in 1492 Granada continued to be a thriving cultural centre, and was embellished with churches and secular buildings constructed in the MUJEDAR and Renaissance styles.

Grand Pressigny. The source in Indre-et-Loire, central France, of a characteristic honey-coloured flint, which was widely traded throughout Western Europe in the Late Neolithic and Copper Age. It was generally traded in the form of large blocks, measuring $c30$ by 10 cm, which served as cores for the production of long blades.

grange. A medieval monastic manor house controlling the estates belonging to a monastery. Granges were first created in the 12th century and are, as a rule, a later medieval phenomenon common to several countries in Western Europe. The farms were run by monks with the assistance of lay servants, and their purpose was to produce food for the mother church as well as for sale in the wider market. Granges range in form from the elaborate monumental farm complexes of the Loire Valley such as Parcay-Meslay north of Tours, to the elegant Piedmont farms of Renaissance Italy and the hill farms of the Pennines in England.

granulation. A technique of decorating gold and silver jewellery. Many small spheres of metal were soldered on to the part to be decorated, giving it a granular texture.

Grass-marked pottery. Most of the pottery of the Dark Age period in western Britain is characteristically covered with 'grass' impressions. 'Grass-marked' pottery occurs in Ulster, the Hebrides and in Cornwall, and it has often been argued that it owes its widescale use to 5th- or 6th-century migrations between these regions. The pottery is crude, and the impressions indicate limited seasonal production which was terminated once wheel-thrown wares were produced during the Saxo-Norman period in Cornwall and Ulster.

Grass-tempered pottery. Crude hand-made ware made in various parts of Frisia in the MIGRATION PERIOD and in certain parts of southern England in the Early Saxon period. Examination of the inclusions in these pots shows that ferns and other organic material besides grass was also used as tempering.

grattoir. *See* SCRAPER.

Grauballe Man. A Danish BOG BURIAL in central Jutland, belonging to the Roman Iron Age, with a radiocarbon date $c310$ ad. Grauballe Man was naked and had clearly met a violent end, his neck having been cut almost from ear to ear. His skin was particularly well-preserved by the chemicals in the peat. It was possible to reconstruct his last meal, which had been eaten immediately before death: it consisted of a gruel made of 63 different types of identifiable seeds.

Grave Creek Mound. *See* ADENA.

Graveney Boat. The well-preserved timbers of an ANGLO-SAXON boat found in 1970 during the drainage of the Graveney marshes in Kent. It is the only vessel of this period from the British Isles which has left more than an impression in the soil, and radiocarbon and dendrochronology have effectively dated it to late in the 9th century. The Graveney Boat was a cross-Channel cargo vessel probably converted later in its life into an estuarine barge with a flat plank keel. It was 14 metres long and well-constructed, with planking sealed by cattle hair. It has been restored and is now on display in The National Maritime Museum in Greenwich.

Gravettian. Named after the site of La Gravette (in the Dordogne, southwest

France), the Gravettian was formerly called Upper or later AURIGNACIAN. In France it is equivalent to the later PERIGORDIAN cultures, which date from approximately 28,000 to 20,000 years ago. A group of central European sites has been attributed to an east Gravettian, but although they are of similar age it is not clear whether they are related or not. Russian sites attributed to the Gravettian are now known to date mainly to the latest part of the Upper Palaeolithic, later than 20,000 years ago. The presence of backed blades or backed points is usually regarded as typical of the Gravettian, but the VENUS figurines have also been regarded as characteristic.

Great Compound. See TEOTIHUACAN.

Great Interglacial. See HOLSTEIN, HOXNE.

Great Langdale. A Neolithic AXE-FACTORY on the side of Langdale Pikes in Cumbria, northwest England. Axes from this factory were widely traded, with the greatest concentration occurring on Humberside and Clydeside in the east of the country. They also reached southeast England, but none have so far been found in Wales or southwest England, which received axes from other factories.

Great Wall of China. Dating as a connected whole from the QIN dynasty (221-206 BC), the Great Wall linked together ramparts built independently during the 4th and 3rd centuries BC by the Eastern ZHOU states of Qin, Zhao, and YAN. Though building materials varied with locality, the Qin wall consisted mainly of rammed earth (HANGTU); it began in eastern Gansu and stretched more than 2000 km along the southern edge of Inner Mongolia to end at Shanhaiguan on the coast of northern Hebei. Several large sections were added during the early HAN dynasty (2nd-1st centuries BC), when the western end was carried as far as Yumen in western Gansu, and between the Han period and the 16th century AD the wall was repaired and elaborated many times. Rebuildings carried out under the MING dynasty were particularly extensive and the stone-faced wall seen today dates from that period.

From the Qin dynasty to the Ming the Great Wall continued to serve the same purpose as the Eastern Zhou walls incorporated in it: these 'monuments to cultural incompatibility', in William Watson's phrase, were erected for defence against the mounted nomads whose attacks on the northern frontier first became troublesome in the 4th century BC (see XIONGNU). The walls that the northern states built at that time to repel barbarians had precedents, however, in many similar ramparts erected by Eastern Zhou states for defence against each other.

Great Zimbabwe. This impressive site, located near Fort Victoria in southeastern Zimbabwe, is by far the largest and most elaborate of many late Iron Age dry-stone constructions to which the Shona name *zimbabwe* (meaning 'stone houses' or 'venerated houses') is applied. After an Early Iron Age phase (see GOKOMERE) the main sequence of occupation began at the commencement of the later Iron Age in about the 11th century ad, when the archaeological material resembles that from GUMANYE. Stone wall construction began around AD 1300, but the best work of this type dates to between the 14th and 15th centuries. Despite claims to the contrary, there is no reason to attribute to this architecture an origin other than a purely indigenous one among the ancestors of the recent Shona population.

It is reasonable to assume that Great Zimbabwe, at least at the period of its maximum prosperity, was the capital of an extended polity. The large quantity of imported luxury items recovered from the site indicates that trade formed the basis of this prosperity: glass vessels and beads, pottery and porcelain were imported, while gold was presumably the principal export. Great Zimbabwe appears to have been at the centre of a network of related sites through which control was exercised over the gold-producing areas; cattle-herding was the foundation of the domestic economy. Shona oral traditions link Great Zimbabwe with the cult of Mbire, their supreme god. In the 15th century the site declined, trade and political power shifting to a more northerly focus near the Zambezi Valley.

Green Gully. A Pleistocene open-air site in southern Victoria, Australia, near KEILOR, occupied between 15,000 and 4000 bc. Stone tools include large side-trimmed and concave flakes similar to those in Tasmania and at KENNIFF CAVE in the same period, and bipolar cores. Bones of two individuals, one male and one female, were found combined in a grave and were dated by radiocarbon on collagen to 4500 bc. The single cranium is female with modern morphology.

Greenland. The Icelandic sagas and histories tell of failed attempts to colonize Greenland in the 970s and how the exiled Erik the Red eventually succeeded in 985. It seems that these years were times of famine and over-population in Iceland and Erik was soon joined by 25 ships carrying colonists, 14 of which arrived.

Erik and one group of settlers founded the Eastern Settlement, while the rest sailed further up the western coast to the Western Settlement. Archaeologists have located several of these earliest farmsteads, where the occupants began some cultivation and animal farming, supplementing their diets by hunting and fishing. Erik's own farm at Bratthalio consisted of a main LONG HOUSE with walls 1.5 metres thick constructed of stone and turf. Inside there was a central conduit and animal stalls with partitions made of whale scapulae. There were also four barns and outbuildings and the remains of a small U-shaped chapel with a wooden gable which was built by Erik's wife after her conversion to Christianity around 1000.

From Greenland voyages were made to the coast of America, and Erik's son was one of the first explorers to reach 'Vinland'.

greenstone. A rather imprecise term, meaning basic igneous rocks that have become slightly metamorphosed. This includes a great many different rocks, some of which have been used as decorative material — including the JADES and SERPENTINES.

Grenzhorizont. A RECURRENCE SURFACE, defined by Weber in Germany, meaning 'boundary horizon'.

Grey ware. The typical ceremonial ceramic ware of MONTE ALBAN, Mexico, is of a fine grey paste and first occurs in the middle PRE-CLASSIC. Grey ware occurs throughout the site's occupation and variations in shape and ornamentation, rather than colour, are the best indicators of change over time. A distinctive ZAPOTEC speciality is the funerary urn which dates to the Late CLASSIC and typically is an unpolished cylindrical vessel depicting an elaborately modelled (usually seated) deity.

grid. Many archaeological sites are surveyed by measuring from a grid, usually in the form of a rectangle of equally spaced points, enclosing the site. *See* SURVEYING.

griddle. A flat ceramic plate used in the final stage of detoxifying MANIOC. After grating and pulping, thin discs of manioc are baked on the griddle into a kind of unleavened bread. Although there are other methods of preparation, use of the griddle is especially common in northeastern South American contexts, where it is considered a hallmark artefact signifying the practice of agriculture.

Grimaldi. A site on the Riviera in Italy, a few hundred metres from the French frontier, with a series of shelters and caves which were mainly investigated in the 19th century. Long sequences of archaeological levels were excavated with many burials and objects of adornment. Two of the burials, the 'negroids' from the lower levels of the Grotte des Enfants (or dei Fanciulli) have been the subject of controversy. First they were thought to be pre-NEANDERTHAL, and when that idea was abandoned in favour of an early Upper Palaeolithic date, they were claimed to represent an early appearance of the negroid peoples, an idea rarely held today.

Grimes Graves. A group of FLINT MINES in Norfolk, eastern England, with almost 350 mine shafts up to 9 metres deep and with radiating galleries. Radiocarbon dates suggest that the main period of use was in the Late Neolithic, c2000 bc (c2500 BC). The mines were mainly supplying material for the manufacture of flint axes and many rough-outs for such axes were found in the mines, as well as tools such as so-called 'antler picks', almost certainly used not as picks but as wedges. A ritual deposit was found in one shaft: a figurine of a pregnant woman, a phallus and several balls, all carved in chalk.

Grivac. A large open site of the STARČEVO and early VINČA periods, situated on a tributary of the Zapadna Morava River in central Serbia, Yugoslavia. Magnetometer survey of the site indicated rectangular house floors arranged in regular rows across the hillside;

through excavation these houses have been dated to the Vinča period, c4375-3980 bc. The slighter architectural remains of the Starčevo occupation are dated c5300 bc, the earliest radiocarbon date yet known from the Serbian Neolithic.

Gromatukha. *See* AMUR NEOLITHIC.

Grooved ware. A British late Neolithic pottery type, its flat-based vessels having straight vertical or outward sloping walls. It is decorated with shallow grooving or sometimes with applied cordons. It was formerly called Rinyo-Clacton ware after two widely separated findspots (Clacton in Essex and Rinyo in the Orkney Islands), but is now known to be widely distributed throughout Britain. It occurs commonly on the great HENGE sites of southern England, including STONEHENGE and DURRINGTON WALLS.

Grotefend, G.F. (1775-1853). German scholar who made considerable strides towards the decipherment of the CUNEIFORM script and, specifically, inscriptions in the Old Persian language written in this script. He presented a paper on his work to the Göttingen Academy in 1802, but it was not published and his work was largely ignored.

Grubenhäuser [German: 'sunken huts']. Most early medieval settlement sites in northern Europe are characterized by two types of building: timber dwellings built on the ground surface which have left traces of post-holes, stake holes and beam slots, and sunken huts or Grubenhäuser. The archaeological remains of Grubenhäuser take the form of rectangular pits sunk into the ground at a depth of between 0.2 and 1 metre; their floor space varies quite considerably. The sunken hut was usually roofed by a lean-to structure supported by one or three posts at either end and a simple ridge post creating a tent-like structure. It seems that many of these buildings had floors, with the sunken area being a kind of shallow cellar.

These sunken huts apparently date back to the Roman period in North Germany and Frisia, when they were used as workshops or ancillary buildings alongside farmhouses. On the continent of Europe, these buildings continued to be used for this purpose until c1000, with sites such as Dienne-sur-Meine in France having many post-Carolingian examples of Grubenhäuser. In England, the first sunken huts were probably employed as short-term dwellings by the migrants. Many late 4th-century examples have been found at MUCKING, for example. Later on, however, they were used as ancillary huts at villages such as WEST STOW, Suffolk. Whether the sunken hut was equally popular in the Middle Saxon period is still open to question, and similarly the question whether the sunken hut is the forerunner of the earliest urban cellared dwellings from Britain and Scandinavia has yet to be discussed. It was without doubt a significant type of building and one that clearly distinguishes early medieval settlements in Western Europe.

gu [*ku*]. *See* RITUAL VESSELS (CHINA).

Gua Cha. A large limestone shelter in Kelantan Province, central Malaya, excavated in 1954 and 1979. The basal level is HOABIN-HIAN, spanning the period 8000-1000 bc, with burials; the upper level (c1000 bc to ad 1000) contains richly provided Neolithic burials with southern Thai (BAN KAO) pottery affinites. The sequence relates to the ancestry of the present *orang asli* (Austro-Asiatic-speaking aborigines) of central Malaya.

Gua Kechil. A limestone shelter in Pahang Province, central Malaya, with a sequence which demonstrates a gradation from a late phase of the HOABINHIAN with cord-marked pottery, into a Malayan Neolithic assemblage which post-dates 2800 bc. *See also* GUA CHA, where the change from Hoabinhian to full Neolithic is apparently much sharper and also later in date.

Gua Lawa. A limestone shelter near Sampung in eastern Java excavated in 1926. The sequence may document a transition from a pre-ceramic assemblage of small hollow-based stone arrowheads (*see* MAROS POINTS of SULAWESI) into a Neolithic assemblage with cord-marked pottery and many bone and antler tools. The site remains undated.

guang [*kuang*]. *See* RITUAL VESSELS (CHINA).

Guarrazar. *See* GOTH.

Guattari Cave. *See* MONTE CIRCEO.

Gudea. *See* TELLOH.

Gudnja. A cave site in a steep valley west of Ston, in southern Dalmatia, Yugoslavia. A five-metre stratigraphy comprises six occupation levels: I, Early Neolithic IMPRESSED WARE; II-III, Middle Neolithic DANILO culture; IV-V, Late Neolithic regional variant of the HVAR culture; and VI, Copper Age. This site has yielded the first radiocarbon dates for the Dalmatian Neolithic: the Impressed Ware occupation dates to c5200-4600 bc, the Danilo levels to c4600-4450 bc.

Guerrero. *See* OLMEC.

gui [*kuei*]. (1) A Chinese Neolithic pottery tripod pitcher. The *gui* shape is characteristic of the east-coast Neolithic (*see* LONGSHAN) and of the HOUGANG II and KEXINGZHUANG II cultures. At first made with solid legs, the *gui* acquired bulbous hollow (LI-shaped) legs at the stage of the upper level at Dawenkou (*see* QINGLIAN'GANG).

(2) [Written with a different character] A bronze RITUAL VESSEL shape, a bowl ordinarily provided with handles. The bronze *gui* was known in the SHANG period but was especially common in Western ZHOU.

'Guinea Neolithic'. This ill-defined term has been applied to a heterogeneous series of industries in the coastal regions of West Africa. Backed microliths akin to those manufactured in earlier times are associated with pottery and with ground stone axe-like and hoe-like implements. One of the few well-described and dated occurrences is at BOSUMPRA near Abetifi in Ghana, where the occupation is dated between the 4th and the 2nd millennia bc. It is generally assumed, but has not yet been proven conclusively, that food-production techniques were being adopted in West Africa at this time.

Guitarrero Cave. A PRE-CERAMIC PERIOD site of long occupation, located at the base of the Cordillera Negra in northern Peru. Stratified deposits have yielded a wide variety of artefacts, both lithic and organic, together with a number of reliable radiocarbon dates. Its earliest level (Guitarrero I) has rendered a date of 10,610 ± 360 bc and contains flaked tools sharing general characteristics with the AYACUCHO complex and with TAGUA-TAGUA. Stemmed points of a similar type to those in LAURICOCHA II were found in the same level. Perhaps of more significance is the presence of a human mandible and other bone fragments which, if dated correctly, represent the earliest human remains yet found in South America. Tooth wear suggests a diet of soft food and thus points to an emphasis on meat and hence to a hunting group.

Guitarrero II has produced a series of radiocarbon dates covering the period c8500-5700 bc and contains bone and wood artefacts, basketry and loosely woven textiles, and the ubiquitous willow-leaf projectile point (*see also* AYAMPITIN). The cave is thought to have been seasonally occupied throughout its period of use, but an ARCHAIC life-style is especially evident in Guitarrero II.

Gumanye. The eponymous site of the initial phase of the later Iron Age of south-central Zimbabwe, dating to about the 11th century ad. It marks a clear break with the preceding Early Iron Age: opinion is divided as to the extent and source of external influence represented by this transition.

Gumelniţa. The eponymous site of the Gumelniţa culture is a TELL located near Olteniţa in the lower Danube Valley, Rumania. Excavated by V. Dumitrescu, the Copper Age deposits were divided into two occupations, Gumelniţa A and B, dated c3800-3200 bc. This subdivision of the culture parallels the partitioning of the closely related KARANOVO V and VI culture in Bulgaria. The Gumelniţa culture represents the climax development of the Neolithic sequence in south Rumania and is defined by nucleated tell settlement, highly evolved copper metallurgy and intensely varied ritual activity. *See also* CĂSCIOARELE.

Gundestrup. Find-spot of a great silver cauldron of the late pre-Roman Iron Age near Aalborg in Jutland, Denmark. The cauldron was found dismantled in a peat bog and is thought to have been put there as a votive offering. It weighs c9 kg and the eight outer and five inner plates are decorated in relief in the CELTIC ART style, with scenes of warriors, gods, heroes and exotic animals and human sacrifice. One of the most important figures is identified as the Celtic god Cernunnos ('the horned one') shown wearing a torc, symbol of status, and flanked by a deer on one side and a wolf on the other. The cauldron was probably imported from somewhere in the LA TÈNE province, perhaps somewhere in eastern Europe, in the 1st or 2nd century BC.

Günz. *See* MINDEL and RISS.

Günz/Mindel. The term for the INTER-GLACIAL erosion interval, envisaged by Penck and Bruckner as separating the Günz and MINDEL GLACIALS. The Alpine sequence is now known to be much more complex than was originally thought, but Günz/Mindel has unfortunately gained wide currency as a general term meaning the antepenultimate interglacial throughout Europe. This usage is still common in archaeological literature, but is better avoided.

Guran, Tepe. Situated south of Kermanshah in western Iran, Tepe Guran has 21 occupation levels, dated *c*6500-5500 bc. In the earliest, aceramic levels there were remains of wooden huts; it is probable that at this stage the site was a semi-permanent winter camp for goat-herdsmen who also hunted gazelle. In later levels, when pottery came into use, permanent mud-brick houses are found and there is evidence of farming: as well as domesticated goats, hulled two-row barley was probably cultivated.

Gussage All Saints. An Iron Age settlement in Dorset, southern England, similar in size and organization to LITTLE WOODBURY. The most interesting evidence from the site is that for metalworking: this small community was engaged in the production of bronze fittings for chariots and harnesses, a specialized activity that implies the existence of other centres specializing in other aspect of vehicle-production.

Guti. The Guti tribe came from the Zagros Mountains, probably in the area of Luristan, western Iran. They invaded and overran the homeland of the AKKADIANS in the reign of Shar-gali-sharri (later 3rd millennium BC), bringing to an end the Akkadian empire. Gutian kings are listed as having ruled Akkad for about a hundred years, but little is known about them beyond their personal names and a few words in texts.

Guweicun [Ku-wei-ts'un]. A late Eastern ZHOU cemetery site near LIULIGE in Hui Xian, Henan province, China. Three large shaft tombs were provided with entrance ramps on north and south, and are similar in construction to far earlier SHANG tombs. The largest of the three, which had an overall length including the ramps of 190 metres, was, however, marked at ground level by a low mound edged with large stones, a new feature modelled on the usages of the northern nomads (*see* SHAFT TOMBS, CHINA). Especially noteworthy is the discovery in this tomb of a number of cast-iron tools, including ploughshares, picks, hoes, shovels, axes and chisels.

Gwisho. A group of hot springs in the Kafue Valley of southern Zambia, the scene of intensive 'Late Stone Age' occupation during the 3rd and 2nd millennia bc. The sites are of particular importance because of the preservation of organic materials in the spring deposits. Grass-lined hollows have been interpreted as sleeping places, and there were traces of post-settings that probably represent wind-breaks. Among the wooden artefacts present in the assemblage were bows, arrowheads, fire-drills and digging sticks. The microlithic chipped stone industry is of the type usually described as 'Zambia WILTON'. Graves at the sites yielded some 35 human skeletons which show that the Gwisho people, despite their relatively large stature, shared many physical features with recent Khoisan-speaking populations. These people's economy was based upon hunting the rich game herds of the Kafue Flats, but a wide variety of vegetable foods was also collected.

Gwithian. Over the last 30 years the parish of Gwithian in Cornwall, southwest England, has been the subject of intensive archaeological research. Among the sites of all periods investigated, some of the most interesting belong to the prehistoric and medieval periods. A settlement site with evidence of two successive timber structures, the earlier circular, the second oval, belongs to the BEAKER period. At a later period, in the Middle Bronze Age, evidence of two successive field systems has been found here. Small square fields of 'Celtic' type (*see* CELTIC FIELD) were cross-ploughed using an ard and finished off with a wooden spade. Both the ard marks and the spade marks, the latter concentrated around the edge of the field, were exceptionally well preserved in blown sand.

The sites of the post-Roman period include a small settlement of circular drystone huts, a shell midden and a late Saxon chapel. The sites cover the sub-Roman (400-950), the early Christian (550-850) and the Late Saxon (850-1050) periods. These classifications have been made on the basis of pottery, which is far more determinate in the Celtic regions than anywhere else in Britain at this time. Gwithian ware and Mediterranean imports mark the first phase, and GRASS-MARKED pottery (associated with Irish missions and settlements) the second. The economy of Gwithian in the early medieval period seems to have been based on mixed agriculture, supplemented by shellfish. The rectangular chapel of St Gocanius is one of the few pre-Conquest buildings in Cornwall and although it is 9th or 10th century in date, it may well be the successor of an earlier Celtic chapel.

gymnasium [Greek *gymnos*: 'naked']. A classical Greek institution that combined athletics training and practice (for men only, except at Sparta) with open house for philosophers and teachers. The Academy of Plato and the Lyceum of Aristotle were both gymnasia. The sports training related to preparation for the various periodic games, and would have a whole group of indoor and outdoor facilities available, ranging from running tracks to an area set aside for wrestling and boxing (*see* PALAESTRA). This combination of health for the body and education for the mind might have seemed to some Greeks to represent an ideal of perfection. One or two Roman writers however had their doubts: worried perhaps at such a concentration of undressed young men and immature young minds, they saw only the chance for moral licence and seditious trouble-making.

gypsum. A soft white mineral, also known as alabaster, used in cements, stucco and, nowadays, in the manufacture of plaster of Paris.

H

Ha'amonga. The Ha'amonga-a-Maui on Tongatapu Island (*see* TONGA) is a huge coral trilithon with two notched uprights supporting a lintel. It was erected, according to tradition, by the 11th Tui Tonga (hereditary chief) around 1200. The monument is unique in the Pacific region.

Habaşeşti. A multi-level settlement site of the Late Neolithic CUCUTENI culture, located west of Iaşi, north Moldavia, Rumania. The main settlement level, of the Cucuteni A3 phase, has a radiocarbon date of *c*3130 bc. The village of almost 70 houses lies on a promontory site, the neck of which is defended by a ditch and palisade. Rich polychrome painted ware is found in many houses; an important discovery is a group of large copper bossed pendants, with affinities in Denmark and Austria.

hacha. *See* SPOUT-AND-BRIDGE VESSEL.

hachas. *See* BALL GAME.

Hacilar. A Neolithic and Chalcolithic TELL site in southwest Anatolia. The earliest settlement, of the 7th millennium bc, was an ACERAMIC NEOLITHIC village, based on the cultivation of emmer wheat, barley and lentils; it is not clear whether animals were also reared. The site was abandoned and re-occupied in the Late Neolithic, early in the 6th millennium bc. The new settlement had substantial rectangular mud-brick houses with doorways. Querns, mortars and braziers were fitted into mud plaster floors, while recesses in the walls acted as cupboards. The kitchen was separated from the living rooms and upper storeys were used as granaries and workshops. Pottery of a high quality developed from light grey and cream colours to red and brown monochrome wares; rare painted decoration occurred. Female figurines of a unique style were also made. The latest phase of this period was burnt *c*5400 bc and when the site was reoccupied it was smaller; houses now had courtyards attached and workshops were of a different design. This settlement was also burnt *c*5050-5000 bc and the Chalcolithic settlement that replaced it was defended by a perimeter wall. Inside were houses, a guardhouse, three potters' workshops and two possible shrines. Fine painted wares, predominantly in red on cream, characterize this phase.

Hadar. A site in northeast Ethiopia, also known as the Afar locality. Hominid fossils found here date back about three million years, and include the most complete early hominid skeleton ever found ('Lucy'), an individual not much over 90 cm tall. This skeleton and a series of skull pieces have been attributed to a new species, *Australopithecus afarensis*, but may be indistinguishable from *A. africanus* (*see* AUSTRALOPITHECUS). Claims of stone tool-making at about 2.7 million years ago have also been made.

Hadda. On the fertile plain of Jalabad in Afghanistan, Hadda was one of the principal Buddhist pilgrimage centres. Pilgrims such as Fa-Hsien (AD 420) and Sun-Yun (*c*520) believed that the Buddha himself visited Hadda, and its innumerable shrines and monasteries contained important relics: part of the Buddha's skull, his cloak etc. By 632, when Hsuan-Tsang visited the site, many of the shrines had been abandoned. Parts of Hadda have been excavated — and looted — as Western collections attest. The most important excavated complex, Tapa Shotor, is a sanctuary containing a STUPA (relic shrine) surrounded by miniature stupas. The shrines were decorated with clay and stucco sculptures, the earliest of which owe much to the hellenizing art of AI KHANUM. Others are closely similar to contemporary GANDHARAN reliefs.

Hadrian's Villa. Near Tivoli, 29 km from Rome, this amazingly extensive and architecturally capricious Imperial villa was built for the Emporer Hadrian over the years 125-135 AD. Some find the choice of site odd, located as it is upon low-lying ground of dubious attraction, and possibly at a disadvantage to the villas belonging to prominent members of Hadrian's court, which dotted the hills of neighbouring Tibur (Tivoli). It may be, however, that a large, relatively flat site was precisely what Hadrian wanted for his adventurous plans. The Emperor certainly gave free rein to the imagination of his designers, and seems to have backed them with an almost unlimited budget. Vaulting and walls alike show a pioneering exploitation of complex angles and curves, while the so-called Naval Theatre (Teatro Marittimo) offers a confusing maze of convex, concave and curviform patterns. The tradition of direct parallels between areas of the Villa and well-known models drawn from, for instance, Athens and Egypt (as in the case of the *Stoa Poikile* and the *Canopus*), should be treated with caution. Hadrian himself was unable to enjoy his villa for long, as ill-health took him south to Baiae, where he died in 138. Excavations date back to the 17th century, and the large number of works of art discovered are now dispersed over the museums of Europe.

Hadrian's Wall. The major and longest-lasting northern frontier to the Roman province of Britain. (For alternative frontiers at earlier and later date, *see* FOSSE WAY and ANTONINE WALL.) In 122 the emperor Hadrian visited Britain, and authorized the construction of this new frontier, stretching from the Solway Firth to the Tyne, a distance of some 117 km (80 Roman miles). Built 122-128 on a line just north of the existing Roman STANEGATE road, the wall was perhaps basically some 4.5 metres high, with possibly an additional 2-metre parapet above that. Some parts were originally constructed in turf, but in time (by about 160) the whole structure was completed in limestone. The wall had 16 forts to house troops, a small fort or milecastle every Roman mile (i.e. 80), and two signal turrets between each milecastle. A ditch in front (some 8.5 metres wide by 3 metres deep) was balanced by one behind with embankment (*vallum*). Forts and supply depots based on the Stanegate offered back-up facilities. At the Solway Firth end a chain of forts strung out for some 64 km down the coast were designed to prevent outflanking. Over the centuries of its use, the wall was refurbished three times, before final abandonment some time soon after 400. There are well-preserved examples of major wall-forts to be seen at Chesters and HOUSESTEADS. For the Stanegate, *see* CORBRIDGE.

Haftavan Tepe. A TELL site in northwest Iran occupied, though not continuously, from the Early Bronze Age to the SASSANIAN period. It has provided a valuable sequence for the prehistory of the area. In the 8th century BC the mound became an Urartian citadel (*see* URARTU) with an attached lower town. It was destroyed either by Sargon II in 714 BC or by the CIMMERIANS. The site was reoccupied in the Sassanian period: a town wall and numerous graves of this period are known.

Haft Tepe. A TELL site near SUSA in southwest Iran. The earliest occupation is dated to the 6th millennium bc, but the most important material comes from the ELAMITE period, in the centuries preceding the apogee of the Elamite empire, in the 13th century BC. A royal tomb of c1500 BC containing 21 skeletons, some covered in red ochre, is an early example of a vaulted tomb. This tomb was connected by a stairway to the main temple which contained many simple burials, some in urns. A brick-paved courtyard in the centre of the temple contained an altar, around which were found fragments of inscribed stelae in CUNEIFORM in the 14th-century BC Elamite language. These have provided details of the temple economy.

Hafun. A peninsula on the eastern coast of Somalia, some 150 km to the south of Cape Guardafui. It provides the best archaeological evidence yet available from the East African coast south of the Red Sea for early trade contact with the Mediterranean world at the beginning of the Christian era, as described in the *Periplus of the Erythraean Sea*. No permanent settlement is attested, but burials contain imported pottery, some of it apparently Hellenistic. The *Periplus* records that spices, gums and ivory were the principal exports.

Hagar Qim. One of the largest of the MALTESE TEMPLE complexes, situated in the southwest of the island. It contains three separate temples, constructed over a considerable period of time. It is unique among the temples in that the softer of the two available local limestones, the globigerina limestone, was used throughout, even for the outer walls and facade, for which the harder coralline limestone was usually preferred; as a result the stones of the outer wall of Haġar Qim have been reduced by weathering to strange and fantastic shapes. The buildings are provided with numerous altars of various shapes and a variety of niches and recesses. Many of the stones have pitted decoration.

Hagia Sophia. Situated in Constantinople, the capital of the Eastern Roman Empire, this is one of the most splendid churches in the Christian world. The present building was erected by Justinian between 532 and 537 to replace Constantine's earlier basilica, which had been destroyed by fire. Its central design was revolutionary at the time; it has three main aisles divided by piers and columns within a square plan, and a large central flattened dome supported by four arches and pendentives inside, and semi-dome outside. For many years the Hagia Sophia was unsurpassed in size and the interior still retains much of its original sumptuous appearance. Its lower walls are faced with polished multi-coloured marbles and the vaults, domes and pendentives are covered with brilliant Byzantine mosaics set in their background of gold. See BYZANTIUM.

Hagia Triadha. See AYIA TRIADHA.

Haithabu. See HEDEBY.

Hajdusamson. Denotes a horizon of Hungarian and Rumanian metalwork hoards (the 'Apa-Hajdusamson' horizon) defined by A. Mozsolics and dated to the later Early Bronze Age, c1700-1500 bc. Whilst the bronze solid-hilted swords, disc-butted and shaft-tube axes and daggers are often richly decorated, the peak of aesthetic skill is reached in gold-working. The Hajdusamson horizon includes many small ornaments (discs, rings, bracelets) as well as extraordinary unique pieces such as the Persinari sword and the Bihar cups. The unique pieces were almost certainly the products of a single workshop, probably located in Transylvania.

Haji. Reddish earthenware used during the KOFUN, NARA, and HEIAN periods in Japan. It is technically very similar to YAYOI pottery, and many authorities disagree over when Yayoi pottery ends and Haji begins. Early Haji pottery is characterized by the appearance of ceremonial vessels that are homogenous throughout a wide area, along with domestic vessels made in local styles. After the wheel-made, kiln-fired SUE pottery was introduced in the 5th century, only domestic vessels were made in Haji ware, and from the 8th century onwards Haji pottery, too, was made on the potter's wheel.

Hajji Firuz. This site near Hasanlu in northwest Iran is the type site of the Hajji Firuz culture, which dates to c5500-5000 bc and represents the earliest known settlement in this area. The settlement seems to have been a village of farmers, who cultivated wheat and barley and kept sheep and goats and perhaps pigs. They lived in mud-brick houses separated by alleys; the houses were square in plan and consist of a single room, partially divided by an internal wall into living, working and storage space. The most interesting finds were the burials: as well as a collective grave of 13 individuals buried over a period of time, 28 massacred bodies distributed in three graves have been seen as the earliest clear evidence of conflict from early farming sites in western Asia.

Hajji Muhammed. An early 5th-millennium bc site near URUK in southern Mesopotamia which has given its name to a type of painted pottery and an early phase of the UBAID culture (Ubaid 2). The pottery is painted in dark brown or purplish black in a 'busy' geometric style. Hajji Muhammed pottery is found also at ERIDU in layers stratified between the earliest 'Eridu' pottery and the fully developed Ubaid culture. It is found over southern Mesopotamia, as far north as RAS AL-AMIYA, near KISH.

Hakataya. A pottery-making tradition of the American Southwest which includes groups of regionally distinct cultures based in the desert environment of the southwestern plateau and the Colorado River basin, such as Cerbat, Prescott, Cohohina and Sinagua. Sometimes known as the PATAYAN, there is considerable disagreement about the real extent and cultural affiliations of the tradition. As with other Southwest traditions (e.g. ANASAZI,

MOGOLLON) the Hakataya is thought to have emerged from the DESERT TRADITION. Dates vary within the period AD 500 to historic times.

Hakuho. *See* HOFUN.

Halaf, Tell. A TELL site on the river Khabur in northeast Syria, close to the Turkish border, which has given its name to a widespread culture of north Mesopotamia and Syria, with radiocarbon dates in the range 5500-4500 bc. It is characterized by a fine painted pottery with designs in black, red and white on a buff ground. The finest polychrome Halaf vessels come from the potter's workshop at ARPACHI-YAH. This site and Tepe GAWRA have produced typical Eastern Halaf ware, while a rather different Western Halaf version is known from such Syrian sites as CARCHEMISH and Halaf itself.

Although no Halaf settlement has been extensively excavated, some buildings have been excavated: the misleadingly named 'tholoi' of Arpachiyah, circular domed structures approached through long rectangular anterooms. These buildings, constructed of mud-brick, sometimes on stone foundations, may have been for ritual use (one contained a large number of female figurines), but other circular buildings on this and other sites were probably simply houses.

The Halaf population practised dry farming (based on natural rainfall without the help of irrigation), growing emmer wheat, two-rowed barley and flax; they kept cattle, sheep and goats.

As well as their fine painted pottery, the Halaf communities made baked clay female figurines and stamp seals of stone; these latter artefacts are often thought to mark the development of concepts of personal property (because at a later date seals are used to produce marks of ownership).

The Halaf culture was succeeded in northern Mesopotamia by the UBAID culture. *See also* HASSUNA, YARIM TEPE.

Halawa Valley. A valley on eastern Molokai, HAWAIIAN ISLANDS, which has been the scene of intensive archaeological research. Major sites include one of the earliest Hawaiian settlements at the valley mouth (c600-1200), and inside the valley are many irrigated TARO terraces which document intensification of cultivation and perhaps political development at a late stage of Hawaiian prehistory (after 1500).

halberd. A metal weapon with a blade like that of a dagger, but mounted at right-angles to the haft and used rather like a battle-axe. Halberds occur quite commonly in the Copper Age of Italy and in several parts of Europe during the Early Bronze Age. Halberd blades on their own can be confused with dagger blades; however, they are frequently stronger and often asymmetrical in outline.

Halfan. A Nubian stone industry, named after the settlement of Wadi Halfa, dating from c23,000 bc. Its sites, characterized by tools made on small blades, appear to have been camps of hunters and fishermen.

half-life. The time taken for half a radioactive isotope to decay. Thus after a time of one half-life has elapsed, one half of the isotope will be left. After two half-lives, one quarter is left; after three half-lives, one eighth — and so on. The most recent determination of half-life for ^{14}C is 5730 years. The original Libby half-life was 5568 years and this has caused some slight complexity. Radiocarbon laboratories have agreed (for consistency) to continue to use the 5568 half-life as a standard, even though it is now known to be incorrect (*see* RADIOCARBON DATING). Therefore dates as quoted by the laboratory are in terms of the 5568 half-life. CALIBRATION tables are so arranged that they automatically correct for this — so the archaeologist usually does not need to worry about it. If, for any reason, it is desired to correct a 5568 to the 5730 half-life, this is easily accomplished by adding the 5568 date to 3 per cent of itself.

Halicarnassus [Bodrum]. An Ionian Greek port on the west coast of Caria, Asia Minor, lying opposite the island of Cos. Possibly a very early foundation (traditionally dated to the 9th or 10th century BC), it was famous in antiquity for its Mausoleion (*see* MAUSOLEUM) and as the birthplace of the 5th-century BC historian, Herodotus. In the classical period it shows an Ionian Greek culture, strongly coloured by local Carian influences. As Persian satrapy, it became the capital of Carian dynasts, one of whom, Mausolus (377-353 BC) was especially responsible for the distinction of its agora, theatre and temples, to which he added his own palace. The fine view afforded by the town from the sea is described by Vitruvius. Its sack by ALEXANDER THE GREAT in 334 BC (for having the impudence to resist) is the last major event on record, after which the town seems to have retreated into obscurity. Virtually all trace of ancient Halicarnassus has now unfortunately disappeared under modern Bodrum. Some sections of the city wall survive, and the site of the mausoleum, the tomb of Mausolus, is known. From its materials a great castle of the Knights of St John was later constructed in the 15th century.

Hallstatt. A site 50 km east of Salzburg, Austria, which has given its name to the earlier Iron Age of central Europe (c700-500 BC). The site of Hallstatt itself consists of a cemetery of some 3000 graves on a mountain slope above the valley; there are also extensive salt mines in the area and a settlement in the valley, largely inaccessible under the modern village. Excavations of the cemetery in the last century have provided the basis for the subdivision of the Hallstatt culture: Hallstatt A and B belong to the Late Bronze Age URNFIELD culture (12th-8th centuries BC); Hallstatt C and D belong to the Iron Age (7th and 6th centuries BC). It was succeeded by the LA TÈNE culture and a few of the latest graves at Hallstatt itself belong to this later period.

The Hallstatt Iron Age culture certainly developed out of the Urnfield Bronze Age groups, but there were a number of important changes: iron technology was introduced and gradually replaced bronze for many tools and weapons; inhumation replaced cremation as the dominant burial rite and settlement in HILLFORTS became more common. The most marked changes, however, appear in the field of social organization: Hallstatt Iron Age society appears strongly differentiated, with chieftains buried in richly equipped graves with four-wheeled vehicles and fine goods of pottery and metal, some locally made, others imported from the Mediterranean civilizations (see HOHMICHELE, VIX). The wealth and status of the Hallstatt chieftains was indeed based in part on trade with the Mediterranean world: in exchange for raw materials such as metal ores, amber and salt and perhaps also perishable products such as skins and textiles, the chieftains obtained fine pottery and metal vessels produced in the workshops of the cities of Greece, Magna Graecia and Etruria. There was also extensive trading within the territory of the Hallstatt culture itself.

Hallur. A site in Mysore, southern India, which has produced evidence of a Neolithic-Chalcolithic culture of the 2nd millennium BC, characterized by one-roomed circular houses, burnished grey ware, an abundant ground stone industry and a few copper objects. A later level has BLACK AND RED WARE, iron objects and a radiocarbon date of c1100 bc (c1400 BC), although many authorities believe this to be too early.

Hal Saflieni. An enormous rock-cut hypogeum of the prehistoric period in the outskirts of Valletta on the island of Malta. The hypogeum, which was constructed by the same population that built the MALTESE TEMPLES, is a complex of many small rock-cut chambers, on three different levels, linked by a series of halls, passages and stairways. The hypogeum was excavated in a natural hill, and covers an area of c150 square metres with the lowest level some 10 metres below the surface of the rock. Many of the chambers are elaborately decorated, often with carved features imitating wooden structures such as beams and lintels; other chambers have painted decoration, usually on the ceilings. Most of the chambers had been used for burial and it has been calculated that some 7000 individuals were buried in the whole hypogeum, over a period of some centuries. The hypogeum may also have been used as a temple and it seems that some chambers, free of skeletal remains, were set aside for ritual. Finds from the hypogeum include much highly decorated pottery and a series of female figurines including one labelled the 'Sleeping Lady' representing a woman wearing a fringed skirt and reclining on a couch with her head on a pillow.

Hama [Hamath]. A TELL site on the River Orontes in Syria which has produced evidence of occupation from the Early NEOLITHIC to c700 BC (and, after rebuilding c200 BC, later occupation in the Greek, Roman and Islamic periods). During the 2nd millennium BC Hama was a large town, but it does not appear in ancient documents until c1000 BC, when it became capital of an Aramaean kingdom. Danish excavations in the 1930s revealed a fine palace of this period, with evidence of ivory carving. The palace ground floor was used for storage while upper floor rooms were used as living-quarters, decorated with red, white and blue plaster with gold leaf ornament. Across the central court was a temple dedicated to the moon god Sin. The city was destroyed by the Assyrians c720 BC.

Hamangia. The Hamangia culture is distributed along the dry Black Sea coast of south Rumania and north Bulgaria, dating from the late 5th millennium bc to c3700 bc. These sites represent the earliest known farming culture in this steppe area; settlements are mostly single-phase, with more emphasis on mixed farming than fishing or hunting. An important landscape feature is the large cemeteries, with up to 300 extended inhumations. Grave goods were unexceptional, but for finely made fired clay and marble figurines — one of the very few instances of figurines found in funerary contexts in southeast Europe.

Hambledon Hill. A CAUSEWAYED CAMP of the early 3rd millennium bc in Dorset, southern England. Extensive excavations have revealed pits containing collections of pottery, flint tools and bone. Human skulls had been placed at regular intervals along the ditch bottom. These finds and the discovery of fragmented remains of many bodies in both the ditch and inside the enclosure have led the excavator, Roger Mercer, to suggest that the site may have been used for exposing the dead, prior to burial in a long BARROW, whether MEGALITHIC or non-megalithic. Another enclosure on the nearby Steepleton Spur may have been a settlement, also of the Neolithic period. Much later there was an Iron Age HILL-FORT on another ridge of this three-spurred hill.

Hamburg. Excavations of an area of about one-third of a hectare were undertaken in the old medieval heart of Hamburg, north Germany, between 1947 and 1959. The southern part of the old town near the river and the cathedral precinct were examined, and archaeologists located the fortified CAROL-INGIAN monastic nucleus which, according to the 9th-century chronicler Rimbert, was attacked by the Danes in 845. Investigations of the *suburbium* also mentioned by Rimbert were equally successful, and showed the existence of a long sequence of buildings with important groups of artefacts related to each period.

Hamburgian. A late glacial culture of Northern Europe. At the site of MEIENDORF near Hamburg and at other sites in north Germany and Holland reindeer-hunters' camps are found which date from about 11,000 bc. Although they have quite a lot in common with the contemporary MAGDALENIAN, they have been grouped under a separate name, Hamburgian. Characteristic tools are shouldered points and stout piercers called *zinken*.

Hamsavati. The original name of the city of Pegu, Lower Burma. The chronicle givers 825 as the date of its foundation by the twin brothers Samala and Vimala as the new capital of the kingdom of Râmaññadesa (i.e. the MON country).

Hamwih. *See* SOUTHAMPTON.

Han [Han]. Chinese dynasty (206 BC-AD 220). Historians divide the Han dynasty into Western Han (206 BC-AD 8), when the capital was at CHANG'AN, and Eastern Han (AD 23-220), when the capital was at LUOYANG, separated by the Wang Mang Interregnum (AD 8-23). In many respects the pattern for later Chinese empires, the Han represented for succeeding generations an image of imperial unity; its name was even borrowed to mean 'Chinese' in the ethnic sense: the population of China is today officially described as made up of Han Chinese and some 50-odd Minority Nationalities.

Next to the rich tombs at MAWANGDUI and MANCHENG, perhaps the most revealing Han archaeological finds are a number of tombs whose wall paintings, decorated tiles and stone reliefs form the earliest substantial corpus of Chinese pictorial art.

An unrelated character also transliterated Han is the name of an Eastern ZHOU state.

Handan [Han-tan]. The capital of the Eastern ZHOU state of Zhao from 386 to 228 BC, probably to be identified with a walled city whose remains lie 4 km southwest of the modern city of Handan in southern Hebei province, China. The massive walls, which enclose an area of about three square kilometers, are built of HANGTU, as are the foundation platforms of a number of large buildings. A cemetery 5 km north of the walled city, excavated in 1957 and 1959, contained six CHARIOT BURIALS and twelve rich tombs, five with human sacrifices.

hand axe. One of the most typical stone tools of the Lower PALAEOLITHIC period. Characteristically it is made on a nodule which has been flaked over both surfaces until it is approximately almond-shaped.Usually one end is more pointed than the other, but the whole tool is normally symmetrical about its long axis. Hand axes first appear between one and two million years ago and they were common in assemblages for about a million years. They continued to be made as late as the last glacial period, especially in the West European 'MOUSTERIAN of Acheulian Tradition'. Generally hand axes are regarded as diagnostic of the ACHEULIAN. The use to which hand axes were put is far from clear, although meat-cutting may have been one of their functions.

Hane. A valley on Uahuka Island, MARQUESAS (Polynesia), with a sand dune site behind the beach which has documented aspects of Marquesan prehistory from initial settlement (c300 ad) to European contact. It is a crucial site for documenting early human dispersal into Eastern Polynesia.

hanging bowls. Thin bronze, shallow bowls found in ANGLO-SAXON graves up until the 7th century, hanging bowls are an important part of a Celtic metal-working tradition which has its origins in the Roman and pre-Roman Iron Age. They have three equally spaced suspension rings, fixed to the bowl by means of escutcheons which are usually decorated in a very distinctive way with coloured enamel and MILLEFIORI, invariably in (Celtic) trumpet and volute patterns rather than Germanic zoomorphic interlace. It seems likely that the bowls were actually suspended by means of tripods, but their exact function is not known.

hangtu [*hang-t'u*]. A kind of rammed-earth construction used for walls, foundations, and SHAFT TOMBS in China throughout the SHANG and ZHOU periods. Earth was packed between wooden forms in successive thin layers, each layer being pounded hard before the next was added. In the Shang city wall at ZHENGZHOU,

which is about 20 metres thick at the base and 7100 metres long, the clearly distinguishable layers are 70-100 mm deep. *Hangtu* walls have been found at only two late Neolithic sites, Chengziyai (*see* LONGSHAN) and HOUGANG, and it is uncertain whether these walls actually pre-date the use of *hangtu* at early Bronze Age sites such as ERLITOU. In the latter part of the Zhou period *hangtu* constructions were often faced with stone. Much of the GREAT WALL was originally built of rammed earth.

haniwa. Large hollow clay objects that were placed on the top, around, or inside burial mounds (KOFUN) in Japan. Early *haniwa* of the 4th century are cylinders with see-through designs, and are considered to have developed out of the tall stands for Late YAYOI ritual vessels of the 3rd century. House-shaped *haniwa* also had a Yayoi prototype, and continued to be made until the end of the 6th century, when *haniwa* production ceased. Other representational forms include boats, weapons and armour, popular during the 4th and 5th centuries, birds and animals frequent in the 5th and 6th centuries, and human figures that were made in the 6th century.

Hao [Hao]. *See* ZHOU CAPITALS.

Harappa. One of the two major cities of the HARAPPAN CIVILIZATION of the 3rd millennium BC. Whereas MOHENJO-DARO is situated in the southern Sind province, Harappa is on the middle Ravi plain of the northern Punjab. Unfortunately the site was largely destroyed during the last century by the extraction of bricks for ballast for the Lahore-Multan railway, then under construction. Smaller than Mohenjo-Daro, Harappa originally covered c43 hectares and may have housed 20-25,000 people. Like Mohenjo-Daro, it consisted of a citadel mound to the northwest and a more extensive group of mounds to the east, representing the ruins of the lower town. The citadel was defended by a wall, about 14 metres wide at the base but tapering upwards; we know virtually nothing about the buildings on the citadel. In the area between the citadel and the river a group of 12 small granaries was excavated; they were arranged in two rows separated by a central passage. The combined floor space of these granaries is close to that of the earliest phase of the large granary on the Mohenjo-Daro citadel. In the same area were at least 18 circular brick platforms with holes in the centre, probably used for pounding grain. Two lines of small oblong dwellings not far away may have housed workmen. The whole area seems to have been used for the preparation and storage of grain and the accommodation of those who worked on it. Another important discovery at Harappa was the so-called R37 cemetery, one of the few known cemeteries of the Indus Valley civilization. Here 57 citizens had been buried individually, in the extended position; with them were numerous pottery vessels, personal ornaments and sometimes toilet articles.

Harappan civilization [Indus Valley civilization]. Name given to the civilization that flourished in Pakistan and northwest India in the later 3rd millennium BC, based on the flood plain of the River Indus and its tributaries. Nearly 300 settlements of the civilization are known: two large cities (MOHENJO-DARO and HARAPPA), a number of smaller towns (including CHANHU-DARO, JUDEIRJO-DARO, KALIBANGAN and LOTHAL) and many villages. The Harappan civilization was characterized by a high level of architectural, craft and technical achievement, but we know little about its social and economic organization and nothing about its military or political history, since although the civilization was literate the script is as yet undeciphered, and we are dependent on archaeological evidence alone for information. Like other early civilizations in Mesopotamia and Egypt, the Harappan civilization was based on the cultivation, presumably with the help of irrigation, of the cereal crops wheat and barley. On some sites, in the later phases, rice was also grown and the cultivation of this crop may have opened up the rest of the subcontinent for food production, since environmentally it is much better adapted to rice cultivation than to that of wheat and barley. COTTON was grown for its fibre and actual cotton cloth — the earliest yet discovered anywhere — was found at Mohenjo-Daro and Lothal. The farmers also kept cattle, buffalo and perhaps also pigs and sheep. Camels, horses and asses were all used for transport and even elephants may have been domesticated. Among the most distinctive achievements of this civilization are the architecture and town planning, with the use of true baked brick for building, and cities and towns laid out on a grid-iron street plan, perhaps the earliest examples of town planning in the world. Among crafts, the most outstanding productions were those of the seal-cutters: thousands of seals have been found, mostly made of steatite and decorated with carefully executed incised designs, usually depicting animals associated with an inscription.

Harappan civilization flourished from about the middle of the 3rd millennium BC; it

Inscribed stone seals of the Harappan civilization

came to an end early in the 2nd millennium, either as a result of environmental factors (especially excessive flooding) or as a result of invasions by ARYAN intruders, or possibly a combination of different factors.

hard water effect. When material that is RADIOCARBON DATED has been buried, groundwater may have percolated into it. Groundwater frequently contains dissolved calcium carbonate, where it has passed through limestones. Such carbonate may crystallize within the sample to be dated. As a result carbon from a source very much older than the sample may be included. Dates from material that has been contaminated in this way will be far too old. Samples such as wood and charcoal may be treated with hydrochloric acid to dissolve away the crystallized carbonate; this eliminates the problem. A real difficulty, however, arises with shell samples, which are themselves made of calcium carbonate. Any attempt to dissolve away the contaminant will result in destruction of the sample. This makes it hard to obtain reliable dates for shell.

Hargeisan. A stone industry of northern Somalia which appears to pre-date the local appearance of true backed-microlith industries. Based upon the production of blades, the Hargeisan (which has not itself been dated) may be related to the EBURRAN occupation of the central Kenyan Rift Valley between the 11th and 8th millennia bc, and/or to contemporary blade industries of Ethiopia, as seen at GOBEDRA.

Hariharālaya [Sanskrit: 'abode of Hari-Harā', i.e. the combined god Vishnu and Siva]. The 'eastern district' of ANGKOR, at present known by the name of Rolûos, situated about 15 km southeast of Siem Reap. The 'Rolûos group' consists of several brick edifices with pre-Angkorian art, as well as monuments dating from the reigns of the first three kings of Angkor, notably the BAKONG, built in 881.

Haripunjaya. The original name of the town of Lamphun, near Chiangmai, in northern Thailand. According to tradition it was founded by a colony of MON emigrants from LAVO (present-day Lopburi) led by the queen Chammadevī; 12th-century inscriptions show a Mon dynasty reigning in Haripunjaya at that time.

Hariri, Tell. *See* MARI.

Harmal, Tell. Located in the suburbs of Baghdad, Iraq, Tell Harmal has been identified as ancient Shaduppum, an administrative centre for the surrounding area, ruled by ESHNUNNA in the early centuries of the 2nd millennium BC before Hammurabi's conquest. This small walled town, covering only c1.7 hectares, was excavated almost completely by the Iraqis in 1945. Excavated buildings include several temples, one with an entrance guarded by life-size terracotta lions; a residential area of private houses and some shops has also been excavated. The site produced a large collection of tablets, mostly administrative, but also literary texts and lexical lists of zoological and botanical terms; a famous mathematical text anticipates Pythagoras' theorem. The ancient name apparently means 'place of writing' and the town may have been a centre for priests and scribes.

harpoon. Barbed spears and harpoons appear at the close of the PALAEOLITHIC and represent an important invention. Generally they were made of reindeer antler, cut into strips and carved with barbs. The harpoons were presumably fixed on the ends of wooden spears in such a way that they came loose after being shot into the animals but remained attached to the shafts by a line. Similar harpoons have remained in use until recent times amongst the ESKIMO and other hunting peoples.

Hasanlu. A TELL site on the south bank of

Magdalenian biserial harpoon

Lake Urmia in northwest Iran. It consists of a citadel, constructed early in the 1st millennium BC on the debris of much earlier prehistoric remains, and surrounded by a lower town. Four buildings on the citadel, facing onto a court and linked to a higher court with further buildings, have been interpreted as a palace complex. In c800 BC the building was burnt down and in its shell were found 21 bodies, alternatively interpreted as human sacrifices or as looters who died when the building collapsed. One of the skeletons held a magnificent gold bowl decorated with mythical scenes in relief. Other rich finds of gold, silver, electrum, glass and ivory have been made at Hasanlu.

Ha Soloja. *See* MOSHEBI'S SHELTER.

Hassuna. A TELL near Mosul in northern Iraq which has given its name to a pottery style represented in the lowest levels on the type site and widely distributed over northern Mesopotamia. It is dated to the 6th millennium bc and in much of the area it is associated with the earliest farming communities known. The pottery is a buff ware with simple shapes and often decorated with incised or painted geometric designs.

At Hassuna six occupation levels were recognized, the earliest without structural remains and often described as a 'campsite'. Later levels have houses built of packed mud, consisting of a number of rooms opening on to a courtyard, in which were ovens and grain bins. Recent work at the sites of UMM DABAGHIYAH and YARIM TEPE have cast new light on the Hassuna culture, which may have begun as early as 6000 bc and lasted for as long as a millennium. The people of this culture were competent mixed farmers, but also depended to a considerable degree on hunting. The very interesting new evidence from Yarim Tepe indicates that they were already experimenting with metallurgy and that pottery-making was a specialist activity (with true pottery kilns). The appearance of stamp seals suggests the importance of private ownership.

The Hassuna pottery style is partly contemporary with the appearance of the finer SAMARRA ware, which subsequently replaced it.

Hastinapura. A site in the upper Ganges Valley of India which is referred to in the Mahabharata (an epic story about a prolonged feud between rival princely families in the Ganges valley) as the seat of the Kaurava kings. The earliest level has OCHRE-COLOURED POTTERY, which is succeeded in Period II by PAINTED GREY WARE. Iron slag appears in the later part of this period, as do domesticated horses. The Period II settlement was destroyed by a flood and the site abandoned for a while. The Period III occupation was a substantial settlement of mud-brick houses associated with NORTHERN BLACK POLISHED WARE and coinage of the later 1st millennium BC. Over this were levels of historical date, down to the 15th century AD.

Hatra [present-day al-Hadr]. A north Mesopotamian desert oasis settlement some 80 km south of Mosul in Iraq. Hatra probably came into existence in SELEUCID times (c300-100 BC) and then flourished as the capital of a little semi-independent Arab state within the PARTHIAN orbit, close to the Roman border, ruled first by 'lords' and then from c150 AD by kings. Three times (in AD 117 and 198-201) it withstood Roman sieges but was finally occupied from c233 AD until it was destroyed by SASSANIAN Persians in 241.

Remarkable ruins survive and excavations in the 1970s by the Iraqis have revealed buildings of mud-brick and limestone: town walls, gates, a large palace, several great temples, houses and tombs, with striking stone statues and reliefs, and Aramaic inscriptions.

Hattusas. *See* BOGHAZKÖY.

Hatvan. The eponymous TELL site for the Hatvan culture, an early Bronze Age group distributed in the Tisza Valley of eastern Hungary in the early 2nd millennium bc. Many of the sites are tells in the Great Hungarian plain, although enclosed hilltop sites are known in the Carpathian foothills. Cremation cemeteries are frequent, often with more than one serving a single settlement; inurned cremations are as common as pit burials. Unusually for this period, Hatvan settlements commonly produce large numbers of fired clay zoomorphic figurines and vases, as well as model cart-wheels.

Haua Fteah. Excavations at this great cave in

Cyrenaica, Libya, have illustrated the most complete sequence of Upper PLEISTOCENE and HOLOCENE industries yet known from any single site in North Africa. The lowest levels have not been investigated, so it not known when the site's occupation began. The earliest industry so far known from Haua Fteah is an enigmatic one referred to as the Libyan pre-AURIGNACIAN, which covers a period of uncertain duration prior to c60,000 BC. Based upon the striking of parallel-sided blades from prismatic cores, it has clear affinities with broadly contemporary industries in Syria, Lebanon and Israel. Its makers exploited both large game animals and seafood resources. Between c60,000 and c40,000 bc the inhabitants of the site produced a LEVALLOISO-MOUSTERIAN industry; but after this period there was a return to blade technology with the DABBAN industry which clearly belongs with the Upper PALAEOLITHIC complex represented in many parts of Europe and the Near East at this general time-depth. The beginning of the Dabban occupation of Cyrenaica seems to have coincided with the onset of very arid conditions in the Saharan regions to the south. The Dabban continued until c12,000 bc, when it was replaced in a manner not yet properly understood by an industry of small backed bladelets here known as the Eastern Oranian, so called in view of its apparent affinity with IBEROMAURUSIAN (Oranian) material from the Maghreb. The microlithic sequence continues with a 'Libyco-Capsian' industry in which evidence for the herding of domestic animals first appears at a level dated to the early 5th millennium bc.

Hawaiian Islands. Situated in the north-central Pacific Ocean, the Hawaiian Islands (Kauai, Oahu, Maui, Molokai and Hawaii, plus many smaller islands) were first settled by Polynesians in the mid-1st millennium AD. Hawaiian valleys often contain profuse remains of HEIAU [temples], dwelling-sites and ancient horticultural systems, and these document the development of the populous and highly stratified society observed by Captain COOK in 1778. See BELLOWS BEACH, HALAWA, HEIAU, MAKAHA, MAUNA KEA, NECKER, PU'UHONUA.

Hazor. Large Palestinian TELL southwest of Lake Huleh in northern Israel, occupied from the Early Bronze Age till the Hellenistic period. In the Middle Bronze Age, c1700 BC, it was a large town covering 72 hectares with a citadel in the southwest corner and surrounded by a rampart with sloping plaster ramp, of the type associated with the HYKSOS.

At a later date the CANAANITES were driven from the city by the ISRAELITES, reputedly under Joshua, c1220 BC. In the 10th century the city was rebuilt by Solomon, who constructed a monumental gateway. This city was destroyed by the ASSYRIANS c734 BC; however, the citadel continued to be used into the Hellenistic period.

he [*ho, huo*]. *See* RITUAL VESSELS (CHINA), LI.

head. a PERIGLACIAL deposit which results from SOLIFLUCTION.

heavy mineral analysis. A technique of PETROLOGICAL ANALYSIS. If rock, ceramics or other mineral-bearing materials are crushed and then mixed with suitably high-viscosity fluid, the minerals in them will separate. Those that sink to the bottom are called the 'heavy minerals', and very conveniently these also happen to be the minerals which are most variable in their occurrence. The particular suite of heavy minerals may thus frequently be used to classify a rock or piece of pot fabric, and compare it with others. In archaeology, the method has mainly been used to classify pottery and identify the source of its raw materials.

Hedeby. Important VIKING settlement in northern Germany. It is situated on a fjord and covers c25 hectares, defended on the landward side by a large earth rampart. Between c800 and 1050 Hedeby was a major trading centre and many imported luxury goods have been found, especially in graves. Excavation has revealed many wooden buildings, well preserved in waterlogged conditions, and evidence of industrial as well as commercial activity.

Heekeren, H.R. van (1902-74). Dutch archaeologist who spent his career in Indonesia and wrote two fundamental books entitled *The Stone Age of Indonesia* (1957, 2nd edn. 1972) and *The Bronze-Iron Age of Indonesia* (1958). Van Heekeren conducted many important excavations, particularly on Sulawesi and Java.

Heian. *See* HAJI, MIRRORS (JAPAN), SUE.

heiau. A prehistoric Hawaiian stone temple, akin to the MARAE of other parts of Eastern Polynesia.

Heidelberg. *See* MAUER.

Heijo Palace. The seat of the government from 710 to 784 in Nara, Japan. The palace, located in the north-central part of the grand capital set in a grid-pattern, covers an area of approximately one square kilometre, of which a little under a quarter has been excavated since 1959. Remains of some 500 buildings, including royal residences, administrative quarters, warehouses and workshops, have been uncovered. Of particular interest are over 20,000 thin rectangular pieces of wood, which served as office memoranda and labels attached to tributes from the provinces.

Helgö. A small island west of Stockholm in Lake Malaren. 20 years of excavations from 1954 revealed several important artisans' houses spanning from the 5th or 6th century to the 9th century. These buildings dotted around the island included evidence of brooch-making and bead-making, and the excavations also brought to light exotic finds such as a 7th-century Buddha from Kashmir, a Coptic ladle, a number of gold coins, and Rhenish pots. All the material points to the island being a craft centre and perhaps a small trading settlement producing jewellery that was subsequently distributed all over central Sweden and possibly as far as coastal Finland. The moulds and debris from the brooch-making provide a great deal of new information about the development of this craft up to the beginning of the Viking period. Present excavations have located the cemeteries of those craftsmen, and field survey shows the existence of a small fortress commanding the island. As yet its relationship with the famous emporium of Birka, founded on another island close by in about 790, remains unclear. Helgö, however, was probably abandoned before the end of the 9th century.

Heliopolis. *See* BAALBEK.

Helladic. Term for the Bronze Age of mainland Greece, equivalent to CYCLADIC in the Aegean islands and MINOAN in Crete. It is divided into Early, Middle and Late Helladic, the last representing the MYCENAEAN period.

Hellenistic. Term commonly used of the generalized Greek, or Greek-dominated civilization of the Eastern Mediterrean and the Near East, from the death of Alexander the Great (323 BC) up to the arrival of the Roman Empire (say 30 BC). A common form of the Greek language, Koine [Greek: 'common'] developed, which was largely indebted to ATTIC Greek.

Hell Gap. A well-preserved, deeply stratified site in eastern Wyoming, USA, with evidence of occupation from c12,000 to 8000 bc throughout the PALEO-INDIAN period. Although cultural material was relatively sparse, the site's great time depth marks it as significant, especially as it relates to LLANO culture sequences.

Hembury. A Neolithic CAUSEWAYED CAMP and Iron Age HILLFORT in Devon, southwest England. The Neolithic site is particularly important because it has produced early radiocarbon dates of c3300-3000 bc (4200-3800 BC) associated with Early Neolithic pottery, greenstone and flint axes and a deposit of charred spelt wheat (by far the earliest occurrence of this type of wheat in Britain).

Hemudu [Ho-mu-tu]. Neolithic site excavated in 1973-4 in Yuyao Xian, south of Hangzhou Bay in northern Zhejiang province, China. The remains cover about 40,000 square metres. Four levels, counted from the top, were distinguished. The upper levels 1 and 2 correspond to the two phases of the MAJIABANG culture; level 2 yielded a radiocarbon date of c3700 BC. Levels 3 and 4 define the Hemudu culture, the earliest known stage of the east-coast Neolithic (*see* LONGSHAN, 2). Two radiocarbon dates from level 4 of c5000 and c4800 BC are the earliest yet obtained for RICE cultivation: in level 4 deposits of rice grains, stalks, and husks were half a metre thick in places, and covered an area of 400 square metres, perhaps a threshing floor. Pigs, dogs, and perhaps water buffalo were domesticated. Hoes or spades made from cattle scapulae, contrasting with the stone hoes typical of YANGSHAO sites, were found in large quantity; stone tools were few and crude.

Timber houses show the use of a mortice-and-tenon technique. The low-fired handmade pottery includes shallow DING tripods.

Hen Domen. One of the many Norman MOTTE AND BAILEY castles in the Welsh Marches, but interesting because excavations here showed for the first time the vestigial remains of the retainers' encampment as well as the lord's timber castle.

henge. A type of ritual monument found only in the British Isles in the Neolithic and Early Bronze Age. They consist of a circular or irregular area enclosed by a bank with a ditch usually but not univerally on the inside. They range in size from monuments c30 metres across like WOODHENGE to the vast late Neolithic enclosures more than 400 metres in diameter, such as AVEBURY and DURRINGTON WALLS. They may have single entrances (Class I henges), two entrances opposite each other (Class II henges) or, in the case of Avebury, four entrances. Internal features also vary considerably: some enclose pits, with or without burials, while others have rings of timbers or timber buildings; 13 examples, including the famous examples of Avebury and STONEHENGE, contain STONE CIRCLES.

Hengelo interstadial. An INTERSTADIAL of the WEICHSELIAN cold stage. It is dated to around 39,000 bp.

Herat. For centuries the largest town in western Afghanistan, Herat stands on the Hari Rud. Already important in pre-Islamic times, it is sometimes identified as the capital of the ACHAEMENID satrapy of Aria and the Hellenistic city of Alexandria Ariana. Herat was captured by the Arabs in 645 and thereafter was ruled by successive Islamic dynasties, including the Ghaznavids (from 1000) Saljuqs (1040) and Ghorids (1175). Taken by the Mongols in 1221, it became the capital of a quasi-independent state. It fell to the TIMURIDS in 1381. With one exception, the principal monuments of Herat were built in the reigns of the Timurid rulers Shah Rukh (1405-47), the son of Timur, and Husain Baikara (1469-1506). To the former belong Musalla, constructed by Gowhar Shad, the wife of Shah Rukh, in 1417 and, just outside the city, the shrine of Gazur Gah, built in 1425-6. To the latter belong the Madrasa of Husain Baikara

and the reconstruction of the Friday Mosque, begun in 1498. Little of the pre-Timurid mosque survives, although restoration has revealed an elaborate Ghorid doorway. These buildings apart, the most importat Timurid monument in Herat is the Mausoleum of Gowhar Shad, who died in 1457.

Herculaneum [Modern Ercolano]. A small but wealthy and sophisticated Roman seaside town 8 km from Naples which, like POMPEII, was damaged in the earthquake of 63 AD and destroyed in the eruption of Vesuvius in 79. For beginnings, we have the option perhaps either of an original Greek settlement, or of an Oscan town onto which a Greek commercial centre was grafted. Etruscan and Samnite influences followed as in the rest of Campania, and Herculaneum finally became a Roman *municipium* in 89 BC. In the destruction of 79 AD, the deposit that reached Herculaneum, unlike the pumice and ash that rained upon Pompeii, was largely a slurry of liquid mud which subsequently solidified into a tufa-life consistency. This mud deposit, accumulating in parts to a depth of 20 metres or more, percolated and filled structures but tended to preserve organic materials, especially timber. The site, which was perhaps something of a promontory between two torrents before the eruption, was literally obliterated by the mud, and became a featureless expanse. This, together with the great depth, must have discouraged immediate attempts at recovery or treasure-hunting. The 18th century onward saw a resolute programme of well- and tunnel-digging, often conducted with great bravado and panache, which led to the creation of an amazingly complex network of underground passages, which might be visited by the intrepid. The subsequent 'more conventional' excavations of the 19th century and the continuing modern excavations have had to face not only the problem of the removal of so vast a deposit, but also the complication and damage caused by these 'miners' and their *cuniculi*.

The general impression is of a town quieter and less commercial than Pompeii, with fishing suggested as its main industry. The absence of the wheel-ruts and stepping stones so common at Pompeii and the apparent use of blocking bollards have led to the suggestion of a traffic-free area for the central zone. The houses are remarkable for the preservation of internal and external structures in timber, and, in some cases, of furniture and fittings.

Herpaly. A regional variant of the trio of Late Neolithic cultures (TISZA, Herpaly, Czöszhalom) found in the Great Hungarian Plain c4000-3400 bc. The Herpaly culture, distributed in the northern Alföld zone, is characterized by TELL settlement and intra-mural burial. The tells tend to occur on narrow peninsulas or on islands, and riverine resources are important in the subsistence economy. Throned figures and both anthro-pomorphic and zoomorphic figurines play a significant part in ritual activities.

Herzfeld, Ernst (1879-1948). German archaeologist who excavated on many sites in the Middle East before World War II, includ-ing PERSEPOLIS, SAMARRA and TALL-I BAKUN.

Hesi, Tell el. TELL site on the Palestinian coastal plain west of Hebron, occupied from the Early Bronze Age to the Hellenistic period. It was excavated in the 1890s first by Sir Flinders PETRIE and subsequently by F.J. Bliss, and these early excavations mark the beginning of stratigraphical excavation in this area. They also saw the beginning of the establishment of an absolute chronology for Palestinian prehistory, through the discovery of imported, datable Egyptian objects in association with local material. Recent excavations by an American team have led to the revision of some of the conclusions, and especially the dates, suggested by the early excavators.

Heuneburg, the. A HILLFORT of the HALL-STATT Iron Age, overlooking the River Danube in Württemberg, southern Germany. The site has five main building phases, the most remarkable of which was the second, when the traditional timber-framed con-struction was replaced by a Greek type of construction, with a bastioned wall built of mud brick on stone foundations. This evidence of Greek influence is reflected also in the finds, which include ATTIC BLACK-FIGURE pottery and wine amphorae, imported from the Greek colony of Massalia (*see* MARSEILLES). The Heuneburg seems to have been the seat of a local chiefdom, the power and wealth of which depended at least in part on trade with the

cities of the Mediterranean. A number of rich burials under barrows occur in the vicinity, including the HOHMICHELE barrow.

Hidatsa. *See* MIDDLE MISSOURI TRADITION.

Hierakonpolis. An important PREDYNASTIC EGYPTIAN settlement located 100 km north of Aswan. The town was of considerable extent: estimates of its population vary greatly, but the figure is almost certainly in excess of 5000. In proto-dynastic times Hierakonpolis was the capital of southern Egypt: important dis-coveries of this period are stone palettes and mace-heads, with carving illustrating the rise of the kings to the divine status they enjoyed in pharaonic times.

hieroglyph. Egyptian hieroglyphic writing was developed about 3100 BC and continued in use with remarkably little change until the 4th century AD. Its meaning seems to have been forgotten soon afterwards and the hieroglyphs were not deciphered until early in the 19th century following the discovery of the bi-lingual inscription known as the ROSETTA Stone. Some 700 signs were employed. The majority of these are ideograms: simplified pictorial representations of the concepts to which their meaning relates. Some of these ideograms also had a phonetic value repre-senting one or more consonants. Vowels were not indicated, so it is often not possible (other than by comparison with related Coptic words) to ascertain the original pronunciation. Ideograms and phonetic symbols were gener-ally combined, for example the word 'depet', meaning a boat, could be written

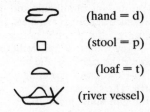

	(hand = d)
	(stool = p)
	(loaf = t)
	(river vessel)

Inscriptions were generally written from right to left, but also on occasion from left to right or vertically. Gaps between words were not indicated. Royal names were enclosed in an oval line or cartouche. Less formal scripts, the so-called hieratic and demotic, were also used and may be traced back to the Fifth Dynasty.

High Lodge. A site close to Mildenhall in Suffolk where distinctive PALAEOLITHIC tools were found in the 19th century, including classic QUINA type scrapers similar to those found in the CHARENTIAN culture of France. The main occupation is from lake clays overlying a glacial boulder clay, but it is now known that sands above these clays have hand axes and other tools, presumably of the ACHEULIAN.

hillfort. Term for a hilltop settlement defended by stone walls or earth ramparts. Settlements of this type occur in many parts of the world at different times, but the term is most commonly applied to sites of the later Bronze Age and Iron Age in Europe.

hippodrome [Greek: 'horse race-course']. Much the same as a STADIUM, but intended rather for horse- than foot-racing. The hippodrome rather than the stadium is the initial model for the Roman CIRCUS, which likewise concentrated on chariot-races.

Hispano-Moresque pottery. Highly decorated ceramics that were produced in the late medieval period by the Moorish potters of Spain. They tend to be plates and jugs with bold semi-abstract designs painted on a creamy background and with a gold lustre finish. These wares were much in demand throughout Europe and, judging from finds in northern Europe, they were widely traded.

Hissar, Tepe. TELL site near Damghan in northern Iran, occupied from the 5th to the early 2nd millennium BC. The earliest levels are characterized by fine painted pottery, decorated with designs of animals and birds, and by the presence of copper artefacts. In the 3rd millennium BC the painted pottery was replaced by a grey ware that has traditionally been interpreted as marking the arrival of intrusive INDO-EUROPEAN-speaking peoples from the north. The site was destroyed in the first half of the 2nd millennium BC.

Hissarlik. See TROY.

Hittites. A people who established a kingdom in central Turkey in the 2nd millennium BC and later extended it into northern Syria. Their first capital was at Kushara, not yet identified, but it was soon moved to Hattusas, modern BOGHAZKÖY. The Hittites did not originate in Anatolia and are thought to have infiltrated from the north. They were INDO-EUROPEAN speakers and indeed Hittite is the earliest Indo-European language to be written down.

The Hittites are known both from documentary and archaeological sources. From the documents we know that they challenged HURRIANS, ASSYRIANS and Egyptians. In 1286 or 1285 BC they fought the Egyptians under Rameses II at KADESH, a battle which was probably indecisive, although the Egyptians claimed victory. From archaeological remains we know the Hittites especially for their relief sculpture, found in the cities themselves and also in rock sanctuaries like YAZILKAYA, and for their inscriptions (in hieroglyphs on their public monuments, although CUNEIFORM was used for adminstrative records). They are also known for their metal-working. They exploited and traded copper, lead, silver and also iron; indeed, they were among the first peoples to use iron, and for a period maintained a virtual monopoly in the new metal.

In c1200 BC the Hittite empire came to an apparently abrupt end, perhaps as a result of some of the folk movements that characterized the whole of the eastern Mediterranean area at this time (see PEOPLES OF THE SEA). After this date Hittite culture survived in the city states of northern Syria, described as Neo-Hittite or Syro-Hittite. These cities, such as CARCHEMISH, KARATEPE, MALATYA and SAKCE GOZU, were finally incorporated into the Assyrian empire in the 8th century BC.

Hivaoa. See PUAMAU VALLEY.

Hjortspring. Find-spot on the island of Als, southern Denmark, of an Iron Age long boat preserved in a peat bog. The boat, c17.5 metres long, was built of planks, not nailed together but tied and caulked with resin; both stem and stern terminated in carved ram's heads. Inside was a mass of weaponry — wooden spears and shields and iron swords, as well as everyday equipment such as bowls, boxes and smith's tools.

Hoabinhian. A major stone tool industry of the mainland of Southeast Asia, with extensions into SUMATRA and perhaps the northern PHILIPPINES. Dated sites range from about 12,000 bc onwards, and overlap with

Neolithic assemblages with pottery and ground stone tools for several millennia after 6000 bc. Best described as a techno-complex with successive cultural accretions, the Hoabinhian cannot be regarded as an archaeological culture or chronological horizon. It is basically a tradition of stone tool manufacture (pebble tools, flakes) which continued even into the 1st millennium AD in remote interior regions. Claims for Hoabinhian horticulture prior to 6000 bc have been made for SPIRIT CAVE in northwestern Thailand, and edge-ground tools and pottery appear in Late Hoabinhian (BACSONIAN) assemblages in north VIETNAM soon after 8000 bc. The majority of Hoabinhian sites found to date are in rock shelters and coastal shell middens. *See also* GUA CHA, GUA KECHIL, LAANG SPEAN, QUYNH-VAN, SAI YOK, SON VI.

hoard. Term for a collection of objects buried usually at one time. Hoards can contain artefacts of any material and any number of different materials, but hoards of metal objects are particularly common. Depending on the circumstances of deposition, the make-up of hoards will vary. For instance, a merchant's hoard will contain objects ready for use, whereas a founder's hoard will often contain large quantities of scrap metal. Many hoards represent the personal property of individuals, buried for safety at a time of threat. Votive hoards, unlike other types, contain objects offered to a deity and not meant to be recovered; hoards of this type may represent not single depositions but accumulations of material offered over long periods of time. Hoards are a useful source of evidence for archaeologists, because they provide considerable quantities of material and, except in the case of some votive hoards, that material represents a true ASSOCIATION (i.e. was in use at one time).

Hochob. *See* CHENES.

Hod Hill. The site near Blandford Forum, Dorset, southern England, of an Iron Age HILLFORT with evidence for numbers of circular huts, the whole being defended by huge ramparts. It was attacked by Roman artillery under Vespasian in 44 AD. The Romans made use of the northwest corner only, and constructed a fort of some 4.5 hectares. They were able to utilize the existing ramparts on two sides while on the other two directions they built new triple ditch-and-turf rampart defences inside the area of the earlier settlement. The timber buildings were intended perhaps for a garrison of some 600 legionaries and 250 auxiliary cavalrymen. The fortification seems to have been damaged by fire *c*52-3 AD and not re-used afterwards.

Hoëdic. A small island off the coast of Morbihan in southern Brittany where a large mass burial of 13 individuals, with antlers placed over it, was discovered. The artefacts were of TARDENOISIAN type and the whole site was a Mesolithic midden or shell mound.

hog-back tombs. These tombs mostly date from the 10th century and are believed to have been developed in northwest England. They take the form of rectangular blocks with pitched roofs, and are usually decorated with INTERLACE and other typical designs. Many scholars believe that the tombs imitate vernacular architecture.

Hohmichele, the. A large barrow close to the HEUNEBURG hillfort in southern Germany. The barrow still stands to a height of 13 metres and covered 13 burials (eight inhumations and five cremations) of the later HALLSTATT Iron Age (6th century BC). Two burials (one containing a man and a woman, the other a woman on her own) had wagons with them and, although the burials had been robbed, there were remains of what had originally been rich grave goods. The most remarkable find is a piece of silk cloth, presumably an import from the Far East, perhaps via the Mediterranean — the earliest documented occurrence of silk in Europe.

Hohokam. An early group of settled agriculturalists in North America. Their core area was in the drainage basin of the Salt and Gila Rivers in the southern Arizona desert. Traditionally 300 BC marks the earliest Hohokam manifestation, though their origin (and their disappearance) is still uncertain. A major debate continues among scholars as to whether or not the Hohokam represent an immigrant Mexican group. Diagnostic traits include small villages of shallow, oblong pit-houses with no formalized community plan, cremation of the dead, plain grey or brown paddle and anvil smoothed pottery (or sometimes painted red on buff). Where the environment allowed, canal irrigation was practised on a grand scale.

The major chronological periods are Pioneer (300 BC-AD 550), Colonial (550-900), Sedentary (900-1100) and Classic (1100-1450). Hohokam dates were originally derived from material found in association with more chronologically sound ANASAZI material, but excavations at SNAKETOWN have largely confirmed this dating scheme. A strong Mesoamerican influence is evident throughout Hohokam history but particularly between 500 and 1200. New types of MAIZE, slab METATES, platform mounds, BALL COURTS, as well as copper bells, mosaic mirrors and other luxury goods all make their appearance.

From 1200 on the introduction of new traits (e.g. PUEBLO building) suggests an influx of new peoples, probably the Anasazi. After 1450 distinctive Hohokam traits have all but disappeared, and continue only as an admixture to other cultural groups. It is possible that the present-day Pima and Papago tribes are Hohokam descendants, but clear continuity has not yet been established.

Holocene. The latest epoch of the QUATERNARY period, starting at 10,000 bp and extending to the present day. This epoch is, in reality, merely the most recent INTERSTADIAL stage of the Quaternary, and the concept of a Holocene epoch is not a very useful one. In Britain, the term FLANDRIAN is used to describe this interstadial.

See Tables 4-7, pages 417-20.

Holstein. A group of QUATERNARY INTERGLACIAL deposits in northwest Europe. They are stratified above ELSTER GLACIAL deposits and are overlain by SAALE glacial deposits (*see* Table 5, page 418). Their exact age is unknown, but they are older than the extreme range of RADIOCARBON DATING (70,000 bp) and can be shown by PALAEOMAGNETISM to be younger than 700,000 BP. In the Netherlands and around the Baltic, a sea level rise caused the deposition of Holstein marine sediments. The Holstein deposits appear to represent two interglacial stages, the younger being distinguished as the Wacken or Dömnitz interglacial. This in turn implies that the underlying Elster deposits represent two cold stages. In spite of all this, the term 'Holstein' is still used by some to imply only one interglacial stage, the 'penultimate' interglacial.

Holuke'a. A replica of an ancient Polynesian canoe, which was sailed from Maui (in the Hawaiian Islands) to Tahiti by traditional Polynesian methods of navigation in a 35-day voyage in 1976. The canoe was 18 metres long, double-hulled and carried 15 men and a cargo of traditional plant foods and livestock. The success of the voyage has thrown important light on ancient Polynesian voyaging and navigation.

hominid. *See* HUMAN EVOLUTION.

Homo erectus. Early form of man found between c1.6 and 0.5 million years ago. Many remains have been found in Java: *see* MOJOKERTO, MEGANTHROPUS, NGANDONG, SAMBUNGMACAN, SANGIRAN, TRINIL. Other examples come from ZHOUKOUDIAN and Yuanmou in China and Tham Khuyen in Vietnam, and there are now fairly numerous examples also from Africa. *See also* HUMAN EVOLUTION.

Homo habilis. Early hominid form of the period 2 to 1.5 million years ago, found mainly in East Africa. Some authorities believe *Homo habilis* to be closely related to the Australopithecines, while others believe it to be different from the Australopithecines and directly ancestral to man. *See also* AUSTRALOPITHECUS, HUMAN EVOLUTION.

Homo sapiens neanderthalensis. Technical name of Neanderthal Man. *See* HUMAN EVOLUTION, NEANDERTHAL.

Homo sapiens sapiens. Technical name of modern man. *See* HUMAN EVOLUTION.

Honaunau. *See* PU'UHONUA.

Hong Kong. Hong Kong was firmly incorporated in the Chinese cultural sphere in the late CHOU and HAN Dynasties (late 1st millennium BC), and prior to this had a prehistory closely connected with that of neighbouring mainland south China. Earliest sites in Hong Kong date from about 3500 BC and belong to Meacham's 'Yueh coastal Neolithic'; these are followed by a Bronze Age culture with geometric-stamped pottery which appears during the 2nd millennium BC. The site of SHAM WAN on Lamma Island has produced a key sequence.

hood stones. *See* MEGALITHS (INDIA).

Hopewell. A widespread Middle WOODLAND culture whose major focus was in southern Ohio, USA, but with sites as far away as Kansas and the Florida Gulf Coast. Sometimes seen as an extension of ADENA, it is characterized by large earthworks, ceremonial burial practices and long-distance trade. Both inhumation (often interment in log tombs) and cremation were practised and were frequently accompanied by rich grave goods. Other cultural traits include deeply incised or rocker-stamped pottery, distinctive broad-bladed points (some clearly ceremonial) and small stone platform-pipes, often carved in zoomorphic shapes.

Both agriculture and hunting and gathering contributed to subsistence activities, but archaeologists disagree as to the relative importance of each. It has recently been suggested that internal variability is so great that Hopewell sites are best considered as local manifestations linked only by pottery styles and limited social interaction. Dates vary considerably but characteristic traits appear in the late centuries BC and come to an end *c*400 AD.

Horgen. Settlement site on Lake Neuchâtel, Switzerland, which has given its name to a Middle Neolithic culture, which succeeded CORTAILLOD in north Switzerland. The characteristic pottery is coarse without decoration or with applied cordons; most vessels are bucket-shaped. Horgen pottery resembles that of the SEINE-OISE-MARNE group; it is found in settlement sites and also in MEGALITHIC tombs.

horizon. In soil science a horizon is a layer formed in a soil PROFILE by soil-forming processes.

When used in an archaeological context, the term implies a spatial but contemporaneous relationship between cultural complexes. It is used particularly widely in North American prehistoric archaeology. Typically art styles or artefacts associated with religious beliefs which achieved rapid and widespread popularity but which had a relatively short life span, are considered horizons, for example the CHAVIN art style. A horizon, in contrast to a TRADITION, normally has a broad geographic distribution, but very little chronological depth.

horn cores. Bony projections from the skull which support horns. The horn itself forms a tight sheath around the core, which is removed for horn working. Large accumulations of horn cores on some archaeological sites appear related to this industry.

Horner. *See* CODY.

Hornsbluff. *See* CODY.

horns of consecration. A term first used by Arthur EVANS to describe the symbol, supposedly representing stylized bulls' horns, which played a major role in MINOAN religion. Usually made of alabaster or other stone, horns of consecration are found in sanctuaries and other buildings; they also appear in artistic depictions.

horrea. [Plural form of Latin *horreum*: 'storehouse, granary']. The large-scale granaries of the Roman Empire, of which classical illustration may be found at Roman OSTIA. Often constructed of brick-faced concrete, and arranged around a central colonnaded court, the industrial nature of their architecture admits a few concessions. Their individual size, frequency throughout the Empire, and above all the complex civil service devoted to their administration, are all eloquent testimony to their importance.

horse. Today's horses all seem to represent one species, *Equus caballus.* The genus *Equus* also includes zebras and ASSES. Three races of wild horse existed until recently: the Mongolian Wild Horse (Przewalski's Horse, *E. caballus przewalski,* or *E. przewalski*), which may still just survive, the Forest Wild Horse of Poland, which became extinct during the 18th century; and the Tarpan, which occupied the steppe of Cental Europe and southwestern Russia. During ancient cold periods (*see* QUATERNARY), horses also occupied the open vegetation which then existed in northern and western Europe. At some sites, horse bones occur in large numbers, and it is likely that they formed a major part of PALAEOLITHIC hunters' diet. With the end of the last glaciation, they disappeared from northwest Europe and became restricted to the temperate grassland and dry shrubland of Central Europe and Asia. Horse bones have been found at several sites in the Near East and Asia where other animals had already been domesticated, but there is no evidence that the horses themselves were domestic. The first evidence for possible manipulation of horse by man occurs in the 4th millennium BC in sites of the TRIPOLYE culture and related cultures of the Ukraine. References to horses and artistic representations of them appear by 2000-1300 BC in Egypt, Mesopotamia, Syria, India and China; chariots also appear at about this time.

horsehoof cores. Domed cores on blocks with flat based striking platforms, heavily step-flaked around their marigins. Both very large and smaller varieties are found commonly on PLEISTOCENE sites in most areas of Australia and on some mid-HOLOCENE sites. It used to be believed that the step-flaked edges resulted from heavy chopping, planing or scraping, but it is now also considered possible that the step-flaking could have resulted from repeated striking to remove flakes.

Horsham. A town in Sussex, southern England. MESOLITHIC flints are abundant on the sandy heaths close by, and include a hollow-based point, sometimes called a Horsham point. This was once considered typical of a Horsham culture or group.

Hoshino. A PALAEOLITHIC site in Tochigi City in central Honshu, Japan. During excavations in the 1960s thousands of tools, mostly of chert, were recovered from 13 layers. Choppers, scrapers, and flakes in the lowest seven layers should be older than 55,000 years, and those in the next two layers over 30,000 years old. Blades and bifacial points in the top three layers date to between 21,000 and 10,000 years ago. The dates are based on radiocarbon and fission track ages of pumice beds betwen the cultural layers.

Hougang [Hou-kang]. Type site of the Henan Longshan or Hougang II Neolithic culture, at ANYANG in Henan province, China. Hougang was the first site to show YANGSHAO, Henan Longshan and SHANG remains in clear stratigraphic succession. This sequence is nowadays believed to result firstly from the transformation of the local Yangshao under influences originating on the east coast to produce a new culture, the Henan Longshan (see LONGSHAN, DAHE); and secondly, from the rise of the Shang bronze-using culture, which was at least in part a local outgrowth of the Henan Longshan. More detailed and revealing stratigraphic sequences are now available at XIAWANGGANG and Dahe. The following radiocarbon dates have been obtained from Hougang: for the (BANPO-type) Yangshao level, c4400 BC, c4200 BC; for the Henan Longshan level, c 2350 BC.

Houjiazhuang [Hou-chia-chuang]. *See* ANYANG.

Houma [Hou-ma]. A city in southwestern Shanxi province, China, where extensive remains of an Eastern ZHOU city have been under excavation since 1956. Houma is believed to be the site of Xintian, capital of the Jin state from 584 BC until 453 BC, when Jin was partitioned by Han, Zhao, and Wei. Several thousand stone and jade tablets found at the site in 1965 are inscribed with the texts of alliances between various Eastern Zhou states, and date chiefly from the early 5th century BC. The most important discovery so far made at Houma is a very large foundry complex whose period of activity is assumed to correspond to the time when Xintian was the Jin capital. Over 30,000 fragments of clay moulds and models for casting RITUAL VESSELS (some in the LIYU style), chariot fittings, weapons, BELT HOOKS, COINS, and other bronzes were distributed over the site in such a way as to suggest that separate workshops specialized in producing particular types of object. The mould fragments make it clear that the basic casting technique used at Houma was still the section-mould method perfected in SHANG foundries a thousand years earlier, as opposed to the CIRE PERDUE method. Nevertheless the moulds and models give evidence of a variety of new techniques for decorating bronze (inlaying with metal or semi-precious stones) and for applying decoration to the mould prior to casting (e.g. replication of pattern units carved on master stamps).

Hound Tor. *See* MANOR, DESERTED MEDIEVAL VILLAGES.

hourglass perforation. Type of perforation found in many prehistoric stone artefacts. Holes are drilled from opposite sides of the artefact to produce a perforation that is biconical or 'hourglass' shaped.

Housesteads. [Roman Vercovicium or, less properly, Dorcovicus]. Wall-fort on HADRIAN'S WALL, dramatically sited roughly mid-way along its length in Northumberland, England. Substantial remains are to be seen of the stone buildings, gateways and ramparts, especially from the 3rd century onward, when the garrison was made up of 1000 Tungrian soldiers from Belgium. The site includes a commandant's house, headquarters building, barrack blocks, granaries, storerooms and the only good example of a Romano-British hospital. There is also a fine military latrine; probably originally equipped with wooden seats, it could accommodate some twenty users. The installation features basins, gutters for the washing of (toilet) sponges, and efficient sewer channels. Outside the fort proper, there is evidence for the shops and houses of the civilian community (*vicus*), and for cultivation terraces.

Howiesonspoort. An ill-defined and poorly understood industry of the southern Cape Province of South Africa, marked by the appearance of small blades and backed tools at a time when most stone industries were still based upon the production of flakes struck from discoidal cores. The evidence for the date of the Howiesonspoort occurrences is not conclusive, but some if not most seem to be over 40,000 years old. In addition to the name-site, the industry has been investigated at KLASIES RIVER MOUTH and MONTAGU CAVE.

Hoxne. A site in Suffolk, East Anglia, of historical importance because in 1797 John FRERE recovered and described hand axes from here associated with extinct animals. In 1956 it was demonstrated that the lake clays had a distinctive HOXNIAN pollen diagram, and ACHEULIAN hand axes were associated with this. In recent research, a higher occupation level with abundant scrapers has been investigated.

Hoxnian. A group of British QUATERNARY INTERGLACIAL deposits named after the site of HOXNE. They occur as isolated patches, related by POLLEN ANALYSIS and the analysis of other plant and animal fossils. Their exact age is unknown, but they are older than the extreme range of RADIOCARBON DATING (70,000 years bp) and can be shown by PALAEOMAGNETISM to be younger than 700,000 years BP. Some Hoxnian deposits are stratified above ANGLIAN GLACIAL deposits, others below WOLSTONIAN glacial deposits (*see* Table 6, page 419). There is some evidence that the Hoxnian deposits represent more than one interglacial. This in turn implies that the Anglian deposits may represent more than one cold stage. ACHEULIAN and CLACTONIAN artefacts are found in Hoxnian deposits. In addition, parts of a hominid skull have been found in Hoxnian gravels at SWANS-COMBE. It used to be thought that the Hoxnian represented only one interglacial (the penultimate), and the term is still used with this meaning. Now that the Hoxnian is known to be more complex, such a usage is questionable; 'Hoxnian' is better confined to the description of a particular group of sediments.

Hradistě. A site situated on the Dyje River in Moravia. It is a well-excavated example of a Slavic stronghold and manorial residence of the 9th-12th centuries.

Hrtkovci. *See* GOMOLAVA.

Hsiung-nu. *See* IVOLGA, NOIN-ULA.

hu [*hu*]. *See* RITUAL VESSELS (CHINA).

huaca. A name derived from the Quechua word meaning shrine, *huacas* were revered or sacred objects. Diverse in nature, ranging from portable amulets to large natural phenomena such as caves and rocks, they were thought by the INCA to have magical or religious powers. For example the Kenko Stone or Huanacauri, a large rock located near CUZCO, was thought to be the petrified brother of the first emperor.

Huaca de la Luna. *See* MOCHE.

Huaca del Sol. *See* MOCHE.

Huaca Prieta. A village site located in the Chicama valley of north-coast Peru with evidence of an early sedentary way of life. Excavated by Junius Bird and dating to the

PRE-CERAMIC PERIOD VI, it has an initial radiocarbon date of c2300 bc. Built on an artificial hill of refuse and other debris, semi-subterranean houses with walls of cobbles set in mud accommodated a population of several hundred. Although fishing was an important part of subsistence activities, Huaca Prieta is notable for its evidence of incipient plant domestication — the earliest in South America (see BAT CAVE for North America). Squash, peppers, lima beans, gourds and cotton are all in evidence and basketry and textiles were produced both by twining and weaving. The site was abandoned before the introduction of either maize or pottery in c1200 bc.

Huahine. See SOCIETY ISLANDS, VAITO'OTIA.

Huai [Huai] **style.** The name applied to a class of surface patterns common on Chinese Eastern ZHOU bronzes of the 6th-3rd centuries BC. Cast in relief, these dense arrays of hooks and curls — Loehr's 'graceful froth of the Huai style' — derive from tight configurations of dragons but verge on complete abstraction. The style owes its name to finds made in and around SHOU XIAN on the Huai River; while by-and-large the Shou Xian bronzes are not early examples, there is some reason to believe that the typical Huai-style patterns were invented in this region. The basis in dragon configurations is a feature that the Huai style shares with the contemporary LIYU style, but while the Liyu patterns stress interlace and contrasting surface textures, the Huai style exploits high relief to obtain a uniformly frothy, or gritty or prickly texture in which interlace plays little role. In its early (6th century) manifestations, the Huai style might be viewed as a Yangzi-region counterpart to the Liyu designs of North China; by the 5th century BC it had been adopted in the north. The most outstanding Huai-style designs, including extraordinary examples from SUI XIAN, belong to the 5th century, which also saw the appearance of stereotyped low-relief versions that enjoyed a lasting vogue as backgrounds for other motifs. Of these standardized patterns the most familiar is Yetts' 'feather-curl', a very common background on MIRRORS of the 5th-3rd centuries BC.

The Western literature of Chinese art and archaeology abounds with varying definitions of the Huai style, most of them broader than that given above. In the 1930s, Bernhard Karlgren took the term to signify a period style applicable to the whole of China for the years c650-200 BC, so that it included many forms of ornament unconnected with the Huai region, such as the Liyu style. More recent definitions equate the Huai style with the art of the lower Yangzi region or, less plausibly, with the art of the CHU state; though narrower in scope, these definitions are open to the same fundamental objection as Karlgren's, namely that they group under a single heading widely different and sometimes quite unrelated designs.

Huanacauri. See HUACA.

huang [huang]. A flat semi-circular or arc-shaped jade pendant. Examples are known from Neolithic sites in China and the shape was made throughout the Bronze Age.

Huangpi [Huang-p'i]. See PANLONGCHENG.

Hua Pan. See LAOS.

Huari. A major site of the MIDDLE HORIZON, located near AYACUCHO in the Mantaro River basin in the Peruvian Andes. Strongly linked to TIAHUANACO, it is thought to have been a secondary centre for the diffusion, possibly by force, of the cultural traits of that city. Early ceramics (Chakipampa A) date to the Early INTERMEDIATE PERIOD and are seen as a blend of Huarpa (a black-on-white geometric style) and NASCA styles. The later Chakipampa B style shows a strong Tiahuanacan influence. Having no formal plan and covering an area of several square kilometres, the type site is a huge conglomeration of 'contour' architecture — that is, there is no alteration of the natural topography. Structures include huge rectangular compounds with multi-storey and subterranean masonry. Unlike Tiahuanaco, there are no megalithic structures and although there is some dressed stone work, cobbles of unformed stone are also widely used. The site seems to have been abandoned some time in the latter half of the Middle Horizon.

Huarpa. See HUARI.

Huasteca. A native group centred on the northeastern fringes of Mesoamerica in northern Veracruz and Tamaulipas provinces of Mexico. Although MAYA-speaking, there is little evidence of cultural contact with the Maya after 1400 bc. The major influences in the CLASSIC PERIOD were Veracruz (*see* EL TAJIO) and TEOTIHUACAN, but the cultural climax of the Huasteca occurs in the Early POST-CLASSIC.

Characteristically, Huastec centres did not develop to the level of centres in other areas of Mesoamerica; the large village, typical of the Pre-Classic elsewhere, is the usual settlement pattern.

The largest of the Huastec centres (at Las Flores and Tamuin) contain only moderately sized pyramids surrounded by a number of housemounds. The monumental sculpture, some with death imagery, is of relatively poor quality but there are some fine representations of QUETZACOATL. The hallmarks of the Huastec culture are structures on a round plan (a relative rarity in Mesoamerica), a black-on-white hard paste pottery, and carved shell ornaments.

Apparently trading partners of the AZTEC, the Huastec are potentially the most likely link between the cultures of Mesoamerica and the southeastern United States. There is, however, very little evidence of this, although carved shell ornaments of the SOUTHERN CULT bear a noticeable resemblance to those of the Huasteca.

Huating [Hua-t'ing]. *See* DADUNZI, QINGLIAN'GANG.

Huaylas. *See* RECUAY.

Huelva. Find-spot in the harbour of Huelva, southwest Spain, of a large hoard of Late Bronze Age bronzes, dated to the 7th and 6th centuries BC. The find, which may represent the remains of a prehistoric shipwreck, contained bronzes of types found in various Mediterranean contexts (e.g. a Cypriot type of FIBULA), as well as types characteristic of the ATLANTIC BRONZE AGE (e.g. CARP'S TONGUE SWORDS).

Huitzilpotchtli. *See* AZTEC, QUETZACOATL, TENOCHTITLAN.

Hui Xian [Hui-hsien]. *See* GUWEICUN, LIULIGE.

Hull. City on the Humber estuary, northeast England. A 12th-century settlement called Wyc de Mitune is known to have existed somewhere close to modern Hull, but the centre of commerce seems to have changed from the mid- to late 13th century onwards, when High Street became the core of the new town. Excavations throughout this town have revealed the archaeological evidence for the port's high standing in Britain's late medieval overseas trade. Most of the houses are brick-built and their cess-pits tend to contain large amounts of imported pottery ranging from western French SAINTONGE wares in the 13th century to 15th-century German stonewares and Flemish redwares. Besides the high number of imported pots, glass and many other objects have come to light, illustrating Hull's prominence in North Sea trade.

Humaita. A lithic tradition based in southeastern Brazil, dated to the 5th millennium bc and lasting into the Christian era. Its earliest manifestation is a rough flake, essentially unifacial, industry although some bifaces do appear, notably the boomerang shape. Clearly hunting oriented (artefacts include flake knives, choppers and scrapers), its earliest manifestation has no projectile points. Biface projectile points begin to appear in the 3rd millennium bc and semi-polished axes and grooved bola stones are added in *c*2000-1000 bc. The complex remains non-ceramic throughout, although ceramics are evident elsewhere in Brazil at the same time. Insufficient archaeological data have kept the chronology vague.

human evolution. The hominids include all species believed to be related more closely to man than to the apes (pongids). Numerous human (and hominid) fossils are now known and conflicting interpretations of them exist. The simplest view is of a single line of species leading to modern man. *Ramapithecus* of the Miocene period (*c*15-6 million years ago) leads to *Australopithecus africanus* or 'gracile australopithecines' of the Pliocene (*c*5.5-2 million years ago) and '*Homo habilis*' of the period 2-1.5 million years ago. Then at about the beginning of the PLEISTOCENE (*c*1.6 million years ago) comes the species *Homo erectus*, originally known from Java and near Peking, but now well-known also from Africa. In the last half million years *Homo erectus* is replaced by *Homo sapiens*, including (in the wider sense used by most students since 1962)

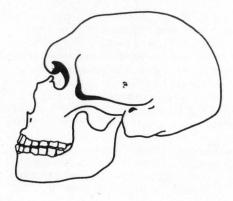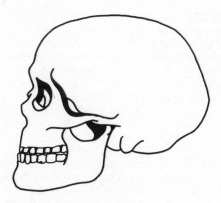

Human evolution: skulls of Neanderthal (left) and Cromagnon man (right)

NEANDERTHAL and pre-Neanderthal fossil men, as well as all modern races and fossils of broadly modern type.

While some extreme views have included all known hominids in the line described above, most modern workers now regard fossils of *Australopithecus* (or *Paranthropus*) *robustus* — 'robust australopithecines' — and related forms as a separate cousin lineage and not directly ancestral to modern man. At various times almost all the other fossil groups visibly different from modern man have also been regarded as separate lineages not ancestral to us. Many workers still regard the European Neanderthals as non-ancestral, and a similar view has been taken of the 'Rhodesian' group (BROKEN HILL man etc), Java and Peking Man and several types of *Australopithecus* including *africanus.* The most obvious changes detectable since the Pliocene seem to have been an increase in brain size from under 500 cc on average to the average of over 1300 cc found today, and a concomitant decrease in the size of teeth and the jaws which support them.

humus. Decomposed organic matter which becomes incorporated into SOIL. Litter from plants is broken down by soil organisms into fine particles, which may then by incorporated into the soil by EARTHWORMS and other soil organisms.

hunebed. Dutch name for the local variety of MEGALITHIC tomb. They consist of rectangular stone chambers with the entrance in one of the long sides, covered by a round or oval mound surrounded by a stone kerb. They were erected in the 3rd millennium bc by communities of the TRB CULTURE.

Huns. Of the many 'barbarian' tribes who threatened the Roman empire during the 4th and 5th centuries, the Huns are almost the most obscure in archaeological terms, but are remembered in all the literature as being the most fearsome and bloodthirsty. Their origins were not Germanic but Asiatic, their later homelands being in northeastern Europe. During the latter part of the 4th century the Huns continually stirred up other tribes to make forays into the eastern Roman provinces, and proved a constant threat to the Romans. During the 5th century, the Romans adopted a policy of employing 'barbarian' mercenaries to defend the empire against potential invaders, and thus under the governor Aetius Hunnish forces were used to defend eastern Gaul from the Burgundians. The most notable period of Hunnish disruption took place under their leader Attila, who invaded Gaul in 451. Visigothic and Roman forces joined to defeat Attila near Troyes, and after Attila's death the Huns were never again a major force in European history mainly because, unlike the Franks, Vandals and Visigoths, they were never able to capture large blocks of imperial territory.

Hunter Island. *See* TASMANIA.

hunting. In the 19th century the view developed that the hunting and gathering way of life still found among some modern primitive peoples had been typical of the earlier stone age or PALAEOLITHIC period. Subsequent research has gone a long way to confirming that before farming was developed some 10,000 years ago, hunting had been a way of life for early man for well over a million years. Not all the food was obtained from hunting: gathering plant foods and creatures like shellfish was also important. Little is known about techniques of hunting during the Palaeolithic. It is thought that at first arduous pursuit on foot may have been a common method, while spearing and trapping were probably developed later. Finally, sophisticated methods like the bow and arrow and the spear-thrower presumably increased the efficiency of hunting.

Hurri. A people known from documentary references and some archaeological sites, who originated in the area of Armenia (southeast Turkey, northwest Iran). They are documented from mid-3rd-millennium BC times, but are better known in the 2nd millennium when they settled in northern Mesopotamia and Syria in some numbers and set up a series of kingdoms, including that of MITANNI. They came into contact with HITTITES, ASSYRIANS and Egyptians and in the second half of the 2nd millennium BC were absorbed by the Hittites and the Assyrians.

Hushu [Hu-shu]. *See* GEOMETRIC POTTERY (CHINA).

Husterknupp. The site in the Rhineland, 50 km from Cologne, of a 9th- and 10th-century fortified MANOR which developed into a feudal castle. Excavations have shown a stage-by-stage evolution from a flat site in the river bend in the 9th century to a timber manorial complex on top of a mound, surrounded by ancillary dwellings.

Huxley's Line. The eastern edge of Sundaland and the East Asian faunal zone during the Pleistocene. The line runs between Bali and Lombok, Borneo and Sulawesi, thence northwards to the west of the Philippines. It marks the southeastern edge of the Asian continent during Pleistocene periods of low sea-level. Often confused with Wallace's Line, which follows the same course, but runs south, not west, of the Philippines, Huxley's Line also

marks (on present evidence) the limit of settlement by hominids before 50,000 bc.

hüyük. Turkish word for an artificial mound, equivalent to the Arabic TELL.

Hvar. Named after the island which boasts the largest number of its sites, the Hvar culture comprises the Late Neolithic and Copper Age sites of the south and central Dalmatian islands of Yugoslavia. In the absence of radiocarbon dates, a 4th millenium to early 3rd millennium bc date seems reasonable. Since the vast majority of Hvar sites are caves in areas of low mixed farming potential, fishing and shell-collecting were presumably the economic mainstays. Copper artefacts are rare, an exception being a bracelet of almost pure copper from Grapčeva Spilja. The pottery assemblage is dominated by dark burnished ware with red crusted decoration.

hyaena. Three species of hyaena survive today: the striped hyaena (*Hyaena hyaena*) of northeast Africa and parts of Asia; the spotted hyaena (*Crocuta crocuta*) of East and South Africa, and the South African brown hyaena (*Hyaena brunnea*). In the past, the spotted hyaena in particular had a far wider distribution. Throughout much of the QUATERNARY, *Crocuta* was common in European caves. Today's *Crocuta* are social animals, forming clans which hunt together and live in one den. This presumably explains the concentration of bones from *Crocuta* and other animals in caves. These 'Cave Hyaena' have been differentiated by some authors as *Crocuta spelaea*, although there is little evidence to support this.

hydria [Greek *hydor*: 'water']. Like the *kalpis*, this is a Greek pot for carrying water. Wider and usually lower than the AMPHORA, the shape was typically broad, with well-defined foot and neck, two horizontal handles (for carrying), and one vertical handle (for pouring). *See* illustration, page 224.

Hyksos. Often described as the Shepherd Kings, these nomadic groups from Palestine entered Egypt towards the end of the Middle Kingdom in the 18th century BC. Subsequently they established a capital at Avaris in the eastern Nile delta and later extended their control further south. In the 17th century BC

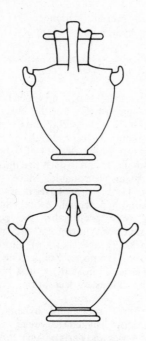

Two forms of hydria

there were several attempts to expel the Hyksos rulers, but their final defeat and expulsion occurred c1567 BC under Amosis, the founder of the Eighteenth Dynasty, and marked the beginning of the Egyptian New Kingdom (*see* DYNASTIC EGYPT). Little is known about the Hyksos; in the documentary record they appear as a military aristocracy with little information provided about their culture. Archaeologically they are recognizable in their Palestinian homeland by a system of defence with ramparts faced by a smooth hard plaster slope, recognized at such sites as HAZOR and JERICHO. The Hyksos are credited with introducing horses and chariots to Egypt, as well as the olive and the pomegranate.

hypocaust [from Greek *hypokauston*: 'heated (space) under']. The Roman system of central heating. Normally the ground floor (probably tiled or mosaic concrete) is supported on low pillars, allowing a draught of hot air from a nearby furnace to circulate in the sub-floor space. Examples are found from about 100 BC onward. The hypocaust is linked in due course to vertical vents of BOX-FLUE tiles, built into the walls at intervals, which carry the warm air up into the upper areas of the house.

Hyrax Hill. Located on the outskirts of Nakuru township in the Central Rift Valley of Kenya, the archaeological site of Hyrax Hill was occupied at two distinct periods. The earlier settlement is attributed to the East African PASTORAL NEOLITHIC complex, and was one of the first sites of this complex to be scientifically excavated. The second phase is of the Iron Age, and includes a series of so-called 'Sirikwa Holes' which are interpreted as semi-subterranean cattle pens constructed by Nilotic-speaking peoples around or shortly before the middle of the present millennium.

I

Iberomaurusian. Previously sometimes known as 'Oranian', this is an industry of the Maghreb dating to final PLEISTOCENE times. Iberomaurusian assemblages are dominated by large numbers of small backed bladelets. The earliest occurrences, as at TAFORALT in eastern Morocco, are of the 14th millennium bc. During the following 2000 to 3000 years the area of Iberomaurusian occupation extended eastwards into eastern Algeria and Tunisia. Hunting was carried out from small temporary encampments: at least in later times shellfish collection was also an important activity. Extensive cemeteries have been investigated, as at Taforalt, and also at Afalou bou Rhummel and COLUMNATA in Algeria. The human population represented was invariably of the robust MECHTA-AFALOU type. Burials were sometimes decorated with ochre or accompanied by food remains or by horns of wild cattle.

Iblis, Tal-i. Located *c*80 km southwest of Kerman in southern Iran, Tal-i Iblis is a TELL settlement occupied in the 5th, 4th and 3rd millennia bc. The earliest occupation, dating to the early 5th millennium bc (Tal-i Iblis 0), is characterized by coarse-tempered red burnished ware made into a variety of simple forms. In the next phase, dated by radiocarbon to the late 5th millennium bc (Tal-i Iblis I), small quantities of painted ware, in maroon or black on a buff ground, appear in a settlement of mud-brick houses, each consisting of a central area of storerooms, surrounded by living rooms with red plaster floors. Domesticated goats were bred and perhaps also sheep and cattle; bread wheat and probably emmer wheat were cultivated; wild cattle, gazelle, onager and horse were hunted. This layer has also produced abundant evidence of copper-working, in the form of hundreds of pieces of crucibles with copper stain; this evidence, along with remains from both SUSA and SIALK, suggests that the communities of Iran were at least as developed as those of Mesopotamia, if not more so, in the practice of metallurgy.

The exploitation of copper and steatite and trade in these commodities to the civilizations of southern Mesopotamia and Susiana in the 4th and early 3rd millennia BC allowed Tal-i Iblis to grow to urban or proto-urban status. Clay tablets inscribed in the PROTO-ELAMITE script demonstrate the connections that linked communities throughout Iran at this time.

Ice Age. Popular term for GLACIAL or GLACIATION.

Iceland. The 9th-century Irish geographer Dicuil suggests that Celtic monks had reached the Faroes and possibly even Iceland by his time, but Iceland was not systematically settled until the Norwegians came to the island in the late 9th century, in the last great wave of VIKING emigration and expansion. The country was rich in fertile land and natural resources, and accordingly the independent farmers flourished. The sagas recount that they grew wheat, raised cattle and sheep and maintained strong trading connections with the rest of the Viking world, to which they exported iron, linen and woollen cloth. From the beginning the settlers established their own unique parliamentary commonwealth based on the law and the power of the individual. It had a central assembly (the *althing*) and regional divisions administered by the local chiefs or *Gooar*.

The archaeology of medieval Iceland is fairly rich because many of the Viking-period farms have been located. Excavations in 1939 revealed several farm complexes in the lava-filled Pjorsadaelur Valley showing the typical farmstead to be a fairly elaborate construction of several rooms with turf and stone walls with wainscotted facing, paved areas, and benches and other turf and wood furniture. A typical house would be a long hall with division into several internal rooms, a kitchen, hearths and outbuildings including dairy and possible lavatory. The form of these buildings is unique apart from a few parallels in the Orkneys. The Icelanders also developed a strong literary tradition; details of their history and way of life have come down to us through their poetry and chronicles but most of all through the unique medieval vernacular prose form commonly known as the Saga. The Sagas first emerged in the 12th century and increased in craftsmanship and output through the 13th century. They tell mostly of family feuds, murderous intrigues and voyages; Njal's and Egil's sagas are perhaps the best known of all these great stories.

ice-wedges. Structures that develop within the permafrost layer of the PERIGLACIAL zone. In the winter, when the ground freezes and contracts, fissures are formed that penetrate into the permafrost. Water percolates in and freezes, and a wedge of ice gradually develops, continuously enlarging the fissure as it does so. When the ice melts, these fissures may be filled with sediment, forming a cast of the ice-wedge. Fossil ice-wedges of this kind are seen in many sections of sand and gravel deposits in Europe. They have been used to reconstruct the extent of the periglacial zone which developed around the DEVENSIAN and WEICHSELIAN ice-sheets. Another feature, similar in form to the ice-wedge cast, is the sand-wedge. This is a frost fissure that has been filled directly with sediment, without the formation of ice. In plan, systems of ice-wedges are arranged in a polygonal network which frequently appears as a crop mark in aerial photographs, alongside features of more archaeological interest.

icon. A form of Christian painting which spread throughout BYZANTIUM and much of the Christian world from the mid-6th century. Based on old traditions of Roman portraiture, the icons were portraits of sacred personages set into panels, always with a frontal pose and an exaggerated spiritual expression, often with large staring eyes directed at the observer. One of the earliest examples in the West is the Madonna from Santa Maria in Trastevere, Rome.

Icons became objects of such devotion that in 726 the eastern Byzantine Emperor and clergy, believing that the worship of images was fundamentally opposed to the teaching of Christ, issued a complete ban on their use. The Latin Church under successive Popes resisted this ban, and until 843 the church was split in the bitter quarrel known as the iconoclastic dispute.

Idaean Cave. Situated on Mount Ida in central Crete at an altitude of 1500 metres, this cave is one of those claimed as the birthplace of Zeus. It was an important cult centre from the late MINOAN period. Inside was a large rock shaped into a stepped altar, while the floor was covered with ash, charcoal, bones and rich votive offerings, including seal stones. The cave remained important at a later period and the most splendid finds are a series of decorated shields from the 8th to 7th centuries BC.

ideogram. *See* WRITING.

Idojiri. A group of about 50 Middle and Late JOMON sites in the mountainous area of central Honshu, Japan. The sites are large clusters of substantial pit houses. Pottery with moulded rim ornamentation, numerous figurines, and curious stone arrangements suggest a well-developed ceremonialism. There are well-worn grinding slabs and chipped stone celts which could have served either for cutting trees or digging soil. Carbonized cakes of vegetable matter were found. It has long been suspected that the inhabitants practised cultivation as well as nut-collecting and game-hunting.

Ife. An important town in Yoruba country in southern Nigeria, whose archaeological antecedents extend back into the 1st millennium AD, although they are only known with clarity from the 11th century onwards. The buildings were of sun-dried brick: their architecture is not known in detail but included open courtyards paved with potsherds set on edge. Ife has yielded a magnificent series of realistic bronze and terracotta human figures, the style of which probably owes at least some inspiration to the earlier NOK tradition. The metal employed in the CIRE PERDUE (lost wax) process by which the bronze figures were made appears to have been derived from a northerly origin, perhaps ultimately from trans-Saharan trade; it may be that the gathering of forest products required for this trade formed the basis of Ife's prosperity. It has been suggested that the bronze-working tradition of BENIN was derived from that of Ife.

Igbo Ukwu. An Iron Age burial site in south-eastern Nigeria that has yielded remarkable evidence for artistic and technological development and accumulation of wealth in that part of West Africa during the closing centuries of the 1st millennium ad. The principal corpse was interred in a deep pit, sitting on a stool surrounded by extensive regalia; the burial chamber was then roofed over and the bodies of attendants were placed above it. Further offerings were deposited nearby. The most noteworthy objects recovered at Igbo Ukwu are the CIRE PERDUE bronze castings — vases, bowls and items of personal adornment — which display an unparalleled delicacy and intricacy of ornament. Domestic pottery and enormous numbers of glass beads were also incorporated in the deposits. The date of the deposit has been the subject of dispute, but the 9th century ad is strongly indicated.

Île Carn. An Early Neolithic PASSAGE GRAVE in Brittany, built of dry stone walling with a corbelled vault to the chamber. Inside were only a few sherds and flint flakes. There is a radiocarbon date of $c3270$ bc ($c4100$ BC).

Île Longue. An Early Neolithic PASSAGE GRAVE in the Locmariaquer area of southern Brittany, situated on a small island in the Gulf of Morbihan. The tomb, built of stone orthostats with a corbelled vault, is a good example of a classic passage grave.

Ileret. Situated on the east side of Lake Turkana [Rudolf] in Kenya, a short distance south of the border with Ethiopia, Ileret has yielded important archaeological sites of two periods. The first group of discoveries, of Plio/ Pleistocene age, is noted here under EAST RUDOLF. The second group dates to the late 3rd millennium bc. Domestic cattle and sheep/goat were represented and these are the earliest sites in East Africa to have yielded incontrovertible evidence for pastoralism. Associated pottery and, especially, stone bowls serve as a link with PASTORAL NEOLITHIC sites of significantly later date in the Rift Valley highlands further to the south.

Illinoian. A group of QUATERNARY glacial deposits in North America; covered by the SANGAMON soil and burying YARMOUTH PALAEOSOLS (*see* Table 7, page 420). It consists mainly of TILLS, the products of large ice-sheets, and has been split up into three substages, the Liman, Monican and Jubileean.

Tills of the Liman and Monican sub-stages are separated by a palaeosol, the Pike soil, which may represent either an INTERSTADIAL or an INTERGLACIAL. A much more weakly developed soil separates the Monican from the Jubileean. It is unclear how many cold stages the Illinoian deposits represent, but it may be more than one. The Illinoian has never been dated satisfactorily.

illuminated manuscript. Medieval handwritten books, decorated with paintings or drawings, usually executed on parchment or vellum. The illustrations themselves fall into several categories: miniatures (small paintings incorporated into the text or border, or occupying a whole page), decorated monograms or initial letters, and decorative borders. Before the year 1000, the books most commonly illustrated in this way were gospels or psalters, while large Bibles and Books of the Hours became more popular after this time. The origins of manuscript illumination are thought to lie in 5th century Coptic Egypt; throughout the succeeding centuries works continued to be produced by many different schools and scriptoria throughout Christendom.

The BYZANTINE illuminators worked very much within the naturalistic confines of Late Antique art using a great deal of gold leaf but lacking the distinctive pictorial monogram. In Western Europe the Hiberno-Saxon school developed out of the Christian-inspired cultural revival in that part of the world. The books were characterized by a wealth of abstract spiral and interlace ornament, and stylized figures, combined with large capitals and whole pages of pure ornament; typical examples are the LINDISFARNE GOSPELS and the BOOK OF KELLS. The CAROLINGIAN and Ottonian schools, which flourished in 8th-century to 11th-century Western Europe were very eclectic, taking inspiration from Antique Byzantine and Hiberno-Saxon manuscripts. Some fine miniaturist schools, such as that at Reichenau, were incorporated within this spectrum, while the decorative monogram continued to be important. In 10th-century England the new monastic reforms laid the foundations for the WINCHESTER school of manuscript art with its preference for naturalistic figures and foliage and line drawings, best demonstrated on the large bibles of the time. As the Gothic period progressed the art of illumination was no longer confined to religious works produced in scriptoria, but was also carried out in the universities. Romances and Bestiaries were among the illustrated books produced at this time. The invention of printing effectively ended the era of manuscript illumination, although many printed books continued to be illustrated by hand.

illuvial horizon. A SOIL HORIZON which has resulted from the deposition of minerals, HUMUS or plant nutrients, washed down from higher up in the PROFILE. *See* ELUVIAL HORIZON.

Illyricum. *See* DALMATIA.

Ilopango. In the late PRE-CLASSIC PERIOD (*c*260 AD), Mount Ilopango in El Salvador was the centre of a catastrophic volcanic eruption. At least two volcanic events, temporally very close together, blasted an estimated 40 cubic kilometres of ash into the atmosphere. Aside from the direct effects of the blast, an area of maximum devastation some 3000-5000 km around the crater was covered with ash to an average depth of one metre. A further 50,000 square kilometres around this core received sufficient fallout to effectively destroy most subsistence vegetation.

These events, it is suggested, caused the local populations (early MAYAN groups) to migrate out northwards and eastwards into the lowlands of central Guatemala and Belize. It is possible that the pressure of this sudden influx of migrants may have given rise to the improved agricultural methods which mark the beginning of the Classic Maya civilization. Certainly, archaeological evidence at BARTON RAMIE (and to a lesser extent at ALTAR DE SACRIFICIOS) indicates a period of noticeable environmental and demographic change which can be roughly synchronized with (and would be appropriate to) such events.

Impressed Ware. Type of pottery that characterizes cultures in the central and west Mediterranean (Yugoslavia, Italy, Sicily, Malta, Sardinia, Corsica, southern France, Spain, Portugal and north Africa) from *c*6000 bc to *c*4000 bc, or later in some areas. The pottery is dark-surfaced and is decorated with impressions made in a variety of different ways: with fingers, sticks or other implements or with the edge of a cardium shell (therefore

often called Cardial Ware). Shapes are generally simple and include bowls and large open-mouthed storage or cooking vessels. In the 6th millennium bc Impressed Ware is found mainly in caves or rock shelters or shell midden sites, many of which had been occupied in the preceding Mesolithic period. On these sites, Impressed Ware is usually associated with a hunting and gathering economy, although there is some evidence for the early appearance of domesticated sheep. After *c*5000 bc Impressed Ware is found with evidence of a mixed farming economy, based on domesticated animals and cultivated plants (both cereals and pulses). By this stage open settlements had become much more common and in Italy these were often surrounded by multiple ditches (the so-called *villaggi trincerati*). Other types of pottery are found alongside Impressed Ware at this stage, including fine red painted ware in Italy. STENTINELLO Ware in Sicily and GHAR DALAM ware in Malta represent specialized versions of Impressed Ware.

Inariyama. A keyhole-shaped KOFUN [tumulus] in Saitama Prefecture, Japan. There are at least three other *kofun* by the same name in different parts of Japan. The one in Saitama has two moats around a mound 120 metres on the longer axis, an impressive structure for an area far away from the centre of *kofun* development. An X-ray examination in 1978 revealed an inscription with 115 characters on an iron sword recovered during the excavation ten years earlier. It referred to a person called Wakatakeru, who is likely to be Emperaro Yuraku of the Yamato court, and a date which can be interpreted as 471 or 531. This is one of the handful of dated inscriptions found from *kofun*, although the date of the sword manufacture does not necessarily indicate the date of the construction of the mound.

Inca. Easily the largest and most powerful political unit in all of prehistoric America, the Inca empire stretched from the Maule River in southern Chile to southern Colombia and supported, at its height, a population of six million. A recognizable entity by *c*1200, the Quechua-speaking Inca were just another group of minor raiders in the Urubamba area of Peru until a decisive victory over the Chanka at CUZCO in 1438. Over the next 38 years they conquered and absorbed the

AYMARA kingdoms, the CHIMU and the CHINCHA and came to control the major population centres of the Titicaca Basin and north-coast Peru. The years 1476-1532 represent the period of continuing Inca dominance (*see* LATE HORIZON).

The empire was divided into four quarters (the literal meaning of the Quechua word for empire, *Tawantinguyu*) and was ruled through a hierarchical pyramid of administrators at the top of which was an absolute ruler, the emperor. Local religions were tolerated, and often local rulers were left in command as provincial governors rather than replaced. The Quechua language, however, was imposed on all conquered peoples. Every societal unit in the empire, down to the smallest *ayllu* (a kin-based village group) paid taxes in the form of labour service (*mita*). An impressive system of roads with way stations (*tambos*) and distance markers and a complex system of record keeping (*quipu*) facilitated administration to a great extent.

Inca subsistence was principally agricultural and included MAIZE, POTATO, MANIOC, COTTON and a great variety of other plants, many of which were grown on irrigated land. Although some hunting took place (e.g. deer and guanaco), there were numerous domesticated animals. The cavy (guinea pig) was bred principally for its meat and the LLAMA and alpaca, though sometimes eaten, were most often bred for wool and for use as pack animals. Inca ceramics were standardized and mass-produced; the diagnostic ceramic is a tall, narrow-necked conical-based jar named an ARYBALLUS because of its similarity to the classical Greek form.

The considerable architectural skill of the Inca is reflected in CYCLOPEAN MASONRY (*see* CUZCO and SACSAHUAMAN), although many buildings were constructed using rectangular dressed stone blocks as well as adobe. The basic dwelling-unit was a cluster of single rooms arranged around a rectangular courtyard and was most often enclosed by a wall. Huge urban agglomerations were not the norm. The trapezoidal doorway, narrowing at the top, and the storage niche are common architectural features; the CHULLPA borrowed from earlier cultures was a common funerary structure.

Viracocha Inca was the creator, culture hero and supreme deity of the Inca, but religion embraced a pantheon of natural gods (earth, sea, thunder etc.). The most actively worshipped were the sun and, by extension, the emperor, who was considered the son of the sun. The Temple of the Sun, built at the pre-Incan CEREMONIAL CENTRE of PACHACAMAC suggests some incorporation of earlier religions. Indeed, it has been argued that the whole of Inca achievement relied heavily on a variety of political, societal and religious infrastructures already in place before their ascendancy (e.g. TIAHUANACO, AYMARA etc).

The arrival of the Spanish in 1532 brought a rapid end to this grand empire. Their apparently easy conquest is legend; however, it was due less to military acuity than to other factors: the fact that the authoritarian nature of the Inca administration was tailor-made for control by a very few; the Spanish were able to capitalize on the disaffection resulting from a recent civil war, and the devastation wrought by imported European diseases on a population with no natural immunity had already considerably reduced resistance.

incensario. *See* INCENSE BURNER.

incense burner. The burning of incense as part of ritual life was a widespread practice in Mesoamerica, from as early as the PRE-CLASSIC PERIOD. Depictions of its use have been found on stelae dating to the MIRAFLORES phase at KAMINALJUYU, and paraphernalia connected with its use have been found in some quantity at many major sites. Usually made from stone or ceramic, there is considerable variety in form, from the simple small candelero (found literally in hundreds at TEOTIHUACAN) to the highly elaborate incensarios of PALENQUE and MAYAPAN. Copal, the Maya word for pine-resin, was widely traded as incense; it appears in the Aztec tribute lists in the Codex Mendoza.

Incense burners also occur in other parts of the world and sometimes vessels of uncertain function have been thought to be associated with the use of incense. For instance, small pots of specialized shapes found in graves of the WESSEX CULTURE in southern England have sometimes been called 'incense cups'.

Inchtuthil. An unfinished Roman fort in Tay, eastern Scotland, built by Agricola during his Scottish campaigns of the early 80s AD. Started about 83, the fort covered some 20 hectares, and was constructed largely of earth and timber. Its buildings include 64 barracks, a commandant's house, officers' quarters and a hospital. About 87-8 the fort was systematically dismantled as part of a planned withdrawal. Besides the deliberate breaking of crockery and glassware, a million or so nails were buried in a pit — presumably to save transport and prevent local re-use.

Indianization. Formerly referred to as Hinduization, denotes the transplantation by peaceful means of Indian civilization into Southeast Asia, or 'Farther India'. This must be understood as the expansion of an organized culture that was founded upon the Indian concept of royalty, was characterized by Hindu or Buddhist cults, mythology and cosmology, and expressed itself in the Sanskrit language; hence it is sometimes called 'Sanskritization' or 'Brahmanization', as Brahmans were its main agents. The process began around the beginning of the Christian Era, lasted for several centuries and created so-called Indianized kingdoms or civilizations which declined in the 13th or 14th century. Recent research has shown that Indianization was limited to a very small proportion of the population and that the indigenous element played a more decisive role in the formation of Southeast Asian civilization than was formerly believed.

Indo-European. Name of the group of languages from which most modern European languages are derived, as are the Indian Sanskrit and its descendants and the Farsi language of Iran. Since it is assumed that the dispersal of the languages of this group must have occurred through large-scale migrations of people, many attempts have been made to identify the carriers of Indo-European languages with groups recognizable in the archaeological record. This is a valid exercise when the groups in question were literate or are recorded in other people's documents, as with the HITTITES and the LUWIANS in Asia Minor, because it is possible to establish that the groups were indeed Indo-European speakers. In the case of non-literate peoples the exercise is a much more tricky one, as the only clues to the linguistic affiliations of prehistoric groups lie in the language of later groups in the area, assumed to be their direct

descendants. Many attempts have been made to document the spread of Indo-Europeans into Europe. One school maintains that the original homeland was in the south Russian steppes (perhaps recognizable in the KURGAN culture) and spread into Europe with the SINGLE GRAVE, CORDED WARE and GLOBULAR AMPHORAE groups. Other authorities feel that there is little evidence for a widespread movement of people at this time and that the dispersal may have occurred at an earlier stage. In general, this line of study is little followed by archaeologists today, because of the problems of correlating linguistic groupings with ethnic or cultural groupings.

Indonesia. *Prehistory.* In political terms, Indonesia is the most southerly and largest portion of Island Southeast Asia. It is divided by the Huxley/Wallace Line into westerly Sundaland and easterly Wallacea, the former being settled by HOMO ERECTUS (especially JAVA man) by almost two million years ago. Later major developments in Indonesia include settlement across HUXLEY'S LINE to reach Australia and NEW GUINEA by 40,000 years ago (early Australoid populations), the development of small flake and blade industries in eastern Indonesia (and in Australia) after 4000 BC (*see* LEANG TUWO MANE'E, TOALIAN), the spread of Neolithic cultures correlated with AUSTRONESIAN expansion after 3000 BC, and spreading bronze metallurgy in the 1st millennium BC.

Classical. The history of Indonesia is difficult to summarize, as almost each of the 3000 islands in the archipelago has its own local history, which may be very different from that of its neighbour. It seems logical to assume that the western part of the archipelago would have experienced INDIANIZATION earlier and more thoroughly than the eastern part, but the earliest Sanskrit inscription and the earliest Buddha image, both dated to about AD 400, were found in BORNEO and CELEBES respectively. However, the first important Indianized states developed in SUMATRA and JAVA from the 7th-8th centuries on, Java becoming more and more the focus of Indianized and, after the 14th century, Islamized Indonesia.

See also BALI, BORNEO, CELEBES, GILIMANUK, HEEKEREN, JAVA, MAJAPAHIT,

Matarâm, Śailendra, Śrīvijaya, Sūlaw-esi, Sumatra, Sunda, Timor, Wallacea.

Indrapura [Sanskrit: 'City of Indra'] (1). In Cambodia, Indrapura was the first capital of the future king Jayavarman II upon his return from Java before he founded the kingdom of Angkor in 802. It has not been identified with certainty, but corresponds probably to the site of Bunteay Prei Nokor, in the province of Thbong Khmum, to the east of Kompong Cham.

Indrapura (2). In Champa, the city of Indra-pura, located in the present province of Quang-name, was the capital of the dynasty bearing the same name, founded by Indra-varman II in 875 and lasting to 986; the capital was then transferred to Vijaya, further south.

Indus Civilization. See Harappan Civiliza-tion.

industrial archaeology. The study of the material remains of past industrial activities, covering ways of making, transporting and distributing things. It can apply to material of any age, but the term is most often applied to post-medieval archaeology, and especially to the archaeology of the Industrial Revolution in Britain and Western Europe.

industry. Set of artefacts, made of a single material, that is thought to represent the products of a single group. An industry may represent one of a group of industries making up a Culture. For instance, the Linear Pottery culture has a distinctive stone industry and pottery industry, as well as characteristic settlement form, subsistence economy, and other traits.

Infiernillo. See Tamaulipas.

Ingaladdi. A sandstone rock shelter in the northwest of the Australian Northern Territory between the Victoria and Daly Rivers. The site is notable for two well-separated stone industries and for art. Lower levels dating between 3000 and 5000 bc contained a typical Australian Core Tool and Scraper assemblage with large, steep-edge flake scrapers and Horsehoof cores. After a sterile layer, the upper sandy deposits con-tained Tula adze flakes, and small unifacial and bifacial points, dating from 1000 bc. The unifacial points included some with denticul-ated margins and others classed as Pirri points. The latter have a wide north-south dis-tribution across arid Australia, but bifacial points have been found only in the north of the Northern Territory. Rock-paintings include Wandjina style mythical beings, animals (some in 'X-ray' style), men on horseback and revolvers. Fragments of Panaramitee-style engravings were found in layers dated 3000-5000 bc.

Ingitkalik. See Cape Krusenstern.

Ingombe Ilede. Located on the north bank of the Zambezi, a short distance downstream of the modern Kariba, Ingombe Ilede was initially an Iron Age settlement of the late 1st millennium ad. Around 1400, however, it was reoccupied by people who were evidently engaged in extensive trade in both copper and gold. It seems reasonable to interpret the site as one where these metals were brought together from their areas of production to the north and south, for transport via the Zambezi Valley to the coast. By the same route large numbers of glass beads and, possibly, Indian cotton cloth found their way into the African interior. It is noteworthy that this evidence for development of trade in the Zambezi Valley coincides in date with the decline of Great Zimbabwe.

ingot. A mass of unwrought metal resulting from Smelting or other extraction processes.

Initial Period. One of a seven-period chrono-logical construction used in Peruvian archae-ology and sometimes employed in other Andean areas. Covering the period 1800-900 bc, its beginning is marked by the first appear-ance of pottery and its close by the occurrence of Chavin materials. Many of the traits that make up the Peruvian cultural tradition (such as intensive agriculture, the widespread use of textiles, and larger and more numerous population centres) occur during this period. See Table 9, page 552.

Initial Series. See Calendar.

insula [Latin: 'island']. In Roman archi-tecture, either (1) an area of a town, typically enclosed by four streets, and probably corresponding to a smaller subdivision on the familiar CARDO/decumanus grid; or (2) a large 'tenement'-type house, or apartment block, as well-illustrated at Roman OSTIA. An *insula* can rise to four storeys, and we learn that the maximum permitted height (probably stipulated because of abuse) was 15 metres. The ground floor was frequently given over to shops. Balconies are quite common, and the number of the apartment is given on the staircase leading to it. Conditions in this type of building, especially at Rome, were often overcrowded, insanitary and disease-ridden.

intaglio [Italian: 'carving']. (1) The process of cutting or engraving a design, usually into a (gem)stone or precious metal; or (2) the artefact so created, which was then characteristically set into a finger-ring, and used as a personal seal.

Integration Period. The most recent period in the chronological continum FORMATIVE, REGIONAL DEVELOPMENT, Integration. Formulated for use in Ecuadoran archaeology by Betty Meggers, it covers the period from AD 500 to 1550 and has been applied to other areas of northwestern South and Central America. Sometimes known as the Late Period, it is characterized by greater cultural uniformity over wider areas and an increase in the hallmarks of civilization, for example urban centres, intensive agriculture and class stratification. The absorption of Ecuador into the INCA empire is the culmination of this trend.

interglacial. Term commonly used to describe the periods of generally warm climate which occurred at intervals during the QUATERNARY period, interspersed between colder periods (*see* GLACIAL). *See* Tables 5-7, pages 418-20.

interlace. A form of pattern that intertwines parallel strands and ribbons, passing them over and under one another alternately. In the 7th and 8th centuries interlace ornament was refined and used to great effect by CELTIC and ANGLO-SAXON metalworkers, sculptors, and manuscript illuminators in intricate combinations of animal and foliate motifs. The artistic tradition was also very prominent throughout the VIKING period.

Intermediate Periods. Part of a chronological construction used in Peruvian archaeology. There are two clearly separate Intermediate Periods (*see* Table 9, page 552). The Early Intermediate Period (200 BC-AD 600) is characterized by the rise of the first great city states, such as MOCHE and NASCA. The Late Intermediate Period (1000-1476) is characterized by the presence of numerous fractionalized corporate units which arose after the decline of TIAHUANACO and HUARI, for instance CHIMU on the north coast and AYMARA around Lake Titicaca.

interstadial. A short period of warmer climate during a GLACIATION (cold stage). *See* DEVENSIAN, WEICHSELIAN, WISCONSIN; *see also* Tables 5-7, pages 418-20.

Intihuasi Cave. A site of long occupation and clear chronological continuity which evidences a way of life similar to the DESERT TRADITION of North America. Located in northwest Argentina, its lowest level (Intihuasi IV) contains willow-leaf points (*see also* GUITARRERO, AYAMPITIN and LAURICOCHA) and other hunting tools in association with MANOS, milling stones and ground stone ornaments. This level is dated, by radiocarbon assay, to c6000 bc. Subsequent levels contain medium-sized triangular points (Intihuasi III), bone projectile points (Intihuasi II) and a ceramic level (Intihuasi I) with an estimated date of AD 750.

Inuit. *See* ESKIMO.

involution. A structure that develops within the active layer of the PERIGLACIAL zone. CRYOTURBATION causes movement within the layer and sorting of its constituents. Involutions formed by this process may consist of tongues or pillars of fine material which extend into overlying sand and gravel, or they may be festoons of coarser material, pulled up into the active layer from underlying SEDIMENTS. Pockets filled with finer material are a type of involution which develops characteristically on the surface of chalk. Involutions are important because they help to define the area of ancient periglacial zones (although involutions are not absolutely diagnostic of periglacial activity). Archaeologists have frequently confused them with archaeological features, and great care needs sometimes to be exercised when excavating sites.

Inyanga. An area of the Zimbabwe eastern highlands, adjacent to the border with Mozambique, which retains evidence for a prolonged sequence of Iron Age occupation. Early Iron Age settlement, related to that at GOKOMERE, is attested at several sites around ZIWA Mountain. Between the 16th and 18th centuries, and perhaps earlier, extensive irrigation works were undertaken. Other stone structures date from the same period, including semi-subterranean structures interpreted as stock pens.

Iona. A small island off the west coast of Scotland. In 563 St Columba and a group of his followers left their Irish homeland to found a monastery on the island; from here they ministered to the spiritual welfare of the Picts and the Irish settlers of DALRIADA, and also directed missions to other parts of Britain and Europe. The vestigial remains of the monastery are earthworks that include a distinctive rectangular vallum or ditched enclosure surrounding the complex. The standing buildings belong to the later medieval Benedictine abbey. The island also boasts a fine collection of 8th-century standing crosses. In the early 9th century constant interference by the Vikings caused the Columban monks to abandon their monastery, and many returned to Ireland.

Ionic. (1) One of the principal regional dialects of ancient Greece, closely related to ATTIC, and characteristic of the so-called 'Ionian' cities of Asia Minor.

(2) In classical architecture, the Ionic order, which emerged after DORIC (perhaps from about 570 BC) in the context of Aegean and eastern Greek settlements. The order typically shows a COLUMN of slender proportions tapering evenly upwards, smoothly fluted with 24 (rather than the 20 of Doric) flutes. The base consists of disc-like roundels surmounted by a cushion-like moulding (*torus*: 'cushion'). The CAPITAL has distinctive end-spirals (*volutes*). Unlike the Doric, the Ionic capital has four distinct sides, only two of which are intended to be conspicuous. On corners this created a problem, and a special corner-version capital was devised with the two 'facing' sides adjacent and linked by an angled *volute*. Above the column, the Ionic order is characterized by friezes of egg-and-tongue motif and dentils.

Ipiutak. The most recent variant of the NORTON tradition, beginning $c1$ AD and persisting in some areas to as late as $c800$. Its major characteristic is a highly developed art style, similar to OLD BERING SEA, which is most commonly expressed in the working of ivory. Projectile points and other stone implements are similar to those of the preceding Norton culture, but other Norton-associated materials such as pottery, ground slate tools and oil lamps are usually missing from Ipiutak assemblages. Excavations at the village site at Point Hope, Alaska, revealed evidence of a settlement of 600 houses. Numerous examples of finely carved ivory were found in the associated cemetery.

Ipswichian. A group of British INTERGLACIAL deposits — lacustrine muds, river terraces, estuarine and marine sediments. They exist as patches of materials containing fossils indicating warm conditions, overlain by DEVENSIAN deposits and also underlain by sediments indicating cold conditions. Individual patches have been correlated by POLLEN ANALYSIS and the evidence of vertebrate fossils. A climate warmer than the present is indicated. Nowhere is there any direct evidence of the underlying stratigraphy, but Ipswichian terraces in the Midlands have been shown to be later than WOLSTONIAN sands and tills. Traditionally, the Ipswichian deposits are supposed to represent a single warm stage, the last interglacial. This may be supported by a pioneer URANIUM SERIES date of $174,000 \pm 30,000$ BP for supposed Ipswichian deposits at Brundon in Essex. Such a date fits in well with the expected age of the last interglacial and with the DEEP SEA CORE oxygen isotope sequence. There is, however, no direct connection between the patches of deposit, and recent discussion of the vertebrate fossil assemblages by which the Ipswichian is correlated has suggested that the deposits may in fact represent more than one interglacial. Further developments are awaited. LEVALLOISIAN and MOUSTERIAN artefacts are found in Ipswichian deposits. *See* Table 6, page 419.

Ipswich ware. A proficiently made type of pottery produced between the 7th and 9th centuries in Ipswich, Suffolk, where kiln debris has been found. The cooking pots and un-decorated pitchers were distributed widely around East Anglia, while stamp-decorated pitchers were traded as far as York and Rich-borough. This ware makes it possible to identify sites of the elusive Middle Saxon period.

Irian Jaya. *See* LAKE SENTANI.

Iron Age. Third age of the THREE AGE SYSTEM, defined by the use of iron as the main material for making tools. The term is still widely used in West Asiatic, European and African prehistory. In Western Asia the Iron Age begins in the later 2nd millennium BC, in Europe during the earlier 1st millennium BC, and in Africa south of the Sahara in the first millennium AD.

Technically we could regard ourselves as still in the Iron Age today, but traditionally the term is not used in this way. Usage varies from area to area: in much of Europe, for instance, the Iron Age is taken to end with the expansion of the Romans, while in parts of Africa the Iron Age continues until the colonial era.

iron and steel. Since the IRON AGE, iron has been the most commonly used METAL. Iron ores are widely available: the most common as rocks are siderite, haematite and limonite. Iron may also be obtained from the 'bog iron ore' precipitated underwater or in boggy water-logged ground. Although iron is much more abundant than copper — it makes up fully five per cent of the earth's crust — its exploitation comes later in history and its technology follows a vastly different course, for reasons inherent in the metal itself. Far more than any other metal in common use, iron is affected in its properties by the techniques used to produce and work it, from the smelting process (which may add alloying carbon) to the final shaping, hammering or heat treat-ment. The exploitation of any metal naturally depends on the cost of producing it and the qualities it can be seen to offer; in the case of iron, however, the most useful properties of the metal are not readily apparent and were only slowly evoked by the ingenuity of generations of craftsmen. The history of iron thus cannot be understood without giving close consideration to methods of production and treatment.

Pure iron melts at 1535°C, a temperature inaccessible before the 19th century AD. Hence in antiquity iron could be reduced from its ore in molten form only if during the smelting process it absorbed carbon from a charcoal fire, thereby forming an alloy with a lower melting point. When the carbon content reaches 3 to 4.5 per cent the melting point falls to about 1150°C, not much higher than the melting point of copper (1083°C) or the temperature of a good pottery kiln. The result-ing alloy, called cast iron or pig iron, is hard and brittle (too brittle to make a dependable sword). In China iron was regularly produced in the form of cast iron from the time of the metal's first exploitation around the 6th century BC (*see* IRON AND STEEL, CHINA). Elsewhere in the world, however, the pro-duction of iron depended on processes in which the metal was never melted but was instead obtained in solid form.

Iron can be reduced from its ore at a temperature well below the melting point to form a spongy mass called a bloom; the bloom can then be welded into a compact mass and purified of slag by repeated forging (hammer-ing while hot). The iron so produced, which does not contain carbon, is called wrought iron; it is both softer and tougher (stronger, less brittle) than cast iron, and it could not be melted in any furnace before modern times. Iron was probably first produced, in the form of wrought iron, as an accidental by-product of lead and copper smelting, for in the ancient Near East the iron ore hematite was often added to siliceous ores of lead and copper as a flux. (A flux is a material which combines with the earthy parts of the ore to form a slag that is liquid at the furnace temperature and easily separated from the metal.) The deliberate production of iron originated perhaps in Anatolia around 2000 BC.

It was probably the process of forging the white-hot bloom that led to the discovery of steel — or rather, to the discovery that careful treatment of wrought iron could improve its properties enormously. Steel is an alloy of iron and carbon containing about 0.3 to 1.0 per cent carbon. It is therefore intermediate in carbon content between wrought iron (no carbon) and cast iron (3 to 4.5 per cent carbon), and in principle can be made either by adding carbon to wrought iron or by removing it from cast iron. In the West, where cast iron does not seem to have been made deliberately before the 14th century AD, the manufacture of steel prior to that time began with wrought iron and added carbon to it by a simple process called cementation: a piece of wrought iron deeply embedded in a charcoal fire is converted to steel by prolonged heating, which allows it to absorb small amounts of carbon by solid-state diffusion. Although smiths stumbled on the cementation process before the end of the 2nd millennium BC, the essential alloying role of carbon was not realized until the 18th century AD: until then 'steel' was simply the name given to a mysteriously fine iron that a good smith knew how to produce. The smith certainly never guessed that his charcoal fire was adding carbon to the iron to form an alloy; indeed, he was more likely to believe that he was purifying the iron in 'the refiner's fire'.

The property that sets steel apart is its response to heat treatment. Like any other metal, steel can be hardened to some extent by hammering (work-hardening); unlike other common metals, it can be hardened dramatically by quenching (rapid cooling from temperatures above red heat, 725°C). The exact compromise between hardness (which entails brittleness) and toughness best suited to any particuar application can then be achieved by tempering (reducing the hardness by reheating to temperatures between about 200 and 400°C). It should be noted that the presence of carbon is essential to these processes: quenching has little effect on pure iron. The difficulty of producing a fine sword by carburizing, forging, quenching and tempering will be appreciated if it is kept in mind that the smith had no way of judging the carbon content of the metal and had only its colour as a measure of its temperature.

Before the mastery of carburizing and quenching, iron could not be made to equal the performance of a good work-hardened bronze, and its use is likely to reflect only the abundance of its ores and the consequent cheapness of the metal. Carburized and quench-hardened, however, iron becomes immensely superior to bronze. In the Near East a few examples of quench-hardened steel can be dated as early as the end of the 2nd millennium BC, but the difficulties of the process are such that it was not widely used until much later. The process of quenching steel was certainly known to Homer, who used it as a simile for the blinding of Polyphemos

(*Odyssey*, Book 9). It might be added that the techniques required to make good steel cannot be borrowed ready made from the bronze workshop: bronze and copper are hammered cold rather than hot (red-hot bronze may even shatter when struck), they do not form alloys with carbon, and quenching has no effect on them (heating copper or bronze anneals it, i.e. softens it, regardless of whether the subsequent cooling is fast or slow).

As long as it was forged from wrought iron by smiths, steel could be made only in fairly small quantities. The proud names given to swords like Excalibur and Durandal hint that steel-making was not an industry but an art — and perhaps also that even the most expert smith could not make two swords alike. Large-scale steel manufacture depends on the production of cast iron, which in Europe dates only from the 14th century AD. The West did not enter the 'Age of Steel' until the 19th century with the invention of the Bessemer and Siemens processes, which are industrial processes for obtaining liquid metal of any desired carbon content by the decarburization of cast iron. In principle these modern techniques were anticipated by many centuries in China, where steel was made from cast iron as early as the last few centuries BC; *see* IRON AND STEEL (CHINA).

iron and steel (China). The earliest iron artefacts known from China are a few blades forged from meteoritic iron (*see* BEIJING, GAOCHENG, XINCUN). Iron does not seem to have been smelted until about the 6th century BC, at which time wrought iron and cast iron appear more or less simultaneously. The iron artefacts of this stage are mostly agricultural tools made of cast iron. A number of such tools were found in a 4th-century BC tomb at GUWEICUN, and 87 iron moulds for casting iron tools have been unearthed at a foundry site of about the same date at Xinglong in Hebei province. From its beginning Chinese iron technology was dominated by cast iron — so much so that in later centuries whole buildings could be assembled from cast iron parts: a 13-storey cast-iron pagoda erected in Hubei province in AD 1061 still stands. The extensive use of cast iron from the time of the metal's first exploitation no doubt reflects the SHANG and ZHOU bronze-workers' habitual reliance on casting and must have drawn heavily on

their expertise (*see* METAL AND METAL-
WORKING, CHINA).

Steel was made in China within a few
centuries of the first known use of smelted
iron. Some was produced by carburizing solid
wrought iron, the only method known to
Western craftsmen, but the Chinese iron-
worker's familiarity with cast iron led him to
explore other techniques as well. Steel can be
made from cast iron by removing carbon from
it; thus prolonged exposure of hot cast iron to
air, which eliminates some of the carbon by
oxidizing it, can produce a serviceable steel.
The oldest steel objects shown by scientific
examination to have been made by this
method of decarburizing cast iron are arrowheads from the tomb of Liu Sheng (*d.* 113 BC)
at MANCHENG, but earlier use of some such
process is suggested by the long steel swords
(*see* SWORDS, CHINA) found at many late
Eastern Zhou sites (e.g. at YAN Xiadu, where
a multiple burial of soldiers contained iron
scale armour and 51 iron weapons). Swords of
the 1st century AD and later sometimes carry
inscriptions describing them as 'steel of 30
refinings' (or 50, or 100). These have proved
to be decarburized cast iron folded and forged
repeatedly to give a laminated structure with
the stated number of layers. In texts of the
period '100 refinings' denotes the best steel.

A second process for decarburizing cast
iron, today the most common method of
making steel, subjects liquid cast iron to the
oxidizing action of air. A third method is to
soak solid wrought iron in molten cast iron,
allowing it to absorb carbon. All three
methods were used in China centuries earlier
than in Europe, a consequence of China's
much longer experience with cast iron.

In the HAN dynasty (206 BC-220 AD) iron
production was a government monopoly. An
ironworks of this period excavated near
Zhengzhou in Henan province, at the site of
the Han city of Xingyang, was identified as
'Henan Prefectural Ironworks No. 1' by the
discovery of moulds that marked the castings
made in them with this inscription. Hearths of
two very large furnaces were excavated along
with 20-ton salamanders (unmanageable
masses of iron that collected in the bottom of
the furnace and were disposed of by burying
them on the spot when the furnaces were
rebuilt). The furnaces are described in the
excavation report as blast furnaces (i.e. driven
by bellows) but are perhaps more likely to have
been pottery kiln-like reverberatory furnaces,
driven by natural draught, in which reduction
of the iron ore, carburization, and melting took
place in slow succession. Because of the need
for a high flame the fuel was necessarily wood
(in later times bituminous coal) rather than
charcoal.

iron pan. *See* PODZOL.

Isakovo. *See* BAIKAL NEOLITHIC.

Īśānapura [Sanskrit: 'City of Lord Siva'].
Capital of king Īśānavarman of CHENLA,
now Cambodia, (*c*616-*c*635) to whom the
effective conquest of FUNAN is attributed. It
has been identified with some probability with
the group of ruins at Sambor Prei Kuk, north
of Kompong Thom.

Isfahan. The second city of Iran, Isfahan
stands on a fertile plain, watered by the
Zayandeh Rud. An ACHAEMENID palace,
known to Strabo as Gabai, may have existed
here. By the early 3rd century, Isfahan was a
PARTHIAN provincial capital and we presume
that it was occupied throughout the SASSAN-
IAN period; indeed, the city's oldest bridge, the
Pol-i Shahristan, is thought to rest on
Sassanian piers. Isfahan fell to the Muslims in
the 640s. The 9th-century writer Ibn Rosteh
reported that in his day it was a round city, like
Firuzabad and BAGHDAD, 3100 metres in
diameter. Two early Islamic monuments
survive: part of the congregational mosque,
which is encased in the existing Friday Mosque
and was found during restoration in 1971, and
the porch of the Masjid-i Hakim. In 1051,
Isfahan was occupied by the Saljuqs, under
whom it flourished and for a time was their
capital. The principal Saljuq monument is the
Friday Mosque, which contains two 11th-
century dome chambers and was rebuilt in its
present form after a fire in 1121. Following the
Saljuq period, Isfahan declined until the
Safavid ruler, Shah Abbas I (1587-1628)
made it his capital. He embarked on a trem-
endous programme of building and the city's
most famous monuments — including the
Maidan-i Shah (begun in 1598-1606),
Masjid-i Shah (begun in 1612 and finished in
1638), Mosque of Shaikh Lutfullah (1603-
17), the Chehel Sotun pavillion and the Ali
Qapu — were constructed by himself and his
immediate successors, in the 17th century.

Ishango. Located in eastern Zaire on the northwestern shore of Lake Edward, Ishango has a long sequence of occupation and represents the southernmost known manifestation of the so-called African AQUATIC CIVILIZATION. A crude stone industry with rare backed microliths was accompanied by bone harpoon heads: those in the lower levels were barbed on both sides, those in the later horizons on one side only. There was no pottery and, although the site has not been precisely dated, the consensus of opinion is that its occupation was early, falling perhaps between the 9th and the 5th millennia BC. The faunal remains from the site indicate a climate somewhat wetter than that which prevails in the region today.

Isimila. A site in southern Tanzania. The most distinctive tools are hand axes and cleavers of African ACHEULIAN type, but two other assemblage types are found, one with picks and the other with small retouched tools. Isimila may have been occupied about a quarter of a million years ago.

isostasy. A state of balance maintained by the earth's crust. Continental crust behaves like a body 'floating' on the denser underlying layers. Loading of one area may cause downwarping of the crust, which is compensated by uplift elsewhere. Removal of the load causes the crust to readjust to its former state. This phenomenon has occurred during the QUATERNARY, due to the development of large ice-sheets. The enormous weight of ice has caused downwarping of the continental crust beneath. At the ice-sheet margins, there was a compensatory uplift. On melting of the ice-sheets, the crust readjusted by uplift in the areas directly underneath and downwarping at the edges. This process is continuing today, for example in northern Europe. Such uplift and downwarping complicate the detailed study of variation in sea level. Thus it is usual to distinguish between isostatic and EUSTATIC sea level changes.

isotopic fractionation. One of the central assumptions of the RADIOCARBON DATING method is that ^{12}C, ^{13}C and ^{14}C are passed around the carbon cycle at similar rates. The three isotopes are indeed chemically very similar, but slight differences between them may cause them to be taken up at different rates by some plants and animals. This is called isotopic fractionation and may cause inaccuracies in the dating. The effect may be tested in the laboratory by measuring the ratio of ^{12}C to ^{13}C, as well as ^{14}C. Both ^{12}C and ^{13}C are stable isotopes and their ratio should therefore remain constant throughout life and after death. If it has changed from the expected value, then fractionation has occurred. Once the degree of fractionation is known, it can be corrected for mathematically by the laboratory.

isotopic replacement. A source of inaccuracy when determining RADIOCARBON DATES from fossil shells. If the ancient material has been buried in sediments subject to percolation of modern rainwater, there may be some interchange of carbon between the calcium carbonate of the shell and the carbon dioxide dissolved in the rainwater. This introduces a quantity of 'young' carbon, rich in the ^{14}C isotope, and can make the date appear to be younger than it is. *See* HARD WATER EFFECT.

Israelites. Although there exists a wealth of documentary evidence for the Israelites in the Bible, they are difficult to identify in the archaeological record. They appear to have been a Semitic people of nomadic origin and are said to have been led by Moses from Egypt to the Promised Land of Palestine. However, archaeology provides little evidence of their entry into the country and, though we have good evidence of Late Bronze Age occupation in many places, there is nothing in the archaeological record to suggest dramatic or violent change and no way to distinguish clearly traditions that can be regarded as specifically Israelite, as opposed to CANAANITE. It appears that they settled mainly in the hill country and that the Canaanites retained control of the coastal area. By the time of Solomon in the 10th century BC they had conquered both Canaanites and Philistines and established a powerful kingdom with its capital at JERUSALEM. This subsequently split into two separate kingdoms of Israel, which fell to the Assyrians in 722 BC, and Judah, which finally succumbed to the Babylonians in 587 BC.

Istallosko. A cave in the Bükk mountains of northern Hungary that has revealed two layers with early Upper PALAEOLITHIC bone tool types. The stone tool assemblage is poor, but radiocarbon dates indicate that the lower level with split based points is earlier than 40,000 bc, contemporary with the earliest known Upper Palaeolithic. A flute was found in the upper level.

Isturitz [Isturits]. One of the longest sequences of PALAEOLITHIC strata yet known was excavated in the Isturitz cave in the west Pyrenean area of southwest France. Several MOUSTERIAN levels were overlain by a long sequence of Upper Palaeolithic levels. Human remains were found and very numerous art objects have been recovered, mainly in the MAGDALENIAN levels.

Itazuke [Itatsuke]. An early agricultural village site in Fukuoka, Japan. Rice paddies outlined with wooden boards, over 100 grains of charred rice, wooden hoes and semilunar stone harvesting-knives were associated with Final JOMON pottery of Yuusu type. Above them was another set of paddy fields associated with both Yuusu type pottery and the YAYOI pottery of Itazuke type. A number of pits located inside and outside a ditch enclosing an area of 100 by 82 metres are probably for storage. There are also Early Yayoi graves and Middle and Late Yayoi occupation levels. Other artefacts recovered from the site include spindle whorls and bronze weapons.

Itza. *See* CHICHEN ITZA, COZUMEL, MAYA-PAN.

Ivolga. A settlement site in southern Siberia belonging to the Hsiung-nu state of the last few centuries BC and first few centuries AD. The settlement covered *c*7 hectares and was defended by four lines of walls and ditches, showing clear evidence of Chinese influence. The community seems to have been based on millet farming.

ivory. A material derived from a greatly enlarged tooth, or tusk, often belonging originally to an ELEPHANT, but sometimes from other animals, such as walrus or narwhal. It has been used since the Upper PALAEO-LITHIC for tools, artwork and other artefacts.

Iwajuku. An archaeological site in Japan, about 90 km north of Tokyo. The 1949 excavation by Meiji University, following the site's discovery by an amateur a few years earlier, provided the first convincing evidence that the Japanese islands were occupied by man during Palaeolithic times. Among the stone tools recovered from the oldest layer of the site were three first described as hand axes. However, they are partially polished on the edges, and radiocarbon and FISSION TRACK DATING suggest that they are about 20,000 years old.

Iwo Eleru. A rock shelter in the forest zone of southwestern Nigeria which has yielded the longest dated sequence of microlithic industries yet investigated in West Africa. Occupation was established by the 10th millennium bc and the chipped stone industry continued for as long as 8000 years with only minor discernible changes. From the lowest horizon a human burial, described as showing negroid physical features, was recovered. In about the mid-4th millennium ground stone artefacts and pottery came into use. It is tempting to suggest that some forms of food production may have been practised by this time, but the evidence for this is restricted to the appearance of microliths bearing edge-gloss or 'sickle sheen' such as may be caused through use to harvest grasses. Further research is needed to illustrate the beginnings of food production in the West African forests, especially the cultivation of yams and other non-cereal crops.

Ix Chel. *See* COZUMEL.

Izapa. Located on the Pacific coastal plain in southern Chiapas, Mexico, the site was first occupied in 1500 bc, possibly by OLMEC-associated groups. Its importance as a major centre, however, came in the Late PRE-CLASSIC when most of its 80 temple-pyramids, courts and plazas were built. It is best known for its unique style of stone carving, which is a chronological as well as cultural link between Olmec and MAYA styles. Olmec beginnings are evident in such designs as the St Andrew's Cross, jaguar motifs, and thick-lipped gods. A stele carved in the Izapan style with the earliest Maya LONG COUNT date has been found at El Baul in Guatamala. The centre's economic base may well have been CACAO, which features in Izapan iconography and was certainly a crop of considerable importance by CLASSIC times.

Izvoare. A multi-level open settlement site of the Late Neolithic CUCUTENI culture, located near Piatră Neamt, in the upper Seret basin, Moldavia, Rumania. Excavated by R. Vulpe, the settlement has four main occupation phases: I_1 a Pre-Cucuteni II level with monochrome and incised wares: I_2 a Pre-Cucuteni III level with bichrome painted wares; II_1 a Cucuteni A1 phase with bichrome painted wares and II_2 a Cucuteni A2 level with trichrome painted wares. Good preservation of complete Cucuteni house plans is found in the later levels.

J

Jabrud. Several rock shelters at Jabrud in the Anti-Lebanon hills of Syria were excavated in the 1930s and seem to provide a long lower, middle and upper PALAEOLITHIC sequence of over 30 layers. The precise significance of the various suggested cultures (Jabrudian, Pre-AURIGNACIAN, NEBEKIAN etc) is far from agreed, and their exact dating is also in doubt.

jade. A general term for a precious stone from which jewellery and other decorative work may be made. The word jade is today applied to two minerals, nephrite and jadeite, which often look similar: greenish in colour, hard and translucent. Although sometimes found in prehistoric Europe and other areas, the two regions where the working of jade was most highly developed are China and Mesoamerica.

China. Only nephrite was worked in China before the 18th century AD; Chinese texts however refer to any similar hardstone worked by the same techniques as *yu* 'jade'. Because of its hardness, 6.5 on the Mohs scale, nephrite can be cut, shaped and polished only with abrasives. This quintessentially Neolithic technology was already well developed in China in the 4th millennium BC; the slow but steady improvement of technique that can be seen in SHANG and ZHOU jades led eventually to an easy mastery of three-dimensional sculpture in the HAN period. At that time the major source of Chinese nephrite was Turkestan; textual evidence to identify the sources exploited in earlier periods is lacking.

At least as early as the 4th millennium BC polished jades were typical mortuary offerings in graves of the east-coast Neolithic cultures (*see* LONGSHAN, sense 2), making their first appearance at sites like QINGLIAN'GANG and BEIYINYANGYING. Some of these mortuary jades are ornaments, others are replicas of tools such as axes or harvesting knives; a few common shapes (BI, ZONG) lack obvious prototypes. The jade shapes copied from tools often depart considerably from the proportions of their functional prototypes, their cutting edges are often unsharpened, and signs of wear are usually absent; it is no doubt safe to assume that objects made in this valuable material, which was probably imported over long distances, served ritual and mortuary purposes above all. The same is evidently true of the refined versions of the Neolithic shapes executed by Bronze Age Shang craftsmen, who added to the repertoire a few shapes copying metal objects (*see* GE). In the Western Zhou period, however, inscriptions on bronze RITUAL VESSELS mention jades as gifts bestowed by the king in ceremonies of investiture, showing that these cult objects had been diverted to play a role in feudal transactions, a shift of function paralleled by the ritual vessels themselves. Jades of the Eastern Zhou period, surpassingly fine in design, were often used for personal adornment, but even at this late stage the mortuary associations of jade remained strong. Han texts recommend powered jade as an elixir of immortality, and jade burial suits like those found at MANCHENG were believed to prevent decomposition.

The Americas. A variety of materials collectively described as jade were coveted for luxury items by groups in Mesoamerica and the American Southwest. Shades of blue and green were especially favoured; its symbolic meaning was water, and hence the source of life itself. Probably the most renowned workers of jade were the OLMEC, but it was a valued commodity in the trade networks of all the major cultures of Mesoamerica (the MAYA, TEOTIHUACAN, TOLTEC, AZTECS etc). A comparative scarcity of raw material sources meant an increasing premium on the material with the passing of time, and early pieces were frequently reworked or maintained as heirlooms. Some scholars suggest that indigenous sources were so few that they could not possibly have met demand; they argue for trans-Pacific contact, with the ultimate origin of some jade being China.

jadeite. A rare mineral, one of two distinct minerals which may be described as JADE. Much of the jadeite prized as a precious stone is green, but the mineral varies widely in colour. One form of jadeite which varies from green to black in colour is sometimes called chloromelanite. Sources of jadeite are known in Burma, Mexico and California. Many prehistoric artefacts in Europe are made from jadeite, but no suitable European sources are known today.

Jain. *See* VAISALI.

Jaina. A Late CLASSIC MAYA necropolis located on a tidal island 50 km north of Campeche in the Gulf of Mexico, Jaina is famous for its high-quality portrait figurines. Its two CEREMONIAL CENTRES at Zayosal and El Zacpool, built of uncut stone and stucco, are clearly of minor importance. The finest of the ceramic grave-offerings are solid and hand-modelled, but even the hollow, mould-made ones are usually embellished by hand. Burials are commonly flexed, wrapped, and sprinkled with cinnabar; a jade bead was commonly put in the mouth to serve as currency in the next world. Some cremations and urn burials (especially for children) also occur.

Jam. A remote valley of the Hari Rud in western Afghanistan, where a spectacular tower, inscribed with the name of the Ghorid ruler Ghiyath al-Din Muhammad b. Sam (1153-1203) was discovered in 1957. The tower is 65 metres high and built of brick. It has an octagonal base and four cylindrical tiers, each narrower and shorter than the one below. The fourth tier is a circular arcade supporting a dome. At the base of the second, third and fourth tiers were corbelled balconies. The interior contains a double spiral staircase. The exterior is covered with geometric, vegetal and epigraphic ornament in brick, some of which is glazed; it includes the complete text of Sura 19 of the Qu'ran. Although usually identified as a minaret (one of the tallest in existence), some scholars regard it as a victory tower. Other sites in the area, which include a Jewish cemetery with tombstones dated between 1149 and 1215, have been taken to belong to the 'lost' Ghorid capital, Firuzkuh, but the identification is uncertain.

Jamestown. The first successful British settlement in America, Jamestown was founded in 1607 by 105 settlers and served for a time as the capital of Virginia. James Fort, as it was first called, was built 15 miles inland from the Chesapeke Bay, on a swampy island in the James River on the site of previous native occupation. A systematic excavation of the town was begun in 1934 and continued intermittently until 1956. Altogether 10 of the total 25 hectares have been studied, 140 structures recorded, and a huge inventory of 17th-century artefacts amassed.

The earliest settlers subsisted by fishing, trade with natives and farming of both local (e.g. maize, squash, pumpkin) and imported staples. Houses from that time were of wattle and daub with thatched roofs, giving way later to structures of locally made brick. Pottery and glassmaking were other local industries. In 1699 WILLIAMSBURG became the capital of the colony, after which Jamestown went into decline and was ultimately abandoned.

Jarlshof. A coastal settlement on the island of Shetland, and one of the richest and most complex archaeological sites in Britain. Stone buildings date to the Neolithic, Bronze Age and Iron Age periods and show continuous occupation throughout the Dark Ages. During the 9th century Jarlshof was settled by a small group of Norse farmers.

Excavations carried out in the 1930s by Gordon CHILDE and continued in the 1950s revealed a complex of levels and many building phases overlying one another. It seems that some time in the 3rd and 4th century several of the Iron Age BROCHS and their courtyards were transformed into Celtic aisled WHEEL-HOUSES accompanied by circular huts. In the 9th century these abandoned Celtic buildings were succeeded by the Norse settlement. Jarlshof is the most distinctive and convincing VIKING village in Britain. The first farmhouse was a stone bow-shaped LONG HOUSE with two rooms including a kitchen with an oven and rectangular hearth. Slightly later another compartment was attached to the main dwelling-house to serve as a byre, while other farmhouses continued to be built in the same tradition. The archaeologists also found evidence of typical Viking industries such as soapstone, bone and metal working. Some of the most interesting artefacts recovered from the Norse levels are a series of slates incised with drawings of animals and interesting abstract decorations.

Jarmo. The type site of the Jarmoan culture, situated in the Zagros mountains in Iraqi Kurdistan. The settlement, of the ACERAMIC NEOLITHIC, has a range of radiocarbon dates, of which the earliest is c6500 bc, and has produced important evidence for early farming in this area. The population cultivated barley, emmer and einkorn wheats and pulses and kept domesticated goats and, at a slightly later date, pigs as well. Hunting of small game and gathering of snails, nuts, fruit and wild grain were also important. Domesticated dogs were kept. Up to 150 people lived in about 25 rectangular houses made of mud-brick or pisé. Clay ovens and grain pits were found and artefacts included flint and obsidian chipped stone tools, stone bowls, clay figurines and — in the upper levels from c5950 bc — also pottery.

Jarrow. The twin monasteries of Monkwearmouth and Jarrow in Co. Durham are two of the most interesting Middle Saxon sites in England. The historian BEDE lived and worked at Jarrow and tells us most about its history. Jarrow was founded on the banks of the River Tyne by Bishop Benedict Biscop a few years after Monkwearmouth and consecrated in 681, according to the dedication stone inside the nave. Both monasteries suffered seriously during the Viking raids of the 9th century and never really recovered. Recent excavations at both sites have proved of great importance. At Jarrow, most of the work was concentrated on St Paul's Church and the adjoining cloister and cemetery, but evidence was also found for glass-making and other crafts. The earliest coloured window glass known in Europe comes from these excavations, and bears out Bede's statement that Benedict Biscop brought glaziers from Gaul to work on his churches.

Jászdózsa. An earlier Bronze Age TELL settlement near Szolnok, in the Tisza valley of eastern Hungary. Thick occupation layers of the HATVAN and FÜZESABONY groups have been found, with well-preserved domestic architecture. Complete rectangular Hatvan house plans have internal divisions with several hearths, whilst the later Füzesabony structures are smaller, with more varied internal fittings.

Jaulian. See TAXILA.

Java. *Prehistory*. A major island of INDONESIA, best known for its remains of HOMO ERECTUS (2,000,000 BC to c300,000 BC). Neolithic and Bronze Age cultures are known but still poorly understood. See GUA LAWA, MEGANTHROPUS, MOJOKERTO, NGANDONG, PACITANIAN, SAMBUNGMACAN, SANGIRAN, SOLO, TRINIL.

Classical. From the 5th century AD a number of INDIANIZED kingdoms, both Hinduist and Buddhist, developed in Java. Their power eventually extended over large parts of the Indonesian archipelago and at times even to the mainland of South East Asia. The Buddhist ŚAILENDRA dynasty, the builders of the BOROBUDUR, became in the late 8th century the suzerain of CAMBODIA, while the predominantly Hindu kingdoms of MATARĀM and KADIRI which followed the Śailendras in Java looked to the east, to BALI. The kingdom of Kadiri was succeeded in 1222 by that of SINGHASĀRI, which completed the conquest of Bali and also reached westward, establishing Javanese suzerainty over parts of Sumatra and the Malay Peninsula. It came to an end at the hands of the Mongol expedition in 1293, but its successor state MAJAPAHIT expanded Javanese power even further in all directions, uniting most of the archipelago under one empire for the first time. When Islam advanced in Java in the 15th and 16th centuries, Hindu-Javanese culture took refuge in Bali, where it is preserved to this day. See also BORNEO, CELEBES, CHENLA, LORO, JONGGRANG, PRAMBANAN, SANJAYA, ŚRĪVIJAYA, SUMATRA, YĀVADVĪPA.

Java man. A convenient term for the fossil men, now attributed to HOMO ERECTUS, from various localities in east and central Java, dating from c2 to 0.5 million years ago, or the early to middle PLEISTOCENE. See SANGIRAN, MOJOKERTO, TRINIL.

Jayamachay. See AYACUCHO.

Jebel et Tomat. A settlement site between the Blue and the White Nile near Sennar in the central Sudan. Small-scale excavations have indicated that sorghum was under cultivation by the site's inhabitants by the 3rd century ad. Covering some five hectares, the site was occupied through the first five centuries of the Christian era by mixed-farming people who supplemented their rare iron tools by continuing the production of chipped stone artefacts. It is possible that the pottery shows a late continuation of the tradition represented at ESH SHAHEINAB.

Jebel Ighoud. A site in northern Morocco where LEVALLOISO-MOUSTERIAN artefacts were recovered in association with fossil human remains of NEANDERTHAL type.

Jebel Moya. Excavated in the early years of the 20th century, Jebel Moya lies in the Blue Nile province of the Sudan, some 60 km east of JEBEL ET TOMAT. Before the excavation of the latter site, the enormous amount of material recovered frm Jebel Moya was difficult to interpret. Both are now seen as settlements broadly contemporary with MEROE, but lying beyond the limit of direct contact with more northerly civilizations.

Jebel Sahaba. *See* QADAN.

Jebel Uweinat. A complex of rocky hills in the eastern Sahara, close to the modern borders of Egypt, Libya and Sudan. Many rock shelters show signs of prehistoric occupation, including abundant rock art. The latter is of particular interest in view of representations of various creatures, including giraffe and ostrich, which are tethered. It is possible to speculate that this feature may be connected with the experimentation in animal control (and, perhaps, proto-domestication) that is attested in Egypt during Old Kingdom times.

Jefferson, Thomas (1743-1826). As well as his many other achievements, the third President of the USA has a claim to being one of the world's first scientific excavators. In 1784 he excavated a prehistoric burial mound on his own land in Virginia. He noted that the burials occurred in a number of different levels and concluded that the process of placing bodies on the ground and then covering them with earth, repeated many times, had produced the four-metre-high mound. His careful observation of the position of the skeletons and the different deposits in the mound anticipated WORSAAE's work in Denmark by half a century and the wider adoption of stratigraphical excavation methods by twice that long.

Jellinge. A site in East Jutland which seems to be the remains of a 10th-century royal palace and burial ground of some importance. Two large barrows have been excavated; one contained a wooden burial chamber and the other nothing. In the cemetery area stand fifty bauta stones, which are part of a ship monument, while in the churchyard itself are two exceptionally fine rune stones outlining the exploits and Christian conversion of the VIKING kings Gorm the Old and Harald Bluetooth. One of the stones depicts the oldest crucifixion scene in Denmark and on the other is a magnificent lion, which was undoubtedly carved by an Englishman — this carving is the inspiration of the term JELLINGE STYLE.

Jellinge style. An art form that takes its name from the Viking site at JELLINGE. Much Anglo-Saxon and Scandinavian art from the 9th century until the mid-11th century is characterized by animal ornament and zoomorphic motifs, which are usually disjointed, stylized and entirely abstract. This kind of decoration was most often applied to jewellery, sculptured crosses and sculptured stones. The complexities of the different styles and their chronologies continues to be the subject of scholarly debate. One such style, known as the Jellinge style, seems to have been developed by Anglo-Scandinavian craftsmen and then reintroduced and perfected in Scandinavia during the 10th century.

Jemdet Nasr [Jamdat Nasr]. Site between Baghdad and Babylon in southern Iraq which has given its name both to a painted ware characterized by red and black designs on a buff ground, and to the period when this pottery was in use. This period falls between the URUK phase and the EARLY DYNASTIC PERIOD and is usually dated to the late 4th millennium BC (*see* Tables 2 and 3, pages 320-21). The period is characterized by increasing populations, the development of more extensive irrigation systems, towns dominated by temples, and the increased use of writing and cylinder seals; increasing trade and more specialization of craft practice are also features of this period. In all these ways the Jemdet Nasr phase represents the direct predecessor of the full SUMERIAN civilization of the Early Dynastic period.

Jenne. A major trading city on the southern margin of the inland Niger delta in southern Mali, the site is traditionally stated to have been established in the 8th century. For much of the next thousand years it occupied an important position in local and trans-Saharan trade. Its antecedents may be traced back in the archaeological record of nearby Jenne-jeno to about the 3rd century bc. By late in the 1st millennium ad Jenne-jeno had grown into a major urban centre some 30 to 40 hectares in extent. Trade with areas beyond the delta is attested throughout its occupation, metal being one of the main commodities involved. The city appears to have been the centre of a fertile and prosperous region. Cultivation of indigenous African rice is attested from the beginning of the Christian era. A series of elaborate anthropomorphic clay statuettes dates, at least in part, from the early centuries of the 2nd millennium ad.

Jericho. Known today as Tell es-Sultan, Jericho lies in an oasis in the Jordan Valley north of the Dead Sea, on a main east-west route. Its long stratigraphy documents almost continuous occupation from before 9000 bc to c1580 BC. At the base of the tell was a NATUF-IAN deposit, associated with a rectangular platform surrounded by stone walls, interpreted by the excavator, Kathleen KENYON, as a shrine. The Natufian deposit was four metres thick in places, but has provided little evidence of other structural remains or of subsistence economy. It was succeeded by PRE-POTTERY NEOLITHIC A levels, with radiocarbon dates in the range 8350-7370 bc. At this stage the settlement covered a surprisingly large four hectares and was surrounded by a stone wall and a ditch, reinforced by at least one massive stone tower. The houses of this period were round and built of mud-brick. The population was already growing emmer wheat, barley and pulses, while the meat portion of the diet was supplied in the main by gazelle, supplemented by wild cattle, boar and goat. It is possible that some of these animals were being herded, although the evidence is exiguous. In the succeeding PRE-POTTERY NEOLITHIC B levels (with radiocarbon dates 7220-5850 bc), rectangular houses with plastered floors and walls were built; an increased range of cultivated plants was exploited and it is possible that domesticated sheep were kept. Evidence of an ancestor cult is present in the form of skulls with facial features restored in plaster and, in some cases, eyes set with cowrie or other shells.

A break in occupation followed the PPNB levels, but there is evidence of some reoccupation in later Neolithic and Chalcolithic times. From the late 4th millennium BC there was a walled town on the site which was continuously occupied until c1580 BC when the settlement, with a sloping plastered ramp of HYKSOS type, was destroyed by the Egyptians. It was probably reoccupied c1400 BC, to be captured by the ISRAELITES under Joshua, but erosion has removed almost all traces of occupation of this period.

Jersey Bluff. *See* KOSTER.

Jerusalem. City sited on the Judaean hills, occupied for more than 4000 years and now the capital of Israel. Many excavations have taken place since the 1860s, but because of the long history of destruction and rebuilding on the site, it has been difficult to reconstruct the development of the city. Sporadic traces of 4th- and 3rd-millennium BC occupation occur, but the first substantial settlement with a town wall belongs to the 2nd millennium BC. The town of this period was on the spur of Ophel, in the southeastern part of the city, and when David captured Jerusalem c1000 BC he retained the existing defences. Solomon built his temple and palace on the higher ridge to the north. In the 8th-7th centuries part of the western ridge was also incorporated in the town walls, though the southeast part of this ridge was not included until the time of Herod Agrippa (AD 40-44), in a second phase of growth after the destruction by the Babylonians in 587 BC and later resettlement. Few early buildings survive; one exception is the rock-cut water tunnel constructed by Hezekiah in the late 8th century BC. Some remains of the Herodian and Roman period also survive.

Jerusalem is venerated not only by Jews and Christians, but also by Muslims, who believe it to be the place where Muhammad began his night journey to heaven. The precise spot is said to be an outcrop of rock in the Haram ash-Sharif, the platform of the Jewish Temple. Between c685 and 691-2, the caliph Abd al-Malik enclosed the outcrop in a shrine, the Dome of the Rock. This is the earliest Islamic building to survive intact and consists of a domed circular chamber, 20.5 metres across, surrounded by an octagonal ambulatory. It is richly decorated with marble, mosaics and beaten metal, which encases the wooden beams. At one corner of the platform stands the Aqsa Mosque which, despite rebuilding in the Crusader and Mameluk periods, contains extensive remains of the mosque of az-Zahir, the Fatimid caliph, who reconstructed it after an earthquake in 1035. The Old City of Jerusalem contains an extraordinary large number of Mameluk buildings: houses, hospitals, bazaars etc.

jet. A hard, black, dense form of coal, which may be cut, polished and used in decorative work. A well-known British source of jet is at Whitby in Yorkshire.

Jhukar. A site in Sind province, Pakistan, which has given its name to a prehistoric culture of the 2nd millenium BC. At the type site and at AMRI and CHANHU-DARO, levels of the Jhukar culture succeed those of the HARAPPAN CIVILIZATION; indeed, some authorities regard Jhukar as a late version of the Harappan, in a phase when urban life had declined or disappeared.

ji [*chi*]. *See* GE.

jia [*chia*]. *See* RITUAL VESSELS (CHINA), LI.

Jiagezhuang [Chia-ko-chuang]. *See* TANG-SHAN.

jian [*chien*]. *See* RITUAL VESSELS (CHINA).

Jiangling [Chiang-ling]. A city in Hubei province on the north bank of the Yangzi River, China. Scattered Western ZHOU finds have been made in the Jiangling district but far more important are extensive Eastern Zhou and HAN remains associated with the CHU culture. The walled city of Ji'nan just outside present-day Jiangling is believed to be the site of Ying, the principal Chu capital from 689 BC until its capture by QIN in 278 BC, when the Chu court removed eastward to settle finally at SHOU XIAN in Anhui. Over 800 Chu burials ranging in date from the 8th to the 2nd century BC were excavated in the Jiangling district between 1961 and 1982, an abundance suggesting that Jiangling was a more important Chu centre, by comparison for instance with CHANGSHA, than was previously supposed.

Especially notable are two 4th-century tombs excavated at Wangshan in 1965, which contained painted LACQUERS of exceptional interest. A number of tombs of the early Han period (2nd century BC) have been found since 1973 at Fenghuangshan within the walls of Ji'nan; the tomb furnishings include lacquers and inscribed bamboo slips.

Jiangzhai [Chiang-chai]. *See* BANPO.

jiao [*chiao, chio*]. *See* RITUAL VESSELS (CHINA).

Jih-nan. The southernmost commandery of the HAN Chinese empire, situated in the central part of present Vietnam. It was in its southernmost sub-prefecture, that of Hsiang-lin, corresponding roughly to the southern part of the present Vietnamese province of Thu'a-thiên, that a native official founded in 192 the independent kingdom of LIN-YI, later to be known by the name of CHAMPA.

Ji'nan [Chi-nan]. *See* JIANGLING.

Jincun [Chin-ts'un]. A village near LUOYANG in Henan province, China, where rich tombs robbed around 1930 yielded 5th-2nd century BC carved JADES and inlaid bronze RITUAL VESSELS, many of which are now in Western collections. Excavations in the Luoyang area since 1930 have unearthed little that is comparable in style or quality to the objects said to come from the Jincun tombs. The name Jincun is often applied to a style of Eastern Zhou bronze décor, also called the inlay style, characterized by inlays of gold, silver, malachite, turquoise, jade and glass.

Jodhpura. *See* OCHRE-COLOURED POTTERY.

Jomon. A Japanese word for 'cord mark', used to describe all pre-YAYOI pottery; the term is also used to describe a period from about 10,000 BC to 300 BC and all the archaeological remains of this period.

There are over 10,000 Jomon sites, and hundreds of pottery types have been defined. These are arranged into regional sequences, correlated into a nation-wide ceramic chronology. It is customarily divided into five segments: Initial (10,000-5000 BC), Early (5000-3500 BC), Middle (3500-2500 BC), Late (2500-1000 BC) and Final (1000-300

BC). The dates are compromises of RADIO-CARBON, FISSION TRACK and OBSIDIAN HYDRATION DATES.

The oldest pottery is not cord-marked, but has appliqué designs of dots or lines below the rim of a plain bowl. Among the dated sites for this phase are FUKUI, KAMIKUROIWA and SEMPUKUJI. Cord-marking appeared about a thousand years later, and about 7500 BC rolling a cord-wrapped or notched stick over the wet surface before firing became a widely used practice. As seen at NATSUSHIMA, there is a clear evidence also for the use of bows and arrows, fishing and shellfish collecting. Some authors reserve the use of the word Jomon for the post-7500 BC remains, preferring to call the earlier ones Mesolithic or Proto-Jomon.

Initial Jomon pots are conical, medium-sized, and simply decorated. They seem to have been used for cooking. Early Jomon saw the increase in vessel shapes, from large storage jars to shallow serving bowls. Decorative designs also varied regionally, and are often very complex, combining cord-marking, incising, punctating and moulding. Pit houses, common throughout the Jomon Period, became quite substantial and were made in large clusters during Early and Middle Jomon. IDOJIRI is a good example of substantial clusters of house remains, with elaborate pottery, personal ornaments and ritual objects. These clusters disappeared from inland by Late and Final Jomon, when population centres shifted to coastal regions. Spectacular developments in pottery, figurines and fishing harpoons occurred then along the Pacific coast of north and central Honshu. The earlier regional diversity of ceramic styles is replaced by a few widely distributed styles, such as the KAMEGAOKA style of the Final Jomon.

Throughout the Jomon Period, sites are not as numerous in southwestern Japan, and pottery is less ornate than in the northeast. The pottery made during the last few centuries of the Jomon Period in Southwestern Japan, particularly in northern Kyushu, is quite similar to the Early Yayoi pottery.

The northeast-southwest contrast seems to be reflected in Jomon physique, although samples of skeletal remains large enough to draw a meaningful conclusion are not numerous. There is also a trend towards large and robust physique from a shorter and gracile population in earlier times.

The Jomon Period began when the deciduous broad-leaf forest was expanding in Japan, and 80 per cent of Jomon sites are located in the area where this environment, rich in edible nuts and game, prevailed in the past. These resources, with fish, shellfish, and sea mammals, were clearly important to Jomon people. In addition, there is increasing evidence that some plants were cultivated. Among them are *Echnochloa* and *Perilla* species. Bottle gourds and mung beans, recovered at TORIHAMA and other sites, are likely to have been brought in as cultigens. Buckwheat and rice are reported as well from Late and Final Jomon sites.

The Jomon Period ended when wet-rice cultivation became fully established. While this was spreading towards the northeast, Jomon cultures continued in northern Honshu and Hokkaido. On the latter island, a way of life essentially similar to Jomon continued as 'Epi-Jomon' until the 8th century.

Jordanova [Jordanów]. A settlement and cemetery site in Lower Silesia, southern Poland, which has given its name to a regional group of the Late Neolithic LENGYEL culture. The settlement had timber houses which were trapezoidal in plan. Cemeteries contain grave goods which include many ornaments and some tools of copper, and objects of Baltic amber. Pottery was incised or painted.

Jorwe. A CHALCOLITHIC site in southern India, consisting of several mounds, but representing a single period of occupation, related to the MALWA complex further north. Metal was in use, but a stone industry based on blades, some microlithic, also occurred. Typical Jorwe pottery is a hard-fired wheel-made red ware, painted in black.

Judeidah. A TELL site in the AMUQ plain of northern Syria. Excavations by the Oriental Institute of Chicago University in the 1930s on this and other sites on the plain established the basic prehistoric sequence for the area..

Judeirjo-Daro. A town of the HARAPPAN CIVILIZATION in Kachi province, Pakistan. The site has not been excavated, but seems to be very large: it occupies *c*25 hectares, which makes it the third largest settlement of this civilization, after MOHENJO-DARO and HARAPPA. Surface investigation suggests that both pre-Harappan and mature Harappan phases are represented on the site.

jue [*chüeh*]. *See* RITUAL VESSELS (CHINA).

Juodkrantė. An industrial site of the Baltic Early Bronze Age, located on the shores of the Baltic in western Lithuania and dated to the mid-2nd millennium bc. An amber-processing workshop was found there in the 19th century, with half-finished pendants and beads, presumably produced for the Bronze Age amber trade to central and southern Europe.

Jutes. The Germanic tribe who inhabited the southern part of the Jutland peninsula in the early centuries AD. According to BEDE, they settled in Kent, Hampshire and the Isle of Wight after the 5th-century invasions of Britain. Unfortunately, the Jutes have proved particularly difficult to trace in the archaeological record. *See* ANGLO-SAXON.

Juxtlahuaca Caves. Located in the hills of Guerrero, Mexico, to the east of Chilpancingo, these caves contain the earliest parietal painting in the New World. Some 1.2 km in from the cave entrance are chambers containing polychrome paintings which because of certain motifs (notably the jaguar and the St Andrew's Cross) have been identified as OLMEC art. Dated to c900-700 BC on the basis of stylistic similarities to the art of LA VENTA, these are the only example of polychrome painting in Olmec tradition. Similar cave paintings have been found in nearby Oxtotitlan.

K

Kabah. *See* PUUC.

Kabambian. An Iron Age industry of the Upemba depression, southeastern Zaire, best known from the excavation of numerous graves, notably at SANGA. The industry appears to have been a direct descendant of the earlier KISALIAN and is dated between the 14th and 16th centuries ad. It is marked by an abundance of copper cross-shaped ingots, of standarized weights, which may have served as a medium of exchange.

Kadero. This important site, located on the edge of the old Nile flood-plain northeast of Khartoum, has recently thrown much new light on the early development of food-production in the central Sudan, previously known only from ESH SHAHEINAB. Kadero was an extensive village, covering some four hectares, inhabited during the second half of the 4th millennium bc. The material culture of the site's inhabitants was comparable with that of Esh Shaheinab, but fishing equipment was poorly represented. Herding was of major importance at Kadero, with domestic species — principally cattle, but with some sheep and goats — accounting for about 90 per cent of the animal bones recovered. There were large numbers of grindstones, and grain impressions on the pottery indicate the presence of wild panicum together with possibly cultivated sorghum and finger millet. Kadero must be regarded as a base settlement of a population which may have occupied several scattered sites, in diverse environments, in a seasonal cycle.

Kadesh [modern Tell Nebi Mend]. Ancient Kadesh is a TELL site on the River Orontes, southwest of Homs in Syria. Occupied from the 3rd millennium BC, it is best known as the site of a battle between the Egyptians under RAMESES II and the HITTITES in 1286 BC. The outcome seems to have been inconclusive; the Egyptians claimed victory but, if anything, the battle may have favoured the Hittites and facilitated peace between the two nations.

Kadiri [Kediri]. The western part of the kingdom of Airlanga of JAVA (1016-1149), which he divided before his death, the eastern part being Janggala. Originally called Panjalu, it became better known by the name of Kadiri (with its capital Daha being the present Kediri) and soon absorbed Janggala, thus becoming in fact the successor to the kingdom of Airlanga. The kingdom of Kadiri lasted until 1222, when it was succeeded by that of TUMAPEL, later known by the name of its capital SINGHÂSARI.

Kafiavana. An important rock shelter in the NEW GUINEA Highlands, with a sequence that commences with edge-ground axes and flake tools of early Australian type (*c*10,000 bc), and then documents trade in coastal shells (from *c*8000 bc) and the appearance of pigs (by 3500-4000 bc). Pigs are not native to New Guinea and were introduced from Indonesia.

Kairouan. *See* QAIRAWAN.

Kakanj. The type site for a Middle Neolithic regional group in north-central Bosnia, located near Visoko in the Bosna Valley, Yugoslavia. Dated *c*4700-4300 bc, the Kakanj culture is typified by monochrome fine wares and decorative elements with affinities in the coastal DANILO culture. The type site comprises working pits, with flint production areas and a rich bone-working assemblage.

Kalambo Falls. The small lake basin above this spectacular waterfall near the southern end of Lake Tanganyika on the Zambia/Tanzania border has preserved a long sequence of archaeological deposits extending from the ACHEULIAN to the Iron Age. The Acheulian horizons so far investigated belong to a relatively late phase of that complex, although it remains possible that significantly earlier material remains inaccessible below the modern water level. The age of the Kalambo

Acheulian deposits is beyond the effective limit of RADIOCARBON DATING (*c*60,000 bc), and may be as great as 190,000 years. Several undisturbed occupation horizons have been investigated: the hand axes, cleavers and other stone artefacts show a consistently high standard of workmanship. Bone was not preserved on these sites, but several wooden objects have survived, some of which show signs of burning and/or intentional shaping. Grass-filled hollows probably represent sleeping-places, and an arc of stones may be the remains of a windbreak or shelter. Pollen preserved in the deposits indicates that the local late Acheulian climate was cooler and wetter than that of today.

The Acheulian at Kalambo was followed by a long series of industries of SANGOAN type. These are associated with radiocarbon dates of between 50,000 and 40,000 bc, but it seems likely that their true age is significantly greater — perhaps around 100,000 to 80,000 years. Mixed rubble deposits overlying the Sangoan horizons contain LUPEMBAN artefacts of *c*30,000 bc, associated with pollens indicating a vegetation closely similar to that of the present. Later, final 'Middle Stone Age' material likewise occurs only in a disturbed context. A fine microlithic industry in the upper levels is dated to the 3rd millennium bc. Early Iron Age occupation of the Kalambo basin appears to have been established by the 4th century ad and to have continued through much of the 1st millennium.

Kalanay. A burial cave on Masbate Island in the central PHILIPPINES, which has produced incised and impressed pottery of a type found widely in Island Southeast Asia and South VIETNAM from *c*500 BC to AD 1000. Kalanay is one of the type sites for Solheim's 'SA-HUYNH-Kalanay' pottery complex. Sa-huynh is in South Vietnam, and this complex is an expression of trade and contact over wide areas during the Early Metal Period in Island Southeast Asia.

Kalemba. A large rock shelter in eastern Zambia close to the borders of Malawi and Mozambique. The lowest levels have not yet been investigated, but a prepared-core industry akin to that of BAMBATA was being produced by *c*36,000 bc. A long series of transitional industries led to the appearance of a true backed microlith assemblage of NACHI-

KUFAN I type by 20,000 bc. The shift to a microlithic industry was accompanied by a change in faunal remains indicating a new preference for hunting small solitary creatures in place of the larger gregarious ungulates which had been favoured in earlier times. Later microlithic occurrences were of the type best known from nearby MAKWE. Kalemba also contains a large series of rock paintings, most of which are believed to be of later Iron Age date.

Kalibangan. A town of the HARAPPAN CIVILIZATION on the Ghaggar River in Rajasthan, India. The main occupation is of mature Harappan type, but the lower levels have yielded pre-Harappan material. In this early phase, beginning *c*2250 bc (2900 BC), the site covered *c*4.5 hectares, and was already fortified and urban or proto-urban in character. An intact ploughed field of this phase has been discovered, indicating that the plough was already in use before the main Harappan period. In the Harappan period, *c*1950-1600 bc (*c*2400-2000 BC) the site consisted of a citadel and a lower town, both defended, and laid out, in the normal Indus Valley pattern, with the citadel to the west of the main town. The lower town was *c*10 hectares in size, the citadel *c*1.5 hectares, to which was later added a residential annexe of approximately the same size, also defended. The lower town was laid out on a grid plan like other Harappan towns.

Kalina Point. *See* GOMBE POINT.

Kalomo. The name of this small township in southern Zambia has been given to the Iron Age industry which flourished on the surrounding plateau and in the adjacent section of the Zambezi Valley from about the 9th to the 11th century ad. The industry probably developed from an Early Iron Age ancestor in the valley and spread to the plateau. Its practitioners were simple subsistence farmers, herding cattle and small stock, cultivating a variety of food crops, making pottery and a few metal tools, and occupying villages beside river valleys or on possibly artificially built mounds.

Kalumpang. *See* SULAWESI.

Kalundu A deep stratified mound site near Kalomo in southern Zambia where KALOMO industry levels overlie those attributed to a distinctive local Early Iron Age variant to which Kalundu has given its name.

Kamakura. *See* MIRRORS (JAPAN).

Kamares Cave. Cave site on Mount Ida in central Crete, used as a sanctuary by the MINOANS. It has given its name to a type of polychrome pottery produced in the Middle Minoan period (early 2nd millennium BC), characterized by red and white decoration on a black ground and among the finest ceramics ever produced in Europe.

Kambuja. The ethnic name of the people who founded the kingdom of CHENLA in present southern Laos, the first kingdom of the KHMERS. Its origin is unknown, but could possibly be seen in another ethnic name, that of the Iranian Kambojas, as there are signs of SASSANIAN influence in the southern part of the Indochinese Peninsula. According to a Cambodian dynastic legend preserved in a 10th-century inscription, the origin of the kings of CAMBODIA goes back to the union of the hermit Kambu with the celestial nymph Merà, names probably related to both 'Kambuja' and 'Khmer'; the names 'Cambodia' and 'Kampuchea' have the same etymology.

Kamegaoka. A JOMON site in Aomori prefecture in northern Honshu, Japan, best known for its Final Jomon deposits with elaborate pottery and lacquered dishes. The Kamegaoka complex, named after the site, is characterized by the widespread appearance of the distinctive pottery style, production of hollow figurines, salt-making out of sea water, and fishing and sea-mammal hunting with harpoons. It was partially contemporaneous with the Early YAYOI Culture.

Kamikuroiwa. A stratified rock shelter on Shikoku, Japan. The pottery from the oldest layer, radiocarbon-dated to the late 11th millennium bc, is essentially the same as those from similarly dated layers of FUKUI and SEMPUKUJI, but is associated with bifacial points rather than with microblades. Incised flat pebbles representing human females were also found. The 20 human and two dog burials in one of the upper layers are among the oldest Initial JOMON burials.

Kamilamba. Named after a site in the Upemba depression of the valley of the upper Lualaba in southeastern Zaire, this is the initial phase of the local Early Iron Age, precursor of the KISALIAN. Dated to between the 5th and 8th centuries ad, it is poorly illustrated by the research so far undertaken, but the associated pottery shows affinities with that from settlements of the same age in the Copperbelt area further southeast.

Kaminaljuyu. A large Highland MAYA centre located on the western edge of Guatemala City. Its earliest occupation is in the Early to Mid-PRE-CLASSIC and is evidenced by artefacts which are strongly OLMEC influenced (for instance the 'squashed frog' motif, kaolin pottery, and pits reminiscent of those at TLATILCO). The most important Pre-Classic occupation, however, is in the MIRAFLORES phase, during which the site shows a marked increase in both area and population. The artistic tradition of this period bears a strong IZAPAN flavour.

The site comprises some 200 scattered adobe mounds, some of which have been built over several times. Tombs, many of which contain luxury grave goods and evidence of retainer SACRIFICE, were sometimes excavated out of previously constructed mounds. A number of the elaborately carved stelae have been deliberately smashed; the reason for this practice is unclear, but it is thought to coincide with the death of the person whom the stele commemorates.

The period *c*200-400 is marked by decline, with some areas of the site falling into disuse. Shortly thereafter, however, there is a regeneration and reconstruction which is accompanied by the influx of vast quantities of TEOTIHUACAN material. TALUD-TABLERO architecture, THIN ORANGE WARE and CYLINDRICAL TRIPOD VASES all occur in increasing quantities, although trade with the CLASSIC Peten centres continues.

The nature of this intrusion is uncertain (there is little evidence for conquest at the site) and though Mexican forms are introduced many elements of style remain Mayan. New construction tends to be less spread-out and is concentrated around the north-central Palengana (a complex of temple-pyramids in uncut stone and adobe) built around a BALL COURT. Rich tombs still continue but grave goods confirm that a Teotihuacan élite has replaced the Mayan as the controlling power.

Surprisingly, sites much closer to Teotihuacan show less influence than at Kaminaljuyu. It is thought, however, that its proximity to areas in which cacao and cotton were grown was a decisive factor in its being occupied.

Kampuchea. *See* CAMBODIA.

Kanam. A site near the Kavirondo Gulf in western Kenya. Early stone tools are reported from Kanam West. A small frgament of lower jaw, found in 1932, was believed to represent a modern type of man with a pronounced chin at a date early in the PALAEOLITHIC. However, the supposed chin seems to be a growth, and today the find is not regarded as significant.

Kandahar. The remains of Old Kandahar, abandoned in 1738, occupy a well-watered position at the foot of a precipitous ridge, near the crossing of the Arghandab in southern Afghanistan. The site contains a series of walled enclosures surrounding the citadel. Nearby, at the foot of the ridge, is a bilingual (Aramaic and Greek) inscription of the MAURYAN emperor ASOKA (273-232 BC). On the crest of the ridge is a Buddhist monastery of the early centuries AD. Excavations showed that a defended settlement, perhaps the successor of MUNDIGAK, already existed in the first half of the 1st millennium BC. In period 2, the citadel was erected and the defences rebuilt on a massive scale, perhaps by the ACHAEMENIDS, who may have established Kandahar as the capital of Arachosia. The defences were rebuilt again in the Hellenistic period. The discovery of a statue-base with a Greek inscription confirms a Greek presence on the site, although its name and foundation date are unknown. The town seems to have been occupied continuously until the 18th century and a large barrow cemetery belongs — surprisingly — to the Islamic period.

Kandanda. Located beside the upper Zambezi River near Sesheke in Zambia, Kandanda preserves an archaeological sequence in which a prepared-core industry that included rare bifacial hand axes apparently continued to a remarkably late date, being replaced by a microlithic industry probably around 1000 bc.

Kandrian. *See* NEW BRITAIN.

Kanem. One of the early sudanic African states which arose late in the 1st millennium AD in the area immediately west of Lake Chad. Its rulers are traditionally believed to have been Zaghawa from the southern Sahara. Kanem has been poorly researched by archaeological methods, but the increase in trade and changes in artefact types which occurred at DAIMA at this time may tentatively be linked with the rise of Kanem.

Kanesh. *See* KÜLTEPE.

Kangaroo Island. *See* KARTAN CULTURE.

Kanheri. A series of rock-cut Buddhist temples, monasteries and brick STUPAS near Bombay, western India, dating to the early centuries AD.

Kanjera. A site near KANAM close to the Kavirondo Gulf in western Kenya. Hand axes of probably ACHEULIAN type were found in the Middle PLEISTOCENE deposits. Very fragmentary remains of three or four skulls were long claimed to be representatives of modern-type man associated with the Acheulian; recent evidence suggests they are post-Pleistocene.

Kansanshi. An ancient copper mine near the modern Solwezi, west of the Zambia/Shaba Copperbelt. Small-scale exploitation of the copper deposit appears to have begun during the Early Iron Age of the second half of the 1st millennium ad. Large-scale workings are not attested prior to the 14th or 15th century. It is noteworthy that this development may coincide with both the rise of centralized states in the Copperbelt area and the opening of a Zambezi Valley trade route to the east coast of Africa, where copper was a significant export (*see* INGOMBE ILEDE).

Kansyore ware. Kansyore Island in the Kagera River on the Uganda/Tanzania border west of Lake Victoria has given its name to an enigmatic type of pottery found at several sites around Lake Victoria and also, apparently, further south in central Tanzania. Similar, but not necessarily related, material occurs in south-central Kenya. The makers of Kansyore ware appear to have been hunter-gatherers, makers of a backed microlith industry. At Nyang'oma near Mwanza,

Tanzania, this pottery is dated to the second quarter of the 1st millennium bc. Elsewhere, as at Gogo Falls in southwestern Kenya, there are indications that it may have continued in use up to the advent of the Early Iron Age makers of UREWE WARE.

Käpää. One of the best-explored sites of the late Mesolithic NARVA culture, Käpää is stratified in a peat bog in Estonia. The thin occupation deposits on slight wooden platforms have radiocarbon dates of c2900-2400 bc. A rich assemblage of bone tools is associated with fragmentary Narva pottery.

Kapovo. A painted cave in the southern Urals of European Russia, mainly important because cave art is otherwise unknown in central and eastern Europe. The representations of MAMMOTH and woolly rhinoceros are the main evidence for its PALAEOLITHIC age.

Kapwirimbwe. An Early Iron Age village site near modern Lusaka, Zambia, dated to about the 5th century ad. The elaborately decorated pottery is similar to that from contemporary Copperbelt sites. Iron-working was a major industry and domestic cattle were herded.

Kara Kamar. See AQ KUPRUK.

Karakellang. See LEANG TUWO MANE'E.

Karako. A village site in Nara prefecture, Japan, which was occupied soon after the YAYOI culture appeared in Kyushu, and repeatedly thereafter. Excavations in the 1920s and 1930s contributed to the understanding of the development of the Yayoi culture. Over 100 dwelling and storage pits contained pottery covering the whole span of the Yayoi period in this area. Organic materials were well-preserved and included baskets, wooden agricultural tools, a bundle of rice plants, melon seeds, nuts, and bones of wild boar, deer, dogs and cattle.

Karanovo. Providing one of the most important stratigraphies for the European Neolithic and Copper Age, the TELL of Karanovo lies in the Azmak valley, near Nova Zagora, central Bulgaria. Excavated by V. Mikov and G. Georgiev, the tell is divided into seven periods. I-II represent the FIRST TEMPERATE NEOLITHIC levels, with regular rows of rectangular houses; III has VESELINOVO levels, with dark burnished and carinated pottery; IV is the Kalojanovec level (very little material of this phase is known outside Karanovo); V represents Marica levels, with graphite painted wares and excised pottery; VI is the main GUMELNIŢA occupation with graphite painted wares and a floruit of copper metallurgy; this is followed by a stratigraphic hiatus and then VII, which is the Early Bronze Age level. Almost all the period designations here have become known as cultures in their own right (e.g. the Karanovo III culture).

Karasuk. The culture that succeeded the ANDRONOVO culture in southern Siberia in the later 2nd millennium BC. Two settlements of large pit houses are known and many cemeteries of stone cists covered by a low mound and set in a square stone enclosure; many of these are in the MINUSINSK Basin. The Karasuk people were farmers who concentrated on sheep-rearing. They practised metallurgy on a large scale: the most characteristic artefact is a bronze knife or dagger, with a curved profile and a decorated handle. They produced a realistic animal art, which probably contributed to the development of the later Scytho-Siberian animal art style (see ANIMAL STYLE.

Karatepe. A small citadel site on the Ceyhan River behind the Adana plain of southern Turkey. It represents a fortified palace built in the 8th century BC by a local ruler, Azitawandas, and occupied for a short time only. The palace is decorated with relief carvings of uneven quality and demonstrating mixed stylistic influences (HITTITE, PHOENICIAN and ASSYRIAN). The most important discovery at Karatepe was the monumental gateway, flanked by lion figures. The figures and the adjoining stone slabs were covered in inscriptions, one in the Phoenician script, the other in Hittite hieroglyphics. This bilingual inscription contributed to the decipherment of the Hittite script and to understanding of the Hittite language.

Karbuna. One of the earliest hoards discovered in the Balkan Neolithic. The Karbuna hoard of 852 objects was discovered in a TRIPOLYE A-B1 pot at an unexcavated site in Soviet Moldavia. The finds include some of the earliest cast copper items (a hammer-axe, a chisel and two plaques) in Europe, as well as large quantitites of copper, shell, marble and bone jewellery. The date of deposition is disputed (c3800 bc or 3500 bc) and the hoard has been interpreted as either a shaman's kit or as a communal ornament collection.

Karim Shahir. An open site on a terrace of the River Zab in Iraqi Kurdistan which has given its name to a culture dated c9000-7000 bc associated with the transition from a hunting and gathering economy to one based on farming. There is little evidence for permanent structures on Karim Shahir sites and most of them were probably occupied seasonally. The economy was based on hunting, with some possible evidence of herding (see Tepe ASIAB, SHANIDAR, ZAWI CHEMI SHANIDAR), while the artefactual evidence also suggests an increased dependence on plant resources: blades with the silica sheen often described as 'sickle gloss', pierced stone balls which might have been weights for digging sticks, and stone axes.

Karkarichinkat. See TILEMSI VALLEY.

Karli. A rock-cut Buddhist temple in the western Deccan, India, of the early centuries AD. It is elaborately decorated like that at BEDSA. The STUPA in the temple is embellished with wooden umbrellas and imitation balustrades.

Kartan culture. A group of stone assemblages with heavy core tools predominating, found on Kangaroo Island and the nearby peninsulas of South Australia. Kangaroo Island, now separated from Australia by a 15-km strait, was joined to the mainland during the PLEISTOCENE. There were no Aboriginal inhabitants at the time of European contact. Of 100 surface Kartan sites on the island, none has been found on the post-Pleistocene coastal dunes. Firm radiocarbon dates are lacking for Kartan assemblages, although radiocarbon estimates of 14,000 bc have been obtained for a possibly subsequent small scraper industry in Seton rock shelter on Kangaroo Island. Kartan tools include semi-unifacially flaked pebbles, waisted blades and large HORSEHOOF CORES, with mean weights of 500 grams, sometimes associated with small quartz flakes. The proportion of core tools in the assemblage is much higher than in other Pleistocene sites.

karum. See KÜLTEPE.

Kassites. A people known mainly from documentary evidence who established a dynasty in BABYLON after the HITTITE raid of 1595BC. They ruled for about four centuries until they were overthrown by an ELAMITE incursion in 1157 BC. They are difficult to identify in the archaeological record, probably because they adopted the language and customs of Mesopotamia. They appear to have entered Mesopotamia from the Zagros mountains to the east and it is sometimes claimed that they were ruled by an INDO-EUROPEAN aristocracy, since they introduced the worship of Indo-European deities, as well as such practices as horse-breeding and riding.

Katoto. An Iron Age cemetery at the southern end of the Upemba depression on the Lualaba River, southeastern Zaire. It probably dates to around the 13th century ad, and is thus broadly contemporary with the KISALIAN cemeteries from a short distance further north. The burials were accompanied by rich and varied grave goods including pottery, copper and iron artefacts, notably an iron gong of a type which has served as a symbol of political authority in more recent central African societies. The presence of sea shells and imported glass beads indicates links with the Indian Ocean coast.

Katun. See CALENDAR (AMERICAS).

Katuruka. An Early Iron Age site in Buhaya, northeastern Tanzania. The pottery, although not yet published in detail, appears to be of the UREWE type known from other parts of the Lake Victoria basin; there was also evidence for the practice of a sophisticated iron-smelting technology. Particular interest attaches to the radiocarbon dates from this and nearby sites: these indicate an age within the last three or four centuries bc. Claims that the early occupation of this site is recalled in extant oral tradition of the region's present inhabitants are not widely accepted.

Kauai. See HAWAIIAN ISLANDS.

Kaupang. A site located on Viks Fjord in Vestfold, Norway. Excavations began there in 1956 when Kaupang was considered the likely site of Skiringssal, a place visited by the merchant farmer Ottar or Ohthere, who came to King Alfred's court. The excavations have revealed a small group of houses focused around a jetty, and it is suggested these are part of a large trading emporium. The pottery, glass and coins from the excavations indicate that the site flourished in the 9th century. Like HEDEBY, LÖDDEKOPINGE, Västergarn and Birka, Kaupang seems to have maintained extensive contacts with the Franks and Slavs as well as sustained links with the Arab world.

Kauri Point. A MAORI PA near Tauranga in the Bay of Plenty, New Zealand, which has revealed several phases of Classic Maori ditch and bank fortification, two with double ditches, from c1500-1750. The interior of the *pa* contained large numbers of sweet potato storage pits.

Kausambi. A site in the Ganges Valley in northern India which was a great urban centre in the early historical period. The earliest defences, dating to the mid-1st millennium BC, were of mud-brick, faced with baked brick. Of the same period is a building interpreted as a palace, with walls of stone rubble. Another early building is a Buddhist monastery where, according to an inscription, the Buddha himself stayed for a time.

Kauthāra. One of the four natural provinces of CHAMPA, corresponding to the plain of present Nha-trang in southern Vietnam. As a 3rd-century inscription shows, the area must originally have been a part of FUNAN, but at least from the 8th century on CHAM was spoken there. To this period also belong several brick sanctuaries in the Nha-trang area, notably that of Po Nagar. *See also* AMARĀVATI, PĀNDURANGA, VIJAYA.

kava. A stimulating beverage made from the chewed roots of the shrub *Piper methysticum* in central and eastern Oceania. *See also* BETEL.

Kazanlik [Kazanluk]. A large Neolithic, Copper Age and Early Bronze Age TELL in the Valley of Roses, Tundža Valley, southern Bulgaria. Excavated by G. Georgiev and R. Katinčarov, the site has a six-metre stratigraphy with two metres of KARANOVO I occupation; VESELINOVO occupation levels; Karanovo V-VI layers (with a stone wall enclosing the site at the end of this period) and an Early Bronze Age occupation. The cultivation of emmer wheat and cattle and caprine husbandry formed the principal economic strategies.

Kechi Beg. A 3rd-millennium BC site in the QUETTA Valley of West Pakistan, which has given its name to a fine quality pottery, buff in colour and painted in black with solid bands interspersed with delicately painted patterns; sometimes red paint is also used to produce a polychrome effect.

Kedah. *See* KUALA SELINSING, MALAYSIA.

Keilor. A site complex in the alluvial terraces of the Maribyrnong River, 16 km north of Melbourne, Australia. Archaeological interest in the site began in 1940, with the discovery of a cranium with modern features and apparently of high antiquity, resembling the GREEN GULLY skull found 3 km away. Complex geomorphology has made firm dating difficult, but the skull is now thought to date from 11,000-13,000 bc. Other finds include stone flakes and hearths possibly 30,000 years old, and the bones of extinct megafauna. Continuing work by the Victorian Archaeological Service is aimed at unravelling the geomorphological problems and testing possible associations between the megafauna and human occupation.

Kells. *See* BOOK OF KELLS.

Kenko stone. *See* HUACA.

Kenniff Cave. A sandstone rock shelter situated in the mountains of eastern central Queensland, Australia. It contains one of the longest and most complete technological sequences for any Australian site. Excavations in 1962 produced a series of radiocarbon dates from 17,000 to 550 bc, the first dates to be recovered for Pleistocene human occupation in Australian from a stratified deposit. Stone tools from the base to the 3000 bc levels comprised steep-edge flake scrapers and cores, including HORSEHOOF CORES. Between 3000 and 500 bc there occurred an unusually wide range of AUSTRALIAN SMALL TOOLS, including PIRRI POINTS, geometric microliths, BONDI POINTS and TULA ADZE flakes, as well as grinding stones. Ochre pellets, some use-striated, were scattered through all levels.

Kents Cavern. This site at Torquay in south Devon, southwest England, is of historic interest because discoveries made here after 1822 suggested the antiquity of man before its general recognition in 1859 (*see* BOUCHER DE PERTHES, MACENERY, PENGELLY). It now seems that late and early Upper PALAEO-LITHIC occupations were present, as well as MOUSTERIAN of Acheulian tradition and an early hand-axe level. The latter may be as early as any known in Britain, perhaps some 400,000 years ago.

Kenya Capsian. *See* EBURRAN.

Kenyon, Dame Kathleen (1906-78). British archaeologist who made major contributions to the understanding of the prehistory and protohistory of Palestine. One of her most important excavations was at JERICHO (1952-8), where she brought to light evidence of a substantial fortified settlement associated with early farming of the 9th-8th millennia bc, as well as elucidating the later history of the site. Another major excavation was conducted in ancient JERUSALEM between 1961 and 1967, and enabled much of the town planning history of this most important city to be documented.

Kephala. A Late Neolithic settlement on a headland on the Cycladic island of Kea, dated to the mid-4th millennium BC. Nearby was a cemetery of graves made of small flat stones in circular or rectangular constructions, each with a number of burials. Children were commonly buried in pottery jars (*pithoi*). The typical pottery was covered with a red slip and decorated by pattern burnishing. Evidence for copper-smelting was found, one of the earliest occurrences in the Aegean.

Kerbschnitt. A technique used for decorating wood or pottery, alternatively called CHIP CARVING.

Kerma. Situated near the third Nile cataract, Kerma was the capital of an apparently independent Nubian kingdom which achieved prominence following a northward retreat of the Egyptians under the 13th Dynasty, c1700 BC. Kerma's trade contacts were wide and

great wealth was accumulated, accompanied by a high level of craftsmanship, especially in pottery. The rulers of Kerma, together with the bodies of many retainers, were buried under huge grave mounds up to 80 metres in diameter. The power of Kerma was already passed when Egypt reconquered Nubia under the 18th Dynasty, c1500 BC.

kernos. A type of terracotta or earthenware dish or bowl, with a collection of smaller cups attached around its upper edge. Examples are found from the Bronze Age onwards, and seem typical in the East Mediterranean area. The use is uncertain, but a ritual association has been suggested.

kettle drum. Name commonly applied to large bronze drums, also known as DONG-SON drums, first produced for an unknown purpose more than two thousand years ago and found throughout Southeast Asia, with the exception of the Philippines and the island of Borneo. These drums, one type of which was still manufactured in Burma in the early 20th century, are generally associated with wealth, power and fertility, and may originally have been part of the regalia of rulers throughout the region prior to INDIANIZATION.

Kexingzhuang [K'o-hsing-chuang]. A site on the Feng River southwest of Xi'an, China. The most important stratum lies above a YANG-SHAO Neolithic level and defines the Kexingzhuang II culture. Kexingzhuang II is the immediate successor to the Yangshao of the Wei River valley; it belongs to a horizon that includes HOUGANG II to the east and QIJIA to the west, and is the Longshan culture of Shaanxi province (*see* LONGSHAN, sense 3).

ZHOU remains at Kexingzhuang, including perhaps a brief occupation just antedating the founding of the Zhou dynasty, lie directly above Neolithic levels. More extensive Western Zhou finds have been made in excavations nearby, for example at ZHANGJI-APO and PUDUCUN.

Kezuo [K'o-tso]. *See* YAN.

Khabur. A tributary of the Euphrates River which provides an important communication route between Mesopotamia and Anatolia. Important prehistoric sites such as Tell HALAF, Tell BRAK and CHAGAR BAZAR have been excavated in the Khabur basin. It has given its name to a distinctive painted ware found in northern Mesopotamia and north Syria in the early 2nd millennium BC. Pottery of this type also occurs in level IB at KULTEPE in Anatolia, indicating wide-ranging trade at this time.

Khafajeh. Identified as ancient Tutub, Khafajeh is one of a number of TELL sites on the DIYALA River in eastern Iraq excavated by an American team in the 1930s. Three separate temples were excavated. The oldest, dedicated to the moon god Sin, had five levels of the JEMDET NASR period, and five of the EARLY DYNASTIC PERIOD. The second temple, named the Oval Temple because it was enclosed by a massive wall which was oval in plan, belonged to the Early Dynastic period also. The third temple, dedicated to Nintu, was also of Early Dynastic date. As well as the temples the excavators found almost 200 ED graves, mostly beneath the floors of houses; some were simple shaft graves while others had constructed chambers, two being built of baked brick and roofed by CORBELLING. The pottery vessels which constituted the main grave goods contributed greatly to the class-ification and subdivision into phases of ED ceramics.

Khami. Located near Bulawayo, Zimbabwe, Khami is one of the most extensive and well preserved stone-built structures erected in that area after the late 15th and 16th centuries AD (*see also* DHLO DHLO). Elaborate and well-built retaining walls produced a series of platforms on which pole and clay buildings were erected. There was evidently much trade contact with the east coast, probably through the Portuguese stations that were established on the Mashonaland plateau to the northeast at approximately this time.

Khandragiri. *See* ORISSA.

Kharga Oasis. *See* NABTA PLAYA.

Khasm el Girba. A modern Sudanese settle-ment on the Atbara River, a short distance downstream of the Sudan/Ethiopia border. Important archaeological sites are known in the vicinity but have not yet been investigated in full detail. At least one extensive settlement site appears to be closely related to the

KADERO/ESH SHAHEINAB complex of the Nile Valley.

Khirbet al-Mafjar. A palatial complex just outside Jericho in the Jordan Valley, attrib-uted on epigraphic grounds to the Umayyad caliph Hisham (724-43). It contained three elements: the South Building, a two-storey mansion, adjoined on the north side by a mosque; the self-contained Bath-house, supplied (as was the rest of the complex) by an aqueduct; and the North Building, which may have been a *khan*, or guest-house. In front of the South Building and the Bath-house was a forecourt with a fountain at the centre. The buildings are particularly important because they are closly datable within a period when the Hellenistic traditions of art and archi-tecture were being transformed for Muslim patrons, and also because they yielded rich collections of stucco, wall paintings and mosaics.

Khirbet Kerak [ancient Beth-yerah]. An Early Bronze Age walled town, covering *c*22.5 hectares, situated west of the River Jordan close to the Sea of Galilee in Israel. It appears to have been occupied throughout much of the 4th and 3rd millennia BC. The town of the EB III phase, of the mid-3rd millennium BC, contains a massive public building, probably a religious structure (although it has been sug-gested, alternatively, that it might have been a public granary). It comprises eight circular stone structures, each containing four radial walls not quite meeting in the centre, all enclosed by a massive outer wall, rectangular in plan.

The site has given its name to a pottery type, characterized by a highly burnished finish, on a slip with sharply defined zones of red, black and light brown colour; it is some-times further decorated with fluting. The pottery belongs to the EB III phase and has a wide distribution in Syria and Palestine. It is usually thought to have originated in northeast Anatolia and may have been distributed either by emigration or by trade.

Khirokitia. An Early Neolithic settlement in southern Cyprus with radiocarbon dates in the early 6th millennium bc. About fifty houses were excavated, of circular 'beehive' type, built of mudbrick on stone foundations. Hearths and benches were found inside and some houses had burials with grave goods (especially stone bowls) underneath the floors. Agriculture was practised and sheep and goats were kept. The culture was aceramic but there was a fine stone industry, using Anatolian obsidian and flint for tools, local andesite for both tools and containers, and Levantine carnelian for beads. The site has given its name to the Early Neolithic culture of the island and is known from several sites. It lasted for rather less than a millennium and was succeeded by a period of some 1500 years when there may have been no population at all, or only a very reduced one, on the island.

Khmer. Ethnic name of the Cambodians and of their language. Its origin is unknown, but it seems to have the same etymology as KAMB-UJA and CAMBODIA. See AUSTRO-ASIATIC.

Khor Musa. A site near Wadi Halfa in the northern Sudan, which has given its name to the final phase of the Nubian 'Middle Stone Age'. Blade tools and burins now accompanied the earlier prepared-core artefacts. It seems probable that the Khormusan industry was broadly contemporary with the DABBAN of Cyrenaica, belonging to the period following *c*40,000 bc when increased aridity rendered the Sahara uninhabitable. Faunal remains from Khormusan sites indicate that both fishing and the hunting of land animals were practised.

Khorsabad [ancient Dur Sharrukin]. Situated 20 km northeast of Mosul in Iraq, Khorsabad was a very short-lived capital of ASSYRIA. Founded by Sargon II (721-705 BC) as a new capital to replace NIMRUD, it lost this role after Sargon's death, when his son Sennacherib moved the capital to NINEVEH. Occupation at Khorsabad continued, but the city was important only during the reign of Sargon. It was almost square in plan, covering *c*300 hectares. The most impressive remains lie on the citadel which straddles the north wall; they include several temples, a ZIGGURAT and a royal palace. Many of the stone reliefs and CUNEIFORM inscriptions excavated by BOTTA in the last century are now in the Louvre.

Khufu [Cheops]. The second pharaoh of the Fourth Egyptian Dynasty, who reigned *c*2580 BC and is remembered primarily as the builder of the Great Pyramid at GIZA. The pyramid,

covering a ground area of 53,000 square metres and rising to a height of 148 metres, is a vivid indicator both of the complex and efficient organization of which the pharaoh was the head, and of the completeness with which the state's resources were under central control.

Kidder, Alfred Vincent (1885-1963). One of the first American archaeologists to employ the scientific method on a grand scale. Using a synthesis of STRATIGRAPHY and SERIATION, he established the first area-wide chronological sequences for the American Southwest. Although DENDROCHRONOLOGY has since refined it, the basic framework still stands today. In 1927 Kidder initiated the Pecos Conference, an event which brought archaeologists together to exchange information and agree on basic standards. It still functions in the same way.

Kidder, however, was not content with the achievements of one career and soon began to apply his talents to MESOAMERICA. He implemented a massive multi-disciplinary study of the lowland MAYA area and laid the basic framework of Maya chronology (*see* UAXACTUN). Kidder more than anyone was responsible for changing American archaeology from antiquarianism to scientific discipline.

Kid-Nun. *See* JEMDET NASR.

Kiev. Capital of the Ukraine, Soviet Russia, Kiev has been the scene of many excavations in recent years. These have shown how in the 8th and 9th centuries a collection of small hamlets comprising sunken-floored workshops, merchant houses and artisans' dwellings gradually amalgamated to form a town. There was also at this time a defensive stronghold surrounded by earth and timber walls that may have contained buildings of a royal nature. By the early 10th century Kiev had developed into an important political centre and a flourishing trading emporium on the route from the Baltic to BYZANTIUM. Byzantine silks, for example, have been found in nearby cemeteries, and the influence of Byzantium is very apparent on local monumental architecture of the 11th to 14th centuries. The cemetery evidence from Kiev has also proved of great interest because several wealthy graves have been found and some have shown that there was a very strong Scandinavian presence in Russia during the 9th and 10th centuries. *See also* KYRILLOVSKAYA.

Kiik Koba. The cave of Kiik in the Crimea was occupied in MOUSTERIAN times. Some NEAN-DERTHAL remains have been found, including foot bones and hand bones, but no complete skulls were recovered.

Kili Ghul Mohammed. A prehistoric site just north of QUETTA in West Pakistan, with four phases of occupation. Period I has 4th millen-nium bc dates (5th millennium BC) and begins with an occupation by farmers who kept domesticated goats, sheep and cattle, and perhaps cultivated a cereal crop. They lived in pisé huts, but did not initially use pottery. In Period II, a crude hand-made pottery was introduced and mud-brick became the normal building material. In Period III black-on-red painted wares and some wheel-made wares occur; in Period IV the beautiful KECHI BEG ware appears, as do the first copper tools. The site of DAMB SADAAT overlaps with Kili Ghul Mohammed IV and continues into the 3rd millennium BC.

Killke. *See* CUZCO.

Kilwa. One of the most southerly of the major trading cities of the East African coast, Kilwa is located on an island off the shore of Tan-zania, some 350 km south of Zanzibar. For three centuries before the arrival of the Portuguese in 1500 it was the leading entrepôt on the East African coast. Extensive excava-tions have yielded a good sequence from the 9th century onwards. The earliest settlement, attributed to the period c800-1200, was a village of thatched, timber-framed houses. The subsistence economy was based on fishing, collecting shellfish and cultivation, including sorghum. The only industries were iron-working and the manufacture of shell beads. Small quantities of pottery from Western Asia and, towards the end of the period, chlorite-schist from Madagascar indicate commercial activity, but on a modest scale; at this stage imported goods are rare compared with the contemporary settlement at MANDA far to the north.

At Kilwa the age of prosperity began c1200. It is marked by the introduction of coins, widespread use of masonry and the construction of the mosque, which shows that the rulers were Muslim. Kilwa came to occupy 100 hectares. In the 14th century the sultan built a spectacular palace, known as Husuni Kubwa, just outside the town. The establish-ment of a wealthy Islamic community is identified with the arrival of the so-called Shirazi dynasty which, according to tradition, came from the Persian Gulf, perhaps by way of Somalia. In the 14th and 15th centuries Kilwa controlled the coast far to the south and grew even more wealthy through its control of the trade in Zimbabwean gold. The arrival of the Portuguese in the Indian Ocean at the end of the 15th century heralded Kilwa's decline.

Kimberley point. A bifacially trimmed stone point with serrated margins and long shallow surface scar beds, suggesting pressure flaking. These points are distributed in the Kimberley region of Western Australia and neighbouring areas of the Northern Territory and northwest Queensland; lengths vary from 2 cm to more than 10 cm. Museum collections contain finely worked specimens made on bottle glass and ceramic telegraph insulators, as well as wooden spears tipped with the points. South of the Kimberleys the point was a trade item and was used as a surgical knife.

Kin. *See* CALENDAR (AMERICAS).

Kings Lynn. Norfolk coastal town on the River Ouse in eastern England which grew in importance from the 12th century to become one of England's busiest ports and markets. It was mostly concerned with North Sea trade and specialized in exporting the wool and agricultural produce of the fens to Flanders and the Baltic countries. The layout and standing buildings of Kings Lynn still reflect this activity and include a remarkable series of tenements, markets, quays, warehouses and guildhalls, among them part of the Steelyard (the premises of the English-based Hanseatic traders) and the large merchant house and warehouse complex of Hampton Court. Other public buildings of the town document the rise of the urban middle classes, with a prepond-erance of lay and friary churches as well as other churches and colleges containing monuments dedicated by wealthy merchants, and the important Tuesday and Saturday markets. During the 14th-century recession in the wool trade Kings Lynn suffered a severe economic set-back, but the town recovered during the 15th century due to a revival of the fishing industry.

Kingston brooch. *See* FILIGREE.

Kintampo. A Ghanaian Neolithic industry which occurs on sites near the forest/savanna woodland margin west of the Volta. Small domestic cattle and goats were herded; oil palm nuts and cowpeas were also exploited and may have been cultivated. Characteristic stone rasps may have been used for grating yams. Substantial village settlements are attested, as at NTERESO. Kintampo Neolithic sites are dated to the second half of the 2nd millennium bc.

Kiowa. A rock shelter in the New Guinea Highlands with a sequence spanning the last 10,000 years, commencing with a pebble and flake industry (with many waisted tools,) and developing with the appearance of polished axes and pig bones between 3000 and 4000 bc. *See also* KAFIAVANA.

Kiribati. *See* MICRONESIA.

Kirjath-sepher. *See* BEIT MIRSIM.

Kisalian. An Iron Age industry of the northern Upemba depression, southeastern Zaire, best known from the large cemetery site at SANGA on the shore of Lake Kisale. The earliest Kisalian appeared around the 8th century ad and the industry reached its full development in the 10th-14th centuries. The rich and varied grave goods at Sanga include finely decorated pottery clearly derived from an Early Iron Age tradition. Fishing and hunting were practised; domestic fowl and goats were also kept. Iron, copper and ivory were worked with considerable skill.

Kisapostag. A regional group of the earlier Bronze Age, concentrated on the middle Danube Valley in south central Hungary and dating to the early 2nd millennium bc. A high proportion of known sites are cemeteries, in which inurned cremation is the characteristic rite. Large cemeteries are known (e.g. Dunaújváros) which served the small settlements in their hinterland. Kisapostag arsenical copper work is relatively rich and from its typological affinities with Únětice metalwork

in Bohemia, Danube-borne exchange networks may confidently be proposed.

Kish. Situated on an ancient branch of the Euphrates River, 80 km south of Baghdad in Iraq, Kish was one of the city states of the SUMERIAN civilization. Occupation began in the JEMDET NASR phase and the city was of major importance in the early 3rd millennium BC. It declined in importance later, but remained in occupation until the SASSANIAN period. One of the most important monuments excavated is an EARLY DYNASTIC palace, one of the earliest indications anywhere in Sumer of the growing power of kings, which was to challenge and eventually overtake that of the Temple organizations during the course of the Early Dynastic period. Important remains still standing at Kish include two temples, one probably dedicated to Inanna, the Sumerian goddess of love, of the 6th century BC.

kitchen midden. Term which might be used to describe any rubbish deposit containing mostly food debris, but most frequently applied to large shell middens left by communities exploiting shellfish on a considerable scale. The term was first used, in its Danish form *kjökkenmödding*, early in the 19th century, to describe the middens of the ERTEBØLLE culture.

Kitoi. *See* BAIKAL NEOLITHIC.

kiva. A structural feature of late culture Southwestern USA communities, such as the MOGOLLON and ANASAZI. Usually subterranean and circular in plan (though some are rectangular), the *kiva* served as a community gathering-place, probably for ceremonial purposes.

Kivik. Site in southern Sweden of a very large Bronze Age barrow. It has a diameter of *c*70 metres and covers a chamber made of dressed stone slabs. Each of the ten slabs was carved on its inner face with stylized figures including ships, a chariot with rider, other human figures, fish, axes and sun discs. The tomb was robbed in the 18th century and no trace of the grave goods survived, but it is thought that it was built in the Middle or Late Bronze Age (later 2nd millennium BC).

Kizilkaya. A middle to late 6th millennium bc Neolithic culture recognized on a few sites on either side of the Taurus mountains above Antalya, in southern Turkey. The culture is known mostly from its pottery, which shows links both with that of Early Neolithic ÇATAL HÜYÜK and that of Late Neolithic HACILAR; it may fit chronologically between the two. Lack of excavated material has inhibited knowledge of the stone industry and of subsistence economy.

Klasies River Mouth. A complex of caves on the south coast of South Africa. Detailed archaeological investigations have been conducted but have not yet been reported in detail. The sequence covers at least the last 60,000 years, and probably longer. A long development of 'Middle Stone Age' shares some features with the PIETERSBURG industries and is interrupted by a phase attributed to HOWIESONSPOORT. The later microlithic phases have not been described but yielded three painted stone slabs of the last millennium bc.

Klein Afrika. An Early Iron Age site in the northern Transvaal, South Africa, dated to about the 4th century ad, which has yielded pottery of GOKOMERE type, akin to that from Zimbabwe.

Knossos. The largest and most important MINOAN palace site, situated near Heraklion on the north coast of Crete. It was excavated by Sir Arthur EVANS between 1899 and 1935

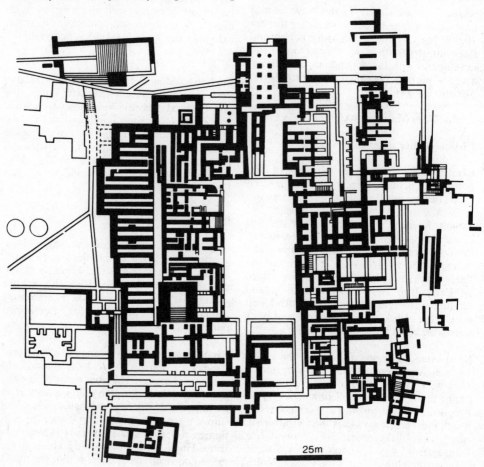

25m

Knossos: plan of Minoan palace

and more recently by other British archaeo-logists, including John Evans and Peter Warren. The earliest occupation on the site was an aceramic Neolithic settlement, in existence by c6000 bc and this was followed by other Neolithic deposits, now with pottery, building up a stratigraphy some seven metres deep.

The Neolithic settlement was succeeded by an Early Minoan one, but little is known about this phase. The first palace was built in the Minoan period, beginning c2000 BC and lasted for some 300 years. It was subsequently rebuilt on a very grand scale, with large banks of rooms of various sorts arranged around a central courtyard; it may have been the complexity of the Knossos buildings that gave rise to the story of the labyrinth later associated with the site. The rooms include public assembly and audience rooms, domestic quarters for the royal leaders, shrines, workshops, storage magazines and archive rooms. The building was at least three storeys high and elaborately decorated with wall frescoes and equipped with water and drain-age systems. Unlike other Minoan palaces, Knossos survived the volcanic eruption of the island of THERA in c1450 BC; however, after this period it was controlled not by Minoans but by Greek-speaking MYCENAEANS from the mainland. Their presence is clearly attested by the tablets inscribed in the LINEAR B script, which characterize this phase (in contrast to the LINEAR A used earlier). The site was finally destroyed probably c1375 BC.

The great palace was surrounded by a sub-stantial town, and although archaeological work has concentrated on the palace itself some houses have been excavated, as well as cemeteries of chamber tombs outside the town itself.

Knoviz. A regional group of the central European URNFIELD culture of the later Bronze Age. The Knoviz group is distributed in Bohemia from c1400 to 900 bc. Few large settlement sites are known, the bulk of material deriving from small farmsteads with pits and post-holes or from cemeteries. The Knoviz group is one of the exceptions to the normal Urnfield rite in that inhumation is more frequent than cremation burial. Hengi-form monuments (see HENGE) and horseshoe-shaped enclosures are occasionally associated with Knoviz pottery at sites such as Čakovice.

Knowth. One of the largest BARROWS in the great late Neolithic cemetery of the Boyne Valley, Co. Meath, Ireland, dating to the 3rd millennium bc (see BOYNE CULTURE). The barrow measures c90 metres in diameter and is made up of layers of turf, stones, clay and earth. It is surrounded by a kerb of stones. The mound covers two PASSAGE GRAVES, opening from opposite points on the diameter; both have long passages and one has a CORBEL-vaulted chamber. Many of the stones of the chambers, passages and kerb are decorated with the incised designs characteristic of this group of tombs. Around the great central cairn were 16 smaller barrows, each covering a tomb of passage grave or entrance grave type.

Excavations have also revealed the remains of the Early Christian royal centre here, belonging to the Northern Brega known from the Irish annals. The settlement of this period was cut into the rock and was undefended. Evidence of crafts such as bone comb making and metalworking has been uncovered. There has been some speculation that the Vikings raided the Boyne tombs during the mid-9th century AD, but it is perhaps more likely that they were raiding not the much earlier tombs, but the contemporary homes of some of the wealthier tribesmen of the region.

Kofun. Japanese term used in two ways: (1) a type of tumulus used for burials in the proto-historic and early historic periods and (2) the period AD 300-700 when these tumuli were in use.

The Kofun period falls between the YAYOI period and the fully historic Nara period and partially overlaps the ASUKA and Hakuho periods of art historians. It was a proto-historic and proto-literate period: contemporary Chinese and Korean records refer to the inhabitants of what is now Japan, and by the 5th century the political élite in Japan was itself making use of writing. KOJIKI and NIHON SHOKI were edited during the 7th century and completed in the early 8th century.

The tumuli — kofun — are the most con-spicuous monuments of the period. Round tumuli of modest size were the most frequent, but square ones were also built. The most spectacular and unique to Japan is a round mound with a rectangular projection, resembl-ing an old-fashioned keyhole in plan. In a few examples the longer dimension of the keyhole reaches more than 400 metres and many mounds are surrounded by one or more moats. The grave itself was in the round part of the keyhole, dug from the top in earlier *kofun*, entered by a passage in the side in later ones. HANIWA were placed on top of and around the mound and occasionally in the passage of the type with side entrance. Very large keyhole-shaped *kofun* were rare in the 6th and 7th centuries, particularly in the Kyoto-Osaka area where they appeared the earliest. New burial practices in the later part of the Kofun period are hundreds of small mounds arranged in clusters and also burials in artificial caves dug into a cliff face. The latter practice continued until the 9th century in outlying areas.

There is no sharp break between the Yayoi and Kofun periods. Early *kofun* (for example TSUBAI OTSUKAYAMA) were built by modifying natural hills, as were Late Yayoi burial mounds. The tall stands for ritual pots placed on the Yayoi mounds could easily be the precursors of *haniwa*. Mirrors, swords and beads, buried in abundance in early *kofun*, apparently had ritual importance, as they did in Yayoi times. HAJI pottery, used throughout the Kofun period, is very similar to Yayoi pottery and farmers lived in the same kinds of houses, using very similar tools.

Technical advances over the Yayoi period include irrigation canals and dams for agricultural fields and other engineering projects, such as the construction of *kofun* and, later, palaces and temples. A larger variety of iron tools was manufactured by blacksmiths. There were also silversmiths who made the ornaments deposited in *kofun* and professional potters began making SUE pottery in the 5th century.

The Kofun period is characterized by the rise of political leaders who initiated and co-ordinated the kind of activities just described. Available records, both archaeological and documentary, suggest that there were many of these leaders in the earlier part of the period on both sides of the Korean Strait. There was then no international boundary nor a clear-cut ethnic division there and the leaders were in frequent contact — sometimes friendly, sometimes hostile — across the Strait. Those in the fertile and well-protected Yamato Basin actively sought new technical and administrative skills on the continent, in order to improve their competitive position over other leaders. Thus artisans came to make new kinds of pottery, ornaments and weapons, and scholars, bureaucrats and Buddhist priests were welcomed at the YAMATO court. The Yamato leaders gained control over much of Japan in the 7th century and moved the capital to Heijo in 710. However 'rebels' and 'barbarians' survived in outlying areas and caused trouble for governments for centuries afterwards.

Koh Ker. Name of a plain *c*70 km northeast of ANGKOR, in northern Cambodia, and the monuments on it. Originally called Chok Gargyar, it was the location of the capital of the kingdom of Angkor for the period 921-44 AD, the so-called Koh Ker Interlude in the history of that kingdom. Its art and architecture form a distinctive style.

Kojiki [*Records of Ancient Matters*]. The oldest extant comprehensive history of Japan. The effort to compile and edit legends and genealogies into a coherent account which would justify the supremacy of the ruling YAMATO house began in the 7th century, and was completed in 712. Written in an old Japanese using the linguistically incompatible Chinese characters, the account begins with a creation myth and covers the events up to the early 7th century.

Kok Charoen. A site in northeastern Central Thailand, dated to the 2nd and 1st millennia BC, which yielded, in addition to occupational remains, more than 60 burials furnished with pottery very similar to that of NON NOK THA. As no metal artefacts have been found at the site itself or in the vicinity, Kok Charoen must be considered to be the largest Neolithic burial site so far discovered in Southeast Asia.

Kokkinopilos. A site in northeast Greece which has produced a surface collection of MOUSTERIAN types. Some leaf points were also found.

Koldewey, Robert (1855-1925). German scholar who excavated the great Mesopotamian city of BABYLON from 1899 to 1914. These excavations were of very fine quality for their time. They exposed many of the major buildings of the city, including the Ishtar Gate, Nebuchadnezzar's Palace, the temple and ziggurat of Marduk and the city walls; they also investigated the stratification of the site. Some of the results of this great work were published in Koldewey's book *The Excavations at Babylon* (1914).

Kolihwa. *See* RICE.

Köln-Lindenthal. Settlement site of the Neolithic LINEAR POTTERY culture in a suburb of Cologne in northwest Germany. Excavations in the early 1930s stripped a large area of the site and much of the settlement was exposed, although the long houses were described as barns and the hollows left where mud for the walls had been dug were interpreted as pit dwellings. Later the site was seen as a typical Linear Pottery settlement, with seven different building phases separated, it was thought, by periods of abandonment perhaps 50 years long, giving an overall period of nearly 400 years of use of the site. More recently still this view of Linear Pottery settlement has been challenged and it is possible that Köln-Lindenthal, like other sites of the culture, was continuously occupied, perhaps for a shorter period than originally envisaged.

Kolomiiščina. A large two-period settlement site of the TRIPOLYE culture, located in the forest steppe zone near Kiev and dated to the late 4th to early 3rd millennium bc. The earlier occupation contains Tripolye B2 pottery associated with a small number of houses. In the second phase a more formal circular village plan of some 25 houses is laid out with a stock-enclosure in the centre. This village is dated to the earlier Bronze Age Tripolye C1 phase; the pottery in the houses shows affinities with the CORDED WARE and Yamnaya styles. Cattle husbandry is the pre-eminent economic activity.

Kolomoki. A large multi-mound site (1.2 million square metres in area) in southern Georgia, USA, which seems to have thrived in the period between the decline of the WOODLAND TRADITION and the emergence of the MISSISSIPPIAN. Its major features are a large flat-topped mound *c*17 metres high (with barely a trace of surmounting structures) and several smaller mounds, some of which contain burials. Elaborately worked funerary vessels and grave goods such as copper ornaments and shell beads attest to ceremonial burial practice. When the practice of retainer SACRIFICE (possibly a Mesoamerican influence) is added to this collection of cultural traits, a unit of notably complex social organization, possibly an early chiefdom, is indicated. Although there is ample evidence of hunting and gathering, there is little indication of agriculture as would normally be expected at a site of such complexity.

Kom Ombo. A riverine plain in Egyptian Nubia. Particular interest attaches to the period around 12,000 to 10,000 bc, when intensive exploitation of local food resources, including wild grasses, seems to have been accompanied by differentiation of three distinct population groups.

Kondane. A rock-cut Buddhist temple in the western Deccan, India, dating to the late 1st century BC or early 1st century AD.

Kondon. *See* AMUR NEOLITHIC.

Kon-Tiki. A balsa raft constructed by Thor Heyerdahl and his companions in 1947 to test the hypothesis that South American Indians could have drifted into Polynesia. The raft drifted from a point 80 km off the coast of Peru for 101 days until it reached Raroia in the Tuamotu Archipelago. The experiment showed that Indians could have reached Polynesia, but modern archaeology has shown that any contacts were only of a minor nature. *See also* EASTER ISLAND, SWEET POTATO.

Koobi Fora. The name now often given to a widely spread group of fossil hominid localities, including ILERET, on the east side of Lake Turkana [formerly Lake Rudolf] in northern Kenya adjacent to Ethiopia. Over 150 hominids in more or less fragmentary state have been recovered from deposits that seem to date between 1 and 2.5 million years ago. At least two lineages seem to be represented in the period between 1 and 1.5 million years ago, *Homo erectus* and *Australopithecus robustus/ boisei*. Earlier fossils may be of the '*H. habilis*' type. Stone tools are found at several levels from the KBS tuff at about 1.8 million years ago up to some later levels where hand axes appear in small quantities.

Koonalda. A huge limestone cave beneath the Nullarbor Plain, South Australia. Bands and nodules of flint in the limestone were quarried in conditions of complete darkness and difficulty of access, up to 300 metres from the cave entrance. From deep excavations in the cave floor, charcoal associated with quarrying debris and utilized flakes has returned radio-carbon age estimates of c20,000-13000 bc. Parietal art (in the form of enigmatic, but regular, 'finger' grooves on soft limestone) and scratches and engravings on harder rock have been dated by covering rock-fall to at least 18,000 bc.

Kootwijk. A MIGRATION PERIOD settlement was discovered near the village of Kootwijk in Central Holland in 1964. Excavations between 1971 and 1974 uncovered a segment of what would have been a very large village dating from between the later 7th and later 10th centuries. The excavators found evidence of 45 post-built houses, 177 sunken huts, 14 animal sheds, and 3 raised grain silos. Kootwijk bears similarities to WARENDORF in the variety of building types, the way in which the buildings overlie each other, and the grouping into units enclosed by a palisade set in a shallow trench. The principal building in each group was a rectangular or boat-shaped long hall, which was often partitioned intern-ally into two or three rooms. At its largest Kootwijk probably possessed 15 or more such farm units. The village lies in a sandy lake basin and as a result of the gradual encroachment of sand over the fields and their boundaries it has been possible to determine not only the types of cereal cultivated here but also the size and shapes of fields and the ploughing techniques used.

Körös. *See* FIRST TEMPERATE NEOLITHIC.

Kosipe. The oldest site with human occupa-tion in NEW GUINEA, Kosipe lies in the Papuan Highlands and has produced waisted stone tools stratified between volcanic ash showers of 19,000 to 26,000 years ago. Such tools continue to occur in other Highland sites (especially KIOWA) until about 3000 BC.

Kostenki. The most important group of PALAEOLITHIC sites in Russia is around the village of Kostenki in the Don basin, near Voronesh. There are more than 20 sites, but the most important are Kostenki I, K XIV (Markina), K VIII (Telman), K XII, K II, K XI (Anosofka II) and K XVII (Spitsyna). Skeletons of CROMAGNON type but mainly immature have been found at sites II, XIV and XV. The basic sequence of strata is similar in most sites on the second terrace. Two buried humuses are separated by volcanic ash and *suglinok*, a kind of loam. These contain the earlier Upper Palaeolithic levels. Above a further *suglinok*, the upper layers contain late Upper Palaeolithic, roughly contemporary with the MAGDALENIAN of France. Numerous art objects have been recovered, and Kostenki I has produced more of the 'VENUS' figurines than any other site in Europe. A number of hut plans are also claimed. Latest Palaeolithic sites are known around nearby Borchevo.

Koster. A site of long occupation located in west central Illinois, USA, and notable for its well-stratified ARCHAIC sequences. Deposits more than 9 metres in depth contain at least 11 distinct cultural levels covering the period c7500 bc to ad 1000. The site served variously as a workshop for stone tools, a deer-butcher-ing camp and possibly as the site for one of the earliest villages in North America. Stone-ground ADZES and MANOS and METATES dated c6400 bc certainly occur rather early.

Ceremonial mortuary practices in the form of extended burials together with incised ceramics dated 200-100 bc indicate a WOOD-LAND component. Later levels, designated the Jersey Bluff phase, contain evidence of increased hunting efficiency (the replacement of the ATLATL by the bow and arrow) and of agriculture (squash and pumpkin remains), and may even have MISSISSIPPIAN associ-ations.

An inundation from the Illinois River in 1979 considerably disturbed the integrity of the site, which has since been back-filled. Further work now seems unlikely.

Kosziderpadlas. Denotes a horizon of metal hoards defined by A. Mozsolics as dating to the later part of the Early Bronze Age (mid-2nd millennium bc) and distributed over Rumania, Hungary, most of Czechoslovakia, southern Poland and parts of Eastern Germ-any. Whilst several types continue in use from the preceding HAJDÚSÁMSON horizon (e.g. disc-butted and shaft-tube axes), new orna-ment types in bronze (ivy-leaf and cordiform pendants, twisted pins and bracelets) abound alongside flanged axes, palstaves and solid-hilted daggers. Smaller scale goldwork is found but the unique pieces of the Hajdúsámson phase are no longer produced.

Kota Batu. The capital of the Muslim Sultanate of Brunei in northern Borneo. The defended palace and sumptuous court were described by Pigafetta in 1521, and excavations at Kota Batu have produced large quantities of imported Chinese and Thai pottery dating from about 1380-1580. The palace was on the bank of the Brunei River and most of the town's inhabitants appear to have lived in pile dwellings built over the estuarine waters. The Brunei Museum now stands on a part of the ancient site.

Kota Tampan. *See* MALAYSIA.

Kot Diji. A site in the Indus Valley in Pakistan, which has given its name to one of a group of pre-HARAPPAN cultures in this area, a variant of the NAL-AMRI group. The Kot Dijian levels underlie a mature Harappan occupation and have radiocarbon dates suggesting a range of c2450-2000 bc (c3150-2500 BC). Kot Dijian ceramics have also been found in early levels at HARAPPA and KALIBANGAN and on a number of surface sites.

Kotosh. An early ceremonial complex located at an elevation of 1950 metres on the eastern slopes of the central Andes above present-day Huanuco, Peru. Four successive major phases designated Mito, WAIRA-JIRCA, Kotosh and CHAVIN run from the PRECERAMIC PERIOD VI through the INITIAL PERIOD and into the EARLY HORIZON. The earliest Mito phase contains, among other structures, the Temple of the Crossed Hands, so called from the decorative motif in mud plaster on the lower walls. Stone tools, some similar to LAURICOCHA II and III, and other artefacts appropriate to an ARCHAIC subsistence pattern also occur in this phase. The first ceramics appear in the overlying Waira-Jirca levels, which have also produced radiocarbon dates in the range 1800-1150 bc. In the following Kotosh phase, radiocarbon dated to c1000-900 bc, there is further construction of platform mounds, new pottery forms (effigy and STIRRUP-SPOUT VESSELS) and inferential evidence of the use of maize (representations on ceramics). Ceramics of the Chavin phase maintain distinctly local characteristics, but incorporate elements of the Chavin horizon art-style. Negative painted vessels of the poorly understood Higueras style occur in post-Chavin contexts.

Kourounkorokale. A rock shelter near Bamako in Mali, West Africa, containing evidence for at least two poorly defined phases of occupation. The crude stone industry was accompanied in the second phase by barbed bone harpoon heads. The site may indicate a westerly representative of the heterogeneous complex of harpoon-fishing adaptations which is attested in the southern Sahara between the 8th and the 3rd millennia bc.

Kow Swamp. A large burial site close to the Murray River, Victoria, Southern Australia, dated to between 11,000 and 7000 bc. More than 40 crania and mandibles show marked robusticity of the fronto-facial regions combined with more modern, but still thick-boned, posterior areas of the crania. Contrasts between the robust Kow Swamp population and the much older but more gracile LAKE MUNGO skeletons pose questions about the derivation of Australian Aborigines from early Indonesian populations in single or multiple migrations, and the possible role of adaptation in human populations to effect morphological change. Both the Mungo and KEILOR gracile crania and the Kow Swamp robust group lie outside the extremes of the range of recent Aboriginal populations. Kow Swamp stone tools consisted of a few small quartz flakes and bipolar cores, similar to finds of the same age at GREEN GULLY.

Krak des Chevaliers. A grandiose castle of the Crusader period and one of the few to have been systematically excavated and restored. It is situated on a hilltop in the Nusairi mountains in southern Syria and is surrounded on all sides by a formidable gradient. The Crusader castle was constructed on top of an Arab fort and its principal phase was built after 1142 by Knights of the Hospital of St John, who kept a permanent force there. Krak has an advanced composite plan consisting of two concentric rings of fortification separated by a moat and lined with circular bastions backed by defensive galleries, which in turn surround a massive internal complex of halls, courtyards, strongholds and chapel. In 1271 the castle fell to the Arabs, who rebuilt extensive parts of it.

Kraków. *See* CRACOW.

Krefeld-Gellep. A large Roman and Frankish cemetery of the REIHENGRABERFELD type situated on the lower Rhine. Among the 2000 excavated burials within the cemetery, one grave of outstanding wealth dated to about 630 and contained a gilded helmet, a sword inlaid with precious stones, three spears and a dagger, axe and shield. There were silver and gilded bridle-trimmings and glass, bronze and gold vessels and tableware. The personal apparel included a garnet-inlaid purse and gold belt-buckle and ring. The circumstances and date of this grave suggest that the occupant may have been a chieftain or the founder of a settlement.

Kremikovci. *See* FIRST TEMPERATE NEO-LITHIC.

Kremlin. The fortified citadel of medieval Russian and Slavic towns. The most famous and best-preserved is the so-called Kremlin in Moscow, which dates to the 14th century, and is a rare stone-built example. Within it lie a variety of palaces, churches and state buildings in a range of styles spanning the 14th-18th centuries.

Krems. A classic LOESS area in Lower Austria; a major soil horizon, possibly of the last INTER-GLACIAL, is called the Krems-boden. The Krems-Hundssteig locality has revealed a very rich AURIGNACIAN-like assemblage in which numerous bladelets and 'Krems' points are found.

Kroeber, Alfred Louis (1876-1960). American archaeologist and anthropologist who made major contributions to both practical and theoretical archaeology in the Americas. His main areas of study in the field were the American Southwest (*see also* KIDDER, A.V.) and Peru (*see also* UHLE, Max) and in both areas he helped establish the basic sequences of development, largely through the SERIA-TION of pottery types. In the field of archaeo-logical theory he showed an early interest in such modern concerns as the explanation of culture change.

Kuala Selinsing. A coastal site in northern Perak, Malaysia, which has produced remains of pile dwellings probably built over a man-grove swamp, burials in canoe-like coffins, and quantities of beads of presumed Indian origin. The site may have been a small trade station of the period AD600-1100, but its exact significance in the process of 'Indianization' in West Malaysia is still only poorly understood; the material seems to be considerably earlier than that found in Hindu-Buddhist sites to the north in Kedah (post-11th century).

Kuban [Koban] **culture**. Denotes (1) a regional variant of the earlier Bronze Age 'North Caucasian' culture group, located in the Kuban Valley of western Caucasia and dated to the mid-2nd millennium bc; (2) an industrial complex of the latest Bronze Age to earliest Iron Age, dated to the early 1st millennium bc and located in the same area. This complex comprises bronze horse harness, shaft-hole axes, pendants, racquet pins and belt-clasps. The heavy concentration of Caucasian bronzes in the amber source zone of east Prussia is taken to indicate an extensive amber trade, the reciprocal results of which are seen in Kuban cemeteries.

Kufa. In central Iraq, Kufa was founded as a garrison by the caliph Omar I in 638. It was a hotbed of anti-Umayyad sentiment. In 749, it served briefly as the capital of the Abbasids, before they founded BAGHDAD. Kufa became a large commercial and intellectual centre, but a series of incursions by the Qarmathians in 924-5, 927 and 937 caused extensive damage and the city declined. By the 14th century it was almost deserted. In 670 the governor of BASRAH, Ziyad b. Abihi, imported masons from Khuzistan to erect a mosque 'that would be without equal'. It was a stone structure with columns 15 metres high supporting the roof without the use of arches — presumably in the tradition of the *apadana*, or hall of columns, as at PERSEPOLIS. Kufic, an angular script often employed for writing the Arabic alphabet, is said — erroneously — to have been developed at Kufa.

Kujavian grave. Name given to a distinctive type of tomb found in Poland during the Neolithic period, associated with the TRB CULTURE. Extended inhumations, usually within a stone built chamber or a trench, were covered by long trapezoidal barrows, some-times surrounded by a stone kerb. Very few of these tombs had more than one burial.

Kuk. A site complex in the New Guinea Highlands, near Mount Hagen, which has produced several systems of swamp-drainage ditches, some up to three metres deep, extending back to about 7000 bc. The major crop grown may have been the AROID *Colocasia esculenta*, and the findings have great significance because they appear to document a totally independent origin of horticulture in the New Guinea Highlands, quite separate from any AUSTRONESIAN influence. *See also* NEW GUINEA.

Kulèn. Phnom (Cambodian: 'mount') Kulèn is a hill in the plain north of the Tonle Sap or Great Lake of Cambodia, about 30 km north of ANGKOR. Under the name MAHENDRAPARVATA it was the place where the founder of the Angkorian kingdom, Jayavarman II, proclaimed its independence from Java in 802, probably so as to claim the title of 'King of the Mountain' (i.e. Universal Ruler), which seems to have been that of the kings of FUNAN before him. There are the ruins of several monuments on this hill, and it also served as a quarry for the sandstone which was used in a number of monuments at Angkor, notably ANGKOR WAT.

Kulkulkan. *See* CHICHEN ITZA, MAYAPAN.

Kulli. A site in the Kolwa region of southern Baluchistan, excavated by Aurel STEIN, which has given its name to a cultural group of the 3rd millennium BC. The site covers c10 hectares and is c10 metres high. The characteristic pottery of this group is wheel-turned and painted in black on a buff or red slip with friezes of zebu cattle, ibexes and other animals, and spiky trees. Clay figurines of women and bulls are found in this culture, as are copper tools and ornaments of lapis lazuli, bone and other materials. Like the related sites of the NAL group, Kulli settlements are associated with evidence of water control and developed agriculture. Mud-brick was used for buildings, but at the type site Stein excavated part of a stone-walled structure which may have been a special building, such as a temple or palace. Cremation was the normal burial rate of this culture; an important cemetery was excavated at MEHI.

Kültepe [ancient Kanesh]. Bronze Age town near Kayseri on the Anatolian plateau in modern Turkey, occupied in the later 3rd and early 2nd millennia BC. Outside the walls of the town, but annexed to it by an enclosure wall, was a commercial colony known as a *karum* where Assyrian merchants established themselves in the early years of the 2nd millennium BC. The Kültepe *karum* was one of several established in Anatolian cities by the kingdom of ASSUR to establish supplies of raw materials, especially metals, needed in Mesopotamia. Early levels in the *karum* area pre-date the arrival of the Assyrians (levels IV and III), but level II (usually dated 2000-1900 BC) and level IB (dated c1850-1750 BC) have yielded some 15,000 clay tablets which have provided a detailed record of the commercial activities of the merchants. The tablets are inscribed in Assyrian CUNEIFORM and represent the earliest writing found in Anatolia. They record day-to-day administration and commercial organization in the colony. The main materials traded were metals (silver, gold and copper produced in Anatolia, tin produced in Mesopotamia) and garments (made in Mesopotamia). The Assyrian merchants controlled the trade between Assur and Anatolia, but they were subject to Anatolian laws and paid taxes to the Anatolian rulers. The *karum* was destroyed by fire at the end of the level II phase and again after IB; after this second destruction the trading colony ceased to exist. Excavations in the *karum* have revealed houses, separated by streets and alleys, and workshops, which suggest that it was also important as an industrial centre for metal-working. The associated city had a double fortification and enclosed a palace complex and other public buildings, including temples.

Kumadzulo. An informative Early Iron Age village site near the Victoria Falls in southern Zambia. Dated between the 5th and the 7th centuries ad, Kumadzulo has preserved the remains of several rectangular pole and clay houses of unusually small size. Bones of cattle and small stock indicate the herding of domestic animals: the presence of grindstones and iron hoes is a strong indication that food crops were also cultivated.

Kumbi Saleh. The extensive ruins at this site in southern Mauritania are very probably those of the capital of ancient GHANA. Excavations have revealed the presence of a stone-built mosque and two-storey houses with ground-floor storerooms. Pottery and glass indicate trans-Saharan trade with North Africa.

Kumtepe. Site in northwest Turkey, overlooking the Dardanelles, 4 km from TROY. Excavations have demonstrated three phases of Early Bronze Age occupation, all earlier than the first settlement at Troy (Troy I), and probably dating to the earlier 4th millennium BC.

Kunda culture. Refers to the eastern Baltic variant of the Baltic forest techno-complex, an adaptation to the mixed deciduous and coniferous forests of the early Postglacial period, c7000-5000 bc. Most Kunda settlements are located at the edge of the forest, near rivers, lakes and marshes. Economic strategies included specialized hunting of the elk (partly aided by the domestic dog), seal-hunting, fishing for pike and other fish. Bone and antler tools were decorated with simple geometric motifs which lacked the complexity of the contemporary MAGLEMOSEAN groups' artwork.

Kuntur Wasi [La Copa]. A site located near Cajamarca, in the upper Pacasmayu drainage in the northern highlands of Peru. Although now largely destroyed, the central structure was a stone-faced triple terraced pyramid topped by a temple. Three-dimensional statues and other carved stone are executed in the CHAVIN style; the characteristic feline motif is common. Other associated features, however, including the ceramics, appear to be a mixture of Chavin and later styles, suggesting that the site may extend beyond the EARLY HORIZON.

Kurgan. The Russian word for 'burial mound' has been extensively used to denote archaeological cultures of the south Russian steppe zone, from the 4th millennium bc onwards. Three forms of burial can be identified: Yamnaya (pit-grave) burial, dated c2400-1800 bc; Katakombnaja (catacomb-grave) burial, dated c2300-1800 bc; and Srubnaya (timber grave) burial, dated c1600-900 bc. It is the thesis of M. Gimbutas that pastoral nomads from the Eurasian steppe invaded the Balkan Copper Age culture areas in four 'Kurgan' waves, thereby putting an end to the Neolithic cycle of cultural development and introducing INDO-EUROPEAN languages to the Balkans.

Kush. The name applied to the area of the Sudanese Nubian Nile Valley which, during and after the pharaonic period, was subject to Egyptian cultural and/or political influence. After a brief florescence centred on KERMA, Kush's main period of independence commenced in about the 9th century BC. In the 8th century, the kings of Kush conquered Egypt and ruled briefly there as the Twenty-fifth Dynasty, being expelled southwards once more after the Assyrian invasion of Egypt in 671 BC. In their homeland, the Kushites' capital was established first at NAPATA near the fourth Nile cataract; about 600 BC it was moved to MEROE, south of the Nile-Atbara confluence. Here, the capital was better situated to exploit trade-routes eastward to the Red Sea and Ethiopia as well as those of the Nile Valley. Timber was also more plentiful and was used to fuel the Meroitic iron industry, which probably began on a small scale in about the 6th century BC. The kingdom of Kush survived into the early 4th century AD, when the final collapse of Meroe was probably due to an invasion from AXUM.

Kushan. A nomadic tribe that settled in Iran, Afghanistan and northern India in the 2nd century BC. Their Indian empire lasted until the 3rd century AD.

Kutikina [formerly Fraser Cave]. *See* TASMANIA.

Kuyunjik. *See* NINEVEH.

Kwakuitl. *See* NORTHWEST COAST TRADITION.

Kwale. A site not far inland from Mombasa in southeastern Kenya, which has given its name to the Early Iron Age industry of that area and adjacent parts of northeastern Tanzania. The highly characteristic pottery, Kwale ware, was being produced from about the 2nd century ad onwards and appears to be derived in some way from the UREWE ware of the interlacustrine region. Pottery akin to Kwale ware occurs far down the East African coast as far to the south as MATOLA in Mozambique and sites in the eastern Transvaal, where it is dated to the 4th century ad.

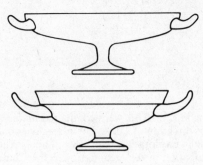

Two forms of kylix

kylix [Greek 'cup'; *cf* chalice]. An ancient Greek drinking vessel. The term was originally used for a cup of any form, but modern scholars restrict it to shallow two-handed stemmed forms.

Kyrillovskaya. A site in KIEV which has produced late PALAEOLITHIC remains, including some ivory bracelets and other pieces carved with a kind of 'greek key' or 'squared spiral' design.

L

Laang Spean. A cave in western Cambodia which has yielded a HOABINHIAN sequence with an appearance of ground stone tools and pottery by perhaps 4300 bc. Hoabinhian tool forms may have continued in use here into the 1st millennium AD.

Labra. *See* PUUC.

labret. A decorative plug inserted into a ready-made incision in the lower lip, like earrings in pierced ears. Although styles vary and labrets were particularly popular in MESO-AMERICA, they occur in artefact inventories from the Arctic to the Andes. They are made from almost any material that is suitably hard, including stone, bone, metal and pottery.

La Centinela. *See* CHINCHA.

La Chapelle. The small cave of La Chapelle aux Saints is in the Corrèze department of southwest France. In 1908 a skeleton of NEANDERTHAL man was found here buried in a level of MOUSTERIAN (QUINA) type. In a famous study by Marcellin Boule, it was made the type specimen of *Homo neanderthalensis*, supposedly an extinct line of human evolution. Boule also initiated the view that this type of man was stooping in posture and essentially different in body structure from modern man. We still recognize significant differences in the skull, such as the large forward-positioned face and very large nose, as well as the long low braincase and brow ridges; but anthropologists now know that the skeleton was little different from that of today. The La Chapelle man was deformed pathologically by chronic osteo-arthritis and other degenerations often found with old age today.

Lachish. The biblical city of Lachish has been identified as the site of the large TELL of Tell ed Duweir, west of Hebron in southern Israel. Early excavations in the 1930s were brought to a halt by the tragic murder by bandits of the director, J.L. Starkey, in 1938. New excava-tions in the 1970s were conducted under the joint direction of Tel Aviv University and the Israel Exploration Society. The earliest occupation in the area, dating to the Chalco-lithic and Early Bronze Age, has been found in caves, used for occupation and burial. The town itself seems to have been first occupied in the later Early Bronze Age and in the Middle Bronze Age a massive earth rampart with a plastered ramp of HYKSOS type was con-structed around the town. This was destroyed, probably by the Egyptians, *c*1580 BC. After this the fortifications went out of use for several centuries and a temple was built at the foot of the mound, with three main phases of use, dating to the 15th-13th centuries BC. Later Bronze Age and Iron Age occupation of the mound was brought to an end by a violent destruction, perhaps to be equated with the campaign of the ASSYRIAN king Sennacherib in 701 BC, which he celebrated in reliefs in his palace at NINEVEH. The city defences were rebuilt and the settlement continued until another destruction by the BABYLONIANS in 588 BC. After this there was some occupation also in the ACHAEMENID and HELLENISTIC periods, but the site seems to have been of only minor importance at this time. One of the most important finds from the site is a dagger, dated to the 18th or 17th century BC with four symbols engraved on it; this is one of the earliest alphabetic inscriptions known. Lachish has also produced a group of incised pottery vessels associated with the temple at the foot of the mound and dated to *c*1400 BC, and a group of incised potsherds found within a guardhouse by the gate and dating to the period immediately before the Babylonian destruction.

La Copa. *See* KUNTUR WASI.

lacquer. The juice of the lac tree, *Rhus verni-cifera*, a natural varnish which hardens on exposure to air. Applied in many coats to a core made of wood, fabric, or cloth-covered wood, it forms a tough and durable protective surface, resistant to water and capable of a high polish. In China lacquered vessels were made as early as the SHANG dynasty. The oldest securely dated examples, a few fragments from GAOCHENG Taixicun (c14th century BC), are decorated in the two staple colours of later Chinese lacquers, black and red. A few other Shang and Western ZHOU examples have been unearthed, but lacquers are found in large numbers only at Eastern Zhou and HAN sites of the 5th century BC and later, when the lacquer industry seems to have flourished on an unprecedentedly large scale. Waterlogged tombs in or near the territory of the CHU state have yielded spectacular finds of perfectly preserved lacquers, including not only vessels, cosmetic boxes and other luxury goods but also musical instruments and even coffins (see LINYI, MAWANGDUI, JIANGLING, SUI XIAN, XINYANG, YUNMENG). These Eastern Zhou and Han lacquers are decorated with painted designs of extreme refinement in which the usual red and black pigments are sometimes joined by green, yellow, brown, white, gold and silver; occasionally they are also fitted or inlaid with shell, bronze, gold or silver. Painted coffins like those from Sui Xian must have been extraordinarily expensive; Han texts say that lacquer vessels were more prized and far more costly than bronze (so that in later periods they came under increasing competition from ceramics). Some Han lacquers carry dated inscriptions that name not only the state-operated factory where an object was made (see CHENGDU) but also all the artisans responsible for the successive stages in its manufacture, attesting a very considerable division of labour. Lacquer production has continued to the present day in both China and Japan, since the Han dynasty relying for decoration more on inlays and carving than on painting.

La Cumbe. *See* CHINCHA.

Lac-viêt [Chinese Lo Yüeh]. Earliest ethnic name of the people of present northern Vietnam, in Chinese sources. Etymologically unknown, it also appears in the name of the kingdom of ÂU-LAC in the 3rd century BC.

laeti. Latin term used under the later Roman Empire (from the 3rd century AD onwards) of barbarians who were settled as farmers by the Roman government, in areas deserted after intrusive raids. They had an obligation, inherited by their descendants, to perform Roman military service.

Laetoli [formerly Laetolil]. A site in Tanzania, part of the same group of PLEISTOCENE and PLIOCENE deposits as OLDUVAI GORGE some 40 km to the north. No stone tools are found, but remains of about a dozen hominids are known. They date from some 3.5 to 4 million years ago; along with HADAR they have been attributed to a new species, *Australopithecus afarensis*, but others have compared them to the previously known gracile species *A. africanus* (*see* AUSTRALOPITHECUS, HUMAN EVOLUTION).

La Ferrassie. A rock shelter in the Dordogne, southwest France. It has a long series of deposits from MOUSTERIAN at the base, including several layers of 'Ferrassie' type or CHARENTIAN with LEVALLOIS flaking, through a long series of Upper PALAEOLITHIC levels. These are PERIGORDIAN I, AURIGNACIAN I to IV, and later Perigordian (with Font Robert points and with truncated elements). The most famous feature is the NEANDERTHAL burials found from 1909 onwards. These comprise an adult male and female of classic Neanderthal type, and some five younger individuals including two newborns. One child was buried under a slab with apparently deliberately carved cup marks on its surface. Another child was buried below one of a series of nine small mounds.

Laga Oda. A rock shelter near Harar in southeastern Ethiopia. A long sequence of occupation has been dated, commencing around the 14th millennium bc, with an industry of small blades including numerous backed elements. This industry appears to have continued into the 2nd millennium ad. Bones of domestic cattle first occur at a level dated to around the mid-2nd millennium bc. The site also contains rock paintings depicting humans, cattle and fat-tailed sheep.

Lagash. An important city-state of SUMER which flourished during the EARLY DYNASTIC, AKKADIAN and UR III periods. For many years it was assumed that the site of TELLOH, excavated by the French, was the city of Lagash itself, but it is now known that Telloh is ancient Girsu, within the state of Lagash, though not its capital. Lagash itself is now identified with the site of Al Hiba, *c*25 km to the southeast.

Lagoa Santa Caves. A system of caves located in the state of Minas Gerais in eastern Brazil with evidence of human occupation during the terminal PLEISTOCENE period. DOLICHO-CEPHALIC human remains and stone tools have been found with bones of extinct fauna such as mastodon, sloth and horse. Although there has been considerable argument over the antiquity and validity of these associations (some archaeologists argue that flooding is responsible for the mixture of cultural and animal material), more recent work has isolated an early tool complex. Called Cerca Grande and comprising bone and quartz projectile points, scrapers and hammerstones, it has produced two radiocarbon dates of *c*7600 and 7000 bc. Earlier radiocarbon dates have been derived from this site, but are sufficiently inconsistent with known data elsewhere to be regarded with some scepticism.

Lagozza. A LAKE VILLAGE near Milan in north Italy which has given its name to a Late Neolithic culture of the late 4th and early 3rd millennium bc. It is characterized by plain dark-surfaced, burnished pottery, usually undecorated; it is thought to be related to the CHASSEY culture of France and the CORTAIL-LOD culture of Switzerland. Its main area of distribution is in north Italy, but Lagozza material has been claimed from some sites in the peninsula. The Lagozza people were mixed farmers and a considerable quantity of plant material was preserved in waterlogged conditions at the type site: as well as wheat, barley, lentils and flax, which were cultivated, a large number of wild fruits and nuts were found, including pears, apples and cherries, nuts and acorns. The animal side of the diet may have involved a concentration on dairy products, as a number of artefacts occur which could have been used for making butter and cheese, including churns, strainers and pottery vessels in the form of perforated funnels which are interpreted as milk-boilers for cheese making. A small number of copper artefacts occur on Lagozza sites, suggesting the incipient development of metallurgy. Some crouched inhumation burials in cists occur.

Lake Arumpo. A large dried lake bed with a clay lunette, formerly a PLEISTOCENE lake in the Willandra Lakes system, western New South Wales, Australia. A radiocarbon date of 33,600 bc has been determined for an occupation layer containing unionid shells and charcoal fragments. *See also* LAKE MUNGO.

Lake Besaka. Several archaeological sites have been investigated in this area of south-eastern Ethiopia. Around the middle of the 2nd millennium bc the local stone industries are marked by an increase in the frequency and variety of scrapers. Stone bowls, akin to those of the East African PASTORAL NEOLITHIC sites far to the south, also occur at this period, which may mark the adoption of a herding life-style.

Lake Hauroko burial. A 17th-century burial of a MAORI woman, found in a cave on an island in Lake Hauroko, southwestern South Island, New Zealand. When found, the skeleton was still sitting on a bier of sticks and wrapped in a woven flax cloak.

Lake Mangakaware pa. A MAORI lake-edge fortification (PA) in the Waikato District, North Island, New Zealand. The site has produced one of the most complete Classic Maori settlement plans known (dated 1500-1800), with remains of palisades, houses, a central open space (MARAE), and many wooden objects from the adjacent lake.

Lake Mungo. A dry lake with a lunette in the Willandra Lakes, a complex of former PLEIS-TOCENE lakes in the arid region of western New South Wales, Australia. Excavation of the lunette has produced the best authent-icated series of radiocarbon dates for the earliest evidence of man's occupation of Australia, from 30,800 ± 1200 bc onwards when the lake was full. Stone tools belong to the AUSTRALIAN CORE TOOL AND SCRAPER TRADITION. Fossilized skeletal remains of three individuals were found, with evidence for ritual cremation 24,000 bc, together with the use of ochre in burial rites. Analyses of the Mungo I and III skeletons show extreme gracility in cranial morphology, resembling the KEILOR and GREEN GULLY fossils and con-trasting with those from KOW SWAMP. Faunal remains in middens around the former shore-line have provided dietary and Pleistocene environmental evidence, while the burnt clays in Pleistocene hearths have been tested by ARCHAEOMAGNETIC and THERMOLUMIN-ESCENCE dating methods. The Willandra Lakes started to dry up c13,000 bc. The appearance of grinding stones in this period suggests an adaptation to wild grain exploitation. Intensive occupation ceased with increasing aridity, although sporadic visits occurred during the HOLOCENE.

Lake Ngaroto pa. An excavated lake-edge fortification (PA) of Classic MAORI date in the Waikato District, North Island of New Zealand. This is one of the largest and deepest sites in the Waikato, being 5400 square metres in area, with deposits up to three metres deep.

Lake Nitchie. A relict lake bed on an ana-branch of the Darling River, western New South Wales, Australia. Excavation of a burial uncovered the skeleton of a very tall man wearing a necklace of 159 pierced teeth of the Tasmanian Devil (*Sarcophilus harrisii*). The skeleton was estimated to date to c4500 bc, and many frontal features of the cranium resembled the robust KOW SWAMP population although combined with a more modern temporal and frontal fullness and height.

Lake Sentani. A lake in northeastern Irian Jaya (NEW GUINEA), noted for a range of tools and weapons of bronze, iron and brass found in burial mounds. These artefacts are undated, but could represent a metallurgical industry established by Indonesian traders in recent centuries. New Guinea has otherwise no ancient metallurgical traditions.

lake village. A type of settlement found quite commonly in prehistoric Europe in areas with many lakes, such as Switzerland and north Italy. They should properly be labelled lakeside villages, since in most cases they were constructed on the shore and not on stilts over the water, as was formerly believed. They were, however, frequently constructed on timber platforms and subsequently rising water levels in the lakes have preserved these platforms and much other wooden material, as well as artefacts of other organic substances such as textiles and bark. Cultures in which lake villages are common include CHASSEY, CORTAILLOD, HORGEN and POLADA.

Lalibela. Located in the Lasta Province of Ethiopia, east of Lake Tana, Lalibela was the capital of the Zagwe dynasty from the 12th century. It is remarkable for a series of subterranean churches elaborately carved from the solid rock, which retain representations of many features known also from the architecture of AXUM in earlier times.

Lalibela Cave. Situated near the east side of Lake Tana, this is one of the very few sites in Ethiopia to have yielded remains of cultivated food plants. In the earlier part of the sequence, dated to the mid 1st millennium bc, scrapers and other stone implements were associated with pottery and with seeds of barley, chick-peas and legumes. It is unfortunate that the site throws no light on the antiquity of the cultivation of any of the indigenous Ethiopian food crops. Later deposits at Lalibela Cave contained Iron Age material.

Lalinde. A small rock shelter on the Dordogne River in southwest France. MAGDALENIAN deposits included a number of important art pieces and a human lower jaw.

La Madeleine. Beside the Vezère River a few kilometres upstream from LES EYZIES in the Dordogne, southwest France, is the large rock shelter of La Madeleine. First investigated in 1864 by LARTET and CHRISTY, it has become the type locality of the MAGDALENIAN stage or culture. Magdalenian IV to VI layers date from approximately 13,000 to 10,000 bc. Very numerous carved art pieces have been found with the stone and bone tools.

Lambityeco. See MONTE ALBAN, ZAPOTEC.

La Micoque. The collapsed rock shelter at La Micoque close to LES EYZIES in the Dordogne, southwest France, has a series of early PALAEOLITHIC levels. The uppermost with hand axes is the type assemblage of the MICOQUIAN industry, while the five lower levels are the type series of the TAYACIAN.

Lamoka. An inland site of the late ARCHAIC period located in the Finger Lakes region of central New York, USA. It is characterized by narrow-stemmed points of a type usually associated with coastal areas and by a well-developed industry in worked bone. Other traits include houses framed with upright poles, bevelled adzes, ATLATL weights, MANOS and METATES and fishing gear. Dates are from c2500 to 1800 bc.

Lamphun. *See* HARIPUNJAYA.

Lancefield. A small swamp near KEILOR, Victoria, Australia, containing bones of an extinct giant fauna representing an estimated 10,000 individuals, dated to c24,000 bc. Six species are represented, but *Macropus titan* bones predominate. A few stone tools have been found in the bone beds indicating that men and megafauna were contemporary in the area, probably for 7000 years. Cut-marks on some bones have been interpreted as the teeth marks of the carniverous predator *Thylacoleo carnifex*, now extinct, and not as the result of human butchering. Evidence of the long association of humans and megafauna at Lancefield does not support the theory that rapid overkill by man led to the extinction of Pleistocene megafauna.

Lan Chang [Lan Xang]. The earliest kingdom of LAOS, founded in 1353. This was the establishment of an eastern branch of the THAI people in a territory which belonged to the by then declining KHMER empire of ANGKOR. The kingdom was formed by the union of the principalities of Muang Chawa (present-day Luang Prabang) and Wian Chan (present-day Vientiane). It was undoubtedly favoured by the weakening of the state of SUKHOTHAI, and included Thai and Khmer elements in its cultural basis.

landnam. A term introduced by the Danish palynologist J. Iversen in 1941, meaning 'land-taking'. It describes fluctuations seen in Danish POLLEN DIAGRAMS, just above the ELM DECLINE. Associated with charcoal layers in lake-edge deposits, there is a fall in the pollen of forest trees, a rise in herbaceous plants and a rise in birch and hazel, followed by a return of forest tree pollen to normal levels. Cereals and weeds of arable agriculture may be present. Iversen suggested that such fluctuations represented temporary clearance of the forest, a period of agriculture (usually pastoral, but with some arable) lasting some 100 years or more, followed by regeneration of the forest. The landnam phases were associated with NEOLITHIC artefacts, but seemed to be of varying date, representing a kind of shifting agriculture. Clearances of landnam type are

also seen in the British Isles, again mostly characterized by grasses and weeds of pasture. Some pollen diagrams show several such phases. They range in date from Neolithic to Bronze Age.

Lang-cā. A newly discovered Bronze Age site at the outskirts of the town of Viêt-trì in northern Vietnam. With about 350 burials it is the most important site of the DONG-SON phase so far discovered in Southeast Asia.

langi tombs. Large square or rectangular earthen tombs on the island of TONGA. They have terraced sides faced with slabs of cut coral limestone. According to tradition, *langi* were the burial places of the Tongan ruling aristocracy. None have been excavated.

Langkasuka. An INDIANIZED state on the Malay Peninsula, the name of which appears (as *Lang-ya-hsiu*) in a Chinese source of the 6th century, asserting that it was founded 400 years earlier; its name reappears in later Malayan and Javanese chronicles. The kingdom must have been situated astride the Malay Peninsula, therefore controlling one of the land transport routes, and was apparently conquered in the 3rd century by Fan-Man, the first king of FUNAN.

Lan Na. An ancient northern THAI principality, centred around present Chiangmai. Founded in the late 13th century, it first bore the names of Yonarattha, or Yonakarattha ('kingdom of the Yüon') or of Bingarattha ('kingdom of the Mae Ping') in the Pali chronicles. Recently the name has also been used to designate a Palaeolithic industry discovered in northern Thailand (the 'Lannathian').

L'Anse aux Meadows. A site on Epaves Bay, Newfoundland, Canada, containing evidence of a VIKING settlement during pre-Columbian times. Material which is anomalous to the cultural setting of the time, such as remains of turf-built houses (which have cognates in GREENLAND and ICELAND), iron rivets, slag, a ring-headed bronze pin and a soapstone spindle whorl, is convincingly ascribed a Norse origin. Supporting documents, such as *Groenlendingabok*, Erik's Saga and the map of Sigurthur Stefansson, also indicate that, around 1000, Norse sailors journeyed to a land west of Greenland, which they called

Vinland. The site has produced a series of radiocarbon dates which fall in the range ad 660-1080, with many clustering around ad 1000. The site mean date is 920 ± 30 ad, which gives a corrected date of c970 AD.

Lanzon. *See* CHAVIN.

Laoguantai [Lao-kuan-t'ai]. *See* BANPO.

Laos. Owing to its rather isolated inland position and recent political conflicts, the prehistory of Laos remains virtually unknown. The best-known sites, investigated in the 1930s, are the MEGALITHS and underground tombs of Hua Pan in the northeast and the more famous PLAIN OF JARS in the north-centre.

In the early history of Southeast Asia, Laos is also practically a void. Only what is now its southernmost part, the Champasak (Bassac) area, played a role as the presumed homeland of the KHMER and the origin of the kingdom of CHENLA in the 6th century. From then on Laos was, albeit marginally, under the political and cultural influence of the Khmers until well into the 13th century, the time of THAI ascendancy. The first Laotian kingdom, that of LAN CHANG, came only into being in the middle of the 14th century, when INDIANIZED kingdoms throughout the region were already on the decline. *See also* ANGKOR, SUKHOTHAI, VAT PH'U.

lapis lazuli. A semi-precious stone of a rich deep blue colour, sometimes flecked with gold. It was a rare commodity, much prized in the ancient Near East, with its main — and possibly only — source situated deep in the mountains of Badakhshan, north Afghanistan. It was widely traded in Mesopotamia, at least from the end of the UBAID period (c4000 bc/ 4800 BC), where it was made into beads, decorative inlays, seals and various forms of jewellery. The sites of Tepe HISSAR and SHAHR-I SOKHTA in eastern Iran seem to have served as entrepôts in the working and distribution of lapis lazuli, which was traded in quantities as far as Egypt. One of the richest collection of lapis lazuli objects was found in the burials at Tepe GAWRA.

Lapita culture. The major archaeological culture of the southwestern Pacific, named after the site of Lapita in NEW CALEDONIA, the Lapita culture spans the area from NEW GUINEA to SAMOA between c1500 and 500 BC, after which it loses coherence. Lapita sites are characterized by homogeneous dentate-stamped pottery, a range of shell goods and stone adzes, and a small but widespread trade in OBSIDIAN, mainly from the TALASEA source on NEW BRITAIN. The culture is almost certainly associated with ancestral Polynesians moving eastwards from Island Southeast Asia (perhaps from the PHILIPPINES), through previously inhabited MELANESIA, to the hitherto empty islands of TONGA and SAMOA in Western POLYNESIA. The culture therefore represents the origin of the Polynesians prior to their settlement of geographical Polynesia.

La Plata. *See* BAHIA.

La Quina. The rock shelter of La Quina in the Charente, southwest France, has revealed MOUSTERIAN and Upper PALAEOLITHIC levels with radiocarbon dates. Human remains from the Mousterian include a female and a child skull regarded as of NEANDERTHAL type. The site has given its name to a type of Mousterian and also a type of scalariform retouch found on scrapers.

La Ramada. *See* CHIBCHA.

larnax [Greek *larnax*: 'box, cinerary urn, coffin']. A terracotta sarcophagus. This kind of coffin enjoyed a brief popularity in the east Greek area c530-460 BC with the 'Clazomenian' examples, which were painted in imitation of contemporary vase styles. Other examples in antiquity are relatively rare.

Larnian. This name has been given to a Mesolithic culture of Ulster, based on sites at Lough Larne. Recently the use of the term has been criticized and restricted in scope, but it is still sometimes used for the late Mesolithic with large flake blades and Bann points, which are heavy pointed flakes sometimes with a rudimentary tang.

Larsa. A TELL site north of UR in southern Iraq, which was one of the city-states of SUMER. It has never been properly excavated, but is well-known from documentary sources. It emerged as a city state during the EARLY DYNASTIC period, but gained in importance after the collapse of the Third Dynasty of Ur (shortly before 2000 BC on the traditional middle chronology; see Table 3, page 000). For some two and a half centuries after this a Larsa dynasty held considerable power, competing with other dynasties based at Isin, ASSUR and ESHNUNNA for control of all Mesopotamia. The dynasty — and the period of Larsa's greatest power — was brought to an end by Hammurabi of BABYLON in 1763 BC.

Lartet, Edouard (1801-73). A magistrate by training, who abandoned the study of law to become a palaeontologist and one of the pioneer PALAEOLITHIC prehistorians of France. Initially on his own, later with the help of his English banker friend Henry CHRISTY, he excavated many of the famous caves of southwest France, including LA MADELEINE, LAUGERIE HAUTE and LE MOUSTIER, published eventually in the volumes of *Reliquiae Aquitanicae* between 1865 and 1875. Lartet devised a system for classifying the material from these caves, based on palaeontological criteria. He proposed four successive periods: the Cave Bear period; the Woolly Mammoth and Rhinoceros period; the Reindeer period and the Aurochs or Bison period. It was an interesting scheme, but difficult to apply and with geographically restricted validity; most scholars preferred the system of de MORTILLET which was based on archaeological criteria (such as tool form) and employed the names of type sites for periods, for example MOUSTERIAN after Le Moustier. Lartet and Christy discovered Upper Palaeolithic decorated objects (MOBILIARY ART) in their cave excavations and the publication of these objects from well-excavated contexts made it easier for some scholars at least to accept the authenticity of CAVE ART when the first wall paintings were discovered in the 1870s.

Las Bocas. Located on a natural opening in the hills of Puebla, Mexico, this site is particularly well known for its hollow figurines and other pottery in the OLMEC style (e.g. babyish features, the down-turned mouth and the jaguar paw-hand motif). Unfortunately the site has been the object of considerable looting because of its valuable figurines. Strategically placed in an easily defensible position at the eastern entrance to the Morelos Plain, Las Bocas is noticeably similar to a site at the other end of the plain, Chalcatzingo. Thus it is thought to have been one of a series of Olmec trading stations. Burials similar to those at TLATILCO further confirm the Olmec connection.

Las Casitas. *See* EL JOBO.

Lascaux. The most famous of all painted caves, Lascaux, near Montignac in the Dordogne, southwest France, was discovered by four boys in 1940. A small number of archaeological finds from inside the cave probably date to the early MAGDALENIAN and include a well-made lamp. A NEANDERTHAL skeleton was found a few hundred metres away at Regourdou. In addition to the very large number of paintings, there are also numerous engravings, and a reasonably complete list of them has been completed. Some of the paintings in the rotunda, especially the bulls, approach life size, which is unusual in cave art. A number of paintings are in two contrasting colours, red iron oxide and black manganese dioxide. Red deer, ox and horse are the commonest animals, and cold-loving species are noticeably absent. Lascaux was closed to the public in 1961 because growth of the alga *Palmellococcus* ('*la maladie verte*') threatened to damage the paintings.

Las Flores. *See* HUASTECA.

Lashkari Bazar. Situated on the Helmand Rud, near the site of Bust in Afghanistan, Lashkari Bazar was the winter retreat of the rulers of GHAZNI. Bust, which overlooks a river-crossing, has a massive TELL, thought to conceal an ACHAEMENID settlement. It was conquered by the Arabs c661, and the 10th-century writer Ibn Hauqal described it as a large and wealthy town. Apart from the tell, the principal monument is a ceremonial arch of the Ghorid period. The palace complex at Lashkari Bazar extends northwards from Bust for more than 5 km. It was founded by the Ghaznavid sultan Mahmud (998-1030), who with his son Masud I (1030-41) built the so-called South Palace. Later rulers added two other palaces. The complex also contained barracks and a bazaar. Lashkari Bazar was sacked by the Ghorids in 1151; it was restored by them, then destroyed by the Khwarezm-shah or the Mongols in the early 13th century. The site stands in an area of low rainfall and the buildings, although of mud brick, are astonishingly well-preserved. Excavations revealed elaborate wall paintings in the South Palace and a fine stucco MIHRAB in an adjacent mosque.

Las Lagunas. *See* EL JOBO.

Late Horizon. Most recent and briefest period of a chronological construction widely used in Peruvian archaeology. Dated 1476-1534, it is the time of INCA power at its height. The early date marks the point at which territorial expansion was virtually complete; the late date marks the passing of control to the Spanish under Pizarro. *See* Table 9, page 552.

La Tène. Situated on Lake Neuchâtel in Switzerland, La Tène is the site of a large votive deposit of bronze, iron and wooden objects found in the shallow water at the edge of the lake and dating to the later Iron Age. It has given its name to the second Iron Age in much of Europe, succeeding the HALLSTATT culture *c*500 BC and lasting until the arrival of the Romans (at different times in different areas). The La Tène culture demonstrates clear continuity from the Hallstatt culture in settlement type, burial rite and many aspects of material culture. Settlement was characteristically in hillforts and from the 3rd and 2nd centuries BC massive OPPIDA occur, some of which (e.g. BIBRACTE and MANCHING) can be regarded as of urban or proto-urban status. As in the Hallstatt culture, there is a notable distinction between the markedly wealthy burials of chieftains and their associates, and burials of other members of society. As in the Hallstatt period also, the chieftains were often buried with vehicles, but these are now usually two-wheeled chariots, rather than four-wheeled wagons. The rich graves, which are concentrated in the Rhineland and on the Marne, continue to include a wide variety of metal and pottery goods imported from the Greek and Etruscan cities of the Mediterranean.

The La Tène period is best known for the art style, known as CELTIC ART, developed by metalworkers in the chieftain's courts from the 5th century BC and used for a wide range of weapons, ornaments and drinking vessels.

The La Tène culture was the culture of the Celtic groups which the Romans encountered in Europe and we therefore have literary sources as well as archaeological evidence (especially in Caesar's *Gallic Wars*). *See also* ARRAS, BELGAE.

Laterza. A cemetery of rock-cut tombs near Taranto in southeast Italy which has given its name to a local Copper Age culture of the 3rd millennium bc. The tombs were used for collective burial and contained grave goods including a few copper weapons, tools and ornaments, bifacially worked flint arrowheads and a variety of decorated pottery bowls and cups, some of which appear ancestral to the APENNINE pottery of the Bronze Age. Other Laterza burial sites are known; these include rock-cut tombs and stone cists and possibly MEGALITHIC tombs (certainly in use by the Proto-Apennine phase that succeeded Laterza). No settlements are known.

Latte. *See* MARIANAS ISLANDS.

Laugerie. On the edge of the village of LES EYZIES in the Dordogne, southwest France and only just above the flood plain of the Vezère River, are a line of rock shelters, of which Laugerie Basse and Laugerie Haute are very important. Laugerie Basse, mainly dug in the 19th century, has a later MAGDALENIAN sequence and very numerous small art objects. Laugerie Haute provided a long sequence with Magdalenian and SOLUTRIAN underlain by the latest stages of the AURIGNACIAN and PERIGORDIAN sequences. A number of radiocarbon dates are available, in the range *c*20,000-16,000 bc for Solutrian and Initial Magdalenian levels at Laugerie Haute.

Laura. *See* EARLY MAN SHELTER.

Lauricocha Caves. A series of well-stratified caves of long occupation located in the highlands of central Peru. They are postulated as summer hunting camps, the associated winter locus being the lowlands (*see* LOMAS) and are seen as part of the seasonal round typical of the ARCHAIC. A radiocarbon date of *c*7500 bc places the earliest period of occupation (Lauricocha I) at *c*8000-6000 bc; this level is characterized by stemless triangular points and stemmed diamond-shaped points. A number of burials indicates a DOLICHOCEPHALIC population, in keeping with early-man groups elsewhere in South America. The willow-leaf points of Lauricocha II (6000-

4000 bc) show strong similarities to points at CHIVATERROS, EL JOBO, AYAMPITIN and elsewhere, and are associated with knives, scrapers and other implements appropriate to the preparation of hides. Later levels contain small points and ultimately ceramics, indicating a change in subsistence, sedentism and possibly agriculture.

Laurion [Roman Laurium]. A hilly area in Attica, Greece, south of Athens and near Cape SOUNION (Sunium), which became important when silver-bearing lead ore was discovered there, probably in the 1st millennium BC. The region developed into a principal mining area, especially in the period from about 483 BC until the end of the 5th century. The mines were closed in the 2nd century AD. The mines, which were state property, were rented out to individual contractors, and worked by slaves who were often maltreated. The general area is still abundant in evidence for ancient mineshafts, surface mining structures, water cisterns, and ore-washeries of the common rectangular and rarer circular types.

Lausitz. The Lausitz or Lusatian culture represents the northeasterly group of the European URNFIELD cultures, occurring in East Germany, Poland and parts of Czechoslovakia. It emerged c1500 BC and survived well into the Iron Age, till c300 BC. Fortified settlements occur, such as the exceptionally well-preserved site at BISKUPIN. The dead were cremated and placed in urns and buried either in flat cemeteries (urnfields) or under barrows. The pottery was of good quality and was often decorated with graphite painted designs and plastic ornament. The bronze industry, of general Urnfield type, flourished; iron was introduced from the HALLSTATT Iron Age culture from the later 7th century BC.

Laussel. A rock shelter near LES EYZIES in the Dordogne, southwest France. A long sequence of MOUSTERIAN and Upper PALAEOLITHIC levels was found under the rock shelter, though the investigation was not up to modern standards. The site is best known for its bas-relief carvings, especially the female figure holding a horn or 'cornucopia'.

La Venta. A large OLMEC CEREMONIAL CENTRE of the Middle PRE-CLASSIC located on an island in the swampy lowlands of the Tabasco Province of Mexico. The site dominated by a large, conical clay PYRAM some 110 metres high. There are numerou other low platform mounds, oriented on north-south axis, which are thought to hav supported élite residences made from peris able materials. A courtyard palisaded wit monolithic basalt columns lies to the north.

The site is best known for its great variety c worked stone, made all the more impressive t the lack of local sources. Carved STELAl altars, colossal stone heads in basalt (th nearest source for this material is some 100 kr away) and three massive mosaic pavements i serpentine laid in the form of a jaguar mask ar among the monumental works. The famou Jade Group, consisting of 16 human figur statuettes and 6 celts arranged in a kind c circular gathering, was buried in associatio with the main building complex. Househol goods are very few and there are only a limite number of burials — although these have ricl offerings of magnetite mirrors, sting-ra spines (see PERFORATION) and worked jade.

The site flourished from c1000-600 bc, bu grew in importance after the abandonment o SAN LORENZO in c900 bc.

La Victoria. An early PRE-CLASSIC village sit located on the Pacific coastal region of Ocos ir Guatemala. The site consists of 10-12 lov mounds built on the swampy substrate a; platforms for houses. Its earliest phase (Ocos dates to c1300 bc and contains OLMEC (o Olmec-influenced) pottery, some of which ha; been traded to other areas of Mesoamerica The late Conchas Phase (800-300 bc) contain; sherds of a unique striped design which ha; also been found in Ecuador, indicating probable ocean trade.

A subsistence based on exploitation of the rich coastal environment was supplemented by terrestrial foods, including some MILP/ cultivation of maize.

Lavo. Former name of the present town o Lopburi in central Thailand, the provincia capital of the KHMER empire of ANGKOR from the 11th to the 13th century. There are severa monuments of Khmer origin in the town notably the Prang Sam Yot. The period is alsc known as a distinctive style in the art history o Thailand, denoting Khmer influence.

Layard, Sir Austen Henry (1817-94). One o

the earliest explorers and excavators in Mesopotamia. Between 1845 and 1851 he excavated at two major sites — NIMRUD and Kuyunjik (NINEVEH) — and brought back many art objects and architectural pieces to Britain, where they are still to be seen in the British Museum. His popular book *Nineveh and its Remains* (1849) aroused wide public interest in the early civilizations of Mesopotamia.

layer. A unit of STRATIGRAPHY. SEDIMENTS and SOILS on an archaeological site are split up into layers by the excavator. In many cases, the boundaries between them are well marked, where deposition of one layer is separated from the next by a clear interval or change in TEXTURE, colour or mineralogy. However, some sequences are not so conveniently split up. Deposition of one layer may merge into another so that boundaries between them are unclear, or a layer may change in composition from place to place. In such cases, it is important that the excavator records exactly what has been found in as objective a manner as possible.

LBK (Linienbandkeramik) culture. *See* LINEAR POTTERY CULTURE.

lead. A soft metal of very low melting point, which was used in ALLOYS or for pipes, roofing etc. Most lead comes from the ore galena, from which SILVER may also be extracted. The first evidence for lead-extraction in parts of Europe is the addition of the metal to BRONZE during the Late Bronze Age. Later, there was a considerable Roman lead industry.

lead glaze. The most ubiquitous type of glaze found on medieval European pottery. The process was invented by the Romans, and involves either dusting the unfired vessel with galena (lead ore) or dipping it into a mixture of lead ore and water. The glaze fuses in one firing. Lead glaze reappeared in Europe in the 9th century in the Loire valley and at Stamford in Lincolnshire; its adoption at these two places has long puzzled archaeologists. The natural colour of lead glaze has a yellowish tinge; after the 13th century copper ore was often added to give a green affect.

Leakey, Louis (1903-72). A Kenyan-born British archaeologist and palaeontologist, who devoted most of his life to unearthing early hominid fossils in east Africa, especially at the site of OLDUVAI GORGE. Among the important fossils found there were those of *Australopithecus boisei* (formerly *Zinjanthropus*) and *Homo habilis*, dating to c1.75 million years ago.

Leang Burung. Two rock shelters in the Maros region of southwestern SULAWESI, Indonesia. Shelter 1 has produced a late TOALIAN assemblage with microliths, MAROS POINTS, and pottery, which dates to the 2nd and 1st millennia BC. However, Shelter 2 produced a much older stone tool assemblage, with possible early Australian and also LEVALLOISIAN technological affinities, dating back to c30,000 bc.

Leang Tuwo Mane'e. A coral limestone rock shelter on the coast of Karakellang, Talaud Islands, northeastern INDONESIA, which has produced a preceramic small blade industry (c3000 bc), followed by the appearance of a NEOLITHIC assemblage by about 2000 bc, probably introduced from the PHILIPPINES.

Lébous. A settlement site of the Copper Age FONTBOUISSE culture in Herault, southern France, dated to the early 2nd millennium bc (mid-3rd millennium BC). The settlement was enclosed by a dry-stone wall, set with circular towers at regular intervals. It was once interpreted as a colony from the Aegean (along with others in Iberia, such as LOS MILLARES and VILA NOVA DE SÃO PEDRO) but this view is not widely held today.

Leczyic. *See* OPOLE.

legion. The principal organizational unit of the Roman army, composed of Roman citizens. The legion changed size and character over the Roman period, ranging from a unit of 3,000 with a property qualification under the early kings, to one of 6,000 in the final century of the Republic. Numbers changed again under the Empire, and from Diocletian onwards (284-316 AD) the legions were increased in number but reduced in size. Each legion was given the standard of the eagle, an identifying number — there were more than 30 under Severus (193-211) — and an honorific title, often based upon the name of the founder. The legion was typically subdivided into ten cohorts, and each cohort into six centuries.

Lehringen. A site near Bremen in north Germany, where organic muds have revealed a POLLEN DIAGRAM of the last INTERGLACIAL. In these muds, a yew wood spear 2.4 metres long and broken into several pieces was found. It passed between the ribs of the skeleton of an ELEPHANT of *Elephas antiquus* type. The tip was finely shaved to a point and hardened in a fire. 27 flakes were found lying around the area.

lei [*lei*]. *See* RITUAL VESSELS (CHINA).

leiwen [*lei-wen*]. A cast background pattern of fine spirals, round or angular, used to set off the motifs in the decoration of Chinese bronze RITUAL VESSELS, chiefly those of the ANYANG and Western ZHOU periods (i.e. *c*13th-9th centuries BC). *See* TAOTIE.

Leland, John (1506-52). British antiquary. In his official capacity as King's Antiquary (a post which unfortunately did not outlive its first and only holder) Leland toured England and Wales describing places of antiquarian interest, including prominent prehistoric sites.

Lelang [Lo-lang; Korean: Nangnang]. A Chinese commandery, located at modern P'yŏngyang, established after the HAN conquest of the Korean state of Chosŏn in 108 BC. Lelang survived as an outpost of the Chinese empire until AD 313. Tombs excavated by Japanese archaeologists on the outskirts of the city contained Han LACQUERS, bronze MIRRORS, and gold filigree work. Some of the lacquers carry dated inscriptions, the dates ranging from 85 BC to AD 102, indicating that they were made in Sichuan in western China (*see* CHENGDU). Trade passing through Lelang carried such Chinese products still further, to Japan.

Le Lazaret. A cave on the coast close to Nice in southern France, with a considerable thickness of deposits from before the last INTERGLACIAL, with ACHEULIAN tools and interspersed beach deposits. A human skull fragment is known, and it has been claimed that a hut was constructed inside the cave.

Le Moustier. The type locality of the MOUS-TERIAN 'epoch' or Middle PALAEOLITHIC, situated on the Vezère River in the Dordogne, southwest France. Upper Palaeolithic levels cover the Mousterian levels in both the classic shelter and the lower shelter. From the lower shelter came a NEANDERTHAL skeleton of nearly mature age found in 1908. Due to controversy over its finding and several poor reconstructions, not to mention its temporary disappearance from Berlin at the end of World War II, the full significane of this skeleton has never been evaluated, but it seems to be unlike most classic Neanderthals.

Lengyel. The type site for a widespread Late Neolithic culture of the 4th millennium bc, distributed from central Hungary to western Austria and from southern Poland to Srem in Yugoslavia. The Lengyel culture is divided into two main phases: the Painted Lengyel, defined by white, red and yellow crusted wares and dated *c*4000-3500 bc, and the Unpainted Lengyel, characterized by knobbed and incised pottery and dated *c*3500-3000 bc. The type site, near Szekszard in western Hungary, excavated by M. Wozinszky, comprises a settlement adjoining a cemetery of some 90 inhumation graves.

Leopards Hill. A cave in south-central Zambia, east of Lusaka. The dated sequence covers the whole timespan of the south-central African microlithic industries, from their appearance *c*20,000 bc, through a NACHI-KUFAN I phase and successive stages, to the appearance of the local Early Iron Age in about the 5th century ad.

Leopards Kopje (Nthabazingwe]. A site near KHAMI, southwestern Zimbabwe. The name was formerly given to the greater part of the local Iron Age sequence, which was believed to reflect a process of internal development. However, recent research has shown that this sequence, like those in neighbouring areas, includes successive Early Iron Age and later Iron Age elements, and the designation Leopard's Kopje is now restricted to the later Iron Age industry which developed in about the 11th century ad. At the name-site large circular houses were excavated. The mixed-farming economy was based upon the cultivation of finger millet, sorghum, ground beans and cowpeas, while cattle were herded in large numbers along with some sheep and goats.

During later phases, from about the 14th century, gold mining and building in stone are attested.

Lepenski Vir. A hunter-fisher-gatherer site in the Iron Gates gorge of the River Danube, on the right (Yugoslav) bank. Excavated by D. Srejović, this site produced a three-level stratigraphy. I-II were Mesolithic levels, dated c5400-4600 bc, with trapezoidal houses (often with red plastered floors), stone hearths filled with fish bones and other refuse, and a remarkable group of stone sculptures — by far the earliest monumental sculpture in Europe. These levels were separated by a sandy level from III, an Early Neolithic occupation in three phases (with no radiocarbon dates), with rectangular houses and pits filled with STARČEVO pottery but a complete absence of the sculpture and architecture of levels I-II. The most significant aspect of Lepenski Vir is the degree of cultural elaboration achieved by sedentary fisher-hunters at a time when agriculture was gradually becoming established in other areas of southeast Europe.

Lepsius, Karl Richard (1810-84). Outstanding German Egyptologist of the 19th century. He followed up the lead of CHAMPOLLION with further work on the decipherment of Egyptian hieroglyphic writing. He also worked in the field and between 1842 and 1855 led an expedition to record the monuments of Egypt and Nubia. The results of this expedition were published in 12 magnificently illustrated volumes entitled *Denkmäler an Aegypten und Aethiopien* (1859).

Leptis Magna [also Lepcis (from Punic *Lpdy* or *Lpqy*)]. Principal city of Roman North Africa in Libya, particularly well-preserved after its 7th-century decline by the intrusion of the desert sand. It was known to imperial Rome as the birthplace of the Emperor Septimus Severus (193-211) whose Latin was apparently marred by a distinct African burr. The settlement was founded probably before 600 BC, by Semitic, Punic-speaking colonists from Phoenicia, who exploited its agricultural and trading potential. Successively Carthaginian (until 146 BC), Numidian (until 46 BC), and then Roman, the town long retained its Punic language, constitution and religion. Roman domination brought great prosperity and expansion under the Empire, until 5th-century Vandals, 7th-century Arabs and the desert brought ultimate decline. The earliest remains are from the Augustan age, and the site is important as evidence for the early development of Roman North African provincial architecture. Notable are the Augustan Old FORUM, MACELLUM and THEATRE; Hadrianic BATHS with marble latrines (126-7 AD); and Severan Hunting Baths and Forum (c200 AD).

Leptolithic. It is well known that blades and blade tools, especially end scrapers, burins and backed blades, are typical of the Upper PALAEOLITHIC. The term Leptolithic has sometimes been used specifically to refer to this type of stone technology, without any necessary implication of age or evolutionary position or human type, such as are inevitably involved in the term Upper Palaeolithic.

Lerma. *See* TAMAULIPAS.

Lerna. Coastal settlement in the Argolid, eastern Peloponnese (southern Greece) occupied in the Neolithic period and the Early and Middle Bronze Age. The Neolithic settlement was followed by a break in occupation and then the site was reoccupied in the Early HELLADIC II phase, c3000 BC. At this stage it was a fortified township, surrounded by a stone wall with D-shaped bastions. Houses, built of mud-brick on stone foundations, include a building known as the House of Tiles, measuring c25 by 12 metres and roofed with stone and terracotta tiles — a very early appearance of this roofing technique. The House of Tiles was destroyed by fire, perhaps c2400 BC; the settlement was rebuilt subsequently in the EH III phase, when MINYAN WARE came into use. The site remained in occupation throughout the Middle Helladic period until about 1600 BC. The latest dateable material comes from two rectangular shaft graves, approximately contemporary with the Shaft Grave B circle at MYCENAE.

Les Combarelles. A narrow tortuous cave just outside LES EYZIES in the Dordogne, southwest France, where a large series of engravings of PALAEOLITHIC animals was discovered in 1901. BREUIL regarded this cave as one of the 'six giants' of cave art.

Les Eyzies. This village on the Vezère River near the centre of the Dordogne, southwest

France, is a natural centre of the rich sites left by prehistoric man in the limestone zone called the Perigord. The chateau and National Museum contains many important finds and underneath it there is a small MAGDALENIAN site, Grotte des Eyzies. *See also* CROMAGNON, FONT DE GAUME, LA MADELEINE, LAUSSEL, LAUGERIE, LES COMBARELLES.

Leţ. A small open settlement of the Early Neolithic CRIŞ culture, the Rumanian regional variant of the FIRST TEMPERATE NEOLITHIC, with later BOIAN and GUMELNIŢA occupation levels. Located in the upper Olt Valley and dated typologically to the early 5th millennium bc, Leţ is a rare example of a multi-level Criş site, with three occupation horizons, each characterized by differing styles of painted wares.

Leubingen. An early Bronze Age chieftain's burial of the ÚNĚTICE culture in Saxony, Germany. It consisted of a lean-to wooden mortuary chamber under a stone cairn, itself covered by a barrow *c*34 metres in diameter. Inside was the burial of an extended elderly male and, place at right angles across him, a second body, of an adolescent, perhaps female. This occurrence is sometimes interpreted as evidence for the practice of SATI. Grave goods included a series of gold ornaments (pins, spirals, hair-rings and an arm-ring), bronze daggers, axes and chisels, stone tools and pottery.

Levallois. A Levallois flake is a kind of special flake removed from a prepared core, sometimes a tortoise core. It took its name from a suburb of northern Paris, where an early example was found. In a more general way, the term 'Levallois technique' is used to describe this method of flaking. The concept of a Levalloisian culture defined by this technique is now obsolete.

Levalloiso-Mousterian. This name has been used for the MOUSTERIAN cultures found at MOUNT CARMEL and other east Mediterranean sites. It was once thought that LEVALLOIS flakes signified a Levalloisian culture, while side scrapers indicated a Mousterian culture, and when the two were found together it was tempting to call the combination Levalloiso-Mousterian. However the idea of a hybrid culture is now rejected and the term should be used with careful qualification, if at all.

Levanzo. A cave in the Egadi Islands off Sicily with fine engravings of animals. It belongs to the ROMANELLIAN group of *c*10,000 bc.

level. A SURVEYING instrument, used in conjunction with a graduated staff to determine height differences. The term is also used to refer to the actual height measurements taken with such an instrument. More generally, archaeologists often use the term 'level' interchangeably with LAYER.

Levkas. One of the Ionian islands off the west coast of Greece, where excavations by DÖRPFELD revealed occupation in several prehistoric periods: Neolithic settlement in the Chirospilia Cave and groups of Early and Middle Bronze Age burials in several locations. The Early Bronze Age burials were cremations in jars or stone cists under round barrows. Grave goods include slotted spearheads and daggers of bronze. In the Middle Bronze Age burials some MINYAN WARE appears.   In the 7th century BC the Corinthians established a colony on Levkas.

Lezoux. A site in Puy-de-Dôme, central France. Important centre for the production of TERRA SIGILLATA or 'Samian' pottery from the 1st to the 4th centuries. Neither the ancient name nor the detailed development of the site is known, but Lezoux appears to be an example of an industrial VICUS. Excavation has produced evidence for workshops, potters' kilns, and stockrooms for storing the unsold production. There are similar production sites at La Graufesenque and LYONS. Gaulish Samian pottery is clearly 'second-generation' to Arretine (*see* ARRETIUM), and local production may have been started originally by Arretine immigrants (*see* LYONS).

li [*li*]. A tripod bowl with hollow legs from China, a pottery shape characteristic of the Henan and Shaanxi LONGSHAN cultures (i.e. HOUGANG II, KEXINGZHUANG II) that in SHANG and ZHOU times was copied in bronze. Several other vessel types have similar bulbous hollow legs. The oldest may be the pottery GUI pitcher, which does not appear among Shang or later bronzes. The *xian* steamer, consisting of a perforated bowl set atop a *li*, first appeared in Henan Longshan pottery, and was made in both pottery and bronze in the Shang period; lobed versions of the *jia* and *he* seem to have the same history (*see* RITUAL VESSELS).

Liangchengzhen [Liang-ch'eng-chen]. *See* LONGSHAN.

Liangzhu [Liang-chu]. Type site near Hangzhou, China, of the Liangzhu culture. Represented at many sites in northern Zhejiang, southern Jiangsu, and Shanghai, Liangzhu is a continuation of the MAJIABANG culture of the same region. Seven radiocarbon dates range from *c*3300 to *c*2250 BC. The Liangzhu JADE industry was very advanced; jade ZONG from Liangzhu sites bear face-like designs that may have inspired the TAOTIE motif. Similar *zong* have been found far to the southwest in Guangdong province at Maba Shixia (Qujiang Xian) accompanying pottery that recalls Liangzhu (and its immediate predecessor, the Songze phase of Majiabang) and QUJIALING.

li ding [*li-ting*]. A name sometimes given to lobed tripods intermediate in shape between LI and DING vessels.

Lifan [Li-fan]. Type site northwest of CHENGDU, China, of a local culture of western Sichuan province characterized by slate cist burials. Grave goods suggest that the Lifan culture flourished in the late Eastern ZHOU and early HAN periods and point to very wide-ranging contacts, including metropolitan China (Western Han coins), the Xindian culture of Gansu (pottery shapes; *see* QIJIA), the ORDOS region (small animal bronzes), and perhaps even Western Asia via steppe intermediaries (glass beads).

Ligor. *See* TAMBRALINGA.

limes [Latin: 'cross-path' or 'baulk between fields']. The term *limes* came to mean a military road with forts and watchtowers, and ultimately a frontier. From the 1st century AD, as imperial boundaries gradually stabilized, frontiers gained permanent garrisons. From the time of Hadrian (117-138) the *limes* could also comprise a continuous physical barrier, such as a wall (in Britain, Germany and Numidia). *See also* HADRIAN'S WALL.

Lincoln [Roman Lindum]. An important Roman COLONIA in eastern England on the main Roman route north. The site on raised ground above the River Witham relates to the intersection of two principal Roman roads, the FOSSE WAY and ERMINE STREET. Limestone of good quality was available from a local quarry. The site shows earlier traces of Iron Age occupation. Roman use was possibly from as early as *c*43 AD, and certainly from *c*60 a turf and timber fortress had come into existence. By about the end of the 1st century a *colonia* was established, with stone walls and tower defences. Pottery kilns have been found, especially concentrated in the area of Swanpool and Bootham, and imply an industrialized production of pottery. Substantial remains survive, mostly from the 3rd and 4th centuries, of walls, baths, mosaic floors and a remarkable stone sewage system. Evidence for an aqueduct seems to show an uphill gradient, which may imply the use of pumps. Three of the Roman gateways are to be seen, including the famous north gate, or Newport Arch, which is currently still used by traffic and pedestrians.

Lindholme Høje. A site on the northern shore of Limfjord in Jutland, used as a grave-field from the prehistoric period until the Viking era. In the 11th century it was overlaid by a Viking village. Extensive excavations, combined with documentary references, suggest that during the 11th century Lindholm Høje functioned as a small trading-post and industrial settlement with four different house-types: an early example of a courtyard house (otherwise only known from Danish military sites), bow and straight-sided long houses, and sunken-floored huts. The sunken huts seem in this instance to have been used only for weaving and other light crafts. One of the most rare and interesting finds was a spoked wagon wheel. It seems that the settlement went out of use around 1100 due to the silting-up of the fjord and continual sand drifts.

Lindisfarne. Island off the coast of Northumberland, northeast England. In 634 King Oswald gave the island to St Aidan and other monks from IONA to found a monastery. The foundation followed the Irish pattern until the Synod of Whitby (664), when Lindisfarne relinquished its Celtic traditions and embraced the Roman style of Christianity. Its most famous bishop was St Cuthbert, who officiated there from 685 until 687. Lindisfarne became a centre for producing illuminated manuscripts (see LINDISFARNE GOSPEL) and works of art of the NORTHUMBRIAN school. In 793 the Danes raided the island — an event which shook the Christian world — and the monastery only functioned intermittently after this disaster. Unfortunately, there are no traces of the earliest buildings; the church, cloister, ranges and walls visible today all date to the Norman Benedictine abbey. However, Lindisfarne's glorious past is reflected in the famous manuscripts that have survived from this age, St Cuthbert's coffin, and some carved sculpture.

Lindisfarne Gospel. This gospel book, written out and painted by the order of Eadfrith, Bishop of LINDISFARNE between 698 and 721, is one of the most splendid Early Christian manuscripts from the British Isles. Its sumptuous decoration shows a slight weakening of the great Irish tradition (see BOOK OF KELLS), but it is an outstanding blend of Celtic and Germanic art — both of which were heavily influenced by Italian figural illustration — and the first great Anglo-Saxon work of this kind.

Linear A. Script used by the MINOAN population of Crete in the period 2000-1500 BC. The signs are inscribed on clay tablets and appear to represent a syllabary. Linear A has not yet been deciphered, but it seems to have developed out of the earlier hieroglypic script of the island. After c1500 BC Linear A was replaced by LINEAR B, used by the MYCENAEANS. Linear A tablets have been found in the palaces of Crete itself and also on the Cycladic islands of MELOS, Keos, Kythera, Naxos and THERA.

Linear B. Script used by the MYCENAEANS after c1500 or 1450 BC and found on clay tablets in the palaces of both Crete and the Greek mainland. Linear B was deciphered in 1952 by Michael VENTRIS, who demonstrated that it was an early form of Greek. It is probable that when the Mycenaeans overran the MINOANS they adopted the script used on Crete, LINEAR A (as yet undeciphered, but certainly not Greek) and adapted it for writing the Greek language. The most important collections of Linear B tablets come from

KNOSSOS on Crete and PYLOS in southwest Greece. They consist in the main of accounts and inventories, which have thrown much light on the organization of the Mycenaean economy and the functioning of the state bureacracy.

Linear Pottery culture. The English name for the German Linienbandkeramik (or LBK for short) culture, sometimes also known as the Danubian I culture. It denotes the first farming culture in central Europe, dated c4500-4000 bc in its core area, lasting as late as 3200 bc on its periphery. The Linear Pottery core area of rapid expansion (c4500-4300 bc) stretches from eastern Hungary to the Netherlands, including settlement concentrations in the Pannonian Basin, Bohemia, Moravia, central Germany and the Rhineland. A second rapid expansion eastwards round the northern rim of the Carpathians, from Poland to the Dnieper, can be dated c4300-4200 bc. Later, in the 4th millennium bc, a slow penetration of modified Linear Pottery culture spread westwards from Holland as far as the Paris Basin.

Most settlements of the core areas comprised timber-framed LONG HOUSES (c8 metres wide and 15-40 metres in length). Linear Pottery material culture is characterized by incised and sometimes painted pottery with linear designs (curvilinear, zig-zig and meander patterns), polished stone SHOELAST ADZES and a microlithic stone industry. Small cemeteries of individual inhumations are common.

The Linear Pottery core groups selected loess-derived soils for agriculture; cattle-husbandry was also significant. Traditionally, Linear Pottery farming has been regarded as of slash-and-burn type, involving cyclic shifts in settlement to allow time for the land to regenerate after exhaustion. It has been suggested that it would take 10-15 years to exhaust all the land around a settlement, which would then be abandoned for up to 50 years before being reoccupied. Recently, scholars have challenged the validity of this model for early farming in temperate Europe, suggesting that with simple techniques of restoring soil fertility, such as allowing animals on the land after harvesting or rotation of cereals with leguminous crops, a long fallow period would have been unnecessary. Moreover, the considerable labour involved in constructing the massive wooden long houses seems inappropriate for settlements destined to be used for only 10-15 years before abandonment.

The remarkable uniformity that characterized the Linear Pottery culture in its core area broke down after c4000 bc and the cultures that emerged — TISZA, LENGYEL, STROKE-ORNAMENTED WARE, RÖSSEN etc — are more divergent in characteristics. *See also* BYLANY, ELSLOO, GELEEN, KÖLN LINDENTHAL, POSTOLOPRTY and SITTARD.

ling [*ling*]. *See* BELLS (CHINA).

Lingtai [Ling-t'ai]. County in eastern Gansu province, China, where nine Western ZHOU tombs and a CHARIOT BURIAL were excavated in 1967 and 1972. Two well-preserved tombs contained bronze RITUAL VESSELS, JADES, and a wide variety of bronze weapons including four short SWORDS. Lingtai is just across the border from Shaanxi province and not so far west as the important Shaanxi site of BAOJI.

Lingyuan Xian Haidaoyingzicun [Ling-yüan-hsien Hai-tao-ying-tzu-ts'un]. The designation sometimes given to the provenance of a Western Zhou bronze hoard from Kezuo Xian, Liaoning province, China. *See* YAN.

Lintong Xian [Lin-t'ung-hsien]. *See* BANPO, QIN SHI HUANGDI.

Linyi [Lin-i]. A county in southern Shandong province, China. In the past decade, at least ten important Western HAN tombs have been excavated in this district, some richly furnished with paintings on silk and LACQUERS comparable to those from MAWANGDUI. A tomb excavated in 1972 at Linyi Yinqueshan contained nearly 5000 inscribed bamboo slips that preserve the texts of a number of late Eastern ZHOU philosophical works and military treatises, some hitherto believed lost, including the *Sun Zi bing fa* ('Master Sun on the Art of War') and related works.

Lin-yi. A kingdom founded in 192 in the southernmost part of the HAN Chinese commandery of JIH-NAN in present central Vietnam. Later it became known as the INDIANIZED kingdom of CHAMPA, which was eventually absorbed by Vietnam in the course of its expansion into the southern part of the Indochinese Peninsula.

lion. The lion, *Panthera (Felis) leo* is today restricted to the open savanna and plains of Africa south of the Sahara. Previously it inhabited much of Europe as well, and even in the 19th century its range covered most of Africa and large areas of southwestern Asia. Fossils of lion occur in European caves throughout much of the later QUATERNARY. Many of the animals represented by these fossils were much larger than the modern lion; some authors differentiate them as *Panthera (Felis) spelaea.*

Lipari. The largest of the Aeolian islands of the Tyrrhenian Sea north of Sicily. Lipari was important in prehistory because it possessed a source of the much-prized volcanic glass, OBSIDIAN; later in prehistory it remained important because of its strategic position, which allowed communities positioned there to control trade routes through the Straits of Messina and up the west coast of Italy. There are important prehistoric settlement sites not only on Lipari, but also on several of the other Aeolian islands, including Filicudi, Panarea and Salina. The most complete sequence occurs on the acropolis of Lipari itself, where excavations by Bernabò Brea in the late 1950s revealed a stratigraphy documenting occupation from the Middle Neolithic to the Late Bronze Age. The site was abandoned some time in the 9th century BC and not reoccupied until the foundation of a Greek settlement by a mixed group of Cnidians and Rhodians in the early 6th century BC.

Lisičići. Refers to a Late Neolithic culture in southern Bosnia, Yugoslavia, dated to the 4th millennium bc. Only the type site, in a steep valley in mountainous terrain, has been widely excavated. The subsistence economy is based as much on hunting as on cattle husbandry and scanty structural remains are known. The ceramic assemblage shows affinities with the Dalmatian Late Neolithic HVAR culture.

Little Woodbury. A palisaded farmstead of the Iron Age (probably beginning in the 4th century BC) located on Salisbury plain, southern England. Excavations by Gerhard Bersu in 1938-9 were among the first to employ the open area approach to prehistoric sites and the results achieved make this still a classic excavation. Bersu identified a single large circular, post-built house, rebuilt several times, four-post granaries and storage pits (both for grain), two-post structures interpreted as drying racks (for hay and straw) and working areas where grain was parched. The site is likely to have been occupied by a small group, perhaps an extended family, who lived by mixed farming, cultivating cereals and breeding cattle, sheep and pig.

Liulige [Liu-li-ko]. A town in Hui Xian, Henan province, China, where many burials of the SHANG and Eastern ZHOU periods have been excavated. The Shang burials, some containing bronze RITUAL VESSELS, belong to the ERLIGANG PHASE. Eastern Zhou finds at Liulige range in date from the 7th to the 2nd century BC, and include one of the largest of Chinese CHARIOT BURIALS, a single pit containing 19 chariots. Tombs of the same period have been found nearby at GUWEICUN in Hui Xian and Shanbiaozhen in Ji Xian.

Liulin [Liu-lin]. *See* DADUNZI, QING-LIAN'GANG.

Liu Sheng [Liu Sheng]. *See* MANCHENG.

Liyu [Li-yü]. A village near Hunyuan in northern Shanxi, China, where a large hoard of bronzes of the 6th and 5th centuries BC was found in 1923. The name Liyu has since been applied to a style of decoration, shared by many bronzes from the hoard and characterized by an interlace of dragons whose ribbon-like bodies are textured with fine meander and volute patterns. Despite the northern location of the Liyu site, near the GREAT WALL, and the borrowings from nomadic art seen on some of the bronzes, such as naturalistic animal motifs, the Liyu style cannot be regarded as provincial in any sense. Its borrowings from steppe art are common to much Chinese art of the period, and recent excavations in Henan and Shanxi, notably at Fenshuiling near Changzhi and at the HOUMA foundry site, show the style to have been a familiar part of the metropolitan caster's repertoire. *See also* HUAI STYLE.

llama. A relative of the camel, the llama was the principal beast of burden in prehistoric Andean societies, although it was also exploited to a lesser extent for its wool and meat. The first clear evidence of its domestication (dating to the INITIAL PERIOD) comes from ceremonial burials in the VIRU VALLEY and from remains at KOTOSH. Able to carry loads of up to 60 kg over difficult terrain, the llama gained economic importance as the basic unit of transportation of goods in the INCA empire, and was also maintained purely as a form of wealth, with the state owning huge flocks. SACRIFICE (sometimes in the hundreds) was quite common.

Llano. The earliest PALEO-INDIAN BIG GAME HUNTING culture. Its chief diagnostic trait is the presence of CLOVIS materials (especially the fluted point) in association with mammoth remains. Typically, sites are located in what was once a boggy lakeshore environment. The type site is located in the eastern Plains of New Mexico at BLACKWATER DRAW (now destroyed by gravel-mining activities). Evidence of the culture, however, exists throughout North America: as far south as Iztapan, Mexico, as far north as Worland, Wyoming, and possibly as far east as DEBERT, Nova Scotia. Dates normally fall between 10,000 and 9000 bc.

loam. A particular TEXTURE in SOIL. When used in soil science, the term has no implications of colour, organic content, or any property other than texture.

Loch Lomond stadial. A STADIAL of the DEVENSIAN cold stage which occurred between 11,000 and 10,000 bp. Small glaciers were formed in the high mountains of Wales and the Lake District and an ice-cap was formed over the highlands of Scotland. The Loch Lomond stadial may be correlated with Godwin's POLLEN ZONE III and the YOUNGER DRYAS.

lock-ring. A small bronze or gold pennanular ring found in the Bronze Age of northern Europe; they may have been used for decorating the hair.

Loddekopinge. An important settlement near Lund in southern Sweden, dating to the VIKING period. Excavations have shown that in the 9th-10th centuries this was probably the site of a fair, to which both native and alien traders came. Plentiful evidence of Slavic traders, for instance, has come to light and it seems that Loddekopinge expanded to a considerable size before it was superseded by Lund.

Lödöse. A small abandoned trading-site in southwest Sweden, and the forerunner of Gothenburg. Investigations brought to light a range of later medieval imported pots from Britain, western France and Denmark, which reveal the port's importance in North Sea trade at the time of the Hanseatic League.

loess. A fine wind-blown deposit, which forms wide spreads in Europe, Asia and North America. Wind erosion was widespread in the PERIGLACIAL zone that surrounded the large QUATERNARY ice-sheets. Material was picked up by the wind from the large expanses of PROGLACIAL deposits at the ice-sheet margins. Erosion and deposition by the wind results in a very high degree of sorting into different PARTICLE SIZES. Loess represents the finer, SILT fraction of this material. Other deposits, known as cover-sand, represent the coarser, SAND fraction and are also found as wide spreads. As well as the thicker deposits of loess, much of Europe was covered by a thinner layer of this material, detectable only by detailed analysis of soils (*see* SOIL ANALYSIS). Soils formed on loess are particularly fertile, and the extensive loess areas of Europe and Asia were centres of early settlement and agriculture.

Loftus, Sir William Kennett (1821?-58). One of the early excavators in Mesopotamia. In the 1850s he excavated several sites, including URUK. The main object of the excavations was to collect antiquities, some of which were transported back to the British Museum.

Lohapasada. *See* ANURADHAPURA.

lomas. In the period *c*6500-2500 bc seasonally occupied camps were set up several kilometres from the sea in the coastal plain of central Peru. In the winter months, precipitation in the form of fog changed this virtual desert into a fertile area of seed-producing grasses. Highland hunters (*see* LAURICOCHA CAVES) descended into these lomas lowlands to exploit this resource as part of an ARCHAIC lifestyle. Milling stones, MANOS, mortars and pestles occur frequently in the assemblages of the later period, which may also have seen some cultivation. By 2500 bc shifts in ocean currents and other environmental factors caused the disappearance of fog precipitation and the lomas was abandoned in favour of permanent settlement at the littoral zone.

Lombards. A tribe of Germanic descent who conquered northern Italy in the late 6th and early 7th centuries. The region was already weakened by the Gothic wars and was left vulnerable in 565 by the death of the Emperor Justinian, encouraging another phase of invasions. Led by their king Alboin, the Lombards crossed from Pannonia into the north Italian regions of Friuli and Veneto, capturing Aquelia and founding a new capital at Milan. Although their territorial expansion extended as far south as Benevento, the Lombards never managed to gain complete control of the peninsula. Many major Byzantine cities fell to them but the Eastern Empire maintained a firm hold in the coastal ports of Ravenna and Venice.

The Lombards always remained somewhat politically disorganized, with control exercised not by central government but through provincial leaders of noble or ecclesiastical status. Nevertheless, their impact was considerable and they imposed distinct cultural traditions on Italy's decaying classical past. This tradition was expressed in the rich inlaid gold jewellery (such as the Monza Cathedral treasure) buried in the tombs of their nobles. New emphasis was also placed on sculpture as a decorative medium for church interiors, a feature found in the nimbed figures adorning the Tempietto at CIVIDALE. This individuality persisted in Lombardic architecture generally and the combination of new sculptural and architectural design played a significant part in the development of the Romanesque style.

London [Roman Londinium]. Capital town of Roman Britain by about 100 AD, probably in replacement for an originally intended capital at COLCHESTER. The site, on a previously unoccupied gravel plateau on the north side of the River Thames, was probably chosen as the lowest crossing point at the time of the Roman invasion in 43 AD. Use began as a supply depot and a trading centre. The location was also convenient as the starting point for the growing network of Roman roads. Burnt and ravaged by BOUDICCA in 60-61 the town soon revived, and capital status brought a large FORUM (Leadenhall Market), governor's palace (Cannon Street), and a 4.5-hectare legionary fort (area of London Wall).

Although damaged by fire again in c125-30, the settlement continued to consolidate its position, and a wall was added to protect its some 134 hectares between 183 and 217. Continuous occupation since the Roman period has prevented anything but piecemeal remains and excavation. Major evidence is collected in the Museum of London, (e.g. marble heads of MITHRAS, Serapis and Minerva from the Mithraeum) and in the British Museum (Tomb of Julius Alpinus Classicianus, procurator of Britain after Boudicca's revolt). A good section of wall may be seen in Trinity Place near the Tower of London, and the MITHRAEUM has been reconstructed to the west of its original site, in front of Temple Court, Queen Victoria Street.

long barrow. *See* BARROW.

Long Count. *See* CALENDAR.

long house. Many prehistoric societies in Europe lived in timber long houses. Among the most famous are those of the LINEAR POTTERY culture, which reach lengths of up to 40 metres. In the later prehistoric and post-Roman periods, the term long house is used to describe a rectangular, aisled building incorporating a dwelling and a byre under one roof, although in some cases the byre is not evident. In a true long house of this type, the human beings and cattle are separated by a through passage with doors placed in the centres of the long sides of the building. Archaeologically, the two halves of the long house are often distinguished by the existence of a hearth in the living quarters, a central drain and sometimes stalls in the byre. The purpose of the long house was to stall stock during the wet winter months, and at the same time to provide additional warmth for the farmers. The long house is known from many parts of Europe from late prehistoric times and continued to be used until recent times, with variations in size, arrangement and fabric according to climate and environment.

Longmen [Lung-men]. A large complex of Buddhist cave temples near LUOYANG, China, begun in AD 495 under the sponsorship of the Northern Wei dynasty (*see* YUNGANG). Construction of temples and images was most active during the first three decades of the 6th century and again in the TANG dynasty from about 650 to 710. The site is dominated by a colossal seated image of the Buddha Vairocana carved under Tang imperial patronage in 672-5.

Longshan [Lung-shan]. A county in Shandong province, China, where a Neolithic site at Chengziyai was excavated in 1930-31. The name Longshan has since been applied in three distinct ways to Chinese Neolithic cultures:

(1) It refers to the culture of the Chengziyai type site, often distinguished as the Classic Longshan or Shandong Longshan. Represented at many Shandong sites including Weifang and Rizhao Liangchengzhen, the Shandong Longshan belongs to the late 3rd and early 2nd millennium BC, and may have survived to a time contemporary with the bronze-using SHANG civilization. A large earthen wall at Chengziyai was built in the HANGTU technique familiar from Shang walls and foundations. A small proportion of Shandong Longshan pottery is a very fine, thinly potted, wheel-made black ware; the Shandong Longshan is therefore sometimes called the Black Pottery culture, and this name has at times been used interchangeably with Longshan in the two broader senses explained below, even though the black pottery itself is essentially confined to Shandong province.

(2) Especially in older publications, the name Longshan is applied to the entire Neolithic tradition of the east coast of China, of which the Shandong Longshan is a late and local manifestation. In this sense the Longshan (or Black Pottery) culture is on a par with YANGSHAO, the other main division of the Chinese Neolithic. More recent literature replaces Longshan in this broad sense with the names of earlier sites (e.g. QINGLIAN'GANG) or substitutes a variety of less inclusive terms; to avoid confusion, the name 'east-coast Neolithic' is here used for Longshan in the broadest sense of the word. On present evidence the east-coast Neolithic was a tradition independent of the Yangshao, centred in the lower Yangzi region. The earliest radiocarbon dates have come from HEMUDU (early 5th millennium BC) together with clear evidence of RICE cultivation. Later stages have been recognized in a series of sites south of the Yangzi (*see* MAJIABANG) and in another, related series in northern Jiangsu and Shandong, where the well-established cultural

succession leads from the Qinglian'gang culture via Dawenkou to the Shandong Longshan (see DADUNZI, QINGLIAN'GANG). The independence of the east-coast tradition from the Yangshao is clearly marked, most obviously in the cultivation of rice rather than MILLET; in the highly developed JADE industry; and in the pottery repertoire, where painted decoration plays a minor role and the very distinctive shapes include a wide variety of stemmed or footed vessels, tripods, and, at a late stage, hollow-legged tripods (GUI). The Neolithic of southeastern and south coastal China, characterized by cord-marked or comb-impressed pottery, may have a common origin with this east-coast tradition or alternatively may depend on some third independent area of agricultural origins (see DAPENKENG).

(3) Lastly, the name Longshan is applied to cultures that differ fundamentally from those mentioned so far. These are the Henan Longshan (HOUGANG II), Shaanxi Longshan (KEXINGZHUANG II) and Gansu Longshan (QIJIA), which are not branches of the east-coast Neolithic but products of its fusion with the local Yangshao traditions of central and western North China. The application of the term Longshan to these Yangshao successor cultures is unfortunate, since it has the appearance of grouping them together with the Shandong Longshan, which lacks any Yangshao component and is simply a late stage of the east-coast Neolithic. The westward movement of influences from the east coast, which did not replace the Yangshao tradition outright but altered it drastically, seems to have begun in the 4th millennium BC and continued through the 3rd millennium (see DAHE). The pottery of the Yangshao successor cultures is unpainted, often cord-marked, and heavily dependent on the east-coast repertoire of shapes. Tripods with hollow legs (LI, GUI, and xian) are prominent, and some of the shapes seem to imitate metal vessels.

Throughout the cultural province of the Yangshao tradition, Longshan remains in this third sense lie above Yangshao (see HOUGANG, MIAODIGOU, DAHE, XIAWANGGANG, KEXINGZHUANG, QIJIA). At a time when radiocarbon dates from the Yangshao site at BANPO were by far the earliest known from the Chinese Neolithic, this stratigraphy was taken by some scholars as evidence that the post-Yangshao cultures of North China evolved out of the Yangshao and then spread east and south, bringing a Neolithic economy to the coastal provinces for the first time. This 'nuclear theory', which entailed the assumption that Neolithic remains on the coast were without exception young, even contemporary with the Bronze Age of North China, made little sense of the cultural differences separating the Yangshao and east-coast traditions. It was decisively disproved by radiocarbon dates showing the high antiquity of sites on the east coast and by stratigraphic sequences established there (see DADUNZI, LUNGSHANOID).

Lopburi. See LAVO.

Loro Jonggrang. A monument of the PRAMBANAN group in the region of Yogyakarta in central JAVA, Indonesia, built c913 by king Daksha as the funerary temple of his predecessor, king Balitung. The largest monument of the group, it is particularly known for its lively Brahmanic relief scenes.

Los Millares. A defended settlement site in Almeria, southeast Spain, which has given its name to the local Copper Age culture of the 3rd millennium bc. Excavations at the turn of the century demonstrated that the site was defended by a stone wall with semicircular bastions, enclosing approximately five hectares, while recent work suggests that there are further defensive walls inside the enclosure, as in the contemporary Portugese sites of VILA NOVA DE SÃO PEDRO and ZAMBUJAL. At Los Millares four small outlying forts also exist and an extra-mural cemetery of more than 80 PASSAGE GRAVES. Grave goods, found with collective burials in the tombs, include pottery, copper tools and weapons, stone tools and a variety of so-called idols, made of stone, bone or pottery; objects of ivory and ostrich-eggshell, imported from Africa, also occur. BEAKER pottery occurs in some of the later tombs and in a second phase of occupation of the settlement. At one time it was customary to interpret Los Millares and similar settlements as colonies from the Aegean. Now most authorities believe the developments represented at Los Millares to have occurred locally. They are thought to indicate the emergence of ranked societies, with élites whose power may have been based on the control of water supplies (perhaps used for irrigation in this extremely arid zone) and sources of metal ores.

lost wax. *See* CIRE PERDUE.

Lothagam. A site at the south end of Lake Turkana (formerly Lake Rudolf) in Kenya. Jaw fragments of what is thought to be a hominid come from deposits some 5-6 million years old (at the MIOCENE-PLIOCENE boundary). The main importance of this discovery is that it fills the supposed 'gap' in the human evolutionary record between four and eight million years ago. *See* HUMAN EVOLUTION.

Lothal. An important port site of the HARAPPAN CIVILIZATION, situated not in the Indus Valley itself, but in Gujarat near the head of the Gulf of Cambay. The town originally covered *c*12 hectares, and was surrounded by a wall; later it expanded outside the wall to cover 24-5 hectares. It had a fortified ACROPOLIS on an artificial mound like other Harappan towns, but in this case enclosed within the main town wall. A mud-brick structure excavated on the acropolis may be the base of a granary like that on the MOHENJO-DARO citadel. The town had the characteristic Indus Valley gridiron street plan and drainage system. As well as comfortable dwelling houses, a bead factory has been excavated and a bazaar where shell-workers, bone-workers, coppersmiths and goldsmiths lived and worked. The most interesting structure is a large rectangular enclosure on one side of the mound, measuring *c*225 metres by 37 metres and faced with baked brick. It had a sluice gate at one end, and is interpreted by the excavator, S.R. Rao, as a dock for ships, although this interpretation has been challenged by other authorities. Radiocarbon dates from Lothal fall in the 1950-1700 bc range (*c*2400-2100 BC).

Lough Gur. A lake in Co. Limerick, Ireland, surrounded by a great concentration of prehistoric sites, including STONE CIRCLES, MEGALITHIC tombs, Neolithic hut foundations and a CRANNOG. One circle, measuring *c*46 metres in diameter, was constructed of stones set edge to edge; BEAKER pottery, which had been deliberately smashed, was found at the bases of the stones.

Loulan [Lou-lan]. A Chinese military outpost in Eastern Turkestan (modern Xinjiang province), founded in the mid-3rd century. Documents of the 3rd and 4th centuries and silk fabrics have been found there.

Lovelock Cave. A late ARCHAIC site in the Humbolt Lake region of west-central Nevada, USA, for which a dating scheme covering the period 2500 bc to AD 500 has been developed. 40 pits containing a total of over 20,000 artefacts indicate that this site was a cache or storage place rather than a living community. Evidence in the form of tule duck decoys, fish bones and marsh-plant seeds imply a culture routinely exploiting a lacustrine environment.

Lowasera. A site lying on an old beach line, 80 metres above the present water-level on the eastern shore of Lake Turkana (formerly Lake Rudolf) in northern Kenya. The beach was formed between the 9th and the 4th millennia bc, during a period when the lake waters stood at a high level and apparently maintained an overflow north-westwards to the Nile. The site was occupied from at least the 7th millennium by people who produced both microlithic and macrolithic implements and depended for their livelihood on fish caught by means of barbed bone harpoons akin to those from EARLY KHARTOUM and related sites. The earlier pottery at Lowasera was of wavy-line style; the later pottery was undecorated. This occupation continued until after the retreat of the lake at the end of the 4th millennium bc.

Luangwa tradition. The general designation applied to a widespread later Iron Age pottery tradition which is attested in much of eastern, central and northern Zambia from the 11th century ad and has continued into recent times.

Luangwa variant. A facies of the SANGOAN industry found in gravel deposits of the Luangwa and tributary valleys of eastern Zambia, marked by large picks and other core tools made from water-rounded cobbles. No assemblages have been excavated *in situ*, nor has the industry been dated.

Lubaantun. A Late CLASSIC MAYA centre, located on the Rio Grande in southern Belize [formerly British Honduras]. Built in the early 8th century on a ridge in the foothills of the Maya Mountains, a considerable amount of fill

(3000 cubic metres) was required to alter the topography sufficiently to allow the site to be completed according to a fixed plan. Although the site consists largely of ceremonial buildings its handy placement, on a navigable river between the mountains and the coastal plain, suggests that it probably functioned as a regional market centre. Furthermore, its proximity to one of the few areas where CACAO grows suggests that control of this much sought-after commodity was its major economic base, and may be the reason why such a considerable investment of labour was made to build the site.

A fairly short-lived centre, Lubaantun was abandoned some time between 850 and 900, probably as part of the general Maya collapse.

Lubbock, Sir John. *See* Lord AVEBURY.

Łubna. The type site for a regional group of the earlier Bronze Age Trzciniec culture, the Łubna group is distributed in central Poland in the early 2nd millennium bc. Stratified settlement sites are rare, with many sites constructed in sandy areas. One of the best-preserved cemeteries is the type site, comprising 29 tumuli over stone-built burial chambers containing inhumation burials. Bronze and gold grave goods were found, with close affinities in the Central European Bronze Age.

Lugdunum. *See* LYONS.

Lukenya Hill. An inselberg in southern Kenya, southeast of Nairobi. Numerous rock shelters and other sites have preserved a long sequence of prehistoric occupation ranging in date from the 'Middle Stone Age' to the later Iron Age. A backed microlith industry was established by the 16th millennium bc and probably long before. A fragment of human skull associated with this industry is stated to display negroid features. The PASTORAL NEOLITHIC sequence at Lukenya, currently under investigation, is of particular interest and complexity.

Lumbini. The birthplace of the Buddha, in northeast India. Archaeological finds include NORTHERN BLACK-POLISHED WARE, which was in use during the period of the Buddha's lifetime. In 249 BC the emperor ASOKA made a pilgrimage to Lumbini — and other Buddhist

holy sites — and set up a commemorative pillar which still survives.

lungshanoid. A term coined to describe Neolithic cultures that supposedly evolved out of the final stage of the YANGSHAO (*see* MIAODIGOU); spread to the east coast of China, there forming the east-coast Neolithic (*see* LONGSHAN, sense 2); and in Henan, Shaanxi, and Gansu evolved into the Longshan cultures of those regions (*see* LONGSHAN, sense 3). The assumption that all the Neolithic cultures of the east coast were late offshoots of the Yangshao tradition constitutes the so-called nuclear theory, which has been abandoned since the publication of radiocarbon dates from east-coast sites (*see* LONGSHAN, sense 3). The term lungshanoid embodies the assumptions of the nuclear theory and should probably be avoided.

Luni. A small but prosperous Roman town on the Ligurian coast of north Italy that specialized in the trade of marbles quarried at nearby Carrara. However, small excavations in the centre of the abandoned classical town have revealed a sequence of post-classical phases that illustrates Luni's 5th- and 6th-century prosperity, and its slow contraction thereafter. In particular, evidence of its Late Roman trading contacts with North Africa and the Eastern Mediterranean have come to light, as have imported soapstones and lead coins of the 7th-9th centuries. Whether the history of Luni is typical of many classical towns now remains to be seen, but these excavations put the Dark Ages in this part of Italy in sharp perspective.

lunula. A crescent-shaped chest-ornament of sheet-gold made in Ireland, Scotland and perhaps Wales during the Early Bronze Age; examples found elsewhere in northern Europe were probably traded from Britain. They were usually decorated with fine incised lines or in relief by the repoussé technique; the form of the decoration has led to the suggestion that it imitates the multiple-strand necklaces of jet and amber that are also found during the Early Bronze Age.

Luoyang [Lo-yang]. A city in Henan province, China. A few SHANG burials have been found at Luoyang but the site evidently had little importance until the ZHOU dynasty established a subsidiary capital there, Cheng Zhou, during the reign of the second Western Zhou king (c1000 BC; see ZHOU CAPITALS). Even so, Zhou remains at Luoyang are not abundant until the Eastern Zhou period (770-256 BC) when the Zhou royal house, having been forced to abandon its Shaanxi capital, resided at Luoyang. Bronzes and pottery recovered from some 270 tombs excavated at Luoyang Zhongzhoulu supply a valuable artefact sequence, described in the excavation report in terms of seven stages, spanning the entire Eastern Zhou period. Particularly rich finds from JINCUN, just northeast of the modern city, belong to the latter part of Eastern Zhou; lesser tombs from the end of Eastern Zhou and the HAN period have been excavated in large numbers at Shaogou. During the QIN and Western Han dynasties the capital returned to Shaanxi (see CHANG'AN), but Luoyang was again the capital during the Eastern Han dynasty and, for the last time, from AD 494-535, when the Northern Wei emperors ruled there.

Lupaqa. See AYMARA.

Lupemban. A stone industry of western central Africa, where it appears to have developed from a SANGOAN predecessor. In its characteristic form, the Lupemban is found in northern Angola and southern Zaire. An important dated occurence is that at KAL-AMBO FALLS on the Zambia/Tanzania border, while related material has been reported from as far to the east as MWANG-ANDA in northern Malawi. In contrast with the Sangoan, Lupemban assemblages are marked by the fine quality of their bifacial stone-working technique on elongated double-ended points and thick core-axes. At Mufo, in the alluvial diamond workings of the Dundo area in northern Angola, and at Kalambo Falls, the industry is shown to cover a time-span from before 30,000 bc until c15,000 bc, with a gradual reduction in artefact size in the former area.

lur [plural: *lurer*]. A large horn of the Late Bronze Age of Northern Europe, with examples from Denmark, Sweden, Norway and north Germany. *Lurer* are among the most elaborate products of the European bronzesmith, made in sections by the lost wax method (*see* CIRE PERDUE), with a long double-curved body and a disc-shaped mouth. Most finds are of pairs of *lurer* from peat bogs; these probably represe   deposits and it seems most likely that these elaborate instruments were mainly for ceremonial use. Experiments have shown that they have a surprisingly large musical range.

Luristan. A region of central western Iran, best known for the bronze industry of the area in the early 1st millennium BC (the so-called Luristan bronzes). The area has produced evidence of early farming sites (*see* Tepe GANJ DAREH, Tepe ASIAB, Tepe GURAN and Tepe SARAB) and of later prehistoric settlement (*see* Tepe GIYAN). Perhaps undue prominence has been given to the later bronze industry, which reached museum collections as a result of persistent looting of tombs dating from the 10th to the 7th centuries BC. The bronzes of this period include weapons, horse bits and trappings, vessels and ornaments, often decorated with designs based on animal and human figures. Iron also appears at an early date in the Luristan tombs. A settlement of the period of the bronzes has been excavated at Baba Jan.

Lusatian. See LAUSITZ.

Luwians [Luvians]. An INDO-EUROPEAN-speaking group in Anatolia, known mainly from references in HITTITE records, from the Hittite Old Kingdom onwards. They appear to have migrated into Anatolia, perhaps from the Pontic steppes in southern Russia, in the 3rd millennium BC and spread through western Anatolia and as far as the Cilician plain. The Luwians are rather difficult to recognize in the archaeological record, but there is some evidence to suggest that it was they, rather than the Hittites, who developed the so-called 'Hittite hieroglyphic' writing system and it seems that by the 16th century BC Luwian had become the dominant spoken language of the Hittite state.

Luzon. See DIMOLIT, PHILIPPINES.

Lycia. An area on the southern coast of Turkey which became a kingdom in the 1st millennium BC. Groups identified as Lycians are mentioned in the 14th century BC AMARNA letters as pirates in the East Mediterranean, and were later among the PEOPLES OF THE SEA who attacked Egypt. Little is known about them in their homeland, although the French have carried out excavations in their capital Xanthos. They spoke an INDO-EUROPEAN tongue, which appears to be a dialect of LUWIAN. Some inscriptions were found at Xanthos in this language, but using an alphabet derived from the Greeks. The Lycians were absorbed into the ACHAEMENID empire in the 6th century BC.

Lydenburg. An Early Iron Age site in the eastern Transvaal, South Africa, dated to about the 5th century ad and noteworthy for the discovery of a series of unparalleled terracotta human heads of up to life size.

Lydia. A small kingdom which appeared in western Turkey in the 1st millennium BC known to the Assyrians as Luddu. By about the 7th century BC it was an important staging post in trade between the Aegean and the oriental civilizations. Its capital at SARDIS became rich, exploiting the gold of the nearby Pactolus River. In the mid-7th century the kingdom, under Gyges, was overrun by the CIMMERIANS, but became powerful again subsequently. The legendary rich king Croesus (560-546 BC) was ruler when Lydia was finally overcome by the ACHAEMENIDS. Sardis subsequently became the western capital of the Persian empire, linked to SUSA by a royal road. The Lydians are known for two achievements in particular: mastery of fine stone masonry, witnessed in the Acropolis wall at Sardis and in the Pyramid Tomb and the Tomb of Gyges in the royal cemetery, and the invention of a true coin currency, which was adopted by both the Greeks and the Persians.

Lyell, Sir Charles (1797-1875). Distinguished British geologist who was one of the chief proponents of the Uniformitarian or Fluviatilist school of geology. In marked contrast to the previously dominant Catastrophist view, this held that all changes which have occurred in the earth's surface must be explained in terms of processes still at work, such as the movements of rivers and glaciers, changes in sea-level etc. Lyell's *Principles of Geology* (1830-33) established the view that the earth had been in existence for very much longer than the 6000 years allowed by the biblical chronology and laid open the way for the later acceptance of the antiquity of man.

lynchet. A step-like feature of the landscape, formed when COLLUVIAL material, eroded as a result of ploughing, accumulates downslope against a field boundary. Series of lynchets may develop up hillsides, marking the boundaries of ancient fields.

Lyngby. Norre-Lyngby in Jutland, Denmark, has given its name to a kind of ANTLER club or 'Lyngby axe', made of an antler stem and branch bevelled to form a sharp edge, possibly for use as a pole axe. These axes date from *c*9000 bc.

Lyons [Roman Lugdunum]. A major Roman provincial town in southern France, a COLONIA, eventually capital of the three 'imperial' provinces of Roman GAUL, and birthplace of the Emperor Claudius. Lugdunum was founded in 43 BC shortly after the conquests of Julius Caesar, where the Rivers Rhône and Saône join, and in an area where we know of two previous Gallic settlements. The site had importance not only because of Agrippa's road system, of which it was to become the centre, but also because of the volume of commercial traffic on the two rivers, which were themselves lines of communication. The initial city, in the area of Les Minimes, shows the familiar colonial grid-plan, and both the CARDO and *decumanus* seem to have been paved with granite. The city enjoyed a rather privileged prosperity under the early Empire, especially under Hadrian, and suffered no real set-back until it was seriously damaged in the war between Severus and Clodius Albinus in 197 AD. A very large number of monumental remains and other Roman evidence have been identified. Notable are the FORUM Vetus (modern Fourvière), the THEATRE (expanded to take up to some 11,000 spectators in Hadrian's time) and the ODEUM. Both the Theatre and the Odeum are interesting for the elaboration of their stages, both featuring a pit and mechanism to take a stage curtain. As many as four AQUEDUCTS were put up to provide for the ever-increasing demand for water, and there are examples of the use of siphons. An industrial area in the Quai de Serin shows potters' kilns and glass and bronze foundries. Evidence such as common names points to links between these potters and those of AREZZO in Italy, and Lugdunum was clearly an important centre for the manufacture and distribution of imperial pottery.

M

Maba Shixia [Ma-pa Shih-hsia]. *See* LIANG-ZHU.

Macassans. In Austrialian archaeology, this term is used to describe monsoon-season visitors from the eastern Indonesian islands (particularly south SULAWESI) to the northern Australian coastline to collect and process sea-slugs (trepang or *bêche-de-mer*). Archaeological evidence consists of stone structures used to support boiling vats, scatters of Indonesian potsherds, ash concentrations from smoke-houses, graves, and living tamarind trees descended from seeds brought by the trepangers. Their cultural legacies to the Aboriginies included metal tools, dug-out canoes, vocabulary, art motifs, song cycles, rituals, and depictions of Macassan praus in rock paintings and stone arrangements. The adoption of Macassan cultural elements was apparently rapid, as the known history of the trepang industry in Southeast Asia indicates that Macassan voyagers to Australia were unlikely to have arrived much before 1700.

macellum [Latin: 'food market, especially for meat']. Roman meat-market, which was often probably combined with, or only a special case of, the general food-market. Some more sophisticated examples have individual architectural features associated with them, such as (at LEPTIS MAGNA and POMPEII) a porticoed enclosed rectangular courtyard, with one or two colonnaded pavilions in the central area. At Pompeii, shops under the portico face inward into the market and also outward into the surrounding streets — presumably reflecting high land values, and the need to maximize on use of shop frontage. At Rome, the Macellum Magnum erected by Nero was apparently a grand-scale example, doubling both the portico and the pavilion into two-storeyed structures.

MacEnery, Father J. (17??-1841). A Roman Catholic priest who excavated in KENTS CAVERN, Devon, between 1825 and 1841. His discoveries of flint tools in association with the bones of extinct animals seemed to prove the great antiquity of man. However, his views were not shared by most scholars of the time and MacEnery never published his work. This was eventually accomplished by William PENGELLY.

Machalilla. A series of early FORMATIVE PERIOD sites in the Guayas and southern Manabi provinces of Ecuador contain the distinctive Machalilla ceramic complex. The chronological position of this complex is a matter of some argument but traded sherds found in both VALDIVIA C and Late TUTISHCAYNO contexts suggest an inception some time in the mid- to late 2nd millennium bc. Artefacts and burial practices imply a sea-oriented subsistence very similar to that at Valdivia; the ceramics, however, though utilitarian in both cases, are distinctly different. Machalilla ceramics, in contrast to Valdivian, are painted (red banded and black-on-white) and figurines here are rare and crudely made. With no known precursors, the advanced nature of the ceramic technology is difficult to explain. Opinion usually divides between a local and a MESOAMERICAN genesis, with insufficient evidence on either side to provide a wholly satisfactory explanation. Wattle and daub fragments in middens indicate that houses existed, but no foundations have been defined.

Machang [Ma-ch'ang]. Named after a site east of Ledu in eastern Qinghai province, China, the Machang culture belongs to the western or Gansu branch of the YANGSHAO Neolithic. It seems to be a late stage or outgrowth of the BANSHAN culture and precedes QIJIA; this sequence is established stratigraphically (e.g. at Ledu) and is consistent with radiocarbon dates from Machang sites, which fall in the latter half of the 3rd millennium BC. Machang pottery is closely allied to Banshan ware, but less fine.

Machu Picchu. Located on a high ridge

between two higher peaks, overlooking the Urubamba River valley in Peru, the so-called 'lost city of the INCAS' was re-discovered by Hiram Bingham in 1911. Machu Picchu was a walled fortified city with a steep stone stairway to its single entrance and was approached via a stone roadway connecting with CUZCO. Amid plazas, cultivation terraces, temples, palaces and residential compounds, one of the most striking buildings was the astronomical observatory. Built on a circular plan (unusual in Inca architecture), its large granite blocks stand in contrast to the surrounding straight-sided structures. Houses were rectangular in plan with high gables, thatched roofs and trapezoidal doorways; house compounds were discrete but not enclosed by walls as in other centres.

Excavations revealed an unusual number of female skeletons buried in caves on the steep rocky slopes, suggesting that the site may have been the refuge of the Chosen Women (Virgins of the Sun).

A pre-Incan presence may be deduced from a number of green schist 'record stones' found in the oldest part of the site, but this is uncertain.

macrofossils. *See* PALAEOBOTANY.

Madagascar. This island in the Indian Ocean off the east coast of Africa was one of the last major tropical land masses to be settled by man: there is no evidence for human presence prior to the 1st millenium AD. The Malagasy language contains both African and Indonesian elements; in the recent material culture the latter element is dominant, and it is generally accepted that the island's first settlers came from Indonesia, perhaps from Borneo. It is evident that they were accomplished navigators, whose livelihood was based on fishing and the cultivation of rice, cocoyams and bananas. Later, probably in about the 11th century ad, Bantu-speaking immigrants from East Africa also arrived; they would have been responsible for the introduction of domestic cattle and cereal crops of African origin. In due course Madagascar became a part of the coastal trade network of the Indian Ocean.

Madai Caves. These caves in eastern Sabah, northern BORNEO, form a large complex like those of NIAH, Sarawak. The main excavated cave is Agop Atas, which has produced an industry of early Australian type dated to 8000 years ago, with an upper pottery sequence (above a sterile layer) dated from 500 bc to the present. The latter may relate to the ancestry of the present AUSTRONESIAN-speakers of the area, the Idahan Muruts.

Mad'arovce. A regional group of the later phase of the Early Bronze Age, distributed in southern Slovakia and dated to the mid-2nd millennium bc. A large number of sites are hill-top settlements fortified by earthen banks or ditches. TELL-like multi-phase settlements are also known from lowland valleys, often with rich assemblages of dark burnished pottery. Mixed burial rites, sometimes inhumation, sometimes cremation, are known from the medium-sized lowland cemeteries.

Madura Cave. *See* DINGO.

Maes Howe. A magnificent PASSAGE GRAVE on Orkney, north Scotland. It is covered by a circular mound 7 metres high and 35 metres in diameter and surrounded by a ring ditch. The tomb is built entirely of a local stone which splits easily into rectangular slabs, giving an impression of deliberate dressing. The central chamber is roofed by CORBELLING and has three additional chambers opening from it, entered through doorways raised about a metre above the floor of the main chamber. Nothing was found in the tomb when it was explored in the 19th century, but a RUNIC inscription tells of the VIKINGS looting a great treasure in the 12th century. Recent radiocarbon dates indicate that the tomb was built in the late 3rd millenium bc (early 3rd millenium BC).

Maeva. A cluster of 25 Polynesian MARAE on the island of Huahine, SOCIETY ISLANDS. Many of the AHU and pavements have been restored, and this is now one of the most visible and impressive *marae* complexes in Polynesia.

Magadha. Kingdom of northern India which flourished in the second half of the 1st millennium BC, when under Chandragupta and, later, ASOKA, it became the centre of the vast and powerful MAURYAN empire.

Magan. Name appearing in Mesopotamian texts of the EARLY DYNASTIC, AKKADIAN and UR III periods. It appears to refer to a land with which SUMER was trading, perhaps situated somewhere in the southern part of the Persian Gulf, either in Baluchistan (on the Iranian side) or in Oman (on the other), or possibly both. Danish archaeologists working at the site of UMM AN-NAR, a small island off the west coast of Abu Dhabi, have suggested that it might be identified with Magan.

Magdalenian. The last major culture of the French Upper PALAEOLITHIC is called the Magdalenian from the type site of LA MADE-LEINE in the Dordogne, southwest France. It dates from approximately 16,000-10,000 bc, according to radiocarbon, and has been divided into six phases. There are no clear distinctive features which identify the Magdalenian as a whole, but certain kinds of harpoon and the 'parrot beak' burin are diagnostic of parts of it. All Magdalenian assemblages have abundant burins, backed bladelets and composite tools, especially composite grattoir-burins, with 'end scraper' at one end and burin at the other.

The Magdalenian is important because of the abundance of sites in western Europe, from Iberia through France to the area north of the Alps and to Czechoslovakia. It has been suggested that the population of western Europe may have reached a new level at this time — possibly a quarter of a million or more. Above all, the Magdalenian is the period of high artistic productivity. The majority of the painted caves and most mobiliary art come from this time. There are at least four sites, including La Madeleine itself, which have produced over a hundred art objects. See also CAVE ART.

Magdalenska Gora. An Iron Age cemetery of the early LA TÈNE period located near Smarje, south of Ljubljana in Slovenia, Yugoslavia. Excavated by the Duchess of Mecklenburg between 1905 and 1914, the cemetery comprises large barrows into which as many as 40 burials are inserted. The rich grave goods include weapons, armour, horse trappings, personal jewellery and bronze vessels, including a complete bronze SITULA.

Magellan Complex. A sequence of human occupation defined from assemblages in deeply stratified deposits at the southern tip of mainland South America, especially Palli Aike and FELL'S CAVE. The earliest assemb-

lage (Magellan I) contains fishtail projectile points, considered a hallmark artefact signifying PALEO-INDIAN activity (*see also* EL INGA). Horse and sloth bones and the remains of three partly cremated DOLICHOCEPHALIC humans, found in association with these points, have produced a single radiocarbon date of *c*8700 bc.

A shift from fishtail- towards willow-leaf points (*see also* AYAMPITIN, LAURICOCHA) occurs in Magellan II (*c*8000-4000 bc). This probable change in subsistence is also confirmed by the disappearance of Pleistocene megafauna (replaced by modern forms) and accompanying widespread climatic change. Magellan III, occurring in the late 5th to early 4th millennium bc, is characterized by the willow-leaf and stemless triangular points and a subsistence base strongly oriented to the hunting of guanaco. The later periods (Magellan IV and V) are ill-defined, but represent a continuing hunting strategy blending into a period of ceramic use which runs well into historic times.

Maglemosean. A Mesolithic culture or group that takes its name from the site of MULLERUP in the Magle Mose, the Danish fenland area on the island of Zealand. The culture was believed to extend from the Baltic across northwest Europe to Britain, and to date to the Boreal period, about 6000 bc at a time when parts of the southern North Sea were dry land. The English sites of this group are now known to be generally earlier than 6500 bc and to constitute the early MESOLITHIC of Britain. Barbed bone points and microlithic tools, especially obliquely blunted points, are typical of the Maglemosean. Flaked flint axes were used in tree-felling and canoe-making.

Magna Graecia. General term applied to the Greek cities of southern Italy and Sicily. Two of the earliest are probably PITHEKOUSSAI (modern Ischia) and neighbouring CUMAE, both of whose foundations are normally attributed to the 8th century BC. This very prosperous 'New World', often more prosperous than their founder cities, consisted almost entirely of commercial ports. Their Greek culture, which is well documented in Greek and Roman sources, seems to have remained localized to a considerable extent in the cities themselves. The whole question of their relationship with the indigenous peoples of the peninsula, whom they must have permanently displaced in many instances, lacks good evidence and is under-researched.

magnetic surveying. One of the most commonly used GEOPHYSICAL surveying methods. The strength of the earth's magnetic field is measured using a MAGNETOMETER. Measurements are made in a grid-pattern of points all over a suspected site. Features buried below ground may have a modifying effect on the strength of the earth's field recorded at the surface. Hearths, kilns and other burned structures may contain large quantities of iron oxide, permanently magnetized by being heated and cooled in the ancient earth's field (*see* PALAEOMAGNETISM). Such structures may show up as a strong 'magnetic anomaly' in the readings of survey. Soil materials often have a somewhat enhanced 'magnetic susceptibility' compared with the subsoil. The fills of pits and ditches may therefore also cause magnetic anomalies.

magnetometer. An instrument used in MAGNETIC SURVEYING to measure the strength of the earth's magnetic field. There are a number of designs, but two are particularly widely used. The proton magnetometer makes an absolute measurement of field strength, but is intermittent in operation: each reading is initiated by the push of a button, and takes some seconds to appear on the display of the instrument. Fluxgate magnetometers work on a different principle, and give a continuous reading, which makes surveying less time-consuming. Most fluxgate machines do not however measure field strength directly. They are GRADIOMETERS, measuring the vertical gradient of the earth's magnetic field, that is, how fast the field strength changes with vertical distance from the earth's surface. Gradient measurements can also be used in archaeological surveys, and in fact have an advantage over absolute measurements. The earth's field strength varies continuously during the day at any one locality. Absolute measurements taken at different times have to be calibrated for this effect if they are to be comparable. Gradient measurements are not affected by this diurnal drift in field strength, and so do not need to be calibrated. Proton gradiometers are also available (*see* BLEEPER).

Mahabharata. *See* HASTINAPURA.

Mahaiatea. The largest MARAE [temple] constructed in Eastern Polynesia, with an 11-stepped pyramidal AHU covering 81 by 22 metres, 13.5 metres high. Constructed by the chieftainess Purea of Papara district, TAHITI, in 1767 and described by COOK, Banks and Wilson in the late 18th century, this structure now has only a few foundation fragments surviving.

Mahavira. *See* VAISALI.

Mahdiya. The FATIMIDS, who conquered Egypt in 969 and thereafter ruled from CAIRO established their first capital at the port of Mahdiya in 902. The town occupied a narrow peninsula barred by a double wall with a single imposing entrance, the Sqifa al-Kahla. Apart from this, the most imposing Fatimid monument is the Mosque of Obeid Allah, built *c*912 and remodelled subsequently. It has a monumental entrance, a courtyard with single arcades on all four sides, and a sanctuary with a T-shaped arrangement of nave and transepts — a plan which anticipates the Fatimid mosque at AJDABIYAH and the mosques of Cairo. Other Fatimid buildings at Mahdiya include part of the palace of Obeid Allah and a naval dockyard.

Mahendraparvata [Sanskrit: 'mountain of the Great Indra']. Original name of Phnom KULÈN, north of ANGKOR in Cambodia.

Maheshwar. A central Indian site, facing NAVDATOLI on the opposite bank of the Narbada River. There is some trace of prehistoric occupation, but Maheshwar became a major site only after Navdatoli was abandoned, in the Iron Age and the medieval period.

Maiden Castle. Hill southwest of Dorchester, Dorset, southern England, on which were built successively a Neolithic CAUSEWAYED CAMP, a long BARROW and a massive Iron Age HILLFORT enclosing nearly 20 hectares. The site was excavated in the 1930s by Sir Mortimer WHEELER and the work here made major contributions to the development of techniques of archaeological excavation and recording, as well as to the understanding of British hillforts. The earliest structure was the causewayed camp, with two concentric rings of ditches on the eastern end of the hill. After this site had gone out of use an unusual bank barrow was constructed, partly over the filled ditches, measuring almost 550 metres in length and originally c1.5 metres high. At the eastern end there was a concave setting of posts and the burials of two young children. Occupation was resumed in the Iron Age, perhaps in the 5th century BC, with a univallate fort on the eastern knoll of the hill; subsequently this was extended to cover the entire hilltop. Inside were huts of stone and timber, some circular, some rectangular, and surfaced trackways between them. In the 2nd century BC the site was twice refortified, ending up as a massive stronghold with double ramparts on one side and treble on the other, and with complex entrances, involving elaborate outworks, sentry boxes and platforms for slingers. Beside one of the sentry boxes at the eastern entrance was a pit containing 22,260 sling stones. In the 1st century BC the site became the tribal capital of the Durotriges. In the Roman campaign of AD 44 Maiden Castle fell to Vespasian's army and the excavated war cemetery of this period contained 38 bodies, one with an iron BALLISTA bolt lodged in his spine. The Romans moved the population to a new settlement at Durnovaria (Dorchester) and Maiden Castle was abandoned. The only later indications of use come from the 4th century, when a Romano-Celtic temple was built on the hilltop, possibly continuing worship of the Iron Age deity.

Maikop. A tumulus cemetery in the northern Caucasus, Russia, dating to the late 3rd millennium bc, which yielded exceptionally rich grave goods comparable to the finds of ALACA HÜYÜK in Anatolia. Wooden and (exceptionally) stone mortuary houses were constructed under the barrows. The richest grave was filled with wooden carts or wagons, copper, gold and silver objects, carnelian and turquoise jewellery and well-preserved textiles with elaborate designs. This 'royal' grave gives its name to the Maikop culture, distributed in the southern Caucasus. Most settlements were located in defensible positions, occasionally girt with stone walls or timber palisades. Slab-cist graves and small barrows were provided for burial of less important individuals.

Mailhac. A series of important Late Bronze Age and Iron Age sites near Narbonne in southwest France, dating from the 8th to the 1st centuries BC. The sites comprise a defended hilltop settlement (Le Cayla) and a series of urnfield cemeteries (Le Moulin, Grand Bassin I and II). The earliest phase (Mailhac I) is represented by a cemetery of URNFIELD type at Le Moulin and the earliest phase of occupation of Le Cayla, with wooden houses and evidence of a mixed farming economy, supplemented by hunting. In the Mailhac II phase of the early 6th century BC, HALLSTATT influences are strong: iron became quite common and a chieftain's wagon burial at La Redorte is of Hallstatt type, although most burials of this period, in the Grand Bassin I cemetery, are still cremations in urns. This period postdates the foundation of the Greek colony at MARSEILLES (Massalia) and Greek and Etruscan imports start to appear in both graves and occupation deposits in this and especially in the succeeding phase (Mailhac III, dated to the later 6th century BC); the burials of phase III are still inurned cremations in the Grand Bassin II cemetery. Phases IV and V are known from the settlement and belong to the Early and Middle LA TÈNE Iron Age. Occupation ended early in the 1st century BC with a burning, probably to be attributed to Roman punitive action after threatened risings in the area.

Mainz [Roman Mogontiacum]. An imperial Roman legionary base and civilian settlement on the west bank of the Rhine, at its confluence with the River Main. A fort was built of timber to house two legions, in the period 18-13 BC, and renewed in stone somewhere between 50 and 100 AD. Between the fort and the river grew up a civilian settlement with port, which, under Domitian, was to become capital of Germania Superior (Upper Germany). There has been only modest exploration of the fort area (although the extent of some 36 hectares is known) and the modern city of Mainz inhibits much work on the civilian evidence. Surviving remains include a great column of the god Jupiter, nine metres high and decorated with reliefs of 28 deities, evidence for a Flavian aqueduct, portions of late Roman wall, and some areas of civil and military cemeteries. The most important material has been collected together in the Mittelrheinisches Landesmuseum in Mainz.

maiolica. *See* ARCHAIC MAIOLICA.

maize. *Zea mays* (maize) is one of the cereal

plants, nowadays grown widely in the USA, Mexico and South America, southeastern Europe and Southwest Asia. It was an important early domesticated food plant in the New World and one of the trio which provided a balanced diet for early American farmers (the other two being beans and squash). The plant originated in the Central Mexican Highlands, where pollen belonging to maize, or one of its near relatives, has been found in cores from Mexico City, dated to between 60,000 and 80,000 bp. The earliest macrofossils of maize appear in the TEHUACAN VALLEY in Mexico between 7000 and 5000 bc. These early finds have very small cobs and kernels and it has been suggested that they come from wild maize. The earliest evidence of its cultivation comes from the succeeding Coxcatlan phase in the Tehuacan Valley (4800-3500 bc). Remains dated to *c*3000 bc were also found further to the north at TAMAULIPAS. Maize first appears in South American contexts on the Peruvian coast in the late PRE-CERAMIC PERIOD VI; its earliest appearance in North America dates to *c*2500 bc (*see* BAT CAVE). Although diffusion from Mesoamerica is the most commonly held explanation for its occurrence elsewhere, independent domestication is still sometimes proposed.

A plant of great variety and versatility, the ancestry of maize is a matter of considerable argument. Some scholars argue that it derives from an extinct wild form (the major proponent of this theory is Paul Mangelsdorf); others (notably G.W. Beale) claim that it derives from a wild grass called teosinte, still indigenous to the Mexican Highlands.

Majapahit [Malay: 'bitter fruit']. Name of the 'last and most glorious' INDIANIZED kingdom of JAVA. Founded in 1292 by king Vijaya, who defeated the Mongol fleet which had come to punish his predecessor, it developed into the most powerful empire of the Archipelago for two centuries until its decline in the face of the advance of Islam. The apogee of Majapahit was reached under king Rājasanagara (1350-89) who, with the powerful Prime Minister Gaja Mada, extended the kingdom's suzerainty to its farthest limits. At this stage he shared power in the whole of Southeast Asia only with the Thai kingdom of AYUTTHAYA, founded in the year of his own coronation.

Majiabang [Ma-chia-pang]. A Neolithic site in Jiaxing, northern Zhejiang province, China, near Shanghai. The name 'Majiabang culture' commonly refers to the descendants of the 5th millennium BC HEMUDU lower-level culture in the region south of the Yangzi near Shanghai. The Majiabang culture comprises two phases, the earlier represented by the Majiabang site itself and the later by the middle stratum at Qingpu Songze in Shanghai. The lower stratum at Songze, belonging to the early phase, yielded a radiocarbon date of *c*4000 BC. The site of Beiyinyangying in Nanjing is classified by some archaeologists with the Songze phase. The successor to the Majiabang culture is the 3rd millennium BC LIANGZHU culture.

Majiabang is sometimes incorrectly read as Majiabin [Ma-chia-pin], an error originating with Chinese archaeologists who misread the simplified character for the place name.

Majiayao [Ma-chia-yao]. Type site of the Majiayao culture, in Lintao Xian in the Tao River valley of Gansu, China. Majiayao remains are found as far west as Wuwei in Gansu and in eastern Qinghai. On the evidence of a few radiocarbon dates, mostly in the latter part of the 4th millennium BC, Majiayao is regarded as the earliest stage of the western or Gansu branch of the YANGSHAO Neolithic. A few primitive metal implements from Majiayao sites offer the earliest hints of a Chalcolithic technology in China. Majiayao pottery designs, perhaps the finest known from the Chinese Neolithic, are painted in black only; most derive from running spiral patterns, though in some of the more attenuated and asymmetrical designs the spirals are well concealed (*see* BANSHAN).

The Gansu Yangshao apparently resulted from a westward expansion of the older eastern branch of the Yangshao, but its exact history remains unclear. Some archaeologists believe Majiayao to be an offshoot of MIAODIGOU, and a phase regarded as transitional between the two, named after the Gansu site of Shilingxia, has yielded a radiocarbon date (*c*3800 BC) in the same range as one obtained for Miaodigou. However, Miaodigou painted pottery designs include sophisticated running spiral patterns whose simpler forms are unknown in the eastern branch of the Yangshao but are staples of the Majiayao repertory in Gansu. It is therefore conceivable that Majiayao arose from some eastern Yangshao phase earlier than Miaodigou (e.g. BANPO) and then in return contributed to the formation of Miaodigou.

Makaha Valley. An important valley on western Oahu, HAWAIIAN ISLANDS, which has been the scene of intensive settlement archaeology to document cultural developments from ad 1100 to 1800. The valley contains well-preserved rainfall cultivation systems in its lower portion, wet TARO terraces in its upper section, and several HEIAU.

Makapan. The limeworks deposit from this locality has produced one of the two main South African samples of *Australopithecus africanus*, the gracile species (*see* AUSTRALOPITHECUS). There are no typical stone tools, but many bone and horn fragments are alleged to have been modified as tools, the so-called osteodontokeratic culture. The hominid remains may date from about three million years ago. The nearby CAVE OF HEARTHS has ACHEULIAN and later deposits.

Makassar. *See* SULAWESI.

Makwe. A rock shelter in eastern Zambia, close to the border with Mozambique. Excavations revealed occupation during the last four millennia bc by the makers of a stone industry in which backed microliths were virtually the only type of retouched implement represented. Traces of mastic provided evidence of the manner in which the various classes of these implements had been hafted.

Malacca. *See* MALAYSIA.

malachite. One of the COPPER ores. This hard, bright green mineral was also powdered and used for personal decoration in various parts of the world.

malae. *See* MARAE.

Malangangerr. *See* OENPELLI SHELTERS.

Malatya [ancient Milid]. The TELL of Arslantepe near the Euphrates River in central Turkey. It has produced important Syro-HITTITE remains of the early 1st millennium BC, including a Lion Gate bearing relief carved mythological scenes and libations to the gods.

Malaysia. Prehistory in West Malaysia (Malaya) commences with a possible Pleistocene assemblage (Kota Tampan), but the first coherent and widespread industry is the HOABINHIAN (GUA CHA, GUA KECHIL). Neolithic assemblages of probable Thai origin appear in north and central Malaya after 2800 bc (Gua Cha, Gua Kechil). The sequence in most of inland Malaya is clearly tied to Aslian (AUSTRO-ASIATIC) ancestry, and Austronesian ('Malay') settlement on the coasts (after 1000 bc, probably from west Borneo) is undocumented archaeologically.

It is not known when the first contacts between the Malay Peninsula and India developed, but it was most likely well before the beginning of the Christian Era. Chinese sources mention petty Indian states as early as the 2nd century AD and the earliest Sanskrit inscriptions appear in the 4th century. By then the northern part of the Peninsula had come under the suzerainty of the CAMBODIA-based kingdom of FUNAN, while a number of independent INDIANIZED kingdoms continued to exist further to the south. One of the more important of these was that of P'AN-P'AN (5th-7th centuries) which served as a relay station between India and the rest of Southeast Asia; *see also* KUALA SELINSING. Soon after the SUMATRAN kingdom of ŚRIVIJAYA came into being in the late 7th century it gained footholds on the Malay Peninsula, and exercised suzerainty over much of the Peninsula until succeeded in the 13th century by the JAVANESE kingdom of SINGHASĀRI and the THAI kingdom of SUKHOTHAI. From the following century come the first signs of the Islamization of the Peninsula. In the 15th century the Islamic trading state of Malacca developed into a major entrepôt of world trade.

For East Malaysia (the states of Sarawak and Sabah), *see* BORNEO.

Malāyu. An INDIANIZED kingdom situated on the east coast of SUMATRA, Indonesia, centred in the region of Jambi. Its name was mentioned in the middle of the 7th century by a Chinese source (as *Mo-lo-yu*) and more information about it was given by the Chinese pilgrim I-Ching later in the same century. It appears that around 690 the kingdom was absorbed by that of *Shih-li-fo-shih* or ŚRIVIJAYA.

Mali. One of the early African Sudanic states,

Mali rose to prominence in the 12th and 13th centuries, when it appears effectively to have taken over from ancient GHANA the control of the BAMBUK goldfields and their links with the trans-Saharan trade. By the 14th century its rulers controlled an extensive stretch of territory including the Songhai country of the middle Niger, and Mali's ruler made the pilgrimage to Mecca. The empire declined in the late 15th century.

Malian [Malyan], **Tal-i**. A TELL site northwest of Shiraz in southern Iran, excavated by a joint Irano-American team in the 1970s. This huge site covers some 400 hectares and has been positively identified from inscriptions as the ELAMITE city of Anshan, located far further east than had been predicted by most scholars. Occupation of the site goes back well into the 5th millennium BC and many buildings of the PROTO-ELAMITE and Middle Elamite periods have been discovered. In the 3rd and 2nd millennia BC the city was clearly a major trading centre (yielding much imported material) as well as the local capital.

Maliq. A large settlement site of the Neolithic, Copper Age and Bronze Age, located in the upland Korçe basin in south central Albania. A four-metre stratigraphy contained four major occupation horizons: I, two late Neolithic building levels with rectangular houses with reed on plaster floors set on timber beams, associated with rich painted pottery; II, two building levels associated with late Copper Age material, the first a pile-dwelling on top of lacustrine sediments, the second a set of rectangular houses on clay floors. Incised and channelled ware is found. IIIA-IIIB represent two Early Bronze Age building levels, IIIC-D a Middle and a Late Bronze Age building level. The Maliq stratigraphy provides the clearest prehistoric sequence yet available from Albania.

Mallia. A MINOAN palace and town site in northern Crete east of KNOSSOS. The town was established in the Early Minoan period, but the palace was constructed in the Middle Minoan period, c2000 BC, and then rebuilt after a destruction — probably due to an earthquake — in the 18th century BC. It was finally destroyed, like the other Minoan palaces, c1450 BC, probably by the eruption of THERA. The palace consists of ranges of rooms around a central courtyard; it is large, but relatively simple in layout. Investigations in the town have explored several Middle and Late Minoan houses, some very well appointed.

Mal'ta. An important site in southern Siberia near Lake Baikal occupied in late PALAEOLITHIC times. There are traces of a dwelling and a burial of a young person of possibly mongoloid affinities, as well as several art pieces.

Maltese temples. The tiny islands of Malta and Gozo in the central Mediterranean south of Sicily provided the setting for the development of an impressive prehistoric architectural tradition of stone temple-building. Between c4000 and 2500 BC the inhabitants of the islands constructed at least 12 major temple complexes, most of which contained two or three separate temples, built in several phases over a long period of time. The temples are built of local limestone in CYCLOPEAN MASONRY and are characterized by a series of apsidal courts or chambers arranged on either side of a central corridor opening from a monumental facade. The whole structure is enclosed by a solid outer wall and the space between this and the building itself filled with stone and earth rubble. Early examples are trefoil in plan, but later temples may have five, six or seven apsidal chambers. Characteristically they have a number of installations which are presumably ritual, including altar-like constructions, niches and port-hole openings. Some of the later temples have decorated slabs, with rows of drilled hollows, but the temples at TARXIEN are unique in having slabs carved with spiral and animal ornament as well as the lower part of a massive free-standing statue of a 'fat lady', often interpreted as a mother goddess figure.

In the past scholars often regarded the Maltese temples as part of a MEGALITHIC complex, showing influence from the east Mediterranean. More recently it has been recognized that the temples are unique in form and construction and are in any case too early to be derived from any east Mediterranean stone architecture. They are now seen as a local development, perhaps representing the visible witness to the man-power capabilities and organizational powers of chiefdom societies. *See also* HAGAR QIM, SKORBA, TARXIEN.

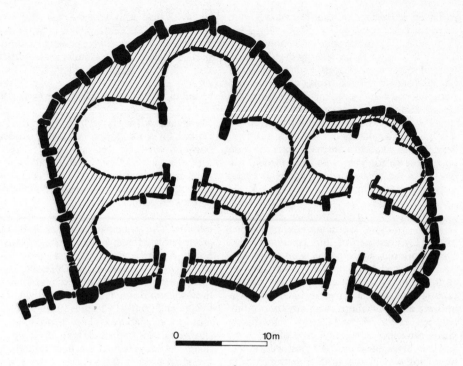

Maltese temples: plan of the Ġgantija temple on Gozo

Malwa. A district of central India which has given its name to a culture complex of the CHALCOLITHIC period (3rd-2nd millennium BC). The characteristic pottery is painted in black on a red or cream ground in exuberant designs including geometric, plant and animal motifs. One of the most important sites of the Malwa complex is NAVDATOLI.

mammoth. A type of ELEPHANT. The woolly mammoth, *Mammuthus (Elephas) primigenius*, evolved from an earlier form of mammoth, *Mammuthus (Elephas) trogontherii*, about a quarter of a million years ago, and was perhaps the largest animal hunted by PALAEOLITHIC man. At European Upper Palaeolithic sites like DOLNÍ VĚSTONICE and KOSTENKI there is little doubt that mammoth were the animals most frequently taken. How they were captured and killed is not known; it is possible that they were speared, as no pit traps have ever been found near their carcasses. At GRAVETTIAN hunters' camp-sites in Moravia and the Ukraine large numbers of mammoth bones have been found, and even

houses built from them. The woolly mammoth spread right across Eurasia into North America, and became extinct *c*10,000 bc.

Mamon. A phase of PRE-CLASSIC developments in the Lowland MAYA area. Dated *c*550-300 BC, it was first defined at UAXACTUN and TIKAL. Although some artefacts of stone and obsidian are included in the complex, it is principally characterized by monochrome pottery, with a 'waxy' feel to it, which comes in a limited variety of shapes — the flat-bottomed bowl is common. Figurines possibly of highland origin (e.g. CHIAPA DE CORZO) are also characteristic. Diversity between sites is notable but there is no construction associated with the complex (*see also* CHICANEL).

Mancheng [Man-ch'eng]. District in Hebei province, China, where very large rock-cut tombs of the HAN prince Liu Sheng (*d*113 BC) and his wife Dou Wan were discovered in 1968. The tombs, each of several chambers, were underground palaces: they openly imitate features of buildings above ground, and many of their sumptuous furnishings were luxury articles used by Liu Sheng and Dou Wan in life. The most remarkable object from Dou Wan's tomb is an inscribed gilt-bronze lamp in the form of a kneeling servant girl. Liu Sheng's tomb contained swords and other iron weapons and also a uniquely fine BOSHANLU censer. Both tombs were provided with large stores of food and wine and escorts of chariots and horses. The bodies of Liu Sheng and Dou Wan were dressed in shrouds made of jade plaques sewn together with gold thread, the first of some dozen jade shrouds thus far recovered from Han tombs.

Manching. An OPPIDUM near Ingolstadt, Bavaria, southern Germany, dating to the Middle LA TÈNE period, 2nd-1st centuries BC. This enormous site covered some 380 hectares, enclosed by a rampart 7 km long of MURUS GALLICUS type. Large-scale excavations in the interior have revealed areas of housing and workshops, with streets running between them. A wide strip immediately inside the rampart was left free of buildings and may have been used for pasturing stock. Manching was clearly both a manufacturing and a trading centre. Crafts practised include iron-working, glass-making, the minting of coins, the working of amber, stone and bone, and some pottery manufacture. Textiles and leather goods were also produced. Pottery made here was exported widely throughout central Europe and long-distance trade is attested by the presence of imported fine wares from the Mediterranean world. Although no public buildings were found in the excavations, they may exist in the large part of the site still unexcavated. On the basis of the size of the site and the evidence for craft specialization and extensive trade, it seems reasonable to classify this settlement as of urban, or at least proto-urban, status.

Manco Capac. *See* CUZCO.

Manda. A site located in the Lamu Archipelago off the coast of Kenya, showing evidence for an urban-type settlement with numerous stone-built houses from the 9th century AD onwards. Stone architecture was more advanced than at the contemporary settlement at KILWA, and imported luxury goods more plentiful. Trade contact with the Persian Gulf appears to have been particularly strong. Local iron-working was well developed by the 12th century, as is confirmed also by Arabic written sources. Despite its prosperous start, Manda's subsequent development did not match that of Kilwa.

Mandan. *See* MIDDLE MISSOURI TRADITION.

Mangaasi. A long-lived pottery tradition of central VANUATU (NEW HEBRIDES), dated to between *c*700 bc and ad 1600. This is a MELANESIAN tradition, with parallels in the northern SOLOMONS and NEW CALEDONIA, quite separate from the ancestral POLYNESIAN LAPITA culture.

manioc. The principal staple of agricultural groups of the forest lowlands of northeastern South America. Probably first cultivated in what is now Venezuela in *c*2000 bc, its use spread west to the coast of Peru and south into the Amazon Basin. It is normally divided into sweet and bitter varieties and the latter requires an elaborate detoxification process (including grating, pulping, draining and finally cooking) before consumption. Many of the tools used in this process survive in the archaeological record, especially juice-catching pots and GRIDDLES.

mano. A hand-held stone implement, used throughout the Americas for milling, grinding or pounding operations. Most often used in conjunction with a METATE, it is a hallmark artefact in defining the economic or subsistence base of prehistoric societies. Its forms vary considerably, from a barely modified cobble to a long cylinder similar in appearance and operation to a rolling pin.

manor. The focal point of the feudal societies that developed throughout Western Europe from the 8th and 9th centuries. The manor reflects the emphasis upon landholding in feudal society, and the relation of the village workforce to the lord who owned the manor. Very few manors have been excavated. The best-known examples are 10th-12th-century sites such as Goltho in Lincolnshire and Sulgrave in Northamptonshire for the Anglo-Norman period, and Wintringham, Lincolnshire, and Hound Tor, Devon, for the later Middle Ages. These reveal that the lord of the manor's dwelling and its associated storage buildings were typically constructed within the local vernacular tradition. The earliest Carolingian and Ottonian manors can be expected to be of a similar kind, but none has yet been found. The small RINGWORKS of the 11th and 12th centuries in northern and western France possibly provide some illustration of the houses of feudal lords; small castles inside fortified villages, as at Rougiers in Provence or in Renaissance villages in Tuscany, may be the best examples to be found without detailed archaeological investigations.

mansio. A kind of Roman lodging-house. Communications throughout the Roman Empire were maintained by the provision along main roads of places to change horses (*mutationes*) and to stay overnight (*mansiones*). The *mansio* can be archaeologically difficult to identify, but is frequently sited near the town gate. It might be a comfortable, centrally heated courtyard house, and it may be that use was restricted to officially approved personnel.

Maoris. The POLYNESIAN native people of New Zealand, whose ancestors arrived about AD 900 from central Polynesia, (possibly from COOK ISLANDS, or SOCIETY ISLANDS). *See* NEW ZEALAND.

Mapungubwe. An Iron Age hilltop site in the Limpopo Valley, northern Transvaal, South Africa. The material from the earliest levels is very similar to that from the nearby site of BAMBANDYANALO. Later developments in the 14th and 15th centuries ad included finer pottery, evidence for the spinning of cotton, and trade in glass beads and gold. The latter material, in the form of thin foil, was used to decorate wooden objects such as bowls, clubs and animal figurines to which it was affixed by means of small tacks. The essentially pastoral economy of earlier times continued, although sorghum and cowpeas were cultivated also.

marae. A stone temple of Eastern POLYNESIA, usually consisting of a stone platform [AHU] in a walled, paved or terraced court.

The word *marae* (or *malae*) also refers to an open space within a village in TONGA, SAMOA and NEW ZEALAND.

Marae comprise important archaeological remains in EASTER ISLAND (here called simply *ahu*), HAWAIIAN ISLANDS (HEIAU) and the

Tuamoto, SOCIETY, COOK, Austral and MARQUESAS ISLANDS. Ancestral forms probably go back to the period of Early Eastern Polynesian settlement, around AD 500. *See* MAEVA, MAHAIATEA, OPUNOHU, TAPUTAPUATEA.

Marajoara. *See* MARAJO ISLAND SITES.

Marajo Island sites. A number of sites on an island group located in the mouth of the Amazon River, which evidence a long sequence of ceramic use. A single radiocarbon date of *c*980 bc relates to the earliest Ananatuba phase which has relatively deep shell middens that imply a long-term stable residence unusual for this area. This, together with abundant pottery, tempered with crushed sherds, suggests an incipient agricultural stage, although direct floral evidence is lacking. Artificial mounds — some used for burial, some for habitation — occur in the later Marajoara phase in company with an unusual ceramic complex. Plain utility wares stand in sharp contrast to elaborate polychrome funerary wares and may suggest a degree of social stratification. Other commonly occurring ceramics include pedestal stools, spindle whorls, LABRETS and tangas (pubic covers). The Marajoa complex survived to some time close to AD 1500 but had already been replaced by a new intrusive group, the Aruans, by the time of European contact.

Marathon. A coastal plain on the northeast coast of Attica and, under classical ATHENS, location of a *deme* (subordinate township). The area shows evidence for some kind of occupation from Neolithic times, through Helladic, continuously to Classical. The area gains most fame as site for the Battle of Marathon (490 BC), in which a Persian invasion was successfully repulsed — the good news of which, tradition has it, was conveyed the 35 km to Athens by non-stop runner. In commemoration, the Athenians erected a funeral mound for their dead, with whom they duly buried much fine pottery, both BLACK- and RED-FIGURE WARE. This evidence provides a useful fixed point for the chronology of Greek vase-painting.

Marca Huamachuco. An important regional centre located in the northern highlands of Peru near the ruins of Viracocha Pampa. The site consists of a complex of circular and rectangular multi-storey buildings in cut stone (10-metre high walls still stand) and is surrounded by a stone wall 1 km long and 4 metres high. Early construction dates to the latter part of the Early INTERMEDIATE PERIOD. The centre appears to have been important as early as HUARI times, and to have had some CHIMU affiliations. It survived well enough to have been revised and remodelled by the INCA.

marching camp. Usually refers to a Roman temporary military camp. The Roman army on the move had a systematic procedure for overnight and short-stay stops. Surveyors laid out a suitable and reasonably flat rectangular site, tent positions were planned and marked, and a ditch and low rampart were quickly dug, usually surmounted by a palisade of stakes. These distinctive enclosures may be identified by aerial survey.

Mardikh, Tell. The modern name of the ancient site of ELBA.

Mari [modern Tell Hariri]. Situated on the middle Euphrates River in Syria, Mari was a wealthy and powerful city in the 3rd and early 2nd millennium BC. The city probably dates back to the EARLY DYNASTIC II period and was occupied until its final destruction by Hammurabi in 1757 BC on the Middle Chronology (see Table 3, page 321). Among the important Early Dynastic buildings are six temples dedicated to Ishtar, goddess of love, while from the Old Babylonian period evidence of growing secular power is seen in the Palace. The Great Palace was repeatedly enlarged during its 400-year period of use before it was destroyed in Hammurabi's campaign.During the reign of Zimri-Lim, last king of Mari, it covered two hectares and had 250 rooms, including an audience chamber and other reception rooms, as well as administrative and residential quarters. The structure demonstrates clearly the multiple functions of the palace as residence of the ruler, place of reception for important guests, centre for the civil service, and tax and storage depot. An archive of some 25,000 tablets has provided invaluable information about the economic organization of the city state and its international relations, both commercial and political. A room near the archive has been interpreted as a school — the only one known from Mesopotamia, although schooling was certainly an important aspect of Mesopotamian society. The Palace is famous also for its mural decorations: both representational pictures and geometric designs were painted directly on a thin layer of mud plaster and represent a new and impressive school of decoration.

Marianas Islands. An island group in western MICRONESIA. Excavations have revealed a sequence starting with settlement c1500 bc, perhaps from the PHILIPPINES (Marianas Redware Phase), and continuing after AD 800 with settings of large coral limestone pillars in double parallel rows (LATTE), which presumably served as house supports. *Latte* pillars with their hemispherical capstones may be up to 5.5 metres high, and village groupings of up to 30 *latte* occur on Guam.

Mariette, Auguste (1821-88). Starting his career in the Louvre, Mariette spent most of his life in Egypt, where he became head of the new Egyptian Antiquities Service in 1858. He excavated many of the most important sites of ancient Egypt, and although his excavations were carried out according to the unsystematic and destructive methods usual in the 19th century he has many achievements to his credit. As well as understanding and demonstrating the importance of the ancient sites of Egypt, he was responsible for the establishment of the National Museum of Egyptian Antiquities.

Maringishu. *See* PASTORAL NEOLITHIC OF EAST AFRICA.

maritime archaeology. *See* UNDERWATER ARCHAEOLOGY.

Markkleeberg. A site just outside Leipzig in East Germany, where gravel pits have revealed gravels earlier than the SAALE ice maximum advance in the region. They contain a cold-indicating fauna of early penultimate glacial date and numerous stone artefacts, especially LEVALLOIS flakes.

Marlik Tepe. A royal cemetery of early Iron Age (late 2nd millennium BC) date, occupying a natural spur overlooking a fertile valley southwest of the Caspian Sea in northern Iran.

A total of 53 graves was excavated in the early 1960s; some contained rectangular stone slabs, on which the body with its grave goods was laid and then covered with earth. The grave goods were rich, including many gold and silver vessels, as well as weapons and jewellery. Characteristic decoration is in relief and portrays mythical animal and human figures; it may represent an early phase in the development of the art of the MEDES. See also AMLASH.

Marnians. Name formerly given to the regional LA TÈNE Iron Age group found in the Marne Valley of northern France and thought to represent a group which invaded Britain in the 3rd and 2nd centuries BC. The view is generally rejected today, although there were certainly close connections between Iron Age groups in the Marne region and the ARRAS culture of eastern Yorkshire.

Maros points. Small hollow-based stone projectile points, often with serrated edge-retouch, characteristic of a mature phase of the TOALIAN industry of southwestern SULAWESI (c4000 BC into the 1st millennium BC). See TOALIAN, LEANG BURUNG, ULU LEANG.

Marquesas Islands. An island group of Eastern Polynesia, first settled c300 AD, and perhaps the first group to be settled in Eastern Polynesia. See HANE, PUAMAU, TAIPIVAI.

Marrakesh. A city built on a fertile plain at the foot of the High Atlas in Morocco. Marrakesh was the capital of two dynasties with possessions on both sides of the Strait of Gibraltar: the Almoravids (1061-1147) and the Almohads (1147-1248). The Almoravids were nomadic Sanhaja berbers from Mauretania. They converted to Islam in 1043 and c1062 their leader Yusuf b. Tashufin (1061-1107) founded Marrakesh as their first permanent settlement. Yusuf invaded Spain in 1090, annexing a substantial area despite strong opposition led by El Cid in Valencia. The Almohads of the High Atlas attacked Marrakesh unsuccessfully in 1130, but in 1147 Abd al-Mu'min captured the town and in the next 20 years took most Almoravid possessions in the Maghreb and southern Spain. Marrakesh contains one major Almoravid monument, the al-Barudiyin Qubba, a domed mausoleum built by Ali b. Yusuf in 1109 or 1117. Of the Almohad period, we have the city walls and the Kutubiya Mosque; its most famous feature — the minaret — was built in 1199.

Marseilles [Greek Massalia; Roman Massilia]. Situated at the Bouches-du-Rhône in the south of France, the city was an important Mediterranean port from the end of the 7th century BC and throughout antiquity. The traditional date of foundation, by Phocaean settlers, is put at about 600 BC. With their excellent harbour, the Massiliotes were already prosperous enough by c535 BC to dedicate a treasury at the sanctuary of DELPHI in mainland Greece. Daughter trading colonies were rapidly established along the coast of Spain (see AMPURIAS), in the Golfe du Lion, along the Ligurian coast, and on Corsica. Trading links were energetically pursued up into many areas of western and northern Europe. Prosperity received only a temporary setback when, in 49 BC, the city had to yield to Caesar after the error of siding with Pompey. Even under Roman rule, the port managed to remain more or less independent, certainly in outlook, and preserved in large measure its distinctively Greek culture. Characteristic of loyal devotion to the Greek deities of Artemis and Apollo are silver and bronze coins minted by the city, which bear their images. Perhaps most interesting among the surviving evidence are the remains of the Roman docks (Musée des Docks Romains).

Marshall, Sir John (1876-1958). Director General of Archaeology in India, who excavated at the HARAPPAN CIVILIZATION site of MOHENJO-DARO in the 1920s. These excavations were published in three fine volumes in 1931, entitled *Mohenjodaro and the Indus Civilization*, but the excavations themselves were inferior in quality to those conducted by the best archaeologists of the time, demonstrating, for instance, little understanding of the principles of STRATIGRAPHY.

Marshall Islands. See MICRONESIA.

Mary Rose. A Tudor warship, the flagship of Henry VIII's fleet, which sank in the Solent, off the south coast of England, on its maiden voyage in 1545. The exploration, excavation and recovery of this ship is the largest UNDERWATER ARCHAEOLOGY project ever undertaken. By the time the ship was raised from the bed of the Solent in October 1982, the project had already cost £4 million and a long programme of conservation and study still remains to be carried out. The *Mary Rose* excavation has not only yielded remarkable information about Tudor equipment (both military and for daily life), but has provided the opportunity for the devolopment of new equipment and techniques for underwater archaeology.

Marzabotto. A rare example of an ETRUSCAN occupation site, 25 km from Bologna, northern Italy. Situated in the Reno valley, it was presumably deliberately set on an important Etruscan trade-route. Two distinct phases may perhaps be separated: a 6th-century BC phase, characterized by plain and rather primitive dwellings, with evidence for metalworking; and a 5th-century stage, in which the city appears to have been laid out afresh upon a grid system. On the flat river terrace there are laid out one north-south axis and three east-west main streets that cut it. The precision of the orientation is striking, and surveying *cippi* have been found at some of the major intersections (*see* CIPPUS). It has been suggested that the use of such a grid system indicates, as so often with Greek and Roman examples, a 'colonial' town; and indeed that the grid system itself is, in general, transmitted along a Greek-Etruscan-Roman line of borrowing. The town shows sophisticated drainage, both road and domestic. Interesting are the workshops, foundries and kilns that border the principal street and imply, perhaps, a provincial settlement with single-minded devotion to trade, pottery and metal-working. To the northwest, an 'acropolis' shows evidence for three temples, fronting south on the same axis as the streets of the town.

Occupation, and possibly destruction, by the Boii (*see* BOLOGNA) in the 4th century BC seems to have brought an end to settlement within the century.

Masada. A hilltop desert fortress beside the western bank of the Dead Sea. It was built by Herod in the 1st century BC as a stronghold against the PARTHIANS and was destroyed in AD 70 by the Romans after a last stand by the Zealots of the First Jewish Rebellion. Most of the excavated remains are the buildings erected by Herod between 37 and 31 BC.

These include two monumental palaces, one built on three terraces.

Masbate Island. *See* KALANAY.

Mas d'Azil. *See* AZILIAN.

Massalia, Massilia. *See* MARSEILLES.

mastaba [Arabic: 'bench']. The name given to the low rectangular superstructures which mark many tombs of the Egyptian Early Dynastic period and the Old Kingdom. Nobles and court officials were buried in tombs of this type, sometimes adjacent to the royal burial place. Initially made of mud-brick, the larger mastabas of more important individuals were in later times reinforced with stone, the latter material also being used on occasion to line the underground burial chamber.

Matarām. A dynasty founded by king Sanjaya in the 8th century in the southern part of central JAVA, Indonesia. The name was applied retrospectively to the kingdom of SANJAYA in the 10th century, as the official name of the country which united the centre and the east of the island under the same authority, so as to indicate that the state was no longer confined to eastern Java.

Matarrah. Prehistoric site south of Kirkuk in northeast Iraq, which has yielded evidence of occupation in the 6th millennium bc, in the phase defined by the use of SAMARRA ware. *See also* CHOGA MAMI, SAWWAN.

Matarrubilla. A large PASSAGE GRAVE near Seville in southern Spain, built in the Copper Age. The tomb was built mainly of dry stone walling and the chamber was roofed with a CORBELLED vault. A number of crouched inhumations were discovered, with rich grave goods including an ivory necklace and a clay sandal.

Matera. A town in southeast Italy which has a large number of Neolithic sites in the vicinity. Some of these are caves (e.g. the Grotta dei Pipistrelli) but many are ditched villages, such as Murgecchia and Murgia Timone. Matera has given its name to a type of Middle Neolithic pottery, decorated with incised geometric designs and encrusted with red and white colouring matter. The site of SERRA D'ALTO is also near Matera.

Mathura. An important religious and commercial centre in the Ganges Valley, India, in the post-MAURYAN period. A distinctively Indian art style developed here, showing contacts with GANDHARA. Images of the Buddha appear from the 1st century AD; the image is always stylized and shown larger than other figures.

Matola. An Early Iron Age site near Maputo on the coast of southern Mozambique. The pottery recovered there is remarkably similar to that from KWALE near the Kenya coast far to the north. Despite the great geographical separation of the two areas, it seems plausible to suggest that there may have been an extremely rapid southward spread of Early Iron Age cultural traits along the eastern coast of Africa between the 2nd and the 4th centuries ad.

Matupi. A cave at Mount Hogo, in the Ituri forest of northeastern Zaire, containing a long sequence of predominantly microlithic stone industries extending back to c40,000 bc; the appearance of true backed microliths is dated prior to 19,000 bc. The site is important both in indicating early settlement of this densely forested region and also as yielding one of the oldest microlithic occurrences in sub-Saharan Africa.

Mauer. The lower jaw found in a sand pit at Mauer near Heidelberg, southern Germany, in 1907 was the first of the pre-Neanderthal fossils to be found in Europe. Although it dates from perhaps 400,000 years ago, it is not very different from the NEANDERTHALS of c50,000 years ago. The teeth are similarly small, but the ascending ramus is very wide. *See also* HUMAN EVOLUTION.

Mauern. The Weinberg caves at Mauern in Bavaria, southern Germany, have revealed two MOUSTERIAN levels, the upper one with abundant leaf points. Above these is an Upper PALAEOLITHIC level. A female figurine has also been found.

Maui. *See* HAWAIIAN ISLANDS.

Mauna Kea. The highest mountain in Polyn-esia, Mauna Kea on HAWAII ISLAND is a dormant volcano, 4204 metres high, with very extensive prehistoric basalt adze quarries, mostly between 3350 and 3800 metres above sea level. The sites include workshops, rock shelters, stone-walled enclosures and shrines; radiocarbon dates from the shelters range from ad 1400 to 1650.

Maupiti burial site. An early Eastern Polynesian burial site on Maupiti, SOCIETY ISLANDS, dated AD 800-1200. Grave goods (adzes, pendants, fishing gear) are paralleled in the MARQUESAS (at HANE), New Zealand (at WAIRAU BAR) and elsewhere in the Society Islands at VAITO'OTIA (at Huahine).

Mauryas, Mauryan. An Indian dynasty which established an empire which flourished from the 4th to the 2nd century BC. The first Mauryan leader, Chandragupta, king of MAGADHA, was responsible for driving the Greeks out of India; his grandson ASOKA who reigned from c270-232 BC is the ruler about whom most is known. At the height of its power the Mauryan empire extended over most of the Indian subcontinent except for the far south. Its capital was at Pataliputa (modern PATNA) in northeast India.

mausoleum [Greek *mausoleion*]. Properly used of the great tomb at Mausolus of HALICARNASSUS but also used of various grand tomb structures. The Mausoleion at Halicarnassus was erected, or at any rate finished, by Mausolus's sister-wife and successor, Artemisia II, shortly after his death in 353 BC. As one of the SEVEN WONDERS OF THE WORLD, it was famous not only for its vast dimensions, but also for the refinement of its decoration and sculptures. Several differing reconstructions have been proposed on the basis of the conflicting reports that survive in ancient authors, such as Pliny. Attributed to the architect Pythius, it seems to have been constructed entirely of white marble, and reached a total height of some 40 metres. It consisted of a massively broad and high plinth, surmounted probably by a temple with IONIC peristyle, this itself topped by a pyramid, and the whole capped with a gigantic chariot-and-horse group designed by the architect himself. Some time before the 15th century it had collapsed due to earthquake damage. Following excavation of the site in 1857 by Sir C. Newton, the colossal statues often identified as those of Mausolus and Artemisia were brought to the British Museum, together with sculpture and frieze details.

Mawangdui [Ma-wang-tui]. A site in Hunan province, China, on the outskirts of CHANG-SHA. Three early HAN tombs were excavated here in 1972-3. Tomb No. 2 belonged to the first marquis of Dai (*d.* 186 BC), a high official of the Han administration. Nos. 3 and 1 are apparently the tombs of his son (*d.* 168 BC) and wife (*d.* shortly after 168 BC). In construction and contents the three tombs are far different from Han princely burials in the north (*see* MANCHENG) and reflect instead the lingering traditions and material culture of the CHU kingdom, which had fallen to QIN less than a century earlier. Each tomb takes the form of a massive compartmented timber box at the bottom of a deep stepped shaft; the shaft was filled in with rammed earth and a mound was raised over it. The contents of Tomb No. 1 were very well preserved: the body of the wife of the marquis, wrapped in silk and laid inside four richly decorated nested coffins, was in good enough condition for an autopsy to be performed. The 180 dishes, toilet boxes, and other lacquer articles found in this tomb are by themselves enough to mark it as exceptionally wealthy. Metal vessels, superseded by lacquers, are conspicuous by their absence; the only bronze object in the tomb was a mirror. Other furnishings include silk clothing, offerings of food, musical instruments, small wooden figures of servants and musicians, and a complete inventory of the grave goods written on bamboo slips. A silk banner laid over the innermost coffin is painted with scenes perhaps meant to guide the dead woman's soul in its journey to the next world. A similar banner was found in the tomb of her son, Tomb No. 3. This was furnished in the same fashion as Tomb No. 1 but contained in addition three more silk paintings and an extraordinary collection of manuscripts, some on silk and some on bamboo slips. Among the manuscripts are the earliest known maps from China, treatises on medicine and astronomy, including comet charts, and important literary texts (the Daoist classic *Dao De jing*, the *Yi jing* or *Book of Changes*, and several texts hitherto believed lost). The contents of Tomb No. 2 are comparable to those of Tomb No. 1 but poorly preserved.

Maya. Centred on southern Mexico and Guatemala, the Maya were the major cultural force throughout the CLASSIC PERIOD. Origins are unclear but Mayan characteristics begin to emerge in the Late PRE-CLASSIC (although excavations at CUELLO have sequences going back to the Early FORMA-TIVE).

Population increase and the introduction of new ceramic and architectural forms (*see* CHICANEL) are accompanied by an artistic transition from OLMEC through IZAPAN to Mayan. These changes are particularly evident in the MIRAFLORES phase of the highland site at KAMINALJUYU. The earliest PYRAMIDS appear at TIKAL and at UAXACTUN and the earliest CORBELLED arches at ALTAR DE SACRIFICIOS.

Classic Maya civilization is traditionally dated from the earliest LONG COUNT date (AD 292) found on stele 29 at Tikal. A curious gap in dating of monuments occurs between AD 534 and 593, probably connected with a realignment of political power after the fall of TEOTIHUACAN.

There are numerous models for the rise of Maya civilization, concentrating mostly on economic control of resources or populations by élite groups.

Classic Maya culture is characterized by an immense investment of labour in construction of ceremonial architecture (*see* TIKAL, PALENQUE, COPAN), a growing differentiation between the élite and the peasant population, proliferation of hieroglyphic writing and an increasing concern for CALENDRICS and ASTRONOMY. These traits reach their maximum expression in the Late Classic. However, the notion of the CEREMONIAL CENTRE settlement pattern supported by MILPA agriculture (both long considered hallmarks of Mayan culture) is now in serious question.

The collapse of Maya culture (in *c*900) is the phenomenon which has inspired a good deal of intellectual enquiry, but its relative suddenness still remains without satisfactory explanation. It is clear, for example, that warfare becomes increasingly common in the Late Classic (*see* BONAMPAK); evidence of widespread invasion, however, is comparatively rare (*see* SEIBAL). Environmental degradation through over-use of arable land was once considered to be a viable explanation, but it has become less believable as more evidence of successful intensive agriculture comes to light. Revolution of the peasantry and catastrophic disease have also been postulated. Evidence remains weak for any single explanation and a combination of at least some of these events seems the most plausible. Certainly there are no Long Count dates after 900, after which time lowland populations dwindled by as much as 90 per cent.

A POST-CLASSIC Maya presence is particularly evident in the northern Yucatan, but it is most usually expressed in a mix with Mexican elements (*see* PUUC, RIO BEC, CHENES, CHICHEN ITZA). The last major Mayan centre was at MAYAPAN, which had its florescence after the decline of Mexican influence.

Mayapan. A late POST-CLASSIC urban centre in the northwest Yucatan in Mexico. Although there is an earlier TOLTEC-dominated occupation in the period 1100-1250, the city emerges as a major centre (and ultimately provincial capital) in the period 1250-1450. Founded by the Itza (a putative Mayan group) after the fall of CHICHEN ITZA, the site, though large (*c*4 square kilometres), represents a noticeable decline in planning, architectural technique and artistic achievement. The major features of the site are the surrounding defensive wall, a central temple-pyramid complex dedicated to Kulculkan (the Mayan name for QUETZA-COATL) and some 2100 dwellings; there is, however, no BALL COURT. The most characteristic artefact is the highly elaborate incensario (*see* INCENSE BURNER). Historic sources indicate that the city's economic base was tribute: hostage-taking as a means of guaranteeing the system was routine.

The end of this relatively short-lived centre was precipitated by internal dissension resulting in the summary execution of the ruling élite (the Cocom); abandonment followed shortly thereafter in *c*1450.

Mazapan. A ceramic style developing out of COYOTLATELCO and first appearing in association with major architecture at TULA, Mexico. A red or orange-on-buff painted ware usually decorated with parallel wavy lines on the inside, it is considered a marker of TOLTEC culture.

Meadowcroft Rock Shelter. A stratified site of long occupation, located 80 km southwest of Pittsburgh near Avella, Pennsylvania. Occupation extends from at least 14,000 bc to historic times. Charcoal samples in the lowest stratum have yielded dates in the range 35,000 to 19,500 bc, although there was no association with cultural material. Flint tools bearing a resemblance to finds at BLACKWATER DRAW and Lindenmeier, for example, the Mungai knife and a carbonized fragment of what may have been a basket, were contained in lower stratum IIA, with radiocarbon dates of 16,350-17,950 bc. Such evidence established beyond reasonable doubt the presence of a human population south of the ice masses in the Late Pleistocene.

mean. A measure of central tendency in a DISTRIBUTION. The arithmetic mean is the sum of all values, divided by the number of cases. Other measures of central tendency include the mode — the most commonly occurring value — and the median — the value in the middle of the distribution's range.

mean ceramic dating. A method devised by Stanley South for arriving at the mean date of occupation of American Colonial sites. It is especially applicable to 18th-century sites, where many distinctive ceramic types may be expected to occur in large numbers. The mean ceramic date is found by multiplying the sum of the median dates for the manufacture of each ceramic type by the frequency of each ceramic type and dividing this figure by the total frequency of all ceramic types. The median date for each type is arrived at from documentary evidence.

Although there are notable shortcomings (e.g. the supposition that the median date coincides with the period of maximum use, and the use of a count of sherds rather than whole vessels) the method has been successfully applied at sites in North Carolina and elsewhere.

Meare. A lakeside village of the Iron Age on the SOMERSET LEVELS in southwest England, which has produced evidence similar to that from the nearby site of GLASTONBURY. The settlement consisted of about 40 round houses built on dessicated peat and with timber and brushwood floors. It was surrounded by a palisade and occupied from the 3rd century BC to the 1st century AD.

Mecca [Mekka]. A caravan town on the route from southern Arabia to Palestine and the birthplace of the Prophet Muhammad, *c*570. The holy book of Islam, the Qur'an, was revealed to the Prophet partly on Mount Arafat, just outside Mecca, and partly at Medina, where he migrated in 622 — an event which marks the beginning of the Muslim era. Mecca is the most important Islamic centre of pilgrimage and all Muslims are supposed to visit the holy places at least once. The focal point of the pilgrimage (*haj*) is the sanctuary which contains the Ka'ba, a pre-Islamic shrine reconstructed in 608. According to Azraqi (*d.* 858), the new Ka'ba was built of alternate courses of stone and wood, a technique alien to Arabia, where timber is scarce, but common in Ethiopia. The Ka'ba was destroyed in the civil war of 683 and rebuilt the following year. Now entirely of stone, it was embellished (according to Mas'udi) with mosaic brought from a church at San'a in Yemen.

Mechta-Afalou. The name given to a human physical type represented in the archaeological record of the Maghreb, especially on IBEROMAURUSIAN sites. Cemeteries such as those at COLUMNATA and Afalou bou Rhummel have yielded large numbers of skeletons, with the result that the physical parameters of the population are exceptionally well known. The people were of medium height, robustly built, and with a mean cranial capacity of *c*1650 cc. Remains from earlier periods suggest that the Mechta-Afalou population was of stock indigenous to northwestern Africa.

Medemblik [formerly Medemelach]. The present town of Medemblik is situated on the Zuyder Zee. A monastery is known to have existed at Medemblik from CAROLINGIAN times up to the later medieval period, while occupation material suggests that there was an ancillary settlement from the later MEROVINGIAN era during the 8th and 9th centuries. Recent excavations have discovered an earthen bank surrouding an area of intensive late 8th- and 9th-century occupation mostly in the form of storage pits. Buildings appear to be lacking, but they may well have been built of turf and thus have not survived in the archaeological record. Contemporary documents state that Pepin the Short incorporated Medemblik in a grant of land given to the Bishop of Utrecht and that the king continued to maintain an interest here.

Medes. An INDO-EUROPEAN-speaking people of northwest Iran, known mainly from classical sources. Between the 8th and the 6th centuries BC they took part in the complicated power struggles that affected Iran and Mesopotamia at this time. In 612 BC, under Cyaxares, they conquered ASSYRIA. Subsequently they were united by marriage connections with their one-time rivals, the Persians, and became partners in the ACHAEMENID empire. Their capital at Ecbatana (Hamadan) has not been excavated, but Median sites have been excavated at GODIN TEPE, Baba Jan and Nush-i Jan. By tradition the Medes are credited with the invention of trousers.

Medicine Lodge Creek. A deeply stratified site located in the Big Horn Mountains of Wyoming, USA, with a date range of *c*8000 bc to historic times. Evidence of a diversified subsistence base of small game hunting and gathering occurs at a time when the BIG GAME HUNTING TRADITION was still widely practised on the Great Plains. MANOS, METATES and remains of fish, gopher and rabbit were found at levels dated from 7500-6500 bc; bone of bison and large game animals is extremely rare. Lanceolate projectile points, similar to those found at MUMMY CAVE, also fall within this date range, but stemmed points typical of the ARCHAIC fall slightly later at *c*6300 bc.

Medina [ancient Yathrib]. An oasis town in western Saudi Arabia, 300 km from MECCA. It is venerated by all Muslims as the place to which the Prophet Mohammad fled from Mecca in 622. This event (the *Hijra*) marks the beginning of the Islamic era. Mohammad built himself a house consisting of a walled compound containing a courtyard, living quarters and, on the south side, a double portico. The Prophet and his followers worshipped here and the building, with its large courtyard and covered hall, became the prototype of congregational mosques, such as those at SAMARRA. The House of the Prophet was rebuilt in 707-9 by the caliph al-Walid, who inserted a niche (the *mihrab*) in the end wall of the portico to indicate the direction one must face while praying. Medina is the second most important Islamic place of pilgrimage, after Mecca.

Medvednjak. Refers to a pair of Neolithic settlement sites on adjoining hills, north of Smederevska Palanka in northern Serbia, Yugoslavia. The first site, as yet unexcavated, is dated to the earliest VINČA phase. The second site, excavated by R. Galović, is 24 hectares in extent and contains two occupation horizons of the Early Vinča phase and a Late Vinča phase. Complete house-plans from the latest level indicate well finished rectangular houses. The domestic assemblages are notable for the association of ritual finds with domestic activities such as spinning, weaving, food storage and grinding.

megalith, megalithic. Meaning literally large stone (from the Greek *megas*, 'large', and *lithos*, 'stone'), the term megalith is generally applied to monuments made of large stone slabs including CHAMBER TOMBS, MENHIRS, STONE CIRCLES and ALIGNMENTS. It is customary to include also in a general category of megaliths monuments of similar type built not with large stone slabs, but with drystone walling and CORBELLED vaults, such as the PASSAGE GRAVES of Brittany and other areas. Some authorities have used the term in a still wider sense to cover monuments built of CYCLOPEAN MASONRY such as the MALTESE

TEMPLES, the NURAGHI of Sardinia and the NAVETAS of Minorca. It has even been used on occasion to cover monuments not built of stones at all, such as rock-cut tombs; these were included because they were thought to be closely associated with megalithic tombs, as part of a 'megalithic complex'.

megalithic monuments. Various types of megalithic monuments have been found in many parts of the world: in Europe, several parts of Asia, Oceania and Africa. In the heyday of the DIFFUSIONIST interpretation of prehistory, many scholars believed that all the groups of megaliths were directly connected and could be taken to indicate the movements of people. This idea is no longer accepted and it is clear that the practice of erecting megalithic monuments arose independently in many different areas at different times and that the monuments served different functions in different communities.

Europe. The largest number of megalithic monuments, and the most extensively studied, occurs in western and northern Europe. Excluded from this account are monuments no longer normally classified as megalithic such as the MALTESE TEMPLES and the NURAGHI, TORRI and TALAYOTS of the west

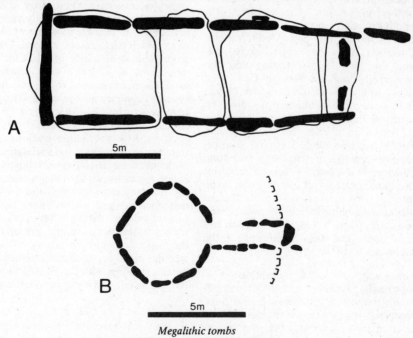

Megalithic tombs
A) Gallery grave B) Passage grave

Mediterranean islands, but the chamber tombs, menhirs, statue-menhirs, stone circles and alignments will be discussed here.

Tombs. Thousands of megalithic tombs occur throughout western and northern Europe, with dense concentrations in parts of Iberia, France, Britain, Ireland, north Germany and Scandinavia. A great number of variant forms exist, but many can be fitted into a simple three-fold classification of simple rectangular chambers (sometimes called DOLMENS), tombs with separate chambers and entrance passages (PASSAGE GRAVES) and longer chambers with no separate passage (GALLERY GRAVES). Simple chambers and passage graves are most commonly found under round BARROWS, while gallery graves are often covered by long barrows. Passage graves in Iberia, Brittany and Ireland are often decorated with usually geometric designs executed by pecking. While some small chambers contained only one or two bodies, the larger tombs of all types were usually used for collective burial, sometimes over very long periods of time (up to 1000 years in some documented cases).

European megalithic tombs were formerly interpreted in terms of the diffusionist view of European prehistory: they were thought to mark the routes taken by missionaries of a 'megalithic religion', spreading west and north from a home in the east Mediterranean. Radiocarbon dates have conclusively disproved this view, demonstrating that the earliest tombs are the Passage Graves of Brittany, with dates in the early 4th millennium bc (mid-5th millennium BC). Indeed by the early 4th millennium BC there were megalithic tombs in Iberia, Brittany, Ireland, England, Scotland and northern Europe. These now seem to represent the earliest stone architecture in the world — several centuries before the appearance of monumental architecture in Mesopotamia or Egypt. Recent studies of megalithic tombs have concentrated not on their origins, but on their function and their economic and social significance to the communities that built them.

Standing stones. As well as megalithic tombs, Europe has large numbers of individual standing stones (MENHIRS) and some in human form (STATUE-MENHIRS). Sometimes menhirs are grouped in rows (ALIGNMENTS) or in enclosures (STONE CIRCLES). Although some

examples may be of early date, the standing stones and monuments of standing stones are in general later than the megalithic tombs, belonging in many cases to the late Neolithic and Copper Age. Simple menhirs occur in many areas, but the anthropomorphic examples known as statue-menhirs are less widely distributed. Female examples shown with breasts and often necklaces occur mainly in Iberia and France and have often been interpreted as mother goddess figures. Other examples shown with weapons and presumptively masculine occur in Corsica, Sardinia and Italy; some areas have both male and female forms.

Whereas unspectacular alignments occur in most areas where menhirs are found, large-scale alignments are known from two main areas. One is Corsica, where impressive examples, incorporating statue-menhirs, occur at Pagliaiu and FILITOSA, and the other is Brittany where the alignments of the CARNAC area consist of three major groups disposed in 10-13 rows, several kilometres in length.

Enclosures of standing stones of various shapes occur in Brittany, but true stone circles (and other geometrical shapes) are found exclusively in Britain where about 900 examples are known. These range in size from very small circles, measuring only a few metres in diameter to massive monuments like AVEBURY which encloses *c*11 hectares. The most remarkable stone circle of all is the unique monument of STONEHENGE. Much recent work has been devoted to the measurement system, geometry and possible astronomical significance of the British stone circles and the Breton alignments; *see* ASTRONOMY (PREHISTORIC EUROPE). Other work has concentrated on the economic and social significance of the monuments and many scholars believe that the immense input of manpower, the central planning necessary and the evidence of mathematical and astronomical knowledge present indicate that the societies of Late Neolithic southern England and Brittany (where the largest monuments occur), were of the type described as chiefdoms, characterized by notable ranking, with the chief at the head of the hierarchy, and by a redistributive economy.

Western Asia. Megalithic monuments are rare in Western Asia as a whole, but a series of megalithic tombs, alignments and enclosures occurs in Israel and Jordan. These monuments are hard to date because the tombs are normally empty when found and standing stones are rarely associated with finds. However most Palestinian archaeologists believe that the tombs are of Neolithic date. CISTS which look rather similar to the megalithic tombs but on a smaller scale are characteristic of the Copper Age Ghassulian culture in the same area (*see* GHASSUL).

India. Megaliths and related monuments of various kinds are found in many parts of India; they are particularly common in the south. The megalith builders seem to have been mainly rice agriculturalists, iron-users and, at least according to traditional studies, speakers of the Dravidian language. The megaliths include many types of funerary monument: rock-cut tombs; hood stones (dome-shaped blocks covering rock-cut burial pits); topikals (plano-convex capstones on three or four boulders, also covering burial pits); megalithic chamber tombs of various kinds (often with PORT-HOLES); stone circles and cairn circles. As well as these burial monuments, MENHIRS are also found. One important site is Adichanallur near the southern tip of the Indian peninsula. Here an extensive urn-burial site (possibly associated with stone circles) covering c45 hectares, was excavated early this century. The rich grave goods include BLACK AND RED WARE, Black polished ware, Red polished ware, iron tools and weapons, bronze vessels and ornaments and a few gold ornaments. Another very important site is Brahmagiri in northern Mysore; here were hundreds of slab cists surrounded by single or double stone circles, of which Mortimer WHEELER excavated six; there were also nine pit circles, four of which were excavated by Wheeler. Both types of tomb were used for collective burial, containing disarticulated and fragmentary skeletons. Grave goods include pottery and many tools and weapons of iron.

Recent work suggests that Indian megaliths were being built and used throughout most of the 1st millennium BC and into the first few centuries AD.

Tibet. There are at least four main types of megalithic site in Tibet: stone circles with one or more central pillars or *rdo-riṅ*; stone circles without any *rdo-riṅ*; single standing stones and alignments. Circles with central *rdo-riṅ* contain either one pillar or three, the central one being taller than the two flanking it. Their purpose is unknown, but they are clearly of ritual significance. There are examples at SPU, Sab-dge-sdins and near Doptakdsong.

Stone circles without a *rdo-riṅ* frequently occur in groups, unlike those with them, which more often occur singly, and this makes a funerary function likely. They are constructed of large boulders.

Single monolithic stelae are found throughout Tibet. G. Tucci found numerous examples along the southern borders. J.N. Roerich found a four-metre high megalith of grey granite surrounded by small cairns of white quartz at Sagadsong in central Tibet.

The most spectacular of the Tibetan megalithic sites are the alignments, for instance at RDO-RIṄ, RATI and DRALANG.

Japan and Korea. Megalithic monuments in Japan and Korea include both tombs, often known as dolmens, and stone circles. The tombs consist of a large stone supported by several smaller stones, placed over a burial pit. The pit is sometimes outlined by vertically placed slabs, making it a burial CIST. In some tombs the dead are placed directly in the pits, while in others they are placed inside ceramic jars which were placed in the pits. The megalithic tombs in Japan have limited distributions both in time (the last three centuries BC, or from the terminal JOMON to the middle of the YAYOI period) and in space (northwestern Kyushu and the adjoining coastal areas of western Honshu). Some pottery and stone arrowheads are the only burial goods found under megalithic tombs in Japan. Several thousand so-called dolmens are known in Korea and have been divided into two types. The northern type, thought to be the earlier (though there is little good dating evidence) consists of a large stone resting on a few large upright slabs. The southern type, usually dated to the first few centuries AD, is similar to the kind found in Japan, with a burial pit.

Most of the stone circles in Japan date to Late Jomon times and are found in northern Honshu and Hokkaido. At Otoe Koyo on Hokkaido, about a dozen circles, 2-5 metres in diameter, were placed over pit graves. At Oshoro Mikasayama, also on Hokkaido, is an oval arrangement of stones, each about one metre high, around a central stone. The longer axis of the oval is about 30 metres. Structures known as 'sundials', with an upright stone at the middle of radially placed horizontal stones, are also known. One of the two at Oyu in northern Honshu, dated to *c*1730 bc (*c*2130 BC) is associated with two concentric circles of many small stone clusters and a passageway made of a double alignment of river cobbles.

Southeast Asia, Oceania. Truly megalithic monuments of the prehistoric period occur in southeast Asia and Oceania (excluding simple dry-stone walled structures and restricting discussion to those using massive stones). They occur in LAOS (Plain of Jars, Hua Pan), west coastal Malaya (slab graves, alignments of uprights), southern SUMATRA (PASEMAH group), central SULAWESI, and parts of POLYNESIA (MARAE, AHU, EASTER ISLAND statues). Recent and ethnographic groups who still construct megaliths are found in Assam, Nias (western INDONESIA), parts of inland BORNEO, and some of the Lesser SUNDA Islands (especially Flores and Sumba). The vast bulk of such monuments in the region probably postdates 1000 BC and functions include tombs, temples, ancestor memorials and status markers for the living.

Africa. Megalithic monuments are not widespread in Africa as a whole, but an extensive series of monuments exists in The Gambia and adjacent areas of Senegal. Most are single circles of standing stones, but other settings are more complex. They appear not to be funerary in function. They are of Iron Age date, belonging mostly to the first millennium ad.

Meganthropus. Name given to a large-toothed hominid of uncertain (probably Middle PLEISTOCENE) age, known only by mandible fragments from SANGIRAN, central Java, Indonesia. The remains could belong to members of a *Homo erectus* population. *See* HUMAN EVOLUTION.

megaron. A building consisting usually of three rooms: a large hall, usually with a central hearth, entered by way of a smaller vestibule, which is itself preceded by a porch. Buildings of this sort formed the central structures of MYCENAEAN palaces, but there are predecessors of generally similar form in the earlier prehistory of Greece, possibly as early as the Neolithic.

megger. A type of RESISTIVITY METER.

Megiddo. A large TELL above the Plain of Esdraelon in Israel, excavated by the Oriental Institute of Chicago in the 1920s and 1930s. The ambitious aim of the project was to excavate the entire mound, layer by layer. This proved beyond the resources of the Institute, even at that period of cheap labour, but strata I to V (*c*350-1000 BC) were completely excavated; below stratum V only restricted excavations were carried out and in only one place was bedrock reached. It was nonetheless a project on a scale rarely repeated. Limited evidence suggests some settlement in the Neolithic and Chalcolithic periods before the township of the Early Bronze Age in the 3rd millennium BC. In the EB III period a wall was added to a well planned town with monumental buildings. It was a heavily fortified city throughout the 2nd millennium BC; it fell to the Egyptians *c*1470 BC but recovered and flourished again as a CANAANITE and subsequently, after *c*1000 BC, an ISRAELITE city. To the 9th century belong a series of palace, shrine and stable buildings. This town was destroyed at the end of the 8th century BC and although the town was rebuilt, its greatest days were over and it had declined into insignificance by the Hellenistic period.

Mehi. A site of the KULLI culture of southern Baluchistan, Pakistan, excavated by Aurel STEIN. The site covers *c*8 hectares and Stein excavated part of the settlement and an adjacent cremation cemetery, with grave goods including copper tools, beads, and female, bull and bird figurines of terracotta. Carved stone vases and other artefacts show connections with the HARAPPAN CIVILIZATION.

Mehrgarh. A series of settlements of the Neolithic and Chalcolithic periods in Baluchistan, Pakistan, important as the earliest farming site known in the area, perhaps dating to before 6000 bc. Subsequent phases in the 4th and 3rd millennia show a developing society, characterized by craft specialization (with specialist production of pottery figurines and beads of semi-precious stones) and extensive trade networks linking Baluchistan with eastern Iran and southern Turkmenistan. Although no HARAPPAN CIVILIZATION phase is represented here, the culture of Mehrgarh provides a plausible local antecedent for this civilization.

Meiendorf. Close to Hamburg, northern Germany, in a glacial 'tunnel valley', the Meiendorf site has late glacial occupation in peaty deposits, with numerous reindeer carcases and stone and bone tools of HAM-BURGIAN type.

Meillacoid [Melliac] **phase**. One of two ceramic series (the other being CHICOID) which emerged from the OSTINOID series. Originating in Haiti, it remained largely con-fined to the western Greater Antilles, although there was some expansion to the west and north. Sites are normally village shell middens, but are often close to good agricultural land implying possible agricultural practice. The pottery which characterizes the series is thin and hard but with a rough surface texture; simple incision, sometimes combined with appliquéd strips is the most common decora-tion. Dates are usually within the period 850-1000, although some sites in central Cuba endured to as late as 1500.

Mejiro. A rock shelter near Old Oyo, south-western Nigeria, where a microlithic industry occurs, without associated pottery, in an undated context. This is one of relatively few presumed pre-pottery 'Late Stone Age' occur-rences yet known in Nigeria.

Mekong River. *See* CAMBODIA.

Melanesia. An ethnographic region compris-ing NEW GUINEA, the Bismarck Archipelago, the SOLOMONS, VANUATU, NEW CALEDONIA, FIJI and minor intermediate groups. Early Australoid settlers reached New Guinea when it was joined to Australia, by at least 30,000-40,000 years ago, and the New Guinea High-lands have a long and stable archaeological sequence extending into the HOLOCENE (KOSIPE, KIOWA, KAFIAVANA). The High-lands may also have seen an independent development of early Holocene horticulture (KUK). The Bismarck Archipelago east of New Guinea was settled before 9000 bc (MISISIL CAVE), but the Solomons, New Cale-donia and Vanuatu were probably first settled by AUSTRONESIAN-speakers about 3000 BC. The later prehistory of Melanesia is complex, but major archaeological entities include the LAPITA culture and the MANGAASI pottery tradition. *See also* POLYNESIAN OUTLIERS.

Melka Kontoure. A site in Ethiopia some 50 km south of Addis Ababa, with many archaeo-logical levels dating from over 1.5 million years old at the base to late PLEISTOCENE times. The earliest levels are of OLDOWAN type, but hand axes appear at first in small numbers and later in dominant quantities in the later ACHEULIAN levels. A few hominid fragments have been found, but it is the long succession of artefact assemblages and living floors which make the site important.

Melos. One of the Cycladic islands in the southern Aegean Sea. The island was import-ant in prehistory, because it possesses a source of OBSIDIAN which was exploited from the Mesolithic period onwards. A campaign of survey and excavation carried out in the 1970s has thrown much light on the prehistoric exploitation of the island. The principal settle-ment was PHYLAKOPI. This site has three major occupation phases: the first is of local Early CYCLADIC type, while the second demonstrates strong MINOAN influence; in the third phase, after the collapse of the Minoans, mainland Greek MYCENAEAN influence dominates.

Meluhha. Name appearing in Mesopotamian texts of the AKKADIAN and UR III periods as a land with which the city states of SUMER were trading. The land is described as a source of gold and it is usually identified as the area of the HARAPPAN CIVILIZATION in western India and Pakistan.

Memphis. An important Egyptian adminstra-tive centre at the head of the Nile Delta. It rose to prominence under the First Dynasty and was traditionally linked with the process of Egyptian unification (*see* DYNASTIC EGYPT). Its major temple was dedicated to the god Ptah. At an early date Memphis saw a major concentration of influence and industries which may be regarded as the appurtenances of political authority. Memphis remained a major centre throughout the dynastic period: under the New Kingdom it was the adminis-trative seat for the northern half of the country. It followed that Memphis was also the centre of a vast complex of court cemeteries, includ-ing the pyramids of the Fourth Dynasty pharaohs at GIZA. From the Fifth Dynasty onwards there was a very marked reduction in the size of the royal tombs, together with the use of materials and techniques which involved a lesser expenditure of effort and resources in their construction. By the First Intermediate period the construction of monumental tombs seems effectively to have ceased: the corresponding structures of the Middle Kingdom are very little known.

menhir. A standing stone. Menhirs may occur singly, in rows (ALIGNMENTS) or in enclosures (STONE CIRCLES). Anthropomorphic examples are known as STATUE-MENHIRS. Menhirs occur in all parts of the world where MEGALITHIC MONUMENTS are known, but they are particularly profuse in prehistoric Europe.

Mercia. The ANGLO-SAXON kingdom of Mercia encompassed most of Central England, bordered by the Welsh Marches, East Anglia, Yorkshire, ancient NORTHUMBRIA and WESSEX, and defended by linear earthworks such as Wat's and OFFA'S dykes. The name is thought to be derived from *Mierce* meaning border folk. Rulers such as Aethelbald, Offa and Coenwulf brought Mercia to European prominence during the 8th and 9th centuries, and during this time the important Mercian School of manuscript illumination and sculpture developed.

Merida [Roman Augusta Emerita]. A flourishing and extensive Roman COLONIA in western Spain, capital of the province of Lusitania (roughly equivalent to modern Portugal). The town, on the right bank of the River Guadiana, was founded by the emperor Augustus in 25 BC for the settlement of veterans from the Cantabrian wars. The modern town betrays the familiar colonial Roman grid layout, with the *decumanus* (*see* CARDO) still identifiable. To the east of the town a complex consisting of theatre and amphitheatre was begun by Agrippa, Augustus' son-in-law. Attractive ruins survive of a Roman bridge (possibly pre-dating the town), a temple of Diana, an arch of Trajan, aqueducts and conduits, a group of structures devoted to MITHRAS and other mystery cults, and a number of rich houses with colonnaded courts and mosaics (including the so-called 'Creation of the Universe'). Gold *tesserae* are found, and some of the sculptures, especially Roman marble portraits, are of fine quality. VISIGOTHIC rule (5th and 6th centuries) has also left some rare evidence.

Merimde. An early village site of farming people on the southwest side of the Nile delta, inhabited late in the 5th millennium bc, broadly contemporary with the FAYUM Neolithic settlement. The oval houses were of insubstantial construction, but by contrast great care and expertise were devoted to the manufacture of flaked stone daggers, knives and concave-based arrow-heads, as well as to the production of polished stone mace-heads and axes. Cereals, notably wheat and barley, were cultivated, and large pottery jars appear to have been used for storing the crop.

Meroe. A site located near the east bank of the Nile about 100 km upstream of its confluence with the Atbara, in the central Sudan. From about 600 BC Meroe was the capital of a prosperous kingdom over which, at least in the early centuries of its existence, the influence of ancient Egypt was extremely strong. Meroe was able to exploit a region of considerable agricultural potential with fairly regular, if not abundant, rainfall. In contrast with more northerly regions, there was also a supply of timber adequate to fuel the smelting of the local iron deposits. By the beginning of the Christian era, if not before, the iron industry had been developed on a considerable scale. Meroitic architecture included temples in the Egyptian style, and royal pyramid tombs. This Egyptian influence gradually diminished: for example, Egyptian hieroglyphs were abandoned in about the 2nd century BC in favour of a local script. The Meroitic language thus recorded cannot at present be understood. The tenuous nature of the link with Egypt is to be appreciated by considering the trade route, which it appears did not follow the inhospitable Nile Valley, but ran along the Red Sea coast. From about the beginning of the Christian era this route was increasingly endangered by local developments, notably the rise of the kingdom of AXUM. By the 3rd century AD Meroe was in decline; its final collapse came at the hands of the Axumites early in the 4th century.

Merovingian. This general name is usually applied to the FRANKISH rulers and their kingdom from the time of Childeric (*d.* 481) until the middle of the 8th century. The name is derived from the mid-5th century Merovech, father of Childeric. The term is used to describe all the archaeological evidence from the western Rhineland to the Atlantic coast of France, and embraces a number of kingdoms such as Austrasia in the Rhineland, Neustria in central northern France, and Burgundia in central France.

Mersin. The TELL of Yumuktepe in the coastal plain of Cilicia, southeast Turkey. The 24-metre deposit contained 33 major levels, starting with an Early Neolithic deposit dated c6000 bc with dark-surfaced wares, some with impressed decoration, and ending with a medieval deposit dated to c1500 AD. A series of nine Neolithic levels was succeeded by a long series of Chalcolithic deposits; the most important architectural remains came from level XVI, in the form of a heavily defended fortress which had been destroyed by fire.

Mesa Verde. An area of ANASAZI occupation in the northern San Juan region of southwest Colorado, USA. Major occupation began in c600 AD, and the population rose steadily until 1200, after which date came decline and total abandonment of the area by the end of the century. The defensive aspect of the PUEBLO III period is epitomized by the cliff-dwellings of Mesa Verde. The most famous of these, the Cliff Palace, is a complex of over 200 rooms and 23 KIVAS built from dressed stone blocks. A variety of other types of site existed, however, the most common of these being the mesa-top pit house village of between 6 and 12 dwellings.

Mes-kalam-dug. A little-known king of the SUMERIAN city of UR, whose richly furnished grave in the Royal Cemetery was excavated by WOOLLEY. His name does not appear in the Sumerian king list and it is therefore suggested that he might have been a local ruler who reigned before the First Dynasty of Ur, perhaps c2650 BC. The most notable find from the deep shaft grave was a helmet beaten from a single sheet of gold and decorated with repoussé work and chased decoration.

Mesoamerica. A culture area originally defined on the basis of shared traits such as the developments of agriculture, urbanization and elaborate ceremonial practice. Centered on the modern states of Mexico, Guatemala, Belize and El Salvador, its northern borders are the deserts of Sinaloa, Durango and TAMAULIPAS. The southern extent is less clearly defined but would certainly include parts of Honduras, Nicaragua and possibly Costa Rica. An immense environmental diversity is enclosed within this area and numerous examples of advanced civilization have developed here (see OLMEC, MAYA, TEOTIHUACAN, AZTEC). In recent years the term has been applied to the geographic area alone, without being limited by the defining traits named above.

Mesolithic. The Middle Stone Age, falling between the PALAEOLITHIC and the NEOLITHIC. The Mesolithic belongs to the early part of the HOLOCENE geological period, after c10,000 years ago (see Tables 4-6, pages 417-9), and is characterized by societies continuing to practise a hunting and gathering economy and using chipped stone tools as in the PALAEOLITHIC period. The term is used widely only in European prehistory. See also THREE AGE SYSTEM.

Mesopotamia. Greek name (literally 'between the rivers') for the land between the Tigris and Euphrates rivers, mainly within the borders of present-day Iraq. This land was the home of the world's earliest civilization, that of the SUMERIANS, and of the later BABYLONIAN and ASSYRIAN civilizations. The chronology of the prehistoric periods is based on radiocarbon dates (see Table 2, page 320). For the historical periods the chronology is based on a combination of documentary sources and calendrical information and there is room for differing interpretations. Most scholars today prefer what is known as the Middle Chronology, but others favour a longer or High Chronology; both are shown in Table 3, page 321. See also BABYLON, ERIDU, GAWRA, HALAF, HASSUNA, JEMDET NASR, KISH, LAGASH, LARSA, MARI, NIMRUD, NINEVEH, SAMARRA, TAYA, UBAID, UR, URUK.

metal. The metals most commonly used in antiquity were COPPER and copper ALLOYS (such as BRONZE), IRON and STEEL, GOLD and SILVER. TIN and LEAD were commonly used as constituents of alloys. See METALLURGY.

metal detector. A device used in ELECTROMAGNETIC SURVEYING, specifically designed for the detection of buried metal objects.

Table 2. Prehistoric Mesopotamia

North	South	Khuzistan (SW Iran)	date bc	date BC
Tepe Gawra	Uruk			
VIII ————	Jemdet Nasr III — Susa C ————		3000 ——— 3800	
	Late Uruk VIII			
	VIII			
XI ————	————	Susa B ————	3500 ——— 4400	
	Early Uruk XV			
XIV ————	Ubaid 4		4000 ——— 4850	
		Susa A		
XIX ————	Ubaid 3 XVIII	————	4500 ——— 5350	
XX				
Halaf	Ubaid 2	Sabz		
	Ubaid 1 ————	————	5000	
Hassuna/Samarra				
			5500	
Umm Dabaghiyah		Muhammad Jaffar		
			6000	
		Ali Kosh ————	6500	
			7000	
		Bus Mordeh		
			7500	

Table 3. Mesopotamia: Babylonian Chronology

Period		High Chronology approximate dates	Middle Chronology
Kassite Period			
		1740 BC	1600 BC
Old Babylonian Period			
		2030	1900
Isin-Larsa Period			
		2140	2000
Ur III			
		2250	2110
Lagash II/Guti			
		2300	2190
Agade			
		2470	2370
Early Dynastic III			
		2780	2600
Early Dynastic II	Uruk sequence I		
		2900	2700
Early Dynastic I	II		
		3100	2900
Jemdet Nasr	III		
		3400 (or earlier)	3100

metallographic examination. A technique of METALLURGICAL ANALYSIS involving the examination of metals under the metallurgical microscope. Samples are taken from metal artefacts, polished flat on one surface and examined under reflected light. This allows study of the crystalline structure of metals, and may yield information about manufacturing processes and ALLOYS.

metallurgical analysis. The study of metals. Metal artefacts and the tools or waste products of their manufacture are examined to reconstruct working processes and the source of raw materials. This may be done by the various techniques of CHEMICAL ANALYSIS, or may involve METALLOGRAPHIC EXAMINATION under a microscope. In the case of COPPER, BRONZE and other non-ferrous metals, such analysis may yield information about ALLOYS, CASTING, COLD-WORKING and ANNEALING. For IRON and STEEL, there may be information about FORGING, CARBURIZATION, QUENCHING and TEMPERING.

metallurgy. General term for metal-working. See ALLOY, ANNEALING, ARSENIC, BLOOM, BRONZE, BRONZES (CHINA), CASTING, CASTING TECHNIQUES (CHINA), CIRE PERDUE, COLD WORKING, COPPER, ELECTRUM, GOLD, INGOT, IRON AND STEEL, IRON (CHINA), LEAD, METAL, METALLURGY (CHINA), METALLURGY (JAPAN), PATINA, PATTERN WELDING, REPOUSSÉ, SECTION-MOULD CASTING, SILVER, SMELTING, TIN.

metallurgy (China). The earliest clear evidence for the use of metal in China is associated with the QIJIA culture of the late 3rd or early 2nd millennium BC, though isolated finds hint at the possibility of much older metal industries (see MAJIAYAO). The exact relationship between the Qijia metal industry and later Chinese metal working has yet to be established. The metal industry encountered towards the middle of the 2nd millennium BC at ERLITOU, on the other hand, is clearly ancestral to the SHANG and ZHOU metalworking tradition, showing already the distinctive character that in the realm of metal technology sets ancient China apart from the rest of the world.

The main idiosyncrasy of the Chinese tradition, a single-minded reliance on CASTING to the exclusion of other methods of shaping and decorating metal, cannot be properly appreciated without some consideration of the used to which metal was put in early China. As elsewhere in the ancient world, BRONZE was used in China for weapons and to a lesser extent for tools, but beyond this there is a clear divergence of traditions, with the bronze RITUAL VESSEL in China holding an importance that the civilizations of the Near East gave instead to sculpture. Metal sculpture may favour or even demand the use of casting; metal vessels do not. Outside China metal vessels have rarely been made by casting because such objects of regular shape are made more easily and more cheaply by hammering, which requires little in the way of workshop apparatus and readily achieves an economical thinness of metal. A variety of factors peculiar to the Chinese scene might be suggested to account for the early Chinese metal-worker's apparent indifference to these considerations of ease and economy: abundant supplies of COPPER and TIN probably lessened the appeal of techniques that conserved metal (see TONGLÜSHAN); precious metals, which demand economical techniques, were little used in China; and an already highly sophisticated ceramic technology could provide the mastery of high temperatures needed for SMELTING and casting, expertise with clays useful in mouldmaking, and perhaps also experience with large and well-organized workshops. At a very early stage lavish royal patronage in China seems to have mobilized the resources necessary for casting on an industrial scale, a conclusion that might almost be argued on the evidence of a single bronze vessel, the SI MU WU FANG DING, found in the Shang royal cemetery at ANYANG and dedicated in its inscription to a deceased empress. Made in a single pour of metal, except for its handles, this vessel weighs 875 kg and is the largest bronze casting known from antiquity. It must have required an enormous foundry, and it is only one of many large Shang and Zhou castings.

The narrow range of objects that early Chinese founders were called upon to produce — weapons, tools, and ceremonial vessels — had a direct bearing on their choice of manufacturing technique. Weapons and tools could be cast in simple bivalve moulds, while vessels could be cast in moulds of more than two sections (in principle only elaborations of bivalve moulds); since vessels have fairly regular shapes, the number of sections required was not inconveniently large. Section-mould casting thus satisfied all the needs of the early Chinese metal-worker, who relied on casting not only for the fabrication of bronze vessels but also for their decoration. The importance of the section-mould technique lies chiefly in the influence it exercised on the decoration that grew up in Shang foundries (see RITUAL VESSELS, CHINA).

Given the limited range of objects they sought to produce, Chinese founders had no pressing need for the CIRE PERDUE or lost-wax method, which is useful in casting very complicated shapes. Though it appeared in the Near East in the 4th millennium BC, the lost-wax method does not seem to have been employed in China until the 6th century BC and even then was used only occasionally as an adjunct to section-mould casting (see XIASI, SUI XIAN); highly elaborated section moulds were still the basis of casting technique at the 6th-5th century BC foundry complex excavated at HOUMA. The contrast between the Chinese and Near Eastern metal-working is sometimes presented as a contrast between section-mould casting and lost-wax casting. This is misleading at best, since the Western metal-worker asked to make a vessel would be unlikely to use the lost-wax process or any other form of casting. What sets Chinese metal-working apart is not the use of a particular casting technique but the use of casting rather than hammering to make and decorate vessels.

The long Bronze Age tradition of casting and neglect of hammering techniques in China — seen even in Chinese COINAGE — strongly influenced the course taken by the Chinese IRON industry from its beginnings in about the 6th century BC; its emphasis on cast rather than wrought iron is completely at variance with the history of iron in the West. As in the case of bronze technology, the contrast is at least in part that of an industrial process organized on a large scale and a craft that can be pursued in small workshops or even by a single smith.

metallurgy (Japan). Metal tools are first reliably documented in Japan as continental imports about the same time as wet-rice cultivation was established in northern Kyushu around 300 BC. By the middle of the YAYOI period, in the 1st century AD, bronze BELLS and weapons that were much larger than their continental prototypes were cast in Japan,

evidently for ceremonial purposes. Stone moulds and the tips of bellows have been found, but no smelting site of this age is known. Tin and copper do not seem to have been mined in Japan until the late 7th century.

Iron axes and sickles replaced the stone counterparts by the end of the Yayoi period c300 AD. Hoes and spades had iron tips by this time. Since these are in styles with no parallel in Korea or China, they are considered to have been manufactured in Japan by itinerant blacksmiths. Here again, we do not known where the ores were mined and smelted. It is possible that the Yayoi people relied on outside sources, and the increasing indications of conflicts between Yayoi communities may be due in part to the competition to secure a supply of iron, for which there was growing demand.

A greater variety of iron implements was used during the next few centuries when large burial mounds (KOFUN) and irrigation canals were built. Quantities of iron weapons and horse-trappings were deposited as burial offerings. Blacksmiths' equipment has also been found in the mounds. Throughout this time there were contacts with the continent, and new techniques for making body armour, for example, were introduced either as imports or by migrant artisans. Smelting sites dating to the 8th century are known and authorities believe that iron smelting was probably practised in Japan in the 6th and 7th centuries.

metate. The base and lower grinding surface of a two-part milling apparatus used in the preparation of plant food (the upper, movable part is the MANO). Made from any suitably hard stone, it comes in a variety of shapes and sizes and is still used in many areas of the Americas. Mostly associated with the grinding of MAIZE, it is a hallmark artefact in the definition of prehistoric subsistence patterns.

Mezin. An open-air site in the Desna valley of European Russia. It has a late PALAEOLITHIC occupation, and art material with squared key pattern carving, in one case on an ivory wrist band.

Miaodigou [Miao-ti-kou]. A Neolithic site in Shan Xian in the western corner of Henan province, China. The stratigraphy at Miaodigou was complicated but two main levels were distinguished. The lower level, Miaodigou I, belongs to the YANGSHAO Neolithic; for this stratum a radiocarbon date of c3900 BC was obtained. The fine painted pottery from Miaodigou I reveals some dependence on earlier Yangshao cultures (e.g. BANPO) but the Miaodigou painted designs, monochrome or painted in black over a red or white slip, are as a rule entirely abstract, only rarely incorporating the simple animal motifs of Banpo pots. Painted ware identical to that from Miaodigou has been unearthed at sites in nearby Ruicheng Xian, Shanxi province, where sherds with designs recalling Banpo pottery are also found. The most sophisticated Miaodigou patterns are obscurely derived from running spiral designs and have close affinities with MAJIAYAO in Gansu.

The Miaodigou II level is sharply different. The pottery is unpainted and includes many shapes virtually unknown to the Yangshao tradition, such as tripods with solid or hollow legs; these are typical instead of the HOUGANG II culture (see LI). The stratigraphy at Miaodigou was for a time interpreted as support for the so-called nuclear theory, but is now taken to show influences from the eastern seaboard intruding on the local Yangshao culture (see LONGSHAN, sense 3).

Michelsberg. A Neolithic culture of the late 4th and early 3rd millennia bc, found mostly in the Rhineland and stretching from Belgium in the north to Switzerland in the south. Connections have been claimed both with the north European TRB CULTURE and with the west European cultures such as CHASSEY and WINDMILL HILL. The Belgian group of the Michelsberg culture shows strong connections with the British Windmill Hill group in such features as ditched enclosures, flint mines and some artefact types, such as leaf-shaped flint arrowheads and antler combs.

Micklegate. See YORK.

microburin. When a small bladelet is removed from a CORE it has an inconvenient thick butt end, which has to be removed before it can be made into a spear tip or barb. It is removed by making a notch and then snapping off the end, which is called a microburin. The name originates from the erroneous belief that these pieces were the same as BURINS.

microlith. A very small stone tool made on a bladelet by the MICROBURIN technique. Microliths were produced in quantity at the end of the PALAEOLITHIC period and especially in the MESOLITHIC. They were shaped by abrupt RETOUCH into various shapes like triangles and crescents, and used for a variety of purposes, including both barbs and tips for spears and arrows. Microliths represent both a versatile and an economic use of raw material: just as BLADES yield more cutting edge than FLAKES per unit weight of raw material, so bladelets improve yet further this advantage, by a factor of something over 100 compared to CORE tools.

Microburin

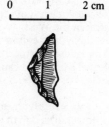

Microlithic triangle

Micronesia. An ethnographic region comprising the PALAU, MARIANAS, Caroline and Marshall Islands, and Kiribati [Gilbert Islands]. The Palaus and Marianas were probably settled from the Philippines after 2000 BC and each has a ceramic sequence throughout prehistory. The eastern groups, mainly atolls, were settled later, perhaps from a LAPITA source in MELANESIA, and pottery production died out after initial settlement (as in POLYNESIA). Physically and linguistically, the Micronesians are close cousins to the Polynesians, although immediate origins are different: Polynesian ancestors appear to have moved through Melanesia rather than Micronesia. See also MARIANAS, NAN MADOL, PALAU, YAP.

Middleburg. A town on the island of Walcharan in the southwestern Netherlands, probably founded as one of the string of BURHS intended to act as refuges for the Flemish population in the times of Viking raids. Those refuges were probably planned by Baldwin of Flanders in the 890s and at Middleburg and Souburg consisted of a simple circular fortress with a massive rampart and ditch. The symmetry of these early fortresses is fossilized in the street plan of modern Middleburg. It has also been argued that these circular forts were the prototypes of the Danish royal fortresses like Fyrkat and TRELLEBORG. Excavations at Middleburg have shown that the town was not properly founded until about 1000, from which time it has developed as a regional centre.

Middle Horizon. One of seven periods within a chronological construction widely used in Peruvian archaeology. Dated AD 600-1000, it is characterized by the ascendancy of powerful regional states, especially TIAHUANACO and HUARI. Although the decline of these two states was followed by a period of more localized political power (see Late INTERMEDIATE PERIOD) it was during the Middle Horizon that the system of state control, exploited to high degree by the INCA, was first laid down. See Table 9, page 552.

Middle Missouri Tradition. One of the village-dwelling, farming traditions of the American Plains, based on the Missouri River drainage especially in the states of North and South Dakota. Although hunting and gathering were part of subsistence activities, the culture is characterized by a specially developed strain of cold-resistant, quick-maturing MAIZE, by the bison scapula hoe, and by permanent dwellings in the form of the semi-subterranean timber and earth lodge. Often palisaded and constructed on high promontories, overlooking a river, villages of over 100 dwellings (e.g. the Huff site) are quite common. Ceramics, though WOODLAND derived, bear evidence of some MISSISSIPPIAN influence, such as shell tempering. The tradition began to emerge in c1000 AD and had disappeared, due to drought and/or alien incursions, by 1500. Historic tribes such as the Mandan, Arikara and Hidatsa (now virtually extinct) are thought to be the cultural heirs to the tradition.

Middle Shang. See ERLIGANG PHASE.

midrib. The raised midline which reinforces the blade of a bronze dagger.

Migration Period. A term applied to the time between the 5th and later 7th centuries when 'barbarian' tribes overran the Roman Empire. The settlements and cultural record of Migration Period Europe are distinctive, and essentially owe their character to the Roman-period tribes in central and Eastern Europe, as well as in Asia.

mihrab. See MOSQUE.

Mikhajlovka [Mikhailovka, Mykhailivka]. A settlement of the Late Neolithic and Bronze Age, located in the lower Dnieper Valley near Nikopol, Ukraine, USSR. Three main occupation horizons have been distinguished: I a TRIPOLYE B2 settlement with shell-gritted, cord-impressed pottery of steppe origins; II a shorter-lived settlement of the Sredni Stog group with sand-gritted pointed-base pottery with comb decoration (USATOVO painted sherds date the layer to the 2nd millennium bc); III a late phase of the Catacomb culture, with sand-gritted, pointed-base pottery and a wide range of copper tools and weapons. Near the settlement was a flat cemetery of pit graves (Yamnaya burial rite).

Mikulčice. A site situated on the River Morava in Czechoslovakia. It is a complex site with stratified deposits going back to the late

6th century, when it was one of the earliest SLAVIC fortified centres. This stronghold consisted of a central nucleus contained within a plank-built palisade, with an additional suburb of workshops and houses. Mikulčice was an important metal production centre, famous for the manufacture of elaborate bronze and gilded spurs. The organic material in these excavated levels is well-preserved and includes part of a large timber bridge.

In Mikulčice's second phase during the early 9th century the defences were refurbished in stone and timber, and a stone church was built. In the latter part of the 9th century there were a series of tribal clashes, and after these disturbances yet more buildings were erected. These include a stone-built palace and a number of churches. These churches display an enormous variety of designs, and include several rotunda buildings, including a rotunda with horse-shoe apses. In most of them, both the interior and exterior walls were covered with plaster, which was typically painted.

Milazzo. A settlement site on the northeast coast of Sicily; it faces the Aeolian Islands and demonstrates close cultural connections with the prehistoric sequence on these islands (*see* LIPARI). It was occupied throughout the Bronze Age. To the Middle Bronze Age Milazzese culture belongs a cemetery of pithos burials (with the dead placed in large jars in the crouched position) while in the succeeding Late Bronze Age phase (Ausonian culture) there was a cemetery of URNFIELD type, characterized by cremations in urns and bronzes of local Urnfield (Proto-Villanovan) type.

Mildenhall. Thistley Green, West Row, 5 km from Mildenhall in Suffolk, eastern England is the find-site of a hoard of 4th-century Roman silver plate, richly decorated with figured reliefs. The 34 pieces include a large dish (roughly 60 cm in diameter) depicting the head of Oceanus, ringed by friezes of sea and other deities revelling; two smaller platters with Bacchic scenes; a *niello* dish with geometric design; a covered bowl with Centaurs; goblets; ladles and eight spoons, five with Christian inscriptions. The quality of the craftsmanship suggests an owner of high rank, and an official of the emperor Julian the Apostate has been proposed. The collection is now in the British Museum, London.

mile fort [or mile castle]. A small Roman fort set at intervals of one Roman mile along a major well-defended frontier (LIMES). On HADRIAN'S WALL examples show a small rectangular plan. A gateway in the wall, with watchtower over, permitted access into an area of offices and barrack quarters for up to about 30 men, and a second gateway (in line) then gave access to Roman territory.

milestone. Roman examples show stones, normally cylindrical, up to two metres high. These were placed along all principal roads, and instances are found from about 250 BC onwards. The stone was typically inscribed to give the distance in (Roman) miles to the nearest major town, and commonly a date of installation, expressed in terms of Republican magistracies, or the years of an Emperor's reign.

Miletus. This ancient settlement on a bay at the mouth of the Meander River in southwest Turkey was inhabited from the 2nd millennium BC. By the beginning of the 1st millennium BC it was an Ionian Greek city, colonizing Black Sea and Egyptian Delta areas in the 7th and 6th centuries BC. Miletus produced philosophers, the classical historian Hecateus and the town planner Hippodamus. Destroyed by the Persians in 494 BC, the city came under Athenian, Persian, Greek and (in 129 BC) Roman control. Impressive ruins survive nearby of the re-built Hellenistic Greek oracular temple of Apollo, and a Roman theatre.

Subsequently, the harbour silted up and Miletus declined, but occupation continued into the early Byzantine period. In AD 263 it survived an attack by the Goths and was refurbished by the Emperor Diocletian. Excavations have shown that between the time of Justinian and the 11th century the city underwent a drastic transformation. Although the Late Antique city was smaller than its predecessor, new Byzantine churches and monumental buildings were erected within its boundaries. The main effort went into building a system of fortifications around the Roman theatre. In effect, the theatre was turned into a castle which became the focal point of a citadel whose walls were lined with square towers;

inside were churches and small houses. In the 10th century the citadel was destroyed by an earthquake but was again rebuilt over the ancient ruins; the small Byzantine town became known as Kastron ton Palation — the castle of the palace.

Milingimbi shell mounds. *See* SHELL MOUNDS (TROPICAL AUSTRALIA).

millefiori. A very delicate and attractive technique developed by ANGLO-SAXON glass and metal-workers, whereby panels of multi-coloured glass were set into a background of metal or enamel. To create the distinctive minute chequerboard or rosette-like patterns, bundles of glass rods of varying cross-section were tied together and heated until pliable; these were then drawn out to great lengths. The resulting thin cord of glass was allowed to cool and was cut into thin slices which were later set into the object to be decorated. Some of the finest examples of the millefiori technique can be seen adorning the SUTTON HOO discoveries — the brilliant reds and blues on the purse lid and shoulder clasps are outstandingly colourful and effective.

millet. A number of cereal plants, belonging to different genera, are described as millets. Broomcorn or common millet (*Panicum miliaceum*) is rarely grown today, but it had a much wider distribution in the past. The earliest finds are from Neolithic central and eastern Europe, spreading into southern Europe during the Bronze Age. Its origin is uncertain, but it is possible that it was first domesticated in China. Foxtail or Italian millet (*Setaria italica*) was almost certainly first domesticated in China: *S. italica* grains have been identified at BANPO dating from the 5th millennium BC. Millet was the chief crop of the SHANG and ZHOU empires, but barley and wheat began to replace it toward the end of the Eastern Zhou period. In Europe, most finds of foxtail millet come from the Bronze Age of the Alpine region. Today it is still widely grown, particularly in China and India. Bulrush millet (*Pennisetum americanum*) is commonly cultivated in the Sahel region of Africa and was probably first cultivated in this area. *Panicum*, *Setaria* and *Pennisetum* are all members of the tribe Panicae of the Grass family. Finger millet (*Eleusine coracana*) belongs to the tribe Chloridae. It is widely grown in central Africa and India, and probably originated in Africa. *See also* AFRICAN FOOD-PRODUCTION.

milpa. A MAYA term meaning literally 'cornfields', synonymous in Mesoamerican archaeology with slash-and-burn agriculture. Depictions on Maya frescos and CODICES coupled with ethnographic evidence of modern-day methods of cultivation in the Maya Lowlands, gave rise to the theory that *milpa* agriculture was the basis of Maya subsistence. Exhaustion of the land by its indiscriminate practice was long held to be a factor in the Maya collapse. Recent thought, however, has tended to the notion that the *milpa* system alone could not possibly support the populations estimated for many of the major centres (e.g. TIKAL). Increasing archaeological evidence of such practices as canal irrigation, terracing and raised fields suggests that more diverse and more intensive methods were, in fact, being used.

Mimbres. A late manifestation of the MOGOLLON cultural tradition of the Southwestern USA, which also evidences a strong ANASAZI influence. It is characterized by an extraordinary ceramic art style which flourished from *c*900-1200. The essentials of the style are complex geometric or fine naturalistic designs painted in black over white slip.

Minaean [Minaeans]. One of the kingdoms of southern Arabia in the 1st millennium BC, contemporary with the SABAEANS, QATABANEANS and HADRAMIS. Its capital city was Qarnāwu.

minaret. *See* MOSQUE.

minbar. *See* MOSQUE.

Mindel. A group of QUATERNARY deposits in the Alps and the valleys of south German rivers. The Mindel consists of MORAINE and related river terraces of PROGLACIAL deposits. It formed part of the classical scheme of four GLACIALS with intervening INTERGLACIALS published in 1909 by Penck and Bruckner. In this scheme, it was held that the Mindel deposits represented the antepenultimate glaciation of the Alps. More recently, it has become clear that the Alpine sequence is much more complicated than had been thought. During the period of time occupied by the GÜNZ, Mindel, RISS and WÜRM deposits, no less than ten world-wide glacials are shown by the analysis of DEEP SEA CORES. The position of the Mindel within the climatic sequence of the Quaternary is as yet unclear. For this reason, the term should only be used to describe a particular group of Alpine deposits. Unfortunately, 'Mindel' has gained wide currency as a more general term, meaning the antepenultimate cold stage throughout Europe. This is still common in archaeological literature, but should be avoided.

Mindelheim. A HALLSTATT C (7th century BC) cemetery west of Munich in West Germany. The grave goods include distinctive melon-shaped urns and wide open bowls, heavily decorated with incised geometric designs, as well as the long sword type to which the site has given its name. Mindelheim swords are made of bronze or iron, are c90 cm long, with a leaf-shaped blade and a pommel on the hilt; they may have been used as a cavalry weapon.

Mindel/Riss. The term for the INTERGLACIAL erosion interval envisaged by Penck and Bruckner as separating the MINDEL and RISS glacials. The Alpine sequence is now known to be much more complex than was originally thought, but 'Mindel/Riss' has unfortunately gained wide currency as a general term meaning the penultimate interglacial (the so-called Great Interglacial). This usage is still common in archaeological literature, but should be avoided.

Minet el Beidha. *See* CANAANITES.

Ming [Ming]. Chinese dynasty (1368-1644).

Minggonglu. *See* ZHENGZHOU.

Minoan [Minoans]. Term for the Bronze Age culture of Crete and the earliest civilization found on European soil, named by Sir Arthur EVANS after the legendary king Minos. Minoan civilization, once attributed to immigration or at least influence from elsewhere, is now thought by many scholars to be a local development. Like its mainland rival and eventual successor, the MYCENAEAN civilization, it was palace-based with a king at its head. In Crete, the first palaces developed earlier

than on mainland Greece, in the Middle Minoan period c2000 BC (KNOSSOS, MALLIA, PHAESTOS). Throughout the first half of the 2nd millennium BC Minoan civilization dominated the Aegean, establishing close trading connections with, or possibly actual colonies on, south Aegean islands such as MELOS (PHYLAKOPI) and THERA (Akrotiri). In the middle of the 15th century BC all the palaces were destroyed, probably by the eruption of the volcanic island of Thera. After c1450 BC only Knossos was reoccupied on a significant scale and this time by Mycenaeans from the mainland. They ruled here for a further half century or so until the final destruction of Knossos, c1400 BC or a little later. The causes of this fall are still disputed but there is no doubt that it marked the end of Cretan prosperity and widespread influence.

Minoan civilization is characterized by a palace-based redistributive economy, with food products, raw materials and manufactured goods collected by and redistributed from the palaces. Writing was developed in response to the adminstrative needs of the palace bureaucracy: the early hieroglyphic script was replaced by LINEAR A, both undeciphered, and eventually, in the period of Mycenaean dominance, by LINEAR B, which was used to write an early form of Greek. Craftsmen reached high levels of technical skill and aesthetic achievement in pottery, metalwork, stonework, jewellery and wall painting (the palaces are lavishly decorated with frescoes). Cult activities normally took place either in hilltop shrines, often in caves, or in small shrines within the palaces, and often involved animals, including goats and especially bulls. Common cult symbols include the double axe and HORNS OF CONSECRATION (stylized bulls' horns). The traditional view of Minoan culture as peace-loving, gentle and artistic has received a jolt in recent years with the discovery of evidence of human sacrifice both at Knossos itself and at the temple site of Arkhanes not far away. However, it is possible that such sacrifices were exceptional, occurring only in times of crisis.

Minusinsk Basin. An island of steppe on the upper YENISEI River in southern Siberia, surrounded by forested mountains. Very large numbers of burial mounds of different periods exist in the area and some 40,000 bronze objects survive in collections — presumably only a fraction of the number originally present. See AFANASIEVO, ANDRONOVO, KARASUK and TAGAR cultures.

Minyan. A wheel-thrown fine grey ware of the Middle HELLADIC period, found throughout the Aegean. Traditionally it has been associated with an apparently violent end to the Early Helladic culture, c2000-1900 BC and the arrival of Greek-speaking peoples in the Aegean. It is now regarded as a Greek product developed during the Early Helladic period.

Miraflores. A complex of cultural materials which define a phase (100 BC — AD 200) of Highland MAYAN sites in the Late PRE-CLASSIC (see KAMINALJUYU). Characteristic artefacts include engraved soft stone and engraved monochrome ceramic vessels and 'mushroom stones' (hollow stones set in an annular base and capped with mushroom-shaped covers). A strong IZAPAN influence is evident in this phase.

Miriwun. A rock shelter in the Ord River valley, east Kimberley region, Western Australia, now inundated by the Argyle Dam. Occupation deposits date from 16,000 bc. Artefacts from the early phase include adze flakes, small denticulated flakes, thick notched flakes, pebble tools, irregular blade cores and amorphous cores. An edge-ground grooved axe was found just above charcoal dated to about 1000 bc, when the late-phase tools appeared. These included unifacial and bifacial points, many of the latter denticulated, while the earlier tool types continued alongside. Preliminary analysis of faunal remains indicates a long-term stability in species exploited, and an apparently stable subsistence pattern for 18,000 years.

mirrors (China). The typical early Chinese mirror is a bronze disc with a faintly convex reflecting surface and cast decoration on the back; it has no handle, being held by a cord tied to a projecting loop in the centre of the back. Such mirrors were not common until about the 5th century BC, but far older examples are known. The earliest are four mirrors found in the tomb of FU HAO at ANYANG (c1200 BC) and two similar mirrors that come from sites of the QIJIA culture and might therefore be some centuries older still. The Fu Hao mirrors differ in decoration from other SHANG bronzes, and

this together with their resemblance to the Qijia specimens hints at a foreign origin for the Chinese mirror. Aside from a few undecorated Western ZHOU examples, the next successors to the Fu Hao mirrors are four from SHANGCUNLING dating from the 8th or 7th century. Two of these are undecorated and the third has decoration more or less Chinese, but the fourth, crudely decorated in thread relief, has parallels in the ORDOS and ALTAI. A century or so later steppe influence is again to be detected in the decoration of round or square 'double-plate' mirrors, which are unusual in being constructed from a back plate of openwork decoration riveted or soldered to a separate reflecting part. By the Warring States period (5th-3rd centuries BC), however, mirrors were common and wholly Chinese in decoration. The decoration is usually cast but occasionally inlaid or painted in LACQUER. Warring States mirrors are found especially often in CHU tombs; 5th century mirror moulds have been unearthed in the north, at HOUMA and YAN XIADU. Dated, inscribed mirrors first appeared in the late Western HAN period (1st century BC). The decoration of Han mirrors generally has a magical or cosmological significance.

mirrors (Japan). Many round imported mirrors and their domestic copies are found from YAYOI and KOFUN graves. They are flat and shiny on one side, with a raised rim and decorative designs and inscriptions arranged around one or more knobs with holes on the other. Most are of Chinese derivation, but several mirrors with geometric designs, which are traced through Korea to northern Eurasia, have been found from Yayoi graves. Domestic production began in the Late Yayoi period (3rd century) and continued throught the Kofun period. The Nara period (8th century) saw the development of domestic styles, initially inspired by Tang mirrors. A number of distinctive styles, later with handles, were made in the Heian, Kamakura, Muromachi and Edo periods.

Misisal Cave. A limestone cave in southwestern NEW BRITAIN, which has yielded OBSIDIAN tools from the TALASEA source, dated to about 9000 bc. The site represents the earliest known evidence for human settlement in the islands east of New Guinea and also the earliest date for the use of obsidian in this region. *See also* BALOF CAVE.

Mi-so'n. An archaeological site in the northern part of CHAMPA, in the present province of Quang-nam, central Vietnam. The site has given its name to the earliest style in Cham art, dating from the 7th century. It is also important for inscriptions of the 5th century, attesting to the oldest known royal linga in Southeast Asia.

Mississippi tradition. The last major cultural tradition in prehistoric North America, the core area of which was the central Mississippi Valley. At its maximum extent it covered most of the southeastern USA and had outposts as far north as Aztalan in Wisconsin. Although there is considerable internal variability, its characteristic traits are the platform mound (frequently built on large open plazas), intensive valley-bottom agriculture, and distinctive shell-tempered pottery. Hunting and gathering persisted as a means of subsistence throughout, but typically sites are located close to rivers on good agricultural land, with the flint hoe being the most common artefact. Defensive works (*see* CAHOKIA, ETOWAH) are also a common feature. Architectural, agricultural and ceremonial traits (*see* SOUTHERN CULT) display undeniable similarities to those of contemporary Mesoamerica, but the true dynamics of this relationship are still unclear.

Mississippian characteristics began to appear in *c*700 and its cultural climax and maximum geographic extent date to 1200-1400 (*see* Table 9, page 552). By the late 17th century, all the major centres had been abandoned. *See also* TEMPLE MOUND PERIOD.

Mitanni. A mid-2nd millennium BC kingdom in the area between the Tigris and the Euphrates in northern Syria. It formed a buffer zone between the kingdoms of the HITTITES and the ASSYRIANS until it fell to the Hittites *c*1370 BC. The population seems to have been mainly HURRIAN, although the rulers may have been INDO-EUROPEANS. The capital — Washukkanni — has not been identified on the ground.

Mithraeum. A small Roman religious building devoted to the celebration of the rites of MITHRAS. The usual layout is that of central nave flanked by two side-aisles. At the far end of the nave, a type of reredos often depicts Mithras in his act of slaying the bull, and the building itself apparently represents the cave of the original story. Symbolism shows the coming of new life from the blood spilt, and the conquering of evil (of which the scorpion is sometimes the agent). The side-aisles are typically raised to form reclining couches for the taking of the sacred banquet. The remainder of the building may be decorated with other episodes from the Mithras story, such as a hunting expedition, his genesis from the rock, and his close alliance and virtual identification with the Sun. Some examples show more elaborate architecture, such as the addition of apse and colonnades (e.g. Walbrook, LONDON).

Mithras. Best known as the saviour deity of the Roman mystery cult of Mithraism, which flourished alongside early Christianity and shows many parallels with it. Originally an old Persian and Indian god of light, truth and the contract, Mithras bore such titles as Lord of Light and Saviour from Death. From the 1st century BC onwards he begins to appear in the Roman world as the god of a mystery cult, and is usually shown wearing the Persian cap and trousers. His disciples, who were exclusively men and often limited to the ranks of soldiers and businessmen, were promised life and happiness after death. As in other mystery cults, the rites were kept secret, and truth and benfits came only to initiated believers, who had to pass through a sequence of seven grades of initiation. These were the stages of the Raven (*Corax*), Bride (*Nymphus*), Soldier (*Miles*), Lion (*Leo*), Persian (*Perses*), Runner of the Sun (*Heliodromos*), and Father (*Pater*). The disciple also underwent baptism, took part in the re-enacting of the sacred meal, and bore the seal of his discipleship on his body. The central sacrificial theme was the *tauroctony*, the slaying of the bull by Mithras in the cave. This event symbolized the giving of life by the shedding of blood, the victory of life over death and of good over evil. Mithraism expanded rapidly from the second half of the 1st century AD, and found capital and provincial representation alike. Particularly strong adherence is seen in the western and northern frontier provinces, the Rhine and the Danube. HADRIAN'S WALL and LONDON offer British examples. *See* MITHRAEUM.

Mitla. Located 40 km southeast of MONTE ALBAN in Oaxaca, Mexico, Mitla was first occupied in the Middle PRE-CLASSIC and was still in use at the time of the Spanish Conquest. Major construction in the Early POST-CLASSIC coincides with the abandonment of Monte Alban, suggesting that it became a new locus for the ZAPOTEC. Constructions include a fortified stronghold, five 'palace' complexes finished in cut-stone and plaster, and elaborate cruciform tombs. Typically, the palace complexes are rectangular patios flanked by long rows of apartment type buildings. Polychrome pottery, mosaic walls and frescos indicate a strong MIXTEC influence in later times. An increasing mingling of Zapotec and Mixtic traits, also reflected at contemporary Yagul, characterizes the whole occupation.

Although considered somewhat anomalous, given the increasingly secular attitudes of the Post-Classic, historical documents suggest that Mitla was a CEREMONIAL CENTRE under the control of a highly influential Zapotec priest.

Mito. *See* KOTOSH.

Mixtec. A culture of the POST-CLASSIC PERIOD centred on the high valleys of Oaxaca, Mexico. The major source of information on the Mixtec are the surviving genealogies (*see* CODEX) which trace their origins back to AD 692. The early period is characterized by a relatively bloodless struggle with the ZAPOTEC for control of Oaxaca (possibly via kin-alliance or other diplomatic means). A major expansion, directed from the capital at Tilantongo, occurred in the 11th century under the ruler 8-Deer whose close ties to TULA imply TOLTEC control.

The Mixtec occupied the great centre at MONTE ALBAN some time before the 14th century (that is, after the Zapotecs had left), but they used it principally as an elite burial place. The extraordinary collection of gold, silver, copper, jade and other materials from Tomb 7 show them to be skilled lapidary- and metal-workers as well as exponents of a complex artistic tradition. A blending of Mixtec and local traditions at CHOLULA produced the Mixteca-Puebla art style, which was a seminal influence in the growth of AZTEC art.

Though the Mixtec were always able to maintain a degree of independence, indeed remnants still survive today, their major power centres, such as Coixtlahuaca and Tlaxiaco, ultimately fell under Aztec control in the early 16th century. Their history overall, however, is a record of increasing fusion with the Zapotec.

M'lefaat, Tell. An open site in northern Iraq of the KARIM SHAHIR phase (undated here, but probably 8th millennium bc). The site contained round and oval sunken houses with stone floors. Finds include a chipped stone industry of Karim Shahir type, lightly baked clay figurines and beads, and fragments of stone bowls. There is little evidence on the subsistence economy: the faunal remains have not been published and no plant remains were found. However, the occurrence of mortars and querns may indicate that cereals were harvested; clay balls, perhaps used as weights for digging sticks, suggest that these were cultivated and not wild cereals.

moas. Extinct New Zealand land birds (*Dinornithidae*) comprising 13 species in 6 genera, according to recent analysis. Moas (a Polynesian vernacular term) were exterminated by early Polynesians in New Zealand between initial settlement (about AD 900) and possibly 1600. The largest species, *Dinornis giganteus*, stood about three metres high. Moa-hunting was once held to be an economic mainstay of the Archaic MAORIS, but it is now clear that large concentrations only occurred in certain regions, especially east coastal South Island.

moated sites. Defended homesteads constructed in great numbers throughout England, Ireland and Flanders during the late medieval period. There was already a tradition of building defensive moats around CASTLES and manorial establishments, and during the troubled years at the turn of the 13th century some wealthier farmers adopted this style of fortification. Other reasons advanced for this development are that in marshy areas a moat provided an extra means of drainage when the climate was deteriorating, and that status-seeking landowners wished to imitate the military and aristocratic classes.

mobiliary art [French: *art mobilier*]. Term used to cover all the portable decorated objects produced in the Upper PALAEOLITHIC of Europe, as opposed to CAVE ART, which covers the paintings, engravings and reliefs found on the walls of caves and rock shelters of the same period. Typical mobiliary art is in the form of decorated utilitarian objects, like spear-throwers and harpoons or sometimes statuettes (*see* VENUS FIGURINES) and engraved plaques. In the case of pieces of limestone with painting or engraving, it is often difficult to know if they were once wall art which has since flaked off. Unlike wall art, which is difficult to date, mobiliary art is usually found in archaeological layers and can therefore be dated. The earliest pieces probably date to about 35,000 years ago and they continued being made throughout the Upper Palaeolithic to *c*10,000 bc.

Moche [Mochica]. A culture having widespread influence, centred on the Chicama, Moche and VIRU VALLEY of north-coast Peru during the Early INTERMEDIATE PERIOD. Structures at the CEREMONIAL CENTRE at Moche include a large, terraced, truncated pyramid (Huaca del Sol) and the smaller Huaca de la Luna, on top of which is a series of courtyards and rooms, some with wall paintings. The major characteristic of Moche, however, is its outstanding ceramic complex, the decoration of which is a rich source of information not only about daily life but about ceremony and warfare. Typically, vessels are mould-made, with red-on-white or buff-on-white designs rendered in a lively naturalistic style. A common form is the STIRRUP-SPOUT VESSEL, but the unique form for which Moche is most famous is the portrait-head vase. Grave goods in gold, silver and copper display a fairly advanced metal-working technology. Incised lines on lima beans have recently been interpreted as a form of non-verbal communication similar in concept to the QUIPU. Developing out of CUPISNIQUE, GALLINAZO and SALINAR, Moche survived into the MIDDLE HORIZON but appears ultimately to have been overtaken by the HUARI culture.

model. In mathematics, the term model has a very precise meaning. STATISTICS can determine a series of hypothetical mathematical 'rules' by which a process or phenomenon may be guided. This set of rules is a 'model' of the way in which the process is thought to work. Models of this kind are tested by applying the rules to a set of information and comparing the outcome with the results known to be obtained by the real process. The rules of the model can then be altered until an appropriate set of results is produced. A model which has been tested in this way may be used to predict the outcome of a particular set of conditions. Prime examples of this are the General Circulation Models used to predict future weather conditions. Models can also be a useful tool for finding out how a phenomenon works.

The concept of formulating a model, testing it and refining it, is frequently applied in a non-mathematical way and this is the way in which it is most often used in archaeology. In this sense it is either synonomous with 'hypothesis' or refers to a number of interlocking hypotheses. A major problem is that all archaeological processes are strictly untestable, because they have already happened; rigorous application of models to archaeology is therefore difficult.

Modjokerto. *See* MOJOKERTO.

Moershoofd interstadial. An INTERSTADIAL of the WEICHSELIAN cold stage. It is dated to *c* 50,000-43,000 bp.

Moghul Ghundai. *See* ZHOB.

Mogollon. An early American agricultural tradition, with its heartland in the mountainous belt on the northern fringe of the basin and range region of Arizona and New Mexico. Immense regional variability in cultural traits and relatively few absolute dates have meant that a satisfactory chronology covering the entire tradition has yet to be worked out. However, the dates *c*300 BC to AD 1400 would embrace most chronological schemes.

The Mogollon seems to have evolved from DESERT CULTURE adaptations, most probably COCHISE Archaic. Evidence of MAIZE and bean horticulture found at BAT CAVE dates to earlier than 2000 BC, but unequivocally characteristic traits, such as plain brown pottery, do not appear until 300 BC. Pottery types such as Alma Plain and San Francisco Red persisted throughout Mogollon history, but the finely worked MIMBRES pottery flourished only from AD 900-1200.

Although the tradition was agriculturally based, hunting and gathering continued to play some part in subsistence activities. Before *c*1000 AD typical communities were small villages of pit houses, located in easily defensible positions such as high mesas. Larger villages often included a communal assembly building (possibly an early KIVA) and sometimes fortifications.

The period 1000-1400 is characterized by rapid change, much of which seems to have been associated with ANASAZI immigration. Surface PUEBLO dwellings replaced pit houses, populations concentrated into larger settlements, and a general movement from north to south occurred. After 1450 Mogollon traits survive mostly as a blend with Anasazi.

Mohenjo-Daro. One of the two major cities of the HARAPPAN CIVILIZATION of the 3rd millennium BC. Mohenjo-Daro, in the upper Sind district of Pakistan, is the largest of all the Indus Valley sites, covering c100 hectares, of which nearly one third has been excavated. Its population has been estimated as around 40,000. Like other Indus Valley settlements, Mohenjo-Daro consists of two parts: a lower town in the east, overlooked by a high artificial mound or citadel on the west side. The fortified citadel, dominated today by a ruined Buddhist STUPA of the 2nd century AD, has produced remains of several important buildings of the Indus Valley Civilization. The Great Bath, measuring 12 metres by 7 metres and 2.5 metres deep, with its associated complex of bathrooms and other rooms, was probably connected with the religious life of the city. Next to the Great Bath is the Granary, a massive structure, covering originally an area of c46 by 23 metres and subsequently extended, which is usually regarded as a state granary for the storage of the collective agricultural wealth of the whole community. The function of other structures on the citadel, labelled by the excavators the 'College' and the 'Assembly Hall', are unknown but their size and impressive appearance suggest that they were important public buildings.

The lower town was laid out on a gridiron plan of streets dividing the area into rectangular blocks. The streets were unpaved but supplied with brick drains and brick-built manholes at regular intervals. Although some buildings may have had an industrial function and a few have been tentatively interpreted as shrines, the vast majority were houses, commodious dwellings consisting of ranges of rooms opening on to a central courtyard. Baked brick was the normal building material

and the houses were built to a high standard, provided with upper storeys and often with a well room and adjoining bathroom, with a drain connecting it to the street drain outside.

Radiocarbon dates from Mohenjo-Daro fall between 1950 and 1650 bc, giving corrected dates for the mature Harappan civilisation here of c2450 to 2000 BC. However, deep soundings have shown evidence of occupation at great depths below the modern flood plain, suggesting that much earlier phases of occupation remain to be investigated. Mohenjo-Daro was abandoned c1600 bc (1950 BC), apparently after a massacre, as in the latest layers groups of skeletons were found lying in houses and in the streets.

Mohra Moradu. *See* TAXILA.

Mojokerto [Modjokerto]. Find-spot (1936) in eastern JAVA, Indonesia, of a skull of an archaic *Homo* child, located 8 metres above a potassium-argon dated pumice of 1.9 ± 0.4 million years. Believed to be the oldest hominid fossil in Southeast Asia, the Mojokerto child is usually classified as *Homo erectus*, but attempts have also been made to classify it in the more archaic *Homo modjokertensis* (or *Homo habilis*) grade. *See* HUMAN EVOLUTION, MEGANTHROPUS.

Mokrin. Type site of an earlier Bronze Age group (PERIAM in western Rumania, Mokrin in north Yugoslavia, Szöreg in south Hungary) in the lowland Banat, dated to the early 2nd millennium bc. The type site, near Kikinda, north Yugoslavia, is, like most other sites in the group, a large cemetery with over 300 graves. The graves are organized in 11 lines radiating from the central area, a possible indication of family groupings. Earlier grave goods occur in the more northerly graves, whilst most of the rich graves, with gold ornaments and imported metal objects, lie further south.

Mokto. *See* PUSAN.

Molfetta. The Pulo di Molfetta is a large collapsed limestone cave near the Adriatic coast in southeast Italy. Adjacent to the Pulo was an Early Neolithic village of small round huts and for this reason the south Italian version of IMPRESSED WARE is sometimes named Molfetta ware. After the settlement had gone out of use, the area was used for a

Late Neolithic cemetery of single graves, two of which have yielded fine painted cups of SERRA D'ALTO type. At a later date, in the Bronze Age, the small caves in the sides of the Pulo and the floor of the depression itself were occupied, perhaps sporadically, by people using pottery of Proto-Apennine and APENNINE type.

molluscs. Soft-bodied invertebrate animals often, but not always, living inside (or bearing) a shell. The phylum Mollusca is divided into five classes: Amphineura (the Chitons), Gastropoda (SNAILS and slugs), Scaphopoda (Elephant's Tusk shells), Lamellibranchiata (bivalve molluscs, such as mussels, clams, oysters), Cephalopoda (octopus and squids). With the exception of the gastropods, most of these groups are aquatic. Shells of gastropods and lamellibranchs are frequently found on archaeological sites. Coastal sites may incorporate deposits bearing large numbers of shells from marine members of these classes. Shells also remain from the exploitation of these animals for food. Large 'middens', consisting mostly of the shells of marine lamellibranchs, are found on Mesolithic coastal sites in northwest Europe. Shells were also used for decoration.

The shells of land snails may also be found incorporated into BURIED SOILS and deposits. These are most useful for environmental reconstruction.

Molodova. The site of Molodova V on the Dniester River in western Russia has some 12 archaeological levels spanning from c45,000 bc to 7000 bc according to radiocarbon evidence, but the occupation was not continous. The Upper PALAEOLITHIC levels do not correspond to cultures known from the classic West European sequence, and there is no general agreement as to which cultures should be recognized in this area.

Molokai. *See* HALAWA VALLEY, HAWAIIAN ISLANDS.

Momil. Located on a large lagoon in the Sinu River in northern Colombia, this site is significant for its evidence of the transition from MANIOC to MAIZE farming. Two major periods are defined. Momil I (ascribed a mean date of c700 BC) contained stone tools, both percussion and pressure flaked, incised and stamped pottery, and circular-rimmed GRIDDLES. By Momil II (dated 100 BC) griddles no longer occur and have been replaced by troughed METATES, similar to those used in Mesoamerica. New vessel forms, hollow figurines and the earliest known occurrence of negative resist painting in Colombia, also appear in Momil II, further implying a new external influence. Faunal remains indicate exploitation of the riverine environment throughout Momil's occupation. The date for the appearance of maize is, however, rather late, suggesting that it did not arrive directly from the north but came indirectly via a southern route.

Mon. A people in mainland Southeast Asia speaking a language akin to KHMER (*see* AUSTRO-ASIATIC). Their origin is unknown, but archaeological evidence indicates that at the beginning of the Christian Era the Mons must have occupied a large territory stretching from Lower Burma through into the southern part of the Indochinese Peninsula. The first historically documented Mon state is the Buddhist kingdom of DVĀRAVATĪ, which appears in Chinese sources of the 7th century and was absorbed into the westward expanding Khmer empire of ANGKOR in the 11th century. Later, the THAI kingdom of AYUTTHAYA absorbed both Mons and Khmers into its population. The equally Buddhist Mon state of THATON in Lower Burma was also absorbed by the southward expanding Burman kingdom of PAGAN in the 11th century, to which it passed on its religion, script and other cultural elements. Although the Mons in Burma, also referred to by the name of Peguans or Talaings, did at times become independent again, they are now only a small ethnic minority centred around the eastern shore of the Gulf of Martaban.

Mon-Khmer. A linguistic family of southern Asia, comprising MON, KHMER, and a number of languages of mountain populations in the Indochinese Peninsula as well as of India. According to recent research, VIETNAMESE is also a member of this family.

Monk's Mound. *See* CAHOKIA.

Monreale Cathedral. This magnificent cathedral, 8 km from Palermo, Sicily, was constructed between 1173 and 1186 by William II, the third NORMAN king of Sicily, and is a splendid reflection both of Norman achievement and the unique nature of Sicilian Romanesque with its combination of Norman, Arab and Greek influences. The massive exterior of the building is plain yet imposing. Twin towers flank the west porch and around the triple apse there is Islamic-style blind arcading in black and white stone. The western and northern porches have finely decorated late 12th-century bronze doors. The interior is covered in sumptuously coloured mosaics set into a background of gold, equal to any in the Byzantine world and dominated by the large portrait in the central apse of Christ surrounded by saints and apostles (including the recently martyred Archbishop of Canterbury, Thomas à Becket). Old and New Testament stories line the area above the nave arcades. On the southern side of the cathedral is a cloister belonging to the 12th-century monastery; renowned for its beauty and delicacy, each of the four corridors is supported on slender paired columns resting on a low wall, and the marble columns are inlaid with bands of coloured mosaic.

Mons Badonicus [Mount Badon]. *See* ARTHUR.

Montagu Cave. Located in the Cape Province of South Africa, about 150 km east of Cape Town, this site is one of the very few African caves to have preserved traces of ACHEULIAN occupation. The Acheulian material was at one time stated to be associated with evidence for the use of fire, but this is now discounted. Later horizons include one containing an industry which has been variously attributed to the HOWIESONSPOORT and and to a PIETERSBURG variant.

Mont Beuvray. *See* BIBRACTE.

Monte Alban. Located in the central Southern Highlands of Mexico, overlooking the valley of Oaxaca, this ZAPOTEC capital is an immense complex of monumental construction. At the heart of the site is a huge plaza (300 by 200 metres) dominated by three central mounds. It is flanked on the east and west by temples, PYRAMIDS and platform mounds; on the

northern and southern extremities are further discrete complexes of monumental building, including a BALL COURT.

Earliest occupation dates to the Middle PRE-CLASSIC (Period I, c500-200 BC) and includes the appearance of GREY WARE, of OLMEC-influenced monumental art (*see* DANZANTES), hieroglyphs and CALENDAR dates. Period II (c200 BC — 200 AD) is characterized by contact with MAYA lowland centres and, later, by the increasing influence of TEOTIHUACAN. In Period IIIa this influence is very strong and is evidenced by TALUD-TABLERO architecture, THIN ORANGE WARE and CYLINDRICAL TRIPOD VASES. By Period IIIb (c450-6/700 AD) Monte Alban was at its height as an independent power, Teotihuacan influence evaporated, and the centre was rebuilt, as indicated above. Elaborate funerary urns in Grey ware make their appearance in this period.

Some time between c600 and 900 (Period IV), the main plaza was abandoned (possibly in favour of MITLA and Lambityeco) and the entire centre fell into disrepair. It was totally abandoned by the Zapotec in c950 although it continued to be used for burials. During the 14th century (Period V), Monte Alban was partially reoccupied by the MIXTEC.

Monte Alban was long interpreted as a CEREMONIAL CENTRE, and although there is much religious and civic architecture, a genuine remoteness in terms of physical accessibility and no obvious natural water supply, recent work has convincingly challenged this interpretation. The survey by Richard Blanton suggests that the centre was part of a much larger urban conglomeration. Hundreds of house platforms, a series of dams, and defensive walls have been identified, as well as common burials and large amounts of everyday cultural debris. The site has also been interpreted as an administrative seat governing a confederacy of small states located in the valley. Population, at its peak, may have been as high as 50,000.

Monte Circeo. The Circeo peninsula in Latium, south of Rome, has several caves with prehistoric remains; Fossellone Cave with several early Upper PALAEOLITHIC levels and Guattari Cave are the most important. In the latter, a NEANDERTHAL skull was found on the MOUSTERIAN deposits, and three lower jaws come from the deposits.

Montelius, Oscar (1843-1921). Swedish archaeologist who wrote many books and articles on European prehistory. He worked first on Scandinavian prehistory, dividing the NEOLITHIC into four periods and the BRONZE AGE into five (divisions which are still retained by many northern prehistorians). He later applied this scheme, with some modifications, to other parts of Europe. His interpretation of European prehistory generally was based on the DIFFUSIONIST view that derived all developments in Europe from the ancient civilizations of the Near and Middle East; this view, often described as *ex oriente lux*, is expounded with great clarity in *Der Orient und Europa*, published in 1899. The diffusionist view, combined with the technique of CROSS DATING, allowed Montelius to construct a chronology for prehistoric Europe based on the historical chronologies of Egypt and the Near East. Gordon CHILDE took over and developed many of Montelius's views and further developed his 'archaeological' chronology, which was accepted until the advent of RADIOCARBON DATING and the tree-ring calibration (DENDROCHRONOLOGY) demonstrated it to be wrong in many respects.

Montelupo. *See* ARCHAIC MAIOLICA.

Monteoru. The type site for a long-lasting Bronze Age culture of the Sub-Carpathian zone (south Poland, northeast Rumania), lasting through much of the 2nd millennium bc. The type site of Sărata-Monteoru comprises a citadel with a long occupation and four large grave groupings in an adjoining cemetery. The citadel was fortified by box-like ramparts and stone walls, with house platforms in the interior. The burial rite is predominantly contracted inhumation, with pottery, bronze jewellery and stone or faience beads as grave goods.

Montespan. The deep central Pyrenean cave of Ganties-Montespan has traces of probably MAGDALENIAN engravings, but it is mainly famous for a modelled clay body of a life-sized bear or bear cub, probably originally covered with a bear pelt and apparently speared in ritual ceremonies.

Monte Testaccio. *See* AMPHORA.

Monthaillou. This village in the French Pyrenees became famous through the research of Emmanuel Le Roy Ladurie into the 13th-century Cathar rising. The modern hamlet nestles around the bottom of a knoll, which is crowned by a small castle. Around the edge of the knoll are the distinctive house-platforms on which must be the remains of the dwellings occupied by the Cathars.

Monza Cathedral. *See* LOMBARDS.

Mootwingee. A rich rock-art site in a range of hills near Broken Hill, western New South Wales, Australia. Human and animal figures in the PANARAMITEE style were pecked prolifically on rock surfaces. Human figures are represented frontally as stick men, or more fully rounded and carrying barbed spears and boomerangs. Other motifs include emus and eggs, kangaroos, sets of animal and human tracks, and radiating lines. Most of the figures are less than 60 cm in size, but a large pecked kangaroo is 1.8 metres in maximum dimension.

moraine. A land form, built up directly by the depositional action of ice. There are many forms of moraine. Flat areas of 'ground moraine' are deposited underneath the interior of a moving ICE-SHEET. 'Hummocky moraine' results from the down-melting of stagnant ice. 'End moraines' accumulate where the ice margin has remained stationary for a period of time. The SEDIMENTS involved in morainic land-forms vary from TILL to ice-contact stratified DRIFT, depending on the mode of deposition.

Morelos. *See* OLMEC.

mortar. A vessel, usually of stone but sometimes of other materials, used in conjunction with a pestle or grinder for crushing up food. Mortars were frequently made of special rocks, which might be traded over considerable distances.

Much study has been devoted to the mortars of the medieval period in Europe. The first stone mortars occur in 8th century DORESTAD and have origins in the Moselle Valley, while the French CAROLINGIANS at this time were using pottery mortars. In the 12th century Caen stone mortars were traded around the North Sea in competition with Quarn and Purbeck stone mortars from central England.

Millstone grit mortars were first used in the 13th century and like the others were widely traded.

mortarium. A Roman mortar, a culinary pottery form. Examples are often stamped with maker's name, and some sophisticated versions are found.

Mortillet, Gabriel de (1821-98). French prehistorian who made major contributions to the study of the French PALAEOLITHIC. He subdivided the sequence into periods defined by tool types and named after type sites. His initial sequence ran CHELLEAN, MOUSTERIAN, SOLUTRIAN, AURIGNACIAN and MAGDALENIAN, though alterations and additions were made later. De Mortillet believed that these periods represented stages in human evolution and were universally valid. This is no longer accepted and de Mortillet's epochs are now thought to represent cultures and to have local validity only. The practice of using type site names, however, proved so useful that it became standard practice and remains so today.

mosaic. A decorative surface composed of small pieces (*tesserae*) of materials such as stone, tile and glass, applied most frequently to floors and bath interiors, but also to walls, ceiling structures and roofs (notably domes). There are some Greek examples found from about the 4th century BC onwards but it is by the Romans that the technique is most vigorously exploited. Under the Empire, the mosaic established a wide-ranging technology leading eventually, for example, to the achievements of the 5th-6th century Byzantine artists at RAVENNA. An excellent collection of mosaics from POMPEII may be seen in the Museo Nazionale at Naples, and a good selection of Imperial Roman provincial work may be seen at the Museum of Le Bardo, outside modern Tunis, Tunisia.

Moscow. A programme of archaeological excavation in the old town of Moscow since the end of World War II has revealed important sites such as the 12th-century predecessor of the cathedral and many simple dwellings dating from the 9th and 10th centuries. These levels were associated with coin hoards as well as preserved organic material such as wooden beds, shoes and clothing. The KREMLIN itself

was found to overlie a settlement of the 1st millennium BC.

Moshebi's Shelter. Located at an altitude of over 2000 metres in eastern Lesotho, close to the borders of Natal and the Cape Province of South Africa, this rock shelter contains c3 metres of archaeological deposit. The two earliest industries represented are attributed to the 'Middle Stone Age': the later of these contains a number of large backed crescent-shaped pieces and other tools which suggest a possible connection with the HOWIESONS-POORT industries. Other sites in eastern Lesotho where related industries have been investigated are Sehonghong and Ha Soloja. The later industries at Moshebi's are of backed microlith type (compare WILTON). At a level dated to the 1st millennium ad pottery is first represented, as are pressure-flaked tanged arrow-heads of a type known from a number of sites in Lesotho, the Orange Free State and the northeastern Cape Province.

mosque [Arabic: *masjid*]. The Islamic place of worship. The earliest mosques were simple enclosures, imitating the courtyard of the Prophet's house at MEDINA of the 7th century AD. All subsequent congregational mosques, whatever their precise architectural form, are essentially similar: large areas, partly covered and partly open, where the community meets for prayer. Mosques usually, but not always, face MECCA, the direction of which [*qibla*] is indicated by a niche [*mihrab*] at the centre of the end wall. To the right, there is a stepped pulpit [*minbar*]. Sometimes a screen [*maqsura*] was erected in front of the *mihrab* to protect the ruler from attack while he prayed. Outside the mosque, the most prominent feature is the minaret [*manar*] or minarets, usually towers, from which the muezzin [*mu'adhdhin*] gives the call to prayer. Most mosques also have facilities for washing. Schools and libraries are frequently attached to mosques, the most famous being the al-Ashar University, CAIRO.

Mossgiel. The find-site of a skeleton with robust cranial morphology on the western plains of New South Wales, Australia, about 160 km north of LAKE MUNGO. Radiocarbon dating of bone carbonate gave an estimate of about 4000 bc.

motte and bailey. An expedient, quickly erected, medieval fortification consisting of an artificially constructed earthen mound — the motte — with a flattened top, surrounded by a ditch with an adjoining separately defended enclosure, the bailey. Several classic examples of motte and bailey castles are illustrated in the BAYEAUX tapestry, with wooden towers and palisades on top of the motte. The motte was connected by wooden drawbridge and gate to the bailey, which contained all the ancillary buildings, usually constructed in timber. It seems likely that the motte and bailey idea originated in the Rhineland during the 10th century and the concept was eventually adopted in central and northern France in the 11th century. It is often regarded as an archaeological expression of feudalism, and this kind of private fortification was certainly used by the Normans to reinforce their political conquests of the British Isles, southern Italy and Sicily. As a result of its widespread use, it is hardly surprising that excavations have revealed many different mound constructions and a variety of timber and stone buildings on the top of the motte.

Motupore. A site on an offshore island near Port Moresby, Papua New Guinea, with an excavated sequence from ad 1100-1700, ancestral to the present AUSTRONESIAN-speaking Motu inhabitants of the region. The sequence documents the development of the specialized ethnographic Motu trading system, in which pottery, shell beads and marine resources were exchanged for sago and wallaby meat from adjacent populations on the Papuan mainland.

Motya [modern San Pantaleo]. One of the three principal centres of Carthaginian Sicily (the other two were at Panormus [*Palermo*] and Soloeis [Soluntum]). The site lay on a tiny island off the extreme west of Sicily, on the north side of the bay of Stagnone. The settlement was founded as a PHOENICIAN colony, probably early in the 7th century BC, and joined to the mainland by a causeway. Excavations since 1906 have revealed stretches of island/city wall with gates and towers, an artificial dock, a temple, houses, and the earlier of two cemeteries. A tophet (shrine) has been found. From the beginning of the 6th century, probably at the time of the construction of the walls, a second cemetery was established on

the mainland of Sicily at Birgi, and the present-day underwater causeway between the two probably dates from the same period. After the destruction of the city by Dionysius of Syracuse in 397 BC, the inhabitants seem to have moved to colonize nearby Lilybaeum, although excavation has shown that a reduced level of occupation continued on the island.

mouflon. *See* SHEEP.

mould. The earliest moulds for casting metal were made of stone. European early Bronze Age stone moulds consist of one main unit, a depression carved into a flat stone surface. Metal would simply have been poured into this depression to make a casting of the desired shape. Such moulds are often termed open moulds, but it is likely that they would have had some sort of cover to cut down the cooling rate and metal loss by oxidation. A number of such moulds have been found, most for producing flat axes. In the Middle Bronze Age, more complicated castings appear, cast in stone moulds consisting of more than one component (piece moulds), and usually made of STEATITE. The PALSTAVES cast in these moulds were much more intricate in overall shape, but spearheads also had hollow sockets cast into them. Moulds for this purpose would have consisted of two main stone pieces forming the outside of the casting, and a clay core to form the inside of the socket. During the Late Bronze Age, piece moulds began to be formed of clay. Such moulds were broken to extract the casting and fragments have been found on archaeological sites. Piece moulds made of bronze appeared first in the Middle Bronze Age and continued into the Late Bronze Age. A complex mould must have provision for pouring in molten metal, for allowing bubbles of gas to escape and to allow for contraction in the metal on cooling. Moulds are designed with a small cup or funnel, into which the metal is poured. This may be connected to the main body of the mould by channels. The mould is filled right up to the lip of the cup. Bubbles can then rise through the mould and accumulate in the cup, away from the main part of the casting. Molten metal in the cup also acts as a reservoir to counteract the effect of metal contracting in the mould as it cools. When the casting is released from the mould, the metal solidified in the cup and in the channels must be trimmed off. These structures, respectively called the feeder or header, and gates or jets, have been found on archaeological sites. Where the various parts of the mould meet, casting seams or flashes are left on the casting. These may be observed on ancient bronze artefacts. Some very complex castings could not be made using piece moulds: these were cast in moulds formed by the lost wax or CIRE PERDUE method. *See also* CASTING, METALLURGY (CHINA).

Moundville. *See* SOUTHERN CULT.

Mount Cameron West. *See* TASMANIA.

Mount Carmel. There are several important caves on Mount Carmel near Haifa in Israel. Tabun Cave has a long sequence of deposits of ACHEULIAN and MOUSTERIAN type; the latter levels include a skeleton of Neanderthal type. The nearly Skhul Cave has burials of eleven individuals, formerly regarded as NEANDER-THALS, but now usually regarded as closer to CROMAGNON, or hybrid or transitional. The Wad Cave has a sequence of Upper Palaeo-lithic deposits with important NATUFIAN levels at the top and on the plateau outside; associated with this are numerous burials.

Mount Do [Nui Do]. An open site near Thanh-hoa in northern Vietnam which has yielded a pebble and flake industry with a few bifaces. Russian and Vietnamese authors have suggested CHELLEAN (early ACHEULIAN) affinities, but these are still disputed.

Mousterian. The term Mousterian, based on the site of Le Moustier in the Dordogne, south-west France, was originally applied to the epoch-making middle division of the PALAEO-LITHIC. Later it came to be regarded as a culture or group of cultures, but it is now used in many quarters in its old sense, referring to the period from the last interglacial through to about 35,000-40,000 bc, when the Upper Palaeolithic begins in Europe and adjacent areas (*see* Tables 5 and 6, pages 418-9). It is generally thought that the Mousterian was the work of NEANDERTHAL man; the evidence now available is mainly but not indisputably consistent with this view.

Several kinds of Mousterian are known, notably the Mousterian of ACHEULIAN tradition, which has hand axes, and the CHAR-ENTIAN, with an abundance of special kinds of racloir or side scraper. There is also a central European variant with leaf points. Less satis-factorily identified are the denticulate Mousterian and 'typical' Mousterian. The people of this time generally lived in caves and hunted such animals as reindeer, horse, red deer and bovines; one species often out-numbers all the others in a way that suggests specialization.

Mousterian industries of North Africa. The earliest post-ACHEULIAN industries in much of North Africa are those designated Mous-terian. In many areas the Acheulian appears to have been brought to an end by a period of exceptional aridity when much of North Africa, away from such favoured places as Morocco and south-eastern Libya, was largely depopulated. It was not until a climatic amelioration, of perhaps about 100,000 years ago, that human settlement is again attested, and it is marked by the Mousterian (or LEVAL-LOISO-MOUSTERIAN) industries. Flake tools were characteristic, notably sub-triangular points and side-scrapers, made on flakes removed from carefully prepared cores. The earliest North African Mousterian is probably that from the Maghreb, from which its Saharan variant, the ATERIAN, is presumably derived. To the east, Levalloiso-Mousterian industries occur in Libya, as at HAUA FTEAH, and at numerous sites in the Nile valley.

Mshatta. Although never finished, Mshatta in Jordan is among the most famous early Islamic palaces. It consists of a square enclosure, 147 metres across, with a single gate in the south side. The interior was divided into three parallel strips running from north to south. The lateral strips were never built, but bonding stones on the inner faces of the enclosure walls provide clues about the intended plan. In the central strip, the gate gives access to a hall, 17.4 metres long, and a small courtyard. Beyond this lies the central courtyard, 57 metres square, to the north of which stands the main building, the only part of the palace to be completed. Here, a triple arch leads to a long basilical hall and a square, triple-apsed throne-room, reminiscent of the bishop's palace at Bosra in Syria, which is attributed to the 6th century. The main entrance and other parts of Mshatta were faced with richly carved stone reliefs, some of which are now in Berlin. The palace is attributed to the Umayyad caliph Walid II (743-4) and presumably work ceased when he died.

Mu'a. The main ceremonial and residential centre of the ruling dynasties of Tongatapu, TONGA, held by tradition to have been in use from the 11th century AD. The site, never excavated, has a core area of 400 by 500 metres defended by an earthwork, and contains numerous house platforms and tombs (LANGI).

Mucking. The combined settlement and cemetery of Mucking in Essex is one of the largest and most extensively excavated Early Saxon sites in England. Mucking is situated on the high gravel terraces of the Thames estuary, and attention was first drawn to it through a remarkable series of crop marks spotted as a result of aerial photography. The excavations have mainly concentrated on the Anglo-Saxon period, uncovering over 100 sunken huts as well as at least two hall houses. The main occupation debris from the site consists of clay loom-weights, great quantities of handmade, grass-tempered pots, and some fine metal-work. The cemeteries contain a mixture of inhumation and cremation burials, including some wealthy graves that possess a full range of Early Saxon jewellery and weapons.

mud-brick. *See* BRICK.

Mudejar. A term used to describe the unique style of art and architecture, part Gothic, part Islamic, which developed in the Iberian peninsula during the Moorish occupation of the 12th-15th centuries. Many of the greatest Mudejar buildings were constructed by Moorish workmen for Christian masters, and were executed in brick, tile and wood. One of the finest examples is the great Mudejar palace of the Alcazar in Seville.

Mufo. *See* LUPEMBAN.

Muhammad Jaffar. *See* ALI KOSH.

Müller, Sophus (1846-1934). Danish prehistorian who succeeded THOMSEN as Director of the Danish National Museum in 1865. A contemporary of MONTELIUS, he worked in the same tradition, building up detailed typological sequences and CROSS DATING them by reference to the historical calendars of the Near Eastern civilizations. He was, however, more aware than Montelius of the possibility of variation in culture among contemporary groups and suggested, for instance, that there were several contemporary versions of the Neolithic of northern Europe. He also made contributions to the development of excavation techniques, especially the recognition of STRATIGRAPHIC relationships.

Mullerup. The type locality of the MAGLEMOSEAN culture of northern Europe, situated in the Magle Mose (or Great Bog) in Zealand, Denmark. The Maglemosean in one of the Mesolithic cultures characterized by axes and microblades, or small tools and points made on microblades. It belongs to the early postglacial period or BOREAL time, *c* 6000 bc.

multidimensional scaling. A technique of MULTIVARIATE ANALYSIS. Points or items distributed in a hyperspace, whose dimensions are a large number of VARIABLES, can be similarly distributed in a space of fewer dimensions. To do this, the technique 'keeps in its mind's eye' two DISTRIBUTIONS: one the original, distributed in hyperspace, and the other distributed in a 'new' space of the required number of dimensions. The points, orginally randomly distributed, are moved about in the new space until the distances between points are similar in proportion to those between points in the original hyperspace. Thus, for example, a group of artefacts, about which a large number of characteristics and measurements have been recorded, can be represented by a two-dimensional plot. As a matter of interest, the reverse is also possible: distributions in a space of few dimensions can be 'unfolded' into space of many more dimensions. Multidimensional scaling is accomplished 'iteratively'. This involves a considerable amount of computing time.

multivariate analysis. A branch of STATISTICS that deals with more than two VARIABLES at once. This is important, for example, when comparing series of skull measurements, the results of CHEMICAL ANALYSIS for a number of elements, or a large number of characteristics recorded about a group of artefacts. In multivariate statistics, the skulls, objects, or whatever, are distributed in a hypothetical space, called hyperspace, or

Euclidean space, which has a number of dimensions equivalent to the number of variables being studied. Some multivariate techniques (e.g. CLUSTER ANALYSIS and DISCRIMINANT ANALYSIS) analyse the DISTRIBUTION of the items under study within the hyperspace, reporting their results as a table or plot. Other techniques (e.g. PRINCIPAL COMPONENTS, DISCRIMINANT FUNCTIONS, MULTIDIMENSIONAL SCALING) mathematically reduce the number of dimensions of the space. Typically, a multidimensional distribution may be reduced to two or three dimensions, after which it may be plotted or analysed by conventional statistics.

Mummy Cave. A deeply stratified site located in northwest Wyoming, USA, containing an almost ideal stratigraphy from which a series of radiocarbon dates was taken. 38 distinct cultural levels, each sealed by sterile alluvial deposits, evidence an intermittent occupation from at least 7300 bc to ad 1580. Subsistence activities were not based on the BIG GAME HUNTING TRADITION normally associated with the Plains area, but rather on a generalized hunting and gathering life-style (*see also* MEDICINE LODGE CREEK). Very little material has been recovered from the thin, lower levels; however, later levels revealed small mammal bones, basketry fragments, MANOS and other material typical of the ARCHAIC. The cave is named from the dessicated body of an adult male who died there some 1200 years ago.

Munda. *See* AUSTRO-ASIATIC.

Mundigak. TELL site on the Helmand River in southern Afghanistan, occupied in the 4th, 3rd and 2nd millennia BC. In the 3rd millennium BC it was a major urban centre, closely related to the great city of SHAHR-I SOKHTA, also on the Helmand River, but over the modern border in Iran. Monumental buildings of this period have been excavated, including a probable temple. Strong cultural connections link Mundigak both to contemporary urban communities in Turkmenia to the north (*see* NAMAZGA-DEPE) and to the cities of the HARAPPAN CIVILIZATION in the Indus Valley to the south. It is likely that the wealth of Mundigak, as of Shahr-i Sokhta, was based largely on trade in LAPIS LAZULI and perhaps also copper.

Munhata. Located on a high terrace of the River Jordan, 15 km south of Lake Kinnereth in Israel, Munhata was occupied in the PPNB phase and has a radiocarbon date of *c*7200 bc. Several different building phases are documented and the architecture is characterized by plastered areas and raised stone platforms; earlier rectangular buildings were later replaced by round ones. The economy seems to have been based largely on wild resources. There is no evidence of crop cultivation, although sickle blades, querns, grindstones and pestles suggest that wild cereals were harvested. The animal side of the economy was based on caprines (possibly herded) and gazelle. After a hiatus in occupation there were three ceramic phases: the Yarmukian, with semi-sunken round huts; the Munhata phase with similar structures and the Wadi Rabah phase with rectangular houses.

municipium. A Roman term of political classification. Originally an Italian town or community in the Republican period, which was granted Roman citizenship without the vote. In the 1st century BC all Italian communities gained this status, with a uniform pattern of local government under four magistrates. Later, *municipium* status was granted widely in the western provinces.

Munsell colour chart. One of several systems used to describe colours accurately. A Munsell chart contains a number of pages, each with many coloured chips glued to it. Colour is assessed by matching with these chips, and is described in standard terms. The colour of any material can in fact be described, but the system is most widely used in archaeology to describe SOILS, SEDIMENTS and pottery FABRICS. Colours described by this method can be instantly understood by others with access to a chart, even if they have never visited the excavation or seen the pottery.

Müsingen. A cemetery of the Early and Middle LA TÈNE Iron Age in the canton of Berne, Switzerland. The 200 or more graves were commonly lined with stone and contained coffins; they were situated on a ridge, and as time passed the cemetery spread from the north end of the ridge to the south. This tomb sequence, combined with the typology of the grave goods, especially the brooches, has provided the basis for the detailed subdivision of the La Tène period in this area.

Munyama Cave. Located on Buvuma Island in Ugandan waters of Lake Victoria, central Africa, the cave contains an early backed microlith industry extending back to c13,000 bc. Small backed bladelets were the most common implements, with end-scrapers and occasional geometrical backed microliths. Backed microliths industries of comparable antiquity are known in East Africa at NASERA and LUKENYA HILL, at MATUPI and, further afield, KALEMBA.

Mureybat [Mureybet, Mureybit]. A site on the middle Euphrates c80 km east of Aleppo in Syria, occupied from c8500 to 6900 bc. The site went through three major occupation phases, beginning with a NATUFIAN village of round huts and expanding to cover some three hectares with both rectangular and round houses. The traditional interpretation of the economy of this site is that it was based entirely on wild resources, specifically on the hunting of onager, aurochs and gazelle and on the gathering of wild einkorn and, to a lesser extent, wild barley, lentils and vetch. Recently, however, it has been suggested that the einkorn, though still morphologically of wild type, was being cultivated, as has been suggested for the earlier site of Tell ABU HUREYRA, only 36 km downstream from Mureybat. This view is supported by the fact that wild einkorn does not grow in the area today and it is thought unlikely that it ever did (Mureybat is less than 300 metres above sea-level and einkorn usually grows at elevations between 600 and 2000 metres.) The other plants might also have been cultivated and the main animals either selectively hunted or actively herded, while hunting, fishing and collecting of truly wild foods continued alongside the newer activities.

Muromachi. See MIRRORS (JAPAN).

murus gallicus. A type of rampart used in Europe during the LA TÈNE Iron Age; it was given this name by Caesar, when describing the OPPIDUM of Avaricum. The ramparts were made of earth and stone with horizontal timber lacing, held together with iron nails. This type of construction used large quantities of timber and iron nails: the *murus gallicus* at MANCH-ING had a circumference of 7 km and is estimated to have needed 300 tonnes of iron nails.

Mwanganda. A butchery site in northern Malawi, unfortunately not dated, where numerous scrapers and a few core axes were preserved among the dismembered skeleton of an elephant. The site is of interest as preserving *in situ* the debris of a single, clearly defined, activity. It has been attributed, on somewhat inconclusive grounds, to the LUP-EMBAN industry.

Mycenae, Mycenaeans. A major citadel of the Greek Bronze Age situated in the Argolid, in the northeast Peloponnese. It was occupied in the Early Bronze Age, but became powerful in the Middle and Late Bronze Age after, it is believed, an invasion by Greek-speaking peoples. Among the most important monuments of Mycenae are the two circles of shaft graves, one inside and one outside the town walls, with their rich grave goods, dated to the 16th century BC; the walls of CYCLOPEAN MASONRY, the palace, including a MEGARON hall and associated houses, belonging to the period after c1400 BC; and the famous Lion Gate, added in the mid-13th century BC. A short distance away from the city are two well preserved THOLOS tombs, wrongly attributed by SCHLIEMANN to Homeric characters and thus labelled the Treasury of Atreus and the Tomb of Clytemnestra; these too belong to the Late Bronze Age (after c1400 BC).

The site of Mycenae has lent its name to the Late Bronze Age civilization of mainland Greece, which represents the earliest civilization to arise on the mainland of Europe. Mycenaean culture owes much to the earlier civilization of the MINOANS of Crete: it was based, like the Minoan civilization, on a palace-based bureaucracy with a king at its head and in its later phase it was, like the Minoan, literate: the LINEAR B script found on clay tablets on Mycenaean sites represents an adaptation of the earlier Minoan syllabary (*see* LINEAR A) to the writing of the Greek language. In many other ways, the Mycenaean civilization differs from that of the Minoans; it was, for instance very much more warlike, characterized by heavily defended citadels and a strong emphasis on weapons as grave goods. In craft skills and art styles, manifest in many spheres, including architecture, fresco-painting, pottery manufacture, metallurgy and jewellery production, the Mycenaeans demonstrate a mixture of Minoan and mainland influence. By c1450 BC the Mycenaeans had taken over KNOSSOS and from this date onwards it is more realistic to think in terms of a combined Minoan-Mycenaean civilization. In this Late Bronze Age heyday of Aegean civilization, its influence spread far outside the Aegean: Mycenean pottery and other goods were traded to the Levant coast of Syria, to Egypt and to the central Mediterranean, perhaps in exchange for raw materials such as metals. After c1200 BC the Mycenaean civilization went into abrupt decline; many sites were abandoned, while others declined drastically in size; the palace bureacracy collapsed and with it went the art of writing and many of the other attributes of civilization, not to be reinstated for several centuries.

There have been many studies of both the rise and fall of Mycenaean civilization. Earlier scholars tended to attribute its rise to outside influence or actual invasion, looking to the earlier civilizations of Egypt and Western Asia for sources. More recently the balance has shifted towards explanations based on local development. In a deservedly famous study, *The Emergence of Civilization*, Colin Renfrew used the systems approach to culture to show how changes in two or more sub-systems of culture might interact to produce an accelerating process of change (examples he gave included among others the introduction of the vine and olive in the subsistence sub-system and the development of metallurgy in the technology sub-system). The abrupt end of the civilization has also given rise to many theories. Some favour external catastrophe, whether invasions of new people from outside (the favoured traditional view) or environmental disaster, such as earthquakes or volcanic eruptions. Alternative views of the decline suggest internal collapse, whether based on slow environmental degradation or social revolution. It is in fact likely that the end of Mycenaean civilization was a complex event, that may have involved more than one of these factors. *See also* KNOSSOS, PYLOS, TIRYNS.

Myrtos. An Early MINOAN settlement in southern Crete, with corrected radiocarbon dates suggesting occupation c2800-2200 BC. It was a village of irregularly grouped buildings on a sloping hillside. There is evidence of relatively complex economic organization, attested by seals and sealings and by evidence of craft specialization. This economy may have been based in part on cultivation of the olive.

N

Nabta Playa. A lake basin near the Egypt/ Sudan border in the desert west of the Nile. Extensive scattered prehistoric occupation is attested from *c*7000 bc. A thousand years later, settlement appears to have become concentrated in larger sites adjacent to the lake shore. Pottery and concave-based arrow-heads now appear and show affinities to those from EARLY KHARTOUM and the FAYUM respectively. Cattle, probably domestic, are now represented in the faunal remains, alongside the wild species that were hunted as in former times. Seeds were well-preserved and include two kinds of barley (one of them domestic), doum palm, date palm, possible sorghum and several weed species indicative of the presence of cultivation. The degree of continuity from earlier times illustrated by this Neolithic phase is noteworthy, as is the early date at which food production is clearly attested. At a broadly contemporary site at Kharga Oasis, some 300 km to the north of Nabta, domestic sheep/goat have also been identified.

Nachikufan. A term describing the backed microlith industries of northern Zambia, with those of some adjacent regions, formerly regarded as forming a distinct complex, of long duration, divided into three successive phases. These Nachikufan industries, named after a large cave near Mpika, were differentiated from their WILTON contemporaries in other areas on the basis of the large numbers of scrapers they contained, and the relative scarcity of backed microliths. They were held to represent an adaptation to the woodland environment of the central African plateau. Recent research has challenged this inter-pretation. The first phase, Nachikufan I, is now seen as a widespread industry, character-ized by the presence of large numbers of small backed blades, of early date; it extends back as early as *c*19,000 bc at such sites as KALEMBA and LEOPARD'S HILL. The later phases are more restricted geographically, and form part of a general continuum of variation among the backed-microlith industries of south-central Africa during the last seven or eight millennia bc.

Nāgarakritāgama. Name of a JAVANESE chronicle, started in 1365 by Prapancha but containing information about court life going back to the early 13th century. *See also* SING-HASĀRI.

Nagyrev. The type site for a regional group of the earlier Bronze Age, distributed in the lowlands of northern Hungary and dated *c*2300-1500 bc. Most known settlement sites are TELLS surrounded by enclosing banks and ditches. Whilst timber-framed houses are common, clay houses with internal partitions are found at TÓSZEG. Burial rites show considerable variation on the basic theme of inurned cremation. Rich grave goods are rare, ocurring predominantly in the Budapest area. A universal pottery form is the one- or two-handled cup with tall funnel neck in black burnished ware.

Nahal Oren. A cave and open terrace site in the CARMEL caves, Israel, occupied from the early Upper Palaeolithic to the PRE-POTTERY NEOLITHIC B (PPNB). NATUFIAN levels show a strong bias towards the selective hunting, or possibly herding, of gazelle and this continued through to the PPNB levels. Although there is no evidence of plant cult-ivation, there was a growing assemblage of processing-tools such as mortars, suggesting that plant-gathering was becoming more important with time. Natufian and PPNA buildings were round houses 2-5 metres in diameter, with central fireplaces. In the PPNB the convention changed to rectangular houses with paved floors; these were sited on the artificial terrace outside the cave, constructed in the Natufian phase. A cemetery of early Natufian date is associated with the site: bodies were buried individually, usually tightly flexed with knees drawn up to the chin; old mortars were used as grave markers. Grave goods sometimes occur and include carved stone and bone work; the most notable example is a gazelle's head.

Nahuatl. Native language of the AZTEC and other MESOAMERICAN groups and member of the Uto-Aztecan language family which is distributed over a large area of northwest and central America. Still widely spoken in the Basin of Mexico, it is the source of a number of words current in the English language, such as tomato and chocolate. It is also the source of the widely used New World term for spear thrower, ATLATL.

Nakada. A settlement site in the western suburbs of Tokyo, Japan, best known for the 79 pit houses of the KOFUN Period. A change in heating and cooking methods was introduced in the middle of the Kofun Period, from a central hearth on the floor to a clay stove built against the wall. Various, but not numerous, iron tools and a simple forge were also found. Curbed beads and clay imitations of bronze mirrors suggest that farmers subscribed to the belief-system symbolized by these objects; *see* MIRRORS (JAPAN).

Nakada [Nagada]. *See* PRE-DYNASTIC EGYPT.

Nal. A cultural group named after the site of Sohr Damb, near the village of Nal in central Baluchistan, Pakistan, related to the KULLI culture further south. The Nal culture probably belongs to the first half of the 3rd millennium BC and both Nal and Kulli settlements are associated with water-control systems which allowed exploitation of alluvial plains for agriculture. The Nal population used copper for many tools and weapons, but continued to use ground stone as well. They made beads from agate and perhaps also lapis lazuli. The pottery, some wheel-made, is decorated with geometric patterns in black paint; red, blue and yellow pigments were often applied after firing. Many burials were excavated on the type site, belonging to a period later than the settlement.

Naletale. *See* DHLO DHLO.

Namazga-depe. A large CHALCOLITHIC and Bronze Age settlement in southern Turkmenia (Soviet Central Asia). The Namazga phases I-III are assigned to the Chalcolithic period (6th-5th millennia BC), while Namazga IV and V belong to the Bronze Age and are dated to the 4th-3rd millennia BC. Already a large village of more than 13 hectares in its first phase, Namazga had grown to cover nearly 70 hectares by Phase V and was truly urban in character, with a high population concentration and separate artisans' quarters, producing evidence of specialist production of bronze, gold and silver goods, and wheel-turned, kiln-fired pottery. The 'proto-civilization' of southern Turkmenia in the later 3rd millennium BC was characterized by two large towns — Namazga-depe and ALTIN-DEPE — and a number of smaller settlements such as Ulug-depe. Other features include a wide-ranging trade network, a high level of craft specialization, marked social differentiation and an incipient writing system, with repetitive symbols incised on flat clay figurines. This incipient civilization never reached the levels achieved by the fully fledged civilizations of Mesopotamia, Egypt and the Indus Valley. Moreover, it was short-lived; for reasons not yet established, but which may be connected with environmental changes, there was a marked decline in the early 2nd millennium BC: Altin-depe was abandoned while Namazga-depe survived only as a small village (phase VI).

Nam-Viêt. An ancient kingdom which comprised parts of present southern China and of northern Vietnam. It came into being in 207 BC, when a Chinese official declared himself king of the southern province of Nan Hai, to which he added the conquered kingdom of ÂU-LAC; its capital was near present Canton and its population must have been overwhelmingly non-Chinese. The expansion of the Han empire put an end to the existence of Nam-Viêt in 111 BC.

Nana Mode. An Iron Age village site in the Central African Republic, dated to about the 7th century ad. Small-scale excavations have revealed pottery decorated by means of a carved wooden roulette. It has been suggested that this type of pottery may have been made by speakers of an Ubangian language.

Nan Madol. Built in a shallow tidal lagoon off the shore of Ponape, Caroline Islands, Nan Madol is the largest single complex of ancient stonework in Oceania, comprising about 70 hectares of basalt platforms, some of a remarkable crib-like construction using prismatic basalt. The most famous structure is the burial platform of Nan Douwas, which contains four pit-tombs within prismatic basalt enclosure walls up to 8.5 metres high. The whole complex is traditionally associated with the Sau Deleur rulers of Ponape, and was presumably constructed several centuries ago, although no exact date is known.

nao [*nao*]. *See* BELLS (CHINA).

Naples. Greek *neapolis*, 'new city' (a name common in antiquity). The principal Greek city of Campania, southern Italy, but probably only of modest size and importance during the Roman period. Tradition gives the settlement as a daughter colony founded by Greeks from CUMAE, and a 7th-century BC date looks plausible. Earlier occupation of this fertile location, framed on one edge by volcanic Mount Vesuvius and by the sulphurous plains of the 'Phlegraean Fields' on the other (*see* CUMAE), is extremely likely, but evidence for this, as for the Greco-Roman city itself, will have been largely obliterated by the intensive development and redevelopment of modern Naples. Sources mention a distinction between Palaiopolis ('old city'), possibly the original Cumaean settlement and to be located in the harbour area, and Neapolis, a newly laid-out and grid-planned larger zone, to which emphasis then switches. Although Naples long preserved its Greek language and institutions, it seems as if any independent outlook was extinguished by the Roman takeover in 326 BC. In the Roman period, Naples was eclipsed by neighbouring Puteoli (Pozzuoli), becoming first a MUNICIPIUM and then a COLONIA. Among the traces that still survive of the Greco-Roman city, stretches of Greek city walling have been identified in several areas, and a portion of 6th-7th century BC necropolis located in the Pizzofalcone region. A 700-metre tunnel on the Via Puteolana, joining Naples and Puteoli, was originally constructed by Augustus' architect, Cocceius. The identification of an Augustan-period COLUMBARIUM on the same road with the tomb of the Roman poet Virgil is intrinsically unlikely. The Museo Archeologico Nazionale (Piazza Cavour) contains an extensive collection of Campanian antiquities, and much material from POMPEII and HERCULANEUM.

Naqsh-i Rustam. *See* PERSEPOLIS.

Nara. *See* HAJI, KOFUN, MIRRORS (JAPAN), SUE.

Naranco. A town near Orviedo in northern Spain. The province of Asturias and Galicia remained an independent Christian kingdom after the Moors had conquered most of the country, and in Asturias a very individual pre-Romanesque school of architecture flourished between the 8th and 10th centuries. The Asturian style owed little to the Byzantine world, being much closer to Carolingian and Anglo-Saxon traditions although it betrays slight influences of Visigothic and Islamic art. One of the finest buildings in this style is the church of S. Maria in Naranco, dedicated in 848 by King Ramiro I. The well-preserved church once adjoined a royal palace and baths; it is constructed in roughly coursed ashlar and has a basic hall plan with internal arcades. The most outstanding feature is the double-storeyed narthex (entrance porch) supported on columns with an upper belvedere. In the nave and crypt are some of the first examples of transverse vaults in Europe. The inset medallions decorating the arcades and other parts of the church are another individual and attractive feature.

Narce. A settlement on the Treia gorge near Calcata in Lazio, Italy, surrounded by extensive necropolis, and probably inhabited from the 12th century BC. Essentially occupation seems to have been by Faliscans, an Indo-European Italic group, and therefore the site is to be associated with their centres at Falerii Veteres (modern Civita Castellana), 9 km away. The town appears to have enjoyed its greatest prosperity under Etruscan domination in the 7th and 6th centuries BC. Material evidence seems in general to follow a local (Faliscan) cultural sequence. Evidence survives for fortification walls, pit and trench burials, and chamber tombs with monumental doorway. The latest material seems to be 4th to (possibly) 3rd century BC. Some tomb material is to be found in the Museo di Villa Giulia at Rome.

Narosura. An important PASTORAL NEOLI-

THIC settlement site near Narok in southern Kenya, occupied between the 9th and the 5th centuries bc. Post-holes suggest the presence of semi-permanent structures of some kind, and the site appears to have covered an area of at least 8000 square metres, although it cannot of course be demonstrated whether the whole area was occupied at one time. A backed microlith industry in obsidian was accompanied by ground stone axes, stone bowls, and pottery with comb-stamped decoration of a type also found on many other Pastoral Neolithic sites and known as Narosura ware. All but 5 per cent of the animal bones recovered were of domestic species, with sheep/goats predominating over cattle. Since the majority of the cattle (in contrast with the small stock) were not slaughtered until old age, it has been suggested that they were kept primarily for milk or blood. Despite the large size of the settlement there is no conclusive evidence for the practice of agriculture.

Narva. The eponymous site of a late Mesolithic culture distributed on and near the Baltic coast of Estonia, Latvia and Lithuania and dated to the 4th-3rd millennium bc. Similar in type to the ancestral KUNDA culture, the Narva economy was based on hunting and fishing, with more tools of bone and antler than stone. Simple pointed-based pottery was adopted by stimulus diffusion from groups further to the south (e.g. the DNIEPER-DONETS group).

Nasca [Nazca]. The dominant pottery style of the valleys of south-coast Peru, during the Early INTERMEDIATE PERIOD. The characteristic polychrome decoration is a continuation of the earlier PARACAS style. Although the two styles are similar, Nasca can easily be distinguished because its colours are set by firing. Favoured motifs are stylized biomorphs (especially the 'cat-demon') and bodyless heads. A monumental quality is discernible in some designs, particularly in the later phases. Defined originally from looted and other unprovenanced materials, a number of Nasca sites have since been brought to light. The principal one, at Cahuachi on the Nasca River, consists of a great adobe temple atop a mound, some walled courts and large rooms, and a number of smaller constructions (probably dwellings). Nasca survived into the MIDDLE HORIZON, when it became fused with the more dominant TIAHUANACO and HUARI styles.

Nasera. A rock shelter on the Serengeti Plain of northern Tanzania, formerly known as Apis Rock, containing one of the longest well-documented archaeological sequencs from any single site in the region. PASTORAL NEOLITHIC material overlies an aceramic microlithic industry dated to about the 6th millennium bc. Below this is an early 'Late Stone Age' horizon including some large implements alongside microlithic types, and a long series of problematic industries prior to 20,000 bc, that may represent a long process of transition from a stone-working technology based on the use of prepared cores to one in which backed microliths were the characteristic end-product. The earliest part of the sequence remains undated, and further details of the industries and their associations are awaited.

Nasik. A rock-cut Buddhist temple in the western Deccan, India, dating to the early centuries AD.

Natal Early Iron Age. The South African province of Natal has revealed traces of the furthest southeastern extension of the Early Iron Age complex of sub-Saharan Africa, which has been linked provisionally with the dispersal of peoples speaking BANTU languages. In Natal, evidence for Early Iron Age settlement is found in the fertile areas of the lower river valleys and dates from about the 4th century ad. It appears that the quality of available grazing land may have been an important factor in the location of settlements. Closely related sites are known from the Transvaal, as at BROEDERSTROOM and LYDENBURG.

Natsushima. An initial JOMON shell midden near Tokyo, Japan, dated to 7290 and 7500 bc. The dated layer contained deep conical bowls with cord-marks made by rolling a cord-wrapped stick over the surface of wet clay. There were also bones of domestic dogs, bone and stone arrowheads, grinding stones, partially ground pebble-axes, bone fish-hooks and eyed needles.

Natufian. A Mesolithic culture of the Levant; dated c10,000-8000 bc; most sites occur in a band c40 km wide along the Mediterranean coast, though some sites occur much further inland, like MUREYBAT in Syria. Caves and rock shelters continued to be occupied, as in earlier periods, but open settlements also occur, including some that continued in use in subsequent periods, such as BEIDHA and JERICHO. Generally, Natufian sites demonstrate greater diversity in economy and more permanent settlement than earlier cultures. Some sites (e.g. NAHAL OREN and Beidha) show evidence of animal manipulation, perhaps herding (of gazelle at Nahal Oren, goat at Beidha), while others such as AIN MALLAHA, show evidence of the harvesting of wild cereals (mortars, pestles and blades showing silica gloss); there is no definite evidence of plant cultivation, but it is possible that it was practised. See also ABU HUREYRA.

Naukratis. A Greek trading settlement on the western (Canopic) branch of the Nile. Sources mention concessional arrangements made by Psammetichus I (663-609 BC), who may have been grateful for support from Greek mercenaries, and later by Amasis (578-525 BC). It looks as if Greek trading and residence on Egyptian soil was a matter for negotiation, with some traders, such as the Milesians and Samians, having separate quarters. There was also a shared administrative building, called the Helleneion, although the basis of participation is far from clear. With the arrival of ALEXANDER THE GREAT (332 BC) and the consequent founding of the new ALEXANDRIA, emphasis seems gradually to have shifted away from Naukratis. Some activity, however, continued, and we have evidence for the minting of silver and bronze coins, and for the existence of a new building programme under the early Ptolemies. By Roman imperial times the site may well have been abandoned, and perhaps was soon as overgrown as it is today.

Navdatoli. A large prehistoric settlement on the Narbada River in Medhya Pradesh, central India, made up of four separate mounds. There were three main phases of occupation. The first, of the 3rd millennium BC, was a village of 50-75 houses, mostly measuring c12 by 6 metres; the occupants were farmers growing wheat and a number of legumes. In Phase II, dated to the late 3rd/early 2nd millennium BC, the houses were smaller, c3 by 2.5 metres — possibly indicating a shift from

extended family to nuclear family dwellings; in the subsistence economy rice was added to the crops grown. In all phases, cattle, sheep, goats and pigs were kept and deer were hunted. Flint blades, some microlithic, were used, but copper was employed for axes. Beads of faience, agate and carnelian occur. The pottery used includes MALWA ware (painted in black on red) and AHAR polycrome ware (in Phase 1 only). In Phase III, which is dated to the 2nd millennium BC, pottery of JORWE type (thin, hard-fired red ware) appears. Subsequently the site was abandoned and its role as a trading centre was assumed by MAHESHWAR on the opposite side of the river.

naveta. A type of megalithic tomb found on the island of Minorca during the Bronze Age (see MEGALITHIC MONUMENTS). It takes its name from its shape, which resembles — a little — an upturned boat. Navetas were built of CYCLOPEAN MASONRY and contained long chambers with corbelled roofs. The best preserved example is ELS TUDONS.

Nawamoyn. See OENPELLI SHELTERS.

Naxos (Greece). Largest of the group of Aegean Islands known to antiquity as the Cyclades (see DELOS), and an important centre for the so-called CYCLADIC culture of the Aegean Early Bronze Age (late 4th to 2nd millennium BC). MYCENAEAN, PROTOGEOMETRIC and GEOMETRIC periods are also well represented. In the period of classical Greece Naxos has a relatively insignificant political history, and is better known for its wines. Naxos marble was a favoured source especially for the sculpture of monumental figures, and the island also conveniently supplied the emery with which to polish the marble. The Cycladic period has left numerous graves, and examples of the characteristic Cycladic idols, but relatively sparse and difficult occupation evidence, some of it probably now submerged. An isolated marble door-frame on the Palatia hill overlooking the modern harbour, is the CELLA door of a 6th-century BC temple, while near Sangri lies the site of a square temple. For the ancient quarries there is no lack of evidence, particularly for the practice of cutting large statues in situ. There are several unfinished figures,notably a colossal archaic statue, male and with beard — possibly a representation of Dionysius, who, tradition has it, was born on

Naxos. In the 8th century Naxos is said to have combined forces with Chalcis in a colonizing initiative to Sicily, where the colony of the same name was founded.

Naxos (Sicily). The settlement of Naxos at Capo Schisò, near Taormina, Sicily, is generally reckoned, following Thucydides, to be the first Greek colony in Sicily, founded by Chalcidians from Euboea in 735 BC. Participation by the Aegean island of Naxos may be a later reconstruction from the similarity of name. Sicilian Naxos itself went on to found daughter colonies at Catana and Leontini. There is evidence in the area for Neolithic huts and Bronze Age settlement. The city seems to have been reconstructed around 460 BC after a serious attack by Hippokrates of Gela earlier in the 5th century. At the close of the 5th century the city was again destroyed, this time by Dionysius of SYRACUSE, in reprisal for assistance to ATHENS in her attack upon his city. The minting of coins afterwards shows some continuing occupation, but the scale was probably modest. Excavations, an area of which is now opened to the public, show sections of perimeter walling, a town plan going back to the archaic period, and a sanctuary area assigned to Aphrodite. Pottery is often distinctive in style, with Euboean and Cycladic reminiscences, and a potters' quarter (vicinity of Colle Salluzzo) reveals kilns, depositories, and antefix moulds. Naxos coins (6th-5th centuries BC) carry a bearded Dionysus with ivy, vine and grape decoration, while later examples have his companion in revelry, Silenus, who is popular also on the local terracotta antefixes.

Nderit Drift. A site on the Nderit River south of Lake Nakuru, Kenya, which preserves a long sequence of alluvial and lacustrine deposits containing several archaeological occurrences which illustrate the precursors of the PASTORAL NEOLITHIC complex. Full details of the sequence are not yet available, but a blade industry of the 11th millennium bc is regarded as a probable ancestor of the EBURRAN, as seen at GAMBLE'S CAVE.

Nderit ware. First discovered at Stable's Drift on the Nderit River, south of Lake Nakuru in the central Rift Valley of Kenya, Nderit ware is a widespread but poorly understood variety of pottery which may pre-date the main florescence of the PASTORAL NEOLITHIC in southern Kenya. It is characterized by finely executed decoration, apparently made by means of repeated impressions of a pointed object such as an obsidian spall; it is also often deeply scored on the interior surface of the vessel. In northern Kenya, apparently related pottery occurs at least as early as the 3rd millennium bc. The pottery associated with the early pastoral sites at ILERET may also belong to this tradition. Further to the south, no occurrences are known which consist only of definite Nderit ware without admixture with pottery attributed to other traditions.

Neanderthal. Quarrying in 1856 revealed a small cave in the Neanderthal or Neander Valley near Dusseldorf in West Germany, and in it a skull cap and some other bones. Similar long low skulls with brow ridges are now known to be typical of the MOUSTERIAN period, perhaps in the range 100,000 to 40,000 years ago, and are often called Neanderthal man. *See also* HUMAN EVOLUTION.

Nea Nikomedeia. A TELL site in Macedonia, northern Greece, occupied in the Early Neolithic period. Of a range of radiocarbon dates from c6200 to 5300 bc, most authorities feel that those between 5800 and 5600 reflect the most likely date of the occupation. Several square and rectangular single-roomed houses were excavated, built of clay and timber. One structure, rather larger than the rest, is interpreted as either a communal meeting house or a shrine: it produced two female figurines, two greenstone axes and about 400 flint blades. The economy was based on mixed farming, with a concentration on the breeding of sheep and goats and the cultivation of wheat, barley and leguminous crops; hunting, fishing and shellfish-gathering also contributed to the diet. Equipment includes plain, painted and impressed pottery and a rather small chipped stone industry. Ground stone artefacts also occur and include axes and distinctive objects interpreted as ear or lip-plugs.

Neapolis. *See* NAPLES.

Nebo. A Late Neolithic site of the BUTMIR culture, located near Travnik, central Bosnia, Yugoslavia, and dating to the early 4th millennium bc. Excavations by A. Benac indicated two occupation phases in the Classic and Late Butmir periods. The large quantities of manufacturing debris on the site may be interpreted as workshop debris from stone and bone tool production.

Necker Island. A small (1 km long) barren and isolated island off the west end of the Hawaiian chain, containing a very large number of prehistoric sites (including 33 HEIAU) for its size. The island may have been visited sporadically from the main Hawaiian chain, or it is possible that it had a resident population of Hawaiians who died out, unable to return to their homeland. The island was uninhabited on European discovery.

Nelson Bay Cave. *See* ROBBERG.

Nemunas River. Located near Šernai in Lithuania, northeast Poland, the mouth of this river is the source of a stray find of a bronze statuette of the HITTITE sky god Teshub. The find has been adduced as evidence of long-distance trade in the European later Bronze Age.

Nene Valley ware. A type of fine pottery, also known as 'Castor', first made around WATER NEWTON (Roman Durobrivae), and appearing from around 150 AD. It is a local ware, made in imitation of the dark, glossy Rhenish wares, and was perhaps the first fine ware to be produced locally in Roman Britain. Its popularity lasted beyond 400 AD.

Neo-Indian. *See* BARRANCOID.

Neolithic. The New Stone Age, following the MESOLITHIC period. Originally defined by the use of ground and polished stone tools (in contrast to the chipped stone artefacts of earlier periods), other criteria were added later: the use of pottery and, especially, the practice of a farming economy. It is now known that these traits did not all appear at the same time in every area and this has given rise to the use of such awkward terms as ACERAMIC NEOLITHIC and PRE-POTTERY NEOLITHIC. The term Neolithic is widely used in Asian, European and African prehistory, but refers to different chronological periods in different areas. In Western Asia the earliest Neolithic societies appear before 8000 bc, while the beginnings of farming occur only several thousand years later in other parts of Asia, in Africa and in Europe. The Neolithic is succeeded either by the CHALCOLITHIC or the BRONZE AGE, depending on the terminology used in different areas and the nature of the archaeological sequence itself. *See also* THREE AGE SYSTEM.

neoteny. The retention of juvenile or foetal features of the ancestral body form into adult life, as in the living axolotl, is thought to be an important mechanism in EVOLUTION, having facilitated certain crucial changes such as the emergence of the first chordates. Modern man has a number of features which seem to be neotenous, at least in relation to the apes and to the kind of common ape-like ancestor we are thought to have. One possible mechanism to explain the emergence of modern morphology, perhaps from a NEANDERTHAL-like ancestor, is therefore neoteny.

nephrite. One of two distinct minerals which may be called JADE. Nephrite is considerably more common than JADEITE, the other 'jade' mineral. It varies widely in colour from white or grey to green, including yellow, blue and black. Sources of the material are known in China, Siberia, Pakistan, New Zealand, the Philippines, New Guinea and Australia, Poland, the Swiss Alps, Italy and Sicily, and North and South America.

neutron activation analysis. A method of CHEMICAL ANALYSIS.

Principle. A specimen or sample is irradiated in a nuclear reactor. In the nuclear reactions that result, stable atoms of the material are transformed into radioactive isotopes. These isotopes start to decay immediately, and emit gamma rays, whose energy is related to the elements present in the sample. The energy and intensity of these gamma rays can be detected, and from this information, the concentrations of different elements may be determined.

Materials. Small objects may be left intact, but larger objects require a sample of 50-100mg to be removed. The technique has been used to analyse glasses (natural and man-made), flint, pottery and metals (as coins).

Applications. Neutron activation analysis has proved useful in determining the origin of flint artefacts, by matching the trace element concentrations with those of flint from various sources. Similar studies have been carried out on obsidian and pottery. Coins can be analysed non-destructively by neutron activation, and the technique has been used widely to investigate their major and minor elements.

New Archaeology. The name sometimes given to the innovations in archaeology associated especially with the names of Lewis Binford in the USA and David CLARKE in the UK and introduced from the late 1960s onwards. The premises of the New Archaeology are the need for both an explicit theory and a rigorous methodology, involving the principles of the scientific method (especially hypothesis testing). Although the proponents of the New Archaeology have been criticized by more traditionally minded scholars for dehumanizing archaeology and their use of 'jargon', they have had wide influence and the basic principles they outlined are now widely accepted.

New Britain. The main island of the Bismarck Archipelago, northeast of New Guinea. Archaeological discoveries include stone pestles and mortars like those from the New Guinea Highlands, an undated industry of waisted flaked tools from Kandrian, and the first discovered LAPITA site (on Watom Island, 1909). Also on New Britain is the TALASEA obsidian source, the most important in the southwestern Pacific and quarried since at least 9000 bc (*see* OBSIDIAN). The island was probably settled by Papuan-speakers from New Guinea before 9000 bc (*see* BALOF CAVE, MISISIL CAVE).

New Caledonia. The largest island of southwest MELANESIA, with an AUSTRONESIAN-speaking population and an archaeological record going back to LAPITA settlement, about 1300 BC. Settlement before this date remains hypothetical but probable. The island is well known for its prehistoric and ethnographic systems of terraced wet TARO cultivation, and also has the richest assemblage of rock-carvings in Oceania.

New Forest ware. Colour-coated fine ware produced in the New Forest area (central southern England) of Roman Britain, in the 4th and 5th centuries AD.

New Grange. One of the largest and most splendidly decorated PASSAGE GRAVES of the Boyne area of Ireland, *c*40 km north of Dublin. The mound has a diameter of 80-85 metres and is *c*11 metres high; it is surrounded by a kerb and an outer freestanding circle of stones, originally 35 in number, of which only 12 survive. The tomb has a very long passage, 19 metres in length, and built of orthostats; the chamber is cruciform in plan and roofed with a magnificent CORBELLED vault. Many of the stones of the chamber, passage and kerb are decorated with pecked geometric designs, characteristic of Irish passage grave art. The central chamber was illuminated at dawn on the winter solstice through a gap left above the entrance — the earliest documented astronomical orientation yet recorded in the megalithic monuments of northwest Europe. Radiocarbon dates indicate that the tomb was built in the mid-3rd millennium bc (late 4th millennium BC).

New Guinea. The largest island of Oceania, New Guinea (800,000 square kilometres) was joined to Australia in periods of Pleistocene low sea-level, and was probably first settled by early Australoids at the same time as its larger neighbour (*see* KOSIPE). New Guinea archaeology is best considered under two headings: the Highlands, totally PAPUAN-speaking, and the coasts, mixed Papuan and AUSTRONESIAN. For the Highland prehistoric sequence in general (totally aceramic), *see* KAFIAVANA, KIOWA, KOSIPE. For horticultural origins early in the Holocene, *see* KUK. Stone mortars and pestles, many of elaborate shape, are also found in the Highlands, but their significance is still uncertain. The New Guinea coasts only have sequences back to 3000-2000 years ago so far (earlier sites probably being drowned by rising sea levels), and the best reported are from Collingwood Bay and south coastal Papua (both with pottery). Some coastal groups had developed elaborate trading networks by the time of European contact (*see* MOTUPORE). *See also* LAKE SENTANI, PAPUAN, SAHUL, SUGAR CANE.

New Hebrides. *See* VANUATU.

New Zealand. The southernmost and (except

for CHATHAM ISLANDS) the only temperate land-mass to be settled by POLYNESIANS (MAORIS). The sequence, beginning c900 AD, is predominantly horticultural in the North Island, grading to hunting and gathering in the colder South Island. Language, economy and technology are fully Polynesian with certain adaptations to a non-tropical environment. There are two archaeological phases: Archaic, c900-1300, and Classic, c1300-1800. The Classic is associated with many earthwork fortifications, a rich woodcarving tradition, and development of the chiefly society observed by Captain COOK in 1769. See DUFF, LAKE HAUROKO, MOAS, PA, PALLISER BAY, SWEET POTATO, WAIRAU BAR.

Nezahuacoyotl. See TRIPLE ALLIANCE.

Ngandong. In 1931 a terrace of the Solo River at Ngandong, central Java, Indonesia, produced 11 skulls and 2 tibiae which are thought today to belong to a late and fairly large-brained population of HOMO ERECTUS. Faunal associations are Upper PLEISTOCENE, and age estimates range from 60,000 to 300,000 years. Solo man has features of earlier JAVA MAN, and has also been regarded as a tropical NEANDERTHAL. See also SAMBUNG-MACAN.

Nhunguza. A later Iron Age site in northern Mashonaland, Zimbabwe, where a large clay-built structure has been interpreted as a court house, with open yard and audience chamber.

Niah Caves. The Gunung Subis limestone massif near Niah in Sarawak, East Malaysia, contains a number of massive limestone caves, used for habitation and burial in ancient times. The most important, called the Great Cave, has archaeological deposits going back to 40,000 years ago, with a pebble and flake industry and human burials in its lower levels. The latter are presumed early Australoid and comprise an isolated skull at c40,000 years (perhaps less) and full skeletons from c15,000 years ago. Upper levels are Neolithic and Metal Age, and appear to date from about 2000 BC onwards.

Niaux. One of the greatest PALAEOLITHIC painted caves, near Tarascon in the Pyrenees, southwest France. The paintings are in black; bison and horse are the animals most fre-

quently depicted. A new gallery discovered in 1970 has hundreds of Palaeolithic footprints.

Nicobarese. See AUSTRO-ASIATIC.

niello. A black paste composed of silver sulphide which was developed by Germanic and Anglo-Saxon metalworkers for infilling the incised pattern on a piece of silver. The inlay was heated after its application to the object, and was then usually burnished or gilded.

Nihon Shoki [Nihongi]. The 'Chronicles of Japan', the first official history completed in 720. The work began in the 7th century with the same objectives as for KOJIKI, but the *Nihon Shoki* is a more lengthy and scholarly attempt written in Chinese, the official written language of the day. Numerous documents, including Chinese and Korean sources, were clearly consulted, and often cited. Beginning with a slightly different version of a creation myth from the one related in *Kojiki*, the chronicles end with the events at the very end of the 7th century. The accounts for the last 100 years of its coverage are probably reliable.

Nimes [Roman Nemausus]. Important town of Roman Gallia Narbonensis (see GAUL) in southern France and at one time possibly its capital. Earlier, Nemausus had been a Celtic settlement, capital of the Volcae Arecomici, and associated with the shrine of a water-deity. The title Nemausus preserves the name of this deity. Under Roman control since 120 BC, the town was given COLONIA status by Augustus, who is credited with the construction of its walls (cf the so-called Porte d'Auguste). Increased importance came with Antoninus Pius, who had family connections with the area, and the city seems to achieve its greatest prosperity somewhere around the end of the 2nd century AD. By the middle of the 4th century, however, occupation appears to have ceased over a large area. Impressive remains from the Roman imperial period include the Tour Magne, an Augustan-period structure of unusual design and uncertain function, being an octagon with internal staircase and semi-circular rooms; the Maison Carrée, a fine, CORINTHIAN-order temple of a pseudo-peripteral type (i.e. the columns of the peristyle are engaged in the wall of the CELLA) which is now used as a museum, but has seen service variously as a fort and as an Augustinian church; the AMPHITHEATRE (Les Arènes); and, at the Fountain Sanctuary, an odd NYMPHAEUM and the barrel-vaulted Temple of Diana. The Augustan period also saw the construction of an AQUEDUCT for the city, built by Agrippa (Augustus' son-in-law), a portion of which is still extant; *see* PONT DU GARD.

Nimrud [ancient Kalhu; biblical Calah]. One of the great cities of ASSYRIA, situated on the Tigris River, south of Mosul; in the last century it was wrongly identified by LAYARD as the site of NINEVEH and his book *Nineveh and its Remains* refers in fact to this site. Unlike many of the cities of Mesopotamia, Nimrud was not a long-lived site occupied from the prehistoric period, but was a new foundation by Shalmaneser I of Assyria in the mid-13th century BC. Its heyday was in the time of Assurnasirpal II (884-859 BC), who made it the capital of Assyria; it remained the capital till c710 BC when the capital was transferred first to KHORSABAD and subsequently to Nineveh.

The walls enclosed c200 hectares and a citadel in the southwest corner housed a ZIGGURAT, a temple dedicated to Ninurta (patron deity of the city), another dedicated to Nabu (god of writing) and a series of palaces. The largest and most important is the Northwest Palace, built by Assurnasirpal II, originally decorated with massive reliefs and with doorways flanked by winged lions and bulls. Many of these sculptures were brought back to England by Layard and are now in the British Museum. In the southeast corner of the city was the arsenal, built by Shalmaneser III (859-824 BC) and yet another royal palace. Perhaps the most famous finds from Nimrud are the delicately carved ivory plaques found in large numbers in the palaces of both the citadel and the arsenal. They may originally have been mounted on wooden furniture.

Nineveh. One of the most important of the ancient MESOPOTAMIAN cities, situated c400 km north of Baghdad on the Tigris River opposite Mosul in Iraq. The site today consists of several mounds, the main one being Kuyunjik. It was occupied from the 6th millennium bc (a test pit beneath the Temple of Ishtar, the goddess of love, produced material of HASSUNA type at the bottom) until it was destroyed by the MEDES late in the 7th century BC. Even after this date settlement continued, but now on the plain next to the river and it subsequently became a suburb of the expanding city of Mosul.

The heyday of the city was in the 7th century BC when Sennacherib made it the capital of ASSYRIA and most of the surviving remains date from this period. They include parts of the city wall, 12 km in circumference, and the great palace of Sennacherib with its splendid reliefs. Some of these reliefs, together with the great archives of CUNEIFORM tablets which constituted the two libraries of Sennacherib himself and his grandson Assurbanipal, were transferred to the Louvre and the British Museum during the 19th century.

Ningxiang [Ning-hsiang]. A county in Hunan province, China, the site of repeated finds of bronze RITUAL VESSELS and large BELLS. These objects date from the latter part of the SHANG dynasty but often differ in style from Shang bronzes found at ANYANG. Many similar bronzes have been unearthed along the middle and lower course of the Yangzi River, suggesting that this region was the seat of bronze-using powers partly independent of the Shang court to the north but indebted for their knowledge of metalworking, and no doubt for much else, to an earlier southward expansion of the Shang civilization that took place during the ERLIGANG PHASE (*see* PANLONGCHENG, WUCHENG).

Nippur [modern Nuffar]. Situated 150 km southeast of Baghdad in Iraq, Nippur was centrally placed in the territory of the SUMERIAN civilization of the 3rd millennium BC. As well as being the centre of a city state, it played a special role in the life of Sumer as a religious city, centre of the worship of Enlil. Nippur was occupied from URUK times to the PARTHIAN period. Important monuments include a series of EARLY DYNASTIC temples dedicated to Inanna, the temple of Enlil and the neighbouring ZIGGURAT, of the UR III period but later converted into a Parthian fortress. Nippur is particularly important to scholars because of its large archives of CUNEIFORM tablets, ranging in date from the late 3rd millennium to the later 1st millennium BC and including both administrative and literary texts.

Nishapur. In the early Islamic period, Nishapur in Iran was among the most important towns of Khorasan; indeed, for a short period in the 9th century it replaced Marv as the regional capital. The town was a major commercial centre, noted for its textiles and visited by merchants from all over Western Asia and Egypt. Nishapur became a capital again in 1037 under Tughril Beg, the first Saljuq ruler. His successor, Malik Shah, made the city a centre of learning, the home of Omar Khayyam, among other famous scholars. It declined in the 12th century as a result of earthquakes (in 1115 and 1145) and looting by Turkish tribesmen (1153). In 1221, Nishapur was sacked by the Mongols, and never regained its former prominence. As a result of excavations by the Metropolitan Museum of Art, New York (1935-9) and much illicit digging, Nishapur's pre-Mongol slip-painted pottery is represented in many western collections.

Nitra. A fortified site in Poland where excavations have revealed traces of the 9th-century stronghold. It seems that within its walls there were workshops producing relics and metalwork that were distributed to other Slavic sites.

Nitrianski Hrádok. A multi-phase defended settlement site of the earlier Bronze Age, located on the banks of the River Nitra, west Slovakia. Little excavation has taken place in the interior. The fort was defended by a double ditch and timber-framed rampart. TELL-like accumulation of material from substantial occupation indicates an occupation covering most of the early 2nd millennium bc.

nitrogen dating. One of the methods of BONE DATING. After burial, the COLLAGEN component of bone gradually decomposes. This occurs at a slow, relatively uniform rate. Bones of similar age, which have been buried under similar conditions, possess roughly the same amount of collagen surviving undecomposed. Nitrogen is one of the essential elements of collagen and the nitrogen content of ancient bone may be used as an index of the extent to which collagen has decomposed. The relative ages of bones from the stratigraphical context can thus be determined by comparison of their nitrogen content.

Njoro River Cave. Dated to c1000 bc, this is one of the earliest well-documented Neolithic sites in southern Kenya. It was a cemetery for cremated burials, each interment being accompanied by a stone bowl and pestle, as well as by numerous hard stone beads and pendants. A finely decorated wooden vessel, such as is often used today to carry milk, was also preserved. The associated stone industry was of ELMENTEITAN type.

Nkope. An Early Iron Age site near the southern end of Lake Nyasa, which has given its name to the variant of the Early Iron Age complex represented in southern Malawi and eastern Zambia from about the 4th to the 11th century ad.

Nkudzi. A later Iron Age cemetery site on the southwestern shore of Lake Malawi (formerly Lake Nyasa), probably dating to the late 18th or early 19th century. The abundant grave goods may be assumed to reflect the material culture available in the area at a time of increasing slave-raiding and coastal trade.

Noailles. The Grotte de Noailles, close to Brive in Corrèze, southwest France, has given its name to a small multiple BURIN. The Noailles burin distinguishes a culture of considerable importance called PERIGORDIAN Vc or Noaillian, dating to c26,000-23,000 bc.

Nogliki I. Settlement of pit houses in the northeast of Sakhalin, an island off the east coast of Siberia, north of Japan. The settlement is regarded as Neolithic (defined by the presence of pottery rather than the practice of farming); the population lived by hunting and fishing and used pottery.

Noin-ula. A range of hills in northern Mongolia near Lake Baikal. KURGANS believed to be tombs of XIONGNU nobility were excavated here by a Russian expedition in 1924-5. They are assigned to the 1st century AD on the evidence of a Chinese lacquer dish inscribed with a date equivalent to 2 BC. The tombs, which were plundered in antiquity, take the form of wooden burial chambers in deep shafts over which earthen barrows were raised. The furnishings left behind by the robbers include lacquers, silks, woollen goods and felt hangings. These are notable for the diversity of their sources: the lacquers and silks are imports from China; a carpet, similar to objects from PAZYRYK in the Altai, is decorated in felt appliqué with scenes of animal combat but also incorporates Chinese designs and even pieces of Chinese silk; and other textiles are Iranian, South Russian, or Bactrian, some showing unmistakably the influence of Hellenistic designs.

Noirmoutier. An island that lies off the coast of western France just south of the mouth of the Loire. The island was colonized by Philibert monks in the 6th or 7th century, and the monastery became an important producer of salt during CAROLINGIAN times. From 842, the Vikings raided the island repeatedly, forcing the monks to flee inland with the remains of St Philibert; there they constructed the church of St Philibert de Grandlieu, one of the finest examples of French 9th-century architecture.

Nok. The name given to the archaeological manifestation of a very early Iron Age settlement on the southern and western slopes of the Jos Plateau in Nigeria. Attention was first drawn to the Iron Age archaeology of this area by the recovery during mining operations of numbers of fine pottery human figurines, some of them life-sized. The detailed and accomplished modelling pays particular attention both to attributes such as beads, stools etc, and also to physical peculiarities or deformities. The associations of these figurines have been demonstrated through the excavation of settlement sites, notably TARUGA, dated between the 5th and 3rd centuries bc. Here, shallow pits with low surrounding walls served as furnaces for the smelting of iron and were associated with domestic pottery and fragments of characteristic Nok figurines. Unfortunately, the local predecessors and successors of the Nok settlements remain unknown, although it is possible that the clay figurines of IFE may be traced to a Nok stylistic ancestry.

Nombe. A rock shelter in Simbu Province, Papua New Guinea. Excavation has revealed a rich cultural sequence from the late PLEISTOCENE to the present, and the basal levels contain waisted blades, pebble tools and several extinct animals, including *Protemnodon* and *Thylacine*. *See also* KAFIAVANA, KIOWA.

Non Nok Tha. A site of major importance in north-central Thailand, with burials spanning the period *c*3500 bc to recent centuries. Like BAN CHIANG, the site has produced evidence for possible 4th-3rd millennium BC domestication of cattle, pig and dog, the cultivation of rice, and the use of copper and bronze. It has been claimed that Non Nok Tha and Ban Chiang have the earliest evidence for bronze-working in the world, but precise dates are still under debate. *See also* BAN CHIANG.

Nora. A Phoenician colony on the promontory of Cape Pula, Sardinia, probably of the 8th century BC. From the end of the 6th century BC Sardinia came under Carthaginian control, and from 238 BC under Roman, becoming a province in 227 BC. Nora seems to have enjoyed particular prosperity under Roman rule, rivalled only by Cagliari (*municipium Iulium*). Decline appears to have come with the 4th century AD. Excavations since 1952 have uncovered a fair area of the city. Evidence survives for a Punic necropolis, an HELLENISTIC tophet (shrine) a temple to Tanit, a THEATRE with a mosaic-surfaced *orchestra*, and Roman bath-buildings, also with mosaic. The northwest shore was lined with a series of luxury houses, including the so-called House of the Atrium.

Noricum. Roman name for an Alpine region, later a province, situated south of the Danube, roughly in the area of modern Austria. Earlier Illyrian in culture, the region came under Celtic influence from the 3rd century BC, and the name Noricum is thought by some to derive from the Celtic Norici centred around Noreia. Becoming a Celtic kingdom, with reasonably friendly relations with Rome, it was turned without resistance into a province about 16 BC. The new province fitted into a pattern, lying east of Raetia and west of Pannonia. The capital was now at Virunum in the Klagenfurt area. Governors seem to have been of middle (equestrian) rank, and commanded auxiliary troops. The area was subdivided into two provinces by the emperor Diocletian (*c*300 AD); Roman rule finally collapsed with German incursions in the 5th century.

Normans. The population of the Duchy of Normandy in northwest France was a mixed race descending from the FRANKS and 10th-century Norse settlers. Under leaders such as William the Conqueror, Robert Guiscard,

Roger of Sicily and Bohemund of Taranto, the Normans effected the conquest of England, Sicily and southern Italy in a volatile period that began in 1063. These military feats were consolidated by the strength of the Norman feudal aristocracy and their skill in erecting strong, expedient fortifications ranging from MOTTE AND BAILEY earthworks to substantial stone CASTLES. The Normans were also the main force behind the Crusades, which began in the 11th century. They promoted the French language and French culture, and the romanesque style of architecture is part of their legacy. By 1200 the Norman conquerors had been absorbed into the countries they ruled, but many of their institutions lasted into the late Middle Ages.

Northern Black Polished ware. An Indian pottery type found on Iron Age sites of the 1st millennium BC. It is a hard, wheel-made, metallic-looking ware with a shiny black surface; the chief forms are bowls and dishes. It suceeds PAINTED GREY WARE in the Ganges sequence and is the main pottery type associated with the GANGES CIVILIZATION.

Northumbria. The Saxon kingdom of Northumbria was founded in the 7th century by the earlier kingdoms of Bernicia and Deira. After the conversion of King Edwin in 626 and the establishment of many major monasteries within the region, Northumbria became a centre of missionary activity and a leading centre for the production of all forms of Christian art. During the later 7th and 8th centuries Northumbria saw a Golden Age, when its schools of art, monumental sculpture and manuscript illumination were of major importance, and their influence was transmitted throughout Britain and other parts of Europe.

Northwest Coast tradition. A collection of prehistoric groups whose common economic base was the exploitation of abundant marine and riverine resources. Centred on the Pacific Coast, USA-Canadian border, the cultural area of the tradition stretches from southeastern Alaska to Northern California. Much information comes from ethnographic studies of historic and present-day groups (e.g. Tlingit and Kwakuitl) but characteristics in the archaeological record include bone and slate hunting tools, stone effigy carving, and wood-working tools (totem poles and elaborately carved long houses are still a cultural feature in the area).

The origins of the tradition are unclear but movement of peoples from the interior (see FRASER RIVER SITES) and an ESKIMO or Asian influence from the North are likely components. Firm dates are extremely rare but defining traits seem to have coalesced between 5000 and 1000 bc and the tradition was clearly established by AD 1000. See Table 9, page 552.

Norton. Sometimes designated Paleo-Eskimo, the Norton tradition embraces the cultural continuum CHORIS-NORTON-IPIUTAK and spans the period c1000 BC to AD 1000. The Norton aspect of this continuum is typically represented by the presence of poorly fired, check-stamped pottery and tools of crude appearance, made from basalt rather than chert. Polished slate implements and oil lamps appear frequently on site inventories. Sites are mostly on, or in easy reach of, the Alaskan coast. Cape Denbigh, CAPE KRUSENSTERN and ONION PORTAGE for example, all have a Norton component.

Novgorod. A city on the River Valkhow about 160 km south of Leningrad in the Soviet Union. Excavations in the medieval town were carried out before and after World War II and proved some of the most remarkable in Europe. Waterlogged conditions have preserved intact a complete sequence of wooden buildings and streets dating from the foundation of the city in the 10th century up to the 18th century. DENDROCHRONOLOGY has made it possible to date accurately the layers of timber streets superimposed on top of each other as well as their relationships to the log cabins either side of them. Particularly interesting are the small factories, complete with collections of tools for metal, wood, leather and glass working. Other important finds from Novgorod include a superb group of medieval textiles, and a unique collection of birch-bark documents which have proved invaluable in understanding the history, trading relationships, and feudal estates of the town. The fortified KREMLIN at Novgorod dates from the 11th century and is one of the earliest to have been given a stone enceinte.

Novopetrovka. See AMUR NEOLITHIC.

Ntereso. The site of a fishing settlement related to the KINTAMPO industry, located to the east of that industry's main area of distribution, in the valley of the White Volta, Ghana. In addition to artefacts characteristic of Kintampo were others, notably bifacially flaked arrow-heads, bone harpoon-heads and fish hooks which may have affinities with sites far to the north, in the southern Sahara. Particular interest attaches to the remains at Ntereso of a rectangular house built of poles and mud daub, incorporating carved wooden mouldings. A wide range of fish was caught, hunting was practised and small goats herded. The site, which dates to the late 2nd millennium bc, was occupied during the dry season and also, perhaps, at other times of the year.

Nubian A Group. The name conventionally given to the earliest fully food-producing society known in the archaeological record of Nubia, late in the 4th millennium bc. The 'A Group' people probably had an indigenous Nubian ancestry, but were much influenced from later PRE-DYNASTIC EGYPT, with which they were evidently in regular trade contact. So far the A Group is known mainly from graves, but some settlement sites have been investigated, as at Afyeh near the First Cataract where rectangular stone houses were built, as well as more insubstantial rural villages. Sheep and goats were herded, with some cattle, while both wheat and barley were cultivated. Luxury manufactured goods imported from Egypt included stone vessels, amulets, copper tools and linen cloth.

Nubian C Group. The conventional designation of the indigenous population of Nubia in the late 3rd millennium BC. There is disagreement as to the exent to which these people were the direct descendants of the preceding NUBIAN A GROUP population, there being apparent connections also between the C Group and contemporary peoples inhabiting the Red Sea hills, east of the Nile. It is clear that this livelihood depended to a large extent on their herds of small stock and cattle, but the importance of cultivated foodstuffs has not yet been adequately demonstrated. Such settlement sites as have been investigated consisted mainly of circular houses with their lower walls of stone. In later C-Group times more elaborate buildings were erected, and there was an increase in the quantity of luxury goods imported from Egypt. Both these developments reached their peak at KERMA.

Nui Do. *See* MOUNT DO.

Nuku Hiva. *See* TAIPIVAI.

Numidia. Homeland in Algeria and Tunisia of the Roman-period Numidae, whose name Roman authors derived from Greek *nomades*, 'nomads'. The Numidae were a group of nomadic Berber tribes, occupying a region of North Africa that corresponds today with the eastern part of Algeria and the western part of Tunisia, excluding the area around Carthage. These tribes achieved a degree of unity under the HELLENISTIC style kingship of their leader Masinissa (*c*240-148 BC) who encouraged them to exchange nomadism for agriculture and urbanism. It was Masinissa who was largely responsible for the notable spread of Phoenician culture into this area, and who by skilful management of his link with Rome was able to bring greatly increased prosperity and stability to his community. In 46 BC Numidia became the Roman province of Africa Nova, and from 30 to 25 BC was once again a client kingdom, this time under Juba II. Subsequently it was incorporated into the large province of Roman Africa, and in a final stage, was again separated off by Severus (193-211 AD) as a distinct area. Ancient literary sources mention Numidia particularly for the excellence of its cavalry (which helped to bring Scipio victory at the battle of Zama in 202 BC; *see* PUNIC WARS), and for its fine marble. While probably not as fertile as regions further east, Numidia seems to have grown wine and olives very successfully on the plain, and horses and sheep were reared on the higher ground. The Saharan region to the south was source for a lucrative slave trade, but a line of forts here suggests that trouble from outsider nomadic tribes was never far away, and it is in the face of incursions from these that Roman administration finally collapsed.

nuraghe, Nuraghic culture. Type of stone tower built of CYCLOPEAN MASONRY which has given its name to the main Bronze Age culture of Sardinia. The earliest nuraghi, built early in the 2nd millennium bc (later third millennium BC) are simple stone towers with internal chambers, but later examples can be very complex, consisting of multiple towers, with elaborate internal rooms and passages, and often form part of larger fortified structures, sometimes defended settlements. Nuraghi continued to be built during the PHOENICIAN and CARTHAGINIAN occupation of the island, right down to the Roman conquest. There are thousands of nuraghi in Sardinia and they remain a prominent feature of the island's landscape today. The Nuraghic culture is associated with a flourishing bronze industry (based on local ores) which in its later stages produced a series of attractive figurines that cast light on a number of both everyday and ritual activities of the Nuraghic population. The MEGALITHIC tombs known as *tombe di giganti* (*see* GIANT'S GRAVE) belong to the Nuraghic culture, as do a number of other monuments including sacred wells. The nuraghi show some similarities to the TORRI of Corsica and the TALAYOTS of the Balearic Islands. *See also* BARUMINI.

Nuzi [modern Yorgan Tepe]. A TELL near Kirkuk in northern Iraq. Excavations in the 1920s explored levels of the mid-2nd millennium BC. A palace and private houses of the 15th to 14th centuries BC were excavated and finds include some 20,000 CLAY TABLETS, mostly recording business transactions.

Nydam. One of the most important archaeological finds of the MIGRATION PERIOD is the bog deposit from Nydam, southern Jutland. Many objects were ritually deposited in this mere over several centuries, and were fortunately preserved by the peaty soil. The most important of these finds was one of three clinker (plank) built rowing boats which measured 21.5 metres long and 3 metres wide, and was propelled by 15 pairs of oars. This boat has received considerable scholarly attention because some believe it would have been typical of the vessels used by the ANGLO-SAXON migrants coming to England in the 5th century. However, its construction would have made this a dangerous journey and it is likely that its use was confined to the tideless sea of the Baltic.

nymphaeum [Greek *nymphaion*: 'sanctuary of the Nymphs']. An inexact term, used of a Roman pavilion or pleasure-house, which could vaguely be characterized as having fountains, statues and flowers; often a fountain with a rich architectural surround.

O

Oahu. *See* BELLOWS BEACH, HAWAIIAN
ISLANDS, MAKAHA VALLEY.

Oakhurst. A cave near George, a short
distance inland from the south coast of the
Cape Province of South Africa. Over three
metres of deposit preserved a microlithic
industry of WILTON type overlying material
without backed microliths and where utilized
flakes and informal scrapers occurred to the
virtual exclusion of other implement types.
Industries related to this latter occurrence are
now known to have been widely distributed in
southern Africa between the 12th and 9th
millennia bc. The name 'Oakhurst Complex'
has been proposed for this material, but many
authorities deny its unity and prefer the term
ALBANY industry for reference to scraper
industries of this type in the south Cape coastal
region.

oats. A group of cereals, members of the genus
Avena. As in WHEATS, there are diploid
species, with two sets of chromosomes, tetraploid with four and hexaploid with six sets of
chromosomes — the results of crosses between
species. Most (but not all) cultivated oats are
hexaploid, and seem to have developed from
A. sterilis, the wild red oat, or Mediterranean
wild oat. Main cultivated varieties include the
common oat (*A. sativa*), found in cool
climates; the cultivated red oat (*A. byzantina*),
from hotter climates, and the large-seeded
naked oat (*A. nuda*), now mostly found in
Southwest Asia. Wild hexaploid species
include *A. fatua* (common wild oat) and *A.
ludoviciana* (sometimes regarded as a subspecies of *A. sterilis*), the winter wild oat.
'Wild oats' (undifferentiated) are present at
early Neolithic sites of the Near East, dating to
*c*6000 bc. This need not imply deliberate
gathering of oats, as the wild oats consistently
grow as weeds amongst wheat crops. Cultivated hexaploid oats first appeared in Bronze
Age Europe.

Obanian. On the basis of some finds from the
now-destroyed McArthur's Cave at Oban in
western Scotland, a Mesolithic culture called
Obanian has been suggested. The antler
harpoons were reminiscent of AZILIAN types,
but the stone tools were too rare for diagnosis.

Obre. Two long-lived and adjacent Neolithic
sites, near KAKANJ, Bosnia, Yugoslavia. Obre
I comprises four occupation horizons, the first
with STARČEVO pottery, dating *c*5100-4700
bc, the next three with increasing quantities of
Kakanj monochrome wares (dated *c*4500-
4200 bc). Obre II represents the most complete development of the BUTMIR culture yet
discovered, with nine habitation horizons in
three main periods (dated *c*4250-3950 bc,
*c*3900 bc and *c*3800 bc). This 1300-year cut
through the Bosnian Neolithic sequence
provides fascinating details on the evolution of
timber-framed architecture (with its increased
size, solidity and number of internal fittings),
subsistence economy (with progressive
reliance on domesticated animals, especially
cattle) and exchange systems (connections
with the Dalmatian coast and north Bosnia
fluctuate throughout the sequence).

obsidian. A black, naturally occurring
volcanic GLASS, from which artefacts may be
made. This brittle material can be easily
chipped to produce implements with an
extremely sharp edge; for this reason and
because of its splendid appearance obsidian
was highly prized by communities in several
different parts of the world. Sources of
obsidian are relatively rare: the most
important ones identified occur in the
Mediterranean islands, Anatolia, the Pacific
islands and the Americas. The outcrops are
few enough and their chemical composition
sufficiently distinct for artefacts to be traced to
a known source by techniques of CHEMICAL
ANALYSIS (especially NEUTRON ACTIVATION
and X-RAY FLUORESCENCE SPECTROMETRY).
Two DATING methods have been applied to
obsidian: OBSIDIAN HYDRATION dating and
FISSION TRACK dating.

Western Asia. A number of sources in central and eastern Turkey were exploited from c10,000 bc onwards and obsidian was traded for great distances from these sources, occurring as far south as BEIDHA in Jordan and ALI KOSH in southwest Iran. A high point in the exploitation of obsidian occurred between 6500 and 5500 bc at the Anatolian site of ÇATAL HÜYÜK, where it was used not only for bifacially flaked tools and weapons, but also for mirrors and beads demonstrating considerable technical skills.

Europe. The most important sources were on Mediterranean islands, especially Melos in the Aegean and Lipari and Sardinia in the Tyrrhenian Sea; another source occurs in Hungary. Obsidian was exploited extensively from c6000 bc to 3000 bc, and was widely traded within the Mediterranean and in eastern Europe. After 3000 bc it generally went out of favour for everyday purposes (perhaps as a result of competition from metal tools) but it continued to be used for prestige objects in some areas, especially by the MINOANS and MYCENAEANS.

Southeast Asia and the Pacific. Obsidian has been quarried and traded by western Melanesians since at least 9000 bc (MISISIL CAVE), with the earliest-used and most important source being that at TALASEA on New Britain. Much later, perhaps during LAPITA times (1st millennium BC) sources in the Admiralty and D'Entrecasteaux Islands near New Guinea came into use, and Talasea obsidian has been found in Lapita sites in NEW CALEDONIA, up to 2600 km from its source. Other Southeast Asian Pacific sources (apparently used on a local basis only) occur in Easter Island, the Lake Kerinci region of Sumatra (in use by 7000-8000 bc at Tianko Panjang Cave), north Sulawesi (in use by 5500 bc at Paso), Java, and Luzon on the Philippines. New Zealand has many sources, the main one being on Mayor Island, with products traded throughout the country from soon after initial settlement (*see* NEW ZEALAND).

The Americas. Obsidian was used throughout the Americas as a medium for stone tools, but in Mesoamerica craftsmen displayed remarkable technical skill in overcoming the material's qualities of hardness and brittleness to produce artefacts of extremely high quality. Items of jewellery, such as ear spools and LABRETS, were worked to delicate thinness,

mirrors were polished to a high finish and the intricate shaping of the enigmatic artefacts known as 'eccentrics' utterly defies the qualities of the medium.

obsidian hydration dating. A method of dating artefacts of OBSIDIAN.

Principles. Surface layers of obsidian artefacts undergo a gradual chemical change as a result of the inward diffusion of water. This 'hydration' commences as soon as the artefact is made and has surfaces exposed to the atmosphere. If the rate of hydration is known, then the thickness of the hydrated layer can be used to date the object. Rate of hydration, however, is also controlled by temperature and the chemical composition of the obsidian. Information about hydration rate must be built up for each region and can be calibrated by FISSION TRACK DATING.

Range. Dates have been obtained in Japan extending back as far as c25,000 BC. Range and applicability depends on the extent to which it has been possible to investigate hydration rate in the area. The technique is therefore limited to those regions of the world which are rich in obsidian.

occupation layer. A term applied by archaeologists to any LAYER that is believed to be an *in situ* accumulation of domestic refuse and other debris resulting from occupation of an area of a site by man. It is not at all certain that all deposits described as occupation layers necessarily originated in that way.

Oc-Eo. A site in southern Vietnam, near the border with Cambodia, thought to have been the main port of the kingdom of FUNAN, built on a Neolithic site. Excavated in the 1940s, it yielded, in addition to objects of local production, a large amount of traded goods not only from India and China, but also from western Asia and even the Mediterranean, dated to between the 2nd and 5th centuries. These finds include Roman coins of Antoninus Pius and Marcus Aurelius.

ochre. A material made of the naturally occurring iron oxide mineral limonite. A variety of colours occurs — yellow, orange, brown, red and black. Ochre has been used as a pigment in cave art and for personal decoration.

Ochre-coloured pottery. An Indian pottery type, found in the Upper Ganges valley. It is a badly fired, thick red ware with an OCHRE wash and is normally found in very worn condition. The earliest date for the ware comes from Jodhpura in Rajasthan with an early 3rd millennium BC date, but in the upper Ganges Valley it has early 2nd millennium BC dates (e.g. at ATRANJIKHERA). It thus seems to be initially contemporary with, but survives later than, the HARAPPAN CIVILIZATION. It has been found in association with a harpoon of GANGETIC HOARD type at Saipai and there are other less firm associations of this pottery type with the Gangetic hoards.

oculus. A decorative motif found on pottery, usually incised, consisting of double circles or spirals, resembling a pair of eyes. It occurs in the Spanish Copper Age, for instance at LOS MILLARES, and is also found in Ireland and northern Europe in the late Neolithic. Indeed similar motifs occur in many different contexts and too much significance should not be assigned to it: an earlier tendency to see in it a representation of a deity is not now widely followed.

Odderade interstadial. An INTERSTADIAL of the WEICHSELIAN cold stage. It has been dated by RADIOCARBON to about 58,000 bp, but this is at the extreme range of the technique and it may be earlier.

odeum [Greek *odeion*: 'music-hall']. The term perhaps originates with the Odeion built by Pericles at ATHENS in the 5th century BC and intended for musical and artistic performances of some kind. This seems to have been a large rectangular building, with a forest of internal columns, and capped by a pyramid-shaped roof. The term is loosely used, however, of many types of roofed hall. Roman examples often amount to small semicircular THEATRES, and are occasionally unroofed.

Odmut. A long-occupied cave site of the Mesolithic, Neolithic, Copper Age and Bronze Age, located in the steep Piva Valley in the Dinaric mountains of Montenegro, Yugoslavia. Seven occupation horizons have been recorded: Ia-Ib, Early and Late Mesolithic levels, dated c8100-6650 bc with a hunting economy based on ibex exploitation; II, an Early Neolithic IMPRESSED WARE level,

dated c5035-4950 bc; III, a level with no radiocarbon dates, containing pottery with DANILO and KAKANJI affinities; IV, a level with Final Neolithic black burnished ware; V-VI, two undated levels associated with Late Copper Age pottery; VII, a level with a radiocarbon date of c1710 bc and Early Bronze Age pottery.

Oenpelli Shelters. A group of five sites in the East Alligator River area of Arnhem Land, northern Australia. Three sites (Padypadiy, Nawamoyn and Malangangerr) are situated on the riverine plain, subject to wet monsoon flooding, while Tyimede I and II lie 22 km away on the adjoining Arnhem Land plateau, 240 metres above the plain in abrupt escarpment country. From 20,000 bc to approximately 3000 bc Malangangerr and Nawamoyn contained similar tool assemblages to Tyimede II (from 4500 bc), consisting of thick flake scrapers with steep edges, HORSEHOOF CORES, stone hammers, grinders, and waisted or grooved ground-edge axes, some of which resembled waisted blades from the New Guinea Highlands, where they are dated to 24,000 bc at KOSIPE. The ground-edge axes found at Malangangerr and Nawamoyn in levels dated to 20,000-16,000 bc are the oldest examples of edge-grinding known in Australia. Similarity of stone tool industries in both plain and upland zones suggested a similarity in economies during the Pleistocene when the sites were 160 km from the sea. The sudden appearance of estuarine species in shell middens of 5000-4000 bc in the Malangangerr and Nawamoyn deposits reflected rising sea levels. About 2000 years later, at all five sites, small stone points and scrapers appeared and continued until the present.

Offa's Dyke. A linear earthwork, 192 km long, built by King Offa of Mercia (*r.* 757-96) as a frontier between his kingdom and the kingdom of Powys. It consists of a large earthen bank and quarry ditch, and runs almost continuously between Treuddy and Chepstow, close to the border of England and Wales. Archaeologists, among them Sir Cyril FOX, have tried to locate secondary timber fortifications on its length, so far without success.

Offa's reign is also noteworthy for the close connections he established between MERCIA and the Carolingian empire — he married his daughter to one of CHARLEMAGNE'S sons — and the introduction of regular coinage based on pennies.

Ofnet. A cave near Nordlingen in Bavaria, best known for the composite burial of 33 skulls of early MESOLITHIC date. Some earlier PALAEOLITHIC deposits are also present in this and the nearby Klein Ofnet cave.

Ogham. A script which occurs crudely inscribed on a group of memorial pillar stones in the Celtic regions of Britain from as early as the 4th century. Usually the memorial consisted of no more than the name and descent of the dead man, and the script was equally simple. The 20 letters of the Ogham alphabet consist of a series of strokes cut across or on either side of a stem line. It was often the custom, particularly in the south and west in Wales and Cornwall, to provide a translation in Latin miniscule and this has proved important for the translation and dating of Ogham. The true origins of the script are believed to be Irish and certainly the Pictish adoption of the script is thought to belong to as late as the 8th century. Unfortunately, the pagan overtones of the Ogham stones caused many of them to be removed or defaced in succeeding centuries even though many undoubtedly commemorate Christian chiefs.

Okhotsk. A late prehistoric culture ot the coastal areas of northern and eastern Hokkaido, Skhalin and the Kurile Islands, Japan. It is intrusive to Hokkaido from the north, co-existed with the SATSUMON culture from about AD 800 to 1300, and then disappeared. The enigmatic maritime hunter-fishermen, who also kept pigs and lived in distinctive hexagonal pit houses, may have become extinct, or have been absorbed by the Satsumon people, or may have withdrawn to the north to emerge in historic times as one of the maritime peoples, such as the Gilyak, the Ulchi, or even the Sakhalin AINU.

Okvik. An early manifestation of the THULE tradition, dating to the early Christian era and named after a site on the Punuk Islands in the Bering Sea. It is characterized by a high art style and by the extensive use of polished slate and organic artefacts, as is the culture with which it is frequently linked, OLD BERING SEA. Recent radiocarbon evidence would indicate that the two were coeval; there is, however, sufficient stylistic difference between the art styles of these near neighbours to call such a proposition into question.

Old Bering Sea. An early manifestation of the western Arctic THULE tradition, often linked with the possibly contemporaneous OKVIK culture. Although both share similar traits — a highly evolved art style, polished slate tools and pottery — the exact relationship between the two is still uncertain. The art style appears to have flourished between AD 100 and 500. Sites have been found on both the Alaskan and the Siberian coasts but the major type site is on St Lawrence Island in the Bering Sea.

Oldbury. In the vicinity of former rock shelters in the Greensand ridge at Oldbury Hill near Ightham, not far from Sevenoaks in Kent, southeast England, a collection of tools of MOUSTERIAN of Acheulian type have been found. They are more abundant than in any other British Mousterian site, but poor by the standards of the caves of southwest France.

Old Copper culture. A unique middle/late ARCHAIC development occurring in the Great Lakes region of Wisconsin and Michigan, USA. Characterized by hammered and ANNEALED copper implements (such as spear points, knives, awls and ATLATL weights) its best-known assemblages are from Osceola and Ocanto. Made from surface deposits of natural copper found locally, these implements were fashioned in imitation of contemporary stone tools. Later cultures, in fact, did not develop metal technology, but reverted to stone use. Radiocarbon dates for the beginning of this culture are the subject of some argument with 5556 ± 600 bc being less favoured than the more conservative 3646 ± 600 bc. There is general agreement that 1500 bc represents the terminal date.

Old Cordilleran culture. A late Pleistocene culture which pursued a generalized hunting and gathering way of life in the high ground of the Pacific Cordilleran Mountains. The characteristic artefact is a leaf-shaped bifacial projectile point (Cascade point) which was first identified from sites in the Cascade Mountains of Washington and Oregon, USA; it has been found as far north as the FRASER RIVER VALLEY as well as down into South

America. Radiocarbon dates from these sites fall between 9000 and 5000 bc with many clustering in the middle of this period. *See* Table 9, page 552.

Old Crow Flats. The site of a PLEISTOCENE fossil-bed on the banks of the Porcupine River in the Northern Yukon, USA. A radiocarbon date in the range 22,000-28,000 bc was derived from redeposited bone material that had probably been altered by man. Although redeposition has destroyed any definite cultural associations this absolute date is among the earliest attesting the presence of early man in the Americas.

Older Dryas. A STADIAL of the WEICHSELIAN cold stage. The Older Dryas dates to between *c*12,000 and 11,800 bp. *See* YOUNGER DRYAS.

Oldowan. Stone tools from Bed I at OLDUVAI GORGE and levels of comparable date elsewhere in Africa are often attributed to an Oldowan culture. In its pure form, hand axes are absent, and it is pebble tools, especially those called 'chopping tools', which are characteristic. The subsequent 'Developed Oldowan' of M.D. Leakey, however, often has tools like hand axes. The true Oldowan belongs to the period *c*1.6 to 2 million years ago, but the Developed Oldowan is later.

Olduvai Gorge. On the edge of the Serengeti plain in northern Tanzania, this is probably the most important PALAEOLITHIC site in Africa. A fine succession of stone tool assemblages from 1.8 million years down to about 10,000 years ago has been partially investigated. Hominid remains include 'Zinjanthropus', now usually compared to *Australopithecus robustus*, and the first fossils to be named '*Homo habilis*', a group now often regarded as ancestors of *Homo erectus*. *H. erectus* and *H. sapiens* are also represented in later levels among more than 40 numbered hominids. Remains of the hunted animals and even a shelter have been recovered in excavations since the 1930s. *See also* AUSTRALOPITHECUS, HOMO ERECTUS, HOMO HABILIS, HUMAN EVOLUTION, ZINJANTHROPUS.

Olmec. A MESOAMERICAN group whose heartland lay in the low-lying swampy areas of the southern Veracruz and Tabasco provinces of Mexico. Since their cultural zenith occurred in the Middle PRE-CLASSIC, they are often proposed as the earliest civilization in Mesoamerica. The CEREMONIAL CENTRE settlement pattern is typical, although an Olmec presence is evident at numerous small sites in Mesoamerica which are presumed to be trading stations.

The Olmec were apparently great traders, but they are particulary noted for the variety and high quality of their art, especially their ceramic and jade figurines. Massive basalt heads depicting thick-lipped men in tightly fitting helmets have been found at all the major centres (*see* SAN LORENZO, TENOCHTITLAN, LA VENTA and TRES ZAPOTES). They are also noted for a distinctive black, white-rimmed kaolin pottery.

Certain elements of style are highly characteristic, including the down-turned mouth, the St Andrew Cross, infantile features and feline motifs. The were-jaguar (the transmutation of man and jaguar) is a constantly recurring theme in Olmec art.

The internal workings of Olmec society are by no means certain but it is clear that the Olmec were controllers of a widespread trade network. None of the elaborately worked stone found at the major centres occurs naturally there; jade, obsidian and even the basalt for the massive heads had to be imported, in some instances over distances of 100 km. On the other hand, unmistakeably Olmec materials have been found as far afield as El Salvador. Figurines have been found at LAS BOCAS, ceramics of all kinds at TLATILCO, cave art (*see* JUXTLAHUACA) and carved jade in Guerrero, and colossal heads in sites in Morelos.

Although San Lorenzo and La Venta were abandoned in the Pre-Classic, Olmec traits persisted well into the CLASSIC PERIOD at such sites as Tres Zapotes and CERRO DE LAS MESAS.

Olorgesailie. An important Lower PALAEOLITHIC site south of Nairobi in Kenya; the area of Mount Olorgesailie was where the Rift Valley was first recognized. One of the richest discoveries of hand axes was made here in deposits of silts of mainly volcanic origin. Baboons were hunted in large numbers. The site was occupied possibly about 400,000 years ago.

Olympia. At Elis in the Peloponnese, Southern Greece, was the sanctuary of Olympian Zeus and his consort, Hera, and the regular venue for the original Olympic Games. Perhaps first attracting use as an earth shrine and oracle (*see* DELPHI and DELOS), the site shows signs of continuous occupation from early in the 3rd millennium BC. The Games were celebrated on a four-yearly cycle, the Olympiad, which came to form the basis of a Greek system of dating. The first Olympiad is dated to 776 BC, but tradition places the commencement of the Games in the 9th century, with ascriptions variously to Heracles or Pelops as founder. Out of regard for the sanctuary and for the pan-Hellenic nature of the Games, a special neutral status was given to the area of Elis, and an armistice (*ekecheiria*) was proclaimed and duly observed for the period of the festivities. Helped by this background, the Games showed an unbroken record of celebration from 776 BC to 393 AD, when Theodosius I abolished them.

The connection between religious rites and ritual games seems to be characteristically Greek. No married women were permitted to be present, and competition was on an individual basis only, with participation limited to free-born Greek-speaking men and boys. Emphasis seems to be upon bodily perfection, and wrestling, rather than racing, was reckoned the finest test of prowess. Competitors participated naked, although there is some discussion by scholars as to what naked means in this context. Apart from purely athletic events there were recitations (one of the most famous being by Herodotus of portions of hiš history), and the emperor Nero had some special musical events staged which he could win. Accommodation for competitors may have been under canvas, or possibly some slept in the open. In 330 BC a hostel, the Leonidaion, was erected and paid for by Leonidas of Naxos. Possibly reserved originally for more distinguished visitors, the building was converted to a residence in the 2nd century AD for the governor of the province of Achaia.

The sacred precinct itself, called the Altis, contains the great temples to Hera and Zeus. The 7th-century BC Temple of Hera competes for the position of earliest monumental temple in Greece, showing construction from mud-brick and timber, with terracotta tiles and antefixes. The Temple of Zeus is a grand-scale concept, put up in the 460s BC, and had elaborately sculptured pediments and metopes. Each victor in the Games had the right to put up a statue (a realistic representation if he had won three events) and gradually a large number of these, and of other votive statues of heroes, gods and kings etc began to accumulate. Many of these competitor statues were probably destroyed for incorporation into the House of Nero before that emperor's arrival — presumably so that he should not feel overwhelmed by the competition!

The dedication of precious votive offerings was a long-standing ritual, practised more obtrusively by some than others. The Spartans attached a gold shield to the pediment of the Temple of Zeus in 456 to commemorate their victory at Tanagra, while excavation has shown that many votive offerings were buried during the alteration of the STADIUM, presumably to make them secure from damage or sacrilege. Eventually this practice took on aspects of the Roman triumph: Mummius, for instance, in 146 BC dedicated 21 gilded shields by attaching them to the metopes of the same temple.

The end of the sanctuary came in 426 AD with the order from Theodosius II for its destruction — damage that was only compounded by earthquakes in 522 and 551. During the 5th and 6th centuries a small Christian community converted the workshop of Pheidias (set up originally for work on the giant chryselephantine statue of Zeus) into a church. Local flooding and landslide left the area more or les untouched until the 19th century.

Olynthus. A classical Greek settlement at Toronaios Bay, Chalkidiki, familar from the speeches of Demosthenes (the so-called Olynthiacs), and of central importance as an example of Greek town-planning and the Hellenic house in the period 430-348 BC. Some late Neolithic settlement is followed after a gap by Iron Age occupation by Thracian tribes, perhaps from about 1000 BC. The 5th and 4th centuries BC saw the classical Greek town caught up in alliances, misalliances, intrigues and wars variously with Persia, Athens, Sparta and Macedon, and it was Macedon that brought final destruction in 348 BC, despite all Demosthenes' efforts to organize Athenian aid. Excavation shows a distinction between an earlier, rather irregular town, and a newer area laid out on a grid plan. Four north-south avenues are crossed by 13 streets, enclosing blocks of mud-brick housing. Many of the houses show an internal courtyard, sometimes colonnaded, and a south-facing dining room. In some cases, a second storey (possibly of bedrooms) is reached by a wooden staircase from the courtyard. The roof is typically pitched and tiled. There are important examples of pebble mosaic floors, some with mythological scenes, and of a bathroom with pottery tub. Inscriptional evidence from the houses gives information on their sale, rental and mortgage. The houses have also produced several coin hoards.

Omo. The Omo River basin is in Ethiopia north of Lake Turkana [formerly Lake Rudolf]. The 800-metre thick Shungura formation spanning the time from over 3 million to under 1 million years ago is of outstanding importance as a basis for dating other sites throughout Africa, because its time-scale is unusually well fixed by PALAEO-MAGNETIC studies and a series of POTASSIUM ARGON dates. Mammal remains suitable for correlation are found at all levels. In addition, hominids are numerous, though unfortunately much less complete than at sites like KOOBI FORA. Stone tools (some possibly as old as 2.5 million years) are known from various levels. Two hominid skulls of late PLEISTOCENE date are also known, but their status and exact date are unclear.

Omori. A shell midden in Tokyo, excavated by Edward S. Morse in 1877. This was the first scientific excavation of an archaeological site in Japan. 'JOMON' is the Japanese translation of the term 'cord-mark' used by Morse to describe the pottery from the site.

onager. A race of Asiatic wild ASS. Sometimes used in a wider sense to mean Asiatic wild asses in general.

Onion Portage. A site with a long strati-graphic record located on the Kobuck River in northeast Alaska. 70 living surfaces, each sealed by a layer of silt, show evidence of human occupation dating from c8000 BC to historic times. Tool assemblages, mostly blades, bifaces and associated cores, from the lowest level (designated Akmak) bear some

resemblance to pre-ceramic complexes in Asia. The overlying Kobuck complex (6200-6000 BC) contained similar tool types but they were of limited variety, suggesting that they represent only a part of a much larger complex. These two levels together are assigned to the Paleo-Arctic Tradition.

A hiatus in occupation of some 2000 years is followed by complexes of the Northern Archaic Tradition, Palisades (4000-2000 BC) and Portage (2600-2200 BC). Immediately overlying these are, in order, the DENBIGH FLINT COMPLEX (2200-1800 BC), CHORIS (1500-500 BC) and NORTON/IPIUTAK (AD 400-800).

The excellent vertical stratigraphy of this site makes it the major reference for all western Arctic chronologies, especially when taken together with the horizontal stratigraphy of CAPE KRUSENSTERN.

opole. A series of centralized territories in Poland between the 7th and 11th centuries. Each *opole* was dominated by a fortified timber citadel which often had large and complex defences; examples of these have been excavated at Leczyic and Szeligi.

Opone. A trade station of the early centuries AD on the coast of the modern Somalia. Mentioned in the *Periplus of the Erythraean Sea*, it is probably to be identified with the modern HAFUN, some 150 km south of Cape Guardafui.

oppidum. A Roman term for a town which served as an administrative centre. Caesar referred to several of the Iron Age settlements of Gaul as *oppida* and archaeologists have adopted the term to apply to all large and complex settlements of the later LA TÈNE Iron Age. These *oppida* are normally defended settlements, often HILLFORTS, and may cover several hundred hectares. Excavations have produced evidence that these sites served as manufacturing and trading centres and many were probably administrative centres also; it is reasonable to describe these communities as proto-urban or urban. *See* BIBRACTE, MANCHING.

optical emission spectrometry. A technique of CHEMICAL ANALYSIS.

Principle. A sample is volatilized or vapour-ized by a spark discharge or laser beam. This also excites electrons within the sample, causing light to be emitted. The wavelengths of this light are related to the chemical composition of the sample. Thus, if the spectrum of light is analysed, it is possible to calculate the concentration of different elements.

Materials. Metals, glasses (natural and man-made), pottery. Between 5 and 100 mg of material are needed.

Applications. Optical emission spectrometry has been used with great success to establish the sources of OBSIDIAN artefacts in the Near East and Mediterranean. This is done by matching the concentrations of TRACE ELEMENTS found in artefacts with those of the obsidian sources. Similar work has been carried out on pottery, although the larger number of possible origins for this material makes sources difficult to establish. The technique has also been used to investigate minor and trace elements in bronze and copper artefacts.

optical square. A SURVEYING instrument, used for setting-out right angles on the ground (*see* GRID).

Opunohu. A valley on Moorea, SOCIETY ISLANDS, which has preserved remains of many late prehistoric structures including MARAE and house foundations. The Opunohu settlement pattern has been used to throw light on the hierarchical society of Tahiti-Moorea at European contact.

opus incertum [Latin: 'irregular work']. Technical term used by Vitruvius (Roman architectural writer, *c*30 BC) to describe the irregular stone surface that was commonly applied to Republican-period walls, as a decorative facing for the concrete inner core.

opus reticulatum [Latin: 'net-like work']. Technical term used by Vitruvius (Roman architectural writer, *c*30 BC) to describe the diamond pattern of square stones that was often used as a decorative facing to an inner rough concrete core. The pattern is popular, roughly in the period *c*100 BC-200 AD.

opus sectile [Latin: 'sectioned work']. Technical term used by Vitruvius (Roman architectural writer, *c*30 BC) of a decorative type of floor or wall surface. In a 'mosaic' made up of relatively large segments, geometric, floral and figured designs are made up from specially cut, thin pieces of coloured marble. The technique is found over the period roughly *c*200 BC-400 AD.

opus signinum. Latin technical term used by Vitruvius (Roman architectural writer, *c*30 BC) of a kind of waterproof plaster, commonly employed to seal walls and floors in bath complexes. The mix was essentially a lime mortar with an aggregate of coarse pieces of broken terracotta.

Oquendo. *See* CHIVATEROS.

oracle bones. Animal scapulae or tortoise plastrons used in ancient China for divination. A few examples have been found at Neolithic sites as KEXINGZHUANG (*see also* DADUNZI). More important are the oracle bones of the 13th-11th centuries BC found in large numbers at ANYANG, for these were often inscribed. The language of the Anyang oracle inscriptions is Chinese; their highly sophisticated script remains the earliest known form of the Chinese writing system, as pre-Anyang inscriptions, perhaps confined to more perishable materials, have not yet been found.

The Anyang oracle bones were prepared for use by drilling cavities in one side; the oracle was somehow read from the crack that appeared in the other side when heat was applied to the cavity. The inscription was carved on the bone after the divination was performed and may have had some commemorative purpose. It ordinarily records a question addressed by the SHANG king to his deceased ancestors, or the response to the question, or even the ultimate outcome of the matter divined about. The subjects of divination comprise a limited range of royal concerns and the inscriptions supply little of the practical or commercial information encountered at an early stage in Near Eastern texts. The Anyang kings enquired chiefly about war, hunting, rainfall, harvests, sickness, their consorts' childbearing, the fortune of the coming week and, above all, sacrifices. From the names of kings mentioned as recipients of sacrifice, scholars have been able to reconstruct a genealogy of the Shang royal house almost identical to that given in much later historical texts, and it was this that secured the

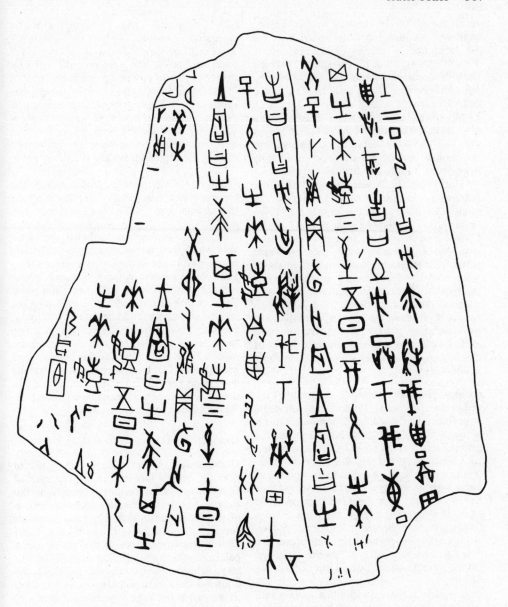

Scapula from Anyang inscribed with the record of several divinations. The subject of enquiry is the fortune of the coming week, and following each enquiry the oracle's prediction and the events that fulfilled it are recorded. This well written and unusually full inscription dates from the reign of Wu Ding, the fourth Anyang king. Height 22 cm.

identification of the Anyang site as the last capital of the Shang dynasty. Apart from the far more limited corpus of inscriptions on bronze RITUAL VESSELS, the oracle texts are the only documents left by the Shang civilization. However, in Shang as in later times the ordinary form of writing is likely to have been brush-writing, of which a few examples survive; no doubt because of the different writing materials and techniques, the oracle texts and the bronze inscriptions differ in calligraphy from brush-writing and from each other.

Until recently it was assumed that the practice of inscribing oracle bones was a monopoly of the Shang court. In 1977, however, excavation of a palace site at QISHAN Fengchucun in Shaanxi province disclosed a large hoard of oracle bones, some of which carry inscriptions showing that divinations were performed at Qishan on behalf of a predynastic ZHOU ruler who was at least a nominal vassal of the Shang king. After their conquest of Shang the Zhou apparently gave up scapulimancy in favour of divination using milfoil sticks and guided by the hexagrams of the *Yi jing* or *Classic of Changes*, a diviner's handbook.

Orange [Roman Arausio]. Augustan COLONIA in southern France, of strategic importance for the control of communications along the Rhône. In the pre-Roman period the general area was occupied by rich and powerful Celtic tribes, notably the Tricastini, who seem to have been prepared to co-operate as much with the newly arrived Romans, as they had previously with the Greek colonists at Massilia (MARSEILLES). Of the Roman town (probably enclosing some 70 hectares), two monuments are particularly well-preserved. The TRIUMPHAL ARCH of Tiberius (perhaps from about 20 AD) is located just outside the old line of the Roman fortifications. It has three arches decorated with relief-work which depicts various military and naval triumphs and processions, together with some mythological themes and floral motifs. During the medieval period the Arch was fortified by the Princes of Orange, and came to be known as the Chateau de l'Arc. The Roman THEATRE is still used for open-air performances in the summer, and can currently accommodate some 7,000 people. Probably constructed in the 1st century AD, the theatre is remarkable for the remains of its stage building, in front of which there still exists the groove for the storing of the curtain. The back wall still stands to a height of some 37 metres, and preserves anchorage points that were probably used for the tensioning of a canvas awning over part of the theatre. A lime kiln near the theatre has produced a notable series of fragments which document various local land surveys and, in particular, describe the terms of confiscation and redistribution that were applied at the time of the original founding of the *colonia*.

Orangia. An important but undated site in the Orange River valley in the extreme south of the Orange Free State, South Africa. The artefacts are analogous to those of the PIETERSBURG complex from further to the north, with which they are presumably broadly contemporary. In the undisturbed levels at Orangia were preserved at least six semi-circular settings of stones, open to the west and some 2-3 metres in diameter. Inside each setting the surface of the gound had been hollowed away, and it seems reasonable to interpret these features as the remains of shelters or sleeping places. Since part of the site has been eroded away, up to 12 of these shelters may originally have been present: assuming that all were in use at the same time, a population of some 20-30 individuals may be indicated.

Oranian. *See* IBEROMAURUSIAN.

Orchomenos. A major Bronze Age site in Boeotia, central Greece. The rocky spur of Orchomenos was occupied throughout the Bronze Age, but, although extensive remains of the Early and Middle HELLADIC periods survive, the MYCENAEAN levels are badly eroded. However it seems that there was a palace or other large building on the hill at this stage, while to the east lies the THOLOS tomb known as the Treasury of Minyas. Some 20 km to the east is the huge Mycenaean fortress of Gla, defended by walls of CYCLOPEAN MASONRY some six metres thick and still surviving in places to a height of three metres. This fortress and a number of subsidiary forts must have defended the eastern approaches to the Copais basin, which, according to ancient literary tradition, was drained and cultivated by the people of Orchomenos in Mycenaean times.

Ordos. A steppe region of western Inner

Mongolia bounded on the south by the GREAT WALL and on the north by the northern bend of the Yellow River. The name is commonly applied to bronze daggers, plaques, and other ANIMAL STYLE metalwork thought to come from the Sino-Mongolian border region: these so-called Ordos bronzes, mostly unprovenanced, are well represented in Westen collections. The distinctive metal culture of the Ordos reaches back as far as the latter part of the 2nd millennium BC, a date fixed by the discovery at ANYANG of knives with animal-head pommels closely related to Ordos types. From that time until the HAN dynasty the Ordos steppe was the home of semi-nomadic Indo-European peoples whose culture can be regarded as an eastern province of a vast Eurasian continuum of Scytho-Siberian cultures. Owing to its position on the northern frontier of China the Ordos was probably the main channel by which Chinese influences were transmitted to the steppes; it was also the route by which foreign elements reached China, especially during Eastern ZHOU and Han (*see* DIAN). The metal plaques that account for a large proportion of unprovenanced Ordos bronzes have parallels excavated from sites in Mongolia dated to the last three centuries BC and tentatively associated with the XIONGNU. The pictorial or narrative compositions common among these plaques, many including human figures, are typical also of Sarmatian metalwork.

orientalizing. Essentially an art history term, used of various periods and cultures in antiquity, when a 'western' production shows evidence for influence from the Near, Middle or Far East. An example would be the borrowing by Greek BLACK-FIGURE painters, notably Corinthian and Athenian, of numerous abstract, vegetable and animal motifs from Syrian and Phoenician art, around 720-550 BC.

Orissa. A district of eastern India, well known for its Jaina rock-cut temples, dating from the 1st century BC and 1st century AD. The best-known examples are at Udayagiri and Khandragiri.

Ornament Horizon. Name sometimes given to a very brief phase of the British Middle Bronze Age, marked by the appearance in hoards of a number of ornaments and tools of Scandinavian and north German type. This influx seems to have given a boost to the native bronze industry, which started producing such forms as twisted torcs, armlets, ribbed bracelets and coiled rings as well as socketed axes and sickles.

Orongo. A village of 48 stone houses with CORBELLED roofs on the rim of Rano Kao volcanic crater on EASTER ISLAND. Famous as the gathering-place for the annual 'birdman' ceremony which took place on the island, the Orongo village was probably built in the 16th century AD and the ceremony itself continued until *c*1867. Adjacent to the village are rock-carvings of birdmen holding eggs. The corbelled houses are unique in Oceania and South American parallels have been claimed for them.

Osa. A stratified settlement of the Late Mesolithic and Early Neolithic, located in a peat bog in the Lubana lowlands on the Piesteně River, Latvia, USSR. The stratigraphy at excavation B comprises three levels: 1 Mesolithic levels with a rich bone and antler industry, with radiocarbon dates of *c*5200-4800 bc; 2 an Early Neolithic occupation with Osa type pottery and similar bone tools, with radiocarbon dates of 3950-3800 bc; and 3 a thin layer of the PIT-COMB WARE group, with a radiocarbon date of *c*2050 bc.

Oseberg Ship. Found under a burial mound in southeast Norway and now reconstructed in the Oslo Ship Museum, the Oseberg Ship is a fine example of a large sophisticated VIKING warship. It was found with most of its timbers intact and its main burial chamber still filled with most of its contents. Among the objects in the chamber were the skeletons of a man, dogs and horses, a chest containing oil lamps and personal items, a wooden bed and a sledge. The ship itself was plank-built and had a pronounced keel, a large mast and a beautifully carved stern.

Oshoro Mikasayama. *See* MEGALITHS (JAPAN).

Osinovoe Lake. *See* AMUR NEOLITHIC.

Ostia. A Roman settlement situated in antiquity at the mouth of the River Tiber, but now inland and up-river. The town was for a long time effectively the port of ancient Rome. Traditional early links with a salt industry are quite plausible, but little trace had been found. The earliest evidence we have suggests a 4th-century BC fort with defences of tufa block and an area of only some two hectares. The foundation is almost certainly Roman, and may be one fort in a series forming a coastal guard for the growing city of Rome. Development through the stage of naval base (probably in connection with the PUNIC WARS) to harbour seems to have been quite rapid. The demands of Rome's growing population, particularly for corn imports, soon boosted the port to an area of some 64 hectares, which were now guarded by new walls (early 1st century BC).

However, the problems created by silt deposits, sandbanks and an advancing coastline, which have today left Ostia well inland, were already making themselves felt. In an enterprise initiated by Augustus, and carried on by Claudius and Nero, a new large harbour was constructed just north of the Tiber mouth, and two canals dug to connect it to the Tiber and thereby to Rome. Experience soon showed that the new harbour was too exposed to the open sea and the weather. After some shipping disasters, Trajan eventually excavated a large hexagonal basin a little further inland (now Lago Traiano) and encouraged the development of a new port in the immediate area — Portus Traiani (later Portus Romae and now Porto). A further canal was dug to the sea, the *fossa Traiana*. This had the effect of separating off a stretch of land that was to become an island necropolis for the new Portus (now Isola Sacra). Whereas it might have been thought that this intense activity which essentially by-passed Ostia would have blighted the earlier port, the reverse is the case. The 2nd century AD proved to be a period of unprecedented prosperity, which has left the most plentiful traces in today's ruins. The new harbours were largely administered through Ostia, and presumably much of the workforce chose to live at Ostia. Pressure on building land brought extensive new building programmes that concentrated in particular on high-density housing. The ATRIUM-type house, familiar from POMPEII, gave way to the new INSULA apartment-block. The *insula* might be up to five storeys high, and the ground floor was often devoted to a row of shops. Unlike Rome, however, where the *insula* also became a standardized unit, there is little evidence at Ostia of slum and squalor. The second century also saw the construction of an AQUEDUCT, and the erection of no fewer than three major imperial suites of public baths, which were in addition to many smaller establishments. The greater capacity of the new harbours had the effect, as so often, not only of facilitating existing traffic, but of attracting yet further amounts of shipping, and diverting it from elsewhere. The need for depositories and warehouses (HORREA) became paramount not only because of a general need for storage, but also because the re-shipping of loads upstream to Rome in smaller vessels required temporary transit storage. The typical warehouse became bigger, upper storeys were added, and the buildings were sometimes equipped with the sophistication of underfloor ventilation.

The increase in trade brought prosperity to many areas of the city. In a double colonnade behind the THEATRE a large number of small offices housed agencies for all the major shipping destinations and types of trade. In the city as a whole over 800 shops are known, and some trades, such as building and ship-construction, show particular signs of a boom period.

The small scale of the theatre, seating perhaps only some 3000-4000 spectators, suggests perhaps that the more urbane of entertainments had little appeal for most of the perhaps 80,000-strong population, and some have proposed the existence of an amphi-theatre. The cosmopolitanism of a thriving port is, however, quite clear in the local proliferation of cults, with representation for Serapis, Isis, Cybele, a Jewish synagogue, fifteen lodges of MITHRAS, and eventually competition from a newly established Christianity.

With the 3rd century AD political instability at Rome combined with an economic recession brought a general decline in shipping. Constantine gave explicit favour to Portus in preference to Ostia, and gave the rival port the grand title of *civitas flavia constantiniana portuensis*. The failure of commerce provoked the emergence instead of a seaside-resort function for Ostia, and expensive houses for the urban rich begin to appear. Even this latter-day use, however, decayed with the general breakdown of imperial administration in the 5th century, and malarial swamps led to further desertion.

Ostionoid, Ostiones. One of three associated ceramic series developed by Irving Rouse and José Cruxent to facilitate cultural comparison in the Greater Antilles area. Seen as transitional to CHICOID and MEILLACOID, the Ostionoid appears in c650 AD in Puerto Rico, where it overlays more elaborate SALADOID materials. Typically, vessels are smooth, finished in red monochrome slip, often with plain tabular lugs. The introduction of new artefacts in the Ostiones phase (for example, petalloid celts, pottery stamps and ZEMIS) indicates an external influence, possibly MESOAMERICAN. The presence of BALL COURTS and YOKES, although not in unequivocal association with Ostionoid material, also seems to confirm this. Agricultural activity is indicated by the presence of GRIDDLES used in the preparation of MANIOC.

ostrakon. Greek term for a pottery sherd, most commonly used of inscribed examples, and in association with the classical Greek voting practice of *ostrakismos* (ostracism), a 5th-century BC political ceremony, notably at ATHENS, in which each citizen could write upon a potsherd (usually in paint or ink) the name of someone whom he wished to see banished. If sufficient votes were cast against one person (the number seems to have been 6,000), the person named would be banished for ten years. The usage of inscribed sherds seems to have spread to Egypt with the Greek conquest, and from the 3rd century BC onwards we have evidence for the practice widening beyond voting, to include religious and magical texts and incantations, educational exercises, tax returns, and letters.

Ostrogoth. *See* GOTH.

Ostrów Lednicki. An island in Lake Lednika which is one of the most important medieval sites in Poland. Excavations began in the mid-19th century and established that the earliest 9th-century settlement lay within natural defences, but that in the early 10th century the site was fortified by a 10-metre high rampart. This rampart had an interesting construction, consisting of a series of boxes formed by horizontal planks bonded internally with clay. In the third phase, at the end of the 10th century, the fort was levelled to make way for the grandiose citadel which was one of the official residences of the Polish rulers. The official secular and religious buildings inside the stronghold consisted of a stone-built palace with an inner courtyard. It had an upper storey and gallery and dome carried on four columns. The chapel had a cross plan reminiscent of Byzantine churches of this date. The wooden dwellings and workshops were concentrated outside the main centre.

Archaeologists claim to have found dramatic evidence of the 11th-century Kievan attacks on Ostrów Ledniki. One timber bridgehead, for example, was burnt, and in the lake muds were found the carbonized remains of a bridge, dug-out boats, and skeletons of men and horses with helmets, swords and other military equipment.

Otakinini. An excavated MAORI *pa* (hillfort) on a small island in the South Kaipara Harbour, North Island, New Zealand. The site has three defensive phases from the 14th-18th centuries AD, and after 1500 its inner citadel was defended by palisades and large raised fighting platforms. Cultural affiliations are Classic Maori. *See also* KAURI POINT, PA, TIRIMOANA.

Otoe Koyo. *See* MEGALITHS (JAPAN).

otoliths. Small calcareous concretions from the middle ear region of fish, quite commonly found on archaeological sites. Otoliths are normally recovered by wet SIEVING of deposits from excavations. Study of otoliths recovered in this way allows the identification of the fish species present on the site. It may also be possible to estimate the size of fish. Microscopic studies of growth layers within otoliths allow estimation of age and even of the season during which fish were caught.

Otomani. The Rumanian equivalent of the Hungarian FÜZESABONY group, Otomani is an earlier Bronze Age culture of the mid-2nd millennium bc found primarily in the lowlands of the Banat as well as the Carpathian foothills to the east, in northwest Rumania. A high proportion of Otomani settlements are artificially or naturally fortified, often by the use of water. Tells are frequent, whilst the type site, near Marghiţa, is a citadel site overlooking the eastern edge of the Hungarian plain. Cemeteries are as yet uncommon, with inurned cremation the principal burial rite. Black burnished ware with bossed decoration on one-handled cups is the most frequent pottery type.

Otranto mosaic. The Romanesque cathedral at Otranto in Apulia, southern Italy, houses a unique treasure — a mosaic pavement that covers the entire nave and aisles of the building from the entrance to the chancel. The mosaic, which was laid between 1163-6, was designed by a priest named Pantaleon and shows certain similarities in its narrative style and colour to the Bayeux tapestry. The central theme is the history of the universe, which is developed around a massive tree running the length of the nave; stemming from its leafy boughs run a myriad of different ideas. The tree is guarded by two elephants at its base and as it climbs it contains a host of characters, both historical and mythological: Alexander the Great with two griffins on one side for example, and the building of the Tower of Babel on the other, followed by the life of Noah and his ark full of animals. Towards the top of the tree is a series of roundels containing the signs of the zodiac and the activities of the months. Various biblical episodes including the Last Judgement are depicted on other parts of the floor, and among them is the rather incongruous figure of King Arthur. Similar mosaics existed at other Apulian Romanesque cathedrals, but this splendid work is the only one to have survived.

Otzaki. A Neolithic TELL site on the Thessalian plain of northern Greece. Early levels have yielded pottery of IMPRESSED WARE type, labelled Pre-Sesklo, but the main occupation belongs to the Middle Neolithic SESKLO culture. This stratum has rectangular mudbrick houses with internal buttresses and abundant painted pottery.

Ousegate. *See* YORK.

Ovčarovo. A TELL settlement and two cemeteries near Trgovište, northeast Bulgaria, with an Early Neolithic occupation with pits and post holes stratified beneath 13 Copper Age habitation levels, dated to much of the 4th millennium bc. After the initial construction of a rectangular wooden palisade enclosure, houses were closely packed into the enclosed space. Some of the houses were two-storeyed; in the upper storey of one house, more than 100 pots were stored. In level IX a unique cult scene was found, in which 26 miniature objects (altars, tables, figurines etc) were arranged as if to depict a shrine. Many ritual objects were incised with simple signs. Both cemeteries date to the Copper Age.

Overton Hill. *See* AVEBURY.

ovicaprid. *See* SHEEP.

Oxtotitlan. *See* JUXTLAHUACA CAVES.

Oxus treasure. A large hoard of gold and silver metalwork found in 1877 on the bank of the Oxus River near the present Afghan-Russian border. The objects include a variety of jewellery, ornamental plaques, figurines, chariot models and vessels. They show a great variety of influences, including ACHAEMENID Persian, SCYTHIAN and even Egyptian, but many may have been made by local Sarmatian craftsmen. The hoard is dated to the late 5th century BC.

oxygen isotope ratio. *See* DEEP SEA CORES.

Oxyrhynchus. An ancient Egyptian town some 11 km west of the Nile on the left bank of the Bahr Yusuf, best known for its papyri texts. Oxyrhynchus was a regional capital, and derives its name from the fish (Greek *oxyrhynchus*: 'sharp-nosed') with which the locally worshipped deity of Seth was associated. Little is known of the town itself save that it seems to have been reasonably prosperous in the Roman period, and developed into a church and monastic centre during the Coptic period. Peculiarly favourable local conditions contributed to the preservation of a large number of fragmentary papyri, mostly carrying Greek texts, that had been written or copied from the HELLENISTIC period onwards. These texts are now of central importance in the reconstruction of the manuscript tradition of a number of major classical authors, including Homer, Pindar and Aristotle. Also included are previously lost works or sections of works, as with Menander, and previously unknown authors, such as the so-called Oxyrhynchus Historian. There are also local administrative documents and a number of scientific tracts, some with illustrations.

Oyu. *See* MEGALITHS (JAPAN).

Ozette. A group of sites located on the western tip of the Olympic Peninsula, Washington State, USA. Three to five centuries ago the principal site, a Makah Indian village, was completely engulfed by a mudslide which preserved several plank houses and their contents. The over 60,000 artefacts recovered, including whale-hunting paraphernalia, weaving equipment and wooden bowls, constitute a splendid NORTHWEST COAST TRADITION assemblage.

Ozieri. A Late Neolithic and Copper Age culture of Sardinia, dated to the late 4th and 3rd millennia bc. It is characterized by the use of rock-cut tombs (*see* ANGHELU RUJU). Artefacts include pottery decorated with incised designs, figurines of marble and occasional copper and silver objects.

P

pa. The MAORI term for a fortified village. Excavated examples, mostly in the North Island of NEW ZEALAND, are of Classic Maori date. Most are defended by ditch-bank combinations or scarped terraces (KAURI POINT, OTAKANINI, TIRIMOANA), but some were built up from swamps or lake beds and defended by multiple rows of palisades (LAKE MANGAKAWARE, LAKE NGAROTO).

Paccaicasa. The earliest stone tool complex of the AYACUCHO Valley which may represent man's earliest presence in South America. Radiocarbon dates of 17,620 bc (± 3000), 14,070 bc (± 1200) and 12,730 bc (± 1400) were obtained from sloth bone found in association with crude stone tools and flakes of volcanic tuff. These early dates have not gained wide acceptance since there is some disagreement as to whether the 'tools' are man-made or the product of some natural action.

Pachamac. A CEREMONIAL CENTRE and home of an oracle, located in the Lurin Valley 17 km south of Lima, Peru. It was probably established in the Early INTERMEDIATE PERIOD and was definitely functioning in the MIDDLE HORIZON. Material from graves associated with the old temple building have defined three ceramic styles. The earliest of these (a polychrome technique known as the Pachamac style) incorporates elements of the TIAHUANACO and HUARI styles. A later building, the Temple of the Sun, was erected by the INCA; its associated buildings contained richly appointed female mummies, some of which bear evidence of ritual strangulation.

Pacitanian [Patjitanian]. A pebble and flake tool industry with a small percentage of bifaces found in valleys in south-central JAVA, Indonesia. Believed to be of Upper Pleistocene date, the industry may have been made by the later *Homo erectus* populations of Java, although such tools have not yet been found in direct association with the Javanese hominids.

See also CHOPPER/CHOPPING TOOL tradition.

Padina. A settlement on the western edge of the Iron Gates Gorge of the River Danube, comprising a late Mesolithic occupation (A) dated to 7400-5800 bc and an Early Neolithic STARČEVO occupation (B), dated to *c*5100-4600 bc. Unlike at LEPENSKI VIR, the Padina site revealed the association of trapezoidal houses with both Mesolithic finds in level A and with Starčevo pottery in level B. Large numbers of Mesolithic and Starčevo burials occur between the houses at Padina: the skeletal type is CROMAGNOID (i.e. the descendants of the local Palaeolithic stock).

Padypadiy. *See* OENPELLI SHELTERS.

Paestum [Greek: Poseidonia]. A Greek coastal settlement in Campania, southwest Italy, some 100 km south of NAPLES, famous today for its three well-preserved Greek temples. There is some occupational evidence for both Palaeolithic and Neolithic settlement, and there is a Copper Age necropolis at Contrada GAUDO, just north of the classical town. Traditional sources ascribe the Greek colony to SYBARIS, and proto-Corinthian pottery suggests a date in the second half of the 7th century BC. Lucanians from the hinterland took and held the town from about 390-273 BC, altering the name to Paiston. From 273 BC, as a Roman COLONIA, the town enjoyed a period of prosperity until problems with silt deposits and the gradual growth of malarial swamps made the area progressively uninhabitable from perhaps the 2nd century AD onwards. There was some early medieval use of the Temple of Athena as a church, but by the 9th century the location was probably deserted, and remained so until the 18th century. Apart from the three great temples, which should probably be ascribed, in chronological order, to Hera (formerly known as the Basilica, mid-6th century BC), to Athena (formerly assigned to Ceres or Demeter, late 6th century BC) and again to Hera (formerly associated with Neptune or Poseidon, mid-5th century BC), there are traces of a number of smaller temples. The surviving town walls are of Lucanian period and later, and the Roman town has left an AMPHITHEATRE, and evidence for a Republican-period FORUM with temple, shops, bath buildings, and housing. A necropolis just north of the town has Lucanian painted tombs of the 4th century BC, and just south of the town is yet a third cemetery where the most interesting tomb is the so-called Tomb of the Diver (c480-470 BC), with 'Etruscan'-style painted decoration.

Paffrath ware. Hard-fired ware with a black finish, made from the 10th or 11th century until the 13th century at Paffrath, a short distance east of COLOGNE. These pots are known from rescue excavations in the 1950s at Paffrath and from finds elsewhere in Western Europe. The best-known products of this centre are the so-called handled ladles — small cooking pots or bowls with a curved handle — which commonly occur on sites in the British Isles and Scandinavia.

Pagan. A city in northern BURMA, close to the confluence of the Irrawaddy and the Chindwin, formed in 849 by the union of 19 villages and originally called Arimaddanapura. Rulers of the Pagan dynasty (1044-1287) dotted the plain with hundreds of Buddhist monuments made of baked brick, which contributed to the deforestation of the area now known as the 'Dry Zone' of Burma. Until its conquest by the Mongols in 1287 Pagan, next to the irrigated rice-growing plain of Kyaukse, was the capital of an expanding Burman kingdom which included the MON country to the south and areas inhabited by THAI peoples (Shan States) in the east. Abandoned as capital ever since, Pagan is now a major tourist attraction.

Paglicci. A cave on the Gargano peninsula on the Adriatic coast of Italy. Recent excavations have yielded a long sequence of Upper Palaeolithic levels of GRAVETTIAN or Epi-Gravettian type. There are engraved objects from several levels, dating back to 20,000 bc, a few cave paintings and some human remains.

pagus. Latin term for the smallest unit of land in the territorial system of Italy: a country area, not a village or town, and to be distinguished from OPPIDUM and VICUS. The inhabitants of this 'locality' were called *pagani*. The later Christian use of *pagani* ('pagans, heathen') may reflect the commonplace cliché of the country bumpkin in urbane literature, or may arise from a reference to their difference of status as 'outside the city' of God, or as 'civilian, non-serving' as opposed to 'Christ-militant'.

Painted Grey ware. An Indian pottery type found over a large part of northern India, with its centre of distribution in the eastern Punjab and the central Ganges Valley. It is fine, wheel-made, thin-walled ware, with a grey surface decorated with geometric designs in red or black paint. The forms that occur most frequently are a shallow dish and a deeper bowl. It occurs in deposits of the later 2nd millennium and early 1st millennium BC, and is apparently associated with the use of iron from an early date. The distribution of Painted Grey ware coincides with the main areas occupied by ARYAN groups at a later date, and excavations have shown that the ware occurs in low levels on many of the sites recorded in Vedic traditions. Many authorities therefore believe that Painted Grey ware was the pottery used by the early Aryans in India.

Painted Pottery cultures. *See* YANGSHAO.

Pair-non-Pair. An engraved cave some 30 km from Bordeaux, western France. 19th-century digging revealed one MOUSTERIAN and several Upper PALAEOLITHIC levels. The engravings are possibly AURIGNACIAN. A flute was found, and there were also human remains.

Palacio. *See* TIAHUANACO.

palaeobotany. The study of fossil plants. Remains of plants may be split into two groups: microfossils, which can only be seen under a microscope, and macrofossils, which are large enough to be seen under modest magnification. Microfossils include pollen, other types of spore, and phytoliths. Macrofossils include such remains as wood, seeds and other tough parts of plant anatomy.

palaeoethnobotany. The study of plants used by man in the past.

Palaeolithic. The Old Stone Age, representing the first and by far the longest period of man's existence, from the first tool-makers 2.5 million years ago to the end of the PLEISTOCENE geological period *c*10,000 years ago (*see* Tables 4-6, pages 417-9). The Palaeolithic was orginally defined by the use of chipped stone tools, but later an economic criterion was added and the practice of hunting and gathering is now regarded as a defining characteristic. The term is used throughout the Old World; the American equivalent is PALEO-INDIAN. The Palaeolithic period was succeeded by the MESOLITHIC. *See also* THREE AGE SYSTEM.

palaeomagnetism. The preservation of the ancient orientation and intensity of the earth's magnetic field, by magnetization of iron oxides in rocks, sediments and archaeological materials (ARCHAEOMAGNETISM). Palaeomagnetism's main importance in archaeology lies in its use as a DATING method.

The earth's magnetic field. The magnetic North Pole is not a fixed point, and it does not coincide with the geographic North Pole. It traces a sinuous path around the Arctic Circle, its average daily position moving some 25 km per year at present. This difference between the Poles is the reason why a compass needle does not point true north (that is, at the geographic North Pole). For any one point on the earth's surface, the angle between magnetic north (the direction in which the compass needle points, towards the magnetic North Pole) and true north is known as the declination. As magnetic North Pole wanders about the Arctic, the declination changes. A compass needle works by lining itself up with the lines of force of the earth's magnetic field, so that as well as registering the direction of these lines of force in a horizontal plane, it follows their dip, or inclination. This inclination is least near the Equator, but as the magnetic poles are approached, it becomes steeper and steeper until, at the magnetic North (or South) Pole itself, it is vertical. This is why magnetic compasses are difficult to use near the Poles, and why compass needles for use at different longitudes need to be balanced differently. In addition to changes in declination, the magnetic pole's wanderings have caused changes in inclination. The distances between any one point of observation and the magnetic pole varies over time, and this gives rise to slight changes in the angle of dip of the lines of force passing through that point.

So-called 'secular variation' in the orientation of the earth's magnetic field occurs in this way over periods of some hundreds of years. But on a time-scale of hundreds of thousands of years, even greater changes have occurred. Periodically, the magnetic field changes its polarity completely — north becomes south and south, north. The 'reversals' appear to happen quite rapidly, and periods of relatively stable polarity — often lasting several hundred thousand years — extend between them. Longer periods of stable polarity are called magnetic epochs; shorter periods are called magnetic events.

In addition to varying in orientation, the earth's field varies in strength, or intensity. Field intensity in fact varies widely throughout the day, but in any one place, there is a gradual change in the average field intensity, over a time-scale of hundreds of years (again called secular variation).

Ancient direction and intensity of the earth's magnetic field may be preserved in three ways:

(*a*) *Thermoremanent Magnetism (T.R.M.).* Alignment of magnetic domains within iron minerals, by heating to above the Curie point (650° C for the mineral haematite) and subsequently cooling. In a lava flow or kiln floor, for example, this preserves the direction and intensity of the earth's field at the date when they cooled down for the last time. Pottery or bricks fired in kilns are also magnetized, but since they are moved after firing, it is impossible to compare the direction of magnetization with that of the present day. Intensity, however, can be compared.

(*b*) *Detrital Remanent Magnetism.* The alignment of clay particles sinking down slowly through still lake or deep ocean water. A block of sediment is magnetized in the direction of the earth's field at the time when it was deposited.

(*c*) *Sun-dried bricks.* The throwing of clay into moulds causes bricks to become magnetized in the current direction and intensity of the earth's field.

Using igneous rocks, independently dated by POTASSIUM/ARGON, and kilns, hearths, pots etc dated archaeologically, it has been possible to reconstruct something of the history of the earth's magnetic field. Subsequently, sequences of igneous rocks, sediments, kilns, hearths, bricks, tiles and pots can have their direction or intensity measured, and so be dated by comparison with the already established sequences.

Range. Archaeological dating by these means (archaeomagnetism) is limited to the period of man's existence that includes the production of pottery, kilns, hearths etc. Furthermore, it can only be applied in those areas where enough work has been carried out to build up adequate sequences. In Britain, for example, a direction sequence is available for the Roman period and for medieval times onwards. Magnetic sequences of this kind are only applicable to one region, perhaps 500-1000 miles across. Dating of more ancient periods (Palaeomagnetism proper) is done by studying reversals. The most recent of these occurred at about 700,000 BP. As an archaeological dating method in Europe, reversals are thus of limited use, but for investigating QUATERNARY deposits, and at the HOMINID sites in Africa, this method has proved invaluable.

Accuracy. This is difficult to quantify. For archaeomagnetism, the degree of accuracy depends upon the way in which the field has changed in a particular region, on the accuracy by which the sequence has been dated, and on the origin of the samples taken for direction or intensity determination. Particular directions and intensities are often repeated in any one sequence, so that there may be a number of possible archaeomagnetic dates for one sample.

Materials. Archaeomagnetic direction measurements are confined to immovable structures, such as kilns and hearths. Many samples are taken to counteract the effects of subsidence. Intensity measurements may be made on any fired, iron-containing material — pottery and brick, in addition to kilns etc. Palaeomagnetic dating has been successfully applied to lacustrine deposits, DEEP SEA CORES and volcanic rocks.

palaeopathology. The study of ancient disease. The palaeopathologist is usually limited to studying diseases that affect the SKELETON. Most work has been done on the pathology of human skeletons, but other animals are increasingly being studied. The following groups of diseases have been regularly diagnosed in skeletons (both human and other animals) from archaeological sites:

(a) dental diseases; (b) diseases of the joints; (c) trauma (fractures and other injuries); (d) dietary deficiency diseases; (e) tumours; (f) inflammatory diseases: general inflammation and more specific conditions such as tuberculosis, leprosy and syphilis in man; (g) congenital deformities; (h) endocrine disturbances. Of these groups, dental disease, disease of the joints and trauma are the most common. A number of additional categories of disease are seen in human skeletons.

Study of the relative frequency of different diseases yields information about both the medical history and biology of ancient populations.

palaeosol. A fossil SOIL, preserved within a sequence of deposits. Palaeosols are widespread within the WEICHSELIAN LOESS sequences of the Netherlands, north Germany and Denmark. They presumably represent a period when cold conditions had ameliorated enough for vegetation to colonize the then surface of the loess and so for a soil to be formed. The INTERSTADIALS of the Weichselian have been reconstructed from the northern European palaeosol and loess succession. Very extensive palaeosols characterize interglacials and interstadials in the North American sequence (*see* Table 7, page 420).

palaestra [Greek *palaistra*: 'area for wrestling', 'wrestling-school']. Latin term often used almost interchangeably with GYMNASIUM, and in a similar way often carrying the additional associations of education and moral training. In its stricter use, the term relates only to training in wrestling and boxing. By the Hellenistic and Roman periods the architectural facilities (which could be public or private) usually took the recognizable form of a rectangular colonnaded court framing a sandy practice-area. Washing and changing rooms were usually provided.

palafitta [plural: *palafitte*]. Italian name for the villages of PILE DWELLINGS found around the North Italian lakes in the Neolithic and Bronze Age. Later changes in water levels have meant that many of these villages are now submerged. *See also* LAGOZZA, POLADA.

Palanga. The find-spot of a stray find of a perforated amber disc pendant on the Baltic coast in Lithuania, Poland. The disc is a skeuomorph of a bone type more common in central Europe and the south Russian steppe zone. The pendant can be dated to the earlier Bronze Age, of the 2nd millennium bc.

Palatine. Principal of the seven hills of ancient ROME, and favoured location in the later Republic and the Empire for magnificent private houses and, ultimately, the sumptuous residences of the emperors. The modern use of 'palace', from Latin *palatinus* (or similar) is commonly traced back to this period. Tradition was convinced that the Palatine hill was the site of the earliest Roman occupation, associating the area with mythical Romulus, whose supposed original thatched hut was carefully preserved until the 4th century AD. Festivals were celebrated, such as the Lupercalia, in honour of the she-wolf which suckled the twins. Some support for an early occupation is given by post-holes of an 'Italic' type house of the Iron Age and two early cisterns (possibly 6th century BC), but the scale of the wholesale imperial building and rebuilding must have destroyed much evidence. Augustus was born on the hill, and started a fashion for imperial residence by buying and enlarging the house of Hortensius. This trend was followed with zest by later emperors, and Domitian took over most of the hill for his amazingly extensive Domus Augustiana, and had the Aqua Claudia aqueduct specially diverted. Later structures included a special emperor's box overlooking the Circus Maximus, and the Septizonium, a monumental facade built solely to screen the southeast corner of the palace.

Palau Islands. An island group in western MICRONESIA, perhaps settled from the PHILIPPINES *c*2000 BC. Its prehistory includes a continuous pottery sequence to ethnographic times, and some large-scale terraced, horticultural and/or defensive hilltop sites. An ethnographic currency of glass beads and bracelet segments, perhaps imported from the Philippines over the past 2000 years, was in use.

Palegawra. A late Palaeolithic site in northern Iraq. The occupation was by ZARZIAN hunters about 10,000-12,000 bc.

Palengana. *See* KAMINALJUYU, TALUD-TABLERO.

Palenque. Located in the forest on the edge of the Chiapas Mountains, Palenque is the westernmost of the great CLASSIC MAYA sites. Famous for its unusual architectural features (pillar and lintel doorways, mansard roofing) and its numerous stucco bas-reliefs, the site displays an unusual regard for the natural topography with only minimal alteration of the land surface to accommodate its many temple-pyramids. A subterranean vaulted aqueduct joins the central Palace complex, with its unique four-storey tower, to the eastern terraces where the Temples of the Foliated Cross, the Cross and the Sun are situated.

The other major construction is the Temple of the Inscriptions which was built to house the cleverly concealed Tomb of Pacal. Discovered by Albert Ruz in 1949, the tomb (dated AD 692 from LONG COUNT inscriptions) contained rich grave goods including jade ornaments, a number of sacrificed retainers and a massive, elaborately carved sarcophagus.

Palenque was among the first major centres to suffer in the general Mayan collapse; it was abandoned in 810.

Paleo-Indian. A general term used in American archaeology for the exponents of the BIG GAME HUNTING TRADITION, but often broadened to include any adaptation that is pre-ARCHAIC. *See* Table 9, page 552.

Palermo. Major city of Sicily, on the northwest coast of the islamd, which has been continuously occupied for two and a half millennia. The Phoenicians established a port on the site, and from the 5th century BC the city was controlled by Carthage. The Romans captured Palermo in 254 BC. With the barbarian invasions of the 5th century AD, it was held successively by Gaiseric, Odoacer and Theodoric. Belisarius reconquered Sicily in 535 and the island remained in Byzantine hands until the Islamic offensive of the 9th century. The Muslims took Palermo in 831. By 902, they had conquered the whole island and Palermo became the capital of a quasi-independent emirate. Ibn Hauqal, who visited Palermo in 973, described it as one of the great cities of Islam. In 1061, the Normans invaded Sicily. They took Palermo in 1072 and completed their conquest of the island in

1091. Most of the 'Islamic' monuments of Palermo were built by the Normans, although pre-Norman work survives in S. Giovanni degli Eremiti and the lakeside palace known as the Favara. The principal Norman monument is the royal palace, which contains the palatine chapel of Roger II (1130-54), with BYZANTINE mosaics and a wooden ceiling painted in the tradition of FATIMID art in Egypt. The other Norman buildings consist of churches (e.g. the Martorana and S. Cataldo) and pleasure domes (e.g. the Zisa and the Cuba).

Palli Aike. *See* MAGELLAN COMPLEX.

Palliser Bay. A bay, at the southern limit of New Zealand's North Island, recently the scene of a large-scale archaeological programme by the University of Otago. Archaic MAORI sites, associated with stone field-boundary alignments, perhaps for SWEET POTATO cultivation, attest a fairly large horticultural population between ad 1100 and 1400. After 1450 the area became depopulated, due to environmental degradation and an adverse climatic change. One major result of this work has been to show that horticulture played a major part in Archaic Maori subsistence. *See also* NEW ZEALAND, TIRIMOANA PA.

palmas. *See* BALL GAME.

Palmela. A Copper Age cemetery of rock-cut tombs near Lisbon, Portugal, which has given its name to a group of the local Copper Age culture and to the so-called 'Palmela point' (probably an arrowhead, made of copper with a wide blade and long tang) which occurs in the tombs. The group, dated to the earlier 3rd millennium bc (4th millennium BC) is a variant of the VILA NOVA DE SÃO PEDRO culture. Grave goods include copper axes and daggers, as well as Palmela points, pottery of various forms (including BEAKERS in later burials) and a range of stone ritual or symbolic objects, including stylized human figures and model tools.

Palmyra. An ancient oasis town near Tadmor in the Syrian desert, important for its inscriptions documenting the caravan trade, and its monuments which blend Greek, Roman and PARTHIAN traditions and art. Occupation is probably continuous since the 3rd millennium BC, but the town achieved prominence in the 1st century BC by exploitation of the caravan trade. Palmyra also prospered by a calculated and self-interested defence of Roman interests in the area — a role which Odaenathus, a local noble, took over single-handed together with command of the Roman eastern army, when the incompetent emperor, Valerian, allowed himself to be captured by the Persians in 260 AD. His second wife Zenobia, having perhaps first poisoned him and his eldest son, went too far with a grandiose scheme of conquests (including Egypt) and with a proclamation of her own son, Vaballathus, as eastern emperor. Palmyra never recovered from Aurelian's punitive attack, but Zenobia lived on at a villa at Tivoli outside Rome. Surviving remains include the great Temple of Bel, senate house, agora, courtyard-type housing and colonnaded streets. Necropoleis surround the ancient town, and contain remarkable tower tombs, some four stories high, and elaborate hypogea.

palstave. A type of bronze axe found in Europe during the Middle Bronze Age. It is characterized by a stop ridge across the middle of the axe and side flanges on the upper (haft) end. Both these features make for more secure hafting of the axe blade by preventing lateral movement and haft splitting. Palstaves were commonly provided with one or two side loops to make binding easier and more efficient.

palynology. The technical term for POLLEN ANALYSIS.

Pampa Grande. A large urban centre in the Lambayeque valley of northern Peru and probably the relocated capital of the MOCHE polity in its closing phases. It occupies an economically strategic position in the neck of the valley; a large river system, a major road and a network of canals also come together at this point. Highly differentiated architecture is scattered over an area of 4.5 square kilometres and structures include masonry platforms, truncated adobe PYRAMIDS, small agglutinated rooms, an extensive network of corridors and large storage rooms. The principal HUACA measures 250 by 180 metres and is 50 metres high. A considerable variety in human face motifs on mould and hand-made neck-jars may have some socio-economic significance as means of identifying either the contents or the owner. Stone tools used in metal-working and small utilitarian artefacts in copper have also been recovered. The peak of occupation for the site was c600-700.

pan [p'an]. *See* RITUAL VESSELS (CHINA).

Panaramitee art. A style of rock art described at Panaramitee in the Flinders Ranges, South Australia, and found mainly in arid regions close to water-holes in South Australia, New South Wales, north Queensland and the Northern Territory. Isolated examples have also been found in northern TASMANIA and near Sydney. The style involves the pecking on rock surfaces by indirect percussion of clusters of hundreds of small figures, usually about 10 cm tall, in outline or in-filled forms. Motifs are limited in range, and it is the relative proportions of types of motifs that are diagnostic of Panaramitee sites. Motifs, in order of dominance, include animal tracks (mainly kangaroo and emu), circles, dots and crescents, human footprints, lizards and other figures, radiating lines and tectiforms (roof shapes). The art is thought to be of considerable antiquity on the basis of still inconclusive evidence of patination, distribution in both Australia and Tasmania, and the absence of stone tool types belonging to the post-2000 bc AUSTRALIAN SMALL TOOL TRADITION. Rock fragments with Panaramitee art have been excavated at INGALADDI from deposits dated 3000-5000 bc.

Pånduranga. An archaeological territory of the kingdom of CHAMPA, corresponding to the present town of Phan-rang (the Vietnamese version of the name) on the coast of southern Vietnam. It became the centre of gravity of Champa from the middle of the 8th century onward. *See also* AMARÅVATI, KAUTHÅRA, VIETNAM, VIJAYA.

Panlongcheng [P'an-lung-ch'eng]. A site of the ERLIGANG PHASE in Huangpi Xian near Wuhan, Hubei province, China. Palatial foundations, tombs with bronze RITUAL VESSELS, and a HANGTU city wall 1000 metres long have been excavated. Despite its location near the Yangzi River, which suggests a provincial outpost, Panlongcheng is culturally indistinguishable from Erligang phase sites

farther north, such as ZHENGZHOU. Bronze-using cultures of the middle and lower Yangzi region contemporary with the ANYANG civilization seem to have been formed in the wake of a pre-Anyang southward expansion of metropolitan SHANG culture documented by the settlement at Panlongcheng (*see* NINGXIANG, WUCHENG).

P'an-p'an. One of the earliest INDIANIZED kingdoms of Southeast Asia, sending embassies to China between the 5th and 7th centuries. Although its name is known only from Chinese sources and its exact location is unknown, it must have been situated on the Malay Peninsula and served as a relay station between India and the rest of Southeast Asia.

pan-pipe lug [French: *flûte de Pan*]. A type of handle found on Neolithic pottery of the CHASSEY, CORTAILLOD and LAGOZZA cultures in France, Switzerland and northern Italy. It consists of cylindrical vertical lugs placed side by side, thus resembling slightly the pan pipe; they were presumably used for suspension.

Pantalica. A Late Bronze Age to Early Iron Age site inland from Syracuse in southeast Sicily, probably occupied from the 13th century BC to the 8th century BC. The site occupied a plateau of about eight hectares, defended both by its position between steep gorges and by walls of CYCLOPEAN MASONRY. That this settlement housed a large community is indicated by the 5000 or so rock-cut tombs in the hillsides around. It may be reasonable to describe the site as a town: although there have been only restricted excavations on the hilltop, at least one public building has been exposed: a large stone built structure described as an *anaktoron* or palace. Pottery and metal goods from the tombs indicate trading contacts with both mainland Italy and the Aegean.

Pantano Longarini. A large wreck of 5th-7th-century date was found in the sea off Pantano Longarini in southeast Sicily. The vessel would have been about 45 metres long and 9 metres at its widest. There were few finds from the excavated remains but the structural details of the boat are a further contribution to the study of BYZANTINE ship-building.

Pantelleria. Small island in the central

Mediterranean south of Sicily. It has a source of OBSIDIAN which was exploited on a small scale in prehistory, reaching north Africa and Malta, but no further afield. The earliest archaeological remains yet discovered on the island belong to the Bronze Age (2nd millennium BC) and include a settlement site at La Mursia on the west coast. Probably to this period also belong the dry stone chambers with CORBELLED vaults known as *sesi* (singular: *sese*). Nothing has been found in these chambers, so both their date and their function is uncertain. Many authorities, however, assume that they were tombs and that they were built in the Bronze Age.

Pantheon. A classical Roman temple originally put up by Agrippa in 27-25 BC, rebuilt by Domitian, and finally radically reconstructed by Hadrian in *c*118-128 AD. The Hadrianic temple consists essentially of a domed rotunda, lit by a central circular aperture to the sky (*oculus*), and fronted by a pedimented portico. These two areas are linked, clumsily some would say, by a box-shaped intermediate structure. The building is technically advanced and constitutes a good example of the adventurous expertise of early imperial technology in concrete. While innovative, the design is also careful, and incorporates several 'fail-safe' aspects. The foundations are some 4.5 metres deep and 10.3 metres wide, and the aggregate used in the concrete is adjusted for context throughout the building — a light pumice, for example, being used near the centre of the dome, where the thickness of skin narrows to about 1.5 metres. There is a frequent use of relieving arches, and the main walls have a complex internal structure into which are incorporated the service corridors and stairs. *See also* ROME.

Papuan languages. The languages of NEW GUINEA and adjacent parts of eastern INDONESIA and MELANESIA. There are today about 750 Papuan languages spoken by about 2.9 million people, and the family is therefore perhaps the most diverse in the world. The Papuan languages presumably descend from the languages of the first settlers of New Guinea *c*30-40,000 years ago, and some linguists claim to be able to trace population expansion and migrations within the New Guinea region from about 15,000 years ago, especially that involving speakers of Trans-New Guinea

Phylum languages, who appear to have spread over much of New Guinea but about 3000 BC. This expansion could be associated with early horticulture and resulting population growth (*see* KUK). Today, no clear relationships between Papuan and Australian languages have survived, due to long periods of mutual isolation, but nevertheless the two groups probably share an ultimate common ancestry.

Paracas. A highly distinctive art style which arose towards the end of the EARLY HORIZON in the south-coast area of Peru, especially in the Ica Valley. Expressed in ornate pottery and elaborate textiles, its earliest phases are clearly CHAVIN-influenced. Subsequently, however, it developed into an independent style which became an antecedent of NASCA. Typically, Paracas pottery is polychrome, decorated with geometric bands and lifeforms in incised outline. Post-firing decoration in bright resin paints is highly characteristic.

There are no large temple structures at the type site (located on a peninsula in the Bay of Pisco) but excavations there by C.J. Tello uncovered numerous fabric-wrapped burials accompanied by rich funerary urns. Surprisingly, this late-phase pottery (designated Paracas Necropolis) was monochrome — a high-gloss cream-white. The associated textiles, in contrast, were bright embroidered polychromes in designs typical of the highly elaborate Nasca art style (e.g. the cat/demon motif).

Paranthropus. *See* AUSTRALOPITHECUS, HUMAN EVOLUTION.

Pararaton ['Book of Kings']. A Javanese chronicle dating from the end of the 15th century, but containing detailed biographies of kings and persons of their entourage, and accounts of the scandals and dramas of the court, ignored by epigraphy, from the beginning of the 13th century on. *See also* NĀGARAKRITĀGAMA, SINGHASĀRI.

Parcay-Meslay. *See* GRANGE.

Parpallo. A cave in the province of Valencia, Spain, with a sequence of SOLUTRIAN and other Upper PALAEOLITHIC deposits below and above. A few engraved art pieces and some human remains are known but the site is mainly famous for the barbed and tanged points which characterize the late Solutrian in this region, and are so similar to Bronze Age arrowheads.

Parthenon. Principal temple on the ACRO-POLIS at ATHENS, dedicated to the maiden (Greek *parthenos*) goddess, Athena. It was built 447-432 BC as the centre piece of Pericles' grand scheme for the Acropolis, by the architects Ictinus and Callicrates, under the supervision of the sculptor Phidias, who contributed the great chryselephantine statue of Athena. The temple is generally considered to mark the highest achievement in the DORIC order of architecture, and to incorporate sophisticated solutions to problems of visual line and spacing. The material is Pentelic marble (from Mount Pentelikon just north of Athens). Much of the sculptured decoration may be seen in the British Museum, London (the so-called ELGIN marbles). After the classical period the building survived various conversions to the function of church and mosque quite well, until Turkish occupying forces decided to use it as a powder magazine. Hit by Venetian fire, the temple exploded into two ruined halves. What remains today of the building is now under attack, this time from the corrosive industrial atmosphere of modern Athens.

Parthia. The Parthians were essentially Iranian Parni tribesmen from east of the Caspian Sea, named after a SELEUCID satrapy (Parthia, Indian Parthava). United by Arsaces in 247 BC they progressively took over Iran and Mesopotamia from the Seleucid Greeks, and established an oriental empire with Greek civilization grafted on. Their culture and location was an important intermediary between the Near and Far East, and profited from a thriving caravan trade. They were famous in the west for their superlative horsemanship. Parthian art and architecture show an interesting hybridization of cultures. They were eventually ousted by a newly emergent Persian dynasty, the SASSA-NIAN, around 225 AD.

particle size analysis. The investigation of the distribution of the different sizes of particles that make up a SEDIMENT, SOIL or similar material. Particles are classified into a number of size grades, normally under such headings as boulders, pebbles, stones, gravel, SAND, SILT

and CLAY. Sand is often split into a number of sub-divisions. Several different systems exist for defining the limits of these categories. These include the Wentworth-Udden scale (used in Geology), the British Standard 1377 system, and the United States Department of Agriculture scale (both widely used in soil science). When describing particle size, it is important to indicate clearly the particular scale used. Particle sizes are normally determined by a mixture of two methods: sieves with very accurately controlled mesh sizes are used to separate the coarser grades; silt and clay are normally determined by an elutriation method. The mixture of particle size grades found in a material is known as the TEXTURE.

Pasargadae. Capital city of Cyrus the Great, founder of the ACHAEMENID empire, sited in the province of Fars in southern Iran, north of PERSEPOLIS. The buildings are scattered over a wide area; they include two palaces, a gatehouse and a square stone tower, as well as a religious area with a large fire altar. Trilingual inscriptions in ELAMITE, Babylonian (AKKA-DIAN) and Old Persian, all in the CUNEIFORM script, occur on the palaces and gatehouse. About one kilometre southwest of the palaces is the tomb of Cyrus, still more or less intact: an impressive rectangular stone chamber with a gabled roof, set on a high stepped plinth.

Pasemah Plateau. The most impressive group of prehistoric megalithic monuments in INDO-NESIA, the Pasemah sites in southern SUMATRA comprise massive slab graves and a rich collection of virtually life-sized anthropomorphic carvings. Stylistic and artefactual associations are Bronze to Iron Age, perhaps *c*2000 years ago, and remote connections with the DONG-SON culture of northern Vietnam and the megalithic cultures of south India are very likely, but as yet unproven. The complex shows no sign of Hindu or Buddhist influence.

Paso. A shell mound on the shore of Lake Tondano in the Minahasa district of northern SULAWESI, which is the best-preserved pre-Neolithic midden to be excavated in INDO-NESIA. Dated to *c*5500 bc, its inhabitants lived on shellfish, hunted the local fauna, and used obsidian flake tools. Paso provides an important TERMINUS POST QUEM for the small flake and blade industries (after 5000 BC) and Neolithic cultures (after 3000 BC) which later appear in the region.

passage grave. One of the main categories of MEGALITHIC tomb in prehistoric Europe, characterized by a funerary chamber and a clearly demarcated separate entrance passage. Passage graves are frequently but not invariably found under round BARROWS; they may be constructed entirely of orthostats with slab capstones or they may incorporate drystone walling and have CORBELLED vaults; the chambers may be round, square, rectangular or polygonal and may have subsidiary side chambers; in Brittany and Ireland some passage graves are decorated with pecked designs. Passage graves occur throughout the area where megalithic tombs occur in Europe, but have a predominantly western distribution. The earliest dated megalithic tombs — in Brittany — are passage graves, dating to before 4500 BC, but in other areas passage graves were still being constructed in the Bronze Age.

Passo di Corvo. A large Neolithic settlement site on the Tavoliere plain in southeast Italy, with a radiocarbon date in the late 5th millennium bc. The site is ditched (of the type known as a *villaggio trincerato*) and encloses about 100 smaller enclosures with C-shaped ditches, which may have contained individual homesteads or compounds. The site has produced evidence of a mixed farming economy and abundant pottery of various types, including IMPRESSED WARE and a variety of painted wares.

Pastoral Neolithic of East Africa. In recent years this ill-defined term has been loosely applied to most if not all of the pre-Iron Age food-producing societies in East Africa. It draws attention to one of the most striking features of these societies which is clearly attested in the archaeological record — their pastoral economy. The term, however, carries the unfortunate implication that pastoralism was the only type of food-production practised; in fact, the evidence currently available is quite inadequate to determine whether or not food crops were cultivated.

The low-lying plains of northern Kenya were occupied by herders in the 3rd millennium bc (as at ILERET and ELE BOR), significantly earlier than any firm attestation of the Pastoral Neolithic in the highlands further to the south. In the latter area, despite claims for the remains of domestic animals in contexts at least as early as the 8th millennium bc, there is as yet no conclusive evidence which relates to a period before the end of the 2nd millennium.

The subdivision of the Pastoral Neolithic in the East African highlands is not fully clear. One entity which stands out from the rest is that known as the ELMENTEITAN industry. For the rest, groupings are less clearly apparent. Several pottery styles are recognized and have been named after sites such as NAROSURA, Maringishu and Akira, but their significance is uncertain, for in no case is the geographical or chronological occurrence of these so-called wares well defined. The pottery styles are not coterminous with any recognized variants in the microlithic industries. The other aspects of the Pastoral Neolithic attested by archaeology show less variation. Disposal of the dead was by burial beneath a stone cairn or between rocks. Stone platters, bowls and pestles, of unknown purpose, occur on most sites. Settlements show a great range of size, as does the relative importance of herding cattle and small stock in comparison with hunting. There can be little doubt that the Pastoral Neolithic archaeological material represents a complex and variable, perhaps seasonally changing, pattern of settlement, the details of which are not yet properly understood.

Pastoral Neolithic settlement is attested as far to the south as the Serengeti Plain of northern Tanzania, but there is no evidence that areas further to the south saw any practice of food-production prior to the Iron Age. Historical-linguistic studies provide indications that some at least of the Pastoral Neolithic peoples may have been speakers of Southern Cushitic languages.

Pataliputa. *See* PATNA.

Patayan. *See* HAKATAYA.

patina. FLINT artefacts buried in some types of soil or sediment may become chemically altered at their surface. This change results in a white, yellow or brown layer called patina forming on the surface of the artefact. The thickness of the patina must in some way be related to age, but it has not been used successfully as a dating method. BRONZE objects may also acquire a patina, which is green in colour and is the product of corrosion.

Patna [ancient Pataliputra]. A city of northeast India, which was the capital of the kingdom of MAGADHA and the MAURYAN Empire in the later 1st millenium BC. Part of the city rampart (reinforced with timber) and a large pillared hall survive. This hall, with its 80 pillars, has frequently been compared to similar halls found in ACHAEMENID Persia and it has been suggested that some Achaemenid craftsmen fled to India after the defeat of the Persians by ALEXANDER THE GREAT.

pattern welding. An effective strengthening method as well as a decorative technique, commonly employed by sword and metal-smiths of the post-Roman period. Wire and strip metal, sometimes in varying combinations of type and colour, were welded together and hammered out to produce a blade with patterned effect. The finest of these weapons are usually attributed to the FRANK-ISH smiths although notable examples are also known from ANGLO-SAXON and VIKING contexts. *See also* STEEL.

Paviland. Goat's Hole, Paviland, on the Gower peninsula of south Wales, yielded a skeleton in 1882. After its study and publication by Dean Buckland, it was dubbed 'the Red Lady'. Further remains and a few stone tools were added in 1912. The skeleton has a radiocarbon date of 18,460 years bp, and may be Proto-SOLUTRIAN. It was covered with red ochre, ivory ornaments and shells.

Pavlov. Close to DOLNÍ VĚSTONICE in southern Moravia, Czechoslovakia, a large settlement of Upper PALAEOLITHIC mammoth-hunters has been found at Pavlov (*see* MAMMOTH). A skeleton and other human remains have been found, as well as hut plans and numerous art objects. The culture has been called Pavlovian or East GRAVETTIAN. The radiocarbon age is about 24,000 bc.

Pazyryk. Site in the ALTAI Mountains of Central Asia where the 'frozen tombs' of nomad chieftains of the 4th and 3rd centuries BC were excavated by Russian archaeologists. In the Pazyryk kurgans the formation of a lens-shaped layer of permafrost beneath the stone-topped burial mound kept the contents of the timber-lined chamber beneath in a remarkable state of preservation. The embalmed, tattooed bodies of the deceased remained intact, along with fragile objects of wood, leather, felt, silks and other textiles (the tombs were looted of more valuable furnishings in antiquity). Two horses in one kurgan wore elaborate head-dresses, saddle cloths, and ornaments or carved wood, all decorated with familiar ANIMAL STYLE motifs. The silks and a bronze mirror are imports from China; other articles show strong ACHAEMENID influence. One saddle cloth decorated in felt appliqué with the animal-combat motif is related in both design and technique to a felt carpet from a kurgan of the 1st century AD at NOIN-ULA. The Pazyryk finds are kept at the Hermitage Museum together with similar material from earlier kurgans excavated nearby at Bashadar and Tuekta (6th-5th century BC).

peat. An accumulation of dead organic matter, mostly from plants, which becomes preserved to a greater or lesser extent, principally by the exclusion of oxygen. Peat forms mostly in BOGS and FENS. The types of plant which produced it vary, as does the extent to which it has been broken down or humified. The importance of peat to archaeology lies in its preservation of PALAEOBOTAN-ICAL evidence, BEETLE skeletons, and other fossils which can be used to reconstruct the ancient environment. *See* ENVIRONMENTAL ARCHAEOLOGY.

pebble tool. The simplest recognized tool types are pebbles or nodules which have been flaked roughly at one end to form a sharp edge. The most typical are CHOPPERS and CHOPPING TOOLS. They are the earliest tool types known in the world and in Africa they are found back to about two million years ago at sites like OLDUVAI GORGE and OMO. Often the pebble tools are of very coarse raw materials, whereas the chopping tools are later made on finer flint-like materials. Pebble tool industries are claimed for other parts of the world, both in Asia and in Europe, but these may be of much later date.

Pećel. A regional variant of the BADEN group, a Late Copper Age culture group in southeast and central Europe. The Pećel group is a late phase of the Baden group, distributed in eastern Hungary in the 3rd millennium bc. Although some settlement sites are known, the majority of Pećel sites are cemeteries, in which cremation burial is as frequent as inhumation.

Pech de l'Azé. Near Sarlat in the Dordogne, southwest France, the tunnel cave and shelter of Pech de l'Azé has been investigated from the 19th century onwards. The levels have yielded MOUSTERIAN assemblages, mainly of ACHEULIAN type. Underneath, there are Acheulian levels with a penultimate glacial fauna with Merck's RHINOCEROS and few cold-adapted forms. Extensive pollen and sediment studies have been conducted, and together with COMBE GRENAL this site is a key to understanding the Mousterian.

Pečica. A long-lived TELL settlement of the earlier and later Bronze Age, located on the lower Mureş River in the Rumanian Banat, near Arad. At least 16 occupation horizons have been distinguished, with one of the clearest evolutionary sequences of pottery development in the Banat. A large collection of stone moulds for metallurgy was found in the upper layers. Most Pečica type sites are inhumation cemeteries, related to the MOKRIN-Szöreg type; these flat graves contained rich grave goods of gold, bronze and faience and amber beads.

Pecos Conference. *See* KIDDER, ALFRED VINCENT.

pediment. Term of dubious but not classical parentage, used to denote the triangular or gable end of a ridge roof, especially with reference to the classical Greek and Roman TEMPLE. In the classical temple, the outline of the triangle is formed by horizontal and 'raking' cornices which carry decorative mouldings. The vertical 'back wall' (*tympanum*) is often decorated with painting, relief or sculpture in the round. Each of the three corners was also faced with a special, visually striking, 'corner-piece' (ACROTERION).

pedology. The study of SOILS.

Pegu. *See* HAMSAVATĪ.

Peiligang [P'ei-li-kang]. *See* BANPO.

Peiraeus. The ancient and modern port of ATHENS, although virtually deserted from the 5th century AD to the 19th century. The fortification of Peiraeus as a secure harbour for Athens dates effectively from early in the 5th century BC, when Themistocles created a navy

of some 200 ships and, to give them guarded anchorage, suggested a switch from the previous use of the unprotected and open Phaleron Bay. At Peiraeus, three harbours were used; on the east side of the promontory lay two small harbours, Zea (present-day Pasalimani) which had boat-sheds of architectural distinction and the Arsenal of Philo (see below); and Munichia (present-day Tourkolimano), which was likewise employed principally for warships. On the west lay the Great Harbour (*megas limen*) of Kantharos (the 'goblet') which seems to have been used rather for commercial purposes. Under Pericles' programme of public works in the middle of the 5th century BC, the town was laid out on a grid-plan by the civil architect, Hippodamus of Miletus. What was felt to be the strategic weakness of the distance of the link between Athens and her port was corrected by the construction of the Long Walls which joined port and city into one defended unit.

Following intense development since Athens was declared capital of Greece in 1834, very little survives of ancient Peiraeus. Sections of the walling may be found, and evidence for some of the ship sheds and a HELLENISTIC theatre. A 4th-century BC inscription gives a full specification for an arsenal by the architect Philo, but no trace survives. A hoard of bronze statuary including an archaic Apollo, discovered in routine drain digging in 1959, may conceivably be part of Sulla's booty after his attack in 86 BC.

Pei Xian [P'ei-hsien]. *See* DADUNZI, QINGLIAN'GANG.

Peking. *See* BEIJING.

Pekin Man. Popular name of the HOMO ERECTUS found at ZHOUKOUDIAN. *See also* HUMAN EVOLUTION.

Pengelly, William (1812-94). Schoolteacher and geologist who excavated at KENTS CAVERN, Devon, in the 1840s and 1850s. He came to the same conclusion as the earlier excavator, Father MACENERY, that tools of early man occurred in association with bones of extinct animals beneath a layer of stalagmite. This association was still not widely accepted, but in 1858 the opportunity arose to test the theory when a new and undisturbed cave was discovered at Windmill Hill, Brixham, also in Devon. Pengelly conducted excavations here in 1858 and 1859 and found the same association of tools and extinct fauna as at Kent's Cavern, also sealed by an unbroken layer of stalagmite. These excavations and those of BOUCHER DE PERTHES in the gravels of the River Somme in northern France played a crucial role in convincing the scholarly world of the great antiquity of man.

Peng Xian [P'eng-hsien]. County in Sichuan province near CHENGDU, China. The most important Western ZHOU finds from Sichuan are several hoards of bronze RITUAL VESSELS from Peng Xian. The vessels date from the very beginning of the dynasty, and some are unusually flamboyant in design.

Peninj. A site on Lake Natron, north of OLDU-VAI in Tanzania. The deposits have yielded a fine lower jaw of *Australopithecus s. robustus/boisei* type (*see* AUSTRALOPITHECUS) some 1.5 milion years old, and an ACHEULIAN hand-axe assemblage from a somewhat later level.

Penkalaotis. *See* CHARSADA.

pennanular brooch. The most common type of dress fastener used in the sub-Roman period; it remained popular in Celtic regions of Britain up until the 10th century. The brooch took the form of an open hoop, with two terminals and a pin backing the hoop, a type well-known in the European Iron Age. There is an extensive typology for these ornaments, and they vary in appearance from plain bronze or iron rings to elaborately inlaid and gilded examples such as the Tara brooch, which was made around 700 in Ireland.

Penrhyn. *See* COOK ISLANDS.

Peoples of the Sea. Name given by the ancient Egyptians to a group of peoples who attacked Egypt in the 13th and 12th centuries BC and were twice defeated in c1219-1218 and c1182 or 1170 BC. They are referred to and depicted on a number of Egyptian monuments, the best-known of which is the temple of Medinet Habu, in the early 12th century BC. A number of different groups are shown and named, and various attempts have been made to identify them with archaeologically known groups. Since they are referred to as coming from

the Aegean and Anatolian areas, plausible identifications include Peleset as Philistines, Lukka as Lycians, and Ekwesh as Achaeans (i.e. Greeks perhaps from Asia Minor and the Greek mainland); more controversial are other identifications which suggest west Mediterranean connections: Shardana as Sardinians, Shekelesh as Sikels (i.e. Sicilians) and Teresh as Tyrsi (or Etruscans).

Perak. *See* KUALA SELINSING.

perforation. Alternatively known as blood-letting, this was a form of auto-sacrifice widely practised by the cultures of MESOAMERICA. Historical sources (e.g. the CODEX Mendoza) indicate that the AZTEC frequently engaged in penitential exercises by causing self-inflicted wounds with maguey thorns. Artefactual evidence in the form of plant thorns, stingray spines, and pointed instruments carved in numerous media has been found with great frequency at sites of almost all of the Meso-american cultures, including CLASSIC MAYA, HUASTEC, OLMEC and TEOTIHUACAN. Physical appendages such as the ear, the leg, the arms and hands (see Room IV of BONAMPAK murals), the penis (inferred from grave associations) and tongue (a relief carving at YAX-CHILAN) seem to have been the most frequently perforated organs.

Pergamum. A culturally important HELLEN-ISTIC Greek city of Anatolia, and capital of a semi-independent local Attalid dynasty. Credited in antiquity with the development of hide as a writing material, its name lived on as *pergamentum* in late Latin, and (probably) modern 'parchment'. The Attalid kings invested much of their wealth in Pergamum, making it a centre for literature, the arts and the sciences. They laid out a dazzling display of fine monuments, and encouraged a local school of sculpture. Their library rivalled ALEXANDRIA. In the Roman period the artistic charms of the town continued to attract, and there was extensive new building and rebuilding. Hadrian, for example, so restyled the Sanctuary of Asclepius that critics debated its candidature as one of the wonders of the world. The round, domed Temple of Zeus Asclepius, probably also Hadrianic, suggests interesting parallels with the PAN-THEON at Rome.

Periam [Perjamos]. The Periam group is the

Rumanian aspect of the Periam-MOKRIN-Szöreg group of the earlier Bronze Age, dated to the mid-2nd millennium bc and located in the lowland Banat in western Rumania. The type site is a tell located near Arad, on a tributary of the lower Mureş and surrounded by a bank and ditch. A 60-cm culture layer yielded a rich collection of domestic pottery and bonework, discovered mostly in large storage pits.

Periano Ghundai. *See* ZHOB.

periglacial. A term describing conditions existing today in high latitudes and altitudes, and known to have existed in a wide zone around the large QUATERNARY ICE SHEETS. In a periglacial zone, part of the ground is perennially frozen. This so-called permafrost layer is covered by a layer which thaws and freezes seasonally, the active layer. Such seasonal changes give rise to several processes, some of which sort the constituents of the active layer and are collectively known as CRYOTURBATION. Other processes involve the movement and re-freezing of water within the layers. A variety of land forms, including INVOLUTIONS, ICE WEDGES and PINGOS, are formed in the active layer and permafrost. During the summer, when the active layer is thawed, it becomes so charged with water that individual particles are lubricated and large volumes of material move down-slope. This process is called solifluction. Rivers are usually seasonal in the periglacial zone, and erosion by frost action is dominant. Wind erosion and deposition is often an important factor, and caused the formation of the huge deposits of LOESS and cover-sands in Europe and Asia. The periglacial zone is of interest because it would have been the environment in which man lived for long periods of time during the DEVENSIAN/WEICHSELIAN cold stage.

Perigordian. In the 1930s, D. Peyrony advocated the view that the AURIGNACIAN or early Upper Palaeolithic in France consisted of a true Aurignacian and a separate stream or line of cultures, the Perigordian, beginning before the Aurignacian but co-existing alongside it down to the time of the SOLUTRIAN. The term, derived from the Perigord region, is still widely used in France, especially because such units as Perigordian IV, Vc and VI are difficult to discuss within the framework of any other

terminology. Nevertheless, some quite important modifications had to be made to Peyrony's ideas. The question of contemporaneity of Perigordian and Aurignacian has been disputed, though some overlap now seems certain. It is not known what kind of man was responsible for the Perigordian, but it is usually assumed that it was CROMAGNON man, at least in the later part. Recently, however, a NEANDERTHAL-like skull has been found with the early Perigordian, or CHATEL-PERRONIAN. Art is found in a few later Perigordian contexts.

peristyle. Classical Greek term for a 'surrounding colonnade'. Confusingly, the term is used of a colonnade running round the outside of a building (as in the classical Greek TEMPLE); of a colonnade running round the inside of a court or room; and also of the court or room itself that contains such a perimeter colonnade.

Perjamos. *See* PERIAM.

Persepolis [modern Takht-i Jamshid]. Capital of the ACHAEMENID empire in southern Iran. It was founded by Darius in c518 BC and completed in the reign of Xerxes. It replaced the earlier capital, PASARGADAE, situated c50 km further south, and was in many ways modelled on it, although incorporating many architectural and artistic innovations. It consists of a stone terrace platform measuring c500 by 300 metres on which were erected a series of monumental palaces and audience halls, as well as other buildings, constructed over a period of some 60 years. The two largest buildings, the Apadana (audience hall) of Darius and the Throne Hall of Xerxes, occupied the centre of the terrace and divided it into two functional halves. The northern area was military and mainly the work of Artaxerxes I, while the southern area contained the Palaces of Darius and Xerxes, the Harem and Treasury areas. Monumental staircases and other areas are lavishly decorated with relief carvings and inscriptions. The reliefs on the Apadana show tribute-bearers from all over the empire bringing gifts to the king; they may show a ceremony which took place at the time of the Persian New Year festival. It seems likely, indeed, that Persepolis was a ceremonial centre and was not regularly

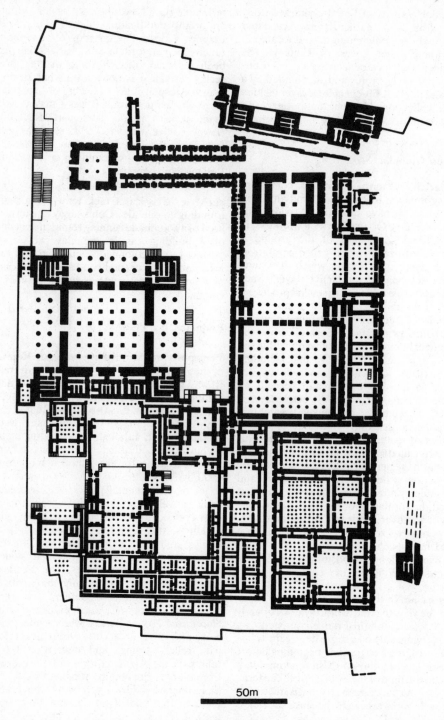

50m

Persepolis: plan

used for dwelling. It was captured and burnt by Alexander the Great in 331 BC.

Six kilometres north of Persepolis is Naqsh-i Rustam, where four monumental tombs were carved in the cliff face; these are the tombs of Darius I and three of his successors. They are also decorated with relief carvings and bear trilingual inscriptions in ELAMITE, Babylonian (AKKADIAN) and Old Persian.

Persia, Persians. Ancient names for the land of Iran and the population that occupied it from at least the 1st millennium BC and possibly earlier. In the middle and later 1st millennium BC the ACHAEMENID empire dominated much of western Asia, until it fell to ALEXANDER THE GREAT in the late 4th century BC. In the 1st millennium AD another great power arose in this area, that of the SASSANIANS.

Peschiera. A LAKE VILLAGE at the southern end of Lake Garda in northern Italy, of the Middle to Late Bronze Age. The site has given its name to a type of knife which has a flanged hilt forked at one end and to the FIBULA of violin-bow form, both dated to the 13th-12th centuries BC.

Peterborough ware. A decorated ware of the British later Neolithic, formerly thought to represent a SECONDARY NEOLITHIC culture, but now believed to have developed directly out of earlier WINDMILL HILL and other styles. The decoration is impressed and is made with bits of wood, bone or pieces of cord. There are three sub-styles: the earliest is Ebbsfleet, the second Mortlake, and the last Fengate. The Mortlake and Fengate styles both show evidence of BEAKER influence, while the flat-bottomed Fengate pots may be the ancestors of the COLLARED URNS of the Bronze Age.

Petersfels. A cave in Baden, southwest Germany, near Lake Constance, with Upper PALAEOLITHIC occupation. Rich MAGDA-LENIAN-type deposits were found here, along with a series of human statuettes and some human fossil bones.

Petra. Dean Burgon's 'rose red city, half as old as Time' was the capital successively of the Edomite and the Nabataean kingdoms of the 1st millennium BC, situated in southern

Jordan. The site was important for trade, situated as it was on the main route between the Dead Sea and the Red Sea. The town is surrounded by mountains and the temples, tombs and other buildings are cut into the red sandstone. Many of these belong to the Nabataean period of the last two centuries BC, though a theatre and temple belong to the Roman period (after AD 106). Little is known of the later history of Petra, although a Crusader fort survives.

Petralona. A cave on the Chalcidice peninsula of northern Greece, which has yielded a virtually complete skull, found in 1959. Once thought to be NEANDERTHAL, it is now seen to be close to *Homo erectus*. Its age is not known, but it is possibly some 400,000 years old.

Petreşti. The eponymous site for a Late Neolithic culture distributed in the upland basin of Transylvania and dated to the early 4th millennium bc. Petreşti settlement pattern is TELL-based, with most occupations preceded by Early VINČA levels in the Mureş Valley. The defining characteristic is a wide range of painted wares, bichrome and trichrome in style, with affinities with the CUCUTENI-TRIPOLYE-ARIUŞD painted wares.

Petrie, Sir William Matthew Flinders (1853-1942). British archaeologist who worked in the Near East and especially in Egypt. He was responsible for introducing scientific excavation techniques into Egyptian archaeology (although his methods fall short of modern standards of care and precision). He excavated and explored many important Egyptian sites. His work in the Pre-Dynastic cemeteries of NAKADA enabled him to develop the relative dating system known as SEQUENCE DATING, a form of SERIATION, using the pottery types found in the nearly 3000 graves of the Nakada cemeteries. His other achievements in Egypt include a survey of the GIZA pyramids, excavation at EL-AMARNA and the discovery of the Greek city of NAUKRATIS. He also contributed to the development of archaeological techniques and his publications include an introduction to the aims and methods of archaeology as well as many works on Egypt.

petrological analysis. Petrology is the study of rocks and minerals. A number of artefacts contain minerals that can be investigated in this way: pottery, stone axes, QUERNS, hones, building stones etc. These may be examined as THIN SECTIONS under the petrological microscope, by HEAVY MINERAL ANALYSIS, or a number of other methods. Work of this kind is chiefly used to determine the source of the materials used.

Peu Richard. A settlement site surrounded by double ditches in Charente-Maritime, central France, which has given its name to a later Neolithic culture in the area, dated to the first half of the 3rd millennium bc. Settlements were generally on hilltops and, like the type site, surrounded by ditches. The subsistence economy was mixed farming. The characteristic pottery is flat-based and decorated with channelled ornament.

Phaestos [Phaistos]. A MINOAN palace overlooking the Mesara plain in southern Crete. Phaestos is the second largest of the Minoan palaces, after KNOSSOS, and has a rather similar early history. Like Knossos, it was occupied from the Neolithic onwards and the first palace was built in the Middle Minoan period c2000 BC. It was destroyed c1700 BC and, although it was rebuilt, it was less important in the succeeding period than its near neighbour AYIA TRIADHA. It was finally destroyed c1450 BC, perhaps as a result of the eruption of THERA. The plan of the palace is like that of the other sites, with a large central court surrounded by living quarters, reception rooms and storage areas; however, it has no frescoes and few fine objects have been found here. No tablets were found and the only writing is on the so-called Phaestos Disc, a clay disc 15 cm in diameter with symbols stamped in a spiral arrangement on both sides. It comes from a deposit dated c1700 BC, which makes it contemporary with the different — but equally undeciphered — LINEAR A script.

Phalaborwa. An area of the eastern Transvaal lowveld, South Africa, where a long Iron Age sequence has been investigated. Both IRON and COPPER were mined here during the final centuries of the 1st millennium ad. From the 11th century onwards the later Iron Age occupation appears to belong to a single developing tradition, perhaps related to that of some recent Sotho groups. Agriculture on terraced hillsides and the herding of domestic cattle formed the basis of the subsistence economy, while mining continued on an increased scale.

Phan-rang. *See* PĀNDURANGA.

Philippi. The site in Thrace, Greece, of two battles in 42 BC when, in the last years of the Republic, Cassius and Brutus were defeated by Antony. Probably originally a Thracian tribal settlement, it had been the object of an unsuccessful attempt at colonization by Thasos in the 6th century BC, and thereafter bore the Greek name of Crenides ('fountains'). It was probably the discovery of the local gold mines that brought back Thasian colonists in 360 BC, who renamed the town Daton. They were closely followed in 356 BC by King Philip II of Macedon, who fortified the town with a great wall, changed its name once again, this time to Philippi, and derived considerable wealth from the mines. After his victory, Antony established Philippi as a COLONIA for his veterans, and the town gained strategic importance from its position astride the military highway, the Via Egnatia, and its proximity to the port of Neapolis. Philippi was important in the early history of Christianity, as is shown by the prominence given to the story of St. Paul preaching there in 49 AD and being consequently imprisoned (*cf* Acts, xvi), and extensive early Christian building. Interesting among surviving remains are a large underground lavatory of Antonine date, and an early Christian BASILICA where an apparent attempt to construct a dome over the eastern end resulted in the collapse of the end wall.

Philippines. *Prehistory*. A firm archaeological sequence commences in the Philippines c30,000 years ago, at TABON CAVE on Palawan Island; claims for Middle Pleistocene sites in the CAGAYAN VALLEY on Luzon are still insecure. Late Pleistocene stone industries grade between HOABINHIAN and early Australian norms, as one moves from north to south through the archipelago. Major Holocene developments include the spread of a small flake and blade technology after 5000 BC, and the arrival and rapid spread of AUSTRONESIAN-speaking horticulturists after 3000 BC. Rich jar-burial assemblages occur in the islands from about 1000 BC (*see* KALANAY); bronze and iron appear late in the same millennium.

Classical. Situated farthest away from India at the eastern rim of Southeast Asia, the Philippines generated no INDIANIZED kingdom, but entered the Chinese trade network in the late 1st millennium AD. For sites with Chinese trade wares, *see* CALATAGAN, SANTA ANA. However, an appreciable number of Indian cultural elements reached the archipelago during the 14th-16th centuries via Indonesian kingdoms, notably the Java-based kingdom of MAJAPAHIT. This is particularly noticeable in Philippine languages and literatures where Sanskrit loan-words and ancient Indian motifs abound. Scripts in use when the first Spanish missionaries arrived were also ultimately of Indian origin.

Philistines. A people who settled in the coastal plain of Palestine (the name is derived from the same source) in the late 2nd millennium BC. They are known mainly from documentary sources, appearing in Egyptian records as one of the PEOPLES OF THE SEA, and in Biblical accounts as a people who drive the CANAANITES out of the coastal plain and eventually became part of the ISRAELITE kingdom under David c1000 BC. They are difficult to identify archaeologically, but excavations at ASCALON explored the Philistine levels on a small scale.

Phimai. A temple made of sandstone near Nakhon Ratchasima (Khorat) in northeastern THAILAND. It was built by the KHMER kings Jayavarman VI (1080-1107) and Dharanindravarman I (1107-1112) of ANGKOR and is of the ANGKOR WAT style. The tower is 18 metres high. Fully restored, the temple is now a tourist attraction.

Phoenicians. Semitic-speaking people, descendants of the CANAANITES, who occupied the Levant coastal plain in the earlier 1st millennium BC. They are not well-known archaeologically in their homeland, though there has been some exploration of their major sites: BYBLOS, SIDON and TYRE. These are all coastal sites with fine harbours and the Phoenicians were known in the ancient world as sailors and maritime traders. They are described as having circumnavigated Africa and, whatever the truth of that, they certainly traded beyond the Pillars of Hercules into the Atlantic, as well as throughout the Mediterranean basin. From the 9th century onwards (or even earlier, according to tradition) they established colonies in the west, including *inter alia* UTICA and CARTHAGE in north Africa, GADES in Spain, MOTYA in Sicily, NORA and THARROS in Sardinia and other settlements in Malta and Ibiza. When the Phoenician homeland was conquered by BABYLON in 574 BC, the western cities (known as Punic), remained a powerful force in the central and western Mediterranean, along with Greeks, ETRUSCANS and ultimately Romans, with whom they engaged in a series of three PUNIC WARS, which led to their ultimate defeat and incorporation into the Roman world in the 2nd century BC. The Phoenicians received a 'bad press' from their contemporaries, the Greeks and Romans, and they have left us few records of their own. They have left few lasting memorials in the form of great works of art or monumental architecture, but they were responsible for one development of enormous long-term potential: the development of an alphabetic writing system (*see* WRITING). This was developed in the Phoenician homeland and diffused to areas in the west Mediterranean: the Greek, Roman, Arabic and Hebrew alphabets are all derived from the Phoenician.

Phongsavadan. The chronicles, only written down in the 19th century, of events which happened throughout the history of LAOS and the Lao-Burmese border area. They are particularly important for the history of the formation of the first Laotian state in the 14th century. *See also* LAN CHANG.

phosphate surveying. Phosphate is one of the natural constituents of the soil. However, it is concentrated by animals, so that excrement, buried bodies, bones and other food refuse can add large quantities of phosphate to the soil of a particular area. Once phosphate has got into the soil, it is usually converted into an insoluble form, so that it does not tend to move down profile nor to be redistributed sideways in the soil. For this reason, settlements and farms tend to leave high concentrations of phosphate in the soil, which often remain stable over long periods, sometimes thousands of years. Soil samples, taken systematically over an area, can be analysed for phosphates. Such surveys have pointed out the existence of settlements, droveways and other features. They are, however, very time-consuming, and may not add much to excavation, or examination of soils. In addition, phosphate varies widely through a soil, and much preliminary work is needed to determine the extent of this variation before a survey's results may be interpreted.

photogrammetry. The technique of SURVEYING from measurements on photographs. Photogrammetry is most commonly used for plotting from AERIAL PHOTOGRAPHS, and many of today's maps are largely produced by this method. Photogrammetry is also carried out using photographs taken on the ground. Most photogrammetrical methods require stereoscopic pairs of photgraphs, taken to exacting specifications, but some plotting can be done on photographs taken with less specialized equipment.

Phrygia. A short-lived kingdom of west central Turkey; it lasted from c750-680 BC, when it was destroyed by the CIMMERIANS. The capital of the Phrygian kingdom was at GORDION. It is known also from rock-cut sanctuaries and burial remains, including rich burials under large tumuli. The Phrygians are thought to have moved into Anatolia from Thrace or Macedonia and to represent an INDO-EUROPEAN aristocracy, dominating an indigenous population. They are referred to in both Greek and ACHAEMENID Persian sources.

Phung-nguyen. A transitional Neolithic-Bronze Age culture of the Red River valley of northern VIETNAM, dated late 3rd to early 1st millennium BC. Rice, pig, cattle, buffalo and chicken all appear to have been domesticated. Pottery has elaborate incised and stamped decoration and some appears to have been wheel-made and kiln-fired. The Phung-nguyen culture also contains the GO BONG, DONG-DAU and GO MUN phases of the north Vietnamese Bronze Age.

Phylakopi. Bronze Age settlement on the island of MELOS in the southern Aegean. The site was important because of the exploitation of the source of obsidian on the island, which remained in demand throughout the pre-history of the area. Excavations at Phylakopi have provided one of the main sources of information about the CYCLADIC Bronze Age. The first settlement on the site belongs to the Early Cycladic Grotta-Pelos culture, but the first town is Phylakopi II, built in the Middle Cycladic period, c2000 BC. The town was destroyed in the 18th century BC, but was rebuilt and flourished again, coming increasingly under MINOAN influence until the collapse of Minoan power in the mid-15th century. Subsequently mainland — MYCENAEAN — influence dominated Phylakopi, as at other sites in the Aegean. Recent excavations at Phylakopi have cast new light on the development of the site; one of the most interesting discoveries is of a modest Mycenaean temple, dedicated apparently to a male deity.

phytoliths. Microscopic bodies of silica that form a skeleton in some plants, notably grasses. Phytoliths have been found in a number of archaeological contexts.

Pianello. An URNFIELD cemetery near Ancona in eastern Italy. The site belongs to the group often labelled Proto-Villanovan and is dated to the 11th century BC. The cremated remains were placed in decorated pottery urns, often biconical in shape, and covered with inverted bowls used as lids. Accompanying grave goods are modest, but simple arc FIBULAE and razors are common. The name Pianello is sometimes used as an alternative to Proto-Villanovan to describe the early Urnfields in Italy.

Piano Conte. A Copper Age culture of LIPARI, traces of which have also been found on the Italian mainland, perhaps as a result of the trade in obsidian from Lipari. In fact the use of obsidian on Lipari itself declined at this time (early 3rd millennium bc), but copper was still rare and many fine tools of flint were produced. The pottery was distinctive, decorated with close-set grooves, producing a corrugated effect.

Picene. Name given to the Iron Age culture of east central Italy, after the Piceni, recorded by classical authors as living in this area. It is known mainly from cemeteries of rich inhumation burials, indicating a markedly ranked society, dating to the 9th-6th centuries BC. There is much evidence of trade with communities on the other side of the Adriatic, in modern Yugoslavia, and with central Europe. Characteristic artefacts include spiral fibulae and fibulae of various kinds threaded with amber beads.

Pictish symbol stones. A unique class of sculptured monument which forms the major part of the cultural heritage of the Pictish people who inhabited northeast Scotland in the Post-Roman period. Although the stones are roughly divided into three chronological categories, their dating remains somewhat tenuous. The Class I stones are roughly hewn, undressed blocks or pillars, inscribed with pictoral symbols of spiral hipped creatures, such as fishes and birds. They are also decorated with strange geometric shapes as well as inanimate objects like mirrors and combs, grouped together in various combinations. The Class I stones are thought to range in date from about the 5th to the 7th century. In contrast, the Class II stones are regularly dressed slabs which exhibit the same range of carvings but with the significant addition of new Christian elements and humans involved in animated scenes. The crosses and 'bosses' of Class II are mingled with NORTHUMBRIAN interlace, which seems to be heavily influenced by manuscript and embroidery art. These slabs were most commonly used as Christian memorials and are often found in churchyards of roughly 8th-10th century date. The Class III stones are in most cases free-standing crosses, decorated with a combination of a distinctive form of interlace as well as some elements of the old motifs. It is likely that these stones date from the 9th century, after the Pictish amalgamation with DALRIADA.

Picts. There is little documentary or archaeological evidence relating to the Picti or 'painted people' who inhabited the northeastern part of Scotland beyond the Firth of Forth in the sub-Roman period. The first reference to the Picts in the Roman annals dates to the late 3rd century although it is certain that they were established well before this, and they probably descend from Bronze and Iron Age tribes. The Picts did not become properly literate until the 6th century, when they began to benefit from their proximity to the Irish settlers of DALRIADA, but the evidence suggests that they spoke a bastardized Celtic tongue. However, a very individual class of monument testifies to the character of this rather mysterious race — the PICTISH SYMBOL STONES carved with distinctive symbols and ornaments. From these memorial stones we know something of the Pictish royal succession and other history.

In 850 the Picts and other native tribes amalgamated with the Scots.

Piedras Negras. A CLASSIC PERIOD MAYA site located in the steep terrain on the Usumacinta River in northwestern Guatemala. A considerable amount of terracing was necessary to accommodate its tightly grouped structures, which include two BALL COURTS and eight sweat baths (*temescales*). It is, however, best known for its superbly carved stelae and wall panels. These art works were the main source in Tatiana Proskouriakoff's seminal study which showed that certain hieroglyphs recorded historical rather than ceremonial events.

Military themes occur frequently in the art of the site (*see also* YAXCHILLAN); and seashells from both the Pacific and Gulf coasts, obsidian and jade attest to widespread trading. The terminal LONG COUNT date for the site is AD 795.

Piestina. A multi-period Neolithic settlement site, situated on a tributary of the Aiviekste River, in the Lubana depression of Lettland, USSR, and dated to the 3rd millennium bc. The occupation floors are stratified beneath peaty deposits. These levels are associated with vegetable- and shell-tempered coarse wares, with barbotine, incised and cord ornament, termed the Piestina style. A rich assemblage of amber buttons, pendants, rings and beads is present, as well as stone, bone and antler tools and weapons.

Pietersburg. A stone industry occurring mainly in the Transvaal, South Africa, although related material is found also further south. It belongs to the general group of industries based upon the removal of flakes from prepared cores and conventionally attributed to the 'Middle Stone Age'. It is differentiated, however, from other contemporary industries of this type by the presence of large numbers of parallel-sided flake-blades. The best sequence showing the development of the Pietersburg industry is at the CAVE OF HEARTHS in the northern Transvaal, not yet published in detail. The chronology is still poorly defined, although it seems probable that industries of Pietersburg type began to be made well prior to 60,000 BC and continued perhaps until after 20,000 bc.

Piette, Edouard (1827-1906). French scholar who excavated Palaeolithic and Mesolithic sites in southwest France in the 1880s and 1890s. He excavated at Mas d'Azil and discovered the Mesolithic culture named after that site — the AZILIAN. He subdivided the Palaeolithic period into three, the Amygdalithic, Niphetic and Glyptic periods, approximately equivalent to the Lower, Middle and Upper Palaeolithic respectively, but this system was never very widely adopted.

pig. All pigs, wild and domestic, are classified as members of the species *Sus scrofa.* Wild pigs still range widely in wooded areas of Europe and Asia and they seem to have been equally widespread in previous warm periods (*see* QUATERNARY). The difference between domestic and wild pigs lies in their build — wild pigs are taller and more gracile — and their faces — domestic pigs have a shorter snout. The latter difference shows up in measurements of cheek teeth. Wild pigs formed part of the diet of Palaeolithic and Mesolithic hunters. The earliest evidence for their domestication occurs at ÇAYÖNÜ TEPESI (7500-6500 bc) in Turkish Kurdistan, but there is also evidence in the upper layers at JARMO (6500 bc), further south in the Zagros mountains.

Pikimachay. *See* AYACUCHO.

Piklihal. Neolithic site in the Deccan, northern India, related to UTNUR. Underlying Iron Age occupation were two phases of Neolithic settlement. The earliest settlers constructed small terraces, probably for habitations and the penning of animals (cattle, sheel and goats were herded) and perhaps for the cultivation of millet. Associated rock paintings depict deer, gazelle and buffalo and it is likely that hunting of these animals supplemented the diet.

pilaster. A rectangular engaged COLUMN — that is, one incorporated as pier or decoration into a wall and projecting partially from it. In classical architecture, a pilaster normally observes the form of one of the architectural orders, such as IONIC or CORINTHIAN.

pilgrim. Throughout the medieval period pilgrimage was considered the highest achievement available to man. To undertake a long and arduous journey in order to worship at the shrine of a famous saint was to earn both spiritual and physical salvation, and the greater the hardship and danger endured, the greater the final reward. To visit the most prestigious shrines such as that of St James at Santiago de Compostella in northern Spain or the relics of Christ in Jerusalem, the travellers, equipped with special guide books, would follow the well-established pilgrim routes, parts of which still exist. These routes were provided with hostels, hospitals, wayside shrines, crosses and bridges and the magnificent churches designed to accommodate the large numbers of travellers. Apart from buildings, the only material evidence which testifies to these faithful are the pilgrim badges: distinctive metal plaques available at the shrine itself and worn by the successful pilgrim as a souvenir and proof of his undertaking: some of the most distinctive of these are the scallop-shell badges from the shrine of St James.

Piltdown. In 1913 the discovery of pieces of a thick skull essentially like that of modern man was announced. It was claimed that the same site at Piltdown in Sussex, southern England, had produced part of a jaw with ape-like features and some PLEISTOCENE or PLIOCENE fossils. Between 1953 and 1955 it was shown that these objects were mostly doctored fakes, and had all been introduced to the site. Meanwhile the task of anthropologists had been greatly complicated, and the idea that the modern shaped skull appeared early in the record had been encouraged, helping to mislead a whole generation of scholars.

Pincevent. A large Upper PALAEOLITHIC open-air site east of Paris at the confluence of the Seine and Yonne. A number of huts or structures have been investigated, and numerous late MAGDALENIAN artefacts and debris of flint and bone have been recovered. The scale of the excavations, and the plotting and refitting of flint fragments as an aid to reconstructing the living conditions, make these investigations an important pioneering attempt.

pingos. Ice-cored mounds that develop within the active layer and permafrost of the PERIGLACIAL zone. Layers of ice may separate out by percolation of water, or form by the injection of water-charged sediment from below.

When a pingo melts, its centre collapses, leaving behind a circular 'rampart' of material. Pingo ramparts have been used to reconstruct the extent of the periglacial zone which developed around the DEVENSIAN/WEICHSELIAN ice-sheets.

Pingsdorf ware. Hard-fired pots made in the villages in the Vorgebirge Hills, west of COLOGNE and Bonn (see BADORF WARE). The earliest example is the Wermelskirchen coin-hoard pot, dated to c960. Pingsdorf ware is characteristically decorated with red paint, and commonly occurs as pitchers with thumb-impressed ring bases; smaller pots, including money-boxes and toys, were also made. The products were exported to all parts of the Rhineland, as well as Britain and Scandinavia. The forms and hard fabrics were later imitated by other potters in Germany, but fell from favour when stonewares were developed in the later 12th and 13th centuries.

Pingshan [P'ing-shan]. A district in Hebei province, China, southwest of Beijing, where two 4th-century BC royal tombs and many lesser burials of the Zhongshan kingdom have been excavated since 1974. Zhongshan, called Xianyu during the first few years of its existence, was a minor state founed in the late 6th century BC by the White Di, barbarians who occupied Chinese territory, adopted a settled way of life, and became thoroughly sinicized (see RONG AND DI). The state was extinguished in 296 BC. The Pingshan cemetery lies near the site of its last capital, Lingshuo.

The two royal tombs at Pingshan are stepped pits of a size and elaboration hitherto unknown among Eastern ZHOU burials (see SHAFT TOMBS, CHINA). The larger of the two, dated c310 BC, was surmounted by a terraced earthen mound that seems to have carried palatial buildings. Among the tomb furnishings, chiefly bronzes and jades, are some unique objects — a bronze sheet bearing a plan of the mausoleum complex drawn in gold and silver inlay, and many other bronzes, including figures of fantastic animals, with extremely refined decoration in the same two inlays. Two bronze ritual vessels are inscribed with texts of more than 400 characters, not cast inside the vessels in the usual fashion but incised on the exterior. These inscriptions, the longest Eastern Zhou bronze inscriptions known, chronicle events in the history of the Zhongshan site. Their language and substance testify to an ardent adoption of Chinese culture, but other objects from the tombs, notably sets of large bronze tridents and a striking sculptural version of the animal-combat theme, recall the barbarian heritage of the White Di. After its fall the Zhongshan kingdom was remembered in the name of a HAN fief: the 2nd-century BC Han prince Liu Sheng, who was buried at MANCHENG, bore the title Zhongshan Wang, 'King of Zhong-shan'.

Pin Hole Cave. See CRESWELL.

pintadera. A small patterned stamp usually of terracotta with a flat, concave or convex stamping surface and often a knob on the back to act as a handle. Pintaderas are believed to have been used to apply painted designs to human skin, as an alternative to tattooing. In Europe they occur in Neolithic contexts in central Europe and Italy; they also occur widely in the Americas.

pipe-stem dating. A means of calculating the date of American Colonial assemblages based on the variation in hole diameters in clay pipe stems. J.C. Harrington first drew attention to the fact that there is a general reduction in hole size over the period 1620-1800; Lewis Binford developed from this proposition a regression equation, thus:

$$y = 1931.85 - 38.26x$$

where y is the mean date for the group and x is the mean pipe-stem diameter for the sample one is attempting to date. The formula works well for the period 1680-1760, but fails to produce satisfactory results when applied to post-1780 assemblages.

Pirri point. An Australian stone tool type, a symmetrical leaf-shaped point, up to 7 cm long, unifacially flaked all over its dorsal surface. The striking platform and bulb of percussion are sometimes removed to produce a rounded, thinned butt. Pirri points have been found distributed widely in inland Australia from South Australia to the Northern Territory and north-western Australia, but have not so far been found south of the Murray River or in eastern New South Wales and eastern Queensland, including Cape York. A component of the AUSTRALIAN SMALL TOOL

TRADITION, the Pirri point dates from about 3000 bc onwards.

pisé. A building material used in constructing walls and floors, consisting of earth or mud rammed into position.

pit. A common feature of archaeological sites. Pits may have been originally dug for storage, to support large posts, or for industrial purposes. When left undisturbed by man, pits erode and fill, in a similar sequence to DITCHES. Frequently, however, they have been used for waste disposal and contain large quantities of food debris, rubbish from hearths etc.

Pitcairn Island. An isolated island in eastern POLYNESIA, settled by Polynesians (perhaps *c*1100), but already abandoned when mutineers from HMS *Bounty* arrived in 1790. Pitcairn is one of many isolated Polynesian islands with a 'lost' population; *see also* NECKER.

Pit-comb ware. A type of pottery widely used in the CIRCUMPOLAR CULTURES of the forest zone of northeast Europe. It was coarse, thick pottery decorated with both pits and comb impressions (hence the name). The commonest forms are round-based bowls.

Pit Grave culture. *See* KURGAN.

Pithecanthropus. Name given to group of early human fossils found mainly in JAVA. These remains are now classified as HOMO ERECTUS.

Pithekoussai [also ancient Aenaria or Inarime; modern Ischia]. A volcanic island off the northern part of the Bay of Naples, and site of arguably the earliest Greek colony in the western Mediterranean. Lying on sea trade-routes to the mainland of Italy, and especially Etruria, the colony was established by Euboean Greeks from Chalcis and Eretria, perhaps some time in the early 8th century BC. The Monte Vico region shows occupational evidence going back to the Bronze Age, and the acropolis shows also Bronze Age and Iron Age material. The island offered good agricultural land and rich deposits, notably of potters' clay, of which it became the principal supplier to Campania. There was also a wide variety of metalworking. The colony's prosperity seems fairly immediate and early, say from about 750 to 675 BC, when many may have joined the early, perhaps daughter colony at CUMAE, opposite on the mainland — although there is some occupational evidence into the 1st century BC. The volcano was active during the classical period, and eruptions and earthquakes may have persuaded many to leave. A large necropolis has inhumation and cremation burials containing oriental trinkets, Egyptian scarabs, and varied imported and local pottery, including, *inter alia*, a Rhodian cup bearing one of the earliest examples of the Greek alphabet, a Chalcidian version written from right to left.

Pitt-Rivers, General Augustus [born Lane-Fox] (1827-1900). British scholar who developed remarkably advanced techniques of archaeological excavation and recording in the last twenty years of the 19th century. He had been interested in archaeology for many years and had already conducted some excavations, when in 1880 he inherited the Cranborne Chase estate in Dorset. From then until his death he conducted excavations on the many prehistoric and Romano-British sites on that estate. These excavations were carried out with great care and precision and meticulously published, with records of details which had been ignored in excavations up to that time, in four splendid volumes, entitled *Excavations in Cranborne Chase*. Pitt-Rivers is known not only for his contributions to techniques of excavation and recording, but also for his ethnographic collections and studies. Adapting the ideas of evolution from biology to apply to technology, he developed typological schemes for artefacts of various types, demonstrating development through time.

Pjorsadaelur Valley. *See* ICELAND.

place-names. The study of place names plays a vital role in medieval studies. The form of the name will often indicate a Celtic, Latin or Germanic origin, and its prefix or suffix may suggest the type of settlement, for instance, hamlet, village, river-side place, woodland settlement, etc. Place-name studies have probably developed most in Britain, where most Celtic, Latin, Early Saxon, Scandinavian and Norman forms have been identified.

Studies in other countries ranging from Eire to Italy suggest that a similar level of analysis is possible, and should prove rewarding.

Plain of Jars. One of the most celebrated site complexes of mainland Southeast Asia, the Plain of Jars in LAOS has about 250 stone burial jars, up to three metres high, together with other megalithic monuments and pottery jar burials. When examined in the 1930s, the jars contained few remains but bones appear to have been cremated, and artefacts include bronze and iron with local and possible Indian affinities. The cultural background remains poorly understood, but the sites appear to predate Hindu/Buddhist influence.

Plano. A widespread late PALEO-INDIAN culture which is subject to considerable local variability. The characteristic unfluted leaf-shaped projectile point appears to have developed from LLANO and FOLSOM types, since Plano materials post-date them in many archaeological contexts. Dating schemes, however, tend to be arbitrary, since the precise relationship of Plano to earlier Paleo-Indian complexes is still uncertain. Plano material has been found at HELL GAP, Agate Basin and Bonfire Shelter, but perhaps the best-known assemblage is the CODY Complex.

Pleistocene. The earliest epoch of the QUATERNARY period, starting some time around two million years BP and ending at c10,000 bp. It consists of a number of warm and cold stages. The Pleistocene was succeeded by the HOLOCENE or recent period. *See* Tables 4-7 pages 417-20.

Pločnik. A large multi-level flat settlement on a tributary of the Južna Morava River, southern Serbia, Yugoslavia, Pločnik gave its name to M.V. Garasanin's Late VINČA (Vinča-Pločnik) phase, now dated to c3950-3300 bc. The site has three occupation levels in a three-metre stratigraphy, the bottom two with Late Vinča pottery, the uppermost with BUBANJ-HUM pottery. Four hoards of copper tools and ornaments have been found at Pločnik, all at a depth corresponding to the Bubanj-Hum assemblage. These shaft-hole axes, chisels, bird-shaft pin and ingot are characteristic of the the late 4th millennium bc and represent one of the earliest metal hoards in the Yugoslavian Copper Age.

ploughmarks. The marks left in the lower HORIZONS of a BURIED SOIL, where a plough has gouged into them in antiquity. Ploughmarks have been found, for example under several British Neolithic monuments and are valuable evidence for ancient clearance and cultivation.

Plumbate ware. A fine paste pottery type widely traded in the Early POST-CLASSIC PERIOD. Its original point of manufacture was on the Pacific coast of Mesoamerica in the vicinity of IZAPA, but since it has been found in quantity in the lower levels of TULA, it also has TOLTEC associations. Its lustrous surface glaze is the result of the action of firing on the metallic compounds which occur naturally in the clay.

podsol. An alternative spelling of PODZOL.

podzol [podsol]. The type of SOIL which characteristically develops under coniferous woodland, moor and heath vegetation, and may develop from BROWN FOREST SOILS or SOLS LESSIVÉS. Most conifers and plants that grow on heaths and moorland produce leaf litter, which is high in chemicals called phenols. These slow down decomposition of the litter and are unpalatable to EARTHWORMS, so that a HORIZON of litter in various states of decomposition accumulates at the top of the PROFILE. In addition, the phenols washed into the horizons below disperse the clay/humus complexes (*see* SOIL). Minerals, humus and nutrients are washed down the profile and become deposited as ILLUVIAL HORIZONS of HUMUS and iron oxides. The latter is often called the 'iron pan'. A bleached, sandy ELUVIAL HORIZON is left at the top of the profile. Podzols develop naturally in areas of high annual rainfall and moorland vegetation, or under coniferous forest, but most of the large areas of podsols in the uplands and lowland heaths of the British Isles were probably at least initiated by man's clearance of woodland during the present INTERGLACIAL (*see* BOREAL and ATLANTIC). In the dampest areas of the uplands, the thick litter layer of the podzols has become waterlogged and colonized by BOG moss and other PEAT-forming plants. The thick 'Blanket Bog' which has grown as a result covers considerable areas of the Pennines and Scotland.

Polada. An Early Bronze Age village near the southern end of Lake Garda in northern Italy which has given its name to a culture covering the southern slopes of the Alps. A variety of settlement types occur, including hill sites and LAKE VILLAGES like Polada itself. These lakeside settlements have produced a large amount of well-preserved organic material, including evidence on the subsistence economy (well-developed mixed farming supplemented by hunting and the collection of wild plant foods) and a range of artefacts of kinds that do not often survive (wooden cups and other vessels and tools such as a saw with flint teeth). The Polada people were accomplished metal-workers, producing a range of tools and weapons showing strong connections with ÚNĚTICE and other Early Bronze Age groups north of the Alps. The pottery was a simple dark burnished ware, but with elbow handles, a form which also occurs on wooden vessels of the time. Dates for the Polada culture begin *c*2100 BC, but mostly fall in the earlier 2nd millennium BC.

Poliochni. A settlement site on the island of Lemnos, in the north Aegean Sea. It has seven successive phases of occupation, spanning the Neolithic to the Middle Bronze Age. In the Early Bronze Age it was a fortified township with stone defences, houses laid out along streets, and evidence of the practice of metallurgy. An associated cemetery of inhumation burials has many with rich grave goods.

Poljanica. A Copper Age TELL located near Trgovište in northeast Bulgaria and dated to the mid-4th millennium bc. Excavated by H. Todorova, the tell has 10 occupation levels, most of which comprise 10-15 complete houses densely packed within a triple palisade. Resembling a Roman fort in outward appearance, Poljanica represents the peak of spatial organization in Balkan tell settlements. The name is also applied to the Early and Middle Eneolithic culture of northeast Bulgaria, related to the BOIAN and Marica cultures.

pollen analysis. The analysis of pollen grains preserved in ancient SEDIMENTS and SOILS. Pollen grains are the microscopic bodies which are released from flowers in enormous quantities in summer. Each grain has an extremely tough outer coat — the exine — which may be preserved for many thousands or indeed millions of years. These exines can be identified: some only to the family, many to genus and a few to the species of plant from which the pollen came. Because of the variation in identifiability, it is usual to talk of 'pollen types' rather than species, etc. The sediments most frequently investigated are PEAT and lake deposits, but the more acid soils, such as PODZOLS, are also analysed. The acidity and anaerobic conditions in these materials inhibit the organisms which would normally be capable of decomposing, or damaging the exine. SAMPLES are taken at intervals through the sediment or soil, using either a coring device or a section, if one is available. Pollen is extracted from the material by chemically breaking down all the other constituents. Each sample is processed separately and the pollen mounted on glass slides; the grains in each slide are identified and the number of each pollen type is counted. These counts are then calculated as percentages (PROPORTIONAL POLLEN COUNTING) or as counts per unit weight or volume (ABSOLUTE POLLEN COUNTING). When all the samples have been counted, a POLLEN DIAGRAM is constructed to show how the relative frequencies of the different pollen types have varied through the depth of the sediment or soil. RADIOCARBON DATES may be taken at intervals up the sequence, and it is possible to reconstruct the history of vegetation in the area around the site where the samples were taken.

Interpretation of pollen analysis is fraught with difficulties. Different plants produce different quantities of pollen; pollen from plants many hundreds of miles away may be blown into the bog or lake where the sediment is accumulating; material eroded from older sediments may be incorporated. But the technique remains the most useful method for reconstructing ancient environments (*see* ENVIRONMENTAL ARCHAEOLOGY).

pollen diagram. A diagram showing the results of POLLEN ANALYSIS. Pollen diagrams consist of a number of graphs, showing the fluctuations of different pollen types through a SEDIMENT or SOIL. The vertical axis of the diagram represents depth through the deposit and is therefore roughly related to time, in the sense that deeper layers will be older than layers above (*see* STRATI-GRAPHY). Each small graph represents the changing frequency of one pollen type, either as a percentage (PROPORTIONAL POLLEN COUNTING) or as an absolute frequency (AB-SOLUTE POLLEN COUNTING). It is often possible to split the diagram up into a number of POLLEN ZONES, each dominated by high frequencies of a particular pollen type, or group of types.

pollen zones. A series of divisions which may be drawn across a POLLEN DIAGRAM on the basis of fluctuations in pollen types. The concept of generally applicable pollen zones was initiated by von Post in Sweden. In Britain, a system of zones was proposed by Godwin in 1940. Godwin's zones were numbered I-VIII. Zone I corresponded to what would now be called the main STADIAL of the DEVENSIAN cold stage, Zone II to the WINDERMERE INTERSTADIAL and Zone III to the LOCH LO-MOND stadial. Zone IV (corresponding to the PRE-BOREAL period) marked the start of the FLANDRIAN INTERGLACIAL and the re-appearance of trees. Zones V and VI (together corresponding to the BOREAL period) showed the gradual development of woodland and forest. Zones VIIa (the ATLANTIC) was the period of domination by deciduous forest; Zones VIIb (SUB-BOREAL) and VIII (SUB-ATLANTIC) marked man's clearance of forest, and the arrival of new tree species.

This scheme was widely accepted and has often been given a significance that was not originally intended. Godwin's zones were applied right across Britain. They became regarded as fixed in time — indeed, pollen analysis has frequently been used as a DATING method. A general scheme like this, however, does not take into account variation in the sequence of vegetation change from place to place. There are often difficulties in applying the zones to pollen diagrams outside southern England, where the system was first applied. RADIOCARBON DATING of the zone boundaries has shown considerable variation in their timing between different sites in Britain. Many palynologists therefore do not now apply this system rigidly to pollen diagrams, but it is still useful as a general guide to the development of British vegetation during the late Devensian and Flandrian.

West has proposed another system, based on the succesion of vegetation during inter-glacials. In West's scheme, all interglacials are divided up into four zones: I Pre-Temperate; II Early Temperate; III Late Temperate; IV Post-Temperate. This is preceded by an abbreviation for the interglacial in question. Thus for the Flandrian there are Fl I (equivalent to Godwin's IV, V and VI), Fl II (Godwin VIIa) and Fl III (Godwin VIIb and VIII). Fl IV has not happened yet. Similarly, there are Ip I-IV for the IPSWICHIAN, Ho I-IV for the HOXNIAN etc.

In recent years, many palynologists have abandoned general zonation schemes and instead have divided their pollen diagrams into 'pollen assemblage zones' (p.a.z.). These are based simply on the pollen fluctuations seen in each particular diagram and can therefore take account of local variation in the history of vegetation.

Polo, Marco (1254-1324). Venetian author of a book of travels dictated to the romance writer Rustichello of Pisa about 1298. With his father and uncle, the merchants Niccolò and Maffeo Polo, Marco spent more than 20 years in the China of Kubilai Khan (*r.* 1260-94) and in travel along the SILK ROUTE. Chinese sources give no evidence that Marco held the important position at Kubilai's court that his book attributes to him, and the quantities of medieval romance freely supplied by Rusti-chello give the book a fairy-tale atmosphere, yet enough of it is demonstrably authentic to warrant the prologue's claim that Marco travelled more widely than any man since the creation. The book does not mention such obvious curiosities as the Chinese script, printing, tea, or the GREAT WALL — omissions possibly explained by the incompleteness of surviving manuscripts — but its account of paper money and admiring description of the city of Hangzhou bear the stamp of first-hand observation. The influence of the book in later centuries may have been as much due to its fictional embellishments as to its authentic substance (and for early readers these two elements were blended inseparably). When the collapse of the Mongol empire closed the land route to China, Marco Polo's narrative kept alive European interest in the fabulous wealth of the East; Columbus owned a copy which he carefully annotated. Accounts of the 13th-century Mongol court at once more factual and more vivid than Marco's were written by the clerics John of Plano Carpini and William of Rubruck, who, however, did not visit China but only the capital of Kubilai's predecessors at Karakorum in Mongolia.

Polonuaruwa. Capital of Sri Lanka from 281 to 1290. The most impressive surviving monuments belong to the later 12th and 13th centuries, and include a series of colossal sculptured figures and a number of temples and monasteries in the so-called Great Quadrangle.

polychrome jewellery. Multi-coloured or polychrome jewellery is characteristically found in cemeteries of 5th-7th century date in southeast England and in continental FRANK-ISH burials. However, the origins of the technique can be traced back to the Scythian and later Iron Age cultures of Eastern Europe. The polychrome effect was achieved by two basic methods; of these, the CLOISONNÉ (or cell) technique was the most intricate and effective. In this case the flat stone or glass gem was placed into a cell built up from strands of metal separated by FILIGREE wire; a piece of stamped foil was placed at the bottom to reflect the light back through the stone and so enhance its beauty. In the second, more commonly used method, both cell and base-plate were cast in one piece with imitation filigree wire. Garnets are the dominant feature of the richest polychrome jewellery and are arranged with combinations of coloured glass, enamels, white shell and NIELLO into settings of gold, silver and foiled bronze. One of the richest collections of polychrome jewellery known is from the early 7th century SUTTON HOO ship burial.

Polynesia. A vast region of islands in the central Pacific occupied by closely related ethnic groups, falling mostly within a triangle with apices at the HAWAIIAN ISLANDS, NEW ZEALAND and EASTER ISLAND. Western Polynesia was settled by AUSTRONESIAN speakers from Island Southeast Asia around 1500 BC (LAPITA culture), and migrations progressed throughout the triangle until New Zealand was reached c900 AD. The Polynesians are a homogeneous population in terms of language and social organization (developed into powerful chiefdoms in the larger islands); and claims for an earlier settlement of eastern Polynesia from South America are no longer tenable. Polynesian economy was based on tuber and fruit horti-culture, with a pre-metal technology; pottery production ceased in Western Polynesia c300 AD and was never present in most eastern Islands nor in New Zealand.

Polynesian Outliers. Communities occupying the 19 small islands to windward (east) of the large MELANESIAN islands of the SOLOMONS, VANUATU and NEW CALEDONIA. Archaeo-logy and linguistics suggest settlement by a back-movement from western Polynesia (SAMOA, Futuna, Ellice) perhaps starting in the 1st millennium AD.

Pomongwe. A cave in the Matopo Hills near Bulawayo, Zimbabwe. At the very bottom of the deep archaeological deposits are a few artefacts which may possibly be of SANGOAN type. Later occupations are attributed suc-cessively to the CHARAMAN, BAMBATA, TSHANGULA and WILTON industries. Inter-stratified between the last two is a horizon containing utilized flakes and crude scrapers to the virtual exclusion of other implement types; dated to about the 9th millennium bc, this industry has been named Pomongwan.

Pompeii. A port and principal city on the Bay of Naples in southwest Italy which was over-whelmed by an eruption of the quiescent volcano, Vesuvius, on 24 August, 79 AD and, as a fortuitous outcome, offers plentiful evidence for prosperous provincial urban life in the 1st century AD. The early history of the settlement is obscure and confused. A DORIC temple of the 6th century BC together with ATTIC BLACK-FIGURE WARE clearly suggests a strong Greek presence, and association with CUMAE, NAPLES and PAESTUM is very plausible. ETRUSCAN influence is also very likely. Takeover by Samnite tribes from the hinterland some time about 420 BC does not seem to have caused any break in the town's civilized prosperity, and the settlement remained Samnite with Oscan language until 89 BC. In that year, Pompeii came under siege from Sulla for its anti-Roman stance in the so-called Social War, and a Sullan COLONIA of veterans was established from 80 BC. Colonial status brought rapid Romanization and an enhanced success, signalled by the advent of sumptuous villas in the vicinity. A violent earthquake in 62 AD caused great damage but apparently no permanent setback in morale. A vigorous programme of rebuilding was put in hand, and in many cases it seems the builders were still busy when the eruption of 79 AD took them by surprise. The deposit that fell was first small pumice and then ash, aggravated later by poisonous gas and rain. Rebuilding would have meant the removal in some places of more than six metres of deposit, and the survivors settled instead for a policy of stripping out everything of value and use that could be reached. Tunnels were sunk, driving in some cases directly through the walls of houses, and it is likely that some of the would-be salvagers were caught by lingering concentrations of trapped gas. The difficulty and danger of this recovery operation probably led quite soon to the total desertion of the site, which remained derelict until rediscovery in the middle of the 18th century.

Of all the numerous surviving buildings, Pompeii is perhaps most celebrated for its ATRIUM-style private houses, often embellished with fine gardens, and decorated internally with elaborate MOSAICS and mural panels. The AMPHITHEATRE is probably the earliest stone-built example that we have, and is interesting for its unsophisticated answers to problems of seating layout and relationship between ARENA and spectators. Of the two THEATRES, the larger is HELLENISTIC (probably 2nd century BC) with later additions and modifications. Features include stage installations for fountain spectaculars, and a large square behind the stage buildings that was probably used as a theatre foyer (or *porticus post scaenam*) in which spectators could stroll and talk. There were at least three major public bath complexes, and there is also evidence for installations in private premises. The Stabian Baths have segregated accommodation for men and women. Religious worship was catered for by the provision, over the whole history of the town, of no less than nine temples. In particular, the Temple of Isis reflects the popularity of the personalized Oriental mystery cults under the early Empire, since the building is one of a small number that had been completely repaired and rebuilt in the interval between the earthquake and the eruption. Another, the Lararium, owes its existence to the earlier disaster, since it is dedicated to the *lares* or proctective deities of home and hearth, with a propitiatory motive.

Pompeian life is further documented by the frequent painted and inscribed notices, or graffiti, which are to be found on both internal and external walls. There often refer to local elections, in which interest was obviously lively, and to events taking place at the Amphitheatre, but personal comments and epigrams also occur. The seamier side of life is represented by gambling den and brothel — although on both of these scholarship is often a little evasive and coy.

During the eruption, both human beings and animals (for instance, a chained-up dog) were encased by the deposit, forming paralysed shapes. Casts made from these give a startling impression of the original victims. There are ancient accounts of the earthquake in Seneca, *Quaestiones Naturales* 6.1.1., and Tacitus, *Annals*, XV.22.4. Pliny the Younger gives a vivid eye-witness account of the eruption in *Epistulae*, VI.16,20. *See also* HERCULANEUM.

Po Nagar. A site of the kingdom of CHAMPA, in the present town of Nha-trang on the coast of southern Vietnam. It is particularly known for its Sanskrit inscriptions recording the late 8th-century raids by seamen from Java who destroyed several temples. A new sanctuary was built at the site by king Satyavarman in 784, and a famous golden statue of Bhagavatī was consecrated there in 918 by king Indravarman III, whose literary and philosophical knowledge is praised in epigraphy.

Ponape. *See* NAN MADOL.

pond barrow. *See* BARROW.

Pont du Gard. Stretch of Roman AQUEDUCT, probably built by Agrippa *c*19 BC to serve the city of Nemausus (NÎMES) in southern France. The aqueduct brought spring water from near Uzès some 50 km upstream. It has been calculated that the down gradient over this whole length is of the order of 1:3000. About 300 metres long and some 50 metres high, the bridge is built of squared stone blocks quarried a short distance upstream. Three tiers of arches are used, the topmost in a stone duct capped by stone slabs. This channel is some 1.2 metres wide and some 1.5 metres high, and access is permitted. Whether by accident or design, the arches observe a system of proportion in a relationship of one unit for the topmost arches, three for the side arches, four for the central ones, and six for the overall height of the bridge. Projecting bosses survive for maintenance scaffolding.

Pontnewydd. A cave northwest of Denbigh, North Wales. Excavations in the 19th century demonstrated that it had been occupied in the Lower Palaeolithic period, but new excavations since 1978 have brought much important new evidence to light and clarified previously obscure issues of stratigraphy and chronology. The site had been occupied by a community using a stone industry of Upper ACHEULIAN type, including artefacts made using the LEVALLOIS technique. Dating by URANIUM SERIES DATING and THERMOLUMINISCENCE suggest dates in the range 170-200,000 years ago, or possibly even older. The most interesting discoveries are several hominid remains, including a tooth showing a marked degree of taurodontism (enlargement of the pulp cavity), a feature that prompts comparison with fossils of NEANDERTHAL type. The only other site in Britain to have produced hominid remains of this early period is SWANSCOMBE.

Popol Vuh. *See* CODEX.

Porodin. A TELL settlement of the Neolithic period, located in the flood plain of the Bitolj basin, Pelagonia, Yugoslavia. Excavated by M. Grbić, the site has a 1.8-metre stratigraphy, including two occupation layers. The earlier, with a radiocarbon date of *c*5170 bc, contains STARČEVO pottery with affinities to Greek Macedonian material (e.g. NEA NIKOMEDEIA); the later level, typologically dated to the mid-5th millennium bc, is characterized by dark burnished ware. In the Starčevo level fired clay house models with chimneys on pitched roofs were recovered.

portal dolmen. Term for a type of MEGALITHIC tomb found in Ireland and western Britain. It is characterized by a rectangular chamber, often with an entrance blocked by a large stone slab and flanked by two large stone slabs forming a sort of porch.

Portchester [Roman Portus Adurni]. A Roman SAXON SHORE fort in Hampshire, southern England, covering an area of some 3.5 hectares. There was some use of the site from the 1st century AD, and traces of timber structures have been found. The surviving Roman stone, flint and tile walls, however, indicate a late 3rd century AD fort that was occupied, with some interruptions, for about a century until 370 AD, when the troops were shifted to nearby Bitterne (Roman Clausentum). The Roman walls still stand some 6 metres high (the battlements are largely Norman), and 14 out of 20 hollow bastions remain. These were floored with timber, probably for the positioning of artillery. The fort seems to have stayed deserted until Henry I saw the strategic advantages of the site and constructed a keep in the northwest corner (*c*1120), and a Romanesque church in the south east angle (1133). Of the great Roman gates, which appear to have been set back in an entrance courtyard for extra protection, the eastern is totally obliterated under the medieval Watergate, but something of the western may be made out inside Landgate.

port-hole slab. A stone slab with a usually circular hole, or two adjacent slabs each with a semi-circular hole, most often found in MEGALITHIC tombs, from western Europe to India. The holes, whether circular, square or irregular in shape, are usually large enough to allow the passage of a human body and generally served to provide restricted entrance to a tomb of part of a tomb.

Portus Adurni. *See* PORTCHESTER.

Poseidonia. *See* PAESTUM.

Post-Classic Period. The Late CLASSIC PERIOD (600-900) in MESOAMERICA saw the fall of many established cultures and the rise of new centres of power (such as TULA, CHICHEN ITZA and TENOCHTITLAN). The Post-Classic Period, traditionally dated from the fall of the Classic MAYA (900) to the Spanish Conquest (1520), is characterized by an increasingly militaristic and secular attitude. This new attitude is reflected in a shift of religious emphasis (for example replacement of QUETZACOATL by Texcatlipoca), increased siting of settlements in defensive locations (TULA) and the rise of military and sacrificial themes in iconography.

posthole. A small pit, made to hold the foot of a post. Many postholes found on archaeological sites contain no evidence of the post or its packing, but in some, a collar of packing stones may still be in position, enclosing a 'post pipe' or even remains of the post itself. Prehistoric sites often have no evidence for structures other than postholes.

Postoloprty. A village in Bohemia, Czechoslovakia, where sites of several periods are known. At one locality a Late Neolithic LENGYEL settlement is known, dating from the 4th millennium bc. Here a timber-framed trapezoidal LONG HOUSE with an antechamber had four domed ovens down the length of its interior; this house has been used to support the theory of LINEAR POTTERY long houses possessing several hearths and, concomitantly, an extended family. At the locality of Žatec, an Early Bronze Age village of the ÚNĚTICE culture was found, comprising over 20 rectangular timber-framed houses.

potassium argon dating. A RADIOMETRIC dating method, developed in the 1960s.

Principles of $^{40}K/^{40}Ar$ dating. There are two main isotopes of potassium, ^{39}K and ^{40}K which exist in a constant proportion in minerals. ^{40}K is radioactive and decays either to the gas argon (^{40}Ar) or to calcium (^{40}Ca), both of which are stable. When igneous rock first solidifies, most of the argon in it has been driven off by the heat. Afterwards, decay of ^{40}K produces ^{40}Ar, which is trapped within the mineral, where it builds up slowly. The rate (half-life) at which ^{40}K decays occurs is known and so the age of the rock may be calculated from the analysed ratio of ^{40}K to ^{40}Ar.

Problem. A source of error in $^{40}K/^{40}Ar$ dates is the possible diffusion of ^{40}Ar into or out of the rock, or retention of small quantities of the gas in spite of the original heating. The former would make the date too young, the latter too old.

$^{40}Ar/^{39}Ar$ dating. A refinement of the analysis technique. It involves a series of heating and measurement steps which enable the problems of ^{40}Ar diffusion and inheritance to be greatly reduced. In this way, it allows the dating of younger rocks than would otherwise have been possible.

Range. ^{40}K has a long half-life ($c1000$ million years) so potassium/argon is most applicable to rocks much older than the archaeological timescale. It can, however be used for rocks as young as 250,000 BP, but becomes inaccurate on younger material.

Accuracy. The probable error of the determination is usually between $\pm$ 10 per cent and $\pm$ 50 per cent of the date.

Materials. Potassium/argon can only be done on volcanic rocks, and then only on certain minerals. It has, however produced useful dating for hominid fossils in OLDUVAI and KOOBI FORA. The palaeomagnetic field reversals are all dated by the method (*see* PALAEOMAGNETISM). In addition, pebbles of particularly characteristic and K/Ar-dated lavas from the QUATERNARY Eiffel volcano have been found in terraces of the Rhine Valley. This has allowed an estimate of the age of the terraces to be made.

potato. An indigenous South American tuber, probably first domesticated in the southern Peruvian Andes around Lake Titicaca. Unlike maize, the potato flourishes at high altitudes (even above 4000 metres) and was the basic staple of many of the societies of the Altiplano, such as TIAHUANACO. The date of its domestication is uncertain, but it was already in use by the INITIAL PERIOD and may have been as early as PRE-CERAMIC PERIOD VI.

pot boilers. The name given to stones which have been heated in a fire; they are often of flint, and characteristically present a white or greyish cracked appearance. They are thought to have been used to heat water for cooking purposes, a practice that is well-documented ethnographically.

pottery. The main constituent of pottery is pot CLAY. This term mainly describes the size of the particles in the material (less than 0.002mm). In practice, however, particles of this size are mostly composed of the clay minerals — in pot clay, usually the mineral kaolinite. The tiny crystals of this mineral are flat and plate-like. When the clay is wet, the crystals are separated by a film of water and the clay is mouldable. When the clay has dried out, the crystals are no longer lubricated in this way and are stacked up against each other rendering the clay hard. These are the properties involved in the first stages of pot-making — moulding and drying. Pots can be built up from rings or coils of clay, pinch moulded, or turned on a potter's wheel. When they have been dried to 'leather hardness', they can have decorations incised, impressed or burnished onto them, or handles and lugs added with a sticky clay adhesive. Drier still, and they are ready for a slip (thin slurry of clay) decoration or coating. When completely dry, the pots are fired. The purpose of firing is to weld the clay particles together. Pure kaolinite melts at 1770°C, far beyond the reach of early kilns. But with the inclusion of impurities which act as fluxes, the clay particles will sinter together at a much lower temperature — 1000 to 1200°C for most ancient pot clays. It is however unlikely that even this temperature was reached in the majority of early kilns. Much of the clay is unsintered, and the pottery is better described as 'baked' rather than 'fired'. Modern potters called this material TERRACOTTA. Kiln temperatures improved in the Bronze Age civilizations of the Mediterranean, in the great Roman factories of Europe, and in medieval times. Glaze coatings are usually added and fired separately, after an initial 'biscuit' firing.

Most pot clay, as it is dug out of the ground, does not consist solely of clay particles. It also contains SAND size (0.02-2mm diameter), particles of minerals or rock fragments. When a pot is made, such inclusions ensure that the clay is not too sticky and does not collapse while drying. Crushed rock fragments or ground-up pottery ('grog') were often added to improve these qualities. Inclusions of this kind also allowed the clay to dry out evenly and to survive firing without damage. PETRO-LOGICAL ANALYSIS of inclusions has been used to trace the source of pot clays and thus reconstruct ancient trade in pottery. Archaeologists usually call fired pot clay the 'fabric' of a piece of pottery. Texture, mineralogy and colour of fabric may be used to describe and classify pottery. Texture and mineralogy may indeed be a result of the origin of the clay, but colour is more often the result of firing. The kiln temperature may not have been sufficient to burn off organic inclusions. Such fabrics may have a black core of incompletely burned carbon. If air was allowed into the kiln, the iron oxides present in most clays will be of the red, oxidized form. If air was excluded, the iron oxides will be in their dark, reduced state. These oxides, and the colour of the fabric, may vary through a pot wall if the kiln atmosphere was not constant.

pou [p'ou]. *See* RITUAL VESSELS (CHINA).

Poverty Point. A site in the Lower Mississippi valley in Louisiana, USA, which rendered radiocarbon dates in the range 1200-100 bc, but has features that are anomalous in the cultural context of the time. Major earthworks include six concentric ridges in a semicircular or octagonal plan (1-2 metres high and 1200 metres maximum diameter), a large mound and a number of smaller features.

A high level of social organization is indicated by the presence of such earthworks, but there is very little evidence of the practice of agriculture, which would normally be expected with such construction. Artefacts, on the whole, are consistent with the Late ARCHAIC, although there are a small number of polished hoes and some crude pottery. The minimal botanical evidence (remains of squash) taken together with the large mound, which is twice the size of its OLMEC contemporary at LA VENTA, is proposed as evidence of a possible MESOAMERICAN connection, although this has yet to be satisfactorily demonstrated. The diagnostic artefacts of the Poverty Point culture are the co-called Poverty Point 'objects', which are small, roughly shaped, hand-moulded lumps of clay purportedly used for cooking in lieu of heated stones. They are found in thousands, both here and at other sites in the Lower Mississippi valley.

Poznan. City in western Poland, one of the centres of the early Polish kingdom established under Mieszko I during the second half of the 10th century. The first Polish bishopric was founded here in 968. Excavations before World War II uncovered the 10th-century rampart; its timber footings were reinforced with rubble. It was for some time the largest defensive work of this kind known from Europe. The excavations also uncovered many relics of the Slavic period, including the tomb of a bishop containing a very fine crozier.

pozzuolana [*pozzolana*]. Properly a volcanic ash found in the locality of Pozzuoli (Roman Puteolum), an Italian coastal town north of Naples. This material, *pulvis Puteolanus* ('dust from Puteolum'), seems to have been recognized by the Romans from the 2nd century BC onwards, especially for its hydraulic properties, and as a constituent of various cements. The natural properties of this and related materials may well have been of central importance in the rapid development that the Romans were able to make in the technology of concrete buildings in the late Republican and early Imperial periods.

Praia das Maĉas. A large Copper Age tomb north of Lisbon in Portugal. In its first phase it was a simple rock-cut tomb. Subsequently it had added to it a PASSAGE GRAVE with partially CORBELLED chamber. A radiocarbon date for the later tomb dates its construction to *c*2200 bc (*c*2850 BC). The tomb contained about 150 burials.

Prambanan. The name of a plain to the east of Yogyakarta on the island of JAVA, Indonesia, studded with stone monuments of the 8th-10th centuries, the so-called Prambanan Group. These monuments are both Buddhist and Hindu; their many inscriptions are a rich source of historical information.

preaching cross [standing cross]. A class of monumental sculpture unique to the British Isles, which probably developed from the 7th century onwards. The tall, tapering cross shaft rested on a plinth or base, and carried a three-armed cross head. Both the cross and the shaft were usually ornamented with Christian figures and other decorative motifs. The origins of the preaching cross are obscure, but probably owe much to Celtic interpretations of Mediterranean crosses and to Iron Age stelae. Many crosses would have been carved in wood, and many would have preceded parish churches.

Preah Vihear. A sanctuary built under the KHMER king Rajendravarman (944-68) of ANGKOR and dedicated to Siva of the Mountain, situated in the Dangrek chain in northern Cambodia on the border with Thailand. It has been described as one of the most beautiful natural sites of the whole of Asia. Claimed by both Thailand and Cambodia, it became a case that went to the International Court of Justice at The Hague; the judgement was in favour of Cambodia.

Pre-Axumite. This misleading name is generally applied to the developed societies of south Arabian origin attested in the plateau country of northern Ethiopia during the second half of the first millennium BC. Although many features of these societies — their stone architecture (*see* YEHA), their Himyaritic

syllabary and their worship of the moon god — may be traced to a homeland in south Arabia, the contribution of indigenous African peoples is more difficult to assess. It is plausible to suggest that the introduction of Semitic speech to an area where Cushitic languages were previously spoken also dates from this time. These societies provided the base from which the kingdom of AXUM rose to prominence during the first centuries AD.

Pre-Boreal. A climatic sub-division of the FLANDRIAN INTERGLACIAL, first proposed by Blytt and Sernander from investigations of Scandinavian lakes and BOGS (*See also* BOREAL, ATLANTIC, SUB-BOREAL and SUB-ATLANTIC). The climate during the Pre-Boreal period represented the start of the Flandrian and was supposed to be Sub-Arctic in character. Von Post's POLLEN ANALYSIS in Sweden showed the Pre-Boreal to be characterized by a mixture of tundra and birch woodland. Blytt and Sernander's scheme, together with Von Post's ideas, were applied elsewhere in Europe and Godwin proposed a similar scheme of POLLEN ZONES for Britain. Godwin's Zone IV corresponded to the Pre-Boreal, and was particularly characterized by the appearance of birch and pine trees.

Preceramic Period. The earliest of a seven-period chronological construction used in Peruvian archaeology. It is usually divided into six sub-periods and is characterized by a variety of subsistence patterns and, as the name implies, a lack of ceramics. Sub-periods I (before 9500 bc) and II (*c*9500-8000 bc) represent a subsistence base exclusively or heavily reliant upon hunting. Preceramic III (*c*8000-6000 bc) is seen as transitional from hunting to hunting and gathering, and IV (*c*6000-4000 bc) as a time of cyclical, seasonal migration (*see* ARCHAIC). The drying-up of the LOMAS and a tendency to sedentism are characteristic of Preceramic V (*c*4000-2500 bc). Large habitation sites, CEREMONIAL CENTRES (e.g. EL PARAISO) and agriculture appear increasingly in Preceramic VI (*c*2500-1800 bc). *See* Table 9, page 552.

Pre-Classic. *See* FORMATIVE.

Predionica. A Late Neolithic settlement of the early VINĈA culture, located near Pristina in Kosova, southern Serbia, Yugoslavia. The first of three occupation horizons has a radio-carbon date of *c*4330 bc. In the earlier excavations of R. Galović, several examples of monumental fired-clay figurine heads were discovered; this prompted use of the term 'Predionica style' for the group of monumental sculptures found in southern Serbia. The main characteristics of the style are abstract modelling with plastic features reinforced by incised lines.

Předmost [Předmosti]. A site near Prerov in central Czechoslovakia, where the largest series of PALAEOLITHIC skeletons ever recovered together was found in 1894. Over 20 skeletons of males, females and children were found in a large communal grave, buried under LOESS. The age of the grave and its archaeological status are poorly fixed, but it is probably around 25,000 bc. Some of the males had marked NEANDERTHALOID features but the overall morphology was CROMAGNON.

Pre-Dynastic Egypt. This stage in the history of the Egyptian Nile Valley intervenes between the florescence of the peasant Neolithic communities represented at MERIMDE and the FAYUM and the formation of the centralized Egyptian state of dynastic times. It covers the period from the early 5th to the late 4th millennium BC. Until recent years, most of our knowledge of pre-Dynastic Egypt was derived from the excavation of numerous graves, and several industries were recognized and ordered, primarily through the typological seriation of the pottery these graves contained. The succession thus established consisted of BADARIAN, Nakada I (Amratian), Nakada II (Gerzean) and Nakada III. New research, aided by a radiocarbon chronology, suggests that these phases were not so distinct as was previously believed.

The initial developments of characteristic pre-Dynastic communities appear on current evidence to have taken place in the section of the Nile Valley immediately south of Asyut, from where their influence subsequently extended both up and downstream. Large settlements were established, notably that at HIERAKONPOLIS, although it is likely that the majority of the population continued to inhabit small rural villages. The food-producing economy, as in earlier times, was based upon the cultivation of emmer wheat and barley and on the herding of cattle and small stock, together with some fishing, hunting and use of wild plant foods.

Changes in settlement patterns were accompanied by, and presumably intimately linked with, important technological developments which strongly suggest the emergence of highly specialist craftsmen able to engage in very lengthy processes. Vessels were carved from porphyry, basalt and alabaster: flaked stone implements were given an unparalleled quality of finish. Rare copper objects found on early pre-Dynastic sites seem all to have been hammered from native copper, and there is no evidence for knowledge of smelting prior to *c*3600 BC. Crafts of linen-weaving, basketry and pottery also flourished.

A clear thread through the history of pre-Dynastic Egypt is the increasing importance of quasi-urban centres accompanied by activity differentiation and social stratification. Many of these centres eventually achieved political control over surrounding areas, resulting in the rise of a series of small states. It was apparently through the success of the rulers of This in establishing their authority over the greater part of the Egyptian Nile Valley, around 3100 BC that the unified kingdom of Ancient Egypt came into being (*see* DYNASTIC EGYPT).

Pre-Pottery Neolithic. Name introduced by Kathleen KENYON to describe early phases of the Neolithic of the Levant, characterized by the practice of agriculture and permanent settlement prior to the use of pottery. From her excavations at JERICHO she identified two phases of the Pre-Pottery Neolithic: the PPNA phase, with radiocarbon dates in the range 8350-7000 bc; and PPNB, dated *c*7000-6000 bc. *See also* ACERAMIC NEOLITHIC.

Prescott. *See* HAKATAYA.

pressure flaking. A technique of flint-working first widely used in the SOLUTRIAN about 18000 bc; it involves removing thin retouching flakes, not by striking, but by pressing them off with a kind of hand-held punch or fabricator. Typically it was leaf-shaped points which were made by this technique and the resulting pieces are very attractive in appearance. Later, remarkable craftsmanship in pressure flaking was achieved by early farmers in Egypt, Denmark and other regions.

Přezletice. An early PLEISTOCENE site just outside Prague, Czechoslovakia, with mammals of CROMERIAN type and an indicated date of c0.7 million years old. A few artefacts testify to man's presence here, and a possible human molar fragment has been recovered.

Priene. A modest Ionian Greek city in western Turkey, close in antiquity to the mouth of the River Maeander, important for its examples of 4th-century BC and HELLENISTIC urban architecture. Priene was probably one of the very early Ionian Greek colonies (traditionally 9th century BC or before), but the early centuries of her existence were never a great success, with constant harassment in particular from LYDIA and PERSIA. Eventually the city was refounded with a shift of site to the present location, some time in the middle of the 4th century BC. The Hellenistic period seems to have brought favour from ALEXANDER and reasonable prosperity, but problems with the silting up of harbour facilities by the Maeander, coupled no doubt with competition from rival MILETUS, contributed toward decline. Excavations, notably a comprehensive series at the end of the 19th century, have revealed extensive evidence for the architecture and layout of the Hellenistic city. The city was ringed by walls with arched gates, and showed a north-south grid plan that was precisely aligned to the compass. The streets centred on a porticoed market place (AGORA), with temples to Asclepius and Athena in the vicinity. An unusual square hall is possibly an assembly hall (*ecclesiasterion*), and a well-preserved Hellenistic THEATRE has interesting stage-buildings. Houses with pillared courtyards are grouped in blocks of eight. A group of inscriptions gives valuable documentary evidence on city life during the Hellenistic period.

Primary Neolithic. Term used by Stuart Piggott to describe the earliest British Neolithic cultures, such as the WINDMILL HILL culture, which were thought to represent intrusive farming groups. He contrasted these groups with SECONDARY NEOLITHIC cultures, which he believed represented acculturated MESOLITHIC groups. The term is sometimes used in a wider manner to apply to early farming cultures in other areas, especially where these are thought to represent intrusive groups.

principal components. A technique of MULTIVARIATE ANALYSIS. Principal components are new VARIABLES calculated from an original, larger number of variables. They are calculated in such a way that most of the variation within the original, multivariate DISTRIBUTION is squeezed into the first few components. So, for example, 90 per cent of the variation within 15 original variables may be compressed into the first three principal components — 70 per cent in the first component, 15 per cent in the second, and 5 per cent in the third. These principal components may then be plotted, or analysed STATISTICALLY. In this way, a mass of information is compressed into a form in which it can be analysed by conventional means. The mathematics of the technique are not particularly difficult, but for speed it is usually calculated by digital COMPUTER.

profile. A section through a SOIL. Soil profiles may be seen in accidental exposures, purpose-dug pits or in the STRATIGRAPHIC sequences of archaeological sites. They consist of a number of layers, or HORIZONS, which result from soil forming processes.

proglacial. The deposition at the edge of an ICE-SHEET or GLACIER. Large volumes of melt water released from the mass carry enormous loads of material eroded by the ice. This material is deposited by streams and rivers, or in ice-marginal lakes. Large spreads of SAND and GRAVEL have been formed in this way.

Prome. *See* ŚRĪKSHETRA.

proportional pollen counting. POLLEN ANALYSIS is often carried out by determining the proportion of different pollen types in each sample. Proportions are usually expressed as percentages of total tree (arboreal) pollen. The advantage of this method is its speed — only a fraction of the grains present in a sample need be counted. Its main disadvantage is that percentages can never indicate actual numbers of grains falling to earth. A change in the percentage of a particular type may indeed be the result of a change in the number of its grains falling on the lake or bog surface, but it could equally well be due to changes in the number of grains of other pollen types. This difficulty is solved by ABSOLUTE POLLEN COUNTING.

Proto-Elamite. The earliest form of writing to develop in Susiana and elsewhere in Iran, so-named because it is assumed to be ancestral to ELAMITE in the same area, although it remains undeciphered. Like the early SUMERIAN writing, Proto-Elamite is pictographic and it may well be derived from the slightly earlier Sumerian script; it was in existence before 3000 BC. Many of the Proto-Elamite clay tablets bear numerical symbols only and it is assumed that is was used for accounting, especially in the context of trade. Proto-Elamite tablets have been found over a surprisingly wide area of modern Iran; examples are recorded from SUSA, GODIN TEPE, SIALK, Tal-i MALIAN, Tepe YAHYA and SHAHR-I SOKHTA.

Proto-geometric. This term defines a phase in the development of Greek painted pottery which succeeded the MYCENAEAN. The style emerged at ATHENS about 1050 BC and lasted until around 900 BC, other regions following suit. Decoration was severely GEOMETRIC and included concentric circles and the use of zigzags and triangles.

proto-maiolica. A tradition of TIN-GLAZED wares made in Sicily and southern Italy from shortly before 1200 until the fifteenth century. The appearance of these wares coincided with the importation of tin glazed pottery from North Africa, particularly the Maghreb, and the origins of the idea may lie there. Typically, these jugs and bowls were painted with various animals or coats-of-arms in a variety of colours before glaze was applied. The best-known proto-maiolicas are from northern Apulia; they were traded extensively to local villages and across the Adriatic to Split in present-day Yugoslavia.

proton magnetometer. *See* MAGNETOMETER.

prytaneum. [Greek *prytaneion*: '(house) of the elders']. The official headquarters of the administration of a typical classical Greek city. At ATHENS, for example, a group of fifty *prytaneis* ('presidents, chief men'), elected by lot and serving for short periods in rotation, acted as committee to the *boule* ('council'). It is not clear whether a distinctive architec-

ture or layout was characteristic. One or two Hellenistic examples seem to show a type of private house, with an inner courtyard ringed by rooms.

sPu. The *dGa-lha* at sPu on the Tibetan border is a megalithic site with three standing stones or *rdo-riṅ*, surrounded by a stone circle. Until as recently as 1950 the site was used as a gathering place for the annual festivals, and libations of butter were placed on the *rdo-riṅ* as offerings to the local deities said to reside within them. Similar sites exist at Doptakdsong near Sa-skya and at Šab-dge-sdiṅs.

Puabi [formerly read as Shubad]. A queen of UR buried in Grave 800 of the Royal Cemetery around the middle of the 3rd millennium BC. In the grave itself were the skeletons of Puabi, adorned with ornaments of gold, silver and lapis lazuli, and an attendant. In the entrance shaft were the skeletons of ten richly adorned women and ten other men, as well as a sledge and the skeletons of the two oxen which had pulled it. Other rich goods in this tomb and its shaft include many vessels of gold, silver and copper, a gaming board and a splendid silver harp, inlaid with shell and red and blue stone.

Puamau Valley. A valley on eastern Hivaoa, MARQUESAS ISLANDS, containing a number of anthropomorphic stone statues up to 2.5 metres high. This is the biggest group of such statues in Polynesia outside EASTER ISLAND.

Pucara. A major urban centre of the Early INTERMEDIATE PERIOD, located in the north Titicaca basin of Peru. The central feature of the site is a CEREMONIAL CENTRE of dressed stone surrounded by a U-shaped enclosure; within its inner court are two subterranean burial vaults. Stone statues, frequently of humans holding trophy heads, are carved in low-relief in the blockish styles of RECUAY and TIAHUANACO. Pottery is typically black-and-yellow on red with colour zones separated by incised lines. Feline and human heads (often modelled) are favoured motifs. The site was abandoned before the zenith of HUARI and the art style is almost certainly a precursor to TIAHUANACO.

Puducun [P'u-tu-ts'un]. A village in

CHANG'AN Xian, China, near the modern city of Xi'an, just across the Feng River from the ZHANGJIAPO site. Western ZHOU bronzes unearthed at Puducun in 1954 include a vessel dated by its inscription to the reign of the fifth Zhou king Mu Wang (10th century BC).

Pueblito. *See* TAIRONA.

Pueblo. A term, from American archaeology, used in two ways:

(1) A contiguous multi-roomed (often multi-storeyed) building complex common in the southwest USA (e.g. PUEBLO BONITO). This building style is especially associated with the ANASAZI tradition.

(2) The more recent of two major chronological periods of the ANASAZI tradition, the earlier being BASKETMAKER. The period was divided into five stages at the 1927 Pecos Conference of Southwesternists (*see* KIDDER). Although perhaps not entirely suitable, this basic scheme still holds today.

Pueblo I (700-850/900) saw an increasing diversity in dwelling types (both pit and surface houses), improvements in ceramic technology and the appearance of the great KIVA. Although small villages were the normal locus of population, a tendency to population accretion was already occurring. Alkali Ridge, Utah, for example, had over 100 structures at this time.

In Pueblo II (900-1100/1150), the Anasazi reached their territorial and population peak. Surface dwellings of masonry became more typical, and pottery decoration more complex. Huge multi-roomed, multi-storeyed building complexes such as PUEBLO BONITO in CHACO CANYON began to make their appearance.

By Pueblo III (1100/1150-1300), the trend to population accretion had resulted in fewer communities with populations concentrated into larger towns, with corresponding loss in territory. These communities were typically in defensive positions, for instance, the cliff dwellings at MESA VERDE.

In Pueblo IV (1300-1600), population concentration caused severe territorial contraction with the virtual extinction of small villages. By 1450 the plateau heartland had been abandoned in favour of settlements to the south and east, mostly along the Rio Grande.

Pueblo V (1600-Present?) is the period of post-European contact. During this time, occupation of Anasazi areas by such tribes as the Hopi and Zuni is well documented. Whether these are the descendants of the Anasazi has yet to be shown conclusively.

Pueblo Bonito. An ANASAZI town or PUEBLO located in CHACO CANYON , northwest New Mexico, USA. Enclosed by high walls, it is a self-contained complex of some 800 contiguous rooms rising four to five storeys, with numerous KIVAS and two large open plazas. Construction commenced in 919 (Pueblo II) and was completed in 1067. The overall D-shaped plan, however, appears to have come about through accretion rather than deliberate planning. The sealing of some outside windows and entrance ways took place in Pueblo III, a period generally noted for the rise of defensive sites. Pueblo Bonito had been abandoned by c1200.

Puerto Hormiga. A coastal site in the northern lowlands of Columbia, which contains an abundance of early pottery in what is essentially an ARCHAIC context. Its major feature is a shell midden in the form of an ovoid ring measuring 72 by 85 metres and 1.2 metres average height, containing fire pits, stone and shell artefacts as well as ceramics. Fibre-tempered pottery, much of it decorated by impression, incision or punctation, has been dated in the range 3090-2552 bc. Thus it is contemporary with or possibly older than ceramics at VALDIVIA to which it may be related. Although these dates are among the earliest ceramics in South America, such advanced techniques suggest that earlier forms, from which these developed, must have existed.

Pulemelei. A massive stone platform, 50 by 60 metres by 12 metres high, on Savai'i Island, Western SAMOA. The Pulemelei is perhaps the largest surviving man-made stone structure in POLYNESIA, and it may once have supported a large community house or temple. The site is undated, but probably postdates AD 1000.

Punapau. A volcanic crater on EASTER ISLAND which was the quarry for the red tuff topknots originally placed on the heads of the Easter Island statues. All statues and topknots were deliberately toppled during tribal wars before 1860.

Punic wars. Name given to a series of wars between ROME and CARTHAGE in the 3rd and 2nd centuries BC. The first (264-241 BC) saw Rome rapidly putting together her first organized fleet of warships. The second (218-201 BC) brought Hannibal's Alpine invasion of Italy and Rome's catastrophic defeats at Trasimene and Cannae. After Scipio's African counterattack had forced Hannibal home to eventual defeat at the battle of Zama in 202 BC, Carthage no longer offered much threat to Rome's control of the western Mediterranean. The third war (149-146 BC) is normally seen essentially as a late punitive reprisal, in which the city of Carthage was destroyed, and her land organized into the Roman province of Africa.

Puntutjarpa. A rock-shelter in the Warburton Ranges of the Western Desert, Western Australia. Uninterrupted dated occupation extends from c8000 bc to the present, as the shelter is still used occasionally by Aboriginal hunter-gatherers. Some changes in stone technology occurred, but the continuing stability in technology, economy and environment at the site has been termed the 'Australian desert culture'. Stone tools in the earliest levels comprised small stone scrapers (micro-adze flakes or thumbnail scrapers), large flake scrapers and HORSEHOOF CORES. Larger adze flakes, similar to the TULA ADZES used now, and seed grinders appeared at 5000 bc. Microliths (BONDI POINTS and crescents) were present from 2000-0 bc, but the earlier tool types persisted until the present, with late addition of flake knives and hand axes. The preponderance of adze flakes reflected the longevity and significance of woodworking in the desert culture.

Pusan. Area of the South Korean peninsula where the prehistoric sequence is relatively well understood, mainly through excavations at the site of Tongsamdong. The first period here, Chodo, is not dated but may be at least partly contemporary with the Early JOMON of Japan. The Chodo culture is ceramic and classed as Neolithic but the economy was based on hunting, fishing and shellfish gathering. The second period, Mokto, has a radiocarbon date of c3950 bc; there is much evidence of fishing and the hunting of sea mammals like whales and sealions. In the third period, Pusan, radiocarbon dated to c3000 bc,

deep sea molluscs were important. This phase was succeeded by the Tudo period, not dated at this site, but characterized by 'comb-pattern' ware. There may have been some limited cultivation at this period, but marine foods continued to dominate the diet. Trade connections with Japan are documented by imported obsidian, probably from Japan, and perhaps also by glycemeris shell bracelets, which were popular in Japan at this time (late Jomon).

Pushkalavati. *See* CHARSADA.

Putun. A Chontal-speaking group inhabiting the delta regions of Campeche and Tabasco on the Gulf of Mexico. Expert seamen and skilled merchants, their material culture evidences some connection with Central Mexico (a connection which is, as yet, poorly understood). Their influence spread throughout the Yucatan Peninsula in the Late CLASSIC PERIOD and it seems likely that they are, in fact, the Itza of historical record (*see* ALTAR DE SACRIFICIOS, CHICHEN ITZA, SEIBAL and COZUMEL).

Puuc. A florid architectural style named after the hill region in north-central Yucatan, Mexico, in which it occurs (*see also* CHENES, RIO BEC). It is characterized by alternating zones of plain and elaborately decorated carving which are made from a veneer of standard pre-cut masonry. Fret- and lattice-designs and round columns are common, with more low, single-storey residential buildings than pyramid-temples. Whether it is a Late CLASSIC development (and hence a delayed expression of the general collapse of the MAYA centres of the Peten) or an Early POST-CLASSIC manifestation of Mexican influence is a matter of some debate. The archetypal centre for this style is UXMAL, but Puuc architecture has been found at Labra, Kabah and Sayil. The style spread all over the northern Yucatan and there are some structures at the great centre at CHICHEN ITZA.

Pu'uhonua. An ancient HAWAIIAN 'city of refuge' located at Honaunau on the west coast of the island of Hawaii. The site comprises three HEIAU (two now reconstructed for visitors) on a rocky peninsula which was defended by a four-metre high stone wall. The complex was traditionally first built around

1450, and served as a refuge to which fugitives could flee for divine protection. One of the original temples was still in use when described by Ellis in 1823.

Pylos. A MYCENAEAN palace near the coast of the west Peloponnese, southern Greece. There was some occupation of the Middle HELLADIC period, but the first palace dates to the LH IIIB phase of the 13th century BC; it was destroyed in LH IIIC in the following century. The palace is well preserved and followed the usual plan, with a central MEGARON surrounded by storage and living rooms; it is unusual in having no defences. The site is particularly important for the archive of some 1200 tablets in the LINEAR B script found in an archive room. The entire collection seems to be the records of the last year of the palace's use before its destruction by fire (which helped to preserve the tablets by baking them) and has thrown much light on the organization of the palace-based economy.

aP'yoṅ-rgyas [pronounced Chong-gye]. Situated near Yarlun in the Dwags-po (Brahmaputra) Valley, aP'yoṅ-rgyas seems to have been the cradle of Tibetal civilization. It is the site of the tombs of the Tibetal kings of the Royal Dynastic period (c620-842 AD) and of their fortified palace. The tombs are natural hillocks on the valley floor, which have been altered to a roughly square plan. There are ten, belonging to eight kings and two princes. The largest is that of Sroṅ-brtsan-sgam-po (c620-649), whose funeral and tomb are described in several Tibetan chronicles. The tomb consisted of a mound standing on a large square base, which was probably used for ritual procession around the mound, and may also have supported ceremonial buildings. The burial was delayed for a year while the tomb was constructed and Sroṅ-brtsan-sgam-po's body mummified and gilded. It was put into a silver coffin and placed on a throne in the central chamber. Belongings and treasures were placed around the king in subsidiary rooms.

High above the valley floor at aP'yoṅ-rgyas and overlooking the royal tombs is the aP'yiṅ-ba-stag-rtse ('Tiger Peak of Ching-pa'), the ancestral castle and palace of the royal dynasty, built by Stab-sna-gzigs, grandfather of Sroṅ-brtsan-sgam.

pyramid. Geometrically, a pyramid is a solid with a base of three of more sides, and sloping sides meeting at an apex. Monumental edifices of this shape, usually with a square base, were erected in two main parts of the world in the past: Egypt and the Americas.

Egypt. The pyramid was the characteristic form of royal tomb during the Old Kingdom and Middle Kingdom periods (*see* DYNASTIC EGYPT). The earliest example is the so-called step-pyramid at SAKKARA, built for DJOSER early in the Third Dynasty c2660 BC. Its six steps rise a total of 60 metres above its rectangular base. This pyramid stood in a large walled enclosure together with a complex of other buildings used in the performance of ceremonies connected with the dead pharaoh's afterlife. By the Fourth Dynasty the true pyramid form of tomb had been adopted, and reached its peak of size and complexity under KHUFU. Built of huge limestone blocks and originally faced with finer material, the pyramid of Khufu at GIZA included in its superstructure two successive burial chambers with elaborately protected access passages. Each pyramid at this period was provided with an adjacent mortuary temple, often linked to a further temple at the edge of the cultivated plain. By the end of the Fourth Dynasty pyramids were constructed to a much smaller size: the earlier ones must have placed a near-intolerable burden on the state's manpower and other resources. In post-Middle Kingdom times pyramid tombs continued to be constructed in the Egyptian style by the rulers of MEROE.

The Americas. Pyramids were constructed throughout the Americas and were usually associated with religious or funerary practices. Since the classic pentahedral configuration does not occur, the less physically specific term 'mound' has become widely used and is virtually synonymous. Furthermore, variety in shape and purpose has led to the adoption of qualifying prefixes such as 'burial', 'effigy' or 'platform'. Constructed entirely of earth or rubble in the earliest instances (e.g. LA VENTA), facings of mud-brick or stone became common with the passing of time. The most common form for American mounds is the truncated pyramid. Structures, often religious, are frequently built on top of the truncated surface (hence the terms temple-mound and platform-mound). Among the best-known constructions are the Pyramids of the Sun and the Moon at TEOTIHUACAN; Monk's Mound at CAHOKIA and Temples I and II at TIKAL.

Pyu. A now extinct Tibeto-Burman speaking population, calling themselves Tirchul, who preceded the Burmans on their southward move into present BURMA. Their kingdom in the Irrawaddy basin was first mentioned in the 3rd century by Chinese sources as that of P'iao. From the 6th century on the capital of the Pyu kingdom of ŚRĪKSHETRA was at Môza (Mawza) near Prome, in Lower Burma. By the 12th century the Pyus were absorbed by the Burmans.

Q

Qadan. A Nubian stone industry belonging to the period of high water levels in the Nile Valley prior to 9000 bc. At this time the content of the various local stone tool assemblages shows considerable variation, and this has been plausibly interpreted as indicating not only the variety of specialized activities which were carried out, but also the differentiation of distinct population groups whose identity and territoriality were reinforced by competition for control of resources. This supposition is strengthened by the evidence for inter-group conflict at the Jebel Sahaba cemetery. Qadan people evidently fished, hunted and consumed large quantities of wild grains.

Qadesh. *See* KADESH.

Qairawan. An important caravan city in Tunisia on the east-west route between Egypt and the Maghreb. It has four major 9th-century structures: the Great Mosque, the Mosque of Three Doors and two massive cisterns. The Great Mosque bears the name of Uqba b. Nafi, the conqueror of North Africa, who built the first mosque at Qairawan, in 670. Nothing of the earliest mosque survives. It was rebuilt first in 695 and later in 724-7 by the caliph Hisham I. The minaret, a stepped tower resembling a lighthouse, may belong to the mosque of Hisham. The mosque was rebuilt again by the Aghlabid ruler, Ziyadat Allah, and his successors, beginning in 836. The 9th-century mosque, much of which survives, had a profound influence on Islamic architecture in the Maghreb. The Mosque of Three Doors (more properly, the Jami Tleta Biban) has a square sanctuary with nine domes, as in mosques at BALKH, SOUSSE and elsewhere. According to an inscription on the facade, it was built in 866. Just outside the town are two polygonal cisterns, 37 and 130 metres across, begun in 860-1.

Qala'at al-Bahrain. *See* BAHRAIN.

Qal'a of the Banu Hammad. The Qal'a, in northeast Algeria, was founded in 1007 as a new capital by Hammad, the grandson of Ziri, builder of the first Sanhaja centre at ASHIR. Excavations began in 1908 and have continued intermittently ever since. The major monuments include the Manar and Lake Palaces and the mosque. The mosque, which measured 61 by 53 metres had a sanctuary with a 'T-shaped' arrangement of aisles and a courtyard completely surrounded by arcades. The minaret displays a combination of oriental and Andalusian ornament. The Lake Palace takes its name from a large pool which was surrounded by porticoes with, on the north side, a suite of rooms for the ruler. The facade of the palace is decorated with distinctive stepped niches. The Manar Palace contained a series of apartments, each with a yard, surrounding a larger central courtyard.

Qalasasaya. *See* TIAHUANACO.

Qal'at Sharqat. Modern name of ASSUR, capital of Assyria in northern Mesopotamia.

Qarnāwu. *See* MINAEAN.

Qasr al-Hayr East. An Islamic site in Syria standing in semi-desert. It consists of two fortified buildings and a bath-house, in an enclosure with conduits which tapped a spring 25 km away and brought rainwater from a nearby wadi. The Small Enclosure is roughly square, 66 metres across, with towers and a monumental gate. The building contains a large courtyard, surrounded by porticos, behind which are vaulted rooms; it appears to be a caravanserai. The Large Enclosure, again roughly square, is 167 metres across with gates in all four sides. This too has a central courtyard with porticos, surrounded by self-contained units, one of which is a mosque. Other units contain dwellings, olive presses and a bath. An inscription from the mosque, now lost, gives the date 728-9 and refers to the site as a town. Although the principal occupation belongs to the 8th century, Qasr al-Hayr enjoyed a modest revival in the 11th and 12th centuries.

Qatabanean, Qatabaneans. One of the kingdoms of southern Arabia in the 1st millennium BC, contemporary with the MINAEANS, SABAEANS and HADRAMIS. Its capital city was TIMNA'.

Qatna. An impressive fortified city east of Homs in Syria. Excavation has found evidence of 3rd-millennium BC occupation, but the fortifications — consisting of a free-standing plaster-faced glacis (bank) — belong to the Middle Bronze Age in the early 2nd millennium BC and were probably constructed by the HYKSOS. The fortifications of this period enclosed more than 100 hectares.

qibla. *See* MOSQUE.

Qijia [Ch'i-chia]. Successor to the YANGSHAO cultures of Gansu, China, named after the site of Qijiaping in the Tao River valley. Qijia is the Longshan culture of Gansu and is related to KEXINGZHUANG II in Shaanxi and HOUGANG II in Henan (*see* LONGSHAN, sense 3). Qijia pottery is rarely painted and often seems to copy metal vessels. Many simple tools and ornaments of copper have been found at Qijia sites along with some described as lead and tin bronze; copper-arsenic alloys are lacking. Qijia metallurgy has been taken by some scholars as evidence of affiliations with cultures farther west, for example in Turkmenia. Four radiocarbon dates for the Qijia culture lie in the range c2250 to c1900 BC. A decorated cast bronze mirror from a Qijia site resembles mirrors from ANYANG (*see* FU HAO) and suggests that Qijia lasted well into the 2nd millennium BC. It was succeeded in the late 2nd or 1st millennium BC by several primitive CHALCOLITHIC cultures including Xindian, named after a Tao River valley site. Xindian pottery is painted with simple geometric, spiral, and scorpion designs and represents the latest and most impoverished survival of the Gansu painted pottery tradition.

Qin [Ch'in]. Name of an Eastern ZHOU state centred in the Wei River valley of Shaanxi province, China, and of the dynasty (221-206 BC) founded after the Qin state had conquered and absorbed the various states ruling the rest of China. The first emperor of the dynasty, QIN SHI HUANGDI, established his capital at Xianyang near CHANG'AN. The Western name 'China' derives from the name of the Qin dynasty which, though short-lived, was the first dynasty to unite under a single rule most of the area since regarded as belonging to China proper.

Qing [Ch'ing]. Name of the Manchu dynasty that ruled China from 1644 to 1911.

Qinglian'gang [Ch'ing-lien-kang]. Neolithic site in Huaian Xian, northern Jiangsu province, China. The name 'Qinglian'gang culture' is often used to designate all or part of the well-defined Neolithic sequence north of the Yangzi River in Jiangsu and Shandong (some authors use 'Huating culture' or 'Dawenkou culture' instead, again with varying degrees of inclusiveness). In Jiangsu this cultural sequence comprises strata at Qinglian'gang, Pei Xian Liulin, and Pei Xian Huating; all three levels appear at DADUNZI in Pei Xian, where the lowest (Qinglian'gang) level yielded a radiocarbon date of c4500 BC. Later stages of the same culture are encountered farther north at sites in Shandong, such as Taian Dawenkou, where the lower level is comparable to Huating while the upper level is directly antecedent to the Classic LONGSHAN of Shandong province.

A few scholars have taken the term 'Qinglian' gang culture' to include not only the Neolithic north of the Yangzi but also the HEMUDU, MAJIABANG, and LIANGZHU cultures in the south; in this broad sense the term signifies more or less the whole of the east-coast Neolithic (*see* LONGSHAN, sense 2).

Qin Shi Huangdi [Ch'in Shih Huang-ti]. Ruler of the QIN state of China (from 246 BC) and first emperor (*r.* 221-210 BC) of the Qin dynasty. Qin Shi Huangdi completed the unification of China begun by earlier rulers of Qin; he standardized the legal code, weights and measures, currency, and script form throughout the country, and built the GREAT WALL to protect his empire against barbarian incursions. His tomb, marked by a tumulus in Lintong Xian, Shaanxi province, is the focal point of a vast mausoleum complex that includes a buried army of life-sized terracotta figures discovered in 1974 and still under excavation. In the pits known thus far the figures of officers, infantry, charioteers, and cavalrymen and their horses are estimated to number about 7000 (*see also* CHARIOT BURIALS, CHINA).

Qinwangzhai [Ch'in-wang-chai]. *See* DAHE.

Qishan [Ch'i-shan]. A district in Shaanxi province, China, just west of FUFENG. The ZHOU people are said to have settled at Qishan several generations before they overthrew the SHANG dynasty, and Qishan remained a major centre after the founding of the Zhou dynasty. A large palace complex discovered in 1977 at Qishan Fengchucun was shown by deposits of inscribed ORACLE BONES to antedate the founding of the dynasty. The tiled roofs of the Fengchucun buildings are the earliest known instance (11th century BC) of this standard feature of later Chinese architecture. Many bronze RITUAL VESSELS have been found in the Qishan area, most of them Western Zhou but some predynastic (i.e. Shang) in date including a few likely to be as early as the ERLIGANG PHASE. *See also* FUFENG, ZHOU CAPITALS.

Quanterness. A MEGALITHIC tomb, usually classified as a form of PASSAGE GRAVE, on the island of Orkney, north Scotland, excavated in the 1970s. Like other megalithic tombs, it had been used for collective burial, but the number of bodies found here was unusually high: remains of 157 individuals were found in the excavated portion of the tomb and, if the same density of remains can be assumed for the unexcavated part, the tomb may originally have housed about 400 bodies. Colin Renfrew has suggested that this represents all the dead of a small egalitarian community, perhaps an extended family, over a period of nearly one thousand years (indicated by radiocarbon dates). The skeletal remains were disarticulated, very incomplete, and showed signs of removal of the flesh before deposition. It seems likely that the bodies had been exposed for some period before burial — a practice for which there is other evidence from the British Neolithic.

Quaternary. The earth's history is divided into 'eras': the Palaeozoic, Mesozoic and Cenozoic. The youngest, Cenozoic, era (starting at 65 million years BP) is traditionally divided into two 'periods': the TERTIARY and the Quaternary. The Quaternary period extends up to the present day and includes two 'epochs': the PLEISTOCENE and the HOLOCENE. These terms may also be applied to groups of deposits, which are described as the Quaternary 'system' and the Pleistocene or Holocene 'series'. The boundary between the Tertiary and the Quaternary is rather badly defined. Estimates for its age range from *c*2.4 million years BP to between 1.8 and 2.1 million years BP. The Quaternary system comprises a number of stages. It also includes deep ocean deposits, which raise a number of separate issues (*see* DEEP SEA CORES). Recent work has shown that both the deep sea and the land deposits of the Quaternary are more complex than had been supposed. The old schemes of alternating GLACIAL and INTERGLACIAL 'ages' are no longer tenable.

See Tables 4-7, pages 417-20.

Quechua. *See* INCA, TARASCAN.

quenching. *See* STEEL.

Quentovic. One of the most important ports on the English Channel in the Early Medieval period. Its coins were first minted in the early 7th century and during the 8th and 9th centuries its mint was one of the most important in the CAROLINGIAN Empire. The settlement is also known from many incidental references made by travellers passing between the northern French kingdom of Neustria and the Anglo-Saxon kingdoms. Despite its prominence, the location of the site has never been found and its actual size, for example, remains unknown. Most historians believe that it lies near Etaples, on the coast to the south of Boulogne-sur-Mer, and Montreuil-sur-Mer in the Canche valley is usually considered to be its 10th-century successor. Quentovic was attacked by the Vikings several times, but its demise is usually attributed to the 10th-century when other more readily fortified sites were preferred to it.

quern. A stone for grinding cereal grains into flour. Throughout most of later prehistory the characteristic form was the saddle quern, in which a hand rubber was pushed backwards and forwards on a concave base. From classical times this was replaced by the rotary quern, in which one stone was rotated on another, either by hand or with the help of animal, water or wind power.

Quetta. The name of a modern town and adjacent valley in west Pakistan. The valley contains a number of important prehistoric sites, the earliest dating to the 5th millennium BC. The most important sites are KILI GHUL MOHAMMED, DAMB SADAAT and KECHI BEG. The Quetta sequence is particularly useful since it links prehistoric sites in Pakistan with those of Afghanistan, like MUNDIGAK, and Iran, such as Tepe HISSAR and Tepe SIALK. The name Quetta ware is given to a black on buff wheel-turned ware, which is found in Damb Sadaat II and contemporary sites.

Quetzacoatl. AZTEC name for the creator god of learning who was also patron of the arts, agriculture and science, among other things. The brother of Huizilpochtli, Texcatlipoca and Xipe Totec, he was, like them, a god of many other aspects, such as the wind god (Ehecatl) and the morning and evening star (Xolotl). He is usually depicted as the feathered serpent. His cult can be seen in many MESOAMERICAN cultures, including TEOTI-HUACAN and MAYA, and may go back as far as OLMEC times. Although an important deity in the early TOLTEC pantheon, a confusion of legend and fact indicates that either Quetza-coatl or a historical figure closely associated with him, the High Priest Topiltzin, was banished from Mexico in c987. Following this, a faction dedicated to the far more militant Texcatlipoca gained control. Although he never regained his exalted position, Quetza-coatl remained 'prominent in the Mexican pantheon. His legendary promise to return from the east became ingrained in Aztec thought. So much so that in 1519 (coinci-dentally a dangerous time in the Aztec CAL-ENDAR) the newly arrived Cortez was for a time regarded as the returning deity. There is little doubt that this psychological element played some part in the fall of the Aztec empire.

Quinzano. A quarry at Quinzano near Verona in northern Italy has several lower and middle PALAEOLITHIC levels and a human occipital skull-bone of perhaps generalized NEANDER-THAL type. Nearby was an open settlement of the SQUARE-MOUTHED POTTERY Neolithic culture and a cemetery of crouched inhum-

ations. The name Finale-Quinzano is some-times given to a variant of square-mouthed pottery named after this site and ARENE CANDIDE (at Finale Ligure).

quipu. A cord from which was suspended a series of knotted strings, used by the INCA as a record-keeping or mnemonic device. Based on a decimal system, the colour of the cord, as well as the size, configuration and placement of each knot, had a special meaning. So complex was the system that a special pro-fessional class (the *quipucamoyac*) grew up to interpret meaning. Used mostly for imperial accounting, the *quipu* may also have been employed to record cultural and historic data; a modified form is still used by some Andean herdsmen.

Quirigua. A CLASSIC MAYA site located 50 km north of COPAN on the Rio Motagua in southeastern Guatemala. Probably at least partly controlled by its larger neighbour (perhaps through kinship ties), its architecture is unprepossessing. The site is notable, however, for its excellent examples of stone carving in the Southern Regional style. Both massive boulder carvings and stelae are un-usually large (stele E for example is nearly 11 metres high). The terminal LONG COUNT date of 810 is carved on a lintel of the main structure.

Qujialing [Ch'ü-chia-ling]. Type site in Jingshan Xian, Hubei province, China, of a rice-growing Neolithic culture of the middle Yangzi region. Five radiocarbon dates from various sites range from c3100 to c2650 BC. At XIAWANGGANG Qujialing remains (radio-carbon dated to c3000 BC) were stratified above YANGSHAO and below HOUGANG II. Qujialing's closest affiliations seem to be with the east-coast Neolithic cultures of the lower Yangzi (*see* LONGSHAN).

Qumran. *See* DEAD SEA SCROLLS.

Quynh-van. A 5-metre deep marine shell midden in northern VIETNAM which has produced a flaked stone industry together with pottery, grindstones and contracted burials, dated to c3000 BC. The industry lacks the normal HOABINHIAN and BACSONIAN pebble and edge-ground tools, but it could be a late and specialized coastal variant of the Hoabinhian. Fauna include deer, cattle, pig, dog and elephant, all presumed wild.

Table 4: Temporal and stratigraphical subdivisions of the Cenozoic era

Time units	Era	Period	Epoch	Age
Stratigraphy units		System	Series	Present day
	C E N O Z O I C	Q U A T E R N A R Y	HOLOCENE	
				0.01 Ma bp
			PLEISTOCENE	
				c. 2 Ma BP
		T E R T I A R Y	PLIOCENE	
				7 MaBP
			MIOCENE	
				26 Ma BP
			OLIGOCENE	
				38 Ma BP
			EOCENE	
				54 Ma BP
			PALAEOCENE	
				65 Ma BP

Ma = millions of years

418

Table 5: The Quaternary stratigraphical sequence in Northwest Europe

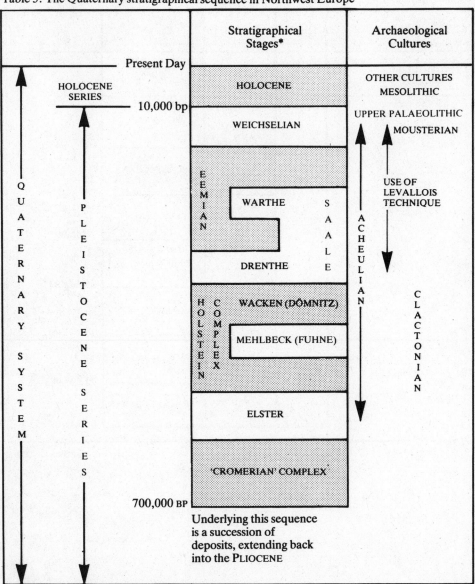

	Stratigraphical Stages*	Archaeological Cultures

Present Day

HOLOCENE SERIES

10,000 bp

700,000 BP

QUATERNARY SYSTEM

PLEISTOCENE SERIES

HOLOCENE

WEICHSELIAN

EEMIAN

WARTHE

DRENTHE

SAALE

HOLSTEIN COMPLEX

WACKEN (DÖMNITZ)

MEHLBECK (FUHNE)

ELSTER

'CROMERIAN' COMPLEX

OTHER CULTURES
MESOLITHIC

UPPER PALAEOLITHIC
MOUSTERIAN

USE OF LEVALLOIS TECHNIQUE

ACHEULIAN

CLACTONIAN

Underlying this sequence is a succession of deposits, extending back into the PLIOCENE

* Stratigraphical Stages are groups of deposits:

Shaded = groups of deposits representing INTERGLACIALS, including marine deposits of raised sea levels and deposits containing fossils that indicate a period of sustained warm climate.
Unshaded = groups of deposits representing COLD STAGES, including glacial and periglacial deposits and landforms, and deposits containing fossils that indicate cold conditions or merely short periods of warm climate (interstadials).

There is controversy about a number of aspects of the information summarized in this table. The vertical axis is meant only to represent stratigraphical relationships and should not be seen as a timescale.

Table 6: The Quaternary stratigraphical sequence in Britain

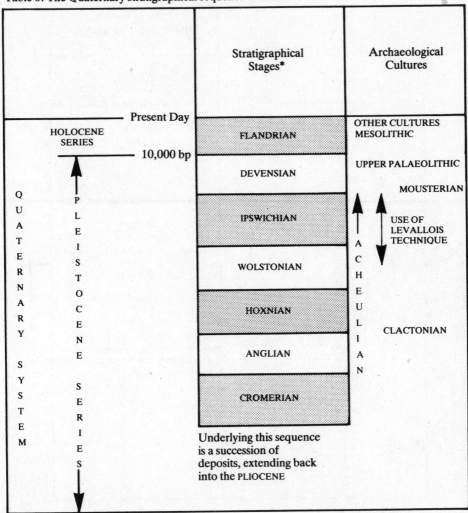

	Stratigraphical Stages*	Archaeological Cultures

Present Day

HOLOCENE
SERIES

10,000 bp

Stratigraphical Stages*	Archaeological Cultures
FLANDRIAN	OTHER CULTURES MESOLITHIC
DEVENSIAN	UPPER PALAEOLITHIC
	MOUSTERIAN
IPSWICHIAN	USE OF LEVALLOIS TECHNIQUE
WOLSTONIAN	
HOXNIAN	
ANGLIAN	CLACTONIAN
CROMERIAN	

QUATERNARY SYSTEM

PLEISTOCENE SERIES

ACHEULIAN

Underlying this sequence
is a succession of
deposits, extending back
into the PLIOCENE

* Stratigraphical Stages are groups of deposits:

Shaded = groups of deposits representing INTERGLACIALS, including marine deposits of raised sea levels and deposits containing fossils that indicate a period of sustained warm climate.

Unshaded = groups of deposits representing COLD STAGES, including glacial and periglacial deposits and landforms, and deposits containing fossils that indicate cold conditions or merely short periods of warm climate (interstadials).

All of the deposits listed in the table are believed to be younger than 700,000 BP but, except for the Flandrian and part of the Devensian, more detailed dating is not possible. Thus, the vertical axis is meant only to represent stratigraphical relationships and should not be seen as a timescale.

Table 7: The Quaternary stratigraphical sequence in North America

		Stratigraphical Stages*
	——— Present Day	
QUATERNARY SYSTEM	HOLOCENE SERIES	HOLOCENE
	——— 10,000 bp	
	P L E I S T O C E N E	WISCONSIN
		SANGAMON
		ILLINOIAN
		YARMOUTH
	S E R I E S	KANSAN
	700,000 BP	Underlying this sequence is a further succession of deposits

* Stratigraphic Stages are groups of deposits:

Shaded = groups of deposits representing INTERGLACIALS, including palaeosols and deposits containing fossils that indicate a period of sustained warm climate

Unshaded = groups of deposits representing COLD STAGES, including glacial and periglacial deposits and landforms, and deposits containing fossils that indicate cold conditions or merely short intervals of warm climate (interstadials).

The vertical axis is meant only to represent stratigraphical relationships and should not be read as a timescale.

R

racloir. *See* SCRAPER.

radiocarbon dating. Developed by Willard
Libby in 1948, the first of the RADIOMETRIC
DATING methods to be applied in archaeology.
Principle. There are three main isotopes
of carbon, ^{12}C, ^{13}C and ^{14}C. ^{12}C and ^{13}C are
stable; ^{14}C is radioactive and decays at a known
rate (*see* HALF-LIFE). At the same time, ^{14}C is
continuously being produced in the upper
atmosphere by a reaction involving cosmic
radiation. Constant decay of ^{14}C is balanced by
constant production. Thus, the ratio of ^{14}C to
^{12}C remains approximately the same throughout time.

Carbon is passed between atmosphere,
oceans and living things in a process called the
Carbon Cycle. Plants take in Carbon Dioxide
from the atmosphere, retain some of it in their
tissues, are eaten by herbivorous animals,
which are in turn eaten by carnivores — and so
on. ^{14}C is chemically not that different from
^{12}C and the two isotopes are passed around the
carbon cycle at similar rates. In this way, the
balance struck between ^{14}C production and
decay in the atmosphere is passed around the
cycle. The ratio between ^{14}C and ^{12}C remains
the same in all living things. The cycle is
stopped by death. When a plant or animal dies
and is preserved, its exchange of carbon
ceases. The ^{14}C which decays is no longer
balanced by new ^{14}C. The proportion of ^{14}C to
^{12}C steadily declines. Since the rate at which
this decay occurs (half-life) is known, it is
possible to calculate how long ago a plant or
animal died from the relative amount of ^{14}C
that is left.

Range. Variable depending on the laboratory.
Most produce dates for the range 0 bp to
c49,000 bp. Gröningen uses a special enrich-
ment technique which extends its range to
c70,000 bp.

Accuracy. Radiocarbon dates are incomplete
without their accompanying 'plus-or-minus'
or probable error. This expresses only the
uncertainties involved in the ^{14}C determination. The date has a 68 per cent chance of lying
within one probable error on either side of the
quoted date, a 95 per cent chance within two
probable errors, or a 99 per cent chance within
three probable errors (*see* STANDARD DEVIA-
TION). Typically, a date of 10,000 bp may have
probable error between ± 50 and ± 250. The
error gets larger with increasing age.

Materials. Anything that has been alive:
wood, followed by charcoal, is best; identifiable plant fragments; skin, leather, muscle
tissue etc; bone — collagen or mineral; shell.

Problems. Various difficulties with samples —
CONTAMINATION and hard water error (*see*
HARD WATER EFFECT). These must be dealt
with by the laboratory. Shell dates suffer
particularly badly from hard water error and
also from ISOTOPIC REPLACEMENT. Most dates
of archaeological age should not be far wrong,
however. Other problems arise from various
failures of the assumptions made by the
radiocarbon method — ISOTOPIC FRACTIONA-
TION and variation in the production rate of
^{14}C in the atmosphere. Isotopic fractionation is
tested for and eliminated by the laboratory.
Archaeologists much themselves correct for
variation in ^{14}C production rate by using a
calibration table (*see below*). A final difficulty
may be encountered in connection with the
half-life of ^{14}C. Laboratories always quote
dates in years bp (in the sense used in this
Dictionary; i.e. uncorrected radiocarbon
years before present, although laboratories
themselves use the capitals BP for this purpose).

Radiocarbon calibration. The adjustment of
radiocarbon dates for the effect of variation in
^{14}C production rate. One of the central
assumptions of the radiocarbon method is that
the rate of ^{14}C production in the upper
atmosphere has remained constant over time.
This assumption is now known to be inaccurate. Comparison of radiocarbon dates with
those provided by DENDROCHRONOLOGY
of the BRISTLECONE PINE tree has shown that
some dates are incorrect by as much as 800

Table 8. Calibration of conventional radiocarbon dates (5568 half-life) after R.M. Clark 1975 (*Antiquity* 49, 251-66)

Radiocarbon date bp	ad	Calendar date AD	BP	Radiocarbon date bp	bc	Calendar date BC	BP
50	1900	—	—	3550	1600	1975	3925
100	1850	1895, 1820	55, 130	3600	1650	2035	3985
150	1800	1685	265	3650	1700	2095	4045
200	1750	1650	300	3700	1750	2160	4110
250	1700	1625	325	3750	1800	2230	4180
300	1650	1580	370	3800	1850	2305	4255
350	1600	1495	455	3850	1900	2385	4335
400	1550	1470	480	3900	1950	2455	4405
450	1500	1440	510	3950	2000	2520	4470
500	1450	1420	530	4000	2050	2595	4545
550	1400	1400	550	4050	2100	2670	4620
600	1350	1375	575	4100	2150	2755	4705
650	1300	1350	600	4150	2200	2850	4800
700	1250	1315	635	4200	2250	2910	4860
750	1200	1255	695	4250	2300	2970	4920
800	1150	1220	730	4300	2350	3030	4980
850	1100	1170	780	4350	2400	3095	5045
900	1050	1070	880	4400	2450	3175	5125
950	1000	1030	920	4450	2500	3245	5195
1000	950	990	960	4500	2550	3310	5260
1050	900	950	1000	4550	2600	3370	5320
1100	850	880	1070	4600	2650	3430	5380
1150	800	815	1135	4650	2700	3485	5435
1200	750	760	1190	4700	2750	3530	5480
1250	700	720	1230	4750	2800	3580	5530
1300	650	685	1265	4800	2850	3635	5585
1350	600	640	1310	4850	2900	3685	5635
1400	550	595	1355	4900	2950	3730	5680
1450	500	535	1415	4950	3000	3785	5735
1500	450	470	1480	5000	3050	3835	5785
1550	400	430	1560	5050	3100	3885	5835
1600	350	390	1560	5100	3150	3935	5885
1650	300	345	1605	5150	3200	3990	5940
1700	250	280	1670	5200	3250	4040	5990
1750	200	245	1705	5250	3300	4095	6045
1800	150	215	1735	5300	3350	4160	6110
1850	100	185	1765	5350	3400	4250	6200
1900	50ad	120AD	1830	5400	3450	4325	6275
1950	0ad	60AD	1890	5450	3500	4375	6325
2000	50bc	0AD	1950	5500	3550	4410	6360
2050	100	95BC	2045	5550	3600	4450	6400
2100	150	160	2110	5600	3650	4485	6435
2150	200	205	2155	5650	3700	4520	6470
2200	250	370	2320	5700	3750	4555	6505
2250	300	400	2350	5750	3800	4590	6540
2300	350	425	2375	5800	3850	4630	6580
2350	400	450	2400	5850	3900	4680	6630
2400	450	490	2440	5900	3950	4760	6710
2450	500	600	2550	5950	4000	4845	6795
2500	550	755	2705	6000	4050	4920	6870
2550	600	800	2750	6050	4100	4975	6925
2600	650	840	2790	6100	4150	5030	6980
2650	700	880	2830	6150	4200	5085	7035
2700	750	925	2875	6200	4250	5130	7080
2750	800	975	2925	6250	4300	5170	7120
2800	850	1030	2980	6300	4350	5215	7165
2850	900	1100	3050	6350	4400	5255	7205
2900	950	1175	3125	6400	4450	5300	7250
2950	1000	1250	3200	6450	4500	5350	7300
3000	1050	1320	3270	6500	4550	5415	7365
3050	1100	1385	3335				
3100	1150	1440	3390				
3150	1200	1495	3445				
3200	1250	1550	3500				
3250	1300	1595	3545				
3300	1350	1650	3600				
3350	1400	1710	3660				
3400	1450	1770	3720				
3450	1500	1835	3785				
3500	1550	1900	3850				

Notes: Calendar dates are rounded to the nearest 5 years.

years. Far from invalidating the radiocarbon method, however, dendrochronology makes it possible to improve it. Calibration tables have been constructed to correct the error for the period from the present day back to *c*5250 bc (6050 BC); it is hoped that future work will allow us to extend the table back a few thousand years further. *See* Table 8, page 422.

radiometric dating. DATING by measuring processes which involve the decay of radioactive isotopes. RADIOCARBON, POTASSIUM/ ARGON and URANIUM SERIES dating employ the known rate of decay, expressed by their HALF-LIVES, as a clock against which to measure time. FISSION TRACK dating similarly employs spontaneous nuclear fission, which also occurs at a known rate.

Raiatea. *See* SOCIETY ISLANDS, TAPUTA-PUALEA.

Raimondi Stone. *See* CHAVIN.

Rajagriha [modern Rajgir]. Indian city of the GANGES CIVILIZATION and capital of the kingdom of MAGADHA. The earliest surviving remains are ramparts of rubble masonry, probably of the 6th century BC. The city was often visited by the BUDDHA and a series of elliptical structures may be the remains of his Jivikarama monastery.

Rajghat. City of the GANGES CIVILIZATION, India. The earliest occupation is characterized by BLACK AND RED WARE and the beginnings of iron technology. The settlement of this period was surrounded by a massive brick rampart. In the succeeding period, after *c*700-600 BC, NORTHERN BLACK POLISHED WARE and copper coins appear. At this stage a channel was excavated to connect the rivers Ganges and Varuna and surround the city.

Ramapithecus. *See* HUMAN EVOLUTION.

Rameses II. A pharaoh of the 19th Egyptian Dynasty, who reigned *c*1304-1237 BC. In the early years of his long reign war was waged both against the HITTITES and in Nubia. Egypt's borders having then been strengthened by military might, fortress building diplomacy, and marriage to the Hittite king's daughter, Rameses' later reign saw the florescence of Egyptian art and monumental architecture, most notably at the great temple of ABU SIMBEL.

rampart. An elongated bank, often forming an enclosure. Combinations of ramparts and DITCHES made up the defences of HILLFORTS in prehistoric Europe. Indications of the construction of the rampart may occur as TIP-LINES, or so-called TURF-LINES, which may represent pauses in the work or, in some cases, different phases of building. Within the body of some mounds and ramparts there are indications of turves included in the building material. Experimental archaeology has shown that ramparts erode to form fans of material spread out from their sides. The profile of the rampart as seen today may therefore bear little relation to its original form. BURIED SOILS are frequently found underneath mounds and ramparts, and this is a source of much information for ENVIRON-MENTAL ARCHAEOLOGY.

Rana Ghundai. A prehistoric site in the Loralai valley of northern Baluchistan, with a stratigraphic sequence beginning with a level with hand-made pottery and chipped stone tools like KILI GHUL MOHAMMED Phase II (4th millennium BC). This was followed by a level with black on red painted ware.

Rano Raraku. An extinct volcanic crater on EASTER ISLAND which served as a quarry for the stone statues which were erected in rows on the many AHU on the island. The rock is a soft andesitic tuff and main usage of the two quarries, one inside and one outside the crater, dates to between AD 1200 and 1500.

Raqqa. City in northern Syria, founded by the Abbasid caliph al-Mansur in 772. It contains a number of important monuments. The city walls, attributed to al-Mansur and reputedly modelled on those of BAGHDAD, were double, with towers at regular intervals. The surviving part of the Baghdad gate shows that it had a four-centred arch surmounted by a band of three-lobed niches resting on engaged colonnettes. The congregational mosque, also attributed to al-Mansur, was a rectangular building, 108 metres long and 93 metres wide, with a sanctuary of three arcades, 15 bays across. A large group of 12th- and 13th-century earthenware with painted ornament under thick alkaline glaze, certainly from

Syria, is known universally as 'Raqqa' ware, although there is no proof that it was made here.

Rarotonga. *See* COOK ISLANDS.

Ras al-Amiya. A small site near KISH in southern Mesopotamia (modern Iraq). It consisted of a small mound, entirely below the alluvium, which was only discovered by accident. Excavations found pottery of HAJJI MUHAMMAD type, now generally regarded as an early phase of the UBAID culture of the earlier 5th millennium bc. Architectural remains were of rectangular houses arranged around courtyards. Occupation continued into the full Ubaid period.

Ras Shamra. *See* UGARIT.

rath. A provincial Irish term (one of many) for the prevalent small RINGWORKS found in many parts of Ireland, and in west Wales. In essence the rath is simply a bank and ditched enclosure — the earthen counterpart of the cashel, the stone-walled fort. A few sites may date to the pre-Roman period, but the majority date to the Early Christian period. Some of these raths were re-used by the Normans as the foundations for small MOTTE AND BAILEY castles, while others, particularly those in southern Co. Clare, continued to be occupied until the post-medieval period. Raths of all sizes are known, ranging from the chiefdom centres like Garranes, Co. Cork, or Clogher, Co. Tyrone (small hillforts in areas without hills) to those sites barely 30 metres across. Most were farms whose occupants were probably one degree higher in status than the lowly persons who inhabited unfortified settlements now recalled in the place-name prefix 'bally' in some parts of Ireland.

Rati. A site in Nag-tshan, northern Tibet, where five 'slab graves' were found when J.N. Roerich visited the area in the late 1920s. Each consists of an oval enclosure c2.75 metres by 3 metres, made of closely set, flat stone slabs and aligned east-west, with a larger stone at the eastern end. This may indicate that the dead were buried facing east. Graves of this sort are quite numerous throughout Tibet and are usually found in groups of two or three on the southern slopes of mountains. According to

Roerich, the only objects found in the Rati tombs were skeletons with long-headed skulls and bronze arrowheads with the trefoil cross-section typical of 'Scytho-Siberian' examples. They show striking analogies with slab graves found in Mongolia, Trans-Baikal and the ALTAI Mountains, some of which have been excavated, and have yielded material belonging to the Scytho-Siberian culture of the 7th-5th centuries BC.

There is also a megalithic ALIGNMENT at Rati, similar to that at RDO-RIÑ.

Ravenna. City on the Adriatic coast of Italy. The 5th century was a period of great disruption in the late Roman and BYZANTINE world as invading barbarians attempted to wreck and destroy these imperial civilizations. Largely for greater security, and to facilitate political and administrative control, the Byzantine empire was split between Constantinople and Italy, which became the western exarchate. In 402 the official western royal residence was moved from Milan to Ravenna, a port on the Adriatic coast which could be more easily contacted and defended by the Byzantine fleet.

Ravenna became of singular importance during Theodoric's reign (498-526) when the emperor initiated the construction of new churches and public buildings, decorated in styles that blended the Eastern and Western art styles of the time. The major buildings are generally built in the tradition of Roman brick, and manifest a variety of forms from the simple cross-domed plan of the tomb of Galla Placidia (450) to the splendid octagonal-domed San Vitale with its flanking towers and pierced apses (526-47), as well as the several large basilicas such as St Apollinare Nuovo and St Apollinare in Classe. The outstanding mosaics which adorn the interiors of this unique group of buildings are undoubtedly the finest collection anywhere in the Byzantine world, and were extremely influential in determining art styles throughout much of Europe and the East in the early Middle Ages. The 5th-century Byzantine influence seen in the vivid gold and blues of Galla Placidia's tomb gave way in the 6th century to Roman-based naturalistic styles best portrayed in the processions of figures in St Apollinare Nuovo, where figures in sweeping robes of oranges and greens are set in a background of shimmering gold.

Rawlinson, Sir Henry Creswicke (1810-95). One of a group of 19th-century scholars who achieved the decipherment of CUNEIFORM and several of the languages written in this script. Rawlinson's particular achievement was the transcription of the massive and almost inaccessible trilingual inscription of the ACHAEMENID period at BISITUN in northern Iran; this led the way to the decipherment of first Old Persian and subsequently also AKKADIAN.

Re. The Ancient Egyptian sun-god, the original centre of whose worship was at Heliopolis near MEMPHIS. At an early date his cult became a nationwide one and remained of importance throughout the Dynastic period. Old Kingdom pharaohs were regarded as sons of Re. Re (or Ra) was frequently identified with AMUN, especially under the New Empire when the priesthood of Amun-Re at Thebes rose to great influence.

Recuay art style. A distinctive pottery style, also called Huaylas, apparently originating in the Northern Highlands of Peru, but for which no major locus of development has been found. It is characterized by a negative resist painting technique, usually of black-on-white or sometimes black- and red-on-white. Designs of stylized life-forms (sometimes elaborately modelled) combined with geometric designs suggest some contact with GALLINAZO and MOCHE. Some monumental stone carving (called Aija) is also ascribed to Recuay; it is characterized by the stiff blockish quality which is widespread throughout the Peruvian Highlands. Recuay flourished in the Early INTERMEDIATE PERIOD.

recumbent stone circle. *See* STONE CIRCLE.

recurrence surface. A division, in PEAT STRATIGRAPHY, which separates well-humified (broken-down) peat from unhumified peat. This represents a change from slower BOG growth in drier conditions to faster growth in damper conditions. Recurrence surfaces are found in raised bogs and blanket bogs, both of which are nourished only by rainfall. It has therefore been suggested that recurrence surfaces are due to a change to damper climate, although other factors of bog ecology seem also to be involved. Recurrence surfaces were first recognized by Weber in German raised bogs. He found a division in all of them that he called the GRENZHORIZONT, dated to between 1000 and 750 bc on archaeological grounds. Similar recurrence surfaces are widely seen in Britain; their radiocarbon dates range from c1200 to 600 bc. Dates in this range are so widespread that these surfaces may indeed by due to a change to higher rainfall (*see* SUB-ATLANTIC). Recurrence surfaces of many dates have been found, often several in one bog, although not so many fitting into one age range.

Red-Figure ware. A phase in Greek vase painting, the inverse of BLACK-FIGURE style, and its successor from about 530 BC onward. Figures are formed in the fired fabric of the pot, against a black background, and with black detail to the inside of the figure. The style lasted at ATHENS until about 320 BC. Other local schools also developed, especially in southern Italy, and continued until c300 BC.

Regional Development Period. Part of a chronological construction used in Ecuadoran archaeology and developed by Betty Meggers. The continuum FORMATIVE, REGIONAL DEVELOPMENT, INTEGRATION PERIOD has also been applied to neighbouring parts of South and Central America. The period runs from 500 BC to AD 500 and is characterized by changes in socio-political organization, art styles and technology, which gave rise to region-wide rather than purely local cultures.

Reichenau. A small island in Lake Constance in southern Germany which is the site of an important CAROLINGIAN and Ottonian-period monastery. Its greatest claim to fame is that it became a flourishing centre of miniature painting at this time. Three impressive monastic churches still remain on the island at Oberzell, Mittelzell and Niederzell, all built to the basic basilican design which typifies the Carolingian period, with later additions. St George, Oberzell, has a particularly fine series of 10th-century frescoes decorating the interior.

Reihengraberfeld [German: 'row-grave cemetery']. A classic form of graveyard found in France, the Low Countries and West German in the 5th-7th centuries. It is normally found by a river on a south-facing slope, usually some distance from a settlement. The bodies were buried in individual trenches in neat rows. As a rule there were no sarcophagi or coffins. The men were traditionally buried with one or more weapons and the women with their brooches, hairpins and other items of dress. In practice, many of the cemeteries show several types of burial, possibly suggesting the presence of different ethnic groups, and in the latest phases there are often fence-lines or ditches isolating small clusters of graves.

reindeer. A number of hunting peoples living in Europe during the later part of the ice ages seem to have specialized in hunting the reindeer, for its bones are much more common than those of other animals on these sites. This is true of a few MOUSTERIAN levels, but it is almost the rule for Late PALAEOLITHIC sites of the MAGDALENIAN and SOLUTRIAN. Reindeer are likely to have lived in large herds, but we do not know whether they migrated widely in western Europe, as they do today in the Arctic, and whether the hunters' camps are seasonal in character is still not clear.

Reinecke, Paul (1872-1958). German prehistorian who was responsible for many typological studies. He is best known for his subdivision of the central European Bronze and Iron Ages, with phases denoted by letters. His system involved eight phases: Bronze A to D (Early and Middle Bronze Age) and Hallstatt A to D (Late Bronze Age and Early Iron Age). It is still widely used today, although usually in modified form.

Reisner, George Andrew (1867-1942). American Egyptologist whose excavations are noted for their high standard of recording. His most important work was in Nubia, where he directed a campaign to survey threatened monuments in 1907-8 and also conducted many excavations, especially in the pyramids and other monuments of MEROE. In Egypt itself, he excavated many tombs and the Valley Temple of Mycerinus at GIZA.

relics. Christianity was governed throughout the Middle Ages by the overriding belief that spiritual virtue could be transmitted through relics (or physical remains) of a person who in life was blessed with miraculous powers. Thus a map of Christendom might be seen in one sense as a constellation of ecclesiastical sanctuaries, each housing some tangible remnant of the Holy Spirit. The most prestigious relics were of course, those of Christ or the Virgin Mary (such as the crown of thorns, the holy shroud, or blood) but they could take the form of almost any part of a saint or in fact any item which had been in contact with the body either in life or after death. Coffins and small objects such as combs, jewellery and clothing were commonly sanctified and subsequently housed in beautiful reliquary caskets or shrines. In many cases pieces of cloth were deliberately laid in the tomb of a saint to imbue the cloth with spiritual power. The finest surviving collection of relics in Britain is the coffin of St Cuthbert with its varied collection of objects now in Durham Cathedral.

Ecclesiastical centres with a good collection of relics were very wealthy, and would be visited by large numbers of pilgrims, especially on saints' days, when the objects were put on special display and sometimes paraded. The temporal as well as spiritual value of relics led to a vigorous trade throughout the medieval period.

relief-band amphora. A distinctive large storage jar strengthened with clay straps or bands, first made in the Rhineland as early as the 7th century and commonly produced at the BADORF pottery centres. It seems that these amphorae were often employed to carry Rhenish wine to other countries, and as a result many amphorae sherds are known from sites in Britain, the Netherlands and Scandinavia. The Badorf amphorae were probably made only until the 11th century, but similar forms were by then being produced in the new pottery centres at ANDENNE and Limburg.

Remedello. A Copper Age culture centred in the Po plain of northern Italy, named after a cemetery of 119 trench graves at Remedello Sotto near Brescia. The grave goods of this 3rd millennium BC culture include copper dagger and HALBERD blades, rare silver ornaments, flint-barbed and tanged arrowheads, and pottery vessels.

Remojades. A CLASSIC PERIOD centre, located southeast of EL TAJIN close to the modern city of Veracruz, Mexico, and noted for its production of ceramics. Best known of these are the mould-made 'smiling face' figurines and small wheeled animals (similar to a child's pull toy). BALL-GAME players and warriors are frequent subjects of the figurines, but women and children are also quite common. Locally available natural outcrops of asphalt were used as paint to highlight some features of the figurines. Examples of wheeled animals have been found as far afield as Nayarit and El Salvador.

rendzina. The type of SOIL which occurs commonly on the softer limstone rocks, especially chalk. Rendzinas are one of a group of soils known as primitive soils. Unlike mature soils, which have three or more HORIZONS in their PROFILE, rendzinas have only a mixed mineral/HUMUS horizon which rests directly on the weathered parent material. They would naturally represent an early stage in soil development. On the chalklands of Britain, however, man's agricultural activities have caused so much erosion of the original BROWN FOREST SOILS and SOLS LESSIVÉS that only the rendzina type of profile is stable.

repoussé. A technique of decorating thin sheet metals by COLD-WORKING. The decoration is raised up from the rest of the sheet using hammer-struck punches on the back. Further work on the design can be done using chisels and punches on the front of the sheet — a technique known as CHASING.

Repton. The church of St Wystan at Repton in Derbyshire, northeast England, with its prominent perpendicular spire appears outwardly to be late medieval in date, but parts of the upstanding masonry belong to the pre-Conquest period. Most interesting is the very fine 8th-9th century crypt, the only English example of that date supported on four central columns. These are embellished with spiral decoration, giving the chamber the appearance of a CAROLINGIAN rather than an English building. Repton is known to be the burial place of the MERCIAN kings, and recent excavations have found evidence of a mausoleum outside the main building, as well as evidence of the Viking encampment of 867.

resistivity meter. The equipment used for measuring electrical resistance in a RESISTIVITY SURVEY. This is generally done through an array of four electrodes, pushed into the ground surface. Despite their name, resistivity meters do not actually measure resistivity, but ground resistance. Resistivity is this resistance, standardized for the distance between the electrodes in the ground.

resistivity surveying. One of the most commonly used GEOPHYSICAL surveying methods. The electrical resistance of the ground is measured with a RESISTIVITY METER. Readings are taken in a grid-pattern of points all over a suspected site. Variation of resistance through a site is caused mainly by differences in the amount of water contained in pore spaces of deposits and structures. Ground resistance may rise to a particularly high level over a stone wall, or fall to a low level over a ditch filled with more loosely packed material, that contains more water than the surrounding subsoil. The outline of features may be seen if the readings are plotted as a plan. Although the technique is generally known as 'resistivity surveying', most archaeological surveys use only the ground resistance, in ohms (Ω). Resistivity is in fact a different quantity: the resistance on a unit lengthed cylinder of material (measured in Ω metres), which should be calculated from the ground resistance readings given by most resistivity meters. However, this distinction is not important in most archaeological work.

retouch. The different types of stone tool recognized by archaeologists are distinguished in part by the nature of the FLAKE or CORE on which they are made, but more importantly by the nature of the secondary flaking or retouch applied to the tool to shape it. There are several types of retouch, of which the two most important are backing or blunting retouch, and invasive or normal retouch. Invasive retouch can be steep or shallow, depending mainly on the kind of edge being retouched; this retouch can also be scaly in character. Backing is most often applied to BLADES and may have been in order to blunt the back or to bring its end to a stout point. Recent evidence suggests that it may have been done to regularize the blade edge to facilitate fixing by resin 'mastic' to a bone or wood shaft. Such a strip of mastic was found in LASCAUX. Notching or toothing is another form of retouch, and the removal of spalls or slivers as in the BURIN technique could be regarded as a further form of retouch or modification. *See* illustration, page 428.

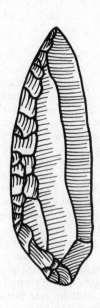

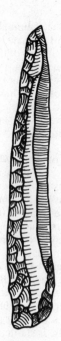

Retouch: backed blade (left) *and backed point* (right)

Rhapta. According to the *Periplus of the Erythraean Sea*, written in the first few centuries AD, this was the southernmost port of the East African coast to which voyagers from the Mediterranean world at that time penetrated. Despite attempts to locate Rhapta's remains, no archaeological evidence for its position has yet been discovered: indeed, nowhere on the coast of the modern Kenya and Tanzania has any definite trace been found of the presence of foreign traders at such an early date. From documentary evidence it seems likely that Rhapta was located in the general vicinity of the modern Dar es Salaam, perhaps in the delta of the Rufiji River.

rhinoceros. Five species of rhinoceros have survived until recently: the Great Indian rhino (*Rhinoceros unicornis*), the Javan rhino (*R. sondaicus*), the Sumatran rhino (*Dicerorhinus sumatrensis*), the white, or grass rhino (*Ceratotherium simum*) and the black, or browse rhino (*Diceros bicornis*). All are almost extinct, or much reduced in numbers. In Africa, rock art and skeletal evidence show that the range of both white and black rhinoceros once extended widely into North Africa. Like the elephant, these species have presumably been restricted both by intensified desertification and the interference of man. Extinct rhinoceroses include Merck's rhino and the short-nosed or steppe rhino, both common in Europe during INTERGLACIALS and becoming extinct at the end of the IPSWICHIAN interglacial. Merck's rhino, *Dicerorhinus kirchbergensis (merkii)* had low-crowned teeth and a horizontally held head, like the black rhino of today. Presumably this was an adaptation (as it is in the black rhino) to browsing in open woodland. The short-nosed rhino (*Dicerorhinus hemitoechus*) had higher crowned teeth and a head and neck especially adapted to reaching the ground. Like the white rhino of today, this animal probably grazed on open grasslands. Merck's rhino and the short-nosed rhino tend to be mutually exclusive in the fossil record. Their relative frequency has been used to distinguish between HOXNIAN and IPSWICHIAN deposits in Britain. The closely related woolly rhinoceros (*Coelodonta (Tichorhinus) antiquitatis*) evolved late in the QUATERNARY period, and was adapted to cold, open conditions. It became common right across Europe and northern Asia during times of colder climate, but became extinct before 10,000 bc.

Rhodes. A large Aegean Greek island off the southwest coast of Anatolia, settled by Dorian Greeks who established three city-states, Ialysos, Lindos and Kameiros. They produced local pottery, which was traded widely in the Greek world. In 408/7 BC they were united into one state, with its capital at Rhodes, a planned city with streets radiating from the harbour. At its wealthiest and most powerful in the period c323-167 BC Rhodes developed a new form of house colonnaded court (peristyle) with one row of columns higher than the others; provided a grand entrance to the Lindos acropolis sanctuary of Athena, and produced sculptures of quality, including a colossus overlooking the harbour (no longer surviving). Under the Romans it prospered less.

Rhodes became important again during the Crusader period, when it was chosen for an important military base. The crusaders first passed through Rhodes in 1097, but it was not until 1309 that the Knights of St John and the Knights Templar captured it from the Genoese and turned it into a strongly defended colony. For the next 213 years it remained in the control of the Knights, and Rhodes town still retains much of the appearance of those times. It was walled by a massive stone enceinte, while inside the knights of different orders built a series of hospitals, palaces and churches. The harbour still retains parts of its medieval defences. In 1523 Rhodes fell to Suleiman the Magnificent.

Rhodesian man. *See* BROKEN HILL.

rhyton [Greek; non-technically a 'drinking-horn']. Technically a ritual vessel found from the Bronze Age onward, and presumably intended for the pouring of libations to the gods. The vessel often shows its association with the drinking-horn by taking an elongated shape. The handle is single, and the mouth at the upper end is often balanced by a hole at the lower end. It is normally presumed that the covering of this aperture by the celebrant would control the pouring of the libation until the right moment in the ceremony. The *rhyton* is often made from precious material, and extensively decorated. The form has animal and other fantastic variations. It is found in the MINOAN and MYCENAEAN civilizations, and also in classical Persia and classical Greece.

Ribbleshead. A rare example of an Anglo-Danish farmstead, founded in the 9th century, high in the Yorkshire Dales. The site consists of a main dwelling-house of typical VIKING construction with stone walls two metres thick faced with limestone, and a paved doorway at either end. The kitchen is housed in a separate building with a hearth, and this contained many animal bones. Among the usual bone objects and domestic rubbish the excavators found a bronze-plated bell.

rice. A group of cereals, members of the genus *Oryza*. There are two cultivated species: *O. sativa* (Asian rice) and *O. glaberrina* (African rice). Asian rice is the more widespread of the two. It was first domesticated from an annual forbear (*Oryza nivara*?) in the region of seasonal monsoonal rainfall which stretches from the Ganges valley of India, through northern Burma and THAILAND, into southern China. The earliest dates for domesticated rice at the moment come from the middle and lower Yangzi region of China, where it was the staple cereal of the Neolithic cultures. It was cultivated at HEMUDU by the early 5th millennium BC, while in the middle Yangzi area clear evidence of rice agriculture dates from the late 4th or early 3rd millennium BC (*see* QUJIALING). Other sites with presumably cultivated rice dated to before 3500 BC include Koldihwa (Ganges valley), BAN CHIANG and NON NOK THA (northern Thailand). In North China the find of rice grain impressions on a sherd from the YANG-SHAO site (Mianchi Xian, Henan province) is isolated and insecurely dated, but rice is mentioned in SHANG oracle texts and rice cultivation was well established in the lower Yellow River valley by the ZHOU dynasty. In Japan, rice must have been introduced as a cultigen, because it is not part of the natural vegetation there. The evidence for rice cultivation includes actual rice grains, impressions of grains and chaff on pottery, planting and harvesting tools, remains of paddy field with water control devices, and pollen and phytoliths from the soil. The earliest evidence is from c1000 BC at a few of the Late and Final JOMON sites in northern Kyushu; it becomes more frequent and widespread after 300 BC, when the YAYOI period began.

The earliest cultivated rice may have been grown in natural swamps or middens, but by at least 2000 years ago many parts of southeast Asia, particularly the lowland riverine plains, were developing terraced or bunded wet-field cultivation. The precise antiquity of wet rice cultivation, however, remains unknown.

Less is known about the history of *O. glaberrina*, but it seems to have developed within West Africa.

Richborough [Rutupiae]. Roman SAXON SHORE fort in Kent, southeast England, covering rather more than two hectares, and sister fort to Reculver (Roman Regulbium); also starting-point for the Roman road, WATLING STREET, to CHESTER via LONDON. In Roman times, the site lay on the coast and not some five kilometres inland as today. Originally bridgehead and supply base for the Roman invading forces of AD 43, the site shows evidence for trenches of this period, and also for timber buildings including granaries. By about 85 a stone residence had been added — perhaps a MANSIO — and housing and shops began to appear. A grand four-way concrete TRIUMPHAL ARCH was erected, decorated with imported marble and statuary. Some time in the middle of the 3rd century the statues were removed, and the monument was converted to use as a signal tower, with three ditches. Later in the same century, the tower was demolished to clear the site for the construction of the Saxon Shore fort, of which partial remains of walls and gate structures survive. The fort was equipped with a military bath-suite, of which the HYPOCAUST survives, and an external AMPHITHEATRE.

ridge and furrow. The fossilized remains of ancient ploughmarks are a common sight in England, having the appearance of long, rounded parallel ridges with alternating ditches. Ridge and furrow is not confined to any particular geographical area and is spread throughout many regions of the country, although 'narrow' as opposed to 'broad' ridge is perhps more common on the chalk downs of southern England. There is no absolute dating for the ridge and furrow fields; a few contentious examples could be Roman in date, while others are as late as the 17th and 18th centuries. However, in general this type of field system is most commonly associated with medieval agriculture and in many cases can be related by maps to the pre-enclosure in-field out-field and furlong patterns of individual villages.

Rigveda. The oldest literary document of India, the Rigveda is a collection of hymns in an archaic form of Sanskrit, sung as part of the Vedic ritual. Although only written down in relatively recent times, it represents an oral tradition originally composed in the later 2nd millennium BC. The Rigveda is of the greatest importance to philologists studying the Indo-European languages and to students of religion studying Hinduism and its immediate predecessor, Vedism; its interest to archaeologists lies mainly in the light it throws on the ARYAN invasions of the 2nd millennium BC and the nature of early INDO-EUROPEAN societies in India.

Rillaton. An Early Bronze Age round BARROW in Cornwall, southwest England, which has produced a gold cup, seen as one of the finest pieces of WESSEX CULTURE craftsmanship. It is made of sheet gold, strengthened with corrugations, and has an s-shaped profile and a single handle. It was formerly thought to be a MYCENAEAN product, or at least show Mycenaean influence, but is now seen by most scholars as a purely local object.

Rim. A site in north-central Upper Volta. A backed microlith industry lacking pottery and ground stone artefacts precedes 3000 bc. From the mid-2nd millennium bc both these elements are present. Stone tool technology continued to be practised until around 1,000 years ago, apparently after the first local appearance of metal implements.

Rinaldone. A Copper Age culture of central west Italy. It is known mainly from funerary sites, which are either collective burials in rock-cut tombs, or single or collective burials in trench graves. The grave goods include copper in relative abundance, made into flat axes, daggers and halberds. Other goods are stone battle axes, fine flint daggers and arrowheads, and a dark burnished ware, in which bottle shapes with lug and tunnel handles predominate. The type site is a cemetery of trench graves south of Lake Bolsena.

Ringerike style. A style of Scandinavian animal ornament which eclipsed the earlier JELLINGE style in the early 11th century. The contorted Jellinge-style beasts were replaced by long-necked serpents and birds, intertwined with spindly scrolled and foliated ornament. Important examples of the style are found on 10th-century metalwork and a few pieces of stone sculpture, but perhaps its most effective use was in manuscript illumination. The Ringerike style may have been introduced to the British Isles by Viking settlers but it was modified and adapted by native craftsmen to decorate a range of very individual objects such as the 11th-century brooch from Sutton, Isle of Ely, and the very important 11th-century churchyard slab from St Pauls, London, which shows a stag-like creature intertwined with serpents.

ringwells. In the GANGES CIVILIZATION of India, wells and soakaways were sometimes lined with pottery rings or whole pots without bases. These are known as ringwells.

ringwork. The most modest form of medieval CASTLE, originating in Germany in the later 10th century. Excavations of several of the hundreds of 10th-13th-century ringworks have shown them to be fortified MANORS of the period. The first ringworks in England were constructed just before the Norman Conquest, around the manors at Goltho, Lincolnshire, and Sulgrave, Northamptonshire; after the Conquest hundreds of ringworks were erected to defend timber and masonry buildings. Excavations have shown some, like Penhallan in Cornwall, to be as late as the 13th century. However, the Normans do not seem to have introduced ringworks to either southern Italy or Ireland.

Rinyo-Clacton ware. *See* GROOVED WARE.

Rio Bec. Southernmost of a trio of architectural styles in the lowland MAYAN north central Yucatan, Mexico, based on the heavy use of uncut stone and stucco (*see also* CHENES and PUUC). Although contemporary with Chenes, it has elements which associate it more with CLASSIC MAYA sites of the Peten. It is characterized by an emphasis on appearance rather than function. Large towers imitating the steep stepped temple-PYRAMIDS of such centres as TIKAL consist entirely of fill which

has been plastered over; the same is true for the whole upper storeys of other buildings. The best example of Rio Bec architecture is at Xpuhil in Campeche.

Rio Seco. A permanent settlement site dating to the PRE-CERAMIC PERIOD VI, located north of the Chancay Valley on the central coast of Peru. The earliest structures were an isolated group of house compounds. Some of these were later filled with rubble and two PYRAMIDS were built over them. These in turn were subjected to a further succession of reconstructions in the form of house compounds, fill, ceremonial buildings and so on. Numerous caches of offerings (including food, cotton, bone tools and sedge matting) were buried in shell refuse around the bases of the pyramids. Rio Seco had a population of 500 to 1000 at its height and was abandoned before the onset of the INITIAL PERIOD.

Ripoli. A Middle to Late Neolithic settlement near the Adriatic coast in east central Italy. A ditch enclosed a number of hut foundations and storage pits. The site has given its name to a type of trichrome painted pottery, decorated with red areas and thin black lines on a buff ground; the most common forms are cups.

Riss. A group of QUATERNARY deposits in the Alps and the valleys of south German rivers. The Riss consists of MORAINE and related river terraces of PROGLACIAL deposits. It formed part of the classical scheme of four GLACIALS with intervening INTERGLACIALS, published in 1909 by Penck and Bruckner. In this scheme, it was held that the Riss deposits represented the penultimate glaciation of the Alps; more recently, it has become clear that the Alpine sequence is much more complicated than had been thought. During the period of time occupied by the GÜNZ, MINDEL, Riss and WÜRM deposits, no less than ten world-wide glacials are shown by the analysis of DEEP SEA CORES. The position of the Riss within the climatic sequence of the Quaternary is as yet unclear. For this reason, the term Riss should be used only to describe a particular group of Alpine deposits. Unfortunately, 'Riss' has gained wide currency as a more general term, meaning the penultimate cold stage throughout Europe. This is still common in archaeological literature, but should be avoided.

Riss/Würm. The term for the INTERGLACIAL erosion interval, envisaged by Penck and Bruckner as separating the RISS and WÜRM GLACIALS. The Alpine sequence is now known to be much more complex than was originally thought, but 'Riss/Würm' unfortunately gained wide currency as a general term meaning the last interglacial throughout Europe. This usage is still common in archaeological literature, but should be avoided.

ritual vessels (China). The bronze ritual vessel is the characteristic artefact of early Chinese civilization and the vehicle of its greatest artistic achievements. At SHANG sites the vessels are found chiefly in tombs, but ZHOU bronzes have often been found in hoards unconnected with burials (*see* FUFENG). Vessels from early Shang tombs are sometimes blackened with soot, suggesting long use in rituals of sacrifice before burial. Beginning in the ANYANG period (*c*1300-*c*1030 BC), vessels were often cast with inscriptions dedicating them to the service of deceased ancestors; hence the sacrificial offerings of wine and food presented in the vessels were connected with the ancestral cult known also from the Anyang ORACLE BONE inscriptions. The practice of providing imposing vessels as mortuary gifts, and perhaps even the ancestral cult itself, originated in the east-coast Neolithic tradition, where some of the Shang vessel shapes have precursors in pottery and where important Shang cultural traits are foreshadowed as early as the 4th millennium BC (*see* DADUNZI, LIANGZHU).

Western Zhou bronze vessels were used in the same rituals of sacrifice but were diverted to serve secular purposes as well. Their often lengthy inscriptions record feudal transactions in which the Zhou king honoured or enfeoffed a vassal lord who thereupon cast an inscribed bronze to commemorate the event. With the collapse of the Western Zhou empire in the 8th century BC these commemorative inscriptions cease to occur, but throughout the ensuing Eastern Zhou period the vessels continued to serve as objects of prestige advertising the wealth and power of a family. At the courts of rival kings and princes they even acquired a symbolic role as emblems of political legitimacy, specific sets of vessels being regarded as prerogatives of lordly rank that embodied a prince's right to rule; these notions must derive from the far earlier use of the bronzes in the ancestral sacrifices performed by the Shang king, who owed his divine authority to his privileged communication with the royal spirits. Overt political symbolism was probably never so important as the sheer wealth that the vessels represented, however, and the increasingly sumptuous Eastern Zhou bronzes, often inlaid with gold and silver, seem to have been luxuries valued more for themselves than for the sake of the rituals they were meant to serve. In its role as luxury object the bronze vessel was displaced towards the end of Eastern Zhou by still more precious LACQUERS, and the bronzes receded into insignificance in the course of the HAN dynasty.

The ritual vessels were made in a variety of shapes whose modern names usually come from inscriptions on the vessels or follow conventions established by scholars of the SONG period. The vast majority of the shapes were already in existence before the end of the Shang dynasty. Shang vessels fall by and large into two classes, tripods (DING, *he, jia, jiao, jue,* LI, *xian*) and ring-footed vessels (*dou, gu, guang,* GUI, *hu, lei, pan, pou, you, yu, zhi,* ZUN). Many of these were made also in rectangular versions, distinguished by the prefix *fang* (*fang ding, fang yi* etc.). For some of the shapes, notably the *ding,* prototypes of great antiquity can be traced at Neolithic sites (*see* HEMUDU). For others, wrought-metal prototypes should perhaps be invoked (*he, jue*), although the earliest bronze vessels yet found in China, four *jue* from ERLITOU, were not hammered to shape but cast. In the Western Zhou period only a few new shapes were introduced (*fu, xu, yi*), but the repertoire of types nevertheless underwent considerable change. The *gui,* a food vessel, enjoyed a special vogue, while certain shapes meant for wine offerings were virtually eliminated, among them some of the very oldest bronze vessel types (*gu, jia, jue*); these changes are consistent with literary evidence for lessened emphasis on wine-offerings in early Zhou. Few new shapes were invented in the Eastern Zhou period (*dui, jian*), and by this time many of the Shang vessel types had fallen from use while the remainder were altered almost beyond recognition.

Throughout the Shang and Zhou periods the ritual vessels were made almost exclusively by casting (*see* METALS AND METALWORKING, CHINA). Since elsewhere in the world metal

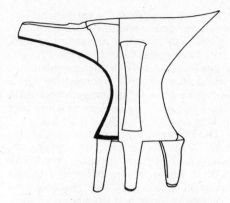

*Bronze jue vessel from Erlitou (3rd stratum),
height 12 cm. This is one of the earliest metal
vessels known from China
(mid-2nd millennium BC).*

vessels have for reasons of economy usually been made by hammering rather than casting, this is an unusual technological habit, and it determined certain characteristic features of Chinese bronzes. First and foremost it meant that since decoration could be so easily supplied in the process of casting an object, the early Chinese metalworker did not rely on techniques for decorating cold metal such as repoussé and inlay. With the exception of a few turquoise-inlaid weapons, Shang and Western Zhou bronzes were both shaped and decorated by casting. Not until about the 6th century BC, perhaps under the stimulus of foreign models, did it become fashionable to supplement cast decoration with gilding or inlays of copper, gold, silver, semi-precious stones, and GLASS (*see* PINGSHAN). Because the bronze decoration was from the first made by casting, it was susceptible to influence from the particular casting method employed by Chinese founders and quickly acquired a special character. The section-mould method, in use already at Erlitou, generally began with a model of the object to be cast; clay was packed around the model to form the mould, which was then removed from the model in sections, baked, and reassembled for casting. The influence of this technique on the bronzes was profound, for the decoration of the earliest bronze vessels was designed so as to fall into self-contained units corresponding to the separate sections of the mould. The most important of the pattern units devised for this purpose — and the most long-lived motifs in

Chinese art — were the TAOTIE and the dragon. Reliance on section-mould casting thus gave rise to a tradition of rigidly compartmented designs; the highly structured decoration of a vessel was moreover almost automatically well-fitted to the vessel's shape, because the shape had necessarily been taken into account in sectioning the mould for removal from the model. The artistic tradition of Bronze Age China owes much of its distinctive character to a sympathetic exploitation of the section-mould technique. It should be emphasized that this technique, best suited to objects of simple or regular shape, was viable only because of the special purpose to which metal was devoted in ancient China, a purpose that seems to have been determined by ritual requirements set already in Neolithic times (*see* METALLURGY, CHINA).

Ritupiae. *See* RICHBOROUGH.

rivet. Rivetting is a method of making joints in metalwork. The rivets are short metal rods which pass through holes in the parts to be joined and are hammered down on either side to hold the joint firmly together. In antiquity, rivetting was used for joint metal sheet, to make such artefacts as helmets or SITULAE. The handles of BRONZE daggers were also often held on by a number of rivets.

Rivoli. A number of sites, including hilltop settlements, in the vicinity of Rivoli, near Verona in northeast Italy, have provided the name for a version of the northern Italian Neolithic SQUARE-MOUTHED POTTERY culture. Agriculture was practised, but hunting and gathering was also important. As well as the characteristic pottery, the sites have produced PINTADERAS, and a fragment of copper — early evidence of metal working in the area.

On the summit of the Rocca di Rivoli is a medieval castle which has been under excavation since 1978.

Rixheim. Site near Mulhouse, Alsace, eastern France, of an Early Neolithic cemetery of the LINEAR POTTERY culture, containing ochre-covered inhumations. There is also an URNFIELD Bronze Age cemetery at Rixheim, which has given its name to an early Urnfield type of sword with a narrow blade and a tang.

Rizhao Liangchengzhen (Jih-chao Liang-ch'eng-chen). *See* LONGSHAN.

Robberg. A cave, on the south Cape coast of South Africa, also known as Nelson Bay Cave. A full account of the long archaeological sequence is not yet available. The initial occupation, of 'Middle Stone Age' type, overlies a beach horizon at some 12 metres above modern sea level which may date from well before 80,000 BC. After a prolonged hiatus the site was re-occupied successively by bearers of the Robberg, ALBANY and WILTON industries the first of which, dating to between the 17th and the 10th millennia bc, and containing diminutive artefacts with few retouched implements, takes its name from this site. As at several sites in southern Africa, the appearance of the microlithic Wilton is marked by a pronounced increase in the proportion of small bush-loving antelope represented in the faunal remains, in contrast with the open-grasslands creatures that were sought in earlier times.

Robin Hood's Cave. *See* CRESWELL.

Roc de Sers. This PALAEOLITHIC rock shelter in the Charente, southwest France, has SOLU-TRIAN and MAGDALENIAN levels with burials in the latter. A line of limstone blocks carved with bas-relief bison, horse, ibex and other figures is one of the rare examples of Solutrian art.

rock art of Africa.

East Africa. Prehistoric rock art is found in several regions of eastern Africa, and several distinct traditions are represented. The area where such art has been executed over the longest period is almost certainly the highlands of central Tanzania. Here, especially in the rock shelters of the Kondoa and Singida districts, it has been possible to establish a long stylistic sequence of naturalistic paintings which shows some similarity to that of the rock art of southern Africa (*see below*) especially Zambia and Mozambique. The animals depicted are exclusively wild and may be shown in outline, with a flat infill, or sketched by a mass of fine lines. Human figures are shown relatively infrequently. Most figures are depicted in isolation, and group compositions or scenes are rare. Later in the sequence are schematic motifs, initially often in red, latterly in white or grey. With the last-named there also occur crude, stylized representations of humans and animals, including domestic cattle. As in southern Africa, there are reasons to attribute the bulk of the schematic and stylized art to the Iron Age, and the earlier naturalistic art to the hunter-gatherers of the 'Late Stone Age'. Around Lake Victoria only the Iron Age series has been recorded.

The Tanzanian area noted above lies to the south of the region formerly exploited by PASTORAL NEOLITHIC peoples; but to the north, in Kenya, it is to this phase that the earliest art appears to belong. This consists of somewhat stylized representations of long-horned cattle in a cave on Mount Elgon. Later art in Kenya, both paintings and engravings, may mostly be attributed to the recent populations or their immediate ancestors: it includes highly stylized figures of camels, cattle etc, together with symbols which may be correlated with those still used in the branding of livestock.

In Somalia and Ethiopia the surviving art is again mainly naturalistic, principally of animals but with occasional human figures. Most of the animals depicted are domestic: it is unclear whether there is an earlier series showing exclusively wild animals. As at Mount Elgon, long-horned humpless cattle pre-dominate: humped beasts and (in some areas) camels are represented only at a late stage in the stylistic sequence.

Northern Africa. Prehistoric rock paintings and engravings are found in numerous areas distributed widely through North Africa and the Sahara. In several of these areas it has been the subject of detailed study, but it has generally proved difficult to relate it to the local archaeological sequences on arguments other than those based on tenuous internal evidence. As is the case elsewhere on the continent, it seems clear that some of the art was the work of hunter-gatherer peoples who had no knowledge of domestic animals, or who at any rate had no reason to make representations of such creatures. This conclusion receives support from the discovery of occasional art objects in IBEROMAURUSIAN deposits and of numerous examples with CAPSIAN associations. It is likely that the earliest mural art consists of the engravings of large wild fauna, notably the giant buffalo Bubalis, represented in the rock shelters of the central Sahara. This art probably extends back to a period before the 6th millennium bc.

In the central and western Sahara the earliest paintings, following the 'Bubalis' engravings, depict strange, often giant, human figures with characteristically round heads. They were followed in turn by both paintings and engravings of the so-called 'bovidian' phase, in which domestic animals and pastoral scenes were the favoured subjects. It is logical to assume that the 'bovidian' art does not pre-date the archaeologically attested appearance of domestic animals in the Sahara, probably about the 6th or 5th millennium bc. The round-headed human figures could then be earlier than this. Subsequent developments show the adoption of the horse and the camel, including light horse-drawn chariots which may have been used for trans-Saharan journeys in the last millennium BC.

Southern Africa. Africa south of the Zambezi possesses some of the highest concentrations of prehistoric rock art known from anywhere in the world, as well as some of outstanding quality. Several regional sequences have been established and in some areas it has been possible to link specific stages of these sequences to events which are independently recorded archaeologically or historically.

The earliest rock art yet known in southern Africa or, indeed, in any part of the continent, consists of stone slabs bearing representations of animals and a human figure excavated at the 'APOLLO 11' CAVE in southern Namibia from levels dating to about the 25th millennium bc. This discovery shows that the antiquity of southern African rock art is of the same order as that of the European paintings. Neverthe-less, it seems unlikely that any of the southern African paintings which survive on the walls of rock shelters are older than a very few thousand years.

In Zimbabwe, a six-phase stylistic sequence of paintings has been established through the study of superpositions. In the first three of these styles the animals depicted are exclusively wild: domestic fat-tailed sheep first appear in style 4. These first four styles are essentially naturalistic. Style 5 consists of schematic designs and style 6 of crude zoomorphs, some of which may be associated with recent rain-making ceremonies. Seen in conjunction with further dating evidence for comparable paintings in Zambia and Malawi,

it is generally accepted that the four-style naturalistic series may be attributed to the stone-tool-using hunter-gatherers who, from style 3 or 4 onwards were contemporary with Early Iron Age farming peoples. Styles 5 and 6 may be attributed to the Iron Age: north of the Zambezi several of the motifs represented may be linked with the religious symbols of recent Bantu-speaking societies.

South of the Limpopo the areas richest in rock paintings are the Brandberg and Erongo Mountains of Namibia, the southwest Cape, the Natal and Lesotho Drakensberg, and the Transvaal. In the latter region, as in parts of the Orange Free State and northern Cape, there are also engravings, largely undated, of excellent artistic accomplishment. It is in the Drakensberg that the greatest variety and development occurs. Probably all the extant paintings are of late date: in the earliest series only wild animals are shown and it is possible to propose direct comparisons with con-temporary work in Zimbabwe and other parts of South Africa. Particular prominence is given in these paintings to the eland, which occupied an important place in the mythology of the San hunter-gatherers. Detailed analysis of the subject-matter of these paintings has enabled them to be interpreted in the light of the artists' cosmology. In the later paintings techniques were developed of using shading in bichrome and polychrome work — to great effect. Iron Age people and their domestic animals are now depicted. In the final paintings representations occur of the European settlers at whose hands the last of the Drakensberg artists were exterminated during the 19th century.

rock-cut tomb. A tomb constructed by excavating a chamber in the natural rock. Rock-cut tombs are entered either directly from a cliff face, or by a vertical shaft from the surface or by a sloping or stepped passage (DROMOS). Rock-cut tombs are found in many parts of the world. They are particularly common in the Mediterranean region, where they occur from the Neolithic to the Iron Age. They may be used either for single or collective burial.

rock shelter. At the foot of limestone cliffs there is often a shelter or protected place where the cliff overhangs, this is a rock-shelter or *abri*. Such sites were frequently occupied by later PALAEOLITHIC man and great thicknesses of deposits built up under them, partly from human debris, but aided by the slow disintegration and fall of the overhanging rock.

Rocky Cape. *See* TASMANIA.

Rolûos. *See* HARIHARÂLAYA.

Romanelli. A large coastal cave in Apulia, the 'heel' of Italy, occupied in the PALAEOLITHIC period. Over a beach of last INTERGLACIAL date came some MOUSTERIAN deposits and a series of Upper Palaeolithic deposits of 'Romanellian' type. There are engraved art objects in these layers and on the walls, and skeletal material is also found in the Romanellian levels. The latter are dated by radiocarbon to *c*9000 bc, and there are some URANIUM SERIES DATES from the lower levels.

Rome. In the Romans' traditional version of the foundation of their capital city, the basic sequence of village settlements, synoecism, rule by kings, expulsion of the kings, and the creation of the Republic, is generally plausible, while the date of 753 BC or thereabouts is not. 2nd millennium BC evidence is of the APENNINE culture, and occurs on the left bank of the River Tiber in the general vicinity of the midstream island (Isola Tiberina). Here there seems to have been a natural fording-point with shallow water, and the island itself may possibly have been reshaped by engineering works. A left-bank location would lie both on the expected north-south route, and would also give a convenient landing for sea and river traffic. The traditional 'Seven Hills' would have given a fallback arc of fortifiable positions. Iron Age evidence is found both on the low-lying ground (such as the area of the later Forum Romanum), and upon the hills themselves (*see* PALATINE). None of the literary sources responsible for the traditional date are themselves earlier than the 3rd century BC (although it is true that they did draw upon earlier archives), and by this period a respectably antique foundation date was essential to the civic pride of any large city. The 6th century BC is ETRUSCAN, when there is evidence for works of city engineering and drainage, and for public works such as the first paving of the FORUM and the Comitium. Later Romans saw the Etruscans as foreigners and

intruders, but Roman indebtedness to Etruscan culture is wide and profound. Although the notion would have been unthinkable to any blue-blooded Roman Republican, it is not impossible that urbanization is hardly earlier than the 6th century BC, and Etruscan at least in organization and inspiration.

The end of the 6th century brought the expulsion of the kings, and the celebration of a republican state. Dynasticism, however, lived on, and Rome never entirely lost that tendency to concentrate power in the hands of a few, competing, aristocratic families. The evolution of democratic institutions with officers such as the *tribuni* and *aediles* appointed to protect plebeian against patrician interests, was slow and contentious. Even so, over the next two and half centuries, Rome achieved an almost linear rate of expansion. With only one serious hiccough — the CELTIC sack of Rome early in the 4th century BC — Rome had managed by the middle of the 3rd century to subdue, or reach favourable terms with virtually all the peoples and cities of the Italian mainland. Rome's new peninsular status offered a direct challenge to Carthaginian supremacy in the western Mediterranean, which was finally resolved in the PUNIC WARS of 264-202 BC.

The sixty years represented by those two wars took Rome into Sardinia, Sicily, Spain and Africa. The following sixty years, say, down to 140 BC, brought Roman territorial expansion or annexation into areas as diverse as southern Gaul, the Dalmatian coast and northern Greece, and Roman influence into Egypt, Syria and the Ionian Greek cities of Asia Minor. But in the final one hundred years of the Republic (say 133-31 BC) aggrandizement was largely overtaken by its own problems, which were essentially three: the maintenance of the borders so far reached, the administration of the provinces within those borders, and the resolution of Rome's own internal political conflicts. Of these three, the first two found scant solution, while the scale of the third overwhelmed the Republic.

At Rome, the land and social reform programme of the Gracchi brothers (133-122 BC), and their violent deaths, struck a keynote for a century of turbulent politics, and near-anarchy. Slave wars, civil wars and war with Rome's Italian allies, were balanced by the emergence of new would-be 'dynasts', such as

Sulla, Caesar and Antony. These pretenders sometimes formed uneasy and unstable alliances, such as the First and Secon Triumvirates. The armed forces, realizing their power, aligned themselves first with one and then another, or in opposing camps. Rome and the provinces became the involuntary stage upon which their rivalry had to be resolved.

The government set up by the surviving victor and peacemaker, Octavian, from 31 BC was careful and calculated, firm and stable. His normally favourable press is probably deserved. Octavian took the title Augustus, which had hallowed associations with Rome's foundation, was careful to call himself only *princeps* ('chief citizen') and, in word at least, to link the senate and people in his actions. In the provinces he was largely content to consolidate existing borders, and a new civil service was set up to improve administration. In Rome he was concerned to restore public security with a fire and police force, and public morale and morality with a new literature for the new age. Historians from antiquity have debated whether he truly intended to restore the Republic when time permitted (as ardent Republicans fervently hoped), or whether his public image was just clever window-dressing for the foundation of a new dynasty. By chance or consequence, the years from 31 BC to the death of Marcus Aurelius in AD 180 were the most continuously successful, stable and prosperous of the whole Roman period.

Even so, not all was joy and light. Of the Julio-Claudian emperors, Tiberius' (14-37) reclusive and arbitrary *distanz*, Caligula's and Nero's excesses, and the reappearance of the army as emperor-maker in 69 (the Year of the Four Emperors), all nearly destabilized what Augustus had achieved. Similarly, what Vespasian (69-79) was able to restore with his Flavian dynasty was thrown into jeopardy by his son Domitian (81-96), whose resort to informers (*delatores*) and a reign of terror, provoked his assassination.

A clutch of five good emperors (Nerva, Trajan, Hadrian, Antoninus Pius and Marcus Aurelius between 96 and 180) secured for Rome her halcyon days. These were in effect appointed administrators and gave the empire a welcome respite from the vagaries of genetic succession. Military operations such as Trajan's annexation of DACIA, and Hadrian's construction of a wall across England (*see* HADRIAN'S WALL), were largely acts of border management. New programmes of public building throughout the empire are evidence for a widely diffused prosperity. It took, however, the wisest of them, the Stoic philosopher Marcus Aurelius, to reverse the trend, and leave the empire to his weak and corrupt son, Commodus.

The 3rd century AD brought economic recession and a return to anarchy and civil war. Among a sea of ephemeral emperors, many once again created by various sections of the armed forces who now began to auction the empire to the highest bidder, a few strong figures stand out for short periods against the storm, notably Septimius Severus (193-211), Aurelian (270-275) and Diocletian (284-305). The civilian emphasis of Augustus' Principate was now replaced by a ruthlessly military autocracy which struggled to hold back raiding bands in virtually all areas of the Empire. The moderate tendency to deify the person of the emperor, which had probably existed from the early empire especially in the eastern provinces, moved all the way to oriental despotism with Aurelian, who took the title of *dominus et deus* ('lord and god'). The recession destroyed financial confidence, brought inflation, and led to a breakdown in the coinage. Although a few lived on in great affluence, the empire now experienced great difficulty in paying for the expensive installations and personnel of its widely diffused army and civil service. Indebtedness and new restrictive economic legislation placed serious pressures for revenue and productivity on tenant farmers and industrial workers, and society moved visibly nearer a feudalistic serfdom.

The policy of Constantine (312-337) took two directions that were to prove long-lasting. First, he confirmed Diocletian's split of the empire into a western and an eastern half by founding a new capital, a second Rome, Constantinople, on the site of BYZANTIUM in 324 (formally dedicated in 330). Secondly, with the Edict of Milan (313), his presiding over the Council of Nicaea (325), and his death-bed baptism, Constantine granted important concessions to the Christian clergy, and gave to the Church the backing of virtual State establishment. This switch to the east was permanent. The new capital soon housed not only the imperial court, but also a Senate, and centralized administration for the army, the law and the church. Investment was particularly directed toward the construction of church and allied buildings, and this major industry gave a new and technical stimulus to architecture. The rapid consolidation by the Church of its new power and prestige brought a structured administration, and influence for its bishops and officers, that changed the social and political make-up of the whole empire.

The eastern empire lasted until the capture of Constantinople by Mohammedan forces in 1453. For Rome itself, however, the 4th and 5th centuries saw a corresponding loss of political favour and power, and a consequent collapse of financial and military investment both in the city and more generally in Italy and the western provinces. Several of the functions of capital were eventually transferred north to Mediolanum (Milan) and northern Italy slowly assumed greater importance. It is significant that Aurelian (270-5) had already seen a need to build a great new wall encompassing not only the seven hills of Rome but also part of the Janiculum, and this was restored several times. The western provinces gradually lost any co-ordinated military protection, and were progressively overrun, Britain by Saxons and Celts, and Gaul and Spain by various Germanic groups. Rome itself was sacked by Alaric the Visigoth in 410 (*see* GOTH) and by Gaeseric the Vandal in 455, and from 476 came under the kingdom of the Ostrogothic leaders who, however, still recognized the eastern emperors.

This picture of collapse, however, needs some qualification, since the exact degree of Rome's dereliction can perhaps be exaggerated. There is growing evidence to suggest that the long-established Roman civilization resisted breakdown and intrusion both at Rome and in the provinces, at least for a considerable time. The advantages of a relatively advanced infrastructure and sub-systems were not necessarily swept aside by the intruders, and the anti-cultural image of the barbarian is contradicted in some cases by evidence for a recognizable continuity into the medieval period.

The visible surviving monuments of ancient Rome are chronicled in E. Nash, *Pictorial Dictionary of Ancient Rome*. All the stone buildings and notably the exposed sculptures have been badly attacked, as at ATHENS, by the corrosive atmosphere of the modern city, and in many cases surface detail is now heavily eroded. The problem is being tackled by a vigorous programme of restoration and preservation by the Italian authorities. *See also* COLOSSEUM, PANTHEON, TRAJAN'S COLUMN.

Rong and Di [Jung and Ti]. Names applied in Chinese sources to nomadic or semi-nomadic tribes who harrassed the northern frontiers of the civilized Chinese states as early as the late 2nd millennium BC. The common expression 'Rong and Di' seems to mean little more than 'barbarians'. Subgroups with names like Northern Rong, Western Rong, Quan ('dog') Rong, Red Di, and White Di are often mentioned, but it is difficult to know how these were distinguished and almost impossible to associate any archaeological finds with them. Chinese histories do however record that in the 6th century BC one of the tribes, the White Di, seized territory in northeastern China and founded a kingdom called Zhongshan, and the tombs of two 4th-century Zhongshan kings have recently been excavated at PINGSHAN.

rongorongo. The ancient script of EASTER ISLAND, carved in boustrophedon fashion on wooden boards. The script has about 120 pictographic symbols and has not been deciphered or traced to any specific outside source. It may be indigenous to the island and could even be of post-European inspiration (it was not recorded until the mid-19th century AD), but owing to the tragic depopulation of the island in the 1860s no one with the ability to read it survived.

Roonka. An open-site burial ground on an elevated terrace beside the Murray river, 50 km upstream from DEVON DOWNS, South Australia. Human occupation debris and two graves were found in deposits dated 16,000-5000 bc, but after 5000 bc the site was exclusively a burial ground. From 2000 bc until the last century it was again a camp-site as well as a cemetery. Over 100 individuals are represented from excavations; a variety of burial methods include dorsal extended, flexed, and vertical shaft graves in which the body was placed erect and later crumpled as the shaft was filled. Some graves contained one adult, others an adult (usually male) with one or two infants, and in others there were two adults. Grave goods were found only in shaft graves and included food animals, ochre, bone and shell ornaments, with stone and bone tools only in the latest phase. The evidence suggests cultural change with varying in-humation practices through time.

Rop. A rock shelter on the Jos Plateau of central Nigeria which has been the scene of several successive excavations. The lower of two main artefact-bearing layers contained rather large crude scrapers and backed crescent-shaped implements, with no pottery. The later horizon contained a backed micro-lithic industry and pottery, but no conclusive evidence for food-production, although the domestic horse appears to have been present. A human skeleton apparently associated with the second industry is dated by radiocarbon to the last century bc.

Roquepertuse. An OPPIDUM of the 3rd and 2nd centuries BC near Aix-en-Provence in southern France, not far from ENTREMONT and (like Entremont) destroyed by the Romans in 123 BC. It has a very well-known sanctuary of the SEVERED HEAD CULT. As well as niches for human skulls, cut into a portico of three stone pillars, were a number of stone statues, including cross-legged human figures, a pair of heads and a goose. Above the portico was a two-faced Janus head. Like other native sites of this period in southern France, Roquepertuse shows a marked blending of classical and native features.

Rosetta. A town at the western mouth of the Nile, famed for the discovery of a trilingual inscription of the 2nd century BC which provided the basic data for the decipherment of ancient Egyptian HIEROGLYPHIC writing. The three scripts are Greek, Egyptian hiero-glyphic and Egyptian demotic.

Roskilde. An ambitious underwater excava-tion in Roskilde fjord was mounted by the National Museum of Denmark in 1962 to retrieve a barrier of sunken ships dating to 1000-1050, deliberately planned to protect the town from enemy raiders. To recover the waterlogged timbers of these VIKING-Age vessels, the archaeologists constructed a coffer dam around the site and then drained it. Later the timbers were injected with glycol to solidify and preserve them. The ships were re-assembled and are now on display in Roskilde Ship Museum.

A range of vessels was recovered from the fjord and includes a knarr, a long-distance, sea-going cargo ship built out of pine and oak and propelled by a sail. The other oak-built merchant ship would probably have been em-ployed in local waters and was propelled by oars and a central sail. The solid oak prow of this smaller merchant ship was found intact and is a fine example of its kind. A third boat known as the warship is a long narrow vessel and resembles those ships portrayed on the BAYEUX TAPESTRY. It would originally have had a sail and provision for 20 oarsmen. This boat showed signs of extensive repairs and contained parts taken from other vessels. Another wreck was 12 metres long and may have been used as a ferry or fishing boat. Lastly, a small portion of a Viking longship was recovered: this would have been crewed by 40-50 men, and is the type of ship used on raids.

Rössen. A Middle Neolithic culture of the Swiss plateau, French Jura and the Rhineland, which developed out of the earlier LINEAR POTTERY culture of the area in the early 4th millennium bc (later 5th millennium BC). It is named after a cemetery site in Halle with 70 burials accompanied by bone and jet neck-laces, shaft-hole stone axes and both plain and decorated pottery. Settlements normally have small rectangular houses, although some long trapezoidal ones demonstrate continuity from the Linear Pottery period.

Rouffignac. A cave in the Dordogne, south-west France, with MESOLITHIC levels (SAUVE-TERRIAN and TARDENOISIAN) at the entrance. Deep inside this large cave system are black paintings and engravings in which mammoth predominates. In default of any conclusive evidence of their antiquity, some doubts have been expressed about the genuineness of this series, but most authorities on cave art have apparently accepted them.

Rough Castle. *See* ANTONINE WALL.

Rougiers. A typical French hill-top village in Provence with a late medieval castle at one end of the promontory on which it sits and a number of clearly defined rectangular peasant dwellings, all within the walls of the *castrum*. Excavations have revealed a remarkable wealth of archaeological finds including nearly 100,000 sherds of local and imported pottery, more than a hundred coins minted between 1177-1420 and a great range of metalwork.

round barrow. *See* BARROW.

round towers. Tall stone towers with conical roofs, known as round towers, were a feature of Irish monasteries from the VIKING period and into the Romanesque. They were usually five storeys high, and each floor was lit by a separate window and had a wooden floor. Because the doors were placed high off the ground it seems that the main function of the towers was as a refuge from Viking and Irish raiders, but they may also have been used as campaniles.

Roy Mata. A chief of the island of Efate, VANUATU, who died c1250 and was buried on a small island called Retoka, off northeastern Efate. His grave, excavated in 1967, was surrounded by remarkable evidence for the mass-sacrifice of 35 retainers, including 11 male-female pairs, of whom the males were apparently buried when stupified with KAVA, while the women may have been still conscious. Many bodies had ankle, wrist and neck ornaments of shells and pig tusks.

Ruanga. An Iron Age settlement in northern Mashonaland, Zimbabwe, where a stone building appears to have been occupied by people related to those of GREAT ZIMBABWE who lived in political authority over a distinct local population.

Rudna Glava. The site of a Late VINČA copper mine, located in the limestone hills north of the Saska Valley in the upland Majdapek area of northeastern Serbia, Yugoslavia. The mine, dated to the early 4th millennium bc, has been excavated by B. Jovanović. The mining technique was to construct platforms on the steep hillside and follow the vertical veins of malachite down, thereby creating empty 'shafts'. Sealed deposits of miners' lamps, antler picks and gabbro mauls have been found at the bottom of abandoned mineshafts, of which there are over 25. No smelting site has yet been discovered near the mine.

Ruicheng [Jui-ch'eng]. *See* MIAODIGOU.

Rujiazhuang [Ju-chia-chuang]. *See* BAOJI.

runes, runic. The runic script is believed to have developed in North Germany or Scandinavia in about the 4th century AD. The alphabet contains 24 characters and is based on Latin. The script developed with regional variations in the ANGLO-SAXON and VIKING kingdoms, for example. Its chief use seems to have been on memorial stones and artefacts, but excavations now commonly uncover runic inscriptions, rather like graffiti, on bits of bonework, metalwork and pottery.

Rupar. A site in east Punjab, Pakistan, which has produced evidence of two phases of the HARAPPAN CIVILIZATION, stratified below an occupation with PAINTED GREY WARE, which was itself succeeded by a level with NORTHERN BLACK POLISHED WARE.

Ruse. A large TELL of the KARANOVO V-VI group (4th millennium bc) located on a major crossing-point of the Danube in northern Bulgaria. Excavations by G. Georgiev and N. Angelov uncovered 11 Copper Age occupation levels in a 3.5-metre stratigraphy. Interspersed between house levels were over 100 intramural burials, mostly disturbed and with scanty grave goods.

Ruthwell Cross. The standing cross now preserved in the interior of the parish church at Ruthwell in Northumberland, northeast England, is considered one of the supreme examples of late 7th-century NORTHUMBRIAN sculpture. It is now partially restored and only one arm of the cross head is original. The main faces of the shaft are clearly divided into separate figural panels portraying biblical scenes and the evangelists with their symbols, all of which are bordered by the Early English 'Poem of the Rood' inscribed in RUNIC. The side panels are filled with the typically Northumbrian inhabited vine-scroll motif.

Rutupiae. *See* RICHBOROUGH.

Ruvanveli dagaba. *See* ANURADHAPURA.

rye. A group of cereals, members of the genus *Secale*. A number of wild species is found today in the Near East. Cultivated rye (*S. cereale*) has been recognized recently on the Anatolian site of CAN HASAN in the 7th millennium bc. Previously the earliest known cultivated rye was from NEOLITHIC sites in central Europe. It was common during the Iron Age in northern Europe, which has remained one of its principal areas of cultivation. Rye frequently appears as a weed of other crops, especially the free-threshing WHEATS, and it may have come into Europe in this way.

Rzucewo. A regional group of the CORDED WARE culture group, located on the shores of the east Baltic in north Poland and Latvia and dated to the turn of the 3rd millennium bc. At the type site, near Gdánsk, large timber-framed houses are known. Most Rzucewo sites are located on sandy soils, with a broad spectrum economy based on deep-sea and fresh-water fishing, the catching of seals and porpoises, the hunting of forest game and some mixed farming.

S

Saale. A group of QUATERNARY GLACIAL deposits in northwest Europe. One of the main features is a complex series of end-MORAINES, demarcating the maximum extent of ICE-SHEETS. These ice-sheets flowed out from centres in Scandinavia, across the bed of the Baltic Sea and into northern Europe and the USSR. The end-moraines are split into two sets: one more eroded and sometimes called the Drenthe moraines (or Dnieper in the USSR), and the other more freshly defined and called the Warthe moraines (Moscow in the USSR). These formations are complex and each seems to represent several 'pulses' of the ice-sheet edge. A bore-hole in northern Germany has shown Warthe deposits to be sandwiched between two sets of marine EEMIAN INTERGLACIAL deposits. So it appears that the Eemian represents more than one interglacial stage and that the Warthe represents a separate cold stage. The Drenthe deposits may represent two cold stages, separated by a third division of Eemian interglacial sediments. The exact age of the Saale deposits is unknown, but they are older than the extreme range of RADIOCARBON DATING (70,000 bp) and can be shown by PALAEOMAGNETISM to be younger than 700,000 BP (*see* Table 5, page 418).

Sabaean. One of the most important kingdoms of southern Arabia in the 1st millennium BC, contemporary with the MINAEANS, QATABANEANS and HADRAMIS. The Sabaean capital was at MARIB.

Sabah. *See* BORNEO, MALAYSIA.

Sabatinovka [Sabatinivka]. In this village near Uljanov in the western Ukraine, USSR, there are several TRIPOLYE sites, the most important being Sabatinovka II (an early Tripolye site of the early 4th millennium bc) and Sabatinovka I (a late Tripolye site yielding a knot-headed copper pin comparable to early ÚNĚTICE metalwork of the early 2nd millennium bc). A later site forms the eponymous site of the Ukrainian aspect of the Nova-Sabatinovka-Bilogrudivka culture, a mid-2nd millennium bc culture found also in north Rumania and Podolia. Most settlement sites are unfortified lowland camps, whose large quantities of ash in domestic debris have inspired the term *zolniki* (ash-pits). Timber-framed houses on stone foundations are organized along streets at sites such as Zvonecka Balka.

Sabouni. *See* AL MINA.

Sabratha [Greek Habrotonon, Roman Sabratha]. A Roman port on the north African coast in Libya, remarkable for its extensive imperial Roman remains. Originally a PHOENICIAN foundation of perhaps the 5th century BC, Sabratha was one of the three cities of Roman Tripolitania. Together with neighbouring Oea and LEPTIS MAGNA, it made up a trio of wealthy trading cities, the 'Tripolis', which were important in linking the Mediterranean sea-routes to the trans-Saharan caravans. It was first annexed by Rome in 46 BC, and subsequently granted COLONIA status in the 2nd century AD. The city enjoyed great prosperity under the early empire, and a trading office of the Sabrathans is found at Roman OSTIA. Sacked by the Austuriani in about 363, Sabratha recovered to enjoy a second but reduced period of prosperity under Byzantine control, when new walls were constructed enclosing a smaller area. Urban occupation seems to have been abandoned after Arab seizure in 643. Interesting among the surviving buildings are the various bath-buildings (one with hexagonal marble public latrine), and the Antonine-period THEATRE, in which the columned stage building has been restored to its full height.

Sabz, Tepe. TELL site in Khuzistan, southwest Iran, which has given its name to a phase in the prehistoric sequence. It succeeds the Muhammad Jafar phase (*see* ALI KOSH), though probably only after a gap; it has radiocarbon dates in the range 5500-5250 bc.

It is characterized by the appearance of painted pottery, buff coloured with geometric designs executed in black paint. The botanical evidence suggests that irrigation agriculture was now practised. Flax was cultivated, as well as emmer and bread wheat, two- and six-row barley, and a variety of pulses. Domesticated goats and some sheep provided most of the meat, although there were a few domesticated cattle also and hunting was still practised, though now on a small scale only.

Saccopastore. A gravel exploitation on the Via Nomentana leading out of Rome has revealed two PALAEOLITHIC human skulls. These are often regarded as early or generalized NEANDERTHALS and are believed to belong to the last INTERGLACIAL. The brain sizes of both skulls are smaller than those of Europeans today, and much smaller than classic Neanderthals. A few stone tools were found with them.

sacrifice. Many societies at different times and in various parts of the world have practised animal or human sacrifice, or both. In the Old World one of the best-known and most spectacular examples comes from the Mesopotamian city of UR, where the Royal Cemetery provided several examples: Grave 800 (Queen PUABI's grave) contained the remains of 11 sacrificed retainers; Grave 789 contained 63 sacrificed men and women, while Grave 1237 (the 'Great Death Pit') yielded no fewer than 74 (6 men and 68 women).

In the New World the practice of animal and human sacrifice was an aspect of almost all MESOAMERICAN cultures, varying from the relatively mild PERFORATION to ritual slaughter on a grand scale. Dating well back into the early FORMATIVE PERIOD, decapitated skeletal remains at El Riego (*see* TEHUACAN VALLEY) can be seen as one of its earliest occurrences (*c*6000-4800 bc). More recent artefactual and iconographic evidence is abundant, as at Tomb 2, Mound E-III-3 at KAMINALJUYU, the temples and BALL COURT at EL TAJIN, the BONAMPAK murals and the ball court at TULA (sacrifice connected with the BALL GAME seems to become increasingly important with the passing of time).

The extreme expression of sacrifice occurs in the POST-CLASSIC, especially under the AZTEC, whose perception of the universe as a continuing battle between the forces of generation and destruction made sacrifice a prerequisite for the continuation of the world. So much so that in the mid-14th century, the so-called 'Flowery Wars' were instituted in which battles with other states (notably Tlaxcala) were set up by appointment; the sole aim was to provide captives for sacrifice.

Many sacrifices, however, were regulated by astronomical events or by a CALENDAR which was studded with dangerous or critical moments. Every year had five unlucky days and a major catastrophic event was likely every 52 years; even the daily rising of the sun could only be assured by human sacrifice.

Aztec sacrifice took many forms. The most common was the opening of the chest with a stone knife and the rapid removal of the still beating heart. An astounding 20,000 victims were despatched in this way in the four days of the dedication of the Great Temple of TENOCHTITLAN. The prescribed method in rituals connected with the god Xipe Totec (god of spring and renewal) was flaying. Captured warriors were often engaged in ritual combat in which they were severely handicapped (for instance, by being shackled or blindfolded).

Recently, scholars have theorized that the practice had a pragmatic rather than religious basis. Most notable among these theories are the use of sacrifice as an instrument of political terror (R.C. Padden) and the eating of human flesh as a dietary supplement (Michael Harner).

Sacsahuaman. An immense fortified complex, built as an adjunct to the INCAN capital at CUZCO, and begun some time after 1438. Thought to have functioned as a storage centre and military garrison in peacetime, it was used as a safe haven for Cuzco residents in times of danger. Its north-facing limestone walls are CYCLOPEAN and the remains of circular-plan towers are still visible. They are built on a zigzag sawtooth plan, front on to an open plaza and run for some 550 metres. The interior structures are built on three rising terraces and include storage and dwelling places, a reservoir and a sub-surface stone conduit supply system. This massive construction represents a considerable investment of labour and is thought to have taken 70 years to complete.

sago. The sago palm (*Metroxylon* sp.) stores large amounts of starch in its trunk prior to flowering. This starch can be washed out from the chopped pith of felled trees, and then cooked into porridge or cakes. Sago was utilized and traded widely around coastal NEW GUINEA and the Moluccas Islands; the palms are native to the area from INDONESIA through to SAMOA. Sago starch was of undoubted importance in early diets in equatorial Indonesia and MELANESIA, but the antiquity of its usage remains unknown.

Sahul Shelf. The shallow ocean shelf between Australia and New Guinea, at its narrowest under the present Torres Strait. The shelf was exposed as dry land at periods of low sea-level in the PLEISTOCENE, and New Guinea and Australia share a linked prehistory until the Torres Strait was finally drowned between 6000 and 4500 BC.

Sa-huynh. An Iron Age culture of southern VIETNAM, dating mainly from the 1st millennium BC and associated with pottery urn burials and rich artefact assemblages paralleled most closely in the PHILIPPINES. The culture may be associated with early Chamic (AUSTRONESIAN) settlement in Vietnam, and appears to be contemporary with, but separate from, the DONG-SON culture of north Vietnam. *See also* KALANAY.

Śailendra. A Mahayana Buddhist dynasty that appeared suddenly in the late 8th century in Central JAVA. Its name ('King of the Mountain') has been seen as the claim to 'Universal Rulership', taken over from the kings of FUNAN; indeed, the Śailendras exercised a sort of hegemony in the region, extending even to parts of the Indochinese Peninsula. In the 9th century, the dynasty left Java for SUMATRA where they continued to hold power at ŚRĪVIJAYA for several centuries. *See also* BOROBUDUR and SANJAYA.

Saint Acheul. *See* ACHEULIAN.

St Gall Plan. A remarkable CAROLINGIAN document, probably formulated after the Council of Inden in 816 and then sent by the Abbot of Reichenau to Abbot Gozbert of St Gall. The plan, drawn in ink on parchment, is an architect's drawing for the rebuilding of the monastic complex. The layout is dominated by the large basilican abbey building with two circular western towers and adjoining cloister. The ancillary buildings are a closely nucleated group, labelled in great detail with instructions on underfloor heating, ventilation and drainage. Many of the domestic ranges and the infirmary would probably have been built in stone with smaller timber latrines and stables blocks. The whole complex has a very orderly appearance, with square courtyards and walkways separating the areas of different function. The St Gall Plan is a unique work epitomizing an ideal 'modern' Carolingian monastic unit, and although it was never fully realized at St Gall it remains an important source of reference for architectural historians and archaeologists.

St Gereon. *See* COLOGNE.

St Ninian's Isle. During the excavation of the small 12th-century chapel on St Ninian's Isle in the Shetlands in 1958 the finest hoard of PICTISH metalwork ever found in Britain came to light. The hoard seems to have been deposited at the end of the 8th century (possibly in response to Norse raids), and included such objects as silver bowls, hanging bowls, spoons, sword chapes and PENNANULAR BROOCHES. The treasure provides strong evidence that the tradition of Pictish metalworking continued into the Early Christian era.

Saintonge ware. A major pottery industry existed in the region of Saintes in western France from the 13th century until recent times. The best-known of these wares are the tall jugs with polychrome glazed decoration which appear to have been traded with western French wine to the English from about 1300. These polychrome jugs frequently occur in English urban contexts, and are also known from excavations as far north as Denmark. The jugs exported were only one of the variety of wares made at centres like La Chapelle des Pots, where kilns and workshops have been excavated.

St Philibert de Grandlieu. *See* NOIRMOUTIER.

St Severin. *See* COLOGNE.

Saint Urnel. Recent excavations at Saint Urnel, near Penmarch in western Finistère,

Brittany, have revealed an extremely large Dark Age cemetery. The hundreds of skeletons found have provided anthropologists with the opportunity of investigating whether the population was descended from British refugees, or whether the isolated Breton community owes more to Gallic origins.

Saipai. *See* OCHRE-COLOURED POTTERY.

Sai Yok. A large rock shelter in Kanchanaburi province, western THAILAND, which has produced a 4.75-metre sequence from a possibly pre-HOABINHIAN industry, through Hoabinhian, to a Neolithic assemblage of BAN KAO type. The sequence is undated, but from its depth the site could have the longest record of Hoabinhian development in southeast Asia.

Sakçe Gözü. A TELL site in southeast Turkey, occupied in the NEOLITHIC period, with a sequence of wares relating the AMUQ and HALAF pottery styles. In the early 1st millennium BC the site was reoccupied and a Syro-Hittite palace erected on the northwest corner of the citadel, decorated with reliefs and inscriptions.

Sălacea. A fortified promontory site of the earlier Bronze Age OTOMANI culture, located near Marghiţa in northwest Rumania and dated to the mid-2nd millennium bc. The principal find is a three-roomed 'temple' of MEGARON-type appearance, unique so far in Bronze Age Europe. In one of the rooms, fired clay altars were associated with clay fire-dogs and vase supports. Outside the temple was the inhumation burial of a child in a pit. Rich ritual finds, together with other unusual burials, typify other areas of the site.

Saladoid, Saladero. The earliest of the ceramic series developed by Irving Rouse and José Cruxent for the purpose of cultural comparison in the Lesser Antilles/Venezuela region. The type site, Saladero, situated on the Orinoco River, rendered a series of radiocarbon dates placing its inception in the early 1st millennium bc. Although Saladoid material is overlain by BARRANCOID ceramics at Saladero, the two continued to flourish concurrently in separate areas until c1000 AD. Characteristically, Saladoid pottery is thin and fine with slight grit temper, and is distinguished especially by white-on-red painted designs. The everted bell, often with tabular lugs, is the favoured vessel form. Vessels connected with the preparation of MANIOC, such as GRIDDLES, are also present at many sites.

Salamis (Cyprus). A principal city of prehistoric and classical Cyprus, situated on the east coast of the island six km from Famagusta. There is a large area of surviving ruins, and an extensive necropolis to the west. The MYCENAEAN settlement was probably at ENKOMI, a short distance inland. Salamis survived into the Roman period, with its characteristic priest-kings, the Teukridae, still possibly in titular control up to the time of Augustus. Under the early Empire there was a large Jewish population. The town was finally abandoned after the Arab raids of 647 AD. Most remarkable are the so-called 'Royal Tombs'. These date perhaps from the Late Geometric period, and feature large *dromoi* (*see* DROMOS). The burial chambers are constructed of large rectangular blocks and have gable roofs, but were generally robbed in antiquity. There is an association with horse-and-chariot funerary rites, and horse skeletons still complete with bit in mouth have been discovered. There are also bronze horse accoutrements, and cauldron and tripod, and ivory furniture. One tombs shows evidence for an original upper beehive structure or THOLOS. Other tombs are rock-cut, and show evidence for rites involving pyres and clay figurines.

Salamis (Greece). An island which straddles and encloses the bay of ELEUSIS to the west of ATHENS. The modern town of Salamis is situated on the western side of the island dominating the Bay of Koulouri. However, the ancient town of Salamis is probably to be located on the eastern side, in the region of the promonotory between Kamatero and Ambelaki Bay. Nothing now survives that can be identified with certainty. The straits formed here between the island and the mainland were the scene for the famous Battle of Salamis (480 BC) in which the invading forces of Xerxes and the Persians were beaten off.

Salcuţa. The eponymous TELL site of a Late Neolithic-Copper Age culture distributed in Oltenia, southwest Rumania. There are four main occupation phases in the tell stratigraphy:I, a short-lived CRIŞ occupation; II-III, five levels of the Salcuţa culture, dated c3500 bc and typified by dark burnished wares and a low proportion of graphite and crusted painted wares; IV, two levels of the Late Copper Age 'Salcuţa IV' group, characterized by unpainted pottery with 'Furstenstich' decoration and with affinities to COŢOFENI and BADEN pottery.

Saliagos. A later NEOLITHIC enclosed settlement now on a tiny island, formerly a promontory adjacent to the Cycladic island of Antiparos. The community that lived here c4200-3700 bc lived largely by tunny fishing, although farming was also practised. Tanged points of Melian obsidian were common, as was painted pottery, with white designs on a dark ground. Parian marble was used to produce stylized fiddle-shaped idols, ancestral to the better known figurines of :he later CYCLADIC Bronze Age.

Salinar. A culture centred on the Chicama Valley of north-coast Peru, at the beginning of the Early INTERMEDIATE PERIOD. Salinar, together with the slightly later GALLINAZO phase, is seen as a transitional culture between CUPISNIQUE and MOCHE. This transition is evidenced in a shift from reduced-fired to oxidized-fired ceramics and in the introduction of new forms and decorative techniques. Salinar introduces the handle-and-spout vessel, although the CHAVINOID STIRRUP-SPOUT form continues. The characteristic decoration is broad white painted bands and dots, sometimes outlined with incision. Life-figure modelling also occurs but the once popular feline motif of Chavin disappears.

Salinas La Blanca. An early FORMATIVE village site located on the left bank of the Naranjo River near Ocos on the Pacific coast of Guatemala, noted for its excellent preservation of vegetal materials. The principal features of the site are two low house-mounds raised above the level of the surrounding swamp, constructed of clay and household debris, and dating to 1000-850 bc. A typical household cluster consisted of the house itself, an outdoor hearth, a number of 'borrow pits' (dug to obtain clay) and a sherd and shell midden. Hunting appears to have played a very small part in subsistence activities, although fish, turtles and other swamp-dwelling fauna were more widely exploited. Large numbers of primitive corn cobs indicate that the population also engaged in some farming.

Salin styles. Name of the Dark Age art styles of northern Europe, first described by E. Salin in his work *Die altgermanische Thier-ornamentik* (1904). During the late 5th, 6th and 7th centuries, much of western European art, from Scandinavia to the Balkans, was pervaded by anthropomorphic designs, probably derived ultimately from naturalistic Roman animal ornament. This ornament was adapted and transformed by the Germanic craftsman into an evolving range of surrealist, abstract expressions. This Germanic animal ornament is most often associated with chip-carved designs on metalwork, but it was imitated to some extent by Christian sculptors and manuscript illuminators. Distinct variations within this Germanic ornamentation gradually developed; these were classified by Salin and are now known as Salin Styles I, II and II. Within these broad categories there are many insular variations, and in ANGLO-SAXON England particularly there is some intermingling between the styles.

Salin Style I stretches loosely from the end of the 5th century until the end of the 6th century, and features crouching quadrupeds which occur in a totally disjointed, abstract way with various parts mixed inextricably together forming a close-knit pattern. This style commonly occurs on the square-headed brooches of Kent for example, as well as the metalwork produced at Helgö in Sweden. This is succeeded by Salin Style II in which the same abstract beasts are elongated into ribbon and tendril designs which are intertwined and interlaced together, losing all concessions to realism. In England the animals were etched in double outline, and the bodies infilled with dots. Style II is seen on many of the gold objects of the SUTTON HOO treasure. In the late 7th and 8th centuries Style III emerged, with its more naturalistic emphasis and less restless designs but introducing a ferocious gripping beast. This was eventually to give way to the VIKING art styles.

Salonae. *See* SPLIT.

Salzgitter-Lebenstedt. An open site in north Germany, 45 km east of Hanover, providing evidence that reindeer and mammoth were hunted by Middle PALAEOLITHIC men. Human skull fragments were found, possibly dating from early in the last glacial period. Some authorities regard this as a key site but its significance remains unclear.

Samaria. Central Palestinian town site which was occupied, after a sporadic Early Bronze Age occupation, from the 9th century BC until the BYZANTINE period. The first six phases of occupation were ISRAELITE and indeed Samaria was the capital of the northern kingdom (Israel) at this time. Excavations have concentrated on the royal palace, which was burned down by the ASSYRIANS when they captured the city in 720 BC, and have also examined the HELLENISTIC fort and Roman temple which occupied the summit of the hill at later dates.

Samarkand. Before the Mongol conquest, Samarkand occupied the site known as Afrasiab, outside the modern city in Soviet Central Asia. Both the old and the new sites benefited from their situation in a fertile oasis at the point where the SILK ROUTE from the West divided, one branch proceeding to China and the other to India. Afrasiab was already the Soghdian capital when ALEXANDER THE GREAT invaded the region in 329 BC, and excavations have revealed abundant Graeco-Soghdian material. A palace of the 6th or 7th century AD, discovered in 1912, yielded wall paintings comparable with the famous paintings from Pendzhikent. The Mongol leader Chingiz-Khan destroyed the water supply and the population moved to the modern site in 1220. In 1375 Samarkand became the capital of TIMUR [Tamerlane] and in 1403 Clavijo described it as a cosmopolitan city with 150,000 inhabitants. The principal monuments of Samarkand are Timurid. They include the cemetery known as Shah-i Zindeh, a group of mausolea for the families of Timur (d. 1405) and Ulugh-Beg (1409-49), built round the Mosque of Kussan. They are noted for their rich tile ornament. Elsewhere in the city, the Mosque of Bibi Khanum, now ruined, was seen under construction by Clavijo. At about the same time, Timur erected the Gur Emir mausoleum (in which he was buried) in the madrasa of Muhammad Sultan.

Samarra. 9th-century city half way between Mosul and Baghdad in Iraq, excavated by Ernst HERZFELD before the First World War. As well as remains of the historical city, Herzfeld found traces of a prehistoric occupation. He was unable to establish very much about the nature or date of this settlement (or cemetery), but he found a fine painted pottery, decorated in black or brown on a light ground with figures of animals, birds, people and complex geometrical designs. This pottery, named Samarra ware after this site, has since been found on a number of other sites, including CHOGA MAMI and TELL-ES-SAWWAN; it is known to date to the 6th millennium bc and to represent a distinct cultural phase.

The site of Samarra was subsequently used for an important Islamic city. Following disputes between residents and foreign troops stationed in Baghdad, the caliph al-Mu'tasim (AD 833-42) decided to establish a new capital. After a brief sojourn at RAQQA, he moved to Samarra in 836. This was a new town, built at astonishing speed. The combination of mud-brick and imported labour made it possible to construct grandiose buildings very rapidly and, by the time the court returned to Baghdad in 882, Samarra sprawled along the Tigris for no fewer than 35 km. Apart from the houses, bazaars etc of the civilian population, successive caliphs built the Jausaq al-Khaqani, al-Mu'tasim's palace (836-42); the Great Mosque of al-Mutawakkil (848/9-52); the Balkuwara palace of al-Mutawakkil (c849-59); the Mosque of Abu Dhulaf, also erected by al-Mutawakkil (860-1) and the Qasr al-Ashiq, al Mu'tamid's palace (878-82). The Jausaq al-Khaqani, the most extravagent complex of all, was larger than Versailles, with walls enclosing 175 hectares of palaces, gardens, slaves' quarters and magazines. The Great Mosque, which measured 240 by 156 metres internally, was the largest ever built. Architectural decoration was lavish, and entire walls were covered with carved or moulded stucco.

Samarra occupies a key position in Islamic studies: its monuments are important for art and architectural history, while the excavations of Herzfeld (1912-13) and the Iraq Government (1936-9) yielded a wealth of archaeological finds which appeared to belong to the period of caliphal occupation (836-82). For 50 years Herzfeld's discoveries dominated the study of early Islamic pottery. However,

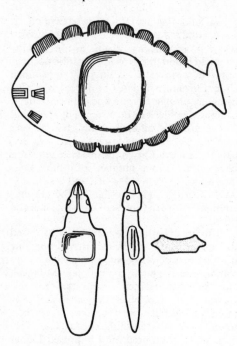

Sambaqui stone effigies

life continued at Samarra after the court withdrew and the mint still functioned in 953. Thus, although we know (from contemporary writers) the dates of the principal buildings, we no longer assume that all the finds are of the 9th century.

Sambaqui tradition. Based on the southern coast of Brazil, the tradition is named after a local term meaning shell midden. Crudely chipped stone tools and a subsistence strategy based on molluscs and fish imply that Sambaqui sites represent an ARCHAIC lifestyle and were therefore only seasonally occupied. Exceptional in this general context, however, are well-finished polished stone effigies (usually of birds or fish) which have a basin-like depression in the back. Probably of ceremonial significance, it has been suggested that these effigies were used in the ritual taking of snuff. An early radiocarbon date of 5800 ± 1300 bc is usually regarded as anomalous since most dates fall in the range 3000-1500 bc.

Sambor Prei Kuk. *See* IŚĀNAPURA.

Sambungmacan. The find-site (1973) on the Solo River, Java, of a calotte of HOMO ERECTUS, with Middle or Upper PLEISTOCENE faunal associations. The calotte belongs to an advanced grade within Southeast Asian populations of *Homo erectus,* perhaps slightly earlier than the population from NGANDONG, further downstream on the Solo River. In 1978 some stone tools were found at Sambung-macan, believed to be the first found in the same context as *Homo erectus* in Java (*see* JAVA MAN).

Samian ware. *See* TERRA SIGILLATA.

Samoa. A major island group of Western POLYNESIA, settled, with TONGA, by LAPITA colonists in the late 2nd millennium BC. Samoa maintains a pottery sequence through the 1st millennium BC, after which pottery manu-facture ceases. As with Tonga, the period since about AD 200 has been aceramic. On the evidence of adze typology, Samoa may have been the source for the first settlers to pene-trate eastern Polynesia, perhaps to the MARQUESAS, in the early 1st millennium AD. The last 1500 years of Samoan prehistory are associated with above-ground monuments, including earthwork forts, earth or stone houses and god-house platforms, and agri-cultural terraces. By the time of European contact, Samoan society was dominated by a partially elective hierarchy of chieftainship, rather different from the patterns of primo-genitural succession prevalent in most other parts of Polynesia.

sample. (1) In statistics, a sample refers to a representative group of objects, cases or items, selected from a larger population. If the selection has been random, the DISTRIBUTIONS within a sample should have similar propor-tions to those of the original sample. The degree to which a sample is truly representa-tive in this way is controlled by two factors: the size of the sample and biasing factors affecting its selection. The larger the sample and the smaller the bias, the more representative the sample. All groups of archaeological material are samples, selected through preservation and choice of site, of an original population of objects, bones layers etc. The problem is always to determine the biases which have operated during selection.

(2) The term sample is also used to describe the small sections cut from artefacts in order to

carry out DATING, CHEMICAL, PETROLOGICAL or METALLURGICAL ANALYSIS.

San Agustin. A group of sites centred in the area of the headwaters of the Magdalena River in the highlands of Colombia. Though pottery, wattle and daub dwellings, and evidence of irrigation and terracing indicate a long cultural sequence in the region, San Agustin is most notable for its mounds and monumental statuary. Earth mounds here commonly have internal stone-lined passageways and chambers, some of which contain sculpture which suggests their use as places of worship as well as burial. Sculptures are rendered in a variety of techniques but are usually free-standing stelae and can be up to four metres high. Two artistic themes in particular are characteristic of these stone works: (1) the anthropomorphic/zoomorphic being with exaggerated feline fangs and (2) the 'alter ego' indicated either by a small figure on the back or head of the main statue or by a man holding a baby in front of him. Though stylistic comparisons are often made with CHAVIN, these themes have strong parallels in OLMEC iconography. Dates are from c550 BC into historic times.

Sanchi. A site in central India with a famous Buddhist STUPA. Excavations have shown that a brick-built stupa of the ASOKAN period was later encased in stone and surrounded by a stone railing. This stupa measured c40 metres in diameter and c18 metres in height.

sand. A term describing the size of particles which go to make up a SEDIMENT, SOIL or similar material. Sand particles are those between 2mm and 0.06mm (BS 1377) in diameter(see PARTICLE SIZE). The term has no implications of colour, organic content or any property other than particle size or TEXTURE.

Sandia Cave. Located in the Sandia Range near Albuquerque, New Mexico, USA, the lowest levels of this site contained a unique tool assemblage. Radiocarbon dates indicating an age greater than 10,000 years are generally disputed but the Sandia level was overlain by FOLSOM material. An association with certain extinct mammals (e.g. mammoth, camel and bison) suggests probable contemporaneity with LLANO, but Sandia has yet to be satisfactorally integrated into other PALEO-INDIAN chronologies.

Sanga. A major Iron Age cemetery beside Lake Kisale in the Upemba depression, southeastern Zaire. The numerous graves that have been investigated are attributed to the KISALIAN and KABAMBIAN industries.

Sangamon. A group of QUATERNARY INTER-GLACIAL deposits in North America (see Table 7, page 420). The Sangamon comprises a range of SEDIMENTS, including organic sediment, but is represented mainly by a PALAEOSOL, which overlies ILLINOIAN TILLS and is covered by WISCONSIN LOESS and tills. This palaeosol can be followed for great distances across North America, and its PROFILE varies from prairie to desert types. It appears to represent one single interglacial, but has never been dated satisfactorily.

Sangiran. The most important locality for INDONESIAN finds of *Homo erectus* in central Java. Rich fossil-bearing deposits of both Middle PLEISTOCENE (Trinil fauna) and Lower Pleistocene (Djetis fauna) have yielded fossils of more than four hominid individuals from each level, including five skulls from the later level of perhaps c0.5 to 0.8 million years ago. Some of the large-toothed fossils from the lower level were once labelled Meganthropus, and have been compared to *Paranthropus (Australopithecus) robustus*. *See also* HUMAN EVOLUTION, NGANGDONG, SAMBUNGMACAN, TRINIL.

Sangoan. The name, derived from Sango Bay on Lake Victoria, Uganda, loosely applied to a rather heterogeneous group of industries in eastern and south-central Africa, and perhaps in West Africa also, following the final ACHEULIAN. Its charactertistic artefacts are massive triangular-sectioned picks and core-axes, together with flake scrapers. Probably the most informative site for an examination of the composition and sequence of Sangoan industries is at KALAMBO FALLS, Zambia. Well-documented occurrences are also known from river gravel deposits near DUNDO in northern Angola. In several regions of Zaire and neighbouring countries the Sangoan appears to mark the first human settlement of the low-lying country now occupied by the equatorial forest. The age of the Sangoan has not been firmly established: it probably lies beyond the accurate range of radiocarbon dating, perhaps as far back as 100,000 to 80,000 BC. The earlier suggestion that the Sangoan tool-kit represents a reaction to a densely wooded environment is not borne out by recent investigations; indeed, the Sangoan may best be attributed to a relatively dry phase when the area of the dense equatorial forests was significantly reduced.

Sanjaya. (1) A Sivaite king of the 8th century in Central JAVA. His earliest inscription dates from 732, and in much later ones he is represented as the founder of the kingdom of MATARĀM and of a dynasty bearing his name. However, his successor reigned under the suzerainty of the ŚAILENDRAS.

(2) The name of an era beginning in 717, but used only in the 10th century.

San Jose Mogote. The largest of a number of village communities which developed in the PRE-CLASSIC PERIOD in central Oaxaca, Mexico, some time prior to 1300 bc. Established in an area where the water table was a mere three metres below the land surface, agriculture was practised by 'pot irrigation', that is, direct watering from a well. Evidence of OLMEC influence becomes increasingly apparent and by c900 bc the village had grown to cover 20 hectares. By this time three areas of social and occupational diversity are apparent: small lower-class residences, public buildings and workshops. Large amounts of debris from 'prized' minerals such as ilmenite, haematite, mica and green quartz, coupled with finished goods of Olmec origin, suggest that San Jose Mogote was a manufacturing site which was part of an Olmec controlled trade system.

Sankisa. A holy Buddhist site in the upper Ganges Valley, India, where the Buddha is said to have descended from heaven. It was visited by the emperor ASOKA in his pilgrimage of 249 BC and retains the commemorative pillar with its elephant capital erected on that occasion.

San Lorenzo. Earliest of the major OLMEC CEREMONIAL CENTRES and a site of long occupation. Located in the open country around the Rio Chiquito in southern Veracruz, Mexico, its main construction, oriented on a north-south axis, rests on an artifically modified salt dome. This plateau has a series of man-made ravines constructed on three of its sides; at the top of some of these massive stone heads had been buried.

The principal features of the site are a large platform mound and a cluster of smaller mounds surrounding what may be the earliest BALL COURT in MESOAMERICA; more than 200 house mounds are clustered around these central features. A system of carved stone drains underlying the site (the longest section is over 200 metres long) is a unique structural feature. Numerous stone heads (the largest is nearly 3 metres high and weighs 25 tons) have been found on the site; most were deliberately mutilated before burial.

The site was first occupied by c1500 bc, but typically Olmec pottery does not appear until after 1250 bc. The site's florescence runs from 1150 to 900 bc, after which it was abandoned by the Olmec. It was, however, occupied by other groups, but it is unclear whether they were responsible for the deliberate destruction which occurred. Some MAMON pottery and evidence of contact with both LA VENTA and TRES ZAPOTES occurs in this late phase. The site was totally abandoned by c400 bc.

San Pedro. Most recent of the chronological periods of the COCHISE culture. Typically, tool assemblages contain seed-grinding tools such as MANOS and METATES, and a variety of projectile points, including the narrow stemmed, side-notched type which first appeared during CHIRICAHUA. Sites generally became larger and more numerous during this period and the increasing appearance of simple pit houses is in keeping with the general trend to settled village life.

Sanskrit. An early INDO-EUROPEAN language, still used in India for religious purposes. The RIGVEDA, the oldest religious document of India, is written in an archaic form of Sanskrit. The discovery in the late 18th century that this language was related to Greek and Latin and many other European languages led to the development of the discipline of comparative philology.

Santa Ana. A very extensive proto-historical burial ground, now in a suburb of Manila, PHILIPPINES, which produced extended burials with large quantities of Chinese monochrome and early blue-and-white pottery of the SUNG Dynasty (probably 11th to early 14th century AD). *See also* CALATAGAN.

Santa Cruz Islands. *See* SOLOMON ISLANDS.

Santa Isabel Iztapan. A kill site in the Valley of Mexico near TEPEXPAN, at which the butchered remains of two imperial mammoths were uncovered in association with flint and obsidian tools. It is important as an indicator of the rapidity with which newly arrived Asian hunters dispersed southward. Its geological context (the Becerra Formation) suggests a Late PLEISTOCENE date which has been confirmed by a radiocarbon date of 7050 ± 250 bc. Artefact associations, however, are something of a puzzle, since stone tools of both the BIG GAME HUNTING TRADITION and the OLD CORDILLERAN TRADITION were found in the same levels.

Santiago de Compostella. *See* PILGRIM.

Santorini. *See* THERA.

Santubong. A complex of open sites on the delta of the Sarawak River in southwestern Sarawak, BORNEO. Most sites date between 900 and 1350 and contain evidence for iron-smelting, large quantities of Chinese pottery, and local pottery of TANJONG KUBOR type. There is a possible Tantric Buddhist shrine at Bongkisam. The sites appear to have belonged to a large entrepôt complex with trade contacts from both China and India during the TANG and SUNG dynasties. *See also* TANJONG KUBOR.

San Vincenzo al Volturno. An important Benedictine monastery in Central Italy, founded early in the 8th century and probably at its largest in the 9th century. San Vincenzo was sacked by Arabs in 881 and the monastery was abandoned. The site was later reoccupied on a smaller scale, and eventually the monastery was taken over by Monte Cassino, 40 km away. A visitor to the site will find the reconstructed abbey of San Vincenzo — rebuilt in a neo-romanesque style — on one side of the River Volturno. On the west side of the river there is a small church with a painted crypt; the paintings are 9th century, and blend Byzantine and Roman styles. Next to this church is another with an altar still in place. To the south runs the main body of the monastery

with, it is assumed, a range of rooms like those exposed next to the second church. The site appears to overlie a late Roman complex, and the remains of part of this complex may be seen behind the churches. Further up the hill behind the monastery is a large cemetery of late Roman (Byzantine) and early medieval date. The remains show this to be an unusual plan for an early medieval monastery, and it is also evident that it was a particularly large complex by the 9th century.

Saqqara. A major necropolis in Lower Egypt, adjacent to modern Abusir and close to MEMPHIS. The pharaohs of the Second Dynasty were buried here in graves which were clearly a development and elaboration of the type of royal tomb constructed in First Dynasty times at ABYDOS. With the passage of time burial chambers were more massively constructed of stone, and eventually hewn from solid rock. During the Third Dynasty this process led to the development of the step pyramids of pharaohs Sekhemkhet and Djoser, each surrounded by a massive walled enclosure some 500 metres in length.

Sarab, Tepe. An early farming site near Kermanshah in the Zagros Mountains of western Iran. The site is at an altitude of 1300 metres and has produced little in the way of structures: it may have been seasonally occupied only, either belonging to a semi-nomadic herding community or representing a summer pasture station of a settled agri-cultural community. Domesticated sheep and goat were kept and there is some evidence for the cultivation of emmer wheat and two-rowed barley. Pistachio nuts and snails were consumed in large quantities. Fine red-burnished and painted pottery occurs, as do stone bowls. The most unusual finds are two female figurines, in the sitting position with bulging thighs and breasts, but without facial features. The site has radiocarbon dates in the range c6000-5650 bc.

Sarawak. *See* BORNEO, MALAYSIA, NIAH.

Sarnate. A settlement site of the Late Meso-lithic NARVA culture, located in the southeast Baltic province of Latvia, USSR. The single culture level has radiocarbon dates of 2950-2550 bc and contains a rich collection of Narva pointed-base pottery and bone implements.

Sarnath. A site in northeast India, famous as the place where the Buddha gave his first sermon. The emperor ASOKA visited the site on his pilgrimage of 249 BC and set up a commemorative pillar, surmounted by a fine lion capital. There is also a small temple, also of the 3rd century BC.

sarsen. A type of sandstone found on the Marlborough downs of Wiltshire, southern England, the remnants of a once much larger deposit from the Tertiary period. It was used by prehistoric man for the construction of MEGALITHIC tombs and for the great STONE CIRCLES of AVEBURY and STONEHENGE, the latter site almost 30 km from the nearest source of this stone.

Sassanian, Sassanians. A Persian dynasty which ruled in Iran from *c* 224 AD when Ardashir Papakan revolted against the PARTHIANS, until 651, when their empire was brought to an end by the Moslems. The Sassanian empire extended from India to Syria; in the west they were frequently in conflict with the Romans. Archaeologically they are known from impressive architectural remains of palaces, temples and fortifications and from rock reliefs. Important Sassanian sites include Bishapur, Firuzabad, Naqsh-i Rustam (*see* PERSEPOLIS) and recent excavations at SIRAF have revealed Sassanian occupation preceding the city of the Islamic period.

sati. An Indian term describing the practice of a widow accompanying her husband to the grave. Archaeologists have sometimes used the term when they believe they have archaeological evidence of this practice: for instance, when a female burial is found in the same grave as a male burial, especially if the female is a significantly younger individual and is placed in a subsidiary position in the grave.

Satsumon. Name given to the HAJI-like pottery made in Hokkaido and northern Honshu, Japan, from about 800 to 1300, and to the culture characterized by this pottery. Satsumon houses are very much like Late KOFUN houses, such as those found at NAKADA in central Honshu. Iron tools were used to grow millet, buckwheat and possibly rice, which supplemented the diet of fish and wild plants. Cloth was woven. The Satsumon culture is seen as the transformation of a JOMON-type culture, which continued late in northern Japan, as the result of the contacts with Haji-using people to the south. Satsumon ceramics were no longer made after the 14th century, when they were replaced by iron pots, but the people who had made them are thought to be the ancestors of the historic AINU.

saucer barrow. *See* BARROW.

Sauveterrian, Sauveterre-la-Lémance. Two rock shelters at this locality in Lot et Garonne, southwest France, have revealed a sequence of MESOLITHIC deposits. Over the late MAGDALENIAN are found AZILIAN, Sauveterrian and TARDENOISIAN layers. A skull buried in Roc Allan is probably Sauveterrian.

Savai'i Island. *See* PULEMELEI.

Sawankhalok. An ancient city in northern THAILAND, known mainly for the celadon-like glazed pottery which its kilns, established in the 14th century, produced for centuries. The ware was exported to countries throughout the region, notably the Philippines and Indonesia. There are also KHMER remains at the site, showing that the area once belonged to the empire of ANGKOR. *See also* SUKHOTHAI.

Sawwan, Tell-es. A 6th-millennium bc site of the SAMARRA phase on the Tigris River north of Baghdad in Iraq. Five building levels have been excavated at Sawwan and by level III the settlement was defended by a ditch and wall except on the west, where the land fell away steeply to the river. Inside the wall were complex T-shaped buildings with up to 14 rooms each. The building material was true mudbrick (while contemporary sites further north used pisé, known locally as *tauf*). A number of graves, mostly of infants, found beneath buildings of level I, yielded a large number of ground stone objects including fine female figurines and bowls of alabaster. The subsistence economy was based on irrigation agriculture (necessary in this arid zone where dry farming could not have been practised): emmer and bread wheat, two varieties of barley, and linseed were grown, probably by flood cultivation on the flood plain of the river. Domesticated animals, including cattle, were kept; a range of wild animals was hunted and fish and freshwater mussels from the river were also eaten. This site, like its contemporary CHOGA MAMI to the southeast, shows an early development towards more complex forms in architecture, subsistence economy and social organization, presaging the development towards urban civilization that characterized the succeeding two millennia in Mesopotamia.

Saxon Shore [Latin: *litus saxonicum*]. The name *litus saxonicum* occurs first in a late Roman historian (*Ammianus Marcellinus*, xxvii, 8.1, concerning 367 AD), but was probably in use earlier. It denoted the southeastern coastline of Roman Britain, from the Wash to Southampton, and probably about 200 AD onwards these areas were subject to raids from Germanic Saxon pirates. The Roman response was the construction of a series of shore forts, built from the early 3rd century. The forts were massive stone structures, defended by projecting bastions, and characterized by narrow gateways. A comprehensive coastal command developed with appropriate communications and administration, and by 367 was under the direction of a Count (*comes*). Remains may be seen at Pevensey, PORTCHESTER and RICHBOROUGH.

Sayil. *See* PUUC.

scapulimancy. *See* ORACLE BONES.

sceatta [sceat]. Small silver coins minted from about 690 until about 790 in the southern English and Frisian kingdoms. Sceattas are distinctive because they were made from pellets which were hammered between two dies, not minted from a flattened piece of metal (as after *c*790 in England). The earliest sceattas are probably those of the Frisian kingdom, and date to the last decades of the 7th century and the first half of the 8th century before the MEROVINGIAN kings came to dominate this area. The kings of Kent almost certainly imitated these silver coins in about 690, and issued them with a variety of designs which are collectively known as the primary series of sceattas. The primary series is virtually confined to Kent and ended about 720. The secondary series include a wider variety of designs which occur over a larger area, south of a line between the rivers Humber and Exe. Secondary sceattas were minted in a number of Middle Saxon kingdoms, probably by bishops as well as kings.

Schela. The eponymous site for the Late Mesolithic group of sites on the Rumanian bank of the Iron Gates gorge of the river Danube, itself located downstream of Kazane Mare on the eastern edge of the gorge. With radiocarbon dates of 6800-5600 bc, the Schela group is directly contemporary with the more elaborate Yugoslav sites of VLASAC, LEPENSKI VIR and PADINA. The Schela group includes cave as well as open sites and, for the first time on the left bank, burials are found, located round a hearth. Intensive plant-gathering and loose herding brought the Schela population to the verge of domestication, although fishing and hunting were equally economic mainstays.

schist hones. Whetstones made of mica-schist from the highly distinctive Eisdborg rocks of southern Norway were widely distributed on all classes of sites all around the North Sea throughout the medieval period. A 9th-century boat carrying these hones was recently found near KAUPANG.

Schliemann, Heinrich (1822-90). German scholar famous for his excavations at the Aegean Bronze Age sites of TROY, MYCENAE and TIRYNS. He spent most of his life in business and made a fortune in international finance before he embarked on work in the Aegean to support his long-held view that Homer's epics were true and that the cities recorded in them, assumed by scholars to be entirely mythical, were real. His excavations at Troy (on and off from 1874 to 1890), Mycenae (1874-8) and Tiryns (1884-5), with their spectacular discoveries of monumental architecture and treasures of gold and silver, aroused immense public interest and considerable controversy. In recent years there have been criticisms not only of Schliemann's excavation techniques, but also of his integrity: it has been suggested that he falsified his site reports to support his theories. Whatever the truth of this, and admitting the many errors and misunderstandings apparent in Schliemann's work, it is nonetheless difficult to deny that Schliemann achieved his main objective — he demonstrated the historical reality of the Homeric world and, in so doing, initiated the development of Mycenaean archaeology.

Scoglio del Tonno. An important prehistoric site which formerly occupied a promontory projecting into the harbour of TARANTO, southeast Italy; it was destroyed, after excavation, when the port was extended in 1899. The site was first occupied during the Late Neolithic by people using SERRA D'ALTO WARE. It was then abandoned but resettled in the mid-2nd millennium BC by a community of the APENNINE BRONZE AGE culture. A great wealth of material of the 14th, 13th and 12th centuries BC was found, including much bronze work, and pottery of MYCENAEAN type. Archaeologists are in disagreement as to whether there was a Myceneaean colony here or whether, as is perhaps more probable, there was a native settlement (perhaps with a small enclave of Mycenaean merchants) trading between the Aegean and the communities of northern Italy and central Europe. As the site has now been destroyed and the excavation records are unsatisfactory, this problem is likely to remain unresolved. After the collapse of the Mycenaean world, the community at Scoglio del Tonno continued to exist and indeed to trade with the Greek world, though on a much reduced scale. It survived until the foundation of the Greek colony of Taras in 706 BC.

Scotti. *See* DALRIADA.

scramasax. A cross between an iron hacking sword and a dagger, with an angled back and single sharp cutting-edge. They commonly occur in MIGRATION PERIOD and ANGLO-SAXON contexts until about the 10th century. These weapons tended to become increasingly elaborate: many were finely inlaid with a variety of metals and some had very distinctive pommels.

scraper. One of the commonest forms of stone tool is a FLAKE with RETOUCH along the edge. This is usually called a side scraper (or *racloir*). A BLADE with retouch round the end is usually called an end scraper (or *grattoir*). Side scrapers are typical of the Middle PALAEO-LITHIC, while end scrapers are typical of the later Palaeolithic. How Palaeolithic tools were used is generally unknown, but a few side scrapers are known from wear studies to have been used for skin preparation. This is also likely to have been the main use of end scrapers, as they resemble tools used for this purpose by recent hunters.

Sdok Kak Thom. A site in northwestern Cambodia, famous for a stele of the 11th century. It bears a detailed inscription relating the foundation of the kingdom of ANGKOR in 802 (for which there are no contemporary epigraphical sources) and its history until the time of writing. *See also* KULÈN.

sea level. The long-term level of the sea varies

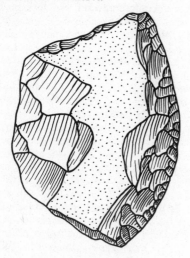

Side scraper (racloir)

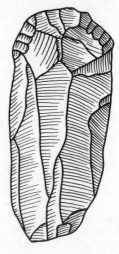

End scraper (grattoir)

in two ways: (1) Changes in the volume of water held in the sea, known as EUSTATIC sea level change; (2) Relative movements of the land surface, resulting from various types of deformation of the earth's crust. Many such forms of crustal deformation are known, but in glacial terms the most important one is ISOSTASY.

Evidence of such seal level variation during the QUATERNARY exists in a number of localities, notably the Mediterranean coasts — particularly Mallorca — and New Guinea. The most recent sea-level fluctuations are shown by deposits and landforms on the coasts of the Netherlands, the Baltic Sea, Scotland, northwest England and several other localities. Additional information is now coming from bore-holes in the beds of the North Sea and Irish Sea.

Sea Peoples. *See* PEOPLES OF THE SEA.

Secondary Neolithic. Term used by Stuart Piggott to describe a number of later Neolithic groups in Britain, characterized by the use of PETERBOROUGH WARE or GROOVED WARE (Rinyo-Clacton Ware). He believed these groups to represent populations of MESO-LITHIC ancestry who had acquired the arts of farming and associated crafts such as pottery manufacture from PRIMARY NEOLITHIC groups, such as the WINDMILL HILL culture, which he thought represented an intrusion of farming peoples from the Continent. This view is not widely held today: the later Neolithic groups in Britain are thought to have developed directly out of the earlier Windmill Hill group and the concept of a Secondary Neolithic in British prehistory is now unfashionable.

secondary retouch. *See* RETOUCH.

Secondary Series. *See* CALENDAR.

section. Term used to describe the vertical site records of an archaeological excavation. It is applied both to the standing vertical face preserving the STRATIGRAPHY of a feature or area and to the drawing of such a face. Advocates of open-area excavation prefer not to have standing sections on the site; instead of drawing sections after the whole area has been excavated, they record the profile of each deposit as it is excavated and construct what

are known as 'cumulative' or 'running sections'.

section-mould casting. *See* CIRE PERDUE; RITUAL VESSELS (CHINA).

sediments. Deposits of accumulated fragmentary material. Some sediments of archaeological sites are directly man-made, deposited as parts of structures or as a result of waste disposal. Other sediments arise from the erosion and decay of structures. In addition, sediments may be affected by SOIL-forming processes. Thus an archaeological site is a complicated sequence of various sediments and SOILS. The study of such sequences is called STRATIGRAPHY. Sediments outside sites are also studied in archaeology, to investigate the changing environment and man's impact on it (*see* ENVIRONMENTAL ARCHAEOLOGY).

seeds. A variety of seeds may be preserved on archaeological sites by CHARRING, as GRAIN IMPRESSIONS, or as a result of waterlogging. They may be the seeds of weed plants, fruits, pulses (*see* BEANS), or the grains of cereals (*see* BARLEY, MAIZE, MILLET, OATS, RICE, RYE, WHEAT).

Segesta [Greek Egesta]. An ancient city in the northwest corner of Sicily west of Palermo, reckoned by traditional sources as home of the indigenous Elymi, and mostly known today for its unfinished 5th-century BC temple, and HELLENISTIC theatre. Earliest occupation seems to have been Iron Age of the 8th century BC. The classical town had an eventful history, shaped by its constant rivalry with its neighbour, Selinus, and by shifting alignments with, variously, Carthaginian, Greek and Roman sources of power. Perhaps the best-documented event (Thucydides VI, 6) is its appeal to ATHENS for assistance (415 BC), which helped to decide Athens to go ahead with the disastrous Sicilian expedition. Later, in 307 BC, the town was sacked by Agathocles with a systematic sadism (which included firing men into the air). Loyalty to Rome in the First PUNIC WAR was rewarded with a grant of the status of *civitas libera et immunis* (free and tax-free). A prosperous but insignificant Roman period seems to have followed.

The city site is on the plateau adjacent to the THEATRE, where the absence of any obvious Roman remains may indicate that the

Roman town shifted nearer its port at modern Castellammare. The 6th-5th century BC Sanctuary shows a *temenos* layout, and evidence for an archaic Doric temple. The surviving 5th-century temple, which stood outside the original city, is usually seen as a distinguished, but unfinished example (it has a colonnade, but no interior *cella*). The query has been raised, however, as to whether some peristyle building other than a temple may have been intended — possibly something more relevant to this indigenous and Carthaginian context.

segmented cist. A type of MEGALITHIC tomb in which the burial chamber is divided into a number of compartments by the use of SEPTAL SLABS or jambs. Alternatively these tombs are sometimes labelled segmented GALLERY GRAVES. Good examples occur in the British Isles among the CLYDE CARLINGFORD tombs.

Segovia [Roman Segobriga]. A local OPPIDUM in central Spain of obscure history before 80 BC, when it came under Roman control, and famous today for its grand-scale AQUEDUCT. Even for the Roman town, information is not plentiful, but the investment represented by this massive structure must presuppose a city of some size and importance. Attributed to Trajan (98-117 AD), the aqueduct system brought water from a distance of some 16 km. The masonry bridge (El Puente) was used to span the final depression before the city, and is in all close to 900 metres long. The central and highest section utilizes two storeys of arches and is nearly 30 metres high. Guadarrama granite is used without mortar, and the blocks are left rough, showing their raising slots. A considerable section was demolished by Moorish attack in 1071 and was finally reassembled at the end of the 15th century. A figure of Hercules in the central niche was then replaced by the Virgin and St Sebastian.

Sehonghong. *See* MOSHEBI'S SHELTER.

Seibal. A Lowland MAYA site, located on a high bluff overlooking the Pasion River in the Peten Province of Guatemala. Although there is evidence of occupation in the Middle PRE-CLASSIC (e.g. Xe pottery and a cache of OLMEC-style jade axes) its period of maximum activity is in the Late CLASSIC between AD 830 and 890. The site is dominated by three groups of ceremonial buildings, built around plazas and connected by causeways. Most of the population, however, lived in small house clusters around these nucleii. The site's florescence coincides with an influx of PUTUN and the receding influence of nearby ALTAR DE SACRIFICIOS; it is therefore likely that Seibal replaced Altar as a trading station. A second influx of foreigners occurred in the Early POST-CLASSIC (*c*930); the appearance of images of TLALOC, serpent motifs and speech scrolls in their iconography strongly implies they were of Mexican origin. Seibal was abandoned by 950, probably as part of the general decline of the Classic Peten centres.

Seine-Oise-Marne [S.O.M.] **tombs.** Group of tombs belonging to the Late Neolithic/Copper Age of the Paris Basin in Northern France. Both rock-cut tombs and MEGALITHIC GALLERY GRAVES occur. The megalithic tombs often include PORT-HOLE slabs, while the rock-cut tombs sometimes have female 'goddess' figures carved on their walls. Collective burial was practised and grave goods include flat-based pottery, flint arrowheads and some daggers of imported GRAND PRESSIGNY flint, beads of callais (a green stone) and copper, both also imported materials.

Seleucid. A Macedonian-Greek dynasty founded by Seleucus I Nicator, one of ALEXANDER THE GREAT's generals, who managed to piece back together virtually all of Alexander's eastern empire after the king's death, to make a domain stretching from Anatolia and Syria to Afghanistan. The dynasty is usually dated from the year 312 BC, when Seleucus I finally established himself at Babylon, and promptly founded his own new capital of Seleuceia-on-Tigris — which in due course was to eclipse Babylon itself, and become a great centre of Greek civilization in the East. Gradually the Seleucid dynasty lost power and territory, notably to the PARTHIANS, and the focus of control moved back west to Syria, where Seleucus I had already in *c*300 BC founded his Syrian capital of ANTIOCH. The Seleucid era was already over when Pompey annexed Syria as a Roman province in 64-63 BC.

Selevac. One of the largest open settlements of the Early VINČA period, Selevac extends over

80 hectares of gently sloping hillside in the Konjska basin, northern Serbia, Yugoslavia. Four occupation levels were detected in the central part of the site, excavated by R. Tringham and D. Krstić and dated *c*4300-3950 bc. In the first two levels houses were rebuilt on their own foundations, creating rapid disposition of debris, but in the last two phases houses were horizontally displaced, leading to more even deposition. Subsistence strategies centred on mixed farming (cattle husbandry and cultivation of emmer and bread wheat). Copper from the RUDNA GLAVA mine was used alongside stone from mountains near the mine.

Semna. A great fort erected beside the Second Cataract of the Nile in Sudanese Nubia, apparently to defend the southern limit of Egyptian pentration under the Middle Kingdom. At least in later times this and neighbouring forts seem to have served primarily as trading stations, ensuring that trade with more southerly regions of the Nile Valley remained in Egyptian hands.

Sempukuji. A very early JOMON site in Nagasaki prefecture on Kyushu, Japan. Recent work at this stratified rock shelter confirmed the association of microblades with linear-relief pottery found earlier at FUKUI, but also revealed an older pottery with discontinuous relief (bean-pattern). Radiocarbon, fission track and thermoluminescence dates in the late 11th millennium bc tend to be slightly younger than the Fukui date.

Senegambian megaliths. *See* MEGALITHIC MONUMENTS (AFRICA).

Senjerli. *See* ZINJIRLI.

septal slab. A stone set on its side dividing a MEGALITHIC tomb into separate burial areas (*see* SEGMENTED CIST). They vary in height from low kerbs to the full height of the chamber; in the latter case they are sometimes provided with PORT-HOLES.

sequence dating. A type of SERIATION combined with CROSS DATING, used in the absence of any other dating method, originally applied by Sir Flinders PETRIE to provide a relative chronology for pottery from PREDYNASTIC EGYPTIAN cemeteries. A series of artefact forms can be built up from their STRATIGRAPHICAL relationships and typology. Petrie assigned numbers, called 'Sequence Dates', to different stages in this series. Artefacts found at other sites were then correlated with the sequence and given a sequence date. The typological series was not calibrated by reference to other dating methods, so the sequence dates provide only a relative and not an absolute chronology.

seriation. The organization of a group of objects into a series, or sequence, on the grounds of their physical attributes. This can be done visually or mathematically. Such series have been used in two ways: (1) To suggest evolutionary trends in, for example, the form of a particular group of arefacts; (2) supposing that a series does indeed represent evolutionary trends, to set up a relative chronology.

Seriation as a mathematical technique is well established. Its application to archaeology, particularly as a DATING method, involves rather far-reaching assumptions and should be approached with care.

Serovo. *See* BAIKAL NEOLITHIC.

serpentine. A mineral occurring in a number of forms. Rocks largely composed of this mineral should properly be called serpentinites, but are often also called serpentines. These rocks are used as a material for decorative work. They vary widely in colour, but the most commonly used varieties are green. Sources are known in Cornwall, Banffshire, Anglesey and Shetland in the British Isles, Ireland, Canada, USA, New Zealand and Afghanistan. The serpentine at the Lizard, Cornwall, was the source of one group of stone axes, used during the NEOLITHIC.

Serpent Mound. A ritual mound located in Adams County, Ohio, USA, and constructed in the sinuous form of a stylized serpent, holding an egg, or possibly a frog, in its jaws. At 386 metres long, 1.2-1.5 metres high, and with an average body-width of 6 metres, it is probably the largest serpent effigy in the world. Although no cultural material has been found within the mound, its proximity to an ADENA village and burial mound testify to its most likely cultural affiliation.

Serra d'Alto. A Late Neolithic village north of

MATERA in southeast Italy. It has given its name to a type of pottery found in abundance here in the 4th millennium bc, characterized by a fine hard buff ware with dark purplish-brown painted decoration and elaborate handles. The commonest forms are cups and jars. The high quality of the ware and the fact that it most often occurs in graves and other ritual contexts suggests that it was produced for special purposes. It was traded over a wide area, occurring in Sicily, LIPARI and in central Italy, but only in small quantities.

Serraferlicchio. Site near Agrigento in southern Sicily which has given its name to a style of pottery current during the Copper Age in the south of the island. It is found mainly in rock-cut tombs and consists of a bright red slipped ware decorated with black paint in geometric designs. Characteristic forms are open bowls and a variety of jug and cup shapes. There are no radiocarbon dates available, but this pottery style should fall within the 3rd millennium bc.

sese. *See* PANTELLERIA.

Sesklo. A Neolithic TELL settlement in the Thessalian plain of northern Greece which has given its name to the Middle Neolithic culture of much of Greece and to the characteristic pottery type, painted in red geometric designs on a light ground. The settlement, dated to the 6th millennium bc, has closely grouped mud-brick houses set on stone foundations, each with its own domed oven.

Seton rock shelter. *See* KARTAN CULTURE.

Seven Wonders of the World. A list was made in the HELLENISTIC period of what were then considered to be the seven greatest wonders of the world. These were normally: (1) the Great Pyramids of Egypt; (2) the Gardens of BABYLON (New Babylonian period, 626-539 BC); (3) the Temple of Artemis (Diana) at EPHESUS (4th century BC); (4) the great gold and ivory statue of Zeus by the sculptor, Pheidias, at OLYMPIA (c450-430 BC); (5) the Colossus of RHODES, a colossal statue to Helios that tradition said straddled the entrance to the harbour; (6) the Pharos (lighthouse) of ALEXANDRIA, built by Sostratus of Cnidus in the early 3rd century BC; and (*i*)

the MAUSOLEUM of Mausolus at HALICARNASSUS (c353 BC).

severed head cult. Among some CELTIC groups in Iron Age Europe, the heads of enemies were collected both as charms and status symbols, probably because the head was believed to be the home of the soul and a symbol of divinity. This practice was elevated to the status of a cult among Celto-Ligurian groups in southern France and sanctuary sites like ENTREMONT, GLANUM, and ROQUEPERTUSE have stone statuary associated with this cult — carved stone heads, headless torsos and pillars carved with severed heads — as well as niches for the display of actual severed heads.

Severn-Cotswold tombs. A group of MEGALITHIC tombs found around the Bristol Channel in southern England. They usually have chambers of GALLERY GRAVE type, sometimes TRANSEPTED GALLERY GRAVES, covered by trapezoidal mounds, usually far longer than required for functional support of the chambers. Other features found include forecourts and FALSE ENTRANCES. *See also* WAYLAND'S SMITHY; WEST KENNET.

sgraffito ware. Glazed vessels prepared first by incising decorations into their surfaces, and then by the addition of paint into these incisions prior to the application of glaze. The result is a fine contrast between the decoration, which is usually bright in colour, and the overall tone of the glazed vessel. BYZANTINE sgraffito wares dating to the 11th and 12th centuries are some of the earliest known from western Europe, but the technique failed to take hold in North European pottery until the end of the Middle Ages and was only established in the 16th and 17th centuries.

shadow marks. An archaeological site may be revealed on an AERIAL PHOTOGRAPH by the shadows cast by earthworks, ditches or changes in slope. Shadow sites are best seen in the low sun of evenings and early mornings.

shaft grave. A type of grave characterized by a deep narrow shaft, with the burials either in the bottom of the shaft itself or sometimes in a small chamber opening from the bottom of the shaft. Shaft graves occur in many parts of the world at different times. Among the most famous are those in Circles A and B at MYCENAE.

shaft tombs (China). The vertical shaft tomb characteristic of Bronze Age China (the SHANG and Western ZHOU dynasties) has two distinctive features. First, its walls step inward on all four sides, part way down the shaft, forming a shelf or *ercengtai*. Second, beneath the coffin or wooden burial chamber in the bottom of the shaft is a small pit, the *yaokeng* or 'waist pit', so called because it lies beneath the waist of the corpse. The *ercengtai* ordinarily carried mortuary offerings, which were also deposited between the coffin and the walls of the shaft or within the wooden burial chamber. The *yaokeng* contained sacrifices meant evidently to serve as guardians: either a dog or, in richer tombs, a man armed with a bronze or jade halberd (GE). Both the *ercengtai* and the sacrificed dog are features anticipated in Neolithic burials on the east coast (*see* DADUNZI). Human sacrifice is a recurrent feature of rich tombs in both the Shang and Zhou periods (*see* ANYANG), and some of the victims, particularly those in Zhou tombs, appear to have been persons of rank.

The largest burials of the type just described are the so-called Shang royal tombs at Anyang Xibeigang. Here the pits were approached by two or four entrance ramps aligned with the cardinal directions and sloping down into the shaft; only one ramp, that on the south side, descended into the burial chamber, the others ending on the *ercengtai*. Tomb 1004 at Xibeigang, average in size, was 12 metres deep; the pit proper measured 16 by 18 metres, while the total north-south length, including the ramps, was about 60 metres. The walls and *ercengtai* of these cruciform tombs were all made of earth pounded hard by the HANGTU technique, and the tombs were filled with *hangtu* to the level of the ground surface.

Monumental shaft tombs comparable to those at Xibeigang have been found at SUFUTUN (late Shang or early Western Zhou), XINCUN (early Western Zhou), and GUWEICUN (late Eastern Zhou). Western Zhou burials in general do not depart from Shang practice, but at Guweicun a new feature is encountered, the burial mound, which was no doubt borrowed from the KURGANS of the steppe mounds (*see also* PINGSHAN). Also first appearing in late Eastern Zhou are tombs in which the burial is located in an annexe cut in the side of the vertical shaft; this construction too is anticipated by far earlier burials in south Russia.

Eastern Zhou burials in the middle Yangzi region — the territory of the CHU state — by and large follow the northern tradition. The coffin was placed in a wooden chamber at the bottom of a rectangular shaft, the shaft sometimes having entrance ramps and an *ercengtai*. In a few large tombs, however, the shaft is entirely filled by a massive timber structure with separate compartments for furnishings and the coffins of attendants; these tombs omit the *ercengtai* and may depart from the usual rectangular plan (*see* SUI XIAN). Chu tombs were often carefully sealed with layers of charcoal and clay and some have been found waterlogged but with their contents exceedingly well preserved (*see* XINYANG, MAWANGDUI).

The tomb of the first QIN emperor (*d.* 210 BC) is covered by a large mound, as were some HAN tombs, but the richest Han tomb so far excavated, at MANCHENG in Hebei province, is a series of chambers excavated from a mountainside. This form of burial, often brick-built and vaulted, owes nothing to the shaft tombs it replaced.

Shahdad. An oasis on the edge of the great Lut desert northeast of Kerman in eastern Iran, which has an important prehistoric site of the later 4th and 3rd millennia BC. A series of floods in prehistoric times destroyed most buildings, but left brick-lined tombs and many artefacts suggesting that Shahdad was an important manufacturing and trading centre in the first half of the 3rd millennium BC (contemporary with the EARLY DYNASTIC period in MESOPOTAMIA). Among the most interesting finds were a number of almost life-size unbaked clay statues found lying in the graves, face to face with the corpses. Both male and female statues occur and are presumed to be actual portraits of the dead people. Metal, both bronze and silver, was locally worked and made into tools, decorated vessels, ornaments and cylinder seals. Other finds include vessels of steatite and alabaster, and beads of agate, carnelian and lapis lazuli. A very early form of writing appears on pottery, sometimes incised, sometimes impressed with seals: some 700 different pictographic symbols have been identified, occurring singly or in groups of up to five symbols. These discoveries indicate wide-ranging trade networks, a high level of craft specialization and the existence of a wealthy élite.

Shahi Tump. A small prehistoric site in western Baluchistan, probably of the 3rd millennium BC, excavated by Aurel STEIN. Three phases of use were recognized: two phases of occupation, followed by a phase of use as a cemetery. The dead were inhumed in the flexed position and provided with pottery vessels, necklaces and other jewellery and sometimes copper objects, including a copper seal. Pottery and other artefacts show connections both with Iranian sites and the KULLI culture of southern Baluchistan.

Shahr-i Qumis. PARTHIAN city in Khurasan, northeast Iran. The remains are spread over a large area, *c*7 by 4 km, and surface survey indicates occupation of some kind from the Iron Age to the Seljuq period; it was finally brought to an end by the Mongol invasion in the 13th century. The size of the Parthian city and its location on a major highway linking Mesopotamia with Central Asia suggests that it might be the Parthian capital known to the Greeks as Hecatompylos, 'The City of a Hundred Gates'. Parthian structures that have been excavated include vaulted mud-brick chambers used for burials (of mixed human and animal — especially horse — remains) and a fortified mansion with six towers, a large courtyard, and a number of long rooms on the ground floor.

Shahr-i Sokhta. TELL site in the province of Sistan in eastern Iran, close to the Afghan and Pakistan borders, which was the site of a vast urban centre of the 3rd millennium BC, covering *c*100 hectares and housing perhaps 20,000 people. The site, which has been under excavation since 1967, has proved remarkably rich, partly because of the environmental conditions which have sealed the occupation deposit under a layer of salt, sand and clay which has preserved the ancient city 'as if kept in a pot of pickles', to quote the evocative phrase of one of the excavators, Maurizio Tosi. As well as abundant structural remains, enormous numbers of finds have been excavated, including literally millions of potsherds and thousands of stone tools, clay

figurines and animal bones. The wealth of Shahr-i Sokhta was due at least in part to its role in the trade in LAPIS LAZULI between its source in north Afghanistan and the markets of Mesopotamia and Egypt. An industrial area produced thousands of unfinished lapis lazuli beads, as well as flint drills and other tools used in their manufacture. Another remarkable aspect of Shahr-i Sokhta is its enormous cemetery, covering some 42 hectares and estimated to have contained perhaps 200,000 burials. Shahr-i Sokhta was occupied from the 4th millennium BC to the early 2nd millennium. Towards the end of this long period, the course of the Helmand River, on which the city depended, changed; this led to the decline and abandonment of this extraordinary settlement.

Shaikhan. *See* CHARSADA.

Shakimu. *See* TUTISHCAINYO.

Shamarkian. A Nubian microlithic industry of the period 10,000-6000 bc, the typology of which shows certain Saharan affinities. By the 6th millennium some of the makers of this industry had adopted a specialized fishing economy using harpoons with barbed bone heads, as preserved at 'Catfish Cave' near the Second Nile Cataract.

Sham Wan. A pivotal site in the prehistory of HONG KONG, situated in a beach ridge on Lamma Island. The levels span the periods from Neolithic (*c*3500 BC) through Bronze Age (*c*1500-200 BC) into TANG times. Much of the prehistoric material relates to that from the neighbouring mainland province of Kwangtung.

Shanbiaozhen [Shan-piao-chen]. *See* LIU-LIGE.

Shang [Shang]. The Shang or Yin dynasty, the first great Bronze Age power in China, ruled the North China plain during the latter half of the 2nd millennium BC. Of the dynasties named in Chinese historical works it is the earliest whose existence has been confirmed by archaeology (*see* ORACLE BONES). The exact dates of the dynasty are uncertain; the various rival chronologies are all based on figures transmitted in historical texts, which cease to conflict only in the ZHOU dynasty at the year 841 BC. Dates proposed for the fall of Shang (the Zhou conquest) vary within limits of about a century; the traditional date of 1122 BC is regarded as too high by many Western scholars, who favour a short chronology that sets the end of the dynasty around 1030 BC. Figures for the beginning of Shang diverge more widely (1766 BC, 1523 BC etc).

The historicity of the Shang dynasty was established by the inscribed ORACLE BONES discovered around 1900 at the site of its last capital, near modern ANYANG. According to later texts this capital was occupied for 273 years, a time known as the historical Anyang period (c1300-c1030 BC on the short chronology). Earlier stages of the culture known from Anyang have been recognized at sites assigned to the ERLIGANG PHASE and, still earlier, the ERLITOU phase (see also GAOCHENG). So far virtually no inscriptions have been found at these pre-Anyang sites; since the few available radiocarbon dates have large error margins, even if the date of the dynasty's founding were known it would be uncertain to what extent these archaeologically defined phases fall within the Shang period. Thus while the type site of the Erligang phase at ZHENGZHOU is generally assumed to have been a Shang capital, some archaeologists have argued that the Erlitou phase falls in the time of the XIA dynasty, traditional predecessor of Shang.

Shangcunling [Shang-ts'un-ling]. Site of a large early Eastern ZHOU cemetery excavated in 1956 and 1957 near the city of Sanmenxia in Shan Xian, western Henan province, China. Inscribed bronzes show that members of the royal family of Guo were buried here. Guo was a small state founded perhaps before the end of the Western Zhou period (771 BC) and extinguished in 655 BC, when its territory was absorbed by the state of Jin. The latter date can apparently be taken as a *terminus ante quem* for the contents of the cemetery, which include well preserved CHARIOT BURIALS and remarkably impoverished bronze RITUAL VESSELS. Finer bronzes of the same period were unearthed in 1953 at Jia Xian Taipuxiang in central Henan.

Shanidar. A cave in northern Iraq at an altitude of 745 metres. A small village site outside, ZAWI CHEMI SHANIDAR, has produced some evidence for early farming at the time of the ZARZIAN, whose levels at the summit of the cave are about 10,000 bc. Beneath early Upper Palaeolithic levels are MOUSTERIAN layers, from which come a series of NEANDERTHAL skeletons, several thought to have been killed by rock falls. One Neanderthal was apparently buried with flowers, the clusters of pollen at the centre surviving. Another had apparently had his arm crudely amputated above the elbow, and lived for some time afterwards.

Shaogou [Shao-kou]. *See* LUOYANG.

Shechem. Modern Balata has been identified as the site of the biblical city of Schechem, near the central Palestinian town of Nablus. There was some occupation in the PRE-POTTERY NEOLITHIC period, but the first town was built in the Middle Bronze Age, defended first by a free-standing wall, then an earth rampart, and finally by walls of CYCLOPEAN MASONRY c2 metres thick. The town was destroyed at the end of the Middle Bronze Age and not re-occupied until the 16th century BC. It was clearly an important city in the Late Bronze Age and it figures prominently in the Amarna letters (*see* EL-AMARNA); however, few buildings of this period have been investigated. This town was destroyed in the 12th century and there was another break in occupation until the 10th century, when it became an ISRAELITE city. This was destroyed by the ASSYRIANS in 720 BC, after which there was intermittent occupation until its final destruction in 101 BC.

sheep. Members of the genus *Ovis*, distinguished from *Capra* (the GOATS) by differences in scent glands, lack of 'beard', the number of chromosomes, and the possession of tightly curled horns, curving around the ears. Goats and sheep may sometimes be difficult to distinguish in the flesh, and skeletons are even more so. Key differences are in the HORN CORES, metapodials and phalanges (see SKELETON). Many researchers, however, do not distinguish between them in archaeological site reports and refer instead to sheep/goat, ovicaprid, caprovine etc.

Classification of the sheep themselves is controversial. All domestic sheep are generally referred to as *Ovis aries*, although it is unclear if they do indeed qualify as a separate species. The surviving wild sheep exist as isolated populations scattered through the remote mountain ranges of the Near East and Asia. Differences do exist between these populations — in horn shape, build and pelage — but there is much dispute about their taxonomic value. Six main groups are generally recognized. (a) *Mouflon*. Recently introduced into the mountains of mainland Europe. The mouflon of Sardinia and Corsica are now regarded as feral domesticated sheep. Usually all classified as *Ovis musimon*. (b) *Urials*. A variable group dispersed through the mountains of Turkey, Iran, Afghanistan, southern USSR, Pakistan and northern India. Some authors include all the variants in *Ovis orientalis*. (c) *Argalis*. Giant sheep of the Himalayas, Mongolia and western Siberia. Again variable, but usually all classified as *Ovis ammon*. (d) *Snow sheep*. Large sheep from Siberia. (e) *Dall sheep*. From Alaska and the northern Rocky Mountains. (f) *Bighorns*. Found in the mountains of the American West.

Most researchers would place the origin of domestic sheep in urial-like ancestors. The argalis, snow sheep, dall sheep and bighorns are unlikely to have been involved. Securely identified sheep bones first appear in the Middle PALAEOLITHIC levels of caves in the Near East. These fossils are not morphologically different from skeletons of modern wild sheep, but at c9000-8500 bc at ZAWI CHEMI SHANIDAR and the nearby site of SHANIDAR CAVE in Kurdistan there are large proportions of juvenile sheep. It has been suggested that this implies manipulation of the sheep by man. The earliest evidence of an actual change in morphology may be the occurrence of hornless sheep at ALI KOSH in the Southern Zagros mountains (before 7000 bc). Sheep seem to have appeared in Europe ready domesticated; they appear in the Aegean before 6000 bc and in the West Mediterranean not much later. The whole question of domestication, like the status of today's wild populations, is still, however, very much under discussion.

Shell Mound culture. *See* SIDEMI CULTURE.

shell mounds (tropical Australia). Found close to the shorelines along the northern Australian coast, especially at Weipa (Cape York) and Milingimbi (Arnhem Land); the steep-sided mounds are up to 10 metres high and consist of accumulations of cockle shells, charcoal, and bone and stone tools. Radiocarbon dates are 500 bc-1200 ad for base deposits of several mounds. Recent ethnographic observations report that the mounds are favoured by Aborigines as wet monsoon camping-sites above the level of insects in the surrounding coastal flats.

Shilingxia [Shih-ling-hsia]. *See* MAJIAYAO.

Shilou [Shih-lou]. A city in Shanxi province, China, on the southward bend of the Yellow River. SHANG bronze weapons and RITUAL VESSELS have been found repeatedly in and near Shilou. These objects date from the AN-YANG period but many are by Anyang standards eccentric in style. Central Shanxi seems to have been the home of a bronze-using power influenced by contact with less civilized populations farther north (*see* ORDOS) and culturally somewhat different from the Anyang civilization — a description that may apply equally well to the nearby ZHOU people before their conquest of Shang.

Shindo. A small spur projecting southwards into the valley of the Kyi Chu River about 8 km east of Lhasa, the capital of Tibet. P. Aufschnaiter discovered and excavated a group of burials there in 1950. He distinguished three phases, each occurring at a different level on the ridge. The first, Horizon A, consisted of flexed burials in rock-cut pits, accompanied by crude, hand-made pottery but no metalwork. Horizon B had two flexed burials in rock-cut pits with much finer hand-made pottery, some of which was decorated, and a few iron artefacts. There was also one larger tomb closed with two carefully dressed stone slabs and containing two skulls, a pile of long bones and vertebrae, three pottery vessels and a wooden bowl with metal lining. Horizon C, on top of the ridge, consisted of two tumuli built of pebbles brought up from the river, with flexed burials, fine wheel-turned pottery with traces of bright red decoration, and a few iron artefacts, including a piece of slag.

About 50 metres from this ridge is a boulder with pecked carvings of animals, probably horses, a chorten, and letters.

Shinto. The native religion of Japan. Its doctrine was only committed to writing by those with nationalistic aims in the recent past, and could only be reconstructed from fragmentary survivals in folk beliefs and court ceremonies, together with the descriptions of myths and rituals in KOJIKI and NIHON SHOKI. The core of belief seems to be that spirits reside in numerous natural phenomena, such as sun, water, fire and mountains, and that it is important to attain ritual purity from pollution. Since Shinto shrines often have a mirror as the embodiment of the deity and share architectural details with the buildings represented in HANIWA and *dotaku* drawings, elements of Shinto probably date back to YAYOI and KOFUN times when mirrors seem to have had ritual significance.

Shirataki. A group of Palaeolithic sites in Hokkaido, Japan. A large number of obsidian, artefacts were recovered during excavations in the 1950s and 1960s. They are divided into two groups, based on radiocarbon and obsidian hydration dates, as well as on the stratigraphy of the Yubetsu river terraces where the sites are located. The older group dates from about 18,000 BC to 13,000 BC, and includes large blades, burins, scrapers, and some bifacial points. There are more bifacial points and micoblades in the younger group, which lasted from about 13,000 to 10,000 BC. The microblades were made by a special technique, called the Yubetsu technique, where a large biface is made into a core which looks like a tall carinated scraper.

Shizhaishan [Shih-chai-shan]. *See* DIAN KINGDOM.

shoe-last adze. A common stone tool found in Early Neolithic LINEAR POTTERY contexts throughout Europe; it is long and thin in shape with a D-shaped cross-section. It might have been used as an adze for carpentry, but it is perhaps more likely that it was an agricultural tool, a sort of hoe.

Short Count. *See* CALENDAR.

Shou Xian [Shou-hsien]. A district on the south bank of the Huai River in Anhui province, China. In the latter part of the Eastern ZHOU period this area was held in succession by the states of Wu, YUE (which annexed Wu in 473 BC) and CHU (which expelled Yue *c*333 BC). Bronzes and MIRRORS of the 6th-3rd centuries BC have been found in large numbers in and near Shou Xian, many of them with decoration typical of the so-called HUAI STYLE. The most important single discovery made in Shou Xian is a tomb of the 5th century BC excavated in 1955. Some of the 486 bronze objects found in the tomb are dedicated in their inscriptions to a marquis of Cai, a state whose rulers took refuge from Chu invasions in the state of Wu in 494 BC and apparently remained in exile at Shou Xian from that time until 447 BC, when the last Cai prince was murdered. Many bronzes of the same period, one with an inscription in which the Cai state is mentioned, have been found in Shucheng Xian 120 km south of Shou Xian; these may be connected with another small principality in this region, the state of Shu (not to be confused with the Shu state in Sichuan province, which is written with a different character; *see* BA AND SHU).

Two centuries after the destruction of Cai, Shou Xian became the last capital of Chu: retreating before QIN armies, the Chu court arrived at Shou Xian *c*241 BC and resided there until the final conquest of Chu by Qin in 223 BC. Inscribed bronzes from a tomb robbed in 1934 at Shou Xian Zhujiaji identify the tomb's owner as one of the Chu kings who ruled at Shou Xian.

Shu [Shu]. *See* BA AND SHU; SHOU XIAN.

Shubad. *See* PUABI.

Shucheng [Shu-ch'eng]. *See* SHOU XIAN.

Shuihudi [Shui-hu-ti]. *See* YUNMENG.

Shungura. *See* OMO.

Shuruppak [modern Fara]. Situated on the bank of the Euphrates River in southern Iraq, Shuruppak was one of the city states of SUMER. Excavations by a German expedition in the first decade of this century uncovered important remains of the EARLY DYNASTIC period. The temples produced a wealth of early documents, including administrative and school texts.

Shwezigon Temple. A great Buddhist monument at PAGAN, northern Burma, housing a copy of the tooth relic of Ceylon. Its construction began in about 1059 under king Anôratha, the founder of the Pagan dynasty, but was not completed until the reign of king

Kyanzittha, half a century later. It contains the latter king's most important inscriptions.

Sialk [Siyalk], **Tepe**. TELL site near Kashan on the Iranian plateau, occupied from the 6th to the 1st millennium BC. The earliest settlement was built of pisé, though no house plans were recovered; painted pottery was in use and some ornaments of hammered copper occurred. In Period II, after c5000 bc, mud-brick architecture appeared, as did fine painted pottery, decorated with stylized animals in dark paint on a light ground. Period III saw the introduction of the potter's wheel, cast copper tools and weapons, and stamp seals. Period IV (late 4th millennium BC) showed strong influence from SUSA, with the introduction of PROTO-ELAMITE writing, accompanied by an increase in wealth. This phase was followed by a break in occupation and the resettlement — represented in cemetery A — is often attributed to intruders from the northeast, who are thought to have been responsible for the introduction of INDO-EUROPEAN languages to this area. The latest occupation of Tepe Sialk, represented in cemetery B and dated to the late 2nd or early 1st millennium BC, saw the first use of iron.

Sidemi culture [Shell Midden culture]. Culture found in the Vladivostok area of eastern Siberia from the late 2nd millennium BC. The population lived in coastal settlements of semi-subterranean houses, which are associated with shell middens. Fish and shellfish were clearly important in the diet, but pigs and dogs were bred for food and it is possible that crops were also grown. Characteristic tools were made of polished slate, though small quantities of iron were also used. The area came under strong influence from Manchuria and China and in the 1st millennium AD it formed part of the Po-hai state.

side scraper. *See* SCRAPER.

Sidi Abd er Rahman. A PALAEOLITHIC site close to Casablanca on the Moroccan coast. A series of pits near the airport has revealed ACHEULIAN levels. These are earlier than the Amirian dune (perhaps 0.5 million years old or 'Mindel') and later than the Saletian dune of about one million years of age. They are associated with ancient beaches of an altitude of 60 metres or less.

Sidon [modern Sarda]. Situated on the coast of Lebanon south of Beirut, Sidon was an important trading centre for Mediterranean trade from the Early or Middle Bronze Age and, with TYRE, one of the two most important PHOENICIAN centres. It was partially destroyed by the ASSYRIANS in 676 BC, but grew to importance again in the ACHAEMENID period. Although it was under Persian rule, the population was autonomous, producing its own coinage — the Persian shekel with a picture of a trireme on the reverse. Because the site underlies the modern town, little excavation has taken place. However, a number of burials of various dates from the 10th to the 4th century BC have been found both in and around the city.

sieving. The practice of sieving SOILS and SEDIMENTS from archaeological sites is now quite common. Sieving each bucket of spoil from the site improves recovery of artefacts, larger bones etc, which may have been missed by trowellers. A relatively coarse sieve is used for this purpose. For lighter soils, dry sieving may be effective, but more clayey material may necessitate the use of wet sieving — washing material through the sieve. Opinions are divided on the cost-effectiveness of carrying out this type of sieving on all spoil excavated from a site.

Wet sieving is also a standard technique for recovering bones, shells, seeds and other biological remains for ENVIRONMENTAL ARCHAEOLOGY studies. Large samples of spoil are removed from selected contexts on the site. These are then gently sieved under water. Mesh sizes of 2 mm, 1 mm and 0.5 mm are commonly used in sieves, the size being dependent on the remains to be recovered. Sand, silt and clay are washed through the sieve, leaving bone and shell fragments, charred material, insect skeletons etc behind, along with pebbles and gravel. These sieved residues are then dried and sorted by hand.

Sigatoka. A beach-dune site on southwestern Viti Levu, FIJIAN ISLANDS, which has produced an important but discontinuous pottery sequence from late LAPITA (500 bc), through a paddle-impressed style (ad 200), into a later, undated level with pottery apparently ancestral to that of the ethnographic present.

Silbury Hill. The largest man-made mound in

Europe, situated near AVEBURY, Wiltshire, southern England. It was built in four distinct phases, but apparently continuously as part of a single constructional process, dated c2600-2300 BC. The final monument was a mound 40 metres high with a base covering c2 hectares, which the most recent excavator, Richard Atkinson, calculates may have required 18 million man-hours to build (other scholars have produced lower estimates). It was for long believed to be an outsize round BARROW, but no burial has been found on any of the five occasions when the hill has been excavated (whether by shafts sunk from the top or by tunnelling from the side). In any case the date of construction now seems earlier than the main phase of round-barrow building in Wessex. Silbury Hill belongs with the phase of large ritual monument construction of the Late NEOLITHIC and, although no evidence survives (as a result of use of the hilltop in medieval times) it is perhaps most likely that there was on the top either a timber sanctuary building or possibly a large stone or timber to serve as a foresight for astronomical alignments.

Silchester [Roman Calleva Atrebatum]. A Romano-British town of some 43 hectares in Hampshire, southern England, remarkable for the detailed information of its complete street plan. Originally a Celtic tribal centre, capital of the Atrebates, the town prospered from the later 1st century AD onwards, and was still in occupation well into the 5th century AD. The site lies some 13 km to the southwest of Reading, and in open countryside. The perimeter walls enclose an irregular octagonal plan. The internal area was totally excavated in the late 19th century, and in parts since, but a general policy of backfilling has left little immediately discernible. The evidence discovered showed a grid-plan of streets oriented north-south, with a remarkably low density of building — although it has been suggested that the early excavations may have missed some timber structures. Some sections of the town seem to have operated as urban farms, but there was also a range of shops and light industrial activities, such as pottery and metalworking. Housing, usually on a foundation of flint masonry, shows variety of internal size, and probably featured timber-frame construction with clay infill, glazed windows and tiled roof. There are several Romano-Celtic temples, two located in a *temenos* beneath the present churchyard. An apsidal structure may be a small early (? 4th century) Christian church. An earth AMPHITHEATRE may be made out. The gilded bronze eagle from the FORUM is kept at Stratfield Saye House, home of the Duke of Wellington, whose estate includes the Silchester site.

silk. The delicate process of rearing the domesticated silkworm (*Bombyx mori*) and reeling silk from its cocoon was first mastered in China. Evidence for sericulture in Neolithic times is so far not conclusive but the silk industry was clearly well established by the ANYANG period (c1300-c1030 BC). The Anyang ORACLE BONE texts include characters for silk, silk fabrics, silkworm, and mulberry tree, and traces of silk fabrics are occasionally found preserved in the corrosion products on SHANG bronze objects that were wrapped in cloth before burial. The silk of these Shang fabrics was reeled, that is, unwound from the cocoon in a continuous filament rather than spun from the short fibres of the damaged cocoon cut by the emerging moth. Patterned weaves (damasks) have been identified in the fabrics from Anyang and clay impressions of silk embroidery were found in two early Western ZHOU tombs excavated at BAOJI Rujiazhuang in 1975. The decoration of a unique bronze vessel of the 6th century BC found in Hunan province depicts silkworms swarming on mulberry leaves. Silk fabric was used as a writing surface at least as early as the 5th century BC (the more usual vehicle for brush writing, used already in Shang times, was bamboo strips strung together to form a sort of scroll). Both manuscripts and paintings on silk have come from CHU tombs of the 5th century BC and later. Especially well-preserved HAN damasks, polychrome weaves, and embroidered silks were found in 2nd century BC Chu tombs at MAWANGDUI (*see also* NOIN ULA). From the Han to the TANG dynasty silk was the main commodity in overland trade with the West along the SILK ROUTE.

Silk Route. The overland route followed by trade between China and the Mediterranean world from the 2nd century BC onwards. The Silk Route began at CHANG'AN and passed up the Gansu corridor through WUWEI to DUNHUANG, where it branched into two main routes across the Central Asian deserts. After crossing the Pamirs the two routes rejoined finally at Merv and continued via Ecbatana and Ctesiphon to Palmyra and the Mediterranean. (West of the Pamirs India was accessible through Bactria.) For centuries the main Chinese export was SILK, a commodity that apparently supplied the Roman name for China, Serica. The institutionalized traffic in silk began in the HAN dynasty (206 BC–AD 220), when Chinese power secured the route through Central Asia, but irregular trade must have followed the same path some centuries earlier, bringing jade from Khotan to China and Chinese goods to the kurgans at PAZYRYK. From the time of Augustus, the Romans spent ruinous sums on silk in a trade in which the PARTHIAN empire of Iran prospered as middleman. The contact with Western Asia is clearly reflected in Chinese art, where foreign motifs like the Parthian shot (a mounted archer turning in the saddle and shooting to the rear) are prominent in the decoration of Han bronzes and lacquers.

Central Asia fell under the control of a powerful Turkish confederacy after the collapse of the Han dynasty and returned to Chinese rule only with the rise of the TANG dynasty (AD 618–907). The cities along the Silk Route and the trade that passed through them continued to flourish despite political changes, however, as SASSANIAN and BYZANTINE coins found in China testify; in the 5th–8th centuries Classical and Iranian motifs were major themes in Chinese decoration (silks, pottery, metalwork) and in Buddhist cave paintings like those at Dunhuang (see also TURFAN, LOULAN). Nevertheless the trade in silk itself began to decline in the 6th century, when according to Procopius (500–565) the technique of raising silkworms was brought to Byzantium. Moreover towards the end of the Tang dynasty the rise of Islamic states in Central Asia put an end to Buddhist civilization there and raised barriers hostile to trade between Europe and the Far East. From the 9th century onwards trade came increasingly to depend on sea routes and the main Chinese export was not silk but porcelain (see CERAMICS, CHINA). Overland commerce revived only briefly during the continent-wide peace that ensued on the Mongol conquests of the 13th century, when MARCO POLO followed the Silk Route to the court of the YUAN emperor Kublai Khan.

silt. A term describing the size of particles which go to make up a SEDIMENT, SOIL or similar material. Silt particles are those that lie between 0.06 and 0.002mm (BS 1377) in diameter (see PARTICLE SIZE). The term has no implications of colour, organic content or any property other than particle size or TEXTURE.

silver. The main source of this metal in antiquity was the LEAD ore galena, in which silver sulphide occurs as an impurity. After smelting the ore, silver was recovered by the process of cupellation, where the lead is oxidized, leaving silver unaltered. Silver is soft, and could be COLD WORKED. In fact, the metal is too soft for most purposes and even ancient silver was often ALLOYED with other metals.

simulation. The use of a MODEL to simulate an observed phenomenon. Models can be used in archaeology to simulate, for example, the DISTRIBUTION of a group of artefacts or settlements. The purpose of this kind of simulation is to suggest the processes involved in creating such a distribution.

Si Mu Wu fang ding [*Ssu Mu Wu fang-ting*]. The largest metal casting surviving from antiquity, a Chinese bronze RITUAL VESSEL cast in one piece except for its handles and weighing 875 kg. Said to have been found in 1939 in the ANYANG royal cemetery, the vessel is inscribed with a dedication to an empress and dates probably from the 12th century BC. It is now in the Historical Museum, Beijing.

Sinagua. *See* HAKATAYA.

Sinai. The peninsula between the Gulfs of Akaba and Suez on the Red Sea. It is a barren desert area and was never important for settlement, but it has sources of turquoise and malachite (exploited both as a colouring agent and for copper) which were sought after by the Egyptians from the PREDYNASTIC period onwards.

Sinan. A district in South Cholla province, South Korea, off the coast of which a sunken merchant ship of the 14th century AD was discovered in 1976. The ship's cargo was Chinese porcelain: some 7000 pieces have been recovered by divers and it is estimated that at least as many more remain to be salvaged. Dated coins suggest that the wreck occurred in the earlier part of the 14th century and the great bulk of the porcelain, mainly celadon and *qingbai* wares (*see* CERAMICS, (CHINA), was certainly of recent manufacture.

Sinanthropus. Early name for PEKIN MAN, now classified as *Homo erectus*. *See also* HUMAN EVOLUTION, ZHOUKOUDIAN.

Singhasāri. Name of the capital of the Javanese kingdom of TUMAPEL. Founded in 1222 by the adventurer Angrok to succeed the kingdom of KADIRI, it became the ruling power in Java. Its art and architecture show a return to the indigenous substratum and a corresponding decline of Indian culture. Historiography also took a different direction, as from now on events at the court are recorded in two chronicles, the *Nāgarakṛitāgama* and the *Pararaton*.

Single Grave culture. Name for the Late NEOLITHIC cultures of Scandinavia, northern Germany and the Low Countries, part of a larger complex extending right across the north European plain and labelled BATTLE-AXE or CORDED WARE cultures; the GLOBULAR AMPHORA culture may also be part of this group. Characterized by the practice of single burial under barrows, often accompanied by a battle axe, amber beads, and pottery vessels including beakers, this group has traditionally been regarded as intrusive in northern Europe because of the contrast with the collective burial in megalithic tombs practised by the earlier Neolithic TRB people in the same area. However, radiocarbon dating has shown that the Single Grave culture was not partially contemporary with the TRB CULTURE, as previously believed, but succeeded it, with dates in the range 2500-2000 bc (*c*3200-2500 BC). It now seems most likely that it developed out of the TRB culture and that the changes in the archaeological record at this time can be explained in terms of changing social systems (more complex social structures and the emergence of elites).

Sippar [modern Abu Habba]. One of the most northerly of the cities of SUMER, situated near the Euphrates River north of Babylon in Iraq. The city was occupied from the EARLY DYNASTIC period and appears to have been an important religious and trading centre. Among the most important finds are

thousands of CLAY TABLETS dating to the Old Babylonian and Neo-Babylonian periods. The great religious enclosure dedicated to Shamash was originally founded by Sargon of Akkad, but little is known about this phase, as it is obscured by the buildings of later periods. The Neo-Babylonian period saw much reconstruction and new building: in the late 7th century BC Nabopolassar not only rebuilt the temple of Shamash but dug a canal linking the city to the Euphrates.

Siraf. In the 9th and 10th centuries Siraf on the Persian Gulf was a leading entrepôt for the maritime trade which brought commodities and luxury goods from South and Southeast Asia, East Africa and the Red Sea to Baghdad and other cities of the Middle East. Despite torrid summers, poor soil and little rain, the city flourished as a market and the home-port for ships which ventured as far afield as Canton in China and Sofala in Mozambique. Siraf, which already existed in the SASSANIAN period, developed round a shallow bay, 4 km across. The heart of the Islamic city consisted of 110 hectares of houses, bazaars and factories built of stone and mortar. A larger area seems to have contained either gardens or *bidonvilles* of huts. Among the buildings disclosed by excavations in 1966-73 are the congregational mosque, houses, a palace, part of the bazaar, the potters' quarter and a monumental cemetery. The principal mosque underwent three main periods of construction between *c*815-25 and *c*1150. The original mosque measured 51 by 44 metres and consisted of a courtyard surrounded on three sides by a single arcade, with a sanctuary three bays deep. It was enlarged *c*850 by the addition of a lateral extension, external washing facilities and other features. In the 12th century, when Siraf was in decline, the mosque was repaired. The houses, some of which had several storeys, differ in detail but share a common plan with a central yard. The palace, which stands in the coolest part of the town, consists of several such units, protected by a wall. Among the finds from Siraf is abundant Chinese porcelain.

Sirkap. *See* TAXILA.

Sirsukh. *See* TAXILA.

Sisupalgarh. An Iron Age city in Orissa, eastern India. The earliest occupation has

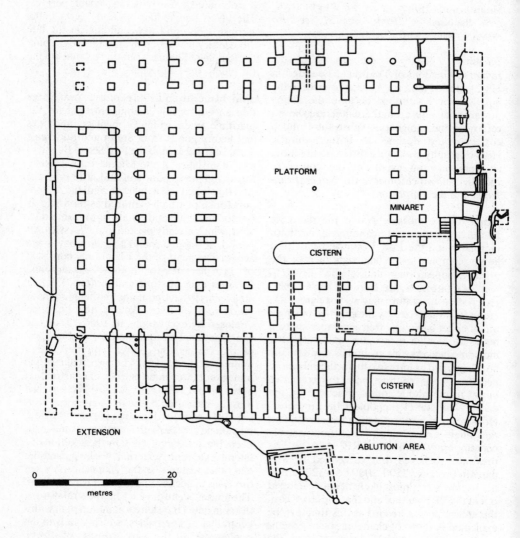

Plan of the Great Mosque at Siraf

BLACK AND RED WARE. In the later 1st millennium BC the city was surrounded by elaborate defensive walls and shows evidence of developed town planning.

Sitagroi. A site in eastern Macedonia, northern Greece, which has produced an important stratigraphy for the chronology of the north Aegean. The 10 metres of deposit begins with a Middle NEOLITHIC occupation dated c4500 bc, and continues into the full Early Bronze Age in the 3rd millennium bc. The site was chosen for excavation by Colin Renfrew in order to clarify the relationships between the cultural sequence in the Aegean and in the Balkans and to establish a radiocarbon chronology for the sequence. The excavation established that finds of GUMEL-NIŢA type, occurring in Sitagroi III, preceded by a considerable period of time finds of TROY I type, found in Sitagroi V. This disproves traditional interpretations, which derived the Balkan Late Neolithic and Copper Age cultures from cultures of Troy I type. It also supports claims for the primacy of southeast European metal-working over that of Anatolia.

site catchment analysis. A method for attempting to reconstruct the economy of archaeological sites, introduced in the late 1960s and early 1970s by E.S. Higgs and his colleague C. Vita-Finzi. A 'site catchment' is defined as the total area from which all the animals, plants and artefacts of which there are remains preserved on the site, are derived. Each group of people living on the site is assumed to have had a 'territory', the area around the site which they habitually exploited. A site territory for a hunter-gatherer group is assumed, from ethnographic parallels, to be an area lying within two hours' walking distance of the site. On similar grounds, the corresponding territory for farmers is assumed to be an area within one hour's walking distance. Territories are determined by walking out from the site along a number of radii. The resources contained within each territory are then assessed by walking over the ground, looking for sources of water, variation in slope, soils, drainage etc. A less exhaustive method, which is widely employed, is simply to draw a 5 km or 10 km circle around the site. These correspond respectively to the one-hour radius and two-hour radius, in 'optimum' terrain.

Many assumptions of site catchment analysis cannot be tested and may be valueless. Particular care must be taken to consider evidence of environmental change in an area. This could give rise to an ancient geography, resources and land use completely different to those of the present day. The technique does, however, place archaeological sites in the context of their surroundings, something that has too often been ignored.

Sitio Conte. *See* COCLE.

Sittard. Settlement site of the Neolithic LINEAR POTTERY culture in Dutch Limburg, Holland. The settlement was surrounded by a palisade and contained a number of timber LONG HOUSES. The houses varied in type, but some of the larger ones were clearly divided into three parts; many authorities believe that the central section was used for living, the southern part for storing grain, and the northern part for stalling animals.

situla. A bucket-shaped vessel made of pottery or sheet bronze. Metal examples, possibly used for serving wine, were common in the HALLSTATT Iron Age of temperate Europe and among related groups in northern Italy. Highly decorated situlae were produced in northeast Italy and traded to other areas (*see* ESTE); the style of decoration found on these situlae and other sheet bronze objects is known as situla art.

Six Dynasties. The period of Chinese history between the fall of the HAN dynasty in AD 220 and the founding of the SUI dynasty in 589. The period takes its name from the six dynasties that had capitals in the south at Nanjing during this time (while North China was ruled by barbarian dynasties). In the course of the Six Dynasties period BUDDHISM came to be firmly established in both north and south; the latter part of the period, together with the subsequent Sui and TANG dynasties, is the great age of Chinese Buddhism. Six Dynasties tombs excavated during the last three decades have contributed notably to the study of ceramics (*see* YUE) and early pictorial art (*see also* HAN, YONGTAI).

Skara Brae. A NEOLITHIC settlement on the

island of Orkney, north Scotland. It was first excavated by Gordon CHILDE in the 1920s, while restricted re-excavation took place in the 1970s. The buildings and internal fittings were all made of stone and survive in remarkably good condition, preserved within a midden deposit and covered by blown sand. In the final phase the village consisted of six or seven houses and a separate workshop, linked by paved paths. Furniture includes beds, hearths, tables, dressers and cupboards. The sea provided much of the food supply, in the form of both sea mammals and shellfish, but sheep and cattle were both kept. Until recently it was assumed that agriculture would not have been possible in the harsh conditions of Orkney, but seeds found by froth flotation during the recent excavations indicate that it was practised, though probably on a small scale only. The settlement is dated to the Late Neolithic, c2000 bc, and the associated pottery is GROOVED WARE.

skeleton. The bony supporting element in the bodies of vertebrate animals. It consists of the axial skeleton — skull (including teeth) and vertebral column — and the appendicular skeleton — ribs, girdles and limbs. The upper (in man) or front (in quadrupeds) limb in mammals consist of the following bones: clavicle and scapula (the pectoral girdle), humerus, radius and ulna, carpals (wrist bones), metacarpals (bones of the palm of the hand) and phalanges (finger bones). The lower or hind limb consists of the following: innominate bones (the pelvic girdle), femur, tibia and fibula, tarsals (ankle bones), metatarsals (bones of the arch of the foot) and phalanges (toe bones). In man, the proportions of these various bones are fairly generalized, but in other animals bones may become eliminated, elongated or strengthened. In the horse, for example, the 1st, 2nd, 4th and 5th digits have been lost and the animal balances on greatly enlarged 3rd metapodials (metacarpal or metatarsal) and phalanges. Similarly, in the ruminants (CATTLE, SHEEP, DEER etc) all digits except the 3rd and 4th have been lost. These animals balance on their 3rd and 4th metapodials, enlarged and fused together, and a cloven hoof formed of the enlarged 3rd and 4th phalanges.

Only broken fragments of the skeleton usually survive on archaeological sites, except in such cases as deliberate burial. For this reason human bones are often studied separately from those of other animals. In the case of most animals, the parts which survive are a function of butchery, and reflect the joints of meat which were brought to the site, cooking, and the robustness of the bones. Thus the bones that survive most often are those which form the refuse of butchery and which are robust. These include horn cores, parts of the large long bones, metapodials and phalanges, and sections of ribs. The fragmentary nature of skeletal material found on archaeological sites makes study difficult. Identification to species may be possible with a considerable number of fragments, but there is always a large pile that cannot be identified. Similar difficulties may be experienced with AGEING and sexing skeletons, and with estimating relative numbers of individuals, proportions of bone fragments from different species, or relative meat weight. See also PALAEOPATHOLOGY, BONE MEASUREMENT.

Skellig Michael. A Celtic monastery precipitously situated on a small rockly island out in the Atlantic, off the southwest coast of Ireland. It is one of the best preserved of the early Irish monasteries although it may be as late in date as the 8th century. The monastic complex includes two rectangular oratories with fine corbelled roofs, a later chapel and a series of terrace walls known as the 'monks garden'; there are also six beehive huts in which the monks lived. The island is known to have suffered Viking raids but the monastery continued to be used until the 12th or 13th century.

Skhul. See MOUNT CARMEL.

Skorba. Important site on the island of Malta, where excavations in the 1960s cast much light on the early part of the prehistoric sequence on the island. Underneath a small trefoil-shaped temple, now in poor condition (see MALTESE TEMPLES) dated c3000 BC was a NEOLITHIC settlement of mud-brick houses on stone foundations of the GHAR DALAM phase. The name Skorba has been given to two successive pottery styles, Grey Skorba and Red Skorba, which seem to have developed out of the impressed pottery of the Ghar Dalam phase and to characterize the later Neolithic phases on the site.

Slavs. The term generally used to refer to the peoples who inhabited an area concentrated in modern Poland, and who by the early middle ages were considered a distinct cultural group. The origins of the Slavs are very obscure though they seem to derive from the Iron Age tribes indigenous to the Oder-Vistula area; they are principally defined by linguistic and place-name evidence rather than by historical or archaeological remains.

small mammal bones. A small mammal is traditionally defined as one which cannot be seen above long grass. This includes a variety of rodents, lagomorphs (hares and rabbits), insectivores and carnivores. BONES of these animals are commonly preserved on archaeological sites, accumulating in drains, pits, wells and other such traps. Identification of teeth and jaws of the smaller animals is relatively easy, but post-cranial material may not be so precisely identified. The composition of small mammal faunas may be interpreted in terms of the environment within and surrounding the archaeological site on which they were found.

smelting. The process of separating METAL from ore. In most cases, this is done by heating in a furnace or hearth. Some metals may melt whilst being smelted, but this is not necessarily part of the process. The main chemical reaction in smelting most of the ores used in antiquity is that of reducing a metal oxide. If the ore was not already in the oxide form, then it was converted by a preliminary process. Most ancient COPPER probably came from oxide ores, which could be smelted by heating with charcoal. The temperature at which the copper oxide was reduced could have been as low as 800°C — the kind of temperature reached in a simple hearth or kiln. In many cases, however, the copper was melted into INGOTS during the smelting operation. This requires a temperature of some 1083°C, which would have necessitated the use of a furnace or hearth assisted by bellows. Careful control of the amount of air entering the furnace would be required for successful smelting. Similar, or lower temperatures would be required for the smelting and melting of GOLD, SILVER, LEAD and TIN, but the melting point of IRON is 1540°C, beyond the range of a simple furnace. Iron could, however, be smelted. The reduction of iron oxide ores can take place at 800°C. If the temperature is increased to some

1150°C, the SLAG melts and can be drained off. This leaves a spongy BLOOM of iron and remaining slag inclusions. The slag within the bloom must then be removed by FORGING. Remains of the smelting process include ingots, slag, TUYÈRES, hearths containing slag and cinder, and more sophisticated furnaces. *See also* IRON AND STEEL.

Smilčić. A multi-level open site of the Early and Late Neolithic located near Zadar in north Dalmatia, Yugoslavia. According to the excavator, S. Batović, there are two occupation horizons: I, an Early Neolithic level with IMPRESSED WARE and scanty architectural remains; and II, 13 occupation phases of the DANILO culture, typologically subdivided into four phases. At one stage, the Danilo settlement was enclosed by a shallow ditch. In both horizons, a broad spectrum economy was utilized, with more cattle husbandry than hunting and shell-collecting.

Smithfield. In early writings on the later stone industries of South Africa, particularly those prepared before the development of radiocarbon dating techniques, reference was frequently made to a group of 'Smithfield' industries, named after a town in the Orange Free State. The unifying feature of these industries, which served to distinguish them from those of the apparently broadly contemporary WILTON, was the almost complete absence of backed microliths and tiny semi-circular scrapers. Further research, coupled with the obtaining of radiocarbon dates, now shows that the old 'Smithfield' concept linked several probably unrelated industries, including that now named ALBANY, several occurrences in the arid interior regions of South Africa, and others dating to the last two millennia on the Cape and Natal coasts.

Smolensk. Excavations at Smolensk in the western USSR have begun to increase our knowledge of early medieval Russia. Stone and timber houses and five churches of the Pre-Mongol period have been discovered; colourful frescoes imitating Byzantine silks were found attached to the lower parts of the church walls.

Smyrna [ancient Izmir]. One of the largest late classical and early BYZANTINE sea ports of western Asia Minor. The early remains are now mostly covered by the modern city and so very little archaeological investigation has been possible, but historical sources have illuminated many aspects of its Byzantine period. The ancient city walls and their inscriptions have been studied and it seems that they were rebuilt and remodelled at various times during and after the 6th century. A new aqueduct was constructed in the 5th or 6th century, while it is apparent that the Roman roads radiating from the town centre were used and maintained throughout this time. Excavations in the classical period AGORA have established that this was also reoccupied. The chronicler Procopius relates that in the reign of Justinian (r. 527-65) the town was rebuilt after an earthquake, with new bath blocks and latrines, while a new mole and lighthouse were constructed in the harbour. Smyrna was captured by the Arabs in 654 and 672, but continued to prosper as an important bishopric and thriving naval and commercial centre until the 11th century.

snails. MOLLUSCS of the class Gastropoda. Many species of gastropod exist, adapted to life in the sea, fresh water and on land. Land snail shells are frequently preserved in BURIED SOILS, the fills of DITCHES, and other deposits over limestone subsoils. They are not preserved in the wet and acid conditions which determine the survival of POLLEN. Conversely, pollen is not preserved in the well-drained, base-rich environment of the lowland limestones, and so land snails fill a considerable gap in environmental reconstruction. The main factor governing snail ecology is water loss. Snails have a variety of strategies for avoiding drying-out during the day. Some spend their lives in water, or in marshy areas; others, the 'shade-loving' species, live only under vegetation cover, often burrowing through the leaf litter on top of the soil. The 'open-country' snails have adapted to life away from dense cover, reducing their water loss by thicker shells, specialized behaviour or physiological mechanisms. In addition, there are 'intermediate' or 'catholic' species that live in a variety of habitats, shaded and open. These include many of the more common species of snail. Using these categories of snail ecology the relative frequencies of shell fragments from different species, extracted from deposits and soils, can be used to reconstruct ancient environments. Snails do

not travel far, and can only be used to investigate local changes in vegetation cover, but the method has been used with success at a number of sites, notably NEOLITHIC monuments on the chalklands of southern England.

Snaketown. An important HOHOKAM site in the lower Gila River valley, Arizona, USA, excavated by Emil Haury in 1964-5. A strong MESOAMERICAN influence is apparent throughout its occupation and architectural features include both the platform mound and the ball court. The site, occupied from the beginning of the Pioneer period to the end of the Sedentary (c300 BC to AD 1100), supported an average of 100 dwellings at any one time. Some time in the 12th century it was abandoned in favour of scattered village sites elsewhere in the valley.

Snettisham. Find-spot in Norfolk, eastern England, of a hoard of fine late Iron Age metalwork, dated to the 1st century BC. The hoard consisted of 58 TORCS (7 of gold, 48 of the silver-gold alloy, electrum, and 3 of bronze), a gold bracelet, and 159 coins (14 of gold and 145 of potin, the copper-tin alloy otherwise known as speculum). Some of the torcs were of very elaborate construction. The finest of the electrum ones was made of eight twisted strands of electrum wire and each strand was itself made of eight strands; the terminals were decorated in relief and one contained a Gallo-Belgic coin of the late 1st century BC.

Soan. The Soan River area in the upper Punjab in India has revealed a larged number of PALAEOLITHIC stone tools. Some series (Pre-Soan) lack hand axes, others have hand axes or LEVALLOIS flakes (Late Soan). Their age is poorly fixed, but is probably over half a million years for some of the material.

soapstone. Another name for STEATITE.

Society Islands. A major archipelago in eastern POLYNESIA, with two geographical sub-groups: Windward (Tahiti and Moorea) and Leeward (Raiatea, Huahine, Borabora, Tahaa, Maupiti). The islands were settled around AD 500 by Polynesians who developed a group of colourful chiefdoms, first recorded by Europeans after 1767. Important early sites include the MAUPITI BURIAL GROUND and the site of VAITO·OTIA on Huahine, and later sites are mainly complexes of MARAE and house pavements (*see* OPUNOHU, MAEVA, MAHAIATEA). The island of Raiatea was regarded as a source of religion and ritual by eastern Polynesians for centuries (*see* TAPUTA-PUATEA), but by European contact this island had fallen under the control of the neighbouring smaller island of Borabora.

Sohar. The principal town of the Batina coast of Oman in the SĀSSANIAN and early Islamic periods. The site had perennial water and enjoyed a plentiful supply of agricultural products, especially dates. The Wadi Jizzi provided a corridor for communications with Buraimi oasis in the interior. Although it lacked a sheltered harbour, the city owed its wealth to maritime trade. It stood on the edge of the monsoon belt and so formed a natural springboard for ships from BASRA and SIRAF bound for the east. (Before the rise of Sohar, Raysut in Dhofar performed this function; after the decline, the role was assumed by Tiz, on the coast of Makran.) The early history of Sohar is obscure, but in the 3rd century it became the centre of the Sassanian enclave known as Mazun. Sohar only became prominent in the 10th century, when Omani merchants were noted in China, the East Indies and Africa. The Omanis emerged as a major political force in 943, when their navy raided Basra, a performance they repeated in 952-3. As a result, the Buyid rulers of Iran and Iraq responded in kind, established a garrison in Oman and in 972-3 attacked and destroyed Sohar.

Sohr Damb. *See* NAL.

soil. Material which has been subject to soil-forming processes. A prerequisite for soil formation is the growth of vegetation. Gradual colonization, first by lichens and then by higher plants causes a parallel build-up of organic matter — HUMUS — in the developing soil. Weathering of the underlying parent material provides finely divided minerals. CLAY minerals form complexes with humus. These complexes act as reservoirs of nutrients, essential to plant growth, which become adsorbed on to their surface. Water from rainfall, entering the top of a soil PROFILE, drains down the soil, taking with it nutrients and sometimes parts of the clay/humus complexes. The type of vegetation, the fauna of small animals that lives in the soil, the type of parent material, the way in which the clay/humus complexes behave, the amount of rainfall and the quality of drainage all go to determine the type of soil that develops.

The study of soils is called pedology. In archaeology, pedology may be applied to soils in a particular region, or it may be used to investigate the BURIED SOILS which are found underneath RAMPARTS and BARROWS. Studies of the way soils have developed may allow a reconstruction of the environmental changes which have taken place. There are many different soil types throughout the world, developing under different climatic regimes and floras, and on various parent materials. Several complicated soil classification systems exist. Amongst the main soil types which an archaeologist is likely to encounter in Europe are the brown earths (which include BROWN FOREST SOILS and SOLS LESSIVÉS), PODZOLS, GLEYED soils and primitive soils (including the ranker and RENDZINA).

soil conductivity meter. One design of ELEC-TROMAGNETIC SURVEYING equipment.

soil marks. Pits and ditches may be revealed on AERIAL PHOTOGRAPHS by the different colour of their fill, in contrast to the surrounding subsoil. Soil marks show up particularly well in ploughed fields, but are sometimes apparent even under a crop.

solifluction [solifluxion]. *See* PERIGLACIAL.

sol lessivé. The type of SOIL which may develop under open vegetation, or under arable fields, normally in areas of relatively low annual rainfall, where the soil may dry out during the summer. Sols lessivés seem usually to have originated from BROWN FOREST SOILS which have been stripped of their protective tree canopy and have had nutrients removed by grazing and cultivation of crops. Under these conditions, CLAY may be washed down the PROFILE to be re-deposited as an ILLUVIAL HORIZON further down. Sols lessivés are often difficult to identify, but they are the dominant soil type of much of lowland Britain, where forest was cleared to make way for agriculture.

Solo Man. *See* NGANDONG.

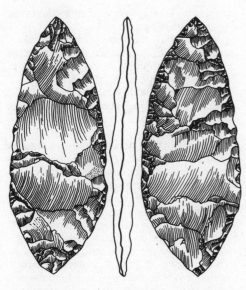

Solutrian pressure-flaked leaf point from France

Solomon Islands. A chain of large islands in the centre of MELANESIA. Dates for earliest settlement remain unknown, but widely distributed PAPUAN languages suggest that the islands were inhabited before the beginning of AUSTRONESIAN expansion into Oceania (c3000 BC). Archaeological sequences are best known from the northern and southern extremities of the chain; the Santa Cruz islands in the south have very fine LAPITA assemblages dating to c1500-500 BC, and the island of Buka in the north has a continuous sequence from late Lapita (c500 BC) through successive localized ceramic phases (similar to the MANGAASI tradition of Vanuatu) to recent times.

Solutrian, Solutré. A site in the Sâone-et-Loire, central France, with PALAEOLITHIC occupation on the slope below a craggy hill. Above MOUSTERIAN deposits come AURIGNACIAN, later PERIGORDIAN, Solutrian (of which Solutré is the name site) and MAGDALENIAN. Only the results of the most recent excavations are at all reliable.

Somerset Levels. The low-lying areas of Somerset in southwest England where marshy conditions led to the formation of peat, which has grown over a period of more than 4000 years. In the process it has preserved remains of human activity, as well as environmental evidence. Peat-cutting exposed remains of ancient trackways in a number of places and in the 1970s a Somerset Levels project was established to investigate the remains preserved by the peat. With the help of techniques such as POLLEN ANALYSIS and RADIOCARBON DATING it has been possible to establish the sequence of development, both climatic and in terms of human usage, in this area. Permanent settlement occurred only on small 'islands' raised above the level of the marsh (e.g. GLASTONBURY and MEARE), but wooden tracks crossed the wet areas. The earliest discovered is the Sweet track (named after the peat-cutter who found it) dated to c2800 bc (c3600 BC); after that tracks continued to be built at various times in the 3rd millennium bc. Subsequently there was a long hiatus in track construction, perhaps because drier conditions made them unnecessary, but with climatic deterioration in the Late Bronze Age there was a new phase of track construction c900-450 bc (c1100-500 BC).

Somme Bionne. A chariot burial of the Early LA TÈNE Iron Age, in the Marne area of France, dated to the late 5th century BC. The burial, presumably of a chieftain, was under a large barrow and was equipped with very rich grave goods, both imported objects and locally manufactured items. The imported items include a Greek RED-FIGURE KYLIX and ETRUSCAN beaked wine flagons of bronze.

Somrong Sen. A 4.5-metre-thick occupation mound near the Tonle Sap Lake in central Cambodia, which has yielded a rich Neolithic assemblage of incised pottery, bone and shell tools and ornaments. The bulk of the deposit predates 1000 BC and it appears that a Bronze Age cemetery may also have been found on the site in the last century, but the finds from this site have been lost.

sondage. A trench of limited area, sunk through the layers of an archaeological site, to make a preliminary investigation of its STRATIGRAPHY.

Song [Sung]. Chinese dynasty (AD 960-1279). During the Northern Song (960-1126) the capital was at Kaifeng near the Yellow River in Henan province. During the Southern Song (1127-1279) it was at Hangzhou (near modern Shanghai), and North China was ruled first by the barbarian Jin dynasty of the Jürched and then by the Mongols, who overthrew the Jin in 1234.

Antiquarian studies flourished in Song China. Large collections of antiques, particularly ancient bronzes, were formed, and Song scholars published many catalogues and epigraphic works, notably *Kaogu tu* (1092), which lists objects from a large number of private collections, and *Bo gu tulu* (*c*1123), a catalogue of the Song imperial collection. From Song times until the first scientific excavations in the 20th century the study of antiquities in China was concerned chiefly with inscriptions. The present-day nomenclature of bronze RITUAL VESSELS is owed largely to the work of Song epigraphers.

Songze [Sung-tse]. *See* MAJIABANG.

Son Vi. The 'Sonviian' stone industry of the Red River valley in north VIETNAM is regarded by modern Vietnamese archaeologists as the immediate predecessor (or an early stage) of the HOABINHIAN. The industry is of late Pleistocene date (radiocarbon dates *c*16,000-9000 bc).

Sopot-Lengyel. Term defined by S. Dimitrijević to denote the later NEOLITHIC sites of Srem, north Bosnia and east Slavonia, Yugoslavia, in the period of *c*4300-3700 bc. The pottery of this group shares affinities with the dark burnished ware tradition of the south Balkans and the incised and monochrome tradition of the north Balkans. While few cemeteries are known, settlement evidence — either from TELLS such as Sopot or open sites — is plentiful and indicates a preference for lowland valleys.

Soroki. A group of short-lived settlement sites of the Late MESOLITHIC and Early NEOLITHIC, located on the middle reaches of the River Dnieper in Moldavia, USSR. The Mesolithic sites, with radiocarbon dates of *c*5500-5400 bc, are 20-cm thick layers with hearths containing layers of shells and fishbones and working hollows. Forest game, especially red and roe deer and pig, was hunted with the aid of the domestic dog. In the Early Neolithic BUG-DNIESTER sites, dated *c*4800 bc, 10-50 cm-thick layers are found, with hearths and shallow pits. The subsistence economy is similar to the preceding Mesolithic, with the addition of some cultivated einkorn wheat and some domesticated cattle and pig.

Sotka Koh. A western outpost of the HARAPPAN CIVILIZATION close to the Makran coast. It is situated on a rocky outcrop and at least partly surrounded by a stone wall.

Soufli. An Early NEOLITHIC settlement in Thessaly, northern Greece. It is especially well known for having produced a rare piece of monumental sculpture depicting a more than life-size woman wearing a skirt and necklace.

Sounion [Roman Sunium]. Byron's 'Sunium's marbled steep' is a classical sanctuary site on a rocky headland some 70 km southeast of ATHENS. It is famous for the standing columns of its mid-5th century BC marble temple to Poseidon, which make a dramatic sight and give the location its alternative title of Cape Kolones. Use of the sanctuary probably goes back to the 7th or 8th century BC, and it was traditionally popular as a refuge with runaway slaves. The Cape offered natural harbouring, but was also vulnerable to pirate and enemy attack, and was fortified in 413 BC by a substantial wall enclosing the headland. A ship shed has been discovered in the vicinity. The local township of Sounion was traditionally reckoned wealthy, and there is evidence for inhabited houses from the 5th century BC to the Roman period. The marble Poseidon Temple was preceded by a limestone version, drums of which are still extant. This earlier structure was apparently demolished by the invading Persians in their attack of 480 BC (*see* SALAMIS). North of the main sanctuary lies a smaller sacred area (*temenos*) which encloses the remains of two modest temples, one dedicated to Athena Sounias, the colonnade of which seems to have been limited to the front and one side only.

Sousse. Islamic Sousse [Roman Hadrumetum] on the Tunisian coast was still a minor settlement in 821-2, when the Aghlabid ruler Ziyadat Allah built the *ribat*, a stronghold for volunteers dedicated to the holy war against the infidel. It is a square fort, 39 metres across, with towers (one of which is a minaret) and a gatehouse. The ground floor contains barracks and magazines; the upper storey includes a mosque. Sousse also possesses one of the oldest free-standing mosques in the Maghreb:

that of Bu Fatata, built in 838-41. It consists of a square chamber divided into nine compartments, as at BALKH, entered through a portico. The facade has a monumental kufic inscription. The town expanded in the 9th century; the Great Mosque was built in 850-1 and by 859 work was in progress on the city wall. The original mosque (subsequently altered) had a courtyard surrounded on three sides by a single arcade, and a sanctuary with a T-shaped plan, as for example at QAIRAWAN. The walls of Sousse enclose a trapezoidal area with maximum dimensions of 730 by 500 metres. The walls are constructed of coursed masonry, and have a curtain with a rampart walk supported on vaulted recesses, and rectangular towers. One tower, however, is a minaret, similar to that of Qairawan.

Southampton. Hamwih (or Hamton), the 8th- and 9th-century predecessor of medieval Southampton, is situated to the east of the later town opposite the Roman site of Bitterne (Clausentum) on the banks of the River Itchen in southern England. Hamwih was discovered in the 19th century by brick-earth diggers. Excavations of the site in 1946-50 revealed a wealth of West Saxon and traded CAROLINGIAN artefacts. Subsequent open-area excavations since the 1960s have demonstrated that Hamwih was a very large Middle Saxon settlement which once covered more than 40 hectares; a drastic economic decline terminated its life in the later 9th century.

Much of the topography of the early town has now been established; it had a gridded street plan, tenement divisions, and several post-built structures including a boat-shaped house. There were also extensive areas of storage pits, at least four cemeteries and possibly two contemporary churches. The unique collection of imported pottery, glass, coins and other traded goods recovered demonstrate its strong contacts with Carolingia, while the rich faunal evidence suggests the economic importance of the local Hampshire basin and marine resources. Contemporary documentary sources imply that a royal site may have existed alongside Hamwih but archaeologists have not yet succeeded in finding it.

South Cadbury. This site in Somerset, southwest England, is one of the more important secular Dark Age sites in Britain. It is essentially an Iron Age HILL FORT with a complex history of abandonment and refortification continuing throughout the prehistoric, Roman and medieval periods. The 16th-century antiquarian John Leyland first recognized South Cadbury's links with the Dark Ages and named it as Camelot, thus initiating its romantic associations with the Arthurian legend (*see* ARTHUR). Extensive excavations between 1966 and 1970 examined both the defences and the interior of the settlement. They revealed that the Iron Age fort was re-occupied and refurbished during the Romano-British period, when a small temple was built. The next phase of reoccupation has been dated by well-stratified deposits of Mediterranean imported pottery to around 470, and during this period the whole settlement was drastically remodelled. The Arthurian defences were very substantial indeed, covering most of the hill top, and consisted of a dry-stone wall with revetment and timber breastwork enclosed in an elaborate wooden framework. The two gateways which covered the original Roman entrances were in the form of raised fighting platforms overlying passageways. The interior of the settlement contained a timber hall measuring 19 by 10 metres, divided by a single partition with a pair of doorways in the long sides. This occupation phase lasted until about 557. The fort was used again in 1010 and 1017 by King Aethelred II and his forces when they were under Danish attack. Further additions and alterations were made to the enceinte at that time, and a cruciform church and a mint were also built.

Southern Cult, Southeastern Ceremonial Complex. A complex of artistic themes and cultural material, often death-related, which occurred over a wide area in the eastern USA, most often in MISSISSIPPIAN contexts. Common motifs such as the hand/eye symbol, the feathered serpent, the skull and long bone, and depictions of SACRIFICE support the frequently postulated idea of a MESOAMERICAN influence. Characteristic artefacts such as monolithic ceremonial axes, effigy jars, and worked shell objects have been found in abundance at the major CEREMONIAL CENTRES at ETOWAH, Georgia, SPIRO, Oklahoma, and Moundville, Alabama. The cult's climax occurred between 1200 and 1400, but it had virtually disappeared by the time of the first European explorers.

Sozudai. A Palaeolithic site in Oita Prefecture on Kyushu, Japan. A few hundred tools, mostly of quartzite, were recovered from a secondary deposit on a marine terrace during excavations in 1964. They include hand axes, scrapers and flakes. The geological age of the deposit suggests that the tools could be as much as 70,000 years old.

spacer plate. A specialized large flat bead with a number of parallel perforations, used to hold apart the multiple strands of complex necklaces. They occur in the European Bronze Age, when they were commonly made of amber, jet or faience. Very similar amber examples have been found in regions as distant as MYCENAEAN Greece, southern Germany and southern England and are often taken as indicators of long range trade.

Spanish Levant Art. A series of rock shelters in the arid region of Mediterranean Spain (the Spanish Levant) has paintings in red and black. The scenes depicted are quite unlike the true PALAEOLITHIC art of the last ice age. There are a number of scenes of hunters chasing their prey, but perhaps the most fascinating are scenes of what seem to be war dances, honey gathering, ceremonies and nature observations, which give some clue of the character of everyday life. The figures are all blocked in as silhouettes in a single colour. This art was probably painted in the period between the end of the last ice age and the arrival of the first farmers and thus is Mesolithic. *See also* ALPERA.

Sparta. A small town in the central Peloponnese, Greece, which in the classical period created the Peloponnesian League and organized the military and financial forces that broke the Athenian empire and subjugated ATHENS (405 BC). Today's remains are very sparse, and offer wry fulfilment to Thucydides' prophecy (Book I) that posterity would never guess at Sparta's power from the meagre remains of her monuments. Although this site has some Late Helladic IIIB material, MYCENAEAN Sparta (if there was such a place) must be elsewhere, perhaps at the so-called Menelaion or Amyklaion. For the early development of Sparta, it is perhaps ironic that much of our evidence should come from the Sanctuary of Artemis Ortheia, which was to become the setting for the ritual whipping of Spartan youth. One interpretation of this and similar archaeological evidence suggests that Sparta is not culturally odd much before the 5th century BC, but rather shares in general Greek trends such as, for instance, participating in the overall aesthetic renaissance, welcoming foreign craftsmen and producing her own distinguished artists. At the end of the 6th century BC, however, imports and exports seem to be interrupted — perhaps heralding the Sparta familiar from 5th-century and later literature. These literary sources themselves split two ways: the hostile critic paints a stereotype that reflects the fear felt by many city-states who saw the Spartan military machine as a force arraigned against civilization; while the admirer tends uncritically to exaggerate the perfection and value of her self-imposed rigour. Some of the elements in Spartan society known to us from these records can, it is true, be seen as a conservative retention of tribal features, or as a venial failure to abandon traditional values and adapt; these would be, for example, the retention of a federated village (rather than urban) structure; of iron-bar currency; of rule by two kings, ephors and elders; of privilege by a few blue-blooded Spartans (Spartiatai) though vastly outnumbered by a subject population of serf-like Helots. But other facets, such as the extremist dedication to physical training and the martial arts, the separation of males to live in communal messes, the flogging of youths to inculcate discipline and physical hardness, the suspicion of music and the arts as decadent and corrupting, the castigation of urban building and improvement as wasteful — all of these suggest a doctrinaire commitment to a consciously imposed frame of idealism. Plato, for example, in the *Republic*, comes near to advocating precisely some of these reforms. The possibility follows that the entire framework, including all the elements categorized as traditional above, was deliberately introduced at the beginning of the 5th century BC as a programme of moral reform, a return to moral values, the whole scheme being justified by reference back to a suitably mythical lawgiver, in this case Lycurgus.

The HELLENISTIC period saw a decline attributable — according to views expressed in antiquity and since — either to a collapse of moral fibre, or as just retribution against barbarism. The early Roman empire saw an unexpected revival, and in the 2nd century AD a weird latter-day re-staging of Sparta's martial and educational rituals, encouraged by the emperor Septimus Severus. A theatre was built for tourists — a kind of moral voyeurism. The town was finally destroyed by Alaric and the GOTHS in 395 AD.

spatial analysis. The analysis of the way in which things, finds, sites etc are distributed in space. A wide variety of mathematical techniques is used for this purpose, many of them looking for patterns and groupings.

spelt. *See* WHEAT.

sphinx. In Ancient Egyptian, Hittite and early Greek art, a representation of a human head on the body of a crouched lion. In Egypt, sphinxes were held to guard temples and tombs from intruders; they often bore the features of a pharaoh and the great rock-cut sphinx at GIZA, 80 metres long and 20 metres high, is believed to represent Khafra [Chephren], the fourth pharaoh of the 4th Dynasty (*r. c*2520 BC).

Spiennes. A flint-mining site of the later Neolithic MICHELSBERG culture in Belgium. These flint mines show strong similarities to the British Neolithic flint mines and were worked in similar ways, with the use of bone and antler picks. Flint from the Spiennes mines was traded quite widely in northwest Europe.

Spina. An important pre-Roman port on the northern Adriatic, now some 10 km inland. Although Greeks were to form a dominant part of the population, the town was probably an ETRUSCAN foundation of the late 6th century BC, belonging to the period of rapid Etruscan northward expansion into the Po Valley. Together with a settlement at ADRIA, to which the Etruscans may have linked it by canal, Spina was a focal link between the markets of Etruria and the Po plain, and Greek shipping in the Adriatic. Cemeteries have yielded large amounts of pottery, especially Athenian RED-FIGURE WARE, terracottas, Etruscan bronzes, western Greek and Etruscan jewellery, faience and amber, which are collected together at Ferrara Museum. The town also kept a Treasury at DELPHI. The site, which is confirmed by aerial photography, shows a town well adapted to the marshy and

flooded conditions, with palisades, earth ramparts and a network of canals. There was a grid plan, and dwellings were of wood, constructed probably on sandbanks supported by wooden piles. Celtic invasion of the north of Italy led to the town's desertion in the 3rd century BC.

Spirit Cave. An important HOABINHIAN site in northwestern THAILAND (*c*10,000-6000 bc), which has yielded many plant remains (BETEL NUT, pepper, GOURD, Chinese water chestnut, amongst others) which have led to suggestions that Hoabinhians in this area may have practised incipient forms of horticulture. The upper layer of the site (*c*6000 bc) yielded pottery and ground stone adzes and knives; these are the earliest convincingly dated Neolithic artefacts from Southeast Asia.

Spiro. A major CEREMONIAL CENTRE of the Caddoan subculture of the MISSISSIPPIAN tradition, the climax of which was *c*1350-1400. Because of its abundance of paraphernalia of the SOUTHERN CULT, it is often linked to the centres at ETOWAH and Moundville, even though it is culturally distinct from them. The site comprised a village and eight mounds, the largest of which had been used for burials as well as a temple platform. Unfortunately its archaeological value has been considerably diminished, since it was heavily vandalized during a period of commercial exploitation in the 1930s.

Spišský Štvrtov. An earlier Bronze Age HILL-FORT of the FÜZESABONY culture, dated to the mid-2nd millennium bc and located near Myšia Hôrka in southern Slovakia. A partly encircling stone wall over 160 metres long defends the site on the east side, where the main entrance is flanked by tower-like bastions. In the fort interior, 26 houses are arranged around a 'village square'. These two-storey timber structures had below-ground chests containing gold and bronze objects. Bronze workshops are known, as well as a ritual area where a rhomboidal stone upright lies near two inurned cremations.

Split. Properly the great palace built by Diocletian (a native of the area), to which he retired in 305 AD, and which subsequently became nucleus for the medieval and modern city of Split in Yugoslavia. This should be distinguished from Salona (some 6 km inland) which had been the prosperous capital of the Roman imperial province of DALMATIA, and earlier still, capital of native Illyricum. Roman Salona shows some imperial-period ruins including evidence for an AQUEDUCT, THEATRE, AMPHITHEATRE and bath buildings. But Salona was an important church centre in the 4th-6th centuries, and is remarkable for its early Christian basilicas (with mosaic decoration) and cemeteries. Although Christian Salona came under the protection of the Eastern Empire, it was attacked and devastated in about 613 AD by Avars and Slavs, when the surviving population fled to the protection of Diocletian's Palace at Split. This was a fortress-style structure with great limestone walls some 20 metres high, 16 towers and splendid gates. These walls enclosed colonnaded streets, a vaulted temple, domed MAUSOLEUM and a residential section.

Spondylus gaederopus. A type of mollusc found only in the Mediterranean, the shell of which was used during the Early Neolithic to make simple ornaments such as bracelets and necklaces. Spondylus shell ornaments were traded from the Mediterranean into temperate Europe, occurring in contexts of the FIRST

A) Stirrup-spout vessels
B) Spout-and-bridge vessels

TEMPERATE NEOLITHIC and LINEAR POTTERY cultures.

spout-and-bridge vessel. A distinctive vessel form popular among southern coastal Peruvian cultures (e.g. PARACAS) with antecedents in the INITIAL PERIOD ceramics of the Hacha complex. Typically it is a closed kettle-shaped vessel, but its defining characteristic is a pair of vertical tubular spouts joined to each other by a strip or bridge. Sometimes, however, one spout terminates as a whistle or as a modelled life figure. It was particularly popular with the NASCA and CHIMU but has been found in many other New World contexts.

Spring and Autumn period. The earlier part, 770-476 BC, of the Eastern Zhou period. *See* ZHOU.

Spy. The first complete NEANDERTHAL skeletons were found during early excavations of the MOUSTERIAN levels of the Spy cave not far from Liège, Belgium, in the 1880s. Both a male and a female are represented, though the bones are damaged and incomplete. It was only after these discoveries that it was recognized that Neanderthal man was associated with the Mousterian.

Square-mouthed pottery. Name given to the type of pottery found in the Middle Neolithic of northern Italy and to the culture in which it occurs. The characteristic shape is achieved by taking a round pot while it is still wet and pinching its mouth to produce a roughly square shape. *See also* CHIOZZA, QUINZANO.

Squier, E.G. (1821-88). American journalist who, together with his colleague E.H. DAVIS, made a study of the prehistoric mounds of the eastern USA. Their book *Ancient Monuments of the Mississippi Valley*, published in 1848, contained detailed description and classification of the mounds, but concluded that they were constructed by a lost race of mound-builders, who had migrated away from the area (perhaps to Mexico), rather than by the ancestors of the surviving American Indians of the area.

Śrikshetra. The ancient name for Prome in Lower Burma, the historical centre of gravity of the PYUS. Here, a Pyu Theravada Buddhist colony existed as early as the 5th century, and a dynasty of Pyu kings bearing Sanskrit names reigned in the 7th and 8th centuries. The architecture of Śrīkshetra shows influences from northeastern India and ORISSA.

Śrivijaya. An ancient SUMATRAN kingdom centred on Palembang, which came into being at the end of the 7th century and developed rapidly. This development may be linked with the dismemberment of FUNAN. First mentioned by the Chinese pilgrim I-Ching as an important centre of Buddhist learning and a relay station on the way to India, it soon controlled both the Sunda and Malaccan Straits and became the dominant power in the region. From the 9th century on the kingdom was ruled by the ŚAILENDRAS; it came to an end in the 14th century.

stadial. A short period of colder climate during a GLACIATION, usually implying the growth of ice-sheets or glaciers. *See* DEVENSIAN, WEICHSELIAN, WISCONSIN.

stadium [Greek *stadion*]. In classical Greece, a track for foot-races and other athletic events, perhaps about 200 metres long, and some 10 metres or so wide. In the Greek examples there is some evidence for a post at the 'far' end and some rounding of the course at this point, while the 'start' seems to have remained square. Seating was probably on raised embankments along the two sides and round the turning end. Confusion often arises with later Roman remodelling, and with the Roman CIRCUS to which the Greek *stadion* is ancestor.

stained glass. Fragments of stained glass have been recovered from excavations of early BYZANTINE churches and the two NORTHUMBRIAN Middle Saxon monastaries of Monkwearmouth and JARROW. The first complete surviving stained glass windows date to the 12th century, when Abbot Suger, in his design of St Denis Priory, made a statement fundamental to Gothic architecture: that the light of God should flow into his house through large glass-filled windows. From this time onwards centres of glass production flourished in Europe, in towns like CHARTRES, Bourges, Paris, Canterbury, York and Lincoln. The basic elements of a stained glass window are pieces of glass fused with colour individually set into lead frames, which are then combined into a design held together by solid lead bars or armatures. The production technique was improved with time, although this was at the expense of aesthetic quality. Early Gothic windows have a rich, carpet-like mosaic quality, enhanced by strong colouring, particularly reds and blues, and a descriptive, narrative quality engendered by the many small circular medallions illustrating bible stories in the main windows. The more open, larger windows of later gothic buildings encouraged a fashion for full length canopied saints surrounded by prominent borders and heraldic motifs. This was combined with a new desire for brighter and lighter windows affected by natural backgrounds, and the invention of silver *grisaille* and pale yellow glass (popular for hair) in the 14th century. By the Renaissance period stained glass was treated much like a painter's canvas, as a medium for full-scale graphic art depicting scenes and events.

stakehole. A small conical hole in the ground, made by hammering in a stake. Stakeholes are a common feature of some archaeological sites and may be distinguished from POSTHOLES mainly by their shape and size.

Stamford ware. Some time during the 9th century the pottery industries centred in and around Stamford in Lincolnshire, central England, started producing the first ANGLO-SAXON glazed ceramics. The Stamford industry, which operated until the 13th century, specialized in glazed, buff fine wares including characteristic spouted pitchers and jugs which were much in demand in England and were sometimes traded abroad.

stamnos. Type of Classical Greek vase, similar in size to the AMPHORA, and likewise used typically for the storage of wine. The *stamnos*, however, is more squat in form, with two horizontal handles. The shape is popular with Athenian RED-FIGURE vase-painters in the period from about 525 to 400 BC, and in Etruria in the 4th century BC.

standard deviation. A measure of the scatter about the MEAN in a DISTRIBUTION. The values of 68 per cent of cases fall within one standard deviation either side of the mean, 95 per cent between two, and 99 per cent between three standard deviations. The plus-or-minus of a

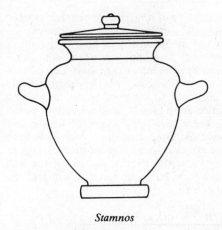

Stamnos

RADIOCARBON DATE works in a similar way to a standard deviation, but is not strictly the same thing and should perhaps be called a 'probable error'.

Stanegate. Roman road in northern England from the Tyne at CORBRIDGE to the Solway at Carlisle, whose construction is attributed to Agricola, c80 AD. Originally a military trunk route, it also acted as line of fortification with forts spaced at intervals of one day's, or half a day's, march. This function was taken over by the construction of HADRIAN'S WALL (122-8) and Stanegate became a service road, providing supply and communications back-up. Its forts then acted as depots.

Stanwick. The largest Iron Age HILLFORT in Britain, situated near Richmond, Yorkshire. It appears to have been constructed entirely in the 1st century AD and is interpreted by the excavator, Sir Mortimer WHEELER, as the capital of the Brigantes tribe, constructed by their leader, Venutius, for his revolt against the Romans after AD 50. The site began as a small fortified enclosure known as the Tofts and not very long afterwards an extension of c50 hectares was added, defended by a stone-faced rampart and a wide flat-bottomed ditch with vertical sides, cut in the solid rock. Still later a further 240 hectares was included in a new enclosure to the south, which was never completed. The whole complex may have been designed to protect not only the people, but also the livestock — including horses — of a basically pastoralist economy. Some time between AD 69 and 72 Stanwick fell to the Romans and the site was abandoned.

Staraja Ladoga. The major north Russian town of Staraja Ladoga was founded in the 10th century on the left bank of the river Volkhow, 20 km from its outlet in Lake Ladoga close to the eastern end of the Baltic Sea. Excavations have revealed that the early town covered at least 9000 square metres and was enclosed by a strong earthen bank. Although Scandinavian material has been discovered here, the Russians firmly contend that the town is Slavic in character and origin. It is seen by many as the precursor of NOVGOROD.

Star Carr. This site in the Vale of Pickering in Yorkshire, northern England, was a lake-side MESOLITHIC camp of MAGLEMOSEAN or Duvensee type dated to c7500 bc. The organic mud deposits ensured the preservation of wooden objects as well as carved bone and antler, especially barbed points, hitherto rarely found in context.

Starčevo. The type site for the Yugoslav aspect of the Early Neolithic FIRST TEMPERATE NEO-LITHIC culture. Starčevo was first excavated in 1928-9 and 1933-5. On the basis of these early excavations, V. Milojčić published a four-fold typological division of the Starčevo culture. This scheme has proved inaccurate in the light of recent excavations at Starčevo, which indicated that the type site was dated entirely to the late phase of the Starčevo culture (c4900-4600 bc).

Staré Mesto. A settlement in the March Valley in Poland. Archaeologists have excavated the 9th-century fortified citadel with its stone-and-mortar church and collection of wealthy graves. During the 10th century, at the time of the Great Moravian culture, Staré Mesto was a great industrial centre, specializing in the production of high-quality gold work. The 10th-century cemetery has proved interesting as it seems to have been used by all the inhabitants, from nobles to peasants.

Staroselje. A rock shelter in the Crimean lime-stone region of the southern USSR. In excavations in 1953 and 1954 MOUSTERIAN levels were removed. Most of the skeleton of a baby of perhaps one-and-a-half years of age was recovered, demonstrating that the general shape of NEANDERTHAL babies' skulls seems to be very similar to modern skull shape. A few pieces of an adult female were also found.

statistics. The study of numerical facts. Artefacts, sites, skulls, items etc are reduced to a series of measurements, analytically determined values or systematic observations which can be represented as numbers. The DISTRIBUTIONS of items with respect to these VARIABLES can then be studied. A wide variety of statistics, quantities summarizing the distributions, may be calculated (e.g. MEAN and STANDARD DEVIATION) and are themselves compared, as representatives of the distributions. This may determine the degree of similarity between distributions. Various statistical 'tests' can also be carried out to determine the 'reality' of any differences or similarities. Best-known of these are the Chi Square test and Student's 't' test. The degree of relationship (CORRELATION) between variables may also be calculated. Most conventional statistics of this kind are carried out on one or two variables. Large numbers of variables can be treated by MULTIVARIATE ANALYSIS.

Any kind of statistics must be applied carefully to archaeological information. Most procedures involve some kind of assumption and clear thought is required as to how valid it may be. Of prime concern is any assumption that the SAMPLE which remains, after the ravages of time and archaeologists, is representative of the original population of artefacts, sites, animals or plants. Archaeology is by its very nature unable to test this and any archaeological conclusions, even if nonstatistical, are subject to uncertainty as a result.

statue-menhir. A standing stone carved to represent the human form, usually in highly stylized form. Although human statues occur in many parts of the world, this term is used only in prehistoric European contexts. They belong in the main to the Late Neolithic/Copper Age, though Bronze Age and Iron Age examples are also known. The main concentrations of statue-menhirs are in Iberia, southern France, Corsica, Sardinia and Italy. Both female and male examples occur. *See also* MEGALITHIC MONUMENTS (EUROPE).

stave construction. A technique popular as a method of church building in Scandinavia from at least the 9th century. Although it was undoubtedly of similar importance in Britain, only one Anglo-Saxon stave church has survived at Greensted in Essex. The staves were made from split logs which were either placed upright into the ground, curved side out, or into a wooden sill. The uprights would be anchored to the roof beams and sill by mortice-and-tenon joints; they slotted together vertically by means of tongue and groove. At Greensted the corner posts were given extra strength by the use of whole logs. In many cases the interior surface of the wall would have been plastered to conceal the timber wall.

steatite. A rock chiefly composed of the soft mineral talc. Also known as soapstone, steatite is easily carved to make artefacts such as bowls and figurines, and is also a convenient material for MOULD-making.

steel. An ALLOY of IRON with carbon. Steel appears in the archaeological record during the Iron Age and was usually produced by CARBURIZATION of wrought iron (*see* IRON AND STEEL). In this process, the iron is heated in a hearth with charcoal to about 800°C. Carbon diffuses into the surface of the metal to make steel. As only the surface is affected, only thin strips of steel could be made by this method. Some Iron Age artefacts are made of piles of such steel strips, FORGED together. Steel for a cutting edge can be further hardened by QUENCHING, where the red hot metal is plunged into cold water (or other liquid). This makes it very hard, but renders it undesirably brittle. The latter effect is counteracted by TEMPERING — gentle heating (*c*200-300°C) in a hearth. The process of quenching and tempering was known from Roman times but early steels must have been rather too brittle for some uses. Many VIKING swords combined the strength of wrought iron with the hardness of steel. They were made of many strips of the two metals, forged together, a technique known as PATTERN WELDING.

Stein, Sir Aurel (1862-1943). Oriental scholar who travelled widely in central and southern Asia, recording a large number of prehistoric, classical and medieval sites in Iran, India, and especially Central Asia (Chinese Turkestan).

Steinheim. A site near Stuttgart in southwest

Germany, where in 1933 a nearly complete PALAEOLITHIC skull was found in a gravel pit. The level in question dates from well before the MOUSTERIAN, possibly from the HOLSTEIN (penultimate) interglacial some 250,000 or 300,000 years ago. The skull is usually classified as primitive HOMO SAPIENS, and as such it is the earliest complete skull of this type.

Stellmoor. A site near Hamburg, north Germany. The organic muds of late glacial and post-glacial date contain an older level (HAMBURGIAN, like nearby MEIENDORF) and a later level of c8500 bc (AHRENSBURGIAN) with tanged points. The later level is also important for a hoard of pine-wood arrow shafts. Both groups were reindeer-hunters.

Stentinello. A Neolithic ditched village site in southeast Sicily, which has given its name to a variety of IMPRESSED WARE that characterizes the Early Neolithic of Sicily and also of Calabria, on the southwest Italian mainland. The pottery forms are simple, consisting mostly of bowls and jars; the decoration is much more elaborate than on most forms of Impressed Ware, with small impressed and stamped designs arranged in careful and often intricate patterns. Stentinello pottery has radiocarbon dates in the 5th millennium bc and almost certainly continued into the 4th millennium.

Sterkfontein. A site on the Witwatersrand near Johannesburg, South Africa, which is one of the most important hominid sites in southern Africa. The main hominid fossil-bearing level of these collapsed limestone cave (Member 4) has produced numerous remains of the gracile species *Australopithecus africanus*, dating from perhaps 2.5 million years ago or more. A later level, Member 5, of perhaps 1.5-2 million years ago, contained a skull of 'habilis' type and stone tools. Since the TAUNG skull is juvenile, Sterkfontein is often regarded as the type population of *A. africanus*, but even this large series may be unrepresentative as most of the remains seem to be female. *See also* AUSTRALOPITHECUS, HUMAN EVOLUTION, SWARTKRANS.

Steward, Julian Haynes (1902-72). American archaeologist and anthropologist who made major contributions to theoretical

archaeology. His main interest was in the study of culture process and for this he drew on both anthropological and archaeological evidence. He edited the monumental *Handbook of South American Indians* (1946-50) and wrote a number of important works, of which the best-known is his *Theory of Culture Change* (1955).

Stichbandkeramik. *See* STROKE-ORNAMENTED WARE.

Stillbay. A site on the Cape coast of South Africa which yielded a poorly defined stone tool assemblage of 'Middle Stone Age' type. The name Stillbay was formerly used over a wide area of southern and eastern Africa to designate industries of this general type. The term has now been replaced by a series of more local designations, such as BAMBATA in Zimbabwe.

stirrup-spout vessel. An ancient American vessel, with precursors in the INITIAL PERIOD, which usually takes the form of a closed globular jar. Its defining characteristic is a hollow loop (or stirrup) of clay attached to the vessel body at both ends with a tubular spout set into it in a vertical plane, usually at its highest point. Common to many Peruvian cultures (e.g. MOCHE, CHIMU), it was greatly exploited by CHAVIN craftsmen, although it has also been found in many other parts of the New World. *See* illustration, page 479.

stoa. Type of classical Greek building, consisting essentially of a long, straight colonnade, with vertical wall (and sometimes rooms) behind and roof over. The colonnade is sometimes doubled, and a projecting wing may be added to either end. Examples occur from about 650 BC onwards. The type does not seem to have been bound to any particular use or purpose, but an association with the presence of teachers and philosophers led for example to the popular Hellenistic and Roman philosophy of Stoicism taking its name from one famous *stoa*, the Stoa Poikile at ATHENS.

stone. One of the first materials to be used for making artefacts. Very fine grained, or glassy stones, such as flint and OBSIDIAN, were shaped mainly by chipping or flaking. Other less brittle stones had to be hammered or chiselled into shape, and then polished.

Precious and decorative stones were also widely used in antiquity, for example, JADE, CHALCEDONY and SERPENTINE. PETROLOGICAL ANALYSIS of stone has allowed the source materials to be discovered. Studies of Neolithic stone axes in Britain have allowed a network of ancient trade to be reconstructed. Hones, QUERNS and building stones may be investigated in a similar way.

Stone Age. The first age of the THREE AGE SYSTEM, defined by the use of stone for tools. *See also* MESOLITHIC, NEOLITHIC, PALAEOLITHIC.

stone circle. Term for a ring of standing stones, either truly circular or near-circular in shape. Stone circles occur in many parts of the world at different times, but in prehistoric Europe they represent a peculiarly British development. About 900 examples are known throughout Britain and Ireland and datable examples belong to the Late Neolithic to Early Bronze Age. The monuments vary not only in size (from a few metres across to the huge monument of AVEBURY, with a mean diameter of more than 400 metres) but in shape, for as well as true circles there are ellipses and other geometrical forms which have been labelled flattened circles and egg-shaped rings. A variant form called a recumbent stone circle and found mainly in Aberdeenshire has the entrance marked by a recumbent stone, flanked by two uprights. Recent work on the stone circles of Britain has concentrated on geometrical and astronomical aspects of the monuments. Work by Alexander Thom has suggested three important achievements of the communities that built the circles: (1) the use of a standard unit of measurement, known as the megalithic yard; (2) the laying out of the monuments according to certain principles of geometry, perhaps including Pythagoras' theorem; (3) the orientation of many of the monuments on astronomical alignments, involving the rising and setting of the sun, the moon and certain bright stars. There has been much discussion about the validity of these claims and there is no agreement on the subject. Many authorities have challenged the concept of the megalithic yard, the use of Pythagoras' theorem and some of the more extravagant astronomical claims. However, even the most sceptical scholar would find it difficult to deny that the monuments were laid out with great care and with much concern for geometry; it is also difficult to deny that some monuments were clearly concerned with celestial events, but it is perhaps more helpful to regard them not as scientific observatories, but rather as temples where astronomical events were exploited and celebrated. *See also* MEGALITHIC MONUMENTS (EUROPE), ASTRONOMY (EUROPE).

Stonehenge. Situated on Salisbury plain in Wiltshire, southern England, Stonehenge is Britain's most remarkable STONE CIRCLE and one of the most impressive MEGALITHIC MONUMENTS anywhere.

Excavations have revealed three major building stages and some subsidiary substages. The first monument, Stonehenge I, was a HENGE monument, consisting of a bank and outer ditch, with a single entrance. Inside the bank was a ring of 56 pits, named the Aubrey holes after the antiquary John AUBREY who first recorded them; some of these pits contained cremations. Outside the monument, opposite the entrance, was a single standing stone, the Heel Stone. It is not known whether there was any structure or other feature in the centre of the monument at this time, as the area is obscured by later structures. Stonehenge I has dates in the range *c*2800-2300 BC.

The monument of Stonehenge II involved the transportation of 82 bluestones from the Preseli mountains of south Wales (unless they had been transported to the area earlier) and their erection in a double circle in the centre of the henge. The entrance of the monument was realigned at this time and the Avenue was also constructed, consisting of two parallel earthworks running from the entrance of Stonehenge to the River Avon 3 km away; it may represent the last part of the route via which the bluestones arrived at Stonehenge. This building phase is associated with BEAKER pottery and is dated to the late 3rd millennium BC.

Stonehenge III consists of three separate building phases in which the monument acquired its final form. Phase IIIA saw the dismantling of the bluestone monument and the transport and erection of the massive SARSEN stones. These were brought frm the Marlborough Downs near AVEBURY some 30 km away. The enormous blocks, originally about 80 in number and weighing up to 50 tonnes, were carefully dressed to shape and then erected in a circle of uprights with a continuous curving lintel and, inside this circle, a horseshoe of five free-standing TRI-LITHONS. This phase also has a date in the late 3rd millennium BC.

Phases IIIB and IIIC represent successive attempts to incorporate the bluestones into the monument. In IIIB an oval of bluestones was erected in the centre of the monument and the remaining stones were probably intended for a double circle outside the main sarsen monument (the Y and Z holes), but this plan was never completed. In phase IIIC, c1550 BC, the bluestones were put in their final position: the previous oval was converted into a horse-shoe of free-standing stones inside the horseshoe of sarsen trilithons and the remaining stones were placed in a circle inside the sarsen circle. This stage — and perhaps the whole of Stonehenge III — belongs in the period of the WESSEX CULTURE and many of the characteristic Wessex BARROWS occur in the region around Stonehenge. It is reasonable to see the phase III monument as a major religious monument of this culture.

The phase IIIC monument does not represent the end of building at Stonehenge. Work in the 1970s showed that although no more construction work occurred in the monument itself, the Avenue was extended in the Late Bronze Age, indicating that it was still revered and probably in use.

Archaeologists — and others — have long been fascinated by this monument, with its evidence of massive manpower input (one calculation suggests 30 million man-hours would have been required for the phase IIIA structure), its architectural sophistication (once ascribed to hypothetical MYCENAEAN architects) and astronomical alignments (see ASTRONOMY). Most authorities now see it as a purely local development, the culmination of a long tradition of similar structures — a temple dedicated perhaps to sky deities, but a monument to the achievements of a non-literate and technologically simple society, probably organized as a chiefdom or as a group of chiefdoms, with a paramount chief or king as supreme authority.

stoneware. Distinctively hard-fired vessels which were first made at Siegburg near Cologne as early as about 1200 AD. Stoneware involved the firing of pots in excess of 1100°C,

at which point the molecules fuse to form a new stronger structure. Stonewares required particular clays, but the technique made possible the production of durable tablewares.

stratigraphy. The study of sequences of SEDIMENTS, SOILS, structures or rocks. Layered deposits are said to be stratified. The sequence of deposition can be assessed by a study of the relationships of different LAYERS. Any one layer can be said to have been deposited at a later date than those which are stratified underneath. Likewise PITS, POSTHOLES, DITCHES or channels which have been cut into lower layers can be said to have been excavated later than the highest layer which they cut. Dateable artefacts found within layers, and layers or structures which are themselves dateable, can be used to date parts of stratigraphic sequences (see TERMINUS ANTE QUEM, TERMINUS POST QUEM). Stratigraphy is the basis of reconstructing the history of an archaeological site. It is also the basis on which the QUATERNARY geological framework of prehistory has been constructed.

Straubing. A regional group of the Early Bronze Age ÚNĚTICE culture found in Bavaria. It is characterized by flat inhumation cemeteries with grave goods such as simple bronze daggers, awls, torcs, cones of coiled wire and amber beads.

Střelice. A small settlement site of the Late Neolithic LENGYEL culture, located in central Moravia, Czechoslovakia, and dated to the mid-4th millennium bc. Among the rich middle Lengyel ritual assemblage was a fired clay house model showing timber posts and a pitched roof with bucrania attached to the gables, the largest group of anthropomorphic figurines in Moravia, and an amphora with human figures and zoomorphic protomes.

Strettweg. A HALLSTATT burial in eastern Austria of the 7th century BC, famous for one of the grave goods: a miniature bronze wagon, possibly a cult object. The wagon frame bears a group of mounted warriors flanking a much larger naked woman, interpreted as a goddess, holding a bowl above her head.

strigil [Latin: *strigilis*]. A narrow curved scraper, made of horn or metal, used by Roman and Greek bathers for the cleansing of the skin. Romans used them particularly in the hot room (*caldarium*) (*see* BATHS, ROMAN), and this task was often performed by slaves.

striking platform. When a CORE is made of stone for the removal of FLAKES or BLADES, it must have a flat surface against which the hammer is struck to remove the blanks. This is the striking platform. Part of it comes away with each flake.

Stroke-ornamented ware. English name for the German *Stichbandkeramik*, which characterizes the Middle Neolithic culture in Central Europe (southern Poland, Czechoslovakia and parts of southern and central Germany). The pottery is decorated with geometric designs, especially zigzags, made by incision in a series of short strokes rather than continuous lines. Stroke-ornamented ware clearly developed directly out of the earlier LINEAR POTTERY during the later 5th and early 4th millennium bc.

Stukely, William (1687-1765). British antiquary who made quite accurate drawings and descriptions of prehistoric monuments such as AVEBURY and STONEHENGE, containing much useful information about features now destroyed. However, he was afflicted with what Stuart Piggott has called 'Druidomania', attributing all pre-Roman monuments to the Druids — a misconception which has unfortunately persisted in popular understanding.

stupa. An Indian burial monument. Stupas were the tombs of Buddhist holy men and often became shrines. Built of brick or stone, stupas are domed structures, surrounded by a decorated railing. The MAURYAN emperor ASOKA is said to have built 84,000 stupas; one of the most famous is at SANCHI. *See also* BUDDHISM (INDIA).

Sub-Atlantic. A climatic sub-division of the FLANDRIAN, originally supposed to be wet and cold, in contrast to the preceding SUB-BOREAL period. The increased rainfall may be attested in Britain by a change in the PEAT stratigraphy of BOGS (*see* RECURRENCE SURFACE). Godwin's POLLEN ZONE VIII corresponds to the Sub-Atlantic in Britain. The start of Zone VIII was originally defined as the appearance of beech and hornbeam in southern England. However, this is of little use in the rest of Britain, where beech and hornbeam do not appear. Vegetation change of a different kind does, however, occur in many areas. During the Iron Age, at dates younger than the change in peat stratigraphy, a large number of POLLEN DIAGRAMS show evidence of intensified forest clearance. Many areas of Britain appear to have been cleared for the first time. These clearings appear mostly to have been permanent, and used for mixed farming.

Sub-Boreal. A climatic sub-division of the FLANDRIAN, originally supposed to be warm and dry, in contrast to a wet and warm preceding ATLANTIC period. Godwin's POLLEN ZONE VIIb corresponds to the Sub-Boreal period in Britain. The zone starts with the ELM DECLINE. Its end is rather ill-defined over much of Britain (*see* SUB-ATLANTIC). Frequencies of tree pollen fall through Zone VIIb, and herbaceous pollen rises correspondingly. This represents man's invasion of the forest in the Neolithic and Bronze Age. This consisted in many areas of temporary LAND-NAM-type clearances, but permanent clearance also occurred in some parts of the British Isles.

Suberde. A small settlement site in the Konya plain of southern Turkey, dated to the later 7th millennium bc. Two occupation levels were recognized, the earlier with traces of hut floors, the later with building of mud-brick and plastered floors. There has been some dispute about the nature of the subsistence economy practised here. There is no information about the plant side of the diet, but some 25,000 animal bones were collected. Sheep and goat were the most frequent, but cattle, boar, red deer, fox and hedgehog also occur. The excavators argued that all the animals were wild and that there was no evidence of even incipient domestication. Other authorities, however, have pointed out that the sheep/goat bones, which constitute 70 per cent of the meat supply in the lower level, 50 per cent in the upper, indicate a high proportion of animals under the age of three. This would be consistent with incipient domestication, before any morphological changes in the skeleton had come about.

Succase. A small settlement site of the RZUCEWO culture, a regional group of the

CORDED WARE culture group dated to the turn of the 2nd millennium bc. Succase lies near the mouth of the River Vistula on the southern shores of the Frisches Hoff in Pomerania, Poland. Several occupation layers are represented by overlapping rectangular timber-framed house-plans. Economic evidence indicates a mixed farming strategy with fishing and hunting. Microlithic flintwork is found associated with an amber industry.

Suchu Island. *See* AMUR NEOLITHIC.

Sue. Bluish-grey pottery used during the KOFUN, Nara, and Heian periods in Japan. A large variety of vessels were made on a mechanical wheel, and fired in a kiln at about 1100°C, with the blue-grey colour resulting from the oxygen-reduced atmosphere in the kiln towards the end of the firing process. The production of Sue pottery began in the Osaka area in the 5th century. Since it is quite similar to the contemporary pottery of Korea, it was probably introduced from there. By the 6th century Sue pottery was mass-produced at many centres, with the emphasis first on specialized ceremonial vessels, then on utilitarian pots and dishes for the elite, and finally on storage and cooking pots for the general population.

Sufutun [Su-fu-t'un]. A site near the city of Yidu in Shandong province where large cruciform SHAFT TOMBS with sacrificial victims were excavated in 1965-6. The Sufutun tombs were similar in construction to the so-called royal tombs at ANYANG Xibeigang and belong either to the very end of the SHANG dynasty or the very beginning of the ZHOU. The tombs had all been looted before excavation, and a large group of inscribed bronze RITUAL VESSELS now divided among several museums is believed to have come from them.

sugar cane. The sugar canes (*Saccharum* sp.) are large grasses which contain a sweet syrup in their coarse fibrous stems. It is believed on botanical grounds that they were first subjected to selection by man in the NEW GUINEA region, by at least an early phase of AUSTRONESIAN settlement (*c*3000 BC).

Sugu. A site in Fukuoka prefecture, Japan, where many YAYOI settlements, cemeteries and workshops, known as the Sugu site group,

are located. The Sugu site proper is a cemetery containing over 200 jar burials. The most famous among them is a grave believed to be that of the political leader of the area. He was buried inside two jars, set mouth to mouth, along with at least 33 imported Chinese bronze mirrors, several bronze weapons, and ornaments of glass, stone and antler. The fine pottery used in the funerary jars is known as the Sugu type, characteristic of the Middle Yayoi (100 BC-AD 100) of Kyushu.

Sui [Sui]. Chinese dynasty, AD 589-618.

Sui Xian [Sui-hsien]. A district in Hubei province, China. A rich burial of the late 5th century BC excavated at Sui Xian Leigudun in 1978 is identified by inscribed bronzes found in it as the tomb of one Marquis Yi of the little-known state of Zeng. A dated inscribed bell contributed to the funerary goods by King Hui of CHU allows the tomb to be dated in or near 433 BC and suggests a close relationship between Zeng and the far more important state of Chu. The furnishings of the tomb can probably be taken to represent Chu material culture; for splendour they are so far unmatched among Chu burials or indeed anywhere else in Bronze Age China. The four timber-built compartments of the tomb contained jades, weapons, suits of leather armour, unique cast gold vessels, inscribed bamboo slips, surpassingly fine LACQUERS (musical instruments, coffins, furniture, vessels), and some ten tonnes of bronze artefacts. The marquis was buried in two nested lacquer coffins held in a 3200-kg bronze frame; 21 single coffins contained female attendants. Among the bronzes are a few highly accomplished lost-wax (CIRE PERDUE) castings (*see* XIASI) and the largest matched set of BELLS yet discovered, a total of 64, nearly all bearing inscriptions concerning musical scales. The bells and many of the other bronzes are decorated in a version of the HUAI STYLE of such extraordinary artistic quality as to seem like an aberration in the generally placid history of that style. A less rich tomb of about the same date as the Marquis Yi's has recently been discovered 100 metres to the west of it.

Sukhothai. An ancient city in northern THAILAND which in the 13th century became the nucleus of a newly emerging Buddhist Thai state, independent of the declining KHMER empire of ANGKOR. Under its greatest king Rāma Khamhaeng (*c*1275-*c*1317), who is also regarded as a sort of culture hero of the Thais, the power of Sukhothai expanded over vast areas of the Indochinese and even the Malay Peninsulas. In the mid-14th century the centre of Thai power shifted south to AYUTTHAYA and Sukhothai ceased to exist as an independent kingdom. It is also known for its ceramic ware, widely exported throughout the region. As cradle of Thai civilization, the site is being organized as a major tourist attraction. *See also* SAWANKHALOK.

Sulawesi. The largest island of eastern INDONESIA, in the intermediate Wallacean faunal region between the SUNDA and SAHUL shelves. Sulawesi may have been beyond the reach of settlement by *Homo erectus*, but there is a possible late Pleistocene industry from CABENGE, and the southwestern peninsula contains many rock shelters with TOALIAN assemblages. Other prehistoric sites include the PASO shell midden in Minahasa and the Kalumpang Neolithic site of the west coast. The Sulawesi Neolithic is poorly understood and the earliest historical kingdoms (Makassar and Bone) are not recorded until after 1600. *See also* LEANG TUWO MANE'E.

Sulgrave. *See* MANOR.

Sulphur Springs. Earliest of three stages of the COCHISE culture, named after a small cluster of sites in southeast Arizona, USA. Evidence of plant food processing (e.g. cobble MANOS) together with split and burnt faunal remains, imply an ARCHAIC lifestyle, although there is an almost complete lack of projectile points. It has been proposed that the poorly understood Cazador complex (which does have projectile points) may be the hunting component of Sulphur Springs, but this association is no more than hypothetical. Sulphur Springs sites have yielded radiocarbon dates from 7300 to 6000 bc.

Sultan, Tell es. *See* JERICHO.

Sumatra. The prehistory of this large island of western Indonesia is little known, but recent excavations at Tianko Panjang cave in Jambi Province have yielded an OBSIDIAN flake industry dating from about 8000 bc, with undated cord-marked pottery in upper layers.

The PASEMAH megaliths may date from the early 1st millennium AD.

Classical. The island may already have been mentioned in the epic *Rāmāyana*, but the earliest sign of Indian influence is the existence, attested for the 7th century, of an important centre for the diffusion of Buddhism in Palembang. It was here that the INDIANIZED kingdom of ŚRĪVIJAYA came into being at the end of the same century, succeeding FUNAN as the dominant maritime power in the region. In the 13th century JAVA established control over the island, spelling the end of Śrīvijaya. However, as Marco POLO mentioned Islam in Sumatra at the same time, Indian culture was soon to vanish from the island altogether. *See also* MALAYSIA.

Sumer, Sumerian. The earliest civilization in the world, which arose in southern Mesopotamia in the 4th millennium BC. The name is taken from inscriptions, where it appears in the title 'King of Sumer and Agade'; it was applied first to the language found on the earliest CLAY TABLETS and later to the whole civilization. *See also* MESOPOTAMIA.

Sunda Shelf. The shallow submarine continental shelf which extends from the Southeast Asian mainland to HUXLEY'S LINE; it supports the islands of SUMATRA, JAVA, BORNEO, Bali and Palawan, which were joined to the Asian continent at times of low Pleistocene sea-level. The eastern edge of the shelf (Huxley's Line) may have been the eastern limit of settlement by *Homo erectus*.

Sungir. An open site of the Strelestsky-Sungir culture some 200 km east-northeast of Moscow, occupied *c*20,000-25,000 bc. It is by far the north-easternmost of the rich Upper PALAEOLITHIC sites, although sites close to the Arctic Circle are known. There is a strong MOUSTERIAN element in the stone artefacts, and the skeletons found buried on the site had such archaic features as large brow ridges. The single and double burial are of outstanding interest for the numerous beads and other grave goods left with them, allowing among other things the reconstruction of many details of clothing.

Sunium. *See* SOUNION.

Sur Jangal. A prehistoric site in the Loralai

Valley of northern Baluchistan, Pakistan. Three major phases of occupation probably belong to the later 4th and 3rd millennia BC. Characteristic blank-on-red painted wares frequently depict both humped (zebu) and humpless cattle; faunal remains from this site indicate that cattle constituted the main domesticated animals here. Other artefacts include female figurines of ZHOB type.

Surkh Kotal. A site in Afghanistan, among the most important monuments of the Kushans, who in the 1st century AD created an empire extending from Bactria to the upper Ganges. The most famous Kushan ruler was Kanishka (early 2nd century), builder of the hilltop fortress at Surkh Kotal, in which the Kushans created a royal sanctuary. The focal point of the sanctuary is a fire-temple in a courtyard with porticos on three sides, occupying the summit of the hill. Below the fourth side is a series of terraces linked by flights of steps. Below the bottom terrace is a stone-lined well. The temple contained sculptures in clay and stone, including three statues of gods or kings. Among the inscriptions from the site is a long text in the Bactrian language, but using cursive Greek letters, giving the name of the a local official, Nokonzoko, and the date 31 of the Kanishkan era.

surveying. Accurate surveying is essential for recording archaeological sites, before and during excavation. At most excavations, horizontal dimensions are measured with tapes, from a 'grid' of known points around the site. Height differences are usually measured using a LEVEL and staff. These dimensions may then be used to plot features of the site as plans and sections. Increasing use is now being made of electronic surveying equipment and PHOTO-GRAMMETRY for surveying sites. *See also* THEODOLITE, TRIANGULATION.

Susa [Susiana]. Major city (Biblical Shushan) in Khuzistan, southwest Iran. The area around Susa, known as Susiana, is contiguous with and very similar to southern Mesopotamia proper (it is sometimes included in the designation 'Greater Mesopotamia') and the development of civilization followed closely related courses in the two areas (*see* Table 2, page 320).

Susa itself was the capital of the ELAMITE state in the 3rd, 2nd and 1st millennia BC, and in the mid-1st millennium it became the administrative centre of the ACHAEMENID empire. It was captured by Alexander the Great in 331 BC, but continued in occupation through the PARTHIAN and SASSANIAN periods and well into the Islamic period.

The site covers two square kilometres and has been excavated by the French with few interruptions since 1897. The tell is made up of four separate mounds: (1) the Acropolis, which has produced most of the prehistoric material from the site, as well as structures of later date; (2) the Royal City which has produced important Elamite remains of the 2nd millennium BC; (3) the Apadana, with its large and impressive Achaemenid palace; and (4) the Artisans' Town, also of the Achaemenid period (and later).

Among the most important individual finds from Susa are the stele of Naram-Sin (of the AKKADIAN period) and the law code of Hammurabi (Old Babylonian period), which had been brought to Susa from BABYLON after an Elamite raid. Both are now in the Louvre in Paris.

Susuya. Site in southern Sakhalin, an island off the east coast of Siberia north of Japan, dating to the last few centuries BC or the first few centuries AD. The site marks the first appearance in this area of a true maritime economy of sea-mammal hunters, using efficient harpoons. It is thought to represent the settlement of a group coming from the north. At a later date this way of life spread still further south into northern Hokkaido (Japan), where it appears in the OKHOTSK culture.

Sutkagen Dor. The westernmost site of the HARAPPAN CIVILIZATION, on the Makran coast, southwest Pakistan. Like other Harappan towns, Sutkagen Dor is divided into a citadel and a lower town. The citadel was defended by a massive wall, not made of brick as in the Indus Valley itself, but of semi-dressed stone. The lower town shows connections with the local KULLI culture.

Sutton Hoo. Perhaps the most remarkable archaeological discovery ever made in Britain is the ANGLO-SAXON ship burial at Sutton Hoo, close to the Suffolk coast. The excavations in 1938-9 concentrated on the largest of a group of mounds which was found to contain the remains of an open rowing boat 27 metres long, with impressions of timbers and clamps surviving. The central burial chamber contained a rich collection of outstanding objects from all over Europe of 4th- to 7th-century date. This type of funerary ritual is known from MIGRATION PERIOD Europe (*see* BOAT BURIAL) and is described in the Anglo-Saxon poem BEOWULF, but it is nevertheless a fairly rare occurrence until the VIKING era. The Sutton Hoo deposit must be regarded as an isolated British example of a pagan burial practice which has survived into the Christian era: many Christian artefacts were among those interred.

Although no traces of a body were discovered, the valuable grave goods deposited in the ship suggest that it commemorates a person of prestige and importance, possible King Raedwald of Essex, who died in 625. The most notable objects among the Sutton Hoo treasure are the items of gold jewellery and armour inlaid with enamels, MILLEFIORI glass, and CLOISONNÉ garnets; there is also the famous gilt-bronze helmet, thought to be an import from Sweden, and the great gold buckle, as well as a fine collection of silver ware; these spectacular finds are now housed in the British Museum. A new campaign of survey and excavation at Sutton Hoo is planned for the 1980s.

Suvarnabhūmi [Sanskrit: 'Land of Gold']. A site or territory on the mainland of Southeast Asia, not identified with certainty, to which the 3rd-century BC Indian emperor ASOKA sent the two Buddhist missionaries, Sona and Uttara. This earliest Buddhist centre was most likely located in MON country either in present Lower Burma or in the lower Menam plain, present-day Thailand. *See also* THATON.

Suzuki. A stratified site in Kodaira City, near Tokyo, Japan. The PALAEOLITHIC materials are of interest, because regularly shaped blades and edge-ground axes were found in the lower layers dated to about 30,000 years ago. A number of piles of burned rock, which seem to have been used for cooking, were also found.

Šventoji I. A Late Mesolithic and Late Neolithic settlement site in the southeast Baltic area, Lithuania, USSR. Stratified in a peat bog are two culture levels separated by a sterile layer: 1, the earlier occupation, of the NARVA culture, with radiocarbon dates of *c*2700-2150 bc; 3, the later occupation of the RZUCEWO group of the CORDED WARE culture group, with a radiocarbon date of *c*1910 bc. Thanks to anaerobic conditions in the peat bog, textiles, wood, fishing, nets, oars, baby cradles and wooden statues of deities have been preserved.

Swanscombe. A site on the lower Thames in Kent, southern England, of major importance on account of the series of river deposits of the 30-metre terrace exposed in Barnfield Pit and elsewhere. These deposits contain useful environmental evidence, including abundant mollusc and mammal remains and large assemblages of stone tools. The Lower Gravels have a CLACTONIAN type assemblage, while the Middle Gravels have ACHEULIAN, with numerous hand axes. Following the Barnfield Pit series comes the 'coombe rock' of BAKERS HOLE, and the channel filling of EBBSFLEET. Swanscombe is best known for the three skull pieces (occipital and two parietals) making up Swanscombe man, usually now classified along with STEINHEIM man as the earliest *Homo sapiens* of archaic type. The skull bones are considerably thicker than those of modern European or NEANDERTHAL skulls.

Swartkrans. A short distance from STERKFONTEIN and in the same valley is the richest hominid site in South Africa. It contains remains of perhaps over 60 individuals of *A. robustus*, the best sample of the robust kind of AUSTRALOPITHECUS. These deposits are later than the main Sterkfontein hominid level, perhaps 1.5 to 2 million years old. Swartkrans has stone tools including rough HAND AXES; a second hominid is present, probably *Homo erectus* or 'habilis', who is more likely to have been the toolmaker.

Swasey. *See* CUELLO.

sweet potato. *Ipomoea batatas*, the sweet potato, is of tropical American origin and is reported from sites in Peru as early as 8000 bc. During the mid-1st millennium AD the tuber was carried by prehistoric voyagers into eastern POLYNESIA and became important in the prehistoric economies of EASTER ISLAND, the HAWAIIAN ISLANDS and NEW ZEALAND. Its further spread took place after Spanish settlement of the New World and since the 16th century it has become of great importance in the economies of the NEW GUINEA Highlands.

Swiderian. A late glacial culture known from Poland at such sites as Calowanie and Swidry Wielkie. Elongated tanged points are typical of these sites, which have radiocarbon dates in the 10,000-8000 bc range. The Swiderian is probably related to other tanged-point cultures of northern Europe known to exist at this time.

Swidry Wielkie. *See* SWIDERIAN.

swords (China). The earliest Chinese swords belong to the Western ZHOU period: examples from ZHANGJIAPO and LINGTAI, only 24-27 cm long, date from the 10th century BC. The Western Zhou sword, a tapering two-edged blade with a flat tang for attaching a grip, is not easily related to swords made outside China and probably derives from older Chinese daggers. It may in turn be the ancestor of the standard bronze sword of late Eastern Zhou times, as a few examples of intermediate form suggest.

The Eastern Zhou bronze sword differs, however, in having a hilt cast in one piece with the blade. It is two-edged and from 40 to 55 cm long. The very distinctive hilt takes the form of a hollow tube or, later, a solid bar with circular flanges that allow the grip to be bound with silk cord; in either case the pommel is a disc. The sword with flanged hilt, sometimes called the classic Chinese sword, was common in the 4th and 3rd centuries BC. Particularly famous examples are the swords of the kings of YUE.

Iron swords first appear around the 5th century BC. A blade of that date from a tomb near CHANGSHA is 38 cm in length, no longer than contemporary bronze swords. Only a century or so later, however, double-edged iron swords with flat tangs average a metre in length. Though it has sometimes been questioned whether these long blades were actually functional, examples unearthed at YAN Xiadu have been shown in recent studies to be made of good steel. The late Eastern Zhou states of CHU and QIN are said to have mastered the production of fine swords, and these are often assumed to have been iron. Many iron swords have been found in Chu tombs, but the weapons found in the mausoleum of the Qin emperor QIN SHI HUANGDI (*d.* 210 BC) were almost all bronze. The tomb of Liu Sheng

(*d.* 113 BC) at MANCHENG contained steel swords and other weapons, and by the 1st century AD forged steel swords of very high quality were made. Some of these HAN swords are single-edged, ring-pommelled sabres, their shape copied from late Zhou bronze and iron knives.

Syäm. Earliest ethnic name of the THAIS (or Siamese) in epigraphy. It appears as the name of an obviously non-KHMER contingent in the imperial army in an inscription at ANGKOR WAT; this interpretation is, however, contested.

Sybaris. Early Greek colonial settlement (perhaps 8th century BC) on the Ionian Gulf in Calabria, southern Italy, proverbial later for the luxury and decadence of its inhabitants, and destroyed by rival Croton in about 510 BC. A new settlement, Thurii, was founded in 443 BC by Pericles of Athens and a group of surviving Sybarites, apparently not on a different site as stated by traditional sources, but over the southern area of the earlier city. After the PUNIC WARS, a Roman COLONIA named Copia was established at Thurii, and occupation seems to have continued until the 4th century AD. Original Sybaris founded daughter colonies, notably at PAESTUM, had widespread trading connections, and issued its own coins. The site was finally identified in the 1960s, and excavations have been made difficult by the degree to which the plain of Crati has sunk below today's sea-level (probably since the Roman period), the presence of metres of silty deposit overlying the ancient evidence, and the constant need for the pumping-out of work which is below the current water table. Pottery and structural evidence supports occupation from the 8th century BC, and for Roman Copia there is an early imperial theatre and some residential material.

Symbolkeramik. Name sometimes given to a type of pottery found in southern Iberia during the Copper Age. The pottery, found at sites like LOS MILLARES, is characterized by incised stylized designs which are thought to hold symbolic meanings. One such design is the OCULUS motif.

Syracuse. A Greek colonial settlement and principal port on the east coast of Sicily, and later capital of Roman Sicily. Earliest occupation seems to be on the island of Ortygia which helps to enclose the Great Harbour, where some early Palaeolithic material occurs. It is likely that a native settlement preceded the arrival of the Greeks, but perhaps not by more than a century or two. The traditional date for the Greek colony is around 734 BC, and foundation is attributed to Corinthians. Early tyrants and leaders extended the power and influence of Syracuse: Gelon against the Carthaginians at Himera in 480 BC, Hieron I against the Etruscans in a naval engagement off CUMAE in 474 BC, and Hermocrates against the Athenian Sicilian Expedition of 415, when large numbers of prisoners were incarcerated in the Latomie stone quarries. Darker moments, however, came with characters such as Agathocles, a sadist of a professional soldier who managed to gain control over most of Sicily (*see* SEGESTA). Siding with Hannibal in the Second PUNIC WAR was a mistake which led to a long siege by Rome, when even Archimedes' brilliant gadgets, such as man-grabbing clamps, could not delay Roman capture. Roman rule of Sicily was undistinguished and poorly organized, with two Slave Wars and the extortions of Verres (chronicled by Cicero) to its discredit. Augustus established a COLONIA at Syracuse in 21 BC and the early imperial period saw a modest return to prosperity. In the early Christian era, Syracuse became something of a religious centre, and there are extensive CATACOMBS. From the 5th century onward, the city's civilization disintegrated under the general chaos of the western empire, and eventually and progressively the surviving population sought refuge in rock-cut housing and churches in the hinterland. Surviving remains include the archaic DORIC temples of Zeus and of Apollo, the Temple of Athena which is ingeniously incorporated into the Cathedral, the Greek THEATRE, and a 3rd-century AD AMPHITHEATRE. Evidence survives also for the amazingly extensive fortification system of Epipolae, a triangular-plan rocky plateau which was unified with the city in some 27 km of walling, with the Fort of Euryalos at the highest point.

Szakalhát. The eponymous site of a later Neolithic regional group of the Alföld LINEAR POTTERY, located in the town of Hódmezövásárhely in southeast Hungary. The settlement has two occupation layers, a level with late Alföld Linear pottery and a level with Szakalhát pottery. For many years Hungarian archaeologists failed to distinguish Szakalhát pottery from pottery of the later TISZA culture; now the Szakalhát group is recognized as a separate entity, distributed in the southern part of the Alföld plain *c*4300-4000 bc. The two main pottery decorative styles — wide incised curvilinear and dark burnished — are often combined on the same vessels.

Szegvar-Tüzköves. A nucleated open settlement of the later Neolithic period, situated near Szentes in southeast Hungary. Two occupation horizons are represented: a SZAKALHÁT (Alföld LINEAR POTTERY) level dated to the late 5th millennium bc and a thick TISZA culture level dated to the 4th millennium bc. Several complete Tisza culture house plans have been excavated, some with bucrania on the gable ends. The most famous Tisza find is the 'Sickle God', a complete, seated, fired-clay male figurine carrying a sickle.

Szeletian. An early Upper PALAEOLITHIC culture named after the cave of Szeleta in Hungary. It is characterized by leaf points, and seems to mark the transition from the Middle Palaeolithic to the Upper Palaeolithic. Indeed, the earlier Szeletian level from the type site could be regarded as MOUSTERIAN, while the upper level is a primitive early Upper Palaeolithic. The culture seems to date from within the period 45,000 to 25,000 bc and is mainly found in north-central Europe, though a possibly related version extends to Britain.

Szeligi. *See* OPOLE.

T

tablets. *See* CLAY TABLETS.

Tabon Caves. A large complex of limestone caves in southwestern Palawan, Philippine Islands, which in combination have produced a sequence running right through the past 30,000 years. Tabon Cave itself has a flake industry of early Australian type dating from 30,000 to 9000 years ago, in association with early Australoid skeletal remains. A simple blade technology appears in Duyong Cave at about 5000 bc and other caves continue through the Neolithic (*c*3800-500 BC) and into a rich jar-burial tradition of the Early Metal Period (500 BC to AD 1000) related to the KALANAY jar-burial tradition elsewhere in the Philippines. Later deposits with Chinese ceramic imports also occur.

Taforalt. A cave in eastern Morocco where a blade industry of uncertain affinities was replaced around the 14th millennium bc by the first of a long succession of IBEROMAURUSIAN phases. A large Iberomaurusian cemetery has also been investigated, the human remains being of MECHTA-AFALOU type.

Tagajo. One of the garrisons maintained in northern Honshu, Japan, for frontier administration. Excavations since 1961 at a site near Sendai identified the ruins of Tagajo, mentioned in historical records in connection with the government's attempts to bring local groups under control. There are outer and inner walls of packed earth, encircling an area of one square kilometre and 10,000 square metres respectively. Inside the walls were several structures, rebuilt four times during the 8th and 9th centuries. Inscribed wooden slips and other documents were also recovered.

Tagua-tagua. A lakeside site in central Chile, 120 km south of Santiago, where stone artefacts in association with faunal remains indicate a PALEO-INDIAN presence at an early date. Bones of mastodon, horse and deer were found in association with cores and flakes from a 'Levallois-Mousterian' type industry. Although no projectile points were found, butchering scars on bone and other lithic evidence strongly suggest that some points appropriate to the BIG GAME HUNTING TRADITION do exist. A radiocarbon date of *c*9430 bc, taken from charcoal which may be evidence of the use of fire drives as a hunting technique, is the base date of the chronology.

Tahiti. *See* SOCIETY ISLANDS.

Taino. An ARAWAKAN group of ZEMI worshippers who occupied much of the Greater Antilles at the time of the arrival of Columbus. Some political organization and social stratification is indicated by the two-tiered system of chieftainship which operated then. The population dwelt, typically, in permanent villages of up to 1000 houses, some of which were built on open plazas which may have been used for the BALL GAME. Cultivation based on slash-and-burn techniques was practised by these skilled carvers in wood and stone. MANIOC was the principal crop, and the pottery most often associated was of the CHICOID series.

Taipivai. A valley on the island of Nuku Hiva, MARQUESAS ISLANDS, famous for a novelized account of the life of its inhabitants, *Typee*, written by Herman Melville in 1846. The valley contains some of the largest stone structures in the Marquesas: megalithic terraced dance floors (*tohua*) and temples, one with anthropomorphic stone statues.

Taipuxiang [T'ai-p'u-hsiang]. *See* SHANG-CUNLING.

Tairona. A culture of village-dwelling farmers who occupied the foothills of the sierras in northeast Colombia during the INTEGRATION PERIOD. These villages had some local control, but the major unit of socio-political organization was a federation under a powerful chief or group of chiefs. Such chiefs resided at one of the larger, more important towns (e.g. Pueblito, see below). A central feature of most villages was a ceremonial building, usually on a platform-mound, and often of dressed masonry. Other features included circular houses with stone foundations (also frequently built on mounds), a well-developed metallurgical tradition and ceramics, both utilitarian (red ware) and ceremonial. The town site at Pueblito has all these features and, in addition, paved streets, the remains of large irrigation projects, and urn burials. Specialized funerary vessels are often modelled with life forms which are markedly similar to MESOAMERICAN motifs: images resembling TLALOC and representations of motifs such as the man-jaguar transformation (see OLMEC) occur frequently. Populations in the thousands occupied Tairona towns and villages at the time of the Spanish conquest, but it is unclear whether these were the prehistoric Tairona or the modern-day Coqui.

Taiwan [Formosa]. The island of Taiwan occupies an important position in the prehistory of Southeast Asia. Evidence for pre-Neolithic settlement is still hazy, but from about 3500 bc a Neolithic culture (Ta-p'en-k'eng culture) enters the island from southern China. This culture has cord-marked pottery and is related to contemporary rice-cultivating cultures on the adjacent mainland. On linguistic grounds it can be correlated with the earliest recognizable phase of AUSTRONESIAN linguistic dispersal into Island Southeast Asia, presumably from southern China. Later Taiwan Neolithic cultures also show close connections with south China and the PHILIPPINES, but little is known about the period following 500 BC.

Taixicun [T'ai-hsi-ts'un]. See GAOCHENG.

Tajin. See TLALOC.

Takamatsuzuka. A small KOFUN [tumulus], about 18 metres across and 5 metres high, in the ASUKA area of Nara prefecture, Japan. The 1972 excavation revealed paintings of human and mythological figures and celestial bodies on the walls and the ceiling of the burial chamber. Close similarities to the SUI, TANG, and north Korean graves were noted. A Tang mirror and some gold- and silver-plated ornaments had escaped the earlier plunder by illicit excavators. A construction date in the late 6th or early 7th century is suggested.

Takht-i Jamshid. See PERSEPOLIS.

Takht-i Sulaiman [ancient Shiz]. This site in the province of Azerbaijan, northwest Iran, was an important religious site in the PARTHIAN, SASSANIAN and Islamic periods. In the Parthian period it was surrounded by a mud-brick wall, while the Sassanians added a further outer wall of stone. To the Sassanian period belong a palace and a fire temple, which was the focus of a great pilgrimage centre.

Talasea. The most important OBSIDIAN source in western MELANESIA, Talasea is located on the Willaumez peninsula of northern NEW BRITAIN. The obsidian occurs from 9000 bc in MISISIL CAVE on southwestern New Britain and was distributed widely in LAPITA times (c1500 to 0 BC) to as far as NEW CALEDONIA, 2600 km away.

talayot [Talayotic culture]. A type of stone tower found only on the Balearic Islands of Majorca and Minorca which has given its name to the local Bronze Age culture. Early talayots were circular and either solid or with a chamber inside; later examples have subsidiary small chambers in the thickness of the wall and some square talayots have upper storeys. They are built of large blocks of dry stone and often form parts of larger settlement enclosures with walls of CYCLOPEAN MASONRY. Their precise function is unknown, but they could have been used as lookout towers or as refuges in times of trouble. Although there are differences of detail, the talayots bear a general resemblance to the TORRI of Corsica and the NURAGHI of Sardinia.

Talgai cranium. The first human fossil found in Australia, discovered heavily encrusted with carbonate in southeast Queensland in 1886. It belongs to the robust group of Australian fossil crania and has not yet been firmly dated, although sediments in which it was found have been dated to 10,000-11,000 bc. See also GREEN GULLY, KEILOR, KOW SWAMP, LAKE MUNGO.

talud-tablero. An architectural feature employed in the construction of MESOAMERICAN stepped PYRAMIDS. It is especially

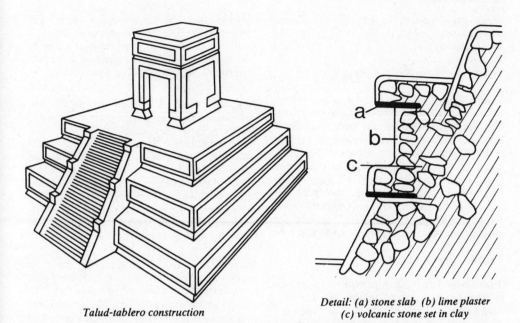

Talud-tablero construction

Detail: (a) stone slab (b) lime plaster
(c) volcanic stone set in clay

characteristic of CLASSIC TEOTHIHUACAN. Each step consists of an upward sloping apron (*talud*) surmounted by a rectangular slab (*tablero*), the outside vertical face of which is usually recessed. Examples occur throughout Mesoamerica; among the best known are the Temple of QUETZACOATL at Teotihuacan, the Palangana Complex at KAMINALJUYU and the temple buildings at CHICHEN ITZA.

Tamaulipas. In the late 1940s an intensive survey of a series of caves in the state of Tamaulipas in northeast Mexico was undertaken by Richard MacNeish. The survey is notable for its evidence of incipient agriculture, but it has since been overshadowed by the much grander TEHUACAN VALLEY Project. The earliest period of the Tamaulipas study was the Diablo Focus which contained crude pebble tools and was designated a pre-projectile point horizon. This is overlain by the Lerma Phase (dated to *c*7000 bc) which contains projectile points similar to those of the OLD CORDILLERAN TRADITION. The following Infiernillo Phase contains the earliest evidence of incipient agriculture. Small amounts of domesticated plants, such as gourds, peppers and pumpkin, were found with wild plants, flake tools and basketry. Later phases contain increasing numbers of MANOS and METATES, flexed, wrapped burials

and other evidence of sedentary village life. Primitive MAIZE has been dated to the period 3000-2200 bc.

Tamaya Mellet. A site located west of the Air Mountains in Niger, where pottery occurs in one of its earliest known Saharan contexts, being dated to *c*7300 bc. The sherds, found in association with barbed bone harpoon heads, are similar to those bearing 'wavy-line' decoration which was subsequently widespread in the southern Sahara and in the Sudanese Nile Valley (*see* EARLY KHARTOUM).

Tambo Colorado. Located in the Pisco Valley in southern Peru, Tambo Colorado is one of the best-preserved walled INCA towns; however, it was most probably strictly an adminstrative centre or military barracks. Constructed in terraces of adobe on stone foundations, traces of red and yellow paint are still visible on the walls. The site divides into two principal areas separated by an open trapezoidal plaza. The northern section consists of a central walled enclosure in the middle of which is a plaza surrounded by residential buildings of varying size. On the southern side is a CEREMONIAL CENTRE and associated buildings. Abandoned shortly after the Spanish conquest, its excellent state of preservation is due to the generally dry climate and the site's remoteness from today's centres of population.

Tambo de Mora. *See* CHINCHA.

Tāmbralinga. An early INDIANIZED kingdom on the eastern coast of the Malay Peninsula, between Chaiya and Pattani, with its centre at LIGOR or Nagara Śrī Dharmarāja, the present Nakhon Sithammarat in southern Thailand. The kingdom may already have existed in the 2nd century and is attested by 6th-century inscriptions. Later it became the most important of the dependencies of ŚRĪVIJAYA on the peninsula and eventually recognized the suzerainty of the Thai kingdom of SUKHOTAI.

Tamuin. *See* HUASTECA.

Tamworth. During the period of MERCIAN supremacy in England in the 8th century, Tamworth in Staffordshire was the site of a royal palace; in the early 10th century it was re-established as a BURH town. Archaeologists have located parts of the burh defences and a gate, and by chance stumbled across a mill which is believed to be part of the 8th-century royal complex. Waterlogged conditions have preserved many of the oak planks of this structure, and thus it is possible to distinguish the joints and pegs which join them, and also to reconstruct the basic outline of the building. The mill consists of two boxes with troughs between them; the upper of these boxes acted as a mill pond and the lower as an outlet channel. Pieces of millstone were found as well as a small piece of iron from the grinding machinery. By Anglo-Saxon standards, the Tamworth mill was a large and sophisticated structure, probably driven by a horizontal wheel; traces of lead frames suggest that it may have had glass windows. Radiocarbon analysis confirms an 8th-century date for the building.

Tang [T'ang]. Chinese dynasty, 618-907. The Tang capital was at CHANG'AN.

Tangshan [T'ang-shan]. A city in Hebei province east of BEIJING, China. Graves of the late 6th century BC excavated in 1953 at Tangshan Jiagezhuang can probably be associated with the Eastern ZHOU state of YAN. They yielded bronze RITUAL VESSELS whose decoration, sometimes executed in copper inlay, borrows motifs from the ANIMAL-STYLE art of the steppes. Pictorial bronzes with similar designs are found mainly in the territories of the northern frontier states, in northern Hebei and Shanxi provinces.

Tanjong Kubor. A coastal occupation site near Santubong in southwestern Sarawak, BORNEO, East MALAYSIA, which has produced a distinctive style of paddle-impressed pottery in association with imported Chinese ceramics of the late TANG and SUNG dynasties (*c*900-1350). Similar sites reflecting trade between Malay communities and China occur commonly on the coasts of northern Borneo, Malaya and possible eastern SUMATRA. *See* KOTA BATU, SANTUBONG.

taotie [*t'ao-t'ieh*]. The principal motif in SHANG and Western ZHOU art, an invention apparently of early Shang bronze casters. The earliest *taotie* are simple face-like designs cast in thread-relief on bronze RITUAL VESSELS of the ERLIGANG PHASE (*c* mid-2nd millennium BC). They consist at first of little more than paired eyes in a vague setting of ornamental lines and may have been inspired by even simpler faces on certain Neolithic jades (*see* ZONG). The elaboration of the *taotie* motif from this sketchy beginning was closely tied to the Shang caster's section-mould technique, which favoured designs falling into self-contained units, each unit corresponding to one section of the mould (*see* RITUAL VESSELS, CHINA). The *taotie* is by far the most important of a number of such pattern units used to decorate the bronze vessels; next in importance is the dragon, which was invented only slightly later and which takes a wide variety of forms having in common little besides the fact that they are always seen in profile while the *taotie* is always seen full-face. During the late Shang and early Western Zhou the *taotie* was at its most 'realistic', more animal-like and less vague than its Erligang-phase ancestors; in the course of the Western Zhou period these 'realistic' images dissolved away, by the 10th century BC arriving at nearly abstract curvilinear patterns of flat ribbons. The art of Eastern Zhou was instead dominated by dragons, often arranged in complex interlacery.

Ta-p'en-k'eng culture. *See* TAIWAN.

Taputapuatea. Traditionally the most sacred MARAE of eastern POLYNESIA, associated with the worship of the god Oro, situated on the island of Raiatea, SOCIETY ISLANDS. The AHU still stands 4 metres high, covering an area of 40 by 7 metres.

Tara. Situated northwest of Dublin in the Irish Republic, Tara is known from the early Irish literary sources as the seat of the High Kings of Ireland before the introduction of Christianity. Archaeological evidence, however, shows that the hilltop was occupied long before this period. The earliest monument is a Neolithic PASSAGE GRAVE, known as the Mound of the Hostages, which produced a mass of cremated bone and many finds of the early 3rd millennium BC. Bronze Age remains from Tara include about 50 single graves with FOOD VESSELS or URNS, mostly with cremations, though one of two inhumations was accompanied by a rich necklace of copper, jet, amber and faience beads. Tara became an important settlement site in the Iron Age and early historic period (last few centuries BC and first few AD). To this period belong a large HILL-FORT (the Royal Enclosure) and a series of smaller forts and burial mounds. The site was a royal capital in the 5th century AD when St Patrick visited it and it remained the seat of the high kingship until about 1000 AD, when it was finally overthrown.

Taranto [Greek Taras, Roman Tarentum]. Greek colonial settlement with double harbour on the Ionian Gulf in southern Italy, traditionally founded in 706 BC from SPARTA. There is evidence for NEOLITHIC, Bronze Age (APENNINE) and MYCENAEAN activity in the general area (see SCOGLIO DEL TONNO). Iron Age dwellers were probably Iapygian, and there is evidence for this period in the mainland area of the city (città nuova). The acropolis of the city was probably situated on the promontory, now città vecchia (which was deliberately converted into an island in the medieval period by the cutting of a canal linking the two harbours). For the 5th and most of the 4th centuries BC the city enjoyed great prosperity, with a widely disseminated pattern of trading, and benefited greatly from the decline of rival Croton. In 433 BC a daughter-colony was established at Heraclea (now Policoro) further along the Gulf. But trouble from the native populations of the

hinterland, especially the Lucanians, was never far away, and the late 4th century saw a series of tussles in which Taranto had no alternative but to pay various foreign kings to come to her aid. The last of these, Pyrrhos of Epiros, was called in to fend off a newly arrived threat, the Romans, who were now taking an active interest in Thurii (see SYBARIS). Pyrrhos soon retired from an unequal contest, leaving Taranto to negotiate its own surrender to the Romans (c275 BC). The city was taken by Hannibal in 213 BC, and soon taken back with punitive vandalization by Rome in 209. Generally, Roman rule brought security and eventually some COLONIAL status with Italian settlers, but Taranto's subsequent history is the modest history of a southern Italian provincial town. Very little survives today since both the Greek and the Roman towns lie beneath the modern city. Numbers of votive and sanctuary terracottas have been collected. Tombs are also found, especially in the città nuova area; these are rock-cut or stone-lined trenches with covering slab, and also chamber tombs with decorated sarcophagi and funerary couches. A fine museum houses a well-displayed collection of material from both the city and the general province.

Taras. See TARANTO.

Tarascan. An independent state of the Late POST-CLASSIC Period centred on the Michoacan Province of West Mexico, and one of the very few to successfully resist AZTEC incursions. Linguistically unrelated to any other MESOAMERICAN group — although there are similarities to the South American language Quechua (see INCA) — the Tarascans claimed a CHICHIMEC ancestry. Their capital, Tzintzuntzan, was built overlooking Lake Patzcuaro, and appears to be a CEREMONIAL CENTRE consisting of a huge platform mound surmounted by five pyramids. Fine jewellery in gold and tumbaga, and well-made tools in copper and bronze indicate an advanced metallurgical tradition. Religion appears to have centred around sun-worship, and included the practices of human SACRIFICE and PERFORATION. The Tarascan state survived into historic times and much of the available information comes from early historical accounts.

Tardenois. Fère en Tardenois, in the Paris basin, is the type site of the Tardenoisian MESOLITHIC group dating to 6000-4000 bc.

Tardiguet. One of the Moroccan coastal localities with early stone tools, near Rabat. The tools are of simple OLDOWAN type without hand axes, the commonest pebble tools being the type called choppers. They belong to Stage 1 of the Pebble Tool culture, and are probably among the earliest cases of tool-making known.

taro. *See* AROIDS.

Tarquinia [Etruscan Tarkhuna, Roman Tarquinii]. Traditionally the earliest of the cities of Etruria (Tuscany), and famous today for its painted tombs. There is an earlier VIL-LANOVAN settlement on the same site. The ETRUSCAN city is important not only for its own civilized eminence and commercial prosperity of the 6th-5th centuries BC, but also for its contribution to early ROME of that city's early kings, the Tarquins, and a cultural and technological heritage. By the 4th century BC Rome was at war with Tarquinia, but even then the Etruscan city managed to hold on to an independent existence a century longer than VEII, and probably did not come under Roman control much before the end of the 3rd century BC. The Villanovan burials are especially rich in bronze artefacts, particularly horse and chariot accoutrements, shields and helmets. The Etruscan painted tombs date from the 6th century onwards, and are usually approached by steeply descending *dromoi*. Probably marked originally by *tumuli*, they show scenes of funeral banqueting and games. The spontaneous gaiety of these scenes later gives way to a more sombre depiction of the demons of the underworld. Sarcophagi occur commonly, and mostly have relief decoration, often with a sculptured reclining figure on the lid. The expense of these elaborate methods of burial was presumably only available to the aristocracy, the rich and officers of state. The city site itself, *Pian di cività*, shows traces of a grid plan, tufa city walls, and the remains of a 4th-3rd century BC temple (the so-called Ara della Regina).

Tarragona [also Kallipolis; Iberian Cissa or Cissis; Carthaginian Tarchon; Roman Tarraco]. An important city of Roman Spain, later capital of the province of Hispania Tarraconensis. There is some prehistoric evidence for settlement, and suggestions of an ETRUSCAN link (perhaps especially in the name Tarchon), but the first easily identifiable occupation is local Iberian, by the tribe of the Cessentani. From 218 BC there is strong association with Rome, particularly in the persons of Publius and Gnaeus Scipio, who captured Iberian Cissa and converted it to its Roman function of base against the Carthaginians and in Iberian campaigns. The town later found particular favour with Augustus, who recuperated there during his Cantabrian wars, and the citizens subsequently dedicated an altar to him and, later, a temple. Imperial Tarraco prospered, only to be sacked by the FRANKS in *c*260 AD and again by Euric in 476. Even so, enough survived to enjoy a final era of importance under Visigothic rule. Despite depredations by the Moors, the Normans and the French, some remains survive, notably of the Republican-period walling, Augustus' palace, an AMPHITHEATRE, a section of AQUE-DUCT (the Devil's Bridge) and a Romano-Christian cemetery.

Tarshish, Tarsis. *See* TARTESSOS.

Tarsus. Prehistoric settlement in Cilicia, southeast Turkey, occupied from the 5th to the 1st millennium BC, with a sequence paralleling that of MERSIN, not far away to the southwest.

Tartanga. An open site on the lower Murray River, South Australia, excavated by H. Hale and N.B. Tindale in 1929 at the same time as their nearby DEVON DOWNS excavation. Artefacts included small cores, scrapers, bone points, grinding stones and TULA ADZE flakes in deposits later dated to 4000 bc. Underlying occupation debris was not dated. Skeletons of two juveniles were found having some cranial features similar to the robust TALGAI skull.

Tărtăria. A TELL site of the Neolithic and Copper Age in the middle Mureş valley, Transylvania, Rumania. Excavations by K. Horedt and N. Vlassa revealed a four-level stratigraphy: I, a thin CRIŞ occupation; II, a TURDAŞ-PETREŞTI level; III, a thick Petreşti-Turdaş level; and IV, a Copper Age COŢOFENI-Petreşti horizon. In a pit cut from level II a ritual assemblage was found containing a cremation, fired clay and alabaster figurines, SPONDYLUS shell bracelets and three fired clay tablets covered with incised signs. These tablets have provoked a controversy over the dating of the VINČA culture and hence, by implication, the validity of radio-carbon dating (some authorities have compared the signs to those found on clay tablets of the JEMDET NASR phase in Meso-potamia, dated to the late 4th millennium bc, almost a millennium later than Vinča/Turdaş dates; most authorities, however, do not find these comparisons compelling). The ritual assemblage has been interpreted as the pos-sessions of a shaman.

Tartessos [Greek Tarsis; ? Phoenician and Biblical Tarshish]. Geographically indeter-minate, Tartessos in southwest Spain was known to early antiquity for its fabulous wealth, especially in tin, bronze, silver and copper, and has given its name to the so-called Tartessian culture of the early 1st millennium BC which is essentially PHOENICIAN with ETRUSCAN and Greek admixture. The town is commonly located at the mouth of the River Baetis (Guadalquivir) but literary sources also tell us that the name applied to a river and a whole region or kingdom. Other writers confuse Tartessos with Cadiz (GADES), or with most or all of Spain. Parallels with Cadiz are attractive, and Tartessos is therefore perhaps to be likewise seen as an early Phoen-ician trading-post, with trading links in tin to Brittany and the Scilly Isles (Kassiterides), and rapidly incorporating in due course the active co-operation of Greek and Etruscan sea-traders.

Taruga. A settlement site on the slopes of the Jos Plateau in central Nigeria where terracotta figurines of NOK type were found in associa-tion with domestic pottery and iron-smelting debris in a context dated between the 5th and the 3rd centuries bc.

Tarxien. One of the finest and most elab-orately decorated of the MALTESE TEMPLES, situated in the outskirts of Valletta, the Maltese capital. It is in fact a complex of four temples, dated to the 3rd millennium bc. Many stone slabs in the walls and courtyards are decorated with relief carvings, in spirals and other curvilinear designs or with animal figures. The most remarkable find is the lower half of an enormous statue of a 'fat lady',

known also from figurines of this period and thought to represent a goddess. After the temples had gone out of use a cremation cemetery of the Bronze Age was excavated in the ruins of the monument. The Bronze Age culture is named the Tarxien Cemetery culture after this site; it is dated c1900 bc at Tarxien itself, but seems to have continued for many centuries.

Tasadays. A small group of forest food collectors, isolated in the rain-forests of Mindanao, PHILIPPINES, and first reported to the world in 1970. The Tasadays have such a simple technology and food-gathering strategy that some investigators thought they could have preserved a pristine pre-Neolithic way of life for many millennia, but linguistic studies suggest that they may instead have descended from an original horticultural population and simplified their culture during about 700 years of isolation.

Tasmania. Part of the Australian continent during the late Pleistocene, the island was separated by rising sea levels which formed Bass Strait about 9000 bc. At the time of European contact Tasmanian Aborigines had a very simple tool kit of stone flakes and core scrapers, pebble choppers, wooden pointed spears, digging sticks, clubs and throwing sticks. They lacked all the post-Pleistocene tools known on the mainland, such as ground-edge tools, adzes, microliths, blades, stone points, spearthrowers, shields and BOOMER-ANGS; the DINGO was also lacking. At sites such as Mount Cameron West, Rocky Cape and West Point, all on the northwest tip of the island, occupation deposits go back to 6000 bc with bone points, stone scrapers and pebble tools among rich faunal deposits reflecting a littoral economy. A notable change occurred about 1000 bc with the disappearance of bone points and evidence for fish exploitation. The Tasmanians were observed by the English colonists to avoid eating fish. Pecked engravings at Mount Cameron West resemble the PANARAMITEE style of central Australia. Firm evidence of Pleistocene occupation has been found in recent excavations at Cave Bay Cave on Hunter Island, just off the northwest coast, with dates of 20,000 bc, when the present island was a hill on the Bassian plain. Very recent discoveries in limestone caves in the Florentine Valley and on the Franklin

River (Kutikina), in the thick rainforests of the southwest wilderness, have dated human occupation to 18,000 bc, a period of glacial maximum climate when the environment was predominantly open sub-Antarctic tundra or cold grassland below mountain glaciers. Fraser Cave contains rich faunal deposits from human meals, mainly wombat and wallaby species, with hearths and dense collections of CHERT flakes. Among the flakes were pieces of impactite, evidence of exploitation of stone sources from a meteor crater 25 km away.

Tassilo Chalice. According to an inscription on its base, the chalice was presented to the abbey of Kreumunster in southern Germany by Tassilo III, Duke of Bavaria between 778 and 788. It is an outstanding and original object, possibly made by NORTHUMBRIAN craftsmen, decorated with a combination of Hiberno-Saxon ornament typical of the period. The chalice is cast in bronze overlaid with gilt and silver NIELLO engravings, portraying Christ in an attitude of blessing, the evangelists and four saints. The cameos are enclosed by bands of dynamic interlace, while all the blank spaces are filled with zoomorphic ornament.

Tating ware. A distinctive later 8th-century pitcher type, always readily recognized because it was decorated with applied tin-foil. These pitchers were widely traded and occur in Swedish graves as well as in HAMWIH and DORESTAD. They were probably made in the Rhineland, but for only one or at the most two generations.

taula. A type of stone structure found on the island of Minorca on sites of the TALAYOT culture of the Bronze Age. It consists of a large stone slab laid horizontally, supported on either a vertical stone slab or on several superimposed blocks. They are often found inside horse-shoe shaped stone enclosures and they are thought to have had a cult function.

Taung. In 1924 the early hominid skull of a child of perhaps six years of age was found at this site in South Africa, and named *Australopithecus africanus*; it was the first AUSTRALO-PITHECUS fossil to be discovered (*see also* HUMAN EVOLUTION). The age of the deposit is unfortunately poorly fixed, and no stone tools are present.

Tautavel. The Arago cave near Tautavel in the east Pyrenees has revealed a considerable thickness of PALAEOLITHIC deposits of pre-MOUSTERIAN date with little stratification. The front half of a skull with heavy brow ridges and robust facial features has been found, as well as two lower jaws, one much bigger toothed than the other. Their date may be about 200,000 years ago.

Tawantinguyu. *See* CUZCO, INCA.

Taxila. A site in Pakistan and a major town in the ACHAEMENID satrapy of GANDHARA, which surrendered to ALEXANDER THE GREAT in 327 BC. It remained important throughout the ensuing MAURYAN and KUSHAN periods, but was abandoned after the Hephthalite incursions of the 5th century AD. The extensive remains of Taxila include Bhir mound, which conceals the pre-Hellenistic town of the 6th century BC and later; Sirkap, an Indo-Greek 'new town' with a rectilinear grid of streets laid out in the 2nd century BC and Sirsukh, another new town founded by the Kushans in the 1st century AD. A number of Buddhist monasteries existed in the vicinity, notably Jaulian, Mohra Moradu and Dharmarajika.

Taya, Tell. TELL site in northern Iraq west of Mosul, subject of a recent survey and excavation project undertaken by a British team led by Julian Reade. The site is a city of the EARLY DYNASTIC and Sargonid periods (mid-3rd millennium BC) and is unusual in that, unlike most Mesopotamian cities, the building material employed was not mud-brick but stone. As a result, and also because the period of florescence seems to have been relatively short, it has been possible to record in considerable detail the plan of a 3rd-millennium BC Mesopotamian city.

Tayacian. Following the excavation of the ancient rock shelter of LA MICOQUE near LES EYZIES-de-Tayac in the Dordogne, southwest France, the layers which probably belong to the penultimate glacial period were assigned to a Tayacian culture. Because this was mainly characterized in a negative fashion, an unfortunate tendency to use this term for any poorly characterized flake assemblage arose; the term is accordingly now out of flavour.

Tehuacan Valley. This high moutain valley, located in southeast Puebla, Mexico, was the subject of a massive multi-disciplinary project aimed at discovering the origins of agriculture in MESOAMERICA. Although particular attention was paid to the transition from ARCHAIC to agricultural ways of life, data was gathered for the whole period from before 7000 bc to AD 1540. The climate is hot and dry normally (and thus conducive to good preservation) but is broken by a short wet season. A number of cave and open-air sites were excavated which were chronologically correlated via stratigraphy (*see* SERIATION), the developmental sequence of plant remains and a series of RADIOCARBON dates.

The Ajuerado Phase (before 6500 bc) is characterized by small wandering groups (4-8 people) engaged in hunting and gathering. In the El Riego Phase (6500-5000 bc) small groups begin coming together seasonally into larger groups but hunting and gathering remains the principal means of subsistence. However, grinding tools, weaving and some plant cultivation (e.g. chilli peppers, avocado and squash) does occur. SACRIFICE, evidenced by decapitated burials, also appears. The Coxcatlan Phase (5000-3500 bc) marks the appearance of larger semi-sedentary groups occupying fewer sites and engaged in agriculture. MAIZE, gourd and beans are among the domesticates and artefacts include MANOS and METATES and improved basketry. A significant change in settlement pattern occurs in the Abejas Phase (3500-2300 bc). Pit house villages occurring along the river terraces are probably year-round dwellings (although cave sites continue to be used in the dry season). New species of plant food, long OBSIDIAN blades and possibly cotton make their appearance and there is an increased reliance on the hunting of small game, although agricultural foods are supplying 20 per cent of the diet by this time.

The later phases indicate progress to a fully sedentary life and include the wide use of ceramics and the domestication of the dog.

Tekkalakota. Neolithic site in the central Deccan, India. Two phases of settlement have radiocarbon dates indicating occupation in the earlier 2nd millennium BC. The earlier phase had fractional burials, but the later had extended burials in interconnected vessels for adults, while children were buried in urns.

tell. An Arabic word meaning mound or hill. In archaeological usage it refers to a mound resulting from continuous settlement by man, in areas where mud-brick is the normal building material. The long accumulation of material from mud-brick houses, successively built and rebuilt, slowly produces a growing mound, with the latest cultural material on the top, the earliest at the bottom. Many of the best-known sites of western Asia are tells, but they occur also in other areas such as in Greece and the Balkans.

Telloh. A TELL site in southern Mesopotamia, excavated by the French between 1877 and 1909. For many years it was thought to be the site of ancient LAGASH, but has more recently been identified as Girsu, possibly a religious centre within the state of Lagash, though not its capital. Telloh has produced a wealth of art objects and CLAY TABLETS, but little attention was paid to the architectural remains in the excavations. Most of the finds belong to the 3rd millennium BC, from the EARLY DYNASTIC, AKKADIAN and UR III periods, and include a large number of CUNEIFORM tablets and many fine statues of Gudea, who was governor of Lagash in the 22nd century BC. One of the most important tablets from Telloh is the so-called 'Urukagina reform text'. Urukagina was the last Early Dynastic king of Lagash (mid-24th century BC on the middle chronology) and the text records a series of sweeping reforms he instituted, directed against a corrupt and overpowerful palace bureacracy.

temescales. *See* PIEDRAS NEGRAS.

tempering. *See* STEEL.

Temple Mound period. The most recent period of a chronological construction relating to the whole of eastern North American prehistory. Formulated by J.A. Ford and Gordon Willey, the periods are, from early to late, PALEO-INDIAN, ARCHAIC, BURIAL MOUND, Temple Mound. The Temple Mound period is divided into two sub-periods: Temple Mound I (AD 700-1200), which covers the establishment and rise of the MISSISSIPPIAN TRADITION, and Temple Mound II (1200-1700) which embraces the cultural zenith and ultimate demise of the Mississippian as well as the continuation (especially in the northeast) of unmodified WOODLAND cultures.

temple-mountain. A form of monument which only occurred in classical CAMBODIA from the 9th to the 13th centuries. It originated from the belief that the main temple of the king, which is the ritual centre of the kingdom and eventually becomes his mausoleum, must be situated on a mountain or at least a hill. The kingdom of ANGKOR was founded on Mount KULÈN, but as there were no other hills in the area north of the Great Lake where the capitals were situated, successive kings built their main temples on artificial mountains, in the form of stepped pyramids. *See also* ANGKOR WAT, BAKONG, BAPHUON, BAYON.

Tenayuca. Located 10 km northwest of Mexico City, near present-day Tlalnepantla, the site, founded in 1224, was the first capital of the great CHICHIMEC leader Xolotl. The huge double temple decorated with a COATLE-PANTLI is a fine example of late POST-CLASSIC architecture and is thought to resemble the Great Temple at TENOCHTITLAN. An altar decorated with a skull and crossbones motif is similar to one at TULA. The temple, first built in c1299, was reconstructed five or six times.

George C. Valliant proposed that these activities coincided with the beginning of the 52-year cycles of the CALENDAR Round, indicating that renewal may have been literal as well as symbolic.

Tenere Neolithic. A variant of the so-called Saharan Neolithic complex, best illustrated at ADRAR BOUS and Arlit near the Air Mountains of Niger, and dating from the greater part of the 4th millennium bc to the first half of the 3rd millennium. Chipped stone implements include backed MICROLITHS, bifacial projectile points and discoid knives. The pottery may have connections with that from contemporary sites in the Sudanese Nile valley, as at ESH SHAHEINAB and KADERO. Both shorthorn cattle and small stock were herded; hunting was also practised. Sites attributed to the Tenere Neolithic contain numerous grindstones, but the only discovery which has been cited as providing firm evidence for plant cultivation is an impression on a potsherd from Adrar Bous that is believed to be from a grain of sorghum.

Tenochtitlan. Capital of the AZTEC empire, founded on an island in Lake Texcoco in the Basin of Mexico in c1345. Expansion was

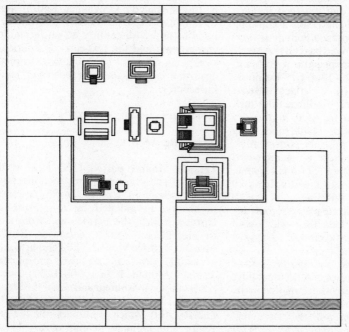

0   100m

The centre of Tenochtitlan in 1520, with main streets and canals

accommodated through a system of land reclamation which was also used as a means of intensive agriculture (*see* CHINAMPA). At its height the city supported an estimated population perhaps as high as 250,000 living in as many as 60,000 dwellings, making it significantly larger than contemporary European capitals. The city was approached by a network of eight major canals, with numerous feeders, and three giant causeways leading north, west and south connected the capital with the mainland. The 16th-century Spanish priest Bernardino de Sahagún recorded that the magnificent city centre comprised 25 PYRAMID-temples with nine attached priests' quarters, seven *tzompantli* (huge racks for displaying the skulls of sacrificial victims), two BALL COURTS, arsenals, plazas and other features. Dominating all were a huge plaza and the twin temples of TLALOC and Huitzilpochtli. At the dedication of the latter an astonishing 20,000 human victims were sacrificed (*see* SACRIFICE).

In the north of this urban conglomeration was the massive market complex of Tlatelolco, at which much of the material exacted through tribute was redistributed. According to Sahagún, the number and variety of goods available almost defied description. The market was open daily and both prices and commercial practice were strictly regulated by a resident court.

Virtually nothing remains of this former glory (although some archaeological remains were discovered during the recent building of the subway in Mexico City). The city was literally flattened in the Spanish siege and its aftermath in 1520.

teosinte. *See* MAIZE.

Teotihuacan. A massive urban centre located in the Valley of Mexico 50 km northeast of Mexico City, and the dominant force of Early CLASSIC PERIOD MESOAMERICA. At its heart is a complex of magnificent architecture including the massive PYRAMIDS of the Sun and of the Moon, the Cuidadela (probably an administrative centre) and the Great Compound which probably functioned as a market place; surprisingly, there are no BALL COURTS. The structures are distributed along a central roadway known as the Street of the Dead.

The site was originally interpreted as a CEREMONIAL CENTRE, but in the 1960s Rene

Millon's long-term mapping project revealed a stunning 21 square kilometres of continuous structures, showing it to be a masterpiece of urban planning.

Teotihuacan has its beginnnings as one of a number of small agricultural settlements dotted around the shores of ancient Lake Texcoco. By the Late PRE-CLASSIC, it had grown considerably (population estimates are as high as 30,000) and appears to have been in competition with a similarly large site at the southern end of the lake (*see* CUICUILCO). After the destruction of Cuicuilco, Teotihuacan expanded to unprecedented dimensions, reaching its cultural zenith between *c*400 AD and 600. Populations, certainly in the high tens of thousands and possibly as high as 200,000, were accommodated in a variety of apartment compounds which evidence some social differentiation. Typically, the 'palace' type dwellings were clusters of rooms around a central open patio which had an altar and sometimes a cistern for water storage. The contiguous rooms of the Tlamimilolpa apartment complexes are by comparison cramped, overcrowded, gloomy and jerry-built and have been called 'slums' by some.

Some areas of the site are clearly industrial and are associated with the manufacture of specific goods. Workshops associated with the production of OBSIDIAN goods and ceramics have been recognized. Of particular interest in this connection is the Oaxacan *barrio* which was an area of the city devoted exclusively to either the importation or manufacture of the goods of MONTE ALBAN.

It would be difficult to exaggerate the influence of Teotihuacan during the Early Classic. Barely a major centre is without some Teotihuacan forms and some (e.g. KAMINAL-JUYU and CHOLULA) seem to have been little more than satellite distribution centres.

Hallmarks of Teotihuacan influence include TALUD-TABLERO architecture, images of TLALOC, CYLINDRICAL TRIPOD VASES, THIN ORANGE WARE and stylized human face masks. Although there is very little massive stone sculpture (except as architectural embellishments), there are literally hundreds of murals. Teotihuacan materials, however, particularly in the later periods, tend to be rather monotonous, and mass-production is clearly a common phenomenon.

The end of Teotihuacan came relatively suddenly. A decline in its influence at other sites was already evident by *c*600, although the city itself thrived until the mid-8th century. Considerable evidence of burning is evident at this time, indicating that the city may have been sacked (possibly by the CHICHIMECS). The city was never rebuilt, but a greatly reduced population lingered on in the ruined city for a hundred years or more. *See* COYOTLATELCO.

tepe. Persian word for an artificial mound, equivalent to the Arabic TELL.

Tepenacs. *See* TRIPLE ALLIANCE.

Tepeu. A Late CLASSIC, Lowland MAYA phase (dated to AD 600-900) defined by a complex of cultural materials but most especially by the polychrome vase. The typical shape is a tall, cylindrical vessel with a flat base. They are decorated with life scenes often involving mythological creatures and commonly have a band of hieroglyphs, usually in the upper register.

Tepexpan. In 1949, on the former shores of Lake Texcoco, near Mexico City, a complete human skeleton, dating to *c*8000 bc, was discovered. There were no grave goods; it was buried face down with flexed legs and was tentatively identified as female. Although recovered from within the Late Pleistocene Becerra Formation its initial dating was regarded with some scepticism because of poor field procedures. Subsequent work, however, including fluorine analysis, has since confirmed this early date.

tephrochronology. A special case of STRATIGRAPHY. Tephra is a general name given to the material ejected from the vent in volcanic eruptions, and covers a wide range of ashes, cinders, bombs etc. Material ejected in this way can spread over large areas, as a dust cloud, or be rapidly distributed through a river system. Layers of tephra may be incorporated into archaeological sites. The volcanic eruptions producing such layers may be dated from historical records, or by such methods as POTASSIUM/ARGON. In Iceland there are several marker horizons of this kind which are used to date sites and structures. Consolidated ashes make up the rocks known as tuffs. At the hominid fossil-sites of East Africa, tuff layers

wihin the sequence have been invaluable for dating purposes.

terminus ante quem. Literally, 'point before which'. A dateable LAYER or structure on an archaeological site, which gives a dating endpoint to the deposition of all the layers below it.

terminus post quem. Literally, 'point after which'. A dateable object found within a LAYER on an archaeological site. All it is possible to say from such a find is that the layer in which the object lies, and all the layers above, must have been deposited at some time after the date of manufacture of the object.

Ternifine. A PALAEOLITHIC site in Algeria, east of Oran. Several jaws of *Homo erectus* type were found here, along with numerous stone tools including hand axes and cleavers attributable to the ACHEULIAN. The fauna is regarded as Middle Pleistocene, but the more exact dating is questionable.

terp. A type of nucleated settlement indigenous to the Iron Age and MIGRATION PERIOD cultures of the Frisian coastlands. These villages were constructed on low mounds as protection against high tides, and these became further heightened by accumulated layers of habitation debris resulting from years of successive occupation. Excavations have shown that terps were densely populated; they contain large numbers of dwellings including buildings in which crafts were practised. The main economic basis of the terps appears to have been derived from stock-raising and fishing with limited cereal production.

Terra Amata. A PALAEOLITHIC site within the confines of Nice in southern France, overlooking the sea, with 11 levels of occupation. Some were under the ancient beach, some in it, and some in a dune over it. The levels are ascribed to the ACHEULIAN, but very few hand axes and few tools at all have been recovered. A THERMOLUMINESCENCE DATE of 240,000 years is available for the site, but its reliability at this early time is uncertain.

terracotta. The material from which most ancient pottery and other fired clay objects were made. Literally, terracotta is 'baked earth'; it is incompletely fired and porous. In common usage today the term is applied to statuary, building materials etc rather than the better fired modern pottery.

Terramara [plural: *terremare*]. A term for both the settlement sites, of which only mounds of rich dark earth remain, and the culture of the Middle to Late Bronze Age in the Po plain of northern Italy. The Terramara population seems to have practised mixed farming. They were efficient metal workers and evidence of bronze-working within the settlements comes from a number of sites. A range of bronze forms was produced, including simple swords, winged axes, double-edged razors and ornaments such as pins and fibulae. Burial was cremation in URNFIELDS. Many authorities believe that the Terramara culture represents an intrusion from Hungary, where rather similar sites and artefacts are known.

terra sigillata [Latin: 'earthenware with relief figures']. Now a general and compendious term for glossy red table ware of the Roman imperial period. *Terra sigillata* is essentially a mould-made pottery, with both plain and relief-decorated examples. Geographic distribution is widespread, with several varieties and provenances. Both form and decoration are predominantly reminiscent of metalwork. Vessels bear the name-stamp of individual potters and workshops. Decorative themes include mythological figures, animals and birds, and foliage. Two principal and common types are: (1) Arretine (*see* AR-RETIUM) approximately 30 BC-50 AD; and (2) so-called Samian, or Gaulish *sigillata*, an industry established in Gaul probably by Arretine migrants, and especially associated with centres at La Graufesenque (Condato-magos), LEZOUX and LYONS. Samian ware is still studied following a classification proposed by H. Dragendorff in 1895-6, and the availability of Samian potters' stamps in dateable contexts gives valuable assistance to the dating of many imperial sites. Generically related or derivative of *terra sigillata* are the late Roman Argonne or Marne ware, and North African (African Red Slip) and eastern red wares.

Tertiary. The Cenozoic era (*see* QUATERNARY) consists of two periods, the Tertiary and the Quaternary. The Tertiary period runs from 65 million to about 2 million years BP and is itself divided into five epochs, the Palaeocene (65-54 million years BP), the Eocene (54-38 million years BP), the Oligocene (38-26 million years BP), the Miocene (26-7 million years BP) and the Pliocene (7-2 million years BP). The Miocene and Pliocene epochs were important in HOMINID EVOLUTION.

Teshik Tash. A PALAEOLITHIC cave in the Uzbekistan republic of the Soviet Union in the west Himalayas, Teshik Tash [hollow rock] has revealed several MOUSTERIAN levels, and the skeleton of a NEANDERTHAL child some 9 years old. He was buried with goats' horns, possibly of ritual significance.

tessera. (1) A small piece of tile, stone or glass, usually a square or cube, typically as used in the construction of MOSAIC decoration.

(2) In the Roman period, various *tesserae* (in the Latin sense of 'ticket' or 'token'), sometimes inscribed, were in circulation for various purposes. These were small, often coin-like tokens of bronze, lead, terracotta and bone.

Téviec. A small island in Morbihan, southern Brittany, France, where the burial of 23 Mesolithic skeletons was uncovered in occupation debris of a TARDENOISIAN settlement.

Texcatlipoca. *See* AZTEC, CALENDAR STONE, POST-CLASSIC PERIOD, QUETZACOATL, TOLTEC.

Texcoco. *See* TRIPLE ALLIANCE.

textiles. Woven cloth. Textiles may be woven from any number of spun fibres, from both animal and plant sources. In the absence of actual textiles, the existence of looms is attested by loom weights and so-called weaving combs. Spinning may be indicated by spindle whorls. Textiles themselves usually survive only in waterlogged or very dry conditions.

texture. The mixture of PARTICLE SIZE grades which make up a SOIL, SEDIMENT or similar material. In soil science, textures are classified into a number of categories, according to the percentage of SAND, SILT and CLAY. As with particle size, overall several different systems of texture classification are in use, including the British Standard 1377 system and the United States Department of Agriculture system. When describing texture it is important to make clear which system is being used.

Teyjat. Two small PALAEOLITHIC caves occupied in the MAGDALENIAN period are situated at Teyjat in the northern Dordogne, southwest France. One has fine line engravings of animals on blocks of limestone. *See also* CAVE ART.

Thailand. *Prehistory.* Archaeology in Thailand is especially active at the present time and recent excavations include HOABINHIAN sites at SAI YOK and SPIRIT CAVE and the two sites of NON NOK THA and BAN CHIANG, which together suggest the presence of rice cultivation, cattle domestication and copper-bronze metallurgy from about 3500 BC, followed by iron metallurgy and wet rice cultivation about 1500 BC. In southern Thailand (BAN KAO, KOK CHAROEN), Neolithic cultures continue well into the 2nd millennium BC and Bronze-Iron Age remains here are apparently related to the DONG-SON culture of VIETNAM (1st millennium BC).

Classical. At the beginning of the Christian Era much of present Thailand was inhabited by the MON people, very early Buddhists; it may even have been in the lower Menam plain that BUDDHISM was first implanted in Southeast Asia in the 3rd century BC. However, by the 3rd century AD the Cambodia-based INDIANIZED kingdom of FUNAN controlled Central Thailand which, in the 7th century, after Funan's dismemberment, became the independent Mon kingdom of DVĀRAVATĪ; peninsular Thailand came under the suzerainty of the SUMATRAN kingdom of ŚRĪVIJAYA. In the 11th century the KHMER kingdom of ANGKOR expanded into the Menam basin and eventually ruled over practically the entire present Thai territory. In the middle of the 13th century the first Thai kingdom of SUKHOTHAI achieved independence, at the northern rim of the Angkorian empire, and in only a few decades reduced the latter to about present CAMBODIA, while at the same time establishing Thai suzerainty over the Malay Peninsula. Sukhothai was succeeded in 1350 by AYUTTHAYA, which became the dominant power in mainland Southeast Asia for more than four centuries and even conquered Angkor itself. *See also* BURMA, HARIPUNJAYA, LAN CHANG, LAN NA, LAOS, LAVO, MALAYSIA, PHIMAI, PREAH VIHEAR, RĀMA KHAMHAENG, SAWANKHALOK, SUVARNABHŪMI, SYĀM, TĀMBRALINGA, U-THÒNG.

Tham Khuyen. *See* HOMO ERECTUS, VIETNAM.

Thapsos. A Middle Bronze Age settlement and cemetery on a promontory near Syracuse in southeast Sicily which has given its name to the local culture of the period. Both settlements and large cemeteries of rock-cut tombs are known, many investigated in the late 19th or early 20th centuries. Grave goods include both local Thapsos pottery, grey in colour with grooved and relief decoration and with many pedestalled vessels, and imported MYCENAEAN pots, mostly of Late HELLADIC IIIA types, datable to the 14th century BC. Many bronze objects occur also and some of these may be Mycenaean imports or local copies. Recent excavations in the Thapsos settlement, not yet fully published, suggest a Mycenaean presence on the site. The Thapsos culture follows the CASTELLUCCIO culture and is succeeded by the PANTALICA culture in the same area.

Tharros [present-day S. Giovanni di Sinis]. PHOENICIAN colony at the northern edge of the Gulf of Oristano in western Sardinia. Built over an earlier NURAGHIC occupation, the town functioned in a network of Carthaginian western Mediterranean harbours, and was particularly important to the MARSEILLES route. The principal period of prosperity seems to have been the 6th and 5th centuries BC, but the port continued under Roman rule from 238 BC and was only abandoned after the Byzantine period. The port installations are now below water. Phoenician evidence includes the largest *tophet* on Sardinia, a temple with engaged DORIC coloumns, and comprehensive remains of the town's water and drainage system. Roman material shows housing in *insulae*, shops, bath buildings and aqueduct installations. Two necropoleis date from the 7th century BC and include rock-cut tombs, some with *dromoi*.

Thatbyinnyu Temple [from Pali *Sabbaññu*:

'the Omniscient']. A large Buddhist monument in PAGAN, northern BURMA, being the principal construction of king Alaung-sithu, built in 1150. Stylistically it marks the transition between the period of predominantly MON and Burman characteristics.

Thatcham. A group of Mesolithic sites is known from the peaty deposits of the Kennet Valley at Thatcham in Berkshire. Dates ranging from over 8000 bc to *c*6000 bc suggest the sites may be of different ages. All seem to contain MAGLEMOSEAN artefacts.

Thaton. An ancient MON city at the mouth of the Sittang in Lower Burma, often identified with SUVARNABHŪMI. Originally called Sudhammavatī, it seems to have been the principal of a number of colonies of Indians from ORISSA, and according to local legend the 5th-century Singhalese monk Buddhaghosa was born and died there. Tradition holds it to be the place of origin of the Mons, although this claim remains to be substantiated archaeologically.

theatre. Examples of the Greek *theatron* (from Greek *theasthai*: 'view') occur from the 6th century BC. Essentially D-shaped, or often rather more than half-a-circle in plan, the Greek *theatron* had three main components: the *orchestra* (central floor, originally used for the procession and dancing of choric odes); the auditorium (Latin *cavea*); and the *skene* (originally perhaps only a temporary structure for the convenience of performers). In early and some classical instances, there was often little specific architecture, and the auditorium was formed from a suitable natural slope. With time, and especially in Roman examples, all these components were developed into greater elaboration, leading to the evolution of an integrated building, a kind of mass-production model that could be erected upon any level site. In these, the *skene* (Latin *scaenae frons*) gradually acquires a stage-like structure, architectural decoration and (probably) a roof; the *orchestra* is often paved and edged; and stone and/or wooden seating is provided, the necessary slope now being created upon a network of masonry and concrete vaults and corridors. Well-preserved examples survive at EPIDAURUS, POMPEII and ORANGE.

Thebes (Egypt). A city on the east bank of the Nile in Upper Egypt, which became the capital of Egypt under the Middle Kingdom and the New Kingdom. It was a centre for the worship of the god Amun, to whom major temples were erected. Opposite Thebes, to the west of the Nile, was the royal cemetery of the New Kingdom known as the Valley of the Kings. In contrast with the practice of earlier times the pharaohs of this time, from the 16th century BC onwards, were buried in carefully concealed rock-cut tombs, the only one of which to have survived with relatively little disturbance into modern times being that of TUTANKHAMUN, a comparatively minor ruler of the late Eighteenth Dynasty. The main burial chamber held a series of gilded wood shrines containing a stone sarcophagus within which were three successive mummy cases, the innermost of gold. Three associated store rooms contained furniture, chariots and other richly decorated possessions.

Thebes (Greece). Principal city of Boiotia in the classical and pre-classical periods, with a legendary history that predates the Trojan expedition. The legendary founder was Cadmus, son of Agenor, King of Tyre. Thebes's external policy always seemed to mistime its opposition to the dominant power of the moment, and its classical history included three near-total destructions — one by ALEXANDER THE GREAT in 336 BC, another by Mummius in 146 BC and a third by Sulla. Whatever may finally have survived these onslaughts is largely covered by the modern town, and excavation is therefore fragmentary and difficult. The Kadmeion, or 'palace of Cadmus', if it exists, might lie under the present city, and enthusiastic identification greeted the exposure of certain early 'palace' structures which were first excavated about 1909. More soberly, this and other structural evidence does suggest dates for occupation in the MYCENAEAN period, while Middle Helladic cist graves, Late Helladic IIIB pottery and LINEAR B tablets also indicate Bronze Age occupation. One rich find of BABYLONIAN cylinder-seals of the 14th-15th centuries BC confirmed for some Cadmus's eastern origins. Structural remains beneath the 'palace' have been dated to the beginning of the 2nd millennium BC.

theodolite. A SURVEYING instrument designed to measure angles. Theodolites are frequently used in archaeology for setting out GRIDS, but they are very versatile instruments and may be used for a variety of other surveying operations (see TRIANGULATION).

Thera [modern Santorini]. Southern Cycladic island c100 km north of Crete. During the Bronze Age there was a thriving settlement at Akrotiri, which came strongly under MINOAN influence, demonstrated by, for instance, the fine frescoes on the walls of the houses. At the end of the Late Minoan A period, c1500 BC, the settlement was abandoned as the result of an earthquake. Some time later an enormous volcanic eruption, greater than that which produced Krakatoa, buried the settlement under some 30 metres of ash and sent shock waves across the south Aegean Sea. Many authorities believe that it was this eruption that brought the Minoan civilization to an end. There is, however, a chronological problem: the destruction of the Minoan palaces on Crete seems to have occurred c1450 BC, some 50 years after the abandonment of Akrotiri and, although there would have been an interval of time between the earthquake and the volcanic eruption, it seems unlikely that it would have been as long as 50 years. Archaeologists and others remain divided on this issue.

Thermi. An Early Bronze Age settlement on the island of Lesbos in the eastern Aegean. Excavations in the 1930s revealed five phases of occupation of the EB I period (4th millennium BC). For most of its life it was an undefended settlement of timber houses, but at a late phase it was defended by a stone wall. It was destroyed some time before 3000 BC, at approximately the same time as sites such as TROY I in northwest Anatolia and POLIOCHNI on Lemnos.

thermoluminescence dating. A method of dating pottery and other fired clay objects.

Principles. All things, both above and below the ground, are being constantly bombarded by cosmic rays and by radiation coming from the decay of radioactive elements in the ground and in objects themselves. Minerals, bombarded by radiation, build up a store of energy within their crystal lattices. This energy can be released in the form of light when the mineral is heated — thermoluminescence [TL]. The longer or more intense the bombardment, the more energy is stored and thus

the more TL is emitted. At the same time, heating releases all the stored energy and the build-up starts afresh. Pottery, which contains mineral inclusions, is fired in antiquity and so starts its life with zero TL. Stored energy starts to build up in the minerals' crystal lattices from this point. Pottery's life above ground is relatively short, so most energy accumulation occurs as a result of radiation bombardment while it is buried in an archaeological site. After excavation, the TL can be determined by heating the sample and measuring the resultant glow. If the rate of bombardment is known, the time elapsed since the pottery was last heated (normally the firing) can be calculated.

Range. Technically unlimited, but dependent upon the occurrence of suitable materials for dating.

Accuracy. The probable error of a TL date is usually between ± 5 per cent and ± 10 per cent. So a date of 5000 BP could have a probable error of up to ± 500 years.

Materials. TL can potentially date any material that contains minerals and which has been heated in antiquity. This includes pottery and other fired clay objects and POT BOILERS (stones heated in a fire for cooking purposes). A number of sherds or stones is needed from each context and the objects should have been buried in a homogeneous layer, at least 300 mm from any boundary of that layer.

Problems. Most of the difficulties with accuracy in TL dates lie in the difficulty of determining the rate of radiation bombardment whilst buried (the Dose Rate). This is normally done by analysing the buried soil and burying a 'dosimetry capsule' on the site, but there are still problems in estimating it accurately.

Thetford. Town in Norfolk, eastern England, which was one of the BURHS created by King ALFRED in the 9th century. Recent excavations have proved successful in locating a large part of this early town. In a peripheral area near the well-preserved Saxon defences, archaeologists located traces of narrow cobbled streets bordered by large and smaller buildings. In the western part of the settlement, substantial rectangular timber buildings were found set within boundary ditches. One of these buildings was 36 metres long while another had a mortared floor; some had cellars and some may have had two storeys, since traces of staircases were found. The industrial workshops were situated near the defences, and among the crafts carried out were metal-working and the production of the mass-produced, wheel-turned Late Saxon pottery known as Thetford ware.

Thin Orange ware. A thin-walled, fine-paste, orange-fired pottery first introduced in the late PRE-CLASSIC PERIOD. It was widely traded all over Mesoamerica and has been found in CLASSIC contexts at KAMINALJUYU, MONTE ALBAN and as far north as Nayarit and Jalisco. It is regarded as evidence of central Mexican influence (especially TEOTIHUACAN), although its probable point of origin is the Valley of Puebla. It should not be confused with the early POST-CLASSIC Fine Orange ware.

thin sections. Microscope sections of rock, ceramics or other materials, which have been ground and polished until they are thin enough to determine the details of crystals and other structures (usually 30 μm thick). Sections of this kind are normally used in PETROLOGICAL ANALYSIS, but may also be used to examine bone and dental tissues. The method necessarily involves the removal of a small sample of material, but the hole which is left can usually be camouflaged successfully. In archaeology the method is most well known for its use in identifying the source of stone axes, but similar work has been carried out with pottery.

This. *See* PRE-DYNASTIC EGYPT.

tholos. A building, most often a tomb, with a circular chamber and CORBELLED vault, often approached by a long passage. In classical archaeology the term can be applied to either temples or tombs; when borrowed by prehistorians it is used exclusively for tombs, of PASSAGE GRAVE type with corbelled chambers. The best known examples are those at MYCENAE, the so-called Treasury of Atreus and Tomb of Clytemnestra.

Thompson, Sir Eric (1898-1975). One of the great MAYAN archaeologists and one of the first to apply ethnology to archaeological problems. Noted for his work in reconstructing the Temple of the Warriors at CHICHEN ITZA and his excavations at LUBAANTUN, RIO BEC and Pusilha, he was the first to establish a chronology for the Belize Valley, based on the SERIATION of ceramics. The first to make the distinction between the CEREMONIAL CENTRE and the less accurate term 'city', his greatest achievement was the correlation of the Maya and Christian CALENDARS. His book *The Civilization of the Maya*, first published in 1927, remains a relevant work today.

Thomsen, Christian Jurgensen (1788-1865). Curator of the National Museum of Denmark in Copenhagen from its foundation in 1816 until his death. Searching for a method of classifying the Danish prehistoric collections, he devised the THREE AGE SYSTEM, envisaging successive Stone, Bronze and Iron Ages. This was the first effective method of dividing up prehistory, and formed the basis of the subsequent development of prehistoric archaeology.

Three Age System. The division of prehistory into three successive ages — STONE AGE, BRONZE AGE and IRON AGE — defined by the main material used for making tools. Although the idea of the three ages had existed as a philosophical concept from classical times, the first person to develop it as a practical system for classifying archaeological material was Christian THOMSEN, who used it as a method of sorting the Danish archaeological collections in the early 19th century and published it in a Guide to the Danish National Museum in 1836. It was the first system devised for classifying archaeological material and has proved of lasting value. Although other systems of classification are used today, the terms for the Three Ages still remain in use as general labels for groups of societies and periods of time.

As the system was used and developed it proved necessary to subdivide and add to the original three ages. Sir John Lubbock (later Lord AVEBURY) suggested the subdivision of the Stone Age into an earlier PALAEOLITHIC (Old Stone Age) period, defined by the use of chipped stone tools, and a later NEOLITHIC (New Stone Age) period, when ground and polished stone tools (and also pottery) came into use. The Palaeolithic was thought to coincide with the PLEISTOCENE geological period and to represent societies living by hunting and gathering, while the Neolithic belonged to the HOLOCENE (recent) geological period and represented communities which lived by farming. Subsequently it was recognized that there were communities in the early part of the Holocene that still lived by hunting and gathering and had a chipped stone technology, and the term MESOLITHIC (Middle Stone Age) was introduced to cover these groups.

The terms CHALCOLITHIC, ENEOLITHIC and COPPER AGE are used — interchangeably — by some authorities to describe communities between the Neolithic and the Bronze Age which used unalloyed copper rather than true tin bronze.

Thule. A tradition, sometimes called Northern Maritime, that spans the period 100-1800 and has its origins along the Alaskan and Siberian coasts. OKVIK and OLD BERING SEA are its earliest manifestations, but whether or not it derived from the earlier NORTON TRADITION is still in doubt. After c1600 the Thule culture spread steadily eastward as far as Greenland, absorbing or supplanting the DORSET CULTURE of the central and east Arctic. Characterized by polished slate tools, impressed pottery and the extensive use of artefacts made from organic material, Thule represents the zenith of ESKIMO decorative art.

Thunderbird. One of a complex of sites at Flint Run, Virginia, USA, and the site of a long exploited jasper quarry. Core fragments, innumerable flakes and broken or preformed tools bear witness to a flint knapping industry of considerable proportions. Occupations from CLOVIS times into ARCHAIC is evident in the stratigraphy, with a near classic Clovis point being found at the lowest level. Evidence of vertical posts in association with living floors (dated to 9000 bc) raises the possibility of this being the site of the earliest house structures in America.

Thuparama. *See* ANURADHAPURA.

Tiahuanaco. Located at an altitude of 4000 metres at the south end of Lake Titicaca in Bolivia, Tiahuanaco was a large urban and CEREMONIAL CENTRE of the MIDDLE HORIZON. Huge megalithic constructions covering an area of c1000 by 500 metres were begun in the Early INTERMEDIATE PERIOD, but occupation of the site, traced throught stylistic similarities with PUCARA ceramics, probably occurred some time in the EARLY HORIZON. Tiahuanacan influence spread over a wide area of the Central Andes and is especially evident because of its distinctive ceramics. Typically, pottery was painted black-on-white on a red polished surface, although later styles employed as many as six colours. Geometric designs were common, but other favoured motifs were stylized life-forms such as the puma, the condor and the serpent. The kero (a flared-rim beaker) is a characteristic form.

Major structures include the Acapana, a platform mound of dressed stone; the Palacio, a double-walled enclosure, and the Qalasasaya, a rectangular sunken courtyard enclosed with monoliths and having a carved gateway. The most celebrated monolith is the 'Gateway of the Sun', which was carved from a single block of andesite weighing c10 tonnes. Representations of the anthropomorphic central figure of the gateway (as well as its flanking winged attendants) have been found on the pottery of many other areas (e.g. PACHACAMAC, NASCA VALLEY).

Characteristically, the monolithic statues of Tiahuanaco have a blockish, stiff appearance but clothing and ornamentation are represented in considerable detail, implying that their source of inspiration may have been motifs on textiles. Articles of bronze, copper and gold suggest that the city may also have been an important metallurgical centre.

Iconographic links with HUARI to the north are such that a strong economic and cultural bond between the two is assumed. The mechanics of this relationship are uncertain but it has been suggested that Huari was a secondary centre, instrumental in the spread of Tiahuanacan traits.

Tianko Panjang Cave. *See* OBSIDIAN, SUMATRA.

Tibava. A cemetery and settlement of the Early Copper Age TISZAPOLGÁR culture, located in the upper Bodrog Valley in eastern Slovakia and dated to the late 4th millennium bc. The site lies near a pass across the Carpathians and the richness of its grave goods supports the notion of a prehistoric 'gateway community', channelling exchange products

Tiahuanaco: centre figure of Gateway of the Sun

and stimulating demand. Over 40 graves have been excavated by K. Andel, who has discovered the largest collection of Early Copper Age gold pendants in the Carpathians, as well as south Polish and Volhynian flint nodules and rich copper finds.

Tiemassas. Set amidst coastal dunes in Senegal, some 80 kilometres south of Dakar, Tiemassas provides extensive undated archaeological deposits adjacent to a lagoon. It is probable that there were several successive occupation phases, at least one of which belongs to a pre-pottery phase characterized by large backed tools and bifacial projectile points. Elsewhere in the region, pottery-associated true backed microlith industries are presumed to be of more recent date.

Tievebulliagh. An area with a number of AXE FACTORIES near Cushendall, Co. Antrim, Northern Ireland. The axe factories were exploited from early in the Neolithic and axes of this particular stone were traded throughout northern Ireland and a few examples reached as far as western Scotland.

Tikal. An important CLASSIC PERIOD MAYA CEREMONIAL CENTRE located in the rainforest of the northeastern Peten province of Guatemala. This massive architectural complex was first occupied in the PRE-CLASSIC in *c*600 BC, as is evidenced by the presence of MAMON ceramics in early CHAL-TOONS. Stucco pyramids, painted in the IZAPAN style and featuring early CORBELLED arches occur in the subsequent CHICANEL Phase. The major occupation, however, is in the Classic Period and Tikal reaches its peak in AD 550; by this time the population had risen to as much as *c*45,000 (*see* MILPA) and the site covered an area of 123 square kilometres.

The core of the site is the group comprising the Great Plaza, with Temples I and II at either end, and the associated North Acropolis complex which covers an area of one hectare. Wide causeways form a triangular link between this, the massive Temple IV (over 60 metres high) in the south and a further temple complex in the west. Thousands of small house compounds surround the centre, decreasing in number with distance from it. A few kilometres to the north and south, great linear earthworks several kilometres long were constructed, probably for defence.

Numerous elite burials containing exotic materials, such as JADE, OBSIDIAN and stingray spines (*see* PERFORATION) occur within the Great Plaza and within some of the temple-pyramids. Commoners, by contrast, are usually buried under their houses. Stelae, many with LONG COUNT dates (including one of the earliest known of such dates, i.e. AD 292) were normally erected in prominent places, such as in front of temples. Some, however, were deliberately destroyed and then buried, presumably after the death of the person to whom they were dedicated (*see also* KAMINALJUYU).

Tikal maintained its cultural peak until *c*770, but a noticeable decline in construction had occurred by 870. By 1000 the site had been completely abandoned.

Tilantongo. *See* MIXTEC.

Tilemsi valley. A northerly tributary valley of the Niger, which it joins near Gao in southeastern Mali. The Tilemsi valley may have been one of the areas through which domestic animals were introduced into West Africa. In the northern reaches of the valley, as elsewhere in the southern Sahara, cattle herders are attested by the 3rd millennium bc. To the south, the Karkarichinkat sites suggest that the initial occupation, by pastoral people, did not take place until early in the 2nd millennium. At the latter sites hunting, fowling and fishing were all practised, but there is no evidence for plant cultivation.

till. A poorly sorted SEDIMENT, consisting of materials carried in ICE-SHEETS and GLACIERS, and deposited directly by the ice. All grades of PARTICLE SIZE may be found, from BOULDERS to CLAY (hence the description of some tills as 'BOULDER CLAY'). Ice does not sort the material it carries and the range of particle sizes, as well as the range of rock types, depends on the geology over which the ice-sheet or glacier has flowed.

Timmari. A hilltop settlement site and associated cemetery near MATERA in southeast Italy. The settlement produced evidence of later Neolithic occupation with SERRA D'ALTO ware, but the main occupation belongs to the Late Bronze Age and Early Iron Age. The associated cemetery is an URNFIELD, of the so-called Proto-Villanovan group, and contained several hundred urns placed in several layers and sometimes marked by small standing stones. The urns contained cremated remains, sometimes of more than one individual, and occasional bronzes of Proto-Villanovan type, such as arc fibulae and razors. The cemetery is usually dated to the 11th and 10th centuries BC.

Timna' [Hajar Kohlãn]. Capital city of the QATABANIAN kingdom of southern Arabia, in the 1st millennium BC Timna' was a walled city occupying *c*20 hectares, occupied from about the middle of the 1st millennium BC to the 1st century AD, when it was destroyed during wars with HADRAMAUT. Among the most important buildings excavated was a great temple with entrance court and rows of columns, near the centre of the city. The site has also produced a number of important inscriptions in the local South Arabian language and script. About 2 km north of the city is a cemetery site with a series of structures made of stone and mudbrick. The tombs have been plundered, but they yielded rich material including sculpture and inscribed tablets, bronze and pottery objects and jewellery.

Timor. An island of eastern INDONESIA, and a possible staging point for early human migrations to Australiia. Timor, with neighbouring Flores, has possible Pleistocene industries, and the presence of two species of *Stegodon* (an extinct proboscid) suggests that early Pleistocene land-bridges may once have reached the island from JAVA. However, the earliest archaeological dated remains come from caves in east Timor, where flake industries date from about 11,000 BC and Neolithic cultures appear after 3000 BC with the introductions of pig, dog and (later) cattle to the island.

Timur, Timurid. Timur (Tamerlane) was a Mongol conqueror of the 14th century who made SAMARKAND the capital of a vast nomad empire extending from Mongolia to the Mediterranean, but centred on Iran, Afghanistan and Soviet Central Asia. Many Timurid monuments, built by Timur himself and his grandson, Ulugbek, still survive in Samarkand.

tin. A relatively rare metal. Deposits of cassiterite, the tin ore, are found in only a few localities. Tin has a low melting point and could easily be SMELTED in a simple furnace. It is one of the major contituents of the alloy BRONZE.

Tingkayu. An open site on the edge of a now dry lake near the MADAI CAVES in eastern Sabah, northern BORNEO. The site has produced many well-made bifacially flaked leaf-shaped knives of chert of a kind previously unknown from Southeast Asia; this industry may be of late Pleistocene date (possibly older than 16,000 bc).

tin glaze. Around 1000 BC the ASSYRIANS discovered that by adding tin oxide to the other ingredients during the process of glazing pottery it is possible to produce an opaque, white enamelled effect. In the 8th and 9th centuries AD Persian and Islamic potters rediscovered this technique, and it was transmitted to Spain, and then to Italy in the 13th century. Afterwards it was copied by potters in France and Holland. The technique was first employed in England at the beginning of the 16th century.

Tintagel. A site in Cornwall, southwest England. Excavations were carried out in the interwar period to investigate the remains on the exposed promontory behind the precipitously positioned 13th-century castle long associated with ARTHURIAN legends. These excavations revealed several complexes of dry-stone buildings, one of which was possibly a church and ancillary structures. Possibly the most important finds, however, were the large quantities of sub-Roman imported sherds of Mediterranean origin. On the basis of these 5th- and 6th-century potsherds the excavator decided that the various complexes were part of an Early Christian monastery of Arthurian date, and any visitor to the site will see an ecclesiastical function attributed to each of the buildings. But academic opinion has recently swung in favour of an alternative interpretation of these much-loved remains, and it has been claimed that many of the structures may be either outbuildings and dwellings associated with the 13th century castle or, less probably, part of an Early Christian stronghold that functioned as a trading port or market rather than as a monastery. Only further excavation will resolve the matter, but the fact that more of these amphorae sherds and imported tablewares have been found on this exposed headland than anywhere else in Britain must be of significance.

tiplines. A term used by archaeologists to describe features of STRATIGRAPHY that appear to indicate where material has been deliberately tipped into a DITCH, PIT or structure on a site. Material tipped in at the edge of ditch spreads out in a fan until it reaches its angle of rest. A sequence of many intersecting fans could build up in the filling of a deep ditch. In SECTION, these fans would be seen as sloping LAYERS, known as tiplines.

Tirimoana pa. An excavated earthwork hillfort on Hawkes Bay, North Island, NEW ZEALAND, with early store pits for SWEET POTATO dated to about AD 1000, followed by the main ditch and bank defences with palisades constructed between 1400 and 1600. The store pits are good evidence that MAORIS grew sweet potatoes from initial settlement of New Zealand. *See also* PA, PALLISER BAY.

Tîrpeşti. A settlement site of the early CUCUTENI culture, located near Bacău, Moldavia, northeast Rumania, and dated to the start of the 4th millennium bc. Tîrpeşti is a characteristic promontory site, the neck of which is cut off by a deep ditch. The remains of ten fired clay house floors have been discovered, associated with a rich Pre-Cucuteni III pottery assemblage.

Tiryns. A strongly fortified MYCENAEAN palace, situated just south of Mycenae itself, in southern Greece. The settlement was occupied from the Early Bronze Age, but the palace and the massive defensive wall were constructed c1400 BC. The defences are among the most impressive surviving Mycenaean remains, constructed of CYCLOPEAN MASONRY, with internal CORBELLED galleries. The palace was of characteristic Mycenaean form, consisting of a central MEGARON opening on to a porticoed court; there are many frescoes showing MINOAN influence. Tiryns was destroyed c1200 BC, like so many of the other Mycenaean sites. There was some later occupation, but on a much poorer level.

Tirzah. *See* FAR'AH (2).

Tisza. Denotes a Late Neolithic culture of the early 4th millennium bc in eastern Hungary, northeast Yugoslavia and northwest Rumania. The Tisza culture represents the peak of nucleated settlement in the Pannonian Basin, characteristically found in large villages of up to 15 hectares. Some 30 such sites are known in Hungary, all near the confluence of important rivers. Cereal production was an integral part of the economy, as demonstrated by the large quantity of cereal storage jars, fired clay bins and granaries in the villages; in addition, local domestication of aurochs is attested, allied to intensive cattle husbandry. The distinctive incised pottery decoration has been likened to woven patterns.

Tiszapolgár. The eponymous cemetery of an Early Copper Age culture in eastern Hungary, northeast Yugoslavia and northwest Rumania, dated to c3400-3200 bc. Whilst tell settlement is rare, most domestic occupations are small-scale and short-lived farmsteads. A major landscape feature is the medium sized inhumation cemetery serving several farmsteads, of which the type site at Basatanya is a notable example. At Basatanya, graves were laid out in rows, suggesting family groupings. Grave goods included copper tools and long flint blades exchanged from north of the Carpathians.

Tjabenge. *See* CABENGE.

Tlacopan. *See* TRIPLE ALLIANCE.

Tlaloc. The Mexican name for the Meso-american god of water and rain, and a deity of great antiquity. Early cognates occur in the PRE-CLASSIC (e.g. the OLMEC god IV) and he has counterparts in numerous other Meso-american cultures such as Chac (Lowland MAYA), Tajin (TOTONACS) and Cocijo (ZAP-OTECS). Images of Tlaloc occur in many cultural contexts over a considerable period of time, for example at COPAN, MONTE ALBAN, KAMINALJUYU and CHICHEN ITZA. During the CLASSIC PERIOD his image appears in numerous media (pottery, wall painting and architectural embellishments) and is one of a group of artefacts which are seen as hallmarks of TEOTIHUACAN influence. Typically he is represented as goggle-eyed with a scroll-edged mouth and often, but not always, wearing flat rectangular headgear.

Tlamimilolpa. *See* TEOTIHUACAN.

Tlapacoya. A site located on an ancient lake in the basin of Mexico, 40 km east of Mexico City, which has produced very early radio-carbon dates for the presence of man. Strata containing hearths, discarded bone of extinct fauna and stone tools in both local andesite and imported obsidian and basalt have rendered dates in the range 22,000-20,000 bc. Such early dates, however, do not fit comfortably with most schemes for the peopling of America and thus are not widely accepted (*see also* VALSEQUILLO RESERVOIR).

There is also a small PRE-CLASSIC village site containing an early pyramid and OLMEC cultural material in the same area.

Tlatchli. *See* BALL GAME.

Tlatelolco. *See* TENOCHTITLAN.

Tlatilco. A village site of long occupation, located in the Valley of Mexico and dating to the PRE-CLASSIC PERIOD (possibly as early as 1500 bc). More than 500 burials have been uncovered here, many containing OLMEC or Olmec-influenced grave goods (e.g. engraved black-slip-on-white vessels and hollow figurines similar to those of LA VENTA and SAN LORENZO). Although there is no monumental stone architecture, low earth pyramids and bottle-shaped pits filled with household refuse (some apparently intentionally buried) indicate permanent residence. Located on an exit point on the western side of the valley, Tlatilco may possibly have been one of a number of stations on an Olmec trade-route linking the heartland in Veracruz with the raw material sources of West Mexico (*see also* LAS BOCAS).

Tlaxcala. *See* AZTEC; SACRIFICE.

Tlaxiaro. *See* MIXTEC.

Tlingit. *See* NORTHWEST COAST TRADITION.

Toalian industry. A microlithic industry from a number of caves in southern SULAWESI, INDONESIA, especially in the MAROS region. The industry develops out of preceding flake industries (perhaps with outside connections) from about 5000 BC and is characterized by small backed flakes and microliths, and well-made MAROS POINTS. The Toalian industry perhaps continued into the 1st millennium AD and overlaps with pottery from the late 3rd millennium BC. *See* LEANG BURUNG, MAROS POINTS, ULU LEANG.

tohua. *See* TAIPIVAI.

Tollan. *See* TULA.

Tollund Man. A BOG BURIAL from central Jutland, Denmark, of the Iron Age. The man's body was well-preserved and was naked except for a skin cap on his head and a hide belt around his waist. Around his neck was a noose of leather thongs, by which he had met his death; he had been either strangled or hanged. Analysis of the stomach contents showed that Tollund Man had taken his last meal 12-24 hours before his death and that it had consisted of a sort of gruel made up of various seeds, both wild and cultivated. *See also* GRAUBALLE MAN.

Toltec. Characterized by militarism and considerable internal dissension, the Toltec were the dominant culture of Early POST-CLASSIC Mesoamerica. Origins are unclear but they probably derived from one of the southward-moving CHICHIMEC groups which migrated into central Mexico after the fall of TEOTIHUACAN. Their capital was established at TULA in *c*960 AD by the ruler Topiltzin. The events of this ruler's life had a major influence, not only on Toltec affairs, but on those of subsequent Post-Classic cultures (*see* AZTEC). Unfortunately, a confusion of legend and history makes it impossible to separate him from the god QUETZACOATL whose banishment resulted in the increased influence of a faction dedicated to the god Texcatlipoca (and hence destruction and human SACRIFICE).

Evidence of Toltec influence (e.g. MAZA-PAN ware, metallurgy, imported PLUMBATE ware and massive architectonic decoration) has been found at many sites, including XOCHICALCO and CHOLULA, but at none more clearly than at CHICHEN ITZA. Historic documents cite an invasion of this northern Yucatan site by (the followers of) the feathered serpent (Quetzacoatl) in AD 987, which coincides with the departure of Topiltzin from Tula. A Toltec presence in Chichen Itza lasted over 200 years and continued long after the fall of Tula.

Numerous fragmented Toltec groups seem to have survived in central Mexico after the destruction of their capital. Such was their prestige, however, that many Post-Classic groups claimed them as ancestors. Most notable of these were the Aztec, who, in order to accommodate a Toltec ancestry, went so far as to destroy ancient codices and rewrite their own history.

tomba di giganti. *See* GIANT'S GRAVE.

Tonatuih. *See* CALENDAR STONE.

Tonga. A major island group of western POLY-NESIA, settled, like neighbouring SAMOA, by LAPITA colonists in the late 2nd millennium BC. Tonga maintains a pottery sequence throughout the 1st millennium BC, after which pottery manufacture ceases; little is known of 1st millennium AD prehistory. After AD 1000 large monuments appear (LANGI, HA'AMONGA), and these relate to the growth of the powerful centralized chiefdoms recorded in the 18th century (the Tui Tonga, Tui Ha'a Takalaua and Tui Kanokupolu dynasties). *See also* MU'A.

Tonglüshan [T'ung-lü-shan]. The site, near the Yangzi River in Daye Xian, Hubei province, China, of an ancient copper mine and smeltery: the name Tonglüshan means Verdigris Hill. The deposits, mainly native copper and malachite, were worked as early as the beginning of the Eastern ZHOU period (8th century BC) and as late as Western HAN (2nd-1st centuries BC). The mine workings cover about two square kilometres. Horizontal galleries branch off from vertical shafts at a depth of 40 to 50 metres; the timber-reinforced shafts and galleries are square in section, ranging from 80 to 120 cm on a side. Tools found in the mine include bronze axes or adzes and, in late shafts, axes, hammers, chisels, and spades of iron. Nearby smelting remains include the bases of seven furnaces, a few 10-kg copper ingots, and slag deposits estimated at 400,000 metric tons (from which a yield of about 10,000 metric tons of copper has been estimated). The Tonglüshan mine workings are the earliest yet known in China.

Tongsamdong. *See* PUSAN.

topikal. *See* MEGALITHS (INDIA).

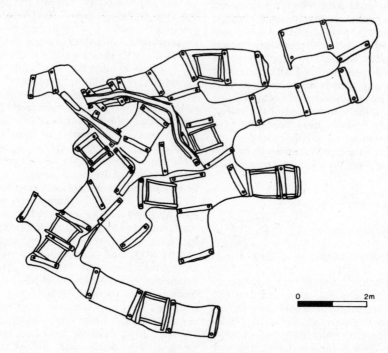

Plan of one section of an ancient copper mine at Tonglüshan.

Topiltzin. *See* QUETZACOATL.

torc [torque]. A pennanular ring, worn as a neck ornament. Torcs appear in the Early Bronze Age of central Europe (*see* UNĚTICE culture), but became particularly common in the later, LA TÈNE, Iron Age. They may be of bronze, but many examples of gold, silver and electrum occur in graves and hoards of the La Tène period. They are often decorated in CELTIC ART style. *See also* SNETTISHAM.

Torcello. An island close to Venice. Excavations around the small abbey revealed an important glass-making centre with the extensive remains of a 6th-7th century kiln that was producing a great range of glass tablewares. How far these glasses were traded is not yet certain, but it seems likely that this was one of the origins of the great Venetian glass industry.

Tordoš [Turdaş]. The largest VINČA site in Rumania, a 65-hectare settlement on the first terrace of the middle Mureş Valley. Transylvania, Turdaş has given its name to the Transylvanian regional group of the Vinča culture. The vast majority of the rich finds from Turdaş derive from surface collections by Baroness Zsofia von Tornia in the 19th century. Test excavations by M. Roska demonstrated a three-metre stratigraphy with a thin CRIŞ occupation level, a thick Vinča horizon and a Petreşti level. Of particular interest is the collection of incised signs, closely related to those at Vinča and BANJICA, and the range of fired clay figurines.

Torihama. A JOMON shell midden in Fukui Prefecture on the Japan Sea coast of western Honshu. Excavations and detailed bio-archaeological analyses have been in progress since 1962. Strikingly rich organic remains, including canoe paddles, bows, axe handles, lacquered wooden combs, basketry, melon rinds and seeds and mung beans, were recovered from an Early Jomon layer dated by a large number of radiocarbon dates to about 3500 bc.

Toro. A Late YAYOI village in Shizuoka, Japan. Excavations since the 1940s have revealed 12 dwellings, 2 storage houses built on piles complete with rat guards, and rice paddies covering 100,000 square metres with a waterway 430 metres long. The numerous artefacts recovered include bronze ornaments, wooden bowls and other kitchen utensils, agricultural tools and parts of looms.

Torralba. Important open air sites of Palaeolithic elephant hunters are known from Torralba and nearby AMBRONA in Soria province, central Spain. The stone tools are of ACHEULIAN type. In addition to *Elephas antiquus*, several other large mammals were present and had clearly been hunted. Traces of fire are amongst the earliest known, possibly c0.4 million years ago.

torre [plural: *torri*]. Stone towers of the Bronze Age of Corsica, found mostly in the south of the island. Built of CYCLOPEAN MASONRY, they measure 10-15 metres in diameter and c3-7 metres in height; normally a narrow entrance opens into a central CORBELLED chamber, sometimes with subsidiary niches. Although the torri are superficially similar to the NURAGHI of Sardinia and the TALAYOTS of the Balearic Islands, they are considerably smaller, too small for effective use for defence or as refuges. This fact, together with the discovery of bones in some torri, suggests a possible cult function.

Torredonjimeno. *See* GOTH.

Torre in Pietra. Just outside Rome, Torre in Pietra is a PALAEOLITHIC site with an ACHEULIAN and a MOUSTERIAN level, both with the bones of hunted mammals. A POTASSIUM-ARGON date of 435,000 years exists, but it is uncertain if this dates from before the first occupation.

tortoise core. *See* CORE.

Tószeg. Providing one of the most important stratigraphies in European prehistory, the Laposhalom TELL near Szolnok in the Tisza Valley in eastern Hungary has long been used as the basis for chronological subdivisions of the Hungarian earlier Bronze Age. Above TISZA and TISZAPOLGÁR levels is a five-metre Bronze Age deposit with four main occupation horizons. I contains layers with NAGYREV pottery, with houses built of clay with internal partitions. II contains layers with HATVAN pottery, with rectangular timber-framed houses, while III-IV consist of levels with

FÜZESABONY pottery and similar timber-framed houses. It should be noted that the sequence of Bronze Age groups found at Tószeg is by no means universal on other Hungarian tells.

trace elements. Elements which on CHEMICAL ANALYSIS make up less than 0.1 per cent of a material. 'Minor elements' make up between 2 and 0.1 per cent, 'major elements' more than 2 per cent. Material from a particular source is frequently characterized by an individual pattern of concentrations of its trace elements. This phenomenon has been used to identify the sources of, for example, OBSIDIAN and flint artefacts.

tradition. A widely used term in North American prehistoric archaeology which implies the persistence of cultural traits through time. It is also used in this sense in Old World archaeology, though the term is less popular in that field. A tradition is most usually regional in scope and always has chronological depth. The term is often associated with an artefact type or assemblage of great longevity, for example, the ARCTIC SMALL TOOL TRADITION, which originated in c4000 BC and some forms of which survived to historic times. A tradition should be understood in contra-distinction to a HORIZON, the internal relationships of which are spatial and coeval.

Trajan's Column. Tall commemorative COLUMN erected in honour of the emperor Trajan (r. 98-117) and dedicated to him on May 18th, 113 AD. The column marks the centre of what was once Trajan's Forum in Rome, one of the important imperial *fora* of the city (*see* FORUM). Composed of 18 massive drums of marble, the column stands some one hundred Roman feet high (29.5 metres) to the statue plinth. The decoration consists of a continuous spiral frieze, commemorating the emperor's triumphs in Dacia (101-2 and 105-6). The column contains an internal spiral staircase.

Tra-kiêu. A CHAM archaeological site in the province of Quang-nam, central Vietnam. It is part of the territory of AMARĀVATĪ, the so-called holy land of Champa, and from this site comes the oldest inscription in the Cham or in any AUSTRONESIAN language, dated to the 4th century. *See also* DÔNG-DU'O'NG and MI-SON.

transepted gallery grave. A type of GALLERY GRAVE in which side chambers open out of the main burial chamber. Characteristic examples occur in the SEVERN-COTSWOLD group of tombs in southwest England, though rather similar forms occur occasionally in northwest Ireland. In a classic work Glyn Daniel identified the source of the Severn-Cotswold tombs in a group of superficially similar tombs round the mouth of the Loire in France, but more recently scholars have regarded these as variant PASSAGE GRAVES, showing no special connection with the English tombs.

TRB culture. Abbreviated name for the Danish *Tragterbecker* or German *Trichterbecher* culture, alternatively known in English as the Funnel Beaker Culture. It is the first Neolithic culture of northern Europe, found in southern Scandinavia, the Low Countries, northern Germany and northern Poland, in the later 4th and early 3rd millennium bc (much of the 4th millennium BC). It is thought by many archaeologists to represent the acculturation of local Mesolithic communities by contact with the LINEAR POTTERY culture groups further south. Settlement sites are not well known, but burials are abundant; these include single burials under DYSSER in Scandinavia and in KUJAVIAN GRAVES in Poland and, a little later, collective burials in PASSAGE GRAVES (*see also* HUNEBED). Pottery includes the characteristic funnel beakers, as well as so-called amphora and flask forms. Other artefacts include ground stone axes and battle-axes, while copper tools appear in the later phases. The TRB culture is succeeded by — and perhaps develops directly into — the SINGLE GRAVE culture.

Treasury of Atreus. *See* MYCENAE.

Trelleborg. A site in southern Zealand and the best-preserved example in Denmark of an insular type of VIKING military camp. Like the similar forts at FYRKAT and Aggersborg which were built at the same time, Trelleborg is composed of a substantial earth-and-timber bank with four timber gates. The internal enclosure is divided into four quadrants each containing four timber, bow-sided LONG HOUSES, in this instance constructed of staves. Trelleborg differs from other camps in that it has a concentric outer defensive bank and an adjoining enclosure, while there are thirteen additional buildings between the two enceintes.

Extensive excavations in the 1930s revealed that Trelleborg was operational some time between the mid-10th and early 11th centuries and that its life was short-lived. The site reconstructions are also very impressive and include a full-scale replica of one of the houses. The origins of camps like Trelleborg with their regular arrangement remain rather an enigma, yet it seems that they were short-lived royal or military settlements. At one point they may even have served as operational bases equipped with barrack blocks for Sven Forkbeard's raids on England. The perfect symmetry of Trelleborg has always attracted attention, as have the origins of this form of fort. Some scholars have looked to the Near and Middle East, but the Flemish forts built as refuges against the Vikings in the 9th century may prove to be the closest model.

Trepang. *See* MACASSANS.

trepanning [trephining]. The surgical removal of a disc or rectangle of bone from the cranial vault. Archaeological examples have been found throughout the world, and are of widely varying date. Trepanations are often well-healed and several may occur on the same skull.

Tres Zapotes. An OLMEC site located west of the Tuxtla Mountains, 160 km northwest of LA VENTA. Surviving well into the Late PRE-CLASSIC, it continued to flourish long after the abandonment of La Venta and SAN LORENZO, even though it was contemporary with them in its early stages. Its Olmec beginnings are evidenced by flat-bottomed, white-rimmed pottery and colossal stone heads; an increased influx of 'foreign' materials characterize the later period. Cut-stone facings on the site's rectangular pyramid, the increasing presence of IZAPAN pottery forms and MAYA-influenced stelae belong to this late period. The site's most important find is Stele C which has the earliest Maya LONG COUNT date yet discovered (i.e. 31 BC).

Trewhiddle. A village near St Austel in Cornwall which was the scene of an important archaeological discovery in 1744: a hoard of metal objects deposited in the latter part of the 9th century. Contained in the hoard were some bronze plaques decorated with an interesting style of NIELLO-inlaid animal ornament usefully dated by association with ANGLO-SAXON coins. The most interesting piece in this collection is a silver chalice standing 13 cm high and ornamented with beaded wire; it is one of two surviving examples from the British Isles.

triangulation. A SURVEYING procedure, by which the position of an unknown point is determined from the dimensions or angles of the triangle it forms with two known points. Dimensions may be measured using tapes, or more accurately with electronic distance-measuring equipment. Angles are normally measured with a THEODOLITE.

Trier [Roman Augusta Treverorum]. Principal Roman city of northeast GAUL, the natural advantages of which were appreciated by emperors as distinct as Augustus and Constantine. Evidence for a tribal sanctuary nearby suggests that the general site was already securely settled by the Treveri, a Celto-Germanic people, well before the town was selected by Augustus for specific promotion. The location was favourable in several respects. First, there was good yet protected access to the Rhine (at COLOGNE, Koblenz, and MAINZ), and use as a supply centre for the armies of the Rhine soon became established. Secondly, communications encouraged trade, notably the Moselle wine-trade, but also, for example, in pottery ('Samian' ware) and textiles. Thirdly, the site was administratively convenient as a link-point for the three provinces of Gallia Belgica (Gaul), and the two Germanies, and a mint was in use from about 296 AD. During the 4th century AD Trier achieved even greater importance as a kind of spiritual and political capital of western Europe. There are notable Roman remains, including evidence for a 1st-century amphitheatre, bath buildings, Constantinian audience chamber and palace, an ornate late Roman gateway (the Porta Nigra), and early Christian churches. During the Roman Christian period souvenirs were mass-produced for pilgrims.

trilithon. Formation of two upright stones supporting a third placed across the top of them as a lintel. Trilithons appear in MEGA-LITHIC monuments of various types, but the most impressive examples are to be found at STONEHENGE, where SARSEN stones, weighing as much as 50 tonnes were used, skilfully joined together with mortice and tenon joints.

Trinil. A locality in east central Java is of considerable historical importance and the find place of the first *Homo erectus* fossil skull, and indeed the first recorded pre-Neanderthal human fossil find in the world (in 1891). The Middle Pleistocene fauna of Java is also called after Trinil. The human remains found in the 1890s included a skull cap, some teeth and five leg bones. *See also* SANGIRAN, NGANDONG, SAMBUNGMACAN.

Triple Alliance. In the Late POST-CLASSIC PERIOD, TENOCHTITLAN, Texcoco and Tlacopan formed a military alliance which became the dominant force in the Lake Texcoco region of the Basin of Mexico. It was actually a formalization of the alliance which had defeated the Tepenacs (the major power at the time) at Azcapotzalco, although Tlacopan (present-day Tacuba and a Tepenac city iself) was included because of its neutrality rather than any active role. The AZTECS rose quickly to control the alliance and absorb the other members, although Texcoco, under its philosopher-king Nezahuacoyotl, became renowned as a centre of culture and learning.

Tripolye. *See* CUCUTENI-TRIPOLYE.

triumphal arch. The triumphal arch seems to be a typically Roman innovation. The archway is normally free-standing and decorative, and erected to commemorate perhaps a military victory, the restoration of peace, or the achievement of other public benefits by an emperor or general. Examples occur from the 2nd century BC, and grow increasingly elaborate under the empire. Consisting of one to three arches, sometimes with intersection, they are commonly decorated with relief panels and attached sculptures. There are good examples at GLANUM, ORANGE and ROME.

Troldebjerg. A Middle Neolithic TRB settlement (*see* TRB CULTURE) on the island of Langeland, Denmark. It has LONG HOUSES c60 metres long, divided up into smaller units. Under the floor was found a votive deposit containing a pot and an axe, placed with its cutting edge pointing upwards.

Trondheim. The great medieval capital of Norway, situated in the centre of the west coast along the ice-free Trondheim Fjord, where it commanded vital land and sea routes to Russia and the rest of Europe. The sagas allege that Trondheim was founded in 997 by King Olav Tryggvason, the Norwegian patron saint, and that the town soon grew to become a flourishing late VIKING trading centre with as many as three royal palaces, several churches and a Thing-place where parliament assembled. Unfortunately, successive rebuilding and a series of severe fires in the 17th century have obliterated most of the timber-built medieval town. Recent excavations, however, have successfully recovered the outlines of a 10th-century hall-type house, an 11th-century church and other smaller buildings, as well as evidence for soapstone, textile and leather-working and other Viking industries.

Troy. The site of ancient Troy has been identified as the modern mound of Hissarlik overlooking the Dardanelles in northwest Turkey. It was identified and first excavated by SCHLIEMANN between 1874 and 1890; further excavations took place in the 1890s under DÖRPFELD and again in the 1930s by an American team under Blegen. Underneath the town of Ilion (Ilium), of the classical Greek and Hellenistic periods, lay seven successive Bronze Age settlements. Schliemann identified the second of these, Troy II, as Homer's Troy, but it has long been recognized that this is in fact much earlier; most authorities today believe that the Homeric city was either Troy VI or VIIa.

Troy I, dated to the 4th millennium BC and perhaps lasting much of that millennium, was a small settlement of 0.5 hectare defended by a mud-brick wall on stone footings. This settlement had 10 building levels, with three major phases. Houses of this period have been excavated, with built-in cupboards and sleeping platforms. Equipment was generally simple, though tin bronze was introduced during the period. The site, along with other sites in the region, was destroyed later in the 4th millennium. Troy II was larger and more wealthy (the so-called 'Treasure of Priam' found by Schliemann comes from this level). The buildings were still modest in scale, but were now of MEGARON form. Troy II lasted from c3000 BC or a little earlier for several hundred years, after which it was destroyed. During Troy III-V (c2600 BC, or a little earlier, to 1900 BC) the citadel gradually grew in size, though the community appears less wealthy than that of Troy II. By Troy VI (1900 or 1800-1300 BC) a new fortification wall enclosed a town of two hectares; this town was wealthy and there is much evidence of trade with the MYCENAEAN centres of Greece. It was destroyed, probably by an earthquake, though some authorities believe that this destruction was that of the Greeks in the Trojan War. Troy VIIa was a poorer settlement, but shows strong evidence of continuity with the previous occupation. It was destroyed in the mid-13th century BC and this destruction is the best candidate for that described by Homer. There were two further occupation phases, VIIb and VIIc, and a final destruction c1100 BC. After this there was a long gap until the foundation if the Greek town of Ilion c700 BC.

Truşeşti. A large settlement and cemetery site of the Late Neolithic CUCUTENI-TRIPOLYE culture, situated near Botoşau, Moldavia, northeast Rumania. Excavated by M. Petrescu-Dîmboviţa, the site comprises almost 100 complete house-plans on a promontory, enclosed on one side by a double ditch. The cemetery containing several dozen graves is located at the narrowest part of the promontory. The houses contained rich pottery assemblages of the Cucuteni A phase.

Trzciniec. The eponymous settlement site of an earlier Bronze Age culture distributed in southeast Poland and the Ukraine and dating to the mid-2nd millennium bc. The type site near Lublin, with a large number of houses with sunken foundations, is but one of a dense distribution of settlements in the Lublin area. Burial types are particularly diverse, with inhumation and cremation, flat and barrow graves occurring in varying combinations. The Trzciniec group is closely related in material culture to the Komarow and Sosnicja groups further to the east, in the Ukraine.

Ts'ai. *See* CAI.

Tshangula. A cave in the Matopo Hills near Bulawayo, Zimbabwe. It contains several layers of archaeological deposit preserving microlithic artefacts and, in the upper levels, sherds attributed to BAMBATA ware. Particular interest attaches to a pre-WILTON horizon where backed microliths are associated with diminutive implements produced by means of a prepared core technique. The alternative names Tshangula and Umguzun have been given to this industry in Zimbabwe, dated at POMONGWE to the 14th millennium bc.

Tshikapa. A mining area in the Lupemba valley, Kasai Province, southern Zaire. Four completely characteristic Early Iron Age pottery vessels of UREWE type are reported to have been found there during mining operations, in an undated context and without further archaeological associations. The discovery has been used as evidence for an early spread of Early Iron Age industries along the southern fringes of the equatorial forest. Recently, however, doubts have been cast as to whether this material really comes from Tshikapa after all.

Tshitolian. Named after the Tshitolo Plateau in southern Zaire, this stone industry was the microlithic successor to the LUPEMBAN. The processes of its development are best seen in the DUNDO area of northern Angola, beginning around the 12th or 13th millennium bc. Tshitolian industries occur also in Congo and Gabon. The most characteristic backed microliths are of a flared triangular shape and may have been hafted for use as transverse arrowheads. Other tool types, more clearly derived from Lupemban ancestors, are small picks and foliate points; the latter types seem to be more frequent on sites located in open plateau environments than in the denser vegetation of the valleys.

Tsubai Otsukayama. One of the earliest large KOFUN [tumuli] in Kyoto prefecture, Japan-Modified out of a natural hill into a keyhole shape about 185 metres long, a rectangular stone-lined grave was dug in the round part of the hill. Among the burial goods were iron weapons and utensils and nearly 40 bronze mirrors. Most of the mirrors were of the same type, probably cast in the same mould. Since this type of mirror has been found from many other *kofun* from northern Kyushu to eastern Honshu, it has been suggested that the mirror was used as a symbol of political alliance and the person buried at Tsuboi Otsukayama was at the centre of this network.

Tuc d'Audoubert. A deep cave system in the central Pyrenees, southwest France, this site has few examples of PALAEOLITHIC cave art, but is famous for the bison modelled in clay, preserved deep in the cave.

Tula. The TOLTEC capital located in an easily defensible position on a major ridge 65 km northwest of TEOTIHUACAN in the state of Hidalgo, Mexico. Founded on an already existing settlement in c960 AD by the priest-king Topiltzin (see also QUETZACOATL), the city grew to cover an area of 11 square kilometres by c1000 and may have supported a population of up to 50,000. At its height it included some 1000 mounds and at least as many low rectangular house mounds, five BALL COURTS, and monumental civic architecture at the southern end of the ridge.

The focus of the civic group is the Temple of Quetzacoatl (pyramid B) which features TALUD-TABLERO architecture, a COATLE-PANTLI on the north wall, a CHACMOOL at the entrance way, six roof-bearing 'Atlantean' figures in stone, and a number of massive carved columns representing warriors. The nearby Temple C bears evidence of savage destruction, as does the so-called Burnt Palace (although some of the burning here was probably associated with ritual).

The earliest pre-architecture phases at Tula are characterized by the presence of COYOTLATELCO ware, but the dominant ceramic occurring after c1000 is MAZAPAN ware. Imported PLUMBATE WARE also occurs frequently. Curiously, although the Toltec are associated with the introduction of metallurgy into central Mexico, no metals have been found.

Tula was destroyed, probably by a CHICHI-MEC group, in either 1156 or 1168 (depending on how one reads the CALENDAR date) when the last Toltec king, Huemac, departed for Chapultepec.

For many years the location of Tula was in doubt. Because it was referred to as Tollan (a more generic word meaning great city), it was often confused with other centres, notably Teotihuacan.

tula adze. A thick, round stone flake, found in Australia, usually about 5 cm long, with a steeply trimmed working edge opposite an obtuse-angled striking platform. Ethnographic examples are set in gum on the end of a wooden handle or spearthrower and used for shaping wooden weapons, tools and utensils. Repeated use necessitates re-sharpening of the edge until the flake becomes elliptical, when it is discarded. In this form, with a heavily step-flaked edge opposite the striking platform and the shorter dimension now the distance between platform and edge, it is termed by archaeologists a 'tula adze slug'. Distribution of tula adzes is restricted to the more arid regions, with INGALADDI at the northernmost extreme and KENNIFF CAVE near the eastern limits, and they have not been found in Victoria or southwest Australia. The oldest examples come from PUNTUTJARPA, dating from 8000-5000 bc levels, and are exactly like those still used by desert Aborigines.

Tumapel. See SINGHASÁRI.

tumbaga. An ALLOY of COPPER and GOLD used in South America. See also CHIBCHA.

tumulus. Another term for a BARROW.

Tumulus culture. Name given to the Middle Bronze Age culture of much of central and eastern Europe, with its centre in southern Germany. It is dated to the mid-2nd millennium bc (earlier 2nd millennium BC). It is defined mainly by the dominant burial rite of inhumation beneath a burial mound, as well as a number of characteristic bronze types, found both in the burials and in hoards. It was formerly regarded as an intrusive culture, but many scholars today see it as developing locally out of the ÚNETICE culture and continuing to develop into the URNFIELD CULTURE of the same area.

Tun. See CALENDAR (AMERICAS).

Tunxi [T'un.hsi], sometimes read Tunqi [T'un-ch'i]. A district south of the Yangzi River in Anhui province, China. Like slightly earlier and later assemblages found in the same general area (see DANTU, WUJIN) finds of late Western ZHOU date unearthed at Tunxi show metropolitan Zhou influence superimposed on the local GEOMETRIC POTTERY tradition and transformed by it. Two burials excavated in 1959 take a peculiar form, each consisting of a low platform built of pebbles, over which an earthen mound was raised. The funerary goods, chiefly glazed pottery, bronze RITUAL VESSELS, and some sort of eccentric local musical instrument, were laid with the corpse on the platform. Most of the bronze vessels are based on Western Zhou prototypes but their geometric decoration copies local pottery. The 71 glazed pots found in the two tombs are of a type represented also at a site further to the east, in Deqing Xian, Zhejiang province, where a burial discovered in 1976 yielded 27 examples. The high-fired glaze of these late Western Zhou wares is comparable to that of the earliest glazed pottery yet known from China, which comes from the SHANG-period site at WUCHENG some 300 kilometres southwest of Tunxi. Glazed pots similar to those from Tunxi and Deqing have been unearthed at metropolitan Western Zhou sites such as LUOYANG and ZHANGJIAPO but in far smaller quantities, and the glazed ware from these more northerly sites may well have been imported from the lower Yangzi region, where glazed ceramics evidently have a long history.

Turfan [Chinese: Turpan]. An oasis city on the northern branch of the SILK ROUTE in Eastern Turkestan (modern Xinjiang province), China. Chinese armies reached the Turfan basin in the 1st century BC; thereafter the city changed hands many times before its abandonment in the 14th century AD. During most of its history Turfan was an important Buddhist centre. Well-preserved Chinese SILKS, documents, and paintings have been recovered from tombs in the area.

turf line. Properly, a layer rich in organic material, which lies on top of a BURIED SOIL profile. It represents the remains of the vegetation which grew on the soil before burial. The term has, however been applied quite widely, and not all 'turf lines' described in excavation reports are necessarily the result of such processes. This distinction is important, because a real turf line, associated with a soil buried in a rampart or other mound, indicates a pause in construction long enough for a soil to have developed. If the dark layer which has been labelled 'turf line' is really only the result of muddy feet, or material tipped into the rampart during construction, then such a pause cannot reasonably be suggested.

Turkana. *See* KOOBI FOBA.

turquoise. A cupro-aluminium phosphate gemstone, sky-blue to pale green in colour, which was highly prized for jewellery in several parts of the world including western Asia, Egypt, Mesoamerica and the American Southwest.

The main Asiatic source lies in northern Iran, whence it was widely traded, especially to Mesopotamia. It was particularly common in the later prehistoric period, for instance at Tepe GAWRA; in the Early Dynastic period turquoise went out of fashion, perhaps because of a preference for LAPIS LAZULI, which occurs in quantities at this time. Sources in the Eastern Desert of Egypt and in the Sinai desert served the Egyptian stone-workers, who used it mainly for beads and other jewellery.

In the Americas, rich deposits occur in Nevada, Arizona and New Mexico, but it is apparently not indigenous to Mesoamerica (purported sources in the Mexican state of Guerrero remain hypothetical). Thus long-distance trade can be inferred from its presence in contexts outside the American southwest; it is, for example, one of the commodities featured in the AZTEC tribute lists in the CODEX Mendoza and was much favoured by the MIXTEC. Some archaeologists, however, propose that it is part of a complex of exotic materials whose ultimate point of origin is China (*see also* JADE).

Tutankhamun. One of the final pharaohs of the 18th Dynasty, whose short reign (c1361-52 BC) saw the return of the capital to THEBES and the re-establishment of the worship of the god AMUN-RE following the EL AMARNA interlude under AKHENATEN. Tutankhamun is mainly known by the chance that his tomb near Thebes is the only burial of an Egyptian pharaoh to have survived into modern times with only minimal disturbance. The value and elaboration of the burial and accompanying grave goods of this relatively young and minor ruler provide a unique insight into the appurtenances of the New Empire kingship. *See also* DYNASTIC EGYPT.

Tutishcainyo. The earliest of the ceramic

phases at a series of sites on Lake Yarinacocha on the Ucayali River in the tropical lowlands of eastern Peru. Although there are no radio-carbon dates from these sites, the distinctive shell or sand tempered pottery decorated by zoned incision has invited comparison with ceramic complexes elsewhere. Radiocarbon dates for WAIRA-JIRCA pottery from the KOTOSH site have helped to ascribe Early Tutishcainyo to the period 2000-1300 bc. A more tenuous comparison with ceramics from MACHALILLA and from the Kotosh phase at Kotosh, have led to a temporal construction of 1300-900 bc for Late Tutishcainyo. Post-Tutishcainyo phases include Shakimu, Yarinacocha, Camaracayu and Caimito.

tuyère. A short tube made of clay, through which the air from bellows can be blown into a furnace, to produce the high temperatures required for metal-working and SMELTING.

Tyimede. *See* OENPELLI SHELTERS.

Tyldal Chair. Discovered in 1879 in the small church of Tyldal in Norway, the Tyldal Chair is a remarkable object hewn out of birch and completely covered with elaborate carved decoration. The carving bears certain similarities to the work of the Early Norman WINCHESTER school, yet its prominent animal ornament interwoven with figures and foliage give it an unmistakeable Scandinavian ap-pearance. There is dispute about the function of the chair but it is in all likelihood an early bishop's throne.

Tyre. Important PHOENICIAN settlement on the coast of Lebanon south of Beirut. Con-tinuous settlement has restricted excavation to the Byzantine and Roman levels and informa-tion about the Phoenician town comes only from documentary sources. It was situated on an offshore island and had a double harbour, linked by a canal, which allowed sheltered anchorage and a safe outlet whatever the wind direction. It appears in ancient documents as a powerful and important trading centre, famous especially for the purple dye made from *murex* shells which was known as 'Tyrian Purple' after this site. It was the parent city of CARTHAGE, which inherited the leadership of the western Phoenician (Punic) cities after Tyre fell to the BABYLONIANS under Nebuchadnezzar in 572 BC. On this occasion the city withstood a 13-year siege before it fell, and in 332 BC there was another remarkable siege by Alexander the Great, who built a causeway to the island from the mainland.

Tzakol. A phase in the early CLASSIC PERIOD which is characterized by a complex of low-land MAYA artefacts. It is especially evident in mass-produced, elaborately decorated polychrome pottery and is frequently asso-ciated with TEOTIHUACAN forms. A common form is the basal flanged bowl decorated with conventionalized designs of human and animal forms.

Tzintzuntzan. *See* TARASCAN.

tzompantli. *See* CHICHEN ITZA.

U

Uahuka Island. *See* HANE.

Uaxactun. A CLASSIC MAYA centre located north of TIKAL in the northeastern Peten province of Guatemala. The central complex consists of a small plaza flanked by long, low palace- or apartment-style buildings and two temple-pyramids. However, the site is best known for its Late CHICANEL stucco decoration in the IZAPAN style, which is especially evident on the beautifully preserved E-VII sub-pyramid. Though never a large centre, a SERIATION of its ceramics laid the basis for the whole of the Lowland Maya chronology (*see* KIDDER). Stele 9 has one of the earliest LONG COUNT dates of the Classic Period (AD 328). The terminal Long Count date for the site is AD 889.

Ubaid. The small TELL of Al Ubaid near UR in southern Iraq has given its name to the prehistoric culture which represents the earliest settlement on the alluvial plain of south MESOPOTAMIA. The Ubaid culture has a long duration, beginning before 5000 bc and lasting until the beginning of the URUK period (*c*4000 bc or later, depending on the chronology favoured). In the mid-5th millennium bc, the Ubaid culture spread into northern Mesopotamia, replacing the HALAF culture. The Ubaid culture is characterized by large village settlements and the appearance of the first temples in Mesopotamia, initially modest in scale, but growing to substantial size, and probably an important economic role, by the end of the period (*see* ERIDU and Tepe GAWRA). Equipment includes a buff or greenish coloured pottery, decorated with geometric designs in brown or black paint; tools such as sickles were often made of hard fired clay in the south, but in the north, stone and sometimes metal were used for tools. There is little evidence of craft specialization or social differentiation.

Overlying the remains of the Ubaid period settlement at the type site was a small but lavishly decorated temple of the EARLY DYN-ASTIC period, excavated by Sir Leonard WOOLLEY in 1922. The decorations included statues and reliefs made in copper sheet on a bitumen base or core, a frieze of figures in shell and limestone inlay, columns covered in copper sheeting and others decorated with mosaics of red, white and black stones. An inscription records that the temple was dedicated to Ninhursag, the Sumerian mother goddess, and was built by A-anne-padda, son of Mes-anne-padda. This latter king is recorded by the King List as the founder of the First Dynasty of Ur; this suggests a date before 2500 BC for this temple.

Ubayama. A large shell midden in Chiba prefecture, Japan, excavated many times since 1893. Pit-houses, human skeletons and Middle and Late JOMON pottery were recovered. Radiocarbon dates of the 3rd millennium bc, the first dates carried out on Jomon materials, were received with scepticism when they were published in 1951, but have since been accepted.

Ubeidiyah. A site in the Jordan valley at Afikim, Israel, where there are a series of PLEISTOCENE deposits with stone tools dated from POTASSIUM-ARGON indications to between 1.7 and 0.7 million years ago. The lower levels are of OLDOWAN type, while ACHEULIAN types appear above. Some tiny skull fragments have also been found.

Udayagiri. *See* ORISSA.

Ugarit. 2nd-millennium BC CANAANITE city at modern Ras Shamra near the Mediterranean coast of Syria. Although securely identified as ancient Ugarit only in the 2nd millennium, the site was occupied from much earlier and the city overlies a series of earlier Bronze Age, Chalcolithic and Neolithic settlements going back to the 7th millennium bc. The city flourished throughout the 2nd millennium, but its heyday was in the 15th to 12th centuries, when it came first under strong

525

Egyptian influence and then under HITTITE dominance. At this stage the town walls enclosed c20 hectares. Commodious family houses have been excavated and a number of important public buildings, including two temples (one dedicated to Baal, the other to Dagon), a priest's library yielding many sacred texts, and a palace with a very large archive of administrative and economic documents. From these we know that Ugarit was a major commercial settlement at this time and must have housed a decidely cosmopolitan community. Not only were there tablets in AKKADIAN CUNEIFORM — the *lingua franca* of trade throughout the Near East — but others, also using the cuneiform script, were in the local language, Ugaritic, and a few others were in Hurrian (*see* HURRI); some seal impressions are in Hittite hieroglyphics. Moreover, the population of Ugarit may be credited with the development of the first true alphabet: simplified cuneiform signs were used for an alphabet of 32 letters, probably in the 15th century BC. The city was destroyed in the early 12th century BC, perhaps by the PEOPLES OF THE SEA.

Uhle, Max (1856-1944). One of the greatest pioneers of South American archaeology and the first to produce an area-wide chronology for Peru, using a synthesis of STRATIGRAPHY and SERIATION. The sheer volume of Uhle's work is astonishing even by today's standards. He discovered the source of NASCA pottery (the Ica Valley), identified the CHAVIN horizon at Ancon, and dug at PACHAMAC, TIAHUANACO and CUZCO as well as numerous small sites in the MOCHE, CHINCHA, CHANCAY and Ica valleys. In addition, he found time to visit other sites in Bolivia, Chile and Ecuador. Not surprisingly, publication did not keep pace with fieldwork, but many volumes of unpublished notes and other records are housed at the University of California.

Uinal. *See* CALENDAR (AMERICAS).

Uioara de Sus. The site of a large hoard of metal objects of the Late Bronze Age, located in the upper Mureş valley in central Transylvania, Rumania, and dated to c1000 bc. The largest known hoard of this period, it contains almost 6000 pieces: weapons, axes, horse harness and ornaments, with a total weight of c1100 kgs of metal. This concentration of metal reflects the intensive exploitation of Transylvanian minerals in the Late Bronze Age; of 360 hoards in Rumania in this period, 320 derive from Transylvania. The site also lies close to one of the richest sources of salt in Transylvania.

Ujjain. A city state of the 1st millennium BC in central India. The earliest phase of occupation is associated with BLACK AND RED WARE and the use of iron; the city of this phase was defended by a large rampart. This phase was succeeded by an occupation with NORTHERN BLACK POLISHED WARE. The city, which occupied several hundred hectares, was an outpost of the GANGES CIVILIZATION.

Ukhaidir. An early Islamic fortified palace in Iraq contained in a rectangular enclosure 169 metres wide and 175 metres long. The enclosure is defended by towers and has gateways on all four sides, the main entrance being to the north. The palace itself adjoins the north wall and is entered through the north gate. The palace is 82 metres wide and 112 metres long. Beyond the entrance is a vaulted hall 15.5 metres long and 10.3 metres high, giving access to a courtyard in front of the reception rooms. The rest of the building consists of a mosque, storerooms and four self-contained *bayts* [residential units]. The walls of the outer enclosure survive to a height of 17 metres and part of the palace is three storeys high. Sir Archibald Creswell, one of the greatest historians of Islamic architecture, concluded that Ukhaidir, which may be assigned to the 8th century on the basis of style and construction, was built by the Abbasid prince Isa b. Musa, in 778.

Ulalinka Creek. *See* ALTAI.

Ulan Khada. A site on the shores of Lake Baikal in southern Siberia. The lowest level is assigned to a 'Preceramic Neolithic' phase, while later levels have pottery and are labelled NEOLITHIC. All levels are associated with a hunting and gathering life-style.

Ulchi. *See* OKHOTSK.

Ulug-depe. *See* NAMAZGA-DEPE.

Ulu Leang. An important excavated rock shelter in the MAROS region of southern

SULAWESI, INDONESIA, with a sequence starting c9000 bc that illustrates the development of the TOALIAN microlithic industry after 5000 BC.

Uluzzo, Uluzzian. Around the bay of Uluzzo, in Apulia, southern Italy, there are several PALAEOLITHIC caves. The most important is Grotta Cavallo, with a series of MOUSTERIAN and Upper Palaeolithic levels. The earliest Upper Palaeolithic levels are the type series of the Uluzzian.

Umbu. A tradition roughly contemporary and co-regional with HUMAITA in southern Brazil, but differing from it by the presence of projectile points at an early date. The most common point form is the elongated triangle, which is often found in association with pounders, anvil stones, bolas and polished axes. By the 2nd millennium bc there is a noticeable decline in the variety of projectile points and the scraper becomes the most common artefact. Although the tradition persisted into the early centuries AD, when ceramics had already begun to appear in northeast Brazil, Umbu remained non-ceramic.

Umguzan. See TSHANGULA.

Umm an-Nar. A settlement and cemetery of chamber tombs on a small island off the west coast of Abu Dhabi on the Oman peninsula. This site, excavated by a Danish expedition in the 1950s, has given its name to an early 3rd-millennium BC culture, which has also been found on sites in inland Oman, including the Buraimi oasis. Sherds of characteristic Umm an-Nar pottery have been found in the lowest levels at Qala'at al-Bahrain on the island of BAHRAIN, below the structures of the first city there. This suggests that the Umm an-Nar culture predates the DILMUN culture of the Persian Gulf, dated to the later 3rd millennium BC. The excavators have suggested that the Umm an-Nar culture can be identified with the land of MAGAN, mentioned in Sumerian documents, but this identification is based on rather flimsy arguments and has been challenged by other authorities.

Umm Dabaghiyah. Early 6th-millennium bc type site of the Umm Dabaghiyah culture, the earliest known culture in the north Iraq plain.

The site is small (less than one hectare), but has yielded some interesting architectural remains: long buildings consisting of rows of small cell-like rooms without obvious means of access, which are interpreted as communal storehouses. Ordinary houses also occur, with evidence of living rooms, kitchens and storage rooms. Some wall paintings have been recorded, showing onager (wild ass) hunting scenes. The importance of hunting in the economy is clearly indicated by the animal remains, 84 per cent of which are made up of two species of wild animals, gazelle and onager, although domesticated sheep, goats, cattle and pigs were also kept. Cereal and pulse remains have been found, but because the area is today an arid gypsum salt covered steppe, the excavator, Diana Kirkbride, has suggested that plant foods were imported (in exchange for animal products, such as onager hides). This is one possible explanation, but as Umm Dabaghiyah is only just outside the area where rain-fed farming is possible today, it may be that slightly different climatic conditions in the 6th millennium bc would have allowed dry farming to be practised then. Pottery is abundant in all the four main phases and includes painted types similar to 'archaic' HASSUNA pottery. Indeed, the Umm Dabaghiyah culture can be regarded as ancestral to Hassuna. Other sites of this culture are YARIM TEPE and Tell es-Sotto further north.

underwater archaeology. This largely self-explanatory term is preferable to the more restricted terms marine or maritime archaeology, since it includes the examination of submerged settlement sites under fresh-water lakes, as well as the examination of harbour works and shipwrecks under the sea. The overall aims and methods of underwater archaeology are the same as those of archaeology in general, but a great number of specialized techiques have been developed to solve the problems of excavating and recording under water and of raising finds from the sea and lake beds, as well as subsequent problems of conservation of materials previously preserved under water. Underwater archaeology is a relatively new branch of the subject, which has grown with the development of the aqualung and other subaquatic equipment since World War II. Its achievements include the examination of

Neolithic villages in Switzerland, Paleo-Indian burials in Florida, classical harbours in the Mediterranean and shipwrecks of many different dates in many different seas. *See also* CAPE GELIDONYA, MARY ROSE, PANTANO LONGARIN, YASSI ADDA.

Únětice. The type site for the principal earlier Bronze Age culture in central Europe, Únětice is a flat inhumation cemetery of some 60 graves near Prague, Bohemia, Czechoslovakia. In cultural terms, Únětice is an umbrella term for several local groups (Nitra, Schlan etc), which between *c*1900 and 1500 bc achieved the technological breakthrough of cast tin bronze metallurgy. Most sites are cemeteries, with inhumation the predominant rite. However, extensive copper mines are known near Salzburg and their products are often found in hoards containing up to 500 items. Although no such sites are known in Bohemia, the Únětice period is often associated with the appearance of princely graves; particularly wealthy burials occur on the periphery of the Únětice distribution (see, for example, LEUBINGEN).

Upton Warren interstadial complex. An INTERSTADIAL of the DEVENSIAN cold stage which occurred between 43,000 and 23,000 bc (45,0000-25,000 bp). It consisted of a very rapid temperature rise to an initial thermal maximum of 41,000 bc (43,000 bp) followed by a temperature decline leading to a lower 'plateau' of temperature lasting from 38,000 to 23,000 bc (40,000 to 25,000 bp).

Uqair, Tell. A TELL site 80 km south of Baghdad, excavated by an Iraqi team in the early 1940s. These excavations uncovered a settlement of the UBAID period and a temple of the URUK period. This temple has a tripartite plan and is very similar to the White Temple in the Anu sanctuary at Uruk itself. It is distinguished by the occurrence of fine polychrome wall paintings with human and animal figures. Fish offerings suggest that this temple might have been dedicated to Enki. A small subsidiary chapel, later in date that the temple itself, contained a fine collection of pots of JEMDET NASR style and four CLAY TABLETS inscribed with pictographic symbols of the kind in use in the Jemdet Nasr period.

Ur [modern Tell el-Muqqayr]. One of the most important cities of SUMER, situated in the south of the country west of the Euphrates River, its walls enclosing *c*60 hectares. Ur was excavated by a joint expedition of the British Museum and the University of Pennsylvania under Sir Leonard WOOLLEY between 1922 and 1934. The earliest occupation of the site belonged to the UBAID period, perhaps *c*5000 BC, and the most flourishing period for the city was the EARLY DYNASTIC PERIOD (*c*3000-2400 BC). To this period belong the celebrated tombs of the Royal Cemetery with their wealth of goods made of gold, lapis lazuli and other precious materials, and their evidence of the sacrifice of human attendants of the dead kings and queens. After a period of decline, Ur flourished again in the time of the Third Dynasty of Ur in the 21st century BC, which saw the final flowering of Sumerian achievement. The founder of this dynasty, UR-NAMMU, built a great ZIGGURAT to the city's patron deity, Nanna, the moon god. The city continued to thrive in the BABYLONIAN period and the Bible claims Ur as the home of Abraham before he left for the west. Later the city declined and was finally abandoned in the 4th century BC.

uranium series dating. A group of related RADIOMETRIC dating methods, based on the decay series of the uranium isotopes ^{238}U and ^{235}U.

Principles. Each of the isotopes decays through a series of radioactive daughter isotopes until a stable isotope of lead is reached. Three daughter isotopes are created and decay with half-lives useful for dating: Ionium (^{230}Th), Proactinium (^{231}Pa) and Radium (^{226}Ra). Several uranium series dating methods exist, most of which apply to ocean-bottom deposits and are not applicable to archaeology. One, however, has recently been applied in a pioneer study to bones from such important sites as CLACTON. This is the ionium deficiency (^{230}Th/^{234}U) method. A small amount of ^{234}U is taken up by animals as they grow and is incorporated into their skeleton (ionium is not taken up in this way). The uranium starts to decay at a slow rate, producing ionium (^{230}Th). The animal dies, the skeleton is preserved, and the uranium continues to decay. The ionium decays also, but there is a gradual net increase of this isotope in the material. Ionium concentration increases steadily with age until, at about

500,000 years, an equilibrium is reached between production and decay. Until this time, the ^{230}Th/^{234}U ratio is a function of age and can be used as a dating method.

Range. The practical early limit for the ionium deficiency method is 300,000 years. Only dates younger than this may be obtained. This range makes the method most useful in geochronology and Palaeolithic archaeology.

Accuracy. As yet, ionium deficiency dates have large probable errors (*see* STANDARD DEVIATION). The dates on bones from the British trial study that are now available are 245,000 + 35,000 or − 25,000 BP, 125,000 ± 20,000 BP; and 174,000 ± 20,000 BP. Errors this size do not matter in such an age range, where any idea at all of date is useful.

Materials. Ionium deficiency has been applied to corals with success. Early trials with bones seem to produce sensible results, but attempts to date mollusc shell have proved unreliable.

Problem. After death and preservation in a deposit, the system must remain 'closed'. That is, uranium must not be lost from the material to be dated. Some adjustment may be made for an 'open system', allowing for migration of uranium, but this still produces difficulties.

Urartu, Urartian. A kingdom that flourished in the early 1st millennium BC in the region of Armenia (i.e. eastern Turkey and adjacent areas of Iran and the USSR). Its centre was in the Lake Van region. The name Urartu first appears in documentary sources in the 13th century BC and the kingdom was in existence by *c*900 BC. It lasted for some 300 years before succumbing to pressures from groups such as the CIMMERIANS, the PHRYGIANS and the SCYTHIANS. The Urartians are known from a number of sites, characterized by their heavily defended citadels: that at Van had to be entered through a rock-cut passage. They adapted the CUNEIFORM script to their language, which is closely related to HURRIAN, and they have left rock-cut inscriptions, some of them bilingual. They were accomplished metalworkers, producing bronze weapons and armour and sheet bronze vessels, including cauldrons with animal heads on the rim, set on tripod stands, which were widely traded in the ancient world.

Urewe ware. The characteristic Early Iron Age pottery type of the interlacustrine region of East Africa. There are good reasons, both typological and chronometric, for regarding Urewe ware as ancestral to the varied wares of the Early Iron Age complex further south. Named after a site in southwestern Kenya, Urewe ware is also attested in southern Uganda, northwestern Tanzania, Rwanda, Burundi and adjacent parts of Zaire. In most areas its appearance is dated to the first three centuries ad, but in northwestern Tanzania, as at KATURUKA, it may be significantly earlier. No local antecedents for Urewe ware are known from the interlacustrine region. Its makers were clearly skilled workers of iron, but so far virtually no direct evidence has been recovered to indicate their subsistence base.

urial. *See* SHEEP.

urn. Name given to any kind of large pottery vessel used to contain the cremated remains of the dead; the term is sometimes extended to cover similarly shaped vessels used for domestic storage purposes. The term is particularly widely used in the European Bronze Age and the name URNFIELD CULTURES, given to the late Bronze Age of much of Central, Eastern and Southern Europe, refers to the characteristic burial rite.

Urnes. The 11th-century church at Urnes in Norway is one of the oldest and finest stave churches in existence. Some of the staves are decorated with Viking ornament in the form of sinuous animals and zoomorphic ribbons including one scene in which a quadruped is locked in combat. The term 'Urnes style' is derived from these decorations; it is the latest of the Viking art styles and it is a type of ornament that occurs a great deal on Scandinavian metal-work from this period and also on Swedish RUNE stones.

urnfield, Urnfield cultures. An urnfield is a cemetery containing cremations placed in urns. The term Urnfield culture or cultures is used to describe the Late Bronze Age groups found over much of temperate Europe, who disposed of their dead in urnfields. The Urnfield cultures are dated to *c*1300-800/700 BC, lasting even later in peripheral areas, and are characterized by a well-developed bronze industry. Many copper mines of this period are known and studies of those in the Mühlbach-Bischofshofen area of Austria indicate that mining was on a considerable scale: one calculation suggests that 20,000 tonnes of crude copper were extracted from the mines of this area over a period of several centuries. The techniques of bronze production also developed in this period: beaten bronze was now produced and used both for vessels and for sheet metal armour, such as helmets, shields and body armour. Mastery of the CIRE PERDUE casting method also characterizes the Urnfield bronze industry. Settlement was often in small HILLFORTS or other small defended settlements. The Urnfield cultures succeeded the TUMULUS CULTURE in central Europe and developed into the HALLSTATT Iron Age culture. *See also* LAUSITZ.

Uruk [modern Warka; biblical Erech]. Situated *c*250 km south of Baghdad, on an ancient branch of the Euphrates River in Iraq, Uruk was one of the major city-states of SUMER. Excavations by German archaeologists from 1912 onwards have revealed a series of very important structures and deposits of the 4th millennium BC and the site has given its name to the period that succeeded the UBAID and preceded the JEMDET NASR period. The Uruk period saw the emergence of urban life in MESOPOTAMIA and led to the full civilization of the EARLY DYNASTIC period. It is not always fully realized how unique the site of Uruk was at this time: it was by far the largest settlement, with the most impressive buildings and with the earliest evidence of writing. It would be true to say that Uruk was Mesopotamia's — and the world's — first city.

It seems to have started as two separate settlements, Kullaba and Eanna, which coalesced in the Uruk period to form a town covering *c*80 hectares; at the height of its development in the Early Dynastic period, the city walls were *c*9.5 km long, enclosing a massive 450 hectares, and may have housed some 50,000 people.

In the heart of the city are two large temple complexes: the Anu sanctuary, belonging originally to Kullaba, and the Eanna sanctuary, dedicated to Inanna, the goddess of love. Both these complexes have revealed several successive temple-structures of the Uruk period, including the White Temple in the Anu sanctuary and the Limestone and Pillar Temples in the Eanna sanctuary. A characteristic form of decoration involves the use of clay cones with painted tops pressed into the mud plaster facing the buildings — a technique known as clay cone mosaic. On the northwest side of the Eanna sanctuary is a ZIGGURAT laid out by Ur-Nammu of UR in the Ur III period (late 3rd millennium BC).

Evidence from the deep trench excavated in the Eanna sanctuary has cast much light on the developments of the Uruk period. The most important of these was undoubtedly the development of writing. The earliest CLAY TABLETS appear in late Uruk levels; they are simple labels and lists with pictographic symbols. Tablets from slightly later levels, of the Jemdet Nasr phase, show further developments towards the CUNEIFORM script of the Early Dynastic period.

The city remained important throughout the 3rd millennium BC, but declined in importance during the later part of that period. It remained in occupation throughout the following two millennia, down to the PARTHIAN period, but only as a minor centre.

Uruk was the home of the epic hero GILGAMESH, now thought to be a real king of the city's first dynasty, and Uruk played an important role in the mythology of the Mesopotamian civilizations to the end.

Urukagina. *See* TELLOH.

Uryudo. One of the many village sites of YAYOI rice farmers who settled in the lowland plains of Osaka, Japan, in the 1st century BC. The cemetery is of interest, because some members of the community were buried in small mounds surrounded by ditches, while most others were interred in simple pits. The difference must be a reflection of some complexity which was developing in Yayoi society. None of the dead, however, were accompanied by rich burial goods, in sharp contrast to the jar burial cemeteries in Kyushu, such as SUGU.

Usatovo culture. The type site for a regional group derived from the Late TRIPOLYE culture (Tripolye C2), distributed in the Odessa region of the south Russian steppe zone. Dated to the mid-3rd millennium bc, the barrow cemetery at Usatovo was one of the richest in the steppe zone and lay next to a stone-built settlement. Crouched inhumations as primary burials were often accompanied by many secondary burials in cists or pits. Widespread contacts are documented by the presence of Baltic amber and Anatolian silver and antimony, and the existence of CORBEL-vaulted tombs with close Aegean affinities.

Ushki Lake. A PALAEOLITHIC site in Kamchatka, northeast Siberia. The lowest horizon (VII) has RADIOCARBON dates of *c*11,650 and 12,350 bc, associated with a small-tool technology including tanged arrowheads. 12 hearths and a burial were excavated in this level: the bones were missing, but red ochre survived, as well as tools, pendants and numerous stone beads. Higher levels yielded a different industry, including bifacial foliate arrowheads, bifacial knives and micro-blades. Level V has a radiocarbon date of *c*8140 bc. The remains of seven dwellings, rectangular, round or oval in plan, are assigned to level VI by the excavator. This is the only Palaeolithic site in Siberia to represent a tundra rather than a forest adaptation.

Ust'-Belaia. A site on the upper Angara River in the Baikal region of southern Siberia, occupied from early in the postglacial period (labelled Mesolithic) into the Neolithic (defined by the appearance of pottery, not farming). The site represents a base camp for a hunting group, occupied over a long period. Finds include large numbers of stone arte-facts, many made on blades. Bifacially worked arrowheads and spearheads occur, and a few ground stone tools, including some slate bayonets. The earliest examples in Siberia of fish spears (leisters) and fish hooks occur on this site. Domesticated dogs occurred; one was found in a ritual burial dated to earlier than 7000 bc.

Ust'Kanskaia Cave. *See* ALTAI.

U-Thŏng. (1) Ancient city in southwestern Thailand which was probably for some time the capital of the MON kingdom of DVĀRAV-ATĪ (7th-11th centuries). (2) A school in the art history of Thailand, denoting Mon origin. King Rāmādhipati, the founder of the kingdom of AYUTTHAYA in 1350, is said to have come from U-Thŏng.

Utica [modern Utique]. In antiquity a PHOEN-ICIAN city on the North African coast, sited at the mouth of the River Bagradas (now Medjerda) in Tunisia. Tradition gives it as the earliest Phoenician foundation, possibly of the 8th century BC. Since antiquity, silting has left the former port isolated some 10 km inland on an alluvial plain. Although playing second fiddle to CARTHAGE for most of its existence, Utica was the favoured survivor in 146 BC when Carthage was destroyed by Rome (*see* PUNIC WARS), and went on to become the capital of the new province of Africa, attract-ing much new blood and finance from Italian merchants. Eventually Utica was again eclipsed, this time by Roman Carthage, and also had to face the growing problems of its receding port and spreading marshlands. Excavation dates from the late 1940s, and has produced evidence for a Phoenician necro-polis, extensive Roman bath-buildings, decorated houses with mosaics, and a possible location for the forum.

Utnur. A Neolithic site in the central Deccan, India, occupied in the 3rd millennium BC. Four major phases of occupation were recognized. The people who occupied the site were primarily cattle-herders, probably living in huts built of branches and brush. Remains of stockades for penning the beasts were found, made of thorn fences initially, but later post-built. Pottery and stone tools were found.

Uvinza. An Iron Age salt-working area of western Tanzania, not far from the eastern shore of Lake Tanganyika. Salt, which was widely traded, was evaporated from the local brine springs. The earliest occupation is marked by Early Iron Age pottery akin to UREWE WARE, dated to around the middle of the 1st millennium ad. The later Iron Age sequence commenced in the 12th or 13th century and has continued into recent times.

Uxmal. A site located 78 km south of Merida in the Yucatan Peninsula, Mexico, which chronologically straddled the Late CLASSIC and the Early POST-CLASSIC periods. It is noted for its impressive architecture in the PUUC style. The principal structures are: (1) the Monjas or Nunnery, a huge quadrangle of single-room cell blocks which encloses a broad masonry patio; (2) the Governor's Palace, comprising a central and two lateral buildings built on an immense 120 by 28 metre stepped terrace (a small BALL COURT is part of this complex); (3) the Pyramid of the Magician, a structure MAYAN in concept, but with some TEOTIHUACAN influence (e.g. images of TLALOC). No LONG COUNT dates are associated with the site but it was abandoned in c1000 after the rise of CHICHEN ITZA.

V

Vădastră. The eponymous TELL site for a Middle Neolithic culture distributed in Oltenia, southwest Rumania, and northern Bulgaria in the late 5th millennium bc. The tell has a long stratigraphy including an AURIGNACIAN level, separated by a long hiatus from two Vădastră culture levels and a SALCUTA culture level (dated to the early 4th millennium bc). Detailed pedological, malacological and palynological analyses provide a clear picture of the Neolithic environment, which fluctuates from drier steppe to damper forest steppe. Large grain storage pits and draught animals for the plough indicate a mixed farming economy.

Vailele. A locality east of Apia, Western SAMOA, which has yielded assemblages from the terminal ceramic phase of Samoan prehistory (c300 bc to ad 200) stratified beneath later aceramic house mounds. The pottery and stone adzes appear to be representative of the culture of the first POLYNESIANS to sail into eastern Polynesia, in the early 1st millennium AD.

Vaisali. One of the cities of the GANGES CIVILIZATION of northern India, famous as the birthplace of Mahavira, founder of the Jain religion. The earliest occupation belongs to the Iron Age, when Mahavira lived (6th century BC) and has yielded NORTHERN BLACK POLISHED WARE and iron artefacts.

Vaito'otia. An important Early Eastern POLYNESIAN settlement on Huahine, SOCIETY ISLANDS, which has produced rich organic and non-organic remains of the period c850-1100. The material culture has close parallels with that of the first MAORI settlers of NEW ZEALAND. *See also* HANE, MAUPITI, WAIRAU BAR.

Valač. A small hilltop settlement of the Late VINČA phase, with a radiocarbon date of c3950 bc, located near Kosovska Mitrovica, Kosovo, south Serbia, Yugoslavia. A single occupation level is known from a 1.2-metre stratigraphy. In contrast to the poor ceramics, each house has a rich ritual assemblage mainly consisting of fired clay zoomorphic figurines known as 'centaurs'.

Val Camonica. An Alpine valley in northwest Italy, remarkable for the abundance of rock carvings found on rock faces throughout the valley. The carvings, thought to date from the Copper Age to post-Roman times, are often superimposed, producing complicated palimpsests, often difficult to disentangle. Scenes include human and animal figures, sometimes engaged in everyday activities such as ploughing or in apparently ritual activities; weapons and abstract symbols also occur commonly.

Valders Advance. The final advance of the WISCONSIN stage of PLEISTOCENE glaciation in North America. The maximum limit of its advance dates to c12,000 bp and its disappearance to c10,000-9000 bp.

Valdivia. A series of Early FORMATIVE PERIOD sites on the central coast of Ecuador with a long ceramic sequence (c3200-1400 bc) which includes some of the ealiest pottery in south America (*see also* PUERTO HORMIGA). RADIOCARBON dates, stratification of midden deposits, and considerable stylistic variation in the highly distinctive ceramic complex have facilitated the construction of a chronology. The periods are: A: 3200-2300 bc; B: 2300-2000 bc; C: 2000-1500 bc and D: 1500-1400 bc. Characteristically, ceramics have a grey body, are smoothly polished and decorated with a variety of techniques, including incision, rocker stamping and appliqué. Decoration is typically only on the upper part of the vessel and all vessels are utilitarian rather than ritual. Periods C and D contained some traded sherds from MACHALILLA.

Other artefacts suggest a sea-oriented subsistence pattern (fish-hooks, sinkers etc), although food grinding implements and deer bone have also been found. Figurines in stone and ceramic appear after Period B with the ceramics usually portraying stylized nude females often with a distinctive 'page boy' hairstyle.

The seemingly 'sudden' appearance of a well-developed ceramic tradition at Valdivia poses considerable problems of origin for South American archaeologists. Some propose a connection with the JOMON tradition in Japan, while others suggest that a native precursor remains to be found.

Valea Lupului. A large open settlement site of the Late Neolithic CUCUTENI culture, near Iaşi, Moldavia, Rumania, with a radiocarbon date of c2750 bc. The single phase occupation produced domestic assemblages of the Cucuteni B3 phase.

Valencoid. The most recent of the ceramic series developed by Irving Rouse and Jose Cruxent for comparison of northeastern South American cultures. The series appears to have evolved from the La Cabrera phase of the BARRANCOID series at a number of sites in the Valencia Basin in Venezuela. Some of these sites have platform mounds. The date for its first appearance is c1000 AD. Typically pottery is coarse and sand- or mica-tempered. Decoration such as appliqué work, rectilinear incision or modelled human faces with coffee-bean eyes indicate a probable ARAUQUINOID influence. Figurines with triangular section, canoe-shaped heads are also characteristic, although they may be an importation from western Venezuela.

Vallhager. A MIGRATION PERIOD nucleated settlement of the 5th and 6th centuries situated on the Baltic island of Gotland just off the coast of Sweden. Its economy was mainly geared towards stock breeding and the extensive post-war survey of the area revealed many cattle droveways and individual farm dwellings enclosed within stone-walled fields. The buildings are typical LONG HOUSES with central hearths, but in this instance it is unlikely that they incorporated the dual function of byre under the same roof. Vallhager shows evidence for some communal buildings, but evidence of craft-specialization seems to be absent.

Vallonnet. A tiny cave close to Monaco in the south of France that has yielded some 11 stone artefacts associated with a fauna datable to c0.9 million years ago. As such it is possibly the oldest well-dated occurrence of man in Europe.

vallum [Latin: 'rampart']. Properly, a heaped rampart of earth as, for instance, around Roman military camps, towns and regional fortifications. These were often topped with stakes. The early English historian BEDE (673-735) also used the term, as is sometimes done today, to describe the whole 'assemblage' of two ramparts and ditch which back HADRIAN'S WALL.

Valsequillo Reservoir. Located south of the city of Puebla, Mexico, radiocarbon assays from this site have produced astonishingly early dates for man's presence in the New World. A date of 36,000 bc for the earliest level seems to confirm the proposition that a migration across the BERING LAND BRIDGE in the warm interstade before the last glacial advance, did indeed take place. A succeeding level, containing bifacial and stemmed points, has been dated 19,850 bc. This later date is supported by similar evidence at TLAPACOYA However, stratigraphic and areal associations at Valsequillo are much less than ideal; consequently these dates are not widely accepted.

Vandals. A Germanic people who in the early 5th century set out from central Europe and ultimately crossed from Spain to invade North Africa, where they quickly succeeded in annexing most of the major towns. They imposed their Arian religion on the native population, and it appears that they upheld many Roman legal and economic practices. The Vandal empire was overrun by the Arabs late in the 7th century.

Văn-lang. A legendary kingdom in present northern Vietnam, ruled by the Hông-bàng dynasty, which is said to have begun in the 3rd millennium BC and was succeeded by the historic kingdom of ÂU-LAC in 258 BC. There is considerable debate over the archaeological basis of these legends.

Vanua Levu. *See* FIJI.

Vanuatu [New Hebrides]. An archipelago in

central MELANESIA, with an AUSTRONESIAN-speaking population and an archaeological record going back to LAPITA settlement about 1300 BC. Settlement before this date remains hypothetical. Important archaeological phenomena include the MANGAASI pottery tradition and the burial site of ROY MATA. Like most parts of Melanesia, the group has a very rich ethnographic record.

Vapheio. A MYCENAEAN THOLOS burial near Sparta, southern Greece, which produced many rich grave goods. Among these were two fine gold cups, decorated in relief with scenes of bulls. These cups have given the name 'Vapheio cup' to this particular shape of drinking vessel, characterized by a flat base, straight flaring sides and a single handle. The form occurs in pottery from the Middle MINOAN period on Crete and became popular among the Mycenaeans in the Late HELLADIC period.

variable. A dimension, quality or measurement that varies.

Varna. The largest collection of pre-Mycenaean gold in Europe was found at the Late Copper Age cemetery of Varna, on the Black Sea coast of Bulgaria. Excavated by I. Ivanov and dating to the mid-4th millennium bc, the cemetery contains over 100 extended inhumations as well as two special grave types: the 'mask' grave (where the skull is replaced by a clay mask) and the 'cenotaph' grave (where grave goods are arranged as if the missing body were present). These grave categories contained some of the richest grave goods: gold sceptres, diadems, pendants, appliqués, copper tools and weapons, stone, shell and bone jewellery. Analysis of the Varna gold indicates two sources, probably in the east Mediterranean and the Caucasus; other exotic items include copper and graphite, Spondylus and Dentalium shells and carnelian and marble.

varves. A form of sedimentation which takes place in lakes marginal to ICE-SHEETS and GLACIERS. Seasonal fluctuations in PARTICLE SIZE and speed of sedimentation take place. During the winter, ice melting is very slow, melt-water streams do not contain much water, and they flow slowly, carrying little material. During the summer, melting accelerates, melt-water streams flow faster and carry more material. In this way, the supply of SEDIMENT to the ice-marginal lake varies with the season. Layers called varves, each representing individual years, can be observed in such lacustrine deposits. Varves can be counted, vary in width according to the year, and may be correlated between lakes. In this way, a varve chronology, similar to a tree-ring chronology (*see* DENDROCHRONOLOGY) may be set up. Such chronologies have been built up for Scandinavia and are used to date the retreat of the WEICHSELIAN ice-sheet.

vase support. Name for a pottery pedestal or ring manufactured to support round-based pottery which would not stand up by itself on flat surfaces. The term is used especially in European prehistory to describe highly decorated incised examples from the French Neolithic CHASSEY culture.

Vat Ph'u. A pre-ANGKORIAN site on a mountain in southern Laos, traditionally considered to be the cradle of the CAMBODIANS. Originally called Lingaparvata, it consists of monuments of the 7th century.

Vedas, Vedism. *See* RIGVEDA.

Veii [modern Veio]. 16 km northwest of Rome, Veii was the most southerly of the principal cities of Etruria, and destroyed by its rival and near neighbour, Rome, in 396 BC. The *ager veientanus* ('territory of Veii') probably extended at one time westward to the seaboard, and northward to Lake Bracciano, but the ETRUSCAN city itself seems to have been concentrated upon a ridge by the River Cremera (now Valchetta). After some intermittent Bronze Age occupation, settlement seems to be established by early Iron Age dwellers (VILLANOVAN) possibly by the 9th century BC, with evidence for huts, and pit and trench burials. The 7th century BC saw early Etruscan chamber tombs, including some painted examples. The main Etruscan habitation area of the 6th and 5th centuries has still not been systematically excavated. What evidence there is suggests a predominantly irregular street-plan, with ample testimony from numerous cisterns and *cuniculi* for the Etruscan preoccupation with hydraulic engineering. The town is surrounded by a number of Villanovan and Etruscan cemeteries. The terracotta life-size group of the 'Apollo of Veii' now to be seen in the Villa Giulia at Rome comes from a local sanctuary, and probably formed part of the roof decoration of an Etruscan temple.

Venosa. An open Lower Palaeolithic site north of Potenza in Basilicata in southern Italy. A hand axe or ACHEULIAN level overlies one with abundant 'side scrapers' (evolved CLACTONIAN, TAYACIAN or CHARENTIAN). The date of these is not well fixed.

Ventana Cave. A deeply stratified site in southwestern Arizona, USA, excavated by Emil Haury. Occupation spans 10,000 to 11,000 years. Materials from the lowest levels, which included CLOVIS/FOLSOM-like projectile points imply generalized hunting activity. The presence of a single MANO, however, suggests some reliance on plant food and possibly represents an incipient ARCHAIC way of life. This lowest level yielded a RADIOCARBON date between 8100 and 10,500 bc. Levels containing materials characteristic of the DESERT TRADITION, especially COCHISE and Aramagosa, are separated from the earlier levels by an erosional hiatus. The firmest date for these upper levels (from geological evidence) is post 5000 BC. The more recent strata contain evidence of the transition from Desert to HOHOKAM and show the cave to have been used into historic times.

Ventris, Michael (1922-1956). Scholar responsible for the decipherment of the LINEAR B script of the MYCENAEANS, showing it to be, to everyone's surprise, an early form of Greek.

venus figurine. One of the most remarkable features of the late PALAEOLITHIC are the female figurines which have been called venuses. They are made in all kinds of material, including ivory, bone, limestone and steatite and are even modelled in clay. Most typically, the figures are large-stomached and large-breasted, and they sometimes have enlarged buttocks as in 'steatopygia'. The heads are featureless and the legs and arms are little emphasized. They mainly date from the period 30,000 to 15,000 years ago and are found from France to Russia. A later series is different in character, being more slender and

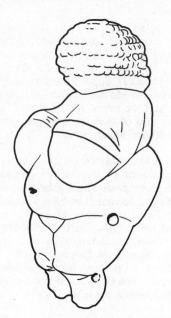

'Venus of Willendorf': Upper Palaeolithic stone figurine

hollow stomached; these later figurines are contemporary with the MAGDALENIAN.

Verkholenskaia Gora. *See* YENISEI.

vernacular architecture. The study of the vernacular architecture of the post-medieval period has developed mainly in Britain. Vernacular architecture comprises buildings belonging to the middle and lower end of the social scale which fall into three main categories, domestic, agricultural and industrial. The study of post-medieval standing buildings has proved an aid to the study of the excavated medieval remnants of buildings and has demonstrated the antecedents of many well-known post-medieval building types.

Verona. Situated on the River Adige in Veneto, northern Italy, Verona was a principal city of imperial Roman Venetia, and has well-preserved monuments from that period. Little is known of the pre-Roman settlement, but an origin as a Celtic foundation of the 5th-4th centuries BC is likely. The town is well-placed in a fertile, wine-growing plain, and Roman imperial prosperity is clearly attested in epigraphical and literary sources. This success attracted not only later Emperors but also, in due course, the LOMBARDS. Noteworthy are an Augustan-period THEATRE and, probably commenced at about the same time, a vast AMPHITHEATRE, possibly second only to the COLOSSEUM at Rome in size and degree of preservation. Recent rescue excavations have explored late Roman and medieval structures.

Vertesszöllos. The travertine deposits of Vertesszöllos, not far north of Budapest in Hungary, have revealed stone tools and traces of fire as well as mammals of late CROMERIAN age, perhaps about 400 thousand years old. Two deciduous teeth and an occipital portion of skull have been found and are attributed either to latest *Homo erectus* or to early *Homo sapiens.*

Verulamium. Present-day St. Albans, Hertfordshire, southeast England. Normally reckoned to be the third largest Roman town in Britain and situated astride WATLING STREET, which it spanned with monumental gateways. Starting as a small fort near Verlamio, the capital of Tasciovanus, King of the Castuvellauni, Verulamium was already by 60 AD a town sizeable enough to warrant the effort of sacking by BOUDICCA. Pre-60 AD shops show construction by wooden frame filled with clay, and traces of bronze-working. The attack of 60 AD seems to have caused only a short hiatus (perhaps some 15 years) and the town was rebuilt, only to be damaged again by fire in the middle of the 2nd century. By the end of the 1st century public buildings had been erected in stone, and now, after the second fire, these are followed by expensive stone-built private houses, boasting fine mosaic decoration. There is evidence also for bath buildings with HYPOCAUST. The 4th century saw mosaics still being laid and repaired, and it looks as if the settlement maintained a Romano-British way of life well into the 5th century. Much of the Roman masonry and tiles was subsequently removed for use in the building of the Abbey dedicated to Alban, who is generally thought to be a Roman soldier martyred sometime early in the 3rd century. Much of the mosaic work is particularly interesting, and some stylistic features suggest perhaps a link with mosaicists at COLCHESTER.

Veselinovo. The eponymous TELL site of the KARANOVO III culture, located near Jambol, eastern Bulgaria, and dated to the late 5th millennium bc. Excavated by V. Mikov, the site has a five-metre stratigraphy with Middle Neolithic and Early Bronze Age occupation horizons. The Veselinovo culture represents an expansion from the Karanovo II phase north to the lower Danube valley, south into the Drama plain and west into the Strumica valley. It is characterized by dark burnished polypod bowls and a great variety of handled vessels.

Vésztö. A TELL settlement site of the Neolithic, Copper Age and Bronze Age, located above the flood plain of the White Körös in Ko.Békés in southeastern Hungary. The six-metre stratigraphy comprises four main occupation horizons: I, a later Neolithic SZAKALHÁT occupation in which there is a long and continuous evolution of the Szakalhát pottery style into the TISZA-HERPALY assemblage; II, the Tisza-Herpaly levels, characterized by a rich cult assemblage in houses and intra-mural burial in wooden coffins; III, an Early Copper Age TISZA-POLGÁR level, also with timber-framed houses and coffin burials; and IV, an earlier Bronze Age level with two massive destruction horizons, with no intra-mural burial.

Vetulonia [Etruscan Vetluna]. A principal ETRUSCAN city and, according to traditional sources, one of the confederation of twelve. Original settlement is perhaps early Iron Age (VILLANOVAN), and it looks as if the city's chief period of prosperity and influence came early, in the 7th and 6th centuries BC. The later Etrusco-Roman and HELLENISTIC periods are obscure. Most interest has concentrated with conventional emphasis upon the cemeteries, although there has been some investigation of the Hellenistic town (see the so-called *scavi città*), and some trial trenches dug. Among the necropolis evidence, we have Villanovan pits, and biconical ossuaries, a type of circular tomb with tumulus which seems to be characteristic of Vetulonia, and some monumental 'THOLOS'-like vaulted examples. The contents have often been rich, including artefacts of gold and silver, and decorated bronze cauldrons. From the Tomba della Pietrera have come the earliest examples of Etruscan stone statuary. The traditional claim, made for instance by Silius Italicus, that the Romans took over such distinctive items as the *fasces* (an axe in a bundle of rods, symbol of authority) and the *sella curulis* (official ceremonial chair of high state officers) precisely from the Vetulonians, is perhaps given some support by the discovery of an axe bound in rods in one of the tombs.

Victoria Falls. This great waterfall on the Zambezi River, on the border between Zambia and Zimbabwe, has cut its way back along a zig-zag series of successive fall-lines. The area is of particular archaeological interest in view of the artefact-bearing gravels which were originally laid down by the river and which have now been left on the lips of the gorges through which the Zambezi presently flows below the Falls. Further archaeological sites are preserved in the sand deposits of the valley flanks both upstream and downstream of the Falls. Pioneer research in this area contributed much to the elucidation of the Stone Age archaeological sequence of south-central Africa. Association of archaeological material with the various stages by which the Falls have retreated to their present position offers the possibility of establishing a chronlogy for the latter process.

vicus. In Roman rural and urban organization, the smallest division of housing, and roughly equivalent, therefore, either to a village or to a suburb. As a village, the *vicus* would be administered by *magistri* or *aediles* elected by the villagers. An urban *vicus* would come under the municipal authorities of the town, with their own representatives — *vicomagistri* at Rome. In military areas, such as along HADRIAN'S WALL, civilian *vici* often grew up next to military forts.

Vidra. A TELL settlement of the Middle and Late Neolithic period, located near Giurgiu in the lower Danube Valley, southeast Rumania. Excavated by D. Rosetti, the site has a four-metre stratigraphy with five main occupation horizons; I, a BOIAN level, separated by a thin silt level from IIA, a Boian-GUMELNIŢA transitional level, including intra-mural burial; IIID, three Gumelniţa levels, the last very poor in finds, the first two with rich metal finds, including gold pendants and copper pins and earrings.

Viet-khe. *See* DONG-SON.

Vietnam. *Prehistory.* Vietnamese archaeo-logy is at present in a very active phase and interpretations change rapidly. Most sites are in the north of the country; Lower Palaeolithic tools are claimed from MOUNT DO and teeth of *Homo erectus* from Tham Khuyen cave. From the end of the Pleistocene there is a lithic sequence from SONVIIAN throught HOABIN-HIAN to BACSONIAN (*c*10,000 to 4000 bc) with pottery and possible horticulture in later phases. Full Neolithic cultures appear after 3000 BC (PHUNG-NGUYEN) and the Bronze Age, terminating in the classic DONG-SON culture, extends from the early second millennium BC to about AD 200, after which northern Vietnam was under Chinese rule (111 BC to AD 939). The Bronze-Iron Age in southern Vietnam is associated with the SA-HUYNH culture and CHAMIC (AUSTRO-NESIAN) settlement. See also DA BUT, DONG-DAU, GO BONG, GO MUN, QUYNH-VAN.

Classical. Vietnamese culture can no longer be regarded as provincial Chinese or even Sinicized; instead it must be seen as a local culture which partook to a certain degree in INDIANIZATION. Having grown out of the Bronze Age of the Red River area, it absorbed Buddhism from India to such a degree that this religion could become, at the end of Chinese rule in the 10th century, the main expression of cultural independence. Expanding steadily towards the south afterwards, and in particular during the Lê dynasty from the 15th century on, into the territory of the Indianized kingdom of CHAMPA, Vietnam eventually absorbed the latter and with it more originally Indian cultural elements, notably in art, music and dress. The southernmost part of present Vietnam having originally been CAMBODIAN territory, more such elements were assimilated when the Vietnamese moved into it. More-over, recent research has shown that the Vietnamese language is basically an AUSTRO-ASIATIC one, the main representative of the MON-KHMER group. *See also* ÂU-LAC, CHIAO-CHIH, CÔ-LOA, DAI VIÊT, DÔC CHÙA, JIH-NAN, LAC-VIÊT, LANG-CA, LIN-YI, NAM-VIÊT, VĂN-LANG.

Vijaya. One of the natural provinces of CHAMPA, corresponding to present Binh-dinh in central Vietnam. Vijaya became the capital of Champa, and its conquest in 1471 by the southward-expanding Vietnamese marked the beginning of the end of this independent kingdom. *See also* AMARĀVĀTĪ, KAUTHĀRA, PĀNDURANGA.

Viking. A collective term used to describe the Scandinavian peoples whose movements made a major impact on much of Europe during the 9th and 10th centuries. The exact origin of this emotive term is keenly debated and no consensus of opinion exists, but in the early Middle Ages it meant a pirate, a robber who came by sea. Nowadays the term Viking is generally used to describe a unique period in Scandinavian history, from *c*790 to 1000, when the many Scandinavian chiefdoms shared a similar material culture and were involved in trading and raiding far beyond the Baltic Sea.

Vila Nova de São Pedro. Strongly fortified Copper Age settlement near Santarém in Portugal. A citadel enclosed by a bastioned stone wall was surrounded by two outer walls, also both with bastions, enclosing a number of huts. The main phase of settlement belongs to the mid-3rd millennium bc (late 4th millennium BC), but there is also a pre-defence phase of settlement, which must be earlier, and a later phase of settlement, associated with BEAKER pottery, which should belong to the later 3rd millennium bc. This site was formerly identified as a colony from the Aegean, but is now recognized as part of a local development in the Iberian Copper Age. *See also* LOS MILLARES, ZAMBUJAL.

villa. Roman country dwelling, probably always with some connection with local agriculture. Early examples may have been in all essentials equivalent to farms, having house, workshops, stables and animal quarters. They seem to have been run either by small farmers in persons, or by slave-farmers on behalf of an absentee landlord. From the 2nd century BC onwards, examples begin to occur which have less emphasis upon farming, and more on the function of country house for the urban rich. It is likely, however, that even lavish imperial versions still retained a 'home-produce' side, even if only to serve the tastes of the owner. Various architectural types occur, two of the commonest being the courtyard house, and a corridor-cum-towers model.

Villanovan. Early Iron Age culture of Etruria and the Po Plain of Italy, named after the site of Villanova, outside BOLOGNA, dated to the 9th-8th centuries BC in Etruria, though lasting to the 6th century in the northern area. Villanovan remains are characterized by URN-FIELD cemeteries containing decorated biconical urns and well-developed bronze objects. These include articles of beaten bronze, often highly decorated, such as helmets, drinking vessels and SITULAE, as well as ornaments such as a great variety of FIBULAE. Villanovan settlements seem mostly to be of village status though lack of excavation makes it difficult to estimate when the onset of urban settlements occurred either in Etruria or in the Po plain. In any case there seems to have been much continuity, as Villanovan villages often underlie the towns of the ETRUSCAN period (e.g. at Bologna and VEII). The Villanovans are often regarded as intruders in Italy, perhaps from central or eastern Europe, but there is little difficulty in seeing them as indigenous. Similarly, although traditional views saw the Etruscans as intruders who displaced the earlier Villanovans, current thinking favours the view that Etruscan culture emerged out of the Villanovan, through 'orientalizing' influences, brought about by trade and other peaceful contact.

villein. *See* FEUDALISM.

Vinapu. The location of two important EASTER ISLAND AHU, one with a seaward face of close-fitted blocks of stone, similar to INCA masonry in Peru, the other of normal Easter Island type. The architectural history of the Vinapu *ahu* suggests that the Easter Island temple structures are of fully POLYNESIAN origin, with a possibility of some fairly late and ephemeral influence from a South American (Inca) source.

Vinča. The eponymous TELL site of a Middle and Late Neolithic culture distributed in east Yugoslavia, southern Hungary and western Rumania and dated *c*4500-3300 bc. Excavated by M.M. Vasić, the tell has a 10.5-metre stratigraphy, comprising I a thin STARČEVO occupation; II nine occupation levels of the Vinča culture with radiocarbon dates of *c*4240 and 3900 bc; III a late BADEN occupation; IV a short-lived earlier Bronze Age occupation; V a large LA TÈNE fortified site; and VI a medieval cemetery. The Vinča levels are distinguished by the early occur-

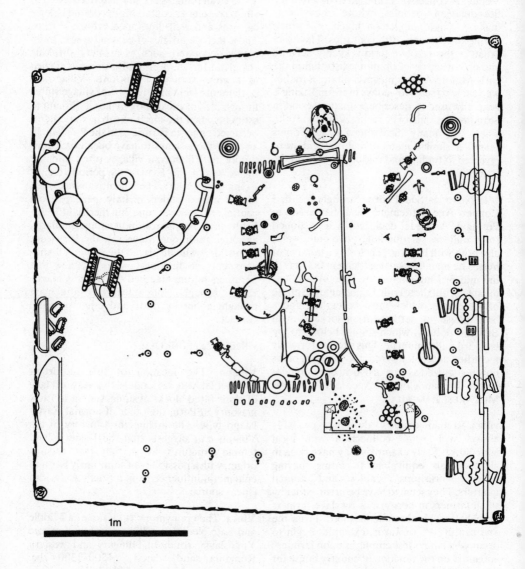

Plan of Hallstatt Iron Age wagon grave at Vix

1m

rence of copper and the wide range of anthropomorphic figurines, numbering over 2000.

Viracocha Inca. *See* INCA.

Viracocha Pampa. *See* MARCA HUAMA-CHUCO.

Viroconium Cornoviorum. *See* WROXETER.

Viru Valley. In 1946 a multi-disciplinary team, headed by Gordon R. Willey, embarked upon a comprehensive project of survey and excavation in this Peruvian north-coast valley. Isolated archaeological work had been carried out in the valley before, but this was the first settlements pattern study conducted in the New World. The settlements pattern approach uses locational and environmental interrelationships between sites (over a broad region) as a means of interpreting prehistoric cultures. The published results were for some time after used not only as a basis for generalizing about other Andean cultures but also as a model for archaeological investigations in other parts of the world.

Visigoth. *See* GOTH.

Viti Levu. *See* FIJI.

vitrified fort. Name given to a type of Iron Age HILLFORT where the stone defences have been significantly vitrified. This has come about through the firing of the timber-laced stone walls which, especially in windy conditions, generated sufficient heat to bring about vitrification. Vitrified forts occur commonly in Scotland, especially in the sites of the so-called 'Abernethy complex' of the northeast. They can be dated to the last few centuries BC and the first few AD.

Vix. A HALLSTATT wagon burial in east central France. The burial, dated to the end of the 6th century BC, was of a woman, accompanied by some of the richest grave goods ever found in a European Iron Age burial. The goods included a gold diadem, an imported ATTIC BLACK-FIGURE cup and ETRUSCAN bronze wine flagons, but the most remarkable object of all is a massive bronze CRATER, with a capacity of nearly 1300 litres. The *crater* is almost certainly of Greek workmanship and is in fact in better condition than any example surviving in the Greek world. It probably reached the Vix 'princess' as a diplomatic gift, travelling up the trade route from the Greek colony at MARSEILLES to central Europe. The burial at Vix is associated with the nearby hillfort of Mont Lassois.

Vladimirovka. A large open settlement site of the Late Neolithic TRIPOLYE culture, situated in the southern Bug Valley, western Ukraine, USSR and dated to the late 4th millennim bc. The settlement consists of over 200 complete house plans organized in concentric rings on a broad promontory. Amongst the rich domestic assemblages of CUCUTENI B pottery were numerous house and shrine models and many fired clay anthropomorphic figurines.

Vlasac. A Late Mesolithic fisher-hunter site located in the Iron Gates gorge of the river Danube some 5 km from LEPENSKI VIR. Three occupation phases are known, with radiocarbon dates of 6000-5500 bc. In each phase, small circular tents are arranged near stone hearths around a central space or platform. Large numbers of Mesolithic burials are known from the site, predominantly extended inhumations of CROMAGNOID physical type with scanty grave goods. The abstract geometric art on bone and antler never approaches the elaboration of the Lepenski Vir assemblage. The economy is based on fishing and the hunting of forest animals, with the aid of locally domesticated dogs.

Vogelherd. A PALAEOLITHIC cave at Stetten near Ulm in southern Germany, with hand axe as well as MOUSTERIAN and Upper Palaeolithic levels. Only the AURIGNACIAN levels were rich in artefacts and bone tools. A few human fragments were found amongst the faunal remains.

Volterra [Etruscan Velathri, Roman Volaterrae]. An important ETRUSCAN city and member of the confederation of twelve mentioned in traditional sources. The naturally defensive position on an elevated ridge some 32 km inland dominates much of north Etruria. Good agricultural land, rich deposits of metallic ores and clay, and the feasibility of salt production all combined to make the site attractive. Occupation is possibly as early as the Copper Age (RINAL-

DONE culture), and seems to be established by the Iron Age, which is perhaps to be dated from around the beginning of the 1st millennium BC. As elsewhere, it looks as if the pattern was one of acropolis settlement subsequently spreading to lower areas, and by the 4th century BC there was perimeter walling enclosing an extensive area. Even as late as the 3rd century BC direct Roman government was evaded by agreement, and the town's individual Etruscan character continued well into the Roman period proper. Volterra is noted for its carved funerary *stelae*, and alabaster urns decorated with mythological scenes. The Roman period itself saw the development of an area to the north of the Etruscan walls, which has left remains of some bath buildings and an Augustan-period theatre.

Vorbasse. A settlement in southern Jutland, Denmark. Excavations have dated its origins to the MIGRATION PERIOD (4th and 5th centuries) when it took the form of a planned village consisting of a series of sturdy LONG HOUSES. Each house was divided into three rooms (living room, stall and barn) with two or three accompanying minor buildings, and each unit was neatly portioned into a square croft and laid out into rows. In the last phase there was also a series of sunken-floored workshops. After its abandonment in the 5th century the settlement was not reoccupied until the VIKING period when there were groups of hall houses and sunken huts for a short period. In the 10th century all this was drastically altered when Vorbasse was turned into three major estates, each of which incorporated a large 'TRELLEBORG type' hall with associated workshops within a large enclosure. It may be that these estates devoted to stock rearing were in some way connected to the JELLINGE royal house.

Voznesenovka. *See* AMUR NEOLITHIC.

v-perforation. A method of constructing buttons which involves drilling two converging holes until they meet at an angle. The technique was used in prehistoric Europe, especially in BEAKER and Early Bronze Age times.

Vršnik. A TELL settlement of the Macedonian Early Neolithic (STARČEVO) culture, located near Štip in the Ovce Polje, Yugoslav Macedonia, with radiocarbon dates of *c*4950 and 4915 bc. Four phases are represented in a 5.4-metre stratigraphy; the material culture sequence leads from a preference for painted ware to a gradual selection of dark burnished wares in the upper levels.

Vučedol. A TELL-like settlement by the River Danube in Srem, north Yugoslavia, is the eponymous site for the Late Copper Age Vučedol culture of northwest Yugoslavia. Excavations by R. Schmidt revealed a 4.6-metre stratigraphy with 8 occupation horizons: I, a thin STARČEVO level; II, a BADEN-PÉCEL level; III, a Baden-Kostolac level with apsidal houses and intra-mural burial; IV-VI, three occupation levels of the Vučedol culture, with rectangular houses, copper-smelting areas and intra-mural burial; VII, a LA TÈNE Iron Age level; and VIII, a medieval domestic occupation. The Vučedol culture is closely related to the Hungarian Zok culture.

Vyadhapura [Sanskrit: 'City of Hunters']. The capital of the INDIANIZED kingdom of FUNAN (2nd-7th centuries). Its exact location has not yet been found, but it is generally assumed that it corresponds to the site of Ba Phnom (i.e. Banam) on the Lower Mekong in Cambodia, the name of which seems to perpetuate that of the kingdom.

Wadi Fallah. Another name for the site of NAHAL OREN.

Wadi Kubbaniya. A site of the 16th millennium bc near Aswan, Egypt, which has yielded remarkably early evidence for the intensive exploitation of cereal foods, at least one species of which is stated to show signs of incipient domestication. Several varieties of grain have been preserved, among which both barley and einkorn wheat have been firmly identified. It is argued that neither crop would have grown wild in the area under the environmental conditions then prevailing, and that the einkorn seeds show physical features indicating cultivation. Enormous numbers of grindstones were preserved at the site, along with typical Nile Valley Late Palaeolithic chipped stone artefacts. If confirmed by future research, this would appear to be the earliest evidence yet available for cereal cultivation anywhere in the world.

Waira-jirca. An INITIAL PERIOD phase from the KOTOSH site, Peru, during which a distinctive pottery style appeared. Although no pottery occurred in the preceding Mito phase, Waira-jirca pottery appeared as a fully developed style. Typically it is a dark brown polished ware decorated with incised geometric designs; its most widely occurring forms are the neckless jar and the open bowl, although some spouted forms do occur. Origins are uncertain but comparisons with ceramics from VALDIVIA and TUTISHCAINYO show sufficient similarities to suggest at least contact and possibly a common genesis.

Wairau Bar. An archaic MAORI burial ground in the northern South Island, NEW ZEALAND, excavated by Sir Roger DUFF. The site is remarkable for its rich grave goods, which include adzes, necklace units and fishhooks, similar to those from contemporary sites in tropical eastern POLYNESIA (HANE, MAUPITI, VAITO'OTIA). Dated to the 11th-12th centuries AD, Wairau Bar has produced perhaps the richest non-organic artefact assemblage of any site in New Zealand.

Waldalgesheim. A chariot burial of the LA TÈNE Iron Age in the Rhineland, western Germany. It contained the bodies of a man and a woman and many fine grave goods of both bronze and gold. Some of these objects were imports, for example a bronze bucket of Italian type, but most were of native manufacture. Many of the locally made objects, such as the gold torcs (neck-rings) and bracelets, were decorated in a curvilinear style and the name Waldalgesheim has been given to the mature La Tène art style of the later 4th century BC. *See also* CELTIC ART.

Wallacea. The biogeographical zone of eastern INDONESIA, flanked by the SUNDA SHELF to the west and the SAHUL SHELF to the east. This zone has never been fully land-bridged and dates of first human settlement are unsure. The first settlers of Australia prior to 30,000 years ago had to cross sea gaps of up to 70 km in this zone.

Wandjina style. *See* INGALADDI.

Wangshan [Wang-shan]. *See* JIANGLING, YUE.

Warendorf. A MIGRATION PERIOD settlement located by the River Ems in Westphalia, West Germany. The excavations represent a palimpsest of individual phases which overlie each other, spanning the latter part of the 7th, 8th and early 9th centuries. The excavations were carried out in the 1950s and uncovered a remarkable range of building types laid out in nucleated groups, each centred upon one long hall. The halls themselves are either rectangular in shape or bow-sided; the bow-sided type has no interior roof supports, but a curved ridge pole and buttresses around the outside. The other buildings in a typical unit consist of barns and outhouses, stables, octagonal- and hexagonal-shaped silos, haystacks, and a variety of sunken huts that were used as workshops. These distinct classes of building make it possible to speculate about the social divisions within the settlement.

Warka. *See* URUK.

Warring States period. The latter part (475-221 BC) of the Eastern Zhou period. *See* ZHOU.

Warsaw. Medieval Warsaw grew up on the left bank of the River Vistula. Excavations in the vicinity of the royal castle located the earthworks of the proto-urban 9th-century fortress, with earth-and-timber ramparts and gateways. The area around the cathedral proved to be the site of the citadel of the 10th-century town.

Warthe. *See* SAALE.

Wasit. Located half way between BASRA and KUFA, Wasit was founded as a new town by Hajjaj b. Yusuf al-Thaqafi, governor of Iraq, in 703-4. Its remains occupy some three square kilometres. The only standing building is a shrine with a monumental portal flanked by minarets, datable to the 13th century. Excavations revealed a congregational mosque with four periods of construction. The earliest mosque, attributed to Hajjaj b. Yusuf, was 104 metres square, with a large courtyard surrounded on three sides by a single arcade and a sanctuary 19 bays wide and 5 bays deep. This plan, which became typical of congregational mosques in Iraq, is often called the 'Iraqi type'. The mosque does not point towards MECCA and there is no concave *mihrab* (*see* MOSQUE), the latter being used first at MEDINA in 707-9. Adjoining the mosque was the Dar al Imara, or governor's palace. The palace rapidly fell into ruin, as later did the mosque, which was rebuilt, perhaps *c*1000, with the same plan, but facing Mecca. The new mosque was rebuilt on two subsequent occasions, perhaps in the 13th century and the 14th century.

Water Newton [Roman Durobrivae]. 25 km from Peterborough in Cambridgeshire, eastern England, this was a large and important Roman pottery town, centre of production for the NENE VALLEY colour-coated fine ware, and find-site in particular (1975) of a hoard of 4th-century Christian silver plate. Accessible today from the modern A1 trunk road, the Roman town was itself cut into two by the Roman ERMINE STREET, upon which the town was probably a staging post. Water Newton grew out of the civilian settlement attached to an early-period Roman fort (perhaps *c*45 AD) sited here with the likely motive of guarding the crossing of the River Nene. Air photography shows a very large expanse (some claim up to 100 hectares) of sprawling industrial development, much of it probably of a shanty nature, of which only some 18 hectares were ever enclosed by defences. This would mark Water Newton as one of the major industrial areas of Roman Britain, attracting with its prosperity a large number of entrepreneur craftsmen, businessmen and service industries. The hoard of Christian silver plate, presumably emanating from a church or private chapel, also indicates a degree of local affluence. Eight items carry the Chi-Rho monogram, and some are inscribed with Christian motifs. The collection, possibly the earliest group of Christian silver known under the Empire, is now kept in the British Museum.

Watling Street. Roman road from RICHBOROUGH to CHESTER in southern and central England, a major trunk route built in the early years of the Roman occupation of Britain. The road runs via CANTERBURY to LONDON; thence it branches north-west to VERULAMIUM, Towcester and WROXETER, and finally turns north to Chester.

wattle. Flexible wooden rods or twigs, used in constructing hurdles and fencing, or as support in a wattle and DAUB wall.

Wayland's Smithy. An Early Neolithic long BARROW in Oxfordshire, southern England, with two phases of construction. The earlier monument covered a wooden mortuary house which contained the remains of 14 individuals. Over this was constructed a much longer trapezoidal mound with a stone kerb and with a megalithic chamber of SEVERN-COTSWOLD type. A radiocarbon date of *c*2800 bc (*c*3600 BC) was obtained from the surface of buried soil underneath the second-phase monument.

Wealden house. A type of timber-framed building, dating from the 15th century;

many surviving examples are concentrated in southeast England. The Wealden house has a distinctive design in which the central open hall is flanked at both ends by multi-storeyed wings; in the purest examples the end storeys are jettied at the front, while the central compartment is recessed. Many of these houses were built by yeoman farmers or householders from the lower to middle end of the social scale.

Weichselian. A group of QUATERNARY GLACIAL deposits in northwest Europe (*see* Table 5, page 418). The main feature is a striking group of end MORAINES, demarcating the maximum extent of the Weichsel ice-sheet. This ice-sheet flowed out from centres in Scandinavia, over the bed of the Baltic Sea and into northern Europe and the Soviet Union (where the moraines are called the Waldai moraines). The final retreat of the ice is marked by a succession of end moraine complexes, whose chronology has been worked out from VARVES. Most of the Weichselian is within the range of RADIO-CARBON dating. Dates vary between greater than 70,000 bp and 10,000 bp, and the Weichselian can be correlated with the British DEVENSIAN. Both Weichselian and Devensian represent one cold stage which probably lasted from about 120,000 BP until 10,000 bp. The ice sheets were probably at their maximum size for only a short period, between 30,000 and 13,000 bp. At other times during the Weichselian, they were probably much less extensive. Outside the ice-sheet margins, great thicknesses of LOESS and COVER-SAND were deposited. Within these deposits is a series of PALAEOSOLS, which have been shown by POLLEN ANALYSIS to represent a series of INTERSTADIALS. Increases in tree pollen have been taken to mark the climatic amelioration of each interstadial. Four interstadials have been recognized in Dutch deposits: AMERS-FOORT, MOERSHOOFD (50,000-43,000 bp), HENGELO (c39,000 bp) and DENEKAMP (c30,000 bp). Three further interstadials were recognized in Denmark: BRØRUP, BØLLING (13,000-12,000 bp) and ALLERØD (11,800-11,000 bp). Another has been identified in north German deposits: the ODDERADE interstadial (c58,000 bp). The stadial between the Bølling and Allerød interstadials has been called the OLDER DRYAS, and the stadial between the Allerød and the end of the

Weichselian, the YOUNGER DRYAS. All the interstadials have been dated by radiocarbon. Amersfoort and Brørup have yielded dates of 68-65,000 bp and 63-61,000 bp respectively, but these are at the extreme limit of the technique and the interstadials may be considerably earlier. Thus altogether eight interstadials have been recognized in the Weichselian of northwest Europe. They are difficult to correlate with the three British Devensian interstadials. The British UPTON WARREN interstadial complex (45,000-25,000 bp) overlaps Hengelo and Denekamp, and the British WINDERMERE interstadial (13,000-11,000 bp) overlaps Bølling and Allerød. LEVALLOISIAN, MOUSTERIAN and Upper Palaeolithic artefacts are found in Weichselian deposits, particularly in the French caves, as are fossils of *Homo sapiens*.

The terms Weichselian, Bølling, Allerød etc should not be applied outside continental Europe, although some archaeological texts still mistakenly use them to describe events of a similar age in Britain.

Weifang [Wei-fang]. *See* LONGSHAN.

Weipa shell mounds. *See* SHELL MOUNDS (TROPICAL AUSTRALIA).

Wessex. Kingdom of the West Saxons established, according to the ANGLO-SAXON CHRONICLE, by Cerdic when he landed on the south coast in the early 6th century AD. It was one of the last ANGLO-SAXON kingdoms to become firmly established, and expanded slowly by a process of conquest to reach its zenith in the 9th century. From then on its house ruled the kingdom of England.

Wessex culture. Early Bronze Age culture of southern Britain characterized by a group of very rich burials under round BARROWS of special types (bell, disc and saucer barrows and enclosures strangely labelled 'pond barrows'). The burials are usually divided into two groups, with inhumation predominating in the earlier Wessex I phase, cremation in Wessex II. These wealthy graves contained objects of gold, copper, bronze (low percentages of tin in Wessex I, high percentages in Wessex II), amber, faience, shale and bone, as well as pottery vessels of special types. Most of these materials are not available in Wessex itself and clearly Wessex was involved in a wide-ranging trade with the continent of Europe. Specific connections with Mycenae, though possible, are not now regarded as having had a crucial role in the development of the Wessex culture. Unfortunately no settlements of the Wessex culture are known and, apart from the barrows, the only monument that may be associated with this culture is the massive sarsen monument of STONEHENGE III (though this association is far from certain). We do not know when the Wessex culture began, but radiocarbon dates for Wessex II burials cluster around 1250 bc (c1550 BC). *See also* BUSH BARROW, RILLATON.

West Drayton. *See* YIEWSLEY.

Western Neolithic. Name given to a group of Early and Middle Neolithic cultures in western Europe, that were thought to be related. The group includes the WINDMILL HILL culture of Britain, the CHASSEY culture of France, the CORTAILLOD culture in Switzerland, the LAGOZZA culture in Italy and the ALMERIAN culture of southeast Spain. Many scholars now feel that these cultures are only loosely connected if at all and that the term Western Neolithic has outlived its usefulness.

Western Zhou [Chou] **period**. The earlier part of the Zhou dynasty, from the fall of the SHANG dynasty (in the 12th or 11th century BC) to 771 BC. *See* ZHOU.

West Kennet. The largest of the SEVERN-COTSWOLD group of MEGALITHIC tombs, situated near AVEBURY in Wiltshire, southern England. The tomb is a TRANSEPTED GALLERY GRAVE with an impressive concave facade, under a massive long BARROW, c100 metres in length. Excavations early in the century and again in the 1950s produced evidence of use for collective burial. The chamber excavated in the 1950s had been filled up to roof level with mixed earth and rubbish, deposited after the final burial in the chamber. The burial deposit has a radiocarbon date of c2600 bc (c3350 BC), while the overlying deposit contains GROOVED WARE and BEAKER pottery, suggesting a date of c2000 bc (c2500 BC) or later.

West Point. *See* TASMANIA.

West Stow. An Early SAXON settlement in Suffolk, eastern England extensively excavated in the 1960s. Situated on the northern bank of the River Nank near a Romano-British site, the Saxon settlement was inhabited between the 5th and 7th centuries, at which time it was surrounded by boundary ditches. In the central area a group of flat-bottomed pits and hollows which may have been animal pens were discovered. The predominant type of building found at West Stow was the sunken hut and, strikingly, only two post-built hall houses were excavated. The range of different sunken huts and their particular arrangement and grouping has added enormously to our understanding of these enigmatic buildings. Although certain types were used for industrial purposes (in most cases for wool manufacture and weaving) others were almost certainly dwellings. Many examples had either one or three post holes at either end of the sunken depression, while several buildings showed clear evidence of plank floors over the hollow. Pottery production appears to have been carried out at West Stow, and one group of wares has been attributed to the so-called Illington-Lackford potter who operated in the late 6th century. The reconstruction of one of the Saxon huts is an interesting example of EXPERIMENTAL ARCHAEOLOGY.

Wharram Percy. A DESERTED MEDIEVAL VILLAGE on the western edge of the Yorkshire Wolds, which has been the site of one of the most important landscape projects in Britain. The Medieval Village Research Group has combined archaeological and historical evidence to document a peasant community between the Early Saxon period and the 16th century.

Wharram Percy is the largest of five nucleated villages combined in one parish. It is first mentioned as a royal demesne with two manors in the DOMESDAY survey of 1086; subsequently the manor was purchased from the Crown by the Chamberlain and Percy families, from whom the village took its name. After replanning the village, the Percys sold it in the 14th century to the Hilton family. Like many deserted villages, Wharram seems to have suffered severely during the economic recession of the 14th and 15th centuries and the later medieval trend towards pastoralism. The manor appears to have declined during the 15th century, when at most 50 people lived at Wharram, and to have been abandoned in the 16th century.

At Wharram, it is possible to see the pattern and layout of the village on the ground: a sunken road that runs through the valley lined on each side by a regular system of mounds (the tofts and crofts of the peasant houses). The isolated upstanding church, as well as a mesh of field systems and land boundaries, are visible. Excavations to date have investigated two complete tofts, the 12th-century Percy manor house, the church and the churchyard, and the vicarage and Saxon settlement area have been sampled. The peasant houses fall into the categories of simple cots and LONG HOUSES (where the dwelling is combined with byre); they were built on low stone walls, or partially timber-framed. One of the most interesting features of these dwellings is that they were invariably rebuilt many times on the same spot and in most cases completely re-aligned. The Percy manor house proved to be a fairly impressive building with an undercroft; built between 1186 and 1190 it too had chalk walls but with dressed sandstone quoins. During the construction of a northern extension to the village in the 13th century the original house was superseded by another. The village church went out of use in the 19th century and its derelict condition provided a unique opportunity for a thorough archaeological investigation of a typical medieval parish church; the ground plan was uncovered, and the walls were stripped to their masonry cores to reveal the complexities of their constructional history. The results of this exercise have proved to be of enormous importance as the church had at least 12 phases of development dating back to the pre-Conquest period, when a small timber building stood on the spot. The fortunes of the church throughout the succeeding centuries reflect those of the village, for as Wharram grew from a small Saxon vill into a large medieval settlement the church grew in size and complexity. As the village population declined after the turn of the 15th century the chancel of the church was shortened and the aisles were demolished.

wheat. A group of cereals, members of the genus *Triticum*. Two wild forms of wheat are found in the Near East today, wild einkorn (*Triticum boeoticum*) and wild emmer (*T. dicoccoides*). A closely related group, the goat grasses (*Aegilops*) is also present in the area. Species of *Aegilops* can cross with *Triticum* and most of the wheats grown today result from such hybridization. Wild and domestic einkorn (*T. monococcum*) are diploid wheats, having two sets of chromosomes. Emmer results from the crossing, at some time in the past, of *T. boeoticum* with *Ae. speltoides*. As a result, wild and domestic emmer (*T. dicoccum*) are both tetraploid wheats, retaining two sets of chromosones from each species in the cross. Other domestic tetraploid species include macaroni wheat (*T. durum*), now grown for pasta. Most of today's wheats, however, are hexaploid, resulting from a further cross, of emmer with *Ae. squarrosa*. The main species in this hexaploid group, all of which are domesticated, are spelt (*T. spelta*), club wheat (*T. compactum*) and bread wheat (*T. aestivum*). Varieties of the latter form the bulk of today's wheat crop. Wild einkorn, and less commonly domestic einkorn, appear in the Near East at such early farming sites as ALI KOSH before 7000 bc. Emmer, both wild and domestic, was much more common than einkorn and has been found on most early NEOLITHIC sites in the Near East. Domestic emmer subsequently spread throughout Europe. Hexaploid wheats appear in the Near East before 6000 bc, as club wheat and bread wheat. Spelt wheat was being cultivated at YARIM TEPE in northern Mesopotamia in the 6th millennium bc. In Europe there are some early (Neolithic) occurrences of spelt, but it became common only in the Iron Age. Einkorn, emmer and spelt, which do not thresh free from the chaff, are called glumed or hulled wheats. Naked, or free-threshing wheats, such as macaroni, club and bread wheat, have a distinct advantage when the crops are processed.

Wheeler, Sir R.E. Mortimer (1890-1976). British archaeologist who made major contributions to the development of excavation and recording techniques. He excavated many sites, both in Britain and abroad, especially in India (including modern Pakistan, then part of an undivided India), where he was Director-General of the Archaeological Survey of India from 1943 to 1947. He also made important contributions to the organization of archaeology in England. In 1937 he founded the Institute of Archaeology of London University, the largest and among the most prestigious archaeological institutions in Britain. He contributed also to the the popularization of archaeology through articles in the press, popular books and especially television programmes. He will probably be best remembered within the profession for his excavation and recording methods. Adopting and developing further the methods of General PITT-RIVERS, Wheeler emphasized the importance of the vertical site record and its importance in constructing the history of the site. The vertical site record is studied through the STRATIGRAPHY of the site and in Wheeler's view the best way to do this was through the study of standing SECTIONS. In order to preserve as many sections as possible, Wheeler advocated the grid or box technique of excavation, in which small areas of excavation are separated by standing BAULKS. This method has generally been superseded today by open area excavation, but the importance of the section is still recognized.

Important sites excavated by Wheeler include MAIDEN CASTLE, STANWICK and VERULAMIUM in England and ARIKAMEDU, TAXILA and CHARSADA on the Indian subcontinent.

wheelhouse. A type of dwelling found in Scotland in the Iron Age and Roman period, taking its name from its form, which is circular, with partition walls running from the outside wall to an open central area, like the spokes of a wheel. They are built in dry-stone.

white pottery. A fairly rare white earthenware made only in the SHANG period and found chiefly at ANYANG, in China. The Anyang white pottery was probably made for ritual or mortuary purposes. Its decoration seldom strays outside a narrow repertoire of incised geometric patterns. Fired at about 1100° C, it is made of almost pure kaolin and is accordingly very brittle; few pots have survived unbroken.

Wichqana. A site in the Ayacucho province of the central highlands of Peru. Dating to the beginnings of the EARLY HORIZON, it is probably antecedent to CHAVIN. The U-shaped ceremonial structure has no examples of carved stone, but is built of stones of alternating size in a similar manner to CERRO SECCHIN. Skulls of decapitated females having the fronto-occipital flattening

typical of Chavin have been found, and bear witness to the practice of ritual SACRIFICE. Pottery is typically thin, brown, pebble-polished with little or no decoration.

Willandra Lakes. *See* LAKE ARUMPO, LAKE MUNGO.

Willendorf. A LOESS site near Krems in lower Austria with nine Palaeolithic levels. The upper five are of Willendorfian or east GRAVETTIAN type including the famous venus statuette (*see* VENUS FIGURINES), while the lower levels were closer to the AURIGNACIAN.

Williamsburg. The site of one of the most extensive restoration projects in North America. Begun in conjunction with a programme of archaeological excavation in 1928, the site has since been developed as a working model of life in the 18th century.

Located on a tidal water peninsula between the York and James Rivers in Virginia, Middle Plantation, as it was then called, was first settled by the British in 1633. On becoming the capital of Virginia in 1699, the town was renamed in honour of King William III and a grid plan of half-acre plots was instituted; structures which did not conform were removed. The College of William and Mary, founded in 1693, and the Capitol building, begun in 1701, were the earliest public buildings and along with the Raleigh Tavern were the first major excavations in the town. Structures of brick as well as wood housed a population of 5-6,000 at its zenith. When Williamsburg's tenure as capital ended, in 1780, the city went into a general decline, although it was never abandoned as JAMESTOWN was.

Wilson Butte Cave. A site of long occupation on the Snake River plain in Idaho USA. It is located on what is postulated as one of the major routes to the interior for migrating PALEO-INDIAN groups. A radiocarbon date of 14,450 bc is regarded as unreliable, but a less controversial date of 12,500 bc from an overlying stratum indicates the presence of man south of the ice at the height of the WISCONSIN glaciation. Overall, a total of six accretional layers covering a period of 10,000 years have been defined at this site. Although artefacts are few, tool assemblages indicate a generalized hunting and gathering way of life prior to the CLOVIS specialization.

Wilton. The name Wilton has in the past been applied somewhat indiscriminately to many backed microlith industries in sub-Saharan Africa. It derives from a small rock shelter on a farm near Alicedale in the Cape Province of South Africa, but industries from as far north-west as Nigeria and as far north-east as Somalia, have, misleadingly, been designated 'Wilton'. The term is still in fairly regular use to denote microlithic industries from Zimbabwe and southern Zambia, but is generally regarded as best restricted to those of the southernmost latitudes of the continent.

The Wilton rock shelter provides a clear demonstration of the development, flores-cence and decline of the eponymous stone industry during the course of the last 6000 years bc. In this area the most characteristic implement type is the tiny semi-circular or 'thumb-nail' scraper; crescent-shaped backed microliths are also present but are significantly less frequent. The faunal remains associated with Wilton industries often show a preference for small non-gregarious creatures, generally those which frequent an environment with fairly dense vegetation. Shellfish and other marine foods were also favoured. A wide variety of vegetable species was exploited for food and for other purposes. Especially in the western Cape, and also in Lesotho, it has been possible to demonstrate a seasonal cycle of settlement. Around the beginning of the Christian era or shortly thereafter the descendants of the Wilton folk acquired domestic sheep and possibly cattle and learned the art of pottery manufacture.

Winchester. The Roman predecessor of medieval Winchester in southwest England was a walled town known as Venta Bulgarum. In the later 9th century the Alfredian BURH with its planned streets and defensive system rose to prominence as the capital of WESSEX; it continued to thrive during the Middle Ages as an important regional centre and the seat of a bishopric.

During the 1960s and 1970s extensive urban excavations concentrated on a range of medieval sites representative of Winchester's history. The Brook Street area was the main cloth-working and industrial part of the town from Late Saxon times until the 14th century.

Here the excavators found a sequence of cottages and shops used for dyeing, fulling and finishing wool garments. This was the first large-scale excavation of a medieval quarter in Britain and a highly influential project in its own right. Possibly the most important excavation took place beside the present Norman cathedral to uncover the earlier Old and New Minster churches. The excavations revealed the evolution of a four-celled 7th-century church to an elaborate structure of 905 with lateral chambers, crypt and westwork. Other important excavations included the project focused upon the 12th-century bishop's residence (the Wolvesey Palace), excavations of the castle, and various smaller investigations to date the city walls.

Winchester Style. From the beginning of the 10th century until the Norman Conquest the Late Saxon kingdom of Wessex was a prominent artistic centre. This renaissance was directed from WINCHESTER, where the building of the New Minster had inspired an artistic tradition based on the revived antique models of CAROLINGIA. The term Winchester Style is applied to a range of categories including manuscript illumination, ivory carving, and stone sculpture as well as, to a lesser extent, metalwork, embroidery and architecture. The new emphasis on naturalistic figure design and acanthus decoration is especially prominent in the sumptuous manuscript, the Benedictional of St Aethel-wold, and the stone angels carved over the chancel arch of BRADFORD-ON-AVON church.

Winckelmann, J.J. (1717-68). German scholar who was an early contributor to the development of archaeology and art history. He is best known for his work on the art of POMPEII and HERCULANEUM, which was uncovered during the 18th century.

Winderemere interstadial. An INTERSTADIAL of the DEVENSIAN cold stage which occurred between 13,000 and 11,000 bp. It consisted of a rapid temperature rise to an initial thermal maximum, followed by a slight temperature decline at 12,000 bp. Thereafter temperature stabilized until 11,000 bp, when it fell sharply at the start of the LOCH LOMOND STADIAL. The Windermere interstadial may be cor-related with Godwin's POLLEN ZONE II.

Windmill Hill. A CAUSEWAYED CAMP in Wiltshire, which has given its name to the Early Neolithic culture of southern England, of the 4th millennium BC. Windmill Hill is the largest of the known causewayed camps: the outer of the three concentric discontinuous ditches has a diameter of c365 metres. The site has an occupation that pre-dates the causewayed camp, dated to c2950 bc (c3730 BC), while the enclosure itself has a date of c2550 bc (c3300 BC). It is thought that the site may have served as a meeting place for fairs and other activities for dispersed communities in the surrounding area.

Winlock, Herbert Eustis (1884-1950). American Egyptologist who excavated at el-Lisht and DEIR EL-BAHARI. He is noted for the high standards of his excavation and recording methods.

Wintringham. *See* MANOR.

Wisconsin. A group of QUATERNARY GLACIAL deposits in North America, stratified above SANGAMON INTERGLACIAL deposits (*see* Table 7, page 420). The Wisconsin stage includes TILLS, SANDS and GRAVELS, which blanket large areas and were deposited by ICE-SHEETS flowing out from centres in the Laurentide shield of Canada. Outside the ice-sheet margins is a sequence of Wisconsin PROGLACIAL and PERIGLACIAL deposits. Most of the Wisconsin deposits can be dated by RADIOCARBON and the stage is broadly correlated by this means with the WEICHSELIAN of northwest Europe and the DEVENSIAN of Britain. All these formations represent one cold stage, which lasted from c100,000 BP to 10,000 bp and directly preceded our present warm stage, the HOLOCENE or FLANDRIAN. Detailed correlation between north America and Europe is, however, difficult. The Wisconsin is best known from the sequence of deposits around the Great Lakes: Huron, Erie and Ontario. Unlike the Devensian of Britain, ice-sheets were present in North America throughout the Wisconsin cold stage. Fluctuations of the ice-sheet edge have been reconstructed by a study of the tills. The sequence has been divided into Early Wisconsin (c100,000-53,000 bp), Middle Wisconsin (53,000-23,000 bp) and Late Wisconsin (23,000-10,000 bp). Periods of glacial advance are seen as STADIALS. The ice-sheets reached their maximum extent during the Late Wisconsin phase. Outside the margin of the ice-sheets, organic and lacustrine deposits have provided evidence for four major INTERSTADIALS: the St Pierre (date uncertain, but beyond the range of radiocarbon), Port Talbot I (date uncertain), Port Talbot II (48,000-42,000 bp), Plum Point (date uncertain).

wolf. *See* DOG.

Wolstenholme Towne. Thought to be the earliest palisaded colonial settlement yet uncovered in North America, Wolstenholme Towne was built on the pattern of similar structures in Ulster, Northern Ireland. Roughly 200 Britons established the colony in 1619 on the James River, 16 km east of JAMESTOWN. Under the direction of Ivor Noel-Hume, archaeological testing and excavation was begun in 1970 and continued for several years. Artefact assemblages indicated a heavy reliance on European imports, but a variety of locally made pottery was found (although a kiln was not). A rare find of closed helmets from 16th-century armour were recovered and restored after an intense *in situ* conservation effort. Charred remains and evidence of the hasty, unceremonious burial of a person whose skull had been split indicate the end of Wolstenholme Towne at the time of a general native uprising in 1622.

Wolstonian. A group of British QUATERNARY GLACIAL deposits (*see* Table 6, page 419). Quite large areas of TILL, SANDS and GRAVELS survive outside the area of the later DEVENSIAN ICE-SHEET. At the type site in the Midlands, Wolstonian deposits overlie INTERGLACIAL deposits that have been correlated by POLLEN ANALYSIS with the HOXNIAN. The exact age of the Wolstonian is unknown, but it is older than the extreme range of RADIOCARBON DATING (70,000 bp) and can be shown by PALAEOMAGNETISM to be younger than 700,000 BP. The Wolstonian deposits appear to represent one cold stage (probably the penultimate). ACHEULIAN and LEVALLOISIAN artefacts have been found in them.

Wolvesey Palace. *See* WINCHESTER.

wombat. *See* DINGO.

wood. On archaeological sites, wood may be

preserved as a result of waterlogging or as charcoal (*see* CHARRING). Both forms may be identifiable.

Woodhenge. A HENGE monument next door to DURRINGTON WALLS in Wiltshire, southern England. Woodhenge is a small Class I·henge with a single entrance. Inside were six concentric rings of wooden posts, not in a circular formation, but in an 'egg-shaped ring' (*see* STONE CIRCLE) representing either a wooden building or free-standing timber posts. At the centre of the monument was a small cairn covering the burial of an infant with a cleft skull — one of the few clear indications of human sacrifice in British prehistory. The monument has a radiocarbon date of *c*1800 bc (*c*2230 BC).

Woodland. A widespread post-ARCHAIC tradition probably originating in the forest environment of the northeast, but ultimately spreading over the whole of the eastern USA as far west as the Great Plains. Its major traits are cord- or fabric-impressed pottery and burial mound construction. Though hunting and gathering are practised throughout, agricultural activity appears to have become increasingly important. To what extent this practice is a characteristic trait is still a matter of argument. Considerable variation between local chronologies precludes a tradition-wide dating scheme, although 1000 BC-1700 AD embraces most. The best-known Woodland cultures are ADENA and HOPEWELL which are usually ascribed to Early and Middle Woodland respectively (also known as BURIAL MOUND PERIODS I and II). The Late Woodland period is characterized by the encroachment of and (especially in the southeast) replacement by the MISSISSIPPI TRADITION. *See* Table 9, page 552.

Woolley, Sir Leonard (1880-1960). British archaeologist who excavated a number of major sites in western Asia, including ALALAKH and CARCHEMISH, but is best known for his excavations at UR in 1922-9, as part of a joint Anglo-American expedition. He excavated many outstanding monuments at Ur, and his discoveries in the Royal Cemetery brought to the notice of the public the astonishing wealth and skills of the SUMERIAN civilization.

Worsaae, Jens Jacob Asmussen (1821-85). Danish scholar, a student of Christian THOMSEN, who was responsible for important developments in both the theory and practice of archaeology. He adopted Thomsen's THREE AGE SYSTEM and his book, *Danmark's Oldtid oplyst ved Oldsager og Gravehöie* (1842; English edition, *The Primeval Antiquities of Denmark*, 1849) was one of the first attempts to write a prehistory of any area; it includes an Appendix with some remarkably precocious comments on excavation techniques and principles.

wrist clasps. A class of metal object frequently found in pagan Saxon graves in the Anglian areas of England as well as on the continent of Europe. They consist of flattened rectangular or triangular pieces of bronze frequently gilded or inlaid with silver and decorated with animal ornament. Their function was to fasten the cuffs of tunics.

wristguard. Alternatively called a bracer, a wristguard is a rectangular stone or bone plaque, perforated at both ends (usually with single or double holes, but an exceptional example from Barnack in Cambridgeshire, eastern England, has nine holes at each end, each with a gold cap). It is thought that it was attached to the wrist of the archer as protection against the recoil of the bow. They occur commonly in BEAKER contexts in Europe.

writing. Writing was developed independently several times in different places and both the writing materials and the types of script show great variation. The earliest true writing developed in southern MESOPOTAMIA in the 4th millennium BC URUK culture. The writing material was clay (*see* CLAY TABLETS) which were first inscribed and later impressed with a stylus to produce the characteristic wedge-shaped signs which have given the name CUNEIFORM to this script. The earliest signs were pictograms ('picture writing', in which the signs represent stylized pictures of the objects in question), but these rapidly developed into ideograms (with the signs being used to indicate not only the original object, but also associated objects or

Table 9: The Americas: Chronological Table

DATE	ARCTIC	NW COAST	SOUTH WEST	PLAINS	EASTERN WOODLANDS	MESO-AMERICA	PERU
AD 1500	Eskimo Tradition				Mississippi Tradition	Post-Classic	Late Horizon
1000				Wood land Tradition			Late Intermediate Period
			South western Tradition			Classic	Middle Horizon
500					Woodland Tradition		
						Late	Early Intermediate Period
AD / BC						Pre-Classic	
						Middle	Early Horizon
1000	Arctic Small Tool Tradition	Northwest Coast Tradition				Early	Initial Period
2000				Plains Archaic Tradition			VI
3000			Desert Tradition		Archaic Tradition	Food Collecting and incipient cultivation	V
4000							Preceramic Periods
5000							IV
6000							
7000							III
8000					Paleo-Indian		II
9000		Old Cordilleran Tradition		Big Game Hunting Tradition			
10,000							I

concepts). By the succeeding JEMDET NASR phase a phonetic element was present, with signs representing a sound as well as an object or idea. The fully developed cuneiform was a syllabic script, with a separate sign for each syllable, but it retained numerous ideograms for use as determinatives (signs used to indicate the classificatory group of a word spelt out in syllabic signs, e.g. a name of a deity would be accompanied by the determinative for deity). Some 2000 cuneiform signs appear in early tablets and even the 'slimmed-down' script of the Babylonian period had between six and seven hundred, of which about 300 were still ideograms. In spite of its manifest awkwardness, cuneiform — perhaps because of its primacy as a writing system — was used remarkably widely (throughout western Asia) and over a remarkably long period (about 3000 years). Initially developed to write SUMERIAN, it was adapted in the mid-3rd millennium BC to write the Semitic AKKA-DIAN. It was later used for a range of other Semitic languages inside and outside Meso-potamia, and for other languages in far-flung regions, including ELAMITE and later Persian in Iran, HITTITE and URARTIAN in Anatolia.

Perhaps as early as the earliest Uruk tablets are examples of the probably related PROTO-ELAMITE script of Iran. The Egyptian HIERO-GLYPHIC script, used for inscriptions on stone, painting on walls and subsequently also writing with a rush pen on papyrus, appears almost as early (well before 3000 BC). There is dispute as to whether the Egyptians developed writing independently or whether the art was diffused from Mesopotamia.

The HARAPPAN CIVILIZATION of the Indus Valley had a writing system of its own, dated to the second half of the 3rd millennium BC; it is found almost exclusively on stamp seals and seal impressions. It has not been deciphered, but as it has nearly 400 symbols, it is assumed to be a syllabic script, since pictographic or ideographic scripts have thousands of symbols and alphabetic ones rarely more than 40.

The first true ALPHABET, with signs for individual letters, seems to have developed in the Levant. There are some indications that this took place in the first half of the 2nd millennium BC, but the first clear evidence comes from UGARIT in the mid-2nd millen-nium, where an alphabetic script of 32 letters was in use; simplified cuneiform symbols were used. Over the succeeding centuries a modified alphabet of 22 letters was developed and, largely through the travels of the PHOENI-CIANS, it spread throughout the Mediter-ranean to the Greeks and other groups. The Phoenician alphabet is in fact ancestral to most of the alphabets in use today, including Greek, Roman, Arabic and Hebrew.

In China writing developed independently, first appearing on ORACLE BONES of the SHANG dynasty. They are inscribed in fully developed Chinese characters. The Chinese still use this ideographic script, which employs tens of thousands of symbols, of which 3000-5000 are in relatively common use.

In Europe the only pre-classical writing occurs in the Aegean in the 2nd millennium BC: the hieroglyphic and LINEAR A scripts of the MINOANS, as yet undeciphered, and the LINEAR B of the MYCENAEANS, used to record an early form of Greek. The use of clay tablets as the writing material suggests that the Aegean writing system was derived from west-ern Asia, where such usage had a long history before the 2nd millennium BC.

The development of writing in the Americas was restricted in extent and scope. It occurred only in Mesoamerica and falls into two main groups: the glyphic writing of the MAYA and related groups, found in inscrip-tions carved on monuments (see CALENDAR), and the pictographic writing of POST-CLASSIC groups such as the Mixtecs and Aztecs, found on manuscripts of bark or deerskin known as codices (see CODEX).

It is interesting to study the context in which writing arose in different areas. In Meso-potamia it was almost certainly developed to cope with the complex bookkeeping require-ments of the temple communities, and a high proportion of Mesopotamian tablets of all periods are administrative documents. The Aegean Linear A and B scripts clearly served the same function in the Minoan and Mycenaean palace organization. An admin-istrative origin could be argued also for Egyptian and Harappan writing, although the evidence is less impressive in these cases. In other parts of the world, however, the context in which writing was developed seems to be ritual: this appears to be the case both for the Chinese oracle bones and for the elaborate calendrical records of the Maya.

Wroxeter [Roman Viroconium Cornovi-orum]. 5 km from Shrewsbury in southwestern

England, Wroxeter was from about 90 AD the large tribal capital (*civitas*) of the Cornovii. The Romans had earlier used the site first as an auxiliary and then as a legionary fortress. The town became the fourth largest in Roman Britain, extending to some 69 hectares. Most of the site still lies unexcavated under open countryside, and excavation has been limited to the central sector. This shows forum, basilica, Roman and Romano-Celtic temples, bath buildings, shops, housing, and an aqueduct. Remarkable are a small open-air swimming pool (demolished by the 3rd century, possibly because of inclement climate), an inscription recording the building of the forum by the *civitas Cornoviorum* in 130, and the 5th-century tombstone of the Irishman Cunorix.

Wucheng [Wu-ch'eng]. A habitation site of SHANG date in Qingjiang Xian, Jiangxi province, China, first excavated in 1973. Familiar Shang bronze weapons, tools, and a few RITUAL VESSELS sugges that the remains belong to the end of the ERLIGANG PHASE and the next few centuries thereafter. Unparalleled at other Shang sites are reusable stone moulds, some inscribed, for casting bronze weapons and tools, and potsherds incised with inscriptions in an eccentric variant of the Shang script. Wucheng is 300 km south of a slightly earlier outpost of metropolitan Shang civilization at PANLONGCHENG and the remains have a distinctly provincial character. Designs stamped on much of the pottery suggest affiliations with the GEOMETRIC POTTERY cultures. A large proportion of the pottery carries a high-fired leadless glaze. Similar glazed pottery has been found only in small quantities at Shang sites in the north such as ZHENGZHOU and ANYANG, and it is possible that glazed ware was native to the Yangzi region, where it figures prominently also in Western ZHOU finds (*see* TUNXI).

Wuguancun [Wu-kuan-ts'un]. *See* ANYANG, CHARIOT BURIALS (CHINA).

Wujin Yancheng [Wu-chin Yen-ch'eng]. Site in southern Jiangsu province, China, of a walled city traditionally identified with the capital of the Eastern ZHOU state of Yan (a different state from the YAN state in the neigh-bourhood of BEIJUNG, written with a different character). Bronze RITUAL VESSELS found at Yancheng in 1957 belong to the late 6th and early 5th centuries BC; stylistic peculiarities suggest that they were made locally and point to connections with earlier bronzes, also of provincial style, unearthed in the same general region (*see* DANTU, TUNXI).

Wun Rok. A large Iron Age settlement mound north of Wau in the Bahr el Ghazal Province, in the Southern Region of the Sudan. Throughout the occupation, which began around the middle of the 1st millennium ad, pottery was decorated by means of a twisted cord roulette. A similar technique of pottery decoration is practised today by several Nilotic-speaking societies. The most important change to be discerned in the Wun Rok sequence was the replacement, in around the 12th century, of the earlier humpless cattle by humped ones akin to those herded by the recent Nilotic-speaking population of the area.

Würm. A group of QUATERNARY deposits in the Alps and the valleys of south German rivers. The Würm consists of MORAINE and related river terraces of PROGLACIAL deposits. It formed part of the classical scheme of four GLACIALS with intervening INTERGLACIALS, published in 1909 by Penck and Bruckner. In this scheme, it was held that the Würm deposits represented only one cold stage, the latest. More recently, it has been discovered that the Würm terraces are the result of more than one glacial advance. They also comprise deposits of several interglacials, including the HOLOCENE. The Würm deposits therefore represent a much more complicated sequence than was at first supposed. For this reason, the term Würm should only be used to describe this particular group of Alpine deposits. Unfortunately, 'Würm' has gained wide currency as a more general term, meaning the latest cold stage (WEICHSELIAN, DEVENSIAN) throughout Europe; this is still common in archaeological literature, but should be avoided.

Wuwei [Wu-wei]. A city in Gansu province, China, the site of a HAN commandery on the

SILK ROUTE at the eastern end of the Gansu Corridor. The 2nd-century tomb of a Han official was discovered at Wuwei Leitai in 1969. Instead of the usual pottery figurines the tomb was furnished with a procession of miniature bronze cavalry, chariots, and spirited horses including the well-known 'flying horse'.

Wyc de Mituno. *See* HULL.

Wyrie Swamp. *See* BOOMERANG.

X

Xanten [Roman Vetera Castra and Colonia Ulpia Traiana]. A Roman legionary camp (or rather successive camps) and a civilian settlement on the Rhine near Wesel and the confluence with the River Lupa (modern Lippe). Vetera I was designed for two legions, and probably predates 12 BC. This Augustan camp had earth ramparts, palisades, timber buildings, a hospital and a quay, with some later stone construction. There was an associated civilian settlement to the northwest. Both were badly damaged during the rebellion of the Batavai in 69-70 AD. Afterwards Vetera II was constructed of stone nearer to the Rhine, and intended for one legion only. The civilian settlement was rebuilt in the period 98-107, and given COLONIA status by the emperor Trajan, becoming Colonia Ulpia Traiana. This subsequently became the principal city of Lower Germany (Germania Inferior). Evidence has been discovered for a rectangular grid street system, town walls, gates, bath buildings, an amphitheatre, porticoed temple, artisans' quarters and housing.

Xemxija. Site of a series of rock-cut tombs on the island of Malta. The tombs are kidney-shaped with a domed roof and are entered via a circular pit. They belong to the so-called Copper Age (but non-metal-using) culture of the 4th millennium BC.

Xia [Hsia]. According to tradition, the first Chinese dynasty. The Xia house is said to have ruled for 471 years and then to have been overthrown by the SHANG. While the historicity of the Shang dynasty has been confirmed by the inscriptions on ORACLE BONES unearthed at ANYANG, the site of its last capital, no such decisive evidence of Xia activity has yet been found. Some archaeologists, however, regard ERLITOU as a Xia site, and archaeological surveys now under way at related sites in western Henan and southern Shanxi have been undertaken in the express hope of identifying Xia remains.

Xiamintum. *See* CHARIOT BURIALS (CHINA).

xian [*hsien*]. *See* LI, RITUAL VESSELS (CHINA).

Xi'an [Hsi-an, Sian]. *See* CHANG'AN.

Xianyang [Hsien-yang]. *See* QIN, CHANG'AN.

Xiaotun [Hsiao-t'un]. *See* ANYANG, FU HAO.

Xiasi [Hsia-ssu]. An Eastern ZHOU cemetery site in Xichuan Xian, southwestern Henan province, China. Nine large tombs, five CHARIOT BURIALS, and 16 lesser tombs were excavated here in 1978. The major finds are all roughly contemporary with Tomb No. 2, whose owner is believed on the evidence of inscribed bronzes to be a minister of the CHU state who died in 552 BC. More than 200 bronze RITUAL VESSELS and BELLS were found in the large tombs and represent Chu bronze-casting of a stage that hitherto was little known since no other tomb or hoard of this early date is firmly connected with the state of Chu. Comparison with the Xiasi finds suggests that bronzes from slightly earlier and later tombs at XINZHENG and SUI XIAN belong to a distinctive Chu artistic tradition even though they cannot be so directly associated with Chu personages.

The Xiasi bronzes include the earliest CIRE PERDUE castings yet known from China, antedating by a century or so the spectacular examples from the SUI XIAN (tomb dated *c*433 BC). At Xiasi the lost-wax method was used to cast the openwork parts of a bronze table from Tomb No. 2 and the flamboyant handles, feet and lid knobs of otherwise sober vessels — the intricate decorative appendages of objects cast in section moulds. This diffident use of the method, far removed from the virtuosity displayed in the Sui Xian bronzes, might be taken to suggest that in the 6th century BC lost-wax casting was still new and not quite fully assimilated.

Xiawanggang [Hsia-wang-kang]. A Neolithic

556

site in Xichuan Xian, southwestern Henan province, China. The clearly stratified remains include levels assigned to the YANGSHAO, QUJIALING (here near the northern limit of its distribution), HOUGANG II and ERLITOU cultures. The continuous evolution said to link the Hougang II and Erlitou levels connects the SHANG civilization of Henan province with its Neolithic predecessors.

Xibeigang [Hsi-pei-kang]. *See* ANYANG, SHAFT TOMBS (CHINA).

Xichuan [Hsi-ch'uan]. *See* XIAWANGGANG, XIASI.

Xincun [Hsin-ts'un]. A Western ZHOU cemetery site in Xun Xian, Henan province, China, where 82 tombs were excavated in 1932 and 1933, among them eight large SHAFT TOMBS. The inscriptions on a few inscribed bronzes suggest that this was a cemetery of the nobility of Wei, a fief established during the reign of the second Zhou king in the heart of the former SHANG territories. The British Museum's *Kang Hou gui*, whose inscription names the first ruler of Wei, is said to have been found in or near Xun Xian. A set of 12 bronze weapons now in the Freer Gallery of Art, Washington, is reported to come from the same district; one of these is inscribed with the name of the same Wei prince, Kang Hou, and two have meteoritic IRON blades.

Xindian [Hsin-tien]. *See* QIJIA.

Xinyang [Hsin-yang]. A district on the Huai River in southernmost Henan province, China. Two large CHU tombs of the 4th century BC were excavated at Xinyang Changtaiguan in 1957-8. Among the tomb furnishings were a set of 13 bronze BELLS and many fine painted LACQUERS. The bells were the first to be found in a large set in good enough condition for the musical scale of the set to be precisely determined; the lacquers included two impressive DRUM stands, the first of these typical Chu artefacts to be unearthed in scientific excavations. Larger arrays of such musical instruments have since been found, for instance in SUI XIAN.

Xinzheng [Hsin-cheng]. A district in central Henan province, China, where an early Eastern ZHOU tomb was rifled in 1923. More than a hundred bronze RITUAL VESSELS and BELLS said to belong to the find are now divided among museums in Beijing and Taibei. The somewhat disparate contents of the hoard, accumulated perhaps by several generations of a noble family, range in date from the late 8th to the early 6th century BC. Many of the bronzes carry dense surface patterns built up of identical small rectangular units of dragon interlace, a form of decoration widely popular in the late 7th and 6th centuries BC (examples were included, for instance, in the LIYU hoard). The name of the site is now attached to these patterns even though the 'Xinzheng style' has no special connection with the Xinzheng region. The most outstanding objects from the tomb, a group of monumental vessels affiliated with CHU bronzes (*see* XIASI), do not carry Xinzheng-style patterns.

Xiongnu [Hsiung-nu]. A large tribal confederation of mounted nomads that dominated the Mongolian steppes during much of the HAN dynasty. Formed near the end of the 3rd century BC, the confederacy reached the height of its power in the early 2nd century BC, when it defeated the YUEZHI. For the next two centuries the Xiongnu harrassed the northern frontiers of China. The Han empire defended itself by means of vast military campaigns alternating with diplomacy; the cost to China of either policy was staggering, the first in men and horses, the second in luxury goods and gold used to buy allies or an uneasy peace. Partly as a result of Chinese pressure the power of the Xiongnu declined during the 1st century BC and in the next century control of the steppes passed to other tribal groups.

Few archaeological remains can be confidently associated with the Xiongnu. The kurgans excavated in 1924-5 at NOIN-ULA near Lake Baikal, robbed in antiquity, are thought to be 1st-century AD tombs of Xiongnu nobility; the silks and lacquers recovered from these tombs can be taken to represent the 'gifts' sent to the Xiongnu by the Chinese court. Aristocratic burials excavated more recently in Liaoning province at Xichagou and in western Inner Mongolia at Aluchaideng and Xigoupan have yielded an astonishing wealth of gold and silver objects unrepresented in the looted Noin-ula tombs. The metalwork from these burials firmly establishes Xiongnu art as a branch of the ANIMAL STYLE with close relatives in the ALTAI mountains and the ORDOS.

The Xiongnu confederacy seems to have embraced a variety of ethnic and linguistic groups, but these remain little more than names recorded in Chinese sources. The Chinese historian Sima Qian (c145-86 BC) gives a description of Xiongnu customs in many ways parallel to Herodotus' account of the Scyths, but he does not clearly distinguish separate tribes and seems to use 'Xiongnu' as a blanket term for the northern barbarians of his own time and those of earlier centuries as well. Some doubt attaches to the hypothesis, suggested mainly by the similarity of the names, that the Xiongnu should be identified with the HUNS who appeared on the frontiers of the Roman empire at the end of the 4th century AD. The racial composition of the Hunnish hordes is no less obscure than that of the Xiongnu confederacy, making it difficult to argue a connection on ethnic grounds; and while one typical Hunnish artefact, the bronze cauldron, has parallels in the Ordos, the negligible role played by the Animal Style in the material culture of the Huns contrasts sharply with what is known of Xiongnu art.

Xipe Totec. See AZTEC, QUETZACOATL, SACRIFICE.

Xochicalco. One of the earliest fortified sites of the Early POST-CLASSIC and a likely beneficiary of the collapse of TEOTIHUACAN (see also CHOLULA). Located on one of a string of hills in southern Morelos, Mexico, the site is positioned to control access to the Balsas River drainage. A strong Teotihuacan influence (e.g. CYLINDRICAL TRIPOD VASES and OBSIDIAN eccentrics) is evident in the site's CLASSIC PERIOD occupation, at which time it was probably a satellite town of that great centre. After the fall of Teotihuacan, however, the site evidences a new complex of cultural influences. Architecture in modified TALUD-TABLERO style, a BALL COURT and MAYAN friezes characterize the centre's new independence.

Xolotl. See QUETZACOATL.

Xpuhil. See RIO BEC.

X-ray fluorescence spectrometry [XRF]. A technique of CHEMICAL ANALYSIS.

Principle. An artefact (or sample, if the artefact is too large to fit inside the chamber of the machine) is irradiated with X-rays. Resultant changes within the atoms of the material cause secondary X-rays to be emitted back. The wavelengths of these secondary X-rays are determined by the elements present in the material. Thus, analysis of the secondary X-ray spectrum allows the concentrations of different elements to be calculated. A development of the technique is the X-ray Milliprobe, which focuses the beam of primary X-rays on a much smaller area, with the specimen outside a window in the chamber of the machine. This allows small areas of objects of almost any size to be examined.

Materials. Since only the surface of the specimen is examined, the method is essentially non-destructive, although in some cases it may be necessary to use a powdered sample. The technique has been employed to examine GLASS (natural and man-made, including GLAZE), pigments, pottery and metals (in coins).

Applications. XRF has been used to identify sources of OBSIDIAN artefacts, by analysing their TRACE ELEMENTS and matching them with those of the sources of the material. The technique has also been used to characterize pottery from its minor and trace elements, and to investigate glazes on the surface of pottery. In its X-ray milliprobe form, the method has been employed for non-destructive analysis of major elements in coins and for examing decoration on the surface of glass beads.

xu [hsü]. See RITUAL VESSELS (CHINA).

Xun Xian [Hsün-hsien]. See XINCUN.

Y

Yaghan. *See* FUEGIAN TRADITION.

Yagul. *See* MITLA.

Yahya, Tepe. A TELL site in the province of Kerman in southeast Iran. It was occupied from the 5th millennium BC to the 3rd, with some later occupation up to the SASSANIAN period. In the late 4th and early 3rd millennium BC it was an important trading centre. The main commodity traded was locally quarried STEATITE (technically actually chlorite, though traditionally labelled steatite), which was in considerable demand in the cities of MESOPOTAMIA. Tepe Yahya was also in contact with the HARAPPAN CIVILIZATION of the Indus Valley and indeed was strategically placed on the overland route between the Indus Valley and Mesopotamia. A group of CLAY TABLETS inscribed in the PROTO-ELAMITE script, clearly inscribed locally since blank and partly inscribed tablets occur, indicates the probable role of this script in the organization of long distance trade. In the later 3rd millennium BC the importance of Tepe Yahya declined, but it is unclear whether this was the result of changing trade patterns in western Asia at this time or of local environmental pressures.

Yala Alego. A site in southwestern Kenya, north of the Winam Gulf of northeastern Lake Victoria, where Early Iron Age UREWE WARE is dated to the first half of the 1st millennium ad and associated with evidence for the working of iron.

Yamato. (1) The name of an old province located in the present Nara prefecture, Japan. (2) The historians' name for the ruling lineage, from which the present Imperial family claims its ancestry, and which developed in the Yamato area. (3) An archaic expression for the Japanese and things Japanese.

The old Yamato Province is rich in archaeological remains of the YAYOI, KOFUN and early historical periods, reflecting important cultural and political developments. There is a reference to a kingdom of Yamatö (which Japanese scholars pronounce as 'Yamatai') in *Wei Chih,* written in China in the 3rd century. It seems to describe Japan in the Late Yayoi period, but the geography is somewhat ambiguous. Scholars have not settled the debate as to whether the kingdom was in northern Kyushu or in the Yamato Basin.

yams. Among the most ancient cultivated tuberous plants of Southeast Asia and the Pacific, yams remain of great importance in NEW GUINEA and MELANESIA, although they have given way to RICE in most parts of Southeast Asia. The two main species, *Dioscorea alata* and *D. esculenta,* were perhaps first domesticated in northern mainland Southeast Asia, certainly before 3000 BC on linguistic grounds, although archaeological evidence for their cultivation is lacking. Independent yam domestication also took place in parts of tropical Africa and South America.

Yan [Yen]. The name of a fief established early in the Western ZHOU dynasty of China in the vicinity of BEIJING and of the independent state that succeeded it in the Eastern Zhou period. A cemetery site at Beijing and isolated finds of bronze RITUAL VESSELS farther north in Kezuo Xian, Liaoning province, are associated with the Western Zhou fief by bronze inscriptions mentioning the Marquis of Yan; other bronze vessels from both places are of SHANG style and must antedate the founding of Yan. There is so far little archaeological trace of the Yan fief much later than the early decades of the Western Zhou period, when its capital was probably at Beijing. The Eastern Zhou city Yan Xiadu ('the Lower Capital of Yan'), capital of the Yan state from 697 to 226 BC, can apparently be identified with a site at Yi Xian in central Hebei. A series of excavations carried out there since 1930 have uncovered a large city neatly subdivided into residential, industrial, and cemetery sectors and including many HANGTU foundation platforms of palatial buildings. Yan Xiadu had an impressive drainage system and was fortified with very large *hangtu* walls. A mass burial of soldiers excavated at the city in 1973 contained a number of late Eastern Zhou iron weapons. *See also* TANGSHAN.

An unrelated character also transliterated Yan is the name of an Eastern Zhou state whose capital was at WUJIN YANCHENG.

Yandunshan [Yen-tun-shan]. *See* DANTU.

Yangshao [Yang-shao]. A site in Mianchi Xian, western Henan province, China, that has given its name to one of the two broad divisions of the Chinese Neolithic, also called the Painted Pottery Neolithic (the other is the LONGSHAN or Black Pottery Neolithic). The Yangshao site itself is an unimportant representative of a late phase. More notable is BANPO in Shaanxi, where radiocarbon dates spanning the 5th millennium BC have been obtained for a village displaying the characteristic Yangshao economy based on MILLET cultivation and domesticated dog and pig. Radiocarbon dates from recently excavated sites in Hebei, Henan and Shaanxi suggest that elements of this economy may reach back to the 6th or 7th millennium BC (*see* BANPO). Yangshao villages have houses with sunken floors or, later, wattle-and-daub houses at surface level. The most typical pottery shapes are bowls, urns and amphorae; tripod vessels are rare and hollow-legged tripods (*xian*, LI, and GUI) unknown. The finest pots carry painted designs while unpainted pots are often cord-marked.

The Yangshao cultures fall into two main regional subgroups. A western branch centred on the Tao River valley in Gansu includes MAJIAYAO, BANSHAN and MACHANG; these are distinguished on the basis of their painted pottery, though continuing discoveries of 'intermediate' types have tended to blur the distinctions. Nearer to central North China is the eastern branch, which is centred in the Wei, Jing and Yellow River valleys and includes Banpo and MIAODIGOU. The earliest radiocarbon dates come from the eastern branch, and stratigraphy at sites in Gansu suggests that the Gansu Yangshao is a westward extension from the older eastern branch (*see* MAJIAYAO).

Beginning in the late 4th millennium BC the Yangshao cultures were transformed by influences moving westward from the east coast (*see* LONGSHAN, sense 3). Chief among their successors were HOUGANG II in Henan, KEXINGZHUANG II in Shaanxi, and QIJIA in Gansu. These cultures were all closely related and all were products of cultural mixing. The characteristic Yangshao painted pottery was virtually extinguished, leaving only a few remote and impoverished survivals (*see* QIJIA).

Yanik Tepe. A TELL site near Tabriz in the province of Azerbaijan in northwest Iran. It is one of the earliest permanent settlement sites in the area, dated to the mid-6th millennium bc. Nine phases of occupation of this early period were recognized, characterized by rectangular mud-brick houses with plastered floors. The earliest pottery was undecorated, but painted wares appeared in the higher levels. Later prehistoric levels overlie the Neolithic deposits and indeed the site was occupied until the beginning of the Islamic period. In the 3rd millennium BC it was a town surrounded by a stone wall and containing round houses and granaries built of mud-brick. The latest structure on the mound is a massive structure, perhaps a citadel, built of mud-brick and probably of the SASSANIAN period.

Yan Xiadu [Yen-hsia-tu]. *See* YAN.

yao [*yao*]. The Chinese word for 'kiln', commonly used to designate the product of a particular kiln, hence any ceramic ware (e.g. YUE *yao*).

yaokeng [*yao-k'eng*]. *See* SHAFT TOMBS (CHINA).

Yap. An island at the western end of the Caroline chain in MICRONESIA, famous ethnographically for its large wheel-shaped discs of stone money, quarried in the PALAU ISLANDS and taken to Yap by canoe, and also for its position at the head of a chain of trade and tribute extending for 1100 km eastwards through the atolls of the Carolines (the so-called Yapese 'empire'). The prehistoric record on Yap is related to that in the Palau and MARIANAS ISLANDS and settlement by makers of Marianas red ware may have taken place in the 2nd millennium BC. The occurrence of child jar-burial suggests later contacts with the PHILIPPINES.

Yarim Tepe 1. A TELL site near the Caspian Sea in northern Iran. The earliest levels have a Neolithic settlement of the Turkmenian DJEITUN culture. Subsequently the site was abandoned and reoccupied in the later 4th millennium BC. It was abandoned again, possibly after a destruction, in the early 2nd millennium. After a long period of desertion the site was reoccupied again in the Iron Age (late 1st millennium BC) and occupied into the late PARTHIAN period, c200 AD. The site of Tureng Tepe, further west, has a similar sequence of occupation.

Yarim Tepe 2. Two TELL sites — labelled Yarim Tepe I and II respectively — 80 km west of Mosul in northern Iraq. Yarim Tepe I is the earlier of the two, with 13 levels of the HASSUNA culture of the 6th millennium bc. Among the most interesting discoveries is evidence of metallurgy, including the smelting of both copper and lead. Pottery manufacture was also highly developed: several large, domed pottery kilns have been found, in clearly marked-out manufacturing areas, suggesting a degree of craft specialization very rare at this period. The houses were of packed mud (pisé or *tauf*) covered in gypsum; they were mainly round and originally separate, but they were gradually added to, making a honeycomb of dwellings with restricted access, probably through the roofs. Some rectangular houses with many rooms were also found. The subsistence economy was based on mixed farming — the cultivation of wheat and barley and the rearing of sheep, goat, cattle and pigs, all domesticated.

The later mound of Yarim Tepe II was occupied in the HALAF period. Many circular houses have been excavated and a rectangular building that may be a shrine.

Yarinacocha. *See* TUTISHCAINYO.

Yarmouth. A group of QUATERNARY INTERGLACIAL deposits in north America (*see* Table 7, page 420). The Yarmouth stage is mainly represented by PALAEOSOLS, overlying Kansan TILLS and buried by ILLINOIAN silts. These soils appear to represent one interglacial, but are not dated satisfactorily.

Yasi Hüyük. *See* GORDION.

Yaśodharapura. The first city in the area of ANGKOR (at present in its southwestern part), Cambodia, founded by king Yaśovarman shortly after his accession to power in 889. For a long time its name was synonymous with the KHMER kingdom itself.

Yassi Ada. Underwater excavations off the Turkish coast near Bodrum have found many wrecks, the most important being a BYZANTINE wreck of the 6th century. The 30-metre vessel was comparatively well preserved and traces of the galley-end and of the cargo holds were found. Amphorae from the excavations have illustrated the trading of later Roman wares and olive oil between North Africa and Anatolia in the Justinian period.

Yasumiba. A late Palaeolithic site in Shizuoka prefecture on Honshu, Japan. Over four hundred microblades made from conical cores were recovered during the 1964 excavation. Carbon from one of the two hearths indicated that the site was occupied about 14,300 years ago.

Yāvadvīpa. Earliest name of the island of JAVA, and possibly also of that of SUMATRA, mentioned in the Indian epic *Rāmāyana*.

Yaxchillan. A CLASSIC MAYA centre located on the Usumacinta River in Chiapas, Mexico. Though there are a number of structures including palaces with ornamented stucco roof-combs and mansard roofing (*see* PALENQUE), temple-PYRAMIDS and two BALL COURTS, the site is best known for its more than 125 carved lintels. Scenes of ceremony and ritual SACRIFICE occur but the dominant artistic themes are military. Though the site may have been controlled briefly by the PUTUN just before 750, it was finally abandoned during the general Lowland Maya collapse.

Yayoi. (1) A type of pottery named after a place in Tokyo where it was first identified in 1884; (2) an archaeological culture characterized by this pottery; (3) a period (approximately 300 BC — AD 300) when this culture predominated.

In Japanese archaeology, the Yayoi period follows JOMON and precedes KOFUN. It is conventionally divided into three parts: Early (300-100 BC), Middle (100 BC-AD 100) and Late (AD 100-300). The dates are based mainly on imported Chinese bronze MIRRORS, because the RADIOCARBON DATES for Yayoi tend to be very erratic.

Yayoi pottery is far less ornate than Jomon ware, but is made and fired in basically the same way. When the pot was being finished, it may have been placed on a stand that was turned by hand, but a mechanical wheel, mentioned in earlier descriptions of Yayoi pottery, was not used. The firing temperature is estimated to be between 700 and 850 degrees centigrade.

Apart from the pottery, the Yayoi culture is characterized by definite evidence of agriculture and the use of metal tools. Rice was cultivated from the beginning in prepared fields with water control devices. Wheat, barley, buckwheat and some varieties of beans and melons were also grown, but wild nuts and fruits, as well as fish, shellfish and game continued to contribute to the diet. Bones of domesticated fowl, cattle and horses have occasionally been reported. Iron utensils were used almost from the beginning, gradually becoming more important. The virtual disappearance of polished stone axes and semilunar harvesting knives from Late Yayoi sites indicates their replacement by iron axes and sickles. Bronze artefacts first appeared as imports from Korea and China in small quantities in Early Yayoi, and in larger numbers in Middle and Late Yayoi. Ceremonial objects in the shapes of weapons and BELLS (*dotaku*) were cast in Japan by Middle Yayoi, and copies of Chinese mirrors in Late Yayoi times.

Yayoi houses were semi-subterranean or built at ground level. Some were raised on piles above the ground. The square or rectangular floor area was most frequently between 20 and 30 square metres. A very large structure, sometimes reaching 100 square metres, was often built among a group of several smaller ones. Such a group formed a small settlement, or several such groups might make up a larger settlement. A series of settlements, a large one with several smaller ones, seem to have formed a community.

The burial practices were varied. The dead were placed in extended or flexed position directly in the ground, or in wooden coffins, slab cists or in ceramic jars set mouth to mouth. In some cases, DOLMENS were built over the graves (*see* MEGALITHIC MONUMENTS, JAPAN). In others, small mounds were constructed and coffins and burial jars were placed inside them. Some of the Middle Yayoi burial jars in northern Kyushu contain an extraordinary amount of imported luxury goods, while others are sparsely furnished.

The Yayoi culture first appeared in northern Kyushu and quickly spread along the coast and river valleys of western Japan. It then moved more gradually into highlands and towards the north, although it never crossed the Tsugaru Strait to reach Hokkaido. The initial spread of the Yayoi culture was probably by population expansion. The later expansion, on the other hand, was the result of the adoption by Jomon people of Yayoi customs, because the Middle and Late Yayoi ceramics of eastern Japan combine Jomon decorative techniques with Yayoi vessel shapes. Many of the cultural items which make up the Yayoi culture, such as cereal cultivation, plain pottery, weaving, and jar and dolmen burials, had been present in northern Kyushu since Late and Final Jomon times. We do not yet fully understand whey these coalesced into the Yayoi culture around 300 BC. In any event, the old idea that the Yayoi people were ancestral Japanese who suddenly replaced the Jomon people does not seem to be an appropriate interpretation.

Yayo. A site 160 km northwest of Koro Toro in Chad, north-central Africa. A skull of early date was found here in 1961, but no stone tools were associated. It may belong to the species *Australopithecus africanus* or 'H. habilis', but was originally named *Tchadanthropus uxoris*.

Yeavering. With CHEDDAR, Yeavering in Northumberland is one of the two sites in Britain most convincingly identified as ANGLO-SAXON palaces, and fortunately both have been competently excavated. Despite difficult soil conditions at Yeavering, the archaeologists were able to distinguish a series of construction and destruction sequences, while the overall plan revealed a group of 20 buildings overshadowed by a large timber fort which seems to have been laid out by King Edwin (*r.* 616-32). In the 7th century there was a dominant timber long hall, from which extended a number of smaller halls at regular intervals; another building has been interpreted as an early NORTHUMBRIAN church. The most unusual and spectacular structure found at Yeavering, however, is the large semi-circular timber grandstand. This was undoubtedly used for meetings and assemblies, and it may have been from its platform that Paulinus preached in 627.

Yeha. A stone-built temple near Adua in northern Ethiopia which is the best preserved example of PRE-AXUMITE architecture. Constructed of well-dressed blocks, it is a double-storey building, 25 metres in length, with tiny windows. It was decorated with sculptures in a typical south Arabian-derived style, and with inscriptions in the Himyaritic syllabary.

Yengema. A cave site in eastern Sierra Leone which provides one of the few stratified sequences of stone industries yet available in that country. Throughout the succession the implements most frequently occurring are crude choppers and flake-scrapers. In a second phase, bifacial hoe-like objects are also present, while in a third phase pottery and ground stone tools are found for the first time. No clear evidence was recovered of the economy of the site's inhabitants. The sequence is not securely dated, but THERMO-LUMINESCENCE tests indicate an age of around 2000 BC for the third-phase pottery.

Yenisei. A river of central Siberia. The Yenisei valley has yielded much evidence of prehistoric occupation, including more than 50 PALEOLITHIC sites, with radiocarbon dates ranging from c19000 to c11,000 bc. The largest and richest site is Afontova Gora II, which has produced evidence of a community living in semi-subterranean dwellings and subsisting mainly on MAMMOTH, reindeer, ptarmigan and arctic fox. They seem to have kept domesticated dogs. Other sites have yielded slab-lined hearths; a layer of this kind with antler harpoons and many fish remains has been dated to c10,550 bc at Verkholenskaia Gora.

The first food production appeared probably in the 3rd millennium BC and a series of Neolithic and Bronze Age cultures are known: AFANASIEVO, ANDRONOVO, KARASUK. This is followed by the EARLY NOMAD period, which saw the establishment of pastoral nomadism. This made possible the first truly effective exploitation of the steppe grasslands and saw the emergence of a wealthy and strongly ranked society.

yi [*i*]. *See* RITUAL VESSELS (CHINA).

Yidu Sufutum [I-tu Su-fu-t'un]. *See* SUFUTUN.

Yiewsley. Just north of London Heathrow Airport, there are a series of gravel pits at Yiewsley and West Drayton. Numerous lower Palaeolithic tools have been recovered here, often rolled. The sequence — from a possible CLACTONIAN and two stages of ACHEULIAN through an Acheulian with LEVALLOIS flaking to the MOUSTERIAN of Acheulian tradition — is one of the longest of its kind in Europe and in part closely parallels SWANSCOMBE.

Yin [Yin]. *See* SHANG.

Ying [Ying]. *See* JIANGLING.

Yinxu [Yin-hsü]. *See* ANYANG.

yoke. (1) The wooden crosspiece fastened over the necks of a pair of oxen or horses and attached to the plough, cart or wagon to be drawn. Remains of yokes are sometimes found in archaeological contexts, for example in HALLSTATT graves in eastern Europe.

(2) In American archaeology, a U-shaped stone, often elaborately carved, and thought to be in imitation of protective belts worn by the participants in the BALL GAME. The yoke is a commonly occurring artefact in MESO-AMERICAN assemblages and has been found at sites in the Caribbean as well as in North and South America.

yong [*yung*]. *See* BELLS (CHINA).

Yongtai [Yung-t'ai]. A Chinese TANG princess whose tomb, dated 706, was opened in 1960 near CHANG'AN [modern Xi'an]. Yongtai's is the best known of several Tang royal tombs excavated during the last three decades in the neighbourhood of the Tang capital. Ranging in date from 630 to 711, these tombs are notable for their wall paintings, some of which are highly accomplished and can be taken to represent the style of the Tang court.

Yorgan Tepe. *See* NUZI.

York. One of England's most historic and best-preserved cities. In 625 the Roman city of York became a bishopric and in the following century under Bishop Alcuin was renowned as a centre for learning and theology. The Minster church was founded in 627; most of the building, with its famous stained glass and chapter house, is 13th and 14th century, but excavations beneath the Minster have found parts of its earlier foundations. Recent excavations on the Micklegate/Ousegate pavement and the Coppergate sites have illuminated the period under Danish rule between 865 and 954. In 883 King Guthfrith became the first Christian Viking ruler, and Anglo-Danish Yorvik developed into an important North Sea trading centre enjoying prolonged commercial success. The Danes colonized a new area between the Rivers Foss and Ouse which centred around their palace and was enclosed by a bank. On several sites waterlogged conditions have preserved timber buildings of the period; some were erected on piles while others rested on stone-filled sleeper trenches. Several examples had mortared floors, but the industrial workshops usually had rafts and planks strewn with brushwood. The walls were mostly woven screens of elder and birch covered in daub, supported by uprights and jointed with pegs. A variety of industries seem to have prospered in Yorvik, including bronze, glass, iron and bone-working and wood-turning. The botanical remains indicate that leather-working and tanning were also important, a process which created considerable squalor.

Recent excavations have also illuminated the character of York's Norman castles, built in 1067-8 after the town was sacked for fostering a revolt against King William. Hundreds of late medieval buildings have also come under archaeological scrutiny, and some of the standing buildings, such as the Merchant Venturer's Hall, rank among the finest medieval structures in Britain.

Yorvik. *See* YORK.

you [*yu*]. *See* RITUAL VESSELS (CHINA). Note that the Wade-Giles spelling (*yu*) for this vessel type is identical to the pinyin spelling for a different vessel type:

pinyin	Wade-Giles
you	*yu*
yu	*yü*

Younger Dryas. A STADIAL of the WEICHSELIAN cold stage. It is dated to between 11,000 and 10,000 bp. It takes its name from a tundra plant called *Dryas octopetala*, fossil remains of which are common in deposits of the stadial.

yu [*yü*]. *See* RITUAL VESSELS (CHINA).

Yuan [Ÿan]. The Mongol dynasty that ruled China from 1279 to 1368.

Yuanjunmiao [Yüan-chün-miao]. *See* BANPO.

Yuanmou. *See* HOMO ERECTUS.

Yubetsu technique. *See* SHIRATAKI.

Yue [Yüeh]. An Eastern ZHOU state in the lower Yangzi region of China whose rise to power was announced by its conquest of Wu in 473 BC; after its defeat by CHU in *c*433 BC Yue in turn disappeared from history. In early texts Yue is celebrated for the fine SWORDS of its kings. Of these legendary weapons eight examples have been found in recent years, not in Yue territory but in Chu tombs: Wangshan Tomb No. 1 at JIANGLING, for instance, contained a magnificent sword whose gold-inlaid inscription names Gou Jian, the king who led Yue in its conquest of Wu. The etched decoration of the Yue swords, like the technically puzzling decoration of certain Chu weapons, displays a metallurgical sophistication unmatched in North China at this time.

The name of the Yue state survived in later times as the literary name for the area around Shaoxing in northern Zhejiang province, where the Yue capital is supposed to have been located. During the TANG period this region gave its name to a glazed stoneware for which the local kilns were famous, and this today is the strongest association of the word Yue. The term 'Yue ware' (*Yue yao*) was until recently often taken by scholars outside China to include not only the Tang ware but also its precursors in Zhejiang as far back as the HAN dynasty; current usage, however, refers to the pre-Tang wares of this important ceramic as 'proto-Yue' or 'green-glazed ware'. *See also* DAPENKENG.

Yuezhi [Yüeh-chih]. An East Iranian tribe of mounted nomads referred to in Chinese sources perhaps as early as the 4th century BC. At that time the Yuezhi evidently inhabited the northern Gansu steppes and the area between the Tianshan and ALTAI mountains; a few stag-shaped bronze finials unearthed in this region may be connected with them. The Yuezhi were defeated in 165 BC by the XIONGNU and driven west to Bactria. One branch of the tribe, the Da Yuezhi, later founded the KUSHAN empire.

Yumuktepe. *See* MERSIN.

Yungang [Yün-kang]. A complex of Buddhist cave temples near Datong in northern Shanxi province, China, constructed between about 460 and 540 under the patronage of the (Tuoba Tartar) Northern Wei dynasty (386-535). Activity at Yungang declined after 494, when the Northern Wei capital moved from Datong to LUOYANG and the LONGMEN cave temples were begun at the new capital.

Yunmeng [Yün-meng]. A district in central Hubei province, China, about 100 kilometres northwest of Wuhan. This region was part of the Eastern ZHOU state of CHU until the Chu capital at JIANGLING fell to the QIN state in 278 BC. 12 tombs excavated in 1975 at Yunmeng Shuihudi belong to the period of Qin occupation (from *c*278 BC to the end of the Qin dynasty in 206 BC). Many of the nearly 200 fine LACQUERS found in the tombs carry inscriptions marking them as products of Xianyang, the Qin capital in Shaanxi province, suggesting that this craft so strongly identified with Chu culture was flourishing in Qin well before the Qin unification of 221 BC. Tomb No. 11, which belonged to a Qin official and dates from 217 BC, contained many books and documents written on some 1100 bamboo slips. The texts include philosophical works and a chronicle of Qin's wars of conquest but are chiefly concerned with a wide variety of legal and administrative matters.

Yuusu. *See* ITAZUKE.

Z

Zagros. Mountain range of western Iran and eastern Iraq, extending from the Taurus Mountains in the north to the Persian Gulf in the south. The valleys and intermontane plateaux of this range provided the setting for the early development of farming. *See* ALI KOSH, Tepe GANJ DAREH, Tepe GURAN, JARMO, Tepe SARAB, ZAWI CHEMI SHANI-DAR.

Zakro. MINOAN palace in eastern Crete. Unlike many of the other Minoan palaces, Zakro did not have a Middle Minoan phase, but was constructed in the Late Minoan period after 1700 BC. The palace was relatively small but had the usual plan, with living quarters, public rooms and storage areas grouped around a central court. Among the finds were a collection of fine stone vessels, of porphyry, alabaster and basalt; tablets inscribed in LINEAR A were found in the Archive Room. Associated with the palace is a terraced town with narrow streets, similar to GOURNIA. The site was destroyed in the mid-15th century BC by the eruption of THERA, which covered the eastern end of Crete with volcanic ash. It was not rebuilt.

Zambujal. A heavily fortified settlement site of the Copper Age VILA NOVA DE SÃO PEDRO culture on the Portugese coast north of Lisbon. The walls measure up to 17 metres in thickness and have circular towers; in the centre is a circular citadel. Sites of this sort were once thought to represent colonies from the east Mediterranean, but are now believed to have developed locally. *See also* LOS MILLARES.

Zapotec. A MESOAMERICAN group centred on the highlands of Oaxaca, Mexico, and the culture most clearly associated with MONTE ALBAN. Origins are unclear but characteristics which are clearly Zapotecan (e.g. GREY WARE) have appeared by the beginning of Monte Alban Period II (*c*200 BC-200 AD) and are fully developed by *c*300 AD (Period IIIa).

Elaborate funerary urns in Grey ware are especially characteristic.

The Zapotec abandoned their capital in *c*950 and appear to have relocated at other centres, such as MITLA and Lambityeco. In the Late POST-CLASSIC, the MIXTEC began to infiltrate Zapotec communities. Although the nature of the resulting struggle is uncertain, the period is characterized by a widespread fusion of the two cultures. Although the Zapotec were able to maintain a degree of independence (some groups still survive today), they ultimately became absorbed into the AZTEC tribute empire.

Zarzi. A cave in northern Iraq which has given its name to the Zarzian final Upper PALAEO-LITHIC culture in which microlithic tools are present.

Zawi Chemi Shanidar. A site of the KARIM SHAHIR culture near the Zab River in northern Iraq, 6 km from the SHANIDAR cave. This open-air site provides important evidence of early stock control, associated with a radiocarbon date of *c*8640 bc. High proportions of imma-ture sheep, especially in the upper levels, were originally interpreted as indicating incipient domestication, but today this evidence is more often taken to indicate stock manipulation, perhaps herding, rather than domestication. Occupation was probably seasonal and plant resources were clearly exploited, as indicated by the occurrence of querns, grinding stones and storage pits. Other artefacts include stone axes and non-utilitarian objects such as worked bone with incised or notched decora-tion. OBSIDIAN from the Lake Van area of Anatolia indicates far-ranging contacts. The site also produced remains of a circular stone structure, perhaps a hut, and 28 burials, 26 of which were associated with a stone platform.

Zayosal. *See* JAINA.

Zebbuġ. A group of five rock-out tombs on the island of Malta. This site has given its name to a

566

phase in the prehistoric sequence of the Maltese Islands, dated to the 4th millennium BC and misleadingly labelled Copper Age, in spite of the absence of any evidence for the use of metal on Malta at this time.

Zelena Pećina. Cave site of the Neolithic and Copper Age, situated above a side valley of the Neretva River near Mostar, Dalmatia, Yugoslavia. Three occupations are known from A. Benac's excavations. Level III is an Early Neolithic IMPRESSED WARE occupation with scanty STARČEVO pottery imports, associated with rare polished stone axes. Level II has an assemblage with HVAR-LISČIĆI affinities and Level I has Furstenstich pottery with similarities to Slavonian material in the Sava Valley.

Zemi. A deity central to the religion of ARAWAKAN groups in northeastern South America and the Caribbean (e.g. TAINO). Represented in both human and animal form, zemis were commonly portrayed on household utensils as well as in loci of worship such as caves or possibly temples built from organic materials. Origins are uncertain but since they are sometimes found in contexts connecting them to the BALL GAME, a MESOAMERICAN derivation is often postulated. However, some types of zemi, such as the trianguloid form 'three pointers', appear to be of local origin and have no Mesoamerican cognates.

Zenebi Falls. A site on the Gaya River, north of the Jos Plateau, Nigeria, where outwash gravels contain a prepared core industry of 'Middle Stone Age' type. A radiocarbon date in the 4th millennium bc for wood from the same deposit is probably not an accurate indicator of the age of the stone industry.

Zengővárkony. A large settlement and cemetery of the Late Neolithic LENGYEL culture, located near Pécs in south Transdanubia, Hungary, and dated to much of the 4th millennium bc. Excavated by J. Dombay, the site consists of clusters of graves interspersed with areas of settlement debris. This pattern is consistent with family groups buried close to where they lived. Over 350 graves are known, mainly crouched inhumations. Whilst not rich, the grave goods include more copper and fine stone artefacts than are known from the settlement.

Zhangjiapo [Chang-chia-p'o]. A Western ZHOU site near the Feng River in CHANG'AN Xian southwest of Xi'an, China. Extensive Western Zhou remains in this area may be connected with the ZHOU CAPITALS Feng and Hao (see also PUDUCUN). Early Zhou finds at Zhangjiapo include modest tombs similar in construction to SHANG tombs, some with YAOKENG, ERCENGTAI, and human sacrifices (see SHAFT TOMBS); CHARIOT BURIALS; bones used in divination, mostly uninscribed; and sherds of glazed stoneware (see TUNXI). The bronzes of a hoard found in 1961, many inscribed, range in date over most of the Western Zhou period.

Zhanguo [Chan-kuo]. The Warring States period, 475-221 BC. See ZHOU.

Zhengzhou [Cheng-chou]. A modern city south of the Yellow River in Henan province, China. Zhengzhou is the site of a large Bronze Age city, probably a capital of the SHANG dynasty. The major part of the occupation predates the ANYANG period and belongs to the ERLIGANG PHASE (named after a type site near Zhengzhou). A rammed-earth (HANGTU) city wall belongs to the earlier of two levels at Erligang, for which a radiocarbon date of c1600 BC has been obtained. The wall is about 20 metres thick at the base and 7100 metres long (as compared with 1000 metres for a similar wall at PANLONGCHENG). House foundations have been uncovered within the walled enclosure. Outside the wall have been found tombs with bronze RITUAL VESSELS, traces of workshops including bronze foundries, and scattered minor sites, some occupied before or after the Erligang phase. The settlement declined sharply in importance after the Erligang phase, when GAOCHENG and Anyang were greater centres.

zhi [*chih*]. See RITUAL VESSELS (CHINA).

Zhob. A valley in northern Baluchistan, Pakistan, with a number of sites of the 4th and 3rd millennia BC, of which the best known are Periano Ghundai and Moghul Ghundai. The so-called 'Zhob cult' phase of the 3rd millennium BC is characterized by goggle-eyed hooded female figurines of a type labelled 'Zhob mother goddesses', bull figurines and some pottery showing connections with the HARAPPAN CIVILIZATION. This phase was succeeded by the 'Incinerary Pot' phase, with burials placed in vessels under house floors, after disarticulation and some cremation.

zhong [*chung*]. *See* BELLS (CHINA).

Zhongshan [Chung-shan]. *See* PINGSHAN.

Zhongyuan [Chung-yüan]. Literally the Central Plain, an area of North China, comprising the river basins and alluvial plains of the Wei River (central Shaanxi province) and the Yellow River east of its confluence with the Wei (southern Shaanxi, northern Henan, southern Hebei, and western Shandong). Capitals of the SHANG, ZHOU, QIN, HAN, TANG and Northern SONG dynasties all lay near one river or the other, and the Zhongyuan area is traditionally and probably rightly regarded as the birthplace of Chinese civilization. The lower Yangzi region can claim equal status as a centre of Neolithic origins (*see* YANGSHAO, LONGSHAN).

Zhongzhoulu [Chung-chou-lu]. *See* LUO-YANG.

Zhou [Chou]. The longest dynasty in Chinese history, founded in the 12th or 11th century BC (*see* SHANG) and surviving until 256 BC. The Zhou period is subdivided into Western Zhou, when the capital was in Shaanxi province, and Eastern Zhou, which began in 770 BC with the transfer of the capital eastward to LUOYANG (*see* ZHOU CAPITALS). In archaeological writings Eastern Zhou is usually taken for convenience to include the years between the final extinction of the Zhou royal house in 256 BC and the founding of the QIN dynasty in 221 BC. Eastern Zhou is then subdivided into the Spring and Autumn (Chunqiu) period, 770-476 BC, and the Warring States (Zhanguo) period, 475-221 BC. These names come from two historical texts, the *Spring and Autumn Annals of the State of Lu* and the *Discourses of the Warring States* (since the former book chronicles only the years 722-481 historians occasionally understand the Spring and Autumn period to refer to this shorter time).

Originally a pastoral people, the Zhou rose to power in the Wei River valley of Shaanxi province, in the process adopting much of the culture of the Shang city-dwellers they eventually overthrew. From their Shaanxi homeland the Western Zhou kings ruled, through vassal lords, an empire that included most of the former Shang territories and stretched to the north-east beyond BEIJING (*see* YAN). Western Zhou sites are scattered throughout this area and are known also in Sichuan (*see* PENG XIAN), northern Hubei (*see* JIANGLING), Anhui (*see* TUNXI), and Jiangsu (*see* DANTU), but are most heavily concentrated in and near the Wei River valley (*see* BAOJI, FUFENG, QISHAN, ZHANGJIAPO, LINGTAI).

Measured against the wealth and splendour of the earlier ANYANG civilization or of the later Warring States period, the material remains of later Western Zhou and the first century or so of Eastern Zhou speak of growing isolation and impoverishment; the inscriptions on Western Zhou RITUAL VESSELS are much concerned with the feudal transactions on which the Zhou king's dwindling power depended. The forced shift of the capital to Luoyang in 771 BC coincided with the dissolution of the Western Zhou empire into a large number of states over which the Eastern Zhou king ruled only in name. The Eastern Zhou period is notable for the appearance of IRON; for an upsurge in the foreign contacts that were eventually institutionalized in the SILK ROUTE (or warded off by the GREAT WALL); and for the rise of brilliant courts in the various states, the most distinctive cultural tradition being that of CHU.

Zhou [Chou] **capitals**. For several generations before their overthrow of the SHANG dynasty, the ZHOU were settled in the Wei River valley of Shaanxi province, China. They are reported in later histories to have shifted their predynastic capital several times, on one occasion to a place that the texts call Zhouyuan, 'the Plain of Zhou' (from which the dynasty may take its name). Zhouyuan was somewhere near modern QISHAN; extensive Zhou remains in this neighbourhood include palace foundations at Qishan Fengchucun shown to antedate the fall of the Shang dynasty by inscribed ORACLE BONES unearthed at the site. Shortly before the conquest the Zhou court moved from Zhouyuan to Feng and then to Hao, twin cities supposed to have been located on opposite banks of the Feng River west of modern Xi'an (*see* CHANG'AN, ZHANGJIAPO).

A few years after the conquest a secondary capital was founded at LUOYANG in the former Shang territories; this new city was called

Cheng Zhou, 'Victorious Zhou'. Throughout the Western Zhou period, however, the chief royal cities remained two in the old Zhou homeland, the Hao capital and a city called Zong Zhou, 'Ancestral Zhou'. This latter name apparently refers to the Qishan area, that is a centre at or near Zhouyuan, and this region is extraordinarily rich in Western Zhou finds (*see* QISHAN, FUFENG).

At the loss of the Wei Valley homeland to invading barbarians in 771 BC, which marks the end of Western Zhou, the Zhou court moved east to Luoyang, where it remained until the end of the dynasty in 256 BC.

Zhoukoudian [Choukoutien]. A locality 42 km southwest of BEIJING [Peking], China, famous for the very numerous human fossils of 'Peking man' found in deposits of possibly 400,000 to 800,000 years ago. Over 40 individuals are represented and most of the bones of the skeleton are known; this has become one of the two fossil populations on which HOMO ERECTUS is based. The first main series was discovered in the 1920s and 1930s. In 1941, when the Japanese were about to attack Beijing, the fossils were packed for transport to the USA but disappeared. New investigations are taking place at Zhoukoudian: more skulls and parts have been found, and a pollen sequence is known. Primitive stone tools — but no hand axes — have been found, along with traces of fire.

Zhouyuan [Chou-yüan]. *See* ZHOU CAPITALS.

Zhuangbo [Chuang-po]. *See* FUFENG.

ziggurat. The name given to the great stepped temple towers of the Mesopotamian civilizations — SUMER, BABYLON and ASSYRIA.

Zimbabwe. Contrary to popular usage, which applies the name to a single site, this term, which is believed to be derived from the Shona, is correctly applied to many stone-built enclosures located in the plateau country between the Zambezi and Limpopo rivers of southern Africa. The major site near Fort Victoria is correctly designated the GREAT ZIMBABWE.

Zinjanthropus. Name originally given to a robust AUSTRALOPITHECUS from OLDUVAI

GORGE. This fossil is now usually classified as *Australopithecus boisei* or *Australopithecus robustus*. *See also* HUMAN EVOLUTION.

Zinjirli. A TELL site in southeast Turkey excavated by the Germans in the late 19th century. It was important during the 2nd millennium BC under the HITTITES and subsequently as an independent city state called Sam'al. It was annexed by the ASSYRIANS in the 7th century BC and then abandoned. The town was surrounded by a wall forming an exact circle c700 metres in diameter. Inside there was a fortified citadel with two palaces inside. The palaces and gateways were decorated with relief carvings and inscriptions in the Syro-Hittite hieroglyphic script.

Ziwa. A local Early Iron Age variant in the INYANGA area of Zimbabwe, closely related to the GOKOMERE tradition.

Ziwiye. TELL site near Saqqiz in Azerbaijan, northwest Iran. It was a fortified city of the local Mannaeans in the 1st millennium BC. Very little scientific excavation has taken place, although the site has been looted over a long period. The most famous discovery is a hoard of gold, silver and ivory objects found in a bath-shaped coffin in 1947 by local villagers, and now dispersed in different museums in Iran and America. The hoard is dated to the late 7th century BC. Many stylistic influences are apparent in the style of these objects: Assyrian, Urartian, Scythian and local.

Zlaty Kun. A cave near Beroun in Bohemia, Czechoslovakia. Two partial skulls from this site are associated with SZELETIAN (early Upper PALAEOLITHIC) artefacts. They are of broadly CROMAGNON type but also have surviving NEANDERTHAL features, as is typical at this time. There are no radiocarbon dates from this site, but dates for the Szeletian generally fall between 45,000 and 25,000 bc.

Zlota. Settlement and cemetery site of the Neolithic-Copper Age in southern Poland. The community lived by farming and the exploitation of nearby FLINT MINES. They lived in simple square houses made of wattle and daub, while the dead were buried in CIST GRAVES. Grave goods include cord ornamented pots, perhaps linked to the

GLOBULAR AMPHORA culture, stone BATTLE-AXES and ornaments of copper and amber.

zong [*tsung, ts'ung*]. A Chinese JADE object made in the shape of a tube with square outer and round inner perimeter. Examples vary widely in size and proportions. *Zong* have been found at both SHANG and ZHOU sites but may have been more common in Neolithic times. The earliest examples come from 3rd millennium BC LIANGZHU sites and are frequently decorated at the corners with schematic face-like designs, often little more than paired eyes. The traditional interpretation of the *zong* as a 'symbol of the earth' is a late invention unsupported by archaeology or early texts. Other suggestions, for instance that it was a container for ancestral tablets or that it was used in conjunction with a jade disc as an astronomical instrument, seem equally irrelevant to the early examples found in Neolithic graves.

Zong Zhou [Tsung Chou]. *See* ZHOU CAPITALS.

Zoque. *See* CHIAPA DE CORZA.

zun [*tsun*]. A word that occurs in inscriptions on Chinese bronze RITUAL VESSELS in the general sense of 'ritual vessel'. It is nowadays used more narrowly to name several specific vessel types, including sculptural vessels in animal shapes.

SUBJECT INDEX

GENERAL

Aceramic Neolithic
acculturation
amphora
antefix
ard
arrow straightener
assemblage
association
astronomy
barrow
battle-axe
baulk
berm
Bronze Age
calendar, calendrics
capstone
carination
celt
Chalcolithic
chamber tomb
chevaux de frise
cist
Copper Age
corbel
counterscrap bank
culture
Cyclopean masonry
demography
diffusion, diffusionist
distribution
dolmen
double axe
dromos
dyke
entrance grave
ethnoarchaeology
evolution
experimental archaeology
false entrance
fire
firedog
fishing
gallery grave
halberd
hillfort
hoard
horizon

hourglass perforation
human evolution
hüyük
industrial archaeology
industry
Kerbschnitt
kitchen midden
Leptolithic
megalith
menhir
Mesolithic
Neolithic
neoteny
New Archaeology
Palaeolithic
palstave
passage grave
pebble tool
pilaster
pintadera
place names
portal dolmen
porthole slab
pot boilers
quern
rampart
rock-cut tomb
sacrifice
sati
segmented cist
septal slab
shaft grave
situla
Stone Age
stone circle
tell
tepe
Three Age System
torc
tradition
transepted gallery grave
trepanning
trilithon
underwater archaeology
urn
vase support
wristguard
writing
yoke

DATING

AD, ad
amino-acid racemization
BC, bc
bone dating
BP, bp
Bristlecone pine
chronology
collagen
contamination
cross-dating
dating
dendrochronology
fission track dating
fluorine dating
half-life
hard water effect
isotoptic fractionation
isotopic replacement
nitrogen dating
obsidan hydration dating
palaeomagnetism
potassium-argon dating
radiocarbon dating
radiometric dating
sequence dating
seriation
stratigraphy
tephrochronology
terminus ante-quem, terminus
    post-quem
thermoluminescence
uranium series dating

MATERIALS

amber
antler
arsenic
bone
brick
bronze
ceramic
chalcedony
charcoal
chert

copper
daub
fabric
faience
flint
glass
glaze
gold
greenstone
gypsum
horn
iron
ivory
jade
jadeite
jet
lapis lazuli
lead
malachite
metal
mud-brick
nephrite
obsidian
ochre
pisé
pottery
sarsen
serpentine
shell
silver
steatite
stone
terracotta
textile
tin
tumbaga
turquoise
wattle

TECHNOLOGY

alloy
blade
bloom
bronze
bulb of percussion
burin
burnish
casting
chasing
cire perdue
cold working
copper
core
crucible
enamel
fabricator
filigree
flake

forging
geometric
gold
granulation
ingot
iron
lead
metal
metallurgy
microburin
microlith
midrib
mould
patina
pebble tool
pressure flaking
repoussé
retouch
rivet
scraper
silver
smelting
striking platform
tuyére

ANALYSIS

atomic absorption
   spectrometry
chemical analysis
heavy mineral analysis
metallographic examination
metallurgical analysis
neutron activation analysis
optical emission spectrometry
particle size analysis
petrological analysis
sample
thin section
trace elements
x-ray fluorescence
   spectrometry

GENERAL
ENVIRONMENTAL

bog
coprolite
domestication
ecology
environmental archaeology
environmental indicators
fen
flotation
froth flotation
peat
sieving
site catchment analysis

GEOLOGY

Allerød interstadial
Amersfoort interstadial
Anglian
Bølling interstadial
boulder clay
breccia
Brørup interstadial
cave earth
Chelford interstadial
coombe rock
Cromerian
deep sea cores
Denekamp interstadial
Devensian
drift
Eemian
eustatic
Flandrian
geochronology
geology
glacial
Günz
Günz/Mindel
head
Hengelo interstadial
Holocene
Holstein
Hoxnian
ice wedge
Illinoian
interglacial
interstadial
involution
Ipswichian
isostasy
Loch Lomond stadial
loess
Mindel
Mindel/Riss
Moershoofd interstadial
moraine
Odderade interstadial
Older Dryas
palaeosol
periglacial
pingo
Pleistocene
proglacial
Quaternary
Riss
Riss/Würm
Saale
Sangamon
sea level
stadial
Tertiary
till
Upton Warren
interstadial

COMPUTING AND STATISTICS

PALAEOLITHIC AND MESOLITHIC (OLD WORLD)

LATER PREHISTORIC EUROPE (post-Mesolithic)

ISLAMIC ARCHAEOLOGY

WESTERN ASIA

SOUTH AMERICA

FURTHER READING

Dating, technology and analysis

Aitken, M.J., *Physics and Archaeology* (Oxford: Oxford University Press, 2nd edition, 1974).

Fleming, S., *Dating in Archaeology* (London: Dent, 1976).

Hodges, H.W.M. *Artefacts* (London: John Baker, corrected edition, 1976).

Tite, M.S., *Methods of Physical Examination in Archaeology* (London: Seminar Press, 1972).

Tylecote, R.F., *Metallurgy in Archaeology* (London: Edward Arnold, 1962).

General environmental, geology and soils

Bowen, D.Q., *Quaternary Geology* (London: Pergamon, 1978).

Evans, J.G., *Land Snails in Archaeology* (London: Seminar Press, 1972).

Limbrey, S., *Soil Science and Archaeology* (London, New York and San Francisco: Academic Press, 1975).

Price, W.L., *The Environmental History of the Near and Middle East* (London, New York and San Francisco: Academic Press, 1978).

Simmons, I. and Tooley, M.J., *The Environment in British Prehistory* (London: Duckworth, 1980).

West, R.G., *Pleistocene Geology and Biology* (London: Longman, 2nd edition, 1976).

Plants and plant remains

Bender, B., *Farming in Prehistory* (London: John Baker, 1975).

Godwin, H., *History of the British Flora* (Cambridge: Cambridge University Press, 1975).

Moore, P.D. and Webb, J.A., *An Illustrated Guide to Pollen Analysis* (London: Hodder and Stoughton, 1978).

Pennington, W., *The History of British Vegetation* (London: English Universities Press, 1969).

Renfrew, J., *Palaeoethnobotany* (London: Methuen, 1973).

Simmonds, N.W. (ed.), *Evolution of Crop Plants* (London: Longman, 1976).

Animals and animal remains

Baker, J. and Brothwell, D.R., *Animal Diseases in Archaeology* (London, New York and San Francisco: Academic Press, 1980).

Bender, B., *Farming in Prehistory* (London: John Baker, 1975).

Brothwell, D.R., *Digging up Bones* (London: British Museum [Natural History], 2nd edition, 1972).

Chaplin, R.E., *The Study of Animal Bones from Archaeological Sites* (London: Seminar Press, 1971).

Ryder, M.L., *Animal Bones in Archaeology* (Oxford: Blackwell Scientific Publications, 1968).

Site technology, sediments and stratigraphy

Barker, P., *Techniques of Archaeological Excavation* (London: Batsford, 1977).

Harris, E.C., *Principles of Archaeological Stratigraphy* (London, New York and San Francisco: Academic Press, 1979).

Limbrey, S., *Soil Science and Archaeology* (London, New York and San Francisco: Academic Press, 1975).

Webster, G., *Practical Archaeology* (London: John Baker, 2nd edition, 1974).

Computing and statistics

Doran, J.E., and Hodson, F.R., *Mathematics and Computers in Archaeology* (Edinburgh: Edinburgh University Press, 1975).

Orton, C., *Mathematics in Archaeology* (London: Collins, 1980).

Palaeolithic and Mesolithic of the Old World

Bordes, F., *The Old Stone Age* (London: Weidenfeld and Nicolson, 1968).

Campbell, J., *The Upper Palaeolithic of Britain* (Oxford: Oxford University Press, 1977).

Clark, G., *The Stone Age Hunters* (London: Thames and Hudson, 1967).

Collins, D. (ed.), *The Origins of Europe* (London: Allen and Unwin, 1975).

Collins, D., *The Human Revolution* (Oxford: Phaidon, 1976).

Kozlowski, J. and S., *Upper Palaeolithic and Mesolithic in Europe* (Warsaw: Polish Academy of Sciences, 1979).

Leroi-Gourhan, A., *The Art of Prehistoric Man in Europe* (London: Thames and Hudson, 1968).

Life Books, *Early Man* (New York: Time-Life, 1966).

Morrison, A., *Early Man in Britain and Ireland* (London: Croom Helm, 1980).

Oakley, K., *Frameworks for Dating Fossil Man* (London: Weidenfeld and Nicolson, 1964).

Palmer, S., *Mesolithic Cultures of Britain* (Poole: Dolphin, 1977).

Pfeiffer, J., *The Emergence of Man* (London: Harper and Row, 1969).

Reader, J., *Missing Links* (London: Collins, 1980).

Wood, B., *The Evolution of Early Man* (London: Peter Lowe, 1976).

Wymer, J., *Lower Palaeolithic Archaeology in Britain* (London: John Baker, 1968).

Africa (including Egypt)

Adams, W.Y., *Nubia, Corridor to Africa* (London: Allen Lane, 1977).

Camps, G., *Les Civilisations préhistoriques de L'Afrique du Nord et du Sahara* (Paris: Doin, 1974).

Clark, J.D., *The Prehistory of Africa* (London: Thames and Hudson, 1970).

Clark, J.D. (ed.), *Cambridge History of Africa*, Vol. I (to c500 BC) (Cambridge: Cambridge University Press, 1982).

Face, J.D. (ed.), *Cambridge History of Africa*, Vol. II (c500 BC-AD 1050) (Cambridge: Cambridge University Press, 1978).

Inskeep, R.R., *The Peopling of Southern Africa* (Cape Town: Philip, 1978).

James, T.G.H. (ed.), *An Introduction to Ancient Egypt* (London: British Museum, 1979).

Noten, F. van., *The Archaeology of Central Africa* (Graz: Akademie Verlag, in press).

Oliver, R. (ed.), *Cambridge History of Africa*, Vol. III (c1050-1600) (Cambridge: Cambridge University Press, 1977).

Oliver, R. and Fagan, B.M., *Africa in the Iron Age* (Cambridge: Cambridge University Press, 1975).

Phillipson, D.W., *The Later Prehistory of Eastern and Southern Africa* (London: Heinemann, 1977).

Shaw, C.T., *Nigeria: its Archaeology and Early History* (London: Thames and Hudson, 1978).

Williams, M.A.J. and Faure, H. (eds.), *The Sahara and the Nile* (Rotterdam: Balkema, 1980).

Prehistoric Europe

Childe, V.G., *The Dawn of European Civilization* (London: Routledge and Kegan Paul, 6th edition, 1957).

Clark, J.G.D., *Prehistoric Europe: The Economic Basis* (London: Methuen, 1952).

Coles, J.M. and Harding, A.F., *The Bronze Age in Europe* (London: Methuen, 1979).

Gimbutas, M., *Bronze Age Cultures in Central and Eastern Europe* (The Hague: Mouton, 1965).

Milisauskas, S., *European Prehistory* (London, New York, and San Francisco: Academic Press, 1979).

Phillips, P., *Early Farmers of West Mediterranean Europe* (London: Hutchinson, 1975).

Phillips, P., *The Prehistory of Europe* (London: Allen Lane, 1980).

Piggott, S., *Ancient Europe* (Edinburgh: Edinburgh University Press, 1965).

Renfrew, C., *Before Civilization* (London: Jonathan Cape and Penguin, 1973).

Renfrew, C., *The Emergence of Civilization: The Cyclades and the Aegean in the Third Millennium BC* (London: Methuen, 1972).

Tringham, R., *Hunters, Fishers and Farmers of Eastern Europe, 6000-3000 BC* (London: Hutchinson, 1971).

Trump, D., *The Prehistory of the Mediterranean* (London: Allen Lane, 1980).

Greece and Rome

Boethius, A., *Etruscan and Early Roman Architecture* (Pelican History of Art), (Harmondsworth: Penguin Books, 2nd edition, 1978).

Brown, D. and Strong, D. (eds.), *Roman Crafts* (London: Duckworth, 1976).

Coarelli, F. (ed.), *Etruscan Cities* (London: Cassell, 1975).

Cook, R.M., *Greek Painted Pottery* (London: Methuen, 2nd edition, 1966).

Cornell, T. and Matthews, J., *Atlas of the Roman World* (Oxford: Phaidon, 1982).

Dinsmoor, W.B., *Architecture of Ancient Greece* (New York: Norton, 1950).

Frere, S., *Britannia* (London: Routledge and Kegan Paul, 2nd edition, 1978).

Hammond, N.G.L. and Scullard, H.H. (eds.), *Oxford Classical Dictionary* (Oxford: Clarendon Press, 2nd edition, 1970).

Nash, E., *Pictorial Dictionary of Ancient Rome* (London: Thames and Hudson, 2nd edition, 1968).

Pauly, A.F. von and Wissowa, G. (eds.), *Realencyclopaedie der classischen Altertumswissenschaft* and supplements (Stuttgart: Druckenmüller, 1893-1972).

Stillwell, R., MacDonald, W.L., McAllister, M.H. (eds.), *Princeton Encyclopaedia of Classical Sites* (Guildford: Princeton University Press, 1976).

Todd, M., *Roman Britain 55BC-AD400* (London: Fontana, 1981)

Travlos, J., *Pictorial Dictionary of Ancient Athens* (London: Thames and Hudson, 1971).

Walker, D.S., *Geography of Italy* (London: Methuen, 2nd edition, 1967).

Ward-Perkins, J.B., *Roman Imperial Architecture* (Pelican History of Art) (Harmondsworth: Penguin Books, 2nd edition, 1981).

Medieval Europe

Archeologia Medioevale. Issued annually by Edizioni all' Insegna del Giglio S.A.S., Via della Querciola 6, Firenze, Italy.

Archéologie Médiévale. Issued annually by Centre du recherches archéologiques médiévales, Université de Caen, 14032 Caen Cedex, France.

Medieval Archaeology: Journal of the Society for Medieval Archaeology. Issued annually by the Society for Medieval Archaeology, University College, Gower Street, London WC1E 6BT.

Zeitschrift für Archäologie des Mittelalters. Issued annually by Rheinland-Vorlag GmbH, Cologne, West Germany.

Chapelot, J. and Fossier, R., *Le Village et la maison au Môyen Age* (Paris: Hachette, 1980).

Dixon, P., *The Barbarian World* (Oxford: Phaidon, 1976).

Hodges, R., *Dark Age Economics* (London: Duckworth, 1982).

Laing, L., *Late Celtic Britain and Ireland, c400-1200* AD (London: Methuen, 1975).

Platt, C., *The English Medieval Town* (London: Secker and Warburg, 1975).

Randsborg, K., *The Viking Age in Denmark* (London: Duckworth, 1980).

Wilson, D. (ed.), *The Northern World* (London: Thames and Hudson, 1980).

Withold, H., *Die Slawen im frühen Mittelalter* (Berlin: Akademie Verlag, 1965).

Islamic Archaeology

Archaeology 24/3, 1971. This edition of this journal is devoted to Islamic Archaeology.

Arts Council of Great Britain, *The Arts of Islam* (London, 1976).

Creswell, K.A.C., *A Bibliography of the Architecture, Arts and Crafts of Islam* (Cairo: American University of Cairo Press, 1961; supplement 1973).

Creswell, K.A.C., *A Short Account of Early Muslim Architecture* (Harmondsworth: Penguin, 1958).

Fehervari, G., *Islamic Pottery* (London: Faber, 1973).

Lewis, B. (ed.), *The World of Islam* (London: Thames and Hudson, 1976).

Otto-Dorn, K., *Kunst des Islam* (Baden-Baden, 1964).

Scerrato, U., *Islam* (London: Cassell, 1976).

World Archaeology 14/1, 1983. This edition of this journal is devoted to Islamic Archaeology

Western Asia

Adams, R. McC., *The Evolution of Urban Society* (Chicago: Chicago University Press, 1966).

Bender, B., *Farming in Prehistory* (London: John Baker, 1975).

Bibby, G., *Looking for Dilmun* (London: Collins, 1969).

Burney, C., *From Village to Empire. An Introduction to Near Eastern Archaeology* (Oxford: Phaidon, 1977).

Doe, D.B., *Southern Arabia* (London: Thames and Hudson, 1971).

Ghirshman, R., *Ancient Persia: from its Origins to the Time of Alexander the Great* (London and New York, 1964).

Kenyon, K.M., *Archaeology in the Holy Land,* 4th edition (London: Ernest Benn, 1979).

Kramer, S.N., *The Sumerians* (Chicago: Chicago University Press, 1963).

Lloyd, S., *The Archaeology of Mesopotamia: from the Old Stone Age to the Persian Conquest* (London: Thames and Hudson, 1978).

Mellaart, J., *Earliest civilisations of the Near East* (London: Thames and Hudson, 1965).

Mellaart, J., *The Neolithic of the Near East* (London: Thames and Hudson, 1975).

Oates, D. and Oates, J., *The Rise of Civilization* (Oxford: Phaidon, 1976).

Oppenheim, A.L., *Ancient Mesopotamia* (Chicago: Chicago University Press, 1964).

Redman, C., *The Rise of Civilization* (San Francisco: W.H. Freeman and Co., 1978).

Roux, G., *Ancient Iraq* (London: Allen and Unwin, 1964

Whitehouse, R., *The First Cities* (Oxford: Phaidon, 1977).

Central Asia and Siberia

Allchin, F.R. and Hammond, N. (eds.), *The Archaeology of Afghanistan* (London, New York and San Francisco: Academic Press, 1979)

Chard, C.S., *Northeast Asia in Prehistory* (Wisconsin: University of Wisconsin Press, 1974).

Gupta, S.P., *Archaeology of Soviet Central Asia and the Indian Borderlands* (Delhi, 1979).

Masson, V.M. and Sarianidi, V.I., *Central Asia: Turkmenia before the Achaemenids* (London: Thames and Hudson, 1972).

Mongait, A.L., *Archaeology in the U.S.S.R.* (Harmondsworth: Penguin, 1961).

Rudenko, S.I., *Frozen Tombs of Siberia* (Los Angeles: University of California Press, 1970).

Tucci, G., *Transhimalaya* (London: Barrie, 1973).

India and Pakistan

Agrawal, D.P., *The Copper Bronze Age in India* (New Delhi, 1971).

Agrawal, D.P. and Chakrabarti, D.K., *Essays in Indian Protohistory* (Delhi, 1979).

Agrawal, D.P. and Ghosh, A., *Radiocarbon and Indian Archaeology* (Bombay, 1973).

Agrawal, D.P. and Kusumgar, S., *Prehistoric Chronology and Radiocarbon Dating in India* (New Delhi, 1974).

Allchin, B. and Allchin, R., *The Rise of Civilization in India and Pakistan* (Cambridge: Cambridge University Press, 1982).

Allchin, F.R. and Chakrabarti, D.K., *A Source-book of Indian Archaeology,* Vol. 1 (New Delhi: Munshiram Manoharlal, 1979).

Bannerjee, N.R,., *The Iron Age in India* (Delhi, 1965).

Davids, T.W.R., *Buddhist India,* 9th edition, (Delhi, 1970).

Fairservis, W.A., *The Roots of Ancient India* (London: Allen and Unwin, 2nd edition, 1971).

Ghosh, A., *The City in Early Historical India* (Simla, 1973).

Gururaja Rao, B.K., *Megalithic Culture in South India* (Mysore, 1972).

Piggott, S., *Prehistoric India* (Harmondsworth: Penguin, 1950).

Possehl, G.L., *Ancient Cities of the Indus* (New Delhi, 1979).

Sankalia, H.D., *Prehistory and Protohistory of India and Pakistan* (Poona, 1974).

Wheeler, R.E.M., *The Indus Civilization,* 3rd edition (Cambridge: Cambridge University Press, 1968).

China

Bunker, E.C., Chatwin, C.B. and Farkas, A.R., *'Animal Style Art' from East to West* (New York: The Asia Society, 1970).

Cheng, Te-k'un, *Chou China* (Cambridge: W. Heffer and Sons, 1963).

Fong, Wen (ed.), *The Great Bronze Age of China* (New York: The Metropolitan Museum of Art and Alfred A. Knopf; London: Thames and Hudson, 1980).

Fontein, J. and Wu, Tung, *Unearthing China's Past* (Boston: Museum of Fine Arts, 1973).

Gettens, R.J., *The Freer Chinese Bronzes*, Vol. II; *Technical Studies* (Washington: Smithsonian Institution, 1969).

Hughes-Stanton, P. and Kerr, R., *Kiln Sites of Ancient China* (London, 1980).

Jettmar, K., *Art of the Steppes* (New York: Crown Publishers, 1967).

Lawton, T., *Chinese Art of the Warring States Period* (Washington: Smithsonian Institution, 1982).

Loehr, M., *Chinese Bronze Age Weapons* (Ann Arbor: University of Michigan Press, 1956).

Loehr, M., *Ritual Vessels of Bronze Age China* (New York: The Asia Society, 1968).

Phillips, E.D., *The Royal Hordes* (London: Thames and Hudson, 1965).

Pirazzoli-t'Serstevens, M., *The Han Dynasty* (New York: Rizzoli, 1982).

Qian, Hao, Chen, Heyi and Ru, Suichu, *Out of China's Earth: Archaeological Discoveries in the People's Republic of China* (New York: Harry N. Abrams, 1981).

Rawson, Jessica, *Ancient China. Art and Archaeology* (London: British Museum, 1980).

Sato, Masahiko, *Chinese Ceramics: A Short History* (New York and Tokyo: Weatherhill/Heibonsha, 1981).

Seckel, D., *The Art of Buddhism* (New York: Crown Publishers, 1964).

Tsien, Tsuen-hsuin, *Written on Bamboo and Silk: The Beginnings of Chinese Books and Inscriptions* (Chicago: University of Chicago Press, 1962).

Wang, Zhongshu, *Han Civilization* (New Haven and London: Yale University Press, 1982).

Watson, W., *Archaeology in China* (London: Max Parrish, 1960).

Watson, W., *Cultural Frontiers in Ancient East Asia* (Edinburgh: Edinburgh University Press, 1971).

Wenwu kaogu gongzuo san shi nian 1949-1979 (Thirty Years of Archaeological Work in China, 1949-1979), in Chinese (Beijing: Wenwu Press, 1979). A survey of important finds in Chinese archaeology, by province and period, with references to excavation reports.

Wertime, T.A. and Muhly, J.D. (eds.), *The Coming of the Age of Iron* (New Haven and London: Yale University Press, 1980).

Willetts, W., *Chinese Art* (Harmondsworth: Penguin Books, 1958).

Southeast Asia

Bezacier, L., *Le Viet-Nam: de la Prehistoire a la fin de l'occupation chinoise* (Paris: edns. A. et J. Picard, 1972). Manuel d'Archeologie d'Extreme-Orient, Première Partie: Asie du Sud-Est, Tome II.

Boisselier, J., *Le Cambodge* (Paris: edns. A. et J. Picard, 1966). Manuel d'Archeologie d'Extreme-Orient, Première Partie: Asie du Sud-Est, Tome I.

Bosch, F.D.K., *Selected Studies in Indonesian Archaeology* (The Hague: Martinus Nijohff, 1961). Kon. Inst. voor Taal-, Land- en Volkenkunde, Translation Series, 5.

Coedès, G., *The Indianized States of Southeast Asia*, ed. Walter F. Vella; translated from the French by Susan Brown Cowing (Honolulu: East-West Center Press and Canberra: Australian National University Press, 1968).

Fox, R.B., *The Tabon Caves* (Manila: National Museum, 1970).

Frederic, L., *The Temples and Sculpture of Southeast Asia*, translated from the French by Arnold Rosin (London: Thames and Hudson, 1965).

Groslier, B.P., *Indochina*, translated from the French by James Hogarth (London: Frederick Muller, 1966).

Le May, R., *The Culture of South-East Asia: The Heritage of India* (London: Allen and Unwin, 1954).

Pisit Charoenwongsa and Subhadradis Diskul, *Thailand* (London: Frederick Muller, 1976).

Smith, R.B. and Watson, W. (eds.), *Early South East Asia* (Oxford: Oxford University Press, 1979).

Suleiman, S., *Concise Ancient History of Indonesia* (Jakarta: Archaeological Foundation, 1974).

Wales, H.G., *The Malay Peninsula in Hindu Times* (London: Bernard Quaritch, 1976).

Japan

Aikens, C. Melvin and Takayasu Higuchi, *Prehistory of Japan* (London, New York and San Francisco: Academic Press, 1982).

Bleed, P., 'The Yayoi Cultures of Japan', *Arctic Anthropology* 9/2, 1972.

Chard, C.S., *Northeast Asia in Prehistory* (Wisconsin: University of Wisconsin Press, 1974).

Ikawa-Smith, F., 'Current issues in Japanese archaeology', *American Scientist* 68/2, 1980.

Koyama, S., 'Jomon subsistence and population', *Senri Ethnological Studies* 2, 1978 (National Museum of Ethnology, Senri Park, Osaka).

Maringer, J., 'Clay figurines of the Jomon Period: a contribution to the history of ancient religion in Japan', *History of Religion*, 14/2, 1974.

Australia

Allen, J., Golson, J. and Jones, R. (eds), *Sunda and Sahul: Prehistoric Studies in Southeast Asia, Melanesia and Australia* (London, New York and San Francisco: Academic Press, 1977).

Edwards, E., *Australian Aboriginal Art: The Art of the Alligator Rivers Region, Northern Territory* (Canberra: Australian Institute of Aboriginal Studies, 1979).

Kirk, R.L. and Thorne, A.G. (eds.), *The origin of the Australians* (Canberra: Australian Institute of Aboriginal Studies, 1976). Human Biology series no. 6.

Mulvaney, D.J., *The prehistory of Australia* (Harmondsworth: Penguin Books, revised, 1975).

Mulvaney, D.J. and Golson, J. (eds.), *Aboriginal man and environment in Australia* (Canberra: Australian National University Press, 1971).

White, J.P. and O'Connell, J.F., 'Australian prehistory: new aspects of antiquity', *Science* 203, 1979.

Wright, R.V.S. (ed.), *Sone Tools as Cultural Markers: Change, Evolution and Complexity* (Canberra: Australian Institute of Aboriginal Studies, 1977). Prehistory and Material Culture Series no. 12.

Oceania

Allen, J., Golson, J. and Jones, R. (eds.), *Sunda and Sahul: Prehistoric studies in Southeast Asia, Melanesia and Australia* (London, New York and San Francisco: Academic Press, 1977)

Barnard, N. (ed.), *Early Chinese Art and its possible influence in the Pacific Basin*, 3 vols. (New York: Intercultural Arts Press, 1972).

Bellwood, P.S., 'The prehistory of Oceania', *Current Anthropology* 16, 1975.

Bellwood, P.S., *Man's Conquest of the Pacific* (London: Collins, 1978).

Bellwood, P.S., *The Polynesians* (London: Thames and Hudson, 1978).

Bellwood, P.S., 'The peopling of the Pacific', *Scientific American* 243/5, 1980.

Fox, A., *Prehistoric Maori Fortifications* (London: Longman Paul, 1976).

Heyerdahl, T., *Early man and the ocean* (New York: Doubleday, 1979).

Howells, W.W., *The Pacific Islanders* (New York: Scribners, 1973).

Irwin, G.J., 'The prehistory of Oceania: colonization and cultural changes', *Cambridge Encyclopaedia of Archaeology*, 1980.

Jennings, J.D. (ed.), *The Prehistory of Polynesia* (Cambridge: Harvard University Press, 1979).

Lewis, D., *We, the Navigators* (Wellington: Reed, 1972).

Steensberg, A., *New Guinea Gardens* (London, New York and San Francisco: Academic Press, 1980).

The Americas

General

Jennings, J.D. and Norbeck, E. (eds.), *Prehistoric Man in the New World* (Chicago: University of Chicago Press, 1964).

Jennings, J.D. (ed.), *Ancient Native Americans* (San Francisco: W.H. Freeman and Co., 1978).

Leone, M. (ed.), *Contemporary Archaeology: A Guide to Theory and Contributions* (Carbondale: Illinois University Press, 1972).

Meggers, B.J., *Prehistoric America: An Ecological Perspective* (Hawthorne, New York: Aldine Publishing Co., 1979).

Schuyler, R.L. (ed.), *Historical Archaeology: A Guide to Substantive and Theoretical Contributions* (Farmingdale, New York: Baywood Publishing Inc., 1978).

Stark, B.L. and Voorhies, B., *Prehistoric Coastal Adaptations* (London, New York and San Francisco: Academic Press, 1978).

Taylor, R.E. and Meighan, C.W., *Chronologies in New World Archaeology* (London, New York and San Francisco: Academic Press, 1978).

Thomas, D.H., *Archaeology* (New York: Holt, Rinehart and Winston, 1979).

Willey, G., *Introduction to American Archaeology*, 2 vols. (Englewood Cliffs, NJ: Prentice-Hall, 1966 and 1971).

Zubrow, E.B. *et. al.* (eds.), *New World Archaeology: Selected Readings from Scientific American* (San Francisco: W.H. Freeman and Co., 1974).

North America

Giddings, J.L., *Ancient Men of the Arctic* (New York: Alfred Knopf, 1967).

Hudson, C., *The Southeastern Indians* (Tennessee: University of Tennessee Press, 1976).

Jennings, J.D., *Prehistory of North America* (New York: McGraw-Hill, 1974).

Martin, P. and Plog, F., *The Archaeology of Arizona* (Garden City, New York: Doubleday/Natural History Press, 1973).

Sturtevant, W.C. (ed.), *Handbook of North American Indians* (Washington: Smithsonian Institution; Vols. 8 and 15, 1978; Vol. 9, 1979).

Mesoamerica

Adams, R.E.W., *Prehistoric Mesoamerica* (Boston: Little Brown and Co., 1977).

Bernal, I., *The Olmec World* (Berkeley and Los Angeles: University of California Press, 1969).

Coe, M.E., *Mexico* (New York: Praeger Publishers, 1977).

Coe, M.D:, *The Maya* (London: Thames and Hudson, 1980).

Flannery, K.V., *The Early Mesoamerican Village* (New York, San Francisco and London: Academic Press, 1976).

Hammond, N. and Willey, G. (eds.), *Maya Archaeology and Ethnohistory* (Austin and London: University of Texas Press, 1976).

Porter Weaver, M., *The Aztecs, Maya and their Predecessors* (New York: Seminar Press, 1972).

Thompson, J.E.S., *Maya History and Religion* (Norman Okla: University of Oklahoma Press, 1970).

Wauchope, R. (ed.), *Handbook of Middle American Indians* (Austin: University of Texas Press; Vols. 2 and 3, 1965; Vols. 10 and 11, 1971).

South America

Bankes, G., *Peru before Pizarro* (Oxford: Phaidon Press, 1977).

Lanning, E.P., *Peru before the Incas* (Englewood Cliffs: Prentice-Hall, 1967).

Lumbreras, L.G., *The Peoples and Cultures of Ancient Peru* (Washington: Smithsonian Institution Press, 1976).

Mason, J.A., *The Ancient Civilizations of Peru* (Harmondsworth: Penguin Books, 1968).

Meggers, B.J., *Ecuador* (New York: Praeger, 1966).

Rouse, I. and Cruxent, J.M., *Venezuelan Archaeology* (New Haven: Yale University Press, 1969).

Archaeologists and other scholars

Daniel, G., *150 Years of Archaeology* (London: Duckworth, 1978).

Klindt-Jensen, O., *A History of Scandinavian Archaeology* (London: Thames and Hudson, 1975).

Lloyd, S., *Foundations in the Dust* (London: Thames and Hudson, revised 1980).

Willey, G.R. and Sabloff, J.A., *A History of American Archaeology* (London: Thames and Hudson, 1974).